The *Opera* of Bartolomeo Scappi (1570)

L'arte et prudenza d'un maestro Cuoco

The *Opera* of Bartolomeo Scappi (1570)

L'arte et prudenza d'un maestro Cuoco

Translated with Commentary by

Terence Scully

University of Toronto Press
Toronto Buffalo London

ISBN   978-0-8020-9624-1

Printed on acid-free paper

Copyright in publication data is available from the National Library of Canada.

This volume is published under the aegis and with the financial assistance of: Fondazione Cassamarca, Treviso; Ministerio degli Affari Esteri, Direzione General per la Promozione e la Cooperazione Cultural; Ministerio per i Beni e le Attività Culturali, Direzione General per i Beni Librari e gli Istituti Culturali, Servizio per la promozione del libro e della lettura.

Publication of this volume is assisted by the Istituto Italiano di Cultura, Toronto.

University of Toronto Press acknowledges the financial assistance to its publishing program of the Canada Council for the Arts and the Ontario Arts Council.

This book has been published with the help of a grant from the Humanities and Social Sciences Federation of Canada, using funds provided by the Social Sciences and Humanities Research Council of Canada.

University of Toronto Press acknowledges the financial support for its publishing activities of the Government of Canada through the Book Publishing Industry Development Program (BPIDP).

Contents

The *Opera* of Bartolomeo Scappi

The *Opera* of Bartolomeo Scappi (1570)

L'arte et prudenza d'un maestro Cuoco

Introduction

*Debbe anteporre l'honor del padrone, & il
suo proprio insieme, & l'utilià del padrone,
a tutte l'altre cose* (Book I, §1)

The early cook

$\mathcal{T}$hroughout the later Middle Ages, the records and accounts of a noble or wealthy bourgeois household show that the personnel who worked in the kitchen were an integral part of the domestic staff and had both a specific status within the hierarchy of the household retinue and clear responsibilities to their superiors under the authority of the household's master. The cook himself, whether alone with that title or one of a pair who shared and alternated the work, had authority over a number of lesser retainers who exercised specific duties in the kitchen: he could recommend that each of them be engaged or dismissed; he directed their activities and instructed them on their duties. The functionary who was the cook's immediate superior varied according to the affluence of the household. In relatively modest bourgeois establishments, that individual might enjoy the intimacy of the master, might perhaps be on roughly the same social level as the master, yet still received wages from the master. In addition to such indoor areas as the master's bed chamber, he had responsibility for the kitchen, for what was supplied to kitchen and what was produced by it and, ultimately, all aspects of the activities there: provisions, equipment, fuel, payment for all purchased supplies, determining menus, organizing the actual serving of prepared dishes and, if he approved, transmitting to the master any recommendations from the cook concerning the kitchen's personnel. He was generally called the household steward, *scalco* in Italian. In larger households there might also be under him a kitchen clerk whose responsibilities would include anything having to do with the operation of the kitchen: personnel, foodstuffs, facilities and hardware, as well as accounting for all kitchen expenses. One way or another the duties of those 'middle managers' could seriously impinge upon the work of the cook.

In large households the cook generally came up through the petty ranks from scullion or pot scrubber to assistant cook and eventually to chief cook. During his rise he may have acquired practical experience in one of the suboffices of the kitchen, the butchery or saucery, as a pastry assistant or roaster. After fulfilling a period of apprenticeship to a master cook, he could be considered for appointment as cook in that or another household. Royal and papal establishments

3

maintained two physically separate kitchens, each with its own foodstuff supplies and personnel: the larger kitchen prepared food for all of the household retainers, the commons, who were entitled to be fed at the master's expense; the smaller one, of more august competence and status, was concerned solely and exclusively with food for the master, his family, and his personal guests.

While early cooks did not have their own guild with its set of regulations, or call themselves professionals, they were in essence craftsmen by the same measure as silversmiths or butchers. By virtue of their special, quasi-esoteric knowledge and abilities, theirs was a closed shop, usually entered at the most menial level and climbed from within as proficiency was obtained and demonstrated. In some form a system of apprenticeship training must always have existed by which an aspirant to the grade of master cook learned by observing, by oral instruction, by doing, and by being corrected. There was, naturally, a rarety of written guidance for a cook; the profession depended, as others in the late Middle Ages and Renaissance, on oral traditions and transmission, and very capacious memories.

A master cook was appointed by the lord on the recommendation of whichever individual was responsible for the household's functioning, normally the household's chief steward. The steward, or *scalco*, nominated a broad assortment of personnel within the various offices of the master's house, recommended their dismissal, directed, personally or through the chief of an office, their day-to-day activities, and determined the conditions of their employment.[1] As Bartolomeo Scappi makes clear near the beginning of Book I of the *Opera*, his ideal cook's contract stipulated not only his stipend but all allowances, benefits and perquisites pertaining to the position. By the sixteenth century a cook was a significant and valued figure among the common retainers of a household, being remunerated at rates comparable to those accorded middle managers today.

A cook exercised authority over the individuals who worked in his kitchen. He had also himself to work cooperatively with other officers. The *spenditore*, or purchasing agent, for instance, was charged with buying foodstuffs, among other things, and delivering them to the kitchen larder. Because that person was charged by the steward and answered to him, the cook had to be assured that his choices in the marketplace were adequate to the requirements and standards of the kitchen. Furthermore, because the steward managed the serving of the lord's meals, which were often long and complex affairs, the cook had also of course to coordinate intricate kitchen work very closely with the unpredictable timing of the steward's demands. We can understand the claim that Scappi makes to his own apprentice in Book I that for a master cook to be truly successful it is more important for him to be master of a steward's work as well.

---

[1] See in Appendix III, below, several contemporary documents that outline the duties of the usual personnel in an affluent household. Passages from Domenico Romoli (1560) are particularly enlightening.

Apart from the obvious requirement of knowledge and ability, a professional cook had also to earn the absolute trust of his employer. To cook for someone – to be in the best position deliberately or accidentally to incorporate some form of mortal poison or the source of a disruptive humour into a well-seasoned dish – implied that the cook personally held his master's health and very life in his hands.[2] To obtain an appointment to his position, and more particularly to retain it, a cook must be worthy of his master's complete and abiding trust.

During the sixteenth century several works were published that dealt with a steward's responsibilities in the household of an aristocrate or prelate. Of those books the most remarkable is *La singolare dottrina ... dell'ufficio dello Scalco* by a certain Domenico Romoli, known also, the title page tells us, as 'Panunto.'[3] Book I of the *Singolare dottrina* is devoted to an outline of the duties both of a steward himself and of those lesser servants for whom a steward is responsible to the master – chiefly the purchasing agent, the master's personal cook (*cuoco secreto*) and the sideboard attendant (*credenziere*). Chapter 3 deals with the master's cook in a noble household, and the interlaced duties of cook and steward; that segment is informative enough to be reproduced in Appendix III.

The repertoire of a late-medieval and Renaissance cook tended naturally enough to exist in his head. As an apprentice he *learned* how to prepare a large or small variety of dishes. Generally speaking, recipes were written down

---

[2] A concrete illustration of that danger is afforded in a 1517 plot conspired by several disaffected cardinals to poison Pope Leo X. On the topic of 'natural' or 'accidental' poisoning during the medieval and Renaissance, particulary by mycotoxicosis and foodborne parasites, see Morton Satin, *Death in the Pot: The Impact of Food Poisoning on History* (Amherst, N.Y.: Prometheus, 2007), 89–117. Lead poisoning continued to be a serious and perplexing problem up until relatively recent times. Contamination was common from lead piping and vessels that contained acidic liquids; lead oxide was regularly relied upon to sweeten wines.

[3] For the full title and bibliographic information of all the principal manuscripts, articles and books referred to in the Notes, see the Bibliography. The date of publication of Panunto's opus is 1560. The author catalogues a sequence of daily menus that he explicitly dates (on folio 32v) as beginning on 10 March 1546. He also lets an old man's nostalgic formula escape his pen as he laments, 'I am surprised to see today that ... , whereas in my day ... ' (f. 6 v). A contemporary of Bartolomeo Scappi, he had been active as a cook himself; now retiring or retired as a steward in a cardinal's household, he is passing detailed practical advice to a certain Francesco Rodolfi who aspires to exercise the same function.

Most books of the sixteenth century were still paginated (properly, foliated) on the right-hand page only, the folio number being assigned in sequence to the *recto* (abbreviated as *r*) or face side of each 'leaf' of paper or parchment; the left-hand page, without a number, is the *verso* (abbreviated as *v*) of that folio. For reference to passages in Scappi's work the present study will always, by default, use the foliation in the 1570 edition; the folio on which a passage appears in the 1581 printing will be enclosed in square brackets where the use of them is not confusing: for example, *masseritie di cucina*, IV, f.328r [1581 f.276r].

and collections made of them primarily for archival purposes, for the benefit or use of individuals in a position superior to the cook himself: the household steward, perhaps with the kitchen clerk if there was one, decided on dishes and planned meals; the master or prince required for his archives a document that would help preserve for his posterity a record of how he had lived, his achievements in gracious living. As a consequence, a remarkable number of medieval recipe collections survive in pristine manuscript copies that were never spotted with kitchen grease, that had likely never passed through a kitchen doorway.

The effects of such culinary dependence upon tradition shows up in written recipe collections. In France there is a sequence of manuscript books derivative from a late-thirteenth-century recipe collection that was apparently known to and elaborated upon by a royal cook called Taillevent. His *Viandier* was copied, and later printed, in a surprisingly long sequence of books with a variety of names and an increasingly corrupted text. In Italy, probably because of a greater number of wealthy, independent and, to some extent, competing courts, somewhat more variety was produced in written recipe books although one or two from the fourteenth century seem to have have exerted some degree of influence on subsequent culinary texts. Across Europe, in Latin and in all of the major languages, traditional collections of recipes were copied or modified from generation to generation, portions of them were variously combined and relatively new collections appeared. By the fifteenth century French cookery looks impoverished, or at least not very innovative, if we can judge by recipe books written during that time, whereas professional Italian cookery has developed a wealthy repertoire of possibilities.

In that fifteenth-century Italian repertoire one tradition emerged, a much more 'modern' – that is to say, newer, more recent – tradition. It is usually refered to as the Martino tradition, even though, much as in Taillevent's case, Maestro Martino de Rossi based his *Libro de Arte coquinaria* almost literally upon an earlier, anonymous recipe collection whose material and single extant manuscript copy relate it to the Catalan court in Naples, *The Neapolitan Recipe Collection*. This work was repeatedly copied, adapted[4] and printed[5] into Scappi's century, the sixteenth, but before expiring it coexisted beside two newer works incorporating contemporary cookery: the *Banchetti* of Messisbugo – intended expressly for the use of household stewards – and the *Opera* of Bartolomeo Scappi.

---

[4] Most notably by Bartolomeo Sacchi, under the pseudonym Platina, in his *De honesta voluptate et valitudine* (c. 1465). This humanistic embroidering on 'Martino' was edited and translated as *Platina, On Right Pleasure and Good Health* by Mary Ella Milham.

[5] Giovanni de Rosselli, *Opera nova chiamata Epulario* (Venice, 1516).

Bartolomeo Scappi

The milieu: Rome in the sixteenth century

$\mathcal{T}$he milieu in which Bartolomeo Scappi lived and worked in the prime of his professional life was that of the paramount court of the western church.[6]   In some respects, secular or ecclesiastic, it was the sovereign court for the whole of Europe. Its constituency was broad; the authority it claimed was superior to that of any secular jurisdiction and, if not enforced by a powerful army, could certainly rely upon spiritual commination. Its self-assurance was rooted in the depth of its organization, its real faculty for gathering wealth, the influence it wielded among the great and small, and in its very perdurability. Only by Scappi's day was that self-assurance being somewhat shaken.

By the middle of the 1400s, the century of the church's Avignonese exile[7] was becoming academic history. Yet the possibility that the church might ever again be other than a Roman institution had left an underlying anxiety in the mind of many Italian clerics. The Great Schism (1378–1417) – during which two separate and distinct papal authorities and successions coexisted in Avignon and in Rome – scarred the end of the Avignonese papacy and was an internecine conflict whose resolution was seen by some as proving the papal displacement merely a temporary aberration. The Schism had, however, confirmed the risk to the church of tolerating any challenge to its central authority. Despite the resolution of the Schism, a factious nationalism had become imbedded in both the sacred and the secular thinking of senior clerics. Conclaves tended thereafter to be riven, or at least tacitly tinged, by conflicts between cabals that were founded in national politics. Electoral ballots were apt to be cast on behalf of Italian and (sometimes) Spanish candidates on the one hand and those representing German, French and English interests on the other.[8]

---

[6] A broad introduction to the time and place is afforded in Partner, *Renaissance Rome 1500–1559*; of particular value for its detailed presentation of ecclesiastical matters is Cochrane, *Italy 1530–1630*.

[7] Otherwise called the Babylonian Captivity, 1309–1408.

[8] Histories of Rome in the sixteenth century necessarily provide illumination on the state, both physical and spiritual, of the church. As well as Partner's work on Renaissance Rome, see Delumeau, *Rome au XVIe siècle*, and the meticulous biographical studies by Hurtubise, 'La "table" d'un cardinal de la Renaissance' and 'Une vie de palais.' Delumeau's work is concerned particularly with conditions of life in and around Rome: roads, inns, buildings, trade, work, coinage,

Apart from such persistent manoeuvring to secure more comprehensive national representation within the Roman church, ecclesiastical authority itself was challenged on several fronts in the fifteenth and sixteenth centuries. The Lutheran reform movement, along with the subsequent counter-reform, stirred a great deal of spiritual ferment yet also encouraged fanaticism and dogmatism on both sides.

In an effort to combat heresy and dissent, the church established the Society of Jesus (1534), founded the Congregation of the Roman Inquisition (1542) and initiated the Index of Forbidden Books (1557). The weapon of excommunication (for example, of Henry VIII in 1533 and 1538) was in ready use. Abuses in religious orders were largely corrected; new orders such as the Congregation of Divine Providence (approved by Clement VII in 1524, later called the Theatines after Cardinal Carafa's bishopric of Chieti), dedicated to poverty and asceticism, were set up.

A few reforms initiated by sixteenth-century popes were aimed at lax procedures in the curia, where simony and corruption were relatively common. Frequently, though, the same popes themselves adopted the inveterate papal practice of dynamic nepotism, investing their teenage (and younger) relatives with a cardinal's scarlet biretta, sinecure and benefits.

The Council of Trent (1545–63) was organized ostensibly to respond to grievances, effect reforms and reconcile differences that had grown among Christians. A few movements, such as that of the *spirituali* guided by Vittoria Colonna and the English cardinal Reginal Pole, attempted to realize one of the initial objectives of the council. Though reform-minded, however, the work of the Council of Trent, pursued despite several suspensions, tended on the whole towards ensuring the legitimacy and hegemony of the Roman church.

The order of the church was being attacked; it reacted in particular instances by forcefully manifesting its sole possession of orthodoxy and indisputable right. The very authority of the pope was questioned with equal persistence and with increasing vigour. In 1527 Rome was sacked and the pope taken prisoner by forces of the Holy Roman Emperor, Charles V. In England in the 1530s Henry VIII's repudiation of papal ascendancy was merely one manifestation of religious dissent extant in Europe since the twelfth century and recently growing. It culminated in the century after Scappi's in France, where Gallicanism denied the pope any authority save in certain matters that were purely ecclesiastic. Furthermore, that authority was severely limited: it was inferior to that of a council, it must conform with the canons of the universal church; papal judgment possessed infallibility only if it was confirmed by the church as a whole. Gallicanism had been condemned in 1512 by the Fifth Lateran Council yet it retained a vigorous and combative life.

---

banking, agriculture and papal finances. He shows that in the second half of the century the city of Rome was beginning to represent by means of noble architectural majesty the power, influence and prestige for which the papacy strove.

Ultimate and supreme authority became of paramount concern for the papal see. That authority was determined and enforced by a series of princes of the church whose spirituality was occasionally of secondary importance to their worldly power and influence. The stresses imposed upon the church demanded men of great, even ruthless, strength. The times allowed that such incarnations of omnipotence were appropriate as guardians and promoters of Christ's truth.

The pontiffs and potentates undoubtedly known to Bartolomeo Scappi are the following:[9]

• Leo X, Giovanni de' Medici (1475–1521; pope, March 1513–December 1521). Second son of Lorenzo the Magnificent of Florence. Cardinal deacon, age thirteen. A Renaissance prince, lover of the arts, 'easygoing and pleasure-loving.'[10] For a number of years during his reign, the pontifical city knew little but a continual round of parties, banquets, country picnics and hunting parties. He burdened the papal see with debts.

• Hadrian VI, Adrian Florensz Dedal (1459–1523; pope, January 1522–September 1523). Rector and chancellor of the University of Louvain; bishop of Tortosa and inquisitor for Aragón, Navarre, Castile and León; cardinal of Utrecht. Ascetic and devout, despised in Rome as a northern 'barbarian.'

• Clement VII, Giulio de' Medici (1479–1525; pope, November 1523–September 1534). A bastard, he was raised by his grandfather Lorenzo the Magnificent. Made archbishop of Florence and cardinal by his cousin Pope Leo X in 1513. As pope he lacked the necessary statesmanship and strength of character to mediate effectively between Francis I of France and the Emperor Charles, both of whom had active designs on Italy. While he vacillated and alternated in his support of each faction, the imperial forces invaded Italy, sacked Rome in 1527 and imprisoned him for six months. Ineffectually he outlawed Luther and excommunicated Henry VIII – both the German Diet and the English church choosing to ignore his edicts. A cultivated man, he was a patron to writers (Guicciardini and Machiavelli) and artists (Cellini, Raphael, Michelangelo).

• Paul III, Alessandro Farnese (1468–1549; pope, October 1534–November

---

[9] See also in the end material of this book, Persons Mentioned in Scappi's *Opera*, a succinct listing of all individuals named either in the preliminary material or named by Scappi in the text itself.

[10] Kelly, *The Oxford Dictionary of Popes*, 258. I am much indebted to this work for fundamental biographical information on the popes who reigned during Scappi's lifetime and whom he likely knew with greater or less intimacy. See also Ludwig von Pastor, *History of the Popes*, vol. 11–2 (Paul III), 13–4 (Julius III, Marcellus II, Paul IV), 15–6 (Pius IV), 17–8 (Pius V), 19–20 (Gregory XIII).

1549.[11]) Although elderly at the time of his election to the pontificate, he worked vigorously on behalf of the church and the aggrandizement of the Farnese family. He was a generous patron of the scholars, artists and writers. 'Under him the Vatican resounded with masked balls and brilliant feasts,'[12] carnival being revived by him in 1536. He approved (1534) the establishment of the Society of Jesus (the Jesuit Order) and of the Congregation of the Roman Inquisition, the central office for combatting heresy. He excommunicated Henry VIII, placed England under an interdiction and encouraged persecution of the French Huguenots.

• Julius III, Giovanni Maria Ciocchi del Monte (1487–1555; pope, February 1550–March 1555). As legate, in 1545 he opened the Council of Trent which sought to impose Roman dogma on all Christians without examining the reforms that some demanded. Typically 'generous to relatives, pleasure-loving, devoted to banquets, the theatre, hunting,'[13] indolent and with markedly worldly interests – including an infatuation with a street juvenile whom he elevated to the cardinalate – Monte supported humanists, artists and musicians (including Marcello Cervini, Michelangelo Buonarotti and Giovanni Pierluigi da Palestrina), spending most of his reign in the luxurious Villa di Papa Giulio just outside Rome. It was his election that required the seventy-one-day conclave that Scappi documents.

• Marcellus II, Marcello Cervini (1501–55; named cardinal by Paul III, 1539; pope for twenty days, April–May 1555).

• Paul IV, Giampietro Carafa (1476–1559; named cardinal by Paul III, 1536; pope, May 1555–August 1559). A conservative, self-willed and authoritarian, a guiding spirit in the Congregation of Divine Providence (the Theatines) and instrumental in Paul III's foundation of the Roman Inquisition; a Neapolitan with an enduring hatred of the Spanish, he stubbornly made war against Spain and swallowed the ignominy of persistent defeat.

• Pius IV, Giovanni Angelo de Medici[14] (1499–1565; pope, December 1559– December 1565). He was legate of Leo X to Henry VIII of England, 1513–14;

---

[11] At the end of his work, after Book VI, Scappi provides a descriptive account of the hours after Paul III's death, of his funeral and of the conclave (29 November 1549–7 February 1550, according to Scappi) at which the cardinals elected his successor. See Appendix I.

[12] Kelly, *The Oxford Dictionary of Popes*, 261.

[13] Ibid., 263.

[14] Of a Milanese family and no immediate relation to the Florentine Medicis. One bare possibility is that Scappi may already have been in the employ of the bishop of Ragusa (Dubrovnik) at the time (1549) in which Giovanni Angelo de Medici was made cardinal by Paul III; it may have been because Scappi was so very competently in this service as cook that he accompanied his master, Cardinal Medichino (as he refers to Giovanni Angelo [Conclave f.a1r]), into the Vatican and was able to observe at first hand the conclave that followed the death of Paul III that very same year. That may have been a very memorable year in his life.

archbishop of Brindisi from 1518; Bishop of Ragusa from 1545; archbishop of Naples from 1549; cardinal, 8 April 1549; dean of the Sacred College of Cardinals from 1553. Formed originally with humanist interests and of a juristic turn of mind, he became a rigid, harsh, reform-minded leader of the Inquisition, establishing (1557) the Index of Forbidden Books; he became aggressively opposed to any reconciliation with the Lutherans, denouncing the peace of Augsburg (1555) that recognized the coexistence of Lutherans and Catholics in the German states. He detested Spanish ascendancy in southern Italy but, like his predecessor, was frustrated by defeat in battle. 'A man admired but dreaded ... as a reformer, the ascetic, self-willed pope laboured with fanatical energy and zeal.'[15] He named Michele Ghislieri to lead the Roman Inquisition.

• Pius V, Michele Ghislieri, Saint (1504–72; pope, January 1566–May 1572; beatified 1672, cononized 1712). Named commissary general of the Roman Inquisition (1551) by Julius III; bishop of Nepi and Sutri (1556), cardinal (1557), and named inquisitor general (1558) by Pius IV. He is noted for his personal and institutional asceticism and for his unflagging persecution of heresy. His Congregation of the Index (1571) harshly punished offending printers and led to a great exodus of them to Germany and Switzerland; in the previous year (the year of Scappi's *Opera*), though, he declared Thomas Aquinas a doctor of the church and had a new edition of his works printed. That same year (1570), in a vigorous struggle for the independence of the church from secular authority, a struggle which alienated most European monarchs, he excommunicated Queen Elizabeth of England and attempted to have her deposed. He was 'single-minded, devout to the point of bigotry, relentless in his persecution of heresy.'[16]

• Gregory XIII, Ugo Boncompagni (Bologna 1502–85; made cardinal by Pius IV, 1565; pope, May 1572–April 1585).

The cardinals and stewards whom Scappi came to know in the course of his professional duties include the following: Lorenzo Campeggio, cardinal bishop of Bologna; Alessandro Casale, priest, chamberlain of Pius V, an executor of Scappi's will; Federigo Donati, personal physician to Pius V; Marino Grimano, cardinal bishop of Venice; Hora, a cleric; Rodolfo Pio, cardinal of Carpi, dean of the Sacred College; and Francesco (di) Reinoso, priest, personal steward and chamberlain of Pius V.

In striving to enhance their common and individual glory most popes and cardinals felt justified in seeking a life of exceptional, even exalted, refinement. For the most part they maintained courts whose worldly magnificence often rivalled

---

[15] Kelly, *The Oxford Dictionary of Popes*, 265.

[16] Ibid., 269.

those of secular princes.[17]   In one way or another the pope, the prelates and the large corps of individuals attendant upon both pope and prelates relied upon the grandeur of the papal court to assure and declare their status.   Symbolic of ecclesiastic power, the pomp, splendour and magnificence of the courts in Rome were founded in large measure upon the foods that were prepared, served and consumed in those courts two and three times each day.   A cardinal's court could employ a household staff of some seventy persons of which roughly half contributed in some way to food preparation or service.[18]

Scappi's life

F ew dates are available by which to fix the time, place or activities of Scappi's life. Most of them are provided incidentally by Scappi himself in his text.   Only recently have additional references to the man been unearthed and the details of his life been a little more fully fleshed out.[19]

   In Book IV, Scappi documents two dinners given in Rome. On f.320r [1581 f.269r], a menu is identified as for a dinner offered in April 1536 by Cardinal Campeggio for the Holy Roman Emperor Charles V.[20] While relatively few notable guests were served, this meal, with its five sideboard servings and seven kitchen servings – each of which averaged more than a dozen different *lean* preparations – must have been an enormous and memorable tour de force for any cook.   Then on f.304r [1581 f.252v], another, lighter meal can be precisely dated to 14 March 1549: this is a collation arranged by the Parisian cardinal Jean Du Bellay (cardinal,

---

[17] In this regard see the finely documented studies by Hurtubise of the rich courts of Alessandro Farnese (1520–89, cardinal from 1534 and vice chancellor of the church from 1535) and of Bernardo Salviati (1508–68, cousin and protégé of Queen Caterina de' Medici of France, cardinal from 1561) in, respectively, 'Une vie de palais' and 'La "table" d'un cardinal de la Renaissance.' By the same author, '"De honesta voluptate" et l'art de bien manger à Rome pendant la Renaissance' argues the primordial importance of food in ecclesiastical courts.

[18] Hurtubise, 'La "table" d'un cardinal de la Renaissance,' 260. *Excluding* salaries, sixty-five percent of the Salviati court's budget in Rome was devoted to food: ibid., 280. Laurioux shows that the role of gastronomy in luxurious Roman life was well established in the previous century. In his *Gastronomie, humanisme et société à Rome au milieu du XVe siècle* see especially chapter 6, 'À la table des papes,' 441–529.

[19] The archival research of Di Schino and Luccichenti, reported in their *Bartolomeo Scappi cuoco nella Roma del cinquecento*, is of particular value in this respect.

[20] 'Dinner given in Trastevere by the Most Illustrious and Most Reverend Cardinal Lorenzo Campeggio of Bologna for His Holy Roman Majesty Emperor Charles V when his Majesty entered Rome in the month of April, 1536, during Lent; to begin with, the board was set with four cloths which were perfumed and worked in various ways and had twelve napkins; with five servings from the sideboard and seven from the kitchen, served on three platters, not counting His Imperial Majesty's platter, with three stewards and three carvers.'

1535–60) as part of a celebration of the birth of a son to the king of France on the previous 3 February.[21]

Because he has stated in his preamble to Book IV that the calendar of menus that follows comprises meals that were 'made by myself' (*fatti da me*), we must suppose that by the year 1536 Scappi was established as a proficient master cook, and that he was in the employ of Cardinal Campeggio 'of Bologna' in some capacity. That position likely lasted up to the death of the cardinal in Rome, July 1539. If that is so, whether his principal kitchen was then in Bologna or, much more likely, in the cardinal's more-or-less permanent establishment in the Trastevere quarter of Rome, the date 1536 is certainly significant in Scappi's life. We may likewise suppose that Scappi's employer by the spring of 1549 was one of the Italians seated at Cardinal Du Bellay's board during the collation that Scappi outlines in Book IV (f.304r [1581 f.252v]). Among the twelve persons, all cardinals, eight were Italians: Farnese, Santangelo, Santa Fiore, Sermoneta, Ridolfo, Pisano, Cornaro and Gaddi.[22] Several of the cardinals' cooks may have assisted in preparing meals on that festive occasion, a celebration whose various activities extended over a number of days. It is not at all certain that Scappi was necessarily in the employ of Cardinal Du Bellay at that time.

We may, however, suppose that, having by 1536 acquired sufficient competence and maturity to be responsible for the complex meal offered the holy Roman emperor, Scappi must have been born near the beginning of the century. Obviously that is pure speculation, but it is not invalidated or weakened by the year of his death: 1577. By the 1560s, when he must have been compiling his *Opera*, Scappi would indeed have reached the peak of his career, would by then have largely trained another cook whose advanced apprenticeship had been entrusted

---

[21] 'Collation given at the end of February at Monte Cavallo, in the hall of the Most Illustrious and Most Reverend Cardinal Du Bellay, at one o'clock at night [that is, one hour after nightfall, about 7:00 pm for the month of March], after which a play in French, Bergamask, Venetian and Spanish was declaimed; with four servings, served on eight platters, with eight stewards and eight carvers' (f.304r [1581 f.252v]). Scappi's recollection of the date of the meal is faulty. However, it should be noted that he invariably dates his collations to 'the end of' each month in his calendar of menus.

[22] Of those eight Italian cardinals, it may be noted that two of the three Farnese brothers, Ranuccio (1530–65) and Alessandro (1520–89: 'Santangelo,' whom Scappi calls Santo Angelo), were seated together, and that the third, Duke Horatio (1531–53) was the principal combattant in the day's mock battles; all were grandsons of Pope Paul III who died later that same year, and whose funeral and the subsequent conclave are so carefully documented by Scappi. Eleven of the twelve cardinals at Du Bellay's table in March 1549 appear as well in Scappi's enumeration of participants in that conclave. (See Persons Mentioned in Scappi's *Opera*, below.)

It is perhaps because of this important culinary activity prior to February of 1550 that Lemaître writes in her *Saint Pie V*, 112, that Scappi was *préfet des cuisines depuis Paul III* and that he had been *en place depuis Paul III au palais pontifical* (360, n. 19). There is, however, no documentary evidence to support that conjecture.

to him – his Giovanni.[23] Both Francisco Reinoso and Giovanni were established in the personal service of Cardinal Antonio (*alias* Michele) Ghislieri and seem to have remained so when he was elected pope as Pius V in 1566, the one as papal steward, the other as an assistant under the direction of Scappi himself. It was then in 1566 that Scappi came to know both the steward and his new assistant, and one imagines that as the austere character of the new pope became more apparent to the papal chef, the friendship of his kindly, helpful superior, the papal chamberlain, became very valuable to him. It was to Reinoso that Scappi dedicated his culinary compendium and it was Reinoso whom Scappi calls at the very beginning of Book I, writing in the plural for both himself and his apprentice, the 'advocate of every good thing we enjoy': *mediatore d'ogni bene che havemo*. Both Reinoso and Giovanni, the two for whom Scappi expresses the warmest affection, came into his life at a time when he would likely have needed something like personal support.

Cardinal Campeggio was born in Milan in 1474 and died in Rome in July 1539, three years after offering to the emperor the grand banquet for which Scappi was at least largely responsible. At another place in his work Scappi writes (Recipe II,149): 'When I was in Venice in the service of Cardinal Marino Grimano … ' That cultured luminary was cardinal between 1527 and his death in 1546, so that – competent cooks with a solidly proven record not being easily come by then or now – Scappi may have been taken up by the Venetian cardinal at some time after 1539, and perhaps immediately after Cardinal Campeggio's death. Within the circle of Italian cardinals who maintained more or less splendid courts in Rome, Scappi's contribution to Campeggio's worldly splendour must have been recognized. It is probable that Scappi remained in the employ of Cardinal Grimano until 1546. He would have acquired most of his extensive knowledge of Venetian cookery during these years in his life.

Other dates mentioned in the *Opera* relate to Scappi's past work. The year 1548 is recalled (mistakenly) twice: in it he made a concentrate for 'Cardinal Pietro Bembo' (mentioned in Scappi's Recipe VI,23, though that date had to be 1547: Bembo died 19 January of that year) and a *sussidio* for the 'Most Illustrious and

---

[23] The name of a certain Giovanni appears in account registers of the Ghislieri household and is qualified as 'personal cook,' *cuoco segreto*, to the family, before Michele Ghislieri became Pope Pius V. (See Firpo, *Gastronomia del Rinascimento*, 21, n. 36.) Di Schino and Luccichenti have identified Scappi's Giovanni with the Ghislieri family's cook, Giovanni Valfredo de Meldula (*Bartolomeo Scappi*, 23 and n. 28; *Il cuoco segreto dei papi*, 19, n. 29, and 23). The same authors (*Bartolomeo Scappi*, 41) note that a Giovanni di Cruce was named personal cook to Pius V along with Scappi. Clearly Giovanni was hardly a novice under Scappi, even though in the *Opera* the latter describes him as young. Scappi's will of April 1571 contains the provision of a bequest to his assistant when he had reached the age of thirty-four (*ibid.*, 23).

A 'Francesco Brinoso' (that is – most certainly – Rinoso) was, or had been, steward also to the Ghislieri family, having entered service there in 1557.

Most Reverend Cardinal Jacomo Sadoleto of Modena *in Rome*' (VI,28; that prelate died in October 1547). The close friendship between the two cardinals may explain that each in turn, in his sickness, called upon the increasingly respected cook of another member of the Sacred College – a cook who happened at both moments of the year to be working in Rome presumably for an ecclesiastic employer.

What we may further infer about Scappi's life towards the end of the 1540s is that at the time of the great conclave of 1549 Scappi was in Rome in attendance almost certainly upon a certain cardinal who was participating in that conclave. In whose employ was Scappi at that time? Had he previously actually been in the household of either Cardinal Bembo or Cardinal Sadoleto, or of each successively? Or had his master on those occasions simply instructed him to prepare the concentrate and *sussidio*, respectively, as a compassionate gesture to an ailing fellow cardinal? We do not know. Certainly he was never in the service of Pope Paul III, whose death and funeral he observes from the outside, as it were, and describes without any subjective commentary about the person who had died. After 1549–50 there were four conclaves that in all probability Scappi had occasion to observe as closely as in 1549; the one that elected Pius IV (in 1559), his future master, lasted a surprising four months,[24] yet to his *Opera* he appends only that early chronicle of the 1549 conclave, an event whose circumstances clearly had made a strong and lasting impression upon him.[25] To repeat, at the time of that conclave it would seem reasonable to suppose that Scappi was working in Rome, even temporarily, perhaps attending one of those cardinals for whom he prepared the collation in March of that same year, 1549: Jean Du Bellay (the host for the celebration), Ranuccio Farnese, Santangelo (Alessandro Farnese), Santa Fiore (Guido Ascanio Sforza), Niccolò Caetani di Sermoneta, Ridolfi (who may be either Nicolò Ridolfo or Rodolfo Pio da Carpi), Francesco Pisani, Andrea Cornaro or Nicolò Gaddi.[26]

---

[24] See Theodor Müller, *Das Konklave Pius IV. 1559 historische Abhandlung* (Gotha: Friedrich Andreas Perthes, 1889).

[25] It might be apropos to consider briefly here the quality of that appended document. The preciseness of the author's observations in 1549–50 is remarkable, given what we might assume to be a two-decade lapse of time before the printing of the *Opera*. It seems that Scappi must have written much of the material on those pages close to the very time the events were taking place. Interestingly, the narrative tenses in the account tend to vary to a surprising extent between an historical past tense and the present. As a faithful and observant chronicle the pages signal the man's narrative interest and skills, and present evidence of his organizational ability; the account hints of later, much larger writing ambitions.

[26] It is particularly interesting to note that the Roman estates of cardinals Grimano (d. 1546), Pio da Carpi (d. 1564) and Du Bellay (d. 1560) were located near one another on the slopes of Mount Quirinal. Evidence exists of strong ties between Scappi (and his apprentice, Giovanni) and one or the other of those cardinals, in particular Grimano and especially Rodolfo Pio da Carpi. It is not beyond reasonable supposition that Scappi was a welcome familiar in all three households.

The rubric of Scappi's Recipe V,80 gives not only the name of the dish, a royal white tourte, but – with evidence of a familiarity with the pope's gastronomic taste and a suggestion of Scappi's own professional pride – adds the qualification 'which used to be favoured by Pope Julius III.' Following the death of Paul III, Giovanni Maria Ciocchi del Monte (1487–1555) was elected pope as Julius III at that very conclave which held such interest for Scappi. The note at the head of Recipe V,80 is in part a testimonial to the tourte's reputation but more importantly suggests that Scappi himself had some occasion, whether in the long term or incidental, to offer that dish to the pope. He does not say. But the implication may be there that del Monte, the cardinal bishop of Palestrina, 'pleasure-loving, devoted to banquets,'[27] *may* have had Scappi in his suite of personal attendants at some time during his reign.

In 1551 Scappi prepared a broth for the Most Illustrious and Most Reverend Cardinal Andrea Cornaro (VI,19); Cornaro died on 30 January 1551. Then we find next in the *Opera* that at the end of April 1564 he made a concentrate for the Most Illustrious and Most Reverend Cardinal da Carpi, Rodolfo Pio (VI,21); Carpi died on 2 May 1564.

Between 1551 and 1564 there seem to be no documented dates for Scappi by which we can fill in that decade of his life. If we look again at the community on Mount Quirinal we may not consider it strange to propose that Scappi's professional association with the house of Rodolfo Pio da Carpi may well have begun soon after the death of Marin Grimano, on 28 September 1546. To pursue the conjecture further, he may have accompanied Carpi to the Du Bellay festivities at the beginning of 1549 and cooked for him later in the year when his master attended the conclave. It would have been while in Carpi's personal service that Scappi witnessed and recorded all the formal arrangements of a papal funeral and a subsequent conclave.

Revealing deep feelings of gratitude, as towards a longtime and considerate master, Scappi begins the first page of his book with a reference to the *fe. me. del Reverendiss. Card. de Carpi Patrone nostro* (' … our patron of blessed memory, the Very Reverend Cardinal da Carpi'), invoking the cardinal's wish that Scappi take Giovanni as his apprentice and teach him a mastery of the culinary craft. Such a request would surely be made only by a master to a servant with regard to another servant. Again, in the preamble to his Book VI, considering a cook's obligation to consider the dietary needs of the sick, Scappi writes, … & *massime con la buona memoria del Reverendiss. Cardinale di Carpi, nelle sue lunghe malatie, come voi sapete* … ('and above all with the Most Reverend Cardinal da Carpi, of blessed memory, during his long illness, as you know … '). The important words are, of course, *patrone nostro* in the first passage: not only does Scappi declare that he

---

[27] Kelly, *Oxford Dictionary of Popes*, 263a.

served Rodolfo Pio as cook but that Giovanni was a member, albeit perhaps junior in mastery of the profession, of the same household. In the second passage it is clear that both Scappi and Giovanni remained in the employ of Rodolfo Pio until his death in 1564.

In 1564, Scappi writes, he prepared frogs for Pope Pius IV in the way the pope was used to eating them (Recipe III,163); often in the same year, 1564, he made a barley gruel for the Sovereign Pontiff Pius IV (VI,57): *Molte volte usava di pigliarne Pio IIII Pontefice massimo nel 64.* Those two recollections seem clearly to establish the arrival of Scappi's career at its zenith. To repeat: towards the end of April 1564, he was providing a sickdish for Cardinal Carpi; the cardinal died on 2 May of that year; that same year he was preparing food in the papal kitchen and was familiar with the pope's taste in dishes. The year 1564 appears as a solid milestone in Scappi's life.

The last date that we possess from Scappi himself and that serves to chronicle his life lacks something in firmness. Depending on where the date is read in the printed text, it is either 27 January 1567 (Book IV, f.168v [1581 f. 133v]) or 17 January 1566 (Book IV, f.186r [1581 f.237v]). On that day Scappi, as the pope's personal cook, was responsible for a banquet on the occasion of Pius V's 'second coronation,' or second anniversary of his coronation.[28] To that anniversary banquet were invited any cardinals who happened to be in residence in Rome as well as ambassadors to the Holy See and local secular dignitaries. In the historical event Pius V, a man of decidedly ascetic inclinations, may have recognized the obligation to offer the first, customarily lavish banquet that celebrated the beginning of his reign – a banquet held perhaps on the date, 17 January 1566, that is

---

[28] It was customary to celebrate a pope's coronation annually by means of a banquet. The first date that Scappi writes for the 'second coronation,' 1567, seems the more probable. In any case the banquet for which Scappi reproduces the menu did not actually take place: the new pope, perhaps in a move dictated by his well documented ascetic austerity, cancelled that supreme gastronomic event. Scappi's disappointment – not to say probable chagrin: he still published what he *intended* for the meal – can only be guessed in the words with which he qualified it: *il preparamento d'un convito* (the *preparation* of a banquet,' f.168v [1581 f.133v]) and *Pranzo preparato ... quale poi non si fece, & si haveva da servire ...* ('a dinner which was *prepared* ... which then was not held ... and was to have served ... ' f.186r [1581 f.237v]).

It is in a sense almost pathetically ironic that the influence of such an austere reformer as Carlo Borromeo (1538–84; cardinal from 1560) should have been exerted upon the tradition of ostentatious papal splendour at the very time that Scappi had a chance to let his culinary skill shine in ever greater universal glory. It is also likely, however, that in the course of Pius IV's six-year pontificate the convivial pope became increasingly swayed by the devout asceticism of his nephew, Borromeo: 'A partir de 1563, Charles Borromée réduisait considérablement son train de vie et les dimensions de sa cour. Il finit par convaincre son oncle, Pie IV, d'en faire autant' (Hurtubise, 'Une vie de palais,' n.45). As pope, Scappi's master reconvened the reformist Council of Trent and ensured it a solid conclusion. Following Pius IV, the election on 7 January 1566 of Michele Ghislieri, as Pius V, brought exceptionally frugal and abstemious convictions to the See of Rome; Cardinal Borromeo exercised an effectual influence upon that election.

printed on f.186r [1581 f.237v] in Book IV. By January of the following year, however, Pius V had sufficiently taken the reins of authority to cancel the annual celebratory banquet, a supreme culinary and gastronomic tour de force of which Scappi had already planned the principal details.

The banquet that was to commemorate Pius V's coronation was to be indeed a long and sumptuous affair. More significantly, the grandiose, demanding menu shows that Scappi was certainly still very much in harness, professionally speaking, in the early years of that pope's reign. The privilege that the pope granted to the Tramezzino brothers on 29 March 1570 betrays no lack of support for his highly proficient cook: he terms Scappi *peritissimus Magister*, 'a most skilled master,' and identifies him as *nunc profectus est nostris intimis Coquis*, 'currently designated our personal cook.'

Concerning the *Opera*, we must bear in mind that the publication date of April 1570 is in all but one respect not too precise a marker about Scappi's life. Printers required up to a full year to set such a long book in type, and Scappi was almost certainly assembling his material over many years. We may imagine the amount of free time – to say nothing of the void of professional frustration – that he must have experienced when Pius V established his abstinent vegetarian regimen at the papal board. Scappi may have been delivering his manuscript to Francesco Tramezzino in Rome by the late 1560s. The publication privilege – a sort of copyright protection granted to the printer – from Cosmo de' Medici (for ten years) is dated 2 January 1570; that from the Senate of Venice on behalf of the Republic (for twenty years), 22 March 1570; and that from Pius V (for ten years), 29 March 1570.[29] The Medici and papal documents state without qualification that Scappi was cook to Pius V on the dates of those documents, both of them

---

[29] The Tramezzino bothers, Francesco and Michele, who benefitted from this multiple protection, were first established as printers in Rome. Following the sack of that city in 1527 both brothers went back to Venice where Michele set up his printery. Within a year Francesco returned to Rome, primarily to maintain the brothers' business and commercial contacts there. He became, in fact, a close acquaintance of several Roman nobles and prelates, people of influence. As it happened, Bartolomeo Scappi himself became one of his friends. (In This Translation and Commentary, below, see a brief discussion of the two Tramezzino printings of Scappi's work.)

The printing establishment to which Scappi entrusted his *Opera* had already in 1560 handled the cookery book of Domenico Romoli (surnamed Panunto), *La singolar dottrina*. Venice had also been the place where Rosselli's *Epulario* was repeatedly printed (between 1516 and 1534), along with the second and all subsequent ten editions (from 1552 up to 1600) of Messisbugo's *Banchetti*. (See the Bibliography.) With Roman printers directly under the eye of increasingly censorious counter-reformists, and devoted particularly to publishing grave juridical and theological matters in Latin, Venetian printers seem to have been more willing to volunteer their services for subjects of as sensually, not to say carnally, mundane a nature as food and cooking. In any case exports of printed works constituted a major source of income for sixteenth-century Venice. In granting a *twenty*-year privilege to the Tramezzinos, the Senate recognized the value of such an enterprise.

issued at the beginning of 1570. After Pius V died in May 1572, his successor, Ugo Boncompagni (Gregory XIII), came to the Vatican with his own personal cook, an arrangement which was perfectly normal. An old man by then, Bartolomeo Scappi must have accepted that his professional life was closed.

Where was Scappi born? His place of birth was likely in the north, in Lombardy, the Veneto or Emilia. The priest of the church of San Giorgio in Dumenza, a commune of Runo (near Lago Maggiore and north east of Luino), recently brought to light the existence of a plaster plaque on the third right-hand pillar of his church. While itself undated, the plaque combines references to both the consecration of the church (26 July 1581) and a bequest for a perpetual mass for the soul of a certain Bartolomeo Sclappi, Lateran count and knight.[30] Despite the misspelling of his surname, given that such bequests were normally made to a church of the donor's birthplace, the little hamlet of Dumenza appears indeed certain to have been Scappi's place of origin.

An archival register in the same church in Dumenza declares that his death occurred *il 13 Aprile 1577 in Roma.* That date and place of death is confirmed in the archives of the Ospedale della Santa Trinità dei Pellegrini in Rome where the entry reads, again, 'at Rome, 13 April 1577.' On the following day, 14 April, he was buried at the church of Saints Vincenzo and Anastasio alla Regola, where the guild chapel of the brotherhood of cooks and pastrymen was located.

And yet he did not account himself a native merely of Dumenza, or of Runo or Luino. In several documents he is qualified in a larger sense as a Milanese. Scappi formulated a testament, dated 10 April 1571, which still survives. In it he calls himself a native of Milan: *Dominus Bartholomeus Scappus Mediolanensis, coquus secretus Sanctissimi Domini Nostri Pii Quinti*: 'Lord Bartolomeo Scappi, Milanese, personal cook of our most holy lord Pius V.' Likewise a registry of deaths for the parish of St Peter in Rome shows, with an inaccurate transcription of the name, *Nicolo Scampi milanese coco di Pio V sepolto alla chiesa di coci a di 14 detto*: 'Nicolo Scampi, Milanese, cook of Pius V, buried at the church of the cooks on the 14 of this month [that is, of April 1577].' Though a revision of his testament, signed 14 May 1576, superseded the earlier one, it has not yet been found. However at least some of its provisions are known from the processes it

---

[30] The text of the plaque reads: *Gregorii XIII Pontificis Maximi signifer Comes Palatinus Lateranensis et Æques Bartolomeus Sclappius ædem hanc perenni dote honestavit obstrinxitque ad unam singula quaque hebdemoda* [sic] *missam duo quoque annualia missarum V Deo Optimo Maximo ac Divo Georgio S. Carolus ædem hanc cum altari et coemeterio dicavit anno 1581 die 26 Iulii Cesar Briuscus nepos et cohæres fecit fieri curato presbitero Baptista Asconino* (reproduced by Pierangelo Frigerio, 'I cuochi dei laghi lombardi,' 81 in *Bartolomeo Scappi il lombardo Michelangelo della cucina*, 70–92). The text of the plaque is found also, with commentary, in Benporat, 'Bartolomeo Scappi, il mistero svelato,' 81; a photograph of the plaque is printed in Di Schino and Luccichenti, *Il cuoco segreto dei papi*, 25.

entailed.[31] Specifically in that document Scappi again declared explicitly the land of his origin: *Ms Bartholomeo de Scappi Milanese Mazzero già di N.S.*[32]

One final particular of Scappi's life is also without any firm date but is nonetheless singular. In the previous text, not from Scappi's pen or that of any civic or ecclesiastical official but from his nephew, is an attribution to him of the function of papal *mazzero*. We must accept the designation at face value, even though the word *già*, 'formerly,' written a year and a half after Scappi's death, may relate the appointment to either of the popes he served, Pius IV or Pius V.[33]

As with the other titles that Scappi apparently claimed – 'Lateran count and knight' – the function of mace bearer was largely honorary. Though the office had to be bought, it carried with it a stipend and a suit of ceremonial clothing. Supposing this last charge of Scappi's to be historically authentic, the investiture must have occured within the last years of his life, along with the other two honours. Certainly none of the three had been bestowed upon the papal cook of Pius V by the year 1570: the author, or the publisher, of the *Opera* would surely have declared on its title page that Bartolomeo Scappi was not *merely* a cook but had possessed himself of some standing at the papal court. Nor would those authorities who granted the printers a publishing privilege, including Pius V himself, likely have failed to cite the dignities that had been accorded the author.

---

[31] Di Schino and Luccichenti, *Bartolomeo Scappi*, 27, n. 38 and 28, n. 39; these biographical data, with others, are reproduced in the first chapter of the same authors' *Il cuoco segreto dei papi*. The authors also point out in that second work (23, n. 43) that had Scappi been married he would likely have arranged for some sort of memorial or bequest to his wife; no mention is made of her in the 1571 will. In that first testament Scappi's universal heir is a nephew, Giovanni Stefano Brioschi. In the second testament, of 1577, a person charged with fulfilling a term of the will is another nephew, by the name of Cesare Brioschi. This is presumably the person whose name appears engraved on the stone plaque mounted in the church at Dumenza. (Bartolomeo's sister, Caterina, married a certain Nazeo Brioschi as well.) Among the three executors named in the first testament is a Monsignor Casale. This personage, a Roman noble and the personal chamberlain of Pius V, had indeed earned the trust and respect of both Scappi and Giovanni. In the *Opera* he appears twice, as a man to whom both cooks felt much gratitude (Book I, preamble), and as a person who had urged Scappi to publish his work (Book VI, preamble).

[32] According to Di Schino and Luccichenti, the sentence is found in a letter dated 4 November 1578 from the nephew Cesare Brioschi: *Bartolomeo Scappi*, 31, n. 47. These are virtually the words pronounced by the parish priest, Giuseppe Parapini, at the re-unveiling of the memorial tablet in his church of San Giorgio of Runo 23 May 1998: *Il presente officio di Messa è ordinato per l'anima di messer Bartolomeo de Scapi, milanese, mazziere di Nostro Signore* (as reported by Massimo Alberini in his preface to *Bartolomeo Scappi il Lombardo Michelangelo della cucina*, 9).

[33] Indirect evidence of the historicity of the appointment is afforded in Scappi's first testament. Among his bequests he directs that a silver mace, engraved with the arms of Pius V and worth 114 *scudo*s, should pass to the eldest legitimate male offspring of his nephew Giovanni Stefano Brioschi. See Di Schino and Luccichenti, *Bartolomeo Scappi*, 29.

The various laurels, *comes palatinus lateranensis, æques* and *mazzero*, must have come from the hand presumably of either Pius V (who died in May of 1572) or, a little less plausibly, his successor, Gregory XIII.[34]

Scappi himself writes of the ceremonial functions of both a cardinal's *mazziere* and papal *mazzieri*, mace bearer(s), in his account of the 1549–50 conclave following Pope Paul III's death (ff.A1r, A2v and A3v [1581 ff.A1r, A2v and A3v]). It was an honorific charge exercised during ecclesiastical ceremonies. Scappi was even careful to ensure that the engraver of the plates for his book included a representation of that official.[35]

Before the recent discovery of documentary evidence about Scappi's life – the fruit of much patient and assuredly exhausting labour by June Di Schino and Furio Luccichenti – a range of proposals had been argued about the cook's place of origin and work. In 1966 Emilio Faccioli proposed that Scappi was Venetian because of certain dialectal traces in his writing.[36] Other scholars proposed Bologna as his homeland.[37] More recently Claudio Benporat reinforced the grounds for that connection.[38] The Bolognese connection in Scappi's life is clear. His work for Cardinal Lorenzo Campeggio, whom he seems deliberately to identify as Bolognese, was historical since it involves the imperial banquet of April

---

[34] The engraved coat of arms which floats alongside the portrait of Bartolomeo Scappi in editions of the *Opera* from 1570 onward shows no sign of anything that might symbolize a Lateran count or knight or mace bearer. Di Schino and Luccichenti point out the office of mace bearer was likely acquired at some moment during the year between the printing of his book's title page (presumably in 1570) and the date of his first testament of 10 April 1571 (*Il cuoco segreto dei papi*, 19, n. 32). In addition to those honours, bought or bestowed upon Scappi, Pope Gregory XIII (14 May 1572–10 April 1585) seems also to have appointed him *mastro di casa*, steward of his household: see Benporat, 'Bartolomeo Scappi, il mistero svelato,' 82.

[35] See the lower right of Scappi's engraved Plate 21 in Appendix II, below, where the office of a cardinal's mace bearer is being exercised at the head of a procession bearing food to a conclave.

[36] Faccioli, *Arte della cucina*, II, 15. Faccioli did not say what peculiarities of dialect he notes in Scappi's language. Luigi Firpo cautioned against placing too much value on such evidence (*Gastronomia del Rinascimento*, 22, n. 38). The typesetters in 1570 and 1581 were likely Venetian themselves in any case.

[37] Firpo (op. cit., 23), for one, cites the presence of a family called Scappi in Bologna – in the seventeenth century. In the introductory essay of his *Bartolomeo Scappi, Opera dell'Arte del cucinare*, vi–xvi, Giancarlo Roversi reviews the bases for the various proposals advanced for Scappi's homeland, Bologna, Venice and Lombardy.

[38] In a brief note entitled 'Bartolomeo Scappi e le sue origini bolognesi,' Benporat adduced several lines by Girolamo Leopardi, a Florentine poet, in a 1613 publication (that is to say, some forty years after Scappi had made his mark on the world), in which he writes concerning Scappi (and soup), 'Che ne lesse in Bologna, e tenne scuola, / In quel suo libro celo manifesta.' (*Appunti di Gastronomia*, 9:5–8.) For Benporat, Leopardi certifies in those lines that Scappi ran a cooking school in Bologna. Nevertheless, the sense of the lines could equally be that Scappi taught by means of his book.

1536 for which Scappi was responsible.[39] In a different sense Scappi's references to Alessandro Casale, also a native of Bologna, are somewhat more personal than professional.[40] In the one case, both Scappi and Giovanni acknowledge an obligation to that cardinal; in the other, Scappi seems gratified that Casale showed enough respect for the cook's work to urge him to give his work to a printer.

Scappi clearly did spend some part of his professional life in Venice, employed, as he says at one point (Recipe II,149), in the service of Cardinal Marino Grimano. Cardinal Grimano died in 1546. At another point (Recipe III,79) Scappi further comments, 'When I was in Venice and Ravenna … ,' suggesting that his stay in Ravenna may have been on the same basis and occasioned by the same circumstances as his life in Venice. His single reference (Recipe VI,23) to Cardinal Bembo, the first historian of the Venetian Republic, qualifies the man with his place of origin, Venice: *l'Illustrissimo & Reverendissimo Cardinale Pietro Bembo Venetiano*. There is something in that qualification that seems intended to magnify the significance of both the cardinal and perhaps also, by extension, Scappi's role in sustaining the venerable man in his last hours.

References to Venetian dishes are far from rare among Scappi's recipes and include *brisavoli alla venetiana, rape alla venetiana, potaggi alla venetiana* and *frittelle alla venetiana*. He is also quite aware of what foodstuffs are available in the fields, fisheries and markets in and around Venice and throughout the neighbouring lands of Chiozza, Brondoli and Comacchio (Recipe III,155) and from the Sile River by Treviso. He is, furthermore, remarkably well acquainted with foodstuffs that customarily arrived from Slavonia (Croatia) to the east[41] and with commercial activity along the upper Adriatic to the west, as far as Senigallia and inland to Ravenna.

There can be no doubt that, to whichever locale Scappi was most indebted for either his early life (and perhaps training) or professional employment, his repertoire of recipes and the experience he garnered and that he so frequently transmits as advice in his *Opera* testify to an exposure to the culinary customs of a broad assortment of Italian regions. The relative importance in Scappi's text of some regions over others may have some significance.

---

[39] The cardinal is mentioned at two places in Book IV (alone), on ff.168v and 320r [1581 ff.133v and 269r], both with regard to the banquet although both mentions contain the explicit qualification of Campeggio as *Bolognese*.

[40] See the preambles to Book I and Book VI.

[41] Note, for instance, Scappi's reminiscence in Recipe III,48: … *Per quel che ho veduto nella Schiavonia* … (See the references to Slavonia in Index 6.) The fact that Giovanni Angelo de Medici (as Pope Pius IV Scappi's employer) was Bishop of Ragusa (Dubrovnik) from 1545 may not be insignificant. For a more complete inventory of dishes that Scappi associates with the Veneto, see the section Scappi's cookery: his preferred processes, dishes, below.

The influence of Bologna is acknowledged in but a single dish in the whole of Scappi's work: *torte d'herbe alla Bolognese* (Recipe V,96). References to Bologna are more those of an inquisitive and observant visitor than of a native or long-time resident who possessed an intimate knowledge of Bolognese taste or custom. Scappi is able (Recipe III,162) to state that frogs abound generally in Lombardy but more so in Bologna: *Per tutta Italia n'è gran copia, ma molto maggiore in Lombardia, che altrove, et maggiormente nel territorio di Bologna* – in which latter place, he adds much as a surprised spectator, they are transported in bags on carts. He further describes their habitat and croaking, rather as if he had been impressed by peculiar phenomena during a sojourn. Similarly he writes of the Bolognese custom of using large pieces of tripe in prepared dishes.

The province of Romagna, centred on Bologna, receives a rare mention, as the source of a cheese, *cascio Romagnolo* (Book IV, ff.289r and 327v [1581 ff.239v and 275r]) and as the origin of a dish called *coppi romagnoli* (Recipe V,85). Scappi notes (Recipe II,136) also that generally in both La Marca and Romagna small birds are stored in millet.

Milan and its environs in Lombardy seem to have provided considerably more experience and education for Scappi. Foods and foodstuffs that are expressly Milanese about which Scappi writes include *mostaccioli milanesi, cervellati milanesi* and *cauli milanesi*, Milanese almonds, Milanese rice, Milanese saveloy – though, as with those foodstuffs that relate to Bologna, it should be borne in mind that, inter-regional commerce being well developed in sixteenth-century Italy, the fact that a cook in a noble household anywhere there could compare and prefer produce from many different quarters of the peninsula, and beyond, is not at all surprising. What is noteworthy is that Scappi knows that the markets of Milan receive and offer a number of preferred foodstuffs: 'Ho veduto,' he writes (Recipe III,161) – 'I have seen in the fish markets of Milan small fish called *marscioni* and in Milan *bottuli*.' A variety of good fish are available in Milan: burbots (Recipe III,129), rudd (III,130), large tench (III,138), large pike (III,146) and large crayfish, (III,176). He writes about a walnut sauce *alla Milanese*. Not imported but raised as a local, domestic product in Milan 'and elsewhere in Lombardy' are storks (II,142).

Perhaps even more significant than his knowledge of Milanese food is Scappi's reference to specific Milanese measures of weight, *libre Milanesi* – as if, perhaps, they were units that he had become accustomed to using. He does not explicitly identify any other regional unit of weight. And, very remarkably, he points out peculiar medical practices in Lombardy, where a sick person is allowed to eat tench (Recipe III,125), and in Milan, where physicians prescribe *zabaglione* for pregnant women (VI,64).

Scappi's reference to Milan's surrounding region, Lombardy, is even more extensive. In his book he offers recipes for *suppa lombarda, riso alla lombarda, torta* and *tortelletti alla lombarda*. He is familiar with local Lombard names for particular fish (III,70) which are known otherwise elsewhere; he is familiar with the Lombard name, *sfogliati*, for the Neapolitan dish called *coppi* (V,49). He provides a recipe (III,253) for which the rubric is only a descriptive *Minestra di fagioli secchi*, but adds a more definite identification by writing, *Tal vivanda in Lombardia si chiama macco*: 'That dish is called *macco* in Lombardy.' Rather repetitively among his recipes, Scappi incorporates varieties of soups and sops *alla Lombarda*. He writes of a Lombard garnish on a soup (II,205). He has a rice dish *alla Lombarda* (II,156), and a herb dish *alla Lombarda* (V,92). He reports (III,162) the practice, apparently unusual, that frogs are eaten whole in some places in Lombardy. And he refers to the manner of making *cascatelle alla Bresciana* (V,150).

Rice is a dependable Lombard product for Scappi (Recipe III,221). Einkorn, he knows, too, is grown in quantity in Lombardy; he is also familiar with the uses to which it is put in Lombardy (II,185; V,88). Lombard rice, he advises, should be preferred (III,221); chub fish from Lombardi are to be favoured (V,187).

Scappi refers to the Milan canal (Recipe III,176) but also has a wide-ranging acquaintance with regional geography, especially concerning the particular places where certain fish are to be found: the lakes Como, Maggiore and Garda, the rivers Ticino, Ambro, Adda, Po, and others (III,125, etc.). He can be very specific in situating the site where the River Adda loops by the town of Pizzaghettone *come l'Ambro passa da Sant'Angelo & Marignano*.

Documentary details about Scappi's life remain scarce and any biography must remain in large measure a sketch. But the *Opera* itself affords much upon which fundamental conjectures about the stages and experiences of his life may be formed. Scappi lets his reader infer a good deal *about* his life's episodes. That he travelled broadly in northern Italy can be understood clearly from his text. Some of his advice – about the rivers yielding the most plentiful fish, for instance, or the best provenance of particular cheeses – may have been acquired at first hand or indirectly. However, it is certain that Scappi did manage at various times in his life personally to observe culinary, agricultural and piscatory practice in an unusually wide range of places. Most of this field experience is likely related to the nature and locale of whatever positions he secured before becoming permanently established in Rome; from practical experience he learned local foodstuffs and cuisines – of Venice certainly, and Ravenna, perhaps of Bologna and, again almost certainly, of Milan. We can guess that during his lifetime Scappi's experience was enhanced by what was for his time an exceptionally rich range of acquaintance with geography and societies.[42] It was Scappi's own intellectual curiosity that

---

[42] See in the Index, below, Part 1, Ingredients, for the foodstuffs that were available and used in the *Opera*'s recipes, and Part 6 for the provenance of specific foods and foodstuffs and for the place names that Scappi had occasion to write, often in relation to his travels. As 'Europe's spice emporium without peer,' Venice offered Scappi and his patron, Cardinal Marin Grimano (II,149), as rich a range of exotic seasonings as was available anywhere in Christendom (Krondl, *The Taste of Conquest: The Rise and Fall of the Three Great Cities of Spice*, 100).

drew upon that experience to the benefit of his professional work, for the formation of his apprentice Giovanni, and even for the education of his reader some four and a half centuries after he so honestly and thoughtfully turned his life's accumulated knowledge into a book.

Scappi's unique situation and daily work

*T*he hierarchical nature of any princely establishment made the security of anyone's position, from the most exalted princes themselves to the least important of their servitors, dependent in large measure upon networks of acquaintances: whom you knew, whom you served effectively, who valued or coveted your service or allegiance. As chief cook to a Venetian cardinal (Grimano), to a Bolognese cardinal (Campeggio), to the dean of the College of Cardinals (Carpi), and to the supreme heads of the church (Pius IV and Pius V), Scappi depended as much as any servant upon pleasing his master, his master's associates and those set in hierarchic authority over him as he exercised his profession.

The only popes whom Scappi seems to have had particularly to please were Pius IV (1559–65) and Pius V (1566–72). Pope Paul III (1534–49) is referred to only in the historical context of his death and the conclave that elected his successor. However, as has been suggested already, Scappi's detailed knowledge of how that conclave functioned – all of its formal arrangements and procedures, even the days on which individual cardinals arrived to join it and when they were absent from it for health reasons – strongly suggests that he had observed that unique and paramount event personally. The elements of it that he describes suggest also that Scappi's viewpoint had in a broad sense been the kitchen; and certain of his detailed observations could have been possible only if he had occupied a relatively important position – perhaps in the retinue of an important cardinal – at that time.

It is natural that Scappi's name has taken on a certain lustre through his close association with the Roman papacy. Yet his life's work, his *Opera*, is rich and historically significant because by 1559 he was professionally ready to serve a pope. Where Scappi matured, the means by which he undoubtedly garnered the most practical experience and developed his natural talents to their acme, was in the service of cardinals of the church. It was the Venetian Grimano, the Bolognese Campeggio, the Modenese and Roman Carpi, and probably others directly or indirectly, who afforded Scappi the chance to satisfy his apparently endless curiosity about foodstuffs and to encourage him in his search for excellence in cookery. To some extent those cardinals helped make Scappi's accomplishments possible.

Scappi's account of the ten weeks that followed the funeral of Paul III is full of descriptive detail, finely observed and carefully noted. He records the sorts and numbers of guards, their functions, when and where they were on duty, the military installations, the special religious services that were held and the processions for them. Yet, even though that exceptional event offered innumerable novel arrangements and routines, for this cook it was in particular the food service to the conclave that mattered, the formal procedures for delivering the dishes from the kitchen and credenza of each cardinal's personal cook to the cardinal himself, safely and without communication. During a conclave the probity and devotion of a cook must have been measured to their highest degree. Scappi makes it clear in his book that those qualities were indeed what he held to be the essence of the best professional cook. In his account of the food service to the conclave of 1549–50, Scappi seems to have been gratified that the various kitchens were able duly to fulfil their grave and exceptional obligations.

Scappi's *Opera*

*O*n the title page of the first edition of Scappi's work, that of Venice, 1570, it is named simply that, the Work: *Opera di M. Bartolomeo Scappi … .*[43]

Interest in Scappi's 1570 book is reflected in the relatively short lapse of time before a second printing was undertaken in 1581 by the same printing house, Tramezzino in Venice. On f.aiiir [1581 f.aiiir], in a statement on behalf of the Venetian Senate which grants Scappi's printer, Michele Tramezzino, a twenty-year exclusive privilege to publish the work, Julius Zambertus refers, interestingly, to the volume as *il libro intitolato Epulario, overo de re coquinaria di Bartolomeo Scappi*: 'the book by Bartolomeo Scappi entitled *Epulario* – that is, *On the Matter of Cookery.*' The word *epulario* is not common, though its Latin root is: *epulæ,* 'a sumptuous meal, feast, banquet; food suitable for a banquet.' That name was, significantly, borne by another earlier recipe collection compiled largely from late-medieval sources[44] by Giovanne de Rosselli. Though rather pretentious, the term meant simply 'food book.' It may be that, if the word was indeed chosen by Scappi, likely as a generic term, it does not eventually appear on his title page because he or his printer felt that it might identify the new culinary work too closely with Rosselli's. It was still desirable in 1570 to distinguish Scappi's new publication from a work that continued up to at least 1579 to enjoy a certain reputation.

In earlier practice the evident relationship between recipe collections can often establish generations within families. Scappi's recipes do here and there echo a good many older recipes, prepared dishes, sauces and beverages found in earlier recipe collections, but usually with substantial modifications in their ingredients or in the manner in which they are elaborated: either Scappi himself or his instructors or some anonymous master cook before him has introduced novelty, has 'modernized' many of those earlier preparations. As an art, cookery survives primarily by change. Very generally speaking, if we compare Scappi's recipes with what we find in recipe collections before his *Opera*, we would be on

---

[43] The Latin word *opera* is a plural (of *opus*), denoting in effect a collective: 'the collected works [of] … '

[44] The *Epulario* of Rosselli (Venice, 1516, with many reprintings and an English translation of London, 1598) is for the most part a rendition, in places an outright copy, of the *Libro de arte coquinaria* of Martino – itself largely a copy and adaptation of an earlier anonymous manuscript cookbook now called the *Neapolitan Recipe Collection.*

the safe side to estimate that more than half of his work is fundamentally original. In a profession that depended, and depends, to such a very great degree upon the faithful transmission of current practice, as a foundation theme upon which variations can be wrought, such a high proportion of recipes of the never-before-seen sort is both significant and impressive.

Its significance lies partly in Scappi's obvious attempt to be complete in his 'recipe collection.' Unlike the traditional cookbooks before Scappi's time, this is not *just* a recipe collection.[45] Meticulously thorough, it deals systematically with every normally edible part of every normally edible animal, fowl, fish or plant – and regularly Scappi points out explicitly just what incidentals he has decided to omit and why. But beyond these bare bones, as it were, of his recipes he also provides culinary advice and commentary. He writes *about* foods and cooking. He helps his neophyte *know – understand* the real nature of – foods and cooking.

Bartolomeo Scappi was by no means unique in his time in writing about food. In sixteenth-century Italy a number of works had been printed that dealt in a variety of ways with foodstuffs, cooking, the organization of meals, their preparation and serving. After Scappi the literature in Italian continued to expand with new works and reprints on the various subjects that concerned food.[46] In a very general way a line may be drawn between printed works that remained essentially late-medieval in their sources and those that reflected a practice that was more 'modern.' Almost without exception those works of a newer, more contemporary inspiration referred to usage in courts, dining halls and kitchens of eminent prelates, particularly cardinals.

Some of the authors of those books were Pantaleone da Confienza (1477) on cheeses; Michele Savonarola (publ. 1508) on the properties of foodstuffs; Giovanni de Rosselli (1516) on traditional Italian recipes; Teofilo Folengo (1521) on a few traditional Italian recipes; Maestro Giovanni (c. 1530) on traditional Italian recipes; Cristoforo di Messisbugo (1549), steward of the Duke Ercole d'Este in Ferrara, on the composition of a formal meal; Giovanni Battista Scarlino (1554) on wines; Sante Lancerio (1559) on wines; Domenico Romoli, alias il Panunto (1560), on a steward's functions; Paolo Giovio (1560) on fish; Vincenzo Cervio (1581) on carving at table; Giovan Battista Rossetti (1584) on a steward's functions; Castor Durante da Gualdo (1585, 1586) on the properties of herbs and other foodstuffs; and Baldassarre Pisanelli (1587) on the properties of foodstuffs.

Working in the household of eminent prelates, Scappi may very well have had access to several of these monographs. Of all of them, the book that is

---

[45] A remarkable exception to this generalization is the *On Cookery* (*Du fait de cuisine*, 1420) of Master Chiquart, into which this chief cook of Duke Amadeus of Savoy put, as an adjunct to his exceptionally detailed recipes, a listing of the ingredients and hardware necessary to prepare a two-day, four-meal banquet that offered both meat and lean dishes.

[46] For a succinct listing of sixteenth-century works on food see the Bibliography.

the most interesting, in part because it contains the greatest variety of material, is the *Singolare dottrina* of Domenico Romoli, generally known as Panunto.[47] Published in 1560, this work is a remarkable 359 folios (718 pages) in length in the 1593 edition. Divided into twelve books, it covers in Part 1, Book I, the responsibilities of household servants, particularly those of the steward or *scalco*; II, the seasonal availability of animals and fowl; III, the seasonal availability of fish; IV, a year's menus; V, recipes; and in Part 2, Book VI, properties of food animals; VII, properties of dairy products, fish, fruits and herbs; VIII, effects on health of various things: foods, beverages, quantity, frequency, order of eating, exercise, moderating humours; IX, properties of herbs and root vegetables; X, properties of legumes, seeds; XI, properties of tree fruits, nuts; XII, properties of spices.

A good deal of Panunto's work is inspired by the traditional late-medieval health handbook or *regimen sanitatis*,[48] itself an evolutionary stage of Greco-Arabic medical analyses of everything that exists and can affect human life and health. Learned adaptations of the foodstuff sections of such treatises were published by Savonarola, Pisanelli and Durante.

Panunto's work likely had little influence upon Scappi, except perhaps in the beginning of the *Opera*'s Book I and the outline of Book IV. Panunto devotes only the 104 pages of his Book V to recipes, whereas Scappi's long work, with the exception of the beginning of Book I and all of Book IV, is wholly given over to a careful instruction in the craft of elaborating a wide variety of prepared dishes. His work is truly a cookbook, an *epulario*. Panunto's is a health handbook written for stewards, whose primary responsibility was the health, welfare, comfort and pleasure of their master. Wherever the material of the *Opera* parallels that of the *Singolare dottrina* we are reminded of Scappi's declaration to Giovanni, his pupil,

---

[47] Or 'Panonto' – that being a preparation consisting of bread, lightly toasted, soaked in grease and fried. That author deals with *pan'unto* in two of his Recipes, V,59 (*Beccaccie arrosto con pan'unto*) and 67 (*Pan'unto con provatura fresca*): these recipes correspond respectively to Scappi's Recipes II,131 (and 229ff, where Scappi calls the preparation *pan ghiotto* or 'gourmand bread') and II,233 (where the toast is soaked in butter and the dish is called a *Butirata*). The preparation is related to a sop, in which the bread or toast that holds a meat is normally soaked in broth.

[48] His Book VIII is a compendium of such treatises, although throughout the whole of his work he insists continually that he is basing himself on the doctrines of, *inter alios*, Bartolomeo Anglico, Martiale, Costantino, Dioscoride, Avicenna, Isidoro, Agostino, Rasis, Plinio, Averrois, Galeno, Aristotile, Plinio, Sant'Ambrosio, Isac, Alberto Magno and, more anonymously, *i Medici, un gran Dottor di medicina* and *i Medici antichi*. To reinforce the learned nature of Panunto's work he or his printer appended, in thirty-two pages, *Un breve et notabile trattato del Reggimento della Sanità*, a precis, its title tells us, of the work of Roberto Groppetio. Concerning the 'scientific' bent in writing about food at this time see Allen J. Grieco, 'La gastronomia del XVI secolo: tra scienza e cultura' in *Et coquatur ponendo*, 143–206. The essay, with its synopses of major texts, underscores the new scholarly activity in Italy directed at analysing the nature of foodstuffs.

that a cook should have acquired such a broad understanding of food, cooking and serving that he could more readily serve as a steward than any steward as a cook.[49] The part of Scappi's Book IV that lists the year's menus may, in effect, be trespassing into the steward's domain. However, like the beginning and end of Book IV, those menus are, from the point of view of a cook, an integral, vital part of what a kitchen can on occasion be expected to be able to do. In a similar way Scappi's brief descriptions of the 'nature' of foodstuffs in their ideal state are designed to aid the cook in his quest for excellent cookery; there is little in Scappi's instruction on foodstuffs that is obviously derived from the physicians' theoretical knowledge – which learned dogma so thoroughly imbues Panunto's treatise. Scappi's counsel is intended primarily as practical advice to the principal food worker: the cook should know when in the year a foodstuff is at its best on the market; he should be able to recognize that goodness, to accept or reject whatever is delivered to the workbenches in his kitchen, to handle and prepare each foodstuff in ways that are most suitable for drawing out and exploiting the best of that foodstuff. And Panunto's survey of the household personnel over which the steward wields authority is naturally limited in Scappi's Book I to comprehensive, entirely pragmatic considerations of a cook's day-to-day working environment and conditions. If the passages dealing with a cook's fair remuneration and treatment had been written in more modern times, we might even think of a job outline drafted by a shop steward.

If Scappi was not content merely to reproduce traditional recipe collections that he may or may not have had at hand, he did take as the framework for his *Opera* what, in the matter of 'cookbooks' over the previous three centuries or so, had become a generic outline. While he never refers to another text, he does, perhaps naturally, adopt the classifications that were common in medieval and other Renaissance recipe collections: food for meat days and food for lean days. He calls them, respectively, his Books II and III.[50] To these fundamentals he makes two significant additions, a chapter on pasta and pastry dishes, Book V, and another on dishes for the sick, sickly and convalescent, Book VI. Neither of those is in essence original: pies and turnovers of one sort or another and filled pasta such as

---

[49] ... *Che piu tosto possa egli* [the cook] *servire nel'ufficio di Scalco, che lo Scalco per Cuoco* (I, §1). If anything, this declaration sounds as if Scappi would like to suggest that Panunto's collection of recipes has no proper place in a book on a steward's responsibilities.

Panunto numbers 135 recipes for meat, lean, pastry and pasta dishes in his Book V. Most of those correspond roughly to dishes set forth in Scappi and usually in somewhat greater detail there. More within the usual scope of a steward's obligations, in his Book V Panunto also inserts an alphabetical listing of the name of dishes that *could* be used in a meal: 203 lean dishes; 360 meat dishes; 16 sauces; 52 *minestre*; 22 'salads'; and 85 'fruits and things served with bread.'

[50] The use of the term 'book' for the divisions of the diverse material that Scappi includes in his work likely reflects the practice in scientific writing of the day.

ravioli are found scattered thinly through the odd medieval recipe collection, as are what we call *pasta asciutta* – that is, tagliatelli, macaroni and lasagne. Dishes for the sick are likewise at least recognized in many early collections, where one or two or half a dozen may be given recipes. Scappi's originality is, again, in assembling extensive assortments of both the pastry dishes and the invalid's foods. He refers to his books usually by name: the Book on Meats, on Fish, on Pastry, for Invalids (or, variably, for the Sick).

Perhaps most unusual in the *Opera* are Books I and IV, the treatises that are not given over primarily to recipes. To a large extent Book I deals with foodstuffs, as do several paragraphs in Book IV. The bulk of Book IV consists, however, of a series of menus, for three sorts of meals and the odd grand formal banquet. Their arrangement in a monthly sequence implies that the reader, if he was a master cook, could feasibly undertake such meals using foodstuffs available at particular seasons throughout a full year, on meat days, lean days and fasting days. However practical such advice might be, Scappi's intention in compiling his Book IV may in large measure have been to document evidence of his own professional ability and his contribution to the magnificent refined life of the prelacy – that at a time during his work for Pius V when his value as a papal cook must have been seriously diminishing.[51]

Among the menus are both outlines of hypothetical meals as well as accounts of the courses and dishes of what actually was served at a specific historic meal. Those detailed menus occupy ff.169r to 327r [1581 ff.134r to 275r] – that is, 282 pages in fine italic type of lists of dishes set out according to the meal (dinner, supper or collation), source (kitchen or credenza) and serving (first to fourth). In the early history of cookery manuals, such an exhaustive catalogue is an exceptional element. Highly valuable portions of both Books I and IV are devoted also to inventories of the gear that is necessary or, at the very least, useful in any first-class kitchen, whether permanent or itinerant. To those outlines of the 'circumstances' or means of cookery (and of baking and of making dairy foods), we can add the historical account, appended after Book VI, of the conclave of 1549–50. Though it bears only tangentially on the role of a papal cook, his kitchen or the serving of his prepared food, it certainly does pertain to the potential duties of a cardinal's cook.

There are six of these books, although Scappi himself occasionally refers to their total as being five.[52] In a preamble addressed to his apprentice, Scappi

---

[51] Even in preparing that pope's normal meals, Scappi had to take into account Pius V's increasing agony of gallstones: for sustenance in his later days he was reduced to relying extensively on plain goat's milk.

[52] In the preamble to Book I that Scappi addresses to Giovanni, the book on pastry (published as Book V) is identified as Book IV; the menus (now in Book IV) are called Book V. That last book, he adds, contains matter on a travelling kitchen (now also in Book IV) and an outline of

declares his overall purpose: with this text he will leave Giovanni a written memorandum of all the high professional standards that he has striven to implant in the youth during his 'apprenticeship.' In these endeavours and practices of a lifetime, he says, lie all the art and skill of a master cook.[53]

Contents of the *Opera*

*T*he full title of Scappi's book reads as follows:

OPERA DI M. BARTOLOMEO SCAPPI, CUOCO SECRETO DI PAPA PIO QUINTO, *DIVISI IN SEI LIBRE.*
Nel primo si contiene il ragionamento che fa l'Autore con Gio. suo discepolo.
Nel secondo si tratta di diverse vivande di carne, sì di quadrupedi, come di volatili.
Nel terzo si parla della statura, e stagione de pesci.
Nel quarto si mostrano le liste del presentar le vivande in tavola, cosi di grasso come di magro.
Nel quinto si contiene l'ordine de far diverse sorti di paste, & altri lavori.
Nel sesto, & ultimo libro si ragiona de' convalescenti, & molte altre sorti di vivande per gli infermi.
Con il discorso funerale che fu fatto nelle essequie di Papa Paulo III.
Con le figure che fanno bisogno nella cucina, & alli Reverendissimi nel Conclave.[54]

Scappi's *Epulario,* or *Opera,* as it was printed twice by the Tramezzino brothers and reprinted many times into the following century, consists of a title page, a series of preliminary documents – three privileges, a dedication and a publisher's promotional blurb – and six books. The books offer recipes, brief disquisitions on particular foodstuffs, menus, the layout of an ideal kitchen and an enumeration of the hardware needed for that kitchen and for cooking when one's employer travels. Each of the books concludes with an index (*tavola*) that

---

a conclave (in the event published quite separately after Book VI, with discrete pagination and no indication of any relation to another part of the *Opera*). In that preamble no mention is made of a Book VI. Those discrepancies suggest that modifications were being made in the volume's contents even as the work was being prepared for its first printing. Given that the typesetting, quire by quire, and printing of a book this size would have taken a good many months, it is understandable that an original project could well have been amplified and altered even in the course of production.

[53] ... *acciò dopo la morte mia in voi rimanessero tutte le mie fatiche, & pratiche, con brevità vi mostrerò in questi cinque* [sic] *libri, in che consista l'arte, et prudenza d'un maestro Cuoco* (f.1r [1581 f.1r]).

[54] This summary of the contents of the *Opera* is based upon an examination of only the first and second printings of the book. For a list of subsequent reprintings and editions of Scappi's work see the Bibliography, below.

itemizes the content of that book. A record of the 1549 conclave and a set of copperplate engravings is bound at the end of each printing of the volume. The name and general subject matter of each of the six books is variously indicated by Scappi.

Book I

• *Opera* title page: *Nel primo si contiene il ragionamento che fa l'Autore con Gio. suo discepolo.*
• Initial preamble to Giovanni: *Nel primo libro vederete in che consiste la prudenza d'un maestro Cuoco, con alcune altre particolarità, & circonstanze molto opportune à tale officio.*
• Rubric to Book I: *Ragionamento, che fa l'autore M. Bartolomeo Scappi, con Giovanni suo discepolo.* Following this preamble, the numbered paragraphs bear individual rubrics: for example, 1. *Delle circonstanze necessarie al mastro Cuoco*; 2. *Del sito, & forma, & disegno d'una cocina, & dell'ordine delle massaritie di questo officio.* Then, following a survey of staple foodstuffs, *Hora verrò con ordine a narrare ogni sorte d'instrumenti, ordigni, & masseritie pertinenti a tal'officio* …
• Table of Book I: *Tavola del primo libro.*
• Preamble to Book V (referring back to the contents of the *primo libro*): … *à conoscere le cose necessarie all'officio del Cuoco.*

This initial book of Scappi's work attempts to deal with whatever bears upon the cook's activities that does not relate directly to specific recipes. Book IV will deal with menus and serving, but the *circonstanze* of the professional cook's life and work involve many other considerations. They include remuneration and living allowances, accommodation and facilities, but the *circonstanze* involve as well each individual's competence in managing the staples of his craft. As Scappi will insist, particularly in Books II and III, a cook's success must rest to a very large extent also upon his skill in recognizing the 'goodness' of the basic raw materials that he will be handling.

Book II

• *Opera* title page: *Nel secondo si tratta di diverse vivande di carne, sì di quadrupedi, come di volatili.*
• Initial preamble to Giovanni: *Nel secondo libro, troverete l'ordine, che haverete ad osservare, per far varie, & diverse sorti di vivande, tanto d'animali volatili, quanto quadrupedi, con la loro stagione, & per fare diversi geli, & sapori.*
• Rubric to Book II: *Secondo libro nelqual si tratta di diverse vivande di carne, si di quadrupedi, come di volatili.*
• III,243: *nel libro delle vivande*: literally 'in the book on prepared dishes.' Scappi seems to consider that Book II is central to his cookbook.
• Table of Book II: *Tavola del secondo Libro.*

• Preamble to Book V (referring back to the contents of the *secondo libro*): ... *à far diverse vivande per li giorni di grasso*. In the same place Book II is called the *libro delle vivande da grasso*.

This Book does indeed deal separately with the preparation of the meats of animals and fowl, foods suitable for meat days. Recipes for a rich series of sauces are incorporated as well into Book II, roughly between 248 and 279; in Book I, §28 Scappi refers the reader also to the *libro delli sapori*, which suggests that we may have a trace here of a modification in Scappi's initial plan.

Book III

• *Opera* title page: *Nel terzo si parla della statura, e stagione de pesci.*
• Initial preamble to Giovanni: *Nel terzo che sarà per i giorni di magro, & quadragesimali, troverete l'ordine da fare diverse vivande di pesci, & conoscere la loro statura & stagione.*
• Rubric to Book III: *Libro terzo di M. Bartolomeo Scappi.* In the following text we read *vivande ... che appartengono alli giorni di magro, et quadragesimali, cominciando dalle stature, et qualità, e stagioni d'alcuni pesci, che alla giornata compariscono in Roma, et in molti luoghi d'Italia ...*
• Table of Book III: *Tavola del libro quadragesimale.*
• Preamble to Book V (referring back to the contents of the *terzo libro*): ... *à conoscer la statura, & stagion di piu sorte pesci, con lo stile che haverete da tener in farne le vivande per li giorni di magro*. In the same place Book III is called the *libro delle vivande da magro.*

Book III has several designations in references to it elsewhere in the *Opera*. Generally it is called the Book on Fish, but it is also called the Book on Lean Dishes and, as in its own table, the Lenten Book. The hesitation may be due to the inclusion, towards its end, of non-fish dishes, particularly of rice, nuts, vegetables, fruits and eggs, preparations appropriate for lean or fasting meals.

Book IV

• *Opera* title page: *Nel quarto si mostrano le liste del presentar le vivande in tavola, cosi di grasso come di magro.*
• Initial preamble to Giovanni: *Il quinto & ultimo, vi sarà di grande utilità, insegnandovi lo stile, che haverete da osservare, in presentare, & servire le vivande, (dopo che saranno fatte) in mano delli Sig. Scalchi*[55] *... & sapere ancora*

---

[55] Scappi's prospectus has identified this book as his 'fifth and last' – the 'fourth' being his treatise on pastry making. After writing *in mano delli Sig. Scalchi*, Scappi continues: *& poi occorrendo sapere servire da un Conclave gl'Illustriss. & Reverendiss. Card. cosi di dentro, come di fuora ...* . In the printed volume this later material on the conclave of 1549–50 will be placed separately after the end of the *Opera* proper.

ordinare diverse massarotte, aspettanti a tal'officio ... [56]

• Rubric to Book IV: *Libro quarto delle liste.*

• Preamble to Book IV: *L'ordine et ... il modo che haverete da tenere nel presentare le vivande cucinate in mano delli signori Scalchi ... ; nell'ultimo ... un sommario di robbe pertinenti alla credenza per tutto l'anno, con un preparamento di masseritie di cucina necessarie a ogni gran Principe, che voglia far viaggio longo ...*

Book IV contains four distinct sections. The first, a preamble, introduces each of the following main topics.

   ○ A preamble about the dining board.
   ○ *Le liste.*
   ○ *Robbe della credenza.*
   ○ *Summario et preparatione di masseritie di cucina per un viaggio che si volesse fare per ogni gran Principe.*

• Table of Book IV: *Tavola del quarto libro dell'imbandire le vivande.*

• Preamble to Book V (referring back to the contents of the *quarto libro*): ... *l'ordine che s'ha da osservar in presentare le vivande in mano de' Scalchi, ordinare diverse masseritie, et insieme à servir ad un Conclave de Reverendiss. Cardinali.*

It becomes apparent from the various preambles that the actual printed content of Book IV is not exactly what Scappi might originally have planned, and that Book VI was not even a part of his original scheme. Furthermore, in this present book, IV, the few meals to which a date actually is or can be assigned suggest that the vast bulk of the book, the series of menus that were feasible throughout each of the seasons of a year, was compiled – like the account of the conclave following the death of Paul III – independently at some point in time long before the *Opera* was published in 1570.

The nature of the menus and Scappi's possible intentions in assembling this very extensive and meticulous listing are complex. Because much of a cook's work depended upon the seasonal availability of foodstuffs, Scappi must have felt that his reader would find a year's sampling of practicable menus useful. In his presentation, under a heading for each month, are regularly found the *pranzo* (dinner) and the *cena* (supper) for (usually) the 8th, the 15th and the 25th day of that month; almost invariably, those are meat meals.[57] At the end of each month are then the same two meals, dinner and supper, for a lean day, any lean day in

---

[56] If Scappi is thinking of lessons that Giovanni will learn solely in this 'fifth and last book,' it would seem that the *diverse massarotte*, 'various furnishings,' may refer either to furniture for a cardinal's cell during the conclave he has just mentioned or, less likely, to the kitchen paraphernalia to be transported when a master is travelling (which he does not in this prospectus anticipate discussing).

[57] A notable exception to that generality is the dinner for 28 October in which the cook has deliberately intermixed meat and lean dishes throughout each of its servings.

that month. The list for most months concludes with a *collatione*, always dated *all'ultimo* (either 'at the end' or 'on the last day') of that month.

Those menus occupy a very large proportion of Scappi's work, some 171 folios (or 342 pages) out of 440 folios in the 1570 printing, some 144 folios (or 288 pages) out of 373 folios in the 1581 printing.[58] Scappi always indicates the number of courses from the credenza (or sideboard) and the number from the kitchen, each course from either source consisting of several, sometimes numerous, preparations. The alternation of kitchen and credenza courses – the so-called *servizio all'italiana* or 'Italian service' – is common but not absolutely regular. In detailing his menus Scappi also notes the number of *piatti* – that is, how many serving dishes or bowls – were to be made up in the kitchen.[59]

The last data that Scappi gives for each meal are the numbers of table attendants, specifically of stewards (*scalchi*) and of carvers (*trincianti*); that number provides again a relative indication of the number of diners. The number of stewards and carvers tends to be identical to the number of serving plates because each pair of attendants, steward and carver, is responsible for what was served to the diners to whom the pair has been assigned.

A supper is less imposing a meal than the noon-day dinner. In his index summarizing the year's menus (reproduced in Book IV, below), using a sort of shorthand, Scappi writes regularly for each day merely that the supper was identical to the dinner in outline: number of courses, number of *piatti*, number of attendants. What shrank for a supper was the overall number of preparations.

---

[58] The present translation of Scappi's *Opera* will offer Scappi's tabulation of his full year of meals and courses, in English, but only a sampling, in Scappi's Italian, of the actual menus themselves.

[59] That number affords a good indication of the number of persons expected at the dining table for the meal. The status of the diners determined how many shared each platter or bowl, two persons being traditionally the norm, but the master and a guest of honour customarily each had his own serving. When Scappi was writing, however, the ratio of persons-per-plate was certainly in a state of flux, at least in a cardinal's house and when national usage is considered. On f.10r of his *Singolare dottrina*, published in 1560, Panunto distinguishes between local practice and the so-called French service in which every single preparation of an entire meal is set out all together, in a single serving, on an oval or circular dining table in a variable number of serving vessels. The French steward will *ordinar tante vivande alla volta, che facilmente si possano servir tutte, infra quattro convitati per ogni servitio di esse*: 'set out as many preparations together as may all of them be served easily, in the ratio of four diners for every serving of a preparation.' By the end of the sixteenth century the sharing of serving dishes and goblets was becoming contrary to proper elegant dining in Italy. On the whole, while each course in a meal for which Scappi was responsible, whether from the kitchen or the credenza, may have offered a large number of preparations to diners at the papal board, the number of diners at that board on an ordinary day seems rarely to have been more than a dozen.

Book V

• *Opera* title page: *Nel quinto si contiene l'ordine di far diverse sorti di paste, & altri lavori.*

• Initial preamble to Giovanni: *Nel quarto troverete il modo da fare diversi lavorieri di pasta.*

• Rubric to Book V: *Libro V Delle paste, di M. Bartomoleo Scappi.*

• Preamble to Book V: ... *l'ordine che v'è necessario tenere, in fare diverse sorte di pasticci, crostate, torte, & altri lavorieri di pasta, cotti al forno, sotto il testo, & fritti.* The last sentence of this preamble indicates which types of pastry (properly 'pasta') will not be found in this book because they have been dealt with in either Books II or III.

• Table of Book V: *Tavola del quinto libro delle paste.*

Book VI

• *Opera* title page: *Nel sesto, & ultimo libro si ragione de' convalescenti, & molte altre sorti di vivande per gli infermi.*

• This book is not mentioned in the initial preamble to Giovanni.

• Rubric to Book VI: *Libro sesto et ultimo. De convalescenti.*

• Table of Book VI: *Tavola di tutte le cose che si contengono nel presente libro de Convalescenti.*

• In Recipe V,237 Scappi has written, ... *Volendone fare d'altre sorti, si vadi al libro intitolato de Convalescenti, separato de questi cinque.* The final phrase of the author's note may suggest that Book VI was hived off from material originally assigned to that Book V or some other; probably as a result of accretion, the sickdishes eventually demanded their own space, a whole additional book.

• In Recipe III,61: *vivande per li convalescenti.* This book represents an enormous expansion of a feature which was standard in late-medieval recipe collections. Those recipe books usually offer a relatively small number of preparations – between two and a dozen – that were suitable for the sick, the sickly, the convalescent and, interestingly, those of finicky appetite. In principal such dishes incorporated foodstuffs that were held by physicians to be readily digestible, nutritious and sustaining of the best bodily humours.

Appendix: On the conclave following the death of Pope Paul III.

• *Opera* title page: ... *Con il discorso funerale che fu fatto nelle essequie di Papa Paulo III.*

• Initial preamble to Giovanni (concerning the 'fifth and last' Book, containing the menus): ... *& piu occorrendo sapere servire da un Conclave gl'Illustriss. & Reverendiss. Card. cosi di dentro, come de fuora,*[60] *& sapere ancora ordinare diverse massaritie, aspettanti à tal'officio* ... .

• Not in the Table to Book VI.

---

[60] The phrase 'both inside and out' evokes the confining doors of a conclave.

While Scappi's division of his material into six books is on the whole simple and comprehensible, it has not been entirely successful. Changes of plan en route and minor accretions have slightly muddied the clarity with which its author may originally have envisioned his *Opera*. Specifically, as first conceived the work comprised five books, a sequence of 'an ideal kitchen with ideal foodstuffs,' 'meats,' 'fish,' 'pastry' and 'menus.' Subsequent additions included the book on food for the sick along with other delicacies, and two miscellaneous enrichments having to do with special arrangements: food service when travelling and procedures for delivering food during a conclave. Of these latter special cases, Scappi appended the first onto his book of menus and decided not to incorporate the second into the *Opera* at all.[61] Neither of those placements for the conclave narrative, in Book IV or as a pseudo appendix, could have been entirely satisfactory.

It may be noted in passing that while Scappi does use both the terms *convalescenti* and *infermi* in identifying Book VI on the title page of the *Opera*, the term he prefers to use, in the rubric to the Book, in its table and in references elsewhere to it, is *convalescenti* alone. It is probable that this preference underscores the cook's deference to the court physicians who alone had the authority, and the responsibility, to prescribe what should be consumed by those who were truly sick.[62] Repeatedly throughout Book VI Scappi warns that even some of those kitchen preparations for convalescents could be served only *secondo la commissione del Phisico* – on the doctor's orders.

It is interesting that, precise and detailed though he normally is as he makes his way through an ordinary recipe, in Book VI Scappi seems painstakingly careful to provide full specifications of ingredients and meticulous descriptions of every step. Recipe VI,11 for a thick chicken broth, being the first of the *brodi consumati* and perhaps the traditional sickdish *par excellence*, is remarkable in this respect.

His collection of recipes for the sick and convalescent shows some attempt at organization, although some of the preparations in that Book VI may, in Scappi's mind, belong merely in a category of pleasant, appetizing and easily digested dishes.

---

[61] As we have seen, a comment in the Preamble to Book V indicates that Scappi initially intended his review of a cook's exceptional responsibilities during a conclave to be part of Book IV, where he deals with those of his duties related to providing both 'ordinary' meals, year in, year out, and meals from an itinerant kitchen. The manner in which that conclave material is printed in its own sequence of folios argues that it had an existence of its own, likely from even before the *Opera* was conceived.

[62] Concerning the role of physicians in an Italian court in Scappi's time see in particular the article by Nicoud, 'Les médecins à la cour de Francesco Sforza.' A cook's role in feeding those whose humoral balance was disturbed could be risky. In the *Neapolitan Recipe Collection*, of more than a century before Scappi, the series of sickdishes contains one of almonds (a food of ideally bland properties) which is indicated *a homo delicato*, 'for a delicate person' (Recipe 31).

A repeated specification of silver and gold for the vessels and utensils in Book VI reminds the modern reader of the reputation that precious metals had long enjoyed in the treatment of illness. Ground gold appears as well there as an ingredient (VI,21).

A very infrequent but curious overlap of recipes occurs between Book VI and previous books.[63] Scappi regularly refers his reader to places elsewhere in which a particular recipe or another dish of a similar sort can be found. He seems to want to make his work as economically efficient as possible, repeatedly directing the reader to 'proceed from that point, following the directions in Recipe ... ' Overall his work reveals a markedly tight organization. In it we can discern an author who is very conscious of the totality of his material and who strives to give it a best arrangement. His prime purpose is utilitarian, to make his book as useful as possible. However, in assembling the material of his appended Book VI, he seems to have been a little less attentive to quasi-repetitions. Those may result from the last-minute rush of revisions and printing schedules, or they may be simply oversights. The very few duplications that turn up in Book VI may still perhaps be explained by a perception that the dishes in that book had a distinctly different function from those presented earlier: Giovanni, needing quick and easy guidance to possible preparations for an invalid, could best be helped by setting out all options collected and presented together.

A final segment of Scappi's *Opera* must obviously be recognized. The extensive set of copperplate engravings are unique for their time. Those plates are reproduced in Appendix II. The series of plates anticipates what the *Encyclopédie* of Diderot and D'Alembert would attempt, with a broader scope of subject matter but in no less detail, almost two centuries later: use graphic art to explain the material tools of a practical trade more concretely than a mere thousand words could ever do. The set of engravings constitutes a meticulous and remarkably comprehensive representation of the conditions in which the cooks of Scappi's time worked and of the devices they handled in their work. If it was not the author himself who arranged to have the illustrations made, he must certainly have worked very closely with the engraver as he portrayed the locales and tools that were so fundamental to Scappi's craft. For virtually every plate, the artist must have had objects before him which he sketched, he must have been able to visit the places that he depicted in such fine detail. The pots and pans (Plates 7–10), the particular knives (Plate 13) and the saddle, spit-turning mechanism and foot warmer (Plates 18–20) had to have been seen, even handled by the engraver. It could only have been Scappi who put those objects in the artist's hand and who showed him the fixtures in his own kitchen.

---

[63] See in particular the pairs formed by Recipes II,267 and VI,192, II,273 and VI,198, III,273 and VI,153.

Furthermore, the correlation between text and the sequence of the pictures is generally so close and so useful to the reader that the composition of each plate must have been prompted by either the author or the publisher. The engravings form a vital adjunct to Scappi's grand plan of making the complex imperatives of a cook's professional service fully understandable. In the translation here, wherever the plates contain an illustration of some article, procedure or arrangement mentioned in Scappi's text, a note will call the reader's attention to that, or a brief mention in the Index will signal it.[64]

- *Opera* title page: ... *con le figure che fanno bisogno nella cucina, & alli Reverendissimi nel Conclave.*
- Initial preamble to Giovanni: ... *& piu occorrendo sapere servire da un Conclave gl'Illustriss. & Reverendiss. Card. cosi di dentro, come de fuora, & sapere ancora ordinare diverse massaritie, aspettanti à tal'officio, come si vedera per i ritratti, & disegni, dove saran tre cucine differenti l'una dall'altra, con gli ornamenti, & masseritie delle camere del Conclave.*

A singular engraving is bound in the *Opera* between the folios of formal privileges and the beginning of Scappi's text proper. A whole page is devoted to a portrait of the papal cook. An ornate frame beneath it contains the identification: 'M. Bartolomeo Scappi.' Undoubtedly an authentic image of the man, the portrait can be seen reproduced in the present book. To the top left of the portrait the engraver shows a coat of arms that was presumably designed exclusively by or for Scappi. The oval medallion, a non-military variety of shield (later favoured by ladies), is set within a florid support, itself suspended on a ribbon, and is divided *per fess* by a horizontal bar: its upper compartment contains a chalice; the lower shows a hound on a taut leash. What holds the leash is, regrettably, not clearly distinguishable, but may be a platter with a mound on it (of some sort of food?). The image of the straining dog probably represents the imperative or hortatory *scappi*, from the verb *scappare*, to escape, take flight. The support extends below the bottom of the shield and splits into into two curling tails, bound together just below the point of the split by two ties. The whole, portrait and shield, is satisfactorily elegant.

Scappi's writing

S cappi's work should be viewed against a background of the practice of his contemporaries and forebears in his profession. By the mid-sixteenth century the traditions of refined cooking were well established. We can better understand

---

[64] Firpo provides a descriptive catalogue of each of the plates in his *Gastronomia del Rinascimento*, 59–68, as do Di Schino and Luccichenti, *Il cuoco segreto dei papi*, 98–126.

Scappi's contribution to the profession by considering what resources he was able to draw upon.

In Italy and across Europe recipe collections had been compiled and copied in manuscript, and latterly printed, for a good three hundred years before Scappi's day. With very few exceptions, however, those cookbook writers were content to remain anonymous, not seeing their work as an occasion to set forth their personal ideas about food and cooking but merely to organize and set out a collection of recipes that enjoyed some degree of approval among a class of people of taste. For the most part, they were not cookbooks as we perhaps might think of them, but merely series of discrete recipes, bare-bone memoranda for the household steward, kitchen clerk or professional cook, none of whom needed explicit indications concerning absolute quantities, heats or times but only a list of the ingredients for a given preparation, its garnish and the method of its cooking. These books were not instruction manuals but rather brief records that documented, in a simple stylistic shorthand, a particular usage at a particular time. Amateurs and housewives did not acquire such recipe collections before the sixteenth century: generally they could not afford them, could not read them and did not need them. In fact, it seems that a good number of such manuscript books of the fourteenth and fifteenth centuries were intended for the library of some potentate who wished to archive an aspect of his family's social history, on the same shelves as account registers and chronicles.

Previous recipe writers relied on their reader's knowledge of common taste and basic culinary procedures; they could afford to abbreviate, to record merely the bare facts of a recipe. If, apart from being testimonials to a house's refinement, those recipes had any practical functionality, it was as an *aide mémoire* for a cook who might be subject to lapses of memory or simply curious about what was done in another kitchen. Early recipes generally indicated neither quantities, heats nor cooking times with any precision. At most, such indications might be relative: a particular spice should predominate; the flame should be low; the pot should boil for the length of three *Our Fathers*. In the *Opera*, however, we find Scappi consistently declaring very precise quantities (by the quarter ounce, half of a quarter of an hour).[65]

Scappi helped make the modern cookbook. After the manner of a Chiquart,[66] he advises his reader on the 'circumstances' of respectable cookery, the pots and pans, knives and grinders, filter cloths and fuel necessary for the successful preparation of good meals. Yet in Scappi the inventory of the kitchen, of *three*

---

[65] For a good number of generations more, while a firewood or coal flame was the usual source of heat for roasting, boiling and baking, it remained difficult for cooks to have an accurate common measure of heat.

[66] Master Chiquart, chief cook of Duke Amadeus I of Savoy and author of *Du fait de cuisine* (1420).

kitchens and their appurtenances, of an itinerant kitchen, of a conclavular serving system, are examined in fine detail. Like Pietro di Crescenzi and Platina,[67] he devotes a good proportion of his writing to setting out the primary qualities *of* the foodstuffs – animal, vegetable and mineral – that will go into the dishes whose elaboration he sketches. Yet what always concerns Scappi is to inform his reader what he has learned to be the 'nature' of each particular foodstuff, particularly when it is at its most excellent for the purposes of the kitchen and dining table, and how to recognize that most excellent state.

A sober objectivity and concision, even terseness, were virtues for compilers of recipe collections in manuscript. Scappi's style is rather different. Its natural manner is remarkably personal; occasionally it verges on the verbose. When his subject slips into the anecdotal, he is clearly the old man reminiscing on the valuable lessons of his life that can be of help to his apprentice Giovanni. His intent is always to foster a more thorough understanding of the foodstuff a cook will be handling and of the procedures he will be following. Illustrations drawn from a long and rich personal experience can properly be a part of the instruction.

Yet Scappi was nipped by the age's scientific bug. He strives to be accurate in distinguishing what he terms 'species' of creature. A freshwater shad, he writes, is a fish similar to the allis shad, but it belongs to the herring and pilchard species; and he goes on to describe the freshwater shad in detail (Recipe III,124). His very precise description of a lamprey (III,90) might have been found in a sixteenth- or seventeenth-century ichthyological treatise.

A curious element in early science is the role of etymology. One of the ways Scappi clearly believes he can penetrate to the real essence of a foodstuff is through an examination of its name. By evoking the supposed etymology of a word, Scappi occasionally proposes to give weight to his lessons about the foodstuff. *Il pesce corbo*, he writes, implanting the fish's shape in his apprentice's mind, *io credo che habbia questo nome, percioche è alquanto corbuto, cioè con il collo arcato* (Recipe III,42).[68] He persists in trying to explain the real nature of things he has handled; he even believes it is worth commenting whenever he has to admit that an explanation eludes him: *Vi son di quelli che sbiancheggiano, et dei altri piu neri, della qual'diversità io non so render la cagione* (III,176).

His basic professional training and his original repertoire were undoubtedly obtained orally on-the-job as an apprentice himself, so that tradition was initially for him in all matters the guiding principle. Yet, as he now composes his *Opera*, he

---

[67] The *Commodorum ruralium* and *De omnibus agriculturæ partibus* of Petrus Crescentius were two of the earliest European books on agriculture, the first reprinted many times after the Augsburg (Johannes Schussler) 1471 publication, the second printed in Basel (Henrichus Petrus) in 1548. The principal work of Bartolomeo Sacchi (1421–81), alias Platina, *De honesta voluptate et valetudine*, was compiled about 1465 and first printed in about 1470.

[68] See also the beginning of Recipe III,108.

writes time and time again that his prime authorities are his extensive experience and other practices he has observed and of which he approves.

With the best scientific attitude, Scappi is an observer. He will include anecdotal information whenever he can vouch for it himself. When he advises, his advice is always established on his own experience: 'I have found that ... '; 'Experience has shown me that ... '; *Trovo per isperienza che ...* As with any true artist and craftsman he has learned what works well – and sometimes where a hidden danger may lie for the unwary; an important part of his job as Giovanni's instructor is to transmit those practical lessons.

Scappi's inquiring mind observes the commercial world about him, beyond his kitchen. When the rayfish is skinned its skin is retrieved and 'used by sword makers and other artisans' (Recipe III,86) – in all likelihood to make tough and pliable scabbards, straps and belts.

But it seems especially to have been the experience of travel that stirred Scappi to be the most observant. For a sixteenth-century commoner he covered a surprising amount of territory and reports on an exceptionally wide range of practices. *Tal vivanda si usa da Peruggini* (III,142); *Non voglio restar di dire come si si accarpiona [il Carpione] nel lago di Garda* (III,122). Writing of oysters in Corsica, he notes, *Io trovandomi nel porto di Brondoli presso Chiozza ne viddi pigliare gran quantità, lequali son molto piu bianche di quelle di Corsica, ma ancho molto piu picciole ... ; Trovandomi in Pesaro vidi un vassello per fortuna sbattere nelle spiaggie, et rivoltarsi il fondo in su, nel qual fondo erano appiccate molte ostreche, et secondo che dicono i pescatori ...* (III,183); *In questi due modi io gli ho veduti in Venetia* (I, §10). And, having journeyed more distantly, he writes about a variety of *fragolino ... che ho veduto nella Schiavonia* (III,48).

His travels and previous sojourns allowed him to indulge in an interesting habit of citing a local name or names for a fish. *Ho veduto nella pescheria di Milano diverse sorti di pesciolini minuti, ove li chiamano marscioni, et in Milano ancho bottuli* (III,161). *Il pesce spigolo ... in diversi lochi è chiamato con diversi nomi, chiamanosi in Venetia* Varoli, *et in Genova* Lupi, *in Roma* Spigoli, *in Pisa et in Fiorenza* Ragni (III,40). In the course of Book III he displays an amazing assortment of names by which fish are variously known in particular localities. For dishes as well: ... *Diverse sorte di crostate, da Napoletani dette coppi, et da Lombardi* sfogliati (V,49).

Venice is a place that Scappi knows well and refers to often. There he experienced the exotic preparation of birds' tongues: *Trovandomi in Venetia al servitio dell'Illustrissimo et Reverendissimo Cardinal Marin Grimano ne furon portate* [that is, *lingue de volatili*] *a sua Signoria Illustrissima di Cipro ... & perciò si può conoscere, che son in prezzo* (Recipe II,149). He even anticipates Giovanni's (and others') scepticism that such things were actually a menu item somewhere. I have seen it, he declares, I myself prepared them. He is quite familar with the Venetian market: of oysters he writes, *Vero è, che in Venetia se ne truovano quasi tutto l'anno* (III,183); of head cabbages, *Son portati in Trevisi et in Venetia di terra Todesca cauli cappucci salati* (II,197). And we have references to particular Venetian preparations: *frittelle alla Venetiano* (V,136); *pottagio alla Venetiana* (III,31 and 40); *brisavoli alla Venetiana* (II,7, 38, 66); *rape alla Venetiana* (II,212); and a certain spice mixture that he calls *spetierie Venetiane* (III,31 and 62).

He was, too, forever entering into conversation with foreigners, gathering information about foodstuffs and cooking practices which he will pass on helpfully to a future cook. He writes of a strange species of fish *de quali per quanto io ho inteso dallo Scalco dell'Illustriss. e Reverendiss. Card. Polo d'Inghilterra, in quel mare si piglia gran quantità, et è a somiglianza dello storione, ma il nome appresso di noi è incognito* (Recipe III, 206).

Scappi is curious about foodstuffs that are available elsewhere and how other cooks, professional or, for instance, simple fisherfolk, go about preparing their dishes. *Nel tempo ch'io mi son trovato in Venetia et in Ravenna, ho inteso da pescatori da Chiozza, et Venetiani, liquali fanno i migliori potaggi, che non si usava di cuocerli in altro modo di quel ch'io ho detto di sopra* (Recipe III,79). He is completely open to these 'foreign' practices, to the possibility of adopting them to the enrichment of his own.[69] By describing them in his book he proposes that, irrespective of their humble or distant origin, they are worthy of the table of the world's most exalted court.

In his preamble to Book I, Scappi says that he has always treated his apprentice with the good will and close personal feelings that are more suitable to a stepson than to a servant. Scappi's reader becomes rapidly aware that he, too, has become Scappi's apprentice, his Giovanni, and that the master's counsel comes to him with that remarkable combination of unlimited curiosity and kindly goodwill.

As a food writer Scappi passes on advice in two distinct areas, his knowledge of foodstuffs and his practice of cookery.

Scappi's practice: tradition and originality

*G*astronomic taste and the cookery that feeds it being in large measure matters of local convention, an equally large part of a cook's work is determined by what has been done before in the milieu in which he works. How that proven practice can be improved further depends upon two factors: the potential of the kitchen, its

---

[69] In her article 'Exotisme culinaire et représentations nationales,' Héraud observes (129) that among European recipe collections of the time those in Italian are especially open to 'foreign' recipes, and most particularly to dishes whose provenance (according to their names) was various regions in the full length of Italy. She could well have recognized as an influence the extraordinary traffic of 'foreigners' from elsewhere in Europe into the Italian peninsula during the late Middle Ages and Renaissance.

facilities and workers; and the initiative of the chief cook. Training and facilities will permit a craft; imagination will foster an art.

Contemporary dining

In Books I and IV Scappi insists that the cook should be cognizant of the steward's functions. Specifically, he should know what happens to the food that he prepares, from the time it leaves his kitchen to the time it is set out properly on the master's dining board. That is, he must know about meals: the genre of meal to be served; table setting for it; the services that comprise it and their sequence; the dishes that comprise each service; the presentation of dishes. Scappi acknowledges that menus and serving lie firmly within the steward's jurisdiction; but, *al Cuoco sarà sempre piu honore di saper servire per Scalco, che il Scalco per cuoco*, adding that as a consequence 'it is nothing if not advantageous for the cook to be knowledgeable also about determining the dishes for the sideboard as well as those of the kitchen' (IV, f.168v [1581 f.133r]). In this respect Scappi distinguishes himself from the two successful food writers of his day: Domenico Romoli (Panunto) and Cristoforo Messisbugo were both stewards in a grand household, as was, later, Giovan Battista Rossetti. Their concern was primarily the presentation of a meal for the lord; the means by which the myriad components of that meal were realized was, traditionally, the province of a 'mechanic,' a plebeian of certain necessary skills but of little learning, cultural refinement or aesthetic taste. For Scappi the supremely competent cook had to understand clearly the nature of every gracious meal he was to prepare, how each dish would contribute to that meal as well as the gastronomic interrelation between the kitchen preparations and the sideboard preparations. He could acquire more prestige, and credit, by knowing the steward's job than if the steward, to do his own job, had to know the cook's. And so, for instance, in his book he will insist upon the season of the year and the provenance of the best of particular foodstuffs – just as Panunto and Missisbugo do. So, too, Scappi's care for a clear organisation of his abundant material and a soberly formal exposition of it.

In most respects Scappi's dishes and meals are generally those that were served and enjoyed in wealthy courts of refined taste throughout the Italian states.[70] The Gonzaga, Medici, Farnese, Este, Sforza and Strozzi families continued to eat the two meals a day that were prepared and eaten in noble courts in the late Middle Ages: the main one, the *pranzo*, just before or at midday and a somewhat simpler one, the *cena*, at nightfall. These might very occasionally be preceded by an elementary breakfast, a bite or two designed solely to stave off hunger; and those meals might also, when the occasion warranted it, be followed by a snack to revive evening activities that went on into the late or early hours. Of the cookery involved

---

[70] For a survey of European food customs and writing at this time see Albala, *Food in Early Modern Europe*, particularly concerning sixteenth-century Italy (118–40).

in the latter 'meals,' there is no evidence; they may have relied on credenza foods, things that were either raw or prepared ahead of time and available either cold or kept warm on a chafing dish over embers.

A third sort of set meal was termed a *collatione*.[71] The etymology of the word – which Scappi may have known but did not take the opportunity to expatiate upon – has to do with 'carrying around with oneself' (Zingarelli) and referred to foods taken standing or walking about; those would be, in essence, finger foods, as distinct from dishes calling for the use of a diner's spoon, fork or knife. By its nature the *collatione* was not originally a formal meal; it called for fewer servitors and was generally more suitable for outdoor locations. By Scappi's day it amounted to a somewhat informal meal often taken outdoors in one of Rome's elegant private gardens.

Outdoor dining seems to have been normal on occasion in the papal court circles. In the preamble to Book IV Scappi gives credit to the steward, Francesco Reinoso, for cleverly placing the table in settings that were compatible with the season, affording shade from a warm sun, shelter from a prevailing breeze, the bubbling of water for the heat, and 'in winter in rooms decorated with a variety of tapestries, sculptures and paintings' (IV, f.168r [1581 f.133r]) – all for the pleasure, *per trattenimento*, of the guests.

Scappi makes a further fundamental distinction between two sorts of food: those dishes that come from the kitchen and are served directly to the dining table, and those things that can be made up or procured and are set out ahead of time on the credenza or dining-hall sideboard. Scappi refers to those two sorts as kitchen foods and credenza foods; the latter he also terms *antipasti et postpasti di credenza*, appetizers and digestives (IV, f.168v [1581 f.133r]) – Scappi's *anti*-being, of course, in the sense of *ante*-.[72] In his menus service from the two sources, kitchen and credenza, tends to alternate.

As is only to be expected, Scappi clearly conforms as well to contemporary Christian requirements in the matter of lean foods and fasting foods. Over the long period of the Middle Ages and Renaissance, the definition of lean foods and of the times when such foods should or must be taken instead of meats varied from century to century and from place to place. According to Scappi's menus in Book

---

[71] In Book IV we translate the elements of a *collatione* that Scappi outlines for 31 May. In France the term is first recognized with the sense of a meal in the *Dictionnaire universel* of Antoine Furetière (1619–88): *le petit repas qu'on fait en haste en passant, quand on n'a pas le loisir de s'arrester*, or *ce qu'on prend en allant coucher, un doit de vin, & des confitures …* Records indicate that in sixteenth-century Italy the collation was somewhat more studied, lavish and impressive; see Benporat, *Feste e banchetti*, 93–9, 'Dalla definizione del convito alla nascita della "collatione,"' where the sumptuous variety of its culinary offerings is apparent.

[72] Concerning the relative sweetness of the initial serving in a refined Italian meal at the time, see Benporat, 'Evoluzione della cucina italiana alla fine del '500.'

IV, for the papal household lean meals were served in principle the day before any day that demanded a high degree of spiritual concentration. On such holy days, though, after due religious devotion had been observed, celebrations were appropriate and could entail plenteous good food; and so those particular holy days became known as feast days. Statutory lean days were fixed primarily for Fridays and Saturdays as a means of bodily and spiritual purification in preparation for the holy day of Sunday; Wednesday might also be a lean day. Furthermore, all forty days of Lent constituted a period of fasting. In a Christian cook's mind, a clear dichotomy had to exist between suitable lean foods and meat foods.

According to Scappi's recipes, meat from animals and fowl was forbidden in dishes for lean meals, as was the broth from boiling such meats; eggs and the dairy foods of milk, cream, butter and cheese were, however, allowed. Book IV contains menus for both a dinner and a supper on the same lean day in July (f.214r [1581 f.174r]) that consist *solely* of eggs and butter. In fasting times – that is, during Lent *giorni quadragesimale* and vigils *giorni di vigilia* – the absence of butter, cheese and eggs, as well as the pleasures of meats and other animal products, strengthened the soul.[73]

Another area in which Scappi's practice conformed very naturally to that of his contemporaries is related to the seasonal availability of foodstuffs. No cook before Scappi nor for several centuries after him could afford not to know how the market could set limits on his work. As we have seen, Scappi insists that his apprentice be aware when things ripen naturally to their most desirable state or the dates between which they may be had on the local (Roman) market. Such information must be an integral part of any cook's knowledge. Since the earliest times cooks recognized that the life of even such a staple as verjuice was subject to natural limitations: it was new if just pressed and used during that summer and autumn, old during the following winter; it rarely lasted in a usable condition through the spring of the next year.[74]

The very lengthy list of menus in Book IV, tracing as they do meals from week to week throughout a whole year, constitutes for Giovanni or any apprentice cook a practical illustration of seasonal limitations and potentials as well as a guide to the standards he will be expected to maintain in loading the papal dining board.

---

[73] See, for instance, Recipe VI,73 where in a lean preparation a meat broth is replaced by fresh butter, which in turn is replaced by sweet-almond oil for a Lenten dish; and III,230 where an herb-and-nut stuffing for an eggplant on a fasting day can include cheese and eggs if it is made for a lean- or meat-day meal. The Easter egg became in time a happy way to mark the end of gastronomic privation.

[74] The verjuice grapes themselves, either whole or in a mash, were usable only immediately following their harvest; by the late autumn the cook would have to resort to alternatives (Recipe II,271; VI,92).

A few preparations that had been common in older Italian cookery are no longer represented among Scappi's recipes: *caldume* (a dish of calf's intestines) and *brodo granato* (a broth with small bits of meat in it) are examples. Yet the genres of dish that Scappi prepares in his kitchen remain largely the traditional ones: *pottaggio, brodo* and *brodetto, zuppa, insalata*.[75] These offered the cook a vast range of possible versions. A pottage roughly approximated what we might include in the word 'stew' or 'soup.' Its varieties depended on the particular ingredients chosen and on their relative consistency: a thick soup was termed a *minestra*; a somewhat thinner soup or thick broth was a *brodetto*.[76] A sop (*suppa* or *zuppa*) was a favourite late-medieval preparation consisting of a firm slice of bread or toast, first soaked in a savory broth, then heaped with bits of virtually any foodstuff in a solid or semi-solid state, and often garnished. The word salad derived from the use of salt, vinegar, oil or acidic citric juice as a preservative, the foodstuff so treated being served cold and plain, without further preparation.[77]

Many variations of the usual types of dough confections are found in the *Opera*: moist and dry pasta, stuffed pasta, turnovers, pies and tartlets. These include *torte, tortelli* and *tortiglioni, tartare, pasticci* and *pasticetti, crostate, cialde* and *cialdoni, ciambelle, ciambellotte* and *ciambelloni, mostaccioli, grostoli, pizze, struffoli, fucaccine*.

In earlier times pies made use of pastry dough – often two or three centimetres thick – as a means to contain a mixture of ingredients while it baked. By Scappi's day a distinction was made between that coarse, but sturdy, flour-and-water pie shell, which a diner or the carver was expected to discard, and a thinner one made of a fine pie dough that incorporated eggs, butter or grease, perhaps with a seasoning; it had a distinct gastronomic appeal in itself. See Scappi's Recipes V,42 and 189 for instances of the use of that fine dough.

Among the pasta preparations gnocchi, lasagne, macaroni, ravioli, vermicelli and *millefanti* remain in good use.[78] According to Scappi, the plain, non-stuffed varieties could be fully dried (*asciutta*) and stored for an extended period – the purpose for which dried pasta was originally designed – but in all cases Scappi's recipes set them to boil in water, broth or milk, or to fry in oil,[79] immediately

[75] See Montanari's survey, 'La cucina Italiana fra Medioevo e Rinascimento.'

[76] Scappi's *brodetto* is still usually a reduced broth further thickened with eggs.

[77] See, for instance, Recipes II,190 for peas; III,207 for tuna, cooked, cooled and cubed, with oil and vinegar; and VI,98 for mallow.

[78] For a quick survey of pasta dishes in late-medieval Italian recipe collections, see Redon and Laurioux, 'La constitution d'une nouvelle catégorie culinaire?,' and Montanari, 'Note sur l'histoire des pâtes en Italie.'

[79] Macaroni, for instance, is normally cooked in water or a broth; if fried in oil and garnished differently, it is called *ferlingotti* (Recipe III,256).

after shaping the dough. At most he prescribes only a short moment for the pasta to sit to absorb moisture or throw off any excess of it. In several places Scappi suggests procedures for stuffing pasta; ravioli is very common among those dishes, although a new name for a similar sort of pasta creation, *tortelletti*, appears just as often. Earlets (*orecchine*, V,44) are a similar sort of small half-round deep-fried pasta turnover that was known to generations previous to Scappi's; they closely resemble the oven-baked yellow pasta turnovers called *offelle* (V,48) for which there is a recipe already by the middle of the previous century in the *Neapolitan Recipe Collection*.

Naturally enough, a good number of other preparations, traditional in Italy and in many other European courts, continue to be made in Scappi's kitchen. The *brodo lardiero* was a relatively simple dish in which pork is boiled slowly, adding its flavour to common spices, a herb or two, fruit, wine or must, the blend occasionally sweetened with sugar.[80] Diners before Scappi's day could similarly have been familiar with versions of a few or all of the following dishes in the *Opera*: *bianco mangnare* (II,162 and elsewhere), *fiadoni* (known in France as *flaons*), *fritelle* and *frittate* (respectively fritters and omelets), *gelatina, ginestrata* (II,160), *giuncata & lattaroli* (V,85), *grostoli* (that is, *crostoli*, V,232), *herbolata* (V,94) and *salviata* (III,284), *marzapane, migliaccio, millefanti* (II,171), *miraus* (II,248), *mostaccioli* (VI,142 and elsewhere), nut pastes – *mandolata, pignocatta, nosetto* and *pistacchea* (VI,217) – *panata, polpette* and *polpettoni*, sausages[81] of many sorts – *salame, salcizza, salciccione, salcicciotto, mortadella, tommacelle, cervellata, sanguinaccio* (II,114) – *suppa dorata, uove ripiene* (devilled eggs, III,273), and *zambaglione*[82] (VI,64).

A few dishes were evidently staples in places beyond the confines of the papal court. The names that Scappi uses for them incorporate the phrase 'after the fashion of': *bove alla Tedesca* (II,12), *trutte alla Tedesca* (III,119), *gattafure all Genovese* (I, §44), *pottaggio alla Francese* (III,148), *alla Romanesca, alla Damaschina, alla Fiorentina, alla Milanese, alla Senese, alla Bresciana, alla Napoletana*. As we have pointed out, the most common of these borrowed or imitated dishes are,

---

[80] For an instance of Scappi's *brodo lardiero* see Recipe II,85. His versions of the dish can be compared with many earlier ways of doing it: in a late-thirteenth-century recipe collection that would become the *Viandier* of Taillevent, Recipe 5; in the *Menagier de Paris*, from the end of the fourteenth century, Recipes 81 and 90; in the Savoyard *Du fait de cuisine* of Chiquart, 1420, Recipes 10, 38 and 78; and in the Italian Martino's *Arte coquinaria*, c. 1460, Recipes 1 and 6. The fifteenth-century Italian manuscript 211 of the Wellcome Institute for the History of Medicine, London, also has an interesting *brodo larderio* at Recipe 34.

[81] Scappi often uses sausages, the smaller ones whole, the larger cut up, as ingredients in his prepared dishes.

[82] A recipe for *zabaglone* is written on a flyleaf of the manuscript containing the *Neapolitan Recipe Collection*.

naturally enough given Scappi's history there, those that purportedly had some connection with Venice.

The survival of many old sauces into Scappi's kitchen is not surprising: *agliata* (II,257), *agrestata* (II,273), *bronegro* or *brodo negro* (II,252), *civiero* (II,249), *galantina* (II,250), *ginestrata* (II,255), *mostarda* (II,276), *salsa reale* (II,267), *salza di pavo* or *salza bastarda* (II,253), as well as perhaps the hoariest pair in European cookery, *peverata* (II,251) and *salza verde* (II,272).

But Bartolomeo Scappi was by no means a strictly traditional cook. Many new or recently new preparations came from his kitchen; many enjoyed enough favour among his patrons that he was confident enough about their worth to give them a place in his book.[83] We find *berlingozzi* (VI,138), *brisavoli* (modern bresaola, II,7 and elsewhere), *capirotata* (II,158, etc), *carabazzata* (II,219), *cascatelle* (V,150), *ciambelle* (V,150) and *ciambelloni* (V,148), *crostata* (V,49 and elsewhere), *fucaccine* (small *focaccie*, V,44), *grostoli* (V,230, modern *crostoli*), *nosella* (a walnut sauce, II,258), *pane stufato* (VI,25), *pasta reale* (V,84), *pizza* (V,121), *sfogliati* (V,49), *crostata* (V, 49), *sussidio* (VI,16 and elsewhere), *tartara* (V,86), *tommacelle* (a variety of croquette, II,107 and elsewhere), *zeppolle* (V,145), *sapore di carotte* (II,260), *sapore di melegranate* (II,264), and sauces made from a fairly wide variety of fruits (II,265ff.).

Of pasta preparations *tagliatelli* are mentioned (II,173 and V,84), although these are apparently a new variety because Scappi explains that they are a sort of lasagne. The new stuffed pasta called *tortelletti* (in one instance *tortellini*), 'miniature tourtes' that look like helmets (II,178), have already been mentioned. And the form of pasta called *sfogliatelle* (V,44), resembling the *orecchine* in final appearance, seems a new preparation.

Readers of modern cookbooks may think it strange that so many of Scappi's recipes, even the more complex ones, have no distinctive name, the equivalent of 'Jane's Ginger Soup' or 'Cottage Delight.' More often than not his recipes have a rubric that begins, 'To make a pie of whitedish ... ' or that reads plainly and simply, 'To make a sauce of quince juice': *Per fare pasticci sfogliati di bottarghe, schinale, schina d'aringhe, e caviale salati in cassa* (V,197). Few modern self-respecting restaurants would offer a dish without a uniquely elegant foreign name: *Potage Botzaris* or *Crépinette Cendrillon*. The dishes listed in the menus of Book IV read for the most part like the recipe rubrics but without the phrase, *Per far*: 'Veal breast, boiled served with parsley over top'; 'Pies of whole goat-kids' heads, deboned and stuffed, one per pie.' Why are Scappi and his professional peers content to name a preparation by only a generic name qualified, usually, with a list of principal ingredients and a cooking method? The answer is not very

---

[83] 'New' is of course a risky word. It would be safer to say that these dishes *appear* not to have been detailed in cookery books of a generation or two before under the same or a similar name.

obscure: proper names help sell a dish and its cook. Scappi's basic repertoire of dishes was prepared for a closed society whose members knew what they liked and let the steward know; the steward would be inclined to transmit his menu choices to the cook not by some abstract name, like *Suprême de béatilles*, that had little in it that was descriptive or precise, but rather by a sufficiently descriptive and generic name. That sort of name was the most useful, culinarily speaking.

An interesting, and perhaps revealing, confirmation of that preference is found in several rubrics which indicate a proper name for a dish: *Per far suppa dorata detta dal vulgo capirotata* (III,266).[84] The *vulgo* are the common people; *they* may have had a reason to tag a dish with a playful or evocative label, but such names had little functional use in the practical workaday world of a professional's kitchen.

Scappi inherited a predilection for a bitter-sweet taste that had been refined by several previous generations of Italian cooks. He will occasionally combine the sources of each flavour and then instruct his cook to check that the balance between the two is what is expected: *... Facendo il saggio piu volte di modo che tal sapore ... habbia del dolce, et dell'agro* (Recipe II,248). His patron's and contemporaries' palate still relished a smooth lusciousness, but enlivened with a tang.[85]

Two traditional serving methods remain in use for Scappi's prepared dishes: solid foods can be presented dressed with a sauce garnish or accompanied by a bowl containing a dipping sauce. Those means of saucing can be alternatives for a given dish: *... con alcuni sporetti in piatti, ò sopra* (Recipe II, 148); or else perhaps[86] complementary: *Si serve asciutta con petrosemolo sopra, & agliata in piatti* (III,86).

The preparations for the sick that appear in early cookbooks tend to rely upon traditional, tried-and-true recipes. For the most, part these are fairly simple, using a few efficacious foodstuffs. Scappi's sickdishes show a proper respect

---

[84] See also *Per far tortelletti con pancia di porco, & altre materie dal vulgo chiamate anno-lini* (II,178); *Per far minestra di zucche & cipolle in diversi modi, dal vulgo detta carabazzata* (II,219); *Per far crostata con cascio grasso, dal vulgo detta butirata* (II,233).

[85] When writing his *Brieve racconto di tutte le radici, di tutte l'herbe et di tutti i frutti, che crudi o cotti in Italia si mangiano* in England in 1614, Giacomo Castelvetro tried to explain the Italian love for the tang of sour, unripe gooseberries rather than when ripe, which preference was 'quite the reverse of you English, who are so fond of sweet dishes ... Your taste for sweet food is probably due to the fact that you never have to endure, as we do in Italy, the loss of appetite caused by the intense summer heat. We like to revive our jaded palates with sharp things ... When gooseberries are not in season we use verjuice, the juice of unripe grapes' (trans. Riley, 71).

[86] Here and there among the recipes it may be advisable to remind the reader that Scappi's 'and' may often be understood as an 'or.'

for tradition – as befitted a household where the best of medical practice was available and, in matters of treating those whose were indisposed, clearly dictated kitchen practice. In Book VI chicken (and other related poultry, especially capon, and some gamefowl), veal and barley enjoy pride of place in a variety of such preparations. Sugar, too, and to a lesser extent egg yolks appear regularly in the recipes for the sick. In all cases, to cook for the sick with those ingredients was to comply with sound medical doctrine, the ingredients having natural temperaments that closely approximated that of human nature: somewhat warm and somewhat moist. For many centuries, physicians had seen them as fundamentally safe foods that could gently moderate and rectify any distemper or wayward tendencies in a person's humoral balance, confirming and strengthening the complexion of his state of good health.[87]

Book VI offers two instances in which Scappi has recourse to an alambic, a distilling flask, in order to extract the essence of a foodstuff. The phenomenon of distillation was well studied in the Middle Ages; stills of several sorts were thoroughly familiar to alchemists and physicians as devices for refining a substance to its fundamental or fifth essence. For some time cooks had had access to distilled alcohols from wine, fruit and flowers (rosewater in particular being a late-medieval kitchen staple), but normally the making and storing of *aqua vitæ* and *aqua ardens* were in former times an exclusive prerogative of a household's pharmacy. Scappi, though, never suggests that access to a still might be a novelty for a cook.

In short, Scappi by and large accepts contemporary gastronomic taste and practises the cookery that satisfied it. Generally speaking, he works within a repertoire of standard generic preparations, adding an uncertain number of specific dishes to specific genres. Much of the substance that Scappi has bequeathed to Giovanni in his *Opera* resides in the manner in which he deals with his recipes: his constant insistence upon possible alternatives and options; his desire to present as large a variety of offerings as possible; his consciousness of the exalted position he occupied, and of the consequent need and obligation to offer a service worthy of that position; and, perhaps above all, his insistence on possessing a thorough understanding of all that touches upon the household's food – not merely in kitchen work but in the marketplace and the dining hall as well, and in the conditions of employment of kitchen personnel. A master cook must be a master of a broad complex of exacting subject matter.

---

[87] The long-established science of the humoral makeup of all substances – of which we shall mention a little more below – continued to be a cornerstone for the medical profession well into the seventeenth century. A contemporary of Scappi's, Baldassare Pisanelli, sustained the erudite dogma with his *Trattato della natura de' cibi et del bere*, Bergamo, 1587 and Venice, 1611. Cautious cooks who were serious about their work and their master's good health had ample guidance from such works and from physicians in the employ of their master.

Material circumstances of Scappi's cooking

It is enough to leaf through the engraved plates that Scappi has accompany his *Opera* to begin to appreciate the real extent of his work. All the bits and pieces of hardware necessary to an ideal kitchen, all andirons and heat shields, the spits and grills, the kettles, pots and pans, the tripods and dishwarmers, the buckets, jugs, cruets and pitchers, the multifarious cutlery, the whips, rasps, rakes, shovels and brooms, the mortars, grinders, sieves and filters, the weigh scales, the candelabras, the crates and hampers – the conglomerate mass of this professional equipment effectively represents the daily labour of a master cook. Installed in its proper setting (see the first plates: the ideal kitchen with its several annexes), this equipment defined and determined the cook's profession. Four hundred and some years later it helps us to grasp more clearly the nature of this sixteenth-century cookery.

In the course of the translation we shall try wherever possible to explain particular items of Scappi's hardware by referring to the plates. A few more general comments might be useful at this point, though, before the reader begins to look at Scappi's text.

Plates 1 and 2 show a very few oil lamps or tallow candles, and few windows in the three walls that are shown; the lighting in a kitchen must have been very dim on dull days or in the morning and evening during the winter.[88] The heat cast off by open fires – to say nothing of the smoke and the steam from long-boiling pots – must also at times have made work in a kitchen difficult.

Pastry makers generally did their work apart from the cooks, as we can see in Plate 2. Scappi's instruction that a dough be made up in such-and-such a way points to the chief cook's necessary authority in all the precincts of his kitchen.

Recipes frequently call for a foodstuff to be beaten with the *costa* of one or two knives. Plate 13 shows a good assortment of knives,[89] some of which have the straight, flat back suitable for beating an ingredient. From the thirteenth century, manuscript illuminations show a cook, a knife in each hand, beating a foodstuff with their spines. The side or flat of most knives is shown in Scappi's engravings to be slightly concave from the back to the cutting edge.

Just as chopping, mincing and grinding were common procedures at some stage in many recipes at that time, so the resultant paste was frequently put through a strainer before the dish was finished. Scappi writes of several sorts of strainer,[90]

---

[88] A variety of candle holders is illustrated on Plates 2, 15, 22 and 27. See also the *bugia* on Plate 23.

[89] As well as for carving, chopping and beating, knives were designed (or at least used) for mixing (II,171). Occasionally Scappi will feel he must specify the use of a slicing knife: *un coltellino che tagli* (VI,55).

[90] We find a *crivello*, *setaccio*, *foratoro*, *stamigna*, and *colatoro*.

of leather, of matted bristles or horsehair, of wool, plain fabric alone, fabric held in a drums or a cone-shaped frame, woven wire sieves, perforated copper or brass collanders. All of these were available in coarse or fine varieties, with large or small holes.

Scappi uses a relative terminology to describe heats: for a gentle heat he speaks of a *foco adagio, foco lento, foco pian piano*, a 'slow flame'; for a moderate heat, a *foco temperato* or *mediocre*; and for a hot heat, a *foco chiaro, gagliardo* or *gagliardetto*, a 'sprightly flame.' He will also distinguish two sources of heat that will contact a food directly: (*brustoliscanosi*) *alle bragie*, 'in glowing coals,' and (*faccianosi finir di cuocere*) *sotto la cenere calda*, 'under hot ash' (II,212).

Ovens, probably shown on the left wall of Plate 1 and on the right wall of Plate 2, may have allowed embers to be set above the baking chamber. In any case the rule in Recipe V,11 – that pies of flaky pastry need a more pronounced heat from above than from below – indicates that bakers could manage their oven's heat rather closely. The purpose of an oven is to cook a foodstuff in a heat that is only relatively dry. When the amount of food is not great, the same end can be achieved by using a pot or pan with a tightly fitting lid such as a *tortiera*, or a *testo*. The latter apparatus was of ancient origin, an earthenware or metal bell, whose top was flat or had a slight depression in which hot embers could be set, that was placed over a food; the food, on a plate or in a pot, could receive heat from below as well by being placed on or over coals and was braised largely in its own juices. (See the note in Recipe II,11.)

Ingredients, foodstuffs available and used

Since classical antiquity, understanding the physical reality of the world depended on an intellectual grasp of the nature and 'properties' of all of its constituent parts. Many physicians, initially Greek, then Arabic and ultimately European, transmitted accumulated lore about the nature of things and of human beings, and the effects of the former upon the latter's human nature.

For the late-medieval cook that physical science implied an obligation to know the peculiar nature of all of the ingredients he handled in his kitchen. From the earliest written recipes in Europe, there is evidence that cooks combined ingredients, chose condiments and cooking methods and garnished dishes in large measure in order to temper the final qualities of a preparation. When Platina,[91] humanist and Vatican librarian, copied Martino's recipe collection, he doubled its volume by inserting a good deal of the conventional scientific data about foodstuffs. Scappi had likely seen a printed copy of the *De honesta voluptate et valetudine* but shows a possible influence of that scholar only in the amount of space he devotes in his own book to the nature of foodstuffs. As a practising cook, Scappi goes much further than Platina, or any earlier cook anywhere in Europe. Not only

---

[91] See n.4, above.

does he examine the nature of the best meats, fowl, fish, fruits and vegetables, as Platina did in a sketchy way, but he also follows the foodstuff through the kitchen, from the time a skinned carcass, a whole fish in brine or an artichoke arrives at the stage at which it can be cut up and cooked. He demonstrates a butcher's intimate knowledge of a carcass as he specifies exactly where a prime or secondary cut of meat is located; he describes how to isolate a fish's 'umbilicus'; he directs the cook's knife to discard all but the desirable part of a carrot.

Most importantly, though, he knows when, at what times of the year, a cook can expect to be able to obtain any particular foodstuff. Sometimes he will refer to the time or times the animal, fish or plant in its natural habitat reaches its most desirable state of 'ripeness'; at other times he will indicate when the cook can count on finding the foodstuff in a local market stall – particularly a Roman one but those of other centres as well. Such practical information is clearly vital for any serious cook: you cannot plan on making a lamb stew except in the spring, a Venetian pottage of sea bass before December or after February, or a dish of lettuce outside of March, April and May.

Refrigerators and freezers do a lot today to obviate that concern about seasonal availability. Scappi's contemporaries still relied on drying (as with raisins and cherries), smoking (as with fish) and salting (as with ham or butter). All three processes entailed driving 'excess' moisture from a foodstuff: early scientists understood quite well that moisture must invariably bring about 'corruption' – rot and spoilage.[92] The process of salting is common, too, in the kitchen when an article is being set aside for later use: *Cosi fresche si accommoderanno in un vaso di terra con sal trito, & fior di finocchio, & vi si lascieranno fin'a tanto che si vorranno cuocere* (Recipe III,149). Though salting was the means of preservation most commonly resorted to, it usually entailed some process of reconstitution that a cook had to incorporate into his handling of the ingredient. A preliminary step, for salted ham (*presciutto*), salted tuna belly (*tarantello*), even salted butter, involved a soaking or parboiling in order to replace moisture and to remove the excess salt.

As we have seen, Scappi was forever concerned that the cook select only the best ingredients, not only those that are most appropriate for a given preparation but those that are in their best natural state. Get, he writes, the blackest, fattiest caviar, which will always be the best (Recipe III,265). Repeatedly he will advise

---

[92] Pierre Laszlo explains that 'salt is toxic to any organism whose concentration of salt is less than the salinity of a mixture applied to it.' Physicians had further long observed that salt was a 'simple technique for asepsis, as a protection against pathogenic bacteria.' *Salt: Grain of Life*, tr. Mary Beth Mader (New York: Columbia University Press, 2001), 4. On the techniques used in the production of salt in Scappi's time, and its commerce across Europe, see S.A.M. Adshead, *Salt and Civilizatin* (New York: St Martin's Press, 1992), 99–111.

how to identify particular foodstuffs and to know when they are at their best.[93] His distinctions between varieties of produce are specific. Squash of several sorts, for instance, can be had and used: common squash or *zucca nostrale, zucca marina, zucca pelosa, zucca savonese* and *zucca turchesca*. Members of the cabbage family that he cooked included broccoli, cauliflower, *cauli cappuci, Milanesi, Bolognesi* and *torsuti* (kohlrabi). Along with the old staples of turnips, leeks and chard, vegetables that may have been novelties in Europe in the previous century are now common in this cookery: artichoke, asparagus (cultivated and wild), broad beans (fava), cardoon, carrot, chickling, cucumber, eggplant, endive, mallow, palm shoots, parsnip root, rhubarb root (a vegetable) and spignel. Liquorice root (*regolitia*, VI,5) retains a quasi-medical use. Missing, even though used in earlier cookery, are smallage (wild celery),[94] chervil, cress (both garden and water varieties), kale, salsify and skirrets – these last having been alternatives in the past for parsnips. Maize had not yet won the favour of noble dining boards although by the second half of Scappi's century it was known as *grano turco* because it was by then grown widely in the near east.[95] Hemp seed and poppy seed, formerly used as agreeable flavourants, are likewise missing from Scappi's recipes.

A good range of fruits in particular make their way through Scappi's kitchen. His cook should be familiar with useful varieties of grape and raisin (*uva schiava, agresta, uva cesenese, uva moscatella* and the *zibibbo*), cherries, dates, figs, gooseberries, azaroles, medlars, mulberries, strawberries, apples (of several varieties), apricots, peaches (freestone or clingstone), plums and prunes; pears are distinguished as being *caravelle, papale, d'acciole, riccarde, ruspe, bergamotte* and *fiorentine*; red currants, jujubes, quince and pomegranates enter one way or another into cooked dishes, garnishes and pastry. Citrus fruits – oranges, lemons, limes and citrons – play major roles in lending the tangy flavour that Scappi prizes; although the newly cultivated sweet orange is mentioned only twice, a semi-sweet variety has some presence in his recipes and the usual bitter variety is used very broadly. Tomatoes, however, are not yet recognized.[96]

---

[93] A useful mnemonic in this regard is passed on to his apprentice: '[A frog's] season begins in May and lasts to the end of October because that's the season of the verjuice grape: while the verjuice grape lasts, frogs are good' (*Mentre dura l'agresto le rane son buone*, III,162).

[94] Italian gardeners will develop a 'cultivated' strain of celery, *Apium graveolens* var. *dulce*, in the seventeenth century from English stocks of smallage, *Apium graveolens* or wild celery.

[95] See Toussaint-Samat, *History of Food*, 172.

[96] See Grewe, 'The Arrival of the Tomato in Spain and Italy.' In the second half of Scappi's century botanists still treated this New World fruit largely as a novel curiosity. Grewe quotes Castor Durante (1529–90): 'They are eaten in the same way as eggplants, with pepper, salt and oil, but give little and bad nourishment' (*Herbario nuovo*, Rome, 1585). See also Pérez Samper, 'La integración de los productos americanos,' 107–10.

In older cookery the preparation of game meats was often accorded just about as much space as the preparation of their domestic counterparts. Scappi does treat stag, deer, chamois and boar but not to the same extent as his predecessors – and also with a suggestion that the young[97] of the wild species is a worthwhile option for a cook. Small game, such as rabbit, is not quite beneath Scappi's notice, appearing in only three recipes;[98] hares are mentioned in seven dishes. Considerably more attention is paid to wildfowl.

Of the domestic meats, Scappi prefers that of male animals, but those that have been castrated. Earlier recipes that specify beef do not distinguish a steer from a cow, as Scappi does. When cooking goat meat earlier recipe writers do not make Scappi's distinction between *becco, capra, capretto* and *caprone*; a *castrone*, a wether or castrated male sheep, provides one of his most commonly used meats. Pork is, as in the past, probably the most useful of all the meats here, partly because of its flavour and partly because it is readily preserved in salt and can therefore be always on hand. The most esteemed meat, however, in the taste of Scappi's patrons is undoubtedly veal.[99] It was the meat of predilection for the wealthy classes: the fact that calves grew into cows and into valuable oxen – the main tractive force in agriculture – put the cost of veal beyond the means of any but very comfortable households.

In an interesting tour de force, a pair of meals, both *pranzo* and *cena* for 15 May (IV, f.180r–182r [1581 ff.144r–146r]), contained only veal as their meat; the rubric for the noon meal proclaims the oddity: *Pranzo … di carne di vitella sola con due servitii di credenza, & due di cocina.* Scappi follows up that particular menu with a sort of appendix (f.182r [1581 f.146v]), labelled simply *Altre vivande che si fanno della carne di vitella*, in which he offers a cook no fewer than twenty-four further recipes for veal by which he could enrich such a veal meal! A few of the *Opera*'s dishes will specify that the veal be of an unweened or suckling animal: *una vitella mongana, una vitella di latte.*

A few foods from the New World are in evidence by Scappi's time. Turkey (Scappi's *gallo d'India*)[100] in particular has a valued role in the *Opera*, cocks,

---

[97] That is, with the tenderer meat. Physicians taught that because of its habitat game was generically warmer and drier than domestic meat, just as castration moderates the desiccation of domestic male animals. The young of any species being naturally more moist than the mature or old animal, the best game meat was necessarily that of younger animals.

[98] A guinea pig (*coniglio d'India*), however, is prepared for eating in almost as many ways: II,95 and V,29.

[99] Early physicians never tire of praising the qualities of veal. The *Regimen sanitatis* of Salerno (thirteenth century) summarizes scientific opinion, found already in Galen and Avicenna, with the line *Sunt nutritive multum carnes vituline*: 'Veal is very nourishing' (l. 80).

[100] The identification of Scappi's *gallo d'India* remains moot. In her article on the use of turkey

hens and pullets being distinguished for appropriate dishes. The Muscovy or musk duck (*anatra d'India*) is also prepared, though in a single dish; brought only recently from South America, it was at that time black with white patches. The guinea pig (*coniglio d'India*) has been mentioned above, yielding a delicate meat. Other New World products, such as potatoes[101] or sweet potatoes, Indian corn (maize), Jerusalem artichokes (brought from Canada only in 1607), and pimentos, are not recorded by Scappi. Chocolate, likewise, is not mentioned.[102]

Fish, crustaceans and aquatic animals are naturally of very great concern to Scappi. The modern reader may indeed feel overwhelmed with the many species mentioned. As Scappi deals with them in extensive detail in Book III, we see particularly clearly how much study he has given to the nature of each, and its sub-species, to its gastronomic value and to its provenance and season. Occasionally he furnishes his reader with one or several various regional names for a fish. Generally he describes distinctive features clearly for identification purposes. Typically he is careful to indicate which fish are exceptionally worthy of being handled in a respectable kitchen: ... *Trutte, dentali, orate, et altri pesci nobili* (Recipe VI,213); and which are not: *Il pesce Palombo ... è pesce indegno di banchetti regali* (III,108).

Because most fish had to be transported some considerable distance, the question of their preservation was crucial to a cook. A summary of the standard means of preserving fish is given in Recipe III,201: Scappi writes that his apprentice must know how to handle *pesci salati, conservati in foglie, & secchi al fumo, & all'aere, & in salimora*. In his *Opera* he carefully describes the cooking procedures for species, fresh or preserved.

As in the past, cooking oils and grease, primarily for frying, came from two sources. Depending on the church's dietetic rules, they were alternatives. They could be either animal fats – pork skin-fat, chicken breast-fat, veal and goat kidney-fat – or vegetable oils – olive oil and various nut oils.

---

in Italian kitchens (*The Oxford Companion to Italian Food*, p. 535) Gillian Riley presents the historical likelihood that Scappi intended the New World bird and not guinea fowl, which had been cooked and eaten in Europe long before Scappi's day. Throughout this translation the very tentative assumption has been made that the relatively numerous recipes using members of the *gallo d'India* family did indeed call for turkey.

[101] These *pomi di terra* were brought from Quito in the 1550s. They appear well established in Francesco Leonardi's six-volume encyclopedia of Italian gastronomy, *Apicio moderno*, of 1790 – long after Scappi's day.

[102] Concerning several of these New World transplants see Pérez Samper, 'La integración de los productos americanos.' Beginning in 1541 the Milanese Girolamo Benzoni spent fourteen years in the New World. Subsequently in his *Novæ Novi Orbis Historiæ id est Rerum ab Hispanis in India Occidentali hactemus Gestarum* ... (published Venice, 1565 and Geneva, 1578) he described how to prepare chocolate in a beverage, but a good century passed before chocolate became popular in Italy.

Before the sixteenth century, Italian cooks had not depended greatly upon milk, in part because in warm climates it did not last more than a day and in part because itinerant milk merchants often succumbed to the temptation to water their product. Throughout the Middle Ages nuts, particularly almonds, yielded a satisfactory substitute for animal milk. Almond milk, almond cream and almond butter were well known and much used substances in the kitchen. For Scappi, however, cow's milk is now a staple, as are the butters and cheeses made from it.[103] Butter, being very largely a domestic product, was rarely used in refined medieval cookery; by Scappi's day, however, it had become commonplace in wealthy kitchens.[104] In part, too, because milk and its products are now permitted in lean-day cookery, Scappi uses all of them very freely. Butter is a preferred cooking medium. Cheese in particular enters into a surprisingly large number of dishes or is used as a garnish.[105] When listing cheese among their ingredients, older recipes are sometimes specific to the extent of qualifying the cheese by 'new' or 'old,' 'moist' or 'dry.' Scappi will also write of a 'fat' cheese, or a cheese that is 'firm' or 'hard,' or that is salted or 'fresh' (unsalted); but usually he will also be more precise, naming the specific variety of cheese that must be used. He will write of *agretti, bazzoto, casciotto, cascio cavallo, fiorita, granito, lattaroli, Maiorichino, marzolino, mozzarella, parmigiano, parmigiano di riviera, pecorino, provaggiole, provatura, raviggioli, ricotta, ricotte fiorite, ricotta pecorina, cascio di riviera, romagnolo, romanesco, sardesco* and *struccoli*. Among fresh cheeses he shows a predilection for provatura; among salted, Parmesan.

The old pan-European herbal staples, sage and parsley, remain in some use, but in Scappi what is evident is the traditional Italian tendency to enrich prepared dishes with an interesting range of herbs. Here and there he will call not only for one or the other of those old herbal staples, and for marjoram and mint,[106] but also for alexanders, bay laurel, borage, bugloss, burnet, clover (as a flavourant), dill, elderflower, elecampane, fennel (Scappi makes great use of the seed), juniper leaves, mugwart, myrtle, nettle, oregano, pennyroyal, poppy (not

---

[103] In Book I Scappi devotes §7 and §8 exclusively to butter and cheese respectively. Both milk products are normally salted in order to prolong their life.

[104] Even Scappi's ideal kitchen has a churn for *latte mele* (honey milk) in its 'dairy room,' Plate 4. Concerning the great use of butter in French recipes of the time, see Philip and Mary Hyman, 'Les associations de saveurs dans les livres de cuisine français du XVIe siècle,' 140.

[105] The seventeenth-century cleric John Ray observed that a fondness for cheese still persisted on the Italian palate: 'They scrape or grate Cheese upon all their dishes even of flesh; accounting that it gives the meat a good relish; which to those that are unaccustomed makes it rather nauseous and loathsome' (*Travels through the Low-Countries, Germany, Italy and France*, 2nd ed., London, 1738; vol. I, February 1664).

[106] Those two herbs are certainly used in earlier cookery but, surprisingly, they *each* appear in Scappi's recipes more than one hundred times.

just the seed), purslane, rocket, sorrel, spinach and chard (these last two chopped up and used as herbs) and wild thyme. More often than not, Scappi will leave the choice of specific herbs to the cook, writing merely that he should include *herbe, herbette, herbicine* or *herbame*, sometimes qualifying these generics with *odorifere, saporite* or *communi.*

Similarly, the traditionally broad use of spices in Italian cookery is continued but with some alterations. Spikenard (an aromatic root), galangal (galingale), mace and cubeb are now missing, for instance. Older recipe collections in Italian show standard spice mixtures, more or less universal in European cookery: pepper, ginger, cinnamon, nutmeg and cloves, along with saffron.[107] In the *Opera* we find those spices as well as anise, coriander and musk. Most interesting are the changes. Sugar, growing in use from the beginning of the fifteenth century, now dominates, and almost collapses, the spice shelf of Scappi's kitchen.[108] It is mentioned in more than 900 of his recipes. The runners-up in popularity are cinnamon and pepper, being drawn upon for more than 600 and 550 preparations respectively, and saffron and cloves, each appearing more than 200 times. Two general comments may be of interest: in cookery elsewhere in Europe, pepper lost ground in aristocratic taste throughout the fifteenth century; and ginger, *the* flavour of medieval European food, has relatively little attraction for Scappi.[109] As with herbs, Scappi often calls for a generic spice mixture, *spezie* and *spetierie.* These terms may designate any spices the experienced cook may care to throw in at his option, or they may refer the cook back to a spice mixture (Recipe I, §26) that, in the best medieval tradition, the cook has made up ahead of time in order to season any dish *a piacere.*

We can also consider the liliaceous bulbs the way Scappi does, as flavouring agents. Onions, spring onions and garlic are chopped (and usually sautéed) into seventy to eighty preparations each, somewhat higher a use than is found in earlier cookery.

---

[107] On spices in common use in Renaissance Italy see Sabban and Serventi, *A tavola nel Rinascimento*, 54. The dominant role that Venice played in the spice trade at this time is examined by Krondl, *The Taste of Conquest*, 27–107.

[108] Transplanted from Egypt into Cyprus, sugar cane became a major crop on the island while it was under Venetian and Lusignan rule. From the fourteenth century Cyprus managed to supply most of the growing European demand for sugar, though Sicily, Malta and Rhodes had a small share of the market.

[109] One further note: grains of paradise (or *grana paradisi*, as Scappi calls it: melegueta pepper, or *Amomum melegueta* for modern botanists), one of the really important spices for early French cooks though of only moderate interest for their Italian counterparts, is named only once (Book I, §26) in the *Opera*, albeit in a general-purpose spice mixture. Curiously, French cookery of the time seems to have remained somewhat old-fashioned by retaining ginger in a 'preponderant' place among spices according to Hyman and Hyman, 'Les associations de saveurs,' 139–41.

A variety of grains are used here. Hard wheat (semolina, *semolella*), spelt, millet, foxtail millet (*panico*), barley, buckwheat and rice are used in various ways, whole-grain or cracked, usually after being steeped for an initial softening. Only wheat (normal soft wheat, *frumento*) and rice are ground and kept on hand as flours.[110] As a thickener that would not colour a dish, starch[111] (*amido*) was also considered to be a sort of flour.

Wines of various sorts played an important role in Italian cooking of the time.[112] In very general terms Scappi mentions *un buon vino* and *vino per bocca*, a good table wine; certain dishes also need, generally, a *vin rosso* or a *vin bianco* – even a *chiaro bianco*, a *bianco dolce* (a sweet white), and wines qualified as *amabile* (pleasant) or *gagliardo* (robust). But then for particular culinary purposes he distinguishes wines according to their origin: most often simply 'Greek wine,' occasionally specifically from Somma or from Ischia, but also (in I, §28) so-called French wine (unqualified, but to which Scappi adds 'and other dark wines'), chiarello (a claret), malvagia, moscatella and trebbiano, a clear Romanescho, a magnaguerra and a lagrima. Along with grape wines he also has several uses for pomegranate wine (II,264 and 270; VI,19 and 189). Only one liquor – in the sense of a distillate of an alcoholic infusion or juice – appears in the *Opera*: *acqua rosa, acqua di rosa* and *acqua di rose*. That so-called rosewater has a history of culinary use that goes back to at least the fourteenth century. Originally prepared for medicinal use,[113] rosewater soon exerted an appeal at the dining board. Its use remains widespread in Scappi. The flavour it lent his dishes forms something of a link with earlier gastronomic taste, but at the same time it points up how other elements of that taste had greatly evolved.

The use of place names to tag the origin of many ingredients – and occasionally even dishes and cooking practices – in Scappi's work is interesting and significant.[114] Among the places that Scappi connects to foodstuffs we find the names of rivers, lakes and seas: Ada, Adriatic Sea, Ambro, Arno, Arpino, Bolsena,

---

[110] See I, §27. For the special use of millet flour and foxtail millet flour, see I, §39 and II,136.

[111] See the note in Book I, §27 concerning starch.

[112] See the article on wine production and service by Aldo Dall'Igna, 'Vini e cantine del cinquecento,' in Marini, Rigoli and Dall'Igna, *Cucine, cibi e vini*, 37–57.

[113] Roses were perceived by physicians as being cool in the second degree and dry in the third – a very high rating for dryness. They could be prescribed as medicinally effective in countering any disease in which the brain was inflamed. Distillation concentrated those properties. The fourteenth-century *Tacuinum sanitatis* (translated by Judith Spencer as *The Four Seasons of the House of Cerruti*, 64) declares that rosewater (*aqua rosacea*) 'provides relief in the summer heat because it does good to *virtutibus et ynstrumentibus sensuum*, the efficacy of the sensory mechanisms which, due to the high temperature, become sluggish.'

[114] Concerning regional foods in Italy see Capatti and Montanari, *La cucina italiana*.

Como, *mare maggiore*, Navilio, Po, Reno, Santa Preseda, Silo, Tesino, Tevere, Tyrrheanian Sea, Vico; of districts, towns and cities: Ancona, Aquila, Argenta, Boccalione, Bologna, Brescia, Brondoli, Cesena (in Romagna), Chiozza (now Chioggia), Cicoriali (?), Comacchio, Consandola, Ferrara, Florenza, Genova, Ischia, Lombardia, Mantova, Marignano, Milan, Naples, Parma, Peruggia, Pesaro, Pistoia, Pizzighitone, Ravenna, Sabina, Salaro, Salerno, Sant' Angelo, Savona, Senigallia, Siena, Somma, Sora, Tagliacozzo, Trastevere, Trevisi, Troiano, Venetia, Verona; and of regions, states and countries: Burgundy, Cyprus, Corinth, Corsica, Flanders, France, Germany (*terra Tedesca*), Greece, India, Liguria, Lombardy, Majorca, Kingdom of Naples (*Regno di Napoli*), Romagna, Slavonia, Spain, Turkey.   Such a remarkable list points up the breadth of Scappi's awareness of the different foods and foodstuffs that were available, but it demonstrates, too, the geographical extent of his knowledge and just how concerned he was to obtain for his kitchen the best of what was available. It is likely evidence, moreover, of the fundamentally international character of the pontifical court and of the wide range of gastronomic tastes that the various Vatican kitchens had to try, though perhaps in only some small measure, to accommodate.[115]   It is evidence as well of how extensively commerce in foodstuffs had developed by the second half of the sixteenth century with, for instance, imports of small preserved fowl from Cyprus (I, §10), cheese, cabbage and barley from 'German lands' (I, §8; Recipes II,197; VI,57) and wines from Greece.   In his *Opera* Scappi shows a broad grasp of the geography of Italy and of proximate European lands, partly because of certain culinary practice that in person he has observed in various localities, including Slavonia (!), but mostly because the trade in foodstuffs has allowed him to learn the provenance of foodstuffs that he has discovered to be better for his purposes and that in turn he recommends procuring.[116]   With several foodstuffs he will distinguish between a 'home-grown,' local variety of the product and a foreign, imported and usually preferable variety: *Trovo esser molte sorti d'uve passe, ma quella di Corinto è assai migliore che la nostrale* (I, §24).   The kitchens of the larger Italian courts had both the means to order such imported foodstuffs and cooks like Scappi with the skills and taste to use them.

---

[115] When a remarkably multilingual entertainment concluded a festive meal, we are reminded how cosmopolitan Rome necessarily was: *Collatione fatta all'ultimo di febraro a Monte cavallo, nella sala dell'Illustriss. & Reverendiss. Card. Bellaia, à un'hora di notte doppo che fu recitata una comedia in linqua Francese, Bergamasca, Venetiana, & Spagnola ...* (IV, f.304r [1581 f.252v]; see the composition of this meal reproduced in Book IV, below). The cook to Pope Martin V was a German, Johannes Buckenhen; many of the recipes in the collection that he compiled – the *Registrum coquine* (1431–5) – end with a notation that the dish just described is appropriate variously for Romans, Germans, Bavarians, Bohemians, English, French, Frisians, Hungarians, Slavs and 'other Europeans,' a spectrum of distinct tastes which a papal cook was obliged to accommodate. See Laurioux, 'Le "Registre de cuisine" de Jean de Bockenheim.'

[116] See, for instance, Recipe III,115 on trout.

The people for whom Scappi cooked enjoyed greater variety in their foods than ever before. Scappi receives his foodstuffs through commercial networks that are more numerous and farther flung than ever before. But it is always clear that his 'foreign' supplies are sought out above all in order to ensure the best result in whatever dish he is preparing: *Essendo mele di Spagna, sarà sempre migliore del nostrale*, 'If the honey is from Spain it will always be better than ours' (VI,206). The generic and varietal range of the foodstuffs is broader in the *Opera* than in any past or contemporary recipe collection from across Europe. As we shall see, Scappi's treatments of those foodstuffs are more varied as well.

Scappi's cookery: his preferred processes, dishes

The richest mine of Scappi's practical experience that can benefit Giovanni lies in the actual activity of cooking. Years of successes and, we imagine, failures in the workplace can often yield instructive lessons to bequeath to a master's apprentice. The master has learned what will work and what will not. In a kitchen the master can teach by doing a specific dish, showing how it is done; he can also distil a universal culinary lesson, write it out and have it printed so that anyone anywhere can adopt a successful procedure, learn to recognize and avoid a pitfall. The injunction, 'Note that ... ,' recurs frequently and usually introduces a generic rule: *Avvertasi però che tal brodo non vuole star fatto, percioche ...* (Recipe II,206); *Habbiasi avvertenza, che tutte le torte fatte di cavoli, richiedeno essere piu presto cotte al forno, che sotto il testo, perche ...* (V,105); *Facciasi cuocere a lento foco, havendo avvertenza di non toccarlo con ferro, perche ...* (VI,56); *Qualunche volta che la pasta della cassa sarà fatta con grasso, sentendo il caldo nel forno, facilmente casca, et però s'impasta solo con l'ova, acqua fredda, et sale, perche quando tal pasta ...* (V,42). Scappi's warnings often seem based upon unfortunate experiences he has observed, perhaps his own; but he will usually try to offer a reasoned explanation of the danger or risk that the experience has taught him. See, for instance, in Recipe III,168 the reason he provides a cook for putting an egg into a ladle of water *before* it is poached; or in Recipe VI,148 the reasons, firstly, for putting an egg into cold water rather than hot and, secondly, for removing it from the boiling water by means of a spoon that has no holes.

Scappi's quantities are precise but, as he is well aware, circumstances vary: a lord's table grows and shrinks, for instance, depending on the current attendance at his court. And so Scappi often resorts to ratios rather than exact amounts: *Per ogni libra d'esse animelle si habbiano sei oncie di ventresca di porco* (Recipe II,50); *Per ogni quantità di cinquanta libre della detta sognia ponganovisi cinque libre di acqua* (II,111); *Per ogni boccal d'acqua pongaglisi un mezo di vino, et una foglietta d'aceto* (III,82). Scappi himself, in his post in the private papal kitchen, is not cooking for the masses. The quantities of ingredients, both foodstuffs and condiments, that he specifies in his recipes are remarkably modest. He seems often to be preparing food for only two or three persons, using only a pound or two of meat, for example, a handful of complementary ingredients, an ounce or half an ounce of spices. What matters is not primarily to feed everyone efficiently but to cook well, delectably and with diversity.

He realizes that Giovanni (and most of his eventual readers) may not in their professional appointments enjoy the ample resources of the Vatican kitchens. Some ingredients may not commonly or occasionally be on hand; some particular piece of hardware may never have been purchased. With regard to ingredients, he indicates the need to be aware of alternative possibilities, when even the most common of them is unavailable: *Et quando non si havesse farina da poter fare la cassa, piglisi* ... (Recipe VI,25); *Et non havendo nocelle adoprinosi pignoli, et pistacchi mondi brustoliti* (II,161). The phrases 'either ... or,' 'or else,' 'instead of,' 'rather than' abound in his recipes, sometimes obscuring the sense of a list to a degree, one would think, that Scappi himself would surely have deplored: *giungendovi,* he writes at one point, *malvagia, overo vin greco, et mosto cotto, over zuccaro con un poco d'aceto rosato, et delle medesime spetierie* (II,8).[117] And, as always, a cook's professional taste and preferences should allow for variants in the ingredients selected: *Se si vorrà sodo senza herbette, incorporisi con rossi d'uova battuti con l'agresto* (III,5); *S'incorpori il brodo con pane grattato, o con mandole peste, overo con uove sbattute* (II,32); *In loco di prugnoli si può cuocere con piselli, ò fave fresche* (III,3); *secondo che si vorrà* (III,9; VI,199).

Selecting an ingredient from among several possible options is often, naturally enough, an æsthetic decision: *Vi si potranno mettere rossi d'uova battuti, et herbicine, ma perche la polpa del fravolino di natura è bianca, comparisce assai meglio senza herbette* (VI,174). Sometimes, though, the reason for a choice will be strictly gastronomic: *Se si vorrà magnare la pasta della cassetta insieme con la compositione, pongasi butiro, ò strutto in essa quando si fa* (Recipe V,42).

Similarly, options are often suggested concerning the nature of the dish the cook can make with a particular mixture he has made up: *Se si ne vorrà far pottaggio* ... *tengasi l'ordine delli potaggi de i pesci inanzi scritti* (Recipe III,86). Alternatives exist, too, depending on the cook's intentions for the dish: *Se si vorrà magnare la pasta della cassetta insieme con la compositione, pongasi butiro, ò strutto in essa quando si fa* (V,42). The same awareness of alternative possibilities is necessary when certain fixtures or utensils are not at hand: ... *et non havendo pignatta, ne forno, si potrà fare nelle stufatore di rame bene stagnata, o di terra* (VI,25); *Si colerà per un foratoro minuto, overo con un pezzo di lino, ponendo in un vaso di legno, overo di terra* (I, §6). Again, it is likely that Scappi's own personal experience, his past practical experience in kitchens with varying equipment and

---

[117] The reader of Scappi's original text has always to remember that his (or his printer's) use of punctuation frequently seems rather arbitrary, having little to do with modern usage, either Italian or English.

supplies, made him conscious of the advisability of being ready to meet any unforeseen contingency and to resort to substitutions.

Scappi is usually careful not to leave doubt or ambiguity in his reader's mind. The word-phrase *cioè*, 'that is to say,' appears readily under his pen, followed by an explanation of what he meant by something he just wrote whose sense, he feared, might not have been all that obvious to his reader. At one point he has written *havendoli fatto bollire in due acque semplici*, 'having boiled them twice in plain water'; then it must have occurred to him that Giovanni or some unknown neophyte cook-apprentice might perhaps not understand *due acque*, so he adds immediately, *cioè mutando l'acqua*, 'that is, changing the water [between each boiling]' (Recipe II,114). Elsewhere: *bene stretta, cioè ammasata insieme* (I, §6); *mosto cotto, cioè sapa* (I, §28); *le zinne, cioè poppe di vaccine* (I,36); *i volatili di meza piuma, cioè li giovani* (I,38); *si segatteranno, cioè scanneranno* (I,39); and innumerable other instances. Scappi is always aware that any misunderstanding about exactly what the cook should or should not do could potentially have drastic consequences.

In the same way he is generally careful to justify his instructions, explaining the rationale for a particular procedure. *Accioche habbia il color vivo, habbiasi apparecchiato un boccal di sugo …* (Recipe II,275); *Accioche l'uove vengano bianche, et belle facciasi purgare il butiro, percioche pigliandosi cosi crudo, anchorche sia fresco, nondimeno v'è sempre dentro latte cagliato, et ricotta, dalche procede, che l'uove vengono rosse, et si attaccano nella padella* (III,270); *Et quando si cuoce in vino si fa per fare piu presto, et per mettere meno pasta nel pasticcio* (V,5). Rarely he will simply assure Giovanni that there is good reason for an action: *Fatta la compositione et passata per lo setaccio, per piu rispetti, pongasi…* (VI,123).

A very large category of observations about Scappi's writing can be grouped under the heading of 'helpful hints' or 'useful tricks.' These are either shortcuts or warnings, advice about particular ingredients or processes that perhaps conceal perils that a younger cook may not be aware of. These are the incidentals of culinary wisdom that a senior cook has garnered from long practice and careful work and that in a few words he can helpfully transmit to a pupil. Pots of a relatively soft metal often had bumps or creases from careless handling; even new ones bore residual hammer marks, it seems, left by the tinker: *Habbia avvertenza, che esso vaso sia liscio, percioche molte volte le battiture del martello che son nel vaso, son ragione, che la vivanda si attacchi* (Recipe II,162). Of the utensils available of various metals, iron ones posed particular difficulties: *… Havendo avvertenza di non toccarlo con ferro, perche l'orzata verrebbe nera, et amara* (VI,56); *… Schiumandosi con un cocchiara di legno, et non di ferro, perche il ferro fa venire la decottione turbida, et amara* (II,239); *Habbiasi avvertenza quando si fa esso maccarone, che lo sfoglio sia infarinato leggiermente, acciò non si attacchi al ferro* (II,175); *Habbiasi quella coccia dell'ostreca, cioè quella parte ch'è piu* *fonduta... & facciasi bollire nell'acqua calda (ilche si fa accioche si conservino piu calde)* (III,185); *Pestisi col piston di legno che non sia amaro come è la noce* (VI,30).[118] Salt gathered at the seashore often contained extraneous material: that salt, he warns, should be very clean *perche se il sale non fosse netto, la carne si empirebbe di terra, et pigliarebbe tristo odore* (II,4). To remove an odour from meat, *vi si potrà far bollire un poco di maiorana nel brodo, ilqual vi si aggiungerà all'ultimo, percioche se bollisse col pisto il farebbe venir nero* (VI,30).

Seasonal influences on recipes are significant for Scappi. He provides Giovanni with practical hints that bear upon the ambient climate: a meat should steep in brine for four days in summer but eight in winter (Recipe II,4); a pie will keep four days in summer and ten in winter (V,36); a pullet is hung for one day in summer and three in winter, *perche tal volatile presto si frolla* (V,37). Likewise, as is often the case and we have seen before, the composition of a mixture will vary according to the season: *la Primavera se gli ponerà uva spina, l'Estate agresto intiero, l'Invernata prugne, et visciole secche* (V,177).

As for Scappi's cookery itself, how he cooked and what his recipes indicate he mostly did – and may have had the most interest in doing – we may make the following observations. First, Scappi seems to have had a liking for closed-chamber cooking. A *testo* or a casserole pot or a deep tourte pan with a closely fitting lid is often the cooking vessel of choice. That sort of cooking affords a continuous self-basting of the food as moisture that evaporates never escapes but condenses again. Moreover, the pot lids were generally flat and allowed embers and coals to be placed on top as well as beneath. The enveloping heat could be moderate, more or less regulated, and prolonged. The process was certainly not invented in the sixteenth century but Scappi does frequently rely upon it.

Many of Scappi's recipes incorporate distinct procedures to be followed depending upon whether the dish is to be eaten immediately – Scappi regularly writes *servasi cosi caldo*, 'serve it hot right from the fire' – or is to be set aside and kept for eating, whether cold or reheated, in a day, a week or a month: ... *servendole con sugo di melangole et pepe sopra, et mostarda in piatti; si serveno freddi con petrosemolo sopra, & sapore in piatti*. This sort of option allowed the kitchen to prepare a certain amount of food ahead of time, provided that the cook understood which foods could be cooked in such a way as to be safely set aside for a subsequent meal. *Servanosi cosi caldi o freddi a beneplacito* (Recipe II,114). *In questo modo durano cotti tre giorni, & piu o meno secondo la stagion de i tempi, & si serveno freddi con petrosemolo sopra, & sapore in piatti* (III,116).

Particular mixtures have more than one specific use. A number of recipes, once a mixture has been compounded, draw the cook's attention to the possible use

---

[118] Compare this with Recipe V,106: 'Then beat it with knives on a table that is not of walnut,' *Poi battasi con li coltelli su la tavola che non sia di noce.*

of that mixture in another dish. The stuffing for a saveloy sausage is an example: a combination of veal, veal kidney-fat, veal liver, salt, pepper, cinnamon, ginger, saffron, cheese, currants, fennel seed and eggs (Recipe II,46), this stuffing is called for in a good number of other recipes that have nothing to do with sausages. Other detailed recipes will make up and cook mixtures that can serve as a main-course dish or be used merely as dressings for some other dish: the *capirotata* of II,159, for instance, the spicy yellow stew that normally will contain sweetbreads, can be used to garnish small spit-roasted wildfowl. Repeatedly Scappi lightens the cook's labour by means of a cross-reference between a recipe that uses or can use a mixture made up in and for another dish.

As was mentioned before, the flavour of pork influences many of the dishes that Scappi prepares. The flavour is an old one in European gastronomy, owing in large measure to the relatively low cost of raising semi-domesticated swine and to the many uses to which parts of the slaughtered pig could be put: blood, bristles, hide, feet, jowls, meat, fat, viscera and bowels. Most usefully, very long traditions had established that pork, whether slabs of bacon or belly or the whole hind thigh, could dependably be preserved by salting. In Italian cooking, *lardo, presciuto, sommato* and *strutto* had also secured for themselves an extensive secondary use, appearing in the form of the most common cooking grease or added into innumerable dishes primarily as flavourants. Pork remained an important foodstuff in Scappi's day. Several of his sham or counterfeit recipes in the book for lean days – see Recipe III,219, for example – are in imitation of pork cuts or products.

The appearance of a dish is important in Scappi's cooking. Among the general rules for good cookery that he offers Giovanni throughout Book I we find two of the more important right at the beginning of the *Opera*: *Le vivande non meno siano saporose, et grate al gusto, che piacevoli, et dilettevoli all'occhio, con lor bel colore, et vaga prospettiva*, 'Dishes should be tasty and agreeable to the palate as well as pleasant and delightful to the eye with their pretty colours and appetizing appearance.'[119] Colours and colourants are indeed mentioned in the *Opera* but seem not to have been quite as important as in earlier cookery. A few preparations, such as *ginestrata* (Recipe II,160, 163, 255; III,223) and *salza verde*[120] (II,272), are named after their colour, but those are survivors from the times of that earlier cookery, as is the ubiquitous *bianco mangnare* (II,162) which, despite its name, is rarely white by the end of the Middle Ages. A reddish-brown or russet (*rosso*) is common in foodstuffs but rarely produced artificially in a dish (II,246). If there is a colour that recurs in Scappi's dishes, for which he or his

---

[119] I, §1.

[120] Scappi's usual colourants for a green hue are rocket (II,272) and spinach juice (V,227), along with the traditional parsley for reinforcement.

master has perhaps a weakness, it might be *pavonazzo*, a 'peacock' hue that is a bluish purple. It is produced by, among other things, carrots or orchil (both seen in II,240 and 246).

These recipes frequently follow a standard progression in their procedure: the meat or fish or vegetable is subjected to an initial parboiling, blanching or searing as a first step in its preparation. The actual cooking follows that preliminary, whether the cooking is by roasting, baking or frying. *Alessati che saranno si potranno ancho soffriggere con lardo, & ponere su la graticola*, 'When [the forequarters of a goat kid] have boiled they can then be sautéed in pork fat and put on the grill' (II,78). 'Sear the meat on a grill (on coals), lard it (coat it with condiments), roast it on a spit.' Scappi never feels a need to explain the purpose of this plumping and sealing of a foodstuff. The steps in the process – parboil or sear, imbue with a flavour, cook, dress and serve – often follow in almost automatic sequence for him.

Certain flavours tend to be preferred when Scappi adds a seasoning to his dishes. Undoubtedly he likes tangy preparations. The citrus fruits help establish that piquancy, but verjuice and to some extent vinegar also help. Not only does sugar frequently provide a counteraction to any excess acidity but it creates as well a deliberate balance between sweet and sour, *agrodolce*, the composite taste that has been mentioned before.[121] The flavour of cinnamon, too, seems to have been enjoyed by Scappi and those for whom he cooked, the ground spice being measured (with careful calculation) into many of the prepared dishes.

As for sauces, a good number and variety of them are provided in the group of recipes placed towards the end of Book II. However, over the decades tastes have changed. From Scappi's assortment of composed sauces, those that were commonplace, even fundamental and universal, one and two centuries before are now missing. Scappi appears to have no interest in the sauces based on the spices ginger (*gengeverada*) or, a little surprisingly, cinnamon (*camelina*).[122] The plain pepper sauce, *peverata*, quite popular in past centuries, is likewise all but ignored by Scappi. For garnishes, his recipes call either for herbs, especially mint and marjoram (in tourtes), or for plain ground cinnamon and sugar. A sharp citrus flavour is preferred in a dressing, especially that of orange juice and pepper, or orange juice combined with (again) cinnamon or sugar or both cinnamon and sugar. The combination of orange juice and sugar recalls again

---

[121] Another instance of this bitter-sweet mixture can be seen in the *agrestata* of Recipes II,273 and VI,198, a sauce that combines verjuice and sugar and is almost a staple in Scappi's kitchen; or the *agretto et dolce* of Recipe III,273.

[122] The fifteenth-century recipe collection in Manuscript 211 of the Wellcome Library for the History and Understanding of Medicine, London, contains no fewer than seven recipes for *salsa camelina*. What seems to have happened by the sixteenth century is that the cold *camelina* sauce has been replaced by a simple, frequently used cinnamon-and-sugar garnish.

the bitter-sweet taste that fifteenth- and sixteenth-century Italian cooks strove to incorporate into their dishes. Verjuice and sugar, perhaps along with bitter-orange juice as in III,273, is a deliberate combination designed to ensure that a dish *habbia dell'agretto & del dolce* (Recipe III,173) in good and proper balance. The honey-and-vinegar beverage known as *ossimele* (VI,206) is a further instance of the same partiality: *Tal liquore vuol bollire pian piano per rispetto dell'aceto. Di farlo dolce, et agro, sarà in arbitrio*, 'That liquid [oxymel] needs to boil slowly because of the vinegar. Whether the sweet or the bitter dominates is up to you.'

Some persistence of earlier culinary logic is evident in Scappi. Fish were considered to have cold and moist flesh, in part because the element in which they existed was itself manifestly cold and moist. In order not to develop phlegmatic humours in a person who ate fish, an early European cook would never boil a fish but would roast or grill it over an open flame and then dress it with a sauce of spices that were held to be of a warm and dry nature. In Books III and V Scappi still steeps his fish in spices or coats them with spices for cooking. Is that practice of his based on a casual tradition or had it a conscious rationale that had over time established it as a gastronomic preference? Scappi does not say. The dishes for the sick in Book VI show some concern for creating foods whose temperament was healthily warm and moist, but the extent to which Scappi was conscious of the underlying reasons behind various sickdish traditions that he inherited is moot. Outside Book VI the only explanations he ever gives for the use of particular ingredients and for the method of cooking them have to do with practical, empirical and gastronomic considerations. In any case, he is not only content to leave to the physician any decision about particular foods for a sick patient, he will even allege for a specific dish (Recipe VI,99) that medical doctors in general (*i Phisici*) hold that certain ingredients, certain initial preparations and certain cooking processes are required to obtain its best effects. When the sick need to eat, the physician is still always the best and most authoritative (not to say canonically reliable) cook.

Cooks in the sixteenth century were generally less aware of humoral properties of the foodstuffs they handled, and of any need to modify them for the health or safety of their patrons, than had been the case in previous centuries. From the earliest recipe collections of the thirteenth and fourteenth centuries, it is apparent that practice in court kitchens was in part determined by the court physicians who watched over the physical well-being of their lord. Specifically, foods whose nature might upset a well-balanced human temperament had to be cooked, seasoned and sauced in such a way as to eliminate or limit any potential dangers. In Scappi, however, the word that had a long-established culinary sense of modifying the temperament of a foodstuff or a mixture, *stemperare* (literally, to dis-temper, to moderate the temperament of something), has now weakened virtually to mean 'to moisten' or merely 'to mix,' with no clear connotation that the agents are chosen specifically to counteract the qualities of the other ingredients with which they are to be mixed. Very rarely the condiment being added is not a liquid: in two instances sugar alone is mixed, by means of the verb *temperare*, 'to moderate [a temperament],' into ingredients of a different nature.[123]   With this semantic shift in traditional culinary terminology we can see that cuisine is evolving in the sixteenth century, that the final effect of a combination of foodstuffs, and not its logic or the theory behind that combination, is what matters in the kitchen and dining hall.

Two verbs with similar meanings abound in the *Opera*: *mondare* and *nettare*. The first has to do with cleaning away anything that is superfluous on a foodstuff – a peel or skin, seeds, fishbones. The second is significant, largely because of the frequency with which it appears in the text. Earlier recipe writers may have presumed that the cook would not process a dirty leg of lamb, but Scappi is overwhelmingly explicit: make sure, he repeatedly instructs Giovanni, that everything is well washed and absolutely clean. Let there be no speck of soil left, no dirt, no blood, not a single hair; wash, rewash, rinse. Keep any smoke away from the pot. Cover semi-prepared dishes with a dust cloth; do the same with whatever has been dished out and is ready for serving. His insistence on immaculateness at every stage of his cookery is characteristic. The principle helps ensure his highest imperative: a good cook must furnish the best of food.

As we have already seen, there is no chauvinism, no Roman prejudice in Bartolomeo Scappi. He is certainly quite aware of what his confrères are doing in court kitchens elsewhere in Rome: *ma noi altri cuochi di Roma pigliamo le trutte mezane* ... (III,116). Yet in a good many places he refers to the practice of other, more distant kitchens. In speaking with the steward of an English cardinal (III,206), for instance, he learns about how in Inghilterra they make semi-salted sturgeon belly (*moronella*) from an Atlantic fish that is larger than a sturgeon, *de quali per quanto io ho inteso* ... *in quel mare si piglia gran quantità*. He frequently associates his dishes with a 'foreign' (that is, extra-Roman) origin, as he does his ingredients. Most often the particular place that we read in conjunction with an ingredient or dishname is the Veneto – undoubtedly a legacy of the time spent cooking there for Cardinal Marino Grimano. He vouches for the foodstuffs available there and sometimes reports on the way they arrive on the Venetian market: *Son portati in Trevisi et in Venetia di terra Todesca cauli cappucci salati con salimora in vasi di terra o di legno* (II,197); *In Venetia* [sea bass] *son piu grandi di quelli di Roma* (III,40); *In Venetia se ne* [mackerel] *trova gran copia, ove son molto migliori di quelli di Roma* (III,65); *In Venetia et in Roma se*

---

[123] In Recipes V,31 and 49 the sugar, warm and moist by nature, is added to vinegar and verjuice respectively, both cold and dry by nature. This is clearly a matter of tempering or moderating the potency of an ingredient. Scappi may now understand the word *stemperare* either as roughly synonymous with *giungere*, 'to mix in,' 'to combine' or, with only a vestige of its earlier sense, 'to bring a mixture to an optimum state.'

ne [cuttlefish] *trovano quasi d'ogni tempo* (III,104); *In Venetia se ne* [oysters] *truovano quasi tutto l'anno* (III,183); *In Venetia nelli cannali se ne pigliano di due sorti* [crabs], *et li dimandano molecche* (III,182). Similarly with culinary preparations: *spetieria Venetiana* (III,31, 62); *brisavoli ... alla Venetiana cotti su la graticola* (II,7); *minestra di rape alla Venetiana* (II,212); *pottaggio di pezzi d'Ombrina alla Venetiana* (III,31); *varie sorte di fritelle, & prima ... frittelle alla Venetiana* (V,136); *Li pescatori da Chiozza, & Venetiani il cuoceno alle bragie, & ancho ne fanno pottaggio con ... spetierie Venetiane* (III,62).

Most interestingly, he writes with expressly first-hand knowledge. His personal testimony, emphasized with the first-person-singular pronoun *io*, reinforces what he writes. *Perche nel tempo ch'io mi son trovato in Venetia et in Ravenna, ho inteso da pescatori da Chiozza, et Venetiani, liquali fanno i migliori potaggi, che in tutti i liti del mare, che non si usava di cuocerli in altro modo* (Recipe III,79). As we have seen, this same declaration of his personal experience in Venice is found several other times: *In questi due modi io gli* [the small birds] *ho veduti in Venetia, portati di Cipro* (I, §10); *Ho veduto in Venetia una sorte di gambari piu piccioli* (III,179); and *Io ho veduto ancho la moronella soda, et asciutta, che assomiglia alla carne salata in Venetia* (III,206). Writing of cranes and their habitat, he notes, *Io ho vedute molte tra le valli di Comacchio & il Pò, & fra gli altri lochi in Argenta, in Baccalione, et Consandola* (II,142).

But then in the same sentence he continues, *In Milano & in altri lochi di Lombardia se ne allevano molte per le case.* As noted above, concerning the places where Scappi may have lived and worked, we find almost as many references to the foods and cookery he has observed in Lombardy and Milan.[124] Scappi writes of *suppa (alla) lombarda* (II,16, 22, 156), *una vivanda di riso alla lombarda sottestata* (II,156, a dish still prepared today), *torta* (and *tortelletti*) *alla lombarda* (V,92 and II,179), *crostate, dette ... da Lombardi sfogliati* (V,49), and *Tal vivande in Lombardia si chiama Macco* (III,253). He comments that buckwheat is used in tourtes and flans in Lombardy (II,185 and V,88) and that a dish of turnip leaves can be served *con agliata sopra come s'usa in Lombardia* (II,205). Dishes connected with the city of Milan include *offelle alla milanese* (IV, f.169r [1581 f.134r]), *mostaccioli alla milanese* (VI,142) and *cervellate gialle milanese* (II,153); he writes of *sanguinacci ... con il brodo come si usa in Milano* (II,110) and *La trutta grossa in Milano si cuoce in questo modo, cioè ...* (III,116).

In several places Scappi measures in Milanese units of weight (Recipe III,115, 138 and 146). Elsewhere (III,161), in the same way as he wrote of his time in

---

[124] As was mentioned before, rice and cabbage from this region are valued ingredients in Scappi's cookery. He also associates a number of other ingredients with Lombardy: *Quel cascio, che in Milano è detto cascio grasso* (I, §8); *In alcuni lochi di Lombardia* [*pesce buco*] *si chiama menola* (Recipe III,70).

Venice, he recalls, as if defending his credibility by offering authentic documentation, that *Ho veduto nella pescheria di Milano* ... ; and in another instance (III,176) he assures the reader that a similar proof is available: ... *come si può veder nelle peschiere di Milano.* He knows – presumably has had experience with – certain medical practices in Lombardy and Milan (III,125 and VI,64). Whether from a long habitation and professional work there or not, it is clear that Scappi has an intimate knowledge of the geography and culinary practice of Lombardy and Milan.

And, of course, he incorporates Roman (local) foodstuffs and dishes into his *Opera.* Roman calves are always 'better' (Recipe II,23) and bigger (II,42); Roman cherries are good (II,259) and better (V,118); Lake Bolsena yields good smelt, tench, pike and eels (III,75, 138, 146, 155); trout can be had from Sora, Arpino and the Tiber, the last also a good place for allis shad (II,50); Civitavecchia has razor clams (III,191); Sabina, Aquila and Tagliacozzo preserve fish in oil, especially tench (III,217); Roman cheese (*cascio romanesco*) is specified in Scappi's recipes. Within Rome itself, freshwater crayfish are caught at the Salaro bridge (III,176). The dishes he qualifies as Roman include *polpettoni alla Romanesca* (II,13, 44), *maccaroni alla Romanesca* (II,174), *cominata alla Romanesca* (II,193), a dish of parsley and other herbs that Roman nobles call *brodo apostolorum* (II,206), and two varieties of fritter that Romans call *Pappardelle* (V,144) and *Zeppolle* (II,145).

By the time he composes his book Scappi is well settled in Rome, declaring (at the beginning of Book III) that the dishes whose recipes he recorded in Book II had been 'proven by myself mostly here in the noble city of Rome' : *sperimentate da me per la maggior parte nell'alma Città di Roma.* He is even thinking of himself as a Roman cook: *Noi altri cuochi di Roma pigliamo le trutte mezane* ... (Recipe III,116), he writes. Yet, most remarkably, given the prejudices of the age and his own exalted status, he never suggests that he possesses any absolute criteria or authority in the matter of contemporary cookery. His book is not proposed as a supreme and final guide for those cooks who aspire to reach the summit of their profession. As he says to Giovanni, he wishes his book to make the apprentice a knowledgeable expert in the art, and custodian of the master's accumulated practical experience in that art. For Scappi, the art was never at any time a finished work. It was forever growing. His experience was constantly nourished from all sides. He knows first-hand the marketplaces of Rome (III,96), Venice and Milan. He not only talks with common fishermen but incorporates their plain, humble cooking practice into his own and his recipes (III,62, 79, 128). He listens to travellers' tales. He consults the mongers of the local *pescarie* and *mercati.* As with his openness to foreign sources for the best of foodstuffs, his cookery is shaped by a curiosity that accepts no parochial bounds. As befits his position at the centre of the Christian world, where a wide range of national cultures met and mixed, he continues to believe that particular routes to excellence can be found beyond that centre. What the apprentice cook learns from his master can always be further enriched by what is done elsewhere. The potential for learning and for improvement is unlimited.

Among all the options and alternatives that Scappi furnishes his junior in his text, all the unsuspected dangers to which he draws his cautious attention, all the helpful tips he proffers, Scappi's principal instruction remains singular and dominant: do honourable work. He concludes his Recipe III,81 by rejecting any mention of a serving sauce 'because,' he declares, 'it is not appropriate that such a noble fish be covered with anything': *percioche alla nobilità del pesce non conviene che sia coperto.* Conversely, in Recipe III,108 he states that the fish called a smooth hound (*pesce palombo*) 'is unworthy of being set on a royal board': *è pesce indegno di banchetti regali.* Those judgments may appear a little arbitrary, yet they point up Scappi's concept of his responsibility to be certain about the quality of both the foodstuffs and the dishes that he could make of them. All that a cook does results from a respect for the various ingredients at his disposal and a keen sense of the profound obligations of his profession. The broad range of foodstuffs and the manifold possibilities of their preparation were abstruse and complex; the need to possess a thorough understanding of both was imperative. But what remains just as important for Scappi, perhaps even more important, is his conviction about the dignity of his work. Whatever is produced in his kitchen must not only satisfy the honour of his master but must reflect a little of that honour upon his cook.

Scappi's legacy

*I*t is impossible to estimate the influence that Scappi's *Opera* has had on cookery during the generations and centuries since its publication.[125] As a consequence presumably of the sales enjoyed by its initial publication and early reprinting, the *Opera* was made available to the public some eight times up to 1646. That number of re-editions is quite exceptional in the early history of Italian cookery.[126]

---

[125] For a brief consideration of Italian cookery of the period, see Benporat, 'Evoluzione della cucina italiana alla fine del '500.' The article is concerned primarily with the make-up of a meal and the waning use of sugar.

[126] It is unfortunate that we cannot point to the very long life enjoyed by the anonymous recipe package now called the *Neapolitan Collection.* None of the subsequent writers who used that collection – Martino, then Platina and then Giovanni de Rosselli – acknowledged his source. In fact the last author's book, *Epulario* (1516), is brazenly qualified as an *opera nova.* The *Epulario* was still being published in 1682 and was translated, here anonymously, into English as *Epulario, or The Italian Banquet* (London, 1598). Maestro Giovanni's *Opera dignissima et utile per chi si diletta di cucinare* (1530) likewise depends heavily upon one or another of earlier recipe collections with their indigenous Italian and Catalan practices. A few recipe collections in both the Italian and French sixteenth century tend to maintain culinary traditions while playing variations upon them and claiming originality.

No other single work had enjoyed such a long life. The only competitor was the *Banchetti* of Messisbugo, which printers made available in eleven printings between 1549 and 1600. However, that work, designed to guide a steward in a noble house, had a somewhat different perspective and offered fewer than a quarter of the number of recipes that Scappi was to publish. No 'new' cookbook became available on the Italian market until 1662 when the *Arte di ben cucinare*[127] of Bartolomeo Stefani, a cook from Bologna in the service of the Gonzagas of Mantua, was published. However, even this work still relies largely for its material upon Scappi's *Opera*.

Some of the content of the *Opera* was spread very tentatively beyond the Italian peninsula in two books: Diego Granado Maldonato, *Libro del arte de cozina* (Madrid, 1599) and Antonius Magirus, *Koocboec oft Familieren Keukenboec* (Louvain, 1612). Each book was published as the translator's own work with no acknowledgment of Scappi's contribution.[128] Scappi's work has also known a few modern reproductions.[129]

Whether the early publications and translations exerted any immediate, perceptible influence on contemporary generations of cooks within or beyond the Italian peninsula is impossible to tell. We can point to similarities between Scappi's recipes and recipes that appear in books published just after 1570. An instance to which we make some reference in our examination of the *Opera* is the *Ouverture de cuisine* of Lancelot de Casteau, written about 1585 and first published in Liège in 1604. The distance between central Italy and the Lowlands may make any gastronomic parallels surprising, but an explanation of the similarities that do exist between the two books is clearly ecclesiastical: one of Lancelot de Casteau's succession of employers was Gerard of Groesbeek, cardinal bishop of Liège.[130] The likelihood that he was among the cardinal's personal servitors during the prelate's travels and while in Rome is tantamount to a certainty.

---

[127] Mantova, appresso gli Osanna stampatori ducali, 1662; repr. Venice, 1690. Facsimile reprint in the series 'Testi antichi di gastronomia' (Sala Bolognese: A. Forni, 1983).

[128] Concerning Granado's book, see Jeanne Allard, 'Diego Granado Maldonado,' *Petits Propos Culinaires*, 25 (1987): 35–41; 587 of the 762 recipes in Granado are translations from Scappi. Concerning Magirus and the question of recipe copying in general, see the article by Henry Notaker, in *Petits Propos Culinaires*, 70 (2002): 58–66, 'Comments on the Interpretation of Plagiarism.' The nature of cookery is, of course, to evolve in large measure as a result of reproducing and then modifying.

[129] Bartolomeo Scappi, *L'arte del cusinare; libro delle ricette per convalescenti, a cura di Ercole Vittorio Ferrario* (Collana Medico-Storica, 3) (Milan: Edizioni Stedar, 1959); this publication reproduces only Book VI. Roversi's *Bartolomeo Scappi, Opera dell'Arte del cucinare* is a facsimile reproduction of Scappi's first Venice edition. A distant derivative of the *Opera* is Grazia Bruttocao, *Un dicembre alla mensa di papa Ghisleri e dei maestri della cucina pavese* (Pavia: Cyrano, 1998).

[130] The history of Lancelot de Casteau's professional employment was firmly ecclesiastic. He

In Rome the occasions were many and endless for the cooks who accompanied a wide assortment of potentates, cardinals not the least, both to bring and to experience culinary and gastronomic novelties, to be influenced by and in turn to influence their counterparts in the diverse national groups that attended the papal court. Rome had, by the nature of the church, a cosmopolitan culture; food and cookery were vital elements of that culture. Scappi himself shared in a gastronomic tradition that was itself, as a collective product, inevitably evolving. What was done in larger, more affluent courts, both secular and ecclesiastical, was bound to carry some weight in lesser courts, and a variety of gastronomic experiences and taste almost certainly gave rise to some degree of emulation in the latter circles. While it is generally difficult in the matter of prepared food to identify distinct influences, now as at any time in the past, it is at least probable that while Scappi worked in Rome and the Tramezzino brothers and later printers published his *Opera*, his influence, great or small, would have carried far.

The papal court at Rome was conscious of being a cynosure for many sorts of standards, and sixteenth-century popes in particular seem to have been determined to include a richly sensuous life among those standards. As their cook, Scappi served his masters faithfully, honourably and enthusiastically. In several places he writes that a dish is made up *secondo la volontã de chi gli fa fare* – that is, that a cook must conform closely to his master's taste. He must apply all of his skill, intellect and devotion to his profession in the service of his employer. As Scappi himself faithfully did.

For Scappi, though, there was always one further criterion: *Questo*, he writes of the adoption of a procedure or the use of an ingredient, *sarà secondo il giuditio del Cuoco*: 'That, according to the cook's judgment.' He writes the phrase or its equivalent much more frequently than he advises the cook to defer to his master's taste or to instructions coming from his master's steward. The phrases *in arbitrio*, 'optionally,' *con giudicio*, 'using discretion' and *secondo il giuditio*, 'as you think proper,' recur innumerable times: *la quantità d'ogni cosa sia ad arbitrio et giuditio* (Recipe II,24).[131] But, even more significantly, Scappi writes explicitly: *secondo il giudicio di chi li farà* (V,129), 'depending on the judgment of the person making them'; and, expressly, *secondo il giuditio del Cuoco* (V,133, 199, 220) and *secondo il giuditio et disegno che haverà il Cuoco* (VI,144), 'according to the cook's judgment and intention.' The final arbiter of professional success lies with the professional himself: the cook must satisfy himself that he has done the best he can. If Scappi left a legacy to European cooking it would perhaps be that. Any individual who is truly a master cook combines his supreme obligation, devoted

---

was also at other times cook to Robert of Berghe, count of Walhain and bishop of Liège; and to Prince Ernest, duke of Bavaria, archbishop of Cologne, elector and, again, bishop of Liège.

[131] See also, for other instances, Recipes II,16, 18, 22, 46, 231; III,92; V,129, 219; and elsewhere.

service to his employer, with a freedom to let his expertise, gained in large part from his own, unique personal experience, guide him in his daily professional practice.

Michel de Montaigne, the observant and highly perceptive French man-of-the-world, recalls a conversation he had in Rome, some time between 1536 and 1555 (while Giampietro Carafa was a cardinal but not yet pope), that was apropos of the subject of 'eloquence' about which he is writing. The other man was an Italian

who served the late Cardinal Caraffa as steward till his death. I made him give an account of his office. He gave me an oration on the science of the gullet with magisterial gravity and composure, as if he had been handling some profound point of divinity. He distinguished for me the difference in appetites: that which a man has before he begins to eat, and that which he has after the second and third course; the means, first, of simply satisfying it, and then of rousing and provoking it; the principle of his sauces, first in general, and then particularizing the qualities of the ingredients and their effects; the differences of salads according to the seasons, those which ought to be heated and those which ought to be served up cold; the manner of their garnishing and decoration to make them agreeable to the eye also. After this he entered upon the order of the service, full of beautiful and important considerations,

> It is a matter of profoundest care
> How one should carve a hen, and how a hare.

And all this swelled out with rich and magnificent words, the very same we make use of in discussing the government of an empire.[132]

This was the period, the setting and the ethos that formed Bartolomeo Scappi, professional cook, and that in turn he undoubtedly helped to mould. As a writer Scappi was an exceptionally literate man, very able to organize his subject matter and impose on it a thoroughly coherent and intelligible expression. We should perhaps expect that of a person who came to dominate the summit of his craft. But Scappi is able also to imbue his subject matter with that frank character of his own human personality. His book is didactic in purpose, yet this master who so willingly and patiently explains any potential obscurity to his apprentice is never condescending.

The reader does from time to time sense a tendency to floridness in Scappi's style, but only briefly and generally only in the conscious formality of the preambles he drafted to each of his books. In the meat of his work, though, in the recipes, he clearly understands the need to write clearly, to avoid prolixity or abstruse terminology that might confuse his young and probably harassed apprentice.

The *Opera* is literally that: the synthesized lifetime work of a master, as refined by experience and intelligence. In the words that he writes to Giovanni

---

[132] *The Essays of Michel de Montaigne*, trans. Jacob Zeitlin (New York: Knopf, 1934); Book I, Chapter 51, 269.

in the opening pages of his Book I, *Sempre [ho] messo ogni mio ingegno per farvi huomo esperto, & intelligente in tal'arte, acciò dopo la morte mia in voi rimanessero tutte le mie fatiche, & pratiche*: '[I have] always set all of my mind to making you a knowledgeable, astute expert in the art, so that after my death all my work and practical experience should remain in you.' Thanks to the *Opera*, every reader has the good fortune to become a Giovanni.

This Translation and Commentary

*T*he *Opera* of Bartolomeo Scappi appeared for the first time in 1570. It came from under a printing press operated in Venice by a well-established publishing duo of the brothers Michele and Francesco Tramezzino. The Tramezzinos were Venetian in origin but apparently first established their careers in the printing and book trades in Rome. Following the sack of Rome in 1527, in which book shops in particular suffered, the pair moved their press to Venice. Michele became the printer there but in the middle of 1528 Francesco returned to Rome to resume his work in the book trade as well as to act as editor for the brothers' Venetian press. The first known volume they produced was a collection of sermons by Girolamo Savonarola in 1536.[133] At its most productive, the Tramezzino press turned out an average of five or six books a year, ranging from chivalric romances to law books. Michele continued to operate the press until 1574; by then he had printed some 243 volumes. The brothers died in 1576 (Francesco) and 1579 (Michele).

By 1570, the Tramezzino output was slowing. Only three books were printed that year: a batch of shorter Latin works by Johannes Spauter and two long vernacular treatises, *La singular dottrina* by Domenico Romoli, concerning the duties of a household steward (a reprint of the Tramezzino's original 1560 publication of the work), and Scappi's *Opera*, on a professional cook's duties and repertoire. On the death of the brothers, the printing and book-selling businesses were inherited by a daughter of Francesco and her nephew, a grandson of Francesco. After 1576, new books from the press usually bore the inscription *Impensis hæredum Francisci Tramezini* or *Per gli heredi di F. e M. Tramezzino*: 'printed by the heirs of the founder(s).' Among the books the heirs undertook to publish in 1581 was a reprint of Scappi's *Opera*. Very little was changed in that second edition. Interestingly, the reprint still appeared under the name of Michele Tramezzino, in all likelihood because the exclusive printing rights (the copyright or *privilegio*) for the book had been granted to the Tramezzino brothers by name, Michele and Francesco. Although the Venetian Senate had accorded a twenty-year copyright, those of the pope and the grand duke of Tuscany were for only ten years, a period that was just passing.

Little of any substance was changed in the 1581 reprinting. Appearing near the foot of the book's title page, the printer's emblem is the same engraved block

---

[133] The personal and professional history of the Tramezzino brothers and their family is still best available in Tinto, *Annali tipografici dei Tramezzino*.

in both printings: in it the lady Sibylla (so identified by a banner beneath her feet) bears a book in one hand and with the other points the way forward; the engraving is bordered on three sides with a text, set originally in italic capitals and in 1581 in roman capitals: *Qual piu fermo e il mio foglio e il mio presaggio*, 'How truer is my page and my foresight.'

The 1570 printing made a graceful book of Scappi's work. However, for several reasons, apparently deliberate or through negligence, the reprinting impaired the book's original attractive appearance. The spacing between letters, words and lines throughout is slightly less generous. The font is a slightly heavier italic. Originally both rubrics and text used the same light italic, whereas in 1581 rubrics and initial words were set in a larger roman font; the effect, whether or not it was desired, seems more to suggest a sober academic tome. In the reprinting an uneven application of ink to a typeset page occasionally mars a series of folios in a sheet with blotches or faintness. And it was perhaps a lower grade of glazed paper used by the Tramezzino press in 1581 that has let letters and lines bleed here and there in the Scappi reprinting.

In appearance a page in the second printing is tighter, too. The font size is slightly smaller so that more text is on a line and on a page. Spacing before and after a recipe's rubric is closed up as well. The 1570 floral spacers between the title of each book and the text are omitted. In the 1570 printing the capital initial of each recipe is large enough to occupy two lines of text, whereas in the 1581 printing the size of the first capital is reduced to nothing more than that of the regular text font. As a consequence of such economies of space, while the first printing required some 440 folios for the *Opera* proper, the second printing squeezed it into 372 folios (including the indices at the end of each book).

Of the large, ten-line illuminated capitals, beginning each of the four segments of the preliminary documents and each of Scappi's six books, four are still in use in the 1581 printing and six are new and in some places of smaller size. In the reprinting the abandonment of the earlier uniformity of style in those ornamented letters suggests a decrease in artistic rigour and oversight at the press, if not a dwindling of available financing.

Overall the impression given by the original printing of the *Opera* is of a careful elegance that paid tribute to its author; in the reprinting something of that elegance has been lost.

That the professionalism of the printery suffered following the death of Michele Tramezzino in 1579 is further apparent. On f.441r of the 1570 printing a *registro* advises the binder about the composition of the volume: *Tutti sono quaderni eccetto il primo alfabetto da a, & A per fino V, che sono duerni*. The first three sheets, bearing the binding numbers a i, a ii and a iii (printed with the title page and preliminary material) are of smaller, half-size paper which, folded once, gave two folios each (*duerni*), six in all. The body of the book is compiled on standard-size sheets, to be folded twice to give four folios (*quaderni*). For the binder's guidance the first two folios of the printed, then folded, sheets show at the lower right [the sheet letter] 1 and [the sheet letter] 2; the first fold would be cut but the second fold would be left so that the two half-sheets, with their four folios, remained nested together. The successive sheets, as the *Registro* declares, are identified by the letters A, B, ... Z, Aa, Bb, ... Zz, Aaa, Bbb, ... Uuu. There are, then, sixty-seven gatherings or signatures in all, excluding the appended narrative about the conclave. The later material, separate from the *Opera* itself, was printed on two half-sheets which were folded once (two *duerni*) to make four folios; the two half-sheets were numbered for the binder A1 and A2. Because the preliminary material and the conclave narrative have no actual folio numbers printed on them, for clarity of reference to each of those pages, the binder's signature number (A 1r, A 1v, etc.) will be used in this translation. The 1581 printing does not bother with a *registro*, though the volume is composed according to the same folding and binding procedures.

A unique, unchanged feature of both printings is the set of fine copperplate engravings. The substantial investment the Tramezzino press made in 1570 having those plates prepared was clearly safeguarded at that time for future use. Subsequent to those plates' second use in 1581, another Venetian printer, Alessandro Vecchi, had to make up his own coarser and less durable woodcuts for his reprintings of the *Opera* in 1598, 1605, 1610 and 1622. Only by 1643 was a third printer of Scappi, Combi, still in Venice, able to revert to the Tramezzino copperplates which, almost seventy-five years after they were originally engraved, he reworked very slightly.

Two printings, then, may be taken as representing what Scappi intended for his book. During his increasingly idle hours between 1569 or so, when he would have delivered his manuscript to his friend Francesco Tramezzino in Rome, and his death in 1577, Scappi may well have begun revisions and eventually annotated his copy of the 1570 volume with corrections or additions. A close collation of the two texts shows that page after page are, however, absolutely identical – even to a perpetuation of the omission of a recipe, whose name appears in the index, and of errors of recipe number in cross-references. The major differences between the two printed texts, rare though they are, appear to be typesetting errors, occasionally corrected in the later printing, more often made by the later printer. Either Scappi did not rewrite anything or make any changes, or else the 1581 typesetter was not informed about them. His pages seem to have been set solely from the earlier printing of the book – and not set with exceptional meticulousness.

This translation attempts to identify differences between the two texts that may possibly have some significance. The sources, for which the translator is grateful to the respective libraries, are: for the 1570 printing, the University of Toronto Library; for the 1581 printing, Harvard University Library.

The translator's difficulties

A few of the slight problems that have arisen in this translation of Scappi's work are due to some extent to the peculiar nature of the original printed text. That is not simply to fix blame elsewhere than on the translator himself for any inanity or obscurity, but merely to point to certain historic factors of which the reader may not be aware. It might not hurt, and it would surely be generous on the reader's part, to keep them in mind.

At some stage in compiling his *Opera*, Scappi inserted the odd recipe into a series of recipes that had already been numbered sequentially within a projected book. That addition is altogether understandable, but unfortunately a certain number of cross-references were already in place according to the previous numbering; the necessary corrections to those cross-references were not always made, a reference that is printed being out usually by one or two numbers. In Recipe VI,189, for instance, the reference to 191 is wrong; it should read 192. The curious reader can try to determine where a particular insertion (never, it seems, a deletion) must have been made. A few references (for instance in Recipe III,149) are clearly incorrect, but it is not altogether clear to which recipe or recipes the reader should have been referred.

Certain errors such as those remain uncorrected in the subsequent edition. Other errors are minor typesetting blunders and, not at all numerous, are corrected in the reprinting.[134] The 1581 typesetter contributes a somewhat more impressive number and variety of *lapsus*, attributable for the most part to inattention.[135] A type of blunder that could bother any contemporary reader – let alone a modern reader – may (again) point to an erosion in the proficiency of the Venice printshop since the death of Michele Tramezzino: the typesetter has made a good number of mistakes by picking up the wrong character from his tray of type boxes.[136]

---

[134] Those 1570 errors, corrected in the reprinting, include, *Sadersco* for *Sardesco*, *palletti ripieni*, 'full posts,' for *polletti ripieni*, 'stuffed chicks,' and *cinamomiti, confetti* for *cinamometti, confetti*.

[135] The Tramezzino reprinting of the *Opera* has wrong or missing letters: *zengevoro* for *zengevero*, *poto* for *poco*, *mondi* for *tondi*, *serviranuo* for *serviranno*, *sacicciene* for *salciccione*, *vero* for *vetro*, *fooco* for *fuoco*. In a few instances words are skipped: *a qui vi porrà cura* for *a chi non vi porrà cura*; and, rarely, a passage is dropped, in V,24 and V,71 for instance. Some errors are attributable to misreading: *latte*, 'milk,' for *lato*, 'side,' *occhi* for *orecchi*, *grassetto* for *grossetto*. A strange negligence, too, in setting recipe numbers (always Roman numerals) and folio numbers (Arabic) correctly seems to afflict the 1581 typesetter.

[136] Wrong letters are set in large part because in the dismantling of a previous page a letter (always, of course, the inverse of its printed shape) is inadvertently dropped into the wrong box: *scbiena* for *schiena*, *paue* for *pane*, *sarauno*, *pcco* for *saranno*, *poco*, *sin a* for *fin a*, *papoi* for *dapoi*, *tropdo* for *troppo*, *chiopi* for *chiodi*. The printer's fingers occasionally stray, too, into a neighbouring box – unless, again, the printer's devil had been lax in replacing used type into the right boxes: *arodo* for *brodo*, *arodetto* for *brodetto*, *gagiano* for *fagiano*. Inattention may account

Scappi refers to his smallest division as a chapter, *capitolo* or *cap.* Overall, that is a satisfactory term, given that many of those paragraphs are not, or not exclusively, properly recipes. Some are descriptions of foodstuffs, some are lists of hardware, some advise on a cook's duties and perquisites. Despite that, I have rather arbitrarily imposed 'recipe' as a uniform translation for most of Scappi's 'chapters.' Books I and IV deal wholly with 'non-recipe' material, however; in Book I the symbol for section (§) is perhaps more suitable than 'Recipe.' Of a similar nature is the difficulty of labelling obvious subsections within a book, particularly, again, in Book IV. Scappi merely juxtaposes successive segments there; as a rubric to the table for the whole of Book IV, he writes only *Tavola del quarto libro dell'imbandire le vivande,* 'Table of Book IV on Serving the Dishes,' which only tangentially implies much other material in the book. In this translation the different parts of Book IV are identified by means of invented rubrics.

In keeping with contemporary practice, Scappi has no noticeable prejudice in favour of short sentences. Often in a long and complex recipe the only period is at the very end. Other punctuation marks – commas, colons, semi-colons – are used in ways that are not consistent with modern English usage and whose sense is occasionally moot. Paragraphing is generally absent within a recipe or long preamble; there are no physical breaks between several discrete topics. In all those matters the translation is concerned primarily with ensuring that Scappi's meaning is understandable.

An apparent peculiarity in Scappi's style appears in many of the lists he compiles. Even though a list may be built of alternatives (options between ingredients or between procedures), Scappi will write, 'A, B *and* C': the meats may be *crude & rostite* (VI,43). The translation usually substitutes an 'or' for an 'and' between a pair of options and at the end of a list of possibilities.

On the topic of lists we should point again to the most remarkable one that Scappi assembled, which is in the middle of Book IV. There, in a sequence of pages that constitute a full third of his book's bulk, Scappi placed his compilation of sample menus for every season of the year. In order to save space and yet provide an overview of this central portion of the *Opera,* this translation will render the entire sequence of months and meals by means of an enumeration (in English) of *servings* (but with no listing of individual dishes), exactly as Scappi himself

---

for other mistakes in typesetting: *levate* for *lavate, zuccaco* for *zuccaro, cotli* for *cotti, troppgo* for *troppo, d pollo* for *di pollo, piedi vitella* for *piedi di vitella, cor* for *corpo*; and repetitions of words and letters: *& et* and *sene se ne* and *botttiglia.* A quick review of his line of type would also have avoided a metathesis such as *tagilsi* for *taglisi.* Correct spacing is as important as a wrong letter, and perhaps easier to spot for a conscientious typesetter: *latte dimand ole* for *latte di mandole.* This catalogue of blunders should not, however, detract too greatly from the enormous credit due the Tramezzino firm for having produced two printings of a very large book, printings which were, overall, neatly composed, legibly inked and pressed, and in which, generally speaking, the type was, indeed, carefully set.

tabulated them in the half-dozen pages of his index to Book IV. That tabulation is merely a synopsis of the kitchen's and the steward's work for the year. However, a selection (in the original Italian) of the menus themselves will also be provided – if only to indicate the sheer labour, week in, week out, that must have entered into preparing the dishes for such long and varied meals.

For reasons that the reader is free to imagine, Scappi strives for a style that is impersonal. In his preambles, addressed directly to Giovanni, he will here and there let himself write 'I,' 'me,' 'myself.' In general, though, he eschews a personal voice, choosing in particular to cast the instructions in his recipes in the passive and in a third-person reflexive, both being similar in effect in Italian. Such a sustained use of passive and reflexive over some seven hundred pages may represent a remarkable effort, and achievement, for a writer – but, handled literally, it is quite untranslatable. The reader is again asked (or, properly, the translator asks the reader) to bear in mind that the fundamental style for which Scappi strives is formal, objective and (until he reflects on some illustrative experiences) impersonal. His intention may have been to imitate a contemporary scientific treatise so that his work on cookery, even if it was in the vernacular, could take an honorable place among the grave, scholarly publications of his day. Despite his probable aim, however, he does sometimes give way to a personal tone, even in the midst of a disquisition on the nature of a particular fish, and write (for instance), 'When I was in Pesaro I saw a vessel accidentally run aground and turn upside down … ' (Recipe III,183), or, 'That was how Pope Pius IV, of blessed memory, used to eat them in 1564 when I was serving him' (III,163). When he does so the change of style makes us realize just how essential the intimate point of view is to Scappi the man. The formal style that Scappi initially adopted for his *Opera* – 'fresh eggs are beaten and are strained, the mixture is taken and is applied … ' – is far from suggestive of a mind and a spirit that were active, curious, open and busy enough to absorb so much of the customs he witnessed; or far from representative of a personality that involved itself with so much obvious ardour in transmitting what he believed in so deeply. He knew, though, the style that a sound scientific document required; a literate man, he tried to satisfy a good part of that requirement.

Some of Scappi's preparations have names that cannot, perhaps even should not, be translated. For the most part, those are generic: *tomamacelle, berlingozzi, fegatelli*. Some are particular bits of hardware, for instance *bastardella*. A description of that dish or pot ('a sort of two-handled, round-bottomed pot or kettle') cannot be repeated every time the vessel is used, and seems more appropriate for a footnote. That will be the usual procedure here: Scappi's term will occasionally be kept, in italics, and explained in a note.

Quantities commonly pose a problem for translators of historic texts. Scappi is usually precise when talking about amounts or quantities. However, while he certainly knew what he meant, and knew which measuring system he was referring to, translating his intentions can give rise to uncertainties. Avoiding potential problems, Scappi depends for many of his quantities upon measurements of weight – the amount of meat, the volume of flour, the ratio of several spices in a mixture.[137] Even though he sometimes measures liquids by volume he will still clarify his meaning by referring to the weight of that unit of measure: take, he writes, *una foglietta di vin* but for safety adds *laquale pesi una libra & mezza* (VI,131). Yet the meaning of even ounces and pounds could vary. I have assumed a pound (*libra*) of sixteen ounces, although Scappi does mention *libre milanesi* of twenty-eight ounces each (Recipe III,115). For Scappi's varied measurements of liquids, I have chosen a litre as the basic measure of liquid volume. The problem there is that the *foglietta*, the *boccale* (four times the volume of a *foglietta*), the *bicchiere* and the *soma* equate only very roughly to some simple amount in litres or fractions of litres. In time the reader may also tire of repeatedly seeing 'two-thirds of a litre' and wonder if Scappi should not have rounded upwards or downwards a little. Of course he may already have done that with his own figures. Alternatively, measurements of distance and size use the very old standards, parts of a normal human body: a foot, an arm (a span), a hand (*palma*) and a finger are the default measures of small sizes; the width of a hand ('a hand and a half long') or a finger's thickness ('four fingers high') become very serviceable rules of thumb. Likewise to indicate anything slender, a very thin layer of dough, for instance, the thickness of a knife blade was universally understood and always close at hand. The translation has tried to retain that wholly corporeal, physical sort of measurement.

The net result of translating Scappi's measurements will, therefore, place before the reader a strange *pasticcio* of metric, imperial and bodily measures.

The translator's intention

*T*wo features of this translation might benefit from tentative justifications. They are the Index and the footnotes.

The Index is a compound table, arranged alphabetically in English (except where no translation of Scappi's Italian is easy or advisable), which lists each of the significant things or actions that Scappi mentions, indicating the location in his *Opera* where he wrote it and transcribing the Italian word or words that Scappi used for it. The catalogue of terms in this Index is by no means complete: its purpose is modestly to help a reader understand and locate items or ideas by which Scappi refers to elements or phases in his cookery, in his kitchen or, from the wider world, in his experience. Even so, not all occurences of a term are noted: if an ingredient, for instance, is used frequently, only one or two of the

---

[137] So indispensable are weigh scales in Scappi's kitchen that he even has them engraved in one of the plates that accompany his *Opera*: see the *Bilanzia* in Plate 12.

first instances of the word will be shown. The word 'passim' will indicate a fairly widespread occurence of a term, sometimes accompanied by number to suggest more concretely the frequency of the term's appearance in the *Opera*.

It is particularly for the overly abundant footnotes that readers deserve an explanation, perhaps an apology. Straining the patience of all but the most indulgent readers (or thoroughgoing stoics or masochists), those tedious notes aim merely to shed slightly more light upon just what an exceptionally bright, curious, capable individual, more than four hundred years ago, held to be really important. Scappi's life was devoted to his work. He had a conviction that to be able to prepare the best food was a supreme honour as well as a supreme charge. As has already been suggested here, he understood that doing that work well demanded a mastery of a surprisingly broad range of skills and knowledge. Few jobs today place such onerous obligations upon a worker.

When we face a new subject all of us are learners. Historical subjects pose obstacles for any learner. The history of food and cookery is not (yet, quite) a field of broadly acknowledged relevance in today's curriculum of general studies. Historic cookery is still indeed something of an arcane subject. It needs some helpful promotion to open up a few of its hidden curiosities, to show a little of the wealth of human experience and ambition that are its components, to say nothing of the gastronomic pleasure that must always have motivated it.

And yet, as far as cookery goes, we all know how to boil an egg. Presumably Scappi did it the same way and for the same purpose – or did he? That is, in part, a central question. What did he do with his foodstuffs, and why?

The notes cannot reasonably explain everything. Nor can a single note attached to a particular instance of an ingredient, a vessel or a procedure be entirely adequate. When an unfamiliar thing or process recurs in Scappi's work, the Index may be helpful. The notes themselves, too, may at least entice a reader to look farther afield in the enormously rich and rewarding subject area of early food and cookery.

To conclude, we may return to one of the difficulties alluded to above. Scappi calls his smallest divisions 'chapters,' a term rendered consistently and sometimes not accurately by the word 'recipes.' The continual mix in the *Opera* of recipes and information or advice arises from Scappi's concept of his profession, from his sense of what he needed to pass on to his pupil. A servant must know his master and his master's taste. Among servants a cook must be aware of all the ways he can influence his master's health and well-being. A cook must satisfy his master's taste by choices from his repertoire of contemporary cookery, his professional experience or his inventiveness. He must do that within the bonds of household authority and finances. The procedures he uses in preparing a dish must depend on the foodstuffs that are available and that he selects. The procedures must further be circumscribed by the potential of his kitchen, the quality of its equipment and of its personnel. A cook must recognize and obviate the strictures of dietary laws, the predictable hourglass and the unpredictable flame.

In sum, a cook's knowledge had to be broad even though his freedom, whether to satisfy his master or merely to create, always had limitations of one sort or another. The broad and disparate areas of experience that a cook might have to draw upon at any moment could not be sorted into discrete departments even for a formal, pseudo-scientific treatise. The terms 'book' and 'chapter' (*librum* and *capitulum*) themselves belong to the scientific style of the day. It was natural for Scappi to pick them up when he arranged the divisions and subdivisions of his own subject matter. Publishing houses and literate readers were used to texts which presented subjects of universal, even eternal, significance in a rational way. The *Opera* is moderately successful in imposing scientifically clear order on an enormously complex body of matter.

Part of the problem with such terminology lies with the modern acceptation of the words 'cookbook' and 'recipe.' Yet Scappi's work is more than a cookbook in a narrow modern sense; his recipes have a broadly instructive purpose that a modern culinary amateur will not expect. The *Opera* aspires to offer an ordered compendium of advice on foods and food preparation such as a professional cook in the most respectable houses and kitchens of his day would benefit from. It is knowledge of both a 'scientific' and a practical kind. Yet the knowledge is not coldly impersonal. It amounts to culinary wisdom. It is particularly a fund of advice gleaned from long experience and passed on with great patience and goodwill, but constantly with the desire to see the office of cook retain all of the burnished respect that Scappi himself was able during his professional lifetime to acquire for it. The *Opera* is a product of intelligence, good taste and wholehearted devotion.

Above all, in his *Opera* Scappi presents a cogent testimonial that, among the really worthy professions exercised by his contemporaries, the office of cook is truly one of serious value. A cook is not merely a technician, a mechanic: he is a craftsman. The knowledge, abilities and responsibilities of a cook verge on the infinite in breadth and degree; he holds life, death and happiness in his hands. A cook is consequently possessed by professional standards that are supremely exigent. Just as his duties are onerous and in a real sense noble, so the treatment of a cook by his employer and superiors must recognize that he is no mere minion or drudge. A dependable cook is exercising a most honourable craft.

I should like to offer my warmest thanks to several individuals who helped very generously to make this a better book. Ken Albala, Antonio Carluccio, Kate D'Ettore, Curtis Fahey, Amy Menary, Gillian Riley, Karen Scott and Martha Wailes all contributed in a variety of substantial ways by offering information, weeding out blunders and generally enriching a book which, had its author not received their generous assistance, would have been even less worthy of its subject,

Bartolomeo Scappi. Production and editorial staff of the University of Toronto Press – Barbara Porter, Ani Deyirmenjian and Suzanne Rancourt – were further painstakingly helpful in improving this publication.

In the protracted elaboration of the whole project I have been, as always, grateful above all else for the constant support and much-tried patience of my wife, Eleanor.

The Collected Work of

Messer Bartolomeo Scappi

Personal Cook of Pope Pius the Fifth

divided into six books.

In the first, the discourse that the author holds
with his apprentice Giovanni.

The second deals with various meat dishes
of both quadrupeds and fowl.

The third speaks of the nature and season of fish.

The fourth sets out the menus for serving dishes,
both meat and lean, to the table.

The fifth contains the way to make various sorts
of pastries and other creations.

The sixth and last book discusses convalescents and
many other dishes for the sick.

With the funeral proceedings in the obsequies
of Pope Paul III.

With the pictures necessary for the kitchen and for
the Cardinals in Conclave.

With a privilege for 20 years granted
by the supreme Pontiff Pope Pius V
and by the Illustrious Venetian Senate.

[f. a ii r]

Pope Pius V

O n my own initiative, and so on.[1] As I have heard that our beloved sons
Francesco and Michele Tramezzino, formerly our publishers in Venice,
will cause to be published at their own expense, a book for the general use of all
– concerning Cookery and the office of Household Steward,[2] and also concerning
nutrition and medicines and things to be given to convalescents, all of which
matters have their own illustrations, and also those things that are needed by
the Cardinals when sitting in Conclave – a book by the most skilled Master
Bartholomeus Scapius, now holding an appointment[3] as our personal cook, not
hitherto printed, in the City of Venice; they intend to be the first to do it. Let that
be known, lest any person print that same work without their permission, which
would place that person in the greatest peril: for we will take action against anyone
found guilty of that. With like intent and certain knowledge, the aforesaid work not
having to now been printed, nor being about to be printed, to the same Francesco
and Michele, if it should be approved by the said City following an inquiry by the
Heresy Office into any irregularities,[4] we grant and concede the printing for ten
years. It is not by anyone whomsoever or in any way whatsoever to be printed or,
by themselves or by others, to be sold or to be kept in their warehouses or elsewhere
for sale, printed or about to be printed, except by the authority of Francesco and
Michele. This applies to each and every follower of Christ, whether within Italy
or beyond, especially to those who are booksellers and printers of books, under
pain of excommunication in the lands subject, directly and indirectly, to the Most
Holy Roman Church; I will furthermore add 200 gold ducats;[5] and in addition
to that punishment the loss of the books every time the deed itself be committed,
each subsequent infraction incurring the same punishment as often as there be
a transgression. Nor let anyone dare, ten years from the printing of said work,
hitherto unprinted, and it being printed by those men Francesco and Michele,
without the permission of the same men, Francesco and Michele during the period
of the said ten years, to print, either by themselves or others, unless printed by

---

[1] The text begins with the words *Motu proprio etc.* As the *etc.* indicates, the phrase *motu proprio* is a set formula; it indicates an act arising from the personal volition of the pope himself, a favour to be granted.

[2] The word *architiclini* translated into contemporary Italian as *scalco*, the individual charged with the operation of a noble household, including all of its ceremonial. A number of books of the time were devoted to the responsibilities of that functionary.

[3] The phrase *profectus est* can also have the sense 'is supremely competent.'

[4] *postquam per inquisitionem officii hæreticæ pravitatis.*

[5] Understand: 'a fine of 200 ducats' as a penalty to be added to the excommunication.

Francesco and Michele; or, if printed, to sell or to have for sale or to display or to possess, as above.

These commands are to all our brothers, the Archbishops, and their vicars in general spiritual [f. a ii v] matters, and to those in the temporal realm of the Holy Roman Church, Legates and Vice Legates of the Apostolic See, and governors of those states that, whenever they may be appealed to on behalf of Francesco and Michele, or are appealed to on behalf of one or the other of Francesco or Michele, affording the protection of an efficacious defence send aid at every request of the said Francesco and Michele against refractory offenders, through ecclesiastical censure, perhaps by some even harsher measure, and that they carry out justice by means of other remedies; invoking also, if need be, the aid of the secular arm, because the matter is difficult to manage; and this present Initiative[6] may be presented anywhere. We wish and decree by our apostolic authority that for this transcript or copies signed by the hand of the same notaries and with the seal of the same Curia, or of persons of confirmed ecclesiastical rank, have full and absolute credence in them, wherever an investigation occurs, in case a copy have more than is in this original, and since absolved from censure to this effect, a signature alone being enough. Declaring null and void whatever other apostolic arrangements and other grants to the contrary, that might otherwise tend to impair all that is set out above in this decree, notwithstanding whatsoever etc.

It is our pleasure that we deliver this, by our own initiative.[7]

Given in Rome at St. Peter's, the 29th of March in the fifth year of our reign.[8]

---

[6] Again, *motum proprium*, the papal action represented by this declaration.

[7] In the text: *Placet Motu proprio M.* The *M.* is likely a scribal abbreviation for *mandamus*, the whole phrase constituting a set formula.

[8] *tertio Kalend. Aprilis.* Pius V was elected on 7 January 1566; the fifth year of his reign began on 8 January 1570.

[f. a iii r]
1570. 22 March in Rogationtide.

L et it be granted to our faithful Michael Tramezzino that no one but he or his consign may throughout our domain print or, if elsewhere printed, there sell, for a period of twenty years henceforth the book titled *Epulario*, or *De re coquinaria*,[9] by Bartolomeo Scappi, on pain of losing the work[10] and paying three hundred ducats, to be divided one-third to the denouncer, one-third to our house of the Arsenal, and the final third to the Magistrate who will execute the indictment.

Charged with overseeing all that our laws require in the matter of printing,

Julius Zambertus

Duc. not.[11]

---

[9] The alternative title, in Latin, and might be translated as 'On Cookery.' It is interesting that of the three privileges only this one granted by the Senate of Venice recognizes Michele Tramezzino alone as printer of Scappi's work, and that the period for which a 'copyright' is granted is *twenty* years, whereas the pope and the duke each guarantee exclusive rights for only ten. Michele was likely well known as a solid Venetian citizen who for three and a half decades had contributed to the economic welfare of the republic. In any case Michele cannily uses Scappi's title page to imply that both Pius V and the Venetian Senate accorded the printer a twenty-year privilege.

[10] The Italian word has an unusual plural form: *l'opere*. The word *opera*, eventually used by Scappi's printer in the book's title, derives from the plural of the Latin *opus* and therefore denotes, as the writer of the present document certainly knew, the collected works of someone. Julius Zambertus is likely referring to all the volumes of the *Opera* that the malefactor might print or sell.

[11] Scappi's title page indicates that the publishers of the *Opera*, Tramezzino of Venice, have received from both the pope and the *Illustrissimo Senato Veneto* a twenty-year exclusive right to print and sell the book. In the present document Julius Zambertus publishes this *privilegio* on behalf of the Senate of Venice. The qualification after his name seems to be an abbreviation of 'Ducal notary.'

[f. a iii v]

Cosmo de' Medici, by the grace of God, Grand Duke of Etruria,[12] Second Duke of Florence and of Siena, Lord of Porto Ferrajo on the Island of Elba, of Castiglione della Pescaia and of the Island of Giglio.

W e decree that no one shall steal the profits of its efforts and the rewards of its watchmen, by the lawful course of this carefully studied privilege, we proclaim publicly, these words of ours having been repeated often, that we utterly forbid all printers, booksellers and others, anyone, for ten years hence to print or cause to be printed or to put up for sale, without the consent and good will of Michele and Francesco Tramezzino, printers in Venice, a book written by Master Bartholomeus Scapius, who is currently chief of the cooks of our most Holy Lord, Pius V, Supreme Pontiff,[13] concerning food and the office of Steward, and also concerning nutrition and effective remedies, and the sure manner and time that ought to be allowed for convalescing, all of which is represented in his engraved figures. But should anyone so dare in any book whatsoever, or should anyone act against these decrees, on them will be inflicted, by our right, for the deed alone a fine of ten gold scudos and the loss of the printed volumes; one part of that fine will be given to the aforementioned Tramezzino printers, the other though to the treasury of the Duke. However forcefully anyone may oppose this decree, its contents will not be impaired in any way whatsoever. We have drawn up this document in good faith and the signature below was written by our own hand, as a safeguard of which we order the apposition of a lead seal.

Given in Florence on the second day in the year of our Lord and of the tidings of the Incarnation 1570, in our first year as Grand Duke of Etruria, thirty-fourth as Duke of Florence and also twelfth of Siena.

Grand Duke of Etruria.

Laeius Titus

Francesco Vintha.

---

[12] That is to say, of Tuscany.

[13] Here in this ducal privilege, the position of *Magister Bartholomeus Scapius* is qualified: *nunc præfectus est Coquorum Sanctissimi Domini nostri Pii Quinti Pontificis maximi.* The phrase has been taken to indicate that Scappi was an overseer of the pope's cooks, although it seems unjustifiable to elevate him to the largely clerical function of kitchen clerk, particularly given that the phrase is not *præfectus est Coquinæ.* In the privilege that he grants the *Opera*, Pius V himself – who should have known – does not call Scappi the *magister coquinæ* or *magister culinæ*, 'master of the kitchen,' as is pointed out above; rather the pope says of him, *nunc profectus est nostris intimis Coquis.* See Laurioux, 'De Jean de Bockenheim à Bartolomeo Scappi,' particularly 305 and 324.

[f.a iv r]

To the Illustrious and Very Reverend Lord Don Francesco di Reinoso,[14] Personal Steward and Chamberlain to His Holiness our Lord Pius the Fifth.

I t is a natural obligation among men, My Illustrious Lord, to help one another, and for each to put his labours at the service of our common life, by revealing to one's fellows whatever he has discovered, either through the contemplation of things or through experience; and so, given that no individual can by himself attend to everything that is both necessary and useful to human life, a person can take advantage of others' labours. Thus is it reasonable to hold that, like malevolent enemies of the common good, those are condemned who, by keeping their secrets hidden, not only refuse to publish them by means of the pen but also prove miserly in their words with other individuals.

Therefore I, desiring to escape any such blame, have in no wise wished to refuse this my present labour for publication, having been so besought by kindly and judicious persons who, judging it apt to be useful to many, have wanted to see it presented for general use. However, since I am now in the service of His Holiness, under the [f. a iv v] authority of Your Lordship, to whom the care of so many Princes has worthily been committed, it seemed to me quite fitting that this work of mine should see the light of day under your ægis also, and that it should have your name as its shield.

Will Your Lordship therefore receive it with that kindness with which you have always treated its Author, who most humbly kisses your hand and commends himself to your good grace.

Your Illustrious and Very Reverend Lordship's most humble and affectionate servant,

Bartolomeo Scappi.

---

[14] This person's name will also be printed in the *Opera* as Rinoso and Reynoso. See a brief biography of this cleric in the listing of Persons Mentioned in Scappi's *Opera*. Born in 1534, he would have been in his early- to mid-thirties as Scappi was writing. Scappi mentions him consistently with respect and in terms that suggest warm personal gratitude. Scappi's eight-hundred-page record of his professional contribution to the Vatican's glory, here dedicated to Reinoso, will be echoed a score of years later when Antonio de Fuenmayor, Canon of Palencia, composed Reinoso's own memoirs of his service as papal major-domo: *Vida y hechos de Pío V*. See Lemaître, *Saint Pie V*, 324.

[f. a v r]

To the Readers[15]

T he main purpose of good authors is usually and properly to compose and publish their work, or to be as useful as possible to the public by offering sound instruction and beneficial precepts, or else by entertaining the Reader in some way either with the subject matter they choose or with their style when they cannot do anything else. It therefore seems to me that absolute glory and true honour are rightly deserved by those who have happily been able to achieve both one and the other of the above purposes; just as, to my way of thinking, it can truly be affirmed has happened with Messer Bartolomeo Scappi, the author of the present work, having taken as his subject a matter so necessary to the body's health and having dealt with it with as great astuteness as any of the ancients; wherein he has managed, as any person of sound intellect can clearly see from the organization of the work itself, to place just as much utility as pleasure for any man willing to read it and use it as need be in his life. And if our intellect learns things easily and as a result prospers through those sciences that, for the industry of a wise and experienced Master, come to be laid out and expounded to it, so ought one to be certain that the rules and precepts of so excellent an author in that art must delight all of the human senses and must maintain and further enhance perfect health in our body, provided we sustain its proper temperament and furnish it with the wise discourse of reason.

Nothing else, then, Gentlemen, is needed to persuade you to read such a worthy work, since by itself it shows you how very useful its reading will prove to be to you.

---

[15] This endorsement, or rather sales pitch, is almost certainly the work of Scappi's Roman publisher and friend, and Venetian printer, Francesco and Michele Tramezzino, respectively. It is unsigned.

M·BARTOLOMEO SCAPPI

Book 1

Discourse That Sir Bartolomeo Holds with His Apprentice Giovanni

T he Most Reverend Cardinal De Carpi, our patron of blessed memory,[i]
having several times commended you to me, saying that I should take you
on as an apprentice and instruct you, to the fullest of my ability, in all that makes up
the very best of my profession, I, desiring to fulfil the commands of his Illustrious
Lordship with good will, accepted you; and, even though you were as yet a youth,
I did not hold your years against you but have always considered you like a son
given to me rather than a servant, having always set all of my mind to making you
a knowledgeable, astute expert in the art, so that after my death all my work and
practical experience, in the service of Our Most Illustrious Lord Hora,[ii] should
remain in you, since you have, I know, reached the age to distinguish between
good and bad (with regard to the work in which I have undertaken to nurture and
instruct you), I am prepared, out of love for the aforesaid of blessed memory, and
out of love for the Very Reverend Lord Don Francesco Reinoso, Personal Steward
to our beneficent Lordship[iii] who furnishes every good thing we have, to give you
fully the directions and procedures to govern you in the functions of that Office,
so that you can with honest craft serve any Illustrious Prince and honour him who,
with so much of his labour, have taken such care that you should come into its
practice having regard for the obligations that you and I together hold toward the
Very Reverend Lord Alessandro Casale[iv] for the favours he has deigned to extend

---

[i] Either Scappi or his typesetter has used the common abbreviation here: *fe. me.* – '*felice memoria*.' In the preamble to Book VI Scappi again indicates, using the same *fe. me.*, that the cardinal
was recently deceased. In Recipe VI,21 he further mentions the cardinal's long illness, writing
that at the end of April 1564 he had prepared a therapeutic concentrate for the prelate's sustenance. At that point he refers to him by name: Ridolfo Pio. The cardinal succumbed to his ail-
ment 2 May 1564. He had participated in the 1549–50 Conclave described by Scappi.

   The phrase *Patrone nostro* seems to indicate that Ridolfo Pio had at some time been in charge
of the papal household, and so was Scappi's (and Giovanni's) superior and director. We learn below that Francesco Reinoso currently occupied the position of personal steward to the pope.

[ii] Scappi will mention this personage, perhaps the kitchen clerk of Pius V, in the present instance
alone.

[iii] See Scappi's dedication, above.

[iv] Alessandro Casale will be mentioned again in the preamble to Book IV. At that point the qualification *molto Reverendo Signor* that we read here has become merely *Reverendo Signor*; he will
be titled there *maestro di Camera di sua Santità*. Casale was Bolognese as was Pius V.

to us in everything we do, and for the favour he has shown us before everyone, and particularly with regard to Lord Don Francesco, who for love of me loves you and holds you in affection. Therefore, in consideration of all that, I shall set out for you briefly in these five books[v] wherein the art and craft of a Master Cook lies;[vi] from which I beg you [f. 1v] never to part, for by past experience I know them to be very necessary for anyone who wishes to reach perfection and to acquire honour in it.

[1581 f. 1v] And so: In the First Book you will see wherein the skill of a Master Cook lies, with a few other specific requirements and compensation[vii] that are fitting and proper for that Office. In the Second Book you will find the procedures you have to follow to make various different sorts of dishes, of flesh, fowl and quadruped, along with the season each is available, and to make different jellies and sauces. In the Third Book, which will be for lean and Lenten days, you will find how to make different dishes of fish, and to identify the fish and know their season.[viii] In the Fourth Book you will find how to make different preparations with dough. The Fifth and final Book will be very useful for you, teaching you how to go about presenting and serving dishes (when they are made up) into the hands of the Steward.[ix] Furthermore, you will see, should the need arise, how to serve a Conclave of Most Illustrious and Reverend Cardinals, both within and without,[x] and how to arrange various furnishings proper to that office, as will be presented in the drawings and sketches where there will be three different kitchens, along with the fixtures and furnishings for the chambers of a Conclave.

1. The requisite conditions for a Master Cook.

It is necessary, therefore, insofar as many long years of experience have taught me, that a skilled and competent Master Cook, wishing to have a good beginning, a better middle and a best ending, and always to derive honour from his work,

---

[v] In the enumeration that follows, the author does not mention Book 6 which offers preparations for the sick or sickly.

[vi] Had Scappi titled his *Works* somewhat more descriptively, he might indeed have chosen these very words: *L'arte et prudenza d'un maestro Cuoco.*

[vii] *particolarità, & circonstanzi.* The latter include not only emolument and such allowances as room, board, livery, and horse but all other perquisites that a master cook can claim by reason of his office.

[viii] As we shall see, for a cook this *stagione* refers primarily to the months during which the foodstuff will be available in the local market.

[ix] This abstract of 'Book V' suggests a preliminary sketch of what Scappi's reader will eventually find in Book IV: the composition of meals.

[x] Giovanni's supposed master may be sitting behind the locked doors of the conclave or, possibly sick – as Scappi reports concerning several cardinals attending the 1549–50 conclave – he may have been allowed to return to his chamber.

should do as a wise Architect, who, following his careful design, lays out a firm foundation and on it presents to the world useful and marvellous buildings. The design of the Master Cook must be the fine and dependable method produced by experience, of which he should have acquired such knowledge that he could serve rather in the Office of Steward than the Steward could serve as Cook. And he must strive to satisfy usual, diverse tastes with delicate dishes. Not least, the dishes should be tasty and agreeable to the palate as well as pleasant and delightful to the eye with their pretty colours and appetizing appearance. The first foundation upon which he will set his main base must be his understanding of and experience with various sorts of foodstuffs so that, for want of anything (it not being available somewhere or in some season), what he cannot make with one ingredient he can make with another one that is available in that place and in that season, so that using that ingredient he can make proper, sumptuous banquets with the main ingredients that are needed. To be worthy of the qualification of shrewd and experienced, he must know[1.1] every sort of meat and fish, and everything else that will be entrusted to him each day, and know how to cut up every sort of quadruped animal and fowl, and to identify every saltwater and freshwater fish, and the cuts and members most appropriate for roasting or boiling or for use in the making of other dishes, and the procedures, and when to use them fresh or to preserve them, knowing the parts most susceptible to deterioration and the most durable, the tastiest and the most delicate. He must also be, if not thoroughly at least broadly, knowledgeable about all the condiments in current use in that Office. And he should know the qualities, the goodness of every sort of liquid, for meat days as well as for lean days, and all sorts of fruits and herbs and their seasons, for that is often necessary. He must be alert, patient and modest in everything he does, and as sober as possible because whoever is without a good deal of sobriety loses patience as well as a natural taste for things. He should place his patron's honour, along with his own, above all else, and his usefulness to his patron above everything else. He should possess a wealth of alternatives[1.2] so that, if need be, with a single ingredient he may know how to make a variety of dishes. Above all other qualities, with regard to humility and everything said above, he should be immaculately clean in his person and should strive to please not only ordinary appetites with his dishes but everyone with his politeness and general pleasantness. First and foremost he should endeavour to understand the nature and quality of the Princes and other Lords whom he will serve, so as to accommodate them as much as he can. He should not rely upon nor

---

[1.1] The verb here, *conscere*, has the strength of 'know intimately,' 'be thoroughly familiar with.' It is not just an intellectual, 'scientific' knowledge but a practical working knowledge of foodstuffs that Scappi insists upon; in his recipes he shows that the first is certainly important but that the second is essential.

[1.2] These *partiti* are variations on a culinary or gastronomic theme, optional dishes, ingredients or procedures.

have complete faith in his assistants, nor any other subordinate, keeping in mind
the old saying that he who places great trust will end up greatly deceived.

2. The location, form and layout of a kitchen, and the arrangement of the furnishings of that Office.

The Cook must know how to design and to construct a kitchen for both
personal and ordinary service[2.1] and to ensure every sort of utensil relating to that
Office, with which I shall deal in the present chapter.

I think, first of all, that the kitchen should preferably be located in a remote
place rather than in a more public area.[2.2] This is for several reasons, particularly
to avoid the distractions that accompany the concourse of people, along with
the dangers, and to avoid annoying those dwelling nearby in the palace with the
noise which is normal in a kitchen. It should be built on a lower floor rather
than a higher, and especially be bright, airy and well proportioned, the throat of
the fireplaces broad and high with wide hoods, those having iron connectors and
ties[2.3] throughout to strengthen them. Some iron fastenings are set into the wall on
which to attach chains, and lower down, set into the wall's buttress,[2.4] articulated
trammels where cauldrons can be hung so they can be pushed forward, in and
out. Near the chimney there should be two sorts of low wall, one hollow with
supporting columns so that a cauldron or frying pans can be set there; hot coals
are put into its open space to keep preparations warm and to finish cooking them.
The other little wall is vaulted, three hands high and four long.[2.5] In the same

---

[2.1] *una cocina tanto secreta, quanto commune.* Working in a household, a professional cook had
two normally distinct responsibilities: they lay firstly toward his employer, for whom he was the
personal or private cook, here *il cuoco secreto*; secondarily they lay toward the other members of
the employer's household, the commons, for whom a kitchen supplied whatever the steward considered to be adequate alimentary sustenance. Scappi was proud to bear the title of *cuoco secreto
di papa Pio quinto*.

[2.2] See Plate 1 of the engravings (Appendix II) for an illustration of most of the details that
Scappi will enumerate in this the main room of his ideal kitchen. The legend in the upper area
of the right wall identifies the room, in fact, as the *Cucina principale*.

[2.3] *staffe di ferro, et chiavi*: masons set these products of the iron monger's forge between the
stones of self-supporting structures, such as these projecting fireplace hoods, in order to keep the
mortared joints stable. The *staffe* were angled pieces for joints under tension, the *chiave* ('nails')
for joints in compression.

[2.4] *nello sperone del muro*: Because a trammel had to be able to bear the weight of a heavy
cauldron, it had ideally to be anchored right through the 'curtain' of a wall and into the exterior
buttress.

[2.5] Neither 'little wall' (*murello*) here is a partition: they are merely series of bridged masonry
supports for the containers of food being cooked or kept warm. The engraving, Plate 1, shows
both sorts: the first one has an upper surface which is more or less square, for a single, larger
pot; the latter one (identified as a *murello per pignatte*) is long, having five openings for coals

kitchen an oven can be made to bake pastries and other preparations of dough. On one side are two water tanks,[2.6] each of which can hold some sixteen thousand litres,[2.7] with their usual piping and drains, suitable for that kitchen. When one is being used let the other be refilled. Around the kitchen two sets of plank shelving should be mounted,[2.8] one three hands wide to hold various utensils placed on it. Likewise, in an airy place on the shelves there should be a set of hooks[2.9] from which to suspend chickens and other meats. Beneath those shelves there should be two large chests[2.10] divided into several compartments, with locks and keys, in which various foods can be kept that are being worked on from day to day. Elsewhere there should be a large chest holding coarse and fine cloths, towels, aprons, straining and filtering cloths, and other materials.[2.11] Besides that, alongside the hearth in the kitchen there should be a light wall – or instead of a wall, some planking – half a rod high so the person doing the roasts can shelter from any excessive heat.[2.12] Moreover, lower down at the rear of the hearth there should be a grill made of fifty heavy iron bars, each of these half a hand in width and four hands high, which must be set firmly in the wall; it is there to protect the wall so that it is not readily harmed. I have found from experience that that sort of grill is much more useful than the stone called leucite.[2.13] On one side of

---

beneath and pots and pans above. Plate 2 also shows a *murello* in the back right. Though Scappi does not say so, the top of these 'walls' has a hole over each bed of coals: the engraver of Plate 2 shows flames spreading up around the base of a pot.

[2.6] In Plate 1, *Conserva*, a cistern or reservoir. Like the one in the adjoining room (Plate 2), it is set into the thickness of the wall above a sink and has two spigots.

[2.7] *cento some*. With a *soma* measuring very roughly 164 litres in Rome, one hundred of them would call for a good-sized tank. At 91 litres to a *soma*, Faccioli calculates 9,100 litres: *Arte della cucina*, II, 17 n.6.

[2.8] Plate 1, upper left and right. In Plate 2 such shelving (in the upper right) is labelled *tavole conficate*, shelves that in this case are supported on brackets.

[2.9] In Plates 1 and 2 these attachments are shown beneath a shelf on the left-hand wall. In the second plate they are identified as *rastelli*.

[2.10] In Plate 1 one of these *credenzoni* can be seen mounted with brackets on a wall.

[2.11] Plate 1 shows such a chest on the right-hand wall. The label that is likely intended to identify it is placed above the broad shelf which is over it: *reduto da pani*. However, the shelf itself seems to bear things that could be fabrics.

[2.12] This fire shield for the spit-turner is clearly pictured in Plate 1. In the etching it is apparently a *tavolone* rather than a *murello*.

[2.13] The iron-grill heat reflector is pictured in Plate 1. The word Scappi uses for an alternative installation is *sperone*, a popular term for a yellowish leucite (*leucite gialla loziale*). Leucite is quite a hard igneous rock, a silicate with a vitreous luster, and seems to have been in common use as a backplate in a fireplace.

the kitchen a short stone column should be set up and stable, on which, as need be, a large mortar can be placed; likewise a large wooden workbench, four hands high and ten long, on which various meats can be cut up.[2.14] There should also be six folding trestle tables,[2.15] each eight hands wide, which can be moved easily from place to place; another one sixteen hands long and six wide which will be used for making up dishes;[2.16] and a similar one of walnut or some other smooth wood to be used for working all sorts of pastry dough on it.[2.17] Besides those, ten other moderately sized tables, each four hands wide, to be used to scrape fish; and likewise ten other larger ones of elm, to be used for beating lard and other things.

In that kitchen there should be blind recesses – that is, armoires[2.18] – where candlesticks and oil lamps[2.19] can be stored. If that kitchen is to be used as a servants' mess, though, there will have to be a large window suitable for such a mess room, with a small wall two and a half hands high where the cauldron can be set so the mess can more quickly and easily be served its dishes; however, that window must always be kept closed except at serving times, and should be four hands wide. In that kitchen, high up, there should be a small chamber of frame construction for the kitchen scullions when they are on duty,[2.20] where they can put pallets and make their beds and put other furnishings appropriate to such a chamber.

[2.14] Plate 1, foreground: to the left, *Colonna col mortaro*; to the right, *bancho*.

[2.15] Scappi's word for an ordinary table is *tavola*, a plank, the same word by which he designates a shelf. We are reminded that tables in the sixteenth century, even dining tables (dining boards), are still basically planks on trestles. In this section Scappi distinguishes a heavier, more solid table as a *banco* or *bancone*, a workbench, as in the previous sentence. It has permanent legs.

[2.16] This would seem to be the kitchen's serving table, its length designed to allow the dishing up of a number of preparations into bowls and platters. The cook and his assistants will work on one side, the servers pick up from the other.

[2.17] It is interesting that Scappi will several times later caution against placing certain foodstuffs on walnut. See Recipes III,219; V,106, 107; VI,22. In VI,30 he explains that walnut is acidic, and in VI,87 that it both turns a foodstuff bitter and darkens it.

[2.18] These will be simply cupboards built into the thickness of the masonry wall and, most likely, closed with a door that has open panels or louvres. See the middle of the right-hand wall in Plate 1.

[2.19] *Candelieri*: see Plates 2 and 15 for this rather tall candle stand; table models are etched in Plate 23. *Lucerne*: Plate 1 shows a multi-flamed oil lamp suspended centrally and high enough in the room to clear the workers' head; a second, smaller, single-flame variety can be hung on a wall bracket (to the left in Plate 1) or from the ceiling (in Plate 2).

[2.20] That is, when they, *gli garzoni della cucina, quando saranno di guardia*, are 'on call' but not immediately needed. A doorway in the middle of the right-hand wall of Plate 1 is labelled 'Boys' chamber': *Camerino per garzoni*.

Apart from that, the same kitchen should have an adjoining chamber on the ground floor[2.21] where pastry,[2.22] sauces,[2.23] whitedish,[2.24] jelly[2.25] and many other preparations needing a lot of space can be worked upon. This chamber needs to be spacious, bright and airy, with window frames in several sections that can be opened or closed as need be.[2.26] Around the walls there should be three levels of plank shelving mounted in the same way as those in the kitchen, on which dough and other things can be set when necessary. Other than those requisites there should be on one side opposite the window a somewhat larger oven than the one in the kitchen,[2.27] with its shovels of wood and iron, and its rag mops,[2.28] with an iron plate to be able to stop up the oven's mouth as need be; the kitchen oven should have the same. To one side of the base of the oven should be a brick tank like a small oven in which water can be heated – ensuring, though, that the vapours issuing from this little oven go up into the same hood as the oven chimney. It would not be inappropriate if those two water tanks provisioning the kitchen should also feed the aforesaid annex by means of two further pipes leading to it and with a rinsing sink nearby. You should check that on the upper range of shelving there is a dough tray or else a kneading trough along with its iron scraper, along with sieves, sifters and lasagna cutters[2.29] for working dough. Besides, in the middle of that room there should be a smooth, flat table fifteen hands long and three and a half wide where all sorts of dough can be worked; and various long and short trestle tables that can be moved from place to place. On one side of the room should be a cabinet ten hands high and six wide, with several compartments that can all be locked holding sugars, spices and other things used daily in the personal food of the Prince. And it would not be bad for there to be

---

[2.21] The room illustrated in Plate 2 corresponds to Scappi's description of this annex. It is identified merely as 'Room next to the kitchen': *Camera propinqua alla Cucina.*

[2.22] Plate 2, middle foreground: *lavorano di pasta*, 'they make pastry dough.'

[2.23] Plate 2, right foreground: *passano sapori*, 'they strain sauces.'

[2.24] Plate 2, left foreground: *la magnar bianco.* For this almond-and-rice preparation see the note in Recipe II,121.

[2.25] Plate 2, middle: *si passa gielo*, 'jelly is strained.'

[2.26] Depending on indoor and outdoor temperatures one or more sections of the windows can be opened. In Plate 2 the three windows that are visible would allow the cook twelve different degrees of ventilation.

[2.27] Pictured in the middle of the right-hand wall in Plate 2 and labelled *forno.* It is larger, of course, because this is the room for pastry making; it is opposite a window perhaps in order to ensure a better draft. In the kitchen proper the oven is to the rear of the left wall.

[2.28] See the creditable representation in Plate 11: *spazzator dal forno.*

[2.29] *lasagnatori.* An iron macaroni cutter with multiple blades is seen in Plate 13.

another one of the same size to hold coarse and fine cloths, boulting and straining cloths, strings, needles and other necessary things.[2.30] In that room proper-sized iron candlestands should be set out in the best locations, where they will not be in the way, and some hooks where lamps and candles can be hung in the evening. Under the vault and reaching the width of the room should be some poles on which to hang fine cloths for covering dough and other unfinished dishes.[2.31] Not less necessary than anything else is a kneading trough for kneading several sorts of dough.

For that kitchen to be fitted out perfectly, I think a little courtyard[2.32] should adjoin it in which at any time fowl can be plucked, large animals skinned[2.33] and various other sorts of work done, especially in summer when the great heat of the kitchen is unbearable. That courtyard should have two sets of hooks mounted on the wall at a place where they can catch the north wind and can be used to hang fowl and other meats.[2.34] Lower down, another set of hooks to hold large animals while they are being skinned, such animals as calves, goats, lambs, wild piglets, wild boar, goat kids and others of the same sort. But mind that fastened to the wall to one side of the hooks there is a row of shelves the same as those in the kitchen for holding various utensils, near which is a large workbench, as broad and as long as the one in the kitchen, of heavy wood, for cutting up various meats. Elsewhere there should be a large plank table sixteen hands long and six wide, on trestles, for preparing various herbs; in summer it can also be used for preparing dishes. Other than those tables, there should be tables, broad and narrow like those in the kitchen, on which slabs of lard can be beaten, fish cleaned, and large and small roasts larded. But it is necessary for all those tables always to be clean and smooth.

In the little courtyard I spoke of, there should be a well[2.35] with a large rinsing sink in which all the utensils can be washed;[2.36] over the sink there should

---

[2.30] Two cabinets are illustrated on opposite sides of this second room in Plate 2.

[2.31] The cloths (at the top of Plate 2) may be draped high on a pole, rather than stored on a shelf or in a closet, perhaps in order to dry after being washed.

[2.32] See Plate 3.

[2.33] A butcher worked under the direction of the chief cook. According to some terms of employment the hides of large animals constituted a perquisite for the cook, to tan and keep or to dispose of at his own discretion and for his own profit. Scappi mentions that particular 'right' in §45, below.

[2.34] These *rastelli*, literally 'rakes,' are a row of hooks, resembling large claws, mounted in a rod which is fastened to a wall. The apparatus is designed to suspend a carcass while it is being butchered. It can be seen in use on Scappi's Plate 3.

[2.35] In the left margin of the engraving (Plate 3) a script identifies a *mezzo pozzo*. This 'half well' may be so called because it is shared, through the wall, with the adjacent room.

[2.36] Plate 3: *si lava piati*, 'dishes are washed.'

be a small roof to shelter it from rain. It would not be a bad idea if that well were connected to the kitchen. Above all, that courtyard needs to be ample in space, cheerful, airy and brick-paved, with a broad gutter that can carry off any filth. That courtyard should always be kept clean, especially in summer, because otherwise it would make a stench in the kitchen, and that would in turn give a bad odour to foods that are daily kept there and would rot them. The courtyard must also be furnished with vessels such as wooden vats and basins for washing fish and meats and many other things, with big cauldrons on tripods for heating water, and several sorts of knives for skinning and dismembering animals and scraping fish and chopping herbs. It would also be very handy if in the courtyard there were a stone wheel for sharpening knives, and a hand-mill,[2.37] somewhat larger than the one in the kitchen, for grinding condiments, making almond milk, and for various other things.

I also think that near that courtyard it would be good to have a small chamber[2.38] for storing oil, rendered fat, butter and all sorts of condiments, for making milk-snow,[2.39] and in summer for storing jelly and whitedish. That little chamber needs especially to be in a cool place, with two windows, one on each side so the air can preserve things better.

[2.37] The *ruota di pietra* for knives is called a *rotatore*, a rotary grinder, in Plate 3. The *macinetta* or hand-mill is not illustrated; it seems to be an alternative to a mortar for grinding spices. There is no other mention of one, either before ('in the kitchen') or later in Scappi's work. It may resemble the nutmeg and sugar graters (*grata noci moschiate, grata zucharo*), though on a larger scale, in Plate 14.

[2.38] The room is illustrated in Plate 4. In the window opening to the left a figure can be seen, surveying the activity below. Given that these four scenes of kitchen work show no other idle individual, we may assume that the engraver has inserted into the last one a representation of someone in authority. Given that the figure does not have the flowing beard seen in Scappi's portrait opposite f. 1r, he may be a generic chief cook, kitchen clerk or even household steward.

[2.39] Scappi mentions this *neve di latte* again in his work in §44, below, and in Book IV at, for instance, ff. 169v and 327v [1581 ff. 134v and 275r]. It was, however, a relatively common preparation, much in vogue by the time Scappi was writing. Scappi's contemporary in Liège, Lancelot de Casteau, offers directions in French for making it: 'Get a pot of fresh cream, four ounces of sugar and four ounces of rosewater; get a clean little whisk and beat the cream hard for half an hour, then let it sit. You will see foam forming like snow on top; take a skimmer, lift the snow out and put it in a dish, with a trencher beneath to let the snow drain. Beat the cream again until you have enough snow. Then set it out in small plates with a sprig of rosemary in it, and serve it like that' (*Ouverture de cuisine* [1604], 123–4). Evidence of the popularity of the preparation is afforded in a second recipe later in the same work (139–40): 'For dry snow.' Ken Albala points out an English recipe for it (consisting of whipped cream, whipped egg whites, rosewater and sugar), called 'A Dyschefull of Snow,' in the *Propere newe Booke of Cokerye* (London: Lant and Bankes, 1545; repr. 1560); ed. Catherine Frances Frere (Cambridge: W. Heffer, 1913).

In the middle of Scappi's Plate 4, which pictures the fourth area of Scappi's ideal kitchen, an assistant is spinning a whisk in an earthenware pot to make this *neve*. See that 'wooden vessel' catalogued in §44.

Near the kitchen I think it is very handy to have another chamber, somewhat larger and at some distance from it, to store supplies, coal, baskets, boxes and other gear used when travelling. And off from this chamber there should be a row of benches with several places,[2.40] and also the drains, which from time to time can answer the natural needs of those in the kitchen. That is done so that men will not have to go far and so, in this matter as in all others, their tasks may be easier.

I have said enough about what is desirable in a kitchen. I shall now turn to examining how to identify, and to preserve, the goodness in every liquid, along with other things which follow below, beginning with oils.

3. To tell how good olive oil is, and how to preserve it.[3.1]

As far as I have been able to find out, there are many kinds of oil – that is, strong and mild, heavy and light, cloudy and clear, pale and coloured. The mild-flavoured, thick kinds are better in dishes and pottages than for frying, but those that are clear and less fatty are better suited for frying than others. Those oils that tend to be palish, made from selected olives and from a first pressing, are perfect; those that tend to be of an orange colour are often heavy. But a good test you can observe is that when an oil froths up while frying it is not very good, and likewise when it spits;[3.2] but when it heats without churning and does not give off a bad smell, then it is the best, as is the case with all other oils. Should you wish to purify oil, heat it in a pan; when it is quite hot put a little bread or uncooked dough into it and leave it there for a fifth of an hour. The bread or dough will draw off the dark extraneous bits and the bad smell, and the oil will be left clean.

To be good, almond oil has to be made from selected Milanese almonds[3.3] and should not be made ahead of time because it turns rancid quickly. That oil tends to be white, and is more suitable for making dishes and for salads[3.4] than for frying.

Should you wish to keep olive oil any length of time, store it in well-stoppered vessels of smooth stoneware or earthenware. You can similarly keep linseed oil

---

[2.40] Scappi is alluding to the need for latrines.

[3.1] Scappi deals with several sorts of oil here, although this rubric implies that the first paragraph refers to olive oil.

[3.2] *quando crepserà*, literally, 'when it cracks, crackles, pops.' That effect is likely caused by the presence of water in the oil.

[3.3] See the note in Recipe II,63 concerning *mandole ambrosine*.

[3.4] These *insalate* are any foodstuff (see Recipes III,204, 207 and 212), though primarily vegetables, that is conditioned or seasoned with oil and vinegar along with, occasionally, sugar and a spice or two. Three contemporary works on salads (in the modern sense) are interesting: Castelvetro's *Brieve racconto di tutte le radici, di tutte l'erbe e di tutti i frutti che crudi e cotti in Italia si mangiano*, and Felici's *Dell'insalata e piante che in qualunque modo vengono preparate per cibo dell'homo* and *Lettera sull'insalata*.

and walnut oil, when made from fresh flaxseeds and from selected, fresh walnuts. In many places in Italy those oils are eaten, but I think they are more suitable for burning than for eating.[3.5] In various seaside places it is usual to make oil from various sea fish, but in Italy such oils are not used for condiments or for frying.

4. To tell how good rendered fat[4.1] is, and how to preserve it.

The fat should be from around the kidney of a freshly slaughtered pig,[4.2] well cooked but not burnt. It should be white and should not have a bad smell. It is best between four months old and a year old. For best keeping, it should preferably have a flavour rather than be tasteless. Just so is that of a goose. The liquid is stored in a wooden or earthenware vessel in a cool place, the better to keep it.

5. To tell how good salted beef fat is from an ox or cow, and how to make it and to preserve it.

Ragnonatica is made from the fat of the above animals. As soon as it is slaughtered the animal is eviscerated and skinned of its membranes, and then the fat is beaten as sausage meat is beaten. For every pound of it mix in two ounces of salt, one ounce of fennel[5.1] and a quarter ounce of crushed pepper. It is stored for a full year in a white linen cloth and in an airy place that is dry rather than damp. It should be very fine – that is, much pounded together[5.2] – so it does not go rancid and take on a bad smell. When you wish to use it, pound it in a mortar along with a clove of garlic and moisten it with a little broth. In this way any sort of herb can season.

[3.5] In his *Brieve racconto di tutte le radici, di tutte l'herbe et di tutti i frutti, che crudi o cotti in Italia si mangiano* (trans. Riley, 93) Giacomo Castelvetro does not indicate any culinary use for walnut oil: 'In Lombardy they make oil from the poorer quality nuts, which they use to light the stables. Poor people and even worthy artisans use it in lamps about the house or on the table. The peasants in the countryside use nothing else for their lamps. This oil is good for various ailments.'

[4.1] *lo strutto.* This grease, from fresh pork kidney-fat, is to be distinguished from the *lardo colato* of §6, below, which is made from salt-pork skin-fat and clarified. To satisfy Christian dietetic rules Scappi frequently replaces *strutto* with fresh butter. Directions for making 'good rendered fat' are given in Recipe II,111.

[4.2] *Lo strutto vuole essere di songia di porco fresco:* variously spelled *sognia, sugna* and, most often, *songia* by Scappi or his typesetter, this is a pure and highly liquifiable fat valued for providing a fine cooking medium.

[5.1] By *finocchio* Scappi will generally mean the seeds from the pod or bulb, ground into a powder. See also the note in Recipe 39, below.

[5.2] If everything in the mixture is reduced to the finest particles, the condiments will mix thoroughly with the fat and can be depended upon to preserve its freshness.

6. To tell how good lard[6] is, and how to make it and keep it.

The slab of bacon fat should have been salted for two months, then it should be beaten like sausage meat. When that is done, it is put into a copper pot with a little water over a low fire, making it liquify. Then it is filtered through a fine strainer or else through a piece of linen, put into a wooden or earthenware vessel and stored in a cool place. That liquid can be used for frying pies and making tortes and dishes, though within a year because after that it will not be at its best.

7. To tell how good butter is, and how to keep it.

Butter should be made from the fat of fresh milk. Although sometimes it has two colours, white and yellow, nevertheless both are good when it is fresh. It is true that butters made at the beginning of March up to the end of May are, I believe, the best, just as are all sorts of cheese.[7] Being white or yellow depends on the grazing land, though. When you wish to store that butter for a long time, you can melt it and gently boil it over a bright fire with a little salt and then strain it, taking the best part and storing it in a cool place in an earthenware or wooden vessel. Above all, the cooked butter should be firm, tending to yellowish. But uncooked butter should be stored in a cool place. When the cooked butter has been in the vessel for four days, make a hole in the bottom of the vessel and, through the hole, move a stick about in the butter so that the whey drains out; then stop up the hole.

8. To tell how good all cheeses are, whether fresh or salted,[8.1] and how to keep them.

About fresh cheeses – they should be made from creamy milk, and do not salt them for more than a day because they would be too strong – I can truly say from experience that those made in Tuscany, called *raveggioli*,[8.2] should be made

---

[6] This *lardo colato* will be used frequently in Scappi's kitchen. It is a salt-pork skin-fat, or bacon-fat, that – unlike its fresh counterpart, the rendered fresh kidney-fat or *strutto* of §4, above – has been clarified and can properly nowadays be called a variety of 'lard.' For a few uses it is less desirable than the rendered fresh kidney-fat because of its residual saltiness, though it may for the same reason have a slightly longer shelf life.

[7] The principle that fresh spring grasses produce the best milk and milk products influences Scappi's advice extensively: for such milk see V,80, cheese, I,8; V,80; VI,155 and 161, and even the young of game animals, II,82 and cow's udders themselves, II,17.

[8.1] Pantaleone di Confienza published a scientific analysis of cheese and cheeses in 1477. Although he gives a surprising amount of space to cheeses produced in distant lands (Savoy, France, Brittany, Flanders, England, Germany) his coverage of his homeland, Italy, is limited entirely to the north. In Part I, Chapters 10 and 12, he examines respectively the nature of new and old cheese, and of fresh and salted cheese: *De diversitate caseorum ex parte novelitatis vel antiquitatis* and *ex parte salsedinis maioris vel minoris* (see the edition by Irma Naso).

[8.2] *raviggioli.* Zingarelli (*Vocabulario della lingua italiana*, 2002) defines today's *raveggiolo* as a sort of squashed, soft, fresh cheese made from sheep's or goat's milk in May or in the autumn.

from creamier milk and are always more tender and moderately salted. But the cheese called 'fat cheese'[8.3] in Milan is brought from German lands in tree bark, and it is good when it is moderately salted, and occasionally it has an exceptional aroma. As for the other salted cheeses, such as Parmesan, Ligurian and March cheeses,[8.4] in my opinion they are quite a bit better when they are made from the beginning of March to the end of June. When cut they give off an excellent aroma and run a bit.[8.5] But some cheeses are transported to Rome from the Kingdom of Naples that are made in various shapes and are called 'horse cheeses,'[8.6] and are not as good as Parmesan.[8.7] It is true that when fresh cheeses are fat, they are as good as fresh provatura,[8.8] although the provaturas of March are better whether fresh or salted. However, the cheese we call Sardinian[8.9] should be firm, white on the inside, although naturally dark. Should you wish to store those cheeses, you have to grease them[8.10] and check on them often, except for the Sardinian.

[8.3] *cascio grasso*. Scappi's recipes often specify a cheese of a relatively high fat content (comparable, in V,65, to provatura), with little or no salting. This is a soft cheese as distinct from a hard cheese: *cascio grasso, & cascio sodo grattato* (V,94). Uniformly I have translated his term *cascio grasso* as 'creamy cheese,' even though in a few instances (II,237; V,67, 139) it is grated. It may be noted that provatura is itself grated in Recipes V,105 and 200 – much, one assumes, as a liver can be grated in Recipe II,109. In Recipe II,162 Scappi writes that cheese is fatter in summer than in winter.

[8.4] *casci salati com'è il Parmiggiano, & di riviera, et marzolini*. Concerning the latter, see Pantaleone, Part II, Chapter 1, *De caseo apellato marcelin*, ed. Naso, 114; see also the note to 'March cheese' in Book IV, f.327v [1581 f.275r].

[8.5] *rendeno perfetto odore con alcune lagrime*: literally, ' ... with a few tears.'

[8.6] *casci cavalli*. Ray has a comment about these particular cheeses: 'In the kingdoms of Naples and Sicily they make a sort of cheese which they call *Caseo di cavallo*, i.e. horse cheese, for what reason I could not learn. These cheeses they make up in several forms; some in the fashion of a blown bladder, some in the fashion of a cylinder, and some in other figures. They are neither fat nor strong, yet well tasted and acceptable to such as have eaten of them a while. The pulp or body of them lies in flakes, and hath as it were a grain one way like wood. They told us that they were made of buffles [buffalo's] milk, but we believed them not, because we observed not many buffles in those countries, where there is more of this cheese made than of other sorts' (*Travels through the Low Countries, Germany, Italy and France*, 2nd ed., London, 1738, vol. 1, February 1664). Today this is a typical southern cheese, made from whole cow's milk. Gillian Riley (*The Oxford Companion to Italian Food*, 84) identifies *caciocavallo* as produced from milk of the *podolica* variety of cow. Zingarelli suggests that this elongated cheese may originally have had the shape of a horse; Ken Albala suggests that the name may have come from the cheese being transported in a horse's saddlebags.

[8.7] Concerning Parmesan cheese, see the note in Recipe II,22.

[8.8] This is an unsalted (i.e., fresh) cheese made from buffalo milk.

[8.9] In the 1581 printing, *Sardesco*; the 1570 typesetter had made the word *Sadersco*.

[8.10] The agent is not specified, perhaps butter.

9. To identify every sort of salami,[9.1] and how to keep it, beginning with fat bacon.

To be good, fat bacon should be firm and moderately salted, and preferably from young, male hogs than from female,[9.2] and fed in the woods rather than in the farmyard;[9.3] it will always be better from a young pig than an old one, as I said. To store it, choose a place that is neither too warm nor too damp because being too warm will make it turn rancid, and humidity will make it ooze and take on a bad smell.

To be good, pork belly and jowl need to be moderately salted and striated on the inside. *Sommata*[9.4] comes from the sow's belly, and particularly when it has milk; it is salted and preserved like fat bacon. It should be a high cut rather than low, and when it is sliced it gives off an excellent aroma.

To be good, prosciutto[9.5] should come from a young pig, not be too salted, and when cut give off a good aroma. Having been well stored and not more than a year and a half old, it will not lose its excellence. If it comes from a young hill pig, it will always be better than any other. Sometimes when they are smoked, hams are cleaned and kept in oil for many days.

All salt beef, when it is removed from the brine, needs to be dried in the sun and open air and stored in a cool, airy place. When it is cut up and gives off a good aroma and is reddish brown, it is excellent. In this way you salt and preserve ox and buffalo tongues. Semi-salted[9.6] meats should be moderately salted; they can be cooked without having been dried but only washed off, being careful that when they are being salted they do not warm up and do not take on a bad smell.

[9.1] For Scappi these *salami* are not just a sort of large sausage but a generic collective name for any meat that has been preserved – traditionally by means of salt, *sal*: in this section, bacon, sowbelly, ham, sausage and baloney. Further on, in §14, Scappi refers to *salami di pesci*, salted cuts of fish. However, in Recipe II,114 *salami* will have an intestine encasing them.

[9.2] Long-established physical theory held that pork was a relatively moist meat; since any male animal is by nature drier than a female of the same species, Scappi's rule here would have the approval of any physician. Given, too, that moisture promotes corruption, effective preserving of a foodstuff requires a thorough drying out – which, in the case of a very moist meat, salt cannot wholly guarantee.

[9.3] *nudrito ... in casa*. Traditionally, domesticated pigs were led by the swineherd onto uncultivated lands where acorns, beech mast and forest herbage constituted their prime, and valued, fodder. Wild or semi-wild animals, well exercised and exposed to the sun and air, are naturally drier than their fully domesticated counterparts.

[9.4] We shall consistently translate Scappi's *sommata* as sowbelly. In Recipe II,101 the author writes that the belly of a sow is better than that of a male pig.

[9.5] *presciutto*. This is a cured ham and is one of Scappi's favourite ingredients.

[9.6] Salted foods are thoroughly dried as a preliminary step, then packed dry in salt; semi-salted foods may be partially dessicated but are kept immersed in a brine.

Sausages, to be good, should be made of young pork and of the loin of young bullocks, and should be moderately salted and firm, and kept the same as prosciutto. It is to be noted that once they are done they can be kept for three months in olive oil, or frequently coated with it, in a place that is not too warm or airy; the same for every sort of mortadella. And when preserved meats are cut they will give off a good aroma, will be reddish brown and will be excellent.

10. Various salted fowl, preserved in oil and rendered fat.

Every salted fowl, such as geese, cranes, wild ducks, barnyard doves[10.1] and other fowl, once they are out of the brine and with the brine well washed off them, are dried in moderate smoke or in the open air. To store them for a long time after they have been hung in smoke, preserve them in oil.[10.2] Fowl that are salted are used more in cool places than in warm, and in places where the meat of quadrupeds is scarce. Ortolans, fig-peckers, and other small birds, after being kept for six days in brine, are removed and put in liquified fat that contains fennel seeds, in an earthenware vessel, letting the lard congeal about the birds.[10.3] Alternatively those small birds can be kept in well salted vinegar that contains garlic, cloves and crushed pepper.[10.4] I have seen them done both ways, and brought from Cyprus to Venice. For best storage they must always be in a cool place.

11. To tell how good pickled tuna back and salted tuna belly are.

Tonnina is the body of the tuna fish,[11] and *tarantello* is the belly of that same tuna. To identify just how good a pickled tuna back is, you should know that it must be firm, be russet-coloured rather than yellow, and give off an excellent aroma; the same with salted tuna belly, but it is somewhat more striated than tuna back. For preserving, all fish should be set in fresh brine: salmon, grey mullet, gilthead, anchovy, sardines, herring, pilchards and shad.

12. To tell how good salted eel is.

Salted eel should be firm, not over a year old and, when cut, be russet-coloured and give off a good aroma.

[10.1] Literally, those fed on acorns: *piccioni di ghianda.*

[10.2] Understand 'olive oil.' This manner of preserving foods was less common than by drying with or without a smoking, but was still in relatively common use in southern Europe.

[10.3] The brine and a thick coating of grease prevented or limited the growth of bacteria.

[10.4] Cloves and pepper were understood to be very dry in nature. A steeping in salted vinegar is properly a pickling.

[11] *il corpo del Tonno.* In Recipe III,208 Scappi will write that *tonnina ... è la schiena del tonno*: it is a tuna's back. Pickling involved a brine, perhaps with vinegar; salting is a drying process. Balducci Pegolotti (ed. Evans, 380) warns merchants that *tonnina* will tend to dry out in the barrels in which it is shipped and therefore the brine should be topped up frequently.

13. To tell how good caviar is.

Caviar is the salted eggs of sturgeon. Good caviar is black and oily, because there are several sorts. That which tends toward a grey-green colour, that is made with the eggs' membrane, does not last as long when cooked as it does uncooked. For eating just as soon as it is made, it is better cooked than raw. To be good it should have all the above-mentioned qualities. Both sorts are stored in wooden or earthenware vessels in a humid place.

14. To tell how good *moronella* is.

As far as I have found out, *moronella* is the belly of a large sturgeon, caught in the Mediterranean[14.1] and salted the same way as tuna belly is done.[14.2] When it is good and excellent it is not rancid but is striated and gives off an excellent aroma. To be stored a long time, none of the above-mentioned salted fish cuts should ever be removed from the vessel in which they were initially put, but must be continuously covered with salt and the brine they ooze, and remain well sealed in a cool, humid place.

15. To tell how good mullet roe is.

Bottarghe are the eggs of a grey mullet or a bass,[15.1] although they can come from a variety of other fish eggs, but the first are the best. Anyone wanting to tell how good they are should know that they ought to be firm, not too old and, when cut, should be russet-coloured. I think the best are medium-sized, rather than the large ones, and come from the Mediterranean.[15.2] They are stored for a long time in bran, though in a cool, dry place.

16. To tell how good a sturgeon back is.

The *schienale* is the salted loin – that is, the back – of a sturgeon. You should know that it must be firm and, when cut, it becomes russet-coloured like a salted dry meat.

17. To tell how good smoke-dried herring are.

To be good, herring should be fat and oily, full of eggs or milt, and above all with a round back, firm and moderately salted; those that are a tawny colour[17] are

---

[14.1] For the sense of *mar maggiore* here, see Recipe III,206 where the Atlantic Ocean seems a more reasonable translation.

[14.2] Further details in the speculation about what *moronella* really is are provided in Recipe III,206. At the end of Recipe III,208, however, Scappi is still somewhat cautiously using the expression *moronella misaltata fatta di pancia di storione*.

[15.1] The modern sense of the word *bottarga*, and apparently what Scappi means, is a patty, compressed, salted and dried, nowadays of mullet or tuna eggs. According to Zingarelli (*Vocabulario della lingua italiana*), *bottarghe* are eaten now either sliced and dressed, or grated on pasta. See also Riley, 63.

[15.2] See the first note in the previous recipe.

[17] *di color leonato*. The proverbial 'red herring' acquired its hue from the smoking process.

the best. They are preserved in barrels, in a place which is neither too humid nor too dry. If, when they are cut open, they turn out to be white and flakey, they are not good; they should rather tend toward a russet colour.

18. To tell how good the fish are that have been soused[18.1] and kept in leaves.[18.2]

Should you wish to know how good a fish is that has been soused and kept in leaves, you must first know that it should give off a good aroma, and secondly that it should tend toward a silvery colour rather than some other hue, though that depends on the fish. But above all, to be good it should be firm.

19. To tell how good a marinated fish is, and one that is jellied.

A marinated fish to be good should be firm and good tasting. Likewise a jellied fish, whether a sea fish or freshwater fish. To store them a long time they should be in a cool, airy place, and well sealed in a vessel.

20. To tell how good honey is.

To be good, honey should be fine-grained, firm, heavy, of a good smell, and with a golden colour. Above all it should be clean. It is stored in wooden or earthenware vessels.

21. To tell how good sugar is.

Although there are several sorts of sugar, nevertheless in our Office the most used are the coarse and the fine. Both should be light and clean, especially on top,[21] because often sugar has all sorts of dirt in it. To store it a long time, it must be kept in a dry place.

22. To tell how good dates are.

To be good, dates should be fresh and of a delicate, sweet flavour, because after six months they go bad.[22]

23. To identify the goodness of shelled pinenuts, hazelnuts, almonds and pistachios.

Pinenuts, hazelnuts and almonds should not be kept beyond a year because they often go bad then. They should be checked often for the rust they leave behind; the same with pistachios. But nuts that have not been shelled can be kept much longer.

[18.1] For this particular preparation of a fish, for which Scappi's verb is *accarpionare*, see Recipe III,122. The cooking involves spiced vinegar. The fish is eaten cold.

[18.2] See Book III for this common practice. Bay and myrtle leaves are preferred, either alternatively or in combination. See §39, below, for fowl that are packed in willow leaves and vine leaves.

[21] Scappi writes *nella cima*, on the peak or summit, suggesting that the form in which his kitchen receives its supply of sugar is a cone.

[22] It is interesting that Scappi suggests no way of preserving dates.

24. To tell how good raisins[24.1] and other dried grapes are.

I think there are many kinds of raisins, but those of Corinth[24.2] are quite a bit better than our domestic ones. Likewise the muscat grape is better than our large grapes. My experience has shown that all white grapes that have small seeds or none at all are better than dark ones.

25. To tell how good dried figs, prunes and dried visciola cherries[25] are.

Dried figs, both in a barrel and on a string, when they are plump and well conditioned and not over a year old, are excellent and best for the kitchen. Prunes as well, both damson and others, when they have been well prepared, in both their drying and their treatment with sugar, can be used in various dishes, as the following books will show in a number of places.

26. To identify every variety of spice suitable for cooking.

Experience has shown me that every sort of spice, when it is fresh and not more than a year old, gives off a good aroma and is much better and flavours any dish better than an old spice. Should you want to use spices in a mixture to be made up ahead of time for use at will in a variety of dishes,[26] I shall tell you the quantity of each that will go into a pound of the mixture, to be used as I have just said. Firstly:

$4\frac{1}{2}$ ounces of cinnamon
2 ounces of cloves
1 ounce of ginger
1 ounce of nutmeg
$\frac{1}{2}$ ounce of grains of paradise
$\frac{1}{2}$ ounce of saffron
1 ounce of sugar.

[24.1] Normally Scappi seems to use the term *uve passe* in the sense of raisins produced locally from common domestic grapes of no specific variety. Here and in Recipe II,261, for instance, they are distinct from muscatel raisins and currants.

[24.2] That is, currants.

[25] Throughout his work, when referring to cherries Scappi almost always names *visciole*, a variety he seems to have preferred, in part because they seem to have kept well in dried form between harvests. Other varieties, occasionally specified by Scappi, are morello (*marasche*) and Roman cherries (*cerase romanesche*). The *Prunus cerasus* (in Italian the *bisciola* tree) produces the visciola cherry which, while classified nowdays as sour, is slightly sweeter than a bitter black cherry such as a morello. The reader is asked to remember that Scappi's cherries always have a tart tang to them.

[26] This is Scappi's version of the late-medieval mixture known simply as 'common spices.'

27. To tell how good every sort of flour is.

Wheat flour, to be excellent, should be culled – that is, the grains of wheat should be picked out from among all other varieties of grain.[27.1] When it is ground a month before it is used, it will be better, especially if done in a mill driven by a good flow of water and when the millstones are not brand new.[27.2] Rice flour should be used as soon as it is ground.

Starch flour[27.3] is better white and less than six months in age rather than older.

To keep those flours: wheat flour should be stored in a cool, humid place; rice flour and starch in a dry place.

28. To identify any sort of wine, both red and white, that is used in various dishes.

Greek wine of Somma, Greek wine of Ischia,[28.1] and Chiarello[28.2] as well, and clear Romanesco – those are the best wines of all to make jelly, as well as to make up dough to be fried on lean days. Magnaguerra, Lagrima and the French wine,[28.3] are quite good for royal sauce[28.4] and other garnishes, as is said in the chapter on it in the book on seasonings; and likewise other dark wines. Must syrup[28.5] – that is, *sapa* – and verjuice[28.6] and vinegar are universally familiar

---

[27.1] In earlier times it was not unusual for grain fields to produce a mix of cereals, whether because various extraneous seeds were accidentally sown with the intended seed or because seeds from other fields or from previous crops germinated there naturally.

[27.2] New millstones were apt to chip, grinding up bits of themselves into the flour.

[27.3] From the fourteenth century on, directions exist in cookery manuals for making *amido*, wheat starch. In essence wheat flour was moistened with water into a paste which was then dried and reduced again to powder, although the procedure could be more complex.

[28.1] The wine that Scappi calls *vino greco* was produced in the region of Naples. It enjoyed a very good reputation and is called for in several of his recipes. The first variety is specified again in II,163.

[28.2] This wine, from Chiarella in Calabria, is described (probably about 1539) in a manuscript that was published by Giuseppe Ferraro, 'I vini d'Italia giudicati da papa Paolo III (Farnese) e dal suo bottigliere Sante Lancerio,' in *La Revista Europea*, 7 (1876), Part 2, 87–116. See Faccioli, *Arte della cucina*, I, 321. Lancerio wrote, in part, of chiarello: *Questo vino è molto buono et era stimato da S. S. e da tutti li prelati della corte*.

[28.3] The vagueness of this reference to a single wine from France may be noted.

[28.4] This *salsa reale* will be described in both Recipes II,267 and VI,102.

[28.5] As Scappi's phrase *mosto cotto* explains, this must, or unfermented grape juice, is boiled or 'cooked' until its sweet, flavourful properties are concentrated. The alternative name that appears here and by which Scappi will also refer to this reduced liquid is *sapa*, a juice that contains the essence of the substance from which it comes.

[28.6] *agresto*. Elizabeth David translates a passage from the *Herbario novo* (1585) of Castore Durante: 'Agresto is the juice of sour grapes, especially that obtained from the fruit of the vine

to people and are used in many different preparations, especially when those are carefully seasoned. The residue – that is, the dregs of a wine cask – is sometimes used in various dishes in place of verjuice. The above-mentioned wines for jelly will always be better from three to four months in age rather than old.

29. All sorts of quadrupeds, domestic and wild, that need to be skinned, or their hair removed, in water or with a flame.

Experience has shown me that most of the quadrupeds that are used can be skinned in hot water while still warm immediately after they have been slaughtered. It is true that domestic and wild hogs could be skinned in a flame, but an ox, calf, wether,[29] goat, stag, hare, fallow deer, large porcupine and bear have to be skinned; however, when those animals are small and suckling, they can have their hair removed in hot water, just as a calf's and goat kid's head and a wether's hooves are cleaned of hair.

30. The meat of some quadrupeds, domestic and game, that can be cooked easily as soon as they have been slaughtered.

All of the above-mentioned animals, young and suckling, just slaughtered, can be cooked easily in various dishes, as is described in the chapters devoted to them in the book on prepared dishes.[30]

31. To keep the above meats.

As soon as they have been slaughtered domestic animals such as an ox, cow and calf have to be bled and fully opened up, and hung in an airy place without skinning them until they are butchered. In that way the meat can be kept quite well and it stays whiter. Wether keeps better when it is skinned, and best when cut up into a number of pieces – although it does darken – and it will be tastier. Domestic pork once slaughtered is preserved with salt. Wild boar, cut open and thoroughly bled, when hung in an airy place, especially a place where it was struck down, can be dried off with a cloth, then sprinkled with salt and stored in an airy place without its being skinned; it can be kept quite well that way. The same can be done with stag, roe deer and any other game animal. If they are to be sent from place to place, though, they are filled with sprigs of rosemary and sage and

---

called *Agresto* ... ' (*Petits Propos Culinaires*, 7 [March 1981], 30). This tangy juice, more generally from early-forming but unripe grapes, has not quite been forgotten in modern cookery. See, for instance, Maggie Beer, *Cooking with Verjuice*, London (Grub Street), 2001. As FitzGibbon says (*Food of the Western World*, 502), its use has generally been supplanted in modern recipes by a 'squeeze of lemon juice.'

[29] The wether is a male sheep that has been castrated before reaching its sexual maturity. As wool-producing animals, sheep were generally held to be too valuable to be raised merely for eating. Furthermore, ewes could be kept as milk producers well into an advanced age. From the sheep family, lamb and wether are Scappi's mainstays.

[30] That is, in Book II.

they are handled in such a way that they do not get warm nor even get wet during the transport. If it is summer you should be careful to put them on the road at the coolest time of day; if the trip is long, as they are brought into the lodgings their inside is dried and rosemary is again put in there, and if not rosemary, then optionally myrtle, juniper[31.1] or nettle.[31.2] The same can be done for hare.

32. To tenderize the meat of the above animals in the shortest time.

An ox or cow, after being slaughtered, with its entrails still in until it has cooled and then is skinned, if put in a warmish place it will become tender. The same is done with all other large meats. And even if you work the animal hard, and then immediately afterwards you slaughter it, if you follow the above directions you will find the meat more tasty and more tender, but it will be darker.[32.1] Domestic pork, the more worked the pig is, then slaughtered and its hair removed immediately with hot water or else the skin taken off as is usually done, the more the meat will turn out to be tender and tasty. If it is a calf or goat kid, or certain young animals, there is no need to tenderize it.[32.2] However, a wether can be cooked, especially roasted, just after being slaughtered because it will always be tastier and juicier than when it has been dead for more than a day. It is true that for cooking in water – that is, by boiling – and for making pastries, the meat should be rather tender; but if it is young, that does not matter.

33. To make the above-mentioned meats cook in the least time.

Meat from old animals is cut into several pieces, and if the pieces are very small they will cook all the more quickly. Set them to cook in an earthenware or a tinned copper pot, tightly sealed, making them boil such that they cannot breathe for two hours,[33] more or less, depending on the size of the meat. Meats that are cooked in wine and with spices will cook quite a bit faster than in water; likewise meats that are cooked in the oven. But meats done on a spit or on a grill will cook much more quickly than in the above ways.

[31.1] 'Juniper goes particularly well with game,' Gillian Riley points out (*The Oxford Companion to Italian Food*, 265). This is the only instance in which Scappi will use this plant, whether leaves or berries.

[31.2] See a reason for the use of nettle in §39, below.

[32.1] Almost a century later an English traveller will describe this same practice in Rome: 'Before they kill their beaffs they put them in a great heat and chase, for the same reason, I suppose, that we hunt deer and bait bulls in England, viz, to make the flesh eat more tender and short, which yet spoils the colour of the meat, and, in some men's judgment, the taste too, disposing it to putrefaction' (Ray, *Travels*, vol. 1: January 1664, 310).

[32.2] By writing *frollare*, presumably Scappi means to tenderize the meat by either method: by hanging (in §31, the traditional, longer way) or by driving, distressing the living flesh (the present, quicker procedure). Regarding the second method, see III,168 on killing a turtle.

[33] Clearly Scappi's disciple would have a problem on his hands if no steam escaped from the pot for any length of time. The pot's seal is only relatively tight.

34. To make every spit-roasted cut from a quadruped stay tasty and juicy.

Roasts of young animals should be seared in the coals rather than plumped in water, so they remain tasty. To begin you have to give them a gentle flame until the heat has penetrated inside the meat. As you see that it is beginning to ooze, then you can give it a more sprightly flame so that the grease and juice heats up and boils within the pith[34.1] of the meat. It should be taken down from the spit slightly undercooked rather than thoroughly done, and that way it will be tasty and full of juice. The meats of old animals, however, need to be cooked slowly.[34.2]

35. How to keep the above-mentioned meats white when cooking them by boiling.

Do as I directed so the animals are fully bled, especially the big ones, and do it in that area that is called the slaughterhouse. Never remove its hide until you are about to boil it because when it is skinned, meat naturally browns and picks up various sorts of filth, especially when it sits on the butcher's table. You should understand that large meats, such as ox and cow, should steep in warm water for three hours and, after being rinsed in clear water, set on the fire in cold water and then boiled gently so that the scum is not broken up: that is done so the blood is purged all the more thoroughly. The same can be done with young animals, but I am of the opinion that a calf, a goat kid and a wether if they are put on the fire in boiling water turn out quite a bit whiter than if they had been in cold water, provided they are carefully skimmed. If you want all meats to stay white, as I said, they must be removed from their bouillon before they are overcooked, and immediately covered with spotlessly clean cloths or with plates, for otherwise they would darken. I shall not speak of game meats, if you wish to boil them, because most of them need to be cooked in the water they have been washed in so as to retain their flavour. Every sort of large domestic meat that can be boiled right after being skinned will stay more tasty than the meat that has steeped, but it will not be as white.

36. Viscera that need to be cooked immediately after an animal's slaughter.

All livers, sweetbreads, lungs, testicles, brains, as well as tripe, can be cooked. Though by nature tougher than the other viscera, tripe can be transported farther than the others. Dugs – that is, cows' udders – especially when full of milk, can be cooked immediately after the animal is killed. A roe deer's eggs can similarly be cooked immediately after the animal is killed; those eggs look like little acorns that are attached to the deer's womb, not more than eight in number and are naturally ring-shaped like a goat kid's kidney; they are removed at the time the

---

[34.1] The word here is *viscere*, plural of *viscera*.

[34.2] Physical theory held that the aging of any creature tended to dry it out. In preparing that meat a cook should avoid further dessicating it by, for instance, an intense cooking over an open flame.

deer is pregnant or begins to become pregnant. The liver of that animal does not have any gall. An unborn roebuck should be cooked just as soon as it is removed from the body, having first been skinned in hot water.

37. Every sort of fowl, domestic and game, that is eaten, which needs to be plucked dry or in water.

Experience has shown me that you can remove the feathers of any fowl in hot water immediately after it has been killed, but game birds are usually plucked dry. This latter is done so those birds retain their flavour, but the same can be done with domestic varieties.

38. Fowl that can be spit-roasted right after being killed and without being left to hang, then used in other preparations.

Every fowl that is partially fledged[38.1] – that is, young ones, not more than a month or two old – can be roasted on a spit and other dishes can be made of them without their being hung. But the fig-pecker, ortolan, turtle-dove, lark, quail, *favaro* dove,[38.2] woodcock, lapwing and teal duck, when they are fat and fresh and are to be roasted on a spit, do not need to be drawn. But if they are to go into other dishes, they should be drawn, though carefully. However, a dovecot dove[38.3] and the domestic sort, a turkey chick[38.4] and the ordinary sort of chick, young partridge and young pheasant need to be drawn before they are mounted on a spit.

39. To keep every sort of fowl, domestic and game.

Hens, capons, for their meat to stay white, are sawn up – that is, they are butchered – and left to sit two days in an airy place bound by their feet and separated from one another. If they are grain-fed and fat, though, right after being killed they are plucked, dry, and left as I said. If it is in summer they are drawn carefully, sprinkling their inside with a little ground salt, ground fennel and pepper

---

[38.1] *di meza piuma*: 'with half feathers,' still showing an immature down rather than being fully fledged.

[38.2] The 1570 printing has *piccione favaro*, the 1581 printing reads *piccione favoro*. An etymology of the former attribute, *favaro*, shows the word cognate with the modern *fabbro*, from the Latin *faber*, a farrier or blacksmith. This bird, among Scappi's list of small wildfowl, may be a species of woodpecker.

[38.3] Scappi writes *piccione de torre*, as if these were wild or semi-wild in contradistinction to the following.

[38.4] *il pollastro d'India*. Gillian Riley points out that guinea fowl had been known in European kitchens for many centuries, though the new-world fowl that received the English name 'turkey' was indeed raised in a few places in Europe in Scappi's day (*The Oxford Companion to Italian Food*, 242; but see as well p. 535). Scappi's compatriots would later call maize, also from the New World, *grano turco*. See also the note to Recipe II,141.

and filling them with nettle so flies cannot nest there. And if it happens that their craw is full of grains of hard wheat or some other food, you must handle the funnel very carefully and use warm water to wash that material out. Then set them in a cool, airy place so they do not touch one another. The same is done with turkey pullets and with any sort of peacock or large pheasant, and any other domestic and game fowl that you want to keep. You should know that in summer a hen and a capon can be kept that way for three days, and a pullet for two. Turkey pullets, which have whiter flesh, become tender more quickly than others and can be kept as long as a capon. A domestic peacock and a wild pheasant, which are to be kept without being plucked or drawn, can be stored in autumn for four days and in winter for eight; when they have been drawn and the bloodiness inside wiped out with a cloth, and the inside sprinkled with salt, pepper and fennel flowers,[39.1] they can be stuffed with nettle and sprigs of rosemary or sage, and they can be stored longer than the other way.

The same can be done with a crane and a wild duck, which, during their season, summer, can be kept for fifteen days. The same can be done with a domestic pheasant and with every other large fowl. But if it is a young partridge or young pheasant – after their bowels have been drawn out, without cutting them, through their natural hole by means of a feather's quill or a small knife – they too are stuffed with nettle, setting them as I said in a cool, airy place, each one apart from the other: that is done so they will not get warm. If anyone should want to send those fowl anywhere, mind above all that they do not press together. Large fowl, just after being killed and drawn, and their inside cleaned of blood with a linen cloth and sprinkled as I directed, can be sent at night or during the coolest hours, especially in summer, arranging them so they do not get wet. Other small birds such as ortolans, fig-peckers and quail can be kept quite well plucked; when quail are neither torn nor bloodied,[39.2] though, in that fresh state they can be sent with their feathers still on, along with other small birds, arranged in baskets in willow leaves or some other leaves, in such a way that they do not bunch together or get wet. Those small birds, especially in the summer, should not be kept for

---

[39.1] Two possibilities are plausible for these *fiori di finocchio*. They may be the seeds formed in the plant's flower head; taken either green or dried they would be ground into flour. They may also refer to the flower's yellow pollen, a saffron-like powder that could be gathered and used as a flavourant. The first is assumed throughout this translation. Our distinction in modern English between 'flower' and 'flour' is orthographic: Scappi and his age still speak of 'flower of flour' (*fior di farina*, a finely ground flour, as in Recipe V,1, for instance; and in V,237 *fior di coriandole*, 'flour of coriander [seeds]'). Scappi uses this sort of fennel flour/flower frequently, sometimes writing, in the singular, *fior di finocchio* ('fennel flour'), at other times using the plural, *fiori di finocchio* ('fennel flowers'). He makes use also of the plant's seeds (whole), panicles, shoots and fronds.

[39.2] That is, lacerated by the hunting birds or dogs. The *stracciate* in the 1570 printing becomes *stracoiate* in 1581.

more than two days; if you want to transport them for a longer time, you pluck them right after they are killed, being careful not to break their skin and, once they have cooled, you put them into millet flour, spaced apart. But if you do not wish to send them abroad but to make use of them on several occasions, instead of in flour they can be kept in vine leaves and willow leaves in an airy place, protecting them from damp air and from west or southwest winds. That can be done with thrush, blackbirds and turtle-doves, which do not have to be drawn. I shall not speak of the domestic dove, duckling, gosling and young cockerel because they have to be cooked right after being killed.

40. To tenderize every sort of fowl, domestic and game.

Experience has shown me that pheasants, partridge and every other fowl become tender more quickly if they have been taken with a bird of prey than if caught in a net or raised domestically, and much more quickly than those that were not drawn for a day. But if they are capons, hens, domestic doves, or turkey cocks, when they have been killed and are still warm, wash them in moderately hot water in the same way as if you were going to pluck them, rolling them around separately, fully feathered and undrawn, in a linen cloth soaked in the same water. Then let them sit under a bunch of hay or some straw, in summer for four hours and in winter for ten, more or less depending on their size and age. Bear in mind that once they've been washed they can also be kept in a warm place covered with some sort of mantle soaked in warm water, in summer for three hours, in winter for eight. In winter you can tenderize them in another way as well, though it takes a little longer: that is, after they have been washed, hang them by their feet in an airy place where the wind blows through; in summer hang them in a warm place. The same can be done with every sort of fowl, young or old, that you want to tenderize.

41. To keep all of the above fowl succulent and with a good colour when they are roasted on a spit.

I think that every sort of fowl has the same quality as any quadruped, and that is always to be succulent when they are mounted on the spit immediately after having been killed. That is because, to the extent they are hung, to that same degree their flesh loses its juice. It is true they will be a little tougher, but they will also be more tasty than those that have been tenderized.[41.1] The same fowl when young call for a more sprightly flame than older ones, and need to be cooked quickly[41.2] and taken off the spit slightly underdone. Coal embers cook roasts somewhat more quickly and give them a prettier colour than other sources of heat.

[41.1] That is, by hanging.

[41.2] Scappi's phrase *in fretta* normally translates 'in haste.' Here he may mean 'soon, without losing any time' (right away after the fowl has been killed and spitted) or 'rapidly' (quickly roasted, as may be suggested by the direction and comment that follow). See the next recipe.

42. To keep domestic fowl white that are cooked in water – that is, boiled.

All domestic fowl that are butchered rather than having their neck wrung will stay whiter when cooked, provided you put them into boiling water. To cook them in less time, when the pot has been skimmed put a lid on it so it cannot let off steam. All of those fowl will always be more tasty and succulent when cooked immediately after being killed, I mean the young ones because the old ones will be more tasty when they become tender rather than cooked right after being killed. All of the viscera and the combs of those fowl, if you want them to be good, have to be cooked when the chicken has just been killed.

[43.]

I shall now turn to an examination of every sort of implement, device and furnishing proper to a kitchen.[43.1] Firstly I shall speak of iron furnishings, beginning with how the andirons should be made that hold the firewood, and also how the iron rods should be made and many sorts of spit-holders which I shall deal with one after the other.

Andirons[43.2] should be large and square,[43.3] with their shaft of iron five hands long and a little more than a hand high, and they should be made in the shape of stars or a moon[43.4] or bow as we usually say, so that a shovel can pass through and withdraw a load of embers. Above all they should have a foot in the middle of their bar to better take the weight of the firewood, and should not weigh less than two hundred pounds a pair.

Big spit-holders should have a hand's width of wicker wrapped around the end so as to be able to lean them against the wall when they are being used. The

---

[43.1] The declaration of a change of subject at this point in his text is not accompanied by a change of number in the sequence that Scappi has so far followed in Book I. It is only later when, changing the style of his kitchen inventory and resorting to a plain listing of the items in it, that he resumes his numbering sequence. To impose a little more clarity in the organization of the material this translation shifts Scappi's §43 from the rubric 'Iron equipment proper for a kitchen' back to this point in his text.

[43.2] Scappi uses alternative words here: *capifochi*, over *cavedoni*.

[43.3] That is, forged square in section.

[43.4] The 1570 edition has *luna*; the reprinting of 1581 shows, interestingly, *tuna*. While not so named, the andiron shown in the upper right of Plate 15 has indeed the form of a crescent moon. The 'star' andiron merely has supports in the shape of a cross. The 'bow' model, in the middle of Plate 15, affords clearance for a shovel to pass under the transverse members between the semi-circular firewood cradles.

double ones[43.5] should have a fork at the bottom end; the lower ones[43.6] should be made in the form of andirons and of the same length but should be flat and lighter than the others, and should have a bearing socket on both sides and teeth like a fork. The iron bars that are to be used across the spit-holders to support cauldrons should be round,[43.7] heavy, nine hands long and divided into three areas, two hands apart, for chains with hooks to be able to attach cauldrons when they're being used. But you should realize that those bars are rarely used except where the fireplace is not [so] furnished, in the way that can be seen in the engraving of an outdoor kitchen.[43.8]

43. Iron equipment proper for a kitchen.
     Andirons of various sorts.
     Large and small spit-holders, with wicker.[43.9]
     Large and small hinged spit-holders – that is, the double sort.[43.10]
     Low spit-holders in the form of andirons, for gentle roasting.
     Round[43.11] bars to go across spit-holders.
     Chains, long and short.
     Braziers, draft-activated and other sorts, large and small, as used by pharmacists.[43.12]

[43.5] See in Plate 16 two sorts of 'single' spit-holders, one of which (*spedera con canna*, the *canna* being the wicker on the curved upper end) is designed to lean against the projecting cheek of a fireplace, and one 'double' one (Scappi's *spedera dopia*), which is free-standing and can carry spits across both the front and back of a fire. In the list of iron articles below, this latter variety will be called *spediere snodate*, 'articulated' (that is, hinged or pivotting) spit-holders, because their arms swing open like a large X.

[43.6] Pictured in the upper left of Plate 15. It is 'lower' in the literal sense that the spits supported on it are closer to the floor and a low fire or embers, and allow a gentle roasting as Scappi will say in § 43. Scappi's fork, whether for use in the kitchen or for dining, always has two tines.

[43.7] That is, the bars are to be round in section.

[43.8] See Plate 6, which shows a pair of the articulated spit-holders, the sturdy iron cauldron-bar across their top and a spitful of various meats roasting at their lowest, coolest level.

[43.9] The wicker, mentioned in the previous section, is wrapped around the upper end of the single-legged variety of spit-holder. The wicker winding is likely intended to reduce any slippage on the wall against which it leans.

[43.10] See the note in § 42.

[43.11] Round, that is, in section.

[43.12] One type of these *foconi a vento/* appears on the left of Plate 11 ('*fuochone*'); in it the low (adjustable?) vent would admit air to regulate the heat. A wooden box with sand in it illustrates another sort of *focone* at the top right of Plate 23. Plate 5 also shows a round fire platform whose label reads *fogone alto*: this might qualify as one of Scappi's *foconi a vento/*, given that the fire's draft, captured and concentrated in a large metal hood, drives a pair of spit-turning mechanisms.

Large tripods, made in a triangle or square.

Lower tripods, a hand and a half tall.

Round tripods for cauldrons.

Four-legged stands[43.13] with a circular opening as can be seen in the engraving of a kitchen in the country.

Round tripods to hold frying pans.

Tourte tripods of various sorts.[43.14]

Tripods, large and small, of various sorts.[43.15]

Spits, very large and square,[43.16] with holes in the middle for mounting goat kids, lambs, and other animals whole.

Spits, large and square, twelve hands long.

Spits made with a driving fan and the chain.[43.17]

Split spits fitted with screws.

Medium-sized spits.

Small spits for birds.

Small skewers, each two hands long.

An iron sampling dipper in the form of a baster, with a long shaft.

Hooks of various sorts for removing meat from a cauldron.[43.18]

Torch stands.

Fire shovels with a wooden handle.

Iron scrapers with a wooden handle for scraping the kitchen clean.[43.19]

A lever scale[43.20] with board beds and hooks, for weighing meats and other things.

Balance scales, like a spicer's, with weights, to weigh out spices.[43.21]

[43.13] *quattropiedi*, of the same general design and purpose as the previous tripods but presumably more stable and able to bear heavier loads. See Plate 6; note the spit supports on the legs.

[43.14] These *trepiedi da torte* are intended to hold lidded tourte pans.

[43.15] See the foot of Plate 16.

[43.16] That is, the bars are to be square in section.

[43.17] This mechanism is illustrated in Plate 5; to the left and across the bottom the engraver offers a more detailed representation of each part of the drive. Plate 19 further illustrates a spit driver with a clock escapement.

[43.18] See the *oncino* in Plate 23 and the *oncino dopio* in Plate 16.

[43.19] These consist of a flat blade at the end of a shaft and seem designed to lift sticky scraps from the floor. The one illustrated at the foot of Plate 14 is labelled *Armiola da raschiare*.

[43.20] On one arm of such a *stadera* a counterweight can be moved to a variety of predetermined positions. It provides a faster though somewhat cruder measurement than the following *bilancie*.

[43.21] See Plate 12.

Cheese graters, hinged, large and small.[43.22]

Tinned graters for sugar.[43.23]

Gridirons with wheels, hinged and otherwise.[43.24]

Cleavers, large and small, for cutting up meat.[43.25]

Large knives for beating.[43.26]

Pastry knives.[43.27]

Skinning knives.

Knives of various sorts with their sheath of boiled leather.[43.28]

Scrapers to scrape tables.[43.29]

Hooks to hang up and take down meat.

Rods, with a knob on the end, for preparing tripe.[43.30]

Iron larding needles[43.31] of various sorts.

Oil lamps of various sorts.[43.32]

Candlesticks, large and small, with a handle.[43.33]

Dough-cutting wheels, both iron and brass,[43.34] and other instruments for working with dough.

Large skillets for frying, with a handle.

Medium-sized frying pans.

[43.22] See Plate 10. The supporting arm is adjustable.

[43.23] A *gratta zucharo* is pictured at the foot of Plate 14.

[43.24] See the foot of Plate 15 for this wheeled grill; the wheelless variety is shown in Plate 23.

[43.25] All sorts of knives are illustrated in Plate 13. The *falcioni* that Scappi mentions here may be one of the *smenbratori* in the illustration.

[43.26] Scappi commonly uses the spine of a knife for the purpose of pounding a foodstuff, perhaps to break up its fibres. In Plate 13, *coltelli mastri da battere*.

[43.27] See Plate 14: *Cortel da pasticier*.

[43.28] An example of this latter item is drawn in Plate 13.

[43.29] See this sort of two-handled draw knife (*raschiatore da banco*) near the foot of Plate 14.

[43.30] See the instrument called *ferro per conciare tripe* in the middle left of Plate 13. The cylindrical knob or *boccolo* scrapes as the rod is withdrawn.

[43.31] Scappi follows this first term, *pillotti*, with a second, apparently more common one, 'that is, *lardorii*.' He will list wooden *lardori* toward the end of §44. See Plate 13 for several varieties of larding needle.

[43.32] Wall-mounted, Plate 1; or suspended, Plates 1 (*lucerna*) and 2.

[43.33] *Candelieri* of various sizes can be seen in Plates 2, 15, 23 and 27. The only candle holder with an apparent handle is the *bugia* to the right of Plate 23. This last is one of the more elegant furnishings of a cardinal's cell during a conclave.

[43.34] An example of this so-called spur or *sperone* can be seen in Plates 14 and 15.

Frying pans for making fritters.

Spoons, round, perforated, medium-sized, a hand and more in width, with a long handle.[43.35]

Spoons, round, perforated, medium-sized.[43.36]

Spoons, perforated, coming to a point for making frittered eggs and for lifting out tourtes.[43.37]

Serving spoons, medium-sized.

Broad spoons to lift out poached eggs.[43.38]

Smaller serving spoons.

44. Copper equipment, tinned on the inside.[44.1]

Large cauldrons of two hundred and four hundred pounds[44.2] each, with their cover.

Cauldrons of one hundred pounds, with their cover.

Cauldrons of fifty pounds and twenty-five pounds, with their cover.

Medium-sized cauldrons of various sorts.

Rimmed pots that fit inside one another, with their cover.[44.3]

Copper pots with two handles.

Two sets of small kettles[44.4] that fit inside one another, each one of which

---

[43.35] See Plate 16. More properly the spoons that Scappi lists in these items might variously be called spatulas, scoops, ladles, dippers and skimmers. It is interesting to note that the spoons illustrated in the engravings have a hook at the end of the handle for hanging from a wall-mounted rod.

[43.36] See Plate 16: *cuchiar forato, cuchiar forato piccolo.*

[43.37] See Plate 16: *cuchiar per ova afritelate.* This sort of 'spoon' appears to be a flat, heart-shaped, holed spatula.

[43.38] See Plate 16: this *cuchiar per ova sparse* is round and slightly dished.

[44.1] Copper is highly malleable and a good conductor of heat, but has three serious disadvantages for a cook: it readily oxidizes when it is heated, giving off flakes of black cupric oxide; exposed to moist air containing carbon dioxide its surface carbonizes with a green coating; and exposed to an acid foodstuff copper will dissolve or 'etch,' giving the food the undesirable copper flavour that Scappi warns his apprentice to avoid (see, for instance, Recipe III,119). Expense being no object in the pope's kitchen, Scappi insists on using tinned copper wherever feasible. Balducci Pegolotti (ed. Evans, 381) wrote that tin came from *Cornovaglia d'Inghilterra* in sheets and was recast into rods in Majorca and Venice.

Not all of this section is devoted to things made of copper.

[44.2] Understand, 'capacity.'

[44.3] Scappi writes *baracchine* in the feminine here; in Plate 9 we can see a *barachino* (masculine) illustrated.

[44.4] *due balle di caldarette* (in the feminine). A 'set' of kettles or cauldrons (in the masculine) is illustrated in Plate 9.

holds eight *caldarette*[44.5] and the largest no more than six pounds.[44.6]

Basins or round-bottomed, two-handled pans,[44.7] – that is, large and small *bastardelle*, for making whitedish.[44.8]

Cooking basins of various sorts.[44.9]

Colanders, large and small, of various sorts.[44.10]

Small colanders – that is copper strainers,[44.11] for straining broths.

Low pots, round and large, with their cover.[44.12]

Chafing dishes of various sorts, with their lid and base – that is, the tiles, both with holes and without.[44.13]

Dutch ovens, large and small, with their unholed base and lid.

Copper sieves, large and medium-sized, for fish.[44.14]

Pitchers, large and small.[44.15]

[44.5] The amount of a *caldaretta* is uncertain. Scappi uses the term only here.

[44.6] We are told in Recipes II,162 and VI,6 that in liquid measure that would be the capacity of one *boccale*, or two and two-thirds litres. The nesting *caldarette* would seem, therefore, to be quite small, having capacities ranging up to something like three litres.

[44.7] Scappi uses two unqualified terms here, *catini, over concoline*, the second being literally a small shell like that of a bivalve. See the *concha* (properly spelled *conca*) in Plate 9.

[44.8] See in the left foreground of Plate 2 the vessel in which an assistant is making *magnar bianco*. He is using a moderately shallow, wide-mouthed bowl.

[44.9] These *bastardelle* are the two-handled round-bottomed bowls of the previous line. They resemble the *concha* of Plate 9 and a modern paella pan, frying bowl or karhai; Scappi relies upon this vessel extensively in his kitchen. For the *bastardella* this translation will consistently use the phrase 'cooking basin.'

[44.10] One *foratoro*, a relatively large, holed pot, is pictured in Plate 9; another, with a handle, is in Plate 10.

[44.11] The word *stamigna* is used also for fabric strainers (and for the fabric itself, a cheesecloth). Here, though, Scappi is referring to the shallow, two-handled pan with holes in a concave bottom, shown (in two versions) in Plate 11: *stamegna di rame* (of copper, inverted) and *stamegna di ottone* (of bronze).

[44.12] Several of these semispherical two-handled copper *conserve*, with their matching lids, are illustrated in Plates 7 and 8. Scappi mentions them also as part of the equipment of a travelling kitchen toward the end of Book IV.

[44.13] Three sorts of these *navicella* can be seen in Plate 8. They may be oval in shape. According to Scappi the (holed or hole-less) plates forming the base are ceramic tiles which he calls *piastrelle*. See a holed *piastrella* at the foot of Plate 10. In Plate 6 (lower left) a *navicela* seems merely a round pan.

[44.14] A shallow *crivello*, with a flat, holed bottom, is in Plate 10.

[44.15] See a metal *cucumo* in Plate 10. The same is shown being warmed in Plate 12.

Tubs, large and medium-sized, for washing meats and herbs.[44.16]
Large, long-handled copper spoons.
Casserole pots, of various sorts, large and small, with an iron handle.[44.17]
Bulls-eye pans, for making large and small frittered eggs.[44.18]
Tourte pans of various sorts, with large and small lids.[44.19]
Skillets, large and medium-sized, for searing and cooking fish.
Lighter skillets for poaching eggs.
Copper sheets for making Milanese *gattafure*.[44.20]
Dippers for taking water from the water-jars.[44.21]
Dripping pans large and small.[44.22]
Bottles[44.23] of various sorts for carrying broths on a trip.
Pewter flasks for carrying vinegar, must syrup and verjuice.
Ring pans for making *struffoli*,[44.24] with their cover.
Pewter syringes for handling butter and other things.[44.25]
Bronze mortars, large and small, with their pestle, for grinding spices.
Filters with their drums,[44.26] for filtering spices.
Mortars of marble and other stone, with their pestle of hardwood.
Gauze filters for straining rice flour.
Horsehair filters for straining ordinary flour.

[44.16] A round-bellied, two-handled *conca* can be seen in both Plates 8 and 9.

[44.17] See two of these in Plate 10. Plate 17 shows a 'Spanish-style' *casola* specifically for making whitedish.

[44.18] Scappi's name for these pans is picturesque: *padelle ad occhi di bove*. See a more pedestrianly named *padella per fare ovi frittolate* in Plate 8.

[44.19] Scappi has used the phrase *padelle da torta* here, while normally throughout his recipes he refers to this pan as simply a *tortiera*. The engravings show a lidded pan of that sort (*tortera con il coperto*, Plate 8), three or four other pans (*tortere*, Plate 9, top) and two which are called 'tall tourte pans' (*padelle da torta alte*, Plate 9, second row).

[44.20] Plate 16 shows (lower left) a long-handled pan (called a shovel) for making this preparation. Scappi does not give a recipe for it, but the dish is described as being a variety of Genoese tourte.

[44.21] Plate 10 shows a *schiumarelo da vetina*, a ladle or dipper, while Plate 12 shows two sizes of *vettine*.

[44.22] See Plate 10 for both the *ghiottole* [sic] and *leccarde* listed here.

[44.23] These capped or stoppered *bottiglie* are of copper and have a carrying handle. One is illustrated at the top of Plate 10.

[44.24] These *boccule* do not seem to be illustrated. For *struffoli* see Recipe V,135.

[44.25] See Plate 13.

[44.26] Plates 14 and 16 (*settacio*) show how the filter cloth is held between two or more 'drums.'

Leather sieves of various sorts.

Pouches for holding and carrying spices.[44.27]

Leather bags made like pouches for carrying flour.[44.28]

Wooden boxes with several compartments for keeping spices.

Straining cone[44.29] for straining jelly.

Straining cloths, coarse and fine.

Serviettes for serving up.

Coarse cloths for keeping prepared dishes covered.

Canvas, each piece two arms in length.

Fabric two rods long for covering meats.

Travelling coffers, with their locks and keys.

Partitioned crates, with locks and keys.

Wicker hampers for carrying kitchen equipment, with locks and keys.[44.30]

Wooden tubs[44.31] of various sorts.

Sets of bellows for stirring up the fire.[44.32]

A mechanical press.[44.33]

Wooden vessels with other devices for making milk-snow.[44.34]

Wooden dough-cutters for making *tortelini*.[44.35]

Shovels of various sorts, of white softwood, with a long handle, for making whitedish.

Rolling pins for spreading dough.

[44.27] The handy arrangement of a number of those bags, with their mouths tied together, is shown in Plate 11.

[44.28] Plate 11: *sachi di corame per farina*. For Scappi the 'pouches' or purses are bags closed with a drawstring around the opening. See the same *borse* made of cloth toward the end of this list.

[44.29] The *calzetta* (in modern Italian a 'hose' or 'sock') is of fine fabric, held open and mouth upward on a standing metal frame and used for filtering liquids. It is illustrated in Plates 2 and 18. An instance of this filter stocking in use can be seen in Recipe II,81.

[44.30] See Plate 17.

[44.31] *schifi di legname*: Scappi may have in mind the *mastello con pesse* and *mastello con piati* of Plate 3, or the *mastelli* of Plate 26.

[44.32] See Plates 16 and 23.

[44.33] Scappi's phrase is *torchio per sussidio*. A *torchio* with pressure screws is shown in Plate 23, a *susidio* in Plate 12.

[44.34] See a reference to this preparation in §2, above. The operation of making *neve di latte*, 'milk-snow,' is shown in Plate 4.

[44.35] Two of these *bussoli*, a small one and a large one, both with a serrated inner surface, are shown in Plate 12 and qualified as being 'for pastry dough.' Recipes for Scappi's various *tortelletti* are at II,177–80.

Copper bottles, large and small, for oil.[44.36]
Tables for dishing out.
Tables for pastry dough.
Large workbenches for cutting up meat.
Small tables for beating.
Hinged tables to take travelling.
Wooden larding needles and skewers.
Needles of various sorts.
Small cloth bags like pouches to hold raisins and almonds.
Oven peels of various sorts.[44.37]
Oven rakes.[44.38]
Oven mops.[44.39]

[45.][45.1] I shall not go on to mention various stamps and moulds that Master Cooks and pastry chefs normally use, of brass, lead and white metal, such as small tubes for pouring jelly, and implements for engraving pastry, with various other wax and wood moulds, because all that will depend on whether the cook cares and can be bothered. It seems to me, though, that it would all be incomplete and open to criticism if I did not review the furnishings and facilities appropriate for a conscientious and competent Master Cook, along with his assistants and scullions; likewise, were I not to deal with what procedure is proper should it happen that more than one Master were in the kitchen, as is the case at great courts where it is usual for cooks to alternate weekly. I say, therefore, that when there are several Masters both have to be equal and have the same authority of that Office. If the one whose turn it is to serve that week does not need the help of his fellow Master, he will enjoy all of the prerogatives and perquisites; but if his companion is helping him, they will both share those prerogatives and perquisites in a brotherly way, recognizing, though, his assistants and scullions according to their station. Should there be a formal contract[45.2] with the Master of the Household[45.3] and the Master

---

[44.36] Plate 10.

[44.37] Plate 11: *pala per infornar*.

[44.38] Plate 11: *raschiator di forno*.

[44.39] Plate 11 shows a rag mop on a shaft. It is labelled exactly as the term appears here: *spazzator dal forno*.

[45.1] In Scappi's text the outline of the conditions of a cook's employment is not particularized by means of a separate number. For greater precision in referring to this final segment of Book I, the translation has assigned a number to it.

[45.2] Scappi's word is *conventione*, an agreement or covenant governing the terms of employment.

[45.3] *il Sig. Mastro di casa*, strangely misprinted in 1581 as *Mastro di causa*.

Steward, then to comply with it they will have to observe the prerogatives and perquisites of the household. As for salary, I shall not speak of it, referring you to the contracts of both parties. With regard to living arrangements, though, I say that the cook shall have his chamber with the pallet furnished, candles and brooms, and firewood in winter just as gentlemen receive. With regard to his food, three pounds of bread per day and four litres[45.4] of wine of at least the same quality as is set on the gentlemen's board. I say nothing of the food allowance because that will depend on the contract; however, at noble courts (excepting those of the Pope, the Emperor and the King, which are free[45.5]) it is usual to give every Master, per day, two and a half pounds of veal or wether mutton,[45.6] and a capon or hen, taken as the dish is being proved in the kitchen;[45.7] on lean days he will receive eight eggs and during Lent two and a half pounds of fish, apart from the assortment of foods taken when dishes are proved. As well as that, for each of his assistants, half of the things listed above. Moreover, he will be allowed his expenses for any mount that must be used for any trip the Master Cook undertakes in the service of his Lord. The assistants, scullions and pastry workers, apart from their furnished room and pallet, should get for their allowance three pounds of bread per day and five and a third litres of ordinary table wine[45.8] and a pound and a half of meat; on lean days, six eggs with the *hors-d'oeuvres*, and during Lent a pound and a half of fish. This arrangement is allowed so they will serve the Lord more faithfully and will endure greater toil submissively. Moreover, the Master Cook should have full authority – without, however, prejudicing the authority of the Master of the Household or of the Chief Steward – to engage and dismiss assistants, pastry workers and scullions, and any other person who is under his orders. Should it become necessary for him – who is deemed of use and service to a Lord – to go travelling, he should be able with authority and propriety

---

45.4 The quantity of the wine allowance is given as six *fogliete*, each *foglietta* being roughly two-thirds of a litre.

45.5 *le quali son libere* – that is, not legally bound by custom or customary law.

45.6 Both options here are esteemed meats.

45.7 The act of assaying or testing a food for its salubrity was often carried out twice, before leaving the kitchen and right at the lord's board. In the kitchen the cook sampled a dish in the steward's presence; occasionally in the hall the steward sampled the same dish in the lord's presence. In both places this tasting was termed, as Scappi writes here, 'la credenza' – a proving of the trustworthiness of the food. In the hall the assay table or sideboard on which the dish was set also became known in time as 'la credenza.' By 1560 Domenico Romoli was able to write that such provings had become *ceremonie* (*La singolar dottrina*, Book 1, Chapter 1, ed. Faccioli, *Arte della cucina*, II, 348).

45.8 *due boccali*, each *boccale* measuring about two and two-thirds litres. The disparity here, the Master Cook receiving four litres of wine and each of the minor kitchen workers five and a third, may be explained by the different quality of the wine allowed each.

to select skilled and reliable men and, while still appropriate for the Office, the lightest and most functional equipment, not overlooking mounts for his assistants, scullions and pastry workers, who have to go on ahead with the first kitchen; and mounts likewise for those who have to remain behind with the second one,[45.9] and he has to arrange that the scullions who will follow on foot will not lack shoes and other things normally given to them, nor the porters who accompany such kitchens, loading and unloading the packs, not forgetting wind-proof torches and their windvane,[45.10] when the kitchen sets out on a journey.

There remain the perquisites to speak about, those that are accorded Master Cooks and that it has always been the custom to accord them. It should therefore be known that by right they receive all the ashes produced in the kitchen, with the obligation, though, of keeping all the coarse cloths, fine cloths and other fabrics clean that are needed in the kitchen; likewise, all the hides of quadrupeds that are consigned to the kitchen and that are skinned, or ordered skinned, by those Masters; likewise, all the feathers of fowls that they pluck or order plucked; likewise, all the feet, necks and heads of quadrupeds that are consigned to the kitchen and skinned, along with all the offal of animals and fish; likewise, all the viscera and gizzards of every fowl, and all the grease that drips from roasts along with whatever is in excess on large cuts of meat; likewise, they receive all the oils and fried grease, with pork rinds and rank bacon.[45.11] And at least once a year, the Masters, along with their assistants and scullions, receive clothing.[45.12]

[45.9] Scappi refers to these different establishments as *la prima cocina* and *la seconda*. It might not be accurate to understand 'primary' and 'secondary' kitchens. As an expedition progressed day by day, the 'first kitchen' would be in advance of the lord, perhaps a rudimentary set-up, adequate only to feed those retainers whose job it was to make an encampment or provisional lodging habitable by the lord and his noble escort. That kitchen, installed in a predetermined locale in advance of the lord's arrival, would likely be obliged also to have a suitable meal prepared for the lord at the end of his day's travel. The 'second kitchen,' with the equipment and personnel that remained always at the immediate service of the lord until he left the current encampment, would follow very closely in his train. See Plates 6 (a camp 'kitchen'), 17, 18 and 25 (equipment for a travelling kitchen).

[45.10] *guida*: late-evening and pre-dawn travel was likely common. The mention of shoes reminds us that the lesser members of a kitchen's personnel usually worked barefoot.

[45.11] Many of Scappi's recipes warn the cook against using preserved pork or sausages that have become rancid. Even the fatty cuts of fish have to be handled circumspectly: see, for instance, the preserved sturgeon belly in § 14, above.

[45.12] These *vestiti* were formal livery that identified a servant as a member of a lord's household. Such a set of dress clothing, stipulated in a contract and furnished by the master of a house, was not worn as an everyday working garment by those in a kitchen.

Book II
Various Meat-Day Dishes, of Both Quadrupeds and Fowl[i]

1. Various ways to prepare an ox's head.

Although it may seem that an ox's head is not much eaten, nor to be counted among the finest foods, nevertheless you can still do it in various ways, and I do think that the head is quite tasty in the ox's season, which begins in the fall and lasts to the end of February. It is true that old oxen become fat in the spring with tender new grass, and in the summer they get fat on oilcakes made of walnut, flax and other things.[1.1] The season for cattle runs from the end of May throughout September, and so too for calves that have been weaned. However, in those seasons you can get the head of those animals immediately after the animal has been slaughtered. When it has been skinned, butchered and washed clean in several changes of water, it can be boiled with prosciutto or *salsiccione*[1.2] that have not turned rancid. When it is cooked, it is served hot with garlic sauce or mustard over it. But should you wish to make several sorts of fricassee with the best parts of the head – that is, the tip of the snout, the brains, the eyes and the jowls[1.3] – that is up to you. When the heads are from mature animals they are much better. And the above-mentioned parts are better after they have been boiled and then fried. They can be dressed with a pepper sauce or with a civet.[1.4]

2. To cook an ox's or cow's tongue in various ways.

The tongue of those animals will always be better when the animal is recently slaughtered and the tongue has been in salt for eight hours, and after washing it in

---

[i] Elsewhere when Scappi refers to this book he calls it the *Libro delle Vivande*, the Book on Prepared Dishes. The rubric here ends with ... *cominciando dal Bove*, beginning with that of an ox.

[1.1] *con il panello di noce, et di linosa et d'altre cose.* Zingarelli glosses *panello* as 'residuo solido di semi oleosi, usato in pani per l'alimentazione del bestiame.' Cattle were fed the caked residue of solids from the bottom of nut and seed presses after the oil was drained off.

[1.2] This latter sort of large sausage is variously spelled *salciccione* and *salcizzone* by Scappi (or by his typesetter). Prosciutto is frequently added to a cooking pot: in Recipe 23 the reason for this ingredient is, at least partly, the salt that it brings to the broth.

[1.3] *et delli polsi.* The sense is conjectural. As a part of an ox's head, the term *polsi* may be related to *borsa* and *borso*, a purse, and describe the pouches of flesh in the animal's mouth.

[1.4] Scappi provides directions for making each of the four sauces that he has referred to here: garlic, mustard, pepper and civet. He has placed them toward the end of this Book II in Recipes 257, 276, 251 and 249 respectively.

clear water and boiling it. Then, when cooked, it is dressed with one of the sauces with which the best parts of the head are dressed in the previous recipe. They can also be done in all the ways listed for a calf's tongue in Recipe 29.[2.1] You should note, though, that boiling them without their having been in salt will make a more useful broth for making sops and thick soups[2.2] than if they had been in salt. But above all they want to be cleaned of that skin – that is, hide – that is on it at its leanest part.

3. To boil every cut – that is, part – of beef, beginning with the breast.

Because the breast is the toughest part of all, it should also be cooked more that any other, and should steep[3] less than any other because by its nature it is light and spongy and always floats. Immediately after being washed, however, the meat should be put on the fire in hot water. To keep it low in the water, tie a cord onto it and to the cord a clean stone or a large ball of glass to hold it under the water. The other cuts should steep longer, especially those that are bloodier. They should be washed in several changes of warm and cold water, and set on the fire in cold water, and should be boiled slowly because as the water heats up, the meat will cleanse itself of its blood. Mind especially that the scum is not broken up, because that scum is heavier than the scum of any other meat; once broken up it sinks into the water and attaches itself to the meat. You must therefore take great care in skimming the pot.

4. To semi-salt[4.1] and boil any side of beef.

I find that the ribs and breast of an ox or cow are more suitable than any other part. Once dead and skinned, without being washed, the sides are cut up into several pieces and put into salt in an earthenware or wooden vessel, which salt must be very clean[4.2] because if the salt were not clean the meat would get

---

[2.1] The reprinting of 1581 shows *al capitolo 90.*

[2.2] The words *minestra* and, rarely, *pottagio* apply to a liquid dish of a thick consistency prepared in a pot and served generally as it comes from the pot. 'Thick soup' will be used throughout as a very rough translation of *minestra.* In a few instances the reader should be prepared to understand 'thin stew.'

[3] *stare in molle.* Scappi's steeping is a means to soften or tenderize a foodstuff. In Recipe 38 cold water is the medium; in Recipe 114, warm water. Compare this steeping with *posto in adobbo,* Recipe 35.

[4.1] On this process, see also I,§9. The term *misaltare* – to semi-salt or half-salt, to brine or to corn (as in 'corned beef') – is used for the soaking of a foodstuff, particularly a meat, in brine but not thoroughly drying it out afterward.

[4.2] In Italy most salt, and the cheapest, was produced by evaporating seawater. Such salt was commonly discoloured with mud; the likelihood was also high of finding sand, bits of vegetation, shell, fish scales and other impurities in one's salt. A cleaner sort was evaporated from salt springs where groundwater had passed through a bed of salt. Those salt beds could also be mined

dirt into it and would take on a bad smell. When the pieces of meat are laid down on top of one another, cover the vessel with a wooden lid[4.3] and on it put a weight that will keep it under pressure until it has made a pickling brine. In summer after the meat has sat there for four days, and in winter for eight, it is removed from the vessel to be cooked as it is, rinsing it in fresh water and cooking it in unsalted water. Make sure above all that it is well skimmed. When cooked, it can be served hot or cold at any time with garlic sauce or mustard in dishes. And should it happen that you want some of it that same day the animal is killed, take a piece of the loin or some other cut and boil it with a lot of salt until it is well cooked. Then serve it in the same way as is said above.

5. To cook the tip of the breast[5.1] – that is, the brisket – of beef in several ways.

I find that the tip of the breast of either an ox or a cow, when they are big and fat, has a brisket – that is, a firm fat – in that tip the same as a wild boar has,[5.2] that is yellowish. When the tip of the breast is thoroughly boiled in salted water, it is taken out of the broth and let cool. With a fine knife you can cut that brisket, which is at the top of the front, into strips the thickness of a knife blade, sprinkling them with wheat flour or gilding them with beaten egg yolk, and frying them in rendered fat.[5.3] When done, they are served hot with orange juice, sugar and cinnamon on top. It can also be done up in all the ways that a cow's udder is prepared in Recipe 6 of the Book on Pastry.

6. To spit-roast a rack of beef ribs.

Although is it not usual to put such a meat on a spit, I nevertheless find that it can be roasted, and especially when it is of a mature age. You take the rack, then, and cut it up into pieces which are no bigger than four pounds. Put each of those into a press[6.1] for four hours with ground salt, fennel or coriander, crushed pepper

---

to extract the mineral directly. The specification of 'ground' salt (*sal trito*, as in Recipe 6) is advisable because salt, like sugar, usually arrived on the market in blocks from which it had to be broken off and granulated more or less finely as needed.

[4.3] It may be that this *coperto* will fit inside the container in order to transmit pressure directly to the meat and salt.

[5.1] This *punta del petto* is the cut lying beneath the throat and between a steer's forelegs, the lower front of its body being like the prow of a ship. It is to this 'pointed' ridge that Scappi refers, explaining himself (and repeating the explanation in Recipe 35) using the term *callo*, brisket.

[5.2] When dealing with wild boar (Recipe 91, below) Scappi will use the presence of a brisket as an indication of its maturity.

[5.3] For the process of making this common cooking medium, rendered pork fat, see I,§4 and Recipe 111, below.

[6.1] *in soppressa*. The mechanism for applying pressure to a foodstuff is identified in Plate 12 as a *susidio*, though the word refers to the product of that press, and in Plate 23, a *torchio*. Here,

and a little beaten garlic. Then mount them on the spit without blanching[6.2] or larding them. It is up to you if you wish to put some sprigs of rosemary among the pieces, or into the drippings some sliced onion which will cook with the grease that drips. When cooked, the pieces of meat are served hot with the onion pieces on top, mixed with a sauce made of vinegar, must syrup[6.3] and common spices.[6.4]

7. To make Venetian bresaola[7.1] of grilled beef ribs.

Get a rack of ribs of a fat ox or cow, of mature age, slicing it apart rib by rib. With the flat of a large knife press each of them, spreading them out a little, and beat them with the spine of that knife on one side and the other: that is done so that the meat will be softer and more tender.[7.2] Then they are splashed with rose vinegar,[7.3] and sprinkled with pepper, cinnamon, salt, fennel flour[7.4] or

---

in the next and a few other recipes the terms *in soppressa* and *sopressare* (Recipe 4) imply only a moderate pressure in order to blend a seasoning into a foodstuff – and not a pressure such as would, for instance, express the juice from that foodstuff as for a *susidio*. See Riley, *The Oxford Companion to Italian Food*, 504.

[6.2] *senza essere rifatti.* Scappi uses the verb *rifare* in a very old, culinary sense of plumping a meat, particularly a meat such as beef that is perceived as being of a dry temperament. When used, that plumping is normally a preliminary step, equivalent to parboiling. Blanching and searing are similar procedures.

[6.3] This *mosto cotto* is must – plain grape juice – that has been reduced by one-half or two-thirds.

[6.4] From the Middle Ages on, culinary spices were generally and most handily classified in two groups: those in common, more-or-less daily use and those whose use was exceptional. For Scappi the common spices seem to have included cinnamon, cloves, ginger and nutmeg: see I, §26. For that mixture the designation *spetierie communi* in recipes is useful shorthand.

[7.1] The end of Recipe II,38 confirms that the distinctive feature of *brisavoli* done in the Venetian style is that they are made of single ribs on which the flesh is beaten. Scappi describes several sorts of *brisavoli* (or *brisauoli*, a *v* always being typeset as a *u*) in Books II and III; see other varieties in Recipes 14, 45, 66, 84 and 99 below, III,16, 17, 39, 86 and 151, and VI,46. See Riley's article on Bresaola in her *Oxford Companion to Italian Food*, 74. Scappi's word, masculine in gender, is likely related to *braciuola* (or *braciola, bragiola*), feminine in gender, meaning today a grilled cutlet (Battisti and Alessio, *Dizionario etimologico italiano*).

[7.2] *piu frolla, & piu tenera.* The verb *frollare* (seen in I, §32 and Recipe II,70) can refer to either the beating or the hanging of a meat in order to tenderize it.

[7.3] This *aceto rosato* is vinegar that has been flavoured with rosewater. Seen also as a flavourant for a garnish in the *Singolar dottrina* of Domenico Romoli, *alias* il Panuto (Book V, Chapter 47), it is in remarkably frequent use in Scappi's kitchen.

[7.4] This *fior di finocchio* is in extensive use in Scappi's kitchen. The fennel bulb was harvested at the time when the seeds in the flower head had fully formed; it was kept on hand in dried form (II,66). See Recipe II,229 where the recipe prefers fresh fennel but, if need be, the cook can fall back on his supply of dried. Fennel commonly appears with other spices, as here, and is likely intended to be used ground up – as flour rather than flower – with them.

coriander.[7.5] Pile them up on one another under pressure[7.6] for six hours, more or less, depending on the time you have. Cook them slowly on a grill, turning them over occasionally, with a slice of pork fat on each so they do not dry out. When they are done, they need to be served with a garnish of vinegar, sugar, cinnamon, cloves and nutmeg on top. You can do the same with a rack of ribs from a wether, a weaned calf and a suckling or free-ranging calf.[7.7]

8. To spit-roast or stew[8.1] loin of beef.

You should make sure above all that the animals are fat, and if they are merely mature they will be a lot better than if they are old. After they have been dead for two days, more or less depending on the season, and the meat has become somewhat tender, take that inner loin which is below the kidney, attached to the ribs, and runs between the tip of the shoulder and the haunch[8.2]: it is quite a bit more tender than the one that is above, which is called a rib loin.[8.3] When it is cut away from the ribs and the purplish membranes around it are removed, to make it stay soft and tender beat it over its full length with a bat, and splash it with malmsey or Greek wine and rose vinegar. Sprinkle it with ground salt, pepper, cinnamon, ginger, nutmeg and cloves ground with coriander or fennel flour, letting it sit in a press with that mixture for three hours more or less, depending on its size. Then get wide and moderately long slabs of pork fat and carefully place them around the tenderloin[8.4] with sprigs of rosemary, binding it all with a cord. Cook it with a very temperate fire, catching the liquid that drips from it. As it is finishing roasting, take it off the spit and serve it hot, dressed with a garnish of the drippings from the pan, vinegar, wine and sugar. But if you want to stew it in a

---

[7.5] *fior di finocchio* over *pitartamo*: presumably this is also the seeds of the plant ground into powder or 'flour'. See also the *fior di coriandole* in Recipe V,237.

[7.6] *facendo stare l'una sopra l'altra ben soppressate.* See the first note in the previous recipe, as well as the verb *sopressare* in Recipe 4, above, where a weight applies the pressure.

[7.7] In Recipe 23 this last, a *vitella camporeccia*, is located *alla foresta*, in uncultivated areas. See also Recipe 139.

[8.1] The verb *stufare* refers to a cooking that takes place in a closed pot or (occasionally) between two dishes: to stew or braise. Often the cooking medium is mainly the liquid already present in the foodstuff. The process is similar to cooking-under-a-bell; it is implied in Recipe 11, below, and explicitly directed in Recipe 43.

[8.2] The *osso mastro* or main bone. Scappi is probably referring to the cut now called tenderloin or fillet.

[8.3] *lombo schienale.* See Recipe II,40 for a more detailed definition of each of these loins. In that recipe this second loin is called simply *lo schienale*.

[8.4] *lombolo*: in British terminology, a fillet of beef. Scappi also uses a diminutive form of the word, *lomboletto*, which expresses the 'tender' nature of the cut.

pot,[8.5] take it down from the spit a little undercooked, remove the rosemary and the fat bacon from around it and put it into a pot or an earthenware stewpot[8.6] with the liquid that fell into the dripping pan,[8.7] mixing malmsey in with that, or Greek wine and must syrup, or else sugar and a little rose vinegar, along with the same spices as are listed above. Stop up the vessel and finish cooking it, occasionally turning it around. When it is done, serve it hot with its sauce over it. You can also put raisins into the stewpot.

9. Another way to roast the above loin.

When the meat has been stripped from the bone and the membranes around it cut away, take the leanest part, boneless, and put it into a press for three hours with the same mixture of spices that is used in the other case, along with fennel flour. Lard it[9] over its full length with rather big lardoons of bacon fat which have been dredged in the above spices; the lardoons will be all over both sides of the loin. On the outer side lard it with very fine lardoons so that it is well covered with those lardoons. Cook it slowly, catching the juice that will drip from it. When it is done, serve it hot with that juice mixed with a little must syrup and vinegar, a crushed clove of garlic and orange juice.

10. Another way to roast or stew loin of beef.

Get the loin with some of its fat, splash it with Greek wine and rose vinegar, and sprinkle it with the above spices and salt. Then set it to cook with a few sprigs of sage around it, stirring the liquid that drips from it. When it is almost done, take it down from the spit, removing the sage, and put it into an earthenware vessel with a spoonful of broth, a quarter of a litre[10] of vinegar, half a litre of must syrup, prunes, muscatel raisins and the grease that has dripped from it, along with onions that have first been cooked under the coals; finish off cooking it with that mixture of ingredients. When everything is done, serve it hot with its broth over the top. Into that sauce you can put a quarter litre of malmsey and some rosewater.

[8.5] The vessel mentioned here is a *pignata* or *pignatta*, the ubiquitous pot, cooking pot, stewpot or braising pot. See Plates 6, 9 and 10. Scappi occasionally qualifies the material of which this vessel is made as *di terra*, 'earthenware.'

[8.6] The alternative vessel is a *stufatoro*, specifically designed for such stewing and made of either earthenware or copper: a copper one is mentioned in Recipes II,94 and III,2. Two models of *stufatoro* are illustrated in Plates 8 (top left) and 9 (lower middle). Each has squat legs to sit close to glowing coals or embers; one has a lid on which coals or embers can also be placed to provide heat from above as well as below.

[8.7] See such a pan called a *ghiottela* in Plate 10.

[9] A useful instrument in Scappi's kitchen is the larding needle. See several of them in Plate 13.

[10] *mezo bicchiero*. The capacity of one *bicchiero*, a beaker, is roughly half a litre.

11. To stew a loin of beef in an oven or to braise it.[11.1]

Get a loin of beef as good as was said before, along with some of the fat and a little of the backbone. After it is cleaned of its membrane, splash it with wine and white vinegar, and sprinkle it with pepper, cloves, ground salt, cinnamon, ginger and with coriander or else fennel flour. Let it sit under pressure in an earthenware vessel for four hours with a little Greek wine or malmsey, must syrup and rose vinegar. Then put it into an oven in the same vessel with that same mixture, adding in a little beaten pork fat and thin slices of prosciutto. When it is half cooked, having turned it over a few times, you add prunes and dried visciola cherries[11.2] into it if it is winter; in summer, though, you can put in the fresh fruit. When it is cooked, it is served hot with the same things and the broth over it.

In the same way you do it braised.

[11.1] *sottestare* and, at the end, *sottestato*. A *testo* was a common cooking apparatus from the time of Cato down to the fourteenth century; it is used repeatedly in the Tuscan *Libro della cocina* and the Venetian *Libro per cuoco*. See in Jacques André, *Apicius, l'Art culinaire* (Paris: Les Belles Lettres, 1974), 164, the note to recipe 131. The *testo* survives, in name at least, to Scappi's day and later, representing a procedure equivalent to braising. See, for instance, Recipes II,43 where the cook can place a preparation *sotto il testo*, 'under a bell' and II,47, *con un testo sopra*, '[cooked] with a bell over [it].' Generally of earthenware, circular, squat and with a relatively flat or concave upper surface, it covered a preparation while the food cooked. Either preheated or covered with live embers, the bell afforded the benefit of an oven's relatively even heat along with the stewing effect of cooking in a closed pot. The verb that Scappi consistently uses, *sottestare* (*sotto-testo-are*), refers generally (but not exclusively) to this under-a-bell cooking procedure; occasionally another vessel, such as a lidded tourte pan, is used with hot coals set on top. The Paris *Tacuinum sanitatis* (produced c. 1380–90, f. 55v; see the edition by Cogliati Arano, black-and-white plate 215) illustrates bread being cooked *sub testo*: a large kettle sits on embers in a fireplace; its flat, recessed lid contains hot coals. Except where Scappi expressly names his *testo*, the present translation refers to the procedure simply as braising; the verb *stufare* (as in the rubric to the next recipe), to stew, is used virtually synonymously. Occasionally a constant and less intense heat can be applied to the bell or to the lidded vessel that acts in the same way, as in Recipe II,43: *si possano sottestare nel forno*, 'they can be braised in the oven'; see also I, §27: *per sottestare* [in a *vaso di terra*] *in forno*; and II,225: *facciasi sottestare al forno ò sotto il testo*. See Barbara Santich, 'Testo, Tegamo, Tiella, Tian: The Mediterranean Camp Oven,' *Oxford Symposium on Food & Cookery 1988: The Cooking Pot* (London: Prospect Books, 1989), 139–42. In the study of the theory and practice of the fifteenth-century physician Giacomo Albini that is presented in 'I medici e l'alimentazione nel tardo Medioevo in area pedemontana,' *Cahiers de Civilisation Alpine*, 8 (1989): 31–45, Anna Maria Nada Patrone interprets the doctor's instruction to cook *inter cineres*, 'cioè probabilmente appoggiata su un *testum* di pietra ollare ó di terracotta posato sulla brace' (38–9).

[11.2] Like the oranges of Scappi's day, cherries had not yet been bred to produce the sweeter varieties we know today. The *visciola*, the cherry that Scappi usually cooks with and is the least bitter in his larder, still has a good noticeable tang to it. See Recipes II,115, 249 and 252 where a distinctly sour cherry, the *marasca* (morello), is combined with the *visciola*.

12. To stew an ox[12.1] loin in the German fashion.

Make sure the loin is from a fat animal, and get a part of the backbone and the fat with it. When it is clean of the membrane and gristle, wash it in wine, vinegar and water, and put it into an earthenware pot with pepper, cinnamon, cloves, nutmeg and ginger, along with bits of prosciutto or pork jowl that is not rancid, filtering the liquid with which you washed it. Add in a little must syrup and put all of that mixture into the pot where the loin is. When the loin has steeped for four hours in the mixture, stop up the pot with a lid, sealing it with dough, and boil it gently for two hours. As it is almost done, add in ordinary raisins and muscatel raisins; finish off cooking it. When it is done it needs to be served hot with the above mixture over it. With that meat you can also cook whole onions that have first been roasted in the coals or parboiled in water.

In the same way you can do up the tip of an ox breast,[12.2] and its ribs and shank, after they have been cut up into several pieces. In winter you can cook partridge, pheasant and other game birds together with the loin.

13. To make fingers[13.1] of beef tenderloin in the Roman style.

Get the leanest part of the tenderloin, with the bones, skin and gristle removed, and cut it crosswise in six-ounce pieces, sprinkling them with ground salt and fennel flour or coriander ground with common spices. Into each piece, set four lardoons of marbled salt pork. Place them in a press[13.3] with that mixture and a little rose vinegar and must syrup for three hours. Then mount them on a spit with a rasher of bacon and a sage or bay leaf between each piece; cook them over a moderate fire. When they are done, they need to be served hot, dressed with a sauce of their drippings together with the compound that exuded from them in the press, which sauce should be somewhat thick and saffron-coloured.

In that same way you can do the loin of free-ranging or suckling calves and of any other quadruped.

[12.1] Previous recipes have been for both ox and cow – i.e., 'beef' – but here Scappi deals specifically with *bove*, the male animal.

[12.2] A cut that elsewhere Scappi also calls the brisket.

[13.1] In Recipe III,38 these *polpettoni* are described as being chunks of whole flesh a handswidth in length and a finger in width (and presumably also in depth). In that recipe the raw fish sticks are beaten a little; here the meat is pressed. These so-called fingers are to be distinguished from the croquettes of the next recipe, even though the two preparations appear occasionally as alternatives. See Francesco Barilli, 'Polpette e polpettone, una storia tutta italiana,' *Appunti di Gastronomia*, 40 (2003), 94–105.

[13.3] This *soppressa* likely does not distort the relative dimensions of the fingers or overly flatten them but merely helps the meat absorb the seasoning applied to it.

14. To make stuffed bresaola[14.1] and croquettes[14.2] from a loin of beef.

Get the leanest part of the loin and cut it up into slices a hand in length, four fingers wide and a knife's spine thick.[14.3] Beat them on both sides with the spine of a knife, splash them with a little vinegar and sprinkle them with fennel flour, ground salt, pepper and cinnamon, piling them up on top of one another for two hours so that they absorb that mixture better. Cook them on a grill with a slice of fat salted bacon on each one: that is done to keep them from drying out. When they have been turned two or three times and you see them colouring, they are served soft like that with orange juice over them, or else with a sauce made of vinegar, sugar, cinnamon and cloves. If you do not want to cook those *brisavoli* on the grill, fry them in rendered fat or lard.[14.4]

Should you wish to make stuffed croquettes, as mentioned, with a knife pound some[14.5] of the loin with the same amount of pork fat and prosciutto, adding in two cloves of garlic, egg yolks, a little cheese, pepper, cinnamon, beaten parsley, mint and wild thyme. With that mixture stuff the *brisavoli*,[14.6] rolling them up like wafer cornets[14.7] and putting them on a spit with a thin slice of pork fat and sage leaves between each one. When they are almost done and taking on a little colour, put them into a pot with a little broth, must syrup, verjuice and raisins, and finish cooking them with the pot stopped up. When they are cooked, they need to be served with their sauce over them. You can also serve them without stewing them, letting them finish cooking on the spit; but they can also stew in a pot or[14.8] braise in the oven, and cook in all the ways that the above tenderloin is done.

15. Various ways to cook lean beef.

The lean meat of a shank of beef can be cooked – that is, braised under cover – and also roasted, and made into croquettes and fingers in all those ways that a

---

[14.1] In Scappi *brisavoli* or *brisauoli*. The name of this preparation in its several occurences may well have had the latter pronunciation. See the note in Recipe 7, above.

[14.2] *polpette*. In a note to Recipe 13 see the reference to the article by Barilli.

[14.3] These dimensions will be for the *brisavoli*.

[14.4] The making of these alternatives is described in I,§4 and §6 respectively. The first is merely a melted fresh fat called *strutto*; the second, called *lardo colato*, is a true lard, clarified and filtered, but made from salted pork fat. They will appear as alternatives in many meat-day dishes.

[14.5] In Recipe III,15 the measurements of a croquette are a handswidth long, three fingers wide and one finger deep.

[14.6] The term seems to be used here, referring to the croquettes, in the sense of small slab of meat.

[14.7] *cialdoni* are somewhat large wafers (*cialde*), normally rolled with some sort of filling within. See Recipe VI,141, for example.

[14.8] Scappi's *et* ('and') is often used between alternatives where we might expect an *o* ('or'). He is merely offering a list of possibilities.

loin is done. If you wish to boil it, follow the directions set out for the breast of beef.[15] It does always need to be thoroughly tenderized, except for beef that is put in brine.

16. Various ways to cook beef feet.

The feet need to be cooked just as soon as the animal is killed, contrary to the meat, which needs to be tenderized. They take a much greater cooking than any other part of the animal. Therefore, after being skinned and cleaned of their nails, they are split into several pieces to better set them out in the pot. You can put prosciutto to cook with them. When the pot has been skimmed well, add in a little vinegar and a little white wine along with common spices and a little saffron – the amount of each at your discretion; close the pot with its lid, sealing it with dough. Boil them slowly on the coals away from the flame for five hours more or less, depending on the age of the animal. When they are cooked they can be served hot with the prosciutto. Of the broth you can make Lombard-style sops.[16] For their sauce you can use garlic sauce or mustard or green sauce, depending on the season. When the feet are to be boiled, they can be done in various ways, just as those of a calf are done.

17. Several ways to cook a cow's udder.

An udder, or dug, needs to be full of milk, and if it is after the cow's first calving it is much better. It needs to be cooked just as soon as the cow is killed because otherwise the milk would go bad; and it will be better in May than at any other time, although in winter more than in summer it is kept raw as well as cooked. If you wish to put the udder to roast on a spit, it is first more than half cooked in water along with prosciutto that is not rancid, then taken out of the broth. When it has cooled, it is stuck with lardoons of pork fat, long and thick, that have been dredged in a mixture of pepper, cloves, cinnamon, ground salt, nutmeg and fennel flour; the lardoons must pass from one side to the other. Mount it on the spit and finish cooking it with a moderate fire, basting it occasionally with rendered fat or lard. When it is almost done, sprinkle it with grated bread, sugar and fennel flour, and with the same spices as are used for the lardoons. When it is cooked it is served hot with orange juice and slices of lime over it.

If you wish to wrap the udder in a caul, when it is boiled in the way that was described, and cooled, you have to sprinkle it with the ingredients mentioned above and then carefully wrap it in a pig's or calf's caul softened in warm water, and set it to cook on the spit. When it is done, it should be served hot with some garnishes over it.

---

[15] The references seem to be to Recipes 8, 9 and 10 for roasting, to Recipes 13 and 14 for croquettes and fingers, and to Recipe 3 for boiling.

[16] For this genre of sop see Recipes 22 and 225, below.

If you want to stew it in a pot, after it has boiled for half an hour in salted water, with the teats tied so the milk cannot escape, remove it from the broth and put it into an earthenware pot or else a copper stewpot in enough broth, mixed with a little vinegar and white wine, to cover it. Add in prosciutto and diced pork fat, sugar and a few whole onions that have first been parboiled, along with pepper, cinnamon, ginger, cloves and nutmeg. Finish off cooking it with the pot sealed, in the same way as the feet are cooked in the previous recipe. When it is done it is served hot. With the broth you can make sops. It can also be cooked under a bell in the oven after it has been well boiled, the way the loin of beef is braised in Recipe 11.

18. To sauté and make various fricassees of a cow's udder.

After the udder has been well boiled in salted water, or else in water with salt pork, let it cool out of the broth. If you want to fry it in rendered fat or in lard, you cut it up into slices the thickness of a knife blade, clearing away the membrane it has around it and flouring them with wheat flour, or else gilding them with beaten egg yolks, sugar, rosewater, cinnamon, saffron and grated bread. However it is fried, it has to be served hot with orange juice and sugar over it, or else with some other sauce. Without being floured or gilded the slices can also be fried with a few thin slices of pork fat and beaten onions; then serve it hot with pepper and cinnamon over top. But if you want it in a fricassee with beaten eggs, you fry it plain, afterward pouring off some of the grease and adding a spoonful of broth tinged with saffron; then add in pepper, cinnamon, sugar, clear verjuice,[18] and beaten egg yolks. The amount of each ingredient depends on the judgement of the cook. When it comes to a boil such that it begins to thicken, it is served with sugar and cinnamon over it.

19. Various ways to cook beef liver.

Although beef liver is not usually eaten or among the more select dishes, neverthless in my opinion it can be prepared in all the ways that a wether's liver can be done. You must, however, get it immediately after the animal has been slaughtered, with the gall bladder removed as well as the membrane that is around the liver. Take the best part of it and cut it up into slices that are as thick or as thin as you like. They need to be fried in oil or rendered fat or lard. When done, they are to be served hot. The slices can also be fried with slices of beaten spring onions.

---

[18] Verjuice, made by mashing verjuice grapes (or any other sour variety of grape or unripe grapes), is frequently used as an ingredient in early cookery with the solids of the grapes still present. In Scappi's dishes we find that *agresto intero* (or *intiero*) as well as the pressed, filtered juice he calls *agresto chiaro* as in this present dish. See both, *agresto chiaro o intero*, toward the end of Recipe 43, below.

If you wanted to spit-roast that liver, though, you could get the best part, as I said, making one-pound pieces of it, sprinkling them with coriander and pepper or else with fennel flour, and wrapping them in the caul of the same animal, which caul must be softened in warm water. When they are done up, mount them on the spit and cook them over a moderate fire. When done, they need to be served hot with some garnishes over them.

20. To make a fricassee of a cow's lungs, blood, kidney and liver.

When the lungs are boiled and well cooked in salted water, they are beaten thoroughly with a knife, or else they are cut up into chunks the size of dice; the same is done with the raw liver and kidney. Fry everything together in rendered fat or lard with beaten spring onions. When they are done, serve them hot the way the liver in the previous recipe is served. If you wanted to fry prosciutto with them, or saveloy sausages,[20.1] they would be better. After being fried they could be done in the manner of a thick soup,[20.2] adding in broth along with beaten fine herbs and thickening it with eggs and verjuice.

In the same way you can also do up the blood after it has been boiled, except for a bull's blood.

21. Several ways to cook beef spleen.

The spleen must above all be fresh, not more than a day old. You carefully make a hole in its middle or on one side so that you can fill it with a mixture of beaten pork fat,[21] garlic, parsley, mint, sweet marjoram, grated cheese, egg yolks and common spices. When it is full you cook it in such a way that the mixture will not come out. You can do it on a spit or in an oven just as the loin is done in Recipe 8; you can also boil it. Then let it cool, cut it into slices and fry those in a pan with rendered fat the way the fricassee of liver is done. When it is cooked, in whichever manner, it is served hot with various garnishes on top.

When it is well cooked and boiled, you can also redo it in slices on the grill.

22. Various ways to cook beef tripe.

The tripe of big animals, even if they are old, will be excellent, but they[22.1] need especially to be cleaned thoroughly in hot water and have any filth cleared out, either by leaving them sitting for ten hours in flowing water, or else in pots, changing the water until their bad smell is gone. You boil them in unsalted water

---

[20.1] *cervellati.* A recipe for making these is given in II,46.

[20.2] This *minestra* is Scappi's thin stew or pottage, for many varieties of which recipes appear throughout his work.

[21] The *lardo* in Scappi was likely salted or from salted pork backs.

[22.1] Scappi always writes tripe in the plural, *trippe.* The English translation may sometimes retain that plural.

until there is no longer any scum, then take them out and rinse them in cold water: that is done so the fat will not drain away. Cut them up into a number of pieces, large and small, whatever you think best, and put them into another vessel with a bit of prosciutto or saveloy and sufficient water, and finish cooking them so they stay white and not too salty and the broth is fat. If they are big pieces it is customary in some places, particularly in Bologna and Ferrara where they are called *cialdumi*,[22.2] to set them out on platters the way Lombard sops are set out – that is, one piece on top of the other with, between each, grated Parmesan cheese[22.3] and slices of provatura[22.4] mixed with common spices – with those tripe you will serve salt pork or saveloy sausages[22.5] – sprinkling fat, saffron-tinged broth on them and setting them to stew in a hot place between two dishes,[22.6] until the cheese and the provatura are absorbed into the tripe. You serve them hot however you like.

But if you want tripe done into thick soups, though, after they have been well cooked and cut up into small bits, that [pottage] can be thickened with beaten eggs and cheese mixed with the above spices, beaten mint, sweet marjoram and parsley. It is served hot with grated cheese and cinnamon on top.

For you to identify the best tripe to take for making those other dishes, to my way of thinking it is the biggest part and the rest of the large intestine; the other intestines are smaller and tougher and more suitable for making sausages than anything else. But when the tripe is from young animals – that is, young steers – all of it can be used.

[22.2] Much earlier the *Menagier de Paris* provided a definition of this term: 'The *chaudun*,' the bourgeois author wrote, 'are the bowels which are called the bowels' mesentery [the caul of Recipe 46, below], and are also the small intestines with which black pudding [*boudin*, blood sausage] and sausages are made; the stomach is part of it' (*Le Menagier de Paris*, ed. Georgine E. Brereton and Janet M. Ferrier [Oxford: Clarendon Press, 1981], 193, line 31). A contemporary of Scappi, Lancelot de Casteau in distant Liège, describes the composition of a variety of large sausage (our 'bologna') that he identifies as Bolognese: *Pour faire saulsisse de Bologne*, the casing, he writes (46), is *des boyaux de boeuf selon la grosseur que voulés avoir les saulcisses*, 'beef intestines of the size you want your sausages to be.' See Scappi's Recipe 103, below, for Bolognese *mortadelle*.

[22.3] Scappi has a predilection for Parmesan cheese, specifying its use more often than of any other variety. In his *Summa lacticiniorum* Pantaleone da Confienza sings the praises of a Piacenza cheese (*casci Placentini*) which, he writes, is very similar to Parmesan cheese and is so called by many people. (Book 2, Chapter 2; ed. Naso, 114–15.)

[22.4] This Roman cheese is made from buffalo milk. The reader is reminded, here and in Recipe 113, for instance, that Scappi's *bufalo* and *bufala* are European animals and not the North American plains animal, bison.

[22.5] The apropos of this detail is not clear. It is set off merely in commas, like so very much of Scappi's whole text.

[22.6] This is a fairly common method of cooking.

23. To boil a calf's head in water and salt.

If you wish the head to stay white, as soon as the calf is slaughtered remove the head from the body and remove its hair in hot water. Bear in mind that if it is from a russet-coloured calf and if the calf was not killed with a mallet, it will always stay whiter. When the head is cleaned of all filth, remove its tongue and put a bit of wood through its nostrils to clean everything out of them. Wrap it up in a piece of white linen so that it cannot come apart, and put it on the fire in a tinned copper or earthenware pot with cold, unsalted water: that is done so the head will clean itself out thoroughly. As it begins to boil, skim it carefully, minding you do not break the scum.[23.1] When that is done, put in enough white salt, or else a piece of prosciutto that is not rancid: that should be enough to salt the broth. To know when the head is cooked, put a foot from the same calf into the pot to cook along with it, because when the foot is almost cooked the head will be done. Then take it out of the broth, undo the cloth and serve it right away with borrage flowers and parsley on top, because if it slips out of the cloth and is not kept covered it will go brownish and will not be as tasty or as pretty.

It will be better to get the head during the calf's season, which runs from April to the end of July, though in Rome suckling calves are always good because they are fed on milk on dairy farms, and in uncultivated areas[23.2] free-ranging calves are suckled by their mothers. When the head is cooked, it can be served with various sauces on it. You can also cook it without a cloth, but it will not turn out as white, and the skin will crack.

24. Several ways to cook the deboned head of a suckling calf.

With the hair removed and the head cleaned as was described above, take out the tongue carefully. Wrap the head in several layers of linen and crush it adroitly with a wooden pestle, being careful not to break the skin. When that is done such that the bones are all broken, take them all out through the neck, turning the head inside out. When the teeth, the brain and the bones have been removed, wash the head in several changes of water, then turn it right side out again – that is, as before with the skin and ears, very clean, outward. Sew up the snout with string. Then make up a mixture of the brain of another calf, kidney-fat and prosciutto, all of that beaten with knives and mixed with grated Parmesan cheese, eggs, pepper, cinnamon and saffron – the amount of each at your discretion and for you to decide. Stuff the head with that. Sew up the hole so the mixture will not come out, and put the head into cold, unsalted water in a large vessel and let it boil gently until the head takes on its proper shape and the stuffing has firmed up. When you

---

[23.1] See Recipe 3, above.

[23.2] *alla foresta.* Land was generally cleared in order to till it for crops. Pasture land normally lay beyond (Latin *foris,* outside) this cultivated area and was deemed the suitable locale for grazing animals. See also Recipe 139, below.

have skimmed the broth, take the head out and put it into cold water. To keep it white, wrap it in a cloth and cook it with a piece of prosciutto as is described above. Serve it the same as above.

If you want it boneless another way, when it is smooth and clean begin to skin it at the lowest part, working adroitly and carefully so that you do not cut the skin, and leaving the ears attached to the skin. Wash the skin and sew up the lowest part and the mouth, and stuff the head with the above mixture and cook it as above. If you want it stewed, though, follow the directions given in the recipe for that.[24]

25. To spit-roast the head of a suckling calf, with or without its skin.

With the hair removed and the head clean, take out the tongue and in place of the tongue put a piece of prosciutto or saveloy sausage; tie up the snout. Boil the head a while in water, then take it out and let it cool in water: that is done so the meat will stay tender in roasting and will not become tough. Then wrap it in the calf's caul or that of a pig, having sprinkled it first with common spices, fennel flowers[25] and salt. Mount it on a spit and roast it over a low fire. When done, serve it up dressed with pitted olives and orange juice.

If you want it skinless, though, when all the dirt has been cleaned off it you can optionally replace the tongue with prosciutto but not blanch the head. Put it on a spit and let it cook over a low fire, basting it with rendered fat or lard into which a clove of garlic has been crushed. When it is cooked, serve it hot on platters, dressed with mustard or some other sauce. If the head is boneless, though, half-cook it first in broth with prosciutto, letting it cool out of the broth. And if you wish to wrap it in a caul or wrap it with strips of pork fat, that is optional; it is still cooked and served as above.

26. To boil or stew a stuffed suckling calf's head.

With the hair removed and the head cleaned in the above way, it is cut up, opening the lower part and leaving the upper part whole. The tongue is taken out as well as the brain. Clean the head very thoroughly in several changes of water, and particularly the passages of the nostrils. Then stuff the void of the brain with a mixture of beaten pork fat and the animal's brain, parboiled and cut up into bits, grated cheese, eggs, sugar, pepper, cinnamon and saffron, along with parsley, sweet marjoram and dried currants. Carefully sew up the neck opening, the snout and the hole at the nape, and boil the head in salted water. To keep it white and prevent the stuffing from leaking out, wrap it in a cloth like the one in Recipe 24.

Should you want to stew it, after it is stuffed put it, without the cloth, into an earthenware or tinned copper pot, with slices of prosciutto that is not rancid, or

---

[24] Recipe 26, below.

[25] *fiori di finocchio*, in the plural: the seed heads of the plant.

else with yellow saveloy sausage,[26] and enough water or broth from some other meat that is not too salty, to that broth adding whole cinnamon, ginger, pepper, cloves and clear verjuice. Stop up the pot so it cannot breathe and set it to cook on the coals away from the flame.

When it is done it is served hot with slices of prosciutto or saveloy sausage around it and with various garnishes in dishes. With that broth you can make Lombard sops and other thick soups. If you want to stew it another way, follow the directions set out above for stewing a loin or a cow's udder.

27. To braise a suckling calf's head [in a pot] in an oven.

With its hair off and the head clean, cleave it through the middle and put it into an earthenware pot in enough broth from another meat – or else in enough water mixed with must syrup and clear vinegar – to cover the head more than half way. With that put in beaten pork fat, diced prosciutto, parboiled onions or garlic, prunes and muscatel raisins, pepper, cinnamon, cloves, nutmeg and saffron – the amount of each at your discretion. Put that into an oven that is not too hot and let it cook, turning it over from time to time. If the head still has its skin on, the pot will need to be covered because the heat of the oven will dry the skin out; but if it has been skinned, you will not need a lid. When it is done, serve it hot with its broth over it.

In that same way you can do up a whole, stuffed head. In autumn instead of prunes you can use visciola cherries with pieces of quince and *carovello* pears;[27.1] in summer, plums and unripe pears, and gooseberries or verjuice grapes.[27.2]

28. To grill the gilded head of a suckling calf.

When cleaned and boiled whole with a bit of prosciutto or else a large sausage that is not rancid, remove the head from the pot and let it cool. Split it in half, separating the halves, leaving the brain. Clean the membrane off the tongue – which is itself split in two. Then coat the head with a mixture of beaten eggs, grated bread, old cheese, pepper, cinnamon, saffron, beaten parsley, mint and

---

[26] Yellow is occasionally a qualification of saveloy, but it is worth noting that in Recipe II,46 for (ordinary) saveloy the list of ingredients includes saffron and egg yolks, and that the caul to encase them is steeped in saffron-tinged water. Milan was recognized as a source of such saveloy: in Recipe II,153 a yellow saveloy is expressly qualified as being Milanese, *cervellate gialle Milanesi.*

[27.1] The Italian name of this pear, as well as a variety of apple, is thought to derive from the French *calville* from the placename Calleville in Normandy. The pear may be similar to the Williams, in North America the Bartlett.

[27.2] By *agresto*, Scappi undoubtedly means the variety of sharp-flavoured, early-maturing grape itself, rather than the juice that is made from it and that is so widely used in early cookery. For the fruit he will normally specify *agresto intiero*, a mash of 'whole verjuice grapes,' but here the fruit is an alternative to *uva spina* or 'prickly grapes,' gooseberries.

sweet marjoram. Put the halves of the head into a skillet in rather hot rendered fat with the half-brain downwards; under the brain first put a little of that mixture so it does not fall out of the head. Use a spoon to baste everything with the mixture. Fry the head so that it browns on one side and the other. When it is done serve it hot dressed with orange juice, slices of lime, sugar and cinnamon.

If you want to coat[28.1] it differently, after it is cooked and cut in two, remove the brain and combine it with the stuffing for yellow saveloy sausage,[28.2] sugar and raisins; then replace it. Then get eggs beaten with sugar, cinnamon, saffron and a little white wine and, with some of that mixture, make a large omelet. When it is done, put a half-head on it – that is, with the brain downwards – sprinkling it with sugar and cinnamon, then adroitly turning up the omelet so that it covers the whole half-head. With a little more rendered fat you can heat it up in the pan on both sides until the stuffing[28.3] is cooked. It is taken out, hot and browned, and served as is described above, with a little rosewater.

When you do not have frying pans that are large enough, you can use tourte pans.[28.4]

If you want it done on a grill, you do not gild it or fry it; it is enough to sprinkle it with grated bread, flour, ground salt, fennel flour, sugar and cinnamon, and then put it on the grill. When each half-head is turned, put a large slice of pork fat on it, or else baste it with a little rendered fat. Make sure the grill is a fine one so the brain does not fall into the coals. When it is done serve it up hot with some garnishes on top. If the heads are very small, they will be quite a bit better for this dish with the skin left on rather than skinned.

29. To spit-roast the tongue of a suckling calf.

Get the tongue along with the sweetbread[29.1] around it and with the windpipe removed; wash it in several changes of water and parboil it. After parboiling, take it and remove the skin around it, and stick it all over with lardoons that have cloves in them. Put it on a spit and roast it over a low fire. When it is done, serve it

---

[28.1] Scappi uses the verb *indorare*, literally 'to gild,' the effect of the egg mixture being uppermost in his mind.

[28.2] For that *compositione* see Recipe 46, below. The saffron and egg yolks in that recipe remind us that saveloy was generally yellow in colour.

[28.3] That is, the calf's brains mixed with sausage, sugar and raisins as above.

[28.4] One of the more common baking dishes in Scappi's kitchen, the *tortiera* is a flat-bottomed, relatively shallow pan, with slightly flared sides and usually with two ring handles. It has a flat lid on which, for baking tourtes and similar preparations, coals can be set in order to apply heat from above as well as below in the manner of an oven. See half a dozen different models of tourte pan in Plates 8 and 9.

[29.1] This particular one of the two *animelle* that Scappi uses is the thymus gland.

hot with slices of lime on top, or else cover it with onion sauce[29.2] or some other sauce.

30. To spit-roast the stuffed tongue of a suckling calf and do it up in several ways.

When the tongue is cleaned of the slime that is around it, make a hole through its upper part near the windpipe, which hole will go along inside the tongue right up to its tip. Then stuff it with a mixture of ground lean meat, pork fat, grated cheese, eggs, garlic, parsley and common spices. When that is done, close the hole with string. More than half-cook it in broth. Then take it out and remove the skin that is around it. Then get a pork caul that has been softened in warm water and wrap the tongue in it. When that is done up in a tight roll and tied with string, put it on the spit and roast it over a moderate fire. When it is cooked, serve it hot with slices of lime over it.

If you want to braise it, though, or to do it in the oven, after it has been stuffed and parboiled and cleaned as directed above put it into an earthenware baking dish[30] with rendered fat or lard, frying it with some spring onions. Add in some broth with prunes and dried visciola cherries, and finish off cooking it. When it is done, serve it hot with its broth over it. In summer you can put verjuice grapes on it and other fruits with a smaller amount of spices than in winter.

You can do likewise with the tongue of a free-ranging or weaned calf. You can also spit-roast those tongues, whether stuffed or not, parboiled or not. And parboil only the leanest part so as to be able to skin it.

31. To grill, gild and make a fricassee of a suckling calf's tongue.

When the tongue has been boiled and cleaned of its skin, if it is small leave it whole; but if it is big, split it in two lengthwise. Sprinkle it with fennel flour, grated bread and ground salt, and put it on a grill with a slice of pork fat wrapped over each part. When it has browned a very little, serve it hot, dressed with orange juice and sugar.

If you wish to sauté it, cut it in slices crosswise after it has cooled, and sauté them with spring onions in rendered fat or in lard. Serve them hot, dressed with those spring onions, pepper and orange juice.

If you wish to glaze it with beaten egg, when it is split lengthwise as was said,[31] coat it with beaten egg, beaten herbs and grated bread, and fry it in rendered fat in such a way that the mixture covers both sides. Serve it hot with orange juice, sugar and cinnamon over it.

[29.2] Scappi's recipe for *civiero* is at Recipe II,249. The Latin for 'onion,' *cæpa*, is at the origin of the Italian generic dish name *civiero* and the French *civet*.

[30] *Ma se si vorrà sottestare … si ponerà in un tegame di terra*: this *tegame*, with its flat or slightly concave lid, can serve the same function as Scappi's *testo*. See the note in Recipe 11, above, and Santich, *Testo, Tegamo, Tiella, Tian*.

[31] This treatment seems to be optional with only the first version of the recipe.

32. To cook the same tongue in various fricassees.

When the tongue has boiled and been cleaned as above, take the best part, which is from the middle back, along with the sweetbread that is around it, cut it crosswise into slices. Sauté those slices in rendered fat; when they are done, pour off most of the fat. Get egg yolks beaten with verjuice, cold meat broth, sugar, cinnamon and saffron, and put all that into the frying pan with the tongue, cooking it slowly away from any smoke, constantly stirring the pan until the preparation has become like a thick, homogenous broth. Serve it hot with sugar and cinnamon over top.

Should you wish to have that tongue differently, when it is sautéed put it into an earthenware or copper pot in enough broth to cover it, along with pepper, cinnamon, saffron, gooseberries or verjuice grapes and finely chopped fine herbs. Bring everything to a boil. Thicken the broth with grated bread or ground almonds or beaten eggs. Serve it hot with cinnamon on top.

33. To boil breast of veal.

Get the breast just as soon as the animal has been skinned, so it will stay more white. Wash it only once and set it to cook in an earthenware or copper pot in sufficient boiling salted water; to keep it down in the water, because by nature a breast will float, follow the directions in Recipe 3 for the cow's breast. When it is cooked but not disintegrating, remove it immediately from the broth because as that meat is cooked with that broth it will absorb it and will lose its flavour and become greenish-grey.[33.1] But when you serve it as I said, it will always be tastier and whiter. With that meat you can serve various garnishes in dishes,[33.2] and parsley.

You can boil all cuts of veal in all those ways, being careful to skim the pot well, particularly when doing the throat. You cook the belly that way, having first stuffed it, however, with cheese, beaten eggs, pepper, cinnamon, saffron and fine herbs. Mind, though, that the belly is beneath the water because it floats easily. If you want to make various dishes from the belly, when it is cooked take it out of the broth, let it cool and cut it into slices with a slender knife, which slices can be fried in rendered fat with or without beaten spring onions. Serve that hot, garnished with orange juice and pepper, or else cover it with some sort of dressing, whether cooked or uncooked. You can also put those slices on the grill, browning them on both sides, and serving them hot with sugar and orange juice over them.

[33.1] This is a peculiar hue, *berettino*, which Scappi evokes several times in his recipes.

[33.2] These are dipping sauces, set out separately. See the same serving in Recipes 4 and 26.

34. To stew or braise the breast of a suckling calf.[34.1]

Get the tip of the breast,[34.2] which is the best cut, and stuff it with the mixture used for the belly in the previous recipe. Put it into an earthenware or copper stewpot which has beaten pork fat and slices of prosciutto in it; also put in pepper, cloves, cinnamon, nutmeg, saffron and verjuice along with enough meat broth that is not too salty, or else water, to cover the breast. Stop up the pot and seal it with dough all around so that it cannot breathe, and set it to cook. When it has been cooking an hour and a half, take the lid off and serve it hot with its broth over top. To cook with this you can put prunes and dried visciola cherries, or parboiled onions or various other things.

In the same way you can do the throat and every other cut – that is, the other parts of the calf.

35. To sauté and make fricassees of a breast of suckling veal.

When the breast has been boiled, whether stuffed or empty, take it out of the broth and steep it for two hours in a mixture of vinegar, must syrup or sugar, cloves of garlic crushed with sweet fennel, salt, pepper, cloves and cinnamon. Then take it out of that mixture and let it drain. Flour it, either whole or cut up into pieces, with wheat flour and fry it gently over the coals in rendered fat or lard, turning it in the pan so that it is thoroughly fried and browned on both sides. Serve it hot, dressed with a sauce made from the same seasoning.

You can also sauté it immediately as it comes out of the broth and is floured, without putting it in any seasoning,[35] serving it hot with any cooked sauce or orange juice or slices of lime – whatever you like best.

Wanting it done in various sorts of fricassee, after it is boiled you can make all of those fricassees that are made with a calf's tongue in Recipe 32. Should you want the tip of the breast – that is, the brisket – in a fricassee, when it has been boiled cut it into thin slices, flour it or gild it with beaten egg yolks, and fry it in rendered fat in the same way that the cuts of tongue are done in Recipe 31.

[34.1] Two verbs appear in this rubric: *Per stufare, & sottestare* ...   Only one procedure is detailed: the verbs are synonymous. The use of a covered pot is the prime requirement.

[34.2] The brisket: see the next recipe.

[35] For Scappi the word *adobbo* that he writes here has the sense of a flavour-enhancing liquid in which a foodstuff may be steeped, specifically in the present case the sweet-and-sour mixture of garlic and spices seen in the first treatment in this recipe. It seems that *adobbo* was originally a lexical borrowing from Catalonia or, less likely, from France. In the early-fourteenth-century Catalan *Libre de sent soví*, a manuscript of which was found in Naples, the verb *adobar* is used in Recipes 1, 41, 152 and 210. The eleventh-century French word *adob* and *adoub* referred to a preparation or garnishing. The Italian term was eventually imported into French in the seventeenth century as *daube*, a cut of meat that has been braised in a seasoning. Scappi's *adobbo* varied its ingredients, as did his *adobbo reale*, or royal seasoning, for which he gives recipes at II,130, V,156 and V,188.

With the same brisket you can make all those dishes that are made with the cow's brisket.

36. To roast that breast of veal, stuffed, on a spit or on a grill.

Stuff the breast with beaten pork fat, fine herbs, garlic, eggs and spices, and blanch it in boiling water. When that is done, take it out, let it cool and stick it with fine lardoons of pork fat that have some little sprigs of rosemary inside them. Mount it on a spit and cook it over a low fire. When done, it needs to be served hot with orange juice or lime juice over it.

Should you wish it on a grill, whether stuffed or empty, boil it until it is more than half cooked then take it out, let it cool and sprinkle it with salt and fennel flour. Put it on the grill with a slice of lard on top to keep it from drying out; finish cooking it. Serve it hot with sautéed spring onions on top, or some other garnishings.

37. Several ways to do the shoulder of a suckling calf.

Not wishing to break the promise I made in Book I to show in how many ways you can cook each of the cuts of quadrupeds, I state that, from my experience, the shoulder of a suckling calf – that is, a calf that is not yet weaned – can be cooked in all of those ways described for doing up the breast of veal.

38. To spit-roast the back[38.1] – that is, the loin cut – of a milk-fed calf.

By the back of a calf is meant from the tip of the shoulder back to the tip of the tail, but the best part for roasting is the loin cut, which goes the length of the animal's loin[38.2] – that is, the fattest part of it, where the kidneys are. When, therefore, it is cut away from the other parts, and reduced to several pieces, you give it a rinse in warm water, then blanch it in boiling water. When it has boiled for a fifth of an hour, take it out and let it cool. Then stick it with lardoons of pork fat that is not rancid, and set it to cook on the spit with a low fire to begin with: that is done so the meat will cook inside and out at the same time. When it is almost done, give it a handful of ground salt and a little more heat. When it is cooked, serve it hot with orange juice over it. Should you wish to sear it on a grill, as soon as it has been skinned put it on the grill to sear without having washed it, sprinkling it right away with fennel flour, crushed pepper and salt. If you want to lard it, that is up to you. You cook it on the spit with a few whole cloves and rosemary tips inside. When done, it is served hot with some sort of garnish over it.

[38.1] Scappi wrote, here and in the first sentence of his recipe, *la schiena*, which elsewhere refers to a rib cut.

[38.2] Scappi distinguishes the cut of meat that he calls *la lonza* from the part of the animal that he calls *il lombo*.

If you want the previous one, the one blanched in water, to stay more colourful than usual, you have to cook it over a coal fire. And before it is put on the spit it will have to steep, already larded, in cold water for half an hour. You can do a free-ranging and weaned calf in all of those ways. If you want the loin to steep in a seasoning, you will have to follow the directions given for the loin cut of wild boar.[38.3] If you want Venetian bresaola, when the ribs are completely separated and beaten with the spine of a knife, you follow the directions given for that of the cow in Recipe 7.

39. To spit-roast the throat of a suckling calf.

To some people it seems a weird and wonderful thing that a suckling calf's throat is cooked on a spit, but experience has shown me that that throat, put on a spit without being blanched or seared, and clean without being washed, sprinkled with salt and fennel flour, is just as tasty and delicate as the loin cut. It has to cook, though, over a low fire. And when cooked it has to be served dressed with orange juice and mustard, or with some other sauce in dishes.

In that same way you can roast the belly after it is stuffed. Bear in mind, though, that a belly should be blanched for stuffing, and then larded.

40. To cook the loin of a suckling calf on a spit and in other ways.

You should know that a calf has four loins, that is, two on each side, like an ox and many other quadrupeds, and two kidneys: the rib loin[40.1] is that which lies over the ribs and beneath the skin, and is round like a cow's inner thigh muscle[40.2] – which is itself good to roast on a spit – and it can be done in all the ways that the above loin[40.3] is done. It runs from the shoulder joint back to the rump joint, and is rather tougher than the one that is under the kidneys, which is shorter. After those loins have been cut away from the ribs, then, and stripped of their membrane, they can be done up in all the ways in which beef loin is done. For spit-roasting, though, any back cut[40.4] has to be rather more tenderized than the other, and has

---

[38.3] Recipe II,91 contains no directions for handling this specific cut of meat but deals extensively with a rib cut from a mature wild boar.

[40.1] In Recipe II,8 Scappi indicates that this *lombo schienale* is higher on the animal than the other loin which he calls the inner one, *quel lombo di dentro*.

[40.2] *il pesce della coscia*. The word *pesce* is so defined by Scappi in Recipe V,5; its elongated round shape doubtless suggested the name 'fish.' The last sentence of the present recipe suggests that some sort of analogy was at work in Scappi's kitchen. The *Dizionario etimologico italiano* of Battisti and Alessio extends the word *pesce* to 'an arm muscle.'

[40.3] Recipe 38? See, however, a couple of sentences further on, the reference back to beef loin (Recipes 8–14).

[40.4] *lo schienale*. Previously in this recipe Scappi has not used this term, called a 'saddle' on smaller animals. He seems to be referring to the 'second' or posterior loin, located above the calf's kidneys, a cut he has just described as round and *alquanto piu duretto*, 'somewhat tougher.'

to be longer in the press than the lower one and larded over its full length with prosciutto, and on its outside larded closely with pork fat. It will turn out to be quite excellent. The same can be done with the inner muscle of a cow's thigh.

41. To spit-roast the kidney of a suckling calf.

Get a veal kidney with the fat it has around it – it must be fresh and not tenderized – and sprinkle it with salt and fennel flour. Put it on a spit and cook it, catching the grease that drips from it. When cooked it is served hot with those drippings mixed with orange juice and sugar, or else with sautéed spring onions.

After it has been sprinkled[41] and coated with a mixture of beaten egg and grated cheese, you can also put it in a caul and follow the same directions for cooking it as are set out for the tongue wrapped in a caul in Recipe 30.

42. To cook the leg of a suckling calf on a spit and in various other ways.

If the leg – that is, the upper leg[42] – of the calf is small, as it is on calves in Trento, which are sometimes less than eighty pounds each, you can roast it whole when it is blanched and larded as is done with the loin. If it is from a Roman calf, though, which is quite a bit bigger, the leg can be split down the middle, and left to sit two hours with pepper, ground salt and fennel flour on it, and then seared on the grill like a game meat. Then let it cool, and lard it – but first the lardoons must be dredged in the mixture mentioned above – all the way through from one side to the other. Cook it on a spit as the loin is cooked. When done, it is served hot with some sort of garnish over it.

If you want it done in the oven, or stewed, follow the directions given for the cow's tenderloin in Recipe 8.

43. To make croquettes and fingers from the lean meat of a suckling calf's leg.

Get the best part, that which has had the skin and gristle removed. To make fingers from it, follow the directions given for fingers made from a cow's loin in Recipe 13.

For croquettes, however, cut the meat rather thinner and shorter and narrower than for the fingers, beating it on both sides with the spine of a knife: that is done to keep it tender. Sprinkle it with a little vinegar, pepper, salt and fennel. Then get a mixture of pork fat beaten with that same lean meat, egg yolks, pepper, cinnamon, parsley and other common aromatic herbs, with a clove of garlic; stuff each of them[43.1] with that mixture, rolling them up like cornets.[43.2] Put them on

---

[41] With salt and ground fennel seed, as above.

[42] The word *zigotto* (and in Recipe 84 *cigotto*) is related to the modern French *gigot* as in 'leg of lamb.' Scappi uses the term to refer to the thigh of both a calf and a wether.

[43.1] That is, each of the croquettes.

[43.2] The *cialdoni* that Scappi refers to here are a variety of rolled wafer. See the same procedure and comparison in Recipe 14.

the spit with a small slice of pork fat between each and cook them, over a sprightly fire to begin with until they are firm. When they are cooked and are somewhat browned, take them down. Serve them hot with some garnishes over them. If you want to put grated cheese in the stuffing, that is optional. When stuffed those croquettes can also be wrapped in a caul just as liver is done, and put on the spit with a bay leaf between each and cooked over a lower fire than above. They are served hot with some sort of garnish over them.

But if you want them stewed, there is no need to put them into a caul. It will be enough for them to be half done to take them off the spit and put them into a cooking pot or stewpot[43.3] in which there is clarified pork fat[43.4] along with verjuice, must syrup, muscatel raisins, pepper, cinnamon, saffron and orange juice; finish cooking them slowly with that seasoning. Should you wish to stew them differently, when they are stuffed and still raw put them into a stewpot in which there is lard or rendered fat, sautéing them slowly and stirring them around so the mixture adheres to them, with enough broth to cover them, along with prunes, dried visciola cherries, gooseberries or whole verjuice grapes depending on the season, and with the same spices as are used above. Finish cooking them, keeping the pot tightly closed. When they are done, serve them with the same broth as above, having put in a handful of beaten herbs just before serving them. In the same way they can also be braised in the oven.

For another way: after the meat has been beaten with the spine of a knife, splash the croquettes with verjuice and sprinkle them with sugar, pepper and cinnamon, letting them sit an hour one on top of the other. Get a tourte pan greased with rendered fat or plain pork fat and make a layer of croquettes without coating them. Over them spread grated cheese, both new and old, mixed with sugar, pepper, cinnamon, saffron and raisins. Then take the same number more of croquettes coated with beaten egg and set them out on the first layer and again put on the same mixture along with some thin slices of provatura. Go on like that, putting down three or four such layers. Cook that in an oven or under a cooking bell[43.5] with a slice of pork fat over the top. When it has been half an hour in the oven, you put on a little broth tinged with saffron and a little verjuice or verjuice mash. When it is done, it should be served hot with its broth. If you would like to put in slices of desalted sowbelly, that is optional.

[43.3] Plates 10 and 8, respectively, illustrate a *pignatta* and *stufatora*. The latter is of earthenware and is made with three stubby feet so that it stands upright when not suspended over a fire.

[43.4] The process for preparing this salted fat is described in I, §6.

[43.5] Scappi writes explicitly *sotto il testo*, under the (cooking) bell. See the note in Recipe 11.

44. To make Roman-style fingers of the above lean meat.[44]

Cut up that meat into six-ounce pieces and lard each piece with marbled prosciutto, or else with pork fat which has first been dredged in fennel flour or coriander, with salt, pepper, cloves, cinnamon and nutmeg, ensuring that the lardoons are right inside the body of the meat – that is, that they cannot be seen on the outside. After the fingers have been in the press for two hours with the above mixture and two crushed cloves of garlic, set them to cook on the spit like the ones made from beef. As they approach being done, you can stew them in a pot the way the above croquettes are done. You serve them hot with their sauce over top. You can do the same with the inner thigh muscle of a weaned calf or cow, after it has been properly tenderized.

45. To make bresaola of lean veal, fried or grilled.

When bresaola are cut up the same as croquettes,[45] and beaten on both sides with the spine of a knife, they are splashed with a little vinegar and Greek wine containing crushed garlic, and sprinkled with fennel flour or ground coriander, pepper and salt, and then set in a press for an hour one on top of the other. To fry them in rendered fat or lard, first flour them, then fry them so they brown a little and they will stay soft rather than dry out. You serve them hot with sugar, cinnamon and orange juice over them; or else dress them with a sauce made of vinegar, sugar, cinnamon, cloves and nutmeg.

But if you want them done on a grill, after they have been sprinkled and been in the press put them on the grill with a thin strip of pork fat for each one, so that the bresaola stay softer, cooking them over a low fire and turning them frequently. The smoke that forms beneath the grill because of the grease that is dripping will give them an excellent flavour and the very best taste. When they are done, they should be served with one of the above-mentioned sauces with which the fried ones are served.

Instead of putting those bresaola on the grill, they can be cooked in a tourte pan greased with rendered fat, with the same thin slices of pork fat on them. They are served with their sauce and orange juice over them.

46. To make saveloy sausages of lean veal and veal liver with veal caul.[46.1]

Get six pounds of that meat, with the bone, skin and gristle removed, and fresh – that is, just after the animal has been slaughtered, so that the meat is much

---

[44] Versions of this recipe for *polpettoni alla Romanesca* can be found in the *Libro de arte co-quinaria* of Maestro Martino, Recipe 19, *coppiette al modo Romano*, and in the *Registrum co-quine* of Jean de Bockenheim, Recipe 3, *copias*.

[45] See Recipe VI,46 and Recipe 14, above.

[46.1] Lancelot de Casteau's *cervelade fin* (48) includes saffron in the sausage stuffing, suggesting that his saveloy are these *cervellate gialle* of Scappi.

juicier – along with two pounds of kidney-fat, skinned. Beat it all together with knives, adding in four pounds of that animal's liver which has first been parboiled and grated with the cheese grater;[46.2] then add in four ounces of ground salt, half an ounce of crushed pepper, one ounce of ground cinnamon, half an ounce of ginger, an eighth of an ounce of saffron, six ounces of grated cheese, six ounces of clean dried currants, one ounce of fennel seeds[46.3] and eight raw egg yolks. When everything has been blended together, add in a handful of beaten mint and sweet marjoram together, and four ounces of cold meat broth. Then get a piece of caul from where it is the thinnest, softened in warm, saffron-tinged water, and coat it with egg yolk. Using that mixture make up saveloy sausages, large or small as you think best. Cook them on a grill or fry them in a pan; they can also be cooked on a spit after they have firmed up on the grill. When done, they need to be served hot. Instead of veal fat, you can use pork kidney-fat.[46.4]

47. To make pear-shaped meatballs from the lean meat and liver of a suckling calf.

Take some of the same mixture as above but without any broth in it and make balls the size of a hard-boiled egg, and put them into a tourte pan which has cold rendered fat in it. Heat it up with a cooking bell over it, adding in enough broth to cover them, with pepper and cinnamon and enough saffron, and gooseberries or else verjuice grapes in summer or verjuice in winter, along with a handful of beaten herbs. Finish off cooking them. Serve them hot. If you want, make them like pears, give them a pear shape by hand, sticking a dry sprig of fennel on top for a stem.[47.1]

From the same composition you can make *tommacelle*[47.2] with a caul of pork or wether, cooking it in the same way you do saveloy sausage in the above recipe, or else in the way you do the meatballs braised in their broth.

[46.2] See the two similar sorts of *gratta cascio* in Plates 10 and 22.

[46.3] *finocchio sgranato.* 'Fennel seeds are gathered in the autumn. We flavour various dishes with them, and eat them on their own after meals' (Castelvetro, trans. Riley, 78).

[46.4] Scappi says in Book I, §4 that this *songia* (elsewhere spelled *sognia* and *sugna*), when taken from a fresh (that is, unsalted) pig, is used for the making of *strutto*, rendered fat. The kidney-fat of calves and wethers is also used in Scappi's cooking.

[47.1] Scappi does not invest as much fantasy in his preparations as earlier cooks, whose whimsical pseudo-creatures and lifelike-but-cooked-and-ready-for-eating animals amused many a diner. Examples of his rather timid essays into an established culinary practice can be seen in Recipes III,160 (*Anguille finte ripiene*) and 219 (*Ricotta & butiro finta*). See Melitta Weiss Adamson, 'Imitation Food Then and Now,' *Petits Propos Culinaires*, 72 (2003): 83–102.

[47.2] See Recipes 107–109, below. Compare also a fifteenth-century recipe for these large, wrapped sausages in the *Neapolitan Recipe Collection*, Recipe 65.

48. To do calf's feet in various ways.

Get the feet as soon as the animal is slaughtered and skin them in hot water, being aware that the forefeet are meatier and better than the hindfeet. When their nails have been removed along with all dirt, boil the feet in salted water. When they are done, split them in half lengthwise and fry them in rendered fat and spring onions; otherwise coat them with beaten egg, grated bread and herbs just as you coat the half calf's head in Recipe 28, and fry them likewise in rendered fat. Serve them up hot with sugar and orange juice over them. If you would like to dress them with green sauce, onion sauce, garlic sauce or some other sauce, when they have boiled and fried just serve them plain garnished with one of those sauces.

You can also put them on a grill after they have boiled and have cooled a little out of their bouillon. Sprinkle them with fennel flour, salt and grated bread, keeping them soft with a thin slab of pork fat over each part. Serve them hot with orange juice over them or else a sauce made of rose vinegar, sugar and cinnamon.

Should you want those feet in a fricassee with beaten eggs, when they have boiled cut them up into small pieces and fry those in rendered fat or lard. Have beaten egg yolks ready, mixed with pepper, cinnamon, saffron, sugar, verjuice and a little cold meat broth; put everything into the pan. Heat it up away from the flame. When it has congealed like a thick broth, serve it with sugar and cinnamon over it.

If you want to spit-roast those feet, when they are half-done boiling, whole, remove them, let them cool, lard them all over with pork fat. Mount them on a spit and cook them completely over a sprightly fire. When done they are served hot with capers[48] over them.

The feet can also be stewed just as the head and breast of veal are done.

49. To roast calf sweetbreads on a spit and on a grill.

Take the sweetbreads and cut them away from the gullet[49.1] and give them a wash in warm water to clear away the bloodiness. If you want them in a caul, cut them up raw into pieces and sprinkle them with pepper, cinnamon, cloves, nutmeg and fennel flour. Get the calf's caul – that is, the thinnest part of it – although a pig's caul would be better; wrap the pieces up in it[49.2] and put them onto a spit, with a slice of salt pork between each. Cook them over a moderate fire. When they are done, serve them hot. Sweetbreads can also be cooked on a spit without

---

[48] *capparetti* in the 1570 printing, interestingly typeset as *capretti* ('goat kids') in the 1581 re-printing.

[49.1] These are the thymus gland in the animal's throat. This sort of sweetbread is not to be confused with sweetbreads of the pancreas, of which Scappi writes in Recipe II,104 and various other places.

[49.2] Scappi intends the caul to be cut up into pieces of a size suitable for wrapping the chunks of sweetbread individually.

a caul but with pieces of sausage through them. When they are about half done, sprinkle them with the same mixture as is used above. It is left optional whether you bring the sweetbreads to a boil before putting them in the caul or on the spit. And, too, after they are cooked without the caul they can be served with various sauces over them.

If you want them done on a grill, when they are cut up into pieces and brought to a boil you mount them onto a wooden stick or iron skewer with a thin slice of salt pork jowl or pork fat between each of them. Finish cooking them that way on the grill, turning them often. When they have browned a little and are cooked, serve them hot, dressed with sugar, cinnamon and orange juice.

50. Various ways to sauté and do the sweetbreads of a suckling calf.

Parboiled or raw, cut up the sweetbreads into small pieces. For every pound of the sweetbreads get six ounces of pork belly, cut into slices, and fry everything in rendered fat or lard. When done, they are served hot with orange juice and sugar over them, or with some other garnish. Instead of pork belly you can fry bits of sage with them, or else thin slices of prosciutto.

If the sweetbreads are parboiled, you can fry them with liver that has been cut up into small pieces. As well, once parboiled and cut into bits they can be done *au gratin* – that is, in a fricassee made with egg yolks and verjuice in the way it is done for the feet.

Should you want to make saveloy sausages of the sweetbreads, when they have been brought to a boil beat them finely with knives, adding in, for every pound of the sweetbreads, four ounces of grated Parmesan cheese, two ounces of soft cheese, half an ounce of cinnamon, half an ounce of pepper and ginger combined, and a quarter ounce of nutmeg, everything mixed together; then add in four ounces of sugar, eight raw egg yolks, enough saffron, four ounces of raisins and a handful of beaten herbs. With the caul of a wether or pig, tinged with saffron, you make up the saveloy sausages and *tommacelle* and cook them. They are cooked and served just as the lean-meat ones are done.[50.1] You can also put in the parboiled brains of the calf, if you are making saveloy sausages with them.[50.2]

51. To make various sorts of pottage of the above sweetbreads.

Get the best part of the sweetbreads and divide them, raw, into several small pieces. Give them a frying in rendered fat or lard, then put them into an earthenware or copper pot with a little of the fat they have been fried in, adding in enough broth to cover them and common spices with a little saffron. Boil them. When they are almost done, put prunes and dried visciola cherries in with them, and thicken the broth with a small amount of almonds ground in a mortar with two leaves of

---

[50.1] Recipe 46, above.

[50.2] The term *cevellata*, saveloy, derives from its original distinctive ingredient, *cervelle*, brains.

spinach, the almonds being moistened with broth and verjuice. At the end, beaten herbs are mixed in. You can also thicken it, when it is cooked, with beaten eggs, grated cheese and herbs mixed together – not forgetting in both cases to add in the spices. When they are cooked however you like, they are served hot in any season.

52. Various ways to cook calf's brains.

When the brains are taken out of the head, remove the membrane and parboil them, cutting them into thin slices and coating them with beaten egg mixed with grated bread and herbs. Fry them in rendered fat or lard. Serve them hot dressed with orange juice, pepper, sugar and cinnamon.

If you want to make saveloy sausages of them with a caul, follow the directions for those done with sweetbreads.[52] If you want to stuff pork intestines with them, or the intestines of the calf itself, when the brains are parboiled grind them in the mortar, for every pound of them adding in two ounces of Parmesan cheese, two ounces of grated fat cheese, three ounces of fresh ricotta cheese, four ounces of sugar, one ounce of pepper and cinnamon combined, three ounces of raisins, six fresh eggs, beaten, and a handful of herbs. With that mixture stuff the veal or pork casings, which must be very clean, and set them to boil in a good meat broth containing prosciutto. When done, they can be served with that broth. And you can recook them on the grill. In whatever way they are cooked, they have to be served hot.

53. Several ways to do calf's eyes.

Boil the eyes and clean away the black in them.[53] When they have parboiled, let them cool and sprinkle them with salt, pepper, fennel flour and cinnamon. Wrap them in the calf's caul, or a wether's or pig's, and set them to cook on a spit with thin slices of pork fat or pork jowl between them. When they are done, serve them hot dressed with orange juice, sugar and cinnamon. Those eyes can be used to make all of the dishes made with calf's sweetbreads.

54. Several ways to cook testicles of a calf, lamb, bull, young buffalo, wild boar, stag and other quadrupeds that are normally eaten.

Get those testicles without their outer and inner skins; they must above all be fresh. To spit-roast them in a caul, bring them to a boil and a little longer[54] in water so they firm up, then follow the directions given for the sweetbreads in Recipe 49.

---

[52] Recipe 50, above.

[53] *privinosi del negro ch'è in essi*: perhaps the iris?

[54] Literally Scappi has written: Have them do 'two boilings.' A single 'boiling' is merely having been brought to a boil.

If you want to put them raw on a spit, though, the spit will have to be very hot when the testicles go onto it: that is so they will grip the spit more tightly, because otherwise they would slip and not turn. Baste them with hot rendered fat or with lard so they will firm up and swell. When they are almost done, sprinkle them with a mixture of flour, ground salt, sugar and fennel flour. When they are done they are served hot.

If the testicles are from a bull, a stag or a wild boar, they can be cut up smaller. With testicles you can make all of the dishes that you make with sweetbreads. You can also fry them in a pan, in slices, with spring onions, prosciutto and other things. I have placed this recipe under the one for calf's eyes because this foodstuff is similarly boneless.

55. To cook the liver of a suckling calf in several ways, beginning with spit-roasting it.

To be good, the liver has to be tender and clean, and has to be of a slightly greenish-grey colour rather than dark, and high rather than low.[55.1] When the membrane around the liver is removed, along with the little nerves that are sometimes in it, cut it into four pieces more or less depending on its size, but the pieces should not be less than a pound each. Parboil the pieces in boiling water, take them out and let them cool. Stick them with lardoons of pork fat dredged in pepper, cinnamon, fennel flour, cloves and nutmeg, doing it in such a way that the lardoons go all the way through. Put them onto a spit which is quite hot so that they will sit there firmly, and set the spit over a low heat, basting the liver pieces from time to time with melted rendered fat. When they are almost done, sprinkle them with flour and grated bread mixed with pepper, cinnamon, cloves, nutmeg and fennel flour. Finish off cooking them. When they are done, serve them dressed with a garnish of rose vinegar, sugar, cinnamon and raisins.

Should you wish it done in a caul, cut the liver up into smaller pieces and, without larding them but only sprinkling them with the above mixture, wrap them in the caul and set them to cook on the spit in the way described above.

Should you want it done as a pasty,[55.2] when the pieces have been larded and mounted on the spit as was said before, half-cook them on that spit. Then get a mixture of beaten egg yolks, rosewater, white wine, flour, sugar, cinnamon, saffron and ground salt; that mixture should be as runny as a pancake batter. With a bristle brush like the one used to glaze pastries, or with a small spoon, spread the batter over the liver, turning it slowly until the batter is set. When it is set,

---

[55.1] *piu tosto alto, che basso*: this last specification may qualify the brightness of the colour, may describe the liver's thickness when lying flat or, most likely, may refer to its location on the animal's carcass.

[55.2] *a foggia di pasticcio*, as in the 1570 printing; remarkably the 1581 typesetter put *a foggia di pistaccio*, 'like a pistachio'!

do the same thing over again. Repeat that several times; the last time, when the batter is quite firm, wrap slices of pork fat and heavy paper around it so the batter will not burn but only browns and adheres closely. When the liver is cooked, take off the paper and pork fat and serve the pieces hot. That dish can be called 'pies on a spit.' If the pieces of liver are roasted without batter, they can be served with sautéed spring onions over them, or else some other garnish, or prunes or dried visciola cherries cooked in wine and sugar.

If you would like to fry the liver in a pan, when the membrane is off it and it is cut into slices flour them and fry them in melted rendered fat or in olive oil. Without flouring them you can also fry them with slices of prosciutto, serving them dressed with pepper, salt and orange juice. That liver can be fried with beaten spring onions, and with sage tips, and with salted pork jowl.[55.3]

56. Various ways to cook the pluck – that is, the lungs[56.1] – of a suckling calf.

When the windpipe[56.2] has been cut away from the pluck with a fine knife, keep cutting along the ridges because often those are full of dirt. When everything is clean and washed, you set it to boil in salted water, needing particularly to skim it very thoroughly and to keep it under the water because by nature it will float. When it is cooked, slice it up. It can be fried in rendered fat as the liver is done, and is likewise served hot with orange juice, pepper and salt over it.

Of it you can also make all those dishes and fricassees, with or without spring onions, that are made with the sweetbreads. If you would like to make a pottage of it, when it has boiled beat it finely with knives, or else cut it up into bits the size of dice. Sauté it with beaten spring onions in melted rendered fat. Put it into an earthenware or copper pot with the same fat along with pepper, cinnamon, saffron and a meat broth, and bring it to a boil with gooseberries or verjuice grapes in summer, or in winter with verjuice. Toward the end throw in a handful of beaten herbs. Serve it hot, dressed with mild spices.[56.3] You can also thicken it with grated cheese and beaten eggs.

57. Various ways to cook the tripe of a suckling calf.

Get the best part of the tripe, which is the small and large intestines; they must above all be clean, turned inside out and rinsed in several changes of water. Set them to boil for a quarter of an hour in unsalted water, skimming them very carefully and watching that they stay under the water or else they darken. When

---

[55.3] As is often the case, Scappi's 'and' may merely be a way of compiling a list of alternatives.

[56.1] In modern Italian the *coratella* includes lungs, heart and entrails – expressly not the sense for Scappi.

[56.2] Here *canaluccio*; compare this with the *gargaruccio*, esophagus, of Recipes V,3 and 8.

[56.3] The composition of these *specie dolci* is never described by Scappi but may be intended to be at the reader's taste and option.

they have boiled, take them out and put them into cold water. Once cooled, divide them up into several small pieces and put those back into another, smaller pot with meat broth that is not too salty and pork jowl that is not rancid: that is done so they will develop their flavour and stay whiter. Finish off cooking them in that broth. When they are done, serve them on platters with cheese and cinnamon over them. At the end, too, you can add in a handful of beaten herbs. And if you have not cooked prosciutto with the tripe, you can thicken it all with eggs and cheese.

That tripe, after being boiled and cut into small pieces, can also be sautéed in melted rendered fat or in lard with beaten spring onions. With that you can make all of those fricassees that are made with the sweetbreads of that same calf.

If you want the tripe fried another way, get the intestines that have been prepared with an iron rod[57] – that is, that have not been cut away from the caul but only cut up – that are very clean, parboiled so they are half cooked, and divided into a number of small pieces. Then take the pieces and coat them with a mixture of beaten egg, rosewater, white wine, saffron and salt, and fry them in such a way that the pieces become like wrinkled fritters. When they are done, they are served hot with sugar and cinnamon over them. They will be better, though, if they are cut up into small pieces while still raw rather than after they have been cooked.

If you want tripe on a grill, when raw and cut up they are parboiled until fully cooked, removed from the broth, cooled and heated up on the grill, being basted constantly with melted rendered fat. They are served hot with strong mustard or some other garnish over them.

58. To stuff the tripe of a suckling calf.

Get the small intestine, which above all has to be clean inside and out, and let it sit a quarter of an hour in a little salt. Then get the other tripe of that calf, which must be clean and parboiled and cut up very small with knives; with it mix pepper, cinnamon, cloves, nutmeg, fennel flour, mint and sweet marjoram. With that mixture stuff the intestine that has been in salt; when that is done, tie both ends and boil the intestine in a meat broth. When it is cooked, serve it hot, or else put it on the grill and serve it the same as saveloy sausage is served.

If, however, you want to stuff that intestine with cheese, eggs, ground walnuts, beaten herbs, raisins and common spices, you will not put it into salt, but it must be very clean. When it is stuffed, put it on the fire in cold water to parboil. When it has taken on its shape and its stuffing has firmed up, finish off cooking it in a good meat broth. Serve it with a garlic sauce over it. You can also stuff the intestine with a mixture of parboiled brains ground in a mortar and moistened with goat's milk, eggs and sugar, adding in pepper, cinnamon, salt and enough saffron – but if you want it white, do not put in any spices – and cook it in the above way.

---

[57] See the *ferro per conciare tripe* in Plate 13.

59. Several ways to cook the above calf's blood.

Although these preparations are not common, they can still be done in various ways, such as the lung is done. As soon as it is taken out of the animal, though, parboil it, unsalted, in a large pot with a lot of water – and put the blood into boiling water because if you put it in cold water, being heavier it will sink to the bottom and stick there. When parboiled, take it out, let it cool, and cut it into slices or into bits. Set those to sauté in a pan with spring onions. Serve it with salt and orange juice over it.

If you want it differently, follow the directions I gave for the calf's lung in Recipe 56.

60. Various ways to cook a wether's head.

Although that head is not more commonly done up than a cow's head, nevertheless for the sake of completeness in dealing with all the parts of a wether, just as I spoke of all parts of an ox, I shall begin with that head cooked in salted water. So, get the head of a wether in that animal's season, which begins at the end of June and goes through February, although in Rome it is available throughout the year; skin it, split it through the middle and remove a particular little hairy white worm[60.1] that it has in its brain, rinse it in several changes of water, cleaning out those little channels;[60.2] remove its teeth, too. Set it to boil as was said in salted water. When it is done, serve it covered with garlic sauce. With it you can make all of the dishes that are made with a cow's head.

You can also spit-roast it whole. However, the head of a large lamb will always be better than that of a wether.

61. Various ways to cook a wether's breast.

If the wether is big and old, hang it for two days in winter and one in summer; if it is young it can be cooked right away.[61.1] To cook it in water, put it into boiling water. If you want to stuff it, do so as directed for the breast of veal in Recipe 33. Make especially sure that it stays under the water in the pot, so that it stays white. When it is done, serve it with green sauce or with some other sauce in dishes.

Should you want to spit-roast it, you do not need to blanch it;[61.2] rather mount it raw on the spit with sprigs of rosemary. If, though, you do want to blanch it, mount it studded with cloves of garlic and pork fat.

[60.1] Scappi's phrase is *un certo bigattello bianco, peloso*.

[60.2] These *canaletti* are probably the nasal passages. See Recipes II,26 and 79.

[61.1] The purpose of hanging animals' flesh – that of game animals in particular, which by nature was believed to be drier than that of domestic animals – is to tenderize the meat. All animals dry out with age, so it was felt that an incipient decomposition was gastronomically advantageous to the older members of a species.

[61.2] Scappi's verb here is *rifare*, meaning generally 'to make plump' and specifically to blanch or to sear depending on whether the operation is done in water or over a flame.

To do it on a grill: more than half-cook it,[61.3] then set it for an hour in a seasoning of vinegar, must syrup, garlic, pepper and coriander, then take it out, flour it and put it on the grill. Otherwise fry it in a pan with melted rendered fat.

62. To make a pottage of a breast of wether.

Take the tip[62] which, being clean, you need not wash, with the belly cut away, divide it into several small pieces and put them into a pot with melted rendered fat or lard. Sauté them gently with beaten spring onions for half an hour; then add in pepper, cinnamon, saffron and enough meat broth to cover them, and cook them. When they are almost done, add in gooseberries or whole verjuice grapes with, in summer, a handful of beaten herbs or, in winter, prunes, dried visciola cherries and verjuice instead. When done, serve them on platters with their broth over them.

In the same way you can also do up the ribs that are under the shoulder, which are much more tasty than any other part of the wether. The same ribs, after being half-cooked by boiling and sprinkled with fennel flour and a little salt, can also be put on a grill.

63. Another way to make a pottage of a breast of wether.

If the wether is old, first parboil the tip of the breast; this need not be done if it is young. Then divide it up into several pieces and sauté them in pork fat or melted rendered fat. When they are done, put them into a pot with enough broth to cover them, adding in the spice mixture of the previous recipe and cooking them on the coals, away from the fire, with the pot sealed. When they are almost done, for every pound of the meat grind up a pound of skinned Milanese almonds[63.1] in a mortar and four ounces of bread soaked in the broth; moisten that with broth and verjuice and put it through a strainer, pouring everything into the pot. Bring that to a boil and keep it boiling until the broth has thickened a little. Serve it hot with mild spices over top. Along with the almonds you can also grind six ounces of grated Parmesan cheese, two ounces of garlic cooked under the coals, and a few spinach tops in order to change their colour.

You can also do it differently, roasting the almonds on a hot shovel,[63.2]

[61.3] In the following recipes the phrase 'by boiling' is added to this instruction.

[62] See the note in Recipe 5, above.

[63.1] These *mandole ambrosine* are a highly regarded variety of sweet almond. They were already named in the *Banchetti* of Cristoforo Messisbugo. They are in common use in Scappi and the only particular variety of almond that he specifies.

[63.2] A *pala focata* (a past participle of the verb *focare*, now *infuocare*, to heat) is frequently used for culinary operations such as browning the upper surface of a preparation. The shovel was at hand for removing ash and embers.

cleaning them and grinding them in the mortar with three ounces of *mostaccioli*[63.3] and four ounces of toast soaked in rose vinegar and must syrup. When everything is ground up and moistened with broth, rose vinegar and must syrup, put it into the pot with the pieces of wether, adding in pepper, cinnamon, cloves and nutmeg, and bring it all to a boil as previously. Serve it hot.

To do it differently, when the pieces are sautéed and put into the pot in enough broth to cover them, also put in raisins and muscatel raisins. When that is cooked, beat egg yolks with verjuice and a little malmsey, adding in pepper, cinnamon and saffron, and put all that into the pot. Bring it to a boil, giving it a stir with a spoon. When it has thickened, serve it on platters with mild spices over top.

You can also do it with those pieces of breast fried, fresh peas and broad beans.

64. To roast a shoulder of wether on a spit or on a grill.

Should you wish to roast a shoulder of wether, it has to be somewhat tenderized, especially if the wether is old. It needs to be put on a spit without blanching, rubbing it with beaten cloves of garlic, and salt, so it will take on their flavour. Before mounting it on the spit you can also stuff it with beaten pork fat, garlic, common herbs, grated cheese, eggs and common spices. Cook it on the spit over a low fire. When done it needs to be served hot.

Should you want it on a grill, first half-cook it by boiling, then sprinkle it with salt and fennel flour. Grill it until it has browned on both sides. Serve it hot with a garnish of rose vinegar, sugar, cinnamon, cloves and a small clove of garlic.

65. To braise, grill or spit-roast shoulders of wether wrapped in a mock caul.[65.1]

Get two shoulders, half-cook one of them on the spit, then take it down and

---

[63.3] These are a sort of fruitcake: see Recipe VI,142. Scappi draws frequently upon a stock of these *mostaccioli*, as if they were a universal kitchen staple, generally crumbling or grinding them before incorporating them into a preparation.

[65.1] A similar reconstructive operation will be given the animal's hind leg as well: Recipe 69, below.

This particular preparation has a solid history in Italian cookery. The *Libro della cocina* has *A empiere una spalla* (Recipe 111); the *Buone vivande*, a *Spalle de castrone ripiene* (Recipe 14); the *Libro per cuoco*, a *Spalle de castron impiete* (Recipe 77); the Wellcome MS, a *Spalla faciata arostita* (Recipe 189); and the *Neapolitan Recipe Collection*, a *Pieno ad una spalla de carnero* (Recipe 78). Two fourteenth-century Catalan works, *De apareylar be de menyar* and the *Libro de sent soví*, describe *Spatle farcide* (Recipe 88) and *Com se ffercex espatla de moltó* (Recipe 8) respectively; and in Latin, the Châlon MS, a *De modo preparandi spallam castronis* (Recipe 62). French recipe collections seem to have picked up the procedure only in the fifteenth century (Vatican MS of the *Viandier*, Recipe 212), although the *Menagier* at the end of the thirteenth, as a justification for *not* giving directions for it, dismisses the preparation entirely, writing *Item des Espaulles de Mouton, quia nichil est nisi pena et labor* – ' ... because it's nothing but a lot of work' (§365). Chiquart likewise (*Du fait de cuisine*, Recipe 88), despite his proclivity to ingenious *entremets* designed to enliven Savoy's banquets, roasts his shoulders of mutton whole, merely colouring them green for effect.

carefully remove all of the flesh. Likewise remove the raw flesh from the other one, taking off the skin and removing the gristle; mind that the shoulder blade of the raw one is not damaged and is not separated from the bone. Then with knives beat both shoulders – that is, the flesh of them, with the skin and gristle removed. Into that meat paste add a pound of marbled prosciutto and six ounces of veal or wether kidney-fat. When all that is well beaten, stir in two ounces of fat cheese, four raw eggs, half an ounce of fennel flour, as much beaten herbs[65.2] as can be held in a hand, two ounces of orange juice tinged with saffron, and three ounces of dried currants. When that mixture has been made up, get a wether's caul, or a pig's – which would be better; it should be very clean and softened in warm water. Spread the caul out on a table and, with it like that, spread on it egg yolks beaten with rosewater: that is done so that when it is heated the caul can better hold the mixture. Put some of the mixture on the caul; on that put the shoulder blade from the uncooked shoulder, with the bone still attached to it; and onto that put the rest of the mixture. Then adroitly wrap the caul so that it goes around twice and so that the leg bone sticks half out of the caul. When it is wrapped up like that, use your palm to give it the shape of a shoulder, and let it sit on a table for an hour. Coat all of its outside with beaten egg yolk, and put the shoulder into a large pan with melted rendered fat or pork fat, giving it a low fire above and below, the way tourtes are done,[65.3] until it is cooked and has browned a little. Serve it hot with orange juice and sugar.

If you want it on the grill, when it is done up there is no need to colour its outside; it is enough to set it on the grill where there are a few sprigs of rosemary. Mind that it's a moderate fire, and turn the shoulder over adroitly – that is, by taking the grill in your hand together with another similar grill onto which you turn it. When it has firmed up, you put a few slices of pork fat onto it to keep it from drying out. When it is done it needs to be served hot with some combination of condiments over it.

If you want it on a spit, though, you have to make the stuffing thicker, and bind the caul with cord even though you will spoil the proper shape of the shoulder that it will have in the previous treatments.

66. To cook a rack[66.1] of wether ribs in various ways.

For boiling, get a rack of wether's ribs that has been somewhat tenderized; for roasting, though, it will not matter whether it has been tenderized provided

---

[65.2] Lancelot de Casteau's recipe for an *Espaule de mouton farcie & rostie* (114) specifies parsley, spinach, marjoram and mint. Scappi's penchant for fat cheese is not shared in Liège, and other minor ingredients vary from those that Scappi uses: egg yolks alone rather than saffron; nutmeg, pepper and aniseed rather than fennel seed, orange juice and currants.

[65.3] A tourte pan normally has a lid, although Scappi calls the present vessel simply *una padella larga*.

[66.1] *schiena*: a slab of ribs. See also Recipe II,7.

the wether is young. For boiling, follow the directions given in Recipe 61 using salted water. For roasting, there is no need to blanch it, but mount it on the spit raw, larded with garlic cloves and tips of rosemary. However, if the wether is lean you can blanch it in water and lard it with small bits of pork fat. For putting on the grill set it to boil until more than half cooked, then take it out and let it cool a little. Sprinkle it with dry fennel flour, ground salt and grated bread, then let it brown on the grill on both sides. Serve it hot dressed with a sauce of rose vinegar, sugar and orange juice. To make Venetian bresaola of this rack, rib by rib, follow the directions given for the cow in Recipe 7.

The loin[66.2] that is under the kidney, even if it is small, can be done up in all the ways given before for loin of veal.[66.3]

67. Various ways to cook a wether's rump[67.1] and tail on a grill.

To be good the rump has to be from a young, fat wether, and preferably a wether that has grazed in the hills rather than on the plain.[67.2] To be done on a grill, boil it first, then take it out, sprinkle it with the same ingredients as are sprinkled on the above rack, and cook it. Serve it as above.

If you want the rump done on a spit, half-cook it by boiling, then mount it carefully, and roast it. When it is almost done, apply a coating of grated bread, sugar and salt. Serve it hot with orange juice over it.

The tail can be gilded with beaten egg yolk. First cook it in salted water, take it out and let it cool. Gild it with the egg yolks and grated bread, and fry it in melted rendered fat or lard. When it is done, serve it hot with cut-up limes, sugar and cinnamon over it. You can also cover the rump with various sauces after it has been cooked, whether by boiling or roasting. And likewise the tail.

68. To boil a wether's leg whole.[68]

A small leg, that has been hung and is from a young wether, will always be better for boiling than a big one from an old wether. After it has hung, wash it in warm water and set it to boil in hot, sufficiently salted water. Then follow the same directions for cooking and serving it as are given for the breast in Recipe 61. If you wish to stuff it, follow the directions below for the braised leg.

[66.2] The cut being discussed thus far is the *schiena*, the back; here more specifically it is a *lombo*, the wether's tenderloin.

[66.3] See Recipe 40, above.

[67.1] This *groppone*, literally 'crupper' or 'haunch,' is likely the English 'fillet' and the French *selle*.

[67.2] *nudrito alla montagna, che al piano*. The distinction is between wild, uninhabited regions and flatter, cultivated ones. Fodder was richer and more abundant where land was not cleared and reserved for crop growing. In a sense the preferred wether could be called 'free-ranging.'

[68] In this and the following recipes for 'wether's leg' (*zigotto*, later *cigotto*: gigot) the modern reader may be tempted to read 'leg of mutton.'

69. To braise a stuffed leg of wether whole.

Get a leg of the good sort described above and beat it with a bat until it separates from the bone in the middle of it, then carefully draw out that bone which is the hollow bone, leaving the knee pad there. Along with the bone remove some of the flesh and beat that with an equivalent amount of pork fat, marbled prosciutto and garlic cloves, adding in pepper, cinnamon, beaten herbs, a few raisins and saffron. Turn the leg[69.1] inside out and slash the inner flesh here and there, being careful not to cut through to the skin. Splash the flesh with rose vinegar and sprinkle on pepper, sugar and cinnamon. Then turn it right side out again, stuff it with the mixture, sew it up with cord, and put it into a stewing pot which has beaten pork fat in it and enough meat broth to cover the leg; add in verjuice, common spices, and prunes and dried visciola cherries. Seal the pot so it cannot breathe, and set it to cook over a low fire for two hours. When it is done, serve it hot with the cord removed and with that broth over it.

If you want to spit-roast it, when it is stuffed half-cook it by boiling, take it out, let it cool, lard it with very small bits of pork fat, and mount it on a spit. Cook it as you do roasts. You can also cook it in an oven, after it is full of the same mixture used to stuff it when stewing it, putting in less broth.[69.2] You can also put it raw on the spit.

70. To spit-roast a wether's leg whole.

To be good the leg needs to be from a young, fat wether. If it is from an old wether, though, hang it; if you do not have time to hang it, beat it with a bat. Without washing it, mount it on a spit, studding it with whole cloves and cloves of garlic. Cook it like that, catching the drippings that will fall from it. When it is done, serve it dressed with a garnish made of rose vinegar and sugar or must syrup, mixed with the drippings.

It can be done differently: when the leg has been skinned and is fairly clean, it is parboiled in salted water, taken out, stuck with cloves and bits of pork fat and set to cook on a spit the way the veal loin is done in Recipe 38. When it is roasted, serve it covered with cut-up limes or with spring onions cooked in the dripping pan with the drippings.

71. Various ways to do up the lean meat of a wether's leg.

If you want to make croquettes, both stuffed and plain, cooking them on a spit or stewing them, follow the directions set out for the veal croquettes in Recipe 43. Of the same meat you can make all the dishes that are made from veal.

[69.1] That is, the skin.

[69.2] The typesetter put an echoic *mentendovi men brodo*, rather than *mettendovi*, uncorrected in the 1581 reprinting.

72. To make a pottage of the lean meat of a wether's leg.

Get the meat of that leg, which should not have been hung for too long, without skin, bone and gristle, and beat it with knives. For every pound of meat get four ounces of the wether's kidney-fat, three ounces of pork fat and two ounces of marbled prosciutto. When everything is beaten together, add in two ounces of clean raisins or gooseberries, or verjuice grapes, one ounce of common spices, and enough saffron. When the mixture is made up, moisten it with cold meat broth and put it to cook slowly in an earthenware or tinned-copper pot. When it is almost done, open it up[72.1] with a spoon and add in mint, sweet marjoram, burnet[72.2] and beaten parsley. When it has come to a boil, serve it hot with mild spices over it. You can also thicken it and colour it with beaten egg yolks.

With that mixture, before it is thinned with the broth, you can make balls and pears the same as are made from veal in Recipe 47.

73. To make pottage from the lean meat of a wether's leg with almond milk.

Take the leg and half cook it on a spit (which is done so it will not lose its juice). Take it down and, while it is still hot, cut away all the meat from the bone, being careful not to take any skin; catch the juice that comes out as the meat is cut. Grind that lean meat in a mortar; for every six pounds of the meat grind with it one pound of shelled Milanese almonds, moistening all that with a meat broth that is not too salty. Put it all through a strainer, adding in a beaker of verjuice along with the juice that came out in the cutting, a pound of sugar, an ounce of cinnamon and half an ounce of pepper. Put everything into a tinned casserole pot and cook it over a low fire, stirring constantly. When it is done and has thickened a little, serve it hot on platters with sugar and cinnamon over it. If you want capon meat with the mixture, or boneless rumps of doves roasted on a spit, put that meat or those rumps in when the mixture is half cooked, then boil everything until it thickens, and serve it in the above manner. You can also grind six ounces of cheese and two ounces of parboiled garlic with the meat. Many people call that composition *capirotata*.[73]

You can do the same with the lean meat of a young wild boar's leg.

[72.1] Scappi wrote, literally, 'Let it break': *rompasi*. His sense may be simply, 'Stir it up.'

[72.2] Scappi's *pimpinella* can designate two varieties of edible herb, *Sanguisorba minor*, salad burnet, or *Pimpinella saxifraga*, burnet saxifage. Both grew widely in Europe since the Middle Ages and were in common use. The first, with a nutty, cucumber-like flavour, had a place in medieval kitchen gardens and was a mainstay in salads. Scappi relies upon *pimpinella* in a number of dishes.

[73] This is a preparation whose provenance appears to be Hispanic. In Cejador y Frauca, *Vocabulario medieval castellano*, *capirotada* is unhelpfully defined as *olla podrida*, 'stew,' an instance of that word's use dating back to 1276. In his *Banchetti* (1549) Messisbugo interestingly offers a recipe for *suppa di capirotta francese* – French *capirotta* sops (ed. Faccioli, *Arte della cucina*, I, 297) – which is similar to Scappi's cheese version of this *pottaggio* but without the garlic that Scappi suggests; see Recipe 227, below.

74. To make a pottage of wether's feet.

Skinned and cleaned, the feet are cut up into small pieces and put on the fire in a pot in enough water to cover them, along with slices of prosciutto, verjuice, white wine, chopped onions, common spices and enough saffron. Then the pot is stopped up and set to boil on the coals away from the flame for three hours. When they are cooked, they are served hot with their broth over them. It is optional whether a handful of beaten herbs is put in at the end.

Those feet can also be done in the same way as the calf's feet of Recipe 48.

75. Various ways to cook every sort of viscera of a wether.

The liver of a wether, the animal having just been slaughtered, has to be prepared in order to be good. Care has to be taken with it, for often it is splotched with certain discolorations which have soil in them. However, if it has no spots, you can do it up in all the ways the cow's liver is done in Recipe 19. And the same for the wether's lung. Its tripe are mostly used for making lute strings; when they are fresh and very clean, though, they can be cooked like the calf's.

76. To prepare every cut – that is, every part – of a goat and chamois.

Get that meat in the proper season, which begins in November and runs to the end of January, because during that time the animals are less smelly and much fatter. To boil it, follow the above directions for wether, and serve it with garlic sauce. If it is a billy goat, though, the hindquarters, stuck with cloves of garlic, can be roasted on the spit; if a wild mountain goat[76.1] – which is a billy goat or a castrated one[76.2] – it is quite a bit better than the previous ones, especially if it is not old. From its flesh you can make all of the dishes that are made above from the wether. The mountain goat is much better in summer and fall, however, than in any other season.

The chamois is an animal that lives on bare hills and resembles a goat but its horns are more rippled and sharper, and it is more agile than a goat. In winter all the dishes made from goat can be made from chamois.

Something of the mystery of this composition's nature remains in Scappi's other recipes that make use of its name: Recipes II,134 (where it is spelled *capirottata* and functions as a garnish), 157 (where a 'bastard' form of it is made), 158 ('common *capirotata*'), 227 ('*capirotata* sops'), and III,266. See also Barbara Santich, 'Capirattata and capirotada,' *Petits Propos Culinaires*, 12 (1982): 70–1. That article refers to two unnumbered recipes in Ruperto de Nola, *Libro de guisados* (first published in 1529; see 71 and 151 in the edition by Pérez: Bibliography, Part 2, *s.v.* Mestre Robert) – but only confirms the difficulty of identifying a genre of preparation with so variable ingredients and uses. The name is related to the French *chivrolée* of earlier years and may derive from the word for wild goat or deer. The fourteenth-century Catalan *Libre de sent soví* (ed. Rudolf Grewe, 123, Recipe 90) offers directions for a similar serving sauce for wild boar, bear, deer (*cabirol*) or any other game meat.

[76.1] Here Scappi uses two terms: *stambecco, che altri chiamano arcibecco*.

[76.2] *il qual'è caprone o castrato.* Scappi seems in any case to rely upon a male mountain goat.

77. To roast goat kids whole on a spit or braised.

To be good a kid needs to be as yet unweaned, because when it grazes its meat is not so tasty but rather woody. Such tiny animals need to be caught at the right time, their season beginning in January up to the end of June, even though in Rome you can find them just about the whole year. If it is small, and unweaned, as I say, after being butchered remove its hair in hot water as is done with a suckling pig. Eviscerate it through its flank or spine, wash it inside and out in several changes of water, and stuff it with a combination of pork fat and beaten prosciutto, mixed with its pluck[77.1] and liver, which must be very clean, along with common spices, prunes, dried visciola cherries, creamy unsalted cheese and eggs; in summer rather than prunes and dried cherries put in gooseberries or whole verjuice grapes and muscatel pears[77.2] and other fruit that is not overripe. When it has been stuffed, sew up the hole,[77.3] or else the spine because it will always do up better using the spine than elsewhere. Mount it on a spit without blanching it, fixing it snugly so it does not slip, and cook it over a low fire. As it begins to feel the heat, grease its skin with pork fat: that is done to keep it from drying out and so it does not burn. If it is skinned, though, when it is stuffed blanch it in water and, when cooled, stick it with fine lardoons of pork fat and cook it over a low fire. Whichever way it is cooked, serve it hot – the skinned one with orange juice and cut olives over top, or else sautéed spring onions; the one with its hair removed, served plain like that. Such little animals do not need their head cut off, nor their feet.

If you want to braise the skinned one, though, when it is stuffed put it into an earthenware baking dish containing melted pork fat and enough broth to half cover it. Into that broth put common spices and, in winter, chopped onions, in summer, other fruits, adding in verjuice or verjuice grapes and must syrup. Set it to cook like that under a bell or in the oven, turning it over from time to time so that both sides get browned. When it is done serve it hot with its enriched broth over it. In the same way you can do up a young stag, a young deer – even an unborn baby deer – in its season, which runs from March throughout May. It is eaten by many lords.[77.4]

78. To boil, roast and make many dishes from every cut – that is, part – of a goat kid, with the exception of the head.

If you want to boil the forequarters of the kid, immediately they are skinned put them on the fire in boiling water. If you want to stuff them with beaten herbs,

[77.1] In Recipes II,56 and V,12 Scappi qualifies *coratella* by saying he means only the animal's lungs. That may well be his intention here also. See also the pluck in Recipes 80 and 105, below.

[77.2] *pere moscarole*, changed with a metathesis of the liquid consonants in the 1581 reprinting to *pere moscalore*.

[77.3] This *buco* has presumably been made in the animal's flank, the other optional place through which to eviscerate it being along its 'schiena,' the spine or back.

[77.4] The singular here, *usato*, may limit the lordly preference to the deer fœtus.

spices, eggs and cheese, that is optional. When they are cooked, serve them hot with green sauce or some other sauce in dishes. Boiled, they can also be sautéed in pork fat and put on the grill.

From them you can make all the dishes that are made from breast of veal in Recipe 33.

However, if you have hindquarters, which require spit-roasting, immediately after being skinned blanch them in boiling water, take them out, let them cook, lard them with fine lardoons of pork fat, then mount them on a spit and cook them. Serve them hot with orange juice over them, or some other garnish. Those quarters can also be stuffed with a mixture composed like the one with which the goat kid is stuffed whole in the previous recipe. You can roast the forequarters the same way.

If you want a pottage of those forequarters, cut them up into small bits and put them first to sauté in melted pork fat in a pot, stirring them often. And follow all of the directions given for the breast of veal in Recipe 34.

In all the above ways you can prepare an unweaned lamb, getting it, though, in its season, which occurs twice a year, in the spring and fall.

79. Various ways to cook a goat kid's head.

Get the head just as soon as the animal has been slaughtered and remove its hair in hot water. Split it in half, washing it in several changes of water, especially those little passages[79.1] that are often full of mucous. To stuff it, dig out the brains and parboil them; when cool, cut them up small and mix them with grated cheese, beaten eggs, common spices, mint, sweet marjoram and beaten parsley, and put that mixture back into the place where the brains were. Join the halves of the head together, binding them with a cord, and set it into a stewpot to cook like that in enough meat broth to cover it by four fingers. With it put a little prosciutto and common spices; in winter also put in some prunes, dried visciola cherries and a handful of beaten herbs; in summer, instead of prunes and dried cherries, gooseberries or else verjuice grapes. Serve it hot with its broth over top.

Should you not wish to stuff the head, you need only clean away the bloodiness and the filth that is in its nostrils, and cook it as above.

To do it on a spit, when it is clean cook it as you do the dehaired goat kid of Recipe 77. To do it boiled or roasted without any bone, when its hair has been removed follow the directions for the calf's head in Recipe 24.

To glaze it and sauté it or[79.2] roast it on a grill, when it is clean – divide the head in two the better to clean it – rejoin the halves and parboil them. When that

---

[79.1] The *canalette* are nasal. In Recipe II,26 for a calf's head Scappi insists on thoroughly cleaning the *canalette delle narici*. See also further on in the present recipe.

[79.2] Scappi wrote 'and' twice for these three procedures. Roasting the head on a grill is an alternative option that he will deal with further on after first telling how to glaze and sauté it.

is done, take them out of the broth and let them cool. Make up a mixture of beaten eggs, cheese, grated bread, beaten herbs, sugar, pepper, cinnamon and saffron, and with that coat both sides of the head. Fry them in melted pork fat or rendered fat. When done in such a way that they are cooked on both sides, serve them hot, dressed with sugar, cinnamon and cut up limes.

To do the head on a grill, when it is parboiled you separate one half of it from the other and clean the tongue. When the head has cooled a little, sprinkle it with fennel flour and salt, and put it on the grill. Onto each half put a slice of pork fat so that it does not dry out. When it is somewhat browned on both sides, serve it hot with a sauce over it made of rose vinegar, sugar, raisins, pepper, cloves and cinnamon.

In all of those ways you can cook the head of an unweaned lamb. With the kid's eyes and the ears you can do all of those fricassees and dishes that are done with those of a calf in Recipe 53.

80. Various ways to cook the viscera of those goat kids.

When the gall bladder has been cut away, the liver can be fried, whole or cut up, in melted rendered fat. It can also be wrapped in a caul and spit-roasted. It is prepared in all the ways that veal liver is done in Recipe 55. The sweetbreads and testicles can be done in all the ways that a calf's are done in Recipe 49. Of the pluck and tripe a pottage can be made as of the calf's in Recipe 56. After having been boiled, the tripe can also be sautéed in melted rendered fat with beaten spring onions, adding in the liver cut up into bits. That is served hot with orange juice and pepper over it. The same can be done with the pluck. But if you want to roast the tripe and pluck on a spit, remove the tripe from the caul[80.1] so it can be cut more easily; slide the tripe down the middle. The intestine comes out whole. Get a small slicing knife[80.2] – on its tip there must be a small ball of hard white wax so that while you are cutting the intestine the knife's point will not catch; also hold the intestine loosely. When the intestine is clean, get the parboiled lung, cut it in long strips and coat the strips with grated cheese, beaten eggs, dry fennel flour, spices and salt. Put the strips on a spit alternating with slices of pork fat, then wind it around – that is, apply the intestine over the spitted slices of lung, beginning at one end and gradually applying it[80.3] until the slices are covered and take on the look of a short piece of yarn. As the intestine is wrapping itself onto the spit, though, sprinkle it continuously with the mixture with which the slices of lung are coated. Cook it over a low fire, basting it often with melted rendered fat. When it is done, serve it hot, dressed with a garnish of vinegar, sugar and spices.

[80.1] That is, from the membrane containing them in the kid's peritoneal cavity.

[80.2] See Scappi's assortment of knives in Plate 13.

[80.3] As the spit turns the intestine winds progressively along it.

If you want it done with the caul, after it is on the spit as described above, get some of that mixture with the beaten eggs and coat the intestines all around with that. Then wrap the caul around them, tying it with a cord. Cook it slowly over a low fire until the mixture is firm. Baste it with melted rendered fat, giving it a sprightlier fire. When it is done, serve it up hot, with cut-up limes over top. When the intestines are from an unweaned goat kid, however, there is no need to split them but only to press out what is inside, which is white.

81. Another way to cook a goat kid's tripe and lungs.

Get the tripe without the caul being cut away from them, and prepare them with a butcher's sharpening file or else with a smooth iron awl – of the sort used to make small filter bags[81.1] with a needle – in such a way that the tripe stay all together with the caul. When the tripe are cut away, wash them in several changes of water; to purge them better, though, when they are washed a second time put the tripe with white salt in a copper colander[81.2] that has rather large holes, and pound it with your hand until you see the sludge coming out through the holes. Again wash them in several changes of water, and set them to parboil in unsalted water along with the small lungs until they are half cooked. Remove the tripe from the broth and cut them up into small pieces; do the same with the lungs and put everything into a pot or some other vessel in enough fat meat broth to cover it, adding in a little prosciutto. When it is cooked, put in pepper, cinnamon, saffron and beaten herbs. Serve it hot with its broth. In summer you can add in gooseberries or seeded verjuice grapes. If you are not putting in any prosciutto, you thicken it with beaten eggs and grated cheese. Along with the tripe, before they are taken out of the broth, you can put the liver cut up into small pieces after it has first been half sautéed.

Those tripe can also be fried coated with egg, and also be cooked on the grill the way a cow's tripe are cooked in Recipe 57.

82. To prepare young roe deer, young stag and unweaned young fallow deer.

Although I mentioned them in the recipe for goat kid[82.1] – saying that when those young animals are to be spit-roasted, their hair can be removed in hot water right after they have been killed and they can be stuffed with the same mixture as that with which the goat kid is stuffed in Recipe 77 – yet it seems to me that the place to deal with them is here. So I say that any of them that are to be skinned before being put on a spit should be basted with their blood: that is done so they

---

[81.1] *calzette*: though not so named, a *calceto* is pictured in Plate 18.

[81.2] See the two sorts of *foratoro* illustrated in Plates 9 and 10.

[82.1] That is, in Recipe 77.

will be tastier. If you want to plump[82.2] the small animals, that should be done by searing them on a grill, not by blanching them in water. They can also be braised and cooked in the oven as the goat kid is done in Recipe 77.

If you want to make a fricassee of them, cut them into pieces, wash them in wine and cook them in that same wine that is used for washing them after putting it through a filter. Add in prosciutto which is not rancid, to make it tastier. When those pieces are cooked, take them out and sauté them with spring onions in melted rendered fat.

If you want to make a larded broth of them, follow the directions that will be given in the recipe for that.[82.3] The season of those animals runs from May to the end of July.

83. To roast a piglet, either domestic or wild.

Just as soon as those animals are killed, remove their hair in hot water and follow all the directions for stuffing and cooking them that are given for the above animals. Their viscera – that is, the liver, tripe and lungs – can be prepared in all of the ways the goat kid's are done in Recipe 80. The season of those animals is twice in a year: fall and when ears of grain are forming.[83]

84. To roast the leg,[84.1] shoulder and loin of a young stag, roebuck and fallow deer.[84.2]

When the above animals begin to graze they are not as good as when still milk-fed up to six months of age, and even up to a year. Their season runs from the end of August throughout December. If you want to roast their leg, shoulder and loin, those have to be hung briefly. When they are skinned and their hair removed, without being washed they have to be rubbed clean with a cloth. They are seared on a grill, then stuck with lardoons of marbled pork fat which have been dredged in pepper, cinnamon, cloves, nutmeg and salt – which lardoons should go through from one side to the other and be rather thick. With its foot left on each one, they

---

[82.2] The verb *rifare* (already used in Recipes 6 and 61, above) has a specific culinary sense of refreshing or restoring. This initial cooking procedure is intended to protect and even enhance the natural qualities of a meat.

[82.3] Recipe II,85.

[83] *il tempo della spica.* See also Recipe VI,168.

[84.1] This *cigotto* (already seen, spelled *zigotto*, in Recipe 42) is properly the upper hind leg of an animal. In this case Scappi directs that the hoof not be severed from the leg.

[84.2] Several later recipes refer back to this and Recipe 85 as being for goat. Either Scappi or his printer omitted goat from this list of animals or the author assumes that the reader will automatically assimilate the domestic animal to its wild brothers: see the beginning of Recipe 87 as well as the end of Recipe 77 for goat kid, suggesting the recipe's possible use also for young stag, young deer and unborn baby deer.

are mounted on a spit. Let them cook over a low fire, catching their drippings. When they are done, serve them hot, dressed with a garnish of rose vinegar, sugar and the above spices along with the drippings.

In the same way you can roast the shoulder and rack of ribs. However, a delicate tenderloin can be done up into all the dishes for which the loin of veal is done. And the lean meat of the leg can go into croquettes and fingers, bresaola[84.3] and all of those preparations that are made with lean veal in Recipe 43.

85. To make a larded broth[85.1] of the breast and ribs of the above animals.

Take the breast or the ribs and divide them in several small pieces, wash them in wine and water, and then filter that washwater and put it into an earthenware or copper pot with pepper, cinnamon, ground nutmeg,[85.2] pork fat and diced prosciutto. Then put in the pieces of meat with a few sage tips, a few raisins, must syrup or sugar, prunes and dried visciola cherries. Set the pot, stopped up, to boil on the coals away from the flame for an hour and a half. Then serve it hot. If into the larded broth you wish to put whole onions that have been half cooked under the coals, that is optional. If you want to make that broth thicker, though not too much so, that can be done with almonds, roasted and ground, or with toast soaked in must syrup and rose vinegar. If you put onions into the broth you can leave out the prunes and dried cherries.

86. Several ways to cook the liver of those animals, which livers have been cleaned of the gall bladder.

The liver of those animals, when cleaned of the membrane that it has around it, can be fried, whole or cut up, in melted rendered fat. It can also be spit-roasted, whole or in small pieces with the caul around them as the calf liver is done in Recipe 55. I do not think any other viscera from those animals are good, except for the eggs of the roe deer, of which I have spoken in Chapter 35 of the First Book.

87. Various ways to cook stag meat.

A stag is quite a bit larger than a goat, even though they are of the same species, but its flesh is somewhat more russet in colour and tougher, tending to the colour of cow's flesh, especially when it is old. To roast it or boil it, or for any other preparation, it has to be hung. If it is fat and has been hung, you can make all those dishes from it that are made with the roebuck, above, getting it in its season, which begins in October and goes to the end of January. The loin, which is under

---

[84.3] See Recipe II,45.

[85.1] A form of Scappi's *brodo lardiero* has a long history in European cookery. Its essence is the flavour of bacon or pork fat. The *Viandier's bouilli lardé* (Recipe 5) is a perfectly elementary version of Scappi's rich dish. See Gillian Riley's *The Oxford Companion to Italian Food*, 78.

[85.2] See Plate 14 for a *grata noci moschiate*, a nutmeg grater.

the ribs and attached to the kidneys, can be cooked in all those ways that are used for the cow's loin in Recipe 8. The animal's testicles are not overly appreciated; if you want to do them up, though, follow the directions set out for those of a calf in Recipe 54. Immediately after the stag has been killed its liver can be cooked in all the ways in which that of the roe deer is done in the above recipe. You can also semi-salt or fully salt its flesh[87] in the way the flesh of an ox is done in Recipe 4. From the lean meat of the upper leg you can make all the dishes that are made from the wild boar in Recipe 91.

88. Various ways to cook bear meat.

The bear has to be young and caught in its season, which is the winter, for even though in July it is much fatter because of its grazing, nevertheless in winter its flesh gives off a less offensive smell. When it is skinned, take its best parts, which are the legs and the shoulders, and let them hang a little. For spit-roasting, sear them on a grill, not larded but only sprinkled with salt, fennel, pepper, cinnamon and cloves. Mount them on a spit and cook them as a goat is done. With that meat you can make all the dishes that are made with a stag, above. The head of a goat, stag and bear are not good and not commonly used, nor is bear[88] meat, though I have prepared it.

89. Various ways to cook porcupine flesh.

Get a porcupine in August because at that time, owing to its feeding, it is very fat, even though its flesh has a less bad odour between October and January. After the animal has been killed let the flesh hang, in winter for four days and in summer for a day and a half. When it is skinned, divide it crosswise and sprinkle the hind half, without blanching it, with the same condiments, with salt, as were sprinkled on the goat's leg in Recipe 84. Stud it with some cloves of garlic and whole cloves and rosemary tips to take away its bad smell. Then set it to roast on a spit, catching the drippings. When it is done serve it up hot, dressed with a garnish of must syrup, rose vinegar, pepper, cinnamon, cloves and the drippings.

You can also roast that animal whole, or do it braised in an oven, if it is stuffed in the way the goat kid is stuffed in Recipe 77. With the forequarters you can make a larded broth the way it is done with a goat in Recipe 85.[89] Moreover, after those forequarters are parboiled and cut up into pieces you can sauté them in

---

[87] The two operations are similar up to the point where the meat, having steeped in a dense brine, is removed. Meat that is *misaltata* can be further prepared and eaten right away. If *saltata*, it is dried and put away for future use; before that use it must normally be desalted to some extent.

[88] Presumably Scappi means the mature animal here – despite the title of this recipe.

[89] Recipes 85 and 84 are for stag, roebuck and deer; there may be an omission of 'goat' from the rubric of Recipe 84. Scappi does, however, tend to view a goat as a domesticated cousin of those other, wild animals. The same reference to the 'goat' in Recipe 85 is found in Recipes 91, 94 and 97.

melted rendered fat and beaten onions. You serve that with verjuice, pepper and cinnamon over top. None of its viscera, except for the liver, can be prepared for eating; when the liver is fresh it can be done like the goat's in Recipe 86.

90. Various ways to cook a hedgehog piglet.

A hedgehog is of the same species as a porcupine. After it is skinned or else its fur removed in hot water, and it is eviscerated, it can be stuffed and spit-roasted or[90] braised in an oven like the above porcupine, catching it in its season, which begins in April and goes throughout the fall, although it is much fatter in July and August because of its feeding.

91. To cook all sorts of wild boar flesh.

If a wild piglet is small it can be done like the domestic piglet in Recipe 83; if it is big, though, it is skinned. Of it you can make all those dishes made of the goat in Recipe 84. But an old wild boar, which has a brisket, has its hair removed in hot water. To be roasted on a spit the legs have to be skinned and seared on a grill and stuck with whole cloves, then set to roast on the spit over a low fire with chopped onions beneath,[91.1] or pieces of quince. A wild piglet's legs can be roasted that same way. Get one or the other in its proper season – the wild piglet from mid-August and the boar from October, both through to the end of February. A rack of ribs from a boar, when the boar has a brisket, is quite a bit better stewed in wine with prosciutto, whole onions, pepper, cinnamon, cloves, nutmeg, raisins, muscatel raisins and sugar, with the same amount again of water as wine. But when the rack of ribs is skinned it can be roasted on a spit with chopped onions beneath, and it will always be tastier – provided[91.2] it has sat for two hours in a press with a little salt and fennel flour, or coriander. But when that rack is from a young pig that does not have a brisket it can be spit-roasted with its hide; it can also be set in a seasoning for four hours before roasting.

With the forequarters and the belly you can make a larded broth and fricassees in all those ways described for the forequarters of a goat in Recipe 85. Of lean meat from the leg you can make all of the preparations that are made from the leg of veal in Recipe 42. You can also cook the rack of ribs along with the brisket, getting a piece of pork throat, which is always bloodier than other cuts, and washing it in white wine and water; the same is done with the rack of ribs which is cut apart into pieces. Then filter that washwater and put it with the meat into an earthenware

---

[90] The text has 'and.'

[91.1] Presumably in the dripping pan, although Scappi does not say so.

[91.2] The phrase here is *ma quando*, literally 'but when.' Scappi writes a succession of three *ma quandos* whose clauses are separated by only a comma. This second clause seems most likely to qualify the preparation that has just been mentioned; the sense of this second *ma quando* must be 'especially if.' The same sort of supplemental conditioning follows the last *ma quando*.

or copper stewing pot, or a cooking pot,[91.3] with crushed pepper, whole cloves, whole cinnamon and crushed nutmegs – the quantities of each depending on the amount of meat there is – adding in marbled prosciutto that has been diced, a little rose vinegar and must syrup, or else sugar, so that the mixture has both a tang and a sweetness to it. Boil that with the pot stopped up and without skimming it except when it is half done, at which time you add in pitted dates, prunes and dried visciola cherries. If you want to put in whole onions that have first been parboiled or cooked under the coals, that is optional. With all that together, finish off cooking. When it is done, serve it hot with broth and other things over top, being very careful that the meat does not fall apart because sometimes the meat is cooked and the brisket is quite tough. Again, you can set that rack of ribs in salt for two days and then boil it in plain water, serving it hot with garlic sauce or mustard over top or in dishes.

Furthermore, after boiling it plain, you can let it cool and cut it apart rib by rib along with the brisket, sprinkling it with pepper and fennel flour. Heat it on a grill until it browns slightly on both sides. Serve it hot with orange juice over it.

Again, you can sauté those ribs with beaten spring onions, and serve them dressed with mild spices and orange juice. In the same way you can prepare that animal's belly. If you want to remove the hair of an old wild boar so that it stays white – whenever that boar is fresh and has been dead for not more than a day, because the hair can be removed more easily then than when it has hung – if you want to remove its hair so it stays white, as I said, put the piece of the boar with its hair downwards in cold water in a kettle large enough for it to be under the water. Heat the water slowly until it boils with the boar flesh in it: that is done so the water can better penetrate the fur. When the water is boiling, take the meat out and adroitly remove the coarse hairs with your hand and the down with a shaving knife.[91.4] Wash it in several changes of water. That way it will stay white. Alternatively, you can remove its hair with fire: singe the coarse hair until you get down to the downy hair; then get a hot iron shovel[91.5] and pass it over the hide, and with the knife shave off the down. When it is shaved, put it into warm water and leave it there for an hour, then shave it again with the knife until you see it white. But the one whose hair is removed in water will be quite a bit cleaner because the roots of the hair will be removed. There are some people who remove hair in limed water – that is, they boil lime in the water; others do it with strong

---

[91.3] For the differences between these vessels see a *stufatoro* in Plates 8 and 9 and a *pignatta* in Plate 10.

[91.4] Two knives designed for scraping are shown at the top right of Plate 13.

[91.5] This is the *pala focata* seen in Recipe 63, above, and elsewhere. Here it is explicitly qualified as being of iron.

lye;[91.6] but done by either of these last two methods it will not be as tasty or as good, because it will always have the stink of the pig's gut.

When they are taken out fresh, the liver, lungs and intestines can be prepared in all the ways the calf's are done in Recipes 55 and 56. The blood when it is fresh can be done in all the ways a domestic pig's is done.

92. To cook a wild boar's head in wine, water, vinegar and spices.

Get the head just after the boar has been killed, remove its hair in hot water in the above way and clean it carefully. Set it to cook in an ample vessel, a tall one rather than squat so it is completely covered, snout upwards, with enough wine, vinegar, water, salt and pepper, the pepper being crushed. Cook it with a sprig of dry fennel to give it flavour. When it is done but not disintegrating, take it out. Then serve it hot or cold as you wish, with oranges in its mouth and with mustard or some other sauce in dishes.

The cheeks are usually cut into slices, browned a little on the grill over a low fire, and served with orange juice or else with rose vinegar and sugar. The snout and ears are also sliced thinly and served with mustard or onion sauce over them. The brains are dug out and sliced thinly, heated on the grill on cardboard coated with rendered fat. The eyes can be done like the cheeks and ears.

93. Various ways to cook every sort of hare and rabbit.[93]

Hare caught with a dog are always more tasty than those caught in a net or by any other means; and they are a lot better in their season, which runs from August to the end of February. In the spring for the most part they are pregnant; I have never been able to distinguish between the male and female because they all bear young and all of them are of both sexes – as I have several times seen looking in their lower parts.

Should you want to spit-roast one, when it has not been too torn by the dogs, clean it, eviscerate it and stuff it with a composition made like the stuffing for the whole goat kid, stuffed and roasted or braised, in Recipe 77. When it has been stuffed, blanch it in water and stick it with fine lardoons of pork fat. Mount it on a spit and cook it. When done, it needs to be served hot with some sort of garnish over it. Stuffed like that it can be braised in an oven.

If you want to roast the hind parts, when they have been skinned and cleaned of their fur rub them with the animal's blood without washing them, and sear them on the grill. Stick them with a few whole cloves and pork fat, and roast them on the spit over a moderate fire. When they are done, serve them dressed with a sauce of rose vinegar, sugar and cinnamon.

[91.6] This *liscia* (today *lisciva*) was a caustic alcaline, potassium hydroxide, made by boiling ashes in water. Its most common use was in the laundering of clothes. Lime and lye were the principal caustic agents available in Scappi's day.

[93] For treatments of rabbit the reader has to pass on to the second half of the next recipe.

94. To sauté and make various fricassees of hares.

When the hare is skinned and eviscerated, take its loin, its ribs and its forequarters, and cut them up into small pieces. Boil them in salted water, then take them out, drain them and fry them in melted rendered fat or salt lard, with or without beaten spring onions. When they are done, serve them with mustard or black broth[94.1] or some other garnish over them.

If you want to make a larded broth with them, cut up the whole hare into pieces, wash them in white wine and water, strain that washwater and put it into a copper or earthenware stewing pot with the cut-up hare. Add in diced prosciutto, beaten pork fat, sage tips, pepper, cinnamon, cloves, nutmeg and a little must syrup and vinegar. Boil everything, keeping the pot stopped up. It is left optional whether you put plums, visciola cherries[94.2] and muscatel raisins into the larded broth. You can also thicken that broth with roasted almonds ground in a mortar, as is described in Recipe 85 for the larded broth of goat.[94.3]

A rabbit is a species of hare. It is found throughout the year because the animal is forever bearing its young, but its season is from May to the end of August. If you want to spit-roast it, the animal's fur is removed just as soon as it has been killed; it is eviscerated. It is stuffed the way a hare is done in the previous recipe. Sear it and cook it like the hare, leaving on its head and hind legs as is done for the whole hare. When it is roasted, serve it hot.

If you do not want it with its skin, take that off and sear the carcass on a grill or in water. Lard it with fine lardoons of pork fat and, without stuffing it, roast it on a spit. To keep it from drying out, tie two of them belly to belly on the spit. When they are done, serve them hot, dressed with a sauce made of rose vinegar, sugar and cloves.

Those small animals can be fried, and done in a larded broth like the hare. The stuffed ones can be braised in an oven like a hare.

95. To prepare a guinea pig and a dormouse.

Some people call a guinea rabbit a piglet[95.1] because it has a sharp snout and

---

[94.1] Scappi's recipe for this *brodo negro* is found at II,252.

[94.2] Usually Scappi explicitly qualifies cherries as 'dried' if he means so. That would certainly be the case for this dish if it were prepared when fresh plums and cherries were not available, in which case the translation should, of course, read 'prunes' rather than 'plums.'

[94.3] As pointed out before, Recipe 85 does not deal expressly with goat. Either Scappi changed the original contents of his Recipe 85 or he equates, generically, the animals that are dealt with in that recipe to a goat.

[95.1] Scappi's Italian for the guinea pig or cavy (of the genus *Cavia*) is *coniglio d'India*, literally 'Indian cony.' In the sixteenth century there was still some mystery about the origins and nature of the rodent, a native of South America. The turkey (called 'Indian fowl') shared the same vague origins: the creatures came from somewhere over in the Western Indies.

small, round ears and a fur that is lighter in colour than our domestic animal[95.2] – and that fur is rather more like a pig's bristles than wool. If you want to spit-roast it, remove its hair in hot water, eviscerate it and stuff it with a mixture like what is used for the goat kid in Recipe 77. Mount it on a spit and cook it over a low fire. You can also roast it empty and braised in an oven.

You can do a dormouse that way.[95.3] It is a small animal with a long furry tail, a sharp snout and sharp teeth; it feeds on chestnuts and walnuts and is born in those trees. Its season begins in October and goes through to the end of February because in those months it is fat. That is the same season as for the guinea pig, although in Rome and elsewhere in Italy they are found throughout the year.

96. Various ways to cook the head of a domestic pig.

If the head is from a small pig, when its hair is removed in hot water and it is cleaned of all filth, you can spit-roast it without taking out its tongue; or you can boil it in salted water. Serve it with garlic sauce or some other sauce. If, however, it is from a large pig, you can cook it in wine, vinegar, water and spices the way you cook a wild boar's head in Recipe 92. You can also split it, uncooked, through the middle and boil it in well-salted water. When it is done, take it out of the broth and let it cool. Then roast it on a grill, serving it hot with some garnishes on it. You can also salt it along with its feet: when it has been in salt for eight days it is washed[96.1] in several changes of water and set it to cook. You can serve it with strong mustard.[96.2] With that head you can make gelatin as is said in the book on sauces[96.3] and gelatins in Recipe 242. The brains can be prepared in all those ways given for calf's brains in Recipe 52. The tongue can be prepared in all the ways the calf's tongue is done in Recipe 29. You can also salt the tongue, like

---

[95.2] That is, a domestic rabbit.

[95.3] Scappi's *ghiro* enjoyed a long gastronomic history in the Italian peninsula. A similar recipe for stuffed dormice (*glires*) is included in the *De re coquinaria* of Apicius (ed. Jacques André [Paris: Belles Lettres, 1974], 105, Recipe 397; Eng. tr. Joseph Dommers Vehling [Chicago: Hill, 1936], 205, Recipe 396).

[96.1] The typesetter of the 1581 reprinting omitted the verb, *si laverà: per otto dì in sale, a piu acque,* ...

[96.2] A century before Scappi's day another Italian cook offered two recipes for mustard, a French mustard and an Italian mustard. The Italian variety is made with mustard seed, ground almonds, must reduced to a sweet syrup, verjuice and, optionally, spices, the whole strained to thicken it. The French mustard has only mustard seed and a tart wine or plain must; of it the anonymous author comments disparagingly, and Scappi would likely concur, that it has 'neither head nor feet' (*The Neapolitan Recipe Collection*, Recipes 121 and 122).

[96.3] Scappi reveals a trace of an earlier layout of his *Opera*. The series of 'sauces' are incorporated into the present book, toward its end. Gelatin is considered related to a sauce because it is used to suspend and garnish other foodstuffs.

the head, and often it is put in the middle of salamis[96.4] when making them. In addition, it is wrapped in intestines and put in salt with those intestines. In summer it is cooked with fresh peas and broad beans. That head needs to be prepared in the pig's season, which runs from November to mid-February, although in some places that are cooler than Rome it begins in mid-September.

97. Various ways to prepare the neck and throat of a domestic pig.

Because these two cuts are the bloodiest and the tastiest, when they are skinned and cut away from the head, they are cut up into pieces. A larded broth is made from them as is done with the goat in Recipe 85. When they are cooked, those pieces can also be sautéed in melted rendered fat with or without spring onions, and served with onion sauce or some other thick sauce over top.

98. Various ways to cook the breast of a domestic pig.

When the breast has been skinned and cut away from the other members, take the best part – that is, the tip[98] – and sprinkle it with salt and dry fennel seed, letting it sit with that mixture for three hours. Roast it on a spit. If it is from a young pig, though, it can be roasted on a grill. Do the same with the ribs that are under the shoulder. When the meat has cooked in any of the above-mentioned ways, serve it hot with sautéed spring onions over top or with any other sauce you like.

But if the pig is very old, the breast will be better boiled in salted water than roasted. When it has boiled it can be served with garlic sauce or mustard or any other sauce you like. After being taken out of the broth, it can also be sprinkled with pepper, salt, fennel flour and grated bread, and then roasted on a grill, and served dressed with a garnish made of rose vinegar, sugar and common spices.

A sow's belly is put into a press for six hours with pepper, cinnamon, cloves, nutmeg, ground fennel seed and salt, then wrapped around in a sugared caul and mounted on a spit. Cook it slowly. It is optional whether you cut it up into pieces. If you want to parboil it first, before putting it in the press, that can be done.

99. Various ways to prepare a rack of ribs of a domestic pig.

If the pig is young, the ribs can be spit-roasted with or without their skin. In the dripping pan have chopped onions which will be cooked with the grease that drips from the roast as it cooks. On the ribs you can put a few sprigs of rosemary. Before mounting the rack on a spit, sprinkle it with salt and ground coriander. You can also set the ribs to steep for a day in a seasoning composed of vinegar, must syrup, cloves of garlic and coriander. Then cook it on the spit in the above way, serving it hot and dressed with a sauce made of the same seasoning.

[96.4] See, at the end of Recipe 103, Scappi's curious comment about *salami* made with pork ham.

[98] Previously also called the *callo* or brisket, the best part of that being considered the lower, fattier part.

If you want to make Venetian bresaola from that rack of ribs, you have to cut it apart rib by rib, beating each rib with the spine of a knife, and sprinkling them with salt, crushed pepper and ground coriander. When they have sat piled one on top of the other for an hour, they should cook on a grill over a low fire, being turned often. When done, they should be served with orange juice or some other sauce over them.

100. Various ways to make a delicate tenderloin of a domestic pig.

When the loin is from a young pig it can be sprinkled with salt, ground coriander and crushed pepper, wrapped in a caul and cooked on a spit. It is served hot with some sort of sauce on it. But if it is from an old pig, it will not be as tender. Nevertheless, both of them can be used for all those dishes that are made with the veal loin described in Recipe 40.

101. Various ways to do pork belly.

When the belly has its hair or hide removed it will sit in salt for three hours,[101.1] then it is boiled in plain water. It is served hot with garlic sauce or mustard over it. From the leaner parts you can make larded broth. From the part that is boiled in plain, unsalted water you can make *tortellini* as is directed in the Recipe for them.[101.2] If the belly is from a young sow, it will be better than from a male.

102. To prepare the leg – that is, the thigh – of a domestic pig.

If the leg is from a young pig, skinned, it can be spit-roasted. From it can be made all the dishes made from the wether's leg in Recipe 68. From the lean meat can be made croquettes, fingers and meatballs, and all the dishes made above from veal.

103. To make mortadella[103.1] from lean meat of a domestic pig's leg, wrapped in a caul.

Get ten pounds of the above meat without any bone, skin or gristle, which meat has both fat and lean. Beat it with knives on a table, adding in eight ounces of ground salt, six ounces of dry sweet fennel, four ounces of crushed pepper, one ounce of ground cinnamon and half an ounce of ground cloves; everything should be well mixed together with your hand. Add in four ounces of cold water, mint

---

[101.1] The 1581 typesetter begins this recipe referring to an 'old pig' and then inserts a negative: *La pancia come sarà di porco vecchio, non farà stare in sale per tre hore, …*

[101.2] See Scappi's *tortelletti* in Recipes 177–180, below.

[103.1] Mortadella (Scappi's *mortatelle*) is the largest of all sausages. Originally made in Bologna, this provenance became its generic name in English in the form 'bologna' or 'baloney.' The Italian word *mortadella* has also migrated into English along with that variety of sausage. For its role in Italian gastronomy, see Riley *The Oxford Companion to Italian Food*, 333.

and sweet marjoram beaten with a little wild thyme. Let that sit in an earthenware or wooden vessel for four hours in a cool place. Get that pig's caul, with any hairs[103.2] thoroughly cleaned off, and softened in warm water. With the mixture and the caul make up mortadelle in the manner of *tommacelle*.[103.3] When they are finished, let them sit in a dry place for two days in winter. Then cook them on a grill, or else in a pan with melted rendered fat. The *tommacelle* can also be cooked on a spit interspersed with bay leaves; and mortadella can also be put lengthwise on a spit surrounded with sprigs of rosemary. Whichever way they are cooked, they need to be served hot.

With that same stuffing mixture[103.4] you can fill pork intestines which have first sat in salt. When they are filled, they can be left sitting for two days in winter, then they can be boiled. After the lean meat has been beaten you can also make saveloy sausages of it using the caul or intestines – for every ten pounds of it putting in a pound and a half of grated Parmesan cheese, an ounce and a half of ground cinnamon, another ounce and a half of ground pepper, an eighth of an ounce of saffron, half a beaker of cool water and three ounces of salt. When you have mixed all that together, you make the saveloy sausage with the caul or the intestines and cook them as above.

You can also make *tommacelle* with it, in a caul, adding in eight ounces of raisins and eight ounces of egg yolk. In winter those *tommacelle* will be much better after two days.

I shall not say anything about mortadella and other salamis that are made from that meat because they have never fallen within my professional concern.[103.5]

104. To cook a pig's 'tasty morsels' – I mean, those of a domestic pig.

The tasty morsels[104] are those that are attached to the throat, in the spot where other quadrupeds have sweetbreads. There are some, as well, attached to the spine close to the kidney. Those tasty morsels can be cooked in all the ways used for veal sweetbreads in Recipe 49.

[103.2] Presumably these *peli* represent any dirt (see Recipe 105, below) the caul may have picked up as it is handled.

[103.3] See the *tommacelle* of Recipes 107 ff.

[103.4] Lancelot de Casteau's recipes for both *Mortadelle* (48, specifying the use of grated Parmesan cheese) and *Sausisse de Bologne* (46; see Recipe 22, above) agree with Scappi in this paragraph.

[103.5] *non è mai stata mia professione*. Scappi means that in his various positions he has never had to make those seasoned and preserved meats. In all likelihood the household *spenditore*, the purchasing agent, would have ordered such supplies from a local tradesman or purveyor.

[104] In a calf the so-called *bocche saporite* are later (V,8) identified as the (upper) sweetbread or thymus gland. The other (lower) sort of sweetbread is that which Scappi identifies as the pancreas.

105. To cook a domestic pig's pluck in various ways.

Although the pluck and spleen are often ground up in a mixture for salami, nevertheless they can also be cooked in all the ways those of a calf are done in Recipe 56. Should you wish to put the pluck into a caul, boil it; get grated cheese, beaten herbs, pepper, cloves and cinnamon, and mix everything with raisins, beaten eggs and saffron. When the pluck is divided in two and cut away from the windpipe, put it into the caul packed around with that mixture. It will seize up in the manner of saveloy sausage.[105] Then put it on a spit or on a grill or in a pan with melted rendered fat.

106. Various ways to roast a domestic pig's liver.

If you want to spit-roast a pork liver in large pieces, when the membrane that is around it is removed, along with the gall bladder. Stick the pieces with lardoons of pork fat that have been dredged in pepper, cloves, cinnamon and sweet fennel, dry and ground. Put them onto a spit and cook them over a low fire. But if you want to put them into a caul with grated cheese and egg, follow the directions for pluck in the previous recipe.

If you want to make small *fegatelli*[106] of it, as are commonly made, cut the liver into several small egg-sized pieces, kneading them with your hand on a table for a quarter of an hour so the blood comes out of them: that is done to make the liver more tender. Sprinkle the pieces with pepper, cinnamon and dry fennel seed, encasing each of them in the fresh caul of that same pig. Cook them on a spit, being careful, though, that when they are put on the spit it is itself hot so that the *fegatelli* will grip it. Between each piece of liver there should be a bay leaf or a sage leaf or a slice of prosciutto. Take them down off the spit when they are a little undercooked rather than too well done. Serve them with salt, pepper and orange juice over them. If you want to keep them from drying out, when they are half cooked take them off the spit and put them into an earthenware or well-tinned copper pot with a little fat broth tinged with saffron, and a little pepper, cloves, cinnamon, and a little sugar or must syrup. Seal up the pot, put it on hot ash and keep it like that for an hour and a half. Then serve them with that sauce hot over them. When they are in the pot, you can put in ordinary raisins and muscatel raisins.

If the liver is from a sow that has just given birth or is pregnant, it will always be better than any other pork liver. In the same way you can also prepare wild boar liver when it is fresh.

---

[105] *si ridurrà*: literally, will reduce (in size) – that is, become more dense, more compact. Recipe 46 speaks of the saveloy stuffing having 'firmed up' (*saranno fermi*) on the grill as it cooks.

[106] Today these small delicacies of wrapped liver often contain more herbs than Scappi's variety, although Scappi's are in contact with bay and sage as they cook.

107. To make *tommacelle* from pork liver.[107.1]

When the liver has been cleaned of its membrane and its little nerves, boil it in unsalted water until the blood has fully drained. Then take it out and put it into cold water, leaving it there until it is firm. Then take it out and grate it lightly with the cheese grater.[107.2] For every pound of grated liver add in two ounces of very clean dry currants, the same amount of sugar, six ounces of raw beef marrow cut up into bits, three ounces of the same pig's kidney-fat from which the skin has been removed and which is diced, four ounces of grated Parmesan cheese, three-quarters of an ounce of cloves, an eighth of an ounce of saffron, four raw egg yolks and a little salt. When the mixture has been made up, get a pork caul with no hairs on it or any other dirt, and that has been softened in hot, saffron-tinged water; with that caul and the mixture make up *tommacelle* the size of a Florentine ball.[107.3] When they are made, coat the caul with beaten egg yolk; let them sit a day before cooking. Do them on a spit or on a grill or in a pan with melted rendered fat. Serve them hot with orange juice and suger over them.

108. Another way to make *tommacelle* with pork liver.

Grate two pounds of pork liver as above. Get a pound each of belly and of jowl fresh from the same pig. When these last have been cooked in salted water, take them out, let them cool and beat them small with knives. Mix them in with the grated liver, adding in six raw egg yolks, a pound of grated Parmesan cheese, three ounces of pitted dates ground in a mortar, four ounces of raisins, one ounce of cinnamon, one ounce of cloves, pepper and nutmeg combined, eight ounces of sugar, sufficient saffron, and beaten mint and sweet marjoram. Make up the *tommacelle* with that mixture and the caul in the way described above. Cook them in a pan with melted rendered fat, and serve them with orange juice and sugar over them.

[107.1] Scappi's three recipes for *tommacelle* differ mostly in the use of another cut of meat along with the liver.

Several antecedents prove that the preparation existed for several centuries before Scappi's day: see the fourteenth-century Italian collections, the *Libro della cocina*, Recipe 141, and the *Libro per cuoco*, Recipe 46. In the Latin *Liber de coquina*, Recipe I,12, a word for sausage, *tomaculum* or *tomaclum*, is used in the diminutive (plural), *tumacella*, in the sense of 'small sausages' (*salcicias*). The dish eventually migrated north from Italy as well. In their secondary ingredients, however, the *Tomaselle de foye* of Lancelot de Casteau (108) do not closely resemble those of Scappi, the Liegeois cook not mentioning fruit but calling for sautéed onions.

[107.2] In Plates 10 and 22 see the *gratta cascia*.

[107.3] In Recipe III,195 Scappi writes that a sea urchin is of the same size as this *palla Fiorentina*. A *gioco di pallone* used a *large*, inflated ball and is still current in Florence. The *palla Fiorentina* that Scappi knew would seem to be a sort of small handball.

109. To make *tommacelle* from the liver and delicate tenderloin of domestic pork.

Get two pounds of pork tenderloin and one pound of pork kidney with its fat still on it but cleaned of its skin and gristle; beat them small with knives. To that add two pounds of grated liver, one pound of pork kidney-fat with the skin removed, a pound of diced salt pork jowl,[109] boiled, a pound of grated Parmesan cheese, an ounce and a half of cinnamon, three-quarters of an ounce of pepper, an ounce of fennel flour, an ounce of cloves, nutmeg and ginger combined, half a pound of raisins and enough saffron. When that mixture is composed, make up the *tommacelle* in the above way. In winter let them sit for two days before cooking. They are cooked in all the ways described above.

With that same mixture you can stuff pork intestines after they have been in salt.

110. To make blood sausages[110.1] from the blood of a domestic pig.

Just as soon as the pig is killed, drain off its blood, and as it is draining put it through a filter or through a fine-meshed strainer: that is done so that hairs and other dirt do not get into the blood. When it has been filtered and is still warm, break it up with your hand because if it coagulates you cannot make black pudding of it. For every six pounds of blood, put a pound of fresh goat's or cow's milk into it – which milk should be somewhat warm – eight ounces of sugar, one and a half ounces of ground cinnamon, half an ounce of cloves, half an ounce of pepper, a quarter-ounce of ground nutmeg, a pound of fresh pork kidney-fat – with the skin off it and cut up into bits – half a pound of very clean dry currants, an ounce and a half of crushed raw aniseed, three ounces of salt and four ounces of onion – beaten and sautéed without burning. Then get large and small pork intestines that are very clean inside and out, and put that composition into the intestines, stuffing them but without bursting them: to make sure they will not burst, for every two handswidths of intestine stuff one and leave the other empty. When they are tied at each end so the stuffing cannot come out, put them carefully one by one into warm water in such a way that the stuffing fills out everywhere, and let them boil for a quarter of an hour. Then take them out. If you want to keep them for more than a day, keep them covered with a white linen cloth in a place that is dry and away from air currents. When you want to use them, warm them up in a broth and then cook them again on a grill. They can also be washed in melted rendered fat so they will not dry out; alternatively they can be kept on a slice of pork fat. They are served hot with mustard or some other sauce in dishes.

If you want them with broth, as is done in Milan, when they have parboiled, take them out of their first broth and put them into another pot with a meat broth,

---

[109] This *barbaglia* is so defined in Recipe V,50.

[110.1] These *sanguinacci* are closely related to the *migliacci*, black pudding, which Scappi mentions at the end of this recipe.

along with a pig's ears and snout – first semi-salted for a day, then cooked. To cook with all that put in some sage, getting a few tips of it. When those black puddings are cooked, serve them dressed with their broth, the snouts and ears. When they have cooled, they can also be sliced crosswise and sautéed in a pan in melted rendered fat and beaten spring onions. They are served hot with pepper and orange juice over them.

If you want to make black pudding, follow the directions given in Recipes 67 and 68 of the book on pastry.[110.2] With pig's blood you can make all those dishes that are made with calf's blood in Recipe 59.

111. To make rendered fat from the kidney-fat of a domestic pig.

In my first book I have shown how to distinguish good from bad in the matter of rendered fat, and how it is kept.[111.1] In the present recipe, I should like to tell how to make that rendered fat. To begin, get the fresh kidney-fat of a pig, cleaning it of its membranes, and cut it up into bits the size of dice: that is done so it will melt better and not burn, which would happen if it were beaten with knives. Put them into an ample kettle, and for every fifty pounds of the kidney-fat put five pounds of clear water into the bottom of the kettle before putting in the fat. Let the fat melt over a slow fire, stirring into it a pound of salt – more or less, depending on the length of time you will be wanting to store the rendered fat. When the fat has melted and boiled for half an hour, pour it off through a filter or fine strainer into an earthenware or wooden vessel, letting it stand until the moisture of the fat and the water have gone to the bottom. Then, slowly, pour it into another vessel of the same sort, minding that only what is on top is poured off.[111.2] Keep it in that vessel in a cool place until you need it.

112. To make rendered fat from the fat of a goose, duck and common hen.

Get a goose that has been freshly killed, plucked and drawn, and fill it with saveloy sausage, and sew up the hole so the stuffing cannot leak out. If you do not want to use saveloy, cut up the flesh of another goose into small pieces and put those into the carcass instead of the saveloy. When it is sewn up, put it without blanching it onto a spit and cook it slowly over a low fire, catching the liquid that falls under it into a clean pot. When the goose is done, so that it does not drip anymore, pour off that liquid through a strainer, adding in a little ground salt if the stuffing was not salted. Keep that rendered fat in a glazed earthenware vessel in a cool place. That sort of rendered fat is more appropriate for making thick soups

---

[110.2] The 1581 printing has *Cap. 67 & 78.*

[111.1] See Book I, §4.

[111.2] Scappi's wording cautions against disturbing the bottom: *avvertendo che il fondaccio non vade giu.* Compare the whole operation here with that which is described in Recipe II,162 for clarifying veal and kid kidney-fat.

than for other dishes. In the same way you can make it from a duck and from a common hen.

You can also make it another way: when those fowl are dead, get their fat, free of any skin, and beat it, or cut it up into bits, or pound it in a marble mortar, and follow the directions for doing it in a kettle with water as pork fat is done in the previous recipe. You can also do it with an alternative procedure, by putting the fat, after it is cut up, into a large glass vessel and putting that into a kettle with cold water, which kettle you set to boil until the fat has liquified. Then filter that with a little salt and keep it as above. You can also do it differently: when the fat is cut up, you put it in a glazed earthenware pot. For every ten pounds of fat also put in half a pound of rosewater and four ounces of ground salt, and let it disintegrate in the pot over a low fire with the pot covered. When it has all disintegrated, let it boil for half an hour, then pour it through a strainer into another earthenware vessel. Keep it as above.

Those sorts of rendered fat can be used instead of butter for making pastry for tourtes and other dough preparations.

113. To cook every sort of salted meat and salami.

The salted leg of a steer or an ox, the nape of an ox belaboured from the yolk[113.1] and the tongue of an ox or buffalo are the most tasty and best parts. Before they are cooked, all those meats need to sit in warm water until softened, and they have to be cooked in water in an ample pot. Sometimes tongues can be cooked in water and wine, but the other parts need to be cooked in water.

Salamis always need to be served cold. If they are semi-salted, though, cook them and serve them as is directed in the recipe for them.[113.2] In the same way prosciutti[113.3] from a wild boar and stag are cooked.

114. To cook every sort of pork salami.

Large salamis and prosciutti can be cooked in water and wine. Yet prosciutti are often cooked with new hay and water, mostly in May: that is done so they will take on the aroma of the new hay. However, before they are cooked they need to sit in warm water so they will stay more tender. When cooked, they are left to cool in the broth where they were cooked, then taken out and cleaned of any rank odour they may have about them.

Salamis have the intestine stripped from them and are served hot or cold as you like.

[113.1] *la coppa del bove affaticato dal giogo.* The *coppa* is the upper area behind the neck proper from which a modern chuck is cut. Until recently, bovines were raised primarily as draft animals; mature oxen and cows became a source of meat only after they ceased being otherwise useful.

[113.2] The reference is likely to the following recipe. See also Book I, §9.

[113.3] That is, here and in the next recipe, the cured hams of certain animals.

Prosciutti of young pigs are sometimes cooked in goat's or cow's milk, having first been set to steep to soften them as above, and having been boiled twice in plain water – that is, with a change of water between boilings – after boiling the first time for an hour, and being more than half cooked the second time. When they are out, skinned and cleaned of all dirt and still warm, put them into a pot where there is enough milk to cover them by three fingers, with two pounds of sugar for every eight pounds of prosciutto. Finish off cooking them the same way. When they are done, serve them hot with sugar and cinnamon over them.

Following the same process you can cook sowbelly, although it is sometimes done on a spit after being desalted. As I have said, mortadella, pork tongues in intestines, salt pork jowl and pork belly are cooked in legumes and herbs, and are served hot. *Salsiccioni* that are not extemely large are sometimes sliced crosswise, heated on a spit and served with orange juice over them.

115. To make various mixtures with which to stuff every sort of commonly eaten animal, quadruped and fowl, for spit-roasting.

Get four pounds of pork fat that is not rancid and with knives beat it finely together with two pounds of liver of a goat kid or of some other quadruped or commonly eaten fowl, and cut it up into small pieces, adding in beaten mint, sweet marjoram, burnet and parsley, four raw egg yolks, an ounce of pepper and cinnamon combined, half an ounce of ground cloves and nutmeg combined, half a pound of prunes, visciola cherries and morello cherries combined – in summer instead of those use gooseberries or verjuice grapes. Mix everything well together. Optionally you can put grated cheese, garlic cloves or sautéed spring onions.

You can also do them in a different way: when the pork fat is beaten with the same amount of lean veal or wether meat or young pork, without skin or gristle, put in with that four and a half ounces of marbled prosciutto, mixing in the above condiments, four ounces of raisins, a few parboiled artichoke hearts[115.1] or field mushrooms[115.2] peeled and well cleaned – or instead of mushrooms, truffles.

You can also make them another way: for every four pounds of beaten pork fat get two pounds of parboiled veal or goat-kid sweetbreads, one pound of the mixture for yellow saveloy,[115.3] four ounces of sugar, four egg yolks, a handful of herbs, nine not-too-ripe plums or else muscatel pears[115.4] without their flower

---

[115.1] The artichoke (*Cynara scolymus*), a variety of thistle, is occasionally used as an alternative to cardoon (*Cynara cardunculus*): see Recipes 120 and 213, below, for instance.

[115.2] The common field mushroom or agaric (in Scappi *prugnolo*) is either *Agaricus pruneolus* or *Tricholoma georgii*.

[115.3] See the note in Recipe 26, above.

[115.4] Concerning these *pere moscatelle* Castelvetro notes: 'Early in the summer come muscat pears ... Although they are a small fruit, everyone likes them because of their musky scent' (trans. Riley, 83).

or stem. Should you not be able to get the above condiments for it, instead of sweetbreads you can use calf, kid or pig brain, parboiled.

In yet another way: with the pork fat beaten, add in two pounds of boiled and grated liver of those quadrupeds, with an ounce of dry sweet fennel, the seed either whole or ground, six egg yolks, four ounces of sugar, a handful of finely chopped herbs, a pound of grated cheese, an ounce and a half of the above spices, and cleaned, parboiled cloves of garlic.

Besides all the above stuffing mixtures you can also make use of all the compositions of which *tommacelle* are made in a caul, as described above in Recipe 103.

116. To make various mixtures with which to stuff various quadruped members and many fowl, which members and fowl have to be boiled in salted water.

For every pound of grated old cheese get six ounces of creamy cheese that is not too salted, three ounces of shelled walnuts ground in a mortar, two ounces of breadcrumb[116] soaked in meat broth and ground in a mortar, three ounces of beef marrow cut up small or else fresh butter, three ounces of cleaned raisins, half an ounce of pepper and cinnamon combined, and sufficient saffron. Combine everything together with eight eggs so that the mixture is neither too runny nor too thick.

You can make it differently: when the cheese is grated, mix it with a pound and a half of parboiled and beaten sweetbreads of a calf or goat kid, or else their brain, adding in an ounce of the same condiments and saffron, and herbs beaten with six eggs. With that mix in gooseberries or verjuice grapes and a little fat broth to keep it moist. Instead of the sweetbreads you can use a calf's udder.

A third way is to grind a pound of shelled Milanese almonds in a mortar with a pound of ricotta, a pound of sugar, an ounce and a half of the above condiments, six ounces of grated old cheese, four ounces of goat's milk, six well beaten eggs and three ounces of butter cut up into bits. If you want that mixture to stay white, put in only ginger and egg whites.

You can follow another process as well: with knives you beat the flesh of four raw capon breasts, a pound of pork fat, two pounds of fresh, parboiled pork belly, a pound of grated dry cheese, a handful of herbs, a pound of fresh cheese, two ounces of the above condiments, half a pound of raisins, six ounces of cleaned truffles, six beaten eggs, sufficient salt, sugar, and saffron at will.

With all of the above mixtures you can stuff a calf's large intestine.

117. To boil all sorts of capons and domestic hens.

For boiling and for roasting on a spit, a capon that is middle-aged – that is, between a year and eighteen months – is much better than one that is very old.

---

[116] The *mollica di pane* is the part of a loaf that is inside its crust, soft bread.

In summer you have to get a capon that has been dead for a day and a half, still with its feathers and viscera; in winter, for four days at the most. Pluck it dry or in hot water, draw it and rinse it inside and out with several changes of water. If you want to stuff it, do it with one of the above mixtures. Then put it on the fire in a pot with boiling water. When it is done, serve it hot with parsley over it.

In the same way you can prepare hens, having trussed up the legs and wings, though, of each of them.

118. To cook the above fowl, capons, hens and pullets in another way in salted water, wrapped in a caul, so they stay white.

When one of those birds has been plucked, drawn and washed in several changes of water, it is optional whether you stuff it with one of various mixtures. Blanch it, though, with its legs trussed and well done up as is usual. Then get a calf's, wether's or pig's caul and wrap it around the bird, tying it with a cord, and cook it in salted water or in a meat broth. When it is done, take it out of the caul and serve it hot with parsley over it. To make the bird tastier you can also cook slices of *salsiccione* or of prosciutto in the caul with it. If you want to stew it in the caul, sprinkle the caul with pepper, cinnamon, cloves and nutmeg. Make up a mixture of beaten pork fat and prosciutto – instead of prosciutto you can use cheese and raw eggs – along with beaten and sautéed common herbs and spring onions. Put that mixture onto the caul, with the bird in the middle so that the mixture completely surrounds it. When it is tied up, cook it in a pot with a meat broth that is not too salty and covers it by two fingers. Add in some of the same condiments, with verjuice in winter and gooseberries or verjuice grapes in summer. When it is cooked, take it out of the caul and serve it with its broth over top.

In that same way, too, you can do a boneless capon.[118]

119. To stew every sort of capon and domestic hen.

Capons and domestic hens, once plucked and drawn, can be stuffed with the mixture outlined in Recipe 116. When they are so stuffed, you put them in a stewing pot with a pound of sliced prosciutto, half an ounce of whole cinnamon, a quarter-ounce of ginger, half a nutmeg, enough saffron, two-thirds of a litre of white wine, a beaker of verjuice, four ounces of plums and visciola cherries together, and four additional ounces of raisins and muscatel raisins together. Into the pot put enough water to cover the capon. Cook it with the pot covered and sealed so nothing can leak out. When it is cooked, serve it with its mixture over top. If that capon is not extremely old, it will have cooked after boiling for an hour and a half.

---

[118] See Recipe 122, below.

120. A different way to stew every sort of capon.

If the capon is old it will be quite a bit better if it is hung briefly.[120.1] When filled with a stuffing as described in Recipe 155, put it into an earthenware or copper stewing pot in enough meat broth or water to cover it by three fingers, along with a pound of saveloy, half a pound of rind from Parmesan cheese,[120.2] very clean hearts of artichokes or cardoons – either of them first boiled or just brought to a boil in water. When the capon is almost cooked, put in gooseberries or verjuice grapes with a little pepper, cinnamon and saffron. When it is done, serve it with slices of bread, sprinkled with Parmesan cheese, under it; around it put the saveloy and the hearts, and splash the bread with a little broth, serving everything hot like that.

You can also stew the capon with turnips instead of artichokes and with turnips and old onions, whole and previously parboiled or cooked on the coals.

If you want that capon dismembered, though, you will not stuff it. When it is plucked and cleaned, cut it up and sauté the pieces in melted rendered fat or beaten pork fat. Then add in enough meat broth to cover them, and finish cooking them in that broth. Half of a quarter-hour before you want to serve it, put in gooseberries and a handful of herbs. If you want to thicken the broth you can do it with clean almonds ground in a mortar, not forgetting, though, to put in the seasonings used above.

If you want a fricassee of the capon, when it is cut up into pieces boil them, take them out and sauté them in a pan in melted rendered fat. Have a mixture ready of egg yolks beaten with verjuice and the capon's broth, cooled, with sugar, pepper, cinnamon and saffron. Pour all that into the pan, heating it up and mixing those ingredients with the pan[120.3] until it takes on the consistency of a thick jellied broth.[120.4] Serve it with sugar and cinnamon over top.

121. To boil all sorts of capon and serve them with various mixtures over them.

If you want a capon to be more tasty and its broth better, cook it in a stewing pot[121.1] in a meat broth with fresh saveloy sausage and half an ounce of ground cinnamon. When it is cooked, take it out and serve it up hot like Lombard sops in

---

[120.1] Recipe 117 suggests a period of between a day and a half and four days of hanging in order to tenderize a capon effectively.

[120.2] *crosta di cascio Parmeggiano.*

[120.3] In both printings, *con la padella.* If not a typesetter's *lapsus* for *con la cocchiara,* 'with a spoon,' Scappi directs that the frying pan be so tipped and moved as to blend everything together.

[120.4] *brodetto congelato.* Scappi does not use this term in the modern sense of a fish soup but only for a thick or thickened broth.

[121.1] Two sorts of *stufatoro* are illustrated in Plate 8.

layers separated by a sprinkling of grated cheese, sugar and cinnamon.[121.2] You can cook *tortellini*[121.3] in that broth and cover the capon with them, with cheese, sugar and cinnamon on top. Besides, you can boil the capon with Bolognese cabbage and mortadella, and serve it with the cabbage and some cut-up mortadella over it. Again, you can boil the capon in plain water, stuffed or empty, wrapped in a pig's or wether's caul to keep it white. When the caul is removed, you cover it with whitedish;[121.4] or with lemon juice topped with pomegranate seeds[121.5] and sugar; or with yellowdish,[121.6] topped with sugar and cinnamon.

122. To boil a boneless capon.

For this dish the capon needs to be big and fleshy, and of middle age rather than old. As soon as it has been killed, it needs to be plucked dry: that is done because after plucking in water the skin does not stay as strong and cannot stand up to the cooking; but if you do pluck it in water, watch that the skin does not break. Draw the capon, leaving its neck and feet on. Wrap it in pure white linen and, with a wooden pestle, crush its bones; then very adroitly remove those bones, turning the capon inside out so you can clean it out thoroughly. Mind that the skin on the wings does not tear, because it is difficult to remove the bones of the wing joints. You can remove the capon's bones another way: when it is plucked, cut it along the spine and, skinning the back, adroitly remove the back and breast bones, leaving the flesh attached to the skin; remove the thigh bones similarly. In a case where the back is to be slit open, you will not draw the bird until it has been skinned.

When the capon has been prepared in either of the above ways, get the flesh from the breast of another uncooked capon, and a pound of prosciutto and pork fat together, and beat those finely with knives, adding in half an ounce of common spices, a handful of finely chopped herbs, two egg yolks and two ounces of grated

---

[121.2] Scappi's *servasi caldo, tramezzato con una suppa alla lombarda* refers to a Lombard predilection for stacking pieces of a foodstuff separated by layers of cheese. See Recipe II,225.

[121.3] See Recipes II,177–180.

[121.4] Scappi's *biancomangiare* has various forms and is incorporated in several genres of dish throughout the *Opera*. Medieval in origin whitedish was virtually universal in early European gastronomy and known by many linguistic versions of its name (including *cibarium album*). It is a distant precursor of today's blancmange. Scappi himself offers several varieties of whitedish: see Recipes II,162, 165 and 167, as well as a lean recipe at III,218. Scappi's most traditional form of whitedish is seen in his Recipe VI,78.

[121.5] Castelvetro notes that pomegranates 'are a very good fruit on their own, and make an excellent seasoning for cooked dishes' (ed. Riley, 127). Scappi rarely incorporates the seeds as a condiment in a dish (see Recipe 244), but relies on them as a savory and pretty garnish. See also the juice so used in Recipe 137, below.

[121.6] See Recipe 160, below, and III,223.

cheese. Stuff the capon with that mixture, pushing it into the wings and thighs; sew it up so that the stuffing cannot come out. With its wings and thighs trussed, put the capon into an ample earthenware or copper pot with cold water and put that on the fire, shaping the capon in it with your hand. Bring the pot slowly to a boil until the capon is blanched, being careful to bind its feet together because if they were not bound it would not turn out with a very good shape. When it has been blanched you can boil it or stew it in all the ways mentioned above. When you want to serve it, remove the binding carefully. Serve it hot.

If you want to roast the capon on a spit, when it has been blanched, deboned and stuffed, take it out of the broth and cool it in cold water. Take it out, wrap it around with strips of pork fat sprinkled with fennel flour, salt, pepper, cloves and cinnamon, and around that a sheet of royal paper[122] which has been greased with rendered fat. Put it on a spit and cook it over a low fire. Instead of using pork fat and the paper, you can wrap the capon in a caul. Again, instead of a caul, you can lard it with fine lardoons, setting it to cook as above. When it is done, serve it hot, dressed with its sauce which is made from rose vinegar, sugar, raisins, pepper, cinnamon and cloves. Be careful that the capon that is to be roasted still has its feet and neck on, and that it is stuffed with that mixture that roasts are stuffed with in Recipe 115.

123. To boil and do up the above-mentioned capon.

When the capon is plucked and drawn, whether stuffed or empty, boil it in a meat broth or else in water with a piece of prosciutto and crushed pepper. When it is done, take it out of the broth and let it drain. Then make several slashes across its thighs, body and breast. Sprinkle it all over, and especially in the slashes, with a mixture of sugar, pepper, cinnamon, cloves, nutmeg and fennel flour. Let it cool. When you wish to serve it, do so with it cold, with cut-up limes over it. Before sprinkling it, you can also splash it with rose vinegar.

124. Various ways to spit-roast a capon.

Whenever a capon is young, it will always be better for roasting than an old one. But if you want to roast an old one, you will have to hang it a while. When it has been plucked and drawn, whether it will be stuffed or empty, blanch it in boiling water, then take it out and stick it with fine lardoons of pork fat. If it is stuffed, though, it does not need that larding. Then put it on a spit and cook it over a moderate fire at the outset; as it begins to drip, give it a sprightly fire so that the

---

[122] During the Renaissance a sheet of the paper known in Italy as *carta reale* measured roughly 44.4 X 61.5 cm. It was produced in various grades and weights, for which the whiteness varied. Finer papers for writing and printing contained a sizing to glaze them, whereas a thicker variety for wrapping, and suitable for the uses to which Scappi puts it (see also Recipe 137, below), was generally coarser. (The translator is indebted to Professor Conor Fahy for that information.)

cooking will not dry it out. If it is not larded, baste it with melted rendered fat or lard. When it is done, serve it hot with orange juice or lime juice over it.

You can also roast a young capon on a spit in the way a pheasant is done in Recipe 136.

125. To spit-roast a capon after it has been half cooked by boiling.

This treatment is rarely done and only when there is a good need for it. When the capon is half-boiled in salted water, whether stuffed or empty, take it out and mount it, hot like that, on a spit. Roast it over a moderate fire, basting it with melted rendered fat or hot lard, and sprinkling it right away with sugar, cinnamon, flour, grated bread and fennel flour. When it has browned enough, serve it hot with cut-up limes over it.

126. Various ways to sauté a capon.

More than half-cook the capon in salted water, quarter it, and let it sit for eight hours in a mixture of white wine, vinegar, must syrup, pepper, cinnamon, cloves, nutmeg, ground coriander and crushed garlic cloves. Take it out, flour it and fry it in melted rendered fat. When it is done, serve it hot, dressed with a sauce of the same seasoning.

After it has been taken out of the mixture, you can also finish off cooking it on a grill without flouring it. Alternatively, the capon, uncooked, can be split along its back and set in salt for two days. Then half-boil it in salted water. Remove it from that broth, cut it up into pieces and sauté them in melted rendered fat or salt lard.

A capon should always be got in its season – that is, the young one from August throughout Christmastide, the old one at any time in the year.

127. To boil or roast common hens and pullets, and turkey pullets.

Get a hen in its season, which runs from October to the middle of March, always excepting any sitting hen; the ones that are grain-fed are good, as Roman poultrymen have them, who pluck them dry as soon as they have been killed. When it has been drawn, a hen like that is boiled in salted water. With it you can make all the dishes that are made with the boiled capon in Recipe 117. The season of a Roman pullet[127.1] begins at the end of June and goes through February. As a pullet it will not lay for six to eight months: as soon as it begins to lay eggs it is no longer considered to be a pullet.[127.2] If you want to boil or roast it, when it has been plucked draw it and carefully remove the bone that is in its breast: that

---

[127.1] As is generally the case, Scappi's 'season' is dated by the availability of the foodstuff – its appearance on the market (in Rome) and its disappearance from that market, vital information for his apprentice Giovanni or any neophyte cook.

[127.2] *Tal volatile non vuol passare sei in otto mesi; percioche come comincia a fare uova, non si intende piu esser pollanca.*

is done so that as it cooks the breast will become better shaped. Boil or roast it, stuffed or empty, just as the capon above is boiled or roasted.

If you want to hang it,[127.3] leave its feet and head on, and then follow the directions given for the pheasant in Recipe 136.

You can also do up a turkey pullet in all of the above ways for doing a domestic pullet.

128. To cook a chick – that is, a small cockerel – on a spit and otherwise.

When the chick is not more than six weeks old, it will be good for roasting. It is plucked dry or in hot water, drawn, and stuffed with beaten pork fat and green fennel, along with its liver, raw egg yolks and common spices, leaving its head and feet on. Sew up the hole so the stuffing cannot come out and blanch it in boiling water. Lard it finely with pork fat, mount it on a spit crosswise or lengthwise and cook it over a sprightly fire. When it is done, serve it with cut-up limes or orange juice on top. It can also be roasted with slices of pork fat around it, the way you do a pheasant.

After it has been brought to a boil in the water, you can let it sit for a day in a seasoning. Then sauté it the way you sauté a capon in Recipe 125. The chick has to be got in its season, from April to the end of June, although in Rome you can find them throughout the year.

With cockerels that are bigger – that is, small roosters – you can make all the dishes that are done with a pullet in the previous recipe. If you want to stew or braise one, though, when it is plucked, whether stuffed or empty, bring it to a boil in water and then sauté it whole in melted rendered fat or lard in an earthenware or copper pan, turning it often. When it is done, put in enough meat broth to cover it, along with pepper, cinnamon and saffron, and a few little slices of prosciutto. When it is cooked and not disintegrating, add in gooseberries or verjuice grapes, or else (depending on the season) plums and visciola cherries, and a handful of herbs. When it is done, serve it hot with its broth over it. You can sometimes thicken the broth with cheese and eggs.

A chick can also be cooked with fresh peas and broad beans in a meat broth that is not too salty and that contains beaten pork fat and mortadella, or else sliced pork jowl or yellow saveloy. When it is cooked, serve it up with its broth and its mixture over it. When the peas are tender, cook them with their shell.

You can cook a cockerel after stuffing it with local squash[128.1] and stuffed

---

[127.3] *volendo affaggianarla* – that is, to treat it as a pheasant, a *faggiano*, in order that it become tender.

[128.1] Scappi's 'squash' or edible gourd is not the spherical variety like a pumpkin, large or small, but the sort with a rounded belly and slightly elongated and bent neck. See the illustration of these *Cucurbite* being harvested in the *Tacuina sanitatis*.

lettuce.[128.2] As well, after having been plucked and drawn, it can be cut up and sautéed with slices of prosciutto or with slices of pork jowl.

129. To spit-roast barnyard or dovecot doves.

Any barnyard or dovecot doves that you want to roast on a spit must be partially fledged ones,[129] immediately after being killed, plucked in hot water and drawn – except for the liver which does not have any gall bladder. They have to be stuffed with a mixture like the one that was made up for the chick in the previous recipe. When that is done, they have to be blanched in water and mounted on a spit without larding. Cook them over a sprightly little fire. They are served a little undercooked rather than overcooked, dressed with orange juice and sugar, or with whatever garnish you like.

The ones that are not stuffed can be larded with pork fat.

130. To cook those doves by boiling or otherwise.

When they have been plucked and drawn, cut off their head, feet and wing tips. If you want to stuff them (which is up to you), do it with the stuffing prescribed for the capon in Recipe 117. Boil them in salted water, and stew them in all the ways in which the capon is done in Recipe 127. If you want them boneless and stuffed, follow the directions given for the capon in Recipe 121. The boneless ones that are stuffed and parboiled can be kept twenty-four hours in a royal seasoning[130.1] made of vinegar, sugar, white wine, coriander, pepper, salt, cloves, nutmeg and cinnamon. After that they are floured and fried in melted rendered fat. When they are done, serve them hot with a sauce made of that same seasoning, along with raisins and muscatel raisins cooked with the seasoning.

If you want to braise the boneless doves in an oven, when they have been stuffed put them into an earthenware baking dish with beaten pork fat. In winter put in prunes and dry visciola cherries, and pieces of apple quince;[130.2] in summer, gooseberries or verjuice grapes, and unripe prunes and other fruit. Also put in common spices, slices of pork jowl that is not rancid, a little white wine, and enough salt-free meat broth or water to cover them. Cook them like that, occasionally turning them over. When they are done, serve them dressed with the same things. In that same way you can do them up still with their bones.

[128.2] For this *lattuga ripiena*, see Recipe II,202 and (for lean days) the end of Recipe III,240.

[129] *di mezza piuma*, literally, 'with their intermediate feathers'; see also Recipe 202. An un-fledged pigeon (or dove) is properly a squab: see Recipe 214.

[130.1] See also a 'plain' *adobbo* at the beginning of Recipe 35. This present prescription for *adobbo reale* seems merely to be a little richer in spices. See also other recipes for the so-called royal seasoning in Recipes V,156 and 188.

[130.2] Castelvetro describes the *mela cotogna* as the best variety of quince, 'rather like a *chrisomele*, as it is sometimes called, because it is small and squat and divided into sections. It is yellow, downy and very much more fragrant than the other kinds' (trans. Riley, 118).

Those fowl will be at their best during their season which, for barnyard doves, goes from April to the end of September and, for those in a dovecot, from the fall to the end of May, although in Rome they can be had throughout the year. Many people hold that doves from Terni are better than from around Rome.

131. To spit-roast jays,[131] stockdoves, small coots, woodcocks and teal ducks.

All of the above fowl have to be plucked dry as soon as they are caught, and seared on the coals without being drawn. A jay can be larded, leaving the acorns in its crop, and the same with stockdoves, but there is no need to lard the others when they are big. When they have been seared on the coals, they have to be sprinkled with salt and fennel flour, then put on the spit and roasted. When done, they are served hot. A woodcock and a teal can be served covered with slices of bread soaked in verjuice and must syrup, which slices of bread were in the dripping pan while the birds were roasting. After all of the above fowl that are drawn have been roasted, they can be served dressed with a variety of sauces.

The season of those fowl runs from mid-September to the end of February.

132. To cook those fowl in a larded broth.

When plucked and drawn, cut off their head and feet and wash them in water and white wine. Filter that washwater and put it into an earthenware or copper pot with slices of prosciutto and pork jowl, common spices, prunes and dry visciola cherries, sage tips, must syrup or sugar, and raisins or muscatel raisins. Into that pot put the fowl, ensuring they are covered with broth. Then close the pot up and set it to boil on coals away from the fire. When they are done, serve them dressed with the same mixture.

133. Several ways to roast and do up turtle-doves and quail.

Get a turtle-dove in its season, which goes from June to the end of November. Right after it is dead, pluck it dry and sear it on the coals without drawing it. Put it on a spit crosswise and set it to roast over a sprightly little fire, turning it rapidly so its grease will not drip off. When it is almost done, make up its crust of flour, fennel flour, sugar, salt and grated bread.[133] When it is done, it is served hot.

To distinguish between a young and an old bird, you should know that the young one has a darker flesh and whiter feet, and the old one white flesh and brownish feet.

You can roast a quail the same way when it is fat. Its season runs from mid-August to the end of October. Although around Rome, and mainly by Ostia and Porto, there are great numbers of quail in the spring yet they are not as good as in their proper season. Sometimes fat quail are semi-salted in salt and fennel flour and left in a wooden or earthenware vessel for three or four days. Then they

---

[131] *piccioni di ghianda*, literally 'acorn-eating doves.'

[133] Scappi omits an explicit instruction to apply this coating, or crust as he calls it, onto the bird.

are sautéed in melted rendered fat with spring onions and served hot with pepper on them. They are also split in half and set in seasoning for a day; then they are floured and fried in melted rendered fat and served hot with sugar and orange juice on them, or with their seasoning hot on them.

134. To cook thrush, blackbirds and larks on a spit and otherwise.

Get a thrush in its season, between the end of September and the end of February. That bird must especially be fresh to be good. Pluck it dry, without drawing it, and sear it on the coals or by the heat of the fire, cutting off its wing tips. Spit it crosswise between bay leaves and slices of pork fat or sausages.[134.1] Cook it over a sprightly fire. When done, serve it hot with orange juice and salt over it.

In the same way you can roast a blackbird and a lark, getting them in their season, which goes from mid-September to the end of January. A thrush has whiter feathers and feet than a blackbird and is preferable to it. After drawing those birds, and roasting them on the spit, they can be covered with onion sauce or *capirotata*[134.2] or whatever other sauce you like. A thinly feathered lark is much better than a thickly feathered one. Those birds when they are drawn can also be cooked in a larded broth and in all the ways in which jays are cooked, the directions for which are set out in Recipes 131 and 132.[134.3] You can do a starling that way, a young pheasant and a coot. A starling in the grape season is fatter than at any other time; but I do not recommend it no matter how fat it may be because it is always bitter.

135. To spit-roast sparrows, robins and other small birds, and to do them up.

In the spring when sparrows, robins and other small birds are young, when they are plucked dry immediately after being killed, and without being drawn, they can be roasted on a spit with slices of pork fat between them. In winter, though, old birds can be cooked in a larded broth the same as a jay is done in Recipe 132.[135]

136. To roast fig-peckers, ortolans and swifts.

Get a fig-pecker in its season, beginning in July and ending mid-October; an ortolan, mid-October to the end of February – which small birds in La Marca and

---

[134.1] Although Scappi writes of the thrush in the singular, the procedure here suggests that, as in the next recipe, several of them on the spit are interspersed with the leaves and fat.

[134.2] See Recipe 73, above.

[134.3] The 1570 text reads *nel capitolo 130 & 131*; the same numbers are reproduced in the 1581 printing.

[135] In both Tramezzino printings, 1570 and 1581, the text reads *nel capitolo 131*.

in Romagna are generally preserved in millet or in foxtail millet;[136] and a swift, which has a big mouth, big wings, small feet and a square head, from the end of April when it is young to the end of June. All three of those small birds, when dead, plucked dry and not drawn, are roasted on a spit, separated by slices of pork fat and sage leaves. A crust of flour, sugar, grated bread and fennel flour is made for them. When they are done they are served hot.

They can also be cooked under the coals wrapped in slices of pork fat, grape-vine leaves and greased paper. But if you want to stew them, and make a larded broth of them, draw them – although in my opinion they are much better roasted on a spit than done any other way.

137. Several ways to spit-roast and do up all sorts of pheasants and old pheasants.

There are two sorts of pheasants: wild ones, called wood grouse,[137.1] and local ones; the wild sort is black like a crow and has brownish eyelids and a smooth beak, and is bigger than the local sort. Many of them are born in the Grigioni and Swiss hills. Their season goes from October to the end of February; in the snowy season they are very fat. The male of the local bird has feathers tending to gold in colour speckled with a bluish purple[137.2] and other colours, its head and neck are bluish purple, its eyelids brownish and its tail, which is long, spotted with black. The female is not so large, her feathers are different from those of the male, being of a greyish colour, and she is much fatter in the fall than at any other time. The season of the local variety, male and female, is from October to the end of February.

After being killed, those fowl have to hang without being plucked or drawn for six days in winter and for a day and a half in summer. They are plucked dry, and drawn, and sprinkled inside their body with salt, fennel flour and pepper. If you want to stuff them with the mixture described in Recipe 115, that can be done. To make shorter work, though, and to keep them from losing their flavour, put into their body a piece of pork fat studded with whole cloves and panicles of sweet fennel, fresh or dry. When they are done up properly – that is, the thighs trussed and the hole sewn up – sear them on the coals or blanch them in boiling water. With that done, stud the breasts with a few whole cloves. Get thin slices of pork fat sprinkled with an amount of ground salt and dry fennel seed that the back of a knife would hold, and place them on the birds, one on the back and another under

---

[136] This *panico* is otherwise called Italian millet. As Book I, §39 directs, it is the ground flour of these grains that is used for this purpose.

[137.1] *galli di montagna*, literally 'hill cocks.' In Book I, §39 this fowl was called a *fagiano di montagna*, 'wild pheasant.' This sense of the word *montagna* refers to uninhabited areas, the hilly (and therefore uncultivated) outback. In Book I, §9 *montagna* also qualifies undomesticated swine: *porco di montagna*. See also Recipe II,67.

[137.2] The name of this peacock colour, *pavonazzo*, derives from the peacock itself, *pavone*.

the belly, joining them so that each bird is wholly covered. Around each bird's slices of fat wrap a sheet of royal paper[137.3] greased with rendered fat. Mount them on a spit and roast them over a low fire. When they are done, take the paper and pork fat off them and serve them hot with royal sauce[137.4] in bowls, or else with pomegranate juice and sugar over them.

The birds that have been blanched in boiling water you can stick with fine lardoons of pork fat, not failing to stud their breast with a few whole cloves and cinnamon sticks. Anyone who wants to keep the neck with its feathers, put the neck and head into a reed tube[137.5] and wrap the tube with paper. As you cook the pheasant, keep a brick by the neck so the heat will not split the reed. Alternatively, put several layers of paper around the neck, and on those layers put another sheet of paper greased with rendered fat or oil because that would be better than sprinkling water on it.

If you want to stew those pheasants or make a larded broth of them, follow the directions given for the jay in Recipe 132.[137.6]

138. To spit-roast and otherwise cook rock partridge, old[138.1] common grey partridge and francolin.[138.2]

Rock partridges are a little bigger than common grey partridges,[138.3] have a greyish plumage spotted with black, and brownish feet and beak. Francolins brought from Sicily and Spain to Rome are the same size as rock partridges and have a greyish plumage. Common grey partridges have rust-coloured plumage, little tail and thicker feathers than the others. All three, though, have the same season as a pheasant.

If you wish to spit-roast the bird, follow the directions for the pheasant in the previous recipe. After it is done on the spit, make a cut along the breast of each one and two cuts on the thighs near the joints, and set them to stew for a quarter of an hour in a mixture of orange juice, lime juice, sugar, rosewater, white salt, seedless muscatel raisins, cinnamon and cloves; stew them over hot coals. Serve them hot with that sauce over them. You can also do them roasted and cut up,

---

[137.3] See the note in Recipe 122, above.

[137.4] For this *salza reale* see Recipes II,267 and VI,102.

[137.5] *un cannon di canna*: the hollow of a large reed. Presumably the brick that will be mentioned either absorbs some of the heat or acts as a shield for the reed.

[137.6] Both printed texts read *nel capitolo 131*.

[138.1] Scappi specifies the mature bird here because the young partridge will be dealt with in the next recipe.

[138.2] This *frangolino* is also known as a black partridge.

[138.3] The comparison here is between *cotorne* and *starne*.

serving them with capers, sugar and cinnamon on them, or else with lime slices and sugar over them.

In the same way you can do a common pullet and a turkey pullet. If you want to stew those three wildfowl and make a larded broth of them, follow the directions for the jay in Recipe 132.[138.4] If you want to boil them with cardoons or Savoy cabbage[138.5] or Bolognese cabbage, when they are half-done on the spit cut off their feet and heat the birds and finish cooking them in meat broth with those cardoons or cabbage, salt pork jowl or saveloy, serving them dressed with the things mentioned above.

139. To spit-roast young common grey partridge, young pheasant and young partridge.[139.1]

The season for the young common grey partridge, young pheasant and young partridge alike runs from mid-July to the end of September, and for the biggest ones from September to the end of November. If you want to roast the small ones on a spit, as soon as they are caught pluck them dry and draw them; leave their head and feet on. Stuff them with a little beaten pork fat, fresh fennel, beaten common herbs, raw egg yolks and common spices – which is done to keep them from drying out. Sew up the hole and arrange their wings and thighs so they are snug. Sear them on the coals. Wrap them, sprinkled with salt and cloves, in a calf or wether caul, or else in slices of pork fat with paper around them. Cook them. When they are done serve them hot.

Young pheasants have darker feet and a longer neck than young common grey partridges and young partridges. Young pheasants appear earlier than young common grey partridges and always have a larger body. Those fowl are always better having fed in the bush than in a yard[139.2]: I say that because some are raised in Rome.

140. To spit-roast a domestic peacock.

The domestic peacock is a well-known bird for its fine plumage; its neck is a bluish purple with a little cap on its head, its tail long and marked with bluish-purple circles, but its feet are rather big and black. White peacocks are found. Their flesh is black, but more tasty than all other fowl.

[138.4] Both printed texts read *nel capitolo 131.*

[138.5] *cavoli Milanesi*: this particular variety of cabbage is still being specified (*choux de Milan*) by the seventeenth-century French chefs, L.S.R. (*L'art de bien traiter*) and Pierre de Lune (*Le cuisinier*), both published in a modern adaptation in *L'art de la cuisine française au XVIIe siècle* (Paris: Payot et Rivages, 1995), 134, 253, 293. See also the note in Recipe 152, below.

[139.1] The first and last fowl here are *starnotti* and *perniconi*.

[139.2] *alla foresta* as distinct from *in casa*, domestically. See also Recipe 23, above.

If you want to roast a peacock on a spit, get an old one between October and February. After it has been killed let it hang for eight days without plucking it and without drawing it; then pluck it dry – although it could be done in water, it is still better done dry so it does not lose any flavour and its skin is not torn. When it is plucked, draw it. Leaving its feathers on its neck and feet, cut off its wings. Clean out the bloodiness inside by means of a very white linen cloth; put one end of a hot iron bar into the carcass through the whole by which it was eviscerated, being careful not to touch the flesh: that is done to remove its moistness and bad smell. To stuff it, use the mixture outlined in Recipe 115, or else sprinkle it with salt, fennel flour, pepper, cloves and cinnamon; into the carcass put panicles of dry fennel and a piece of pork fat that is not rancid, studded with whole cloves or pieces of fine saveloy. Blanch it in water or sear it on the coals. Stud the breast with whole cloves. (The breast can also be larded or wrapped in slices of pork fat as is done with the pheasant in Recipe 136.) Roast it over a low fire, preserving the neck with its feathers as is done with the pheasant. Serve it hot or cold as you wish, with various sauces over it [or] in dishes. You can also, for a fine effect after it is cooked and cooled, coat its breast with egg yolks or honey, and the thighs likewise; onto that stick candied pinenuts, candied cinnamon sticks and candied aniseed. When it is served set a scented flame in its mouth.[140.1]

You can do it differently: when the peacock is dead, skin it right along the breast bone, leaving the skin attached to the head, wings, tail and feet. When the empty carcass is cooked, let it cool. Fit it up with an iron rod in the centre of a small board, in the shape of a half-moon, that rod gripping the carcass in its middle;[140.2] another rod fitted onto the half-moon, which goes straight to the neck; another half-moon one, lower than the first, which goes back to hold up the tail; and two other light iron rods shoved into the thighs. Then spread the skin adroitly over the carcass of the peacock, doing it in such a way that the neck, tail and feet are fixed on the bars, and that it has in every respect the appearance of being alive. In its carcass you can put a variety of living birds, and in its mouth a flame made with alcohol and camphor or other substances. The little board should be surrounded with small branches of myrtle or boxwood. You should put a hole

---

[140.1] A traditional artifice in wealthy European kitchens let an animal or fowl be served in a lifelike state but with a flame burning in its mouth. The flame was normally fed, as Scappi suggests further on, by wads of alcohol- or camphor-soaked cotton – the camphor providing a pleasant scent to offset any other odour that singed flesh might produce. See the same alcohol-and-camphor fire-breathing peacock in the *Neapolitan Recipe Collection*, Recipe 69, of more than a century before Scappi.

[140.2] The *mezza luna* seems to be a sort of snug, half-round cradle of curved rods mounted on a wooden stand. The various parts of the metal skeleton that Scappi describes will be either impaled in the peacock's members or hidden by its skin and feathers.

into the carcass under the wing so that, when the Carver is about to cut, the birds can come out.[140.3]

Medium-sized peacocks can be roasted like the pheasant in Recipe 136, and small ones like the young pheasant in the previous recipe. Old ones when they are roasted can be kept in winter eight days, even up to twelve days, and in summer, three, because their flesh is less inclined to spoil[140.4] than that of any other fowl. Of a peacock's viscera the only good thing is the liver, which is small and of a bluish-purple colour. The gizzard is the tastiest and best among all fowl; it is boiled, let cool, stuck with fine lardoons of pork fat and finished off on a spit. Alternatively, after being half cooked by boiling it is cut in half and fried in melted rendered fat along with the liver.

141. To roast turkey cock and turkey hen, which in some places in Italy are called 'Indian peacocks.'[141.1]

A turkey cock and turkey hen are much bigger in the body than an ordinary peacock, and the cock can spread its tail like the peacock. It has a black and white plumage, wrinkled skin on its neck, and on the top of its head a fleshy crest which,

---

[140.3] Until that moment the wing, of course, will conceal and close the hole. During a meal the *trinciante* or carver stood facing the dining table and diners and distributed the contents of a serving dish onto the trenchers of the individuals whom he was assigned to serve. His major task was to dismember and debone joints or pieces of meat, and reduce those pieces to something close to bite size; he sliced cheese and pies, and peeled fruit. For a few more details on a carver's duties see the passage by Liberati in Appendix III.

[140.4] Scappi wrote *è men corruttibile*, an interesting persistence of the very old humoral theory that excessive moisture causes corruption. All living creatures tend naturally to dry out as they age, and peacocks are considered to be by nature a dry-fleshed species. Earlier recipes for peacock go so far as to state that, even though the cooked bird has been kept so long that its outer surface is becoming mouldy, beneath that mould its meat will still be quite edible: see, for instance, the *Viandier* of Taillevent, Recipe 50.

[141.1] Consistently Scappi qualifies the members of the species we now call 'turkey' with the phrase *d'India*. In the present rubric he writes, *il Gallo, & la Gallina d'India, liquali in alcuni lochi d'Italia si dimandano pavoni d'India* – 'Indian peacocks.' Ten years before the *Opera* Panunto assimilated his *galline d'India* to peacocks in delimiting their season (*Singolare dottrina*, Book 2, p. 25 in the edition of Venice: Bonfadino, 1593) but, undoubtedly for want of any information among his scientific authorities, he does not go on to describe the turkey's gastronomic qualities. While guinea fowl were well known on European dining tables, by the phrase *gallo d'India* Scappi is almost certainly referring to the turkey. Columbus reported seeing 'an enormous number' of those fowl on Jamaica (in the Indies) on 6 July 1503; Hernán Cortés (1485–1547) wrote of many such 'wild hens' in Mexico. By the middle of the sixteenth century in European barnyards and marketplaces there was uncertainty about the origin of the bird, having only just in Scappi's day been introduced into Europe by the Dutch. See Gillian Riley, *The Oxford Companion to Italian Food*, 535. The turkey was in fact beginning gradually to displace the goose on European tables of the late Renaissance. It is probably significant that Scappi mentions a domestic goose – a mainstay of late-medieval gastronomy – only once in his work (II,150).

when the cock gets angry, swells up and covers its whole snout; on some of them
that crest is a russet colour mixed with bluish purple. Its breast is broad; on the
tip of that there is a herringbone of bristle, like a pig's, among the feathers. Its
flesh is much whiter and softer than that of the common peacock and it is hung
for a shorter time than any similar fowl.

If you want to spit-roast it, do not let it sit for more than six days in winter
before being drawn, or in summer for more than two. Pluck it dry or in hot water
– as the turkey hen is also to be plucked. Then, when it is drawn, prepare its breast
because there is a bone there that is a bit higher than in other fowl: cut away the
skin on one side of that bone and skilfully remove the flesh from the bone; cut the
tip of the bone with a shaving knife[141.2] and sew the skin up again. If you want
to stuff it, use one of the stuffings of Recipe 115. Cut the wings away, leaving
the head and feet. Blanch it in water, then let it cool. Stick it with fine lardoons
of pork fat, although if it is fat, and stuffed, there will not be any need for that
larding; you will have to stud it, though, with a few whole cloves. Mount it on
a spit and cook it slowly, that bird cooking much more quickly that a common
peacock. From the breast you can make croquettes and meatballs and all those
preparations that are made from the lean meat of milk-fed veal in Recipes 43 and
47. The same, too, for the flesh of a turkey hen and an ordinary peacock, but
immediately after they have been killed because having hung they do not turn out
as tasty. The turkey cock and hen have the same season as an ordinary peacock,
yet in Rome they can be found throughout the year. Their viscera are done like
those of the ordinary peacock above.

142. To spit-roast a crane and cook it in several ways.

A crane is a big bird, with a long neck, tall feet and little tail; its plumage is
greyish, its legs are slender and coal black, its feet have sharp claws and its beak
is rather long and sharp. It is first seen in Italy in October and is around until the
end of February, those months being its season. If you want to roast it on a spit,
hang it, unplucked and undrawn, for six days after it has been killed. Pluck it dry,
draw it and cook it like the common peacock in Recipe 140.[142.1] When it is done
serve it hot or cold as you like, although it is better cold than hot.

You can do a heron and a bittern in the same way, being of the same species;
their plumage is different, though, and they are not migratory.

You can also roast a stork, which has white feathers, a neck and beak which
are much thinner and longer than those of a crane, and long, russet-coloured legs;
but it does not have a tongue. For the most part it feeds on snakes; it makes its nest
of dry bits of wood in high old walls, preferably in swampy places rather than in
elevated, dry places. I have seen many of them between the valleys of Comacchio

---

[141.2] *con un coltello che rada*: see the sharp points of the two *coltelli da raschiare* in Plate 13.

[142.1] The two Tramezzino printings read *nel Cap. 139*.

and the Po and elsewhere in Argenta, Boccaleone and Consandola.[142.2] In Milan and elsewhere in Lombardy many are raised domestically. Storks are born at the end of May and begin to be good in August, those being much better than fully mature ones. Storks come into Italy at the end of April and stay to the end of October.

If you want to make a larded broth of stork, follow the directions given for the jay in Recipe 132.[142.3] A crane is best when it is boiled in water, spices and prosciutto – in which broth lasagna is then cooked – and served with grated cheese and cinnamon on top.[142.4] If the crane is dismembered after being cooked, it can be covered with that lasagna.[142.5] The crane's gizzard and liver, if they are fresh, are done up like those of the peacock in Recipe 140.[142.6]

143. To spit-roast wild geese and cook them in several ways.

To be good a wild goose has to hang undrawn and unplucked for at least four days. It is then plucked dry and, when drawn, is roasted on a spit. It is cooked in all the ways set out above for the crane. It is much better in winter than in summer or any other time, that being its true season. You find likewise many varieties of wild geese, of both land and marshland, small and large, but the best ones are always those with white and russet feet that feed in the countryside, rather than those with black feet that feed in marshes and swamps.[143]

144. To spit-roast wild ducks and cook them in several ways.

I think ducks are of several sorts: big and small, diverse by plumage and by feet. But the best sort are those with a russet-coloured beak and feet because they feed in the countryside; those with a black beak and feet, that feed in marshlands, are not so good. However, all of them share the same season, between October and February. Those fowl are best during extremely cold weather. And generally all of them are happiest in damp, swampy places.

[142.2] Interestingly each of these three towns, Argenta, Boccalione and Consandolo, by the flat marshlands of the Po estuary called the Valli di Comacchio, lies on the road between Ravenna and Ferrara. We may conjecture that Scappi travelled that road at some time during his service to Marino Grimano of Venice. Compare where he writes in Recipe III,79, 'When I was in Venice and Ravenna ... '

[142.3] The two printed texts read *nel Cap. 131.*

[142.4] Modern punctuation in this sentence can obviously alter its sense considerably.

[142.5] See Recipe 145 where a fowl is dressed with other sorts of pasta.

[142.6] Both printed texts read *nel Cap. 139.*

[143] The bias against waterfowl is rooted in an old humoral theory that distrusted any overly humid or paludal influence.

To roast them, follow the directions given for the crane in Recipe 142.[144.1]
To make a larded broth of them, follow the directions for jays in Recipe 132.[144.2]
To cook them differently, once they are plucked and drawn remove their neck and
feet and put them into a pot in enough red wine, and a little vinegar, to cover
them, together with cut-up prosciutto, pepper, cinnamon, cloves, nutmeg, crushed
ginger, sugar, sage tips and large muscatel raisins. Seal up the pot so it cannot
breathe. Boil it for an hour and a half, more or less, depending on the age and size
of the ducks. When they are done, serve them dressed with their broth. Along
with those ingredients you can cook large whole onions, and prunes and dried
visciola cherries.

However, the ducks that are to be done in a larded broth and in the above way
do not need to be hung: rather they are best right after they are caught. They are
washed with the same wine and vinegar. When that washwater has been filtered,
cook them in it with the same ingredients as above: the preparation will be all the
tastier.

Every variety of those fowl, while still unfledged, can be roasted on a spit
and made into all those dishes that are made of a young partridge, especially in
the spring.

145. To boil poultry-yard geese and ducks and do them in various dishes.

Old poultry-yard ducks are very tender between October and Christmastide,
which is when their proper season is. They have to be plucked, either dry or in
water, and be left to hang undrawn for three days, more or less, depending on the
relative coolness or warmth of the place. Draw them, wash them, remove their
neck, wings and feet. If you want to stuff them with grated cheese and eggs along
with their fat and common spices, that is a possibility. Cook them in salted water
or in a meat broth. When they are done, serve them hot with garlic sauce or some
other sauce in dishes. If you want you can also cover them with macaroni or
tortellini,[145.1] or else with rice.

If you want to stew them, cut them up into pieces and, when those are washed,
put them into a pot with verjuice, prosciutto cut up small or fine saveloy, and some
of the condiments in the previous recipe ground up with a little saffron. Cook
them with the pot sealed tightly. They have to be served hot, covered with their
broth.

In all of those ways you can do up a domestic duck, and a Muscovy duck,[145.2]
which is bigger and darker than our local one. From the breast meat of a goose or

---

[144.1] Both printed texts read *nel Cap. 141.*

[144.2] Both printed texts read *nel Cap. 131.*

[145.1] For varieties of Scappi's *tortelletti*, see Recipes 177–80, below.

[145.2] *l'anatra domestica et d'India.* The latter is also called musk duck in modern Italian, *anatra
muschiata* or *anatra muta.* It had been introduced into Europe from South America by the middle
of the sixteenth century and had at that time a black plumage with white splotches.

duck you can make all those dishes that are made from a turkey cock in Recipe 141.

In the above ways you can also do a swan, which is much bigger than a goose, has a longer neck, extremely white plumage and a black beak. Many of the above wildfowl are found on the banks of the Po. In the winter, after they have been hung, they can be roasted on a spit the way a crane is done in Recipe 142.

146. To spit-roast goslings and ducklings or cook them in various ways.

While domestic goslings and ducklings are still unfledged, as in May while their feathers are still yellow, they can be roasted on a spit and cooked in all the ways that a chick is done in Recipe 127. But the larger ones, from the beginning of July through September, as soon as they have been killed are plucked, in hot water or dry, and are drawn because their intestine and liver are larger than in other fowl of that sort; besides, they go bad quickly and so they need to be cooked just as soon as the birds have been killed. When their neck and wings have been cut off, stuff them with one of the mixtures set out in Recipe 115. Blanch them in boiling water. Having trussed their feet on their rump, put them on a spit and cook them without larding them. When they are almost done, sprinkle them with ground salt, grated bread and fennel flour. When cooked, serve them hot with some garnishes in dishes. And if those garnishes and ducks are on the fatty side, you will not need to give them that sprinkling.

If you want to stew them in an oven, when they have been stuffed with a few garlic cloves, put them into an earthenware vessel containing beaten pork fat, cut-up prosciutto and cleaned garlic cloves, along with enough meat broth or water to half cover them, along with pepper, cinnamon, cloves, nutmeg and ground ginger. Cook them in the oven, turning them over from time to time. When they are almost done, you can put in gooseberries or verjuice grapes, and unripe plums.

Those fowl can also be cooked otherwise, as in La Marca: when they have been stuffed, their breast and thighs stuck with a few whole cloves, and are mounted on a spit, have the oven at a moderate temperature, not too hot. In it set two little spit holders or an arrangement of bricks on which to place the spit, letting its crank stick out the mouth of the oven, and with a dripping pan under the roast with chopped onions in it. Cook the fowl like that, turning them often and keeping the oven's heat moderate. When they are done, serve them garnished with the onions mixed with vinegar and must syrup. That is how you can do piglets, capons and other roasts.

If you want the above fowl steeped in a seasoning, if they are small and unfledged, when they are plucked and drawn split them in half and leave them for six hours in a seasoning of vinegar, must syrup, salt, crushed garlic cloves, pepper, cloves, coriander, cinnamon and ground nutmeg. Then remove them. But if they are big, boil them before putting them into the seasoning. Then cook them as above.

They can also be roasted on a grill after being boiled, the small ones split in half, the large ones in quarters, then sprinkled with fennel flour, grated bread and salt. Serve them hot with rose vinegar and sugar over top of them.

If you want to stew them in stewpots[146] with gooseberries or verjuice grapes or some other things, follow the directions given for the domestic dove in Recipe 130.

147. Several ways to cook all sorts of necks, wings and feet of the above fowl.

The necks, wings and feet must above all be fresh[147.1] – that is, the necks cleaned of blood, the follicles of the wings cleaned, and the feet cleaned of their outer skin. When they are clean and washed in several changes of water, the necks of geese, ducks, hens, goslings and capons can be stuffed with the same mixture as is used for the bodies of those birds, then boiled, braised in an oven and stewed with prosciutto and other ingredients as is done with their bodies. But if you want to roast those necks on a spit, when they have been stuffed and blanched in water they are let cool, larded with fine pork fat, put on the spit and cooked. When done, they are served with any garnishes in dishes or over top of them. Wings and feet can be parboiled with the *magone* – that is, the gizzard[147.2] – and sautéed in rendered fat with spring onions. Other fricassees can be made of them.

But wanting them in pottages, there is no need to parboil them. Rather, cut them up into pieces and put them into a pot with beaten pork fat, ground spices and sliced pork jowl, in enough water to cover them by three fingers. Cook them. When they are almost done, throw in gooseberries or verjuice grapes, and beaten common herbs. You can also thicken the broth with beaten egg yolks.

148. To spit-roast gizzards of goslings, geese, cranes, domestic peacocks and turkey hens, and to make various fricassees of them.

The gizzard of a domestic peacock and turkey cock are the most tasty of all birds' gizzards; if they are removed just as soon as the birds have been killed, they will be even tastier. If you want to roast them on a spit, more than half-cook them in salted water, then mount them on a slender spit, basting them with rendered fat and turning them slowly. Make up a mixture of flour, beaten egg yolks, sugar, saffron, rosewater and salt, giving it the consistency of a fritter batter; as the gizzards are cooking, baste on enough of that mixture that a crust is formed. Let them finish cooking until the batter is quite solid. Get very hot melted rendered fat and with a spoon brush it over them, then quickly sprinkle on fennel flour. Take them down and serve them hot with lime slices over them. You can also, after

---

[146] These are the earthenware *pignatte* shown in Plates 9 and 10.

[147.1] For Scappi the word *freschi* here connotes pure, unsullied.

[147.2] Scappi has used a regional word, *magone*, which he then clarifies with the more standard term for a fowl's gizzard, *ventricello*. The next recipe has *magone* alone.

they have been parboiled and are cool, stick them with fine lardoons of pork fat and cook them on the spit. When they are done they can be served with orange juice over them, or else covered with any of a variety of sauces.

They can also be split in half after they have been parboiled. Finish cooking them on a grill with a thin slice of pork fat to keep them from drying out. If you want to make a fricassee of them, follow the directions given for wings in the previous recipe.

149. Various ways to do tongues of ducks and domestic and wild geese.

Some people think it is pure fantasy to say that it is customary to cook fowls' tongues in various ways, yet I say that when I was in Venice in the service of the Most Illustrious and Most Reverend Cardinal Marin Grimano some were brought from Cyprus to his Illustrious Lordship immersed in rendered fat in boxes and earthenware vessels, and in seasoning in other containers; so you can judge whether they are esteemed. Should you wish, therefore, to do them up, as they are removed fresh from the mouth of those fowl you arrange them in an earthenware vessel with ground salt and fennel flour,[149.1] and leave them there until you are ready to cook them. If you want to keep them in boxes, take them out of the vessels and let them dry, then place them in the boxes in layers, sprinkling them with fennel flour. When you wish to cook them, bring them to a boil in water and the membrane on them will lift off. Finish cooking them on a grill or fry them in melted rendered fat. They can also be cooked on the grill without being parboiled. If they are fresh they can be cooked on the coals with a little salt on them. But there is no need to parboil the ones that have steeped in seasoning;[149.2] rather, just flour them and fry them in melted rendered fat. Serve them with a garnish of that same seasoning over them. The same is done with any that have been preserved in rendered fat.

Those tongues can make all the fricassees and pottages that are made with the necks and gizzards of the chickens above. To preserve them they need to be done in winter.

150. Several ways to cook the liver of geese, goslings, ducks, peacocks, turkey cocks, capons, hens and every other sort of fowl.

Among those livers, that of the capon and the common hen are the most excellent, followed by the goose's and gosling's. Any liver, to be good, needs to be removed and cooked immediately after the fowl has been killed. The larger ones can be made into *fegatelli*[150.1] in the caul of a goat-kid, wether or pig, and cooked on a spit interspersed with a few thin slices of pork fat and bay or sage

---

[149.1] This is a liquid mixture, a seasoned brine: see below.

[149.2] That is, the tongues that have not been dried out for storage in boxes.

[150.1] See Recipe II,106.

leaves. They can also be fried in rendered fat after being floured or not, with thin slices of prosciutto. The smaller ones can be sautéed in capon fat. Of all of the aforesaid livers you can make various fricassees with gooseberries or verjuice grapes. In whichever way they are cooked, they need to stay a little undercooked rather than overcooked.

The liver of the domestic goose that Jews raise is extemely big and weighs two or three pounds.[150.2] Just as soon as the bird is killed it is removed and immersed in warm cow's milk for a day, changing the milk twice: the liver swells in the milk and, when cooked, becomes tenderer. It needs to be wrapped in a caul and cooked whole on a spit, although you will have a great deal of difficulty to make it firm up. When it is done, it is served hot. If you do not want it done on a spit, it is floured and cooked in a pan containing melted rendered fat, being turned occasionally; otherwise it is cooked in that caul in the pan. It is served hot dressed with orange juice and sugar. You can also cut it into slices, flour them and fry them in rendered fat.

From those livers you can also make *tommacelle*, as is said for pork liver in Recipe 107.

151. To cook a chicken's unlaid eggs, tripe and blood in several ways.

Unlaid eggs without their shell can be done into all the *pottaggetti* and thick broths[151] into which the necks in Recipe 147 are done. With the fowl just killed, their tripe can be cooked as a thick soup like the goat-kid's tripe in Recipe 81, although cooking gives them a greenish-grey colour. After that of a goose and a gosling, a chicken's blood is the best; you can make small black puddings of it and use it in various ways like the pork blood in Recipe 110.

152. To prepare a dish of various ingredients called, in Spanish, *olla podrida*.[152.1]

This preparation, *oglia potrida*, is named thus by Spaniards because it is

---

[150.2] This seems to be early evidence of the production of *foie gras*. In the 1390s the *Menagier de Paris* directs how to fatten a goose in three days: feed it hot crustless bread soaked in cheese curds or 'lean milk' (247, §240). By 1651 La Varenne will have half a dozen recipes for *foie gras*. In 1614 Castelvetro comments in a note about the grain millet: 'I swear I have seen [geese] in Venice, fed on a mash made from millet, that weighed forty or fifty pounds or more, whose livers were as big as calves' livers and pale as snow. The Jews fatten up enormous quantities of geese, since they eat them instead of pork, which is forbidden them in the Laws of Moses' (trans. Riley, 103).

[151] The first preparation here, *pottaggetti*, is a particularly dainty sort of pottage; the second, common *brodetti*. Both culinary genres will be extensively treated in Book VI, the first in Recipes 48–50 and 162 ff., the second from Recipe 12 on. As their presence in Book VI (dishes for the sick) implies, each is considered by nature and composition to be a particularly delicate, digestible and nourishing food.

[152.1] Scappi writes, here as below, *oglia potrida*. The sense of the Spanish name *olla podrida* is literally a *pot pourri* or 'rotten pot': it is a pot of mixed ingredients so well cooked that they are disintegrating. As this dish combines meat and vegetables, we would not today be far wrong

made mostly in earthenware stewpots called *oglias*,[152.2] and *potride* [*sic*] means a variety of well cooked ingredients. To make that preparation, get two pounds of salted, marbled pork jowl, four pounds of desalted sowbelly, two pig's snouts, two ears, four feet split in half and semi-salted for a day, four pounds of wild-boar meat with its brisket fresh, and two pounds of good *salsiccioni*. When everything is cleaned, cook it in unsalted water. In salted water in another copper or earthenware pot also cook six pounds of wether rib, six pounds of salted veal kidney-fat, six pounds of fat beef, two capons or hens, and four fat domestic doves; remove from the broth whatever of all those ingredients is cooked first without disintegrating; set it aside in a vessel.[152.3] In another earthenware or copper pot, in the broth from the above meats, cook two hindquarters of a hare, cut up into pieces, three partridges, two pheasants or two wild ducks, large and fresh, twenty thrush, twenty quail and three rock partridge. When the above things are cooked, strain and mix the broths together, minding that they are not too salty. Then get peas, brownish-red chickpeas[152.4] and white chickpeas that have soaked to soften them, cleaned garlic bulbs, chopped old onions, hulled rice, shelled chestnuts and parboiled haricot beans. Cook all of that together in the broth. When the vegetables are almost done, put in kohlrabi, Savoy cabbage,[152.5] yellow rape, and saveloy or sausage. When it is all cooked and rather more thickened than broth-like, stir it up so that everything blends together, testing it from time to time for its saltiness. Into that add pepper and cinnamon. Then set out great platters and put part of the mixture on them without the broth: get all the large fowl, quartered, and the large meats, and the salami sliced, leaving the small birds whole; divvy those up onto

---

in calling it a stew. In the Spanish Netherlands Antonius Magirus copied Scappi's version of the preparation, making several substitutions for southern ingredients: *Koocboec oft familieren Keuken-boec*, 1612, 46. He prefaces his translation with the comment that this dish is 'the best I have ever tasted: *het beste dat ick ete.*' See Schildermans and Sels, 'Una traduzione olandese,' 72–3. Lancelot de Casteau, writing around 1585, is likewise familiar with the dish and, with Scappi, gives his recipe for it the rubric *Un pot pourry dict en Espaignolle Oylla podride.* His ingredients are at least as numerous as Scappi's and would need as enormous a cauldron.

[152.2] Scappi is familiar enough with the authentic Spanish term to reproduce the proper Spanish plural, *ollas*. Concerning the 'exotic' element in this and other recipes in Scappi, see Héraud, 'Exotisme culinaire,' particularly 124. It should also be remembered that Spanish influence was strong at the courts of high prelates in Italy, and that the Castilian Francisco Reinoso was personal steward to Pius V and the person to whom Scappi dedicated his *Opera*.

[152.3] Clearly Scappi intends that each meat be taken out of the cooking pot as soon as it is cooked but not overcooked: there will be a little more simmering to come for everything.

[152.4] Scappi specifies that these first chickpeas are *rossi*, this normally being a russet colour.

[152.5] For Scappi this is *cauli Milanesi*, 'Milanese cabbage.' Castelvetro describes *verzotti o cavoli lombardi* – 'green cabbage [modern Italian *verza*] or Lombard cabbage.' He also writes that it is gathered after the first frosts. In Recipe 198, below, Scappi mentions its crimped leaves. See also Recipe 138, above.

the platters over that mixture. On top of that put some of the other mixture with the saveloy cut into pieces. Make three layers like that. Get a spoonful of the fattest broth and splash it over top. Cover everything over with another platter and let it sit in a warm place for half an hour. Serve it hot with mild spices over top. That preparation is more common in winter than at any other time. The partridge, pheasants, thrush, ducks and quail can be not only boiled but also roasted on a spit, then right afterwards cut up. Instead of the capons and hens you can boil fat domestic geese and ducks, and of those ducks or geese take only the rump and breast. If you want to make that dish in the summer, get the meat that is available. Instead of hare, get a kid's hindquarters roasted on a spit and cut into pieces. That dish can be made with a variety of more or fewer ingredients, entirely at your discretion.

153. To prepare a dish of hard wheat with various other ingredients, in the Moorish style, called *Succussu*.[153.1]

Get white Regno hard wheat[153.2] that does not smell badly and is clean of dust. Put it through a fine colander[153.3] or a fine sieve. For every pound of sieved semolina get six ounces of fine flour in another pot. Put the semolina into an amply large wooden vessel; stir it around there with the palm of your hand, splashing it by means of a small brush with warm water tinged with saffron, and sprinkling it occasionally with flour. Repeat this until the flour is used up and the semolina has turned into granules like millet or foxtail millet. Sieve those granules through a fine colander into another wooden vessel which is much larger and shallower; let them sit there for an hour and a half. Then grease the palm of your hand with a good-smelling oil of sweet almonds or olives, lightly stirring the granules until they become as shiny as millet. Have an earthenware or tinned copper cooking pot on hand, and six pounds of fat beef cut up into half-pound pieces, four pounds of cut-up wether ribs, two pounds of sliced salt pork jowl, and

---

[153.1] In Arabic the preparation is called *kuskus* which, using the French, English spells couscous. The preparation is still made with fine grains of semolina. See Magali Morsy, *Le monde des couscous et recettes de couscous*, 2 vols. (Aix-en-Provence: Edisud, 1996); and Perry, 'Couscous and Its Cousins.'

[153.2] *semolella del Regno*: the 'kingdom' that Scappi refers to here is likely that of Naples and Sicily. See Serventi and Sabban, *La pasta*, 56f., on the historically large role of Sicily and Sardinia in the making and shipping of various sorts of pasta; and at 64, on the shipping of hard wheat. (See also the note on Scappi's Neapolitan pizza in Recipe V,73.) Scappi's specification of 'white' likely implies that all trace of the grain's hull or husk and the bran have been removed: see Recipe 170, below.

[153.3] Scappi's *foratoro* is illustrated in the accompanying engravings in Plates 9 and 10. This filtering is intended to clean out any remaining hull and to remove any mineral grit – from either the grain field, the threshing yard or the millstones – that might contaminate the flour; in Recipe 186 the process is called *sabbionarsi*.

a quartered capon; cook all of that in water. When those meats are almost done, put in yellow Milanese saveloy, an ounce of pepper and cinnamon combined, and enough saffron. Finish off cooking everything with the vessel tightly lidded. When the meats are all done, take them out of the broth and put them aside in a warm place. Strain the broth and put it into a large-bodied earthenware or copper stewpot with a narrow mouth. Get another pot[153.4] which has holes from the middle down like a colander, and put the granules of semolina into it. Seal up the pot with its lid so it cannot breathe and put that holed pot with the semolina in it into the top of the one with the broth,[153.5] watching that all of the holed part is fully in and that it does not touch the broth – because if it touched the broth the preparation would not work. Seal all around with dough. Boil the broth pot on the coals away from flames until the semolina grains are cooked by the steam from the broth. They need, though, to be on the heat at least two hours. Then take the holed pot off the broth pot, remove its lid and take out the semolina, which will be like a ball. Put it into the first, wooden vessel, gently breaking up the semolina, which will be bunched together, so that it becomes like it originally was – that is, in granules. Then get a platter like the one for the *oglia putrida*[153.6] and on it put a portion of those granules with a portion of the cooked meat, and over that meat put the remainder of the semolina granules, sprinkling the first and last layers[153.7] with grated cheese, sugar and cinnamon. When everything is dished out onto the platter, get a spoonful[153.8] of fat broth from the meat pot, with a little fresh butter in it, and pour that over the preparation. Cover it with another platter and let it stand for an hour on the hot coals.

In that same way you can do *millefanti*[153.9] cooked in the broth, putting them on the platter with the meat cooked and cut up as above.

154. To prepare a thick rice soup in the Damascene style with various meats.

Get new Salernitan or Milanese rice that does not smell badly, clean it and wash it in several changes of warm water; let it drain. Have fat, strained broth on hand in which the following are cooked: six pounds of ribs from a fat wether, three pounds of veal ribs, a capon, two fat doves, quartered, and four pieces of

---

[153.4] The cooking pot called a *pignatta* is normally of earthenware, hence Scappi's comparison of the present *pignatta sbusciata* to a metal *foratoro*.

[153.5] The cook now has a form of double boiler.

[153.6] The Spanish *olla podrida* of the previous recipe.

[153.7] In both printings the word is set as *vaso*, perhaps in error for *suolo*.

[153.8] Scappi's kitchen stirring spoons were, of course, much larger than today's tablespoon.

[153.9] This is an old preparation consisting of granules made from ordinary flour. Scappi's directions for making it are in Recipes 171 and 172, below.

fresh fine saveloy. Get a cast-copper cooking basin[154.1] and put two bowlfuls of broth into it; boil it on the coals away from the flame. Into that put a bowlful of rice and a quarter [-ounce][154.2] of crushed pepper, and boil the rice until it begins to swell up. Then put in four ounces of white chickpeas[154.3] and four ounces of shelled dry chestnuts that have first been cooked in meat broth. When the rice has absorbed all the broth, stir it with a wooden spoon or spatula, adding in eight ounces of melted fresh butter and not failing to stir it. When you see it swollen up, again add in another eight ounces of butter. When the mixture has absorbed the broth and a part of the butter and is firm, get a platter and put half of the mixture in it,[154.4] spreading it out and sprinkling it with sugar and cinnamon. On that put the cooked meat of the quadrupeds and fowl and the cut-up saveloy; cover those with the remainder of the mixture. Get four ounces of melted butter and sprinkle it over the top. Cover all that with another platter and let it sit for an hour on the hot coals or in a moderately hot oven. Then serve it hot.

155. To prepare rice flour, from which you can make various hot thick soups.

Get rice from Salerno or some other place, not over a year old and not smelling badly. Remove all dirt from it, wash it in several changes of warm water and have it go back and forth between two wooden vessels containing warm water – that is, pour it slowly several times from one vessel into the other – until the sand is out of it and stays at the bottom of the vessels. Let it sit in warm water for an hour, then take it out and let it drain. Grind it in a marble mortar with a wooden pestle. When ground, sift the flour through a fixed filter of gauze or horsehair. If, though, you want to dry the rice before grinding it in the mortar, that is optional; however, grinding it wet there will be no need to sprinkle it with water as you do when it is ground dry. With that flour you can make whitedish, and you can make other dishes as is set out in their respective recipes.

156. To prepare a rice dish in the Lombard style, braised, with chicken flesh, saveloy and egg yolks.[156.1]

Get rice which is cleaned as above and cook it in a broth that has cooked

---

[154.1] The *bastardella* is a relatively heavy recipient, usually with two handles. Its rounded bottom makes it useful for cooking delicate foodstuffs that need stirring, usually over a moderate heat. At this point in his recipes Scappi begins to specify its use fairly often. See Book I, §44 and in Plate 9, 'Concha.'

[154.2] In the context, the phrase *un quarto di pepe* (in both printings) would be understood implicitly as 'a quarter of a bowlful of pepper' – here, we should hope, *not* Scappi's intention.

[154.3] Chickpeas appear to have been a popular commodity in Scappi's day. Castelvetro writes, 'On summer evenings after supper, our good ladies sit around in droves on their doorsteps, and when they see the countrywomen coming home from the fields with baskets full of tender young chickpeas, they buy quantities of them just for fun, to nibble at raw' (trans. Riley, 102).

[154.4] Scappi writes 'into the bottom' (*nel fondo*). His *piatto* usually has a good dish to it.

[156.1] Two far-from-plain versions of risotto.

capons, geese and saveloy. When it is done such that it is firm, take a portion of it and put it on an earthenware, silver or pewter[156.2] platter. Sprinkle it with cheese, sugar and cinnamon, and on the rice put a few dollops of fresh butter and capon breast and goose breast along with finely chopped up saveloy. Then sprinkle on cheese, sugar and cinnamon. Repeat, building up three layers of it.[156.3] On the topmost pour melted fresh butter, and sprinkle on the same mixture. Put it into an oven that is not too hot, leaving it there for half an hour until it browns a little. Splash rosewater over it and serve it hot.

You can do that rice another way. When it is cooked, grease the platter with butter and on that put slices of fresh unsalted provatura sprinkled with sugar, cinnamon and grated cheese, and on that put the rice. On the rice put raw fresh egg yolks, the number of them depending on the amount of rice there is, having first made hollows in the rice in which you set the yolks. Over those yolks again put the same amount of sliced provatura sprinkled as before with sugar, cheese and cinnamon. Then cover that with as much again of rice. In that way you can make up two or three layers. On the last put a little butter. Set it on hot coals or in the oven as before. Serve it hot.

157. To prepare a bastard *capirotata*.[157.1]

In a mortar grind two pounds of cleaned Milanese almonds with two breasts of spit-roasted capons and three ounces of breadcrumb[157.2] soaked in malmsey or Greek wine. Moisten everything with four pounds of cold meat broth and put it through a strainer, adding in six fresh egg yolks, raw. When it is strained, put the mixture into a cooking basin of red copper with six ounces of muscatel malmsey,[157.3] one pound of sugar, one ounce of ground cinnamon and half an ounce of cloves and nutmeg together. Boil everything on the coals away from the fire, stirring continuously with a spatula until it thickens a little. Get ten doves or

---

[156.2] Scappi wrote *stagno* here and elsewhere in his work; properly the word means tin. Scappi has no distinct term for pewter, which was certainly in use in noble Italian dining halls and kitchens. Given that pewter was normally eighty per cent or more tin at this time, with the balance lead, it seems probable that the author often used 'tin' to mean 'pewter.' See Recipes II,174, 241 and 247, for instance.

[156.3] See the typical 'Lombard' layering in Recipes 22, 121 and elsewhere.

[157.1] For evidence of the long history of Scappi's *capirotata* see the note to Recipe 73, above. The qualification *bastarda* may distinguish this version of the preparation as a 'plain' or 'basic' one; compare this with Recipe II,73, which uses the roasted lean meat of a weather's leg, and Recipe 159, which uses roasted capon breast.

[157.2] That is, the soft, crustless part of bread.

[157.3] The next recipe offers an option between muscatel or malmsey: *malvagia garba, o moscatella*. In Recipes II,163 and 249, however, Scappi confirms that *malvagia moscatella* is a distinct variety of wine.

four wild ducks roasted on a spit, and take the flesh and rumps of those doves or ducks and put them, sprinkled with sugar and cinnamon, on a platter. On top of them put the mixture, letting it sit for a quarter of an hour on hot coals or in a moderately hot oven. Serve it hot with sugar and cinnamon over it.

With that mixture you can garnish a variety of roasts.

158. To prepare another *capirotata* to garnish a variety of roasts.

In a mortar grind a pound of roasted Milanese almonds – that is, toasted on a shovel or in a frying pan – along with a pound of currant raisins, two ounces of fine Neapolitan *mostaccioli*,[158.1] and a veal kidney roasted on a spit with its fat, or else with the flesh of a wild duck roasted on a spit. When everything has been ground up together, moisten it with four pounds of cold broth and half a pound of verjuice, and put it through a strainer or filter, adding in an ounce of cinnamon, half an ounce of pepper, an ounce of cloves and nutmeg together, diluted orange juice,[158.2] a pound of smooth malmsey or muscatel, two pounds of sugar and one pound of seedless muscatel raisins that have first been brought to a boil in wine and sugar. Then set it to cook in a cooking basin or casserole pot on the coals, stirring constantly until it thickens a little. Have ready slices of bread toasted on the grill and ten fat dovecot doves roasted on a spit and quartered or six quartered partridge. Arrange the slices of toast, sprinkled with sugar and cinnamon, in a dish and on them put the quarters of fowl with a portion of the mixture. In that way make up two or three layers. Cover the dish and let it sit for half an hour on hot coals or else in an oven. Serve it hot with sugar and cinnamon over top.

With that same mixture you can garnish a variety of spit-roasted fowl.

159. To prepare a mixture popularly called common *capirotata*.

Get two pounds of Parmesan cheese or of good, creamy Ligurian cheese, and one pound of creamy cheese that is not too salted, and grind them in a mortar with ten garlic cloves that have first been parboiled, and the breast meat of two spit-roasted capons. When everything is ground up, add in ten raw egg yolks and a pound of sugar, and blend cold meat or chicken broth into all that – cold, because if that broth were hot it could not blend in nor, because of the cheese, could it let the mixture be strained as it should be through the strainer or filter. When it has been strained, put it into a well tinned cooking basin or casserole pot, and make it rather thin, cooking it on the coals away from the flame. Add in an ounce of cinnamon, half an ounce of pepper, half an ounce of cloves and nutmeg combined, and enough saffron. As the mixture cooks, stir it with a wooden spoon or a spatula until it thickens. When it is done, try it. Then get sautéed veal or goat-kid sweetbreads, stir everything together. Serve it dressed with sugar and

---

[158.1] See the note in Recipe II,63, above.

[158.2] *sugo di melangole di mezo sapore*; the alternative is *di sapore forte*, seen in Recipe II,279.

cinnamon. Instead of the sweetbreads you can put in the tip of milk-fed veal breast,[159.1] boiled and a little sautéed.

That mixture can be used to cover thrush and other small birds that have been roasted on a spit.[159.2]

160. To prepare a yellowdish[160.1] that can be served either as a thick soup[160.2] or as a garnishing for various meats.

Get twelve pounds of goat's or cow's milk fresh that day, and put it through a filter with fourteen ounces of rice flour made that day as is directed in Recipe 155,[160.3] two pounds of fine sugar, one ounce of cinnamon, a quarter-ounce of ginger, half an ounce of pepper, and saffron and salt in sufficient amounts. Put it all into a tinned cooking basin or casserole pot. Cook it on a tripod or a brazier[160.4] with a coal fire, constantly stirring with a wooden spatula. As it begins to boil, put in six ounces of fresh dates and four ounces of dry figs – both dates and figs chopped up small – five ounces of shelled pinenuts that have softened in cold water for seven hours, five ounces of seedless muscatel raisins, five more of very clean currant raisins. Those ingredients are not to be ground all together but separately, the hardest ones first.[160.5] The raisins are to be put in when the yellowdish is almost cooked. When it is cooked so that it is thick, serve it hot or cold as you like, dressed with sugar and cinnamon.

If you want to cover roast meats with it, keep it more liquid.

In winter that dish can be kept four or five days. If you want to make it with almond milk and starch,[160.6] follow the directions given in Recipe 222 in the book

---

[159.1] That is, its brisket.

[159.2] See the slender spits, identified as *Spedi per uceleti*, in Plate 13.

[160.1] This *ginestrata* had been well known in cookery across Europe for several centuries when Scappi inherited it. It was named after the plant *ginestra*, broom, the brilliant yellow of whose flowers must have inspired its first cooks. The earlier versions of the dish were simpler, the saffron enjoying a more significant role than Scappi in his list of ingredients seems to give it with the phrase *zafferano a bastanza*. In Recipe II,255 see the plant *ginestra* used to define the colour yellow. A lean version of the preparation is offered in Recipe III,223.

[160.2] This is the culinary genre that Scappi calls a *minestra* and that he has mentioned in Recipes II,2, 20, 22, 26, 112, 151, 154 and 155. He will explore its range of possibilities in the next group of recipes.

[160.3] In the text of both printings, 1570 and 1581, *Cap. 154*. The same error – one number too low for the correct recipe – is found also in Recipe 162, below. At some late moment in the preparation of his manuscript Scappi has inserted a recipe into the series before the present Recipe 155.

[160.4] This *focone* can be seen in Plate 11, *fuochone*. It consists of a metal drum on legs that contains hot coals, for a relatively controlled heat, and a grill.

[160.5] The person working the pestle is to allow the hardest ingredient the longest cooking time.

[160.6] See Book I, §27.

on fish.

161. To prepare a hazelnut dish.

Get three pounds of hazelnuts – that is, filberts[161] – shelled or roasted on a shovel and cleaned with a coarse cloth; grind them in a mortar along with a pound and a half of spit-roasted veal loin. With that meat you also grind kidney-fat or flesh of spit-roasted fowl and beef marrow. When everything is ground up, moisten it with a cold meat broth that is not too salty. Put it through a strainer or fine filter and into a tinned cooking basin or casserole pot, mixing in a pound and a half of sugar, four ounces of verjuice, two ounces of smooth malmsey, one ounce of cinnamon, one ounce of pepper, ginger, cloves and nutmeg together, and three ounces of rosewater. Cook everything as for the yellowdish in the previous recipe. When it is done, serve it garnished with sugar and cinnamon.

That mixture can be used to cover spit-roasted fowl, sweetbreads and fried liver. If you do not have hazelnuts, you can use shelled and roasted pinenuts or pistachios.

162. To prepare a thick soup of whitedish.

Get twelve pounds – that is, two Roman jugs[162.1] – of fresh, creamy goat's or cow's milk, and put it through a filter with twenty-two ounces of new flour from Salerno or Milan rice and made as directed in Recipe 155.[162.2] When filtered, put it into a tinned cooking basin or casserole pot, being careful that the pot is smooth because often the hammer marks on it cause food to stick. Put the container with its milk on the fire – that is, on a tripod or a brazier – and stir it with a spatula. As it begins to heat up, put in a little salt and the breast of a hen killed that day, boiled and combed out like hair, which strands can be beaten in another vessel with another beaker of milk before being put into that container. If you want, you can pound them two or three times with a pestle in a marble mortar; afterwards beat them again with milk so that they pull apart from one another. Put them into the basin with three pounds of fine sugar, being sure to stir it continuously until it is cooked. To tell when it is done, lift the spatula and if the whitedish sticks to it and makes a thread and is transparent, then it's cooked. I have found by experience that when that dish is firm and does not smell of the flour, you can take it off the tripod. Then you beat it for a quarter of an hour with the spatula, adding in half a pound of rosewater, keeping the pot on the coals, though. And when the whitedish is like its name says it should be, a lustrous white, its taste consistent

---

[161] Scappi uses two words here, *nocelle* and *avellane* respectively, to designate the same nut.

[162.1] This size of the *boccale* in Rome is confirmed in Recipes VI,6 and 206. Each of the two *boccali* would therefore contain 2.7 litres of water, for a total of roughly five and one-third litres. See a *boccale* in Plate 24.

[162.2] In both editions, *Cap. 154.*

with its fine appearance, you can serve it, hot or cold as you wish, with sugar over it.

If you want to cover capons or a boiled calf's of kid's head with that preparation, keep it runnier. If the milk is not creamy, as is the case in winter, for every two and two-thirds litres[162.3] of it put in four ounces of fresh butter washed in several changes of water; in summer to make the whitedish thicker, instead of butter put in the melted kidney-fat of a calf or kid, clarified[162.4] with water after it has been melted – that is, when it is ground in a mortar and the membrane around it removed, it is liquified in a stewpot with a little water and, when melted, it is poured off through a filter into a very large pot full of cold water and the fat will come to the surface; when congealed, take it out of that water and put it into different water. When the whitedish is almost cooked, add that fat into it. And take care to follow the serving directions given above.

If you do not have time to draw the chicken breast into strands, pound it in a marble mortar, sprinkling it continually with milk. When it has been pounded, moisten it with that milk and, without straining it, put it into the pot. For grinding, capon breast will always be better after having hung a little while than right after it has been killed. If you do not have a mortar, beat it with knives on a white table of elmwood, sprinkling it with milk and being careful that it is exposed to as little air as possible because air will brown and toughen it.

163. To prepare a yellowdish or *zabaglione*[163.1] with fresh egg yolks.

Get the yolks of fifteen eggs laid that day, beat them with ten ounces of muscatel malmsey or Greek wine from Somma, filter that with eight ounces of cold chicken broth, eight ounces of fine sugar and three-quarters of an ounce of ground cinnamon. Cook that in a tinned copper cooking basin or a casserole pot along with four ounces of fresh butter, stirring constantly with a spoon until it thickens. Serve it with sugar and cinnamon over top.

You can also do it alternatively: put it into a small kettle of tinned copper or a squat pot, then put that on the mouth of a pitcher[163.2] which is full of boiling water so that the small kettle or pot touches the water. Seal up the pitcher's mouth and keep it tightly closed, leaving it like that for half an hour until it has thickened. Serve it hot with sugar and cinnamon over top.

[162.3] Again, Scappi's measure is a *boccale*.

[162.4] *purgato*.

[163.1] See Scappi's *zambaglione* (*sic*) also in Recipes VI,64 and 67. The modern *zabaglione* or *zabaione* is described by Zingarelli as a frothy cream made from beating egg yolks with sugar, adding in a liqueur-like wine (such as marsala) and cooking that in a double boiler. A version of the preparation is found already in the *Neapolitan Recipe Collection*, Recipe 220.

[163.2] The *cucumo* is a copper or earthenware flask with a neck and single handle. It is illustrated in Plate 10.

164. To prepare a thick soup of whitedish with starch and steeped pinenuts.

Grind two pounds of shelled Milanese almonds in a mortar, and moisten them with ten pounds of cold meat broth that is not too fatty or too salty. Put that through a filter along with a pound of freshly made starch flour, two pounds of fine sugar and enough salt. Put it into a casserole pot and cook it like the whitedish of Recipe 162.[164] When it is almost done, put in eight ounces of filtered lime juice and six ounces of shelled pinenuts that have been softened in cold water. When it is cooked, put in four ounces of limes with their outer peel and seeds removed and cut up into pieces, which limes have soaked in rosewater for two hours. When everything is stirred together, serve it hot or cold as you like, with sugar over it.

165. To prepare a thick soup of whitedish with breadcrumb and Milanese almonds.

In a mortar grind a pound of shelled Milanese almonds with a pound and a half of breadcrumb soaked in meat broth and a boiled chicken breast, and moisten that with four pounds of the broth in which the bread soaked; put all that through a filter. Cook it like the previous preparation with a pound and a half of sugar. When it is almost done, add in four ounces of rosewater and finish off cooking it. When done, it is served hot or cold with sugar on top. Into that dish you can also put a beaker of verjuice but no less broth. And it would be done like a yellowdish if, in addition, it had pepper, cloves, cinnamon, nutmeg and saffron.

166. To prepare a thick soup of starch in a meat broth.

Get a pound of starch and set it to soak in six pounds of cold chicken broth; filter it. Add in a pound and a half of sugar and a little salt, and cook it in a casserole pot or a cooking basin the way you do whitedish as in Recipe 162.[166] When it is almost done, add in four ounces of rosewater and three ounces of melted chicken fat. Serve it hot or cold with fine sugar over the top. Optionally it can be either thick or thin. If you want it done with almond milk, for every pound of almonds you put in six ounces of starch moistened with five pounds of cold meat broth.

167. To prepare an impromptu[167] thick soup of whitedish.

Cook two pounds of very clean rice with twelve pounds of cow's or goat's milk, two and a half pounds of fine sugar and enough salt, so that it is thick. Put that through a filter and add in three ounces of rosewater and four ounces of veal

---

[164] In both editions: *nel Cap. 161.*

[166] Once again the two texts have *Cap. 161.* However, in the next recipe both strangely show the correct reference: *Cap. 162.*

[167] *all'improvista* – that is, that can be done on short notice. Whitedish being one of the universally common and traditionally favoured preparations, it would be useful for any cook, particularly at a cosmopolitan court, to be able to do it quickly for unexpected guests. See also Recipes VI,15 (for a chicken broth) and VI,76 (for another whitedish).

or goat-kid kidney-fat, melted and purified as is described in Recipe 162. Heat it up in a casserole pot, and serve it hot or cold as you wish, with fine sugar over it.

168. To prepare thick white soup of ricotta.

Get four pounds of fresh ewe's or cow's ricotta, made that day and creamy, with two and half pounds of fresh butter, and put it all into a cooking basin with two pounds of sugar, three ounces of rosewater and three more ounces of starch moistened with six ounces of fresh goat's milk. Cook it in a casserole pot or a cooking basin like the whitedish of Recipe 162. Serve it hot, dressed with fine sugar. If you want it like a yellowdish, put in pepper, cinnamon and saffron.

169. To prepare a thick milk soup popularly called Hungarian Soup.[169.1]

Get six pounds of fresh goat's or cow's milk, twenty fresh, beaten eggs, enough salt, an ounce of cinnamon and a little saffron; filter everything with a pound and a half of fine sugar. Put it into a copper or earthenware pot which has been greased with six ounces of firm fresh butter. Cover the pot and put it into a big casserole pot with water to cook it. When it has cooked so that it is almost like curdled milk,[169.2] have it served either hot or cold as you wish. If you want it white do not put in any cinnamon or saffron.

You can also do it differently with twenty egg yolks, four pounds of milk, four ounces of orange juice, one ounce of cinnamon, half an ounce of ginger, a little saffron, two ounces of rosewater and a pound of sugar. With everything put through the filter, cook it as above.

170. To prepare a thick semolina soup with goat's or cow's milk.[170.1]

Get two pounds of white hard wheat,[170.2] cleanly hulled and even better washed, and five and a third litres[170.3] of goat's or cow's milk, a pound of fresh butter and enough salt. Cook it slowly on the coals in a casserole pot or a cooking basin. When it is almost done, put in a pound of sugar and four ounces of rosewater. As it cooks it is immaterial whether you stir it with a wooden spoon or spatula.

[169.1] *Minestra di latte volgarmente chiamata Ongaresca.* Used later to fill a pie, it is prepared for lean-day consumption in Recipe V,42.

[169.2] Scappi's Italian word here, *giuncata*, is related to the English word junket: in cheesemaking, in order to produce curds the whey was squeezed from the clots between mats of reeds (Latin *juncus*).

[170.1] This recipe is an interesting forerunner, with even more interesting variations, of today's semolina pudding.

[170.2] As before, this is not ground flour but the whole grains from which the chaff has been removed. It is the *semolella* that Scappi has written in his recipe's rubric. See other uses for this sort of wheat and flour in Recipe V,153, For the qualification white, see also Recipe 153, above.

[170.3] Each of the two *boccali* that Scappi uses to measure a liquid contains twelve pounds or roughly two and two-thirds litres.

When it is done, serve it hot or cold with sugar over it. In the same way you can do it with a fat meat broth, and combine cheese and eggs with it.

171. To prepare a thick soup of flour and grated bread, commonly called *mille-fanti*.[171.1]

Get ten ounces of flour and eight ounces of grated bread, sieved, and mix them together along with a quarter-ounce of ground pepper. Get four fresh egg yolks and a beaker of cold water tinged with saffron, beaten together. Spread the flour out on a table, splash the beaten egg on it and mix it gently with knives or with a little wooden pallet in such a way that the flour becomes like tiny little balls. Put those tiny balls through a sieve or strainer into a tourte pan, without putting your hand into the sieve.[171.2] Put the pan with the ones that have gone through into it by themselves onto hot ash the way tourtes are done with a hot lid over them[171.3] and leave them like that until they dry out. If you do not have a lid, put them into an oven that is not too hot. Because the mixture will always be damp, wait till they have dried but not burnt. Then take them out of the tourte pan onto a table because in open air the grains will firm up. Put them back into a very clean strainer or a fine filter and sieve off the excess flour. Have a fat broth ready and boiling, and put the *millefanti* into it, every pound of them needing six pounds of broth. When they are cooked, serve them with grated cheese and cinnamon over them. In the same way you can cook them in goat's milk or with butter and water. They can also be kept for three or four months after they are made in the tourte pan.[171.4]

If you want to make a lot of them, take whatever is left in the strainer or the sieve and put it back on the table, sprinkle it with flour and beat it lightly with knives; while beating turn it upside down several times until it looks well beaten, then put it through the strainer. In drying that, follow the same directions as above.

172. To prepare *millefanti* from flour for keeping.

Get flour that was ground under the August moon because it is more durable, in an amount for the quantity you want to make of the *millefanti*; spread it out on a big wide board. Get warm salted water and with a millet whisk[172] sprinkle

---

[171.1] The sense of the name, 'a thousand pageboys,' is interesting, describing as it does the tiny elongated granules of flour that are the basis of this dish. See also Recipe 153, above. The fifteenth-century *Neapolitan Recipe Collection* offers an earlier version of the preparation in its Recipe 19: *Milli Fanti in Menestra*.

[171.2] That is, without exerting pressure on the material being sieved.

[171.3] *con il coperchio caldo sopra*: Plate 9 shows several *coperchi per tortere* designed to hold live coals or embers on the top of the pan.

[171.4] See the following recipe.

[172] *una scopettina di mellica*. The stalk used for this purpose is either of common millet or sorghum. For the grains of millet in this same sentence Scappi writes *miglio*.

the water on the flour, turning it around with the pallet as is done with the other ones until everything turns into granules the size of millet grains. Then put them through a sieve onto another board and dry them in the sun, carrying on the same way until all the flour is used up. When they have dried, sieve them with a fine filter so the excess flour on them is removed. Put them back on the board and let them sit another day in the sun. Then put them away into little bags or wooden vessels for a whole year.

If you want to make a thick soup of them with a meat broth or milk, follow the directions given above.

173. To prepare a thick soup of tagliatelle.[173.1]

Work two pounds of flour, three eggs and warm water into a dough, kneading it on a table for a quarter of an hour. Roll it out thin with a pin and let the sheet of dough dry out a little. With a cutting wheel[173.2] trim away the irregular parts, the fringes. When it has dried, though not too much because it would break up, sprinkle it with flour through the sifter so it will not stick. Then take the rolling pin and, beginning at one end, wrap the whole sheet loosely onto the pin, draw the pin out and cut the rolled-up dough crosswise with a broad, thin knife. When they are cut, broaden them. Let them dry out a little and, when they are dry, filter off the excess flour through a sieve. Make up a soup of them with a fat meat broth, or milk and butter. When they are cooked, serve them hot with cheese, sugar and cinnamon. If you want to make lasagne of them, cut the dough lengthwise on[173.3] the pin, and likewise divide it lengthwise in two, and cut that into little squares. Cook them in the broth of a hare, a crane or some other meat, or in milk. Serve them hot with cheese, sugar and cinnamon.

174. To prepare a thick macaroni soup in the Roman style.

Make up a dough with a pound of flour, four[174.1] ounces of white breadcrumb which has soaked in warm goat's milk, four egg yolks and two ounces of sieved sugar. When it is ready and not too moist, and has been kneaded on a table for half an hour, make a sheet of it with a rolling pin, leaving that sheet a little thicker than the previous one. Let the sheet dry. With an iron or wooden roller,[174.2] cut macaroni. When they are made, let them dry out. If you want to cook them in plain water, do that in a large pot with a good lot of water and enough salt; put the

---

[173.1] This ribbon pasta, *tagliatelli* as Scappi writes it, is akin to the narrower fettucine and seems to have been native to Bologna, where it remains popular. Scappi uses the pasta again in Recipe V,84. See Riley, *The Oxford Companion to Italian Food*, 376.

[173.2] See varieties of this *sperone* in Plates 14 and 15.

[173.3] *Sic.* The rolling pin need not have been removed.

[174.1] The number *quattro* is omitted in the 1581 printing.

[174.2] This *ruzzolo* is likely of the same design as the *ferro da maccaroni* illustrated in Plate 12.

macaroni in when the water is boiling because, put into cold water, they will sink to the bottom. That is a dough for making every sort of drawn pasta.[174.3] When they have boiled for half an hour, see if they are tender enough; if they are not, let them boil until they are thoroughly done. When done, have at hand a silver, pewter or earthenware platter broadly sprinkled with grated cheese, sugar and cinnamon, and set with slices of fresh provatura. Put some well drained macaroni onto that and on it in turn sprinkle cheese, sugar and cinnamon, with slices of provatura and lumps of butter. In that way make up three layers. Splash rosewater over it all, cover it with another platter and let it sit on hot coals or in a moderately hot oven for half an hour. Serve it hot.

175. To prepare a thick macaroni soup with an iron rod.

Make up a dough similar to the one above but firmer, and sweeter with sugar; colour it with saffron. Spread the dough out, making sheets the thickness of the spine of a knife. Let it dry up – that is, dry out – and cut it in strips half a finger wide and four fingers long. Get an iron stiletto[175.1] – that is, a needle a handswidth long, like what is used to make birettas[175.2] – and put it on the strips so that it lies over the full length of the strip, and with the palm of your hand give it the shape of macaroni,[175.3] so that the dough goes right around the iron stiletto; then draw out the stiletto. Let the macaroni, now hollow, dry. When making that macaroni, make sure that the sheet of dough is lightly floured so it will not stick to the iron rod. When they are dry they can be cooked and served like the ones above. Note that these as well as the ones above can be cooked in a fat meat broth or else in milk and butter.

176. To prepare a thick soup with macaroni called 'gnocchi.'

Get two pounds of flour and a pound of grated and sieved white bread; make a dough of that with a fat broth that is boiling, or with water, adding in four beaten egg yolks as you knead the dough. When it is done in such a way that it is neither too firm nor too runny, but has been made exactly right, take a walnut's amount of it. Sprinkle the back of a cheese grater[176] with flour, put the dough on the grater

---

[174.3] *pasta tirata*: any variety of *pasta asciuta* produced by extruding the dough into strands.
In Recipe 176 pasta is drawn out through a screen. Dried pasta afforded a cheap and dependable way to stock food over time and as a hedge against scarcity.

[175.1] This *stiletto* is literally a small stylus originally used for writing in wax. Scappi's fine iron rod is the forerunner of the modern fusilli pin.

[175.2] That is, as worn by a priest. For such a *beretta da prete* see Recipe V,132.

[175.3] That is, roll it up.

[176] Two models of the same sort of *gratta cascio* are illustrated in Plates 10 and 22. The front has the cutting protrusions whereas the back has the indentations Scappi will use to give a rippled surface to his gnocchi. See also Recipe III,253.

and make the gnocchi with it. If you do not have a cheese grater, make them on a table, drawing the gnocchi out nicely with three fingers. Put in as little flour as possible so they stay soft, and be careful not to handle the dough because it will get too runny. When they are made up, let them sit awhile, then cook them in a fat broth that is boiling, or in water, in a big pot. When they are done, set them out in dishes with cheese and provatura – both grated and not too salted – sugar, cinnamon and lumps of fresh butter the way macaroni are set out in Recipe 174. And let those, too, stew between two dishes on hot coals.

177. To prepare tortellini[177.1] with capon flesh.

In a mortar grind the flesh of two capon breasts that have first been boiled with a pound of boneless beef marrow, three ounces of chicken fat, and three ounces of boiled veal udder; when everything is ground up, add in a pound of creamy cheese, eight ounces of sugar, one ounce of cinnamon, half an ounce of pepper, enough saffron, half an ounce of cloves and nutmeg together, four ounces of very clean currant raisins, a handful of mint, sweet marjoram and other common aromatic herbs together, four fresh egg yolks and two with their whites. When the mixture is so made up that it is not too salty, get a rather thin sheet of dough made of flour, rosewater, salt, butter, sugar and warm water, and out of that dough, with a cutting wheel or dough cutter,[177.2] cut out large or small tortellini. Cook them in a good fat broth of chicken or some other meat. Serve them with cheese, sugar and cinnamon over top. In the same way you can do it with the flesh of spit-roasted turkey hens and peacocks, and of pheasants and partridges and other commonly eaten fowl, and also of veal loin roasted on a spit with kidney-fat.

178. To prepare tortellini, popularly called *anolini,*[178.1] with pork belly and other ingredients.

Get four pounds of fresh pork belly, without its skin, and boil it so it is well done. Take it out of the broth and let it cool. Beat it small with knives, watching that there are no bones or skin in it. Get the same amount again of well cooked calf udder[178.2] and beat it with the other, along with a pound and a half of lean young pork half-roasted on a spit or else boiled with the belly. When everything is

---

[177.1] This pasta dish, whose name means 'little tourtes,' is a sort of stuffed ravioli.

[177.2] *con lo sperone, o bussolo.* A *sperone* can be seen in two models in Plates 14 and 15. Two sizes of *bussolo*, designed expressly for cutting out dough for *tortelletti*, are illustrated in Plate 12. The circumference of the round blade appears fluted like a modern pasta jagger.

[178.1] Here *annolini* and below, *anolini.* The modern forms of the word are *anolini* or *agnolotti.* In Scappi they are a filled dumpling; nowdays they are a sort of oblong ravioli. Lancelot de Casteau knows them, calling them *agnoilen* in two recipes for them (79–81). He serves them as does Scappi dressed with cheese (specifically Parmesan) and cinnamon *comme les rafioules,* like ravioli.

[178.2] *zinna di vittela.* For Lancelot de Casteau the recipe calls for *tetin de vache,* 'cow's teat.'

beaten together, add to it a pound of grated Parmesan cheese, another of a creamy cheese, six ounces of provatura or of some other fresh cheese – grated and not too salty – eight ounces of sugar, one ounce of ground cinnamon, three-quarters of an ounce of pepper, another three-quarters of cloves and nutmeg together, six ounces of very clean currant raisins, ten ounces of elecampane root – first cooked under the coals or boiled, then cleaned and ground in a mortar – eight beaten, fresh eggs and enough saffron. When the mixture is made up, get a sheet of dough made as above and with it make the tiny *anolini* like haricot beans or chickpeas, with their little edges overlapping[178.3] so they look like *cappelletti*.[178.4] When they are made up, let them sit awhile. Cook them in a good meat broth. Serve them with cheese, sugar and cinnamon over them. In winter those tortellini can be kept for a month more or less, depending on the warmth and dampness of the location.

In the same way you can also make them with the skinless belly of a wild boar or its young.

179. To prepare a thick, Lombard-style soup with herb tortellini.

Get chard or spinach, chop it up small and wash it in several changes of water. Press the water out of it, sauté it in fresh butter and set it to boil with a handful of aromatic herbs. Take that out and put it into an earthenware or tinned copper pot, adding in grated Parmesan cheese and a creamy cheese in the same amount, pepper, cinnamon, cloves, saffron, raisins and enough raw eggs. If that mixture is too moist, put in grated bread; if too dry, a little more butter. Have a sheet of dough made up the way that is directed in Recipe 177, and make tortellini of various sizes, cooking them in a good meat broth. Serve them garnished with cheese, sugar and cinnamon.

180. To prepare tortellini with fresh peas[180] or haricot beans.

When the peas or beans have boiled in a meat broth, grind the amount of them you want in a mortar and put them through a strainer or filter. With them put egg yolks, pepper, cinnamon, cloves, nutmeg, sugar, a few spring onions beaten and fried in butter, and grated creamy Parmesan or Roman cheese and a little fresh ricotta or provatura. Make up tortellini out of that with a sheet of dough like the one above. Cook them in a good broth. Serve them with cheese, sugar and cinnamon over them. If you want to make them with dry legumes, soak those first, then cook them well.

[178.3] *& conjunti con li lor pizzetti.* As for a modern filled dumpling the circumference of the little circles is lifted and joined together in purse- or pouch-like fashion.

[178.4] Originally, and still in Scappi's day, a *cappelletto* was a semi-spherical steel helmet or, in leather, a sort of long skullcap formed by sewing together a series of triangular segments. Zingarelli indicates that today's pastry *cappelletto* is characteristic of Emiliano cookery.

[180] Peas and beans were staples throughout the year. Out of season the most common vegetables were still these legumes, but dried, so that many older recipe books offer procedures for either the 'fresh,' 'new' peas or beans, or the dried sort. See the end of this recipe.

181. To prepare a thick soup of ravioli without a casing.[181.1]

In a mortar grind two fresh provaturas or else two pounds of a creamy cheese with a pound of grated Parmesan or Roman cheese, six eggs, half an ounce of cinnamon, a quarter-ounce of pepper and enough saffron. When everything is ground up together add in a handful of beaten herbs or, instead of herbs, chard finely cut up and, after the juice has been pressed out of it, sautéed in butter. When the mixture has been made up, make ravioli of it without a casing – that is, sprinkle the table with flour and take a walnut-amount of the mixture, and shape them with your hand so that each is a finger's width in length. Cook them in a good broth. Serve them dressed with cheese, sugar and cinnamon.

If you want them white without herbs, put a little grated bread into the mixture. They should not be in the broth too long because they will spoil. Every sort of ravioli, except those made with meat, can be cooked in water and butter and eaten on Fridays and Saturdays.[181.2] You can also put some ricotta into the mixture.

182. To prepare a thick soup called *cianciarelle*.[182]

Beat twelve eggs with a pound of flour, pepper, cinnamon and saffron, and put all that through a strainer into a pot where a fat broth is boiling. When it is cooked, serve it hot with cheese, sugar and cinnamon over top. Into the mixture you can also put grated cheese.

183. To prepare a thick soup of *vivarole*.[183]

Beat ten eggs along with a handful of well beaten herbs, grated bread, pepper, cinnamon, saffron and grated Parmesan cheese. Then get a boiling, fat meat broth; moisten the mixture with a cold broth, and quickly put it into the boiling broth. Seal up the pot and let it sit sealed until the preparation rises to the top. Serve it with fat broth, and sugar, cheese and cinnamon over it.

184. To prepare a thick soup of rice or spelt in meat broth.

Get good rice that has been cleaned the way it is done for making rice flour in Recipe 155.[184.1] Put it into a pot in enough broth to cover it, the broth being cold.

[181.1] An Italian ravioli (*gravioli*) made with cheese is mentioned at the beginning of the fifteenth century in the 'B' recipe book of *Due libri di cucina*, ed. Boström, Recipe 55.

[181.2] For lean days as a counterpart to the meat dish see the sturgeon ravioli, Recipe III,6.

[182] In Scappi's day *cianciare* had the sense of 'to joke, to jest.' These *cianciarelle* are, in effect, little jests, little drolleries.

[183] The sense of the designation *vivarole* is not clear. Zingarelli glosses the archaic word *bìvero*, that dates from the beginning of the fourteenth century, as 'castoro,' beaver; the word is related to the idea of 'dun-coloured.' See the same dish name in Recipes III,285 and VI,65, where both times it is qualified as a popular designation, and Recipe VI,66.

[184.1] Both printings show *capitolo 115*.

When the rice has absorbed some of the broth, add in an adequate amount of hot broth, with yellow saveloy sausage to flavour it. When it is cooked like that you can combine it with beaten eggs, grated cheese, pepper, cinnamon and saffron. On the other hand, wanting to serve it plain without those additions, serve it by itself with cheese, sugar and cinnamon, and with a little fat broth over top.

In the same way you can cook spelt, but it will not matter whether you put it into hot broth. If you want that rice differently, follow the directions set out at Recipe 221[184.2] in the book on fish.

185. To prepare a thick soup of einkorn or hulled barley.

Einkorn is a much larger grain than that from which bread is made; in Lombardy a lot of it is found and used for making tourtes and flans, as I say in the Book on Pastry in the appropriate recipes.[185] Cull through it, then, and clean it of dust and set it to soak in warm water for ten hours, occasionally changing the water. Set it to cook in a cold fat meat broth in a tinned copper or earthenware pot, adding to it yellow saveloy or ordinary sausage or else a piece of salt pork marrow to flavour it. Then add in cinnamon and saffron, cooking it on the coals away from the flame with the pot stopped up. Boil it for no less than two and a half hours. Serve it with cheese and cinnamon over it. That soup should be quite thick.

In the same way you can make it with hulled barley, which needs to boil a lot more than the einkorn, although both of them do call for a long cooking. Both of them can be combined with cheese, eggs, pepper, cinnamon and saffron.

186. To prepare a thick soup of cracked millet or foxtail millet.

Get cracked millet[186.1] or foxtail millet, although the latter is much better and tastier than ordinary millet. Clean any dust and other dirt from it – that is, clean

[184.2] Again, both printings are in error, showing Recipe 220. A similar preparation for spelt but designed for lean days is outlined in Recipe III,222.

[185] See Recipe V,88 for another use of this rather coarse grain, the oldest cultivated variety of wheat in Europe. The identity of this *formentone* (and in Recipe V,47, *formento grosso*) is not certain. Scappi thinks it may not be familiar to his reader, describing it here as having a grain that is larger than that of normal wheat, needing to boil at length though not as long as barley, and being commonly used in Lombard tourtes and flans; in V,88 again as being larger than wheat, needing a four-hour steeping in warm water, and being in 'quite' common use in Lombardy; and in VI,57 as being yellowish in colour. For comparison we might think of corn (maize), newly introduced into Europe and having very much smaller kernels than today's varieties.

[186.1] Being *infranto*, cracked or thrashed, the millet grains would have the darker hull and bran removed from the white inner grain. Albala regrets the loss to most modern tables of the rich nutty flavour of millet, the grain now generally relegated to a use as bird seed (*Cooking in Europe 1250–1650*, 119). He suggests that corn (maize), which Scappi would have regretted not knowing, would turn this dish into its modern equivalent.

it of any grit the way hard wheat is done[186.2] – and put it into an earthenware or tinned copper pot with a meat broth. Cook it along with saveloy or a piece of salt pork jowl to heighten its flavour. When it is done, combine it with grated cheese, beaten eggs, pepper, cinnamon and saffron. Those grains can also be cooked in goat's or cow's milk the way semolina is done in Recipe 153. Also, after they are cooked in broth and are fairly firm, they can be taken out of the pot and let cool on a table or in another wooden or earthenware vessel. When they have thoroughly cooled, cut them into slices and sauté those in fresh butter in a pan. Serve them hot, dressed with sugar and cinnamon.

187. To prepare a thick soup of chestnut flour.

Get four pounds of chestnut flour, which is sweeter and has fewer filaments in it than any other flour. Get eleven litres[187] of fat goat's or cow's milk and put it, with the flour mixed into it, into a cooking basin, cooking it the way the whitedish in Recipe 162 is done. If you want to put sugar into it, that is optional, but do not forget to put in enough salt. When it is done, put sugar and cinnamon over it and serve it hot or cold as you like.

When it is cooked you can also let it cool, slice it and fry it in rendered fat or butter, and serve it dressed likewise with sugar and cinnamon.

Some people, after it is cooked in a meat broth or in water, make black puddings with it on chestnut leaves or vine leaves, cooking them under a bell or in an oven. And of the one that is cooked with milk mixed with cheese, egg yolks and spices they make tourtes.

188. To prepare a thick soup of fresh peas or broad beans in a meat broth.

Get fresh peas in their season, which in Rome goes from the end of March throughout June – as is that also for fresh broad beans. Shell the peas and put them into an earthenware or copper pot with fat broth and pork jowl in slices. Boil them until they are almost cooked. Put in a handful of beaten anise and parsley and finish off cooking. If you want a thicker broth, grind up a little of the cooked peas, put that through a strainer and mix it in among the whole peas, adding pepper and cinnamon. Serve them with the slices of pork jowl.

With peas you can also cook stuffed goat-kid heads,[188] their hair removed, and young cockerels, doves, young goslings and ducklings.

You can also do peas in a different way: after they are cooked in broth they can be combined with eggs, cheese and spices.

Beans can be done in all the above ways.

[186.2] In Recipe 153 Scappi specifies that the grains of semolina be finely sieved of any extraneous matter and therefore, as in Recipes 153 and 170, be 'white.'

[187] Four *boccali* would amount to ten and two-thirds litres or just under twenty-four pounds.

[188] Scappi may well intend that *ripiene* ('stuffed') apply only to the bird that the word follows, *anatrine* ('ducklings'), rather than to every item in the list. See Recipe 79 for directions on preparing a stuffed head of a goat kid.

189. To sauté fresh peas, with or without their pod.

If you want to sauté peas in their pod, take the tenderest ones and cut off their flower end[189] and their stem end, and parboil them in a good meat broth. Take them out, drain them and sauté them in rendered fat or melted pork fat. Serve them dressed with orange juice and pepper. Along with those peas you can sauté a clove of garlic and parsley, both beaten.

With the sautéed peas you can garnish young cockerels and other spit-roasted fowl. If you do not want them with their pod, shell them, parboil them and sauté them as above. You can do shelled broad beans the same way.

190. To stew unshelled peas.

Get the tenderest peas, as I said before, and with their stem removed put them into an earthenware or copper pot containing beaten, melted pork fat and sauté them slowly, stirring them around from time to time. Then add in a meat broth mixed with pepper, saffron and cinnamon. Boil them in that broth, stirring rapidly. As they finish cooking,[190] throw in a handful of beaten fine herbs. When they are done, serve them with their broth over them. Along with those peas you can stew salt pork belly cut up into small pieces, or else marbled prosciutto.

If you want to make a salad of them, all they need is to be cooked in the broth and served dry with pepper and vinegar over top. If they are cooked in water, put oil on them.

191. To prepare a thick soup of dried peas.

Set the dried peas to soak in warm water for six hours. Put them into an earthenware or copper pot with an unsalted meat broth, slices of prosciutto and mortadella, and cook them. To thicken the broth grind up some cooked peas, put them through a strainer and then in with the others. Add in pepper, cinnamon and beaten common herbs. When they are cooked, serve them hot.

You can do white chickpeas and brown chickpeas after they have soaked,[191.1] and likewise common vetch[191.2] and dry, unshelled broad beans and lentils and haricot beans. Moreover, with those last four legumes you can cook semi-salted pig's snouts, ears and feet, and whole garlic, and also doves and other fowl

---

[189] That is, the lower end, opposite the stem end. See the same qualification used for a squash in Recipe 221.

[190] See this final addition of herbs in Recipe 194 also. In Recipe 202 Scappi indicates that they function (at least in part) as a thickener.

[191.1] Presumably the chickpeas are also in a dried state.

[191.2] Also known as chickling in English. Its seeds are the size of small peas. See this legume also in Recipe III,252.

that have been under oil,[191.3] noting, though, that the beans and lentils must be parboiled and should not be soaked.

192. To prepare a thick soup of split chickpeas in meat broth with other ingredients.

Get split chickpeas that are brown because the other sort are not good split, clean them of any dirt and wash them in several changes of warm water. Put them into an earthenware or copper pot in enough cold meat broth to cover them by three fingers, and boil them slowly on the coals away from the fire. Using a wooden spoon, skim off the white scum that will form. Get the rind, snouts and ears of salt pork, which should be very clean and well cooked in unsalted water; cut all that up into small bits. When the chickpeas are half-cooked, put in those bits along with a spoonful of fat broth tinged with saffron, and finish off cooking. At the end throw in a handfull of beaten herbs. Serve it in dishes with cinnamon over top. With those chickpeas you can also cook yellow saveloy and mortadella of pork liver.

You can also cook split lentils the same way.

193. To prepare a cumin dish[193.1] in the Roman style.

Get four doves either from a dovecot or wild, and a domestic or wild duck – although for a dish like this wildfowl will always be better than the domestic variety; with them put two snouts and two ears of pork, and a pound and a half of salted jowl from the same pig. Those snouts and ears should have sat softening in warm water and should especially be very clean; the pork jowl should be cut into thick slices. With all that put four pounds of beef ribs. Put everything into an earthenware or copper pot and cook it in water, skimming it well. When those meats are cooked, half a quarter of an hour before you will be wanting to serve them put in four ounces of ground cumin, more or less depending on the taste of the person for whom it is intended; immediately stop up the pot so it cannot breathe and set it to boil. The meats and everything else are served hot. If you want to do it on a lean day, instead of the meats put in a big pike or a cod. Romans eat a dish like that in the winter the same as Spaniards do the *olla podrida*.[193.2]

[191.3] That is, preserved in olive oil. In Book I,§10 Scappi has described this as a common optional process.

[193.1] Scappi's *cominata* had a European history going back to at least the end of the thirteenth century. The earliest version of the *Viandier* of Taillevent contains recipes for three *comminees*, of poultry (Recipe 12), of fish (Recipe 75) and of almonds (Recipe 13). The collection known as *Les Enseingnemenz* (ed. Carole Lambert, 'Trois réceptaires culinaires médiévaux,' Ph.D. thesis, Université de Montréal, 1989), from a decade or so later, has both the fowl and fish versions of the dish (Recipes 28 and 48).

[193.2] Scappi's version of this *oglia putrida* was given in Recipe 152.

194. To prepare a thick soup of kohlrabi in meat broth with other ingredients, cooking it in various ways.

Get kohlrabi between April and the end of May, during which time it is more tender, although it is available up to the end of October. Clean off its bulb,[194.1] cut it into bits and put them into an earthenware or copper pot with some broth that is not too salty, along with beaten pork fat, cut-up pork belly and salted pork tongue. Cook everything together, it being optional if you want to put in some leaves of that kohlrabi. When it is done, if you have not put[194.2] the leaves into it, put in a handful of beaten herbs with a little pepper. Serve them hot with the other ingredients on it.

You can do it another way: when the kohlrabi bulb has been parboiled in a broth, beat it very small on a table with knives and put it into an earthenware or copper pot with fat broth, pepper, cinnamon and a little melted pork fat to flavour it. Finish off cooking it, thickening it with eggs, grated cheese and saffron. Serve it hot, dressed with mild spices.

If you would like to stuff kohlrabi whole, get the tenderest ones, parboil them in a good broth, take them out and let them cool. Make a hole in their middle and stuff that hole with a mixture of lean veal and marbled prosciutto, beaten and mixed with cheese, eggs, common spices,[194.3] garlic cloves and beaten common herbs. Cook all that in a tourte pan with melted pork fat and enough broth to half cover it; heat it from below and above like a tourte. When it is done serve it hot.

You can braise artichoke hearts the same way.

195. To prepare a thick soup of cauliflower in a meat broth.

Get a cauliflower, which has two seasons, spring and fall. Remove it from its stem in several pieces, wash it repeatedly in water and put it into a boiling meat broth. Let it boil a quarter of an hour with yellow saveloy and at the end, just before you will be wanting to serve it, put a handful of herbs in with it. Serve it hot.

With that cauliflower you can garnish boiled capons, sprinkling grated cheese and cinnamon over top.

196. To prepare a thick soup of head cabbage.

Get the head variety of cabbage in its season, which lasts from July to the end of November. To be good that cabbage needs to be white, firm and heavy. Remove the upper leaves and take the whitest part, cutting it into large or small

---

[194.1] Scappi's word is *rapa*, whose sense is normally 'turnip.' He is, of course, referring to the plant's bulbous rhizome. The same term is used in Recipe 213.

[194.2] *poste.* In the reprinting this word became *peste*, 'ground up.'

[194.3] Directions on compounding a mixture of *spetierie communi*, much used in the following recipes, are given in Book I, §26.

pieces as you like. Wash it in cold water and put it into a boiling meat broth with beaten pork fat, salt pork jowl and mortadella. Give it lots of room to boil rather than constricting it. When it is done serve it hot with the other ingredients, and with grated cheese, pepper and cinnamon over top. That cabbage must be taken out just as soon as it is cooked because if it stays in the broth it will become brown and bitter. You can also bring it to a boil in plain water before putting it into the broth.

197. To prepare a thick soup of salted head cabbage.

Salted head cabbages[197] are brought to Treviso and Venice from German lands in brine in earthenware or wooden containers. Taken out of the brine they are washed repeatedly in water and set to soak. Then they are parboiled in plain water, removed and cooled in more water. They are cooked in a broth of fat beef with crushed garlic buds. When they are done, they are taken out, dried and dressed with garlic sauce.

After having been cooked in the broth, they can also be sautéed with beaten garlic and spring onions in melted rendered fat. They are served with pepper and fennel flour over them.

198. To prepare a thick soup of Savoy and Bolognese cabbage[198.1] in a meat broth.

Get the cabbages in their season, which lasts from the end of September throughout February. To be good they have to be white and firm, although some are found with a brown and blood-red middle which are the very best. Remove their outer leaves and take the best part cut into pieces depending on the size of the cabbage. Wash them and set them to cook in a pot containing a meat broth boiling with beaten pork fat and yellow saveloy. When they are almost done, put in the tips of fresh fennel or else the panicles of dry fennel. When they are done, serve them hot with saveloy over top. With that cabbage you can also cook partridge and pheasants after they have been half roasted on a spit. You can garnish boiled capons, hens and ducks with it, putting cheese and cinnamon over top.

You can cook any sort of cabbage that way, especially the sort that comes into Rome that has a wide, tender rib. Generally speaking, all varieties need to be boiled freely with the pot open. Small cabbages, the ones you see in September, are cooked in bunches like broccoli in the spring.

---

[197] These *cauli cappucci*, as in the previous recipe, are likely Savoy cabbage, *Brassica oleraceai*, var. *capitata*, Subanda group. They have a relatively compact head of wrinkled leaves.

[198.1] The Savoy variety of head cabbage that Scappi specifies is probably that of the previous recipe. It is likely that the Bolognese variety has a somewhat loose bundle of leaves of a bulk sufficient to contain a number of chicks.

If you want stuffed Savoy cabbage, when they have been cleaned and stuffed and the heart[198.2] is still whole, bring them to a boil in water, take them out and put them into cold water. When they have cooled, press the water out. Stuff their middle, leaf by leaf,[198.3] with a mixture of lean veal or pork beaten with the same amount of marbled pork fat, with a little prosciutto added to that, along with grated cheese, raw eggs, pepper, cinnamon, saffron, a crushed garlic clove and beaten parsley. When the heart[198.4] is stuffed, wrap it around with a large cabbage leaf that has first been brushed with warm water. Bind the heart round about with a string so the stuffing cannot slip out, then cook it in a fat broth with salted pork marrow. When the cabbage is large, in its middle you can put deboned, stuffed chicks mixed in with that stuffing. When it is cooked, serve it hot right after releasing the leaf with the marrow around it.

199. To stuff cabbage leaves with a compound called *nosetti*.[199]

Get big cabbage leaves of the sort that have a thick, broad rib, and cut that rib away. Brush the leaves with hot water and put them one on top of the other in layers of three, sprinkled with cheese. Make up a mixture of walnuts ground in a mortar together with a few shelled almonds, garlic, and bread soaked in broth with the broth well squeezed out. When everything is ground up, add in beaten mint, sweet marjoram and parsley, pepper, cinnamon, enough saffron, raw eggs and a few raisins. Put that mixture on the top leaf, and roll all three leaves from the bottom upwards and tie them up like a ball. Cook that in a fat meat broth with saveloy. When it is done, take it out of the broth, remove the string from it and serve it with the saveloy.

With that same mixture you can stuff the Bolognese and Savoy cabbage of the previous recipe. Also with the previous stuffing and with the one here you can stuff head cabbage, having first parboiled them, then make a hole in them going up through their foot. When that hollow has been stuffed with the mixture, along with a little of the foot that was dug out, close up the hole with a large leaf, brushed with hot water, from the cabbage. When the head has been bound up, put it into an earthenware or copper pot that is not too big and contains a fat meat broth, beaten pork fat, pieces of prosciutto, salt pork tongues, a piece of salted veal kidney-fat, some other cut of beef, and wether loin. Into that add pepper, cinnamon, cloves, nutmeg, saffron and fennel seed, and close up the pot so it cannot breathe. Cook

---

[198.2] *caspo*, 'core,' later mistakenly copied as *capo*, 'head.'

[198.3] *a foglia per foglia*: the 'stuffing' is to be inserted between individual leaves rather than packed into a centre cavity.

[198.4] The word *caspo* is again erroneously set as *cuspo* ('point') by the 1581 printer.

[199] This *nosetto* is, as is apparent, a complex mixture of ground walnuts, bread, garlic, herbs and spices. See Scappi's use of it also in Recipe V,101.

it on the coals away from the flame. When it is done, serve it hot on a platter dressed with cheese and cinnamon, along with the meats that were cooked with it cut up and arranged around the platter.

When the head has been stuffed you can wrap it in the caul of a wether, a calf or a pig instead of leaves, serving it afterwards without the caul.

200. To prepare a thick soup of squeezed cabbage in the Roman style.

Get the whitest parts of Savoy or Bolognese cabbage and more than half cook them in a meat broth. Take them out, squeeze the broth out of them and on a table pound them small with knives. Then put that into a casserole pot or a cooking basin with melted pork fat. Sauté it slowly, turning it over often, and adding pepper and cinnamon into it. When that is done, put in a little fat meat broth that is cold, in which yellow saveloy has been cooked, and finish off cooking it in that broth so that it is thick rather than thin. When it is done it can be served hot like that, or else[200] with cheese and cinnamon over it.

With that cabbage you can also cover stuffed chicks that have first been stewed together with some other meats, or roasted on a spit.

201. To prepare a thick soup of new cabbage sprouts,[201.1] new haricot beans and other ingredients in a meat broth.

Get whatever variety of cabbage sprouts you like and cook them in a good meat broth. Put in some fresh haricot beans which have first been parboiled in water. Put some beaten pork fat in with them, some semi-salted pork snouts and ears, wether loin, beef and mortadella. When everything is cooked, serve platters of it with the same things underneath.[201.2] Before the cabbage is put into the boiling water, its leaves have to be separated or cut up small.

202. Various ways to prepare a thick soup of lettuce in a meat broth.

Get lettuce in its proper season, between March and the end of May, although in Rome you can get it throughout the year. Clean it and take the whitest part of it. Wash that in several changes of water and parboil it in boiling water. Take it out and beat it on a table with knives, or else cut it in four. Cook it in a fat meat broth with gooseberries or verjuice grapes. At the end put in a handful of common herbs; if you do not want herbs, thicken it with beaten eggs and a little cold broth. Add in pepper, cinnamon and saffron. Just as soon as the eggs go in, give them a stir with a spoon so they do not set. Serve it hot.

---

[200] *Sic*, in both printings. Has Scappi or the 1570 typesetter omitted a first suggested garnish?

[201.1] Today these *cavoletti* might be called Brussels sprouts. See a previous mention of small cabbages in Recipe 198, above. The first sentence of the recipe suggests that Scappi is thinking of them only as small young cabbages.

[201.2] *le medesime robbe* seem to be beans and miscellaneous chunks of meat. See the end of the next recipe.

You can do endive the same way, getting it in its season between the beginning of September and the end of February.[202]

If you want to stuff the lettuce follow the directions for Savoy cabbage in Recipe 198, not forgetting to put gooseberries or verjuice grapes in the stuffing. In the pot along with that lettuce you can cook liver mortadella or saveloy, salt pork jowl, slices of salted sowbelly, stuffed chicks and partially fledged doves. When everything is cooked, serve it hot with those things on top and with its broth.

203. To prepare a thick soup of various common herbs in a meat broth along with other things.

Get chard, borage, bugloss, mugwort,[203.1] dill and other delicate herbs in the spring, which is their proper season; cut them up fairly small and wash them in several changes of water. Put them into an earthenware or copper pot with well ground pork fat and sauté them slowly in that fat because herbs like that will make their own broth. Turn them over often with a wooden spoon. When they have been well sautéed and greatly reduced, add in fat broth with cut-up pork jowl and either sowbelly[203.2] or pork belly cut up into slices, and a few liver mortadelle, or some other sort. Cook everything like that, ensuring that it is not too salty. When it is done, serve everything hot, with pepper and cinnamon over top.

If you want to thicken the dish with eggs and cheese, take out the meat and put in gooseberries, let it come to a boil and thicken it with beaten eggs and grated cheese mixed with common spices. Serve it in dishes or bowls. With those things you can also cook spring onions, beaten and sautéed, and fresh peas and broad beans. In winter when those herbs are much tougher, you can parboil them first in water, then take them out, squeeze the water out of them and beat them with knives. Cook them with big onions that have been beaten with them, a meat broth, raisins and common spices. After that, blend in cheese and eggs as above.

204. To prepare a thick soup of spinach in a meat broth.

For the spinach to be a much tastier and juicier herb than any other, and also so it will cook more quickly, it should be sautéed in melted pork fat rather than cooked in a broth. And so, too, it should be got in its season, which in Rome goes from October to the end of March. You should remove its ribs, taking the tenderest part, and wash that in several changes of water. Cut it up small and sauté

---

[202] Castelvetro writes that in the autumn 'crisp, white endive [*indivia*] begins to appear and lasts all through the winter. ...When endive is not available we use the tender, green leaves and shoots of chicory [*le più tenere folgie della cicorea verdi*]' (trans. Riley, 105; Castelvetro's manuscript text can be read in Luigi Firpo, *Gastronomia del Rinascimento* [Turin: Unione Tipografico-Editrice Torinese, 1973], 155).

[203.1] *herba bianca*: *Artemisia vulgaris*, in English otherwise called artemisia or St John's wort.

[203.2] Sowbelly is normally kept on hand in a salted state. See Book I, §9.

it with spring onions in melted pork fat. When it is done, put it into a pot with yellow saveloy, pepper, cinnamon and enough broth to cover it; finish off cooking it with seedless muscatel raisins or else ordinary raisins. Serve it hot with pepper and cinnamon over it. You can also put a little vinegar and must syrup in with it.

205. To prepare a thick soup of rape greens.

Get rape leaves in the period between July and the end of September while they are much more tender. Cut them up small, as they are cut up for tourtes, washing them in several changes of water. So their smell will not be so bad or so strong, give them a boiling in plain water, take them out and put them in a cool place. When you bring them out again, squeeze the water out of them and put them in an earthenware or copper pot containing beaten pork fat or else salted steer kidney-fat, adding in enough meat broth to cover the leaves, along with salt pork belly and semi-salted pork snouts and ears. Cook all of that together, being careful that the soup is not too salty. To reduce its saltiness, the ears and snouts can be parboiled before being put in. When the soup has been cooked to a thick stage rather than brothy, serve it dressed with pepper and cinnamon. Alternatively, serve it as is done in Lombardy, without its broth but with a garlic sauce over it.

206. To prepare a thick soup of parsley and other common herbs called Apostles' Broth[206] in Roman courts.

Get a meat broth in which yellow saveloy, salt pork jowl and wether loin have boiled and tinge it with saffron mixed with pepper and cinnamon; in summer also put in gooseberries or verjuice grapes. When all that has cooked, get well cleaned and washed parsley, along with other herbs, chop them up finely and put them into the broth. When it begins to boil, serve it immediately on slices of bread, with the meats cut into pieces on the plate. Note, though, that that broth should not stand after being made up because the parsley would lose its colour. This dish is common in Rome in summer. It is optional whether you blend in grated cheese and beaten eggs.

207. To prepare a thick soup of wild fennel shoots in meat broth.

Take the whitest and tenderest part of fennel in its season – in Rome from the fall to the end of March. Wash it in several changes of water and put it together in clumps which you cook in a good meat broth with semi-salted pigs' feet and heads, pieces of wether loin and beef loin. So the broth will have a little body, put in breadcrumb that has soaked in that broth and gone through a strainer. When the fennel is cooked, serve it with the other things over top.[207]

---

[206] *brodo apostolorum*, an interestingly playful mixture of Italian and Latin. Where food was concerned, the pope and his cardinals were not sanctimonious.

[207] As is usually the case, the recipe that Castelvetro remembers from his life in Modena is somewhat simpler than Scappi's treatment. 'The young shoots [of fennel] make an excellent Lenten dish, cooked in water and eaten with oil, salt and pepper. This tastes delicious and is incredibly healthy as well' (trans. Riley, 78).

With that fennel you can cook hens, pullets, capons, doves and other fowl. You can also cover boiled capons and geese with it, sprinkling grated cheese, cinnamon and pepper over top.

208. To prepare a thick soup of parsley root.

Get parsley roots from the end of September to the end of March, that being their season. Scrape them and core them; wash them and parboil them in boiling water, from which you then take them and put them into cold water. Whether you cut them up into pieces or beat them with knives is left optionally to you. Cook them in a broth that is not too salty. When they are done, you can mix in beaten eggs along with verjuice or else grated cheese. You can also serve them plain with their broth.

If you want to cover boiled chickens with them, however, when their core is removed cook them whole without cutting them up, the way the fennel above is done, and with the same ingredients as for the fennel.

In the same ways you can also do rhubarb roots,[208] which have no core, getting them, though, in the same season as the above parsley roots.

209. To prepare a thick soup of leeks and big onions in a meat broth.

Leeks show up in November and last throughout March; big old onions show up in August and go until the end of March. From both of them take the whitest part, clean it and parboil it in hot water, out of which you then take it and put it into cold water. When both are removed from that water, let them drain and finish cooking in the same way as the fennel shoots are done, with the same meats as in Recipe 207. If you want to beat them small with knives, when that is done sauté them in melted pork fat and then finish cooking them with a meat broth, blending in beaten eggs, grated cheese and common spices. After they have been parboiled whole in water you can also stew them with capons or with other wildfowl, or with the loin of a wild boar that has its brisket, along with meat broth and slices of salt pork jowl, desalted pork loin and yellow saveloy, and verjuice, pepper, cloves, cinnamon, nutmeg, saffron and sugar. When they are done, serve everything together on platters.

210. To prepare a thick soup of garlic in meat broth with other ingredients.

When the cloves of garlic are clean there should be as many cloves as from fifty bulbs. Parboil them, changing the water often so they lose their strength, and finish cooking them in a good meat broth that is not too salty, along with slices of pork jowl and desalted sowbelly. Just before you want to serve it, throw in a handful of herbs. If there is no salted meat in it, you can blend in cheese and eggs, not failing to put the spices in the one and the other. With them you can garnish and cook doves, cockerels and other fowl, serving them with grated cheese and cinnamon over the top.

---

[208] See Recipe VI,101.

211. Various ways to prepare a thick soup of turnips and rapes in a meat broth.

Get the turnips or rapes in their season, which runs from October to the end of February. Clean them and slice them. Besides, if you can get yellow turnips, scrape them; if they are small, leave them whole and wash them. Cook them the way the fennel is done in Recipe 207; alternatively, do them in a meat broth with beaten pork fat. When cooked, they can garnish boiled capons, with cheese and cinnamon over top. With turnips you can cook dried fennel seeds.[211.1] Before serving them put in a handful of beaten herbs. Serve them dressed with their broth and pepper. You can also cover them with garlic sauce, or serve them dry covered with that garlic sauce.

After being parboiled, those turnips can also be beaten small with knives and cooked with broth and eggs, blending in cheese and eggs.[211.2]

212. To prepare a Venetian-style thick soup of turnips in meat broth.

Get turnips that are not woody, and roast them on glowing coals; finish cooking them under hot ash. When they are done, clean them and beat the best parts finely with knives. Put that into a tinned copper or glazed earthenware pot in enough fat broth made from beef – I mean [broth with] the grease that comes to the surface when the meat cooks – to cover it. Boil it in that broth slowly until the turnip has absorbed most of the grease, stirring it gently from time to time. First mix in pepper, cinnamon and enough saffron, blending everything together. When it has been there a quarter of an hour, serve it hot, sprinkled with rosewater. If the broth is not all that fat, put in some fresh butter.

In the same way you can do up quince and any sort of big apple that is not too ripe. Into that preparation you can put a little sugar.

213. To prepare a thick soup of cardoons and artichokes in meat broth with other ingredients.

Get cardoons in their season, in Rome beginning in mid-September and lasting to the end of March. Take the tenderest and whitest parts of them because any that are brownish and light in weight are not good. Clean them and set them to steep in cold water for at least three hours, changing the water: that rids them of their bitterness, and as they twist in it they get more tender. You do the same with the tenderest part of the stalk. Let them cook in a fat meat broth the way fennel is done in Recipe 207; it is optional whether you parboil them first in plain water. When they are done, cook them with those meats. When cooked in broth alone with yellow saveloy, they can garnish boiled capons, hens and other fowl, with cheese, sugar, pepper and cinnamon over top.

[211.1] Fennel seeds form in clusters, which Scappi calls *pannocchie*, or panicles, here and in Recipe 198. See also Recipe 229, below.

[211.2] The double mention of eggs is found in both texts.

Those cardoons can also be stewed with various salted meats and fowl the way onions are done in Recipe 208.

You can cook artichoke stalks in the same ways, having first parboiled them and cleaned the fine hair off them. Get them during their season: in Rome from mid-February to the end of June. If you want to stuff artichoke stalks after they are parboiled and then braise them, use a stuffing made like the one for stuffing the kohlrabi bulb in Recipe 194.[213] They are cooked with the same procedure as for that bulb. The stalks can also be heated on the grill after they are stuffed. Sometimes artichokes are cooked whole in broth and, split in two, are sautéed, put on a grill and basted with melted pork fat. They are served dressed with pork fat and rose vinegar.

214. To prepare a thick soup of truffles with chicks and other ingredients.

Get the truffles in their season, from the end of September up to the end of March.[214] Clean off any sand on them and cook them in wine or water. Take them out, peel them and put them into a cooking basin or casserole pot with melted pork fat in it. Sauté them gently, adding in pepper, cinnamon, meat broth, verjuice and orange juice. Then get tiny chicks, stuffed and wrapped in cauls and half-roasted on a spit. Put them, without the caul, in with the truffles to finish cooking. When they are almost done, thicken the broth with shelled Milanese almonds that have been ground in a mortar with truffles that have been cooked under embers and peeled. Before serving it, mix in a handful of aromatic herbs. Serve it hot.

You can also cook shucked oysters with those truffles. You can also do squab instead of little cockerels. That preparation is better tangy with spices and with some verjuice in it.

215. To prepare a thick soup of common field mushrooms[215] and other sorts of mushroom.

Get field mushrooms (which are the most delicate of all mushrooms) in their season, in Rome between the end of February and the middle of May. Clean off the skin that is around them, and especially any sand on their stalk, and wash them in several changes of water. Put them into a casserole pot where there is melted pork fat, pepper and cinnamon, and sauté them lightly with nothing else because as they cook they make their own broth. When they have boiled a little, put in

---

[213] The number 193 was typeset here in both the 1570 and 1581 texts.

[214] In 1614 Castelvetro describes rooting for truffles under the snow. 'The biggest truffles are about the size of an egg, but some are as big as a quince. Truffles are not as spongy as mushrooms. There are two kinds; one has black flesh, like charcoal, and the other is pale. Both of them have a rough, black skin. The black truffles are the best and the most expensive. They sell for more than half a golden *scudo* the pound. They are mainly found around Rome. The pale ones cost less, and large quantities are to be had in Lombardy' (trans. Riley, 143).

[215] See Recipe II,115.

some yellow saveloy or slices of marbled prosciutto to cook with them, adding a little good meat broth. Before serving them, put in a handful of beaten herbs, a little grated bread, verjuice, pepper, cinnamon and saffron, and bring it all to a boil. Serve them hot with the saveloy on top.

If you want to braise them, and make other preparations from them, follow the directions given in Recipe 261 of the book on fish.

216. To prepare a thick soup of chicory with meat broth.

Get chicory during April up to the end of May, because its stalk is more tender and white; from May to the end of September get the tips, which are called 'buds'[216.1] in Rome, and the leaves and roots from September to the end of February. From the stalks clean away the harder ribs, taking the tenderest parts, and wash them in several changes of water. Parboil them in water. When they are done, take them out and put them into cold water. Take them one by one, put them on a table one on top of the other and cut away the upper tips leaving the whitest part. Arrange them in a copper or earthenware baking dish with a broth in which prosciutto or salt pork jowl has boiled, and add in pepper, cinnamon and a little verjuice or gooseberries.[216.2] Toward the end add in a few beaten herbs.

Of the buds take the tenderest part, wash them and make small bunches of them which, after first parboiling them, you do like the stalks. Of the leaves take the tenderest parts, wash them, parboil them and, when that's done, put them into cold water. Then take them out, beat them small with knives and cook them in the same broth and spicing as for the above stalks. The roots are scraped and cored, then parboiled, cut into bits and cooked like the stalks. All the above preparations are to be served hot.

217. To prepare a thick soup of asparagus in a meat broth.

Get domestic asparagus in its season, beginning in April and ending in October (just as wild asparagus in Rome begins in the fall and goes to the end of April).[217.1] Without parboiling the domestic variety, take the tenderest part of them and cook them in a meat broth with a few thin slices of prosciutto. At the end put in a handful of beaten herbs with a little pepper, cinnamon and saffron, along with gooseberries or verjuice grapes. Serve them hot with their broth.

If you want, blend in eggs, cheese and common spices. When they are over half-cooked take them out and beat them with knives. Finish off cooking them in fat broth, adding in gooseberries or verjuice grapes along with the eggs beaten with grated cheese.

216.1 *mazzocchi.*

216.2 An implied direction here obviously is, 'Let the chicory cook by boiling in that.'

217.1 We are again reminded that for Scappi 'season' usually refers to availability on the market.

You can cook wild asparagus in all the above ways, having first parboiled it. And the same, too, with hops[217.2] – that is, by roasting them; or nettle.

218. Various ways to prepare a thick soup of local squash[218.1] in a meat broth.

Get a local squash in its season, from mid-May to the end of September. To be good it has to be sweet and tender – some people, testing its sweetness at the stalk and finding it bitter, do not take the squash; hairy squash are always sweeter than others. Scrape it and, if it is large, remove its core, which you do not do with the smaller ones, or anything else; in fact it is enough to cut it up into chunks the size of dice and wash them well. Put the diced squash into an earthenware or copper pot in melted pork fat, sautéing them gently. Add in enough meat broth that is not too salty, to cover them, along with a few slices of marbled prosciutto or salt pork jowl. When the squash is cooked, put in gooseberries or verjuice grapes, and at the end a handful of beaten herbs with pepper, cinnamon and saffron. Serve it in bowls or dishes. If you would like to blend beaten egg yolks diluted with verjuice into it, that is possible.

Squash that are to be stuffed should not be large; rather, when they are scraped, large ones are divided into pieces a handswidth in length. The inside is dug out adroitly, watching that you do not cut all the way through; to be able to core it better, you can first bring it to a boil in water whole. When it is cored, stuff it with a mixture of grated cheese, eggs, sugar, gooseberries, parsley and cinnamon. Close up the hole with the other piece. Set it to cook in a pot of a suitable size, in a good meat broth with slices of sowbelly or with cut chunks of salt pork jowl. With that squash you can cook small cockerels and squabs. When done it is served hot with the same things over top.

You can also make another sort of thick soup of it with onions: cut the squash and onions into several pieces and stew them in various ways, with various meats, as leeks and onions are done in Recipe 209.[218.2] Otherwise you can cook squash in a broth by itself with beaten pork fat and verjuice grapes, and at the end a handful of common herbs.

In that same way you can do cucumber, which has the same season as squash.

219. Various ways to prepare a thick soup of squash and onions, popularly called *carabazzata*.[219.1]

The squash and onion are cleaned and well parboiled in water so that the

---

[217.2] In all likelihood what are intended here are the tender shoots of the hop plant.

[218.1] The term 'local' identifies a crook-neck squash. In Recipe 220 Scappi will deal with so-called Turkish squash.

[218.2] *nel Cap. 208*: Scappi likely intended Recipe 209 here. The 1570 typesetter had put *i porci, et le cipolle*, 'pigs and onions'; in 1581, *i porri, et le cipolle*, 'leeks and onions.'

[219.1] The name of this dish is Spanish, deriving from *carabazza*, the Spanish word for Scappi's *zucca*, squash. The Spanish name would seem to suggest a Neapolitan source for Scappi's dish.

onion, which is much harder, is thoroughly cooked. Take them out of the water and put them into a strainer and strain them through it. Get grated Parmesan cheese and fresh provatura and grind them in a mortar, moistening them with cold broth. Put that through the strainer into a casserole pot or a cooking basin where there is melted rendered fat as well as the squash and onion. Boil it all gently on the coals, breaking up the squash and onion with a wooden spoon and stirring constantly; add in a spoonful of very fat broth or fresh butter, and fine sugar. When it is cooked, so that it is thick rather than thin, serve it hot, with sugar over it and sprinkled with rosewater.

You can also do the soup another way: after the squash and onion are more than half cooked in meat broth with prosciutto or salt pork belly in it, take them out and beat them with knives on a table that is not of walnut,[219.2] and sauté them in a frying pan in rendered fat or else in melted pork fat, breaking them up with a wooden spoon. When they are done put them into a cooking basin with fat broth. Then get egg yolks beaten with verjuice and mixed with pepper, cinnamon, sugar and saffron; put everything together into the basin and bring it to a boil, constantly stirring it with a spoon. Serve it dressed with sugar and cinnamon.

You can also do it differently: after they have sautéed well, finish off cooking them in enough goat's or cow's milk to cover them, along with sugar.

220. To prepare various thick soups of Turkish squash.

Get Turkish squash in its season, which begins in October and goes to the end of April. When it is cleaned of its rind and its insides, cut it into pieces and parboil it. Then beat it with knives and cook it in a good meat broth. Blend in grated cheese and beaten eggs. You can also do it with onions the way the local ones above are done.[220] Note that squash is much better if it is firm. For keeping, it has to be in a dry, airy place; and there cannot be a hole anywhere in it because the air will make it rot. You can make dried rinds of Savona squash that way, after which they are parboiled in hot water and steeped in cold water.

221. To boil and oven-bake the above squash whole, filled with various stuffings.

If you want to boil the above squash, clean their rind very carefully, watching that you do not break it. Make a round hole in either the flower end or the stem end, setting aside the little round you cut out, and neatly remove the insides with long hooked blades.[221.1] When it is cleaned out, fill it with a stuffing made of lean veal or pork beaten with the same amount again of pork fat and prosciutto, adding in cheese, egg yolks, raisins, common spices and saffron. Get small cockerels or

---

[219.2] See Scappi's warning in Recipe VI,30 that the nature of walnut will affect a foodstuff.

[220] Scappi is referring to one of the variations in the treatment of the local variety of squash, *le zucche nostrali* of Recipe 218.

[221.1] Scappi writes: 'with iron rods, with a hook, that cut.'

small squab, deboned and stuffed, and put them into the squash with the stuffing. When it is full, stop up the hole and put the squash into a pot of a size in which it cannot move about, in enough broth to more than half cover it, and with slices of prosciutto or salted pork belly: that is done so the squash can have some flavour and not be insipid. Into that broth put pepper, cinnamon and saffron. Cook it on the coals, keeping the pot closed up so it cannot breathe. When it has boiled a while, until the stuffing has firmed up, add in more broth and finish cooking it. When it is done, use the pot itself to drain off the broth and carefully slide the squash onto a platter, serving it hot with the ham or pork belly around it.

You can also stuff that squash with milk, beaten eggs, sugar and marbled prosciutto that has been diced.

You can also do it differently: when the hole has been made without the rind being removed, dig out the insides and adroitly plaster the inside of the squash, bottom and sides, with slices of marbled prosciutto. Take bits of raw yellow saveloy or else some of the stuffing mixture and put a layer of it on the bottom. Get small squab, small cockerels, small quail and other small birds – all drawn, their bones crushed, and sprinkled with pepper, cinnamon, cloves and nutmeg – and put them one by one into the squash, settling them with the same saveloy mixture. As a finish, on top of those birds and to cover all the stuffing mixture, put a slice of veal sprinkled with the above spices. Then plug up the hole with that part of the gourd you removed. Wrap sheets of paper around the squash and bind its mouth with cord. Put it in an oven that is less hot than for bread, and set it in such a way that it gets a moderate heat evenly all around it. It should be on a copper or earthenware sheet without sides to it: that is done so that, when it is baked, the squash can be taken out without breaking it. After it has been in for two hours, more or less depending on its size, take it out, undo the paper, unplug the hole[221.2] and put in another stopper of uncooked rind with a few leafy branches attached to it. Serve it hot.

In that squash you can make an *olla podrida*, having, however, cooked the legumes as directed for the *olla podrida* in Recipe 152.[221.3]

222. To prepare a thick soup of melons in a meat broth.

Get a melon in its season – July to the end of August, although in Rome they can also be had in September. Mind that it is not overripe. Remove its rind and its seeds, and take the best part, cutting it into bite-sized pieces. Put that into a cooking basin where you have fresh butter or melted chicken fat in which you cook it. When it is done put it through a strainer so that any seeds are caught; it

[221.2] The text reads, *turisi il buco*, which is identically the phrase used previously after the squash has been stuffed: 'Plug up the hole.'

[221.3] Peas, chickpeas and beans are the *ligumi* that Scappi refers to for that typically Iberian dish.

is put back into that basin with a little broth and gooseberries or verjuice grapes, and boiled. Thicken it with beaten eggs and grated cheese.

You can also cook that melon in a broth. When it is done, break it up with a spoon and blend in eggs, cheese and spices as above. If you do not have gooseberries or verjuice grapes, use plain verjuice.

223. To prepare a thick soup of quince in a meat broth.

Get a quince in its season, which begins at the end of August and goes until the end of November, even though in Rome you can sometimes find them in February. Pare it, core it, cut it up and put it into a pot in enough broth to cover it, along with a little verjuice, sugar, pepper, cinnamon and nutmeg. Cook it. When it is done, serve it hot with its broth.

You can also beat it small with knives after it has cooked, and blend cheese and eggs into it.

224. Various ways to prepare a thick soup of eggplant in a meat broth.

Get eggplants between July and the end of November, which is their proper season. Peel off their rind, which is a purplish colour. If you want to stuff them, half parboil them, take them out of the water and let them drain. Make a hole in their stem end; what you remove you beat small with pork fat, common herbs and garlic cloves, adding in grated cheese, beaten walnuts and common spices, raisins and saffron. Stuff the eggplants with that. Stand them against one another in a suitably sized pot in enough broth to more than half cover them; in that broth there should be chunks of pork belly and sowbelly, pepper, cinnamon and saffron. Boil them until the stuffing is firm. Add in enough broth to cover them wholly, and a handful of herbs, and finish cooking them. Serve them hot with that broth.

If you want them in various other thick soups, follow the directions set out for the squash in Recipe 218. If you want to braise them in an oven, stuff them with a different mixture made up of lean veal or pork beaten with pork fat and mixed with eggs and spices. Arrange the eggplants in a baking dish which has enough broth to more than half cover them, along with beaten pork fat and common spices, and set them to cook in the oven. If you want to do them another way, follow the directions given in Recipe 228 in the Book on Fish.

225. To prepare Lombard-style sops[225.1] with meat broth.

Get white bread sliced to the thickness of a knife blade, remove its crust and braise it in an oven or under a cooking bell. Get a fat broth in which beef, capon and saveloy has been cooked. Arrange the slices of bread in a dish, sprinkle them with grated cheese, sugar, pepper and cinnamon, and on that put a few little slices of provatura or a creamy cheese that is not too salty. Make up three layers like

---

[225.1] The generic nature of this preparation has already been indicated in Recipe II,22. See also the end of Recipe II,205. The next recipe is another *suppa alla Lombarda*.

that. Over top of that pour the above broth, which should not be too salty, until everything is thoroughly soaked.[225.2] Cover it with another dish and let it sit for a quarter of an hour in a hot place. Serve it hot, dressed with thinly sliced saveloy, sugar and cinnamon.

226. To prepare Lombard sops with meat broth interspersed with capon flesh and skins and other ingredients.

Lay out the bread in dishes as before, sprinkling it with cheese, sugar and cinnamon, and on them put thin slices of provatura. Upon that put boiled capon meat, sliced with the skin, rumps of boiled, deboned doves, boiled goat-kid eyes, divided in two, and cooked saveloy sliced crosswise. Sprinkle cheese, sugar and cinnamon on that, then put as many more slices of provatura or some creamy cheese on the bread slices. Continue like that, making up three layers. Pour a broth that is not too salty over it several times until it is quite soppy. Cover it and let it sit as described above.

You can also alternate slices of sowbelly, desalted and boiled, and cow's udder, and well-boiled *salsiccioni* cut into slices, and lamb testicles roasted on a spit and then cut into slices.

227. To prepare *capirotata* sops with fat meat broth.[227]

Get a spit-roasted veal kidney with its fat, and ember-roasted livers of goslings and capons; beat the kidney with knives after the livers have cooled a little. Grind the livers in a mortar with the spit-roasted breast of a pheasant or capon, or of a wild duck. Moisten all that with a cold, fat broth, and put it through a strainer. Put it all into a cooking basin with a pound of sugar, half an ounce of cinnamon, a quarter-ounce of pepper and half an ounce of cloves and nutmeg combined. Cook the mixture over a low heat on the coals, stirring constantly and adding in a beaker of verjuice. Then get slices of bread dredged in egg yolks beaten with rosewater tinged with saffron, and sauté them in melted butter or rendered fat. When they are fried, but not burnt, make a layer of them in a dish. Sprinkle them with sugar and cinnamon, pour the cooked mixture over them; repeat, making up two or three layers. It is served hot, sprinkled with sugar and cinnamon.

With the livers you can also grind hard-boiled egg yolks, and garlic cloves that have first been boiled, and a little Parmesan cheese.

228. To prepare sops of roasted almonds and other things.

Get a pound of Milanese almonds that have been roasted on a fire shovel and well cleaned with a coarse cloth; grind them in a mortar with four ounces of apples, twenty chicken livers roasted on the coals, and two ounces of *mostaccioli*.

[225.2] *insuppata*: literally, 'soppy.'

[227] The lean version of this dish, Recipe III,266, is called gilded sops, with the name *capirotata* indicated as a popular appellation for it.

When everything has been ground up together, moisten it with cold meat broth and strain it. Into it put a beaker of verjuice, a pound of sugar and an ounce and a half of pepper, cloves, cinnamon and nutmeg combined. When everything has been blended together so that the mixture is thin, cook it in a cooking basin as the preparation above is done. Then have ready the slices of bread dredged in eggs,[228.1] fried in butter or rendered fat and set out in the dish as above, and make sops as in the previous recipe.

You can also make them differently with only capon livers ground in a mortar with raisins, *mostaccioli* and raw egg yolks, moistening those things with broth, malmsey and verjuice, putting that through a strainer[228.2] and cooking it as above with sugar and spices. It does not matter whether the bread is dredged and fried or not.

229. To prepare *crostate*[229.1] – that is, gourmand bread[229.2] – with spit-roasted veal kidney.

Get slices of day-old bread the thickness of the spine of a knife and toast them on a grill. Get veal kidney, with its fat, roasted on a spit along with the loin. Cut a little of the tenderloin away from the loin; let it cool a little, then beat it very small with knives, along with mint, sweet marjoram, burnet and fresh fennel – not having any fresh, use the little dried flowers[229.3] – and add in pepper, cloves, cinnamon, nutmeg, sugar, egg yolks, orange juice or verjuice, and enough salt. When the composition is made up, spread it out over the slices of toast. Put the covered toast into a tourte pan without the slices touching one another. Apply heat

---

[228.1] The previous recipe, upon which this one seems to be modelled, makes use of beaten egg yolks, rosewater and saffron for its 'French toast.'

[228.2] This *stamegna* may be either the shallow metal colander pictured in Plate 11 or, more likely, a straining cloth as is used in Recipe 243.

[229.1] The generic name of this preparation, *crostata*, which here (and in Recipe III,265) designates another sort of open-faced sandwich or canapé, apparently derives more from its final 'crusted' appearance than from any close relation to the usual *crostate*, a sort of pie for which we find two series of recipes in Book V beginning at Recipes 49 and 198. The modern version of the genre often translates as 'tart.' To avoid a misunderstanding of what he intends by *crostate*, Scappi provides them with an alternative, clarifying name: here *pan ghiotto*, in V,49 *coppi* and *sfogliati*. The present variety of *crostata* has a history going back to at least the *Neapolitan Recipe Collection* (Recipe 94, *Crostata de caso, pane, etc.*), Martino's *Libro de arte coquinaria* (Recipe 10) and the Latin collection now at Châlons-sur-Marne (Bibliothèque municipale, MS 319, Recipe 133, *De crostata piscium*).

[229.2] *pan ghiotto*: perhaps, more approvingly, 'gourmet bread' or 'delectible bread.' Scappi's qualification *ghiotto* is cognate with the English word 'glutton.'

[229.3] And the seed panicle, understood. Castelvetro writes that the fresh 'flower' was commonly consumed: '[In summer] young, sweet fennel bulbs appear, which we eat raw with salt after meals' (trans. Riley, 78).

to the top of the lid[229.4] and hot coals under the tourte pan, leaving it until the bread has absorbed a little of the grease and the mixture has firmed up. Serve it hot, dressed with orange juice, sugar and cinnamon. You can also put fresh butter of melted pork fat into the tourte pan so the bread will be greasier.

You can also cook it on a grill over a low fire, heating the top with a hot shovel or else with a tourte-pan lid.[229.5]

230. To prepare *crostate* – that is, gourmand bread – with salted pork jowl or prosciutto.

When the bread is cut as above, fry it in butter or in melted pork fat. Get slices of salt pork jowl or prosciutto and sauté them in a pan with beaten spring onions and tips of sage. When they are done, put a little vinegar in with them, and must syrup or sugar, and pepper and cinnamon; heat them up. Have the slices of bread already set out in a dish and soaked with a little hot grease; on top of them put the jowl or ham along with the other ingredients. Serve it hot.

231. To prepare those *crostate* or gourmand bread with calf brains and sweetbreads.

Boil the brains and sweetbreads. When they are done, take them out and sauté the sweetbreads well in rendered fat or melted pork fat. Beat them small with knives along with mint, sweet marjoram, burnet and fresh fennel, stirring the brains into that along with pepper, cloves, cinnamon, nutmeg, saffron, grated cheese, sugar, raw egg yolks, orange juice or verjuice, and enough salt – the amount of each ingredient is whatever seems best, at your discretion. Get slices of bread dredged in egg yolk and sautéed in butter or rendered fat. When they are fried, take them out and let them cool a little. Spread the mixture over them and, covered like that, set them out in a tourte pan that has butter or rendered fat in it. When they are arranged, give them some heat from below and above as was done with the other ones, or else put them into a very moderate oven. When the mixture has set, serve them hot with orange juice and sugar over top.

232. To prepare gilded bread fried in butter or rendered fat.

Get twenty beaten egg yolks, six ounces of finely grated bread, three-quarters of an ounce of cinnamon, three ounces of sugar, three ounces of rosewater and a little saffron, and mix all that together with very finely beaten herbs. Get crustless fresh bread sliced the thickness of a knife blade, dredge the slices in that mixture, fry them in butter or rendered fat and serve them hot with sugar and cinnamon over them and splashed with rosewater.

[229.4] See Plate 8 for a *tortiera* with its lid.

[229.5] That is, after first heating up one or the other in the fire. See the same procedure in Recipes II,63 and III,269.

233. To prepare a *crostata*[233.1] with creamy cheese, popularly called a *buti-rata*.[233.2]

Get crustless square slices of white bread that have been braised. Get a silver platter or a small baking dish of copper that is well tinned inside and out; the platter or dish should be greased thickly with six ounces of fresh butter. On that butter put some of the bread, and on the bread put small slices of fresh unsalted provatura or some other creamy cheese. Sprinkle that with sugar and cinnamon; onto the cheese put the same amount of butter again. In that way build up three layers like the first one. Give it heat from below and above as you do with tourtes, but moderately, and more on top than beneath. When it is braised, serve it hot with sugar and cinnamon over it.

You can also do that dish with the slices of bread gilded and fried and set out as above. You can also sprinkle them with sugar and leave off the cinnamon. And you can do it without provatura but with only bread, without heating it.[233.3]

234. To prepare omelets with various ingredients on a meat day.

Beat ten day-old eggs. Get six ounces of marbled prosciutto, diced, and three ounces of onions that have been cooked under the coals and beaten small. Sauté both of those in melted pork fat. With the eggs put in three ounces of creamy cheese, half an ounce of pepper and cinnamon together, and finely chopped common herbs. Put everything together in a pan containing the ham and onions and make the omelet. Serve it hot with orange juice over it.

235. To prepare a layered omelet.[235.1]

Beat fourteen eggs. Get a spoon that will hold two eggs, fill it with beaten egg and make a small omelet the size of the pan – which pan should not be much larger than the dish in which the omelet is to be set. When the little omelet is made, set it in the dish – minding that, to do it well, it is enough for the bottom of the pan alone to be greased with rendered fat. Sprinkle the omelet with sugar, cinnamon and nutmeg, splash it with orange juice and set small slices of provatura or a creamy cheese on it, and on that little chunks of butter, cloves of garlic that have steeped and been crushed, and raisins. Cover that with another omelet. Go on making omelets, putting one on top of the other until all the egg is gone.

[233.1] Again this is not the pastry *crostata* to which a good number of recipes are devoted in Book V, but rather a variety belonging to the open-faced-sandwich genre that Scappi has just termed *pan ghiotto* (Recipes 229–31).

[233.2] This name means 'buttery' or 'buttered.'

[233.3] The phrase *senza scaldarla* applies to the *crostata* itself.

[235.1] *Per fare frittata doppia*: that is, a 'double' omelet, although at two eggs per layer likely about seven omelets high. See also the next recipe.

To do it another way, instead of the provatura you can spread out a mixture of saveloy with beaten mint and sweet marjoram – not overlooking, though, to splash them with orange juice and to sprinkle them with sugar and cinnamon.

When the omelet is done, finish cooking it the way tourtes are done. Note, though, that it has to be cooked[235.2] on silver dishes or else in small tourte pans.

236. To prepare a layered omelet with veal or kid sweetbreads and other things.

Get a pair of veal sweetbreads, or else two pounds of goat-kid sweet-breads,[236.1] with the testicles and scrota cut away so that only the sweetbreads are left, and cook them in salted water. When the calf's sweetbreads are cooked, cut them up into chunks, but leave the kid's whole.[236.2] Sauté them in rendered fat or in melted pork fat. When they are done, take them out and beat them small with knives. Get fifteen eggs, well beaten with half an ounce of cinnamon, a little pepper, sweet marjoram and grated creamy cheese; mix everything in with the sweetbreads. Make the omelet in rendered fat or butter. When it is done, serve it hot, splashed with rosewater and orange juice and sprinkled with sugar and cinnamon. If you do not have sweetbreads, use the brains of those animals. Into that omelet you can put a beaker of milk.

237. To prepare an omelet of pig's blood or kid's blood.

Pour out two-thirds of a litre of blood from one of the above animals, put it through a strainer and mix it with a third of a litre of goat's milk. Get fifteen beaten eggs, spring onions beaten and fried, a little creamy cheese, pepper, cinnamon, cloves and nutmeg, mint and sweet marjoram, and enough salt. Mix everything together and make the omelet. Serve it hot with sugar and cinnamon over it.

238. To prepare an egg omelet another way.

Get fifteen well beaten eggs, four ounces of boiled salt pork jowl, four ounces of salted pork rinds[238] – very clean, boiled and cut into bits along with the jowl – three ounces of spring onions, beaten and sautéed, half a pound of provatura and grated cheese together, two ounces of finely grated bread, three ounces of finely chopped beef marrow, three ounces of sugar, one ounce of cinnamon, half an ounce of pepper, another half-ounce of cloves and nutmeg together, a little finely chopped mint and sweet marjoram, and four ounces of goat's milk. Make an omelet of that, watching that it does not stick. You should know that if there is no sugar in it, it will not stick in the pan. That omelet should be soft, and served hot with sugar, cinnamon and orange juice over it.

[235.2] That is, the final heating of the omelet stack has to be done in covered dishes on the coals or in an oven.

[236.1] The pancreas is intended here under the term sweetbreads, *animelle*.

[236.2] The instructions are intended to cover whichever sweetbreads, calf or kid, are used.

[238] *cotiche salate.*

Hereafter are directions to be followed for making various jellies and sauces, for lean days as well as meat days and in Lent.

239. To prepare jelly from wether's and calf's feet.

Get[239.1] forty forefeet of a wether and six of a calf,[239.2] fresh, their skin and all dirt cleaned off. Remove the bone – that is, the hollow bone where the marrow is – and divide them up into chunks the size of a walnut, washing them in several changes of clean water. Put them into a new stewpot that has first soaked and does not have a bad smell to it, or else into a tinned copper pot, either of which is able to hold up to sixteen litres;[239.3] along with those chunks put in eight litres of white wine, two and two-thirds litres of new verjuice and the remainder pure water. Boil everything gently over a coal fire, away from the flame, skimming it with a wooden spoon and not an iron one because iron will turn the decoction cloudy and bitter. When it has boiled and reduced by two-thirds, try it out with a beaker – that is, put a little of the decoction in the beaker and put the beaker in cold water or in a cool place; if, after sitting there for half an hour, the decoction has jelled and is set, take the pot off the heat and put the decoction through a strainer. If it does not jell,[239.4] let it go on boiling until, trying it again, the decoction in the beaker does jell. When it is strained into an earthenware or tinned copper pot – though earthenware is better than copper – carefully remove the fat on top, then put it into a smaller cooking pot, a fine, clean one without a bad smell, along with two-thirds of a litre of white vinegar, two pounds of sugar, an ounce and a half of ground cinnamon, three-quarters of an ounce of ground round pepper,[239.5] the same of finely cut up white ginger, and a quartered nutmeg. Boil everything for half a quarter of an hour. Then put in six beaten fresh egg whites, giving it a stir. As those whites come to the surface, have a small fabric cone filter[239.6] ready, or

---

[239.1] The 1570 typesetter has exceptionally marked this segment of Book II by placing an ornamented initial letter P, five lines high, followed by italic capitals on the word 'get': P*IGLINSI*. More frugal with space the 1581 printer makes no distinction in setting this initial word.

[239.2] Here and in the recipe's rubric wether and calf are in the singular: twenty wethers and three calves will give up their forefeet for this dish.

[239.3] That is, six *boccali*. The following two measures are also expressed in *boccali*.

[239.4] Understand: in the beaker, during the test.

[239.5] This *pepe tondo* is just the usual peppercorns, as distinct from long pepper, but blackened by drying. See Balducci Pegolotti, ed. Evans, 360, where the fourteenth-century Florentine tells the merchant what to do if his shipment of round pepper should become damp; on page 42 Evans defines *pepe tondo* as black pepper, being the fully ripe, dried berries; it still has its darkened outer skin, making it distinct from white pepper and more pungent. Scappi does not qualify pepper as 'round' elsewhere.

[239.6] A *calza* or *calzetta* is illustrated in Plates 2 and 18; the engraver identifies the aparatus only indirectly by its function: *gielo*. (In modern terms one might refer to the jelly at this stage

a white cloth bag like the one pharmacists[239.7] use to strain their decoctions, and filter the decoction through the bag several times until it becomes clear. Put it in a cool place to jell in beakers, in dishes or in other vessels. Beneath that jelly you can put capon or other meat, boiled or roasted as you like. If you want the jelly decoction to turn out less fatty, take only the skins and ligaments[239.8] of the feet, which will take up less space and less wine and vinegar will go in, though quite a few more feet.

240. To prepare jelly from goat kids' feet and head, and with feet, back, wings and legs of capons.

Get forty feet and four heads of goat kid; clean the hair and all dirt off everything. In the feet remove the hollow bone where the marrow is; in the heads, the brain and eyes; everything is cut up into a number of pieces. Then of capons get twenty feet and four backs along with the wings and legs. Their breasts are boiled in salted water (then that decoction is put over them, as will be shown). When everything is clean and washed, put it into an earthenware cooking pot a little smaller than the one above, with five litres[240.1] of sweet white wine, two of water and one of verjuice, and boil it until it has reduced by two-thirds, not failing to skim it. Test it with a beaker as in the previous recipe, and put it through a strainer. So that the decoction will stay clearer, remove any fat from it as it strains. Put two-thirds of a litre of vinegar into it, with two pounds of sugar, an ounce and a half of crushed cinnamon, half an ounce of crushed pepper and ginger together, and two ounces of crumbled *mostaccioli*. Boil it in a smaller pot for half a quarter of an hour, putting in six fresh, beaten egg whites. When it has boiled so that the egg whites have risen to the surface, strain the decoction through the bag as in the previous recipe. When it is strained, put it into dishes or other vessels to jell together with, under it, the meat[240.2] of the above capons. You can colour it with

---

in its preparation as 'aspic.') In Book I, §44 Scappi has listed a *calzetta per passar gelo* as necessary to a well furnished kitchen. In Recipes II,265, VI,3 and 190 the fabric is described as being coarse white wool: the fabric is, literally, a filter, this word deriving from the word 'felt' which is compressed animal hair such as sheep's hair. In the present book, Recipe 155, a filter is made of horsehair.

[239.7] By Scappi's time the word *spetiali*, which means literally 'spicers,' was a designation also for pharmacists, those who mix and sell medicinal spices and herbs. See also Book I, §43.

[239.8] Normally these *nervi* are anything that we might generally call gristle in a meat.

[240.1] Two *boccali*: more precisely five and a third litres, or twelve pounds.

[240.2] That is, the breast mentioned previously.

carrots[240.3] or orchil.[240.4]

241. To prepare jelly from wether's and calf's feet, with which you can fill various moulds and egg shells.

Get the feet of a wether and a calf; if it is in the months of April or May, instead of a wether's get a lamb's. Clean them of their hair, remove their bone, wash them in several changes of water and put them to boil in an earthenware or copper pot with enough white wine and water, in equal amounts, to cover them. Cook them until the decoction is reduced by more than half, not neglecting to skim it. When you have tried it in a beaker, so that the decoction makes a firmer jelly than previous ones, take it off the fire, put it through a strainer, removing the fat, and put it back into a pot. Add in a strong vinegar, ground sugar and fresh, beaten egg whites, and boil it. When the egg whites come up floating, be ready with the bag[241.1] into which you have put ground pepper and cinnamon, ground *mostaccioli* and ground ginger. Put the decoction through it several times until it is clear. If anyone wants to put nutmeg and whole cloves into the bottom of the bag with the other spices, he can do so. When it is strained, test it, because it should have a pleasant flavour rather than bitter. Let it sit in earthenware vessels until it has chilled. If you want to fill wax or tin moulds with it, grease the moulds with newly made sweet almond oil, and fill them with the jelly, which should be cool rather than warm because if it is warm it will take the oil off the mould and the oil will not stay on them. However, if you want to fill earthenware or glass containers with it, or small pastry tubes, little white-metal squares or egg shells, put it in warm, and when those containers are filled put them into a cool place to jell.

If you would like to have several colours in a single container or in an egg shell, put in some of one colour and let it jell, then on top of that put in a little white

---

[240.3] In Recipe 246, below, the carrots have steeped in vinegar before being used as a colourant. The colour they yield, though, is not the orange that might be expected. In early Europe the skin and flesh of the carrot had a deep purplish hue, which a steeping in vinegar would enhance. In the middle of the fifteenth century the *Neapolitan Recipe Collection* used scrapings off carrots to produce in a fish jelly the same colour as Scappi's purplish-blue *pavonazzo*. William Woys Weaver writes that the Dutch later crossed this carrot, a long slender root that originated in Afghanistan, with the lemon carrot to produce the common modern orange-hued carrot (*Heirloom Vegetable Gardening* [New York: Holt, 1997], 125).

[240.4] The word *tornasone* was erroneously typeset here as *tomasone* in both Tramezzino printings. For the colour that orchil makes see the note in Recipe 246, below.

[241.1] This *sacco* is a frame-suspended fabric filter, already mentioned in Recipe 239 as being of the sort *che adoperano gli spetiali per passere le loro decottioni*. It is made along the same lines as the cone-shaped filter in the same recipe and in Recipe 244; in both places this bag and the *calza* or *calzetta* are alternative tools for filtering a jelling liquid. The apparatus is shown in Plate 2 and bears the caption, *si passa gielo*: 'jelly is strained.' See also Plate 18.

jelly made with water and almond milk or with starch, then when the white has
jelled put in the other colour on top cold – because if it were warm it would melt
the other ones. You can use that procedure for any other mould with the exception
of wax and pewter ones. It will always look better if you separate colours with a
white layer, because if a purplish colour and a reddish brown are jelled together
they are hard to distinguish.

That jelly can be put through a syringe. When there are several colours mixed
together and then put through a syringe, you can make lines of it around a dish,
which lines will be of mixed colours. With a syringe you can make knots and
crosses[241.2] and other ornaments depending on the whim of the person doing it.
You can also use cardboard moulds in which various sorts of animals have been
cut out. You put a stiffened mould[241.3] – that is, an empty one – on a plate and
carefully, with the syringe, you will shape up the jelly that will remain in the
dish.[241.4] That can be done with any jelly that is setting. And you can work any
similarly moulded jelly with gold and silver implements.

242. To prepare jelly from pigs' snouts, ears and feet.

Get twenty pigs' feet, six pounds of fresh pork rinds with the fat off, four
snouts and four ears; wash and clean everything. Boil it in a cooking pot with
eight litres of white wine, eight of water and one and a third, more or less, at your
discretion, of vinegar. When you have skimmed it with a wooden spoon, put in a
little salt, an ounce of crushed pepper, an ounce of cinnamon, an ounce of ginger
and two nutmegs. Boil it all together. When the ears and snouts are a little less
than done, take them out and finish cooking them[242.1] in another pot with wine,
vinegar, pepper and enough salt, so they'll be more tasty. When the decoction is
cooked, do the test described in the previous recipes. Skim off all the fat with a
wooden spoon and strain the decoction. When that is done, put in two and a half
pounds of sugar, half a pound of firm honey and eight well beaten egg whites,
bringing it all to a boil as in the previous recipes and then putting it through a
bag. When it has been strained, have the ears and snouts already split in two
and arrange them carefully in dishes the bottoms of which are covered with three
fingers of set jelly; then fill up the dishes with cold jelly[242.2] so that the ears and

---

241.2 *si potranno far gruppi, croci.*

241.3 *la forma fermata.*

241.4 Scappi's directions are not quite as clear as we might wish and present a difficulty or two.
In particular there may be some doubt about the sort of mould he is describing, whose shape is
incised or engraved (*intagliato*) in (on, through?) cardboard; yet it is on the serving plate that the
jelly is shaped, using a syringe.

242.1 No mention is made of removing the pigs' feet from the pot. By what appears later, they
remain where they are in order to finish cooking.

242.2 This second dose of liquid has not yet jelled, though: in the previous recipe Scappi has
explained that a warm liquid would melt the first layer of jelly.

snouts are held between the two jellies. In the interval between jellies, with the
ears and snouts you can put the feet, which have been cooked separately from the
jelly in the same way as the snouts and ears are cooked. It has to be a deep dish,
or else use an earthenware baking dish or a shallow basin. When the jelly has set
and is firm and you want to take it out of the pot, warm the pot in hot water[242.3] so
that the jelly warms, then quickly flip it over into a dish, large or small depending
on the depth of the jelly, because that way the jelly will rise up above the dish. If
on the inside by the ears and snouts you would like to put cleaned almonds, that
is optional. For a decoration around the dish put bay leaves. That jelly needs to
be somewhat acidic, and give it a tang with spices.

243. To prepare jelly from pigs' feet, snouts and ears, interspersed with slices of
mock salami,[243.1] with a decoction made as before.

After the decoction has been made, get six pigs' ears and four snouts that have
been cooked in wine, vinegar and water with spices – that is, pepper, cinnamon,
cloves, nutmeg and ginger, and enough salt. In another pot cook four carrots –
that is, spignel roots[243.2] – or else parsnips, I mean the brownish kind, with wine,
vinegar, water and pepper. When the ears and snouts are cooked, take them out
and let them cool a little on a table until they can be cut like strings. Do the same
with the carrots. Combine three strips of ear with one of carrot, and with those put
a few little dry fennel flowers, crushed pepper and a boiled capon breast cut up
like the snouts. When everything is laid out together like a little bundle, put it into
a cloth or a bit of straining fabric and twist it a couple of times so that it takes on
the shape of a long sausage,[243.3] and tie it with a cord, leaving it tied up like that.
When you want to use it, have little square pans of white metal on hand, or else
little round earthenware baking dishes, with a layer of set jelly in them. Untie the
salciccione from the cloth, and cut it crosswise in thin or thick slices as you like
and set out the slices in the square pans or small baking dishes, or else in dishes
or in other more suitable vessels with the same amount of jelly on top of them so
that the slices are held between the two layers of jelly. When it is set, if you want
to take it out of the vessels, follow the directions given above using warm water.

If you want to do it differently, cook the capon breast with the snout and
ears and, when they are done, cut them up as small as dice. Do the same with
the carrots. Mix shelled almonds in with those things. Before they cool off,
blend everything together with pepper, cinnamon, cloves, nutmeg, fennel flour
and a little rosewater. Quickly put everything onto a thin cloth and form up the
salciccione. Use them as before.

[242.3] In the next recipe this water is described as being 'warm.'

[243.1] *salame finto.* For similar 'pseudo' foods see also Recipes III,160 and 219.

[243.2] *gniffe.* The umbelliferous plant *Meum athamanticum* was for some time cultivated for its
squat edible root.

[243.3] *salcicciotto*: as the recipe's rubric suggests, a sort of elongated salami.

244. To prepare a quick jelly from wether's and calf's feet in any season but mostly in winter.

Get thirty wether's feet or fifty lamb's feet, and four calf's feet. Boil them in a pot with ten and a half litres of lightly salted water, skimming it. When they are almost done, stir them with a wooden spoon so they disintegrate as you stir. Let them go on boiling a little, then put the decoction through a filter or strainer into a vessel with a narrow mouth so the fat will come to the surface. When the fat is skimmed off, put the decoction back into another pot along with the feet which are in the filter, having removed all the tiny bones that have been cut away. When it has boiled half an hour, do the test; if it sets so that it is firm, strain it into a basin or a small earthenware dish and let it sit in a cool place until it has set. Then take off the fat on top with hot water and put the jelly into another pot, watching that you do not let any sediment go in – that is, whatever has settled to the bottom. For every pound of jelly put in an ounce and a half of sugar, five ounces of white wine and two and a half ounces of vinegar, mixing everything together with beaten fresh egg whites. When the decoction is stirred up so that it becomes frothy, put the sugar and vinegar into it that it needs; let it sit with two ounces of crushed ginger and one ounce of white ginger infusing in it. Then boil it again in the pot until the egg white comes to the surface. Put it through a cone filter or through a little fabric bag[244] the way the other jellies are done and put it into a beaker or dishes or other vessels. Into that jelly you can put pomegranate seeds, and you can decorate it with good pinenut kernels. You can set out that jelly in all the ways and forms that the others are done in. If you do not have time to infuse the cinnamon and ginger in the vinegar, put the ground spices into a bag when you do the straining.

245. To prepare jelly from wether's feet.

Get fifty wether's feet that have been well cleaned of their skin and bone, and cook them in a stewpot with thirteen litres of water. When they are done, and well skimmed, strain the decoction, take off its fat and let it jell in an earthenware vessel. When it has set, again take off the fat using hot water. Then take the clearest part of the jelly, leaving the dregs at the bottom. For every pound of jelly, get two and a half ounces of strong white vinegar, two and a half ounces of Spanish honey, one ounce of old verjuice, four and a half ounces of Greek wine or some other sort of clear white wine, two well beaten egg whites, a quarter of an ounce of ground cinnamon, and half an ounce of ground pepper, cloves, ginger and nutmeg combined. Mix everything together and bring it to a boil in another pot. Then pour it through a bag filter. When that has been done, put in shelled, soaked pinenuts, shelled almonds and thin slices of quince that have been cooked in wine. Set everything to jell together. Serve in dishes.

---

[244] See Recipe 239 for both sorts of filter.

246. To prepare clarified jelly from sea fish and freshwater fish.

From among sea fish, get conger, sea bass and umbra; among freshwater fish, get eel, pike, tench and carp. Get each of those fish live; leave its scales on, gut it, wash it, remove its teeth and skin and put it into a pot in enough water and wine to cover it by two fingers, along with a little clear verjuice, whether old or new. Boil it until you cannot skim it anymore. Then put in ground pepper and cinnamon – the amount of each at your discretion and depending on the amount of fish you have. Finish off cooking it. Break the fish apart with a wooden spoon so that everything is broken up, being careful, though, that it is not boiling too strongly, or that it is not too salty. Test it with a beaker the way you do with meat jellies.[246.1] When it is done, let it all sit for half an hour with a little white vinegar in it. Then put it through a filter or strainer, squeezing everything through. Carefully lift off the fat that has risen, and taste that it is not too salty, that it is sharp and tangy with spices because that jelly does not need sugar. Then put in the egg whites and boil them with the decoction until those egg whites float up. Then filter it several times through a fabric cone filter until it is clear. Put it over eel flesh in dishes or other vessels to set in a cool place. You can put shelled almonds and pinenuts softened in cold water into that jelly.

If you want to colour any of the above clear jellies, use saffron for yellow, carrots that have steeped in vinegar for a peacock blue,[246.2] and orchil, which is a Levantine spice, for a russet,[246.3] and other colours.

247. To prepare quince jelly.

Get fresh pear quince,[247] which are better and juicier than apples. Remove the fine hair on them without paring them; quarter them and remove only their seeds and the hard part that is in there. Put them into a casserole pot in enough clean water to fully cover them, and boil them over a low coal fire until they are well cooked – bursting, that is – being careful that they should not be stirred, only skimmed with a wooden or silver spoon. Then pour that decoction through a piece of fine straining cloth or else through a white towel, squeezing it a little. For every pound of decoction put in a pound of fine sugar. Boil it all again over a low fire until it is thoroughly cooked – not failing to do the test on a plate or a pewter disk.

[246.1] See Recipe 239.

[246.2] See the note in Recipe 240, above.

[246.3] Scappi assumes that, with enough vinegar in it, the jelly will be sufficiently acidic for the orchil (the lichen known scientifically as *Gozophora tinctoria*) to turn it dark red. Otherwise, and specifically in the presence of alkalis, orchil will produce a blue colour.

[247] *pere cotogne.* 'There are three kinds of quince. The best is the apple quince [*mele cotogne*] .... The second sort is much bigger and called 'pear quince' on account of its shape. It is more succulent and pulpy and not as good as the others, less downy and aromatic. The third kind is called 'bastard quince' ... ' (Castelvetro, trans. Riley, 118).

248. To prepare *miraus*[248] that can be used as a sauce or a garnishing for various spit-roasted fowl and quadrupeds.

Get two pounds of Milanese almonds toasted on a hot shovel or in a frying pan, and rub them with a coarse rag and clean off any burnt area. Grind them in a mortar with three ounces of fine musk-flavoured Neapolitan *mostaccioli*; moisten that with two pounds of malmsey, verjuice and orange juice combined, and eight ounces of broth, putting everything through a filter or strainer. Add in a pound and a half of sugar, an ounce of cinnamon, half an ounce of pepper, and half an ounce of ground cloves and nutmeg combined. Cook all that in a cooking basin, stirring it until it thickens and trying the sauce several times to see whether it is cooked and not burnt, that it has some sweetness and some bitterness. When it is done, take it down and let it cool. As a sauce serve it with sugar and cinnamon over it. If you want to use it to garnish fowl or hares or other game roasted on a spit, keep it a little on the thin side.

You can also make that sauce without putting any broth into it; however, instead of the broth use an equivalent amount of the above [liquid] ingredients.

249. To prepare a *civiero*[249.1] that can be used as the previous preparation.

Get two pounds of prunes that are not oily, two pounds of dried visciola cherries and morello cherries together,[249.2] one pound of raisins and six ounces of toasted white bread. Put everything into an earthenware pot with two and a half pounds of a robust wine and two pounds of must syrup, one and a half pounds of vinegar, an ounce of crushed cinnamon, half an ounce of pepper, half an ounce of ginger, half an ounce of cloves and nutmeg together, and two ounces of fine musk-flavoured *mostaccioli*[249.3] ground up. Boil it all together slowly for an hour on the coals with the pot stopped up. Then put it through a filter or strainer and put it back into a casserole pot or a cooking basin with four ounces of muscatel malmsey, three ounces of orange juice and two ounces of rosewater. Let it come

---

[248] A typically Catalan dish known as a *mirausto* was adopted in Italy in the fifteenth century through the influence of the Aragonese kingdom of Naples. See the *mig-raust* in Recipe 54 of the fourteenth-century Catalan *Libre de sent soví*. Scappi's version of this sauce is generally that found in the *Neapolitan Recipe Collection* at Recipe 37 (*Mirausto alla Catalana*) which is likewise expressly intended for roasted fowl. Scappi will again examine a *miraus* in Recipe III,20.

[249.1] The name for this sort of semi-liquid dish or, as here, sauce derives from the French *civet*, which had a range of variant spellings in Old French including *civé, civié* and *civier*. This was originally a stew whose determining ingredient was onion (Latin *cæpa*) – an ingredient absent among the many that Scappi calls for in his own *civiero*.

[249.2] It seems that the *visciole* alone are not enough to give this dish the tang Scappi wants, so he combines them with a distinctly sour cherry, the *marasca* or morello. See the same combination in Recipe 252, below.

[249.3] These *mostaccioli muschiati* are in fairly common use in Scappi's kitchen.

to a boil. Include a little sugar if it is not sweet enough. Take it down, let it cool, and serve it with sugar and cinnamon over it.

   If you want it for garnishing fowl and game roasted on a spit, keep it on the thin side. Serve it with sugar, cinnamon and candied pinenuts over top of it.

250. To prepare a sauce popularly called galantine[250.1] that can be used as a sauce[250.2] or a garnishing for spit-roasted fowl and quadrupeds.

   Get a pound of dried currants, grind them in a mortar with six hard-boiled egg yolks, three ounces of *mostaccioli* and three ounces of bread toasted on the coals and soaked in rose vinegar; moisten all that with six ounces of malmsey and four ounces of verjuice. Put it through a filter or strainer, adding in a pound of sugar, three ounces of semi-sweet orange juice,[250.3] half an ounce of ground cinnamon and one ounce of ground pepper, cloves and nutmeg together. When it has been strained, heat it in a casserole pot, then let it cool. When it is cold, serve it as a sauce, with sugar and cinnamon over it. If you want it for garnishing fowl and game roasted on a spit, keep it thinner with a little lean meat broth.

251. To prepare a pepper sauce[251] that can be used like the one above.

   Get a pound of grated bread or of crustless bread toasted on the coals; put it into a pot with eight ounces of must syrup, a pound of a lean meat broth or water, four ounces of vinegar, an ounce of cinnamon and another of ground pepper, cloves, nutmeg and ginger combined. Cook that. When it is done put it through a filter or strainer, adding in six ounces of sugar and three ounces of malmsey. Bring it again to a boil in a cooking basin, then take it down and let it cool. As a sauce, serve it with sugar and cinnamon over it, splashed with rosewater. To use it to garnish fowl and game quadrupeds roasted on a spit, keep it thinner with a little broth.

[250.1] The earliest records of a galantine date from the very beginning of the thirteenth century when the proteins in animal hooves or on the skins of certain fish caused a spicy mixture to jell. The words *galantine* and *gelatin* are cognate. Scappi's *galantina*, whether for dipping or for garnishing, will not be a jelly although for both uses relatively thick. The phrase *dal vulgo detto* in the rubric suggests that the sauce was well known by 'ordinary' people; there are, however, few cold sauces like this one.

[250.2] The term *sapore* here seems to imply a dipping sauce served in a separate bowl.

[250.3] As the section 'Things for the Sideboard' in Book IV will show, three varieties of orange were available to Scappi: *forti*, the normal bitter orange, *di mezo sapore*, the semi-sweet, and *dolci*, the still-rare sweet orange. See also Recipes 270 and 279, below. The present preparation is not to have too much of the bitter tang that orange juice would normally give Scappi's dishes.

[251] The use of pepper in a liquid dressing goes back to the earliest extant manuscript recipe collections. What is remarkable about Scappi's *peverata* is the relatively minor role that pepper plays there among all the other spices. On the pepper sauce in Italian cuisine, see Riley, *The Oxford Companion to Italian Food*, 390.

252. To prepare a black broth[252.1] that can be used like the preceding sauces.

Get two pounds of quince, pared and cut up, one pound of raisins and one of prunes, two pounds of muscatel raisins and Slavonian raisins[252.2] together, another pound of visciola cherries and morello cherries together, six ounces of bread toasted on the coals, eight ounces of Greek wine, two pounds of must syrup, two pounds of red wine, three-quarters of an ounce of ground pepper, one ounce of cinnamon, another ounce of nutmeg and cloves together, and three ounces of ground *mostaccioli*. Put all of that into a pot and boil it on the coals away from the flame, with the pot covered. When it is cooked, put it through a filter or strainer, adding in four ounces of orange juice. If it is not sweet enough, put in some sugar and heat it as above. Then take it down and let it cool. As a sauce, serve it with sugar and cinnamon over it. However, it you want it for garnishing wild fowl roasted on a spit, keep it thin with a little broth.

253. To prepare a sauce of toasted Milanese almonds, called peacock sauce.

Get a pound of Milanese almonds toasted on a fire shovel or in a pan; they should be quite clean. Grind them up in a mortar with a pound of clean currants and eight hard-boiled egg yolks. If it is a meat day, include six chicken livers cooked on the coals; on a lean day, fish livers; and add in two ounces of *mostaccioli* and four ounces of toast soaked in vinegar. When everything is ground up together, moisten it with verjuice and a little meat broth or fish broth depending on the day. Put it through a filter or strainer, then put it into a tinned casserole pot with a pound of sugar, three-quarters of an ounce of ground cinnamon, three-quarters of an ounce of pepper, cloves and nutmeg combined. Cook it, adding in a little orange juice. When it is done, let it cool. Serve it with sugar and cinnamon over it. If you do not want to use a meat or fish broth, use malmsey instead. You can garnish roasts with this sauce.

In the same way you can make bastard sauce[253] into which you add more spices.

[252.1] In Recipe 94, above, the *brodo negro* for small game is optional; it is probably the *bronegro* called for in Recipe III,20. The fourteenth-century *Libro per cuoco* in Recipe 56, *Savore negro a cengiaro* ('black sauce for boar'), gives a sauce that combines ground wild-boar meat, burnt toast, vinegar, pepper, grains of paradise and ginger; the recipe's anonymous author summarizes the sauce's character by writing that it is 'black and bitter.' See also the *salsa negra* in Recipe 274 (shown as 261) at f.103v of the Wellcome Institute for the History of Medicine, WMS 274.

[252.2] These *uva schiava* are described in the *Dizionario etimologico italiano* as white with a round seed. In the first decade of the thirteenth century Pietro de' Crescenzi devotes a long paragraph to this grape in his *Liber ruralium commodorum* in the chapter entitled *Delle diverse qualità di viti*. He describes the grape as juicy, mild in flavour and transparent. It was cultivated around Brescia and Mantua. Messisbugo lists it among other fruits likely intended to be eaten raw. See Faccioli, *Arte della cucina*, I, 4 and 269.

[253] *salza bastarda*. See the *capirotata bastarda* of Recipe II,157.

254. To prepare a sauce of raisins and other ingredients.

In a mortar grind a pound of raisins with six ounces of toast soaked in red wine and vinegar, two ounces of *mostaccioli* and three ounces of shelled hazelnuts; when all of that is ground up, moisten it with the same red wine and vinegar and put it through a filter. That done, put it into a tinned casserole pot and also put in ground pepper, cinnamon, cloves and nutmeg – all of which make up one ounce, though there should be more cinnamon than anything else. Cook it, adding in a little malmsey and orange juice. When it is done, serve it hot with sugar and cinnamon on top.

255. To prepare a sauce of a broom colour[255.1] with shelled almonds.

In a mortar grind a pound of Milanese almonds with six ounces of crustless bread soaked in verjuice, three ounces of pinenut paste[255.2] and six raw egg yolks; when that is ground up, moisten it with orange juice, verjuice and a little trebbiano or muscatel, and put it through a filter. Put that into a casserole pot with a pound of sugar, adding in a combination of ground pepper, cloves, cinnamon and nutmeg, an ounce and a half of them all together, though with more cinnamon than the other spices. Cook it like the previous sauces. Serve it either hot or cold as you like, with sugar and cinnamon over it.

256. To prepare a sauce of apples and onions.

Get a pound of apples without paring them, only seeding and coring them. Grind them in a mortar with four ounces of large onions that have been cooked under the coals, four hard-boiled egg yolks and three ounces of crustless bread soaked in rose vinegar and red wine. When everything is ground up together put it through a strainer and into a casserole pot with four ounces of orange juice, a little verjuice and must syrup, and half a pound of sugar. Cook it. Serve it hot or cold as you like, with sugar and cinnamon.

As well, cooked garlic cloves are an optional alternative to the onions.

257. To prepare a garlic sauce[257] with fresh walnuts and almonds.

Get six ounces of fresh, shelled walnuts, four ounces of fresh Milanese

---

[255.1] For many centuries across Europe a dish with a yellow hue was conventionally named *genestrata, ginestrada* and *genesté* (see Recipe II,121 and elsewhere) after the brilliant yellow blossoms of the broom or Spanish broom bush. Here in Scappi (and in modern Italian) the plant is *ginestra*.

[255.2] This *pignocatti* is a sort of sweetened confection of ground pinenuts. Scappi uses it in roughly a dozen recipes.

[257] An *agliata* had been known from at least the time of Apicius and can be seen in the earliest recipe collections of the late Middle Ages. Either almonds or walnuts are commonly ground with the garlic; the combination here of the two is an interesting variation. Castelvetro gives a simpler version of Scappi's recipe: garlic and walnuts, with bread and enough lean meat broth to make 'a liquid like the pap they give to little babies.' He then describes how it is used back home in Italy: 'Prudent folk eat this sauce with fresh pork as an antidote to its harmful qualities, or with boiled

almonds and six parboiled garlic cloves or one and a half raw ones. Grind that in a mortar with four ounces of crustless bread soaked in a meat or fish broth that is not too salty. When that is done, put a quarter-ounce of ground ginger into it. The sauce being well ground, there is no need to strain it but only to moisten it with one of those broths. If the nuts are dry, set them to soak in cold water until they have softened and can be shelled. Into that sauce you can grind a little turnip or kohlrabi that has been well cooked – in a meat broth if it is a meat day.

258. To prepare a sauce called *nosella*.

In a mortar grind a pound of shelled walnuts that are not rancid with six ounces of shelled almonds, six ounces of crustless bread soaked in a meat or fish broth, and three garlic cloves. When it is all ground up, moisten it with one of those broths. Without straining it, put it into a casserole pot with an ounce of mild spices, a little saffron and a little finely beaten rosemary, mint and sweet marjoram. Bring everything in the casserole to a boil. When it is cooked, serve it hot or cold as you like. More often than not that sauce is used to garnish fried frogs[258] or snails and certain fish boiled in water. You can also garnish sautéed veal or kid sweetbreads with it.

259. To prepare a sauce of fresh visciola cherries or of other fruit.

Get four pounds of fresh Roman cherries that are not too ripe, and cook them in a pot with two-thirds of a litre of verjuice, two ounces of fine *mostaccioli*, four ounces of breadcrumb, a little salt, a pound of sugar and an ounce of pepper, cloves, cinnamon and nutmeg together. When it is done, put all of it through a strainer and let it cool. Serve it.

You can do gooseberries and mulberries[259] the same way.

---

goose, an equally indigestible food. Serious pasta eaters even enjoy *agliata* with macaroni and lasagne. It is also good with boletus mushrooms … ' (trans. Riley, 92–3).

[258] Likely the whole frog, perhaps gutted and deboned, as in Recipe VI,167. See the note in Recipe III,162. Scappi does a few times specify only frogs' legs in a preparation.

[259] These *celsi* are relatively rare in early European cookery. They do turn up, though, in two Italian recipes of the fourteenth century (*Anonimo Meridionale, Due libri di cucina*, Book 'A,' Recipes 122 and 130) and in two Latin recipe collections of the same period (both edited by Mulon: *Tractatus*, Recipe I,16 *Moretum*, and *Liber de coquina*, Recipe V,11 *De composito lumbardico*). The first two recipes are for a sauce (qualified as *optimus ad confortandum stomacum*) and combine mint juice, pomegranate wine, mulberry juice, sugar and cinnamon. The *moretum* is a confection of mulberries, honey and wine, and, according to the recipe's author, remains good for at least four years.

Castelvetro notes that there are two varieties of mulberry, the sweeter white – 'not much esteemed (except by silly women and small children)' – and the larger black – 'with a sour-sweet flavour which is most agreeable and wholesome. We also serve them for dessert in the form of mulberry paste' (trans. Riley, 71).

260. To prepare a carrot sauce.

Get the most coloured part of carrots[260] that are very clean, and more than half cook that in water. Then take it out, put it into an earthenware pot and, for every pound of carrots, put in six ounces of sugar, four ounces of quince, half an ounce of cinnamon, a quarter-ounce of pepper and a quarter-ounce of cloves and nutmeg together. Set everything to boil together with two-thirds of a litre of verjuice and four ounces of rose vinegar. When it is cooked, put it through a strainer. That sauce needs to be rather thick. When is it strained, let it cool and serve it.

261. To prepare a raisin sauce.

Get clean, well washed raisins and grind them in a mortar. For every pound of them put in three ounces of fine *mostaccioli*, three ounces of marzipan paste[261] or else thin slices of bread soaked in rose vinegar, eight ounces of fine sugar, half an ounce of cinnamon and a quarter-ounce of cloves and nutmeg together. When everything is ground up, put it through a strainer, having first moistened it with white vinegar and orange juice. Then serve it up in dishes with sugar on top.

You can do seedless muscatel raisins and other dried grapes the same way.

262. To prepare a sauce of raisins and prunes.

Get a pound of raisins and another of very clean and well washed prunes, put them into a pot with two litres of wine, two litres of vinegar and three ounces of *mostaccioli*. When that has cooked, put it through a filter. Then add in half an ounce of ground cinnamon, an ounce of pepper, cloves and nutmeg together, and a pound of fine sugar. Serve it in dishes. That sauce lasts a few days.

263. To prepare a sauce of Milanese almonds.

Grind a pound of Milanese almonds with white breadcrumb that has been soaked in verjuice. Strain it, having moistened it with verjuice and lime juice. Add in six ounces of finely ground sugar,[263] a quarter-ounce of ground ginger and a little salt. Serve it right away because it goes bad quickly.

264. To prepare a pomegranate sauce.

Get a pound and a half of clarified pomegranate wine and a pound of sugar and boil the mixture over a low coal fire until it is cooked – which you can tell by

---

[260] See Recipe 240, above, for the 'peacock' hue of Scappi's carrots.

[261] *Marzapane* is so common in Scappi's kitchen and so simple a preparation that he mentions its composition only incidentally: see Recipe V,229.

[263] See Plate 14 for a *grata zucharo*, a sugar grater.

a test done with a globule.[264] Above all make sure the sugar is fine; and boil it slowly. It is then kept in jars of glass or glazed earthenware.

265. To prepare red-currant sauce.[265.1]

Get red currants, which are like red grapes; seed them and take the best ones leaving aside any that are bruised;[265.2] wash them. Set them in enough clear water to cover them by three fingers and boil them until the berries have burst. Strain the decoction while it is still hot, and filter it through a cone of coarse white twill until you can see it is as clear as a ruby. For every pound of that filtered decoction add in one pound two ounces of sugar. Boil it slowly in a casserole pot, stirring it constantly because of the sugar which will easily burn[265.3] – which will happen with any other sauce when a person is not paying attention.[265.4] When it has boiled for half an hour, test it; if it is beginning to get sticky[265.5] take it off the fire immediately, putting it into a glazed earthenware pot. When it has cooled you can make up beakers out of it because it sets quite easily, just like jelly; for that reason it can more readily be called a jelly than a sauce.

266. To prepare a sauce with the residue of the above red currants.

Take what is left in the strainer and boil it for half an hour in water and wine in a casserole pot, adding *mostaccioli* into it. Filter it, putting in sugar and a little salt and mild spices. Serve it however you like.

267. To prepare royal sauce.[267.1]

Get three pounds of fine sugar and two-thirds of a litre of white vinegar without any pinkness to it, a third of a litre of white wine and a little whole cinnamon. Put everything to boil in a new, glazed pot until it begins to cook; keep the pot covered so it cannot breathe. To know when it is done, put a little of it on

---

[264] Scappi is referring to a confectioner's age-old test in the cooking of a syrup. The same test is evoked a little more explicitly in Recipe 267: a deposited blob of syrup does not spread when it is touched. Recipe 270 suggests that boiling should reduce this very sweet 'pomegranate-wine sauce' by two-thirds.

[265.1] The text of this recipe is virtually identical with what will be printed in Recipe VI,190.

[265.2] *maccato* here; *ammaccato* in Recipe VI,190.

[265.3] *brusciare* here; *abbrusciare* in Recipe VI,190.

[265.4] The 1581 typesetter leaves out the negative here.

[265.5] The verb here is *viscare*, in Recipe VI,190 *invesciare*.

[267.1] See also Recipe VI,192. A sauce very similar to this *salza reale* was recorded more than a century earlier in the *Neapolitan Recipe Collection* at Recipe 118: *Salsa regale*. In his *Dictionarie of the French and English Tongues*, of 1611 but defining French usage of the late-sixteenth century, Randle Cotgrave writes of *Sauce reale*: 'Venison sawce made of red wine Vineger, whole Cynnamon, Cloves, and Sugar boyled together in a pipkin, unto the consumption of almost their halfe.' The sauce might be described as bitter-sweet, spicy and thick.

a plate or a disk;[267.2] if it makes a tight globule that does not spread when you touch it, it is cooked. Then serve it cold. Be careful it does not burn because it has to be taken down just as soon as it makes that glob, as was said. When it is cooking it is optional whether you put nutmeg and whole cloves into it. And instead of cooking it in a pot you can do it in a casserole.[267.3]

268. To prepare a quince-juice sauce.

Grate a quince lightly with a cheese grater without paring it, and press the grated quince in a straining cloth until nothing more will come through it. Put that into a large carafe. Let it sit there for six hours until the coarse matter has settled. Take the clearer liquid and put it into a casserole or glazed pot. For every pound of juice, put in eight ounces of sugar, two ounces of vinegar and one ounce of Greek wine. Cook it the way the above royal sauce is done with a quarter-ounce of whole cinnamon, half an ounce of nutmeg and four whole cloves.

269. To prepare an apple-juice sauce.

Get apples and grate them the same as above without paring them, and follow the same directions as above to obtain a juice and to clarify it. Into it add a little vinegar and white wine. Take the clearest part of it and, for every pound of juice put in eight ounces of sugar. Cook it like the quince juice above, with the same spices.

270. To prepare a sauce of orange juice and lime juice.

Get four ounces of lime juice and a pound of bitter or semi-sweet orange juice[270.1] and set the clearest of it to boil with a pound of fine sugar, a quarter-ounce of whole cinnamon and two whole cloves. Give it the cooking set out in the previous recipe for the sauce of pomegranate wine[270.2] so that it is reduced by two-thirds.

271. To prepare a sauce of new verjuice grapes.

Get four pounds of new verjuice grapes, seeded and washed, and cook them with a beaker of strained new verjuice. Add in two ounces of *mostaccioli*, a pound of sugar, a little dry breadcrumb, two ounces of strong vinegar, a quarter-ounce of whole cinnamon and two whole cloves. When it is well cooked, put everything through a strainer.[271] That sauce is served cold. It spoils quickly.

[267.2] A *tondo* was mentioned in Recipe 247 where it is qualified as being of pewter.

[267.3] Both of these cooking pots, the *pignatta* and the *cazzuola*, can be seen in Plate 10 of the engravings. The second is identified as a *cazzolo con il manico sbusiato*: a casserole pot with a hollow handle.

[270.1] Scappi distinguishes here and elsewhere between juice that is *forte* and *di mezo sapore*, normally bitter and semi-sweet juice respectively.

[270.2] Recipe 264, above.

[271] The reader is reminded that, unless Scappi indicates that his *stamigna* is the shallow metal colander seen in Plate 11, he is referring to a fabric strainer.

272. To prepare green sauce.[272]

Get parsley, spinach tips, sorrel, burnet, rocket and a little mint; chop them up small and grind them in a mortar with thin slices of toast. It is optional whether you put in almonds or hazelnuts, though for the sauce to be greener you should not. When that is ground up, put in pepper and salt, moistening it with vinegar. If it is thoroughly ground up, there is no need to strain it. It can be made in the same way with vine sprouts – that is, grape-vine tendrils.

273. To prepare a verjuice sauce.[273]

Get strained new verjuice and breadcrumb that has been soaked in that verjuice, and put that through a strainer. Add in a little sugar, saffron, pepper and salt, and set it to cook so that it becomes like a thick broth. With that verjuice sauce you can garnish fried dishes, and you can serve it as an accompanying sauce.

274. To prepare a black-grape sauce.

Get black grapes that are rather firm, and they should be of the variety called *gropello*[274.1] – that is, a Cesena grape[274.2] – that are reddish-brown on the outside. Soak[274.3] the bunches and set them to boil[274.4] for an hour in a casserole pot over a low fire. Then take the juice that those grapes will themselves have made and strain it. For every pound of juice, put in eight ounces of fine sugar and boil it again in a casserole pot, skimming it. Toward the end add a little salt and whole cinnamon into it and boil it slowly until it is cooked. When it is done, put it into glass vessels or glazed jars for keeping.

275. To prepare a sauce using the flesh of the same grapes.

Take what is left in the casserole pot, along with the small amount of juice that is there,[275] and boil it with a little vinegar, stirring continuously with a spatula

---

[272] A green sauce had a long history before Scappi's day, although its composition, relying upon parsley, was usually very much simpler than Scappi outlines. Albala (*Cooking in Europe 1250–1650*, 126) points out that Scappi's sauce, a 'combination of savory, sour, and bitter herbs,' resembles a modern pesto.

[273] *agrestata* is nowadays a beverage made with verjuice and sugar.

[274.1] In 1596 Andrea Bacci (*De naturali vinorum historia* [Rome: Niccolò Muzi]) will write: *In Franciacorta* [an area of Brescia province south of Lake Iseo and between the Oglio and Castagnato Rivers, known today for its wines] ... *è celebrato il vino Groppellio, trato dalle uve Groppelle, così denominate con voce dialettale, in quanto gli Italici le chiamano in tal modo a causa dei loro racemi accumulati in un solo grappolo, di color rubicondo* ... ' ... so called because their racemes are entwined in a single cluster.'

[274.2] *cesenese*: a grape and wine from Cesena in Emilia on the Savio River.

[274.3] *suaghinosi* – literally, soften them.

[274.4] *Sic.*

[275] Scappi is referring back to the previous recipe in which the grapes on being 'boiled' have exuded their juice.

– that is done so it will not stick to the bottom. When you can see that it is cooked and quite thick, put it through a filter. Then into that put ground pepper, cinnamon, nutmeg and cloves and a little salt, stirring everything together. In order to give it a lively colour, have at hand two and two-thirds litres of the same grape's juice that has been boiled with sugar for three-quarters of an hour. Mix everything together making it as thin or thick as you like.

276. To prepare a sweet mustard.[276.1]

Get a pound of grape juice, another of quince cooked in wine and sugar,[276.2] four ounces of apples cooked in wine and sugar, three ounces of candied orange peel, two ounces of candied lime peel and half an ounce of candied nutmeg; in a mortar grind all the confected ingredients together with the quince and apples. When everything is ground up, strain it along with the grape juice, and into all that add three ounces of culled, clean mustard seed, more or less, depending on how strong you want it. When it is strained, put in a little finely ground salt and sugar, half an ounce of ground cinnamon and a quarter-ounce of ground cloves. If you do not want to grind up the confected ingredients, beat them small. If you do not have any grape juice, you can do without it by using more quince and apples that are cooked as above.

277. To prepare a cherry sauce.

Get fresh, pitted visciola cherries and put them into a pot of tinned copper or glazed earthenware. Set them to boil dry[277] like that, slowly, without stirring them. When they have burst fully open, pour them into a strainer without pressing them, the juice they've exuded being all you want. For every pound of that juice, put in a pound of fine sugar, half a quarter-ounce of whole cinnamon, a quarter-ounce of ground pepper, cloves and nutmeg combined. Boil all that together, skimming it with a wooden or silver spoon. Let it boil until it forms a globule, testing it as is done for the royal sauce in Recipe 267. It is kept in glazed earthenware jars.

278. To prepare a sauce with the flesh of visciola cherries.

Take the cherries that are left in the strainer, above, and boil them with a little white wine and vinegar, adding in ground *mostaccioli*. Put everything through the strainer. Into that strained matter put finely ground sugar, ground cinnamon, ground cloves and a little salt, and boil all that again if it is to be thin; if it is to

---

[276.1] This recipe is repeated in VI,199. Grape juice was commonly called 'must'; the etymological sense of the word 'mustard' (as a sauce) is 'burning grape juice,' the heating agent being, of course, mustard seed. Scappi's mustard has come a long way from its origins – even to the (optional) point of leaving out any connection to grapes.

[276.2] As made by Recipe 268 perhaps.

[277] *Sic.* As in Recipe 274 no liquid should be added to the pot.

be thick, though, there is no need to do that. For use that same day that sauce is served cold; however, if it is reboiled, it can be kept longer.

If you want to make it with visciola cherries from which you have not extracted the juice, do not put any wine or vinegar into it.

279. To prepare a sauce of quince with orange juice.

Get a pound of pared, cored quince, another pound of finely ground sugar and half a pound of clean water. Cut up the quince into pieces and cook them. Then test the decoction, and if it forms a globule that does not spread, take the quince down. Into the decoction put three ounces of bitter or semi-sweet orange juice and bring it to a boil, skimming it only once with a wooden or silver spoon. Then take it down and serve it cold. You can also put a stick of whole cinnamon and two whole cloves to boil with it. That sauce is kept in glazed jars and lasts for a year, though it becomes like jelly. If you want it to be thick, put the pieces of cooked quince through the strainer with the decoction itself, adding in ground pepper, cloves, cinnamon and nutmeg.

280. To do morello cherries in jelly.

Get ten pounds of fresh morello or visciola cherries that were picked that same day; they should not be bruised. Leave half their stalk on them and make up small bunches of them with ten cherries to a bunch. Get a casserole pot with a pound of clean water and put the morellos into it. As it begins to heat, put in ten pounds of finely ground and sieved sugar and boil it slowly, skimming it with a spoon. When the morellos have burst and are all the same colour, take them down and put them into a dish and let them drain. Boil the decoction by itself until it begins to cook, not failing to skim it. Do the test on a plate and, if it makes a globule that does not spread when you touch it, take it off the fire. Undo the bunches of morellos and set them in beakers or in silver dishes with the decoction, which should be warm, over them and put them in a cool place to jell.

You can do visciola cherries that way. In the same decoction you can cook some fresh damson plums.[280]

281. To cook apples with sugar.

Roast apples. Take them off the fire and pare them, leaving the browned area on them. Get a casserole pot with melted and clarified sugar in it and put the apples in it. Boil them slowly, skimming them. When they are cooked, take them out of the sugar and put them into silver dishes. Let the decoction boil, testing it: if it makes a globule,[281] take it off the fire. Pour it, warm, over the apples, and put it in a cool place to jell.

---

[280] The English name of this variety of plum is cognate with Scappi's *prugne damascene* and relates the fruit to its supposed origin in Damascus, whence it was brought to Europe by early crusaders.

[281] Understand, perhaps: ' … that does not spread when you touch it … '

You can do the same thing with various other fruits. If you want to do pears such as the muscatel, boil them first in water and then finish cooking them with the sugar. They are served up as above.

End of Book Two

Book III
Dishes Proper for Lean and Lenten Days[i]

S ince I have previously dealt with various dishes for meat days, proven by myself in the noble City of Rome for the most part, I must now pass to an examination of those that are proper for lean days and in Lent, beginning with the appearance, nature and seasons of a few fish that are today seen in Rome and in many places in Italy, which have to be prepared in the ways described in the recipes for them. However, before I speak about dressing them, it seems to me appropriate to mention a few peculiarities that, from long experience and practice gained in this Office, I have found to be true. You should, therefore, know that sea fish are much better than those from ponds, rivers and lakes; that fish caught among rocks are more tasty than those from dead waters; that all sea fish that come into freshwater to feed are more delicate, when they are gutted, than any other; and that, in order to be good, more than anything else any fish must be fresh – except for the sturgeon which, when big, should be left awhile before being made into food. Similarly, every fish intended for frying, for grilling and for sousing in vinegar,[ii] should be of a moderate size rather than too big. And all fish that you intend to use for making jelly, for preserving in vinegar and for salting must be alive.

---

[i] The rubric here reads merely *Libro Terzo di M. Bartolomeo Scappi*. The rubric to the table at the end of Book III reads *Tavola del Libro Quadragesimale*, Table of the Lenten Book. As we see in Recipes 4 and 8, for instance, a good number of the recipes that Scappi includes in this book of lean preparations furnish a meat-day variant as well.

[ii] *accarpionare*: a useful term referring to the generic manner in which a carp was conventionally prepared in Scappi's day. See Recipes 52 and 122, below; Scappi indicates there that the procedure is applicable to any freshwater fish, though limited to fish of two pounds and under.

[Sea fish]

1. The appearance and season of a sturgeon.[1.1]

The sturgeon is a big sea fish, long, covered with a skin that tends to a dark green. It has five lines the full length of its body from its head to the tip of its tail, rather like a saw, and the underside of its belly is flat and white. It has a broad tail in the shape of a chicken's wing.[1.2] It has very few guts, mainly the male, which is sometimes full of milt just as the female is of roe. Its liver is whitish and is sweet. It has a single, slimy intestine. It has no bones, large or small, and its backbone is hollow cartilage in which a tiny cord or nerve passes from the head down to the tail. Its head and eyes are small in comparison to its overall size. It has a long snout, like the bow-ram of a galley. Its mouth, under its snout, has no teeth or jaw bone, and it uses its mouth more for sucking than for eating. Attached near its mouth are two small, white barbels; when the snout is cooked and the cartilage[1.3] hits the ground, it bounces like a Florentine ball,[1.4] as does that of its back. Its season begins in the month of March and goes to the end of August; when you get one it is good for the whole year. Many are caught in the Stellata near Ferrara, at which place the Po branches in two, one of which goes to Francolino and the other skirts the walls of Ferrara. By nature that fish swims against the current. It is better when it is caught in large rivers than in the sea.

To boil sturgeon in salted water, or else in wine and salted water.

In my experience I have found that sturgeon is better boiled in plain salted water than in wine. Therefore you have to get it when it is cut up into pieces,[1.5]

[1.1] In neither of the Tramezzino printings is there a number with this rubric. The recipe numbered 1 is the following paragraph. Given that in the remainder of this Book III the description and 'season' of other fish are either incorporated into the first recipe for preparing that fish or receive a numbered paragraph of their own (as is the case in Recipe 34 for tuna), Scappi's first recipe number is in this translation moved back to include the description and season of the sturgeon.

Scappi allots more space to the sturgeon and the ways in which a sturgeon can be prepared than to any other fish. It must have been one of his preferred fish. In the various ways he handles it, the sturgeon serves in some respects as a generic model for several fish that follow it here.

[1.2] The description becomes a little garbled in the 1581 reprinting: *ha la coda larga à foglia alaidi pollo.*

[1.3] Scappi seems to be referring to the cartilaginous process that forms the sturgeon's jaw.

[1.4] A sort of small handball. Further on, in Recipe 195, Scappi writes that the size of a sea urchin is that of *una balla Firentina* (*Fiorentina* in the 1581 printing).

[1.5] Though not explicitly indicated, these pieces appear to be transverse slabs of rather large size: where Scappi's *pezzo* might equate to a relatively thick modern 'steak,' this translation will use the word 'slab.' Later we see that each piece contains a section of the fish's backbone.

preferably a little tenderized[1.6] than too fresh, and wash it carefully in warm water. When it is cleaned of its slime, take out the cord or nerve in the cartilage of its back because cooking would make it stay tough and would make the slab break apart; when it is out and the slab is well cleaned, put it on the fire in cold, salted water – that being done so that any dirt will come out. Then skim it and let it boil slowly for an hour more or less, depending on the size of the slab. It is served hot with parsley over it. You can dress it with a number of sauces, at your option.

If you want to cook it in wine and salted water, after it is skimmed, put crushed pepper, cinnamon, ginger and nutmeg in with it. When it is cooked you can serve it hot or cold, dressed with a sweet mustard or any other sauce you like in dishes. Note that the belly is the fattest and tastiest part of the fish. The head, whole or cut up, can be cooked the same way.

2. To stew slabs of sturgeon in white wine, verjuice, vinegar and water.

Get ten pounds of sturgeon divided into three slabs and put them into a copper or earthenware stewpot[2.1] containing five and a third litres[2.2] of white wine, one and a third litres of verjuice and two-thirds of a litre of vinegar, so that the sturgeon slabs are covered by three fingers of liquid. Into that put two pounds of ground sugar, an ounce of ground cinnamon and pepper together, half an ounce of cloves and ginger together, a quarter-ounce of nutmeg and four old onions, quartered and first boiled in water. Stew everything with sufficient salt and with six ounces of ordinary raisins or muscatel raisins. Boil everything slowly for an hour, more or less depending on the size of the fish, with the lid on the pot so it cannot breathe. When it is done, it is served dressed with its own broth and the onions on top. If it is for a meat day, you can put pieces of pork jowl or saveloy in with it. Instead of the onions you can use yellow rape,[2.3] following the above directions for cooking.

3. Various ways to prepare a sturgeon pottage[3.1] with various ingredients.

Get six pounds of sturgeon, wash it in warm water so that all the slime on

---

[1.6] By the terms *frollo* and *frolletto*, literally 'soft' or 'tender,' Scappi usually means the natural softening that accompanies the aging of a dead animal or fish before it is cooked. For the same effect the game animals of Book II are hung.

[2.1] A *stufatoro* is illustrated in Plate 8.

[2.2] Scappi indicates in Recipe II,162 that a *boccale* equates to two and two-thirds litres (or six pounds, according to Roman measure) of liquid. Here the recipe calls for two *boccali* of wine. In any case, if he had indicated a ratio for the liquids here, it would have been 8:2:1.

[2.3] *navoni gialli*. See also Recipes 242 and 253, below, and V,33.

[3.1] A pottage of fish is a counterpart to a meat or fowl pottage. The principal ingredient, in the present case sturgeon flesh, is cooked in a pot along with some sort of seasoning and served up with some of the hot broth. A *pottaggio* differs from a *zuppa* or sop mainly in that the latter is served, often with garnishes, on a slice of bread or toast which has been soaked in a complementary liquid, usually that broth. In this Book see Recipes 31 (which is not actually called a sop) and 257 ff.

it is cleaned away, and rinse it in several changes of cold water. Get a casserole pot containing a pound of onions, well beaten and sautéed, and two beakers of white wine and one of verjuice; put the sturgeon in, adding enough water to cover it. Boil it without skimming it. When it is almost cooked, put in enough pepper, cinnamon and saffron; and when it is ready for serving, put in a handful of beaten herbs. In summer, instead of verjuice use gooseberries or verjuice grapes; in winter, prunes or dried visciola cherries.

Anyone who does not like any of the above things can cook it in enough water, white wine and butter,[3.2] or else sweet olive oil, to cover it. When it is almost done, he can add in six ounces of grapes and six ounces of ground almonds, moistened with verjuice, along with the same spices, and finish off cooking it. Serve it hot as above.

It can also be cooked in water, oil, salt and common field mushrooms,[3.3] using the same spices with a little verjuice and a handful of beaten herbs. Leaving out the verjuice and instead of the mushrooms, it can be done with new peas and broad beans. You can do the head, whole or in pieces, the same way.

4. Another way to prepare a pottage of sturgeon slabs.

With the sturgeon cut up into several slabs as above, take enough of it to make up the dishes you want to prepare. It is better to skin them, sautéing them in sweet oil or butter in an earthenware or tinned copper pot, turning them occasionally so they are sautéed on both sides. Then get onions, finely chopped and sautéed, put them into the pot with the sturgeon, sautéing it all together a little. Then add in enough water to cover it by three fingers, along with a little verjuice, a little white wine, and enough pepper, cinnamon and saffron. Finish cooking it, minding that it is not too salty. If you want that pottage to be thick, you can put into it a few ground almonds moistened with the broth; if you do not have almonds, breadcrumb soaked in the broth and sieved. At the end put in a handful of beaten herbs, though that preparation should be made to be slightly bitter and the broth attractive in colour, being neither too green nor too yellow.[4] In summer, instead of old verjuice use gooseberries or verjuice grapes. For meat days, instead of oil

---

[3.2] The prevalence of butter in these lean preparations throughout the whole of Book III is noteworthy. It had only recently been approved by the church as a 'lean' grease. Scappi does not indicate any need to wash the butter of its salt, normally added to butter to keep it, so he may feel that the addition of a slight saltiness – rather as salted pork cuts provided in the meat recipes – to certain fish dishes is desirable.

[3.3] These *prugnoli*, also called agaric in English, are used in meat-day preparations and pastries in Book VI and in Recipe 262 of the current Book. In Recipe II,215 Scappi calls them the most delicate of all mushrooms.

[4] This combination of green and yellow, known as 'gaudy green' in Old English, has a long and venerable history in late-medieval cookery.

and butter, use rendered fat or clarified lard. You can also put pork jowl or pork belly or prosciutto into it. Instead of bread or almonds you can thicken the broth with beaten fresh egg yolks, or with hard-boiled egg yolks ground in the mortar with four walnut halves and moistened as above. The head, whole or in pieces, can also be done like that.

5. To prepare a thick soup[5.1] of sturgeon flesh.

Get eight pounds of sturgeon – that is, four from the belly and the rest from elsewhere – and two pounds of salted tuna belly that has macerated to soften it and to wash out much of its salt; beat everything together with knives in the way veal is beaten. When that is done, put it into a casserole pot containing oil or butter and sauté it slowly, stirring it with a spoon and breaking it up so it becomes like beaten meat because it will tend to bind together. Add in a little broth that is not salty from a sturgeon or some other fish, or else enough water to cover it, along with pepper, cinnamon and saffron; finish cooking it with a few raisins. Just before the time to serve it, put in a little beaten herbs, a few gooseberries or verjuice grapes or else verjuice. If you want it thick without herbs, thicken it with egg yolks beaten with verjuice, and a few other hard-boiled egg yolks with a whole clove inside each one. Serve it in dishes with the same egg yolks on top, being careful not to break them, and sprinkling sugar and cinnamon over top of them. During a time of fasting they do not take eggs.[5.2]

6. A different way to make a thick soup of sturgeon flesh.

Get eight pounds of sturgeon, partly from the back, the rest from the belly, skinned. Cook it in salted water and grind it in a mortar with a pound of almonds and another of sugar, or else two pounds of marzipan paste, six raw fresh egg yolks, pepper and cinnamon to taste, and a little salt. When those things are all ground up, add in six ounces of currants.

You can make ravioli with that mixture, flouring them and cooking them in a good broth made with fresh butter or oil, or in a good meat broth, depending on the day. They are served in dishes and dressed with cheese, sugar and cinnamon.[6] You can also put beaten mint, sweet marjoram, burnet and parsley into the mixture.

7. To prepare another thick soup with the above mixture.

When you have made up the mixture in the above way, squeeze it all into a ball and put it, without flouring it, into a small kettle in a fish broth that is boiling,

---

[5.1] This is the *minestra* of which many varieties have been seen in Book II.

[5.2] *... et essendo vigilia non si adoperarenno uova.* A cook distinguished carefully between the normal lean days of a week and fasting days (*vigilia*) that prepared a Christian for the devotions of a high feast day. In the fasting meals that Scappi prepared, butter, cheese and eggs in particular were forbidden. In Recipe VI,174 he will remind his apprentice: *Si sarà giorno di magro, et non di vigilia, vi si potranno metere rossi d'uova.*

[6] See the similar preparation and presentation of *ravioli senza spoglia* in Recipe II,181.

because if it were not boiling the ball would sink to the bottom and fall apart: boiling holds it up and keeps it together. When it has boiled for an hour, take it out of the broth and put it into silver dishes[7.1] or into some other fine vessel, breaking the ball with a spoon and making it look like beaten meat. Then get three ounces of orange juice, two of verjuice, four of the broth it was cooked in, tinged with saffron, three of sugar, and four of butter or else two of oil; mix it all together until everything is blended.[7.2] Serve it hot. However, if you want to set the ball aside whole, make a sauce for it out of those same ingredients; when the ball is served sprinkle the sauce over it hot.

That same mixture can be made into a variety of shapes, round, square, and with the appearance of saveloy.

You can also make the mixture differently: after it is cooked in a long or square shape, cut it crosswise into slices the width of a finger and put it into silver dishes dressed with butter or sweet olive oil, orange juice, sugar, cinnamon and a little of the broth it was cooked in, making sure, though, that that sauce is rather sweet. Then cover it with another dish on top and put it on the dishwarmer[7.3] or on embers. After it has sat there a little while, serve it with sugar and cinnamon over it.

8. To braise[8.1] slabs of sturgeon.

Get ten pounds of sturgeon cut crosswise into slabs each of which is at most the thickness of a finger: that is done so they will cook quickly and stay moist. Stack the slabs on top of one another for half an hour, having first sprinkled them with pepper, cinnamon, cloves, nutmeg and salt; then set them out in a tinned copper or iron tourte pan containing a pound and a half of sweet olive oil or butter. With that put two-thirds of a litre of must syrup,[8.2] a beaker of vinegar and another of verjuice, a pound and a half of well washed prunes and a pound of muscatel

---

[7.1] The plural is used here: *in piatti.*

[7.2] *incorporata*: normally Scappi uses this word in the sense of 'thickened, consolidated.'

[7.3] The *scaldavivande* – properly a 'food warmer' – is a metal bowl holding hot coals on which a dish of food is set to finish cooking slowly or to keep warm. One model is illustrated at the top of Plate 17, along with two sizes of plates or baffles that are designed to fit snugly into it and perhaps hold hot coals on top of them: *Schalda vivande con le sue piastreli.* See also the *navicella*, or 'little boat,' in Plate 8.

[8.1] The verb that Scappi uses here is *sottestare*. It is seen often in Book II and implies the use of a cooking bell or a covered dish or pan: see the note in Recipe II,11 for Scappi's reliance upon that sort of equipment. The translation 'braise' normally refers to such a method of cooking, although in the instances that Scappi writes *stufare*, to stew, as in Recipe 2, above, a stewpot or heavy tourte pan with a lid is normally used. Braising can also be effected in an oven.

[8.2] Often used in Scappi's kitchen, this *mosto cotto* is grape juice reduced by up to two-thirds.

raisins. Cook them the way tourtes are done with heat above and below,[8.3] or else in an oven. When they are done, serve them hot with the same mixture over them. For meat days, instead of oil or butter use rendered fat with those slabs. You can stew pieces of desalted sowbelly with those same ingredients.

9. Another way to braise slabs of sturgeon.

Get ten pounds of sturgeon, more or less depending on how much you want, cut as before. Sprinkle the slabs with the same spices as previously and with salt and fennel flour, and set them to cook in oil or butter the way the others are done, turning them over a few times. When they are almost done, pour off the excess oil or butter and mix the more solid part that is still in the tourte pan[9] together with orange juice, sugar and currants, bringing it to a boil. Serve the fish with that sauce over it. Whatever the season it needs to be served hot.

10. To braise slabs of sturgeon that have sat in a seasoning.

Get ten pounds of sturgeon cut as in the previous recipes, setting it to macerate for three hours in a mixture of two and two-thirds litres of must syrup, sufficient salt, three ounces of ground coriander, an ounce and a half of ground pepper, an ounce of ground cinnamon and three crushed garlic cloves. When they have macerated for that time, take the slabs out and set them in a bell to braise in oil or butter in a tourte pan as before. When they are cooked, take them out of the dish, having boiled some of the seasoning they have macerated in, mixed with the liquid that was left in the pan. Serve them with that sauce over top. And if you want to put Slavonian raisins or muscatel raisins to stew with all that, that is optional.

11. To grill slabs of sturgeon.

Get three pounds of sturgeon cut as before, noting that anyone who wants to skin the fish can do so, although if the skin is left on it holds the fish together. Stack the slabs on top of one another, having first sprinkled them with fennel flour, pepper and salt, and put them into a pot containing oil; let them sit in that oil for half an hour so they are well macerated in the oil. Have sprigs of rosemary or myrtle ready, dipped in that oil and then put on a grill and put the slabs on those sprigs: that is done so the fish will not stick to the grill. Place them in such a way that they do not touch one another. Give them a gentle fire, turning them over a few times. With the same oil in which they have macerated, mixed with vinegar and must syrup or sugar, baste them with a sprig of parsley until they have cooked, so they will take on the flavour of the mixture. Be especially careful not to expose them to an intense heat. That fish will be all the better for cooking with the smoke from the grill caused by the sauce with which the fish has been basted. Serve it

---

[8.3] A *tortiera* is a lidded vessel, suitable for braising: see Plate 9.

[9] What Scappi means by *quella parte piu grossa* is apparently the sludge of spices, salt and fennel flour.

hot, dressed with the same sauce and raisins cooked in wine and sugar, or else with orange juice and sugar.

12. To prepare *tommacelle* of sturgeon flesh.[12.1]

Get ten pounds of a skinned sturgeon, partly from the back and partly from the belly. On a table beat it small with a knife, adding in four pounds of desalted tuna belly, mint, sweet marjoram, a little wild thyme, three ounces of pepper, cinnamon and nutmeg ground together, six ounces of finely ground sugar, a pound of clean currants and ten ounces of raw roe from the sturgeon itself. Of all that make a mixture from which you form balls the size of a Florentine ball[12.2] and a little less; shape them like *tommacelle* with your hand so that some are round and some flat. Flour them and put them into a tourte pan with oil or butter and cook them with heat above and below, turning them over. When they are done, they are served hot with orange juice and sugar over them.

If they are not for a lean day, instead of tuna belly use either desalted sowbelly or pork fat and prosciutto, and instead of sturgeon roe, raw egg yolks. Cook them as before, in rendered fat.

13. To make pears out of braised sturgeon flesh.

Get the same mixture as in the preceding recipe for *tommacelle* and with the palm of your hand make little pear-shaped balls of it with a little stem on top so they look like pears. Flour them and put them into a baking dish or tourte pan in which there is enough oil or butter for the pears. Give them a little heat above and below until they have firmed up. Remove the excess oil or butter and put in enough water and verjuice to cover them, along with pepper, cinnamon and saffron. Boil them for half an hour, adding in a handful of beaten herbs and a little must syrup or sugar. Serve them hot with their broth over them.

14. To prepare saveloy from sturgeon flesh.

Get five pounds of the whitest part of sturgeon belly, skinned, and five pounds from the back; beat them together small with knives, along with two pounds of salted tuna belly – skinned, cleaned and reconstituted[14.1] without being desalted – eight ounces of fennel flour, an ounce and a half of crushed pepper, if you can get any carrots, six ounces of the darkest part of them,[14.2] diced and cooked in wine, six ounces of soaked pinenuts, one ounce of ground cloves and nutmeg

---

[12.1] This recipe begins a series of pseudo-meat preparations, inherently amusing subterfuges in themselves but particularly attractive for anyone who has had enough of eating fish *qua* fish on lean days.

[12.2] In Recipe 194 this is equated to the size of a sea urchin.

[14.1] *levato*, literally 'raised,' as the dried tuna belly is soaked and expands.

[14.2] See Recipe II,246 where the dark part of Scappi's carrots is used to make a peacock blue colour.

together, another ounce of cinnamon, three ounces of olive oil and a little beaten wild thyme, either fresh or dried. Let that mixture sit for a day in a very clean vessel in a cool place; it should be covered so it can better blend together. Then form the mixture into saveloy sausages, large and small, whichever you like, and put them on an oil-greased sheet of paper on a cutting board and leave them in the chimney to smoke for a night: that is done to give them a smell of charcuterie.[14.3] When it is time to cook them, grease another sheet of paper with oil and turn it over on itself in the shape of an oil lamp;[14.4] cook the saveloy on that paper on a grill. When they are done, serve them hot from the grill, dressed with orange juice and sugar.

You can also do saveloy just as soon as the mixture is made up, flouring them and frying them in a tourte pan the way the *tommacelle* are done.[14.5]

If it is for a meat day you can use Parmesan cheese instead of salted tuna belly.

15. Various ways to make stuffed croquettes with sturgeon flesh, cooked on a spit or stewed.

Get ten pounds of sturgeon flesh, partly from the belly and partly from the back, and cut the leanest part into croquettes a hand in length, three fingers wide and a finger deep. Pound each of those twice with the back of a knife; sprinkle them with fennel flour, salt and pepper, and brush them with a little verjuice. With the remainder of the belly make up a mixture as follows: beat it small with knives the way sausage meat is done, adding in cinnamon, nutmeg and cloves ground together, two ounces in all, four ounces of verjuice, half a pound of sugar, enough saffron and salt, six ounces of currants, a handful of beaten common herbs – that is, mint, sweet marjoram and burnet, with a little wild thyme – and with all that make up the filling. Stuff the croquettes with that, rolling them up like wafer cornets.[15.1] Then put them on a spit interspersed with bay or sage leaves and cook them the way other roasts are done, with a sprightly flame so the stuffing does not fall out or they end up dry. Take the grease that falls into the dripping pan and mix it with verjuice and sugar, making a sauce with which the croquettes are served when they are done.

If you want to stew the croquettes when they are still raw or after they have half cooked on the spit, put them into a tourte pan or an earthenware stewpot with

---

[14.3] *l'odore del salume*: *salume* is a collective term for any seasoned pork product, including sausages.

[14.4] What Scappi intends may be a flattened roll with a depression on top.

[14.5] See Recipe 12, above.

[15.1] These *cialdoni* are common enough that Scappi can refer often to their shape. A recipe for a variety of them is at VI,141.

prunes, dried visciola cherries, water, salt, oil or butter, and some of the same spices that are used before in the stuffing. Finish cooking them with heat above and below like tourtes.

Together with the remainder that was beaten you can also put a pound of desalted tuna belly.[15.2] Those croquettes can be cooked with fresh, shelled peas. And after being cooked on the spit they can be served dressed with a variety of sauces. In the same ways you can do the flesh of tuna, corb, big sea bass and anchovy when those fish have been skinned.

16. To prepare sturgeon bresaola,[16] cooked and braised.

Get ten pounds of sturgeon flesh from the marbled area near the belly. Cut it the way you cut croquettes; beat the pieces with the spine of a knife, sprinkle them with salt, pepper and fennel flour. Put them into a tourte pan with oil or butter in it, one on top of the other and, between each, the same mixture that is used to stuff the croquettes in the recipe immediately above – or else use beaten herbs, raisins and spices. Set them to cook with heat below and above, having first put in enough water and verjuice to cover them. When they are done, put a little cinnamon and saffron on them and a handful of beaten herbs. In summer, instead of verjuice use gooseberries or verjuice grapes. Serve them hot with the same broth over them.

17. To fry sturgeon bresaola.

Get ten pounds of sturgeon flesh cut as above, beat the pieces a little with the spine of a knife and sit them in a mixture of oil, salt, pepper, verjuice, cinnamon and fennel flour. Then flour them and fry them[17.1] in oil or butter, or else in rendered fat depending on whether it is a meat day or lean day. When they are cooked, serve them in dishes with orange juice and sugar over them. The same can be done with any that have been in seasoning.

18. To spit-roast pieces of sturgeon.

Get ten pounds of skinned sturgeon flesh – more or less depending on how much of it you want – and cut it into pieces of two pounds each. Get five pounds of salted tuna belly, skinned and completely desalted, that has sat in cool water for four hours; cut it lengthwise the way you cut pork fat for larding roasts. Coat

---

[15.2] Scappi is referring back to the point at which a cook is beginning to assemble the ingredients for the *compositione* or mixture that uses whatever of the sturgeon belly was left over after the croquettes were cut from it.

[16] *Brisavoli* are varieties of braised preparations. The modern treatment prefers tender beef although Scappi has several derivatives for fish, including Recipes 17 and 151, below. See also Recipes II,7 and VI,46.

[17.1] The verb and reflexive object, *friggasi* in the 1570 printing, are missing in the 1581 text.

those strips with fennel flour, pepper, cinnamon and a little sweet oil[18.1] or butter; coat the pieces of sturgeon similarly. Lard the pieces with the strips, put them on a spit and let them cook over a low fire. In the pan that will catch the drippings,[18.2] put a little verjuice, sugar and white wine. When they are done, serve them hot with their sauce over them.

19. Another way to cook pieces of sturgeon.

Get ten pounds of sturgeon flesh and cut it into pieces the size of a hen's egg. Let them sit for two hours in the mixture of Recipe 10 for braised sturgeon, then put them on a spit alternating with slices of salted tuna belly that has macerated. Cook them, basting them from time to time with oil and that same mixture. When they are done, serve them with their drippings over them.

20. To cook pieces of sturgeon differently.

Get as much skinned sturgeon flesh as you want and cut it as above into pieces which you leave to macerate in a mixture of pepper, cinnamon, oil, verjuice and salt. Then put them on a spit and cook them, catching their drippings in a pan. When they are done, get fresh spring onions, beaten and sautéed in oil or butter or rendered fat, depending on the day; mix the onion with the drippings and with that same mixture in which the pieces have macerated. The sturgeon is served dressed with that sauce and sugar and cinnamon.

After macerating, those pieces can also be put on a spit and cooked the way an eel is done,[20.1] making their crust out of flour, sugar and cinnamon. They are served hot with sugar and orange juice over them. Furthermore, after being cooked they can be served with an onion sauce or *miraus* or *bronegro*[20.2] over them along with steeped pinenuts.

21. To fry sturgeon flesh so it looks like young lamprey.

Get ten pounds of skinned sturgeon belly, which is the best part, cut into pieces the length of a palm and the thickness of a knife blade. With those pieces make strips like strings with a knife and put them to macerate for two hours in a seasoning or else in a mixture of oil, verjuice, fennel flour and salt. Flour them and fry them in oil or butter or rendered fat, depending on the day. Serve them with orange juice and sugar over them.

If you want them to look like young lampreys, though, dress them with onion sauce and serve them with candied pinenuts over them, or else with sugar and

---

[18.1] Olive oil understood.

[18.2] The shape of this dripping pan, *iotta*, is suggested in the *ghiottela* of Plate 10.

[20.1] See Recipe 156, below.

[20.2] For an onion sauce (*civiero*), see Recipe II,249; for a *miraus* on meat days, Recipe II,248; for a *bronegro*, the *brodo negro* of Recipe II,252.

cinnamon. After being fried, they can also be served with fried spring onions over them, or a garlic sauce or green sauce,[21] or else with some other sauce depending on the season.

22. Several ways to cook sturgeon intestines.

As I said at the beginning, a sturgeon has only a single intestine, which is slimy and rust-coloured, and it is quite a bit tougher than the rest of the sturgeon; it has a lump in its middle. Slice it lengthwise; with a knife dig out whatever is in it, and with a little salt clean off whatever is on the outside. When it is very clean, wash it, cut it into pieces and put them into a cooking pot or some other vessel with verjuice, spring onions, beaten and sautéed, water, salt and a little white wine. Boil that gently for three hours; at the end, just before serving, add in a handful of beaten herbs, pepper, cinnamon and enough saffron. Serve them with pepper and cinnamon over top.

You can also boil the intestine in salted water alone until it is well done. You can cut it up into pieces as above and make a pottage of it with the same ingredients; instead of water, put in some of the broth it was cooked in. And, too, after it is boiled, sauté it and dress it with various sauces. Otherwise, after it is boiled sauté it in oil, having first floured it, and serve it with orange juice and pepper over it.

23. Several ways to cook sturgeon milt and liver.

If you want to make a pottage of the milt, get it and boil it in plain water (which is done to be able to cut it better), take it out of the boiling water and put it into cold water. Cut it into small pieces. Make a pottage of it with the liver itself cut up into pieces, as is done with the intestine in the preceding recipe. In summer instead of verjuice, use gooseberries and verjuice grapes. You can also thicken the broth with ground almonds or else fresh egg yolks beaten with a little verjuice – that depending on the season.

If you want to fry the milt, you can parboil it and fry it, serving it with orange juice, salt and pepper over it. The same can be done with the liver, without being parboiled, cutting it up into slices. Furthermore, after they are fried they can be dressed with one of several sauces.

In all those ways you can prepare sturgeon roe, after it has been parboiled and cut into small pieces.

24. To prepare caviar of sturgeon roe, which can be eaten just as soon as it is made and also kept for many days.

Get sturgeon roe between April and the end of May because at any other time the eggs are not as perfect; the blacker they are, the better. Very carefully remove the membrane they have around them, minding that you do not break them. Then

---

[21] Scappi gives a recipe for *agliata* at II,257, and for *salza verde* at II,272.

put the amount you want of them into vessels of clean, fine-grained wood. For every pound of roe put in half an ounce of salt and an ounce of sweet olive oil, and mix everything together carefully without breaking the roe. Then get a box three palms wide, more or less depending on the amount, four fingers high and an arm in length; in particular it must be very smooth. Put the roe into it – that is, the amount that will fit in it – and put the box into an oven after bread comes out of it, or with the oven heated to that temperature; let it stay there until you see that it is beginning to give off a little cream. Then take it out of the oven and stir it up, top to bottom, with a wooden spatula, doing that several times until the roe are cooked and have become black and pasty. Test it several times. When it is cooked, it can be kept in a glazed earthenware vessel for a few days. But if you want to eat it hot, that can be done, putting it on slices of bread and serving it with orange juice and pepper over it.

To keep it you put a little cloves and nutmeg into it, with a little oil in the bottom of the vessel and on top. Keep it in a cool place, checking it occasionally, because if it is not kept covered with oil it will go mouldy. About raw caviar, made with salt and kept in barrels whose bottoms are holed so the brine can run out, I will not say anything because it is not used in courts.[24]

25. To prepare an omelet of sturgeon roe and hen's eggs.

Get a pound of fresh sturgeon roe, grind it in a mortar and put it through a strainer or filter. Get ten well beaten hen's eggs with a small amount of beaten herbs, pepper, cinnamon and salt, and a little milk or water, and make omelets of that the way other ones are made. Serve them garnished with sugar, cinnamon and orange juice. They can also be made without hen's eggs, with a little breadcrumb.

26. To prepare an omelet of sturgeon roe done into caviar.[26]

Get six ounces of sturgeon-roe caviar, grind it in a mortar with four ounces of walnuts that are not rancid, and another four ounces of some other fish's roe. Moisten all that with half a beaker of water, adding in an ounce of grated bread and a small quantity of beaten herbs. Make omelets of that in oil, stirring the mixture with a spoon because it will tend to stick. Serve it with orange juice, sugar and cinnamon over top. If you do not have other fish eggs, you can do it without, or else you can do it with hen's eggs as above.

27. Several ways to cook a small sturgeon.

I am of the opinion that a *porcelletta* is a small sturgeon, even though in the spring, during its season, you can see big and small ones of them. Those that are caught in the Po, the Tiber and in the other big rivers are much better than those

---

[24] That is, in refined, high-class cookery.

[26] See also Recipes 24 and 205.

caught in the sea or in salt pools,[27.1] because the river sort are cleaner and whiter; the ones from the sea and salt pools tend toward a dark green. All small sturgeon have the same markings as a mature sturgeon, and therefore when they are of a larger size you can make the same dishes with them as with a mature sturgeon. When they are smaller than four pounds each they are cooked whole in salted water, though you have first to remove the nerve they have from head to tail as you would with a mature sturgeon,[27.2] and to skin them.

You can make several sorts of pottage with them. When they are skinned, you can roast them on a spit, cut up like an eel, making a crust for them. Put the medium-sized ones to boil, skin them, flour them and fry them; serve them dressed with any of a variety of sauces. They can also be cooked on a grill, with or without their skin. The smallest are fried with or without their skin; they are served with orange juice, salt and pepper over them.

28. The appearance and season of a corb.[28]

The corb is a sea fish and it readily swims up large rivers in which it cleanses itself of its saltiness and fattens itself. Its head is big with two white stones in it; its eyes are big, its scales coarse, white and broad, its flesh whiter and more tender than that of a sturgeon. It cooks more quickly. Its proper season begins in May and goes to the end of August, although in Rome they are found practically always.

29. To cook a corb's head.

Get a head that is above all fresh and that is cut off as is done in Rome with a handswidth of the body; above all it should be well scaled. The mouth, where the teeth are tiny, should be well cleaned out and the gills well washed. Cook it in salted water, unseasoned, as a sturgeon is done. Serve it like that, whole, garnished with parsley or flowers. For its sauce it needs a white sauce or green sauce.[29]

It is also cut up into pieces and cooked in water, oil, salt, pepper, cinnamon and saffron, adding in gooseberries or verjuice grapes with a handful of beaten herbs. In that same way you can also cook all the other parts of the corb's body.

[27.1] These *stagni*, ponds, are bodies of sea water trapped behind dunes along low-lying coasts. Fishing their tranquil waters would have been relatively comfortable.

[27.2] See this *nervetto* mentioned in Recipe 1, above.

[28] The *ombrina*, a corb, umbra or umbrine, is a very large Mediterranean fish resembling a perch or sea bass. Its average weight is about thirty pounds.

[29] Each of these would be a dipping sauce to accompany the fish in bowls.

30. To cook pieces of corb 'starched.'[30.1]

Get twelve pounds of corb and make two slabs of it,[30.2] scale it, wash it in clean water and set it to cook in earthenware or copper pots in four litres of white wine, one and a third litres of white vinegar, and properly salted water. When it has been skimmed, add in an ounce of crushed pepper and cinnamon together, and a quarter of an ounce of crushed nutmeg. When it is done, take it out of the pot onto a table and sprinkle it with sugar on every side; let it cool. Serve it cold like that; for serving, it needs a raisin sauce with it, made with fine *mostaccioli*.[30.3]

31. To prepare a Venetian pottage of pieces of corb.

Get ten pounds of corb cut crosswise into two slabs, scale them and wash them well and put them into a copper or earthenware pot with eight ounces of oil and five pounds of malmsey or white wine, two pounds of water, half a pound of verjuice, three ounces of sugar, one ounce of Venetian spices,[31] and four ounces of muscatel raisins. Cook everything together over a low fire. Keep the pot closed, watching that the fish does not disintegrate because, as I said before, it takes very little cooking. Serve it hot on slices of bread with its broth over it.

With the rest of the corb's body you make all the dishes you do for a sturgeon. The same for its milt, its liver and its intestines. The roe is boiled; of it you make a pottage and all the dishes you do with that of a sturgeon, except for caviar.

32. The appearance and season of a salmon.

Very few fresh salmon come into Italy, though a good number of salted ones, large and small, are imported.[32.1] It looks the same as a brown meagre, with the same scales; its flesh is russet-coloured in winter like a trout. Its season goes from May to the end of July. I hold for certain that that fish is called 'salmon' because of the way it leaps in the water.[32.2] It is, like the sea bass, both a sea-fish and a freshwater fish. With it you can make all the dishes you do with a brown meagre and a sea bass, just as you make various pottages of its gut and fry it as you do that of a sea bass.

[30.1] *pezzi d'Ombrina in salda*: the word *salda* is very old in the sense of a starch for fabric. In this treatment the slabs of fish are given a firm coating of sugar that 'fixes' them. In Recipe 41 a small corb, whole, can be treated the same way.

[30.2] *due pezzi*: The following recipe specifies that the pieces are 'cut across the fish.'

[30.3] See Recipe II,261.

[31] In preparing a dish of braised oysters, the *Neapolitan Recipe Collection* (Recipe 213) directs the cook to garnish them with verjuice and strong spices ... *specie forte – he cusi se fa a la Veneciana.*

[32.1] In Recipe III,209 Scappi writes of *il pesce salmone che è portato di Fiandra, et dalli confini di Borgogna, et da molti altri lochi in Italia, salato in barrili con salimora.* While not in great use by Scappi, it appears more often in Book V than in the present collection of lean recipes.

[32.2] Scappi seems to associate the 'sal-' of *salmone* and *saltare*, to jump.

33. The appearance and season of a leer fish.

A leer fish is a fish whose head and tail resemble those of a bonito; it is covered with a smooth skin and tends to a deep blue in colour. On its spine it has certain pointed prongs, not too sharp nor too long. Its belly is whitish. It is smaller than a sturgeon or a tuna. Its flesh is whiter than that of a sturgeon and many people are fooled, accepting it instead of a sturgeon because of its whiteness. Its season begins in April and goes to the end of September. The same dishes are made with its flesh as with the sturgeon's, and likewise with its insides, excepting caviar and the roe.

34. The appearance and season of a tuna.[34.1]

A tuna is big and round in shape and is covered with a dark greyish skin; its flesh is russet coloured, rather more darkish than any other colour. When it is cooked a sort of slit opens up in it like flakes. From part of the back of the tuna is made pickled tuna back, and from the belly is made salted tuna belly.[34.2] I believe that the name *tarantelo* derives from Taranto, in which town a lot of the latter is made. The proper season for tuna begins in May and goes throughout the autumn, though in Rome it is found during most of the year.

35. To cook a tuna head.

Get the head of a tuna and cut it the way it is done in Rome with a handswidth of the body; in particular it must be fresh because otherwise it will not be enjoyable, having the most horrible odour of any fish's head. It goes bad very readily; for that reason it has to be cooked in wine, vinegar, salt, water and crushed spices. It has to be served cold rather than hot. For a sauce it needs a strong mustard.

You can cook the rest of the tuna's body the same way when it is cut up into several pieces.

36. To braise or grill slabs of tuna.

Because I think that tuna flesh is better braised or grilled than with any other preparation, get the skinned tuna slabs and let them sit two hours in a seasoning made of vinegar, white wine, must syrup, pepper, ground coriander, a crushed garlic clove and salt. Put the slabs, which should be two fingers thick at the most and six pounds each, into a tourte pan or baking dish in which you have sweet olive oil, and cook them like tourtes with heat below and above. When they are almost done, add in a little of the seasoning in which they have macerated. When they are done, serve them with their sauce over them.

[34.1] Much of the tuna consumed in Italy was caught in Sicily, and most of that preserved there too. See Henri Bresc, *Un monde méditerranéen. Économie et société en Sicile, 1300–1450* (Rome: École Française de Rome, 1986), 261–73; and Maurice Aymard and Henri Bresc, 'Nourritures et consommation en Sicile entre XIVe et XVIIIe siècle,' *Annales. Économies, Sociétés, Civilisations*, 30 (1975): 592–9.

[34.2] Respectively *tonnina* and *tarantello*.

The slabs that are to be roasted on the grill will be of the same size and thickness. They are sprinkled with salt, fennel flour and pepper. They are put into a pot with oil, and when they have sat in that oil for an hour, they are taken out and set to cook on the grill the way the sturgeon slabs were done before in Recipe 11. Then they are served hot with the same sauce as for the sturgeon. Those slabs that macerated in the seasoning can also be grilled, and served hot with that same seasoning over them.

37. Another way to braise slabs of tuna.

Get six-pound, skinned slabs of tuna and put them into a good-sized baking dish or tourte pan with prunes, dried visciola cherries, and spring onions beaten with oil,[37.1] white wine, verjuice, pepper, cinnamon, cloves, enough salt and a little water tinged with saffron. Finish cooking them[37.2] with heat below and above the way tourtes are cooked. Serve them hot with the same broth over them.

In all the above ways bresaola[37.3] can be done, and croquettes, stuffed or not,[37.4] made with tuna flesh.

38. To prepare fingers of tuna flesh, stuffed and cooked on a spit.

Tuna flesh being (as I said above) much more russet-coloured than that of any other fish, because of that colour it tends to resemble the flesh of newly weaned animals; for that reason fingers are made of it as well as the other preparations described above. Take, then, the leanest part and cut the fingers a handswidth in length and a finger wide, and beat them four or five times with the spine of a knife. Sprinkle them with fennel flour and salt. Have a mixture made up of fresh tuna belly, which is the fattest part of the tuna, and salted tuna belly that has been softened, to the amount of a third of the fresh belly, and beat them together as with a sausage,[38] adding in aromatic herbs. If it is not a fasting day, instead of the salted belly you can use grated cheese and raw egg yolks – along with pepper, cinnamon, cloves, nutmeg and saffron; garlic is an option if you want to put it in. Stuff the fingers with that mixture and set them to cook on the spit, occasionally basting them with garlic and verjuice mixed with must syrup. When they are done, serve them hot with their sauce over top of them.

[37.1] *cipollette battute con oglio.* We may wonder whether the text, which is the same in both printings of 1570 and 1581, should have read *cipollette battute soffritte con oglio,* 'beaten onions sautéed in oil,' as in Recipe 22, above, and frequently elsewhere.

[37.2] This phrase is normally used when the cooking process has been interrupted for some other procedure.

[37.3] See Recipes 16 and 17, above.

[37.4] See Recipe 15, above.

[38] This particular variety of 'beating' is mentioned also in Book I, §§5 and 6; Recipes III,115, 153, 160; V,3; and VI,27.

With that tuna flesh are made all the dishes that are made with sturgeon. Likewise with its insides, excepting caviar which cannot be made from its roe.

39. The appearance and season of a bonito.

A bonito has the same appearance as the tuna; its tail is split into two sharp points, up and down, and it has the same skin as a tuna. It is very good in its season, which begins in March and goes to the end of June, more or less, depending on the weather. With big ones you can make all the dishes that are done with tuna. The medium-sized and small ones you can fry and grill. If you want to make croquettes and bresaola of a bonito, whether big or small, get one that is fresh, skin it and cut it lengthwise. Of its flesh make bresaola, macerated in a seasoning and then stewed and cooked on a grill. You can also make croquettes of them, and thick mashed soups of all the sorts that are made with sturgeon.[39] You can also fry those bresaola after they have macerated and serve them with various sauces over them. If they have not macerated, serve them with orange juice and pepper over them. Note that in the month of May they are usually found to be full of milt.

40. The appearance and season of a sea bass.

A sea bass is yet another sea fish; in various places it has various names: in Venice they are called *varoli*; in Genoa, *lupi*; in Rome, *spigolo*;[40.1] in Pisa and Florence, *ragni*. In Venice, though, they are bigger than the ones in Rome. They have larger scales than a brown meagre; the underside of their belly is white and has two fins, their tail is not split, they have two fins on their spine, one with a point, the other without. Their season is between the beginning of December and the end of February because at that time they are full of milt and roe. When they are caught in large rivers like the Tiber and Po and other rivers, they are at their best and are very white, like silver. The ones caught in the sea or in salt ponds are not as good; those have a dark patch on their back.

The smallest ones, taken in the spring, are good throughout July, and are fried and grilled. The big ones, when scaled and gutted, are cooked in salted water, whole or in pieces depending on their size, the way sturgeon is done; their milt and roe are set aside. You can also do a Venetian pottage of them as is done with the corb in Recipe 31, and other pottages as in Recipe 4. You can also cook them in wine, vinegar, water and spices the way trout is done in Recipe 115. The medium-sized ones are soused in vinegar or marinated as a carp is done in Recipe 122.[40.2] With the tail fat, which is the most compact and bone-free part, you can make croquettes stuffed with beaten, bone-free sardines, which croquettes can be roasted on a spit or grilled or braised.

---

[39] See Recipes 5–7, above.

[40.1] Scappi uses this name, *spigolo*, in the present recipe and elsewhere.

[40.2] Both printings show Recipe 121. For each of the two processes, sousing and marinating, see also Recipes 46 and 52.

41. The appearance and season of a small corb.

The small corb is a fish that greatly resembles a sea bass but its head is higher up, its eye bigger, its scales less dense and its flesh much softer than those of a sea bass. When they are not over three pounds they make excellent eating, and at their best, are particularly suitable for sousing in vinegar or marinating or cooking 'starched'[41] as pieces of a big corb are cooked in Recipe 30. Pottages are made with it, and all the dishes that are made with a sea bass in the preceding recipe and a brown meagre in Recipe 42. Its season begins in May and goes to the end of July, although in Rome they are usually found throughout the year.

42. The appearance and season of a brown meagre.

I believe that a *corbo* has that name because it is a little curved[42.1] – that is, its neck is arched – and it has a dark shadow on its back, but that is much blacker on the ones caught in the sea or in salt pools, those not being as good as the ones that are caught in the mouths of rivers and that have smaller scales than the sea bass and a firmer flesh. They have two stones in their head like the corb,[42.2] though not so large. Their season goes from May to the end of July. In Rome you can usually find them during the whole year. A brown meagre, large or small, can be prepared in all the dishes that are described for the sea bass in Recipe 40.

43. The season and appearance of a gilthead.

You find large and small giltheads. The good ones have small scales, are silvery and have a line from their head to their tail; on their side by the tail there is a dark blotch; their tail is split. Of teeth they have four sets, two lower and two upper, and very strong, as strong as a man's, as other fish of the same species also have. Their season begins in November and lasts until the end of April.

44. To grill gilthead.

Get fresh gilthead, whether from the sea or a salt pool or any other water, and they should still be with their scales. Gut them, wash them well and put them for two hours in a mixture of oil, salt, vinegar and fennel seeds. Put them on a grill and cook them over a moderate fire, basting them with the same mixture in which they have steeped. Turn them from time to time so they will get well cooked. Serve them hot, dressed with the same sauce.

If you want to fry them, scale them, clean out their insides, wash them well and sprinkle them with salt so they will be tastier. Flour them and fry them in olive oil. Serve them hot, garnished with sliced lime or else with orange juice.

---

[41] For the last preparation see Recipe 30, above.

[42.1] As an amateur etymologist Scappi sees a relation between the fish's Italian name and an adjective, *corbuto*, 'humped.'

[42.2] See Recipe 28.

45. To cook gilthead in a pottage.

Get fresh gilthead, scale it, gut it, wash it and put it into an earthenware or copper pot with oil, wine, water, verjuice, salt, pepper, cinnamon and saffron; additionally, in winter, prunes and dried visciola cherries or spring onions, in summer, gooseberries or seedless verjuice grapes. Set it to cook and, at the end, just before serving, put in a handful of beaten herbs. If you want the broth to be a little thick, do it with ground almonds.

46. To souse, marinate and preserve giltheads in vinegar.

For sousing, marinating or pickling in vinegar, get giltheads that in size are not more than three pounds each. Those that you want to souse, gut them and at your option scale them, but have them sit in salt for half an hour. Flour them and fry them in olive oil. When they have cooked, put them into a vessel where there are bay leaves or myrtle leaves, and on top of the giltheads put vinegar boiled twice with salt and pepper. Then take them out of that vinegar and set them on other, dry myrtle leaves. Serve them hot or cold as you like, with sugar and rose vinegar over them.

If you want to marinate them, after they have been fried as above put them into an earthenware pot containing vinegar, white wine and must syrup in equal amounts, with enough salt, pepper and saffron, all boiling, and leave them there. Serve them hot or cold as you like.

If you want to preserve them in vinegar,[46] grill them without scaling them; let them cool, then put them into an earthenware vessel, one on top of the other with fennel seeds between each of them. Boil them in a little vinegar with must syrup or sugar, pepper and ground cloves; that sauce should be bitter rather than sweet. Let the sauce cool, then splash it over the giltheads in the vessel. Keep it covered, and leave it in a cool place.

In the same way you can do sea bass, brown meagre, gudgeon and sea bream; similarly done are medium-sized dentex and pieces of sturgeon, grilled without being scaled.

47. The appearance and season of a dentex.

The biggest dentex that can be seen anywhere are found on the shores of Slavonia. As with the gilthead, that fish is cooked into gelatine in water, vinegar, wine and saffron. Those that are brought to Rome are somewhat smaller, with darker scales and their head and teeth are peculiar in that they are set in a jaw like a man's, and in front they have four teeth like a hare's; an old gilthead is like that, too. The ones from Slavonia are called crown dentex because around their snout they have a marking that looks like a crown. However, the gilthead does not

---

[46] The procedure that begins here is called 'cooking into gelatine' in the next recipe. The fish is preserved by being encased in a 'jelly.'

have that marking and the dentex has a broader belly than the gilthead. Its proper season begins in October and goes until the end of April. It is cooked in all the ways the gilthead is done in the previous recipes.

48. The appearance and season of a sea bream.

The sea bream that comes to Rome is not too big; when they are fully grown, by what I have seen in Slavonia, they do not go above twenty pounds. They are called *frauli*[48] and look like a dentex, and are very delicate. The ones brought to Rome, though, look similar to a freshwater perch. Their scales are dense, they are a little humped, have big eyes with a yellow spot in them, have firm white flesh and few guts. For the most part they have milt in them. They have a line the length of their back like the gilthead, and their tail is less split than the gilthead's. Their proper season is from December to the end of May, although in Rome they are found practically throughout the year. That fish tends to a golden colour and is transparent.

49. Several ways to cook a sea bream.

I find the sea bream less viscous than any other fish because, as I said above, their flesh is firm and white; for that reason in the book on Foods for the Sick[49.1] I have included many dishes for doing that fish.[49.2] I say, besides, that it is done in all the same way as the gilthead. I will not speak about its insides because it has extremely few, as I said above.

50. The appearance and season of shad.[50.1]

A shad is a widely known sea fish that naturally enters into big rivers such as the Po, the Tiber, the Arno and the Oglio. However, those of the Po are much better than all the others. Those that are caught in the valleys of the Comacchio are very big but not so good, and in those places they are called *chiepe*. Their season extends from February to the end of May. They do not have a tongue but they do have a multitude of very fine bones. Their tail is split. The ones from the sea and from salt pools are greenish and are not so good and the ones caught in rivers, which are very white. Their intestines are removed through their mouth so as not to contaminate any roe or milt they have; those intestines have a swelling

---

[48] The name that Scappi uses in the rubric and the recipe for the sea bream is *fragolino*, a diminutive. Here *fraulo* seems a popular pronunciation.

[49.1] The title by which Scappi headed his Book VI, and by which he refers to it here, is the *libro de i convalescenti*: the 'book for convalescents.'

[49.2] The main entry for *fragolino* in Book VI is Recipe 174, although it can also be done in ways set out for several other fish.

[50.1] This *laccia* is the saltwater shad, *Alosa alosa* (allis shad) or *Alosa fallax* (twait shad). The freshwater shad, Scappi's *agone*, will be dealt with in Recipe III,211.

with two projections rather like a fork.[50.2] Shad from the sea and pools breed little worms in their pouches, that is, their gills. That fish needs a thorough cooking because it is much more fleshy than any other fish of its sort. If it has been dead more than a day its head begins to darken near its gills and it makes those worms; for that reason it has always to be cooked fresh. It is boiled in salted water like the sturgeon in Recipe 1. It is served dry[50.3] with parsley over it, or in dishes with a white sauce or green sauce.

After it is cooked its roe can be taken out of it; they are like mullet-roe cakes[50.4] and are washed in a little water so the flour can coat them better. They are fried in oil or rendered fat or butter, depending on whatever day it is. They are served with orange juice and salt on them. Their milt is eaten with a white sauce, although often it is fried.

Sometimes that fish is cooked in a meat broth with slices of prosciutto. A pottage is made of it whole – it is rarely cut up into pieces because of its milt, eggs and bones – in the way that is done with the sea bass, having first scaled it as is said in Recipe 40.

51. To roast shad on a grill or on a spit.

Get shad fresh and cleaned of their intestines and gallbladder, with the roe and milt left in; and clean the gills of their hairy growth. When they are washed, without being scaled, put them into a pot where there is oil and salt, turning them over so they are completely coated with it; leave them in it for an hour so they can better pick up the salt and be more tasty. Then put them on a grill and cook them slowly over a low fire because they need a thorough cooking as was said above. Turn them over often and baste them with oil and vinegar. When they are done, serve them hot with a garnish made of vinegar and must syrup.

If you want them on a spit, take them after they have been in the oil and salt, and fasten them onto a spit with two split canes per side, lengthwise; and between the spit and the cane[51] there should be big bay leaves or sprigs of rosemary or

---

[50.2] Both types of *forcina*, a sturdy iron kitchen variety, with which Scappi and his apprentice would be very familiar, and a more delicate dining fork of silver (see Book IV, folios 327r and 328v [1581 ff.275r and 276v], as well as Plates 13 and 23), had two tines. Scappi is careful to distinguish the second sort by specifying that, when travelling, the cook must have spoons *per minestrare*, for serving, and 'clean' forks *per porre su la tavola*, to set on the dining board (IV, f.328v). In his painting 'Marriage Feast of Nastagio degli Onesti,' Sandro Botticelli (1445–1510) chose to indicate the elegant refinement of the occasion by placing such dining forks in the hand of the two ladies in the left foreground of his scene.

[50.3] That is, not made into a *minestra* or a *zuppa* but just the fish is served with a garnish.

[50.4] See Recipe III,216 for an idea of these flattened blobs of salted roe called *bottarghe*. The same is done with grey mullet roe in Recipe 59.

[51] *tra lo spedo et la canna.* What is implied here is that insulation be placed on both sides of the fish, against the spit and against the cane.

sage so that the shad do not stick to the spit; likewise between the shad and the cane. Cook them over a low fire, basting them with a light sauce made of vinegar, must syrup, salt, pepper and fennel flour. When they are done, serve them with the same sauce over them.

They can be roasted another way: after they have steeped in oil and salt, take and bind each one of them in four half-canes, that is, one at the back, one along the belly and one on each side. Leave a long piece of cord which is tied to all the canes and fasten it in a place close to the fire with the head of the cord upwards. Cook them like that, and when you want to turn them around, twist the cord, basting them from time to time with oil mixed with orange juice and sugar. When they are done, serve them hot with that same sauce over them.

52. To souse and marinate shad.

Get shad that are not too big, preferably with milt rather than roe – which you can determine by squeezing the umbilicus,[52.1] which will show whether the fish are with milt or roe, though you can also tell because the ones with milt have a sharper, thinner ridge along the belly. If you wish, scale them. Having cleaned them and washed them well, as directed above, prick them all over with the tip of a knife. Leave them for an hour with a little salt over them, then flour them and fry them in good oil over a moderate fire to firm up their flesh. When the ones that are to be soused in vinegar are cooked, have a pot ready with vinegar, sugar, pepper and enough salt boiling in it; when the shad are taken out they are put into a vessel[52.2] with bay leaves or myrtle leaves under and over them, and pour the boiling vinegar over that twice, immediately taking the fish out of the vinegar and setting them to drain on some other leaves of myrtle or bay. Serve them hot or cold as you wish, because they will last at their best for ten days.

For those that are to be marinated, as soon as they come out of the pan, put them into an earthenware or wooden vessel large enough to hold them and a mixture[52.3] composed of vinegar, must syrup or sugar, pepper, cinnamon, cloves, wine, salt and enough saffron, everything boiled together. With it hot like that, pour it over the shad, leaving them in it until you want to serve them. That way there has to be both bitter and sweet. You can do shad braised or in an oven, after they have been scaled in the way that tench are prepared in Recipe 141.

[52.1] Scappi's *bellicolo* designates, variously, the fish's anus, rectum or intestine. Wherever in Books III, V and VI he uses the term, the translation will keep Scappi's word as 'umbilicus' or 'umbilical.'

[52.2] This is another container than the one that has just been mentioned.

[52.3] The macerating compound is prepared and boiled separately and then poured around the fish.

53. The appearance and season of a grey mullet.

Grey mullets are of many sorts: big ones have a flat head and are called *migliaccini*; medium-sized ones have a round head and are broad; and smaller, marbled ones, the best ones, are of a round shape, are born in the sea and in salt pools, and by their nature enter into large rivers. In Venice they are called *cefali di buon budello*, 'good-bowelled grey mullets'; in the valley of Comacchio, *letregano*; and in Tuscany, *muggini*.[53.1] It is a sea fish and a freshwater fish, although the best of the whole species are the ones that are caught in river mouths and in clear waters. The season of the small ones begins in the middle of August and goes to the end of February, although in Rome you can get them at almost any time.

54. To grill large grey mullets – that is, *migliaccine*.

Get a big grey mullet with a flat head and gut it through its gills, leaving in its roe and without scaling it. Wash it in several changes of water and put it in a mixture of oil, salt, fennel flour and vinegar, leaving it there for half an hour. Then put it on a grill and cook it over a low fire, basting it with the same mixture it steeped in. When it is done, serve it with raisins cooked in must syrup, and some of the same mixture. If the grey mullets are without roe, because they are often full of a black filth – mostly the ones caught in the pools at Hostia and Città Vecchia – flush out their inside several times with clear water and stuff it with shelled and crushed walnuts mixed with grated bread, pepper, raisins and a clove of garlic; if it is not a fasting day, include egg yolks beaten in with those things. When the mullets are stuffed, cook them on a grill. Serve them with that same sauce over them.

After they have been grilled plain, you can also keep them in vinegar as a gilthead is preserved in Recipe 46.

55. To spit-roast large grey mullets.

Get large grey mullets, scale and gut them, and cut them up into pieces like an eel. Set them for an hour in a pot containing verjuice, salt and pepper. Put them on a spit with a bay leaf or a sage leaf between each piece, and cook them over a low fire, basting them with the mixture in which they have steeped. When they are done, serve them with that same mixture which has been boiled, and with a little pepper and cinnamon over top.

If you want to fry them, slice them along the backbone as tench are done, leaving their gut in if it is good. Flour them and fry them in sweet oil. Serve them hot, garnished with sautéed parsley, pepper and orange juice. They can also be fried whole, making a few slits crosswise on them so they can cook better. After they have fried you can also souse or marinate them, either whole like that or else cut up as is described in directions for the gilthead, Recipe 46.

[53.1] The 1581 typesetter put *maggini*. In Recipe 213 Scappi repeats that *muggine* are found in lakes. The grey mullet tolerates very low salinity and thrives even in freshwater.

56. To prepare a pottage of large grey mullets.

Get a grey mullet rather from the sea or caught in a river than from a salt pool because it will always be better; and above all it must be fresh. Scale it; for any from a pool, gut it, wash it well. If you want to cut it up into pieces, that is optional. Put it into a copper or earthenware pot in a little white wine, oil, water and a little verjuice, along with pepper, salt, cinnamon and saffron. Set it to boil slowly. At the end, before serving it up, put in a handful of chopped herbs. When it is done, serve it with its broth over top. With that pottage you can put beaten spring onions, visciola cherries, prunes and raisins, depending on the season. You can also thicken the broth with ground almonds or else with grated bread.

57. To cook medium-sized and small grey mullets on a grill and in several ways.

If the grey mullets – that is the *muggini*[57] – are 'good-bowelled,' there is no need to gut them nor even to scale them but only to wash them and set them for half an hour in a vessel in oil, vinegar, salt and fennel flour. Grill them over a low fire, basting them with the same mixture in which they have macerated. Serve them hot with the same ingredients as for serving the large grey mullets in Recipe 54.

If you want to keep them and fry, marinate or souse them, follow the directions in Recipe 46 for the gilthead preserved in vinegar. And if you want to make pottages of them with onions or herbs or other ingredients, follow the directions in the previous recipe, having first scaled and gutted them.

58. To fry the entrails of a grey mullet and make a pottage of them.

Get the intestine of a grey mullet at the time it is fattest, and above all it must be fresh and clean of any filth; cut away that lump, which is properly a nerve. Flour it and fry it in oil. Serve it hot with orange juice, pepper and salt over it. If you want to make a pottage of it, cut it up into pieces and follow the directions given in Recipe 56 for making a pottage of large grey mullets.

59. Several ways to cook the roe of grey mullet.

Get the roe fresh, of which the membrane is not broken. Parboil them in salted water and, without separating them, flour them and fry them in oil. Serve them with orange juice, salt and pepper over them. They can also be cooked on a grill if you have first parboiled them, basting them with oil. They are served hot as before. If you want them in a pottage, when they are parboiled, cut them crosswise in thin slices and make a pottage of them with broth of another fish the way the pottage of a large grey mullet is made in Recipe 56. If you want to make mullet-roe cakes of them, follow the directions given for making mullet-roe cakes

---

[57] It is interesting that Scappi clarifies the name *cefali* by using the Tuscan name that he provided for the fish in Recipe 53, above.

from sea-bass roe in the recipe for it.[59] And keep in mind that in all the above ways the roe can be prepared raw.

60. The appearance and season of a red mullet.[60.1]

A red mullet is not a very big fish, rarely being above two pounds. There are two species of them, one as red as fire and the other a violet and brownish grey. The red one is the better, especially those caught on Roman shores; it has very few entrails, is round and has a curved head like a pig. It has two pendants under its chin and for that reason in Venice they are called *barbari*,[60.2] and in a few other places *rossignoli*.[60.3] The violet one has bigger scales and it is not so good to eat because it is caught in ponds and marshes and it often has a lot of filth in its gut. Its proper season is from July to the end of March, though in Rome they are found almost year-round.

61. To cook red mullets on a grill and otherwise.

If the red mullets are from a salt pond, gut them through their umbilicus with a knife, leaving the liver, which is their goodness. With others when they are fresh there is no need to gut them. Coat all of them, though, with a little salt, fennel flour and oil without scaling them. Put them on a grill and cook them in the way described for the grey mullet in Recipe 57. Serve them hot with orange juice together with the same mixture, hot, with which they were coated.

If you want them fried, scale them, flour them and fry them the way other fish are fried. Serve them hot with orange juice, pepper and salt over them.

Because that fish is very delicate and less viscous than others, I have found that a variety of thick soups can be made with them, and other preparations for convalescents, as I have set out in the Book for the Sick.[61] Something similar can be done with the gilthead and the sea bream, which I think are best for convalescents.

---

[59] Recipe III,216. We see there that a six-day compression of the salted roe results in these *bottarghe* or 'cakes.' One evening in 1661 Samuel Pepys revelled in *botargo*, which he described as 'sausage made from the eggs and the blood of the mullet.'

[60.1] Scappi's word for this fish is *triglia*, which he will treat in this and the following recipe. In the seven previous recipes he has offered a rich variety of ways to do up a *cefalo* or grey mullet. In Recipe 137, below, see also a *roviglione*, the freshwater mullet that Scappi describes as being small, greenish and with big scales.

[60.2] That is, 'barbarians,' likely also a play on the words barb, barbel or beard.

[60.3] That is, 'nightingales,' the first syllable of which evokes the fish's reddish colour.

[61] In Book VI there is no recipe devoted primarily to *triglia*, red mullet. However, Scappi writes that procedures for preparing several other fish can be extended to a red mullet. See also the note to Recipe VI,174 for sea bream.

62. The appearance and season of a goby.

A goby is a round, smooth fish, without scales, tending to a tawny colour, in which it resembles a freshwater burbot. It is a sort of *marscione*[62.1] – that is, one of those tiny fish that in Rome are called *capi grossi* or big heads. It has a big liver. Many of them are caught between Chiozza and Venice; they do not go above two pounds each; few come to the shores by Rome. Their proper season begins in September and lasts to the end of May. It needs to be cooked fresh because it spoils quickly. The fishermen of Chiozza and Venice cook it on coals; they make a pottage of it, too, with malmsey and water and a little vinegar and Venetian spices.[62.2] It is fried in oil like other fish, and is served hot with orange juice over it.

63. The appearance and season of a gurnard.

The gurnard is round in shape, rather long[63.1] and is not so thick that it goes above six pounds. Some of them are russet-coloured, with a big, squarish head without any flesh, big eyes and thick, stiff brows, a palish mouth and tiny teeth; under its chin it has two barbels like a red mullet[63.2]; behind its head it has two sharp spurs. The tip of its tail is very fine, and its belly white, streaked with reddish brown. Its flesh is white and somewhat firm; on lean days it is used to make whitedish and you can make various dishes of it for convalescents, as I've said in the Book for Convalescents. There are some other gurnards that have a large mouth like a hook and a back armed with bony scales like a sturgeon: those fish are called tub gurnards[63.3] and many more of them are found on the Roman shores than anywhere else. Their proper season begins in October and goes to the end of May.[63.4]

64. To cook gurnard plain.

A gurnard needs to be cooked in salted water rather than any other way. Gutted and well washed, it is served dry[64] with parsley over it, accompanied by a

---

[62.1] The fish that Scappi mentions here may be a *Lebetus scorpioides*, four centimetres in length, whose English name is 'diminutive goby.'

[62.2] See Recipe 31, above.

[63.1] Scappi's name for this fish is *pesce cappone*. Members of the *Triglidæ* family vary in length between twenty-five and sixty-five centimetres. Later, in Recipe 113, he will deal with a similar fish which he calls *scorfeno*.

[63.2] Scappi describes a gurnard's armoured head well; technically, though, rather than barbels the gurnard has three free pectoral rays that have modified into feelers.

[63.3] *lucerne*. The smaller fish of this species, *lucernette*, are mentioned in the next recipe.

[63.4] This last sentence seems to apply to Scappi's whole family of gurnards.

[64] See the note in Recipe 50.

white sauce in dishes. When they are big, bring them to a boil in salted water and take the flesh from the back, with the skin and bones removed, and make various sorts of pottage of it. That flesh can also be floured, fried, and served with orange juice and salt over it. The small ones, called *lucernette*, are fried whole.

65. The appearance and season of a mackerel.

A mackerel is a sea fish and without scales. They are found in abundance in Venice where they are much better than in Rome. The French call the fish *maccario*.[65] It is broad and smooth, sulphur and blue in colour, and has a split tail. Its season begins in April and goes to the end of September; in Rome they can be had at almost any time. In Venice they are not larger than three pounds and in Rome, one and a half at most.

66. Several ways to cook a mackerel.

A mackerel needs to be done on a grill or braised, as a grey mullet is done, as mentioned before, rather than any other way, although you can fry it and make a pottage of it and cook it in all the ways the grey mullet is done. When it is fresh there is no need to gut it.

67. The appearance and season of a horse mackerel.[67.1]

A horse mackerel, too, has no scales and looks like a mackerel, though it has sort of little dotted lines over its full length; its belly from the umbilicus back has thistle-like spines; its tail is similar to the mackerel's.[67.2] But a horse mackerel is not so good. Its season goes from May to the end of November, and in Rome you can find them almost year-round.

68. Several ways to cook a horse mackerel.

A horse mackerel has to be fried in oil and[68] grilled rather than done otherwise. It is not gutted. If it is big and you should want to cook it differently, follow the directions for the grey mullet in Recipe 54.

---

[65] An Italian rendition of the French *maquereau*. Scappi's interest in the term may have to do, as fairly often is the case, with popular etymology: the words *maccarello* and *maccario* meant gigolo or pimp, but because the mackerel (masculine) was thought to accompany the herring (feminine) as it migrated, the sense of the word came to be extended to designate that first fish.

[67.1] Otherwise called a scad in English. A letter *v* normally appears typeset as a *u*, hence *pesce suero* (here and in the next recipe and elsewhere) can be read as *pesce svero*.

[67.2] 'Superficially [the horse and jack mackerels] resemble the Mackerels and Tunas ... Horse Mackerel, Scad ... : *scales* small and easily rubbed off; *lateral line* has a row of 69–79 wide bony scales each with a point on their rear edge; *fins* ... anal fin long and has 2 isolated spines situated in front of it ... ' (John and Gillian Lythgoe, *Fishes of the Sea: The Coastal Waters of the British Isles, Northern Europe and the Mediterranean* [Garden City, N.J.: Anchor Press Doubleday, 1975], 211).

[68] As is often the case, Scappi's 'and' may well be an 'or.'

69. The appearance and season of a saupe.

Although a saupe is not much to be recommended, mention can nevertheless be made of it because of its pretty body: it is embellished with certain yellow lines, but its main colour is violet. Its belly is broad, narrow at the tip of the tail; it has sharp spines on its back. Its proper season begins in July and goes to the end of December; in Rome, though, they are found at almost any time. It is done up in all the dishes in which the gilthead and sea bream are done, as previously set down in Recipe 49.

70. The appearance and season of a bogue.

A bogue is not too big; it is white and scaly. In some places in Lombardy it is called a *menola*.[70] Many of them are brought from Genoa to Milan in vinegar with an argentine (which is a smaller fish than a sardine) in myrtle leaves. Its season goes from the beginning of March to the end of June, though in Rome they are found at any time mixed in with small fish. More than any other fish that one is useful for frying. Many people, though, grill it without scaling it, and serve it dry with orange juice and salt over it.

71. The appearance and season of saltwater and lake sardines.[71.1]

A saltwater sardine and a lake sardine are of the same species. It is a small fish and is not bigger than two ounces, although *sardoni*[71.2] are found that are larger and of the same species. All of them have a little fin on their back and are of a sky-blue colour which tends toward a silver. They have only one bone,[71.3] which goes from their head to their tail; they have very few entrails and very few scales. When they are kept for too long, their head goes brownish red and their belly bursts. It is an excellent fish, especially when it is caught in its season, which goes between October and the end of April, though in Rome you can find them throughout almost the whole year.

72. To grill or braise sardines.

Get fresh sardines and, without scaling them, wash them and set them for half an hour in a vessel containing oil, must syrup, salt, pepper, fennel flour, and verjuice or vinegar. Then get a little stick or a slender iron pin, skewer them through their eye and put them on a grill, beginning with their back downwards;

---

[70] This is the *Mæna mæna*, the so-called 'blotched picarel' (*sic*), according to Lythgoe, *Fishes of the Sea*, 206.

[71.1] To judge by the variety of preparations that Scappi offers for this fish, his *sarda* must have been one of the more commonly handled in his kitchen.

[71.2] These *sardoni* do not appear to be a distinct variety of fish but only an augmentative of *sarda*: large sardines.

[71.3] *resca*. The word derived from Latin *arista*; the modern Italian is *lisca*, a fish bone.

baste them with that mixture they have steeped in, turning them a few times until they are cooked. Serve them hot with the same sauce.

They can be cooked that way on folded paper: it should be made like an oil lamp.[72.1] Before they are put on the paper it should be greased with oil or butter or rendered fat depending on whichever day it is. Cook them without basting them, turning them occasionally. Serve them hot as above.

If, after they have been in the above mixture, you want to braise them, put them into a pan or earthenware baking dish where there is oil or butter or rendered fat, depending on the day; give it heat below and above as for a tourte. Just before they are done, add in some of that steeping mixture so they are almost covered with it; finish off cooking them. Serve them with that same sauce over them. They are done braised like that also with prunes and dried visciola cherries, or else with gooseberries and verjuice, or else with raisins and beaten herbs, or else with spring onions alone, adding in their seasoning. They are also stewed deboned, splitting them in half.

Various dishes are made of them in the Book for Convalescents.[72.2]

73. To fry, souse and marinate sardines.

Get fresh sardines, scale and wash them, set them on a table mixed with a little white salt, then flour them and fry them in olive oil because it will always be better than rendered fat or butter. When they have fried, serve them garnished with orange juice or sliced limes or fried parsley. And after they have fried, they can be kept in bay leaves or myrtle leaves.

If, after they have been fried, you want to marinate them, put them into vinegar with sugar or must syrup in it along with saffron, and keep them in that marinade until you want to serve them. In summer instead of vinegar you can use verjuice thickened with egg yolks or breadcrumb. And also, after they have been fried, they are dressed with green sauce.

74. To prepare fishballs and other preparations with sardine flesh.

Get fresh sardines and scale them and, still raw like that, remove their head and the bones they have in their middle and beat them with knives.[74] Along with every pound of sardines beat three ounces of salted tuna belly that has soaked enough to soften it, and a handful of herbs; to that add three-quarters of an ounce of pepper, cinnamon, cloves and ground nutmeg combined, three ounces of grated bread and three ounces of raisins. When everything has been mixed together, make balls of it and pears. Cook them the way the sturgeon ones are done in

---

[72.1] See the same procedure in Recipe III,14.

[72.2] Recipes VI,171–3.

[74] As we have seen before, the plural here is deliberate. A cook did this work (of making a coarse fish paste) more efficiently with a knife in each hand, its spine downward.

Recipe 13. If it is not a fasting day, however, instead of salted tuna belly and grated bread put in three egg yolks and three ounces of grated dry cheese. With those balls you can put some spring onions, beaten and sautéed.

You can also do it differently: instead of beating them with knives, grind them in a mortar with three ounces of softened pinenuts. When they are ground up, add in orange juice, beaten herbs, raisins, sugar and the above spices. When the mixture is made up, you can make balls out of it and a tourte and other things depending on your imagination and the season.

75. Smelt from the sea or a lake, and its season.

A sea smelt and a lake smelt are found; all are very small, and so transparent and very white that you can see their backbone. They are the most excellent of all sea fish. Their season begins in November and goes to the end of February – that is, for those from the sea. For the freshwater ones it is from April to the end of August. A great many are caught in the Lake of Bolsena. They are better fried than in any other preparation. Above all they have to be fresh. They are served with green sauce in dishes.

76. The appearance and season of an anchovy.

An anchovy is a much smaller but longer fish than a sardine. In Genoa and Milan they are called *inghioiù*. It is a very white fish and has only one bone. Its season is the same as a sardine's. It is prepared in all the ways a sardine is done in Recipe 72.

77. The appearance and season of a poor cod.[77]

A poor cod is much smaller than a smelt; twenty of them do not weigh an ounce. It has no bones or scales; when it is sold in Rome it actually looks like white goo because it is all stuck together. But it is excellent to eat when it is caught in its season, which begins in December and goes to the end of April, more or less depending on the weather. They are done up in all the ways smelt are done, although in Rome for the most part fritters are made with them the way they are made with parsnips.[77.2]

78. The appearance and season of a turbot.

Among flat fish the best is turbot, which is broad and round; under its belly it is very white and on its back black with some diamond-shaped nodules.[78] Its

---

[77] Scappi's *pesce ignudo*, 'naked fish,' is a *Trisopterus minutus* or *Gadus capelanus*; in English it is also known as a Mediterranean cod. It grows to only some twenty or twenty-two centimetres. Nowadays Italians call that fish *pesce mudo* (which could well be a form of the name Scappi uses for it), as well as *asinetto, busbano, cappelano* (this word related to English 'capelin'), *figarotto, merluzzetta* and *mormoro* – showing that Scappi's contemporaries were not unique in having a number of local names for a particular fish.

[77.2] See Recipe V,234.

[78] Those *punte* will be called *punture* in the next recipe.

mouth is a slit beneath, in the white part; its eyes are on top. Its snout is pointed and low; it has little tail. In size it does not go above forty pounds, though normally they are of eight or ten pounds. The best to be had are the ones caught in the Adriatic Sea in the Gulf of Ravenna. Their proper season begins in November and lasts throughout the year. Another species of them, of a greenish-grey colour and less pointed, are also found; more of those are brought to the fish markets in Rome than of the black ones, though their season is the same as of the black kind.

79. To cook a turbot in a pottage.

Experience has shown me that turbot is better in a pottage than in any other way, particularly if it is big. Take it, remove the black skin from its top and gut it through its upper side; alternatively, if you do not want to skin it, wash it in hot water, removing the sliminess on top along with the tubercles. Cut big ones into pieces, though the medium-sized and small ones can be left whole. Put it into a tinned copper or earthenware pot with enough oil, malmsey or white wine, verjuice and water to cover it by two fingers – because whenever those fish are cooked immediately[79] with a very simple mixture they are better – adding in enough mild spices and salt. Boil it slowly because it needs a thorough cooking. Given that when it is whole it is difficult to flip it over without it breaking apart, it has to be cooked with a lid on, like tourtes. When it is done, serve it hot, dressed with its broth and sautéed onions. You can also make the broth thick with ground almonds; with them put prunes, dried visciola cherries and raisins. However, because at the time I was in Venice and Ravenna I understood from the fishermen of Chiozza and Venice, who make the best pottages, that along all the seashores no other way is used to cook them than what I described above, I believe that they are more successful with them than cooks for the reason that they do them the very instant they have caught them.

80. To grill a turbot.

Get a turbot that is preferably medium-sized or small rather than too large so it can be better cooked. When it is gutted, it is optional whether you skin it or not; then wash it and set it in a vessel for an hour in vinegar, salt and must syrup or sugar. Put it on a grill – if it is skinned, put sprigs of rosemary dipped in oil under it[80] – and cook it over a low fire, turning it over and basting it with the mixture in which it steeped. When it is done, serve it with that same sauce, hot, over it.

81. To fry a turbot.

Get a turbot and, if it is large, skin it and divide it up into pieces; if it is a medium-sized or small one, leave it whole. When it is gutted, wash it and sprinkle

---

[79] *a stretto.*

[80] In Recipe 11, above, Scappi explains that the oiled herb will keep the fish from sticking to the grill.

a little ground salt over it, flour it and fry it in olive oil. Serve it hot with orange juice over it.

You can also first let it macerate in royal seasoning[81] then flour and fry it. Furthermore, after it has been fried you can souse and marinate it the way a gilthead is done in Recipe 46. I shall refrain from saying that after it has been fried it is covered with a variety of sauces, because it is not appropriate that such a noble fish be covered with anything.

82. To do a turbot in jelly.

The larger a turbot is the better it is. Get it as directed above, gut it, wash it, divide it into several pieces, especially removing the skin and fins.[82] Put the pieces into a large-bottomed earthenware vessel with water, white vinegar, white wine and enough salt; there should be enough of the mixture to cover the fish by two fingers. For every two and two-thirds litres of water put in one and a third litres of wine and two-thirds of a litre of strong vinegar. Skim it with a wooden spoon – which is done because otherwise the jelly would turn dark. When it is skimmed, put into it some well ground pepper, cloves and ginger together with a little saffron, and finish cooking it slowly. When the fish is done, put it into a silver vessel which can hold the decoction with the fish under it. Into that decoction put cleaned and chopped Milanese almonds. Put it in a cool place to jell. Then serve it thus jelled. You can also divide the pieces of fish up among several dishes with the same decoction over them. It is optional whether you put a little sugar over the decoction, though to keep it for a few days it would be better without sugar: it should be acidic rather than otherwise.

In that way you can make jelly with a sea bass, a dentex, a rayfish, a sea eel and a medium-sized young sturgeon provided the fish are alive because when they are not fresh they are no good. They do not have to be scaled.

83. The appearance and season of a flounder and a sole – that is, a *linguattola*.

A flounder, too, is a flat, round fish, though not quite as large as a turbot. Its upper skin has the colour of a sparrow[83] and for that reason it has its name; it is white under its belly. Its mouth is the reverse of a turbot. Its proper season goes from November to the end of April. For the most part it is caught in the Adriatic Sea, particularly in the Gulf of Brombo, which is close to Chiozza; and many are caught by means of a certain device that is called a harpoon, made like a fork. A sole – that is, a *linguattola* – too, is a flat fish and of the same colour as the

---

[81] For the composition of this *adobbo reale* see perhaps Recipe II,130 (for meat) or V,156 and V,188 (for fish).

[82] These *ale*, literally 'wings,' refer specifically to the fish's pectoral fins.

[83] Once again Scappi tries to explain the appropriateness of a name: here *passero*, the bird, has influenced the name of *passera*, the fish.

flounder, though darker and longer, and has fewer bones; its mouth is the opposite of a flounder – that is, it is on the left. The ones brought to Rome are much longer and bigger than Adriatic ones. However, both of those fish can be done up the same way as a turbot after they have been gutted and skinned.

84. The appearance and season of a John Dory.

A John Dory, too, is numbered among the flat fish. It is not too large; the ones that are brought into Rome are not more than ten pounds. They have sharp spines on their back, a big mouth, big eyes and a small tail; they have many bones and little flesh. They are of a blue colour mixed with white, and are smooth, scaleless and large-bellied; they have quite a lot of entrails. In the area of their belly they have certain round, black and white marks that look like eyes, two per side. Their proper season goes from January through to the end of May. They are done up in all the ways a turbot is done, except that you cannot make jelly with them because they have little flesh.

85. The appearance and season of a rayfish and a monkfish.

A ray, too, is among the flat fish. There are two different species of them: those with two tails and those with one. Some are called skate[85.1] which have a pointed, coarse tail; others are called *occhiali* because on their back they have markings that look like eyeglasses[85.2] and are of several colours. The true ray, though, is the large one. Many of them are caught in the Adriatic Sea and are much better than the ones caught on shores by Rome, and their skin is not as coarse as the other ones. Under their belly they are very white; their snout is like a night-flying bat's. They have a big greenish-grey liver that is not very good. Their proper season begins in March and lasts through November. The same holds for the monkfish, which is of the same species.

86. Several ways to cook rayfish.

A ray is much better than a smooth hound and has a firmer flesh. It is more appropriately cooked in salted water than any other way. It is served with garlic sauce. It is skinned, and sword makers and other artisans use its skin.[86] The flesh is cut up into pieces and boiled, as I said, in salted water. It is served dry, garnished with parsley and with garlic sauce in dishes.

[85.1] Scappi's word for the rayfish itself is *ragia*. Here his *ragine* is likely a variety of skate.

[85.2] That is the literal sense of the word *occhiali*. Spectacles were known in Europe since the thirteenth century. The name *occhialine* remains in modern Italian dialects for the *Raja miraletus* (Linnæus, 1758), a brown ray, which has several other common names: *quattrocchi, raya quattrocchi, picara quattrocchi, raya liscia, picara liscia*. It measures only up to some 60 cm in length, which is why Scappi writes in the next phrase, *ma la vera ragia è la grande*.

[86] The *spadari* may have made scabbards or hilt wrappings from the rayfish skins, and the *altri arteggiani* perhaps made garments or purses.

If you want to make a pottage of it with beaten fresh onions and dried visciola cherries, prunes and other ingredients, follow the directions written above for fish pottages.

With its flesh you can make fingers and bresaola done the way sturgeon is done in Recipe 15. After the flesh has been cut into bresaola and has macerated, you can also flour and fry it in good oil. And after the flesh in two-pound pieces has boiled, let them cool, flour and fry them. Serve them garnished with various sauces, or else with boiled garlic cloves and sautéed parsley, pepper and orange juice over them. If that fish did not have the odour it has it would be excellent for making jelly the way that is done with the turbot.

When the other rayfish and *occhiali* are small they are skinned and fried whole; medium-sized ones are made into a pottage.

What has been said about a rayfish is also done with a monkfish.

87. The appearance and season of a garfish.

A garfish is a long, round, smooth, scaleless fish; it is of a sky-blue colour. It has a small head and a long, thin jaw like a stork. It has few entrails. It is excellent, especially in its season which begins in September and goes through May. In Rome the biggest ones are not more than two pounds.

88. To cook a garfish on a grill or spit, braised or fried.

Get a garfish, which above all must be fresh, and gut it. Set the one you want to grill in a vessel with oil, salt, pepper and fennel flour for an hour. Take it out, put it on the grill and cook it over a low fire the way a grey mullet is done. Serve it hot, dressing it with vinegar and must syrup mixed with the sauce in which it macerated.

The one you want to roast on a spit is cut up into rounds the way an eel is done, except for its tail and head. After it has macerated in the above mixture, spit the pieces or rounds interspersed with bay leaves or sage leaves, and cook it the way an eel is cooked with a crust.[88.1] Serve it hot, with orange juice and sugar over top.

The one that is to be braised is done up like a *ciambella*;[88.2] the same is done with the one to be grilled. Whether you leave its head on is optional. Put it into a tourte pan or earthenware baking dish containing oil, must syrup and a little verjuice, enough pepper, cinnamon and salt, and a little fennel flour. Cook it with heat from below and above like tourtes. When it is done, serve it hot with its broth over it.

[88.1] See Recipe 156, below.

[88.2] That is, wound around in a circle or spiral: as Recipe 94 says, *in rotoli*, rolled up. Directions for making the ring-shaped dumpling cake are in Recipe V,148. See, too, Recipe 157 where an eel also is done like a *ciambella*.

The one that is to be fried can be cut in rounds, too, or done up like a *ciambella* as above, leaving its snout on and sticking it all the way through, from one side to the other.[88.3] Flour it and fry it in olive oil. When it is done, serve it hot, dressed with orange juice, lime slices and salt.

After it has been fried, you can also marinate it the way a grey mullet is done in Recipe 57.

89. To prepare several sorts of pottage of garfish.

Get the biggest garfish you can, that is fresh, gutted and well washed. Cut it up into small pieces without taking its head, and make a pottage of it in all the ways done with the fish dealt with above.

90. The appearance and season of a lamprey.

Lampreys are of several species: from the sea, river, lake, shore and springs, but all of them are slimy, scaleless and boneless. They all have seven holes per side near their gill, and big ones have two feathery fins near their tail, one on top and the other beneath. They have few entrails. In colour they resemble an eel; they have a few spots around their body like leopards. Their mouth is for sucking, and it is hard to pull them away from wherever they have attached themselves; they have a great number of teeth and their eyes are small. The best are caught in the Tiber, the Po and the Arno. Young lamprey caught in the Tiber are excellent; they are sky-blue in colour and small, no larger round than a little finger and not too long; they have a white underbelly. Lamprey from a spring are much smaller, with some black on them, especially those caught in the state of Milan. All of them have the same season: from February through to the end of May; if you can find them, though, they are good at any time. In springtime many of them are full of eggs, and the big ones, too.

91. To spit-roast large lampreys.

Take a big lamprey without draining its blood, and clean off its slime with water that is not too hot. With a tiny little knife, through its umbilicus remove a small intestine[91.1] that runs from its tail up to its head. It is optional whether you take out its gallbladder because it is wickedly tiny[91.2] and not the trouble it is in other fish. However, when you want to drain its blood, first kill it in lightly salted

---

[88.3] *si farà trapassare da banda a banda.* It seems that the long needle-like snout (*il becco*) of the garfish is to penetrate the body wound around it.

[91.1] *un budelletto.*

[91.2] The 1570 printing had set the phrase ... *cavare il fiele ... perchioche è fiel picciolo.* In 1581 the typesetter seems not to have appreciated – or understood – the pun for he put ... *cavare il fiele ... perchioche ha il* [*sic*] *fiel picciolo.*

malmsey or white wine,[91.3] then drain the blood into that same wine, washing off its slime as directed above. If it is extremely large, skin it like an eel – and if you do, there is no need to wash off its slime. Slice it into slabs as is done with an eel and let them sit for an hour in a vessel with a little salt, fennel flour, oil and verjuice. Spit them with a bay or sage leaf between each piece, and cook them over a low fire. When they are almost done, make up a batter of grated bread, flour, cinnamon and sugar.[91.4] When they are done, serve them dressed with a sauce made of the blood[91.5] and the mixture in which it was killed, adding in pepper, sugar, cloves and cinnamon. You can also serve it without a crust and with only the sauce.

92. To braise large lampreys.

Get a lamprey which, being preferably alive, you will kill in a pot containing salted malmsey; drain its blood and combine it with the mixture in which it died. Gut it and, with that same malmsey in which it died, wash the area where the blood was drained from. Wash away its slime in hot water. When that is done, into each of its holes put a whole clove and a cinnamon stick, and in its mouth a nutmeg, or else a quarter nutmeg depending on its size. Then wind it up in a spiral like a *ciambella* and put it in an earthenware or copper pot where it cannot unwind itself and cover it over, by three fingers, with olive oil or sweet-almond oil or butter, and salt. Cook it slowly with heat below and above. When it has been boiling for a quarter of an hour, more or less depending on its size, drain off the oil gradually so that the thicker dregs remain on the bottom with the lamprey. Then

---

[91.3] This method of killing a lamprey had long been advocated by physicians. A lamprey being by nature cold and moist in the second degree, medical logic taught that the process of making it safe, or safer, for human consumption should begin even before it was dead: wine, warm and dry in the second degree, would be efficacious in tempering the lamprey's dangerous qualities. See, for instance, Maino de' Maineri (Magninus Mediolanensis), *Regimen sanitatis* (Louvain: Johannes de Westfalia, 1482), f.53v: *Salve reverentia utentium, iste piscis* [the *lampreda*] *est valde periculosus, quamvis sit ori saporosus. Horum enim piscium in aqua similis est generatio generationi serpentum in terra. Unde multum dubitandum est que non sint venenosi. … Bonum est etiam propter eorum viscositatem que submergantur in vino optimo vive.* Despite all culinary precautions when preparing lampreys, Maino still concludes, *Inter omnes pisces pessimi sunt et minime comedendi.* In Scappi's treatment salt would help the drying and warming process. Lamprey and other eels were usually subjected to a cooking that dried them and in which the heat was most direct.

[91.4] This batter is, of course, then basted onto the pieces of lamprey to form a crust around each one. See the same procedure with an eel, Recipe 156, below.

[91.5] In recipes from as early as the beginning of the fourteenth century, cooks are instructed to set aside a lamprey's blood, in part because it was held to be the essential goodness of the creature.

get a sauce[92.1] made of roasted Milanese almonds that have been well ground in a mortar with a little *mostaccioli* and raisins; moisten those things with the blood and the malmsey in which it died, adding in pepper, cinnamon, cloves, nutmeg and sugar – everything judiciously; make the mixture as thin as almond milk. Put it into the pot the lamprey is in; shake the pot with your hand so the dregs of the oil will thicken. Finish off cooking with that sauce, adding in a little verjuice and orange juice. Serve it hot, with sugar and cinnamon over it. If you do not want it whole, cut it up into pieces. You can also serve it cold, although it will always be better hot.

I do not want to go on talking any more about a large lamprey, although it should be cooked in various pottages, and on a grill, and fried, and done up in all the preparations that are made with an eel in the recipe for it, because I think that fish is better in those two ways described above, as well as in pastry (as I say in the Book on Pastries[92.2]), than in any other way. And you should know that you can remove the teeth from the large ones.

93. To grill young lamprey.

Get young lamprey and kill them in a sweet white wine. Take them out of the wine, remove the slime on them in warm water and wash them. Then drain their blood, catching it and setting it aside mixed with orange juice so it will not coagulate. Set the lamprey for a quarter of an hour in a vessel containing oil, pepper, salt and a little verjuice or vinegar; arrange each of the lampreys like a small *ciambella*.[93] Then take them out, put them on a grill and cook them, turning them over, and basting them with the above mixture. When they are done, serve them hot, dressed with a sauce made of those ingredients in which they steeped together with their blood and orange juice, sugar and cinnamon – which sauce should be slightly thick and sweetish. The thickening can be done with strained raisins.

You can also cook them on a spit after they have been wound, as was said, into *ciambelle*, and skewered with a slender iron skewer. Then tie the skewer, with the lampreys on it, onto a rather big spit and cook them like large lampreys. Serve them with the same sauce over them.

[92.1] A sauce specifically formulated for cooking and garnishing a lamprey is standard in late-medieval cookery. Invariably it combined liquids and spices whose humoral nature was warm and dry. By the early fifteenth century the lamprey sauce prepared at the court of Savoy used a complex mixture of spices: see Chiquart's *Du fait de cuisine*, Recipe 4. Scappi's lamprey sauce is further described in Recipe 158, below.

[92.2] Recipes V,178 and 202.

[93] *una ciambelletta*: that is, as we saw in the previous recipe, wound around itself in a spiral.

94. To braise young river lamprey.

Get the lamprey as was set out in the other recipes, do them up in rolls and put them into a copper tourte pan or earthenware baking dish with enough oil to half-cover them, and salt and fennel flour. Sauté them for a quarter of an hour with heat from below and above. Pour off the oil slowly, leaving the thicker dregs with the lampreys. Turn them upside down and add in verjuice, a little malmsey or white wine and the blood diluted with the same wine, a little sugar, cloves, cinnamon and a few currants. Boil everything together with the young lamprey for a quarter of an hour. Serve them hot, with the same mixture over top of them.

They can also be braised with only fennel flour, oil and salt without draining their blood. They are served dry[94] like that with orange juice, pepper and sugar over them.

95. To marinate and souse young lamprey.

Take the lamprey without draining their blood; clean them with warm water as above and let them sit for a quarter of an hour in a vessel with a little oil and salt. Then flour them and fry them. When they are done, put them into a pot containing a mixture made up of clear verjuice, sugar, white wine, a little vinegar, pepper, cinnamon, cloves, nutmeg and saffron, which mixture has boiled and is boiling when you put the young lamprey into it. Stop up the pot and leave them in it until you are ready to serve. Then serve them either hot or cold as you like.

If you want, though, to souse them, there is no need to put in verjuice or saffron, but rather vinegar, sugar and wine. And when they have fried, put them into that boiling mixture along with bits of a few bay or myrtle leaves. Serve them with sugar and rose vinegar over them. The marinated ones and soused ones are kept for five days.

Big ones are done up that way. You can also make pottages of them with gooseberries, prunes, dried visciola cherries and finely chopped herbs or else beaten spring onions; and do them in all of those pottages in which a turbot is done in Recipe 79.

The tiny ones from running streams are fried and served hot with sautéed parsley and orange juice on them – having first been killed in wine.

96. The appearance and season of a moray eel.

A moray is a fish the length of a lamprey but of a different colour, tending more toward tawny and black; it is speckled with various colours. It is a very slimy fish. In Rome for the most part it is sold on the Sant'Angelo bridge along with other fish from stagnant waters. Its flesh is soft and whitish. Its entrails are similar to those of an eel. It has a variety of fine bones in it. Its season goes from November to the end of March.

---

[94] See the note in Recipe 50.

97. To braise moray eels.

Get morays fresh, gut them and hang them by their head on a hook and with two canes or sticks, one on each side of the body tightly; then, beginning at the head and pulling repeatedly, work your way down to the tail. It can be done differently by beating the morays with a bat. Skin them, cut them into pieces and set them to braise in a pot or baking dish with very little water, oil, verjuice, mild spices, spring onions or herbs, and must syrup. If you do not want to skin them, clean them in warm water.

They are also done on a spit and in various other ways like a lamprey.

98. The appearance and season of a conger eel.

A conger is of the same species as an eel although it is a sea fish. However, its head is bigger, and down to its middle it is bigger, than an eel. It is white under its belly and sky blue elsewhere. It is quite good when it is caught during its season, which begins in December and lasts until the end of March.

99. To spit-roast a conger eel.

Take a conger and skin it as you do an eel. Gut it, cut it into rounds and roast it on a spit the way lampreys are roasted in Recipe 91. And in all the ways an eel is prepared you can also prepare that conger.

100. The appearance and season of a squid.

A squid is the opposite of many other fish because it has neither blood nor scales, and has only one bone in its back, a transparent one, like a dagger. It has a number of tentacles and coarse white hairs.[100] Its body resembles a pointed purse. In its body it has a small bladder full of a black liquid. Its eyes are hard and its beaked mouth is hard and blackish. It is white and very good in its season, which goes from November to the end of March. In Rome the tiny ones are much better for frying than the big or medium-sized ones.

101. To fry or make a pottage of squid.

Get a small squid and take out the bone it has in its back; cut out its eyes. Check the hairs closely because they are sometimes full of sand; wash them in several changes of water, bearing in mind that it will turn out much better if those hairs are cut away from the body because there is often sand at their base. When they are cut off, give the squid a little salt and fry them in olive oil. Serve them hot, dressed with orange juice and pepper. Be careful that in the oil in which they are fried you do not fry pastries or anything else that should be white, because their small bladder bursts during the frying and colours the oil.

If you want them in a pottage with the same flavour as their bladder, when they are washed and cleaned as above, the small ones are put into an earthenware

---

[100] *crini bianchi*: in Recipe 102 Scappi will call these hairs the squid's *barba* or 'beard.'

or copper pot with oil or butter and sautéed slowly. Afterwards add enough water to cover them, along with mild spices and beaten, sautéed onions or beaten herbs, raisins and verjuice, depending on the time of year. If you do not want it with their black sauce, first take out their small bladder and boil them in water; rinse them in cool water and make up the pottage as directed above.

They can also be served after they have fried, with various sauces over them.

102. To prepare a pottage of big squid.

Take the squid and remove the bone that is in its back, removing the membrane around it, too. Split it down the middle, remove its beard, eyes and beak along with the sand that is often found there. Keep the little bladder, full of the black liquid which is its fecundity.[102.1] When it is clean, divide it up into several pieces, put them into a copper or earthenware pot with oil and sauté them slowly. Add in enough water to cover them, along with common spices; let them cook well because they need a thorough cooking. When they are almost done, get malmsey or some other white wine, and verjuice mixed with the black liquor in the little bladder; put everything including the squid into it and give it four boilings.[102.2] Then serve it. If you want the broth thick you can do that with ground almonds. And you can put beaten herbs and raisins in with the squid.

103. To prepare a pottage of stuffed squid.

Get a medium-sized squid – that is, one that is neither too big nor too small – cleaned as above. Parboil its tentacles in salted water. Set its little bladder aside. Fill the squid's body with a mixture of grated Parmesan cheese, raw egg yolks, grated breadcrumb, chopped herbs, pepper, cinnamon, raisins and saffron. However, if it is a fasting day, instead of the cheese put in almonds or walnuts or hazelnuts, ground up with a little bread soaked in verjuice and mixed in with the same ingredients as above. When the squid is stuffed, put it into an earthenware or copper pot with oil or butter and enough water to cover it, adding in its beard cut up into small pieces. Boil it all slowly, adding in enough common spices and salt. When it is almost cooked add in finely chopped herbs, or else thicken the broth with ground almonds moistened with white wine, verjuice and a little saffron. If you want to give it a black colour, dilute the liquor in the little bladder with some of the same broth.

After the squid is stuffed, you can also boil it an hour in salted water, gently, so the stuffing does not leak out. Then take it out of the broth and, still hot, flour it and fry it in oil or butter. When it has fried, serve it with orange juice and sugar over it, or else cover it with any of a variety of sauces.

[102.1] Scappi's term for the squid's ink is *liquor nero*, which he states is the creature's *grassezza*, its semen. In sixteenth-century Italy the word *liquore* still carried a connotation of a liquid that was a distillate of some property, occasionally, as here, a vital essence.

[102.2] By giving a preparation a single boiling, a cook merely brings it to a boil. Four boilings, *quattro bolli*, amount to a cooking that is still relatively brief.

104. The appearance and season of a cuttlefish.

A cuttlefish is a white fish and is cartilaginous like a squid; it is put together like a white leather purse. Like a squid it has no blood. Its beak is like a little owl's. It has certain tentacles like an octopus. In its back it has a white bone which goldsmiths use to form rings. They are much more numerous in the Adriatic than in the Tyrrhenian Sea. There are small ones and big ones; the big ones are sometimes brought salted from Slavonia to Venice, and likewise from Genoa to Milan, but they are much better fresh. Their proper season begins in the middle of January and lasts to the end of March; in Venice and Rome they are found almost anytime.

105. To cook cuttlefish in a pottage.

Get a fresh cuttlefish and remove the bone in its back and the tentacles that stick out, leaving only the purse;[105.1] set aside a small bladder which is in its body that is full of a dark substance like ink. Split the cuttlefish down the middle and with a knife remove[105.2] the cartilage[105.3] all around inside and out. Wash it in several changes of cold water and warm water so it becomes as white as calf's tripe. Divide it into several little pieces and put it into an earthenware pot or some other vessel with olive oil or butter, finely chopped spring onions, a little water, pepper, cinnamon and saffron, with a little white wine or verjuice. Cook it vigorously because they need a thorough cooking. Be careful they are not too salty, and at the end put in a few beaten herbs. But if you want to give them a dark colour with the substance that is in the small bladder, there is no need for any herbs; rather it will be enough to dilute that blackness with a little white wine or verjuice. Bring it to a boil. Then serve it with mild spices over it. In with that cuttlefish you can put its tentacles after they have been cleaned and washed and cut up into pieces.

If you want to stuff it, when the bone is out and the tentacles removed wash and fill it with a mixture made up of cheese, eggs, grated bread, raisins, beaten herbs, pepper, cinnamon and saffron; on fasting days, instead of cheese put in ground almonds, and instead of hen's eggs, raw roe from another fish, along with the other ingredients used to stuff other fish. When it is full, put it into a baking dish with enough water and oil that it is just barely covered, and boil it gently until the stuffing has firmed up and the cuttlefish has swollen. At that moment add in verjuice and water tinged with saffron, and enough pepper, cinnamon and salt. Cook it for two hours, more or less depending on its size. Serve it with the same broth over it.

[105.1] Scappi keeps the image of a *borsa* which he has already used in Recipes 100 and 104.

[105.2] *levinosi*, erroneously typeset as *lavinosi*, 'wash,' in 1581.

[105.3] The word is in the plural, *le cartilagine*, referring to the cartilaginous processes of the boneless creature. Nevertheless, Scappi does write *l'osso* later.

106. The appearance and season of an octopus.

An octopus is slimy and its body is like a bit of tripe; it is whitish like a cuttlefish and has many tentacles with certain little twisted tubes with which it sucks up water – they are white like the mane of a white horse. It is not very pretty to look at, nor good to eat because it takes a long cooking. Its proper season is from January to the end of April, although in Rome they can sometimes be found out of season.

107. Several ways to cook an octopus.[107]

Take an octopus, cut into it, gut it and cut it up into several pieces like tripe. Take the tenderest part, beat it with a heavy rod, and wash it in salted water to remove any slime. Put it into an earthenware pot with sautéed onions and oil, and cook it slowly with a lid on so it cannot breathe, because an octopus makes moisture by itself. When it is almost done, add in verjuice and spices with a little saffron. If there is not enough broth, add in a little water.

Also cook an octopus in salted water, then cut it up into pieces. Flour them and fry them in oil. Serve it dressed with some sort of seasoning or else with pepper, salt and orange juice.

108. The appearance and season of a smooth hound fish.

It is my belief that the smooth hound took its name from its eggs, which are as big as those of a wood pigeon.[108] The fish has a flat head and a big belly that decreases in size toward its tail; it is covered with a rough, greenish-grey skin; from its middle back it is round. Its flesh is white and soft. As a food it is unworthy of a royal board. Its season begins at the end of December and lasts to the end of May; in Rome you can find large numbers of them. Likewise for a dogfish, which looks much like a smooth hound.

109. Several ways to cook a smooth hound.

Take a smooth hound, skin it and gut it; and if you do not want to skin it, clean off its slime with warm water. Cook it in water, salt and pepper. When it is done, serve it dressed with a garlic sauce.

If you want it in a pottage, cut it up into pieces and sauté them with beaten onions, oil and salt, adding in enough white wine, verjuice and water along with pepper, cinnamon and beaten herbs. Also, if you want it braised, do that with prunes and dried visciola cherries, vinegar and must syrup. After it is skinned it

---

[107] Quoting A. Petronio in his *Del viver delli Romani et di conservar la sanità* (1592), Sabban and Serventi (*A tavola nel Rinascimento*, 127) write that 'il polpo è considerato un "pesce libidinosissimo e per questo è forse incitativo al coito."'

[108] Scappi's etymology is certainly influenced by the single name shared by both the fish and the fowl: *palombo*. In his text he distinguishes *pesce palombo* from *palombo volatile*, a stockdove or wood pigeon.

can be fried. Serve it dressed with any of a variety of sauces or with orange juice and sugar.

I will not speak of its entrails because everything except the liver is thrown away. The liver is fried and served garnished with cloves of garlic and sautéed parsley. Its roe, too, is done the same way.

110. The appearance and season of a cod.

Cod is a fish of a green-grey colour, with a big, flat head and big, sharp teeth in its mouth; it is long in the body with very small scales. It is not much esteemed fresh around here. They are dried on Spanish shores and brought to Italy cut apart, those being much bigger and better than the ones from Rome's shores. Their proper season goes from August to the end of March.

111. Several ways to cook fresh cod.

Take a scaled, cleaned cod, cook it on a grill and fry it like the horse mackerel in Recipe 68. If it is big, make a pottage of it as is done with the grey mullet in Recipe 56.

112. Several ways to cook dried cod.

Get dried cod and soak them in warm water for eight hours more or less, depending on their size for, even though some people pound them with a rod to make them tender, nevertheless I do not advise that, it being better to let them soften by themselves, as experience has shown me. They are parboiled, and when that's done you can make a pottage of them with beaten onions. Otherwise you can cook them in a broth made of oil and spices. They are served dressed with a garlic sauce or some other sauce.

And if you want to fry them, they are floured and then fried, being served with orange juice and pepper over them and with mustard in dishes.

They can also be done in a pottage in oil, white wine verjuice, water, prunes and dried visciola cherries along with the cod after they have been parboiled. The broth of that pottage is thickened with ground almonds and beaten herbs, adding in pepper, cinnamon and cloves because that fish likes spicing.

113. The appearance and season of a short scorpion fish.[113.1]

A scorpion fish has a big head and sharp points on a number of places on its body; it resembles a young burbot[113.2] because of its large mouth. It has skin rather than scales, and two appendages in front. There are several sorts of them: large and small, of varying colours, black, greenish-grey, the best tending to a russet. Their season begins in September and lasts to the end of April. A great

---

[113.1] Scappi's name for this fish is a *scorfeno*; scientifically it is perhaps a *Scorpæna porcus*.

[113.2] *marcione*. The burbot is a member of the cod family. See Recipe 129 in the section on freshwater fish below.

many are found in the salt pool of Civitá Vecchia. The fish needs to be done in salted water or else in wine, vinegar and spices more than any other way. However, if you want to do other preparations with it, follow the directions given for the gurnard in Recipe 64.[113.3]

114. The appearance and season of a green wrasse.[114.1]

In shape a green wrasse looks like a tench, though in colour like a parrot.[114.2] It is caught in the pool of Civitá Vecchia along with many other fish that are hard to recommend. That fish is fried and pottages are made of it as of a rayfish in Recipe 86.[114.3]

I must not overlook writing of the appearance and season of a swordfish, even though they are brought into Rome only very rarely. That fish is somewhat bigger than a tuna, and I am of the opinion that it is the king of tunas because in its forehead[114.4] it has a bone three hands long like a sword, but its skin is whiter than a tuna's; its flesh is white and firm like that of a sturgeon. It has the same season as a tuna and is on the market with a tuna. The swordfish makes the same prepared dishes as a tuna.

[Freshwater fish]

115. The appearance and season of a trout.

A trout is a freshwater fish; by its nature it always goes with the current. There are several sorts of trout, black and white and speckled, but the best are the ones speckled in black and russet. They are caught on the banks of fast-flowing waters. Those from Sora and Arpino are good though darkish in colour; those caught in the Tesino and Tiber are white, but most excellent. Those caught in Lakes Maggiore and Como are very big and sometimes go beyond forty Milanese

---

[113.3] That recipe being for Scappi's *pesce cappone*, a fish of an appearance somewhat similar to that of a scorpion fish.

[114.1] While Scappi does not mention the swordfish here in this rubric nor in the Table at the end of this Book III, he does devote a distinct paragraph to it under this rubric CXIIII. The swordfish, which he relates culinarily to the tuna, concludes the section on sea fish and appears to have been appended.

[114.2] Again Scappi expands upon the fish's name, *il pesce pappagallo*, in order to help an apprentice cook identify the fish by comparing its markings to those of a parrot, *il pappagallo volatile*.

[114.3] Scappi has forgotten to mention the time of year during which this fish is available on the market. Because a salt pool is relatively calm, shallow and reedy, its yield in fish could be consistently high though not, as Scappi writes repeatedly, of the more gastronomically valued species.

[114.4] *nella fronte*. His statement that the swordfish was rare in Rome might explain this error, unusual for Scappi, in descriptive detail: the 'sword' is not like a unicorn's horn but is an elongated upper jaw.

pounds, which are twenty-eight ounces to a pound. Their scales are minute and their underbelly is white; their flesh is more a russet colour in winter than in summer. The season for the average-sized ones is from October through to the end of December.

116. To cook trout in water, salt, wine, vinegar and spices.

Experience has shown me that average-sized trout are better cooked in wine, vinegar and water, salt and spices than any other way, although they can also be done in salted water the way a sea bass is done in Recipe 40. In Milan a large trout is done that way – that is, it is scaled, gutted and cut crosswise in round slabs two fingers thick. Those are washed and put into a copper pot that they call a *caldaro* and that has a broad bottom,[116] and they arrange the slabs side by side: that is done because, if they were piled up, when you took them out they would break up. Enough white wine is put in to cover them by two fingers, and sufficient salt, and they are left to boil gently. The white scum that forms on top is skimmed off. When you see that the slabs begin to rise and make rings sort of like a lady's breasts, they are done. Then, one by one and very carefully, they are taken out and put on a small board to cool. That way they will last for three days, more or less depending on the season and weather. They are served cold with parsley over them and a sauce in dishes. They are also cooked that way in salted water, vinegar and wine; and when they are skimmed you add in crushed spices.

However, we Roman cooks get average-sized trout; we scale and gut them and cook them whole in wine, vinegar and spices. When they are done we take them out and, wanting to serve them hot, we keep them in white cloths. And we make various pottages with them the way they are done with a sea bass in Recipe 40.

117. To fry and souse trout.

Get trout that are not more than two pounds each, and above all they must be fresh, and caught in clear waters or in rivers. Remove their fine scales and gut them. Make a slit along their full length; let them sit for an hour between two boards with a little ground salt under and over them, with a weight on top pressing them. Then clean the salt off them, flour them and fry them in oil. When they are done, souse them with vinegar, pepper and a little wine, and with bay or myrtle leaves, the way a carp is done in the recipe for that.[117] They are kept for fifteen days in the same leaves, and are served cold with rose vinegar and sugar over them. Sometimes they are warmed up on a grill or in oil in a pan and served with the same garnish over them.

---

[116] In Scappi's kitchen a *caldara* is a familiar round-bottomed cooking container for large amounts of a liquid suspended over a fire. The Milanese variant, which we might translate as 'kettle,' with a wide, relatively flat bottom, is illustrated in three versions in Plate 7.

[117] See Recipe 122, below, and perhaps 132.

118. To cook trout that have macerated, on a grill and otherwise.

Take the trout and, if they are big, cut them crosswise in slabs two fingers thick and let them sit for six hours in a mixture composed of vinegar, coriander, pepper, oil, salt, garlic cloves and must syrup. Then take them out and let them drain. Grill them with a few sprigs of rosemary or sage under them, basting them with the mixture they have steeped in. When they are cooked, serve them hot, dressed with that same mixture heated up.

If you want to fry them, when they are out of the macerating mixture and drained, flour them and fry them in oil. When they are done, they are served hot with a sauce in dishes.

If you want to braise them, put the slabs into a tourte pan or an earthenware vessel whether they have macerated or not. In the pan there has to be fennel flour, oil and enough salt and pepper. Those that have macerated[118.1] are cooked like a tuna in Recipe 37 with prunes and dried visciola cherries, with a little verjuice and must syrup added in. Serve them with their broth over them. Those that have macerated are braised plain, and[118.2] just with oil and some of that mixture. Small and medium-sized trout can be done whole in all the above ways.

119. To cook trout in the German fashion.

If the trout is big, take pieces of it as above and set them in an earthenware or tinned copper pot with enough malmsey or white wine to cover them by two fingers, along with pepper, cinnamon, cloves, nutmeg, sugar and a little vinegar. Make the mixture so it is both sweet and bitter. Put in a little fresh butter as well. Boil everything without skimming it. When it is cooked, serve it with slices of toast under it and its broth over it. Some people put the toast and slices of citron peel[119.1] to boil together with the fish; however, because I know that when a lemon is boiled it makes a dish bitter, and that bread obstructs the intestines, even though it thickens a broth, I think it is more decent[119.2] to serve it up the other way. That dish has to be cooked rapidly so that it turns out tastier and picks up less of a copper taste.[119.3] You can cook the small and medium-sized ones in the same way either whole or cut up into pieces.

[118.1] *Sic:* there is no negative here or in the next sentence.

[118.2] This 'and' may be intended as an alternative 'or.'

[119.1] *fette di limoncelli cedrati.* See also Recipe 148, below. In Recipe VI,210 Scappi gives directions for candying citron peel.

[119.2] Scappi's interesting word here is *civilmente: è piu civilmente servito.*

[119.3] As we see in many recipes (for instance, Recipes 4, 8 and 79 in this Book), the inner surface of copper vessels is often coated with tin, the purpose being to obviate a contamination of a food's flavour.

120. Several ways to cook trout entrails.

Of the entrails of trout I think only the roe are good, and even that they are excellent, especially the ones from Lakes Maggiore and Como which are as big as peas. If you want to make them into thick soups or sops, using hot water free them from the membrane that's around them so they are separated. Bring them to a boil in plain water, or else put them raw into an earthenware or copper pot with oil or butter and enough water, or else broth in which the trout has been cooked, to cover them by three fingers; to that add pepper, cinnamon and a little saffron. Boil them for a quarter of an hour, because they take little cooking. Just before serving them, put in a handful of finely chopped herbs and a few gooseberries or verjuice. If, optionally, you want to thicken the broth, do so with ground almonds or grated bread.

To make sops of them, however, there is no need for the broth to be thickened. They are served with slices of toast beneath. If the trout is fresh, its intestines are opened and washed with oil. They, too, can make little pottages as is done with sturgeon intestines in Recipe 22.

121. The appearance and season of a salmon carp.[121]

There is a difference between a trout and a salmon carp. A salmon carp is a little whiter and has a few russettish speckles on its body; its snout is smaller and very delicate; it has tiny scales, few entrails, and tends to a silvery colour, especially the one that's caught in Lake Garda, which is the best in Italy, because it is found in very few other places. The biggest salmon carp is not more than four pounds. Its season begins in October and goes to the end of April, though if you can find any they are good anytime.

122. To souse a salmon carp in vinegar.

A salmon carp being so delicate and exceptional, I cannot leave aside telling how they souse one at Lake Garda. You should know, therefore, that as soon as they are caught, the large ones are gutted without scaling them, though small ones are not; a slit is made along their side and they are coated, live, with ground salt. Then the salt is cleaned off them and they are fried in a kettle full of oil. As each one floats up in the oil so that it is fried and not burned, and is white, it is taken out and set aside for the oil to drain off. It is dumped into a pot containing white vinegar that is boiling, with a little salt, and left there for a fifth of an hour. Then it is taken out, let drain and cool, and put into wooden crates with bay, boxwood or myrtle leaves; that way they can be kept a number of days. They are transported

---

[121] Along with their Italian counterparts, some modern English taxonomists name this fish (*carpione* in Scappi; scientifically *Salmo carpio*) a 'Lake Garda carp' or *carpione del Garda*. This seems to be one of Scappi's preferred freshwater fishes. Apart from the series of recipes that follows here, it is dealt with also in Recipe 202.

to various places throughout Italy and are served with rose vinegar and sugar over them.[122.1]

In that same way you can souse a fish called grayling[122.2] and the freshwater shad of Lake Como and elsewhere and every other sort of freshwater fish that is not larger than two pounds. You can also marinate those fish the way a gilthead is done in Recipe 46. Some of those salmon carp are brought to Rome, but they are not as good as in those places right by Lake Garda. They can also be soused without putting them into vinegar, only having them sit in a pickle for twenty-four hours. When they have cooled, they are set aside.

123. The appearance and season of a grayling.

A grayling is not very big: all told it is not more than three pounds. It is white like silver, has tiny scales, and a goldenish blotch by its gill. It has few entrails which are never removed when it is cooked. It is caught in two rivers, the Adda and the Ambro, though more in the Adda, a river in Lombardy that loops by Pizzighettone, as the Ambro passes by Sant'Angelo and Marignano. Its season runs from May to the end of August. It is cooked in all the ways a salmon carp is done above. And pottages are made with it as with a small trout.

124. The appearance and season of a freshwater shad.[124]

A freshwater shad is a fish similar to the allis shad, but it belongs to the herring and pilchard species. It is silvery, with a forked tail and tiny scales. Great numbers of them are caught in Lake Como. Salted ones are taken everywhere in Italy. Their proper season begins in April and lasts until August. They can be done up in all the ways a shad from the Tiber and a salmon carp from Lake Garda are done.

125. The appearance and season of a perch.

A perch, too, is a freshwater fish; numbers of them are caught in the Tesino, in Lake Maggiore, and in various other lakes in Lombardy. That fish does not reach the fish markets in Rome like the grayling and freshwater shad mentioned above do. A perch resembles a sea bream in its scales and colouring, though those scales are higher and its head is not as curved. Its flesh is very white. Sometimes it is full of eggs, especially in the summer. Lombard physicians allow their sick to have it,[125] along with salmon carp and grayling, provided it is not bigger than a pound and a half. Its season goes from September to the end of May.

[122.1] See also Recipe 202, below.

[122.2] The flesh of the grayling is highly esteemed among freshwater fishes in Europe. Scappi will devote the next recipe to it and mention it again in Recipe 125.

[124] This *agone* (*Alosa lacustris*) is a freshwater counterpart to the allis (or twait) shad seen above in Recipe 50 among sea fish. The salted variety of a freshwater shad is dealt with in Recipe 211.

[125] See Recipe VI,176; Book VI also recognizes perch as suitable in a sickdish in Recipes 35, 114, 174 and 180.

126. To cook a perch on a grill and in other ways.

Get the perch without it having been scaled but only with the gallbladder removed. Cook it on a grill as a gilthead is done in Recipe 44.

If you want to fry it, though, scale it, noting that generally that fish is scaled with hot ashes. When that is done, gut it except for its roe, if it has any, which are good. Then fry it as is done in Recipe 46.

You can also do it up in all the ways a gilthead is done. Large ones need to be boiled in salted water, or else they are made into a pottage the way a turbot is done in Recipe 78.

127. The appearance and season of a chub.

A chub has many other names: in some places it is called *strigie*, by the people of the Po, *alberi*, and in Rome *squalme*. A large number of them are caught in the rivers Adda, Ambro and Tiber. It looks like a grey mullet but is whiter and its scales are somewhat bigger. In season its entrails are very fat. That season begins in April and goes to the end of October; in Rome they can be found anytime. They can be done up in all the ways a 'good-bowelled' grey mullet is done.[127]

128. The appearance and season of a barbel.

This fish is called a barbel because it has two white feelers under its chin. It is a rust colour on its back and under its belly, white; it has minute scales, and is more slimy than not. It has very few entrails at any time except the spring when they are full of roe; that roe is very bad, though. They are caught in the Po, Arno, Tiber and various other rivers. Fishermen on the Po make pottages of them and fry them and grill them, the way the fishermen of Chiozza and Venice do with a grey mullet and a goby, in Recipes 56 and 62. Its season goes from May to the end of September, though you can rest assured you can eat it from September to March, during which time it is best.

129. The appearance and season of a burbot.

No large burbot are brought to the fish markets of Rome, but only those fingerlings that are called *capi grossi* or *marscioni*, which are of the same species. A burbot is slimy, without scales and of a tawny colour. It has a big liver, of which fritters are sometimes made and which is fried, but few other entrails. A great number of them are brought into Milan but they are not very big. Its season begins in September and goes through to May. It is done up in all the ways a goby is done in Recipe 62.

---

[127] This *cefalo di buon budello* is mentioned in Recipes 53 and 57.

130. The appearance and season of *carpina* – that is, a carp.[130.1]

Medium-sized carp are not brought to the fish markets of Rome because more of them are found up toward France than in other provinces, although in Mantua and Ferrara many of them are found; they are called *bulbari* and *carpina*. There's a reason for calling a carp *reina* because they are extremely delicate, especially their flavour. It is a large, slimy, roundish sort of fish with a round mouth and scales as big as those of a corb, though they tend to a golden colour. It has a large head with tiny teeth, and is rather shadowy on its back. Many are born in the Lake of Mantua and in the Po. It is true that Milan receives many of another species that is called rudd[130.2]: they have a broader belly; in the Lake of Peruggia they are called beaked carp;[130.3] likewise those of the Troiano, which is close to Ostia and is a port. They are excellent when caught in their season, which goes from February to the end of August.

131. To cook a medium-sized carp – that is, a *reina* – plain or in a pottage.

Take its head along with a handswidth of its body, which is the best part of that fish. Scale it, clean it and cook it plain in salted water the way a corb's head is done in Recipe 29. Serve it garnished with parsley and other flowers and with a side dish of white sauce.

With its body you can make a pottage when it is cut up into pieces with spring onions, white wine and spices. And you can also do it in all the other ways you do a turbot, and a sea bass in Recipe 78. Serve it dressed with its broth.

132. To cook a medium-sized carp in wine, water, vinegar and spices.[132]

Cut it into rounds four fingers thick and cook those in white wine, vinegar, spices and water as you do a trout in the recipe for it, Recipe 116. Serve them hot or cold, with various sauces in dishes. You can also cook it in plain salted water, and serve it the way its head is served. Above all it has to be scaled and gutted.

133. Another way to cook a medium-sized carp.

Take it without it having been scaled but only gutted, and cut it up into slabs that are not too thick. Set them to macerate for two hours in a mixture of vinegar, salt and pepper, garlic cloves and sweet fennel seeds. Then get a big casserole pot or some other vessel, with wine and a little salt and pepper boiling in it, and put

---

[130.1] *Reina.* The end of Recipes 140 and 141 tell us that a *carpina* is a medium-sized *reina*. This latter name is still used today for a carp in Tuscany, Emilio Romagna, Venetia and Umbria. For the word *carpina*, which incorporates a diminutive, this translation (awkwardly) qualifies 'carp' with 'medium-sized' here and in the following recipes.

[130.2] *scardue.*

[130.3] *lasche.*

[132] Compare this process with the sousing described, for instance, in Recipes 46, 95, 117 and, particularly, 122.

those pieces into it one by one. When they are cooked, take them out carefully, watching that you do not break them. Take off their scales and let them drain. Serve them hot or cold, sprinkled on top with sugar, cinnamon and a few herbs. You can also cover them with any of a variety of sauces.

In the same way you can do a corb, a dentex, a sea bass, a brown meagre, a pike and any sort of rudd, medium-sized carp or beaked carp.

134. To grill, braise or fry a medium-sized carp.

Get a medium-sized carp, scale it, gut it and cut it up crosswise into slabs a finger thick. Grill it, braise it or fry it as is done with the tuna slabs in Recipe 36. The same can be done with medium-sized and small ones without scaling them.

135. To cook the milt and roe of the above medium-sized carp.

Take the milt that is firm and very white and perfect, and make all those preparations of it that are made with a corb's or sea bass's milt. Its roe are greenish; you bring them to a boil and cut them up small and make pottages of them with a variety of ingredients. The intestines are rarely eaten.

136. To cook that fish's tongue.

A *carpina*'s tongue is highly esteemed, as well as the cartilage that is in the brain. The tongue is taken raw out of the head with a part of the throat. If you want to make a pottage of it, with raisins, muscatel raisins, spices, verjuice, water, white wine and beaten herbs, that can be done.

In my opinion, though, better than in any other preparation it is parboiled in salted water, then sprinkled with fennel flour, coated with oil and grilled. That is served with orange juice and pepper over it.

137. The appearance and season of a freshwater mullet.[137]

A freshwater mullet is a small fish, the largest of them not more than half a pound. It has big scales and is greenish. Those caught in fast-flowing waters and near Rome and in the Tiber are much whiter and better than others, and are full of eggs, especially when they are caught in their season. That season comes twice in a year, fall and spring. Mostly the fish is cooked, without being scaled or gutted, on the coals or on a grill. It is also fried in oil like other small fry. It is served hot.

138. The appearance and season of a tench.

A tench is a slimy fish with small scales and various colourations. The lake variety are yellowish, mostly in winter; those from swamps, blackish; river ones, whitish. The ones from Lakes Bolsena and Troiano are much more delicate, but even more so the ones that are sometimes found in the Tiber and the Po, mainly

---

[137] This fish is Scappi's *roviglione*, a freshwater mullet. See Recipes 53–61, 212 and 213 for the several saltwater and freshwater species of mullet. The *Cambridge Italian Dictionary* translates *roviglione* as gurnard, a fish that seems to bear little resemblance to the one that Scappi describes.

when they are caught in their season. That begins in March and goes to the end of August; and, for the males, from September through February. To distinguish between the male and the female, look between the two fins under the belly because on the left the male has a thing sticking out the thickness of a knife blade and the female does not; also, the female has a bigger umbilicus. In Milan very large ones are brought from Lakes Maggiore and Como that weigh thirty Milanese pounds. However, the ones brought to Rome from Tagliacozzo and the lakes of Vico and Santa Preseda are considered the best, except for those caught in the Tiber and Po. The head of the large ones is more delicate than the body.

139. To grill a tench.

Take a tench, which must above all be fresh, and scale it in hot water or else with hot ash so that it stays white. Cut it open along its back and carefully take out its spine. Cut away all its fins and, having gutted it, turn its skin inwards. On that skin put a mixture made up of ground walnuts, grated bread, its intestines with the gallbladder removed, beaten herbs, pepper, cinnamon, raisins and a little oil or butter. Tie the tench up with a thin cord so the mixture will not leak out. Coat it with oil, salt, vinegar and must syrup. Instead of vinegar you can use verjuice. Cook it on a grill, turning it often and basting it with that same sauce. When it is done, serve it dressed with the same sauce, having first untied it. It is not a bad idea, when the tench is put on the grill, to put a few sprigs of rosemary under it so it will not stick. On meat days you can stuff it with cheese and raw egg yolks along with the above mixture; and you can also stuff it with the mixture used for saveloy sausage. Do not fail to put its intestine, with the gallbladder removed, into the stuffing.

140. Two other ways to grill a tench.

Get a tench that is large rather than small, and in winter male rather than female. Without using hot water scrape it so thoroughly that not a scale remains; skin the whole body carefully, leaving both the head and the tail attached to the skin. Take the tench's flesh without any bones and beat it small along with a little salted tuna belly which has soaked to soften it, mixing everything with the mixture of the previous recipe. Turn the skin back and stuff it with that mixture. Cook it carefully, with a few sprigs of sage or rosemary bound around it, basting it with the same mixture as was used to baste the fish previously. When it is done, serve it hot with that same sauce over it.

If you want to do it differently, when it has been scraped and cut open, leaving its intestines in if they are big, let it macerate for two hours. Then take it out, flour it and fry it in oil. When it is half done, remove it from the oil without letting the oil drain off it and put it on the grill, basting it with the same macerating mixture. Serve it hot, dressed with sugar and pepper.

You can do a *carpina*, that is, a medium-sized *reina*,[140] that same way. And you can choose not to turn the skin back when you first grill it.

141. To braise a tench.

Get a tench in one of its seasons.   Scrape it, making it white, and wash it thoroughly; gut it and remove its teeth through its gills. If its intestines are big,[141.1] slit them open; when they are washed, cut them up into pieces and mix them into the same mixture with which the above fish are stuffed, adding in a clove of garlic and a few prunes and dried visciola cherries or sloe berries.[141.2] Stuff the tench with that mixture, sewing the hole up so the mixture cannot leak out. Then put it into an earthenware or copper pan of an adequate size, along with enough oil, water, white wine and verjuice to cover it by a finger, adding in salt and common spices with a little saffron, and prunes and dried visciola cherries if it is in the winter; in summer or springtime, gooseberries or verjuice grapes or beaten spring onions. Braise it under a bell or in an oven as tourtes are done. When it is cooked, serve it hot with its sauce over it.

You can do a *carpina*, that is, a medium-sized carp, that same way. The skin on the head and tail can also be braised; it should be stuffed with the same mixture.

142. To cook a tench in a pottage and in various other ways.

Get a clean tench, scaled and gutted, and if it is large cut it up into slabs; put those into a casserole pot with oil, white wine, water and salt, along with beaten old onions that have been parboiled. If it is small, it is not parboiled. Into that add common spices and saffron. Cook it with a small amount of broth rather than with too much, so it will be tasty and better. At the end, before serving it, put in a handful of beaten herbs. Serve it hot with its broth over it.

If you want to cook it with freshly shelled peas or beans, when the peas have been half cooked in a very good broth put the tench, whole or in bits, into a pot where the peas are and finish cooking the peas with the tench, adding in spices and beaten herbs. It can be done that way on either a meat day or a lean day. When a tench is not more than a pound or two at the most, you can also cook it in salted water. Serve it with oil, verjuice or vinegar, pepper and saffron over it. That dish is eaten by Peruggians.

---

[140] For the *carpina* and *reina* see Recipe 130, above.

[141.1] *grassi*: literally fat; here enlarged, presumably full of digesting matter.

[141.2] The translation of the last ingredient here is proposed very tentatively. Scappi has written *prugnoli*, a word that can designate either *Agaricus pruneolus*, agaric, the common field mushroom, which Scappi uses fairly often and calls the most delicate of all *fonghi* (II,215); or the fruit of a *Prunus spinosa*, a sloe or wild plum bush. In the present context a fruit seems appropriate, yet in all of Scappi's work it would be the only occasion in which he has used it. Furthermore, he himself, normally so cautious about clarity in his writing, must have been aware of the ambiguity this word presented if his optional ingredient here was, in fact, the fruit rather than the mushroom.

143. To fry, marinate and souse tench.

Get a tench that is not more than three pounds; scrape and clean it. Slit it along its back, leaving its viscera[143] in if it is male; but if it is a female, which is sometimes full of eggs, remove those eggs. Sprinkle a little salt on the tench and let it sit for a third of an hour. Clean the salt off fully, flour the tench and fry it. Serve it hot with orange juice, pepper and salt on it.

If you want to marinate it, have verjuice ready, or else white vinegar, and must syrup or else sugar, pepper, cinnamon, saffron and raisins, that mixture having been brought to a boil. When the tench has been fried, put it hot into an earthenware or wooden container with the boiling mixture over it. Let it sit there for two hours, then serve it hot or cold as you will. If you want to souse it, follow the directions for a salmon carp in Recipe 121.

144. To do up a tench in jelly.

Get a tench live without it having been scaled but only gutted, and its barbels and teeth removed because its teeth make it bitter. Wash it well, cut it up into slabs and put them into a pot with enough water, white wine and vinegar, the same amount of each, to cover them by a finger, and enough salt. Boil it gently. When it has been skimmed with a wooden spoon, put in pepper, cinnamon and saffron and finish off the cooking, but do not let the pieces disintegrate. Then put the tench into an earthenware or wooden container with its broth over it, and put that, with a few cleaned, slivered almonds in it, in a cool place to jell. When it has set you can serve it in pieces or whole, whichever you like.

In that same way you could do a carp without scaling it. But if you want the jelly clear – that is, transparent – of those two fish or any other in another way, the recipe is found in the book on jellies and sauces, Recipe 246 on fish jellies.[144]

145. To cook a tench's entrails.

Take the entrails[145] of a tench when there are no roe in them, which entrails are as good as any I have found, along with those of a grey mullet, particularly when they come out of a fresh fish. They are fried right away and served dressed with orange juice, pepper and salt. However, tench roe are not very common in preparations because they are extremely tiny; but when their membrane is not

---

[143] The first sentence of Recipe 145 makes it clear that for Scappi the word here, *budelle* (in the plural), normally 'bowels' or 'intestines,' includes all viscera, with any milt or roe that may be there.

[144] Scappi does not offer a book devoted to *geli e sapori*. However, a segment of Book II beginning with Recipe 239 bears a rubric identifying its subject as 'various jellies and sauces.' Recipe II,246 does indeed deal with a clarified fish jelly. See also the appended portion of Recipe VI,213 which for fish jelly similarly refers back to Recipe 246 'in the Book on Fish.'

[145] The word that Scappi uses here is *budelle*. Previously, in the recipe's title, the word is *interiori*, his general term for any and all internal organs.

broken, they can be boiled. You can make small pottages with them, and they can be fried the way they are done with roe from other fish.

146. The appearance and season of a pike.

A pike is a very well-known fish, long and round in shape; its mouth has a row of sharp teeth, especially the big fish. Those big ones are caught in various lakes, such as those of Peruggia, Bolsena and Vico. However, those that are caught in Lakes Maggiore and Como are bigger and are sometimes over one hundred and twenty pounds, Milanese weight. All are covered with greenish-grey scales and are shadowy over their full length. They are white under their belly. Their flesh is firm, particularly on their back. A pike's umbilicus is big and very delicate; it is the fattest part. I think, though, that when a pike is eight pounds or less it is best. In Mantua and Ferrara the ones caught in the Po are highly esteemed. When they are not more than half a pound they are called *zangarini*. Pike caught in rivers are much better than those caught in lakes or in swamps. The season for the big ones begins in September and lasts to the end of April; for the small ones, from May to the end of August.

147. To cook a pike plain and in other ways.

Get a pike that above all is fresh, because if it is not it is not too good or too healthy. If it is big, cut it into slabs without scaling it, wash it in several changes of water and put it into a tinned copper or earthenware pot with plain salted water. Cook it so it is tasty rather than insipid. When it is done, take its scales off so it is left white. Serve it either hot or cold, whichever you like, garnished with parsley and various flowers.

It is also cooked in wine, vinegar, water, salt and pepper, like a trout in Recipe 115. On a meat day it is cooked with pieces of prosciutto and a meat broth.

148. To cook pike in a pottage in the French fashion.

Get a pike, which in French is called *brucel*;[148.1] it should be alive and not more than ten pounds. Gut it without scaling it, and cut it up into medium-sized slabs. Have a casserole pot on hand with white wine, sugar and vinegar in it – that is, for every pound of wine, four ounces of sugar and two of vinegar – and enough salt; boil the pot. When it is boiling strongly, put the pieces of pike into it and keep it constantly shaken up with the pot handle so the pieces of pike move about in the wine. Add in fresh butter, ginger,[148.2] cinnamon and nutmeg, with pepper and cloves, everything ground together, and each in an amount determined by your taste. Stir this mixture several times until you see it beginning to thicken,

---

[148.1] The word is Scappi's approximation of the French *brochet*. He may have heard the word for a small pike, *brocherel*.

[148.2] An occasion for the use of ginger is rare in Scappi. That spice and, generally, the number of spices that are combined here, are rather typical of earlier French cooking.

always keeping a sprightly fire under it. Then take it immediately out of the pot, dish it up and serve it hot. You can put some muscatel raisins to cook with that. With the pike you can make all the pottages that are made with tench.

In the same way you can cook half-pound, descaled slabs of corb, and slabs of medium-sized carp and sea bass and large trout; however, with those fish and the ingredients for boiling, you have to put slices of toast and pieces of candied lime peel. You can also cook all of the above fish in wine, vinegar and sugar, and pieces of peeled quince, red apples, pitted dates, muscatel raisins, ordinary raisins, ground common spices and sweet almond oil or butter. Serve it with bread under it in the above way.

149. To spit-roast or grill a large pike.

Get a large pike, gut it through its mouth and stuff it with a mixture made up like the one with which a tench is stuffed and grilled in Recipe 140. Mount it lengthwise on a spit, fixing it onto the spit with canes on either side. Roast it over a low fire; do not baste it until the skin is no longer firm because it would swell out too much and you'd run the risk of it bursting open. When it is almost done, baste it with a pickle made of vinegar, must syrup, pepper, dry fennel and oil. When it is cooked, serve it whole like that or in pieces, as you like, with a little warm pickle over it.

You can also cook it on a grill after it is stuffed. If it is scraped, you can braise it in an oven the way a tench is done in Recipe 141. And if you want to cut it up into slabs and grill it, or braise it in an oven, or macerate it, follow the directions for a sturgeon in Recipe 11.

150. On frying a pike.

Get a pike and, if it is big, scale it, gut it and cut it crosswise into slabs one finger thick; if it is two or three pounds, split it along its back as a tench is done; if they are one pound or those very small ones that are called *ciangarini*,[150] leave them whole. All of them have to be scaled, though, and gutted. Take the pieces of a large pike and set them to macerate for two hours. Flour them and fry them in oil. The tail is split as is done with a tench. When they have fried, serve them hot with sautéed parsley over them. They can also be fried without having macerated. The medium-sized ones and the small ones can be done the same way. After they are fried, they can be soused and marinated. The small ones can be served with verjuice sauce over them.

151. To prepare bresaola and croquettes of pike flesh and cook them in several ways.

Take the back of a large, fresh pike that has been scaled, skinned and deboned; cut it lengthwise and make bresaola and croquettes of it. For cooking them follow

---

[150] In Recipe 146 spelled *zangarini* and described as being no more than half a pound in weight.

the directions given for a sturgeon in Recipe 15. With that flesh you can make thick soups, fishballs and pears the way they are done with a sturgeon in Recipes 5 and 13.[151]

152. Several ways to cook a semi-salted[152] pike belly.

Get the belly of a large pike when it is fresh and, without scaling it, set it in salt for three hours. Then cook it in water with a little salt so it stays tasty. When it is done, scale it and serve it garnished with a strong mustard sauce or a garlic sauce.

You can also cook it with fresh peas, and make all of the pottages that are made with sturgeon belly in Recipe 3. The same belly can be braised in an oven and grilled like the pieces of tuna belly in Recipe 36.

153. To prepare large sausages of pike flesh.

Get raw pike flesh, without scales, skin or bones; for every pound of it, also get four ounces of raw salted tuna belly that has soaked and is not too salty, and it, too, is without skin or bones. Beat both of those the way sausage meat is beaten, for every pound of that mixture adding in half an ounce of fennel seed, half an ounce of crushed pepper, half an ounce of wild thyme either dry and powdered or fresh and beaten, an ounce of oil, an ounce and a half of vinegar, two ounces of salted tuna belly from the biggest part, diced, two ounces of carrots from the darkest part, cooked in wine and diced,[153.1] and one ounce of shelled Milanese almonds; make up a mixture of all that. Have a little linen bag on hand, shaped like a large sausage, and fill it with that mixture in such a way that it is firm; tie it tightly. Give it a brief boiling[153.2] in red wine, then take it out and let it drain. Hang it in smoke for six hours. When you want to cook it, undo the little bag and cook it on a grill, coating it with oil. Then serve it hot, either cut into pieces or whole.

However, when you want to serve it just as soon as the bag is filled, and you have only just brought it to a boil in the wine, there is no need to smoke it.

You can do trout flesh and fresh tuna flesh that way, as well as sturgeon flesh. From that mixture, without the carrots and almonds, you can make *tommacelle*, cooking them like the sturgeon ones in Recipe 12.

---

[151] The 1581 typesetter changed this reference to *Cap. 5 et 8.* Pear-shaped balls are made of other fish paste also in Recipes 74 and 193.

[152] For another view of this process see Book I, §9.

[153.1] Elsewhere (Recipes 240 and 246) this darker portion of a carrot has been used to give a preparation a peacock-blue colour.

[153.2] Literally, 'bring it to three boilings.'

154. To cook pike entrails.

In a pike I think only two of the viscera are good: the roe and the liver, popularly called *milza*,[154] because it is long; it has a very big gallbladder attached to it, which is removed. The liver is floured and fried. It is served with orange juice and pepper over it. The roe is cooked the same way when the upper membrane is not broken. Also, after they have been in a vessel with a little oil, salt, ground fennel and pepper, they can be grilled or cooked on heavy paper under hot ash. They are served hot with orange juice over them.

When the pike has milt, the intestines can be done up in a pottage after they have been thoroughly cleaned and washed, the way the milt and intestines of a sea bass are done. And along with those intestines you can cook the liver and the roe.

155. The appearance and season of an eel.

An eel is a round, slimy fish, longer than a lamprey; it has two fins near its gills. It is of a dark colour, whitish under its belly. It has only one bone, which runs inside from its head down to its tail. It is caught in lakes and marshes more than in running waters, and is the opposite of all other freshwater fish because, when rivers are in spate, they go into the sea and feed there and some of them die there: you can see the truth of that for yourself because in the city of Comacchio, which is surrounded by salt marshes, they catch a great number of them, and those are the best of any place in Lombardy; salted ones are carried throughout Italy. The large ones, which have a flat head, are called *miglioramenti*, and the smaller ones, *buratesti*. In Rome the best ones are from Lake Bolsena, as well as the tiny ones that are caught in springtime in the Tiber and that are whiter. However, the proper season for large eels is from October through to Feburary. That fish is heavier than any other, which can be seen by the fact that eels are always on the bottom, whether alive or dead.

156. To spit-roast eels.

Get a large eel, skin it, gut it and cut it in rounds. So that it is tastier, set it in a vessel containing a little oil, salt and dry fennel flour. Mount those round pieces on a spit, separating them with bay or sage leaves, and cook them over a low fire. When they are almost done, sprinkle them with a mixture of flour, grated bread, sugar and cinnamon until that forms a pretty crust. There will be no need to baste them because they are greasy in themselves. They are served hot with orange juice over them.

157. To braise and grill eels.

Get an eel and, having first skinned it, cut it up into big pieces – that is, round slabs; small eels are wound around like *ciambelle*. Put the slabs into a tourte pan containing oil, salt and fennel seed; braise them with fire below and above for half

---

[154] This word normally designates the spleen.

a quarter of an hour. Pour off the excess oil, adding in a little white wine, must syrup, verjuice, pepper, cinnamon, cloves, and prunes and dried visciola cherries that have soaked in cool water; finish off cooking the pieces of eel. When they are done, serve them dressed with the same sauce. They can also be braised with beaten spring onions. When they are braised plain, by themselves, they can be done up with a lamprey sauce the way a lamprey is done in Recipe 92.

If you want to grill them, skewer the pieces of a large eel and only heat them thoroughly in boiling oil; it is optional whether you flour them first so they do not stick. Cook[157] them over a low fire, basting them with a pickle made from vinegar, must syrup and salt. When they are done, serve them garnished with cooked raisins along with the above pickle.

There is no need to parboil the small ones in oil, nor to flour them, but only to cook them in the shape of *ciambelle*. Serve them with orange juice and pepper over them. If you do not want to skin them, remove their sliminess with hot water before cooking them.

158. To cook large eels inside out in wine.

Skin the eel, divide it in two along the back ridge the way a tench is split, taking out its bone and gutting it, and let the two halves sit coated with a little salt and pepper for half a quarter-hour. Roll up each of these halves into a wheel, leaving the back outward; stick two slender canes through them, or else tie them with a bit of string. Put them into a casserole pot with red wine, vinegar, sugar, pepper and cinnamon; boil it. When they are cooked remove them, and serve them hot or cold, whichever you like, with a sweet mustard sauce over them. However, if you want to cover them with a lamprey sauce made of almonds, raisins, sugar, *mostaccioli* and spicing,[158.1] do not let them cook fully in the wine but take them out, drain them and untie them. Put them into a pot where there is enough sweet oil to cover them, and sauté them slowly in the way set out in Recipe 92. When they have been sautéed, pour off the excess oil, leaving the thick part of it that is on the bottom. Put the sauce, which should not be too thick, into that and bring it to a boil with the eel. Serve it hot, sprinkled over top with sugar and cinnamon. You can also take it out of the oil after it has been sautéed, having cooked the sauce in another pot, and serve it in dishes with that sauce over top.

Additionally, you can do it differently so it looks really like a lamprey: skin it, split it lengthwise, carefully remove its spine, then put the halves back together again with a few stitches of thread, and wind it around. Leave it for two hours in a mixture of vinegar and wine in equal amounts, sugar, pepper, cinnamon, cloves and nutmeg – which is done so that the eel will firm up and take on the colour of a lamprey; and do not fail to put half a nutmeg into that eel's mouth, and to stick a

---

[157] That is, 'on a grill.'

[158.1] In the lamprey sauce of Recipe 92 the spices include pepper, cinnamon, cloves and nutmeg.

few whole cloves into its head. After it has steeped the above length of time, take it out and half cook it snugly in a pot[158.2] with enough olive oil to cover it. Then pour off the excess oil, leaving the thicker dregs. Then make up a seasoning with roasted almonds, raisins ground in a mortar, and that mixture in which it soaked. Finish off cooking it in that seasoning. You can also do it without skinning it. If it is skinned and its spine removed, turn it around in its skin and cook it with the skin as above.

159. To fry, souse, put into a verjuice sauce and marinate large, medium and small eels.

If the eel is large, skin it and cut it into round slabs two fingers thick and cut the rounds open, removing the spine. Set them to macerate for two hours. Flour them and fry them. Serve them hot with orange juice and sugar over them.

Cut apart into up to four pieces they can also be fried, without having macerated. After being fried they can be soused, marinated and put in verjuice as is directed for a small pike or a medium-sized eel. It is enough for a small eel to be cleaned in hot water, cut into pieces and fried as above.

160. To prepare stuffed mock eels,[160.1] cooked in several ways.

Get a large, fresh eel and skin it, minding that the umbilicus is not broken – rather leaving a little flesh[160.2] around it – and leaving the head as well as a finger-width of the tail attached to the skin. Take the eel's flesh without the spine and beat it like sausage meat; to every pound of that flesh add four ounces of salted eel flesh or else salted, fat tuna belly that has soaked, and make up the same mixture as is made in Recipe 153 for the pike sausage. Stuff the eel's skin and cook it on a grill or in red wine, or fry it as above.

161. To fry fingerlings.

In the Milan fish market I have seen various sorts of small little fish, where they are called *marscioni*, and in Milan *bottuli*, too, and by other people *guselletti* and *lucide*, that are tiny with a white underbelly and speckles by their gills like lampreys. Tiny black lampreys are often mixed in with them. Between January and the end of March they can be found in great numbers, and likewise crayfish[161.1] that have shed their shell[161.2] – that is, tender, like tender crabs in Rome; and

---

[158.2] *facciasi meza cuocere in un vaso stretto*: Scappi's notion is that the pot not be so big as to let the eel unwind.

[160.1] The qualification in this rubric, *anguille finte*, points to the clever way in which the cook will restore the cooked, stuffed eel to an apparently life-like state.

[160.2] Most of the eel's flesh is about to be removed and mashed.

[161.1] Scappi will later distinguish between sea crayfish (*gambaro marittimo*, i.e., lobster) and freshwater crayfish (*gambaro d'acqua dolce*).

[161.2] Scappi's term here is *mutati*, literally 'moulted.' See Recipes 169 and 176.

from April through to June there are huge numbers of them. They are floured and fried, and served like smelt and sardines.

[Frogs, turtles]

162. The appearance and season of a frog.[162.1]

A frog is a little animal with four legs and no tail, green and yellow in colour and white under its belly. They are born in freshwater and swamps, and they make a variety of cries. Everywhere in Italy there is an abundance of them, though many more in Lombardy than elsewhere, and most of all around Bologna; there they are transported on carts in sacks. That little animal has a big liver with which you can make a fritter. Its season begins in May and lasts to the end of October because that's the season of the verjuice grape: while the verjuice grape lasts, frogs are good.[162.2]

163. To fry frogs and do them in verjuice sauce.

Cut off a frog's head – which has a big mouth – and cut away, too, the tips of its feet up to the first joint. Steep it in freshwater for eight hours, changing the water – that is done to clean them out, to make them swell up and whiten them. Take them out of the water. For frying, arrange their legs under them; or else cut the thighs away from the backbone, taking the bone out of the leg; flour them and fry them in oil. Serve them hot with a little ground salt over them. Above all, when they are fried do not cover them, or keep them after they have been fried, because they will harden and get woody and lose their goodness. You can also fry parboiled garlic cloves and parsley with them, and dress them with that garlic and parsley, along with pepper and ground salt. That was how Pope Pius IV, of blessed memory, used to eat them in 1564 when I was serving him.

After they have been fried plain and only floured, they can be kept, warm from the pan, in a verjuice sauce made of new verjuice and egg yolks, as is set out in the recipe for it.[163.1] They can be served hot or cold as you like. Also after being fried they can be served with garnishes, in dishes or over top of them, made of fennel tips, basil, garlic cloves, breadcrumb soaked in verjuice, salt and pepper. They can also be covered with garlic sauce, or walnut sauce made in the Milanese way.[163.2]

[162.1] 'Frogs are another Italian viand which we in England eat not. These they usually fry and serve up with oil. At Venice they eat only the loins and hind-legs, as also at Florence, and that upon fish-days. In some places of Lombardy they eat their whole bodies, and besides their frogs are of a larger size than ordinary. Their flesh shews white and lovely as they lie in the markets skinn'd, and ready prepared to be fried' (Ray, *Travels*, vol. 1, February 1664, 347).

[162.2] *mentre dura l'agresto le rane son buone*: Scappi's dictum has a proverbial ring to it.

[163.1] This *agrestata* is found in Recipes II,273 and VI,198.

[163.2] Directions for a walnut sauce (*nosella*) are in Recipe II,258, although it is not qualified there as 'Milanese.'

164. To prepare a thick soup of boneless frogs.

Take the frogs after they have steeped and bring them to a boil in plain water; remove them from the hot water and put them into cold. Take the flesh from the thighs and put it into a casserole pot which has butter or oil in it, and sauté that flesh with a little beaten spring onion, adding in a little of the plain water in which the frogs cooked, gooseberries or verjuice grapes, and mild spices with a little saffron; at the end, add a little beaten herbs as well. When it is cooked, serve it hot. If you do not want to put in spring onions, use ground almonds or grated bread to thicken the broth. You can do it the same way if the bone is left in the legs.

165. The appearance and season of a sea turtle.[165.1]

A sea turtle is much larger than a tortoise,[165.2] and is of such a size that small wheels are made from its shell. It has the same markings, made up of squares, as the land variety. It has a singular[165.3] smell to it. Its season begins in the spring and lasts throughout the fall. Sometimes the size of some of them brought into Rome is such that a porter can barely carry one.

166. Several ways to cook a sea turtle.

Take the turtle, cut off its head and carefully remove the meat from the shell, watching out that you do not break the eggs or the gallbladder which is attached to the liver. The eggs that have a shell are cleaned, and the other eggs are removed from the viscera. Both sorts will be fried: the ones that have a shell will be made into omelets mixed with herbs, but the others will be fried the way a tortoise's eggs are done. The meat has to be parboiled before it is fried, although if you want to make it into a pottage raw, cut it up and put it into a pot with beaten onions, oil, vinegar, wine, water, salt and a lot of spices, which will remove its bad smell. The liver is fried the way a calf's liver is done.

Of its flesh and its liver you can also make various pastry dishes, as is said in the book on pastries.[166]

167. The appearance and season of a tortoise and a freshwater turtle.

There are various species of turtle: tortoises and freshwater turtles. The best, though, are the tortoises, because freshwater turtles are black and have a tail; the

---

[165.1] 'Land tortoises are accounted with [Italians] a better meat than sea-tortoises, and are commonly to be sold in the markets. They are eaten by those orders of friars whose rule obliges them to abstain from flesh, as Carthusians, Carmelites, &c.' (Ray, *Travels*, vol. 1, 346).

[165.2] For a more extensive comparison see Recipe 167. Scappi deals with three varieties of *tartaruga*, each qualified according to its habitat: the sea turtle, the freshwater turtle and the land tortoise.

[165.3] Scappi's descriptive word is *extravagante*.

[166] Recipe V,180.

ones that are caught in the country around Rome are marked on their back with squares like a chessboard and have only a stump of a pointed tail. Of both of those varieties the female is always better than the male. To distinguish which is which, you have to know that the male has a convex belly while the female's is high and smooth; moreover, females are much heavier than males. The season for the females begins in February and lasts to the end of May because during that time they are usually full of eggs; for males it begins in June and lasts throughout the fall.

168. Various ways to cook turtles.[168.1]

Get a female turtle, which is always better than a male as I said above, just as the one that is freshly caught is better than the one that has been shut away at home. Cut off its head and let the blood drain out. If you want to remove it raw from its shell, that's your choice; however, I have found it better to kill it in a pot of salted water which is slowly heated until it boils, keeping it covered so the turtle cannot get out: as it struggles it will tenderize. When it is dead, let it continue to boil until it is tender. If you want to know when it is cooked, touch its feet: if they feel tender, it is done. Remove it from the hot water and cool it in cold water. Take it out of its shell; separate its eggs from its liver because those eggs have a shell like a wood pigeon's; use great care in removing the gallbladder from the liver because it is enclosed in the highest place of the liver and can hardly be seen.

The eggs with shells are fried together with the liver, and served dressed with sautéed parsley, orange juice, salt and pepper. You can also fry the meat the same way, and all of it can be covered with various sauces. Of the meat you can make pottages and other dishes that are mentioned in Recipe 166 for a sea turtle. However, from all the ways I have tried there is no better or suitable cooking for a turtle than frying it as above.

You can also make pastry dishes with it, as is said in the Book on Pastry.[168.2]

[Crustaceans and molluscs]

169. On bloodless fish.

Having, up to this point, spoken of various fish and, among others, of three that have no blood, I do not want leave out speaking of many other species that are bloodless, beginning with a lobster;[169.1] in Rome and in Venice it is called a

---

[168.1] This recipe would seem to consist of treatments applicable jointly to tortoises and fresh-water turtles.

[168.2] Recipe V,180.

[169.1] Scappi uses the same generic term, *gambaro,* for a lobster (*gambaro grosso marittimo,* a large saltwater crayfish), dealt with here and in the following recipes, and for a (freshwater) cray-fish (*gambaro d'acqua dolce*), to be taken up in Recipes 176 ff., below.

'lion crayfish' and a common lobster.[169.2] There are two sorts of this lobster, one larger than the other, both smooth and both with the right leg[169.3] bigger than the left. The smaller is speckled with blue, greenish-grey and black markings. Both have the same season: from October to the end of April. Another lobster follows closely on that one and is called a spiny lobster,[169.4] but it is somewhat smaller and on its back from the middle forward it has sharp spines; it has a smooth tail, and two spurs that point forward with two long, round tails that project from its front part. The female has a larger breast and tail than the male. Those lobsters do not have the big claws a 'lion' lobster has. The body of a spiny lobster is russet-coloured and hard, with sharp spines; the male likewise. It has the same season as the 'lion' lobster. In the spring spiny lobsters are found that have shed their shell.

170. Several ways to cook the above lobsters.

Take the lobsters and on each one stop up the hole in its tail.[170] Put them into a pot containing salted water, or else wine, pepper, vinegar and salt. If a spiny lobster has eggs in it, it has to be washed well because it is often full of sand. When they are cooked, shell their tail and claws, taking out a little nerve that they have in the middle of their tail. Serve them with pepper, vinegar, sweet oil and salt over them.

171. Another way to cook those lobsters.

Take the flesh from the tail and claws of the lobsters after they have been cooked in one of the above ways, cut it up into little pieces and make a pottage of it with oil, herbs, spicing and a not-too-salty broth of some other fish. In the spring add in gooseberries.

You can also do it another way: after the flesh is cut up, sauté it in oil with beaten spring onions. Add in water, wine, verjuice and salt and enough spicing; finish off cooking it. At the end, before serving, put in a handful of beaten herbs. Serve it hot, dressed with mild spices.

172. To prepare a thick soup of the flesh of those lobsters.

A spiny lobster will always be better than the other two lobsters.[172] Get a spiny lobster's flesh after it has been cooked in wine or water; beat it small with

---

[169.2] These alternative designations are respectively *gambaro Lione* and *astrisi.* The modern Italian *astice* is scientifically an *Homarus vulgaris*, a common lobster.

[169.3] *la gamba destra.* Later in the recipe Scappi will write *branche* for the lobster's claws.

[169.4] *locusta*, the French *langouste*.

[170] See Recipe 180, below, for the reason for that precautionary step.

[172] Recipe 169 examines different varieties of Scappi's saltwater crayfish. The present recipe deals with a *locusta*.

knives and, after that, sauté it in oil or butter, adding in a little fish broth. In the spring put in gooseberries; in summer, verjuice grapes; in winter, raisins. After it has boiled for a quarter of an hour, thicken it with egg yolks the way you do with thick meat-paste soups. On fasting days use ground almonds or grated bread rather than eggs. You can thicken all the above pottages the same way.

173. To prepare *tommacelle*, fishballs and pears from those lobsters' flesh.

Get the flesh from the tail and claws of the lobsters and, raw, beat it small. For every pound of it, put in three ounces of boneless, salted eel flesh, along with common spices, raisins, a little sugar, oil or butter, beaten mint, sweet marjoram and wild thyme. With this mixture make up *tommacelle*, pears and fishballs they way they are done with sturgeon flesh in Recipes 12 and 13. Cook them the same way.

174. To fry the flesh of those lobsters.

Get the flesh after the lobsters have been boiled, cut it up into finger-sized pieces, rinse them in water, flour them and fry them in oil or clarified butter. Serve them dressed with sautéed parsley, orange juice, pepper and salt. After they have been fried they can also be served dressed with garlic sauce, green sauce[174] or some other sauce.

175. To cook stuffed spiny lobsters.

Get a spiny lobster, which is the best and tenderest of all lobsters,[175.1] as I said above.[175.2] Boil it in salted water. Take out its tail flesh and clean its body, leaving the shell whole. Beat the flesh small and make up a mixture like the one for the *tommacelle*. Alternatively with that beaten flesh, grated cheese, eggs and herbs. Stuff the shell with that mixture.

If there are two lobsters,[175.3] encase the stuffed shell in the empty one, bind them and fry that in oil or butter. When it is cooked, serve it hot with garnishes in dishes. You can cook it also on a grill. However, if there is just a single spiny lobster, set aside the belly which has been taken out of its shell. When the shell is stuffed, you cleverly put the belly back in its place, placing a small slice of bread at the front, tying it with a cord so the belly cannot slip out into the mixture. Cook it on the grill. Serve it as above, having undone the cord.

---

[174] A very common sauce, used already above in Recipes 21, 29, 50, 73, 75 and as often in the remainder of Book III. Directions for it are given in Recipes II,272 and VI,197.

[175.1] Here Scappi uses what in Recipe 169 he has called a Venetian term, *astrice*.

[175.2] Recipe 172.

[175.3] That is, if you use the flesh from two lobsters and stuff only one of them.

176. The appearance and season of the freshwater crayfish.

A freshwater crayfish is quite well known. In some places in Italy they are very large, in Milan particularly so, and also in the country around Brescia and Verona. In the River Sile that flows by Treviso, though, and throughout the whole of that region, they are much larger than any others; on occasion I have weighed some at half a pound. Despite that, the ones caught in Ponte Salaro near Rome are very good though they are not of the size I spoke of. Some species can be had that do not change colour in cooking, becoming russet-coloured as is generally the case; some become whiter, others darker. I cannot explain just why there is such diversity among them, but I'm certain that the ones I mentioned from the River Sile and the Milan canal and Ponte Salare are the best of every other sort. All crayfish, male and female, have eight small feet and two big ones. The female has a broader tail and breast than the male, and a small channel in its breast which is narrower in the male and is covered with certain hairy little tentacles. For the male the season begins in May and lasts through August; for the female, from September through April. Both, however, are better at a full moon than with no moon. Sometimes in the fall they shed their shell,[176] as you can see in Milan fish market where they corner the market on them as they do in Rome with tender crabs.

177. Several ways to cook freshwater crayfish.

In my opinion a crayfish is much better cooked in water, salt, wine, vinegar and pepper, and vigorously rather than stewed slowly as for a broth, and they have to be cooked rapidly, letting them skim themselves in the boiling, and turning them in a casserole pot. When they have boiled for a quarter of an hour and have become seasoned, take them out and serve them, hot or cold, whichever you wish and however they are served at the sideboard,[177.1] with vinegar and pepper in dishes.

With the tail and claws of a crayfish you can make all the pottages and dishes that are made with the 'lion' lobsters[177.2] and spiny lobsters above, even though in the spring and fall their tail and claws make a broth turn yellow. When you make a broth of them it should be tasty, and should have the flavour of the crayfish.

---

[176] In Recipe 161 Scappi calls these *gambari mutati, cioè teneri*, 'crayfish that are moulted – that is, tender.'

[177.1] Scappi intends this preparation for presentation among the simpler, often cold, foods available from the dining hall's *credenza*. In former days this *credenza* functioned in the original, etymological sense as a 'proving' table, where food from the kitchen was set out and tested for anything suspicious or harmful before being served to the master, his family and guests. See the note in Book I, §45 where *la credenza* is, in fact, such an assay.

[177.2] Recipes 170–75. Scappi has written here *gambari lioni*, literally 'lion crayfish,' a Roman designation of large saltwater crayfish according to Recipe 169.

Grind the body in a mortar, moistening it with warm water. Put it through a filter and take that water, which will be russety in colour and flavourful, and with that make the pottage by whatever is the easiest way.

You can also stuff the shell the way a spiny lobster is done in Recipe 175, and fry the tail and with it make all the dishes that are made with 'lion' lobsters and spiny lobsters, taking out that little nerve they have along their tail.

178. The appearance and season of a prawn.[178]

A prawn is a saltwater crayfish that has a large tail and few tentacles; it has certain small, very slight horns on its front, and its tail is divided on each side with a jointed, hairy shell. That sort of crayfish has a lot of flesh and is very good, particularly in its season, from February through May, although in Rome they can be found at just about any time. It needs to be cooked in seawater, though they are also good when they are done like freshwater crayfish. With their flesh you do all the dishes that are done with the flesh of the freshwater crayfish.

179. The appearance and season of squill fish[179.1] and saltwater shrimp.[179.2]

Squill fish are small saltwater shrimp; I think they got that name from the way they jump when they are touched. They are greenish-grey in colour, and more fleshy and better than shrimp, though they share the same season with those crayfish. Such little creatures need rather to be fried in oil than done up in some other preparation. Shrimp are smaller, are more shiny and have a tougher shell; when alive they leap into the air and at night they shine like candles. Those little creatures have a lot of hairs; at times they are full of eggs. Their season begins in November and goes to the end of April. Being found in places where there is seawater, they are cooked in that same water with fennel seed and pepper; alternatively, in freshwater and salt. When the shell is removed from the tails of squill fish and shrimp, you can make all the *pottaggetti* with them that you do with freshwater crayfish.

In Venice I've seen a smaller sort of crayfish, called *gambarucci* in Rome and *biava* by many cooks. Because they are so small, in terms of weight a thousand of them barely amount to a pound; and the same with the freshwater ones. Both sorts are fried because they are not good in any other preparation. They have the same season as the others.

180. The appearance and season of a hermit crab.

A hermit crab has a round shape and is covered with a rough shell; its front part has two sharp pincers.[180.1] All species of crab have little tail, although this

---

[178] This *spannocchia*, *Penæus kerathurus*, is *canocchia* and *mazzancolla* in modern Italian and *caramote* in French.

[179.1] *squille*: *Squillidæ*.

[179.2] *gambaretti di mare*, literally 'small crayfish.'

[180.1] The word here is *spine*, quills.

one has a slightly longer one and the female has a longer one than the male. They produce their eggs under their tail; those are russet in colour. In Venice they are called *granchievoli*. People often make looking-glass ornaments out of their shells. They have round, rough legs with several joints; the end of their feet is forked. A lot of them are caught off the shores of Anchona and Senigallia.[180.2] The males are at their best in their season, with a full moon, between October and the end of April; females, between May and the end of August. That crab is cooked like a 'lion' lobster or spiny lobster, having its tail hole and mouth first stopped up with cotton wadding: that is done because when they boil they would fill with water and not taste as good. They are served hot or cold, whichever you like. They do not have big legs but, as I said, very slender, split feet. Their goodness lies in their viscera rather than in their flesh.

181. To braise hermit crabs.

Take a crab and either open it raw or else bring it to a boil in hot salted water – stopping up its mouth and body before putting it into the water. Get marrow from four of those crabs to stuff a single one, mixing into it pepper, cinnamon, sugar, raisins and beaten herbs; if you want to add in egg yolks and grated cheese, they are optional. Stuff the shells with that, then braise them in a baking dish containing butter, with more heat on top than beneath. Then serve them hot, dressed with orange juice and pepper.

182. The appearance and season of various sorts of crabs.

There are various sorts of crabs. Three sorts are brought into Rome: the first is marsh crabs; the second is hog crabs, which are larger and much darker, and have rather big legs and a round body like the marsh ones; and the third sort is tender crabs – that is, those that have shed their shell. Two sorts are caught in the canals in Venice: they are called *molecche*, which are like the shell-less crabs, and *macinette*, which are very tiny; some are caught that have a big, hard shell. All the hard-shelled ones share the same season, beginning in October and going through May; the *molecche*, though, and the shell-less ones begin in April and go to the end of May, and occasionally you can find some in Rome through to the end of September.

The hard-shelled ones are cooked in wine like crayfish; in Rome, though, they are cooked mostly on the coals. The tender ones are fried in oil and butter. You can make pottages with them as you do with common crayfish tails in Recipe 177. Various pastry dishes are made of them, as is said in the Book on Pastry.[182]

[180.2] Spelled *Sinigaglia*: located just to the north of Ancona.

[182] Recipes V,182 and 206 are for tender (i.e., shell-less) crabs alone.

183. The appearance and season of oysters.

An oyster in Corsica and on the beaches of Ancona and of Chiozza is quite well known by those two seas because there are more of them there than anywhere else. Happening to be in the port of Brondoli near Chiozza, I saw a large number of them gathered in; they are much whiter than the Corsican ones but also much smaller. Those from Corsica are sometimes brought to Rome in not too fresh a state. When I was in Pesaro I saw a vessel accidentally run aground and turn upside down, and a great number of oysters were stuck on its bottom. According to fishermen, the sea current in which oysters breed travels from place to place. Sometimes they attach themselves to one another, more than six of them together. Their season goes from December to the end of April, though it does happen that in Venice you can find them for almost the whole year.

184. To cook oysters on a grill, in an oven and in other ways.

Get a fresh oyster, wash it, taking off the dirt and sand on them. Note that if you can detach them from one another, those that are attached are the better ones. Put them on a grill and cook them. When they are done, take off the first shell and cut them away from the other shell with a small knife. Serve them hot, dressed with the water they have in them and orange juice and pepper. The same procedure is followed with any you cook in an oven, which is done when you have a good number of them. To do them more quickly, they are also cooked in a meat broth or water, and are served in the above way. Be very careful, though, not to overcook them because they will get tough and will lose their goodness.

185. Another way to cook oysters.

Put the oysters on a grill and, as they begin to open up,[185.1] take them off immediately and collect the water that is in them, which is their goodness. Scoop the oysters whole out of their shell, cutting away the muscle, which is tough, and taking the whiter part. Grind the darker part, which looks like tiny tripe, in a mortar with spinach tips, moistening that with the water taken from the oysters and adding in orange juice and pepper. Set the whiter part in a casserole pot to sauté in a little oil or butter. When it is done, add in the part that was ground in the mortar. Then get the oyster shell – that is, the deeper one – clean it thoroughly inside and out, and boil it in hot water: that is done so the oysters will stay warm. As soon as the shells are taken out of the water, they are set out on a dishwarmer,[185.2] or else in a dish containing hot coals. Into those shells put the whiter, sautéed part of the oysters along with their sauce, dividing them up among the shells so that each one gets four of them. If you do not want to put them on the shells, serve them in dishes on thin slices of bread.

[185.1] Scappi's verb is *fiatare*, 'to breathe.'

[185.2] See the *schalda vivande con le sue piastrele* in Plate 17, and also Recipe 7, above.

They can also be served each in its own shell. When the oysters have been scooped out of the shells, sauté them in butter and serve them dressed with their own juice, along with orange juice and pepper.

186. To braise oysters.

Take an oyster that is barely warm, and scoop it from its shell, with its juice. Have a frying pan ready with butter or a sweet oil in it, a small bud of garlic, beaten mint and sweet marjoram, pepper and cinnamon. Put the oyster into the pan, adding in its water, filtered, and a little malmsey and verjuice. Cook it in an oven or braise it under a cooking bell like a tourte. Serve them hot on slices of bread.

187. To grill oysters with paper.

Take an oyster scooped from its shell as above and set its juice aside. Have writing paper ready that is greased with oil or butter and, after the oyster has sat for a quarter of an hour in oil with fennel flour and pepper, put it on the paper with a little oil over it, or some other liquid. Cook it, having put the paper with that oyster on a grill, turning it over on the paper. When they are done, serve them dressed with a sauce made of sugar, orange juice, pepper and the oyster's juice. It is optional whether you put some thin slices of bread under them.

188. To cook oysters [available] in a seasoning.

Oysters are brought into Rome from Corsica in a seasoning because, as I said before, they are rarely transported fresh. Those oysters are floured and fried, and served with orange juice and sugar over them. With them you can make all the dishes that are made with fresh oysters. If they are too salty, let them steep in warm water.

189. To fry oysters.

Get a shelled oyster, flour it and fry it in olive oil. Serve it with orange juice and pepper over it, or else with a sauce made up as in Recipe 187. After it has fried you can cover it with green sauce or any other sauce. You can do pastry dishes with it as is said in the Book on Pastry.[189]

190. The appearance and season of various clams and cockles.[190.1]

The clams that are popularly called St. James clams are much bigger than Roman cockles. Both of them have certain tiny ducts;[190.2] their outer surface is shaped like a shell. Both have the same season, from October throughout April.

---

[189] Recipes V,184 and 207.

[190.1] Cockles: *gongole*, modern Italian *vongole*; scientifically, *Cardium edule*. The clams of this first recipe are *cappe di san Iacomo*.

[190.2] *hanno certi canalletti*: Scappi's meaning is not clear.

On the shores and in the ports of Genoa and in various other places, large numbers of them are found. All of them are prepared in the same dishes as oysters when they are bigger. The cockles that come into Rome, however, are taken for the most part in Porto. They are cooked on a shovel, or else they are made into a thick broth[190.3] with or without their shells, as is done with telleens.[190.4] I think, though, that they are much tastier cooked with a net – that is, if they are put into a little string bag – but above all they have to be fresh and clean. Then get a squat earthenware or copper pot full of boiling water with salt and pepper, and dunk the net with the cockles in it two or three times until they show signs of opening. Serve them hot with pepper on them.

In that same way, too, you cook the ones caught in the Adriatic Sea that are called clams.

191. The appearance and season of razor clams.

Razor clams are of two sorts: white and black. In some places they are called *spoletti*.[191] They are covered with a smooth rippled shell half a palm's width, more or less, in length, depending on their size. They look like a small reed and in that reed is the clam which is long rather like a ligament. A large number of them are caught in the port of Cività Vecchia, and near Chiozza, too; few are brought to Rome, though. They are caught with an iron fork, but those caught in a net are better because they are not so full of sand. They are tougher than a cockle. Their season begins in October and goes to the end of April.

192. Several ways to cook razor clams.

Get razor clams that are alive, because otherwise they are worthless, and let them steep for two hours in saltwater or salted freshwater that is slightly warm: you do that to get the sand out of them. Take them out of the water, coat them in oil and cook them on a grill. When they have opened fully, bathe them in oil mixed with orange juice and pepper. Serve them hot.

If you want them in a pottage, bring them to a boil; alternatively, when they are half cooked on the grill remove them from their shell and make a pottage of them. Braise them the way oysters are done in Recipe 186.

They can also be fried after they are taken out of their shell. Those are served garnished with sautéed parsley and orange juice, or else dressed with a variety of garnishes. And you can make a variety of pastry dishes with them, as is said in the book on pastries.[192]

[190.3] Scappi's term is *brodetto*, nowadays generically a fish preparation. In the present recipe a reasonable translation of the word might be 'chowder.'

[190.4] See Recipe 193, below.

[191] A *spoletto* is a bobbin or a weaver's shuttle. This regional name for the clam is likely suggested by its shape.

[192] Recipe V,207.

193. The appearance and season of limpets, *poveraccie*,[193.1] telleen clams and mussels.

Limpets are little creatures covered with a single shell, and when they feel heat they come away easily from their shell. On the outside they are rough and on the inside a violet colour; their flesh is very tasty. They are cooked on a grill and braised the way oysters are cooked and braised in Recipe 186. *Poveraccie* are smoother and tend to a violet colour; their flesh is very tasty. They are cooked on a grill and in all the ways the mussels are done in Recipe 190. In some places telleens are called *calcinelli*[193.2] because they are white. When telleens are fresh their flesh is very tasty. They are cooked in all the same ways as *poveraccie* are done. Mussels are not brought to Rome. In Genoa they are very numerous, resembling telleens but with the violet colour of a *poveraccia*. They are cooked like cockles. Along with those there are many other little shell creatures about which I could go on at great length. All of them have the same season: from October to the end of April; in Rome, however, they are found practically year round, except for mussels.

194. To cook telleens with or without their shell.

Get telleens that have been thoroughly cleaned of any sand, and merely braise them in hot water until they can be dug out with the tip of a knife: if they are taken out raw, the prepared dish will be more savoury but will taste more of sand. For that reason they are taken out of their shell, as I said, and are put into a casserole pot or some other vessel with oil and beaten fine herbs, pepper, cinnamon and saffron, with a little verjuice and water. Boil them. When they have come to a boil, serve them in dishes on slices of bread.

If you want them with their shell, though, after they have been cleaned of sand they are put into a pot – of copper rather than iron, and earthenware would be much better for that purpose. Along with the telleens, put in oil, white wine, a little water, pepper, cinnamon, saffron, beaten fine herbs and enough salt; there should be enough of everything to cover them. Bring them to a boil; as soon as the telleens have opened you will know they are cooked. Serve them hot on slices of bread in dishes.

In that same way you can do *poveraccie* and mussels, and the *ballari* from Ancona which are a species of sea snail.[194]

[193.1] *poveraccie*: striped Venus. The word is typeset as *peverazza* and *peverazze* in this recipe, as *paverazze* in Recipes 194 and V,207, and as *poverazze* in Recipe V,185. Modern Italian (singular) is *poveraccia*. Bearing the scientific name *Venus gallina*, this mollusc is a variety of mussel.

[193.2] This regional name (scientifically, *Donax*) for a particular variety of *tellina* translates into English as wedge shell.

[194] The precise identity of these creatures remains unknown. From other evidence the *Dizionario etimologico italiano* of Battisti and Alessio suggests they are a phosphorescent fish, an unlikely

195. The appearance and season of a sea urchin.

A sea urchin is a little creature, round in shape and the size of a Florentine ball,[195.1] spiny like a hedgehog[195.2] which goes after chestnuts, and black in colour. In its middle it has a round mouth covered with dense hair. The only good thing in it is its marrow, which is yellowish. When it is clean the little creature is cooked on a grill with a little oil and pepper in its mouth. When it is done it is served hot. You can also stuff it with various mixtures after it has been cleaned as above; then grill it or braise it, whichever you wish. Its season goes from January through April.

196. The appearance and season of snails – that is, sea snails.

There are two sorts of snail but only two are usually eaten. Both have four round horns with a tiny ball on top; they are slimy, have no eyes and leave behind a trail wherever they go. Both have a screw-shaped shell; one is bigger than the other, the bigger ones being of a rusty colour for the most part, although some of them are white. They are gathered twice a year, in the fall and spring, and are kept during the whole summer when they have been purged. The smaller ones are gathered from July through the fall on vine leaves and other vegetation. Just as soon as they have been picked up, you make a pottage of them following the directions in Recipe 200.

197. To purge and keep snails.

Get large snails between February and the end of May, and between August and mid-October, during which time the air is temperate. Purging them, though, cannot be done until after the month of July. At that time put them into a good-sized, damp room where there are faggots or branches from bushes or briars, and let them go where they want, cleaning the room frequently of their excrement because any stench will kill them. When they have spent the month of November in that room, finding themselves closed up there they will be purged.[197] Then they are put into barrels or other containers and kept in a cold place the whole winter. You also find them, purged, on old walls in the country and in various other slimy places.

198. Various ways to cook snails.

If the snails are caught in the spring, let them sit for two days in an earthenware or copper pot containing a little goat's or cow's milk, or even without any milk.

---

conjecture given their association here with clams and mussels, and in some of the menus of Book IV again with clams.

[195.1] *una balla Firentina*: the surprising spelling is changed in 1581 to *Fiorentina*.

[195.2] The Italian for both creatures is *riccio*.

[197] The snails 'purge' themselves in preparation for hibernation. See Scappi's comment in Recipe VI,166 that snails are *piu purgate* in the winter.

Keep the pot covered because the snail will mostly stick to the pot's lid and sides. Then take them out of that pot and put them into another one, leaving them there for twenty-four hours. After that wash them in warm water and cook them in their shell in water, salt, pepper, cinnamon, saffron, pennyroyal and other beaten fine herbs. If you do not want them in their shell, parboil them and dig them out. Take the best part of them and make a pottage of them as above or else with beaten spring onions. You can do stored snails in the same way.

If you want to do stored snails on a grill, though, steep them in warm water until their covering has softened, and wash them in several changes of water. Put them into a little oil, salt and pepper, and cook them on the grill. Serve them hot without any other sauce.

The ones that were purged with milk you bring to a boil; draw them from their shell, clean out the last substance in them,[198] and put them back into their shell with oil, pepper and salt. Set them to cook on the grill the way the others are done. You can also cook them without parboiling them, but they will not be as good.

199. To fry snails and do them up in various ways.

Get snails in the spring, parboil them, draw them from their shell and clean their filth off them. To keep them at their fullest length, put them on the fire in cold water with the pot covered; give them a moderate fire until the water is boiling. When the lid is taken off you will find most of the snails out of their shell, but that will not be the case if they are put into hot water first. Draw them out of their shell, then, as was said, put them into a perforated copper or earthenware pot with ground salt, and beat them for a quarter of an hour until the muck comes out. Then wash them in several changes of water, flour them and fry them. Serve them with sautéed parsley and garlic cloves that have first been parboiled and then fried. Alternatively, when the snails have been fried, serve them dressed with green sauce or one of various other sauces.

If the snails are stored ones, though, parboil them, draw them from their shell and fry them.

200. To prepare a pottage of tiny white snails.

Steep tiny white snails in warm water and carefully wash away any sand on them. Put them into a pot with enough warm water to cover them by two fingers, and boil it gently with the lid on. When you see that the snails are out of their shell, add in oil, pepper, salt, cinnamon, saffron, beaten fine herbs, garlic cloves and verjuice, and boil them for a quarter of an hour. Then serve them in dishes with their broth. That sort of little snail loves pennyroyal, especially the ones from Rome.

---

[198] In writing *cavandone l'ultima materia che hanno* Scappi probably means whatever the snails may have eaten that they have not yet excreted while closed away in the container.

[Dishes of preserved fish]

201. How to serve various salted fish,[201.1] and to prepare them.

I must not forget to deal with certain sorts of fish done in salt, preserved in leaves, dried in smoke, in the air and in brine,[201.2] as well as their names, and how they are prepared and served at the respected tables of great princes. I begin with the salmon carp of Lake Garda which is preserved as is said in the recipes for it and for other soused fish,[201.3] and likewise with the bogue and the argentine that are carried – soused and preserved in leaves – from Genoa to some places in Italy.[201.4]

202. [Salmon carp.][202]

A salmon carp is most often served cold dressed with vinegar and sugar, but it can also be reheated on a grill or fried again in oil and served the same way. All seafish and freshwater fish that have been soused and are not bigger than two pounds, or three at the most, are similarly served.

203. [Bogue, argentine and other fish.]

A bogue, an argentine and other fish that are not bigger than four ounces, or six at the most, that are carried, soused and in myrtle leaves, from Genoa to various places in Italy, are served cold and dry, and only splashed with rose vinegar and sprinkled with sugar.

204. [Sturgeon back.]

Salted sturgeon back[204.1] is brought from Alexandria in Egypt to Venice and other places in Italy: it is the loin of sturgeons that has been salted and smoke-

---

[201.1] The qualification *salati* in Scappi's phrase, *diversi pesci salati*, could be understood as 'cured' and, more generally, 'preserved.' The section deals with fish that were killed and treated in some way to keep them a length of time before arriving in a kitchen.

[201.2] Salt was used as a preservative for fish in several ways. The fish could be dried *all'aere*, as Scappi says, and packed in salt; they could be immersed in brine, *in salimora*, and transported in strong barrels; and to that brine vinegar, sometimes wine, could be added – a pickling – in order to limit the growth of bacteria. Elsewhere (for instance in Recipe 217, below) Scappi mentions preserving in olive oil, a monounsaturated fat that, containing antioxydants, tends not to go rancid.

[201.3] The procedure for 'sousing' or 'carping' (*accarpionare*) a fish is outlined in Recipes 46, 52 and elsewhere.

[201.4] The practice is also mentioned in Recipe III,70.

[202] Recipes 201–7 have no rubrics, merely their recipe number. The rubric that is placed ahead of Recipe 201 was probably intended to cover the initial recipes in this series. The Table at the end of Book III skips also from Recipes 201 to 208. The sousing of fresh salmon carp has already been described in detail in Recipe 122, above.

[204.1] See this *schinale* in Book I,§16 also.

dried. It is served in a salad.[204.2] It is also served dry, cut up into thin slices with orange juice and oil over it. The best tends to a good russet colour like salted newly weaned veal. It is also cut into long thin slices and is warmed up on a grill.

205. [Caviar.]

Caviar[205] made from sturgeon roe is brought from Alexandria and other places on the Mediterranean by merchants who have cornered the market for it; they bring it in casks along with other salted foods. It is served on warm slices of toast with orange juice and pepper over it.

206. [*Moronella.*]

Semi-salted sturgeon belly[206.1] is brought to Italy in barrels of brine from the Mediterranean. Some people hold that it is made from the belly of a bigger fish than a sturgeon, of which, according to what I understood from the Steward to the Illustrious and Very Reverend Cardinal Pole of England, a great number are caught in that sea.[206.2] It looks like a sturgeon, but its name is unknown by us. I have made it of a sturgeon belly in the way I shall set out here. Take the belly near the umbilicus and, without skinning it, cut it into pieces. Salt it with coarse salt the way salted tuna belly[206.3] is done. It is kept in a cool place. When you want to cook it, steep it, changing the water several times, and then cook it in water. Serve it as you do salted tuna belly. In Venice I have also seen hard, dry sturgeon belly which resembles salt meat. To cook that I learned that it is soaked in warm water for twenty-four hours, changing that water several times. It is served as above.

207. [Salted tuna belly and smoked tuna belly.]

Salted tuna belly[207.1] is made from the belly of a tuna, which is the fattest part, salted with coarse salt; likewise smoked tuna belly.[207.2] Either of them is served in a salad. But first it is set to soak in warm water, then it is put into a pot in cool water. To desalt it better, bran is put to boil with it. When it is cooked it is taken out and put into cool water, changing the water several times. It is served

---

[204.2] See, for instance, the end of Recipe 207.

[205] See Recipe 24, above.

[206.1] See *moronella* also in Book I, §14.

[206.2] *in quel mare* – that is, in the English sea.

[206.3] This *tarantello* was commonly available in contemporary fish markets. Larger households apparently prepared their own. Scappi certainly seems adept at curing *moronella*.

[207.1] *Tarantello.* See also Book I, §11.

[207.2] *Sorra* is the same salted tuna belly as is used for making *tarantello* but that has been further processed by smoking in the way that sturgeon back and herring are done (see Recipes 204 and 210). The term *sorra* may derive from the russet colour that such smoking imparts and that survives in the phrase 'red herring' or the French *hareng saur*.

cubed in chunks of a moderate size, dressed with oil, vinegar, must syrup or sugar, and raisins cooked in wine.

208. To prepare a pottage of salted tuna belly or smoked tuna belly.

Get salted tuna belly or smoked belly, desalt it and half cook it as is done in the previous recipe. Skin and debone it, cut it up into chunks and put them into a pot with sautéed onions, prunes, dried visciola cherries, oil, white wine, a little vinegar, water and must syrup; that mixture should be enough to cover the tuna chunks by three fingers. Add in pepper, cinnamon, cloves and nutmeg with saffron, and finish off cooking them. At the end, as you are about to serve, put in a handful of beaten fine herbs. Serve it hot in dishes with its mixture over it.

You can do *tonnina*,[208.1] which is tuna back, that same way, and semi-salted *moronella*[208.2] made from sturgeon belly.

209. Several ways to cook a salmon.

Get a salmon that is brought salted in brine in barrels from Flanders, from the borders of Burgundy and from many other places in Italy. Cut it into pieces and set them to soak. Cook it like salted tuna belly and make a pottage of it following the directions in the next recipe.

210. To cook white salted herrings and smoke-dried herrings.

Herrings resemble freshwater shad and are brought in brine in barrels into Italy from Flanders and France by the Rhine River. When you want to cook them, let them soak for thirty-four hours, changing the water. You can also boil them in plain water. Serve them dressed with garlic sauce.[210]

Dried herrings, after being salted, are hung in smoke until they take on a golden colour. Good ones are shiny. All are full of roe or milt; the best are considered those with milt because their back is bigger. Some are of another, smaller and whiter species and are called pilchard; those are smoked. When they are to be served, all their heads are cut off; they are opened along the back, coated with oil and heated on a grill. They are served dressed with oil and vinegar.

211. To cook and serve salted shad[211.1] and large sardines.

Freshwater shad is generally brought salted from Lake Como in barrels in coarse salt. They are cooked and served like salted white herrings. Large sardines are brought in brine in barrels from the sea of Genoa to various places in Italy.

[208.1] See Book I, §11. This tuna back is pickled in brine.

[208.2] See Recipe 206, above.

[210] See Recipe II,257.

[211.1] These *agoni* (*Alosa lacustris*) are freshwater shad, as distinct from Scapi's *laccia* (and *lacie*), a saltwater or allis shad seen in Recipes III,50 ff.

They are washed in vinegar like anchovies – that is, *anghioie*[211.2] – and are served uncooked like that, dressed with oil, pepper, vinegar and oregano.[211.3] With those two fish, large sardines and anchovies – that is, *anghioie* – you can make fritters and *pottaggetti*, too, after they have been desalted a little.

212. To cook and serve salted grey mullets.

Get salted grey mullets,[212.1] scale them and soak them until they have lost a good deal of their salt. Cook them in water and oil, a little verjuice and spinach leaves. Serve them hot with pepper over them.

They can also be cooked another way after they have been desalted: fry them in oil, and serve them with a sauce made of rose vinegar, sugar and cooked raisins. Again, without being scaled but only desalted, they can be cooked on a grill, serving them with a sauce made of vinegar, must syrup, pepper and verjuice. They can be cooked, too, in a pottage the way salted tuna belly is done.[212.2]

White salted herring can also be cooked those same ways, and large salted shad from Lake Maggiore, and every other salted fish, having first been desalted and parboiled like tuna belly. They are served as well in a salad with cooked raisins, vinegar, oil, pepper, and sugar or else must syrup. I will not speak about fish that are preserved in vinegar because I deal with them in their own place.[212.3]

213. To cook and serve salted eel.

Good salted eels are brought, salted and dry, from the same places as mullets – that is, from the valleys by Comacchio. Big ones are skinned, cut up into pieces and cooked in plain water. They are served deboned in dishes with vinegar, oil, must syrup and oregano. The same is done with small ones. Small ones are also done on a grill, and with heavy paper under the coals. They are served as above.

214. To prepare a pottage of large salted eels.

Take an eel, skin it, cut it into rounds and give them a boiling[214] in plain water. Then take them out and put them into another pot containing leeks that

---

[211.2] That name, we were informed in Recipe 76, is the common Genovese and Milanese designation of *alice*, anchovies.

[211.3] This *origano* (*Origanum onites*), a perennial Mediterranean herb chosen only to garnish a few of Scappi's fish dishes, is distinct from the *maiorana* (*Origanum maiorana*, sweet knotted marjoram) that we see Scappi use, usually in combination with mint, in a large number of other recipes.

[212.1] Scappi clarifies by using a second name for this fish: *li muggini cioè cefali*. In Recipe 53 he has explained that the first word is the Tuscan equivalent of the second.

[212.2] See Recipe 207.

[212.3] See Recipes 46 and 122 for two instances.

[214] What Scappi says is to let it boil a very little more after it has come to a boil: *facciasi trare due bolli.*

have been sautéed in oil, adding in water, spinach leaves, pepper, saffron and a little verjuice. Boil all that. Serve it hot, dressed with its broth. They can also be cooked with Bolognese cabbage and other sorts of cabbage with oil and often with fresh legumes.

215. To cook large salted and smoked pike.

Take a pike and soak it in warm water, scale it and cut it up when it is thoroughly softened. Comb out the pieces of flesh into strands, with the bones removed. Put them back to soak in warm water because if you leave them without moisture they will dry out and lose their goodness. Have at hand a pot containing onions sautéed in oil or butter, along with pepper, cinnamon and saffron; put the combed-out pieces of pike into that together with a little white wine, verjuice and water; there should be enough of the liquid to cover everything by two fingers. Boil it. When they are almost cooked, get some ground toast that is moistened with must syrup – instead of toast you can use roasted almonds or hazelnuts – and with that thicken the broth a little. When it has come to a boil, serve it. In the same way you can do dried cod, dried dogfish and *migliaccina* – that is, a large grey mullet – salted and dry. You can also cook them in plain water after they have soaked and been scaled. They are served covered with oil, vinegar and oregano, or else with garlic sauce or mustard.

216. To prepare mullet-roe cakes[216.1] with sea-bass roe

– even though it is not usual in Italy to make mullet roe cakes from sea-bass roe, because cakes of sea-bass roe are generally brought from the Mediterranean where there are huge sea bass, and from Slavonia and elsewhere where they are made from mullet roe, which is better.[216.2] Sea-bass roe normally comes encased in crude wax. To prepare them, Roman cooks get the sea-bass roe in January and are very careful not to break the membrane around it; they leave the fish's stomach attached. Salt the roe and put them on a cutting board or in an ample earthenware pan, covered with a weighted-down trencher or some other cutting board for six days. After that they take them out, give them the shape of mullet-roe cakes and put them where smoke can play on them. They should not get too warm because they would turn rancid. They are left there for ten days until they have absorbed the smoke, then they are kept in bran or in oil. When cooks want to serve them, they cut them into thin slices and serve those dressed with lime juice and oil.

Cakes of grey-mullet roe are made the same way.

[216.1] These *bottarghe* are 'cakes' in the sense of each being caked in a relatively flat, thin mass, here as a result of compression.

[216.2] The concessive conjunction, *Anchorche* (with that capital letter), with which Scappi begins the text of this recipe links its first clauses grammatically to the rubric – even though the rubric itself ends with a period. Scappi's eagerness to communicate his experience is stirred irresistibly by the rubric alone.

217. To cook tench that have been preserved in oil.[217]

In the territories of Sabina, Aquileia and Tagliacozzo they preserve many fish in oil, especially tench – that is, the males caught in winter and gutted. Those are salted and left in salt for three days more or less, depending on their size. They are washed in wine and, after they have dried in the open air, put whole into large jars full of oil. When they are wanted for cooking they are set in warm water and washed. You can make a pottage of them the way it is done with salted tuna belly in Recipe 208. Generally they are cooked with cabbages and legumes.

The same is done with trout and other fish that are kept in oil.

218. To prepare whitedish with fish flesh.

Get two pounds of shelled Milanese almonds that have soaked, grind them in a mortar and make milk of them with cold water. In all there should be six pounds of that milk.[218.1] Then get two pounds of boiled, deboned pike back, or else two pounds of gurnard flesh, and grind it in a mortar, moistening it with a pound of its broth that should not be too salty.[218.2] Put everything through a strainer together with the almond milk, adding in six ounces of well-sieved rice flour, two pounds of finely ground sugar and enough salt. Cook it in a casserole pot on the coals away from the flame so it will not pick up any smoke, stirring it continuously with a wooden spatula. When it is almost cooked, add in five ounces of rosewater and finish off cooking it. When it is done, serve it, hot or cold as you like, in dishes with fine sugar on top.

You can also make a tourte of it by adding in a little more rosewater and sugar; for every two pounds of the above mixture add in six ounces of softened pinenuts and four ounces of raisins. Make up the tourte with two crusts, one on the botton and the other on top in overlapping strips[218.3] or with other embellishments. With that mixture you can also fill various pastries, as you can see in the Book on Pastry.

[Dishes other than of fish]

219. To prepare mock ricotta and butter from almonds.[219]

Get two pounds of almonds, shelled in cold water; they should have soaked in that water for twelve hours. Grind them in a mortar, moistening them with

---

[217] Scappi uses a phrase here that we have seen elsewhere: *tinche sotto oglio.*

[218.1] Recipe 220 confirms this ratio of 1:3 for whole almonds to finished milk.

[218.2] Scappi is still dealing with salted, dried fish.

[218.3] The phrase 'made like a slatted shutter' (*fatto a gelosia*) is effectively descriptive. This form of upper tourte shell is used repeatedly in Book V.

[219] The creation of fake foods has a long culinary history. In medieval and early modern Europe the practice owed its popularity in part to Christian strictures against foods from certain animals and in part to the pleasure of make-believe. For a survey of medieval counterfeit cookery see Melitta Weiss Adamson, 'Imitation Food Then and Now,' *Petits Propos Culinaires*, 72 (2003): 83–102.

reduced pike broth so that what is ground becomes like milk. Put that through a strainer, adding to it three ounces of finely ground sugar, three ounces of flour starch and four ounces of rosewater. Put it into a casserole pot with salt and cook it, stirring constantly with a spoon until it thickens. When it is firm, take it out. Splash a ricotta mould with rosewater and put the almond mixture into it. Leave it in a cool place until it is quite cold. Then serve it garnished with sugar and flowers on top.

You can also do it another way: grind the almonds and sugar, moistening them with a reduced pike broth in which rice has been cooked. There is no need to put it through a strainer, provided it is thoroughly ground up. When it is moistened, reduce it so the mixture is firm and, without cooking it, put it into the moulds and let it cool. Serve it with sugar on it. If you want to strain the mixture, grind with it a little rice cooked in that broth.

That mixture can be used to make a pseudo butter, colouring it with saffron and then putting it into a straining cloth washed with rosewater and letting it sit in a cool place. Serve it with sugar on top.

220. To prepare a thick starch soup with almond milk.

Get a pound of fresh, white starch and moisten it with nine pounds of milk made from three pounds of Milanese almonds. Put it all through a strainer and put it into a well tinned copper pot with a little ground sugar and a little salt. Cook it over a coal fire[220.1] the way whitedish is done, stirring it constantly with a spatula. When it is almost done, add in six ounces of rosewater. When it is done, serve it hot or cold, whichever you wish. Whether you make it thin or thick is up to whomever has ordered it. Sometimes you can put the flesh of a gurnard into it, or of a pike, ground in a mortar after they have been boiled and deboned.

You can cook hard wheat[220.2] the same way, although it needs more cooking than starch.

221. To prepare a thick rice soup with almond milk or oil.[221.1]

Get rice from Lombardy or Salerno, hull it and wash it in warm water. So that it will stay whiter and cook more quickly, soak it for an hour in warm water. Take it out and let it dry in the sun or in the heat of the fire far from the flame so

---

[220.1] A coal fire could be trusted to give a constant and, if needed, low heat. Furthermore, the smoke from a wood fire was a threat to the delicate flavour of such a preparation as this almond-cream dish.

[220.2] This *semolella* is used in Recipes II,153, 170 and 186. Scappi does not call it a flour; it may come into his kitchen as hulled grains, rather like the rice and spelt (and barley, millet and panic) of the next two recipes.

[221.1] In Recipe II,184 Scappi likely intends the present Recipe 221 as a variant for the thick rice soup of that earlier preparation, even though the reference there is to a Recipe 220. The next recipe, 222, will provide a lean alternative to the spelt preparation also of Recipe II,184.

it will not darken. Set it on the fire in an earthenware or copper pot in enough water to cover it. When it has absorbed the water, gradually put in almond milk and sugar and finish off cooking it so that it ends up firm. When it is done, serve it with sugar and cinnamon over it.

You can also serve it sometimes as yellowdish,[221.2] having strained it with more sugar and ground cinnamon and saffron, and cooking it again with a little rosewater and malmsey.

If you want it with oil, though, all you need to do is put it into the pot with oil, water, salt and saffron, and at the end add in a few fine herbs or sautéed spring onions. No matter how it is done, that thick soup should be served hot.

222. To cook spelt in almond milk or oil.

Get spelt, clean it and wash it in warm water and put it on the fire in a pot with warm salted water. When it has absorbed the water, put in almond milk with sugar, and finish off cooking it like the rice. Serve it hot with sugar and cinnamon over it.

If you want it in oil, follow the directions in the preceding recipe.

You can cook culled barley in the same ways. I will not go into cracked millet or cracked foxtail millet because they need to be cooked in meat broth or butter rather than oil.[222]

223. To prepare yellowdish.[223.1]

Get four pounds of shelled Milanese almonds, grind them and make up twelve pounds of milk from them. Strain that with fourteen ounces of rice flour and into it put an ounce of ground cinnamon, half an ounce of pepper, salt and enough saffron, six ounces of cleaned dates that have boiled in wine and been cut up small, six ounces of dried figs cut up small, another six ounces of soaked pinenuts and four pounds of finely ground sugar. Cook all that as the whitedish of Recipe 218 is done. When it begins to thicken, put in six ounces of seeded and finely cut muscatel raisins that have soaked in white wine, and six ounces of very clean currants. Finish off cooking it. When it is is done – that is, when you see it as thick as whitedish – add in a pound and a half of smooth malmsey or muscatel, and bring it to a boil again with the wine in it. Serve it, hot or cold as you wish, in dishes and dressed with sugar and cinnamon.

You can make a tourte with that mixture by adding a little pinenut paste and ground *mostaccioli*. The mixture should be somewhat thinner. To put it into a

---

[221.2] See Recipe 223, below.

[222] The reader is reminded that the present Book III deals with dishes appropriate for meals on lean or fasting days. In a number of these recipes Scappi will also offer alternative provisions in case a dish is specifically for a fasting day or for a day in Lent.

[223.1] Scappi's meat-day *ginestrata* is at Recipe II,160.

tourte pan with its pastry shell, you follow the directions found in the Book on Pastry.[223.2]

224. To prepare *cipollata*.[224.1]

Get old,[224.2] white, sweet onions and parboil them in water. Take them out and pound them with knives. When that is done, sauté them in very good oil; for every two pounds of beaten onion put in a pound of Milanese almonds that have been made into milk – which milk should have become four pounds[224.3] – along with a pound and a half of sugar, half an ounce of pepper, an ounce of ground cinnamon, a quarter-ounce of ground nutmeg and three ounces of rosewater. Cook that mixture in a casserole pot over a moderate fire, adding in a little verjuice. When is it done and is rather firm, serve it in dishes dressed with sugar and cinnamon.

You can make tourtes with that mixture by adding raisins and beaten fine herbs. It has to be served hot.

225. To prepare a thick soup of common squash[225.1] during Lent.

Take a squash, scrape it and dice it. Put some finely chopped onions with it and put them into an earthenware or copper pot with oil and no water. Sauté them gently, stirring, because they will produce water on their own. When they have reduced, add in enough water to cover them by two fingers, along with pepper, cinnamon, saffron and enough salt. Boil that. When it is almost cooked, put in gooseberries or verjuice grapes, and beaten fine herbs; finish cooking it. Serve it in dishes with pepper and cinnamon over top. With that squash you can cook pieces of tench or large pike.

You can do bryony[225.2] the same way, although it would be better to parboil them before sautéing them. On days that are not fasting days you can use butter instead of oil and thicken it with beaten eggs.

[223.2] Scappi seems to have forgotten, however, to include a tourte of yellowdish in his Book V. See Recipe V,146.

[224.1] The dish name comes from the Italian word for onion, *cipolla*.

[224.2] Recipe 228, below, contains a reference to this Recipe 224 that suggests Scappi may have intended to include an alternative procedure here for fresh spring onions as well as for the old (i.e., dried) onions he uses here.

[224.3] This would be a somewhat watery almond milk.

[225.1] Scappi's phrase is *zucche nostrali*. The qualification *nostrale* implies 'home-grown' or 'local' as distinct from 'foreign' or 'imported.' The squash discussed in this and the following recipes is the ordinary, everyday crook-neck squash a professional cook could find available in his kitchen garden, at his local market or from local suppliers.

[225.2] *zucche marine*: probably *Tamus comunis* of the squash family, whose tender shoots are eaten.

226. To stuff common squash during Lent.

Get a soft, sweet squash that is not too big, scrape it and cut it in rounds the width of a hand. Dig out the seeds from one side[226.1] in such a way that the hole does not go through to the other side, and fill the excavation with the mixture described in Recipe 229[226.2] for stuffed and sautéed eggplant. If it is not a fasting day,[226.3] though, stuff it with cheese, eggs, finely chopped fine herbs, gooseberries or verjuice grapes. Stop up the hole in the squash with a small bung of squash, making that tight with a bit of reed. Cook it in a stewpot[226.4] with water, salt, oil or butter, pepper, cinnamon and saffron, keeping its lid on tight. When it is almost done, to thicken the broth on a fasting day put in ground almonds moistened with the broth; on a non-fasting day, use beaten eggs, not forgetting verjuice and beaten fine herbs. Serve them hot in dishes with their broth over them.

227. To fry common squash.

Get a soft squash that is smaller than the one above, scrape it gently and cut it into slices crosswise. When that is done, sprinkle ground salt on them and let them sit a little while on a board. Then carefully squeeze out the moisture in them, flour them and fry them in oil. Serve them hot, dry, with sugar on top. Alternatively, dress them with ground verjuice grapes, fresh fennel tips, a garlic clove and pepper – if you do not have fresh verjuice grapes, use old ones. You can also cover them with a little sauce made of basil tips and sweet fennel and hazelnuts, the whole moistened with verjuice.

You can do bryony the same way when it is cut into thin slices and parboiled in salted water; likewise the dry rinds of Genoese squash and of 'cane fish' (as it is called in Rome), which 'fish' is the tips of marsh reeds that are brought in February and March by chicory dealers to the fish markets of Rome.[227]

[226.1] *da una parte.*

[226.2] This recipe number appears in both the 1570 and 1581 printings, though 230 seems more likely.

[226.3] Dishes prepared in Lent assume a fasting diet, which excludes cheese and eggs in particular. Many of Scappi's Lenten recipes will offer a 'non-fasting' variant.

[226.4] See the engraving of a *stufatoro* in Plate 8.

[227] ... *pesce canedo, (che cosi è detto in Roma) qual pesce è cima de cane di valle, che sono portate del mese di Febraro, et di Marzo nelle Pescarie di Roma da Cicoriali.* The phrase *pesce canedo* seems to have been an imaginative local name for the edible panicle or spikelets at the top of a particular variety of cane. The sense of Cicoriali is also uncertain. If the word refers to people, they might be producers or wholesalers of chicory. If it is a place on the sea or by marshy ground, from which the 'cane fish' are brought, Antonella Salvatico has suggested that the word may refer to an area in Sabina near the River Turano, called *de Ciconialis* and meaning an association of nobles.

228. To cook squash rinds, popularly called *zazzere*.[228.1]

Dried squash rinds are brought to Rome and various other places from Savona in small bound bundles the way bunches of lute strings are tied. They are very white and look like fine strips of white leather. When they are cooked a pound of them will make five servings. To cook them, you parboil them in boiling water, then you cut them into small bits and make a thick soup of them with beaten spring onions the way you do with the fresh ones in Recipe 224. However, they are much better after they are cooked and have fried without onions, being coated with a garlic sauce made with walnuts and almonds.[228.2] After they have been parboiled they can also be sautéed with parsley and herbs and beaten cloves of garlic. They are served with pepper and orange juice over them.

In the same way you can do wild parsnips that have been parboiled, or dried turnip rinds or dried melon rinds.[228.3] Note that they have to be put into boiling water on the fire because in cold water they would not cook.

229. To braise eggplant – that is, *pomi sdegnosi*.[229.1]

Get eggplants that are not too ripe or too bitter, and clean off the purplish skin they have – although you do find white ones – and cut them lengthwise into several pieces. Let them steep for half an hour; discard that water and set them to boil in a pot in fresh water that is lightly salted. When they are well cooked, take them out and let them drain on a table. Have an earthenware baking dish or a tourte pan ready with oil; carefully flour the pieces and make a layer of them in the pan. Get beaten mint, sweet marjoram, burnet and parsley, and beaten fresh fennel tips or ground dry fennel along with crushed garlic cloves, and scatter all that over the layer of eggplant, as well as enough pepper, cinnamon, cloves and salt; splash verjuice on that and sprinkle it with sugar. Repeat, making up two or three layers. Cook it the way a tourte is done.[229.2] When it is done, serve it hot in dishes with the broth over it. If is not a fasting day you can put slices of provatura

---

[228.1] Literally this word means long locks of hair.

[228.2] See Recipe II,257.

[228.3] *et le scorze di rape, et di melloni secche*.

[229.1] This name, an alternative to *molignane*, means literally 'haughty fruit.' On the earliest Arabic use of eggplant (at least 825 A.D.) see Perry, '*Būrān*: Eleven Hundred Years in the History of a Dish.' Recipes for eggplant (or aubergine) are found in European cookery only by the middle of the fourteenth century: see the Catalan *Libre de sent soví*, Recipe 149 for *Albergínies ab let de amelles* (ed. Rudolf Grewe, 166–7); and, in Italian, the *Neapolitan Recipe Collection*, Recipe 33 for *marignani* (ed. Scully, 50, translation, 180). Scappi has enough regard for the vegetable to devote four recipes here to its preparation, along with a further one at V,109. The present dish may be a precursor of *parmigiana di melanzane*, though without sweet oranges.

[229.2] This is Scappi's abbreviation for applying a moderate heat from above and below to a covered pan.

or ordinary cheese and grated bread between each layer; and, instead of oil, use butter.

230. To cook stuffed eggplant in Lent.

Get eggplants and peel them. Through their small end dig out the inside – which can be done most easily after bringing them to a boil in hot water. Take that and beat it with knives along with aromatic herbs, old walnuts and almonds, both ground, a little grated bread, pepper, cloves, cinnamon, and a small clove of garlic, ground up, adding in a little oil and verjuice. Stuff the eggplants with that mixture and set them on end, their opening upwards, in a pot of a suitable size. In that pot there should be oil, water, salt, saffron and some of the above spices, with enough liquid to come more than halfway up the eggplants. Seal up the pot and boil it gently. When they are almost cooked, add a little grated bread and beaten fine herbs into the broth, ensuring that the broth has a spicy tang and a touch of bitterness. When they are done, serve them hot with that broth over them.

If you want to cook them in an oven, though, there is no need to peel them; only stuff them either with that mixture or else with oil, verjuice, salt, pepper and a small clove of garlic, and bake them. When they are done, peel them very carefully without breaking them. Alternatively, cut them through the middle and lift out the best part with your knife and serve that hot, dressed with orange juice and pepper. If it is not a fasting day, you can put grated cheese and eggs into the stuffing.[230]

231. To fry eggplant in Lent.

Peel the eggplants, slice them and parboil them in water; let them drain on a table. Flour them and fry them in good olive oil. When they are done, serve them dressed with pepper, salt and orange juice, or else with a sauce made of verjuice, basil and garlic. They can be dressed also with a garlic sauce made using walnuts, or with green sauce, or with some other garnish.

232. To prepare a thick soup of eggplant in Lent.

Peel the eggplants and parboil them. When that is done, drain off the water, beat them with knives and sauté them in oil with spring onions in an earthenware or tinned copper pot. Add in salted water, pepper, cinnamon, saffron and, toward the end, a handful of beaten fine herbs and a little almond milk and verjuice. When they are cooked, serve them in a thick soup with cinnamon over top. If it is not a fasting day, instead of oil use butter, and instead of almond milk, beaten eggs, grated cheese and spices.

---

[230] Scappi's versions of stuffed eggplant can be compared with a simpler, less expensive version that Castelvetro is familiar with in family cooking. 'Cut them open down the middle, hollow them out and fill them with a mixture of the chopped pulp, breadcrumbs, egg, grated cheese, sweet herbs and butter or oil, and bitter orange juice. Then either grill them over charcoal, or stew them gently in an earthenware pot or a tinned copper dish' (trans. Riley, 74).

233. To braise whole onions in Lent.

Get sweet white onions; the bigger they are the better. Parboil them in salted water so they get well cooked. Take them out, let them cool and drain. Prick them a little with the tip of a knife so the water can better get out of them. When they have drained, wash them in a little cold water, flour them and put them into a shallow tourte pan with enough hot olive oil to more than half cover them. Give them a gentle heat above and below, stirring them occasionally. When they are cooked, serve them dressed with sugar and cinnamon. Alternatively you can dress them with garlic sauce or green sauce.

If you want them stuffed, though, before they are parboiled you make a hole in their middle that does not go all the way through, and you fill them with the mixture outlined in Recipe 229 for stuffed eggplant. Without flouring them set them to braise in oil with a little verjuice, water tinged with saffron, and salt, pepper, cinnamon and a handful of beaten fine herbs. Serve them with that broth. If it is not a fasting day, add cheese and eggs into the stuffing and cook them in butter. It will always be better to bring them to a boil in water before stuffing them.

234. To prepare a thick soup of onions and leeks mixed together for a Lenten day.

Get an old onion, peel it and cut it up into pieces; take the whitest part of a leek; parboil them. Then remove them from the bouillon and let them drain. Beat them small with knives and sauté them in olive oil, adding in pepper and cinnamon. When they have sautéed, put in saffron-tinged water and boil them in an earthenware or copper pot. When they are almost cooked, put in almond milk that is not too thin, along with a little verjuice and a handful of beaten fine herbs; finish off cooking them so they thicken a little. If it is not a Lenten day you can thicken them with beaten eggs and grated cheese. Serve that hot with spices over it.

235. To prepare a thick soup of salted mushrooms.

Soak a salted mushroom for eight hours, changing the water; the last water should be warm. Test the mushroom and, if it has no salty taste, cut it up into small pieces, putting them into a pot with olive oil and beaten spring onions. Sauté them gently, adding in pepper, cinnamon and saffron. When it is slightly undercooked, put in almond milk that is not too thin and has been moistened with a little verjuice, along with a handful of fine herbs and a few raisins; let it finish cooking. Serve everything together hot, with mild spices over top.

236. To fry salted mushrooms.

Desalt the mushroom as in the previous recipe, flour it and fry it in oil. When that is done, serve it with some sugar and orange juice over it, or else cover it with green sauce or garlic sauce or any of various other garnishes.

237. To cook dry broccoli.

Get broccoli between February and the end of March, with its leaves removed. Take the tenderest part of it that has not flowered. Boil salted water. With the broccoli done up into little bunches,[237.1] put it into that boiling water. Do not overcook it but take it out and put it into dishes. Then get boiling oil and drip it hot with a spoon over the broccoli, adding orange juice, pepper and a little of the broth in which it was cooked. Serve it hot because otherwise it is no good. You can also sauté a crushed clove of garlic in the oil to flavour the broccoli.[237.2]

Whenever you need to hold it back for an hour or two, put it into cold water after it has parboiled and leave it there until you want to recook it. Green broccoli is kept the same way and it will not take on a bad smell. It is served in the above way.

238. To cook cabbage in oil, water and salt.

Get dark crispy cabbage, which is the best sort, which is better cooked in oil than in pork fat, as are young cabbage sprouts;[238] from either of them take the best parts and put them on the fire in boiling water with oil and salt. Cook them only a little. Serve them like the broccoli of the previous recipe.

You can cook every sort of cabbage that way except for head cabbage.

239. To cook cauliflower.

Take a cauliflower and cut it away from the stalk making several bits. Wash it and cook it the way broccoli is done in Recipe 237.[239] Serve it the same way, although it takes less cooking.

240. To cook stuffed Savoy cabbage in Lent.[240]

Get a cabbage from which the harder leaves have been cleaned away and bring it to a boil in water. Then take it out and put it into cold water. Have a mixture ready, made up of old walnuts that are not rancid, ground with a small clove of garlic, breadcrumb soaked in hot water, mint, marjoram, burnet and parsley, those herbs beaten, raisins, pepper, cinnamon and a little salted eel flesh

[237.1] Borage flowers are bound up the same way in Recipe VI,88. See also Recipe II,198.

[237.2] 'Some prefer to cook [broccoli] with a few cloves of garlic, which gives them a wonderful flavour' (Castelvetro, trans. Riley, 54).

[238] What Scappi is saying in part is that, if you cannot (on a lean day, a fasting day or a Lenten day) use pork fat as a cooking medium, then the best cabbage and sprouts to choose for cooking in olive oil are the dark, crispy sort.

[239] The type in both the 1570 and 1581 printings is set as *capitolo 235*. It would seem that by this point in his Book III Scappi had made a late insertion of a second recipe, so that his reference number is now too small by two. Compare this present dish with what is prepared in Recipe II,195.

[240] Compare this with Recipe II,198.

which is cooked and ground in a mortar. Stuff that mixture between each of the leaves toward the middle of the stalk. When the stalk is full, wrap it around with a large cabbage leaf brushed with hot water and tie it with a string. Cook it in water with oil and salt. If you want to make the cabbage's broth thick, put grated bread into it, and a handful of beaten fine herbs, pepper and saffron. If it is not a day during Lent, you can add cheese into the stuffing and some eggs, and instead of oil, butter.

You can stuff the stalks of lettuce that way, thickening the broth with ground almonds instead of grated bread.

241. To cook a stuffed kohlrabi bulb.[241]

Get a bulb of kohlrabi that is not woody and, without peeling it, better than half cook it under hot coals. Then take it out, peel it, make a hole in its middle and fill it with the above mixture. Braise it the way the stuffed onion of Recipe 232 is done. Instead of cooking it under the embers or coals you can also parboil it. Mind particularly, though, that the bulb is of a young kohlrabi.

242. Another way to cook a bulb of kohlrabi.

Get the bulb, peel it, cut it into slices and put it into a boiling broth composed of water, salt, oil, pepper and saffron. Cook it vigorously rather than slowly. When it is done throw in a handful of fine herbs and a garlic sauce made with walnuts and breadcrumb,[242.1] and the kohlrabi bulb all together and moistened with that same broth. When it has all come to a boil serve it with pepper over top.

You can prepare artichoke hearts, cardoon stems, cole and yellow rape[242.2] the same way.

243. To prepare a thick soup of wild fennel.

Get fennel in its season (which is indicated in Chapter 207 in the Book of Prepared Dishes[243.1]) – what I mean is those white sprouts that form at the foot of wild fennel plants. Remove the outer skin and take the tenderest part, wash them and make up a bunch of them like broccoli and put them into a pot containing oil, water and salt. Cook them well. To thicken the broth put in some crustless bread that has soaked in the broth and been sieved. Add in pepper, cinnamon and saffron. When they are done, serve them hot with their broth over them. If it is

---

[241] Scappi's word for the swollen stem of the *Brassica oleracea gongylodes* is *rapa*, a word which in modern Italian translates as 'turnip.' He sees no confusion in referring to the *rapa di cauli torzutti*. Castelvetro writes, 'The leaves [of kohlrabi] are quite nice, but the so-called root, really the base of the stem, is absolutely delicious' (trans. Riley, 108).

[242.1] See Recipe II,257.

[242.2] See other uses for these *navoni gialli* in Recipes 2 and 253, below, and V,33.

[243.1] *nel libro delle vivande nel Cap. 207*: Recipe II,207.

not a fasting day, put Parmesan cheese crusts in to cook with them; and instead of oil, put in butter.

You can do a thick soup of their fronds,[243.2] too, with finely chopped onions.

244. To sauté spinach, as well as to cook it in other ways.

Get tender spinach leaves, wash them and let them drain. Get a frying pan with very hot oil in it and put the spinach in with very little salt, stirring it around with a spoon and beating it. When it is beaten and cooked, add in raisins, pepper and cinnamon, either orange juice or verjuice, and a little must syrup; bring it all to a boil. Serve everything together hot.

If you want it in the Florentine fashion, put the spinach leaves into a pan after they have been washed and drained, without oil, and sauté them and beat them with a spoon. Drain off the water and add in oil, salt, pepper, vinegar, must syrup and raisins. Put everything into a pot and let it finish cooking slowly with the same sauce. When it is done, serve the spinach hot or cold as you wish with its sauce over it.[244.1]

If you'd like it differently, when the spinach leaves are rather big, parboil them in boiling water. When they are done, take them out, squeeze the water out of them and make them into big balls. Those balls can be kept from one day to the next. When you want to serve them, they are sautéed in oil with beaten spring onions, with salt, pepper and raisins added in. They are served hot with verjuice or orange juice over them, and must syrup.

They can also be cooked as a thick soup the way other fine herbs are done.[244.2]

245. To prepare a thick soup of chard, borage and bugloss.

Get chard and borage and other fine herbs chopped up the way they are done for a tourte,[245] and put them into a copper or earthenware pot with oil. Sauté them gently, because they will make their own water, stirring them with a spoon. If they do not have enough broth, add in a little water with a little pepper. You can also thicken the broth with a little thick almond milk. They can be cooked with beaten spring onions; and in the spring and summer you put in gooseberries or verjuice grapes. You can also take the midstem of those two herbs and make up bunches of them the way broccoli is done in Recipe 236; parboil them in water, then finish off cooking them in a broth made of water, oil, pepper, saffron and gooseberries

---

[243.2] *barbe*: the plants' feathery tips, literally 'beards.'

[244.1] Castelvetro (trans. Riley, 50) describes a similar practice in Modena: 'Another way is to cook the spinach first in plain water, drain it, chop it very fine with a large knife, and finish cooking it on a low heat in a pan with oil or butter, seasoned with salt, pepper and raisins; this makes a really delicious dish.'

[244.2] A reference perhaps to some of the following recipes.

[245] See Recipe V,94, for instance.

or verjuice grapes. You can also thicken the broth with ground almonds or grated bread.

You can do endive in all the above ways. You can also use leeks instead of the spring onions.

246. To prepare a thick soup of chicory.[246.1]

Get chicory tips, which is the tenderest, whitest part; when they are well washed make bunches of them as with the broccoli. Boil them in water until they are almost done, then put them into cold water and leave them there a quarter of an hour. Take them out and put them into an ample copper or earthenware pot with oil, water, pepper, saffron and raisins, and finish off cooking them. It is optional whether you thicken their broth, using ground almonds or grated bread.

Chicory root can be done the same way, having first taken off its core and its tips, which in Rome are called *mazzocchi*;[246.2] with those tips, though, you will not put almonds. Chicory leaves have to be parboiled and beaten, and cooked following the same procedure.

247. To prepare a thick soup of wild or domestic asparagus, and of hops.

Take the tenderest part of wild asparagus and wash it and make bunches of it, which you parboil. Then you cook them like the chicory tips in the preceding recipe. Domestic asparagus and hops[247] are done the same way, but there's no need to parboil the domestic asparagus; it is enough to cook it with the broth and to add in beaten fine herbs.

248. To fry hops.

Take the tenderest part of the hops and bring it to a boil in water. Then flour it and fry it in oil. Serve it dressed with sautéed parsley, orange juice, pepper and salt.[248]

The tops of chicory can be fried the same way, and the little stalks of borage. And add in beaten fine herbs.

[246.1] See also Recipe II,216.

[246.2] Still today the word *mazzocchi* designates the long, silvery-white, tightly folded leaves that form the top sprouts or shoots (the *cime* as Scappi has just called them) of a chicory plant, usually eaten in a salad.

[247] For Giacomo Castelvetro (trans. Riley, 50) in 1614 a usual preparation of hops remains similar: 'We never eat them raw, but serve them as a cooked salad. We wash the hops thoroughly and then cook the desired amount in water with a little salt, drain them very well and serve them in a clean dish seasoned with salt, plenty of oil and a little vinegar or lemon juice and some crushed, not powdered, pepper.'

[248] Castelvetro continues his description of the usual ways of preparing hops at home in Modena (see the previous note): 'Alternatively, once the hops are cooked we flour them and fry them in oil and serve them sprinkled with salt, pepper and bitter orange juice.'

249. To prepare a thick soup of fresh peas or beans.[249]

Get peas in their pods, shell them and put them into a pot with olive oil, salt and pepper. Sauté them gently, adding in enough water, tinged with saffron, to cover them by two fingers. When they are slightly underdone, grind some of them in a mortar, moistening them with that same broth, and put them back into the pot with a handful of beaten fine herbs. Bring it all to a boil and serve it hot.

You can do fresh chickpeas the same way, having first parboiled them and let them sit a quarter of an hour in cool water. Fresh beans are also done that way.

250. To prepare a thick soup of brown chickpeas.

Get brown chickpeas[250.1] that have been cleaned of any dirt and put them to soak in clear lye that is not too strong,[250.2] or in warm water with a little wood ash in a cloth; let them soak in a warm place for six hours. Then take them out and wash them in clear water, being careful that the lye is not too strong, as was said, because the skin of the chickpeas would burst and they would take on the taste of that lye. Then take them out of that and wash them in warm water and put them into a pot with oil, salt and a little flour mixed up with a spoon, and enough water to cover them by four fingers or more. Cook them with sprigs of rosemary and sage, whole garlic cloves and pepper. Serve them in bowls. If you want them without flour or oil, put finely chopped herbs with them just before serving. If you want to cook the chickpeas in order to have the broth, though, there is no need for them to soak; it is enough to clean and wash them well and to put them into a glazed earthenware pot with plain warm water. You sit that pot for six hours on hot coals, keeping it covered. When you want to cook them, take off the thin scum that will have formed on top and cook them in that same water, adding in a little oil and salt. To give them a flavour add in a few twigs of rosemary as well.

251. To prepare a thick soup of split chickpeas.[251]

Get split chickpeas, clean them and wash them in warm water. Put them on the fire in an earthenware or tinned copper pot in warm water, salt, oil and peeled garlic cloves. Cook them slowly away from the flame. Just before serving, it is optional whether you add in a few beaten herbs.

252. To cook large dried broad beans and common vetch.[252]

Dried broad beans and vetch are cleaned and soaked in lye as in the above Recipe 250. They are washed in several changes of water and cooked in oil, water

---

[249] See also Recipe II,188.

[250.1] These *ceci rossi* are garbanzos that, when dried, turn brownish naturally.

[250.2] This *lescia* is a common alkaline agent made by boiling wood ash in water. It is used also in Recipe 252, below. See Recipe II,91 where the *liscia* has to be caustic.

[251] See also Recipe II,192.

[252] *cicerchie*. Chickling, chickling vetch, lath or grass pea (*Lathyrus sativus*) is a leguminous plant of the genus *vicia*, which is best known for the broad bean. Castelvetro writes that vetch

and salt. When they are just about cooked, add in sautéed onions and beaten fine herbs, pepper and saffron.

Dried peas are cooked the same way, first soaking them in warm water, though, rather than in lye.

253. To prepare a thick soup of dried haricot beans.

Clean the beans, wash them in warm water and parboil them in water until they are almost cooked. Then put them into a pot with oil, salt and a little flour mixed in with them, and peeled dry chestnuts and cloves of garlic, adding in enough water and a few sage tips. Finish off cooking them, adding pepper, cinnamon and saffron. Serve them as a thick soup. With them after they are parboiled you can put some rice and yellow rape so they cook together, and also some gnocchi made on a cheese grater.[253.1] In Lombardy that dish is called *macco*.[253.2]

254. To prepare a thick soup of dried lentils.[254]

Clean any dirt off the lentils and put them into a pot with warm water; remove any that float and boil the rest in the same water. While they are boiling, with a large, holed spoon lift out any that rise to the top and put them into another pot: that is done so that the sand that sometimes gets into their little hole will come out and drop to the bottom of the pot. Put good lentils into a pot with oil, salt, a little pepper, saffron, water and a handful of beaten fine herbs; finish off cooking them. For the dish to be good, make the broth rather thick. Cloves of garlic can also be cooked with them, and big pieces of tench and pike.

255. Several ways to make and cook macaroni for a day in Lent.[255.1]

Get a pound of fine flour and a pound of grated bread that has been put

---

'tastes rather like chickpeas. We cook them the way we do beans, but they are considered a rather common food, for they generate wind, bad blood and considerable melancholy' (trans. Riley, 103).

[253.1] The procedure is described in Recipe II,176. See also Recipes 255 and 256, below. Two models of *gratta cascio* are illustrated in Plates 10 and 22.

[253.2] The preparation still exists. Zingarelli defines the word as a *vivanda grossolana di fave cotte in acqua e ridotte in poltiglia* – a plain preparation of beans boiled down to a mush (*Vocabulario della lingua italiana* [Bologna: Zanichelli, 2002]).

[254] Presumably Scappi did not share Castelvetro's low opinion of lentils, which the latter qualifies as 'one of the most, if not the most, unhealthy vegetables one can eat, except for the broth, which, they say, is a miraculous drink for children with smallpox. In general lentils are eaten only by the lowest of the low' (trans. Riley, 102).

[255.1] '*Paste* made into strings like pack thread or thongs of white leather (which if greater they call *Macaroni*, if lesser, *Vermicelli*) they cut in pieces and put in their pots as we do oat-meal to make their *menestra* or broth of, much esteemed by the common people. These boiled and oiled with a little cheese scraped upon them they eat as we do buttered wheat or rice. The making of these is a trade and mystery [i.e., a craft]; and in every great town you shall see several shops of them' (Ray, *Travels*, vol. 1, 346).

through a fine sieve, and make up a dough with boiling water and olive oil mixed with a little saffron. On a table make the dough so it is not too firm, but well mixed together. When it is warmed up make the gnocchi – that is, macaroni – on the cheese grater[255.2] and put them to cook in lightly salted boiling water. When they are done, take them out and put them into an earthenware or wooden vessel, putting on them a garlic sauce made with ground walnuts, cloves of garlic, pepper and breadcrumb that has been moistened in hot water. Mix everything together and serve it garnished with pepper and cinnamon.

If, however, you want to make macaroni spread out with a rolling pin, make the dough a little firmer and let the sheet of it sit on a table a short while. Cut it with a pastry wheel[255.3] into rectangular strips or some other way, however you like. Cook them in salted water and serve them like the ones above. Anyone who wants to can also cover them with green sauce.[255.4]

256. To prepare macaroni and fry it in oil, which is popularly called *ferlingotti*.[256.1]

Get a pound of fine flour and another of milk of either shelled pinenuts or almonds, warm and with sugar in it; also get three ounces of breadcrumb soaked in that milk, three of sweet-almond oil and four of white wine. Make all that into a dough like the one above. Out of it make the gnocchi – that is, macaroni – on the back of the cheese grater or on a table.[256.2] Fry them in oil and serve them with sugar over them. The same can be done with any made of the same dough rolled out with a pin and cut with a wheel.

257. To prepare sops with various dried fruits.[257]

Get prunes and let them soak in warm water. After that cook them in white wine with sugar, cloves, nutmeg and cinnamon ground together. When they are

---

[255.2] The dough is pushed through the holes of the cheese grater. The same process is used in the following recipe.

[255.3] This *sperone* is literally a spur. It resembled a modern pastry wheel or pizza cutter. The circular blade could have a zigzag circumference for ornamenting the rim of a pie shell: see Plates 14 and 15.

[255.4] See Recipe II,272.

[256.1] This is the only instance in his *Opera* that Scappi will refer to *ferlingotti*. A modern version of *ferlingotti* is made of grated cheese, breadcrumb moistened in goat's milk, eggs, sugar and flour. The dough is flattened in small rounds (like small coins?) which are fried in lard, then dressed with sugar. The term may derive from *ferlingus*, in Old Italian *ferlino*, 'piccola moneta usata nel Medioevo, la quarta parte del denaro; nome generico di piccola moneta' (Battisti and Alessio, *Dizionario etymologico italiano*) – a coin of little value.

[256.2] If this dough is to be worked on a table Scappi could very well have directed that the cook avail himself of a macaroni rolling cutter, illustrated in Plate 13.

[257] This and the following dishes are lean-day variations of the meat sops that occupy so large a place in Book II. In early cookery it was entirely normal to use fruit with or in place of meat.

done, have slices of toast ready in dishes and put the prunes on them with the decoction. Serve them hot with sugar over top.

You can also do dried visciola cherries or halved dates or dried figs the same way.

258. To prepare sops with raisins.

Get raisins and cook them as above. Grind the same amount of uncooked raisins in a mortar with a little *mostaccioli*, moistening that with the decoction of the cooked raisins. Put it through a strainer and then bring it to a boil, adding in some of the same decoction if it is too dry. Soak slices of toast in that same liquid and put the raisins under and over the toast, along with the liquid. Mind, though, that the toast does not get too sodden. Serve it hot with sugar over top.

You can do the same with seeded muscatel raisins and other sorts of raisin.

259. To prepare sops of muscatel pears and various other pears, of apples and of quince.

Get muscatel pears, remove their flower and bring them to a boil in water. Then cook them in wine and ground sugar, whole cloves and whole cinnamon. Bergamot pears and riccardo pears are roasted; then peel them in hot wine so they end up coloured, and cook them whole or in slices like the muscatel pears. You can also give them a boiling after they have been roasted.

Apples, which are much softer than pears, are roasted and are cooked as above either whole or cut up in slices. Russet apples need more cooking than red apples,[259] but in cooking them follow the directions given for bergamot pears. When the above fruit has been cooked, get slices of toast, set them out in dishes and put the fruit with its decoction on them.

You can cook quince, too, the same way.

260. To prepare sops of various fresh fruits.

Get fresh visciola cherries or morello cherries, pitted, and cook them in a little wine, and sugar, cinnamon and butter, because they make juice on their own. When you see that the visciola cherries or marachino cherries have burst, take them out and put them into dishes on slices of toast that have been sautéed in butter. Morello peaches that are not too ripe are peeled, sliced and cooked in the visciola or morello cherry juice with a little white wine, sugar, cinnamon and cloves. When they are done, but not disintegrating, you make sops with them the same way as with the visciola cherries. Freestone plums that are not too ripe are peeled, either in hot water or not, and split in two. Damson and other varieties of

---

[259] Here *mele ruggine* are compared with *mele appie*. The usual phrase by which Scappi designates apples throughout his work is *mele appie*. It is uncertain precisely which variety of apple he means, but the qualification *appio* (or *appiolo*) refers to a bright red colour. Except where a distinction is necessary, the translation of *mele appie* shows merely 'apples.'

plum are left whole and are brought to a boil in white wine, sugar and cinnamon. They are served in dishes on slices of sautéed toast, with their decoction over them. Azaroles[260] and apricots can be done the same way.

261. To prepare sops of various dry and fresh legumes.

Take dry peas and cook them following the directions in the recipe for a tourte of them,[261] and grind some of them in a mortar. Put that through a strainer with the richest broth and put it into a casserole pot, adding pepper, cinnamon, beaten fine herbs and a little oil in which spring onions have been sautéed. When you have slices of toast ready and set out in dishes, put the strained peas on them together with a little of the whole peas. If, however, you want to serve the sops without whole peas, leave the spring onions in the oil or mix them in with the strained peas. Serve them hot with cinnamon on top.

You can also do white chickpeas and split chickpeas the same way without straining them but cooking them as is directed in Recipe 251. And lentils, too.

262. To prepare sops of field mushrooms and other commonly eaten mushrooms.

Get common field mushrooms that have been scraped and cleaned of any sand. If they are big cut them up into pieces. Scrape them and set them to soak so the sand will come away more easily and leave them better. Remove that from the water and put it with oil into a casserole pot or an earthenware vessel; sauté it gently because it will make its broth by itself. For every pound of the field mushroom that is sautéed, grind up four more ounces of some that is uncooked and that has soaked with half an ounce of spinach tops, moistening it with water and a little verjuice, and adding in pepper, cinnamon, a little saffron, enough salt, and a little finely chopped herbs. Put everything into the casserole pot with the sautéed mushroom and cook it. Taste the broth that it has a somewhat toasted flavour and is tangy with spices. Then have slices of sautéed toast ready, the thickness of the spine of a knife, put the mushrooms on them and serve that hot.

In the same way you can do any sort of edible mushroom, such as morels, brittlegills[262] and others.

---

[260] *lazzarole*: the bitter-sweet berry of a variety of hawthorn bush, *Cratægus azarolus*, that grows prolifically in Mediterranean regions. Messisbugo lists this fruit among dates, pears and apples. Castelvetro writes, '[It] is not yet known beyond the Alps. The azarole is beautiful to look at, delicious to eat, and good for you as well ... The fruit is the size of a walnut, or smaller, and at first sight you would take it for a nice plump cherry. It has a sour-sweet taste, and is an incredibly effective thirst-quencher for patients suffering from a raging fever. Doctors use it to reduce fever.' The azarole bush had long been native to Italy, yet Castelvetro adds, 'It is grown from scions of red apples grafted on to the wild plum' (trans. Riley, 118).

[261] Recipes V,91 and 224.

[262] *rossignoli*: an agaric of the genus *Russola* with a bright pinkish hue on its cap.

263. To prepare sops of large, fresh parasol mushrooms.[263.1]

Get those mushrooms, cut away their stalk, peel and wash them and put them into a tourte pan[263.2] with high sides or into a casserole pot, with oil, crushed cloves of garlic and enough salt; sprinkle them with pepper. If they are in a tourte pan, cook them with fire below and above; in a casserole pot, though, keep turning them over. Into that add beaten fine herbs and a few raisins. Grind the best part of the stalks in a mortar, moistening them with verjuice and saffron-tinged water, and put that in with the other and finish off cooking it. Then have slices of sautéed toast ready in dishes and on them put the mushrooms with their decoction.

You can do artichoke stalks the same way after they have been parboiled in water. However, they are always better stuffed with raisins and grated bread, pepper and cinnamon, and then braised with oil, adding in water and verjuice. Furthermore, you can do artichoke stalks, boiled and ground in a mortar, with pepper, cinnamon, saffron and a little finely chopped herbs. And when they are cooked, serve them on slices of toast. You can also do cardoon stalks that way, when they have been boiled and cut into slices.

264. To prepare sops of truffles.[264.1]

Get truffles that are free of sand and leave them under hot coals for half a quarter of an hour, or else give them a brief boiling[264.2] in wine and pepper. Peel them, cut them up small and put them into a pot of glazed earthenware or tinned copper along with enough sweet oil to cover them, and a little salt and pepper. Sauté them gently, adding in a little orange juice,[264.3] or else a little verjuice and must syrup; finish off cooking them. Then have thin slices of toast ready that have been sautéed in oil and soaked in a boiled mixture of white wine, orange juice,

---

[263.1] These *funghi castagnoli* are, literally, 'chestnut-coloured mushrooms.' Without naming them Castelvetro describes them as coming 'at the end of summer; they are very wide on a long, thin stalk. Some are white on the outside and russet-coloured [*rosseggiante*] on the inside, but not as firm or tightly closed as the field mushrooms; others are a very dark, chestnut brown [*castagnicci*]' (trans. Riley, 128). In Recipe V,223, Scappi writes of another variety of mushroom that grows in the woods at the foot of a chestnut tree, which he describes as tending to an orange colour.

[263.2] Scappi's *tortiera* is lidded and normally shallow.

[264.1] 'In Lombardy and other parts of Italy, *tartufale* ... are accounted a choice dish, held by naturalists to be incentive of lust. The best of all are gotten in Sicily, and thence sent over into Malta, where they are sold dear' (Ray, *Travels*, vol. 1, 346).

[264.2] Scappi writes, literally, 'Give them four boilings.'

[264.3] Scappi's procedure is echoed in 1614 by Castelvetro: 'Truffles should be wrapped in damp paper and cooked in the coals for about a quarter of an hour. Then peel them just as you would a baked apple or pear, cut them up very small, and finish cooking them in a pan with oil, salt and pepper. ... They are good to eat as they are, with just some lemon or bitter orange juice' (trans. Riley, 143).

sugar, cinnamon and cloves. Put the truffles on the toast along with the broth in which they cooked. Serve them hot, minding that they are neither too highly seasoned nor too insipid.

265. To prepare *crostate*[265] of cooked or raw caviar, with slices of toast.

Get the blackest, fattiest caviar, which will always be the best, and spread it on slices of toast. Put that toast into a tourte pan, sprinkling a little pepper, orange juice and a drop of almond oil over the caviar. Cover the pan with a hot lid. When the toast and caviar have been thoroughly heated, serve them hot.

266. To prepare gilded sops, popularly called *capirotata*,[266.1] in Lent.

Get Milanese almonds toasted on a fire shovel but not burned; remove any discoloration on them with a coarse cloth. Grind them and, for every pound of almonds, put in six ounces of raisins, three of muscatel raisins, two of *mostaccioli*, one of cinnamon and one of candied orange peel. When everything is ground up in the mortar, along with a pound and a half of sugar, moisten it with sweet orange juice,[266.2] malmsey and verjuice; put it all through a strainer, making the mixture runny. When that is done, put it into a casserole pot and bring it to a boil, stirring. Have slices of toast ready, sautéed in almond oil or in good olive oil, and make the sops. With that sauce you can also cover a variety of fish that have been grilled, braised or boiled.

I shall not write about sops made with the guts of the above-mentioned fish, in particular with trout roe, having said enough about them in the recipes devoted to them.

[Egg dishes]

Having written about various dishes for days that are not fasting or Lenten days, I now come to deal with egg dishes and days that are not fasting days.[iii]

---

[265] Of the two varieties of preparation called *crostate*, the present recipe is for the sort of canapé or open-faced sandwich seen in Recipes II,229 ff. rather than for the pies of Book V, Recipes 49 ff. and 198 ff.

[266.1] See Recipe II,227 for this dish on a normal meat day.

[266.2] *sugo di melangole dolci*. This is one of only two instances in the whole of his *Opera* in which Scappi expressly mentions sweet oranges. In Book IV see also the section 'Things for the Sideboard.'

[iii] All the dishes in this Book III are primarily for lean days. As we have already noted, the dietary restrictions for fasting days and during Lent were slightly more stringent than for ordinary lean days, the prohibitions extending to include not only the flesh of animals and fowl but their 'products' as well: eggs, butter and cheese. Elsewhere in his *Opera* Scappi provides a fair range of preparations designed expressly for those fasting or Lenten days. See, for instance, Recipes II,239 ff.; III,225, 226, 230–4; V,154, 159, 208; VI,69, 73, 125.

267. To cook eggs for drinking.[267.1]

Get eggs laid that day and in them make a hole no bigger than the head of a pin. Put them in a pot full of water that has boiled, remove it away from the fire and keep it covered until a little of the egg white has come out of the hole. Touch that white and if it is quite firm the egg will be cooked. You can tell whether it is done another way: boil an egg the length of time for a *Credo*, then tap it with the spine of a knife and if it withstands the first tap it is done. If it is not done, the shell breaks easily. You can also tell if, after it has been in the boiling water for the length of that *Credo*, you put the egg on a table and it spins – that is, if it turns around and rotates – then if it spins it is cooked. The fourth way of telling is, after it has been in boiling water for that *Credo* take it in your hand and tighten your fist, and if the heat is such that you cannot keep the egg in your hand it is certainly done. An egg cooked in the heat of the fire has to be turned often; when it begins to sweat and the drops run you can take it out because it will be done. When you serve you have to watch that you break it gently the distance of a knife's thickness down from the top and keeping the knife tip upwards: that is done so that, when the egg is opened, the milky liquid will stay in the shell.[267.2] Put a little sugar and salt on it.

268. To poach eggs in plain water.

Get a casserole pot or some other vessel with boiling water. Break an egg into a spoon that is not holed, which has a little cold water in it. When the water in the pot boils, put the egg into it and take the pot off the heat so it does not boil too strongly because there is a danger you'd break the egg. The water is put in the spoon to keep the white together with the yolk. Whether you make it soft- or hard-boiled is up to you. Take it out with a non-holed spoon because otherwise the egg white will slip into the holes and it will easily break apart. Serve it hot with salt, orange juice and sugar over it.

If you want to make sops of it, however, cut bread in thin slices and sauté them in butter. Put them into a dish and soak them with a sauce made of verjuice, sugar and cinnamon. On those slices of moist bread put the eggs with the rest of their sauce. You can make sops of them also with slices of bread fried in butter and sprinkled with sugar, cheese and cinnamon and soaked in a broth made with butter, water, sugar and spices. Serve the eggs on the slices and sprinkle it with sugar, cinnamon and grated cheese.

You can also poach eggs in goat's milk or cow's milk, serving them on thin slices of bread fried in butter with cheese, sugar and cinnamon over top. You

---

[267.1] If Scappi's dish name, *Uova da bere*, is accurate, these eggs are apparently soft-boiled and perhaps to be 'drunk' directly from the shell.

[267.2] ... *accioche scoprendo l'uovo, il latte rimanga con esso*. Scappi is, of course, referring to the uncongealed egg white.

can also poach eggs in white wine with sugar and cinnamon, serving them on butter-fried slices of bread and sprinkled with sugar and cinnamon.

269. To braise eggs in a baking dish or in dishes in the French manner.

Get an earthenware baking dish with clarified, melted butter in it that is not too hot; break the eggs into it. Cook them with fire below and above. As they begin to whiten, sprinkle them with salt, sugar and cinnamon. Serve them in a little baking dish[269] with a little orange juice and sugar over them. They can be served the same way in silver dishes and in little baking dishes of tinned copper or of silver. You can also cook the yolk without the white. The small baking dishes and plates are heated by means of a hot shovel on top or else with a hot lid from a tourte pan.

270. To cook fried eggs[270.1] in a frying pan with butter.

In order for the eggs to become good and white the butter is clarified, because when you use it unclarified, even though it is fresh, it nevertheless always has some clotted milk and ricotta in it; because of that it causes the eggs to darken and stick to the pan. When the butter has been clarified, melt it slowly over a low fire. When it is melted and not too hot, break the eggs into it, holding the pan up by its handle so the butter covers the eggs. Cook it slowly, preferably over the coals, splashing that hot butter over the yolks with a spoon until you see that the yolk is coated. Then when the egg looks like a marzipan *calzone*[270.2] take the egg out with a sharp spoon. Serve it with orange juice and sugar over it. If you want them cooked more, turn them over with the spoon.

271. To fry eggs with sprigs of rosemary in them.

Heat butter in a frying pan and break eggs into it. Immediately lay the sprigs lengthwise and push the eggs together with a spoon, making them look like saveloy sausages[271.1] with the sprigs held within them. They are served hot, dressed with orange juice and sugar. Alternatively they can also be cooked in

---

[269] This *tegametto*, specified for serving here and further on (where optionally it is of metal), is a smaller version of the ceramic *tegame* in which the eggs have just been cooked.

[270.1] *uova affrittellate*, properly 'frittered eggs.'

[270.2] Scappi is referring to a turnover of thin pastry, fried in oil. His *calicione*, a small turnover, was already described in the first half of the fifteenth century: see the *Neapolitan Recipe Collection*, Recipe 160 for *calisoni boni*. Today's *calzone* is a *disco di pasta da pizza, farcito con mozzarella, prosciutto, pomodoro e ingredienti diversi secondo le regioni, ripiegato a metà e cotto al forno oppure fritto* (Zingarelli, *Vocabulario*).

[271.1] Presumably they are to set with a roughly cylindrical shape. Scappi's image suggests the eggs must first have been scrambled.

a bull's-eye pan.[271.2] And in both those ways they can also be cooked with oil instead of butter.

272. To cook hard-boiled eggs in butter or oil.

Cook eggs in their shells in water such that they are not too hard. Then take them out of the hot water and put them into cold water, shell them and immediately flour them. Fry them in melted butter or oil. When they are done, serve them garnished with sugar and orange juice, or else cover them with garlic sauce[272] or some other sauce.

273. To cook stuffed eggs.[273]

Cook eggs as in the previous recipe, but they should be firmer. Shell them, split them in two lengthwise, and dig out the yolk. Grind it in a mortar with sugar mixed with raisins, pepper, cinnamon, raw egg yolk, a little salt, orange juice, and beaten mint, marjoram and burnet. Fill the hollow of the egg white with that mixture, then put the eggs, with their filling upwards, into a shallow, lidded tourte pan with enough butter to half cover them. Cook them with fire under and over them. When the mixture has set, serve them dressed with a sauce made of verjuice, sugar, orange juice and cooked raisins. Alternatively, when they are slightly undercooked, pour over them a sauce made of ground almonds with a little breadcrumb and raw egg yolk moistened with verjuice, sugar, and cinnamon. Bring everything to a boil together, tasting it to see that it is both bitter and sweet. Then serve it rather hot with the sauce over it and sprinkled with sugar and cinnamon.

274. To prepare little tubes of stuffed eggs.

Beat eggs. With the amount of a single egg make an omelet that covers the whole bottom of the pan, and sprinkle it with sugar, cinnamon and crushed skinned pinenuts that have soaked, raisins cooked in wine, and crumbled hard-boiled egg yolks. Roll that omelet up like a rolled wafer. Then make another omelet of the same size and thickness, sprinkling it with sugar and cinnamon; put the filling on that one and roll it up so that it ends up several layers thick. Cut them this way and that into pieces and put those into an earthenware or silver dish with butter, sugar, rosewater and orange juice; bring them and that sauce to a boil. Serve them hot, sprinkled with sugar and cinnamon. You can also add grated fresh cheese into the

---

[271.2] *la padella fatta ad occhi di bove*: the bottom of this sort of pan is dimpled concavely to hold eggs. See the illustration of the *Padella per fare ovi frittolate* in Plate 8 of the engravings, and the *Padella ovata* in Plate 9.

[272] Directions for an *agliata* are found in Recipe II,257.

[273] Perhaps a variety of 'devilled eggs.' See also Recipe VI,153.

filling. And if you want them a green colour,[274] do that with a juice of pressed herbs.

275. A different way to prepare little tubes, by sautéing.

Get eggs and make an omelet as above. Then make a mixture of hard egg yolks ground in a mortar with marzipan paste[275.1] and creamy cheese mixed with pepper, cinnamon and raisins, and fill the omelet as above. Have eggs beaten with a little rosewater and coat the little tubes with that; fry them in melted butter. Serve them hot with sugar and cinnamon over them. If you do not want them that big, but rather like fritters, take the little tube out of the pan and immediately cut it up into tiny bits[275.2] coat those pieces with beaten egg, flour them and fry them. Serve them with sugar and cinnamon over them.

276. To prepare double omelets.

Get ten eggs and beat them with a little rosewater, plain water and enough salt, and make ten omelets similar to the small cylindrical ones. Lift each one out with a cutting board or disk the size of the pan and put it into a tourte pan or a rather large silver dish. On it sprinkle sugar, cinnamon, orange juice, wine-cooked raisins, thin slices of fresh provatura or else a grated creamy cheese, mint and marjoram, doing the same with each of the ten omelets, one after the other. Over the omelets put a little melted butter, sugar and rosewater, and serve them hot. Instead of plain water when you are beating the eggs you can put in a beaker of goat's or cow's milk.

277. To prepare an omelet with beaten fine herbs and other things.

Get eight eggs that are two days old and beat them – they are better for an omelet than fresh ones because the fresh ones harden it, and it does not turn out as yellowish as with the other ones. When they are beaten, add in a beaker of goat's milk, beaten mint and marjoram, a little crumbled *mostaccioli*, crushed skinned pinenuts that have soaked, and truffles cooked in the coals and cut up small.[277] With that mixture make omelets in butter, turning them over so they are done on both sides. Serve them hot with sugar, orange juice and cinnamon over top.

---

[274] *& volendosi de color verde*: Scappi's syntax allows that either the omelet pieces ('them') can be green or their stuffing (change that 'them' to 'it,' referring to the filling).

[275.1] Scappi does not give a recipe for *pasta di marzapane*.

[275.2] Scappi's word here is *bocconcinelli*, a double diminutive. A modern sense of *bocconcino*, a diminutive of *boccone*, is either a 'small bite-sized piece' or, more specifically today, small balls of fried ricotta cheese or mozzarella. (See Zingarelli, *Vocabulario*, and Riley, *The Oxford Companion to Italian Food*, 57.) Scappi may intend to suggest 'dainty' morsels; in his next instruction he refers to the pieces merely as *essi bocconi*, 'those bite-sized pieces.'

[277] As in Recipe 264, above.

278. To prepare ordinary omelets.

Get six eggs and beat them with a little salt and three ounces of plain water. Put them through a strainer and make an omelet of them in butter the usual way. Serve it with sugar, cinnamon and orange juice or verjuice. Instead of the water you can put in almond milk. And if you want it green, get juice from spinach tops and chard; into that green add sugar and cinnamon. Into ordinary omelets you can also add a little grated bread. In the months of April and May put in elderflower.

279. To prepare an omelet in water, popularly called a 'tourte in water.'[279.1]

Get ten fresh eggs and beat them – for they are better for that purpose than other ones – and put in a little plain water so it will be softer. Put that through the strainer to remove the tread.[279.2] Then get a pot with boiling salted water and butter, pour the eggs into it and cover the pot a little while until the eggs become yellow. Gather it into a ball with a holed spoon, then take it out and put it into a collander to let the water drain off. Serve it hot, dressed with sugar, cinnamon and orange juice or verjuice. If you want it white, instead of the water put in a beaker of goat's milk; and if you want it green, put a beaker of chard and spinach juice in with the eggs at the very moment the broth boils – because if the juice remained too long with the eggs it would lose its colour and would not be as green. Instead of the juice you can use fine herbs beaten small or else elderflower.

280. To poach egg yolks in sugar.[280.1]

Get sugar liquified with rosewater and put it into a baking dish or a silver dish. Into that sugar pour egg yolks and cook them with heat from below and above. Serve them in that vessel with cinnamon and musk water.[280.2]

281. To cook frittered eggs in small silver baking dishes without butter or oil.

Smear a small pan or dish with a little white wax[281] and put eggs on it. Cook them with a hot shovel, because they need to be done with heat from above rather than from below so the wax will stay on the bottom. Serve them dressed with salt, orange juice and sugar.

[279.1] *torta in acqua.*

[279.2] *... per rispetto della calcatura dell'uova.* This, the tread or chalaza, is, as the *Oxford English Dictionary* defines it, 'each of the two membranous twisted strings by which the yolk-bag of an egg is bound to the lining membrane at the ends of a shell, and kept near the middle of the albumen, with the germinating point uppermost.'

[280.1] In his *Cuisinier françois* (Chapter 8, Recipe 80) of 1650, François de la Varenne gave the name *œufs mignons,* 'darling eggs,' to eggs cooked in a sugar syrup. La Varenne garnishes them with orange-blossom water and musk.

[280.2] The beginning of Book VI gives recipes for various medicinal potions, but neither *acqua di rose* nor this *acqua muschiata* are among them.

[281] This *cera* is not, of course, the modern petroleum-based product but edible beeswax, white because it has been purified.

282. To poach eggs on a shovel.

Heat up a shovel and when it is very hot grease it with a pork rind and smear it with white wax or else with oil, and immediately break the eggs onto it. Cook them with another shovel[282.1] over top, or else in the heat of the fire. Serve them with salt, sugar and orange juice on them. For lazy people[282.2] the eggs can also be broken onto embers.

283. To cook soft eggs[283.1] – that is, *barbagliate*.[283.2]

Get an earthenware or silver baking dish containing butter that is not too hot and break eggs into it. Put a little salt on them. As they begin to heat up, start breaking them with a wooden stick or a silver spoon, stirring them slowly. Add in verjuice, orange juice and sugar. When they have firmed up a little, serve them hot with rosewater and sugar over them.

284. To prepare a sage dish.

Beat ten eggs and mix a beaker of sage juice and spinach juice into them, straining everything. Add in a little salt, sugar and cinnamon. Then have a frying pan ready with melted butter in it and cook the mixture in that, stirring with a spoon. When it is slightly less than cooked, add in a little verjuice. Serve it hot, dressed with sugar and cinnamon. You can also cook it like the soft eggs – that is, *barbagliata* – of the previous recipe.

285. To prepare a thick soup popularly called *vivarole*.[285]

Get ten eggs and beat them. Have a broth ready, made of butter, salt, water, pepper, cinnamon and saffron, and in it spinach, chard, mint and marjoram, all finely chopped up as for a tourte. When that broth has boiled a little while with the herbs, mix a little grated bread and cheese into the beaten eggs and pour that into the broth, giving it a stir with a spoon. When it comes to the surface, serve it, hot.

[282.1] Presumably also pre-heated.

[282.2] *per persone svogliate*: these persons would be any cooks who might not want to bother with the heated shovels, Scappi's preferred procedure. Alternatively, though not convincingly, the *persone* might be diners who had no appetite or interest in their food.

[283.1] *uove tenere*. Clearly Scappi is making scrambled eggs.

[283.2] Literally, 'stammering, confused, mixed up.' See Sabban and Serventi, *A tavola nel Rinascimento*, 227: *Barbaglia poteva indicare la gola del maiale ... o avere il significato di mescolare*.

[285] See a meat-day version of this preparation in Recipe II,183. The sense of the term seems to be 'little beavers,' referring perhaps to the type of hat.

286. Another way to prepare a thick soup of eggs with milk.

Beat ten fresh egg whites with three pounds of that day's goat's or cow's milk and put it through a filter or strainer. Put that into a cooking basin[286.1] with four ounces of sugar and four of butter. Then cook it slowly on the coals, stirring it with a wooden spoon until you see the mixture sticking to the spoon and that it has set. Then have an earthenware baking dish or a tourte pan ready, greased with butter, and put the mixture into it. Then put in, whole, the yolks left over from the whites, separating them from one another so they are two fingers apart. Then cook the mixture the way tourtes are done, with little heat from below. When you see that it is beginning to set and is thickening the way a *tartara*[286.2] does, sprinkle it with sugar, cinnamon and rosewater, and finish off cooking it. When it is done, serve it hot. When you do not have any milk, get two pounds of verjuice and the rest[286.3] water, but put in more sugar, and follow through as before.

End of Book Three[i]

[286.1] This basin is a *bastardella*, a moderately deep, round-bottomed pot; see Recipe II,154. Its use for heating and stirring the present delicate mixture is appropriate.

[286.2] See Recipe V,86. This is a sort of custard.

[286.3] That is, one more pound of liquid.

[i] At the head of the Table to this Book III, Scappi calls it the *Libro quadragesimale* – that is, the 'Book of Lenten Foods.'

Book IV

Preparing Meals

[Preamble]

[f. 168r; 1581 f. 133r]

Having up to this point shown you how to prepare various sorts of dishes, both for meat days and for Lenten days, I will not, as I promised you in Book I, neglect to inform you about the order and procedure to be followed in setting out cooked dishes into the hands of the Lords Stewards, because you will not always encounter the kindness and graciousness of Reverend Don Francesco Reinoso, personal Steward of Our Lord, nor even of the Reverend Provost of Mondevi, Lord Giovanni Paldeo, both of whom, out of regard for me, hold you in their regard and have faith that you will zealously carry out everything I have shown you. I shall tell you all that because you will often have to deal with stewards whom their masters have installed in their Office more as favour than for any experience they might have of that function; yet, despite that, those masters confer that charge only when they recognize their cook's experience and capability. To that end I made the present Book, where I shall not overly strain myself showing you how and with what formal order a table has to be arranged for guests; not least importantly, you should be aware of the seasons of the year, for you have seen quite well how felicitously Reverend Don Francesco has had it set in springtime in cheerful locations that are sheltered from the breeze, in summer in airy, shaded places where there is lots of bubbling water, in the fall in a temperate location with an eastern exposure rather than northern, and in winter in rooms decorated with a variety of tapestries, sculptures and paintings to please guests; and always has the table of a length proportionate to its width, so that the attendants can set out and remove courses easily and those who are serving food or drink can move around [f. 168v] freely and without inconvenience to their lords. I shall draw up a list, though, of the things that can be served from month to month, things normally eaten in Italy and particularly in the City of Rome, with some *antipasti*

381

and *postpasti*[1] from the sideboard,[2] the Steward's domain. But, as I said in the First Book, it will always be more honourable for the cook to know how to serve as Steward than for the Steward to know how to serve as cook; so it is nothing if not advantageous for the cook to be knowledgeable also about determining the dishes for the sideboard as well as those of the kitchen, so that if in winter it happens that warm or cold dishes from the kitchen are served at the beginning with sideboard dishes, that will not mean that the order [1581 f. 133v] of the menus is being disrupted because whatever is done is for the pleasure of the table guests.

By means of those menus I shall in the present Book show a variety of formal and informal meals[3] that I have made, for either meat days or lean days, beginning with the month of April and going through the whole year. Some are with veal alone, some a sturgeon alone, some freshwater fish alone; other dinners

---

[1] The first are appetizers or hors d'œuvres – properly *ante-*, 'before' (that is, before the prepared kitchen dishes, and in contradistinction to *post-*, 'after'); the second, Scappi's *postpasti*, are either digestives or desserts. The menus show that Scappi's *antipasti* include marzipan biscuits, Neapolitan *mostaccioli* and sugared ricotta (folio 169r [1581 f. 134r]). His *postpasti* include such things as 'unlimited' candied seeds, nuts, fruits (*conditi et confettioni a beneplacito*, folio 170r [1581 f. 136r]). As constituting a course in a meal these foods can properly be understood in the literal sense of 'des-sert' – a serving as the table is finally cleared. Sweetened foods, because of their approximation to the human temperament, had long been held to benefit digestion.

[2] Scappi's word is *la credenza*. See the note in Recipe III,177. In the sense in which the word is normally used by Scappi – a serving table bearing the comparatively simple, usually cold foods served up from it – *la credenza* functioned in much the same way as the modern 'buffet.' However, the latter word, with its etymology of 'wine bar,' may today have connotations of liquid refreshments which would not be apropos in the context of the *Opera*.

[3] *diversi conviti, e colationi*. Etymologically the word *collatione* at one time designated a meal taken standing or walking around; the sense of the word is 'that which is carried with oneself.' In principle the meal would consist of finger foods rather than foods requiring personal cutlery or a trencher service at one's table. See the article by Hurtubise, 'La "table" d'un cardinale de la renaissance,' where he writes (274–5) of 'collations en plein air,' open-air collations, and indicates that, up to the time of Pius V, guests at such meals could include eminent courtesans. Scappi's *liste* of menus contain only ten meals that he terms *collationi*, all (regularly from May to February, excluding Lent) dated, without exception, the end of the month. One was set in a garden in Trastevere (May, folio 192r [1581 f. 155r]); one offered by Giovanni Ludovico Pio, brother of Rodolfo Pio, cardinal of Carpi, in the latter's vineyard at Monte Cavallo (according to the Table, June, folio 204v [1581 f. 167v]); another in a vineyard (August, folio 226r [1581 f. 185v]); and one (February, folio 304r [1581 f. 252v]) is expressly set indoors, again at Monte Cavallo but this time *nella sala dell'Illustriss. & Reverendiss. Card. Bellaia* (Jean du Bellay), at 7 p.m., with theatrical entertainment following. (Roman time measured the hours of a day from sunset, so that, depending on the season of year, in August one and two o'clock would be approximately today's 19 and 20 hours.) Table cloths, napkins and cutlery (spoon, forks, knives) are occasionally mentioned. Two of the collations follow vespers, three are combined with dramatic presentations; three begin at 'one o'clock' and one at 'two o'clock' in the evening (the latter being *a due hore di notte*, Roman time – that is, at two hours after sunset). For a *collatione* there is no distinction between kitchen foods and *credenza* foods: see the menu for the May *collatione*, below.

and suppers are with eggs and butter alone, others with pasta alone and for Lent alone. In addition to them there are a banquet offered on a Lenten day in April of 1536 by the Most Illustrious and Most Reverend Cardinal Lorenzo Campeggio of Bologna for his Holy Roman Majesty, the Emperor Charles the Fifth;[4] and a lean-day banquet prepared for 27 January 1567 for the second coronation[5] of Pius V, Supreme Pontiff.

At the end you will find a summary of the kitchen equipment needed by every great Prince who wants to travel extensively with his court, along with the arrangements any chief cook will have to make in managing every one of his underlings, and the constant hard work he will have to put into keeping his assistants, pastry makers, scullions, porters, glass workers and others moving along in proper order. But that will always be with the knowledge of the Chief Steward.

---

[4] *la Cesarea Maestà di Carlo Quinto Imperatore.*

[5] The date here is open to some question. On folio 286r [1581 f. 237v] the menu for that banquet begins with the printing of a different date: *alli 17 di Gennaro 1566 in giorno di Venere.* Michele Ghislieri became pope as Pius V on 7 January 1566. Normally a High Mass and coronation (with a banquet) would follow on the first convenient Sunday. The latter banquet date of Friday, 17 January 1566 might in fact be that of the joyous festivity still related to the election.

However, that 'initial' coronation was a relatively minor affair; at the banquet that rounded out the celebration only those attended who happened to be present at the Vatican or in Rome immediately after the new pope's election. Subsequent banquets were normally arranged as a regular festive event on the anniversary of that coronation. A second 'coronation' banquet was customarily scheduled to mark the end of the first year of the new pope's reign; to it invitations could be sent throughout Christendom, and particular guests of the new pope, ecclesiastic or secular, could have time to travel to Rome. The banquet marking the *seconda incoronatione* of Pius V was more likely to have been set for the date that Scappi writes in the present passage, 27 January 1567. In any case, undoubtedly planned by Scappi's kitchen long in advance, that banquet was never actually held. Here on folio 168v [1581 f. 133v] Scappi writes *il preparamento d'un convito*; later, on folio 286r [1581 f. 237v] he writes, 'Dinner prepared for the second coronation of the Supreme Pontiff Pius V, ... which then did not take place; it was to be served in eleven dishes ... ' Apparently the anniversary celebration was cancelled after the kitchen's plans for it were well advanced. We may suppose that the Vatican kitchens may already have been feeling an effect of the rigorously ascetic personality of Michele Ghislieri.

[f. 330v; 1581 f. 278v]

Table of the Fourth Book
On Preparing Meals[6]

Month of April

Dinner[7] on the 8rd of April, with two Credenza courses and one Kitchen course, served in two plates, with two Stewards and two Carvers.

Supper[8] with the same order as the dinner.

Dinner on the 15th of April, with two Credenza courses and two Kitchen courses, served in three plates, with three Stewards and three Carvers.

Supper with the same order as the dinner.

Dinner on the 25th of April, with three Kitchen courses and two Credenza courses, served in five plates, with five Stewards and five Carvers.

Supper with the same order as the dinner.

Dinner on a lean day in that month, with two Credenza courses and two Kitchen courses, served in two plates, with two Stewards and two Carvers.

Supper with the same order as the dinner.

Month of May

Dinner on the 8th of May, with two Credenza courses and two Kitchen courses, served in three plates, with three Stewards and three Carvers.

Supper with the same order as the dinner.

Dinner[9] on the 15th of May, of veal alone, with two Credenza courses and two Kitchen courses, served in four plates, with four Stewards and four Carvers.

Supper with the same order as the dinner.

Various other dishes made with veal.

Dinner on the 25th of May, with four Credenza courses and four Kitchen courses, served in seven plates, with seven Stewards and seven Carvers.

---

[6] As mentioned in the Introduction, the material translated at this point is in reality Scappi's index to the whole set of exemplary menus which constitute by far the major portion of Book IV. Following this translated synopsis a small sampling of the actual menus will be printed in their original language.

[7] The menu for this meal is reproduced below. It will be noted that Scappi's year begins in April with Easter.

[8] The menu for this meal is reproduced below.

[9] The menu for this meal is reproduced below.

Supper with the same order as the dinner.

[f. 331r] Dinner on a lean day in that month of May, with four Credenza courses and four Kitchen courses, served in eight plates, with eight Stewards and eight Carvers.

Supper with the same order as the dinner.

Collation[10] arranged at the end of May on a Friday in Trastevere in a garden.

[1581 f. 279r]

Month of June

Dinner on the 8th of June with two Credenza courses and two Kitchen courses, served in two plates, with two Stewards and two Carvers.

Supper with the same order as the dinner.

Dinner on the 15th of June with only one Kitchen course and two Credenza courses, served in four plates, with four Stewards and four Carvers.

Supper with the same order as the dinner.

Dinner on the 25th of June with four Credenza courses and four Kitchen courses, served in ten plates, with ten Stewards and ten Carvers.

Supper with the same order as the dinner.

Dinner on a lean day in that month with two Credenza courses and two Kitchen courses, served in six plates, with six Stewards and six Carvers.

Supper with the same order as the dinner.

Collation arranged at the end of June at Montecavallo in the vineyard of Cardinal di Carpi, Ridolfo Pio, by Sir Gio. Lodovico, brother of that cardinal.

Month of July

Dinner on the 8th of July with only one Kitchen course and two Credenza courses, served in three plates, with three Stewards and three Carvers.

Supper with the same order as the dinner, with one more Kitchen course.

Dinner on the 15th of July with two Credenza courses and two Kitchen courses, served in four plates, with four Stewards and four Carvers.

Supper with the same order as the dinner, with only one Kitchen course and two Credenza courses.

[f. 231v] Dinner on the 25th of July with two Credenza courses and two Kitchen courses, served in eight plates, with eight Stewards and eight Carvers.

Supper with the same order as the dinner.

Dinner on a lean day in the above month of July, made with eggs and butter alone, which can be given in any month, served on five plates, with five Stewards and five Carvers, with two Kitchen courses and two Credenza courses.

Supper with the same order as the dinner.

Collation arranged at the end of July on a Sunday after Vespers, with three courses served in seven plates, with seven Stewards and seven Carvers.

---

[10] The menu for this meal is reproduced below.

[1581 f.279v]   Month of August

Dinner on the 8th of Auguest with only one Kitchen course and two Credenza
   courses, served in three plates, with three Stewards and three Carvers.
Supper with the same order as the dinner, with one more Kitchen course, optionally
   whether salad is served although usually not when melons are served.
Dinner on the 15th of August with two Kitchen courses and two Credenza courses,
   served in six plates, with six Stewards and six Carvers.
Supper with the same order as the dinner, with only one Kitchen course.
Dinner on the 25th of August with three Credenza courses and three Kitchen
   courses, served in ten plates, with ten Stewards and ten Carvers.
Supper with the same order as the dinner.
Dinner on a lean day in the above month of August, with two Credenza courses
   and two Kitchen courses, served in seven plates, with seven Stewards and
   seven Carvers.
Supper with the same order as the dinner, with one more Kitchen course.
Collation[11] arranged at the end of August in a vineyard after Vespers on a lean day,
   with three courses served in five plates, with five Stewards and five Carvers.

                           Month of September

Dinner on the 8th of September with only one Kitchen course and [f.332r] two
   Credenza courses, served in two plates, with two Stewards and two Carvers.
Supper with the same order as the dinner.
Dinner on the 15th of September with only one Kitchen course and two Credenza
   courses, served in four plates, with four Stewards and four Carvers.
Supper with the same order as the dinner.
Dinner on the 24th of September with two Credenza courses and three Kitchen
   courses, served in ten plates, with ten Stewards and ten Carvers.
Supper with the same order as the dinner.
Dinner on the 28th of September on short notice, served with two Stewards and
   two Carvers, in two plates.
Supper with the same order as the dinner.
Dinner in that month on a lean day, from which Dinner the Supper will be made
   up, with two Credenza courses and two Kitchen courses, served in eleven
   plates, with eleven Stewards and eleven Carvers.
[1581 f.280r] Collation arranged at the end of September on a meat day, with
   three courses served in nine plates, with nine Stewards and nine Carvers.

---

[11] The menu for this meal is reproduced below.

Month of October

Dinner on the 8th of October with two Credenza courses and one Kitchen course, served in three plates, with three Stewards and three Carvers.

Supper with the same order as the dinner.

Dinner on the 15th of October with two Credenza courses and two Kitchen courses, served in four plates, with four Stewards and four Carvers.

Supper with the same order as the dinner.

Dinner on the 21st of October with two Credenza courses and two Kitchen courses, served in five plates, with five Stewards and five Carvers.

Supper with the same order as the dinner.

Dinner on the 28th of October, a combination of meat and lean, with two Credenza courses and four Kitchen courses, which Dinner will be used again as Supper, with eight courses and antipasti and postpasti, served in eight plates, with eight Stewards and eight Carvers.

[f. 332v] Supper on a lean day in the above month, with three Credenza courses and four Kitchen courses, which Supper can be used as Dinner, served in nine plates, with nine Stewards and nine Carvers.

Collation arranged at the end of October on a Friday at one hour[12] of the evening, served in three plates, with three Stewards and three Carvers.

Month of November

Dinner on the 8th of November with only one Kitchen course and two Credenza courses, served in two plates, with two Stewards and two Carvers.

Supper with the same order as the dinner.

Dinner on the 15th of November with two Credenza courses and two Kitchen courses, served in three plates, with three Stewards and three Carvers.

Supper with the same order as the dinner.

Dinner on the 21st of November with two Credenza courses and two Kitchen courses, served in five plates, with five Stewards and five Carvers.

Supper with the same order as the dinner.

Dinner on the 28th of October, with three Credenza courses and four Kitchen courses, served in ten plates, with ten Stewards and ten Carvers.

Supper with the same order as the dinner.

Dinner on a lean day in the above month, which can be used for Supper, [1581 f. 280v] with three Kitchen courses and two Credenza courses, served in three plates, with three Stewards and three Carvers.

Collation arranged at the end of November on a meat day at one hour[13] of the evening, after which a comedy was presented entitled *Gl'Ingannati*, with three courses, served in seven plates, with seven Stewards and seven Carvers.

---

12 That is, for October, at roughly 7 or 8 p.m.

13 Again, at roughly 6 or 7 p.m.

Month of December

Dinner on the 8th of December with only one Kitchen course and two Credenza courses, served in two plates, with two Stewards and two Carvers.

[f.333r] Supper with the same order as the dinner.

Dinner on the 15th of December with two Credenza courses and two Kitchen courses, served in four plates, with four Stewards and four Carvers.

Supper with the same order as the dinner.

Dinner on the 25th of December with three Credenza courses and three Kitchen courses, served in eight plates, with eight Stewards and eight Carvers.

Supper with the same order as the dinner.

Dinner on a lean day in the above month of December, which can be used for Supper, with four Credenza courses and four Kitchen courses, served in thirteen plates, with thirteen Stewards and thirteen Carvers.

Collation arranged at the end of December at two hours[14] of the evening, after which a comedy by Plautus was presented entitled *Il Pseudolo*, with four courses, served in ten plates, with ten Stewards and ten Carvers.

Month of January

Dinner on the 8th of January with only one Kitchen course and two Credenza courses, served in three plates, with three Stewards and three Carvers.

Supper with the same order as the dinner.

Dinner on the 15th of January with two Kitchen courses and two Credenza courses, served in five plates, with five Stewards and five Carvers.

Supper with the same order as the dinner.

Dinner on the 25th of January with three Kitchen courses and four Credenza courses, served in seven plates, with seven Stewards and seven Carvers.

Supper with the same order as the dinner.

Dinner[15] prepared for the second crowning of Pius V, Pontifex Optimus Maximus, on the 17th of January 1566 on a Friday, with four Credenza courses and two Kitchen courses, which then did not happen, and was to be served in eleven plates, with eleven Stewards and eleven Carvers, not counting the [1581 f.281r] Supper made for the end of January with four courses, served in six plates, with six Stewards and six Carvers.

---

[14] That is, for December, at perhaps 7 or 8 p.m.

[15] The menu for this meal is reproduced below.

[f. 333v]

Month of February

Dinner on the 8th of February without game animals,[16] with two Credenza courses and two Kitchen courses, served in two plates, with two Stewards and two Carvers.

Supper with the same order as the dinner.

Dinner on the 16th of February with two Credenza courses and two Kitchen courses, served in three plates, with three Stewards and three Carvers.

Supper with the same order as the dinner.

Dinner at the end of February on a day before Lent,[17] with three Credenza courses and four Kitchen courses, served in ten plates, with ten Stewards and ten Carvers.

Supper with the same order as the dinner.

Dinner on a lean day in the above month, of eggs, butter and cheese and pasta, without fish, not counting the salad and condiments, with two Credenza courses and two Kitchen courses, served in seven plates, with seven Stewards and seven Carvers.

Supper with the same order and the same dishes as the above dinner.

Collation arranged at the end of February at Montecavallo in the hall of Cardinal du Bellay at one hour[18] in the evening, after which a comedy was presented in French, *bergamasco*,[19] Venetian and Spanish, with four courses, served in eight plates, with eight Stewards and eight Carvers.

Month of March

Dinner on the 8th of March with only one Kitchen course and two Credenza courses, served in two plates, with two Stewards and two Carvers.

Supper with the same order as the dinner.

---

[16] *senza salvaticine.*

[17] *in giorno di Carnovale.*

[18] For the month of February that time might be about 7 p.m. The whole menu is reproduced below.

[19] Scappi's *Bergamasca* is the dialect spoken in the town and province of Bergamo, near Milan. It has been defined as vulgar Latin grafted onto native Lombard Celtic. Eight of the cardinals attending the meal were Italian; of them two, Santa Fiore and Cornaro, were closely related to Milan: Guido Ascanio Sforza ('Santa Fiore') belonged to the foremost family of that city and Andrea Cornaro was bishop of nearby Brescia. Two others of the eight cardinals, members of Pope Paul III's family, the Farnese, Alessandro ('Sant'Angelo') and Ranuccio ('Farnese'), also had ties to the upper Po valley. The four languages of the *comedia* may have been those of the eight cardinals' homelands. The actual menu of this historic collation is reproduced below.

Dinner on the 15th of March with two Kitchen courses and three Credenza courses,
   served in six plates, with six Stewards and six Carvers.

Supper with the same order as the dinner.

Dinner at the end of March with four Credenza courses and four Kitchen courses,
   served in ten plates, with ten Stewards and ten Carvers.

[f. 334r] Supper with the same order as the dinner.

Dinner in the above month on a lean day, with a sturgeon alone, which you can
   serve in any month in Rome and other places where it can be found [1581
   f. 281v] almost always, with two Credenza courses and two Kitchen courses,
   served in five plates, with five Stewards and five Carvers.

Supper with the same order as the dinner.

In Lent[20]

Dinner on the 16th of Lent with two Credenza courses and two Kitchen courses,
   served in three plates, with three Stewards and three Carvers.

Dinner on the 18th of Lent with two Credenza courses and two Kitchen courses,
   served in four plates, with four Stewards and four Carvers.

Dinner on the 30th of Lent with four Kitchen courses and three Credenza courses,
   served in nine plates, with nine Stewards and nine Carvers.

Dinner arranged in Trastevere by Cardinal Lorenzo Campeggio Bolognese, for the
   Holy Roman Emperor Charles the Fifth when the Emperor entered Rome in
   the month of April 1536 on a day in Lent, served in three plates, with three
   Stewards and three Carvers, not counting the plate of the Emperor.

Dinner on Good Friday without any sort of fish, fresh or salted, except for the
   salad, with three Credenza courses and three Kitchen courses, served in four
   plates, with four Stewards and four Carvers.

---

[20] No suppers are listed for this period of fasting and penitence; only five generally simple dinners are catalogued.

[A Sampling of Menus[1]]

[f. 169r; 1581 f. 134r]

Pranzo alli VIII d'aprile con due servitii di credenza, & un di cucina servito a due piatti con due Scalchi, & due Trincianti.

Primo servitio di credenza

[Prepared dish or foodstuff]	[Quantity]	[Servings]
Biscotelli di marzapane	nu. 12	piatti 2
Mostacciuoli Napoletani	nu. 12	piatti 2
Ricotte passate er la siringa servite con zuc- *caro sopra*	lib. 3	piatti 2
Presciuto cotto in vino tagliato in fette, servito *con sugo di melangole, & zuccaro sopra*	lib. 6	piatti 2
Offelle alla Milanese	nu. 12	piatti 2
		piatti 10

Primo & ultimo servitio di cocina

Frittelle fatte con sugo di sambugo servite *calde con zuccaro sopra*	nu. 60	piatti 2
Animelle, & fegato di capretto fritto servite *con sugo di melangole, & pepe sopra*	lib. 6	piatti 2
Teste di capretto indorate, & fritte, servite con *limoncelli tagliati, & zuccaro sopra*	nu. 12	piatti 2
Coratelle di capretto involte in rete, arrostite *nello spedo servite con sugo di melangole,* *& zuccaro sopra*	nu. 4	piatti 2
Pasticcetti sfogliati pieni di vitella battuta	nu. 12	piatti 2
Polpette di vitella arrostite allo spedo servite *con il suo sapor sopra*	nu. 36	piatti 2
Piccioni di torre ripieni stufati con prugne, & *visciole sacche, et fette di presciutto serviti* *caldi con il lor brodo sopra*	nu. 12	piatti 2

---

[1] The translation of merely a small plateful of Scappi's many menus is intended to give a taste of their nature and, particularly, a *soupçon* of the enormous amount of work for which, day after day throughout the year, Scappi was responsible. An interesting overview of noble meals in sixteenth-century Europe is offered in Albala, *Eating Right in the Renaissance*, 184 ff. The right-hand columns in Scappi's menus show the quantities prepared of each food (the units are *lib.*, pound(s), *nu.*, number) and the number of servings set out on all tables (*piatti*, platters, *tazze*, cups, *per sorte*, of each variety); totals appear at the end of each serving.

Pollanche nostrali affaggianate con limoncelli tagliati sopra	nu. 6	piatti 2
Mezi capretti di dietro arrosti allo spedo con fette di limoncelli sopra	nu. 2	piatti 2
[f. 169v]		
Trippe di vitella alessate servite con cascio, & cannella sopra		piatti 2
Lonza di vitella arrostita nello spedo servita con sugo di melangole sopra	lib. 20	piatti 2
[1581 f. 134v]		
Olive di tivoli	nu. 100	piatti 2
Capore d'uva passa, & di mostacciuoli		piatti 2
Gelo di piedi di capretto in piatti		piatti 2
		piatti 36

Secondo, & ultimo servition di credenza

Torte di salviata	nu. 2	piatti 2
Torte bianche	nu. 2	piatti 2
Carciofani cotti serviti con aceto, & pepe	nu. 12	piatti 2
Carciofani crudi serviti con sale, & pepe	nu. 12	piatti 2
Pere, & mele di piu sorti	nu. 48	piatti 2
Casci marzolini di due libre l'uno spaccati	nu. 2	piatti 2
Casci Parmeggiano in fettuccie	lib. 4	piatti 2
Mandoline fresche spaccate servite su le foglie de viti	nu. 200	piatti 2
Neve di latte servita con zuccaro sopra		piatti 2
Cialdoncini fatti a scartocci	nu. 150	piatti 2
Ciambellette di monache	nu. 150	piatti 2

Levata la tovaglia, & data l'acqua alle mani, si muteranno le salviette bianche.

Stecchi in piatti con acqua di rose	nu. 12	piatti 2
Finocchio dolce fresco	lib. 2	piatti 2
Marzette di fiori profumati	nu. 12	piatti 2
Conditi, & confettioni a beneplacito		piatti 2
		piatti 32

Cena con il medesimo ordine del pranzo.[2]

Primo servitio de credenza

Insalata di lattughetta, & fiori di borragine		piatti 2

---

[2] This is the evening meal of the same day, 8 April.

[f. 170r³]

Insalata di mescolanza		piatti 2
Insalata di sparagi		piatti 2
Insalata di piedi di capretti	nu. 24	piatti 2
Giuncate servite con zuccaro sopra		piatti 2
Salciccioni cotti in vino tagliati in fette, serviti freddi	lib. 4	piatti 2
Capponi sopramentati serviti freddi con capparetti sopra	nu. 6	piatti 2
Sapor di prugne		piatti 4
Fiadoni di farro serviti freddi	nu. 6	piatti 2
		piatti 20

[1581 f. 135r]

Primo, & ultimo servitio di cocina

Petto di vitella alessato servito con petrosemolo sopra	lib. 20	piatti 2
Anatrelle ripiene arrostite allo spedo servite con pedon di carciofani stufati sopra	nu. 6	piatti 2
Piccioni domestici in brodo lardiero	nu. 12	piatti 2
Agnelletti picciolini pelati, ripieni arrostiti allo spedo serviti con melangole tagliate sottili sopra	nu. 2	piatti 2
Spalle di castrato arrostite allo spedo servite con limoncelli tagliati sopra	nu. 2	piatti 2
Teste di capretti stufate con piselli con la scorza, & gola di porco	nu. 6	piatti 4
Pasticci di lomboli di seccaticcia serviti caldi	nu. 2	piatti 2
		piatti 22

Secondo & ultimo servitio di credenza

Torte d'herbe alla Lombarda	nu. 2	piatti 2
Torte di prugne secche marzapanate	nu. 2	piatti 2
Cardiofani cotti serviti con aceto, & pepe	nu. 12	piatti 2
Carciofani crudi serviti con sale, & pepe	nu. 12	piatti 2
Piselli teneri con la scorza alessati, serviti con aceto, & pepe		piatti 4
Mandoline fresche spaccate servite su le foglie de viti	nu. 200	piatti 2
Pere, & mele di piu sorti	nu. 40	piatti 4

[f. 170v]

---

³ This number was set as 169, repeating the previous folio number.

Cascio marzolino spaccato	nu. 4	piatti 4
Cascio di riviera	lib. 4	piatti 2
Neve di latte		piatti 4
Cialdoni fatti a scartocci	nu. 150	piatti 4

Levata la tovaglia, e data l'acqua alle mani, si muteranno salviette bianche, & si servirà

Finocchio dolce fresco	lib. 2	piatti 2
Stecchi su le foglie de viti	nu. 12	piatti 2
Mazzetti di fiori profumati	nu. 12	piatti 2
Conditi, & confettioni a beneplacito		piatti 2 per sorte
		piatti 44

[f. 180r; 1581 f. 144r]

Pranzo alli XV di Maggio di carne di vitella sola con due servitii di credenza, & due di cocina, servita a quattro piatti, con quattro Scalchi, & quattro Trincianti.

[Primo servitio di credenza]

Fraole suacate servite con zuccaro sopra	nu. 8	piatti 4
Cerase Romanesche	lib. 10	piatti 4
Sfogliatelle piene di bianco magnare	nu. 20	piatti 4
Capi di latte serviti con zuccaro sopra	nu. 20	piatti 4
Butiro fresco passato per la siringa servito con zuccaro sopra	lib. 6	piatti 4
Mostaccioli Napoletani	nu. 20	piatti 4
Calicioni cioè spoletti di marzapane	nu. 20	piatti 4

[f. 180v]

Pasticci di vitella di sei libre per pasticcio serviti freddi	nu. 4	piatti 4
Lomboli di vitella sopramentati con pitartamo, arrostiti allo spedo, serviti freddi con melangole tagliate sopra	lib. 24	piatti 4
Brisavoli di coste di vitella alla Venetiana cotti su la graticola, serviti freddi con sugo di limoncelli, et zuccaro sopra	lib. 20	piatti 4
Sapor d'uva passa, et di mostaccioli		piatti 5
		piatti 45

Primo servitio di cocina

Cervellate d'animelle, et fegato di vitella con la rete, arrostite allo spedo, servite con zuccaro, et sugo di limoncelli sopra	nu. 12	piatti 4

[1581 f. 144v]

Crostate d'animelle di vitella con uva spina, e zuccaro, servite con cannella, et zuccaro fino sopra	nu. 4	piatti 4
Frittura d'animelle, et fegato di vitella, servita con sugo di limoncelli, sale, et pepe sopra	para 4	piatti 4
Polpettoni di vitella ripieni arrostiti allo spedo, serviti con il lor sapor sopra	nu. 12	piatti 4
Trippe di vitella alessate, servite con cascio e spetierie sopra		piatti 5
Lingue di vitella alessate, et poi involte in rete arrostite allo spedo, servite con limoncelli tagliati, et zuccaro sopra	nu. 12	piatti 4
Lingue di vitella alessate, tagliate in fette in-dorate, con uove fritte nella padella, servite con melangole tagliate, et zuccaro sopra	nu. 4	piatti 4
Pasticci piccioli sfogliati di lingua di vitella con fette di presciutto, et grasso di rognon di vitella, serviti caldi con zuccaro sopra	nu. 20	piatti 4
Crostate sottestate con fette di pane coperte di rognon di vitella battuto, che prima sia stato cotto nello spedo con il suo grasso, overo con la lonza, servite con sugo di melangole, et succaro sopra	nu. 20	piatti 4
		piatti 37

[f. 181r]

Secondo servitio di cocina

Ponta di petto di vitella alessata, servito con petrosemolo sopra	lib. 24	piatti 4
Sapor bianco d'amandole		piatti 5
Brisavoli di polpe di vitella tramezati con cas-cio, uova, et uva spina sottestati	lib. 15	piatti 5
Pasticci di lomboli di vitella di sei libre per pasticcio	nu. 4	piatti 4
Gelo di pie di vitella in piatti		piatti 4
Cervellate di sangue di vitella passato il sangue cosi caldo mescolato con bocconcini di grasso, cipollette fritte, zuccaro, et fior di finocchio, et un poco di latte, et piene le budelle fatte cuocere come quelle di porco	nu. 8	piatti 4

Mortatelle fatte di polpe, et grasso di vitella, et presciutto, involte nella rete, et fritte, servite con sugo di melangole, et zuccaro sopra	nu. 12	piatti 4
Pasticci di vitella di sei libre per pasticcio serviti caldi	nu. 4	piatti 4
Pottaggio di giuntura di vitella	lib. 12	piatti 5
		piatti 39

[1581 f. 145r]

Secondo servitio di credenza

Torte di ricotta	nu. 4	piatti 4
Torte herbolate	nu. 4	piatti 4
Carciofani cotti serviti con aceto, sale, et pepe	nu. 20	piatti 4
Piselli teneri alessati con la scorza, serviti con aceto, sale, et pepe	lib. 8	piatti 4
Carciofani crudi serviti con sale, et pepe	nu. 20	piatti 4
Pere, et mele di piu sorti	nu. 60	piatti 4
Cascio Parmeggiano in fettuccie	lib. 6	piatti 4
Scafi teneri con la scorza	nu. 150	piatti 4
Mandoline fresche spaccate	nu. 200	piatti 4
Casci marzolini di due libre l'uno spaccati	nu. 4	piatti 4
Neve di latte servita con zuccaro sopra		piatti 5
Cialdoni fatti a scartocci	nu. 200	piatti 4

[f. 181v]

Ciambelle di monache	nu. 150	piatti 4

Levata la tovaglia & data l'acqua alle mani si muteranno le salviette bianche, & si servirà

Finocchio fresco dolce	lib. 3	piatti 4
Stecchi profumati	nu. 20	piatti 4
Mazzetti di fiori	nu. 20	piatti 4
Conditi et confettioni a beneplacito		piatti 4 per sorte
		piatti 69

[f. 192r; 1581 f. 155r]
Collatione fatta all'ultimo di Maggio.
In giorno di Venere in Trastevere in un Giardino.

Era posta la Tavola, con tre tovaglie, adornata con diversi fiori, & frondi, la Bottiglieria con diversi vini dolci, & garbi, la Credenza ben fornita di varie sorti di tazze d'oro, d'argento, di maiolica, & di vetro; e prima che fosse data l'acqua odorifera alle mani, fu posto sotto ciascuna salvietta una ciambella grossa, fatta con latte, ova, e zuccaro, & butiro, & fu servita à otto piatti, con otto Scalchi, & quattro Trincianti, & ogni volta che si levò la tovaglia, si mutò salviette candide, e per li conditi si messe forcine d'oro, e d'argento con coltelli; per le confettioni si messe cocchiari, & à ogni ser[f. 192v]vitio si messe su la tavola sei statue di rilevo in piedi, le prime erano di zuccaro, le seconde di butiro, e le terze di pasta reale, & tal collatione fu fatta dopo il vespro, con varie sorti di strumenti, & musiche.

Primo servitio con le prime statue di zuccaro
Diana con la luna in fronte, con l'arco, & cane al laccio, con cinque Ninfe.
Prima Ninfa con un dardo in mano.
Seconda con l'arco, & la faretra.
Terza con viola.
Quarta con cornetta.
Quinta con un ciembalo.

[1581 f. 155v]

Condite in zuccaro asciutte di piu sorte a beneplacito	lib. 16	piatti ò taze 8
Cerase palombine	lib. 24	piatti 8
Fraole suacate, servite con zuccaro sopra	lib. 16	piatti 8
Uva fresca conservata	lib. 24	piatti 8
Melangole dolci monde, servite con zuccaro sopra	nu. 60	piatti 8
Mostaccioli Napoletani	nu. 40	piatti 8
Spoletti di marzapane	nu. 40	piatti 8
Morselletti di pasta reale, lavorati in piu modi	nu. 40	piatti 8
Pignoccati freschi	nu. 40	piatti 8
Ciambelle di monache	nu. 400	piatti 8
Capi di latte serviti con zuccaro sopra	nu. 40	piatti 8
Butiro passato per la siringa, servito con zuccaro sopra	lib. 12	piatti 8
Giuncate in frondi, servite con zuccaro, & fiori sopra	lib. 40	piatti 8
Bottarghe tagliate in fette, servite con sugo di limoncelli, & zuccaro sopra	lib. 6	piatti 8

Schinale acconcio	lib. 6	piatti 8
Aringhe acconcie	nu. 40	piatti 8
Tarantello acconcio	lib. 10	piatti 8
Alici acconci	nu. 120	piatti 8
Insalate di sparagi		piatti 8
Insalate di capparetti, uva passa, & zuccaro	lib. 8	piatti 8

[f. 193r]

Insalata di cedro tagliato in fette, servito con zuccaro, & acqua rosa		piatti 8
Insalate di lattughe, & fiori di borragine		piatti 8
Pasticci di trutte, di sei libre per pasticcio, serviti freddi	nu. 8	piatti 8
Focaccine fatte con butiro	nu. 40	piatti 8
Olive di Spagna	nu. 40	piatti 8
Orecchine sfogliate piene di riso Turchesco	nu. 40	piatti 8
		piatti 208

Levossi la prima tovaglia, & dettesi l'acqua odorifera alle mani.

Secondo servitio con le altre sei statue di butiro

Uno Elephante con un castello su la schiena.
Hercole che sbranava la bocca al lione.
Il gran villano di Campidoglio.
Un Camello, con un Re moro sopra.
Un'alicorno che habbia il corno in bocca al serpente.

[1581 f. 156r]

Il cignale di Meleagro con la frezza in petto.

Piselli teneri alessati con la scorza, serviti con aceto, & pepe	lib. 16	piatti 8
Carciofani cotti, serviti con aceto, sale, & pepe	nu. 40	piatti 8
Tartufali cotti con olio, sugo di melangole, & pepe	lib. 18	piatti 8
Cardiofani soffritti con butiro, serviti con sugo di melangole, & pepe	nu. 40	piatti 8
Tartufali crudi, serviti con sale, & pepe	lib. 10	piatti 8
Palmette Napoletane acconcie	nu. 16	piatti 8
Pasticci di pere Riccarde, di tre per pasticcio	nu. 40	piatti 8
Pere guaste, servite con zuccaro sopra	nu. 80	piatti 8
Pere moscarole, o d'altra sorte crude	lib. 24	piatti 8
Visciole palombine	nu. 24	piatti 8
Raviggioli Fiorentini	lib. 16	piatti 8

Cascio Parmiggiano in fettuccie	lib. 16	piatti 8
Scafi teneri con la scorza	nu. 260	piatti 8

[f. 193v]

Casci marzolini spaccati di due libre l'uno	nu. 8	piatti 8
Amandole fresche spaccate su le foglie di niti	nu. 400	piatti 8
Uva fresca dell'anno passato conservata	lib. 24	piatti 8
Neve di latte, servita con zuccaro sopra		piatti 8
Cialdoni fatti a scartocci	nu. 350	piatti 8
Ciambellette di monache	nu. 200	piatti 8
Marroni cotti alle bracie, stufati nelle rose,	nu. 300	piatti 8
serviti con sale, zuccaro, & pepe sopra		
Composta di rape	lib. 16	piatti 8
Composte di carote	lib. 16	piatti 8
Composta di citrioli	lib. 16	piatti 8
Composta di finocchio marino	lib. 16	piatti 8

Levossi la tovaglia, & dettesi l'acqua alle mani, & si mutò salviette candide, cucchiari & forcine.

Terzo, & ultimo servitio con l'ultime statue

Paride con un pomo d'oro in mano.

Pallade ignuda.

Giunone ignuda.

Venere ignuda.

[1581 f. 156v]

Helena Troiana, adornata di veste, & capelli d'oro.

Europa sul toro, con le mani alla corna.

Cedri sani conditi	lib. 16	tazze 8
Limoncelli conditi	lib. 16	tazze 8
Melangoletti conditi	lib. 16	tazze 8
Cocomeri conditi	lib. 16	tazze 8
Meloni conditi	lib. 16	tazze 8
Cocuzze condite	lib. 16	tazze 8
Pere condite	lib. 16	tazze 8
Noci moscate condite	lib. 16	tazze 8
Noci nostrali condite	lib. 16	tazze 8
Persiche condite	lib. 16	tazze 8
Arbicoccole condite	lib. 16	tazze 8
Visciole siroppate in tazzette	nu. 40	piatti 8
Gelo di cotogne in scatoline	nu. 40	piatti 8

[f. 194r]

Scatoline di cotognata	nu. 40	piatti 8

Scatoline di copeta	nu. 24	piatti 8
Fucaccine di cotognata	nu. 24	piatti 8
Scatole d'anaci confetti di due libre l'una	nu. 8	piatti 8
Scatole di confetti grossi di due libre l'una	nu. 8	piatti 8
Scatole di folignata confetta, di due libre l'una	nu. 8	piatti 8
Scatole di seme di mellone confetto di due *libre l'una*	nu. 8	piatti 8
Scatole di coriandoli confetti	nu. 8	piatti 8
Scatole di mandorle confette di dua libre l'una	nu. 8	piatti 8
Scatole di pistacchi confetti, di dua libre l'una	nu. 8	piatti 8
Scatole di pignoli confetti di due libre l'una	nu. 8	piatti 8
Finocchio confetto in pannocchie	lib. 16	piatti 8
Mazzi di fiori lavorati il pie d'oro, & di seta	nu. 40	piatti 8
Stecchi profumati con acqua rosa in piatti	nu. 40	piatti 8

in tutto tazze 88. piatti 128

[f. 226r; 1581 f. 185v]

Collatione fatta all'ultimo d'Agosto in una Vigna dopò il Vespro
in giorno magro, con tre servitii, serviti a cinque piatti,
con cinque Scalchi, & cinque Trincianti.

Primo servitio

Mostaccioli Napoletani, & Romaneschi	nu. 30	piatti 5
Pignoccati freschi	nu. 30	piatti 5
Morselletti di marzapane	nu. 30	piatti 5
Calicioni di marzapane	nu. 30	piatti 5
Cacchiatelle fatte con ova, latte, & zuccaro	nu. 30	piatti 5
Insalata di lattughetta, & fiori di borragine		piatti 5
Insalate di capparetti, uva passa, & zuccaro	lib. 4	piatti 5
Insalate di citrioli, & cipollette		piatti 5
Torte di prugne marzapanate	nu. 5	piatti 5
Trutte d'una libra l'una accarpionate, servite *con limoncelli tagliati & zuccaro sopra*	nu. 5	piatti 5
Uva fresca di piu sorti	lib. 18	piatti 5
Olive di monte Rotondo	nu. 300	piatti 5
Pasticci di corvi di sei libre per pasticcio, *serviti freddi*	nu. 5	piatti 5
Sfogliatelle piene di bianco magnare	nu. 30	piatti 5
Capi di latte serviti con zuccaro sopra	nu. 30	piatti 5

piatti 75

[f. 226v]

Secondo servitio

Parsiche duraci mone in vino bianco	nu. 60	piatti 5
Persiche apertore monde in piatti	nu. 60	piatti 5
Pere, & mele di piu sorti	nu. 100	piatti 5
[1581 f. 186r]		
Prugne damaschine monde, servite con zuccaro sopra	nu. 150	piatti 5
Melloni bianchi, & rossi	nu. 10	piatti 5
Casci marzolini di due libre l'uno spaccati	nu. 5	piatti 5
Olive di Spagna	nu. 180	piatti 5
Melangole di mezo sapore, monde, servite con succaro sopra	nu. 40	piatti 5
Nocelle fresche monde, servite su le foglie de viti	nu. 400	piatti 5
Noci nostrali fresche, monde, state in vino rosso	nu. 180	piatti 5
Marroni arrostiti, stufati nelle salviette con acqua rosa, serviti con zuccaro, pepe, & sale sopra	nu. 200	piatti 5
Neve di lette, servita con zuccaro sopra		piatti 5
Cialdoni fatti a scartocci	nu. 250	piatti 5
Ciambellette di monache	nu. 200	piatti 5
		piatti 85

Terzo, & ultimo servitio

Cialdoncini fatti di mollica di pane, & zuccaro	nu. 500	piatti 5
Ciambellette d'ova, & zuccaro	nu. 300	piatti 5
Finocchio dolce verde mondo il gambo	lib. 5	piatti 5
Mazzetti di fiori profumati	nu. 30	piatti 5
Stecchi su le foglie de viti in piatti	nu. 30	piatti 5
Conditi, & confettioni a beneplacito		piatti 5 per sorte
		piatti 30

[f. 286r; 1581 f. 237v]

**Pranzo preparato per la seconda incoronatione di Pio Quinto
Pont. Opt. Max. alli 17 di Gennaro 1566 in giorni di Venere, con
quattro servitii di Credenza, & due di Cucina, quale poi non si fece;
& si haveva da servire à undici piatti, con undici Scalchi,
e undici Trincianti, eccettuando il piatto di sua Santità.[4]**

Primo servitio di Credenza

Noci d'India, & nostrali confette asciutte	lib. 22	piatti 11
Scorza di cedro, & di melangole confette asci-	lib. 22	piatti 11
utte		
Polpe di cedro confetta asciutta	lib. 22	piatti 11
Melloni confetti asciutti	lib. 22	piatti 11
Persiche confette asciutte	lib. 22	piatti 11
Pignoccati freschi	nu. 55	piatti 11
[f. 286v]		
Pezzi di pistacchea	nu. 55	piatti 11
Calicioni di marzapane freschi	nu. 55	piatti 11
Mostaccioli Napoletani	nu. 55	piatti 11
Morselletti di marzapane in piu foggie	nu. 55	piatti 11
		piatti 110

Secondo servitio di Credenza

Biscotti Pisani con malvagia in bicchieri	nu. 55	piatti 11
Capi di latte, serviti con zuccaro sopra	nu. 55	piatti 11
Pesce salamone salato acconcio in insalata	lib. 17	piatti 11
Cedro tagliato in fette, servito con zuccaro,		piatti 11
sale, & acqua rosa		
Tarantello acconcio in insalata	lib. 17	piatti 11
[1581 f. 238r]		
Muggini di Comacchio acconi in insalata	lib. 18	piatti 11
Capparetti con uva passa, zuccaro, & aceto	lib. 17	piatti 11
rosato		
Caviale acconcio in piatti con sugo di melan-	lib. 17	piatti 11
gole sopra		

---

[4] The banquet that Scappi feels compelled to document here – among meals that historically did
take place – was to have been a long and lavish affair (prepared by a master cook at the very
height of his professional life) to honour Pius V at the end of his first year of wearing the tiara.
The kitchen was to have outdone itself by delighting guests with live birds within castles, the
pope's coat of arms formed in a variety of dishes and his effigy on red and yellow jelly. Though
unquestionably disappointing for Scappi, it is perhaps not too surprising that that pope, 'devout
to the point of bigotry' (Kelly, *Oxford Dictionary of Popes*, 269), ascetic, and zealous for reform
of any excess, should have cancelled such an extravagant display of decadent sensuality as is outlined here.

Fucaccine fatte con butiro piccole	nu. 55	piatti 11
Carpioni accarpionati, serviti freddi, con zuc- *caro, & aceto rosato sopra*	lib. 55	piatti 11
Cardi stufati in insalata	nu. 22	piatti 11
Orecchine piene di bianco magnare	nu. 55	piatti 11
Schiene d'arringhe acconcie in insalata	nu. 55	piatti 11
Olive di Spagna	nu. 220	piatti 11
Uva frasca conservata	lib. 33	piatti 11
Schenale acconcio in insalata	lib. 11	piatti 11
Fiadoncelli pieni di pignoli, & uva passa, & *zuccaro*	nu. 55	piatti 11
Alici acconci in insalata	nu. 165	piatti 11
Pasticci di trutte di 6 libre per pasticcio, serviti *freddi*	nu. 11	piatti 11
Gelatina in quadretti, con polpe d'anguille *misaltate cotte in vino sotto*		piatti 11
Carote acconcie in insalata		piatti 11
Bottarghe tagliate, & anguille di Comacchio *salate acconcie in insalata*	lib. 22	piatti 11
Trutte cotte in vino alla Milanese, servite *fredde con viole sopra*	lib. 66	piatti 11
Cefali stati in adobbo reale, cotti su la grati- *cola, serviti freddi, con zuccaro & cannella* *sopra*	lib. 55	piatti 11
		piatti 264

Primo servitio di Cucina

Offelle sfogliate alla Milanese	nu. 55	piatti 11
Regni di sua Santità fatti di pasta, lavorati in *piu modi*	nu. 11	piatti 11
Castelli di pasta pieni d'uccelletti vivi[5]	nu. 11	piatti 11
Armi di sua santità piene di varie materie	nu. 11	piatti 11
Lamprede grosse arrostite allo spedo, servite *con limoncelli tagliati, & zuccaro sopra*	lib. 33	piatti 11
Orate grosse cotte su la graticola, servite con *suo sapore sopra*	lib. 44	piatti 11
Teste di storione, & d'ombrina cotte in bianco, *servite con petrosemolo, & fiori gialli, &* *rossi sopra*	lib. 11	piatti 11

---

[5] The delight of discovering live birds within a pie (as at the top of f. 324r) was almost common-place by the sixteenth century. Here the pastry is in the form of castles; on f. 324v the live birds are found within clean napkins set before each diner before digestives are served at the end of the long and opulent banquet that honoured the Emperor Charles.

[1581 f. 238v]

Sapore giallo, & rosso, l'impresa di sua San-tità		piatti 18
Pasticci di calamari piccioli, d'una libra per pasticcio	nu. 55	piatti 11
Crostate di tarantello dissalato, & latte di spigole	nu. 11	piatti 11
Crostate d'alici, anguille, & tarantello	nu. 11	piatti 11
Tomaselle di sarde fresche, et tarantello, mescolato con caviale	nu. 121	piatti 11
Polpette di storione di quattro oncie l'una, arrostite allo spedo, servite con uva passa cotta in vino, & zuccaro sopra	nu. 121	piatti 11
Pezzi di porcellette d'una libra l'uno, arrostiti allo spedo	nu. 55	piatti 11
Cannoncine d'ova alla Fiorentina di due ova l'una, ripiene di uva passa, zuccaro, & cannella	nu. 55	piatti 11
Rossi d'ova fresche cotti, in piatti d'argento, con [f. 287v] *butiro, ferviti con zuccaro, cannella, et acqua rosa sopra*	nu. 110	piatti 18
Ravioli senza spoglia, serviti con cascio, zuccaro, et cannella sopra	nu. 330	piatti 18
Linguattole grosse cotte su la graticola, servite con limoncelli tagliati sopra	lib. 55	piatti 11
Triglie grosse cotte su la graticola, servite con capparetti, & zuccaro sopra	lib. 55	piatti 11
Pasticci di spigole di 6 libre per pasticcio	nu. 11	piatti 11
Rombi in pottaggio	lib. 44	piatti 11
Trutte cotte in vino, et spetierie, servite con fiori sopra	lib. 66	piatti 11
Calamari ripieni in pottaggio	lib. 33	piatti 11
Torte di bianco magnare, con sugo di mele appie	lib. 11	piatti 11
Gelo di lucci in boccone, di colore rosso, e giallo		piatti 11
Sgombri marinati, serviti con suo sapore sopra	lib. 44	piatti 11
Bianco magnare in piatti, con grani di melegranate, & fiori gialli sopra		piatti 11
Pasticci di lamprede, di quattro libre per pasticcio, con suo sapore dentro	nu. 11	piatti 11
		piatti 343

Secondo servitio di Cucina

Frittelle di pesce ignudo d'un'oncia, & mezza l'una, servite con zuccaro sopra	nu. 220	piatti 11
Fravolini fritti sbruffati d'aceto rosato, & zuccaro sopra	lib. 44	piatti 11
Sarde senza spina fritte, servite con petrosemolo sopra	lib. 66	piatti 11
[1581 f. 239r]		
Ceriole sottestate con fiori di finocchio, sale, & pepe	lib. 44	piatti 11
Linguatole, & passere fritte, servite con zuccaro, & capparetti sopra	lib. 44	piatti 11
Fiadoncelli ripieni di polpe d'anguille fritti	nu. 55	piatti 11
Triglie grosse fritte, servite con limoncelli tagliati sopra	lib. 44	piatti 11
Rombi, & carpioni fritti, serviti con melangole [f. 288r] *tagliate sopra*	lib. 44	piatti 11
Olive di Tortona con zuccaro, & sua salimonia sopra	nu. 230	piatti 11
Uva fresca conservata	lib. 33	piatti 11
Ova affittellate in diversi modi, servite con sugo di melangole, & zuccaro sopra	nu. 110	piatti 11
Frittate d'ova, d'otto ova l'una, verdi, & gialle, servite con acqua rosa, zuccaro, & sugo di melangole sopra	nu. 11	piatti 11
Cervellate fatte di sarde battute, & code di locuste	lib. 33	piatti 11
Spinaci soffritti, acconci con aceto rosato, uva passa, & zuccaro		piatti 18
Corvette, & trutte fritte, servite con melangole tagliate sopra	lib. 66	piatti 11
Pasticci di panza di tonno, di cinque libre per pasticcio, con suo sapor dentro	nu. 11	piatti 11
Lumache fritte coperte di salza verde	nu. 200	piatti 11
Gambarelli, cioè squille maritime, fritti, serviti con sugo di melangole, & sale sopra	lib. 44	piatti 11
Sgombri, et suere fritti, serviti con limoncelli tagliati sopra	lib. 55	piatti 11
Pasticcetti di code di gambari nostrali, di trenta per pasticcio	nu. 55	piatti 11
Palamide sottestate, servite con sua salza sopra	lib. 66	piatti 11

Cedri tagliati in fette, serviti con sale, zuccaro, & acqua rosa sopra		piatti 11
Ginestrata per minestra, servita con zuccaro, et cannella sopra		piatti 11
Tinche riverse ripiene, cotte su la graticola, servite con prugne, et visciole secche cotte sopra	lib. 66	piatti 11
Lucci grossi ripieni cotti allo spedo, serviti con suo sapore sopra	lib. 66	piatti 11
Crostate di mele appie, et zibibo senz' anime, et mostaccioli	nu. 11	piatti 11
Calamaretti fritti piccoli, serviti con melangole tagliate sopra	lib. 44	piatti 11
Gelo schiavone di dentale		piatti 14

[f. 288v; 1581 f. 239v]

Maccaroni Romaneschi, serviti con cascio, zuccaro, & cannella sopra		piatti 11
Suppe di padelle, cavate della scorza	nu. 1000	piatti 11
		piatti 344

Terzo servitio di Credenza, mescolato con robbe di Cucina

Ostreghe cotte su la graticola, & cavate in piatti, servite con suo brodo, sugo di melangole, & pepe sopra	nu. 220	piatti 11
Ostreghe cavate, stufate, servite con fette di pane sotto	nu. 320	piatti 11
Suppe di gongole, & telline cavate	nu. 1500	piatti 11
Granchi di valle, o di mare cotti alle bracie	nu. 300	piatti 11
Locuste, & astris, cioè gambari lioni di mare, cotti in vino, & spetierie, serviti mondi, con aceto, & pepe sopra	nu. 22	piatti 11
Gambari femine cotte in vino, serviti con aceto, & pepe	nu. 300	piatti 11
Frutte di pasta in diversi modi		piatti 11
Pasticcetti di pere, di tre pere per pasticcio	nu. 55	piatti 11
Pasticcetti di cotogne d'un cotogno l'uno	nu. 55	piatti 11
Torte di dattili, & pignoli mondi	nu. 11	piatti 11
Torte di mele appie, & mostaccioli	nu. 11	piatti 11
Gelo in forme di mezo rilevo		piatti 11
Cardi serviti con sale, & pepe	nu. 11	piatti 11
Tartufoli stufati con olio, sugo di melangole, & pepe	lib. 22	piatti 11
Tartufoli crudi, serviti con sale, & pepe	lib. 18	piatti 11

Pere caravelle cotte al calore del fuoco, servite con folignata sopra	nu. 55	piatti 11
Cotogno cotte allo spedo, servite con zuccaro, & acqua rosa sopra	nu. 55	piatti 11
Olive Napoletane	nu. 330	piatti 11
Pere guaste, servite con folignata sopra	nu. 120	piatti 11
Uva fresca conservata	lib. 33	piatti 11
Pere, & mele crude di piu sorte	nu. 165	piatti 11

[f. 289r]

Casci marzolini Fiorentini di due libre l'uno spaccati	nu. 22	piatti 11
Limoncelli di cascio Romagnolo	nu. 22	piatti 11
Raviggioli Fiorentini secchi	lib. 22	piatti 11
Cascio maiorichino	lib. 22	piatti 11
Raviggioli freschi	lib. 22	piatti 11

[1581 f. 240r]

Cascio Parmeggiano in fettuccie	lib. 22	piatti 11
Butiro con ricota pecorina passata		piatti 11
Provature fresche marzoline	lib. 22	piatti 11
Cascio cavallo Napoletano	lib. 22	piatti 11
Neve di latte, servita con zuccaro sopra		piatti 11
Cialdoni fati à scartocci	nu. 800	piatti 18
Ciambellette di monache	nu. 700	piatti 11
		piatti 361

Levata la tovaglia, & data l'acqua alle mani, si muteranno salviette candide con coltelli, cucchiari, & forcine.

Quarto, & ultimo servitio di Credenza

Finocchio dolce verde mondo il gambo	lib. 11	piatti 11
Stecchi profumati in piatti	nu. 55	piatti 11
Condite siroppate di piu sorte, libre 22 per sorte	lib. 22	piatti 11 per sorte
Confettioni bianche di piu sorte, in scatole di tre libre l'una	nu. 11	piatti 11 per sorte
Cieli di cotogne in scatoline, figurate, & non figurate	nu. 55	piatti 11 per sorte
Cotognate muschiate, in scatole di quattro libre l'una	nu. 11	piatti 11
Grani di mele granate in tazze, con zuccaro fino sopra	lib. 22	piatti 11
Mazzetti di fiori lavorati il piede d'oro, & seta	nu. 55	piatti 11
		piatti 88

[f. 304r; 1581 f. 252v]

Collatione fatta all'ultimo di febraro a Monte cavallo, nella sala dell'Illustriss. & Reverendiss. Card. Bellaia, à un'hora di notte doppo che fu recitata una comedia in lingua Francese, Bergamasca, Venetiana, & Spagnola, con quattro servitii, servita à otto piatti; con otto Scalchi, e otto Trincianti.[6]

---

[6] Both Antonio Buonaccorsi, secretary to the Cardinal d'Este, and François Rabelais, physician and secretary in Rome to Cardinal Jean du Bellay from 1547 to 1549, wrote reports of the festivities organized by Du Bellay on 14 March 1549 to celebrate the birth of the Duke of Orleans, the fourth child of Henry II and Catherine of Medicis on the previous 3 February. Despite Scappi's dating of this *collatione* at the end of February, Scappi's menu is almost certainly what was eaten at Du Bellay's celebration, or was at least intended for it. We have to accept Scappi's statement on f. 133v that he was 'responsible' for preparing it since it is among the 'formal and informal meals that I have made.' In both descriptive accounts of the day a dozen pages are absorbed by the sham battle that was scheduled to take place on the Tiber on Sunday, 10 March and the land combat – the narrative consists particularly of listings of the noble individuals who participated in it – in the large square in front of Du Bellay's palace the following Thursday; a disappointingly lean paragraph or two is then allotted to that evening's grand banquet, and even less space to the theatrical entertainments with which the day ended. Rabelais's description of the meal is reproduced here (as translated by Donald M. Frame):

'It was already getting late and a good time for supper, which, while His Excellency took off his armor and changed his clothes, as did all the valiant champions and noble combatants, was set in such great sumptuosity and magnificence that it could efface the celebrated banquets of many ancient Roman and barbarian emperors, indeed, even Vitellius's table and cuisine, so celebrated that it came to be a proverb, at whose banquet were served a thousand cuts of fish. I shall not speak of the number and the rare species of the fish served here; it is much too excessive. To be sure, I *will* tell you that at this banquet were served more than one thousand five hundred pieces of pastry, I mean meat pies, tarts, and *darioles*. If the foods were copious, so were the drinks numerous. For thirty puncheons of wine and a hundred and fifty dozen servings of light white bread lasted hardly any time, not to mention the other common white bread. And so my said Most Reverend Lord's house was open to all comers, whoever they might be, all that day.

'At the first table of the middle room were counted twelve cardinals, to wit: The Most Reverend Cardinals Farnèse, di Santangelo, Santa Fiore, Sermonetti, Ridolfi, Du Bellay, de Lenoncourt, de Meudon, d'Armagnac, Pisano, Cornare, Gaddi. His Excellency Signor Strozzi, Ambassador from Venice. Ever so many other bishops and prelates.

'The other halls, chambers, galleries of this palace were all full of tables served likewise with bread, wine, and victuals. When the tablecloths were taken up, for washing hands were offered on the table two artificial fountains all interwoven with fragrant flowers, with compartments in the old style. The top of these flamed with pleasing redolent fire, composed of musk-scented brandy. Below, by various channels out came Angel Water, naphtha water. When Grace had been said to honorable music, by Labbat with his great lyre was recited the Ode … composed by my said Most Reverend Lord.

'Then, when the tables were cleared and put away, all the lords came into the main hall, which was all decked and adorned with fine tapestries. [And other entertainments were offered.]' Donald M. Frame, ed. and trans., *The Complete Works of François Rabelais* (Berkeley: University of California Press, 1991), 799–800; the *Sciomachie* is found at 788–801.

In 1549, 14 March fell on a Thursday but, with Ash Wednesday falling the day before and Easter Sunday not until 21 April, Cardinal du Bellay must have obtained a special dispensation to serve his guests such rich and meaty fare during Lent.

Primo servitio

Fiori de cedro conditi	lib. 16	piatti 8
Scorza di cedro condita	lib. 16	piatti 8
Pere di piu sorti condite	lib. 16	piatti 8
Noci moscate condite	lib. 16	piatti 8
Persiche condite	lib. 16	piatti 8
Noce nostrali condite	lib. 16	piatti 8
Melloni conditi asciutti, & cosi tutte le so- *prascritte*	lib. 16	piatti 8
Mostaccioli Napoletani	nu. 40	piatti 8
Calicioni di marzapane	nu. 40	piatti 8
Biscotti Pisani con malvagia in bicchieri	nu. 40	piatti 8
Pignoccati freschi	nu. 40	piatti 8
Ciambelle grosse, fatte con ova, zuccaro, & *latte*	nu. 40	piatti 8
Sfogliatelle piene di bianco magnare	nu. 40	piatti 8
Capi di latte, serviti con zuccaro sopra	nu. 40	piatti 8
		piatti 112

Secondo servitio

Ricotte passate per la siringa, servite con zuc- *caro sopra*	lib. 20	piatti 8
Pasticci di caprio di sei libre per pasticcio, *serviti freddi tagliati in fette nelle casse*	nu. 8	piatti 8
Lingue di bove salate, cotte in vino, tagliate in *fette*	nu. 8	piatti 8
Mostarda Francese		piatti 8
Pavoni nostrali con chiodi di garofani in petto, *serviti freddi*	nu. 8	piatti 8
[f. 304v]		
Olive de Spagna	nu. 240	piatti 8
Uva fresca conservata	lib. 240	piatti 8

Presciutto cotto in vino, & poi sfilato, servito
  con uva pas[1581 f. 253r]*sa, capparetti, &*
  zuccaro sopra
	lib. 16	piatti 8

Capponi sopramentati serviti freddi, con fiori *di bugolossa sopra*	nu. 24	piatti 8
Gelo di colore d'ambra alla Spagnola		piatti 13
Salciccioni cotti in vino, tagliati in fette	lib. 12	piatti 8
Bianco magnare in forma di mezo rilevo		piatti 8
Pezzi di cignale col callo, cotti in vino, serviti *freddi*	lib. 40	piatti 8
Sapore d'uva passa fatto con mostaccioli		piatti 13

Teste di rufalotto cotte in vino, servite fredde con orpelle adornate, & fiori sopra, & fuoco profumato artificioso in bocca	nu. 8	piatti 8
Fagiani arrostiti allo spedo, serviti freddi con zuccaro, & capparetti sopra	nu. 16	piatti 8
Cedro tagliato in fette, servito con sale, zuccaro, & acqua rosa sopra		piatti 8
Ventresca di porco salata, involta nella rete, arrostita allo spedo, servita fredda, con sugo di melangole, & zuccaro sopra	lib. 40	piatti 8
Corone di pasta alla reale piene di crema	nu. 8	piatti 8
Gelo di grugni, & orecchi di porco alla francese		piatti 13
Ginestrata alla Ferrarese, servita con zuccaro, & cannella		piatti 13
		piatti 193

Terzo servitio

Pasticci di cotogne di quattro per pasticcio	nu. 8	piatti 8
Torte bianche marzapanate	nu. 8	piatti 8
Pasticci di pere, de tre pere per pasticcio	nu. 40	piatti 8
Torte cannellate alla Venetiana	nu. 8	piatti 8
Pasticci d'ostreghe, di quattro ostreghe per pasticcio	nu. 40	piatti 8
Ofelle alla Milanese	nu. 40	piatti 8

[f. 303r[7]]

Carciofani crudi, serviti con sale, & pepe	nu. 40	piatti 8
Cari crudi, serviti con sale, & pepe	nu. 24	piatti 8
Pere caravelle, cotte al calore del fuoco, servite con zuccaro sopra	nu. 26	piatti 8
Pere, & mele crude, di piu sorte	nu. 160	piatti 8
Cascio Parmeggiano in fettuccie	lib. 16	piatti 8
Casci marzolini di due libre l'uno spaccati	nu. 12	piatti 8
Arme di pasta di piu sorte, piene di gelo, & di bianco magnare	nu. 8	piatti 8

[1581 f. 253v]

Olive di Bologna	nu. 240	piatti 8
Uva fresca conservata	lib. 24	piatti 8

---

[7] On the first folio of a new gathering (whose signature is Ccc), this number 303 in the 1570 printing along with the next, 304, repeat numbers on the preceding folios. The first 304 was, furthermore, typeset as 104.

Tartufoli stufati con olio, sugo di melangole, et	lib. 16	piatti 8
pepe		
Tartufoli crudi, serviti con sale, et pepe	lib. 16	piatti 8
Ostreghe cotte su la graticola, fervite con sugo	nu. 260	piatti 8
di melangole, et pepe		
Pasticcetti di mele appie di quattro per pastic-	lib. 40	piatti 8
cio		
Un lavoriero di pasta voto fatto con la siringa		piatti 8
		piatti 193

Levata la tovaglia, & data l'acqua alle mani, si muteranno salviette candide.

Quarto & ultimo servitio

Neve di latte servita con succaro sopra		piatti 13
Cialdoni fatti à scartocci	nu. 300	piatti 8
Ciambellette di monache	nu. 250	piatti 8
Finocchio dolce verde mondo il gambo	lib. 6	piatti 8
Stecchi in piatti con acqua rosa	nu. 40	piatti 8
Cedri sani conditi	lib. 16	piatti 8
Polpa di cedri condita	lib. 16	piatti 8
Scorza di cedro, condita	lib. 16	piatti 8
Pere moscarole, condite	lib. 16	piatti 8
Persiche condite	lib. 16	piatti 8
Melloni conditi	lib. 16	piatti 8
Cetrioli conditi	lib. 16	piatti 8
[f. 303v]		
Gambi di lattuga, conditi	lib. 16	piatti 8
Cocuzze piccole sane, condite	lib. 16	piatti 8
Lazzarole condite	lib. 16	piatti 8
Melangoletti conditi	lib. 16	piatti 8
Limoncelli conditi	lib. 16	piatti 8
Scafi freschi conditi	lib. 16	piatti 8
Piselli freschi conditi	lib. 16	piatti 8
Nespole condite	lib. 16	piatti 8
Mandorlette verdi condite	lib. 16	piatti 8
Zengevero condito	lib. 16	piatti 8
Radiche di finocchio condite	lib. 16	piatti 8
[1581 f. 254r]		
Radiche di petrosemolo condite	lib. 16	piatti 8
Confetti bianchi in scatole, di tre libre l'una	nu. 8	piatti 8
Coriandoli confetti in scatole, di tre libre l'una	nu. 8	piatti 8
Anici confetti in scatole, di tre libre l'una	nu. 8	piatti 8
Pignoli confetti in scatole, di tre libre l'una	nu. 8	piatti 8

Mandorle confette in scatole, di tre libre l'una	nu. 8	piatti 8
Arancetti confetti in scatole, di tre libre l'una	nu. 8	piatti 8
Bergamino in scatole, di tre libre l'una	nu. 8	piatti 8
Cannella confetta in scatole, de tre libre l'una	nu. 8	piatti 8
Cotognata in scatole, di tre libre l'una	nu. 8	piatti 8
Gelo di cotogne in scatoline piccole	nu. 40	piatti 8
Visciole in gelo	lib. 16	piatti 8
Mazzetti di fiori profumati	nu. 40	piatti 8
		piatti 293

[f. 320r; 1581 f. 269r]

Pranzo fatto in Trastevere dallo Illustriss.
& Reverendiss. Cardinale Lorenzo Campeggio Bolognese alla
Cesarea Maestà di Carlo V. Imperatore, quando sua Cesarea Maestà
entrò in Roma del Mese d'Aprile, 1536, in giorno Quadragesimale;
prima fu posta la tavola con quattro tovaglie profumate,
& lavorate a diverse foggie, con dodici salviette;
con cinque servitii di Credenza, & sette di Cucina, servito a tre piatti;
con tre Scalchi, e tre Trincianti,
eccettuando il piatto di Sua Cesarea Maestà.

Primo servitio di Credenza.

Biscotti Pisani, et Romaneschi, con malvagia *in tazzette d'oro*	nu. 12	piati 12
[f. 320v]		
Morselletti di marzapane, lavorati in diversi *modi*	nu. 12	piatti 3
Pezzi di marzapane indorati	nu. 12	piatti 3
Mostaccioli Napoletani	nu. 12	piatti 3
Calicioni di marzapane freschi alla Venetiana	nu. 12	piatti 3
Pignoccati freschi	nu. 12	piatti 3
Melangole di mezzo sapore monde, servite con *zuccaro sopra*	nu. 24	piatti 3
Fucaccine fatte con olio d'amandole dolci, *zuccaro, & latte di pignoli*	nu. 12	piatti 3
Zeppolle alla Romanesca, cioè fritelle di ceci *rossi, zuccaro, zibibbo, uva passa, & dattoli*	nu. 48	piatti 3
		piatti 36

Primo servitio di Cucina, arrosto sottile

Lamprede grosse, arrostite allo spedo con sua *crostata*	lib. 12	piatti 3

Pezzi di storione scorticati, arrostiti allo spedo, coperti di bronegro, serviti con pignoli confetti sopra	lib. 12	piatti 3
[1581 f. 269v]		
Laccie cotte su la graticola, servite con zibibbo sens' anime cotto in vino, & zuccaro	lib. 18	piatti 3
Lampredozze di Tevere sottestate, servite con suo sapor sopra	lib. 40	piatti 3
Carpioni accarpionati, serviti freddi, con aceto rosato, & zuccaro sopra	lib. 15	piatti 3
Trute marinate, servite con sua marinatura, & zuccaro sopra	lib. 15	piatti 3
Suppe di prugnoli d'una libra per piatto		piatti 3
Pasticci di lamprede grosse, con suo sapor dentro, de quattro libre per pasticcio	nu. 3	piatti 3
Crostate di latte, & fegato d'ombrina	nu. 3	piatti 3
Olive Candiotte	nu. 72	piatti 3
Uva fresca conservata	lib. 12	piatti 3
Polpe di pesce battute in forma di pollastri	nu. 12	piatti 3
Frittelle di marzapane piccoline	nu. 250	piatti 3
[f. 321r]		
Gelatina di pesce in forma di mezzo rilevo		piatti 12

Secondo servitio di Cucina pottaggiera.

Pezzi di storione in pottaggio con prugne, & visciole secche	lib. 15	piatti 3
Porcelletti di dattoli in pottaggio	lib. 20	piatti 3
Calamaretti in pottaggio con zibibbo senz'anime	lib. 9	piatti 3
Lamprede grosse sottestate con suo sapor tagliate in pezzi	lib. 9	piatti 3
Rombi in pottaggio alla Venetiana	lib. 12	piatti 3
Torte d'amido con sugo di mel'appie	nu. 3	piatti 3
Polpe di pesce battute, fatte in forma di pesce	nu. 12	piatti 3
Pasticci di laccie di sei libre per pasticcio, serviti caldi	nu. 3	piatti 3
Trutte cotte in vino, & spetierie, servite calde con viole sopra	lib. 20	piatti 3
Torte marzapanate, servite con pignuoli confetti sopra	nu. 3	piatti 3
Frittelle di pasta reale in piu forme		piatti 3
Crostate di sarde senza spina, & tarantello, & pignuoli mondi	nu. 3	piatti 3

Casse di pasticci di pasta reale fritte, & poi piene di riso Turchesco	nu. 12	piatti 3
Gelantina di pesce in bocconi di color d'oro	nu. 12	piatti 3
Pezzi di luzzo grosso in pottaggio alla Tedesca	nu. 18	piatti 3
		piatti 46

[1581 f.270r]

Terzo servitio di Cucina, alesso

Teste di storione alessate in bianco, servite con viole pavonazze, & gialle sopra	nu. 3	piatti 3
Pezzi di storione alessati in bianco, serviti con petrosemolo sopra	lib. 20	piatti 3
Lucci grossi alessati in bianco, spogliati della pelle, coperti di miraus, serviti con pignoli confetti sopra	lib. 18	piatti 3
Trotte cotte in vino, & spetierie, servite con [f.321v] pimpinella sopra	lib. 18	piatti 3
Pasticci di lamprede grosse di tre libre per pasticcio con sua salza dentro	nu. 3	piatti 3
Pasticci di panza di storione, di quattro libre per pasticcio con sua salza dentro	nu. 3	piatti 3
Pastelle fatte con latte di pignoli, et d'amandole, & zuccaro	nu. 12	piatti 3
Corone Imperiali piene d'amido	nu. 3	piatti 3
Torte di piselli fatte con mostaccioli Napoletani	nu. 3	piatti 3
Bianco magnare fatto con polpe di lucci, servito con zuccaro fino sopra		piatti 6
Paste ripiene fatte con armi di sua Cesarea Maestà	nu. 3	piatti 3
Testo di gielo bianco indorato	nu. 12	piatti 12
		piatti 48

Secondo servitio di Credenza.

Cardi mondi, serviti con pepe, & sale	nu. 6	piatti 3
Mandorle fresche spaccate	nu. 140	piatti 3
Noci state in mollo monde	nu. 60	piatti 3
Pere papali	nu. 24	piatti 3
Ciambellette	nu. 72	piatti 3
Dattoli stufati	nu. 72	piatti 3
Pere stufate in zuccaro	nu. 24	piatti 3
Pasticcetti di pere, di quattro pere per pasticcio	nu. 12	piatti 3

Cotogne cotte in vino, zuccaro, & cannella, servite intiere con tresia, cioè folignata sopra	nu. 12	piatti 3
Torte di prugne, & visciole secche	nu. 3	piatti 3
Visciole secche, stufate in vino & zuccaro	lib. 6	piatti 3
Diverse paste vote		piatti 3 per sorte

[1581 f. 270v]

Gelo in quadretti con tarantello dissalato sotto		piatti 3
Ricotte d'amandole fritte		piatti 6
Finocchio dolce verde mondo il gambo	lib. 3	piatti 3
		piatti 45

[f. 322r]

Levata la tovaglia, & data l'acqua alle mani, si muto salviette candide, con coltelli & forcine, & cacchiatelle, & ciambelle grosse sopra le salviette.

Primo servitio di Credenza

Tarantello acconcio con olio, aceto, et origano	lib. 6	piatti 12
Alici acconcie con olio, aceto, et origano sopra	nu. 60	piatti 12
Caviale in piatti, servito con sugo di melangole sopra	lib. 8	piatti 12
Carpioni accarpionati, serviti freddi con aceto rosato, & zuccaro sopra	lib. 24	piatti 12
Schiena, et latte d'aringhe acconcie	nu. 12	piatti 12
Fiori di borragine in insalata		piatti 12
Fiori di cedro in insalata		piatti 12
Capperini, et uva passa in insalata	lib. 6	piatti 12
Fiori di rosmarino in insalata		piatti 12
Sparagi in insalata		piatti 12
Lattughette in insalata		piatti 12
		piatti 132

Primo servitio di Cucina

Triglie arrostite su la graticola, coperte di suo sapore	lib. 12	piatti 3
Linguattole grosse cotte su la graticola coperte di suo sapore, et grani di melegranate sopra	lib. 12	piatti 3
Pezzi di tonno cotti su la graticola, serviti con uva passa cotta, et suo sapor sopra	lib. 15	piatti 3
Spigole grosse ripiene cotte su la graticola, servite con sugo di melangole sopra	lib. 18	piatti 3

Cefali grossi cotti su la graticola, serviti con limoncelli tagliati, et zuccaro sopra	lib. 18	piatti 3
Uva fresca conservata	lib. 9	piatti 3
Pezzi d'ombrina sottestati asciutti, serviti con olive spaccate sopra	lib. 15	piatti 3

[f. 322v]

Sapor rosso in piatti		piatti 6

[1581 f. 271r]

Polpe d'anguille, & triglie battute, formate a modo di teste di capretto	nu. 12	piatti 3
Teste grosse di pesce salmone diffalate cotte in vino, servite con petrosemolo sopra	nu. 3	piatti 3
Pasticci di corvi di sei libre per pasticcio serviti caldi	nu. 3	piatti 3
Pasticci di tartarughe di terra di tre per pasticcio	nu. 3	piatti 3
Torte di tarantello dissalato, uva passa, & zibibbo	nu. 3	piatti 3
Torte di pere riccarde	nu. 3	piatti 3
Gelatina Schiavona		piatti 6
		piatti 51

Secondo servitio di Cucina pottaggiera

Pezzi d'ombrina in pottaggio di bronegro	lib. 15	piatti 3
Calamari grossi ripieni in pottaggio con cipollette battute alla Venetiana	lib. 15	piatti 3
Spigole in pottaggio con prugne, & visciole secche	lib. 12	piatti 3
Orate grosse alessate in acqua, & sale, coperte di salza verde	lib. 15	piatti 3
Carpioni freschi con uva passa, & herbuccie	lib. 12	piatti 3
Fravoline alessate in bianco, servite con sapor sopra	lib. 12	piatti 3
Crostate d'interiori di tartarughe di terra	nu. 3	piatti 3
Pasticci di spigole di sei libre per pasticcio, serviti caldi	nu. 3	piatti 3
Melangole piene di dattoli, & zibibbo stufato	nu. 24	piatti 3
Butiro d'amandole contrafatto in quadretti		piatti 3
Frittate d'ova di storione, di due libre d'ova per frittata con herbicine	nu. 3	piatti 3
Gelo di pesce in cannoncini di piu colori		piatti 6
		piatti 39

[f. 323r]

Terzo servitio di Cucina

Teste d'ombrina alessate in acqua, & sale, *servite con viole sopra*	nu. 3	piatti 3
Astris, cioè, gambari lioni di mare cotti in *vino, serviti mondi la coda, et le zanche,* *quali furno inorate, & argentate*	nu. 3	piatti 3
Spigole alessate, servite con sapore bianco, & *grani di melegranate sopra*	lib. 12	piatti 3
Corvi alessati serviti con maiorana sopra	lib. 15	piatti 3

[1581 f. 271v]

Merluccie alla Spagnola alessate coperte di *mostarda*	lib. 6	piatti 3
Spalle di castrato contrafatte, fatte di polpe *di pesce, cotte su la graticola, servite con* *zuccaro, & sugo di melangole sopra*	nu. 3	piatti 3
Pasticci di pezzi di tonno, serviti caldi, di sei *libre per pasticcio*	nu. 3	piatti 3
Pasticci di pezzi d'ombrina, di sei libre per *pasticcio, serviti caldi*	nu. 3	piatti 3
Torte di polpe d'anguille, & spinacci	nu. 3	piatti 3
Fritelle di pasta di marzapane fatte in arme *diverse*		piatti 3
Compositione di ricotta d'amandole con- *trafatta formata in tartarughe, indorate, &* *argentate*	nu. 12	piatti 3
Gelo con polpe di pesce salmone salato sotto, *che pareva presciutto*		piatti 3
		piatti 39

Quarto, & ultimo servitio di Cucina

Fravolini fritti coperti di viole gialle	lib. 12	piatti 3
Triglie grosse fritte coperte di viole rosse	lib. 12	piatti 3
Olive di Spagna	nu. 72	piatti 3
Uva fresca di piu sorte conservata	lib. 9	piatti 3
Lampredozze di Tevere fritte, servite con melan- *gole tagliate sopra*	nu. 48	piatti 3
Calamaretti fritti, serviti con limoncelli tagliati *sopra*	lib. 9	piatti 3
Pescie passere fritto, servito con capparetti, & [f. 323v] *zuccaro sopra*	lib. 12	piatti 3
Spigole d'una libra l'una fritte, servite con *grani, & sugo di mele granate sopra*	lib. 12	piatti 3
Pasticetti di prugni d'una libra per pasticcio	nu. 12	piatti 3

Ginestrata per minestra, servita fredda con zuccaro, et cannella sopra		piatti 12
Gelatina fatta in forme di stelle di mezzo rilievo, di colore d'oro		piatti 6
Code di locuste fritte coperte di sapore di visciole, servite con arancetti confetti sopra	nu. 6	piatti 3
Spinacci soffritti acconci con uva passa, aceto, et mosto cotto		piatti 6
Torte di caviale	nu. 3	piatti 3
Broccoli acconci alla Napoletana, serviti caldi, con olio, sugo di melangole, et pepe sopra		piatti 12
		piatti 69

[1581 f. 272r]

Levata la seconda tovaglia, & data l'acqua alle mani, si muteranno salviette candide lavorate in diverse foggie.

Secondo servitio di Credenza di robbe di Cucina

Ostreghe cotte su la graticola cavate in piatti, servite con sugo di melangole, et pepe sopra	nu. 48	piatti 3
Torte di preugne, et mele appie	nu. 3	piatti 3
Torte di pere carovelle	nu. 3	piatti 3
Pasticci di cotogne d'un cotogno per pasticcio	nu. 12	piatti 3
Crostate di prugnoli	nu. 3	piatti 3
Gelo con pesce vivo sotto		piatti 6
Code, et zanche di gambari monde, servite con aceto, et pepe	nu. 120	piatti 3
Pasticci di pedoni di carciofani di dieci per pasticcio	nu. 3	piatti 3
Suppe di telline cavate di 500 per piatto		piatti 3
Pesce patelle cavate, & poi sottestate, fervite con sugo di melangole, & pepe	nu. 300	piatti 3

[f. 324r]

Pasticci pieni d'ucelli vivi	nu. 3	piatti 3
Vermicelli di butiro contrafatto		piatti 3
Statue diverse di marzapane		piatti 3
Cialdoni di piu sorte	nu. 900	piatti 3
Ciambellette di piu sorte	nu. 500	piatti 3
Tartufali crudi serviti con sale, et pepe	lib. 6	piatti 3
Tartufali stufati con olio, sugo di melangole, et pepe	lib. 8	piatti 3
Carciofani crudi, serviti con sale, et pepe	nu. 12	piatti 3
Carciofani cotti, serviti con aceto, et pepe	nu. 12	piatti 3
Cardi serviti con sale, & pepe	nu. 6	piatti 3

Palmette Napoletane, servite con sale, et pepe	nu. 6	piatti 3
Pistacchi mondi	lib. 6	piatti 3
		piatti 69

Levata la tovaglia, & data l'acqua alle mani si mutò salviette con forcine d'oro, & d'argento.

Terzo servitio di Credenza

Finocchio dolce verde mondo il gambo	lib. 3	piatti 3
[1581 f. 272v]		
Stecchi profumati in tazze d'oro	nu. 12	piatti 3
Mazzetti di fiori con garofali profumati	nu. 12	piatti 3
cedri sani conditi	lib. 6	piatti 3
Polpe di cedro condite	lib. 6	piatti 3
Scorze di cedro condite	lib. 6	piatti 3
Pere moscarole condite	lib. 6	piatti 3
Pere di piu sorte condite	lib. 6	piatti 3
Grisomole condite	lib. 6	piatti 3
Persiche condite	lib. 6	piatti 3
Melloni conditi	lib. 6	piatti 3
Cetrioli conditi	lib. 6	piatti 3
Coste di lattuga condite	lib. 6	piatti 3
Cocuzze sane condite	lib. 6	piatti 3
Lazzarole condite	lib. 6	piatti 3
Melangoletti conditi	lib. 6	piatti 3
[f. 324v]		
Limoncelli conditi	lib. 6	piatti 3
Carciofani conditi	lib. 6	piatti 3
Scasi teneri conditi	lib. 6	piatti 3
Piselletti teneri con la scorza conditi	lib. 6	piatti 3
Mandorlette fresche condite	lib. 6	piatti 3
Nespole condite	lib. 6	piatti 3
Gengevero condito	lib. 6	piatti 3
Cerease marine condite	lib. 6	piatti 3
Radiche di finocchio condite	lib. 6	piatti 3
Rediche di cicorea condite	lib. 6	piatti 3
Radiche de boragine condite	lib. 6	piatti 3
Radiche di cardi condite	lib. 6	piatti 3
		piatti 84

Levossi le salviette, & se ne rimesse dell'altre candide con diversi uccelletti vivi dentro con cochiari d'oro, & d'argento.

Grani di melegranate con zuccaro sopra in	piatti 3
tazze d'oro	

Confetti grossi bianchi	lib. 6	piatti 3
Coriandoli confetti lisci	lib. 6	piatti 3
Coriandoli confetti gricci	lib. 6	piatti 3
Mandorle confette	lib. 6	piatti 3
Anaci confetti	lib. 6	piatti 3

[1581 f. 273r]

Pistacchi confetti	lib. 6	piatti 3
Pignoli confetti	lib. 6	piatti 3
Bergamini confetti	lib. 6	piatti 3
Seme di mellone confetto	lib. 6	piatti 3
Arancetti confetti	lib. 6	piatti 3
Cannella confetta	lib. 6	piatti 3
Folignata confetta	lib. 6	piatti 3
Finocchio dolce confetto in pannocchie	lib. 6	piatti 3
Cotognata in scatoline	nu. 12	piatti 3
Fucattine di cotognata alla Genovese	lib. 6	piatti 3
Gelo di cotogne in scatoline	nu. 12	piatti 3
Visciole in gielo in tazzette di vetro	nu. 12	piatti 3

[f. 325r]

Levata la tovaglia, & data l'acqua alle mani, si servì sul tapeto

Stecchi profumati	nu. 12	piatti 3
Mazzi di fiori lavorati il piede d'oro, et d'ar-gento	nu. 12	piatti 3
		piatti 60

A questo pranzo furno diverse musiche con diversi suoni.

[Things for the Sideboard]

[f.327r; 1581 f.275r]

I realize, Reverend Lord Don Francesco, that, in order to put on the aforesaid formal meals, it is necessary that the sideboard – in addition to fine and coarse cloths and towels,[1] salt dishes,[2] gold and silver knives, forks[3] and spoons, several sorts of candlesticks, gold and silver dishes, basins and jugs,[4] along with dishes, bowls and cups of porcelain, majolica and other sorts of earthenware for salads,[5] fruit and other cold things – should be furnished with those things – that is, with all

---

[1] *tovaglie, mantili, salviette*: these fabrics could be translated as serviettes, dust covers and napkins respectively.

[2] In wealthy households these salt-cellars were traditionally valuable artefacts. In about 1540 Benvenuto Cellini was commissioned by Hippolito d'Este, cardinal of Ferrara, to design and carve such a salt-cellar. The artist himself transmitted the themes proposed by two of the cardinal's learned advisers: 'Messer Luigi had suggested that I should fashion a Venus with Cupid, surrounded by a crowd of pretty emblems, all in proper keeping with the subject. Messer Gabriello proposed that I should model an Amphitrite, the wife of Neptune, together with those Tritons of the sea, and many such-like fancies, good enough to describe in words, but not to execute in metal.' Cellini's own design, eventually cast in gold for the French king, Francis I, incorporated other symbolism: 'I modelled two figures, considerably taller than a palm in height, which were seated with their legs interlaced, suggesting those lengthier branches of the sea which run up into the continents. The sea was a man, and in his hand I placed a ship, elaborately wrought in all its details, and well adapted to hold a quantity of salt. Beneath him I grouped the four sea-horses, and in his right hand he held his trident. The earth I fashioned like a woman, with all the beauty of form, the grace, and charm of which my art was capable.' In one hand the earth goddess held a cornucopia 'overflowing with all the treasures I could think of.' Beneath the figures he sculpted a diversity of fishes, animals and shells. 'What remained of the oval I filled in with luxuriant ornamentation.' (*The Autobiography of Benvenuto Cellini*, tr. John Addington Symonds [Garden City, N.Y.: Doubleday, 1946], 249.)

[3] Unlike the forks that Scappi has mentioned in his previous books, which are kitchen implements (see particularly Book I, §43 and §44), these are clearly part of the table cutlery and are smaller, lighter versions of their two-pronged kitchen counterparts. While such dining forks do turn up in the inventories of late-medieval French nobility (Louis d'Anjou, 1368; King Charles V, 1379), they continued through the Renaissance across Europe to be regarded as a contrivance of somewhat over-dainty Italian eating practice. See also below, f.276v.

[4] An ornate hand-washing basin and ewer are illustrated in Plate 23 of the engravings: *boccalle con il bacile*. Concerning the important role in a sixteenth-century house of vessels made of precious metals, see Valerie Taylor, 'Banquet Plate and Renaissance Culture: A Day in the Life,' *Renaissance Studies*, 19 (2005): 621–33.

[5] These *insalate* are foods that have been pickled or dressed in vinegar and oil (see Book I, §3), with sugar and spices occasionally.

sorts of them whether confected, dried or in a syrup – with jellies, visciola cherries, morello cherries, quince and quince pastes, Neapolitan and Roman *mostaccioli*, several shapes of marzipan creations, pinenut paste, pistachio paste,[6] little goblets[7] and other sugar confections, Pisan, Roman and other sorts of biscuits, always rolled wafers and small *ciambelle* of raw dates, pistachios, pinenuts and Milanese almonds, dried figs of various sorts, white confections, several sorts of olives and small capers, compote of fennel and other fruits, dried grapes – that is, ordinary raisins, Slavonian raisins, *passarina* raisins,[8] currants, muscatel raisins [f. 327v] – fresh, preserved grapes, pomegranates, quince, sweet, semi-sweet and bitter oranges,[9] citrons, small Neapolitan limes and juice limes; caravella pears, papal pears, *acciole* pears, riccardo pears, rough pears, bergamot pears, Florentine pears and other sorts of pear, red apples, pink apples, russet apples and other sorts of apple, March cheese,[10] Florentine *raviggioli*, Romagnola cheese, Roman cheese, Ligurian cheese,[11] Majorcan cheese, fresh and dry *caciocavallo*, March provatura and other sorts of cheese; in spring, summer and fall, milk curds,[12] cream tops, fresh butter, ewe's milk curd cheese,[13] fresh mozzarella, milk-snow. For meat

---

[6] See Recipe VI,217.

[7] *coppete*: see the *calicione di marzapane* in Recipe III,270.

[8] These are a small grape left to dry and shrink on the vine and producing a sweet wine called *passita*. The 1570 printing reads … *uva passa, uva Schiava passarina di Corintho, zibibbo* … ; the 1581 printing has … *uva passa, uva Schiava, passarina, di Corinto, zibibbo* …

[9] Of the three varieties of orange that were available in Scappi's day, the most recently developed, the sweet orange, is still very rare in the *Opera*. It is mentioned here as a whole fruit for eating; the only other use of it is for its juice in Recipe III,266.

[10] For the cheeses mentioned here, and others, see Book I,§8. Pantaleone di Confineza deals with March cheese in his Book II, Chapter 1 (ed. Naso, 114): '*Caseus marcelinus* is commonly called Florentine cheese because it is made around Florence, in Tuscany and the Romagna. They are large rounds, a big arm in depth and span or semi-cubit in diameter. They are quite clean and translucent, of a lemon, waxy colour, at their best in summer. For the most part they are made of sheep's milk, with perhaps some cow's milk mixed in. They are quite solid, with no holes. They are most tasty when moderately hardened over time … They are a delicate cheese and are transported far; I have eaten some in France.'

[11] *cascio di Riviera*.

[12] These *giuncate* are made of a freshly curdled milk and were usually formed, stored and carried in reed (*giunco*) baskets. The Italian word is at the origin of the modern English junket. In Recipe V,85 the curds are also known as *lattaroli*.

[13] *ricotte fiorite*. Domenico Romoli (Book 7, Chapter 44) assimilates *fiorita* with cream-tops and curdled milk (i.e., *giuncata*), warning that they are the most difficult to digest of all milk products and, unlike other cheeses, should be eaten at the beginning of a meal (ed. Faccioli, *Arte della cucina*, I, 383).

days, cold salami,[14] – that is, *salsiccioni*, mortadelle, prosciutto, sowbelly, salt ox tongues, buffalo tongues and pork tongues, semi-salted cow meat, salted steer meat,[15] *sambudelli*[16] salt pork belly and jowl. All of those salami have to be cooked, although *salsiccioni* and fat prosciutto are sometimes served uncooked in thin slices, and mortadella and *giambudelle* are served hot or cold, whichever you like. Big cold pies of roe deer, wild boar, wild piglet and veal, and any other sort of domestic or game quadruped that is normally eaten. Likewise, big cold pies of common peacocks and turkey cocks, cranes, pheasants, grey partridge, wild quail, common pullets and turkey pullets, capons and other fowl. And pies of large cold salami, of prosciutto, sowbelly, *salsiccioni*, mortadelle and *barbaglia* – that is, salt pork jowl.

For lean days the sideboard should be furnished with salted tuna belly, smoked tuna belly, salted salmon, smoked herring and white salmon,[17] anchovies, large sardines, [1581 f. 275v] salted eels from any lake, salted sturgeon belly and back, mullet caviar and sturgeon caviar, pickled gilthead and grey mullet,[18] soused salmon carp, large trout and grey mullets – that is, smoked *migliaccine*[19] – brown meagre, trout, sea bass and any other fish in leaves,[20] old giltheads and chunks of salmon marinated with royal marinade[21] and served cold with muscatel raisins over them, big cold pies of such sea fish as sturgeon, tuna, grey mullet, sea bass, brown meagre, corb, bonito, allis shad and other sea fish. And the same big cold pies of large trout, salmon carp and pike, large eels, Slavonic jelly and other large fish done in jelly. It will be furnished with fresh fruit according to

---

[14] The term *salame* is a generic composite for any meat, a cut or ground-up meat, that has been preserved, usually in salt.

[15] Only the meat of the female and the castrated bovine animals was considered moist enough to undergo the salting process. The meat of a bull or ox dried out as the animal worked in the open drawing a plough or cart; to eat such beef if it were salt-dried would be dangerous.

[16] In Scappi's text, *giambudelle*. These sausages are listed among other varieties in Messisbugo's *Banchetti*: *Salami di porco ... salsiccioni, zambudelli, mortadelle ... sanguinacci bianchi e rossi, tomaselle, salsiccia rossa e gialla, migliazzo* (ed. Faccioli, *Arte della cucina*, I, 267). Scappi uses all of these basic varieties of sausage. The *Dizionario etimologico italiano* of Battisti and Alessio dates the word (which combines *sangue*, blood, and *budello*, bowel) from before 1742 (in Pistoia) and glosses the sausage as a *biroldo*.

[17] Recipe III,210 indicates that these *aringhe bianche* are plain, salted herring, untinged with smoke. The best smoked herrings, Scappi advises us in I,§17, will be of a russet colour.

[18] These *orate, & cefali in aceto* are dealt with in Recipes III,46 and III,54 respectively.

[19] See Recipe III,215.

[20] *di foglia*: preserved in plant leaves as in Book I,§18 and Recipes III,52, 73 and 117.

[21] The *Opera* does not explain what this *marinatura reale* is. A *marinatura* in Recipe III,73, however, is composed richly of vinegar, sugar, must syrup and saffron – the last a regal colourant.

the season: in April, strawberries, fresh little almonds, artichokes, Neapolitan palm-leaves; in May, as well as the above fruit you can serve visciola cherries, *palombino* cherries, Roman cherries and muscatel pears; in June, add apricots, mirabelle plums, mulberries and fresh hazelnuts; in July, [f.328r] add white and brown melons, cleaned fresh figs, fresh grapes such as muscatel and others, and fresh walnuts that have steeped in red wine; in August and September to the July servings are added pears and apples of every variety, azaroles, roasted chestnuts,[22] clingstone and freestone peaches, peeled and unpeeled; from October to March, as well as the above, peeled truffles are served, and sorb apples;[23] in November, ripe medlars.

---

[22] A century later John Ray wrote of Italian food, 'Chestnuts roasted and the kernels served up with juice of lemon and sugar are much esteemed. ... Roasted chestnuts are a great part of the diet of the poor peasants in Italy' (*Travels*).

[23] These *sorbe* are also known as service berries. Of them Castelvetro writes, 'Sorb-apples are picked at the beginning of the autumn while they are still sharp, and put to ripen in straw or hung in bunches from nails. They have the same taste as medlars but are very astringent and not so pleasant' (trans. Riley, 126).

[Kitchen Equipment when Travelling]

[1581 f. 276r] Catalogue and preparation of kitchen equipment for a trip that any great prince might wish to make.[1]

G iven that up to here in these four Books I have provided fully detailed directions needed for making various plates and for setting them out, as well as an exposition of things for the sideboard, I think it would be just as useful to list the equipment and arrangements to be adopted when travelling with any great Prince. Therefore, the Master Cook who is concerned for the honour of his Office, before setting forth has always to select the lightest and most practical equipment and, above all, to have experienced, reliable men around him as assistants, under-cooks, scullions, pastry workers, and robust young porters to be able to load and unload; each of those individuals has to be furnished with a mount and every other requisite appropriate to his station; and the scullions, who will travel on foot, should not be without footwear and tunics[2] as is usual in any court, especially those in Rome. Concerning the equipment (as I said above), having taken the lightest, you will have prepared two leather-bound chests, small or large, partitioned inside, four strongboxes,[3] three sets of hampers[4] and two sets of iron-bound cases, as are usual.

To transport those things you need, for the chests, a large horse on which the chests will go, with one assistant who will always have to go ahead with the Master Cook, and two other assistants: that is done so the assistant can choose the most convenient place for cooking, for setting up fireplaces, for [f. 328v] bringing wood and water, for setting up the tables even though the outriders[5] have gone on

---

[1] See the outdoor kitchen represented in Plate 6. A detailed analysis of the logistics involved in the lengthy travels of a fourteenth-century noble is presented by Paweł T. Dobrowolski in 'Food Purchases of a Travelling Nobleman: The Accounts of the Earl of Derby, 1390–1393,' *Food and Foodways*, 2 (1988): 289–308. An important portion of the life of a medieval or Renaissance noble was spent travelling. During such excursions a major preoccupation of the lord's steward was to feed not only the master but the whole of the master's retinue. For Henry of Bolingbroke, Earl of Derby, the bulk of daily expenses while away from home was devoted to food and its preparation.

[2] These *boricchi* are a relatively long vestment of coarse wool.

[3] Two sorts of Scappi's *forziera* are illustrated in Plate 24. It is a lockable trunk or case.

[4] See the *ceste* hung up out of the way on a wall in Plate 3; and the full and empty views of the *ceste per viaggio per portar masseritie* in Plate 17. These are called *para* ('pairs,' a plural) be-cause they are borne on two carrying shafts.

[5] *gli forieri*: commissaries with the responsibilities of a modern quartermaster.

ahead to assign lodgings for the Master Cook and the others. It is always better
that that assistant and the Master Cook, who will have gone ahead, be foresighted
and painstaking enough to get the key to their lodgings because often in the press
of the court they lose out,[6] from which many an argument arises. After that, he
should take care that the kitchen he chooses is ample, that the chimney be of a
good size and with a high, broad opening and above all clean because otherwise
the fire would easily go up it and make the kitchen smell bad and even the food
taste bad with the smoke and dirt that would fall out of the chimney; with such
great vexation it would be impossible to carry on; so it would not be bad to have
two chimneys. Near that kitchen try to have a chamber where the hardware can
be unloaded as it arrives; [1581 f.276v] strive in particular to ensure that water
and wood that are to be used are located close to the kitchen. It would not be
bad either for their horses to have a place apart from the others so as to be able to
mount up and ride on to the next lodging. When all that is done and a good fire
has been lit and all containers filled with water, he will open his chests, unpacking
serviette and dust cloths and all sorts of spices that he will have with him, along
with some cold foods that are sometimes carried in those chests for the Prince's
personal consumption. Besides that, in those same chests there should be thread,
a needle, cord, paper, pewter flasks full of verjuice, vinegar and must syrup, silver
serving spoons, clean knives and forks to be set on the table, woollen bags for
straining jelly and even some small canvas bags containing spelt, rice, almonds,
various sorts of raisins, pinenuts, pistachios and melon seeds; all those things are
brought in those chests so that there will be no delay either at the larder or at the
pharmacy,[7] and so the Prince will be all the more quickly served. It is necessary,
moreover, for the larder and the stores to restock whatever runs short.

It would not be bad to have two flat bottles, tinned inside and out, to carry
chicken broth, should there be need of it, reduced and plain,[8] or else almond milk.
Apart from that he must not fail to take along iron bars with locks and keys to
be able to place them on the doors of the rooms where the stores are to be kept.
[f.329r] The assistants and under-cooks will always have their knife case fully
equipped at their horses' saddle bow;[9] on the same horses' crupper a pair of leather

---

[6] *si trovano spogliati*: the force of Scappi's phrase is, 'they find themselves done out of a
lodging.'

[7] This *spetieria* is the storage place for valuable herbs and spices in an affluent household.

[8] *consumati, et non consumati*. The most likely use for chicken broth would be to compose a
food to sustain someone who falls ill along the way.

[9] See the saddle, with its complex of compartments, illustrated in Plate 18. The text above that
engraving reads: 'An empty saddle for journeys, with many compartments for carrying both kitchen and credenza foods, which saddle is put on a big horse and mounted by the assistant who
always has to go ahead.' The large sheath for a set of knives (*cortelliera*) of which Scappi writes
is shown in Plate 13 (*coltellera*).

bags to handle any need. In the chests will be ironware[10] with nails, hammers, pincers in order to be able rapidly to drive nails in a wall for the equipment. In the four strongboxes, which will be carried by two mules, for the needs of the whole kitchen, its cleanliness and neatness, there will be serviettes, long aprons, straining cloth, canvas,[11] broad linen cloth, shirts and other clothing to be able to change clothes and be unsoiled.[12] Into the three sets of hampers will always be put the bigger equipment, such as[13]:

Stone mortars.

Large and medium-sized cauldrons, with their lid.

Large and medium-sized tourte pans.

Conserve[14] and chafing dishes[15] of several sorts, with their base and lid.

Large and small cooking basins[16] with their lid.

Casserole pots with a hollow iron handle.[17]

Large two-handled deep basins[18] for washing utensils and meats.

Large cooking basins[19] – that is, tinned basins for making whitedish.

Large and small skillets with a long iron handle.

Deep pans for poaching eggs.[20] Large and small pots.[21]

[1581 f. 277r] Copper straining pans[22] for fish.

Nested straining pans[23] – that is, colanders[24] of several sorts.

---

[10] Plate 24 shows a hammer and tongs with the legend *ferriera*. The leather pouch that seems to be with them is not one of the *sportine* in which the text says they are to be carried.

[11] This utilitarian fabric was probably still made of hemp.

[12] Scappi's word describing his cleanly dressed kitchen workers is *delicati*.

[13] Some of the following items appear listed in Book I, §43 and §44. See the notes there as well.

[14] See a variety of these *conserve*, which resemble a modern lidded gratin pan, in Plates 8 and 11. The lower half of a *conserva* looks much like a *bastardella* or *conca* (listed below).

[15] *navelle*: a misprint? See the *navicelle* in Plates 7 and 8.

[16] *bastardelle*: they resemble the *conche* of two lines further on.

[17] Scappi's *cazzuole* (see Plate 11) are round-bottomed.

[18] See the *conca* in Plate 9.

[19] The same *bastardelle* as above.

[20] See the long-handled, flat-bottomed *bolsoneto per far ova* in Plate 10.

[21] An example of these *cuogome* can be seen in Plate 10 where it is called a *cuccumo*.

[22] A *crivello* is illustrated in Plate 10. It is a shallow two-handled pan with flared sides and flat, holed bottom, rather like a goldminer's pan.

[23] These *crivelli recolti* may be a nested set of strainers. See Plate 10 for a single unit.

[24] The *foratoro* pictured in Plate 10 seems to have an inner basket strainer as well as the simple outer holed pot which has already been shown in Plate 9.

Bull's eye pans for making fried eggs.[25] Dripping pans to be held under a roast – that is, *giottole* and *leccarde*.[26]

Large spoons with an iron handle for taking broth.[27]

Copper stewpots with their lid.[28]

Large and small oil bottles.[29]

Large and small Dutch ovens of copper.[30]

All of this copper equipment should be packed up by itself, separate from the ironware.

The ironware to be packed is the following:

Large and small tripods for cauldrons.[31]

Triangles for tourte pans.

Large and small chains for fastening to the chimney as need be.

Large and small grills.

Large and medium-sized skillets for frying.

[f. 329v] Large and medium-sized omelet pans.

Large hinged cheese graters.

Skewers to skewer small birds and other things.

Bronze mortars for grinding spices.

Cleavers, hatchets and lever scales of several sorts.

Oil lamps and iron candlesticks.

Into the two cases are put the following things:

All the iron spoons, with holes and without.

Small cheese graters.

Macaroni cutters, of brass and wood.[32]

Several sorts of large wooden pestles.

A pestle for grinding spices.

A small box[33] to hold the spices, with their keys.

---

[25] See in Plate 8 the pan with multiple depressions on a supporting stand. Plate 9 shows a smaller *padella ovata* of the same sort.

[26] Both of Scappi's dripping pans are in Plate 10: the rectangular *lecarda* and the oval *ghiottola*.

[27] See the two sizes of serving ladle (*cuchiari da menestrar*) in Plate 10.

[28] A lidded and a non-lidded *pignatta* are shown in Plate 10.

[29] *bottiglie*: Plate 10, *butiglia*, clearly a container for travelling.

[30] These may normally have three feet, a tripod, fastened to them: Plate 7, *Forno di rame có li trepiedi*.

[31] See the *treipiedi* at the foot of Plate 16. Many of the following articles are mentioned in Book I and are illustrated among the engravings.

[32] *Ruzzole ... per far maccaroni*: see the *ferro da maccaroni* toward the foot of Plate 13.

[33] The word *cassetta* is singular; perhaps an error.

A bristle strainer.

Leather straining pans[34] for flouring fish.

Canvas for the scullions.

Leather bags for holding flour.[35]

Other canvas bags to be used as needed.

Several sorts of knives.[36]

Scrapers[37] for scraping tables.

[1581 f. 277v] Several sorts of pastry wheel.[38]

Wafer irons.[39]

Several sorts of moulds, in metal, wood, lead and wax.

Wooden dough cutters for making ravioli.[40]

Brass candlesticks.[41]

Rolling pins for dough. Wooden cups for holding sugar. Leather purses, German-style, for holding spices.[42]

Small hanks of cord. Rag paper.

Large and tiny needles.

A bellows.[43]

Copper jugs[44] for stewing.

All the small kettles, chafing dishes and other pots, tinned inside and out, are put into those cases.

A pewter syringe with a variety of holed disks inside for ejecting butter and other things.[45]

---

[34] As noted above, the *crivello* illustrated in Plate 10 is a holed metal pan.

[35] See Plate 11.

[36] A wide variety of knives can be seen in Plate 13.

[37] In Plate 14 the *raschiatore da bancho* ('workbench scraper') looks rather like a drawknife.

[38] Plates 14 and 15.

[39] See the illustration whose legend is only *per fare cialde* in Plate 16.

[40] Two sizes of *bussolo per pasta* are etched in Plate 12.

[41] A variety of candle holders is illustrated in Plates 2, 15, 23 and 27.

[42] Plate 11 shows several small purses, *borse per spetie*. Their arrangement in a circle with their mouths tied together may be Scappi's *alla Tedesca*, 'German style.'

[43] Plates 16 and 23: *soffietto*.

[44] Plate 24 shows an ordinary *boccale*, Plate 23 a more ornate one.

[45] See Plate 13: *Seringhe*. The left end in the illustration may show one of the exchangeable *piastrelle* or disks. At the lower right of plate 10 is pictured a large flat holed plate also called a *piastrella*.

Things that have to be put on a pack animal:

Several sorts of folding tables with their chains and trestles.[46]
[f. 330r] Tables to beat on.

Two wooden cases, made as to hold a torch stand, full of large and small skewers and their larding needles for larding a roast.[47]

Articulated spit-holders.[48]

Other spit-holders with a tube on top.[49]

Low spit-holders and spit-holders made in a post.[50]

Andirons and fire shovels.[51]

If you want to put utensils not listed here into chests, hampers, cases or horse packs, look in the book that illustrates furnishings, where you will find all the equipment needed both when travelling as well as for a permanent location. That equipment has always to be split so that half of it goes on with the assistants and the other half stays at the current lodging; it will alternate like that day by day. It is up to you whether in the hampers or horse packs you carry a small press[52] to make an invalid's broth[53] and an iron torch stand to hold a torch during evening work. Most especially, immediately on his arrival at the lodging, the chief cook will promptly find out from each person under his authority what things they are bringing and what they do not have. At the right time and place he will send on those who are to go ahead, and urge those who are to stay that, as soon as the noon or evening meal is over, they check all of the equipment against their inventory, that everything is packed up and, particularly, that the porters [1581 f. 278r] have plenty of cord to tie up the cases and other equipment; and he will ensure that the porters are well dealt with. Thus will the Prince be well served. In addition to those porters, I think it is highly necessary to have four watermen, with their mounts and locked water casks, to transport water for the kitchen. It would not be bad either to have with them two trustworthy men who are experienced in kitchen work who, should one of the masters or assistants fall ill, could fill in. I shall not speak

---

[46] See this standard sort of plain table illustrated in Plate 25.

[47] See the open *forciera* in the middle of Plate 24.

[48] This double, hinged aparatus is illustrated in Plate 16.

[49] See the *spedera con canna* also in Plate 16. It is designed to lean against a wall.

[50] This first, 'low' variety may be the *spedera* in Plate 15. The second variety, an upright shaft, free-standing on a tripod base, is also engraved in Plate 16: *baston di fero a foggia di spedera*.

[51] Types of *capifochi* and a *pala* are in Plate 15.

[52] *torchietto*; a *torchio* is shown in Plate 23. A similar apparatus is named for its product, *susidio*, in Plate 12.

[53] Various sorts of *sussidio* are described in Recipes VI,16–18, 28 and 29.

about the riff-raff hangers-on who will always be attached to the court because that is the business of the masters[54] to select trustworthy people who are quite thoroughly known to the officers. And those watermen, when they are on the road and their horses are not laden with their ropes and other necessary apparatus, will carry the scullions' personal packs, the kitchen needing not less than eight mules so that when travelling they can alternate when laden ones become exhausted or unfortunately shoulder-weakened or lame, as often happens.

End of Book Four

---

[54] Scappi does not identify just who either the *ragaglieri* (minor servants?) or the *mastri* (officials with broad authority?) might be.

Book V
of Messer Bartolomeo Scappi
On Pastry

Just as in my First Book I have shown how to tell what is needed for the Office of Cook; in the Second, how to make various dishes for meat days; in the Third, how to recognize several sorts of fish and their seasons, along with the procedures to follow in preparing them for lean-day dishes; and in the Fourth, the way to set out dishes for delivering to the Steward, and to arrange various furnishing as well as to serve a Conclave of Most Reverend Cardinals;[i] so, in the present Book, which is the Fifth – dedicated as well as the others to the Reverend Signore Don Francesco Reinoso, Personal Steward of Our Lord – I shall proceed to set forth for you (as you shall see) the methods you must follow in making various sorts of pastries, *crostate*, tourtes and other dough preparations,[ii] whether baked in an oven, braised or fried. In this Book I shall not deal with stuffed or braised pasta or pasta that is boiled in broth, milk or water because I have written about them in both of the Books on Prepared Dishes, meat and lean.

[Pies *en croûte*]

1. To prepare a pie of an ox tongue in a pastry wrap.[1.1]

Get a fresh ox tongue and parboil it in salted water until it is well cooked. When it is done, take it out, skin it and let it cool. Sprinkle it with pepper, cloves, cinnamon, ginger, nutmeg and salt – the amount of the spices being at your discretion. Get wheat flour that has been sieved coarsely so that only the bran[1.2]

---

[i] Scappi did not write about arrangements for a conclave in that Book IV, but rather advised about organizing an itinerant kitchen. For his outline of chamber furnishings and food service for a conclave, see Appendix I.

[ii] Scappi has a single generic word for things made of flour dough: *pasta*. In this and the next sentence he is trying to define the content of the present Book V as being what we would call 'pastry' and, much more loosely, 'pies.'

[1.1] Within the genre of 'pie' Scappi occasionally distinguishes two subgenres: *in cassa* or *in cassetta*, which is literally 'in a case' or 'in a box,' which we shall usually render as *en croûte*; and *in sfoglio*, 'in a (single) sheet (of dough)' or 'in a pastry wrap.' The latter is what Scappi has written in the rubric of the present recipe. Some of Scappi's 'wrapped' pies are quite large turnovers, the filling being relatively solid. Both sorts of pie are free-standing. Later in this Book V he will deal with pies formed and baked with the support of a pie plate.

[1.2] *semola*. Scappi has no particular use anywhere for bran alone.

is left in the sieve, and make up a dough with unsalted cold water – because if you make dough with warm water and salt it rises and bursts easily,[1.3] and is not as good, especially in summer; in winter, though, when there are those very cold spells, it is enough for the water to have lost its chill, because being too cold is as bad as being too warm. When the dough is made up, it should sit on a table for half an hour. Punch it with your fists, or else knead it, until the dough becomes rather pasty and compact. Roll out a round sheet of that dough, half a finger thick, and on the sheet set slices of pork fat a hand in width, sprinkling the fat and the dough with the above spice mixture. Put the tongue on the fat, with another layer of fat on top of it, sprinkled again with those spices and with water or else with beaten egg whites. Moisten the dough all around its edge and enclose the tongue in the middle by drawing the upper part over to meet the lower, giving it an oval shape[1.4] like *ofelle*.[1.5]

Put the pie into an oven hot enough to do bread, and bake it. If you want to colour it with water tinged with saffron before putting it into the oven, that is optional – because if you use eggs for that, the pie will colour too quickly. When the pie is made with the coarse flour I said above, though, it will by itself become quite a bit darker than if made with finely sieved flour. Therefore, when it is done take it out of the oven and, if you have not coloured it already with saffron or eggs, grease it immediately with a pork rind and that will colour it. That pie stands air better than it would if the dough were made with fine flour, because a shell that is made with fine flour, warm water, salt and fat bursts when exposed to air, and that is not a pretty thing to see. But if the pastry is to be eaten,[1.6] such dough would be better than the first one. Therefore, if you do not want to serve it right out of the oven but you still want it hot, keep it covered with a cloth so the shell will not break; it will stay hot for an hour. In summer that pie can be kept for three days, and in winter for eight.

If you want to do a raw tongue in a pie, remove its skin in hot water and let it steep for eight hours in a seasoning made of vinegar, salt, white wine, oregano, must syrup, cloves of garlic and pepper. Take it out, let it drain and stick it with pork fat over its full length, which fat should be sprinkled with the above spice mixture. Bake the pie as above, minding that the raw tongue is freer – that is, it

---

[1.3] That is, when the free-standing pie or turnover is filled, the shell will not be as strong. See further on and in Recipes 11 and 43 for particular instances in which Scappi does, however, direct that warm water be used for pastry dough.

[1.4] *et venga ovata*, literally 'egg-shaped.' See also Recipe 44, below.

[1.5] Recipe 48, below.

[1.6] Cooks of earlier centuries generally assumed that a pastry shell functioned primarily as a container for a foodstuff while that foodstuff baked; it was to be discarded when, at the table, the pie was 'opened.' See, however, the end of Recipe 42 and the middle of Recipe 189.

must have more room within the pastry shell – because when that tongue warms up it swells and lifts the dough; if it does not have enough room it will easily break the shell. Just as soon as the pie begins to rise, make a hole in the middle of its top[1.7] with a hook or the handle of a spoon and let it finish cooking.

2. To prepare an ox tongue *en croûte*.[2.1]

Get a fresh tongue and more than half cook it in salted water. Skin it, slice it into rounds and stick those rounds with prosciutto or else with salted pork jowl. Sprinkle them with pepper, cinnamon, cloves and ginger, all ground together with salt. Then have a pastry shell ready, the dough made up with sieved flour, cold water, eggs and salt, and a little rendered fat; the shell should not be too thin, and should be thicker at the bottom than at the top. Put some thin slices of pork fat on the bottom and, on them, the rounds of the tongue, prunes, dried visciola cherries with a little sugar and the same spice mixture. Cover the pie with an upper shell the size of the bottom shell – because if it were the same size as the opening the dough would buckle and easily burst. When it is covered, colour it with beaten eggs or with saffron-tinged water. Bake it in an oven. When it is done, serve it hot.

If you want to put a raw tongue into a pastry shell, though, make the shell of coarse flour, as is said in the preceding recipe, and let it sit for half a quarter of an hour. Have the tongue sliced into rounds and skinned and, when the rounds have either steeped in a seasoning composed as in the preceding recipe or else been in a press with salt and spices, put them into the pastry shell on some thin slices of boneless salted pork belly. Sprinkle them with that same spice mixture and cover the pie, pricking it in the middle. Bake it in the oven, making the hole as directed in the above recipe. When it is almost done, take a spoonful of the seasoning and put it into the pie through that hole; finish off baking it. For the rounds of tongue that have been in a press, though, instead of that seasoning put in must syrup, vinegar and orange juice.

You can do up a fresh cow's tongue and a buffalo cow's tongue[2.2] in all the above ways.

[1.7] This pricking of an upper crust is usual when making all pies except, apparently, those made of flaky pastry: see Recipe V,12. As in the next recipe, a hole was also occasionally used toward the end of the baking process in order to add a seasoning to the filling.

[2.1] Scappi's phrase is *in cassa*, literally 'in a case' or, as we might say, 'in a crust.' This pie is not a turnover but a round, free-standing pie whose dough has enough tensile strength to contain a relatively mobile filling and whose sides, for more strength, occasionally slope inwards.

[2.2] This is the south European buffalo, not a bison. Scappi will cook various other parts of this buffalo: see Recipe 35, for instance. The soft cheese provatura is from the milk of the same animal.

3. To prepare a pie of ox cheeks, eyes and snouts.

Get the snout, take off its skin in hot water and remove the pupil from its eyes; cut the snout in two. The cheeks are beaten small with the same amount of pork fat, as sausage stuffing is beaten, mixing in pepper, cinnamon, cloves, nutmeg and salt. Those spices are likewise sprinkled on the eyes and snout. Have a pastry casing ready, made of the dough described in Recipe 1; into it put the beaten cheeks, and on that a little sautéed spring onion; arrange the eyes and snout there with the same amount of sautéed spring onion on top. Cover the pie over and bake it in an oven. When it is almost done, put a little verjuice and must syrup into it through the hole.[3.1] When it is done, serve it hot. Along with the spring onions you can further add in prunes and dried visciola cherries.

In the same way you can do the part of the sweetbread that is attached to the gullet,[3.2] as well as parboiled brains cut up into small chunks and with slices of prosciutto.

4. To prepare a pie of ox loin.

Get an ox loin from beneath the ribs and beneath the kidneys, which is more tender than the loin from above the ribs, which is round and is called the back loin;[4.1] clean away the membrane around it and the gristle, and pound it with a bat[4.2] or the spine of a knife over its full length: that is done to tenderize it. When it has been pounded, sprinkle it with rose vinegar and stick it with pork fat all along it. Let it sit for two hours in a mixture of pepper, cloves, cinnamon, ginger, salt and nutmeg.[4.3] Put it into a sheet of dough made up of coarsely sieved flour as is said in Recipe 1, with slices of pork fat under and over it the way the tongue is set in Recipe 1. Bake it in an oven as above. When it is done it can be served hot or else kept, in summer for four days, in winter for eight.

Alternatively you can first let the loin steep in the seasoning, and do it in every way a tongue is done. In the same way you can do a back loin[4.4] whenever it is cleaned of skin, gristle and bone.

[3.1] As is normal and mentioned in the previous recipe, a small hole is put through a pie's upper shell, partly so steam will not burst the shell and partly to allow the addition of a final seasoning toward the end of the pie's baking.

[3.2] This would be the thymus gland rather than the pancreas.

[4.1] *s'adomanda lombolo schinale*.

[4.2] In the context of pastry making a *bastone* generally refers to a rolling pin.

[4.3] There is no mention of a liquid medium for these condiments. In Recipe 26 this spice mixture will be referred to as an *adobbo*; it can be applied to a meat by means of a press also.

[4.4] This 'back loin' is the *lombolo schinale* that Scappi mentioned before and is *sopra le coste*.

5. To prepare a pie of the flesh of an ox's upper hind leg.

Take the lean meat of an ox's thigh, which should not be too tenderized[5.1] nor too fresh – because when it is tender it has little juice, and being too fresh it turns out tough, so that in summer it should not be more than a day old and in winter, two. Pound it with a bat and lard it with marbled pork fat. Let it sit for a day in seasoning like the tongue or else in a press, with pepper and salt; if you put it in a press, though, do it in an earthenware or wooden container so that the blood will not be lost. Have a sheet of pastry or else a casing ready,[5.2] made of coarse flour as is described in Recipe 1; when the meat is coated with the above spice mixture, put it onto the sheet or into the shell. However, if it has been in a press baste it around with its blood to which is added a little more of the spice mixture. Cover the pie over and bake it with a lower heat[5.3] than is used above, not forgetting to make a hole in its top. When it is done, it is served hot or cold as you wish. Whenever the ox or cow is middle-aged it is better for making pies than when it is decrepit.

You can do another part of the thigh the same way, the part called the *pesce*,[5.4] which is on the inner side. Sometimes it is more than half cooked in wine, water and vinegar, with spices, before being put in pastry. When it is pounded a little with a bat and done up like the loin in the previous recipe, it will be quite a bit better than if cooked in wine. When you do cook it in wine, that is done in order to speed things up and to put less dough in the pie.[5.5] Nevertheless, however it is baked it can either be served hot or set aside.

6. To prepare a pie of a cow's udder.

Get a cow's udder before it has its first calf; tie its teats with cord so no milk leaks out and boil it in salted water until it is well done. Take it out of the broth, let it cool, cut away the teats and skin it, sticking it with pork fat, or fat prosciutto, that has been dredged in pepper, cinnamon, cloves, ginger and nutmeg. Have a sheet of dough[6.1] ready, made up as in Recipe 1, with slices of pork fat on it. Sprinkle the dough and pork fat with the above spice mixture and sugar; do the same with the udder – that is, put the udder on the sheet of dough, and over it

---

[5.1] *frolla*, tender or softened, usually from the meat having hung or been beaten.

[5.2] The sheet of dough would make a pastry wrap (as in Recipe 1); the shell or *cassa*, an *en croûte*, free-standing pie (as in Recipe 2).

[5.3] Literally, a 'slower' fire: *piu lento fuoco*.

[5.4] This is the two-branched inner muscle of the upper leg, so called because it looked like a fish.

[5.5] The pie shell can be thinner because the boiled meat is apt to be less fluid as the pie is baking.

[6.1] Scappi has written *lo sfoglio* (rather than *cassa*): this is apparently to be a turnover variety of pie. See the last sentence for the *in cassa* alternative.

again put slices of pork fat and the spices.[6.2] Bake it. When it is almost done, pour a beaker of verjuice or raisin sauce[6.3] through the hole on top and finish off baking it. If you intend to keep the pie, though, you do not need to put in either the verjuice or the sauce.

You can do an udder that way *en croûte* either whole or cut up.

7. To prepare a pie of a suckling calf's head, boneless and stuffed.

The head is skinned in hot water just as soon as the calf is slaughtered: that is done so it will stay whiter and so the bones can be removed more easily. Remove the tongue. When that is done, wrap the head in several layers of linen and with a pestle beat on the cloth to break up the head bones; take out those bones carefully. Invert the head, so that the inside is outward, sewing up the front parts with string; wash it very well in several changes of water. Then get a mixture of beaten veal combined with grated cheese, eggs, raisins, pork fat, pepper, cinnamon, cloves and finely chopped herbs; stuff the head with that mixture and sew it up with string so the stuffing cannot get out. Put it into a casserole pot in cold water and bring it to a boil. When you see the head back in its proper shape, take it out and let it cool. Then have a pastry shell ready, shaped like a boat,[7.1] its bottom is lined around with slices of coarse pork fat sprinkled with pepper, cloves, cinnamon, sugar, ginger and nutmeg. The head is likewise sprinkled and put into the shell; on it put a broad slice of pork fat and another slice of veal, to keep it moist. Sprinkle everything with those same spices and salt. If the head's ears[7.2] cause a problem, slice them at the nape so they can be fitted into the pastry shell. Cover it over. Bake it in an oven. When it is done, serve it hot. If you do not want to crush the bones, take them out the way that is done in Recipe 24 of the Book on Prepared Dishes.[7.3] Furthermore, you can put the head into a pie without stuffing it and without removing its bone but only cleaning all filth out of its nostrils and removing its tongue and teeth. You can also do it like that when it has been skinned. The smaller the head is, the better it will be.

[6.2] We have to understand that the dough is then wrapped over and sealed, and a small hole made in its top.

[6.3] Directions for making this *sapor d'uva passa* are found in Recipe II,261.

[7.1] *fatta a navicella*: here the literal sense of the word, not the cooking vessel. See also Recipes 22, 28 and 29.

[7.2] The 1581 typesetter skipped two letters and put 'eyes' here (*gli occhi della testa*); the 1570 printing has 'ears' (*gli orecchi della testa*). In Recipe 22 we find a similar direction concerning a calf's ears.

[7.3] In the recipe that he names 'Several ways to cook a milk-calf's head without its bone,' Scappi suggests peeling the skin away from around the bone, beginning at the severed neck.

8. Several ways to make a pie of a suckling calf's tongue.

Get the tongue and half cook it in a broth of some other meat, or else in salted water. Take it out, remove the skin from around it and let it cool. Cut it crosswise in slices, thick or thin as you prefer. Do likewise with the sweetbreads it has around its gullet[8.1] that are called 'tasty morsels.'[8.2] If you want to sauté them first in a little rendered fat before putting them *en croûte*, that is optional. Have a pastry casing ready, made of sieved flour the way that is set out in Recipe 1, and put the tongue into it dredged in pepper, cloves, cinnamon, saffron, sugar and either gooseberries or verjuice grapes; in winter, instead of gooseberries or verjuice grapes, use orange juice, prunes and dried visciola cherries. Cover the pie over, and bake it in an oven. If you want it with raisin sauce or some other sort of sauce, after it has been in the oven for half an hour put the sauce into it through the hole in its top, and bake it. If you are using that sauce, though, you will not put in either prunes or dried visciola cherries.

That tongue can be put into a pie whole, having cut it across so it can be rolled up; otherwise slit it lengthwise in two. However, if the tongue is to be served cold, put it into a pie whole, without a sauce and without anything else but with more spices, salt, and either slices of prosciutto or of pork fat. In that same way you can do the tongue of any sort of quadruped mentioned in the Book on Prepared Dishes. If you want to do it with a flaky pastry, though, follow the directions for flaky dough for the flaky-pastry pies of a suckling calf's sweetbreads in Recipe 11, below.

9. To prepare a pie of calf's sweetbreads.

Get the sweetbreads just as soon as the calf is killed and wash them in several changes of water, removing the blood they often have about them. Take the best part of them and cut it up into egg-sized pieces. Sprinkle them with pepper, cinnamon, cloves and nutmeg. Also get prosciutto, diced, with some fat and lean in it, and either beef marrow or beaten calf kidney – that is, the kidney's fat. Have a pastry casing made up, either large or small depending on the amount of the sweetbreads, and onto its bottom put the beef marrow or the beaten fat and a part of the prosciutto; on those put the sweetbreads with the other things again, adding in gooseberries or verjuice grapes or else raisins – depending on the season. Cover the pie over and bake it in an oven. Serve it hot. If you want the pie with a sauce made of raw egg yolks, sugar and verjuice, there is no need to put in gooseberries or verjuice grapes or raisins. You can also give the sweetbreads a boiling before they are cut up, though I find that they are tastier when put in raw. And instead of the beef marrow or beaten fat on the bottom of the pie you can put saveloy or finely ground sausage meat. In the fall and winter you can put raw peeled truffles with the sweetbreads; and in spring, some common field mushrooms.

[8.1] That is, the thymus gland.

[8.2] *bocche saporite.*

10. To prepare a pie of suckling calf's sweetbreads, beaten.

Get the best part of the sweetbreads, cleaned as in the above recipe. Give them a brief boiling in salted water, and beat them, though not too much, with knives, adding in small chunks of beef marrow and a little prosciutto, fat and diced. Mix in nutmeg, cloves, pepper, cinnamon and a little sugar and saffron; with that, in spring gooseberries, in summer verjuice grapes, in winter raisins. Have a pie casing ready of dough made up of fine flour, egg yolks, a little rendered fat and salt; into that put the filling heaped up in the shape of a pyramid: that is done in order to hold the upper shell up. Cover the pie and bake it in an oven. When it is almost done, through the hole in its top you can put in beaten egg yolks with verjuice and a little broth. When it is baked, serve it hot. That pie needs to be baked slowly. If it browns too much, cover it with a doubled sheet of rag paper.[10] You can do the same with other pies when they get too browned.

11. To do a suckling calf's sweetbreads in flaky-pastry pies.[11.1]

Get fine flour and make up a dough with egg yolks, warm water,[11.2] salt and a little rendered fat; the dough should be soft rather than hard, and should be well kneaded. Roll it out into a thin sheet, elongated rather than broad, and grease it all over with melted rendered fat that is not too hot. Beginning at a narrow side of the sheet, roll it up, making a round roll the size of a man's arm. Mind particularly that it is compact and can be cut. Then cut the roll into slices two fingers thick. Have some other firm, well kneaded dough ready, made of fine flour, egg yolks, water and salt, without any fat, and of that dough make a *coppello*[11.3] – that is, the bottom of the pie shell – which should come up almost the full height of the flaky pastry,[11.4] because without it the flaky pastry would not stand up, and the liquid would leak out in the baking. Now, having the little shell made, into it put a mixture made up like the one in the previous recipe,[11.5] following the same

---

[10] This *carta straccia* is used frequently by Scappi in hot conditions where a pliable protective covering is needed. Ordinary paper from wood pulp without linen would become too brittle, perhaps smoulder, and flavour the pie.

[11.1] Scappi's qualification for this sort of dough is *sfogliato*. The adjective is a derivative of *sfoglia*, a foil or layer, or, as still today, a sheet of (pasta) dough. 'Puff pastry,' that today uses butter, may occasionally be a fair translation, but 'flaky' has the virtue of being close to Scappi's sense and will be so used consistently in this translation.

[11.2] See Scappi's comment in Recipe 1 about the tendency of warm pastry dough to puff up.

[11.3] Scappi's term was for a cupel, a shallow, flat-bottomed cup-like vessel normally used by gold- and silversmiths for assaying and separating precious metals from dross.

[11.4] The ambiguity that Scappi has left is whether the 'wheels' of flaky pastry that will form the inner wall of the pie are set flat or on edge. We may reasonably guess they are set on edge; when the coarse outer pastry is peeled away on the dining board, an interesting mosaic remains. See also the end of Recipe 18, below.

[11.5] That was a composition of sweetbreads, marrow, ham, spice and fruit.

directions for heaping the filling high and firm so that the upper crust, made of the same flaky dough, can puff up better as it bakes. Before putting it into an oven, grease the pie with melted rendered fat, preferably cold rather than hot so it will adhere to the dough better. Then put it into the oven, which should be extremely clean. Grease its bottom. The oven should be moderately hot, though hotter on top than on the bottom so the flaky pastry can open up. As it begins to puff up, without taking it out of the oven grease it with rendered fat by means of a small feather[11.6] tied to the end of a stick; do that two or three times. When it is baked, it should always be served hot sprinkled with sugar. It is optional whether you put into it a little of that sauce that is added in the preceding recipe. Whenever you have a low-domed oven it is always better for baking pasties because pies of flaky pastry always prefer a sprightly heat from above rather than from below.

You can make the dough differently, like pastry chefs in Rome do it; that dough is not as good as the one described above, but it looks better than it tastes. Mix fine flour with warm water and salt, and make it softer than the above. Sometimes two people make this dough – that is, one who holds the dough in his hands and another who pulls on it, as lasagna is made with a pasta frame, and he greases it with rendered fat. To manage those pastry dishes better as they bake, they keep a piece of dry firewood burning at the mouth of the oven; if the oven is not quite hot enough they put some embers at its mouth. Turn the pie around, and do not fail to look at it often because a pie like that bakes quickly, and if it is too browned it will not be pretty or very tasty.

You can do parboiled calf's brains that way, cutting them up into small chunks, along with the stuffing for yellow saveloy[11.7] or else the beaten fat of a calf's kidney, together with raw *salsiccione* grated with pepper, cinnamon and sugar, and a few gooseberries or raisins and beaten mint.

12. To do calf's pluck in a pie shell of flaky pastry or plain pastry.

When a small pastry shell is made up in one of the above ways, get the pluck – that is, the lungs[12.1] – of a calf, boiled and finely beaten with the kidney-fat of the calf and a little diced prosciutto. Mix everything together with pepper, cinnamon, saffron and either gooseberries or verjuice grapes. Put it into the small shell following the directions in the above recipe for sweetbreads.[12.2] Cover the

---

[11.6] *pennello*. See, in Plate 2 of the engravings (lower right), the *penelo per indorar pastici*. Since its origin, *pennello* (diminutive of *penna*, a pinion feather) has undergone a semantic shift from its literal meaning to more generalized senses of a pastry brush and any (large) bristle paint-brush. The same fine brush is used again in Recipe 48, below.

[11.7] See Recipe II,46 for this mixture.

[12.1] See Book II, Recipes 56 (where the same explanation – *la coratella, cioè il polmone* – is made), 77, 80 and 105 for other uses of a calf's lungs.

[12.2] In that recipe for a pie shell within a pie shell, the cook makes a strong outer support for the flaky-pastry shell.

pie over and set it to bake. When it is almost done, if it is not of flaky pastry put a sauce into it made with broth and saffron or else with beaten eggs and verjuice, there being no gooseberries or verjuice grapes in it. If the pie is of flaky pastry, you will not put that sauce into it, though, until just on the point of serving. When it is done, it always needs to be served hot. Sometimes spring onions, beaten and sautéed, can be put into those pies, and beaten herbs; and instead of gooseberries, raisins.

13. To do calf tripe in a pie shell.

With the tripe clean and cut up the way it usually is, cook it well without salt and with only a piece of prosciutto that is not rancid. When it is done, take it out and let it cool. Then have a pastry shell made up out of fine flour and egg yolks, as in Recipe 1; put the tripe into it along with the stuffing for yellow saveloy. Onto that mixture set thin slices of provatura and grated Parmesan cheese, beaten mint and marjoram, pepper, cinnamon and saffron; on top of that put the cold tripe interspersed with the same mixture. The last layer should be of thin slices of provatura and grated cheese. Cover the pie over and bake it. It is always served hot.

You can do cow's tripe the same way, and the small intestine. If you do not have saveloy stuffing, put in beef marrow and a little finely beaten prosciutto.

14. To prepare a pie of calf liver.

Get a liver that is tender, and preferably greenish-grey rather than black. Cut away the gallbladder and the membrane around it. Lard it all over with marbled pork fat or else with pork jowl, which lardoons should be coated with pepper, cinnamon, cloves, ginger, sugar and nutmeg; coat the liver similarly. Then have a pastry shell made up of fine flour as in Recipe 1. To keep the liver moist, put either slices of pork fat or the stuffing of yellow saveloy onto the bottom of the shell and around its sides; the same is done over the top of the liver. That done, cover the pie over and bake it. It needs to be served hot just as soon as it is done, because if it sits it hardens. If the piece of liver is bigger than two pounds, it is enough for it to be in the oven for three-quarters of an hour; if it is cut up into small pieces, though, it needs less time.

You can do the liver of a domestic pig or a wild boar the same way, as well as their testicles with the outer skin removed. If you do not have saveloy stuffing, grind up some lean veal[14] together with raw prosciutto.

15. To prepare a pie of a suckling calf's leg.

If the calf is small, take the whole leg,[15.1] but if it is big you can cut the leg up into several pieces; remove the membrane[15.2] that is around it. It is optional

---

[14] Recipe II,46 tells us that saveloy sausage is made mainly from lean veal and veal liver.

[15.1] This 'leg' is the *coscia*, properly only the upper hind leg or thigh.

[15.2] Scappi uses the word *pellicina* here rather than *pelle*: 'tender skin'?

whether you leave the bone in. Let it steep for three hours in a mixture of pepper, cloves, cinnamon, nutmeg and salt; likewise the lardoons with which it is to be stuck. However, if you want to sear it on the grill, that is optional, because by searing it the juice stays in the meat, the meat swells up and as it cooks the pastry is not at such a risk of bursting. So, whether it steeps in the mixture or is seared or not, stick it all over with pork fat. Have a round sheet of dough made up of coarsely ground flour, as is said in Recipe 1, and put the meat on the dough with slices of pork fat under and over it, sprinkled with the same spice mixture, and brush the dough with beaten egg or water. Close it over and crimp its edge all around, and prick a hole through which it can breathe when the time comes. Colour it with beaten eggs or with water tinged with saffron; alternatively, after it has baked and is still hot you can still colour it with a pork rind. That pie cannot take too intense a heat. If the piece of meat is of six pounds, it wants at least two and a half hours to cook, though more if the leg is whole. To keep it from darkening too much on top put sheets of rag paper on it. When it is done it can be served hot or stored, in summer for four days and in winter for eight. You should note, though, that when it is to be stored, more salt and spices are put in; and especially that the hole on top and any ruptures are to be sealed up, because when the air gets into a pie it quickly goes mouldy and rots. It should be kept in a dry place that is neither too damp nor too warm.

16. To do stuffed fingers of veal in a pastry shell.

Get lean veal that has had its skin, bones and gristle removed, and make fingers of it. Stick it with lardoons as directed in the Book on Prepared Dishes in Recipe 43.[16.1] Then have a pastry shell ready, made of fine flour and egg yolks as in Recipe 1 and put the fingers into it with prunes and dried visciola cherries and a few thin slices of salted pork jowl, sprinkled with the spice mixture of the previous recipe. Cover the pie over and bake it. If you want to put some seasonings into it through the hole, that is up to you.

Similarly you can do small stuffed croquettes as is said in the Book on Prepared Dishes at Recipe 43, adding in gooseberries or verjuice grapes or raisins. You can also have the fingers steep in a royal seasoning[16.2] before they are stuffed.

17. Another way to prepare a pie of stuffed veal croquettes.

When the croquettes are stuffed with the mixture used for doing that in the Book on Prepared Dishes, Recipe 43, half cook them on a spit. Have the pastry shell ready and into it put a little beaten veal mixed with sugar and spices; on that

---

[16.1] Recipe II,43 is for making croquettes and fingers (*polpette & polpettoni*) from the lean meat of a suckling calf's leg. In Recipe III,38 Scappi says that the fingers are small slabs of whole, beaten (but not ground) meat roughly one hand long and one finger thick and wide.

[16.2] See the *adobbo reale* at Recipe II,130.

put the croquettes. Cover the pie over and bake it. When it is almost done, put into it through its hole a sauce made of ground raisins and *mostaccioli* moistened with orange juice, verjuice and a little broth tinged with saffron, and sugar; let it finish baking. It is served hot.

In that way you can do croquettes of the lean meat of any quadruped dealt with in the Book on Prepared Dishes. Instead of the beaten meat you can put in pork fat and[17] beaten prosciutto.

18. To do beaten veal in a pie shell of plain or flaky pastry.

Get the lean meat with the bones, skin and gristle removed; for every pound of that meat get four ounces of kidney-fat. Cut the meat up into four-ounce pieces and bring them to a boil in salted water at least until the blood is purged from them. Then take them out and beat them small with knives; likewise beat the kidney-fat, with the membrane removed. Then mix everything together lightly, adding in gooseberries or verjuice grapes or raisins, and salt, pepper, cinnamon, cloves and ginger. Have a pastry shell ready, made of fine flour as in Recipe 1 and put the filling into it, heaping it up like a pyramid so the upper shell will be raised. Cover the pie over and bake it. When it is almost done, through the hole in its top put in a flavouring made up of broth, saffron, verjuice and sugar. When it is done baking it is always served hot. Sometimes whole, hard-boiled egg yolks, with a clove inside them, are put into that pie.

You can also do it with the meat raw, without parboiling it: after it has been beaten and mixed with the fat, for every pound of the meat mix in three ounces of cold broth or water, two ounces of gooseberries or verjuice grapes – and in winter, raisins and verjuice – making the mixture neither too thin nor too thick. For that filling the shell should not be of flaky pastry; if you do want it to be of flaky pastry, make the bottom of the pie of the firm dough and enclose most of the flaky pastry round about with that[18]: that is done so the broth that the filling makes will not leak out. Sometimes you can put truffles and field mushrooms into that pie.

19. To do beaten loin of veal in pie shells.

Get the loin along with the kidney and blanch it in water. Stick it thickly with lardoons of pork fat that have been coated with a spice mixture; put a few whole cloves into the loin. More than half cook it on a spit. Then take it down and very carefully remove the flesh from the bone, catching in a dish the juice that will drip from it. With knives beat the flesh and the kidney small, mixing in with them, for every pound, three ounces of fine saveloy stuffing if it is in season;

---

[17] It should be remembered that Scappi's *et* is often his way of including an alternative and should be read as 'or.'

[18] Presumably the more substantial lower crust is meant to be turned up a little around the flaky pastry wall.

if it is not, instead of that stuffing, use diced salt pork jowl, beaten fine herbs and gooseberries or verjuice grapes or raisins, the last depending on the season, along with the spice mixture used for the other pies, above, and a little sugar. When everything is mixed together, put that filling into the pie shell and bake it in an oven. When it is almost done, take the juice that has dripped from the meat when it was taken off the bones and mix it with orange juice, verjuice and a little broth tinged with saffron, and put that into the pie through the hole on its top. Bake it. When it is done it should always be served hot. With that filling you can make flaky-pastry pies and stuffed small flans, fried in rendered fat and baked in an oven. Additionally, you can put in finely cut-up prunes or peeled truffles.

20. To do calf's feet in a pastry shell.

Boil the calf's feet in salted water so that they are thoroughly cooked. Take them out and let them cool. Have a pastry shell ready, made of sieved flour and eggs, as set out in Recipe 1. On the bottom and around the sides put thin slices of pork fat so the feet will not stick to the shell, and very thin slices of veal. Put the feet in, with a spice mixture, sugar and beaten herbs, and either gooseberries or verjuice grapes. Over top of all that put thin slices of prosciutto and veal. Set it to bake. When it is almost done, through the hole on top put in a flavouring made of broth tinged with saffron, verjuice and sugar; finish off baking it. It is served hot.

In the same way you can do the feet of a pig, a wether, a goat kid, a lamb and the feet of any other sort of quadruped.

21. Several ways to make a pie of a wether's leg.

When the leg is skinned, cut it from the loin so that it comes away round. If it is of a young animal it will be better than from an old one. Lard it on the inside with pork belly or marbled pork fat that has been coated with pepper, cinnamon, cloves, nutmeg and salt. Have a sheet of dough made with coarsely sieved flour, as directed in Recipe 1, with slices of pork fat on it, and put the leg on those slices with a similar layer of slices on top of the leg. Make up the pie, not forgetting to sprinkle the leg with the same spice mixture. If you want to sear it first on a grill, that is a possibility. Bake it and serve it hot. If you want to keep it, put more salt and spices into it.

If you want to stuff it, beat it all around with a bat[21] at least until it softens, and carefully cut away the bone from the flesh – that is, the bone in its middle, leaving the knee cap. Fill it with a saveloy stuffing and such other ingredients as are mentioned in Recipe 69 of the Book on Prepared Dishes, on stewing a stuffed leg of wether. If you do not want to sew it up again, sprinkle it with pepper, cloves, ginger, nutmeg and salt, and wrap it in the wether's caul and set it onto the sheet of dough without blanching it; under and over it put chopped onion or else cut-up

---

[21] The word *bastone* is the same as for a pastry rolling pin.

quince and other fruit. Cover the pie over, leaving lots of loose dough, and bake it in an oven. When it begins to swell up, make a hole on top with a hook. When it is done, serve it hot because it is not as good when cold. That pie should be in the oven for three hours more or less, depending on its size.

The same can be done with the legs of every other quadruped. With the flesh of that leg you can make fingers in pastry, beaten the way it is done with veal in Recipe 16. Furthermore, you can put it into a pie if the leg were boiled but not thoroughly cooked and, hot like that, sprinkled with the same spice mixture, sugar and salt. When it has cooled put it onto a sheet of dough with slices of pork fat under and over, baking it as above. When it is almost done, through the upper hole put in a sauce made of toasted almonds, *mostaccioli*, hard-boiled egg yolks and raisins, moistened with verjuice, orange juice and sugar. When done, serve it hot.

22. To prepare a pie of a goat kid's head.

Get the head fresh, its hair removed in hot water, washed in several changes of water and very clean – most especially in its nostrils. It is optional whether you leave it whole or not. It is better for it to be cut apart from below; in no case, though, should its upper skin be cut. Remove its gullet and windpipe, parboil them and cut them up into small bits, mixing in beaten pork fat, grated cheese, eggs, beaten mint and marjoram, gooseberries or raisins in with them, along with pepper, cinnamon and saffron. Put all that into the hollow where the brain was and close up the head with a stick or else sew it up with string. Give the ears a slice next to the nape of the neck so they will fit in better. Have a pie shell ready, made of fine flour like the other one, in the shape of a boat and lined likewise with thin slices of pork fat and lean goat-kid meat. Into it put the head, sprinkled with pepper, cloves, cinnamon, ginger, salt and nutmeg, and on that more thin slices of pork fat and meat so the head will not stick to the dough. Cover the pie over and bake it in an oven. When it is done, serve it hot.

If you want it boneless, follow the directions given above in the recipe for a boneless calf's head.[22]

23. To put the eyes, ears and testicles of a goat kid *en croûte* or in flaky pastry.

Get the ears when they are very clean, give them a boiling in salted water, take them out and cut them up into small pieces. Get the eyes and testicles, also raw, mixed with diced pork belly. With the ears add in gooseberries, finely chopped fine herbs, and some of the same spice mixture used in the above chapter. Put all of that into a pastry shell and bake it in an oven. When it is almost done, put a seasoning of beaten egg yolks, verjuice and sugar into it through the hole and finish off baking it. When it is done it is always served hot. If you want it in

---

[22] Recipe 7.

flaky pastry, parboil everything and put it into a shell of flaky pastry with the same spices and following the same procedure. Bake it as the pie of a calf's sweetbread is done in Recipe 11.

In both of those ways you can do small tripe, after they have been thoroughly cleaned and parboiled, and sweetbreads and lungs, too.[23]

24. To prepare pies of a goat kid's quarters.

Get the hindquarters or forequarters of a goat kid, as you prefer, and cut them up into small pieces. Sprinkle them with the spice mixture described in the recipe for the head of a goat kid. With those pieces you put, in winter, slices of prosciutto, with prunes and dried visciola cherries, and pork fat either diced or beaten with knives; splash all that with a little verjuice. In summer, instead of those things, gooseberries or verjuice grapes.[24.1] Have a pie shell of fine flour ready, as set out in Recipe 1, and into it put the pieces of meat and the other ingredients sprinkled with the same spices and enough salt. Cover the pie over and bake it. When it is done, it needs to be served hot.

If you want the hindquarters in a dry pie,[24.2] sear them on a grill or blanch them in water, stick them with small lardoons of pork fat, sprinkle them[24.3] with the same spice mixture, and stick whole cloves into them. Make the pie with flaky pastry the way it is done for a hare in Recipe 27, below – although my experience has been that a goat kid is quite a bit better when it is done in the above way. The one that is done dry in pastry can be served hot or set aside, in summer for two days and in winter for four.

A suckling lamb can be done in all the above ways.

25. To do the quarters of a roedeer in a pastry wrap.

Get the hindquarters of a deer, leaving the feet with their hair on them. When they have hung a while[25.1] they will be quite a bit better. Clean them with a cloth so no hair[25.2] or dirt is left on them, because they are not washed. Sear them on a grill over a low fire. Then have a mixture ready of pepper, cinnamon, cloves, ginger and nutmeg all ground coarsely together, and salt, and while they are hot –

---

[23] All of those additional organs are presumably from a goat kid.

[24.1] For the 1581 printing the typesetter's eye skipped from 'verjuice' to 'verjuice' in these last two sentences and omitted the text between.

[24.2] A *pasticcio asciutto* is lacking any added liquid such as a sauce or verjuice or fresh fruit. See Recipe 39, below.

[24.3] Often the lardoons are dredged in the spices, but here the text states that it is the meat that is so coated.

[25.1] Scappi writes: When they have tenderized somewhat, *quando saranno alquanto frolletti.*

[25.2] Except around the feet: see further on.

so they can better take the spices – sprinkle them with some of that mixture. When they have cooled, stick them all over with rather large lardoons of pork fat which have been coated with the spice mixture. Then have a round sheet of dough ready, or two smaller ones, made of coarsely ground flour as explained in Recipe 1, and on it put slices of pork fat that are four fingers wide and the thickness of a knife. On the slices and the dough put the deer quarters with slices of pork fat again on top of them and sprinkled with the spices. Cover it with a sheet of dough making the pie and leaving the foot and its hair outside. When the pie is closed up, wrap the foot and hair in rag paper so they will not scorch as the pie bakes. Give it a colour as you do other pies and bake it in an oven. When it is done, serve it either hot or cold as you like.

You can do a deer's back and forequarters the same way. Among its viscera I do not think anything is suitable for a pie except for the eggs of a doe, which are rather like ringed acorns; they can be done up like the calf sweetbreads in Recipe 11. The liver should rather be fried than done in a pie. In all the above ways you can do the quarters, both the forequarters and the hindquarters, of a fallow deer, fawns, and a chamois.

26. To do a stag's leg in a pie.

Given that a stag is considerably bigger than a deer, and that its flesh is considerably tougher and darker, after it is skinned take the hind part, cleaned of hairs and all other dirt and cut it up into large or small chunks depending on what your pie will take. To make it tenderize more quickly, let it soak in a seasoning like the loin of beef in Recipe 4, or else have it sit in a press with that spice mixture. Stick it with fat prosciutto or else with salt pork jowl, and sprinkle it with the spice mixture, coarsely ground, of the preceding recipe, and salt. Put it onto a sheet of dough like the loin of Recipe 4. Bake it in an oven, giving it its colour at the right time. When it is done it can be served hot; if you want to keep it, put in more salt and spices.

You can do the shoulders[26.1] of a stag the same way, leaving the feet on them as is done with the deer; likewise the back. Of its lean meat you can make pies of fingers and croquettes, beaten,[26.2] in all the ways that are done with veal in Recipe 16. Yet if you do the fingers of stag meat in a pie and want to serve it hot, you put in sautéed beaten onions along with prunes and dried visciola cherries.

27. Several ways to make a hare pie.

Take a hare and skin it, leaving its head and hind legs with their fur; without washing it, sear it on a grill. Stick it with whole cloves and pork fat, and sprinkle it

---

[26.1] The initial part of this recipe is for the stag's *coscia*, literally 'thigh' or upper hind leg. This extension to the recipe deals with the fore leg and, clearly, the whole of it.

[26.2] Recipe II,43 instructs the cook to beat this meat in order to tenderize it.

with pepper, cinnamon, cloves, ginger, nutmeg and salt. Then have two sheets of dough made with coarsely sieved flour as explained in Recipe 1, with some slices of pork fat on the sheet[27.1] and set out the hare on that, belly downwards, its hind legs and head protruding from the open pie, the head fastened to a stick to support it.[27.2] On the hare's back again slices of pork fat sprinkled with the same spices. Cover the hare over with the other sheet of dough and make the pie with the head and hind legs remaining outside. Put it in an oven, having wrapped the head and feet in rag paper, and bake it. When it is done it is served hot or cold as you wish.

You can also do only the hindquarters. And the forequarters can be done *en croûte* the way a goat kid's quarters are done in Recipe 24. If you have trouble, though, in making the pie with the head hanging out, cut it off; when the pie is done, get a stick and put it through the hare's mouth and out its neck, and join it to the pie where it belongs. The same thing can be done with the tip of the tail, not forgetting to wrap it in rag paper while the pie bakes.

28. To do a common rabbit whole in a pie.

Take a rabbit, skin it and cut off its head and feet. Eviscerate it; wash it in several changes of water. Stuff it with a mixture of beaten pork fat, prosciutto and the rabbit's liver with the gallbladder removed, beaten mint and marjoram, prunes and dried visciola cherries and raisins, or else gooseberries or verjuice grapes, depending on the time of year, along with pepper, cinnamon, cloves, nutmeg, a suitable amount of salt, and raw egg yolks. When it is stuffed, close the hole and sprinkle the rabbit with that same spice mixture. Without searing it, put it into a pastry shell made like a boat, with some slices of pork fat under it and drawing up its legs. On top of the rabbit put slices of pork fat again sprinkled with spices. Cover the pie over and bake it in an oven. When it is done, serve it hot.

If you do not want to stuff the rabbit, sear it on a grill or blanch it in water; stick it all over with lardoons of pork fat. That way, without stuffing them, you can do two of them together done up *en croûte* breast to breast, following the same directions as above for putting them in a pie. You can also do them with their head and feet as hares are done in the previous recipe.

You can do young hares in all those ways, except for washing them. If you want them cut up, follow the directions for doing a goat kid in Recipe 24.

29. To do guinea pigs in a pie.

A guinea pig needs to have its fur removed in hot water the way piglets are done, or else skinned. Eviscerate it, stuff it and cook it the way a common rabbit is done. Make up a pie the same way. And if you want to put some seasonings in through the hole in such pies – which pies are shaped like a boat – that is optional.

[27.1] *sopra esso sfoglio*, in the singular: the second sheet, a covering for the pie, appears later.

[27.2] When served the fully extended hare will appear to be running.

You can do a dormouse in the same way. If you want to do bear meat in a pie, follow the directions set out for a beef pie,[29] or the stag pie in Recipe 26. Likewise, if you want to put a porcupine into a pie, follow the directions given for a young wild boar in Recipe 30. For a hedgehog, do as for the guinea pig.

30. To do the leg of a young wild boar, or other swine, in a pastry wrap.

If the young boar is small, it is skinned only as far as the foot joint. Clean it with a cloth, as the deer is cleaned in Recipe 25. If you want to sear it on a grill, do so. If it is fat there is no need to lard it other than with a few whole cloves, then sprinkle it with salt, pepper, cloves, cinnamon, ginger and nutmeg. Put it onto a sheet of dough made up of coarsely sieved flour, as in Recipe 1, with a few thin slices of prosciutto under and over it. Cover it over, making the pie, making sure the legs with their hair stay outside. Bake it in an oven. Be careful that as the pie bakes the shell does not burst, because that sort of meat is quite a bit more moist than that of a deer and it makes more juice. When it is done it can be served hot or set aside.

If it is a fully grown wild boar, though, for cooking it follow the directions given for the stag in Recipe 26. With lean meat from a young wild boar, and the loin and back, you can make all the pies that are made above with veal. In all those ways you can make pies of domestic pork.

31. To prepare a prosciutto pie.

Get the cured ham of a young male pig, a ham that is not rancid. Let it soak for six hours in warm water, then boil it in water in a roomy cauldron. When it is half cooked take it out and remove its skin and anything else it has around it. Put it back into another pot with enough wine, water and vinegar, tempered with sugar, to cover it, along with ground pepper, cinnamon and cloves; boil it for a quarter of an hour. Take it out and let it cool. Have a sheet of dough made up of coarsely sieved flour as in Recipe 1. Sprinkle the ham with pepper, cloves, cinnamon, ginger, nutmeg and sugar, and put slices of lean veal or pork around the ham so that it is completely wrapped up. Put it on the sheet of dough and make up the pie. Bake it in an oven. When it is done, serve it hot or cold, whichever you wish.

You can do a sow's belly – salted, that is – the same way.

32. To prepare a pie with any sort of large *salsiccione*.

Boil the sausage in enough water in an ample pot: that is done to remove the salt in it and to soften it. When it is half cooked, take it out, let it cool, and wrap lean pork or veal around it. Then have a shell[32.1] made up in the shape of a boat

---

[29] The reference is probably to either Recipe 4 or 5.

[32.1] In this and the next dozen recipes the term that Scappi uses for the pie shell is *cassa*: the meats will be baked *en croûte*.

the length of the sausage. Into it put the sausage sprinkled with sugar and a little cloves and cinnamon. Cover the pie over and bake it. When it is done, it can be served either hot or cold. If it is to be served hot it can have any sort of raw funghi and[32.2] parboiled artichoke or cardoon hearts put into it.

33. To prepare a pie of any sort of mortadella.[33]

Wash the mortadella in warm water and put it, raw, wrapped in fresh pork or veal and sprinkled with sugar, *en croûte*. Cover the pie over and bake it. Serve it hot or cold, whichever you like. With the mortadella you can put some yellow rape that have merely been brought to a boil in water, as well as some fresh beans. If the mortadella is made with liver, though, cook fresh peas with it, or else cardoon hearts beaten with peeled truffles. Those pies should be served hot.

34. To prepare a pie of any sort of saveloy or fresh sausage, with various other things.

Get fine saveloy sausages and put them whole *en croûte* along with parboiled artichoke hearts, peeled truffles, big muscatel raisins and fresh field mushrooms. Cover the pie over and bake it. When it is almost done, add in a little verjuice and beaten egg yolks through the hole. When it is finished, serve it hot.

You can do any sort of sausage that way. If you do not want the sausage whole, cut it up. In the same way you can do oysters when they are out of their shell.

35. To prepare a pie of testicles of a bull or other quadrupeds.

Get the skinned testicles right after the animal has been slaughtered and parboil them in salted water. Then remove the membrane they have on them, and cut them across. Then make a pie of them the way it is done with calf sweetbreads in Recipe 9.

The procedure is the same for testicles of an old buffalo, of a domestic or wild boar, and of a large lamb. You can also put them raw *en croûte* with prosciutto cut up small, or else with saveloy or sausage stuffing. You can do goat-kid testicles along with their scrotum the same way. If you want to put a sauce into the pie when it is almost done, that is up to you. Pies like that always need to be served hot. A young bull's testicles are always a lot better than a mature bull's. Those of a young buffalo can also be done that way.

36. To do common peacocks, turkey or other fowl in pies.

Take a peacock that has hung a while and pluck it dry. Cut off its wings and leave its neck with the feathers on. Draw it and, without washing it, clean away the

---

[32.2] This & is possibly to be understood as 'or.'

[33] This is the rather thick Bolognese sausage that in English, from its place of origin, is now popularly called bologna or, cavalierly, baloney.

bloodiness inside with a cloth. Sprinkle it with pepper, cloves, cinnamon, nutmeg and salt. Inside, to keep it moist, put a little salted pork jowl or pork fat and a few panicles of dried sweet fennel. Tuck the legs in. Sear it on the coals or blanch it in water, although on the coals is better, watching that the neck is not harmed. When that is done, and the bird has cooled a little, cut its feet off and stick a few whole cloves along its breast and thighs. Then have a sheet of dough ready, or a shell, made of coarsely sieved flour as in Recipe 1, with enough slices of pork fat on the bottom of it to hold the peacock's breast; then sprinkle the bird all over with the above spice mixture and put it in, breast down, with as much pork fat again over its back. Cover the pie over in such a way that the head is outside, still attached and erect, wrapped in rag paper.[36] Bake it in an oven with a low heat. When it is done, you can keep it in winter for ten days and in summer for four.

You can do a young turkey the same way, having cut away its breast bone because otherwise it could not fit into a pie. Those two fowl can be stuffed with that mixture used for them in the Book on Prepared Dishes at Recipe 115. In the same way you can do a large wood grouse, which is black and has russet eyes; and a crane, too, and wild geese.

37. To do a turkey pullet in a pie.

Get a young pullet, hung for one day in summer and three in winter, because fowl like that become tender quickly and have quite a whiter flesh than a peacock's; pluck it dry and draw it. Cut off its neck and stuff the bird with yellow-saveloy stuffing, along with truffles or artichoke hearts, parboiled and cut up small, and sweet fennel seed, fresh or dried. Close the hole up and blanch the bird in water, or sear it on the coals. Cut off its wings and feet, and put it into a pastry shell with, under and over it, slices of pork fat, sprinkled with the same spices as are used for the peacock. Cover the pie over and bake it in an oven. If you intend to serve it hot, when it is almost done, through the hole add in a sauce made of vinegar, sugar, white wine, cinnamon and cloves – or else any other seasoning you like.

You can do a young domestic peacock the same way.

38. To prepare a pie of any sort of pheasant or partridge, young or old, or capon, gosling or duck.

To serve pies of the above fowl cold, the head and feet have to be fresh and protruding with their feathers still on. To be served hot, though, all that is needed is that the wildfowl generally be a little tenderized. Once they are plucked and drawn, they can be stuffed with any of the stuffings that are used when they are put to roast as directed in the Book on Prepared Dishes, Recipe 115. Then they are

---

[36] It is a little surprising that there is no suggestion that the peacock's tail be preserved in order to make an even more impressive serving. That practice was common in earlier centuries. See Recipe II,140.

put into the pie shell and baked. If you want to put in some royal sauce[38] before serving them, that is an option.

Young partridges and young pheasants take less cooking and less salt than the others. In that way you can do capons, pullets, young domestic ducks and goslings. If the pies are for keeping, though, you put in more salt and spices, and no sauce of any sort.

39. To do thrush, quail or other small birds in a pie.

All those fowl need to be fresh, plucked dry and drawn. Their neck and feet are cut off. They are sprinkled with salt, pepper, ginger, cinnamon, nutmeg and cloves, and put into a shell with slices of pork fat and beaten veal or pork under them, along with raisins or muscatel raisins or prunes or dried visciola cherries. Cover the pie over and bake it in an oven. When it is almost done put a sauce into it made of prunes and visciola cherries[39.1] or raisins, *mostaccioli* and orange juice. However, if you want to serve it dry, you would not put in any sauce.

You can do turtledoves and woodcocks the same way, and any other sort of small gamebird. Waterfowl[39.2] need more spices than others because of their smell.

40. To do fig-peckers, ortolans and swifts in a pie.

If those three small birds are fat, there is no need to draw them, yet if you want to, only the bowel is removed with the tip of an awl or a stick. When they have been plucked, dry, and singed, they are put into a pastry shell containing the stuffing of fine saveloy or of fine sausage, or else lean veal beaten with prosciutto and pork fat. With the small birds you put truffles or else cardoon or artichoke hearts, parboiled and cut up small and mixed with the spices of the preceding recipe and a little sugar. If, however, you can get fresh field mushrooms, put them in instead of truffles or cardoon hearts. Cover the pie over and bake it. When the birds are almost cooked, through the hole on top put a little verjuice or orange juice tinged with saffron, and finish off cooking them. It is served hot.

If they are other sorts of small gamebirds, they all have to be drawn and their legs and feet removed. And instead of mushrooms, put in prunes, dried visciola cherries, raisins and beaten aromatic fine herbs, following the above directions.

41. To do any sort of dove and cockerel in a pie.

Domestic doves, immediately they are killed, need to be plucked in hot water and drawn and their bones broken; it is optional whether you cut off their wings and head. Cockerels and young pullets, when drawn, have their breast bone

---

[38] Recipe II,267.

[39.1] Here and in Recipe V,165 the qualification *secche*, dried, is probably intended.

[39.2] Properly marsh fowl, *uccelli di valle*.

removed and the neck and feet cut away. If you want to stuff either of those fowl you can use the mixture detailed in the Book on Prepared Dishes at Recipe 115. Then sprinkle them with the same spices and put them into a shell containing veal kidney-fat, beaten, and thin slices of salted pork marrow; add in gooseberries or verjuice grapes in summer, though in winter, prunes and dried visciola cherries and raisins. When the birds are set out in the shell, cover the pie over and bake it. When it is done, serve it hot. It is optional whether you put any garnishes in through the top hole.

Jays, young wood pigeons and other similar small birds are done the same way if you want to serve them hot. If you want to serve them cold, though, follow the directions for the pheasant above in Recipe 38.

42. Various ways to make milk pies.

Make up a small pastry shell[42.1] with well sieved flour, eggs, salt and water; the height of the shell should be in proportion to its size. When it is made, let it dry out so it will hold the filling better. Get ten egg yolks, beaten, with two beakers of fresh goat's or cow's milk, six ounces of sugar, two ounces of rosewater, half an ounce of ground cinnamon, all mixed together, with a few raisins and enough salt. Put the small pie shell into an oven empty and right away put enough of the filling into it to cover its bottom to the depth of a finger. When that filling has thickened, put in some more with a little melted butter; repeat that several times, continuing up the shell by a finger each time. It will then be baked. Take it out and colour the shell. Serve it hot with sugar and rosewater over it. You can also do it with both whites and yolks of eggs, but the filling will not keep in as firm a state as with the yolks alone.

It can be done differently with a small shell made as above: get some *tartara*, made up as in Recipe 86, and some sage-dish[42.2] or else Hungarian Soup[42.3] as made in Recipe 169[42.4] of the Book on Prepared Dishes. When the thin liquid[42.5] of the filling has been drained off, mix in raw eggs, more sugar, a little verjuice and raisins with what is left. Pour the filling into the shell and bake it in the oven. When it is done, serve it hot with sugar and *folignata*[42.6] on top. If you will be wanting to eat the pastry itself along with the filling, put butter or rendered fat into

---

[42.1] *cassetta* throughout this recipe. This seems to be for an open-faced custard pie.

[42.2] For this *salviata* see Recipe III,284.

[42.3] Because of its main ingredient, this preparation is qualified as a Hungarian 'milk' dish in Recipe II,169.

[42.4] Erroneously typeset in both editions as 168.

[42.5] *siero*, the whey of the milk.

[42.6] This decorative garnish may be a sugared almond, a *dragée*, native perhaps to the town of Foligno. See it again in Recipe 48, below.

it when it is made up, although whenever pastry dough is made with fat it tends to collapse when heated; it is made, therefore, with only eggs, cold water and salt, because when that sort of dough heats up it hardens and holds a filling better.

43. To put whitedish into a pie shell of flaky pastry or not.

Make a dough of fine flour with egg yolks, a little rendered fat, salt, sugar and rosewater, and the rest[43.1] warm water, doing it in such a way that the mixture is quite stiff. Make up a shell[43.2] that is either big or small, tall or squat, whatever you like; when it is done, let it sit a while, at least until it has firmed up, and fry it in rendered fat, being careful that the fat is not too hot when you put the shell in the pan and that the shell does not stick. To keep the hollow in the shell, get a chunk of wood like a pestle that is as big as the shell and set the shell on the wood[43.3] and fry it like that: as it heats up it will draw away from the wood. When it is fried, take it out and let it drain. Then fill it with whitedish,[43.4] put it into a tourte pan[43.5] and set that into an oven. When it has heated up, take it out and serve it dressed with sugar and rosewater.

If you want the pie to be of flaky pastry, roll out the same dough as above into a sheet and roll it up and cut the pie's shell, doing it as you do for the calf's sweetbreads of Recipe 11.[43.6] For the present pies, though, instead of doing a bottom of coarse dough, do the bottom with the same dough: whitedish, being compact, will keep the shell from bursting. When it is filled up like a pyramid, cover it over and bake it in the oven the way other flaky-pastry pies are done. When it is baked, serve it hot with sugar and rosewater over top. With the whitedish you can mix as many beaten egg whites as you put yolks into the pie shell, fresh ricotta and more sugar.

44. To prepare earlets[44.1] and little napoleons[44.2] full of whitedish.

When the lump of flaky-pastry dough is made in the above way, cut the roll

---

[43.1] Understand: the rest of the necessary liquid.

[43.2] Scappi uses the word *cassa* in the diminutive: *cassetta*.

[43.3] The pastry shell to be fried blind is inverted over the end of the round segment of wood which is little longer than the depth of the pie shell.

[43.4] See Recipes II,162 ff. and III,218.

[43.5] The pie shell being of indefinite size, Scappi does not intend the pan to support the sides of the pie. Rather the pie remains free-standing and is baked with the pan's cover over it.

[43.6] There the roll is cut into slices of layered dough two fingers wide, which slices form the sides of the shell.

[44.1] *orecchine*, a diminutive of *orecchie*, ears. These are a sort of smaller turnover, standing ear-shaped with their sealed oval edge upward.

[44.2] *Sfogliatelle* is apparently a Lombard name: see Recipe 49, below.

crosswise in thinner slices less than for a pie.[44.3] Carefully grease your hand with melted rendered fat and spread each chunk out, making it like a small flatbread,[44.4] and doing it in such a way that the layers do not run into one another.[44.5] In the centre of that little flat cake, where it is the least layered, put a glob of whitedish mixed with fresh ricotta, beaten fresh egg white and steeped pinenuts. Brush the sheet with a little egg white so that both parts can be joined together. Give the earlet an oval shape in the manner of *offelle*.[44.6] Grease its top with melted rendered fat and fry it in some of the same fat that is not too hot. There should be enough of it in the pot for the earlet not to sink. If you do not want to fry it, bake it in an oven, either in a tourte pan or merely on paper. Serve it hot with sugar over it.

It can be done in another way: first make up a round sheet of dough, like a small trencher board, the dough not being flaky pastry. In its middle heap a little pyramid of whitedish and on that put another sheet, this one of pie pastry and big enough to cover it all, with egg white brushed on its underside. Crimp its rim around its circumference. Fry it or cook it as above. It is served hot with sugar over it. In the same way you can do whitedish and rice, cooked with sugar and goat's milk, and yellowdish.[44.7]

45. Various ways to make pies with a cream filling.

Crema is a French term; it is made of fine flour, milk and eggs. So, get two-thirds of a litre of fresh goat's or cow's milk and mix it with four ounces of sugar, four ounces of fresh butter, a little rosewater and enough salt. Put that on the fire in a casserole pot. When it begins to boil, get a further third of a litre of milk with four ounces of fine flour and six beaten eggs; mix everything in with that flour and pour it into the casserole, stirring until it thickens. Then take it off the fire and put it into a fine filter, let it drain, and put it into an earthenware or tinned copper pot with a little more sugar and rosewater. If you want to add in raw egg yolks, that is an option. Have a small pie shell made up, either of flaky pastry or not, and fill it with that mixture. Bake it in an oven and serve it hot.

[44.3] In Recipe 11 Scappi says the slices should be two fingers thick.

[44.4] A *fucaccina*, a small *focaccia*.

[44.5] That is, in order that the adjacent layers or leaves of this *pasta sfogliata* remain separate. The next sentence suggests that the centre of the round will likely be where pressing the dough has most fused the layers.

[44.6] Cf. the direction in Recipe 1, above. The pie called an *offella* is a small, sweet focaccia made of flaky pastry.

[44.7] The bright yellow of the bush called broom (*ginestra*: see Recipe II,255) gave its name to this preparation, *ginestrata*, whose predominant feature is its colour. See recipes for it at II,160 (for meat days) and III,223 (for lean days).

With that filling you can make all those preparations that are made with whitedish; and you can fill Imperial Crowns and Royal Crowns, having first baked the crowns in the oven.[45] Those crowns are filled more to impress guests with their prettiness than for any other reason. When they are filled give them a quick heating in the oven, serving them either hot or cold as you please, with sugar over top. The mixture can also be used to fill various heraldic arms, both hand-made and moulded.

46. To prepare a pie of goat's milk and either sowbelly or cow's udder.

When the udder or sowbelly has been cooked in water so it is not too salty, cut it into slices or dice it. Then get goat's milk and, for every two-thirds of a litre of it, ten beaten fresh egg yolks, half an ounce of ground cinnamon, one ounce of ground ginger and half a pound of sugar. Have a pie shell made up with firm dough and, when it dries out, put it into the oven with a little of that filling in it. Mix the sowbelly or udder, cut up as directed, with the above ingredients, adding in softened pinenuts, and go on gradually filling the shell with that mixture. Bake it, serving it hot with fine sugar and rosewater over it.

In the same way you can make a pie of ricotta – that is, by mixing fresh ricotta with sugar, egg yolks, rosewater, cinnamon, raisins or pinenuts that have been shelled, softened and crushed. A pie like that always needs to be served hot.

47. To prepare four-cornered pies, popularly called flans,[47.1] of various grains.

Cook coarse wheat[47.2] in a fat meat broth. When that is done, get Parmesan cheese and fresh cheese, the same amount of each and, for every pound of cooked wheat, use a pound and a half of cheese, sufficient saffron, four ounces of raisins, one of cinnamon, half an ounce of pepper and three ounces of softened pinenuts. And when the grain has cooled, mix everything together. Then get a sheet of dough made with fine flour, egg yolks, rosewater, salt and warm water, kneaded so it is firm like the dough of big pies. For every pound of dough get eight ounces of butter, and gradually blend that into the dough, constantly kneading, until all the butter is absorbed into the dough. When the dough has become pasty and smooth, make a round sheet of it the thickness of a knife; make the sheet as large or small as you want. Put the filling in the centre of the sheet, and push the sheet

---

[45] It may be that these names describe pie shells with appropriately carved rims, the first perhaps somewhat larger and more detailed than the second, both baked blind.

[47.1] *i quali dal vulgo sono chiamati Fiadoni.* The term *fiadone* has a long history, going back to Old High German *fladen* and, from that, a late Latin formation, *fladonem*, a flat cake a little like the modern Italian *focaccia*.

[47.2] *formento grosso.* Scappi's phrase is a variant of the *formentone* he writes below and elsewhere. In all cases he seems to mean einkorn. As the title and the variants toward the end of the recipe indicate, this is not flour but the grains of wheat themselves.

together making four corners and giving it the shape of an oil lamp.[47.3] Colour it all around and on top with beaten eggs and saffron. Put it into an oven with a good heat from above so the dough will set more quickly, and bake it. If you do not want it to get too browned, put a sheet of rag paper over it. When it is done, serve it hot. It can also be served cold or reheated in the oven or on a grill.

If you want to make flans on a non-meat day, cook einkorn[47.4] in cow's or goat's milk, with butter. In the same way you can make flans with hulled barley, rice and spelt, and even with cracked millet and foxtail millet. And you can do it with only Parmesan cheese, a moderately soft cheese,[47.5] sugar, spices and raisins.

48. Various ways to make *offelle*.[48.1]

Get a pound of fat Parmesan or Ligurian cheese, and four pounds of cow's cheese – that is, a fairly soft cheese that is not salted – and grate them. Into that put twelve fresh eggs, more or less, depending on what you want, minding that the mixture is neither too thin nor too thick. With that also put in half a pound of clean raisins that have been brought to a boil in water or wine; and six ounces of sugar, one of ground cinnamon, and enough saffron. Then have some dough made of fine flour and the same amount, by weight, of butter, and salt, cold water and rosewater. Of that dough take the size of a small orange and spread it out with a rolling pin that is no more than two hands long;[48.2] make the sheet of dough round and half the thickness of a knife blade. Brush it all around with beaten egg white. In its centre put three ounces of the filling, and close up the *offella* the way *tortelli*[48.3] are done. If you want to crimp it all around, that is up to you, although

---

[47.3] Plate 1 shows a *lucerna* with three flames; it presumably had three spouts, as well as a fourth for filling it. A smaller, common, single-burner sort of lamp is pictured in the same Plate mounted on a wall bracket (to the left); in Plate 2 this more modest lamp reappears hung above (and probably barely illuminating) the pastry workers.

[47.4] *formentone*, as in Recipes II,185 and V,185.

[47.5] *bazzotto*: see Recipe 141.

[48.1] These *offelle* are small focaccios or flat breads. See Recipe V,1 where their shape is described as *ovata*.

[48.2] A rather longer pastry pin can be seen near the centre of the engraving of Plate 1 and, in use, in Plate 2. Unlike a common modern rolling pin, Scappi's is longer, is tapered slightly to each end and is worked from the middle.

[48.3] Scappi never describes *tortelli*, the word being a diminutive of *torta*. Castelvetro describes them: 'Our ladies make *tortelli* with this purée (of fava beans: see Recipe 98, below), seasoned with pepper, which are really delicious. They take a sheet of very thin pastry and cut out round shapes with a glass or a wooden cup, and put a spoonful of the purée on each one, adding a few raisins if desired. Then they fold each one up and make a neat little edging with their fingers and sprinkle them with flour ... They fry them in oil, and some send them to table sprinkled with honey or sugar. These crisp little morsels are so light they never fear for their precious teeth' (trans. Riley, 60). Scappi's Recipes 177–80 give directions for making an even smaller sort of

if it has been brushed with egg whites there will be no need to. Colour it with saffron-tinged water and put it to bake in an oven that is somewhat hotter from above. When it is almost done, colour it again with a small brush and beaten egg yolks. Immediately put a candy on it – that is a candied almond[48.4] – and let it sit in the oven with some sheets of rag paper over it until it is done. Then take it out and serve it hot.

You can also do it another way, by putting as much marzipan paste[48.5] into the filling as there is cheese, along with softened, shelled pinenuts. With that filling you can make little lamps[48.6] and small flans, both covered and open-faced.

[*Crostate*]

49. To prepare various sorts of *crostate*,[49.1] which Neapolitans call *coppi* and Lombards napoleons,[49.2] beginning with a cow's udder.

When the udder has been boiled in salted water, so that it is thoroughly cooked, take it out and let it cool. Cut it into very thin slices. With that put the same amount of boiled, desalted sowbelly and slices of fresh provatura. Have a tourte pan ready, greased with rendered fat or butter, with a rather thick sheet of dough made with fine flour, rosewater, egg yolks, butter and salt. On that sheet of dough put two other thin ones greased with rendered fat or butter, and sprinkle

---

them, *tortelletti* (modern *tortellini*).

[48.4] *se li ponga sopra tresia, cioè folignata.* This *tresia* – in 1581 the word is typeset as *tresi* (though still with a singular verb) – is likely a spelling of *treggia*, a small confection, specifically, as Scappi himself explains, the candied almond (*folignata*, a dragée) in Recipe 42, above.

[48.5] Recipe 73 includes an alternative composition for the cook who finds himself without marzipan paste.

[48.6] *lucernette.* See the *lucerna* in the previous recipe. The shape of a *lucerna* is again evoked in Recipe VI,142.

[49.1] This preparation is not the *crostata* that Scappi describes in Recipes II,229f. and III,265, which is a sort of canapé. Here, Recipes 49–65, 127 and 198f., this is a variety of pie, supported in a tourte pan and hence relatively broad and low. The features that distinguish it are its flaky bottom crust and the so-called *tortiglione* or 'twist,' a pastry band, likewise of layered, flaky pastry, around its upper circumference (see Recipes 122f.). The bottom crust is the same size as the pan in which the pie is made up (see Recipe 217, below); the twist, sitting on the bottom crust, forms the outer wall of the pie. That twist will occasionally be used as an appetizing touch on ordinary tourtes. The name *crostata*, 'crusty,' may relate to the importance of the layered shell, the lower one and sometimes the upper as well, or to the role of sugar, caramelized between each of the layers of the flaky shell and the twist (where a combination of sugar and cinnamon are common), hardened and crispy when it is used as a garnish on the hot upper surface. Significantly, Scappi calls that finishing glaze of sugar a *crostata* (Recipes V,67, 73 and passim).

[49.2] *sfogliati.* The diminutive, *sfogliatelle*, is mentioned in Recipe 44. See also Recipe 217.

them with sugar. Make the twist[49.3] of flaky pastry all around and not very big. On the last sheet of dough set a layer of slices of provatura sprinkled with sugar, cinnamon and raisins, and beaten mint and marjoram; on that layer put little lumps of butter and some of the udder slices and of the sowbelly; continue doing the same up to three layers, covering the last with another sheet of somewhat thinner dough. On that sheet put some strips of flaky pastry, slitting the twist all around with the tip of a hot knife. Carefully, with a greased hand, put waves into the flaky pastry, or else cut it into lacework with a knife. Put it into an oven and bake it, making sure to grease the flaky pastry with rendered fat or melted butter so it will puff up better. When it is done, serve it hot.

Into that pie shell you can put some gooseberries or else seeded verjuice grapes. And if you want it more pleasant tasting, before putting it into the oven put half a beaker of verjuice tempered with sugar into it. Alternatively you can cover it with only a rather thick sheet of pastry and in the middle of that make a small hole as in pies; when it is baked, take it out, put it on a plate and, through that hole, put in a little saffron-tinged broth, verjuice and sugar. Serve it hot.

50. To prepare a *crostata* of a suckling calf's sweetbreads and other things.

Get the best part of the sweetbreads and boil that with the same amount of marrow or salt pork jowl;[50] slice both thinly. Then have a tourte pan ready, lined with three sheets of pastry as above, with rendered fat or melted butter brushed between each one and with sugar and cinnamon sprinkled there, and with the pie's flaky-pastry twist all around. Onto that layered pastry put small lumps of beef marrow, and gooseberries or raisins, and on top of that the cut-up marrow and sweetbreads, and a little beaten mint and marjoram. If you have not put in gooseberries, then splash on verjuice and orange juice. Sprinkle that with pepper, cloves, cinnamon, nutmeg and sugar. Cover it all over with another three thin sheets of pastry, with rendered fat or butter brushed between each; alternatively, use a single, somewhat thick sheet of dough with a few strips of flaky pastry on top. Slash the twist with a knife tip, and grease the strips and twist with rendered fat so they will puff up better. Bake it in an oven or braise it. Serve it hot with sugar on top.

[49.3] A *tortiglione* is a common decorative adjunct wrapped around the wall of Scappi's pie crust. See the end of Recipe 132 where Scappi values a *tortiglione* for its aesthetic contribution to his *pizze*: ... *et il tortiglione sfogliato incirca per fare che sia piu bella.* The Italian word means literally a spiral. This pastry confection was often, as in Recipes 122 f., below, prepared to be eaten by itself. Recalling the procedure for making flaky pastry as it is outlined in Recipe 11, we may imagine that a ribbon of layered dough, perhaps rolled across its width, is given a continuous twist lengthwise and then set around the top or sides of the pie shell. Two of the tourte pans (*padelle da torta alte*) illustrated in Plate 9 show wide rims which could support such a decorative pastry twist.

[50] Here and in Recipe 56 Scappi explains his term *barbaglia* by adding *cioè gola di porco salata.*

51. To prepare *crostate* of goat kid's sweetbreads, eyes, ears and scrotum with testicles.

With the above things half boiled in salted water, have a tourte pan ready, lined with the three layers of dough, with rendered fat or melted butter brushed between each, and with the flaky-pastry twist all around as directed above. On that pastry put beaten kidney-fat of a calf or goat kid mixed with sugar, cinnamon, pepper, cloves, nutmeg, either gooseberries or raisins, and marbled prosciutto, diced. On top of all that put the eyes, with the black pupil removed, along with the other things[51] and over that spread the same mixture as was put beneath, in the same amount. Then get beaten fresh egg yolks combined with orange juice, verjuice and broth, and sprinkle that on top. Cover the pie over right away with the other layers of pastry and the flaky-pastry strips, following the directions for greasing the flaky pastry. Bake it like the previous one, serving it hot with sugar and rosewater on top.

52. To prepare a *crostata* of spit-roasted calf's kidney and loin.

Get the part of a veal loin where the kidney is attached and blanch it in water. Stick it with lardoons of marbled prosciutto that is not rancid, and more than half cook it on a spit. Take it down and, while it is still hot, remove the flesh from the bones so that the meat has no skin or gristle in it. Beat it small on a table with knives; then in with it mix mint, marjoram, burnet, pepper, cinnamon, cloves, nutmeg, sugar and pinenuts that have softened, and truffles, skinned, parboiled and finely cut up. Then have a tourte pan ready, lined with layers of pastry and with its flaky-pastry twist all around as was directed above. Into it put that filling, which should be splashed with verjuice and orange juice. If you want the *crostata* double, into the middle of the filling put a sheet of dough the size of the baking dish, fried in rendered fat, and put as much of the filling above it as under it. Cover it all over with the three pastry layers, with butter brushed between each, or else with only a single one that is a bit thicker with some strips of flaky pastry on it. Grease it and bake it in an oven as above.

In the same way you can do it with the flesh of turkey hens, pheasants, capons and other large, spit-roasted fowl, mixed with spit-roasted veal kidney or else beef marrow, along with the other ingredients listed above. If you want to make a tourte of that, add in cheese and eggs, with a beaker of milk, and serve it hot with fine sugar over top.

53. To prepare a *crostata* of calf's tongue and other things.

Cook the tongue well, which should be fresh. When it is done, remove the skin on it and cut it crosswise into thin slices. Have a tourte pan ready, greased with rendered fat or butter, lined with three sheets of thin dough with rendered

[51] The viscera listed in the recipe's title.

fat or butter brushed between each, and sprinkled with sugar and cinnamon, and with its flaky-pastry twist all around. On the dough put thin slices of fresh, unsalted provatura, finely chopped mint and marjoram, gooseberries or raisins, and a *salsiccione* that is not rancid, grated. On those things put the tongue slices sprinkled with pepper, cloves, cinnamon, nutmeg and sugar; if there are no gooseberries in it, splash some verjuice and orange juice on it. Cover it all over with a rather thick sheet of dough with strips of flaky pastry on it. Grease it, arrange the twist, and bake it in an oven. Serve it hot.

You can put that same filling into small flans made with royal dough[53] and bake them in the oven.

54. To prepare a *crostata* of doves' croupions and flesh.

Get young doves, half roast them on a spit, take them down and let them cool a little; take the flesh from their breast and croupion. Have a tourte pan lined with the sheets[54] of pastry and the flaky-pastry twist around it, greased and sprinkled as above. In the pan make a layer of fine saveloy or sausage on the topmost layer of dough – and if you do not have either, use beef marrow cut up small with salt pork jowl; on that, place the doves' flesh and croupions sprinkled with sugar and the spices listed above, adding in gooseberries or seeded verjuice grapes, or, if in winter, orange juice and verjuice, and raisins or seeded muscatel raisins. Cover it over with the sheet of dough and the strips of flaky pastry; brush it with rendered fat or butter. Bake it in an oven or braise it. Serve it hot with sugar on top.

That *crostata* can also be made with doves without removing their bones. Boil the doves, then quarter them and sauté them in rendered fat with beaten spring onions, adding in orange juice. When they are done, put them into a tourte pan with the same ingredients and following the above directions. In that same way you can do any sort of dove, turtledove, young cockerels, goslings or ducklings.

55. To prepare a *crostata* of fig-eaters, ortolans and swifts.

Take those small birds when they've been plucked and cleaned and, with a knife dig out their little bowels and split the birds in two. Then get veal kidney, spit-roasted and beaten with knives and, along with that, prosciutto finely cut up with mint, marjoram and a little fresh wild thyme. Have a tourte pan ready, greased with butter or rendered fat and lined with the three layers of dough and with the flaky-pastry twist around it. Onto the dough put the mixture along with truffles, skinned and finely cut up, or else field mushrooms, together with the quartered birds. Sprinkle everything with pepper, cloves, cinnamon, nutmeg and sugar, adding in gooseberries or seeded verjuice grapes, or else raisins, depending

---

[53] See Recipe 84, below, where *pasta reale* is made with fine flour, rosewater, sugar and butter.

[54] Undoubtedly Scappi uses the plural to indicate the three thin layers of pastry dough, with grease or butter between each, that he specifies for other *crostate*.

on the season. Over the birds put as much again of the same mixture as is under them – splashing them with orange juice and verjuice if you have not put in any gooseberries or verjuice grapes. Cover it over with three sheets of dough and with butter or rendered fat brushed between each and fashioned into various shapes.[55] With the tip of a hot knife slash the twist; brush it with rendered fat or melted butter so it will puff up better. Bake it in an oven or braise it. Serve it hot with sugar and rosewater over it.

You can, moreover, do the small birds whole. And if you do not have kidney or prosciutto, use the stuffing for yellow saveloy or else for fine sausage. In that same way you can do unlaid eggs and chicken livers.

56. To prepare a prosciutto *crostata*.

Get a cured ham of a young pig, and if it is from the hills[56.1] it will be quite a bit better. Let it steep in warm water, then cook it in water. When it is done, let it cool, then cut it into thin slices and steep them in white wine and sugar for four hours. Have a tourte pan ready, lined with three layers of dough and with its twist around it. On the dough lay out slices of unsalted provatura sprinkled with pepper, sugar, nutmeg, cloves and cinnamon, adding in beaten mint and marjoram, and raisins and seeded muscatel raisins. On that put the slices of prosciutto and sprinkle them again with the same spices and sugar, putting onto that as much again of the same things as were put beneath. Splash that with a little verjuice and orange juice. If you want to set a fried layer of pastry across the middle,[56.2] that is optional. Cover it all over with a sheet of dough that is somewhat thick and put some strips of flaky pastry on that. Brush it with rendered fat or melted butter. Bake it as above, and serve it hot with sugar and rosewater over top.

You can do salt pork jowl and sowbelly that same way, both of them first boiled, and slices of raw mortadella, and well cooked *salsiccioni* also.[56.3]

57. To prepare *crostate* and pies of various fruits, beginning with the mushroom

---

[55] *lavorati a diverse foggie*: It is regrettable that Scappi was not more explicit in detailing what these shapes might have been. Elsewhere he will specify a latticework top and a series of over-lapping slats as in a jalousie.

[56.1] By *porco giovane ... di montagna* Scappi means the animal which has been allowed the relative freedom, in the care of a swineherd, of browsing in nature, particularly on freshly fallen acorns. Because flat land was preferred for cultivation, the word *montagna* came also to mean the outback, the wilderness.

[56.2] As in Recipe 52, making a 'double *crostata*.'

[56.3] Three times in this sentence Scappi's 'and' may well be an 'or.'

called a common field mushroom.[57.1]

Get field mushrooms in their season, as is stated in the Second Book, on Prepared Dishes, at Recipe 215.[57.2] Clean away the skin on them; in particular clean off any sand on their stem – steep them in water for a quarter of an hour so the sand can better be cleaned off them; take them out and let them drain by themselves. Have a tourte pan ready, lined with the three sheets of pastry dough and with the flaky-pastry twist around it. On the uppermost sheet put a little provatura and grated dry cheese, beaten mint and marjoram, and lumps of beef marrow; sprinkle everything with sugar, pepper, cloves, cinnamon and nutmeg. On that set out the mushrooms, and on them put the same amount again of the previous mixture and spices. Splash that with verjuice and orange juice. Cover it over with three more thin sheets of dough, greased with rendered fat or butter between each, and bake it in an oven or braise it. Serve it hot with sugar on it.

In the same way you can do morels and other soft autumn mushrooms. You can put that filling into pie shells,[57.3] whether of flaky pastry or not.

58. To prepare *crostate* and pies of truffles and other things.

Get truffles in their season, as is said in the Second Book, on Prepared Dishes, at Recipe 214;[58] clean off any sand on them. Bring them to a boil in wine or broth, or else half cook them under hot coals. Then skin them and cut them up in small pieces, mixing in with them the same amount of field mushrooms and beaten mint and marjoram, lumps of beef marrow and pepper, cinnamon, cloves, nutmeg, sugar and orange juice. Make up the *crostata* as for the field mushrooms above.

You can also do it with the same ingredients as are used with the mushrooms. The filling can be used for pies with or without flaky pastry.

59. To prepare a *crostata* or pie of artichoke or cardoon hearts.

Get artichokes in their season, as is said in the Second Book, on Prepared Dishes, at Recipe 213,[59] and cook them in a meat broth or in salted water. Take the heart, which is their best part, and clean it well. If it is big, slice it and make the *crostata* or pie of it with the same ingredients as are used with the field mushrooms. You can do the same with boiled cardoon stems cut into slices.

[57.1] These *prugnoli* (also called agaric in English) are the variety of mushroom most commonly used by Scappi. In the recipe he refers back to he calls them 'the most delicate of all mushrooms.' He has already called for their incorporation into several previous dishes in this Book V.

[57.2] This number reads 214 in the two printed texts of 1570.

[57.3] These *pasticci in cassa* are in a pastry casing – that is, the free-standing pies that Scappi dealt with earlier.

[58] This number reads 213 in both printed texts.

[59] This number reads 212 in both printed texts.

60. To prepare a *crostata* or pie with fresh peas.

Get tender, fresh, shelled peas in their season, as is said in the Second Book, on Prepared Dishes, at Recipe 188.[60.1] It is optional whether you bring them to a boil in a fat broth; however, if they are tender there is no need to. Have a tourte pan ready with its layers of pastry and its twist around it, and put the peas into it mixed with fresh provatura and a dry cheese, grated, and beaten mint, marjoram and parsley, with a few lumps of butter in it, sprinkled with the spices and sugar that were listed in the preceding recipe; to that add egg yolks beaten with verjuice. Cover the pan over with a rather thick sheet of dough with a few strips of flaky pastry on it. Bake it in an oven or braise it. Serve it hot with sugar on it. Instead of grated cheese you can use the stuffing of fine saveloy or sausage.

You can do fresh, tender beans the same way, having first brought them to a boil in salted water. And you can also put them into a pie prepared *en croûte*.[60.2]

61. To prepare an apple *crostata* or pie.

Get red apples, either pare them or roast them in the coals, and cut them into thin slices. Stew them a little in an earthenware or copper pot in fresh butter, sugar and a little malmsey or white wine. When they are done, take them out and make a *crostata* with them, with slices of fresh provatura under and over them, sprinkling them with sugar and cinnamon. Put a few lumps of butter and seeded muscatel raisins in with that.

You can do pink apples and russet apples the same way, and several sorts of pear and even muscatel pears,[61] too, when they are cut in two. Red apples and muscatel pears can be put into a *crostata* raw as they are without being stewed if you have sliced them very thin.

62. To prepare a quince *crostata*.

Get a quince in its season, as is said in the Second Book, on Prepared Dishes, at Recipe 223[62.1] and roast it in the coals. Then peel it in wine or water and slice it thin. Then have a tourte pan ready with its three sheets of pastry dough and its twist of flaky pastry around it. Sprinkle it with sugar, cinnamon and cloves; set the quince slices on that, along with seeded muscatel raisins or ordinary raisins, and lumps of butter. Sprinkle everything with Neapolitan *mostaccioli*, ground and powdered, and sugar and cinnamon. Cover the pan with a rather thick sheet of dough with a few strips of flaky pastry on it. Bake it in an oven or braise it. Serve it hot with sugar and rosewater over it.

[60.1] This number reads 187 in both printed texts.

[60.2] *pasticci in cassa*. See Recipes 2 and passim, 154 ff., for that sort of standing pie.

[61] These *pere moscarole* were called *pere moscatelle* in Recipe II,115. The word *moscarolo* is a dormouse and may have been used as a descriptive term for this variety of pear.

[62.1] In both texts the recipe number is printed as 222.

In with the quince you can add slices of fresh dates that have been brought to a boil in wine and sugar and have been cut up small; likewise, shelled pistachios or pinenuts, softened, and a few thin slices of fresh provatura or Florentine *raviggioli*.[62.2]

63. To prepare a peach, apricot or plum *crostata*.

Get a peach that is not too ripe; if it is hard it will do quite a bit better than if not. Peel it and cut it into slices. Have a tourte pan ready, lined with its three sheets of dough and its twist around it, greased with butter or rendered fat, and sprinkled with pepper, cloves, cinnamon, nutmeg and sugar, and with raisins and crumbled Neapolitan *mostaccioli*. On all that set out the peach slices and on top of them put the same ingredients as are under them. Cover the pan over with three thin sheets of dough, with rendered fat or butter brushed between each; sprinkle that with sugar and cinnamon. Bake it in an oven or braise it; it does not take too much cooking because it would disintegrate into a broth. Serve it hot, dressed with sugar and rosewater.

With those ingredients you can also add in provatura or grated cheese.[63]

64. To prepare a *crostata* of visciola or morello cherries, strawberries, gooseberries or fresh verjuice grapes.

Get visciola or morello cherries that are not too ripe, without their stalk; pit them. Have a tourte pan ready with three layers of dough and wash the top one with beaten egg white, immediately sprinkling it with sugar: that is done so the juice will not penetrate into the pastry. Let it sit a while, then get the visciola cherries, having coated them with sugar, cinnamon and musk-flavoured Neapolitan *mostaccioli*, crumbled and mixed with beaten egg yolks: that is done in order to hold everything together. Put it all into the pan and cover it over with three very thin sheets of dough that have been fashioned in various ways.[64]

You can do gooseberries, new verjuice grapes, seeded and peeled, and strawberries the same way. The filling can also be used when the pie is prepared *en croûte*.

65. To prepare a turnip *crostata*.

Get a turnip in its season, as is indicated in the Book of Prepared Dishes at Recipe 211,[65.1] and cook it on the coals. When it is done, peel it, leaving the

---

[62.2] This is a sort of fresh, soft cheese from sheep's or goat's milk. It has been mentioned already in Book I, §8.

[63] Scappi forgets to deal expressly with the apricots and plums listed in the recipe's rubric.

[64] As in Recipe 55 Scappi leaves us wondering just what these decorative *diversi modi* might have been.

[65.1] In both texts the number is printed as 210.

browned area on it; cut it up into slices the thickness of a knife blade. Have a tourte pan ready, lined with its three layers of pastry and with its twist around it, the bottom of the shell sprinkled with sugar and cinnamon. On the bottom set out slices of fat provatura or a creamy cheese; on them lay down a layer of turnip slices, sprinkling them again with the same spices and sugar; and put a few lumps of fresh butter or beef marrow on them. Cover the turnip with the provatura or cheese again and repeat to make three layers like that in all, sprinkling the topmost one with sugar and cinnamon. Cover everything over with strips of flaky pastry like a shutter's slats.[65.2] Bake it in an oven or braise it the way the others are done, and serve it hot with sugar over top.

Into that *crostata* you can add grated Parmesan cheese if there is no salted provatura in it.

[Tourtes[*iii*]]

66. To prepare a veal tourte.

Get that part of a loin of veal that has the kidney attached to it,[66.1] and roast it on a spit without larding it. When it is almost done, take it off the spit, let it cool, lift the flesh from the bones and remove the hide and gristle from it. On a table beat the meat and kidney small with knives, adding to them mint and marjoram; for every pound of beaten meat add in four ounces of a creamy cheese and two ounces of a dry cheese, both of them grated, three fresh eggs, sugar, pepper, cinnamon, cloves, saffron, and nutmeg according to your taste, and orange juice. Then have a tourte pan ready, lined with a sheet of dough made with fine flour, egg yolks, sugar, butter, rosewater and salt. Put the filling into that and cover it all over with another sheet of pastry in strips like shutter louvres or with bumps. You can put a beaker of goat's or cow's milk[66.2] into that filling. Bake it in an oven or braise it, and serve it hot with sugar and rosewater over it.[66.3]

[65.2] *fatte a gelosia* is Scappi's imagery: 'made like a jalousie.' The parallel strips overlap a little like the louvres of a window shutter, so making a relatively continuous upper crust that can breathe, rather than a top that is either open-faced or sealed.

[*iii*] A *torta* is a relatively shallow pie made generally with both an upper and a lower crust of plain pastry in a *tortiera*. The upper shell can occasionally be cut decoratively, in part so any steam can escape; the pastry of the lower is sometimes 'rather thick.' For varieties of the tourte pan, which usually is covered with a lid, see Plates 8 and 9. Characteristically the filling of a *torta* is rich with cheese and eggs; see Recipes VI,116 ff. for tourtes without cheese.

[66.1] In Recipe II,38 Scappi has carefully distinguished the *lonza* as a part of a veal *lombo*.

[66.2] Lancelot de Casteau's *Tourtes de veau à la cresme* uses cream rather than cheese in mixing this pie's filling: *Ouverture de cuisine*, 35.

[66.3] This sort of glazing will be common on top of Scappi's tourtes.

In the same way you can do a cut of fresh pork loin, domestic or wild, half roasted on a spit, and the tenderloin, too, of those animals, and the leg meat of a wether.[66.4] Instead of the kidney, use beef marrow or boiled calf udder. In summer you can put in gooseberries or verjuice grapes; in winter, raisins.

If you want to make ravioli, whether with a dough casing or not, when the meat is beaten grind it in a mortar and add in more dry cheese, more eggs, and more sugar and spices. Make ravioli of that with a casing or not, cooking it in a broth of a fat capon or of some other meat. Serve it dressed with cheese, sugar and cinnamon.[66.5] You can do veal sweetbreads that same way, and well boiled cow's udder, too.

67.   To prepare a tourte of a domestic pig's blood, popularly called blood pudding.[67.1]

Get the blood immediately after the animal has been slaughtered and, still warm, put it through a strainer for hairs and any other dirt, stirring it so it does not coagulate. For every four pounds of blood, put in a pound and a half of grated creamy cheese, six ounces of grated dry cheese, one ounce of cinnamon, half an ounce of pepper, three-quarters of an ounce of nutmeg and cloves combined, a quarter-ounce of ground ginger, a pound of sugar, beaten mint, marjoram and other fine herbs, a little spring onion, beaten and sautéed, a pound of beef marrow or else that pig's kidney-fat,[67.2] without its membrane – the marrow or the fat cut up into lumps – one-third of a litre of milk, four beaten egg yolks, and four ounces of very clean raisins. Then have a tourte pan ready with a rather thick sheet of dough in it, without the twist; into it put the filling, which should be somewhat runny rather than thick. Bake it in an oven or braise it with a low heat. When it is almost done, give it a glazing of sugar and cinnamon. Serve it hot.

[66.4] This *zigotto di castrato* is the upper hind leg.

[66.5] Lancelot de Casteau's *Raphioulles* (*Ouverture de cuisine,* 78) are similar: a dough of white flour, eggs and butter encasing a filling of ground cooked veal, beef grease, eggs, grated Parmesan cheese (expressly), cinnamon and nutmeg; boiled; served dressed with grated Parmesan and cinnamon. The preparation may have been anticipated in Chiquart's *Mortoexes* (Recipe 56); and earlier in the *guanti, cioè ravioli* of the *Libro della cocina,* 35 along with the *de gantis* (*tales tortelli vocantur ganta*) of the *Liber de coquina,* 411–12, Recipe III,9. Remarkably the earliest appearance of ravioli is in an Anglo-Norman collection of the late thirteenth century: '*Ravieles.* Get fine flour and sugar and make up a dough. Get good cheese and butter, and cream them together; then get parsley, sage and scallions, chop them up finely and put them into the filling. Put grated cheese both under and over the ravioli; put them in the oven.' Constance B. Hieatt and Robin F. Jones, 'Two Anglo-Norman Culinary Collections Edited from British Library Manuscripts Additional 32085 and Royal 12.C.xii,' *Speculum,* 61 (1986): 859–82; MS 'A,' Recipe 8, 863.

See also Scappi's 'casingless' ravioli of Recipes II,181 and III,6.

[67.1] *migliaccio*: the mixture originally included *miglio,* millet flour.

[67.2] This *sognia* or *sugna* is the fat immediately under a pig's hide and around its kidney, the source of the rendered fat so commonly used in Scappi's cooking.

You can stuff intestines with that filling, cooking them the way blood sausages[67.3] are cooked. You can also do it without a pie shell: into the pan put rendered fat or butter, heating it up hot before the filling is put in: that is done so it will not stick.

68.   To prepare another tourte of pork blood, popularly called white blood pudding.[68.1]

Get four pounds of blood, strained as above, two pounds of goat's or cow's milk, four well beaten eggs, three ounces of fine flour, mint, marjoram, raisins and a pound of sugar. When everything is mixed together with the spices mentioned above, make a tourte with it in the above ways. With those two mixtures you can fill *tartare*[68.2] in the French style; serve them hot with sugar, cinnamon and rosewater over them.

69.   To prepare a tourte of a calf's brain and sweetbreads.

Calf's brains have to be fresh and need to be parboiled in salted water. For every pound and a half of brains, get six ounces of the calf's sweetbreads, parboiled and beaten small with knives, along with three ounces of marbled prosciutto and a good handful of fine herbs. With those ingredients mix in four ounces of creamy cheese and another four ounces of a grated dry cheese, six eggs, a beaker of goat's milk, half an ounce of cinnamon, six ounces of sugar, half an ounce of pepper, three ounces of softened, crushed pinenuts, and three ounces of raisins. Make a tourte with that mixture, with a pastry shell below and above, and bake it in an oven or braise it. Instead of calf's brains, you can use pig's brains and goat kid's sweetbreads.

With that filling you can fill small pastry shells made with royal dough[69] and fired the way the ones with whitedish are done in Recipe 43.

70.   To prepare a royal tourte[70] with pheasant and partridge flesh.

Of those fowl get the breast meat that has first been more than half roasted

---

[67.3] *sanguinacci.*

[68.1] *migliaccio bianco.*

[68.2] Messisbugo's recipe for a *tartara* combines twenty fresh, beaten eggs, fifteen beakers of milk, five ounces of sugar, half an ounce of cinnamon, saffron, four ounces of raisins and half a pound of butter; it is baked in a pie shell and garnished with four ounces of sugar. Scappi's *tartara* of Recipe V,86, below, is a sort of crustless or shellless tourte.

[69] See Recipe 84, below.

[70] A *torta reale*, of which Scappi offers several versions in this and the following recipes, seems to consist in particular of a paste of almonds (with or without other nuts), spices, eggs (usually yolks) and fat (usually thick cream or cheese), all considerably sweetened. The various fillings are varieties of marzipan custard. For his *Pasta reale* Lancelot de Casteau (*Ouverture de cuisine*, 64) does not make a pie in the normal sense but rather combines ground breast of capon (see the option below), powdered sugar, cinnamon and rosewater, and then, in rounds two fingers wide and half a finger thick, dries that in an oven.

on a spit, skinned and with any gristle removed. Grind it in a mortar; for every pound of flesh, also grind with it four ounces of marzipan or else three ounces of shelled Milanese almonds, a pound of fine sugar, an ounce and a half of fine musk-flavoured *mostaccioli* and six fresh uncooked egg yolks. When everything has been thoroughly ground up together, add in half an ounce of ground cinnamon, half an ounce of cloves and nutmeg combined, a quarter-ounce of ginger, four ounces of rosewater and four ounces either of butter or else of beef marrow, ground in a mortar to keep it soft. With that filling make a tourte with a lower and upper pastry crust, the upper one made like shutter louvres. Bake it in an oven or braise it with a low heat. Serve it hot with sugar and rosewater over top.

You can do it the same way with capon flesh.

71. Another way to prepare a royal tourte with the above meats.

When the flesh of two pheasants or four partridges has been half roasted on a spit and then ground in a mortar with a pound of Milanese almonds, six ounces of either fresh pork kidney-fat or beef marrow or fresh capon fat, six ounces of softened pinenuts and three ounces of fresh pitted dates – when all of that has been ground up so that nothing remains whole (the best thing would be to put it all through a colander), add in six raw egg yolks, a pound of ground fresh ewe's cheese, a pound and a half of sugar, three ounces of apple juice, an ounce of ground cinnamon and an ounce of cloves, ginger and nutmeg combined. With that mixture make a tourte with a flaky-pastry twist around it and cover it with a sheet of pastry[71] made like shutter slats or otherwise. Bake it in an oven or braised. Serve it hot or cold as you like, with sugar and cinnamon over top.

72. To prepare a tourte with capon breast.

Get two large, fleshy capons that have hung a little while and boil them in salted water. Take the breast meat, skinned and without gristle, and grind it in a mortar with six ounces of softened pinenuts, a pound of fresh ewe's-milk ricotta, four ounces of a creamy cheese, six fresh eggs, and four ounces of butter. When all of that has been ground up together, put in six ounces of very clean currants, a pound of fine sugar, three ounces of rosewater, and an ounce of cinnamon – although if you want it white put in ginger in place of cinnamon. With that filling make a tourte, with the twist around it and covered over with another sheet of dough made like shutter slats, or else of flaky-pastry dough. Bake it in an oven or braise it. Serve it hot with sugar and rosewater over top.

---

[71] The words *intorno, & cuoprisi con un sfoglio* are missing in the 1581 edition as the typeset-ter's eye jumped between the words *sfogliato* ('flaky') and *sfoglio* ('sheet') in the 1570 printing.

73. To prepare a royal tourte with dove flesh, which Neapolitans call 'lady's lips pizza.'[73.1]

Get the flesh of three doves half roasted on a spit, with the skin, bones and gristle removed, along with the flesh of three boiled doves. Grind it all up in a mortar with four ounces of peeled dates, eight ounces of marzipan paste and four ounces of ground beef marrow – grind it all so finely that it can go through a colander. If you do not have any marzipan paste, use six ounces of Milanese almonds shelled in cold water and four ounces of fine sugar. Into all that add six fresh cream tops[73.2] – if you do not have cream tops, a pound of fresh curds of ewe's milk. When everything is put through the colander, put ten fresh uncooked egg yolks into it and four more ounces of fine sugar along with an ounce of cinnamon and half an ounce of cloves and nutmeg together. Have a tourte pan ready, lined with a sheet of somewhat thick dough, and with its flaky-pastry twist around it, made with fine flour, egg yolks, sugar, butter, rosewater and a suitable amount of salt. Put the filling into the pan in such a way that it does not come up too high. It is optional if you wish to bake it with an upper shell made like a shutter's louvres, although it looks better open-faced and[73.3] with only a glazing made of melted sugar and rosewater. Bake it in an oven as marzipan is done. When it is baked, serve it hot or cold as you like.

[73.1] *pizza di bocca di Dama.* A distinction of most of the so-called royal tourtes (generally Recipes 73–80) is to contain thick cream (or fresh cheese curds or fresh ricotta) instead of, or as well as, ordinary cheese: these are richer custards. In its use of various cheeses, eggs and cream this pizza of Scappi resembles the four pizzas found in the Lucano manuscript (1524) in a general way; see the note in Recipe 128, below. In the edition of the manuscript by Süthold, Recipe 86 for *Picza reale*, the final recipe in that collection, calls for five varieties of fresh cheese, three of ricotta cheese, eggs, almonds, rosewater and sugar. The 1524 pizza has no meat, however, but may optionally include musk. (The modern *boca di dama* is described by Riley in *The Oxford Companion to Italian Food*, 57.)

In a dialogue dating from the beginning of the 1600s Vincenzo Giustiniani had a chauvinistic Neapolitan exclaim, 'Our monks make things that will raise the dead, specifically lady's-lips tourtes, *mostaccioli*, boxed morsels of rose sugar and many other confections that give pleasure throughout the world': *Le nostre monache fanno cose che suscitano li morti e particolarmente le torte di bocca di dama, le mostaccioli e zuccheri rosati in piezzi e in barattoli, e molte altre sorti di conserve che per tutto il mondo si mangiano per regalo* (*Discorsi sulle arti e sui mestieri* [Florence: Sansoni, 1982], 154). It is perhaps no coincidence that Sicily was recognized as the foremost producer of hard wheat at the time, even shipping it far beyond the Mediterranean world. Scappi will offer a series of various other possibilities in the *pizza* genre from Recipes 128 to 132, below.

[73.2] *capi di latte.* A recipe for making these is given at VI,145. A single cream top probably consists of the cream that will form on top of one *boccale* (two and two-thirds litres) of cow's milk, in Scappi's day unlikely more than a quarter of a litre or one cup. The term *capo di latte* was in use in cookery from the fourteenth century: see the anonymous *Libro per cuoco*, Recipe 134, *chavo de late* (ed. Faccioli, *Arte della cucina*, I, 105).

[73.3] This 'and' likely has the sense of 'or.'

You can put a little musk-flavoured *mostaccioli* into that tourte. When the filling is well ground up, there is no need to sieve it. And if you want it to have a bit of sweetness, put in a little malmsey, orange juice and more sugar.

74. To make a royal tourte of pinenuts, almonds and other things.

Skin a pound of Milanese almonds that have been softened in cold water for eight hours, then grind them in a mortar with the same amount of shelled pinenuts that have been softened in cold water for six hours. When they have been ground with two pounds of fine sugar, add in eight fresh cream tops or else a pound and a half of fresh ewe's-milk curds; if you do not have either of those, get fresh mozzarella, although the cream tops will always be better. Into all that add six fresh, beaten egg yolks, four ounces of apples well ground in a mortar, a grain of musk,[74] half an ounce of ginger and a little rosewater. If you do not want it to be white, instead of ginger put in cloves, cinnamon and nutmeg. Have a tourte pan ready with a rather thick lower shell of royal dough, and its twist all around made of fine flour, sugar, butter, rosewater and enough salt. Put the filling into it so that it does not come either too high or too low. Bake it in an oven like marzipan, making a glazing of sugar and rosewater for it. Serve it hot or cold as you like.

75. To prepare a royal tourte with various fillings.

Get six ounces of shelled Milanese almonds that have softened in cold water for eight hours, six ounces of pinenuts that have been softened, four ounces of peeled dates, four ounces of shelled pistachios and three ounces of seeded muscatel raisins. When everything has been thoroughly ground in a mortar, add in three ounces of breadcrumb[75.1] soaked in goat's milk and put it all through a strainer, adding in five pounds of fresh milk and two pounds of ground sugar. Mix everything together so that it is smoothly liquid, and put it all into a casserole pot. Cook it over a low coal fire so that it thickens, stirring constantly with a wooden spoon. Into it add an ounce of cinnamon, half an ounce of cloves and nutmeg together, four ounces of fresh butter and two ounces of rosewater. When it is all cooked, take it out of the pot and add in six fresh egg yolks and four cream tops or else six ounces of ewe's curds – and if you do not have either, put in ricotta. Make up a tourte as above with that filling. Serve it hot or cold as you wish. When you take it out of the oven brush it with musk water.[75.2]

---

[74] Musk, a secretion of the musk deer, was an item of commerce listed in the fourteenth-century *Pratica della mercatura* of Pegolotti (ed. Evans, 422). One preferred source was Tibet. Musk is also used in Recipes 227, below, VI,139, 142 and 143, and in the flavouring of a sort of *mostacciolo*. See, too, the *acqua di muschio* of III,280, V,75 and VI,139.

[75.1] Here and elsewhere *mollica di pane* is bread without its crust: crumb of bread. 'Crumb' is not plural unless the crumb is expressly broken into bits.

[75.2] This *acqua muschiata* is not dealt with among the medicinal potions at the beginning of Book VI; see, however, Recipe VI,139.

76. To prepare a royal tourte with whitedish.

Get two pounds of whitedish made with capon flesh, rice flour, goat's milk, two cream tops[76.1] and sugar, in the manner directed in the Book on Prepared Dishes at Recipe 164.[76.2] With that put in eight fresh egg whites, beaten, six ounces of sugar, two cream tops, half an ounce of ground ginger and two ounces of rosewater, and mix everything together. Make a tourte of it the same way as above, and serve it hot or cold as you like.

In that tourte you could put some shelled pinenuts, softened and ground. And you also cover it with another sheet of pastry made in lumps or like shutter louvres. With all of the fillings of the above tourtes you can make tortellini,[76.3] and fry them in rendered fat or in clarified butter.

77. To prepare a tourte of ricotta with elderflowers and other things.

Get six ounces of pinenut paste ground in a mortar with two pounds of fresh ricotta of ewe's or cow's milk, adding in eight fresh egg whites, a pound of sugar and three-quarters of an ounce of white ginger. When everything is ground up, put it through a colander. Into that put three ounces of elderflower that has soaked in goat's or cow's milk. Make a tourte of that filling, covering it with a sheet of pastry made like shutter slats, and bake it like the ones above, with a glazing of sugar and rosewater.

You could also put some softened pinenuts into the filling, and creamy cheese with a bit of salt in it. And you could bake it without a pastry shell, having prepared the tourte pan, though, with very hot melted butter before the filling is put in. It is baked in the oven with its sugar-and-rosewater glazing. Serve it hot or cold as you wish. If you want it to be coloured, put in eggs, both yolk and white, and instead of ginger, cinnamon.

78. To prepare a royal tourte of cream tops and other things.

Get ten cream tops and two and a half pounds of fresh ricotta, four ounces of grated creamy cheese, four ounces of softened, ground pinenuts, a pound and a half of sugar, two ounces of crumbled Neapolitan *mostaccioli*, an ounce of cinnamon, half an ounce of nutmeg and cloves combined, and six fresh eggs. Make a tourte with this filling the way it is done with whitedish in Recipe 76; serve it the same way.

79. To prepare a royal tourte of ricotta, a creamy cheese and apple juice.

Extract the juice from four apples and strain it. Then get a pound and a half of fresh ewe's-milk ricotta that has been softened in goat's milk for four hours

---

[76.1] For these *capi di latte* see Recipes 73, above, and VI,145.

[76.2] Both printed texts show *cap. 163*.

[76.3] These *tortelletti* are a relatively small stuffed pasta somewhat like large ravioli. See recipes for them in II,177–80 and in 229, below.

and been well ground in a mortar; also get three ounces of pinenut paste, ten well beaten egg whites, a pound of sugar and three-quarters of an ounce of ginger. Mix everything with the apple juice and make a tourte of that filling, with a sheet of dough on the bottom or without one, in the way outlined above. Instead of apple juice you can use quince juice. When it is baked, serve it hot or cold as you like.

80. To prepare a royal white tourte, favoured by Pope Julius III.[80]

Get two pounds of fresh provatura, made that day, and grind it in a mortar so that it becomes like butter. Add in two pounds of fine sugar, three ounces of rosewater, three cream tops made that day or else a beaker of cream, and fifteen fresh egg whites. Put all of that through a strainer. Have a tourte pan greased with cold butter and sprinkled with flour, and put the filling into it. Bake it slowly with a low heat, more from on top than from below. When it is almost done, make its sugar glazing. Before taking it out of the oven give it a glaze with egg whites like marzipan. Serve it hot or cold as you wish.

If that tourte is made in May it will be better because of the provatura and the milk. You can also make it with a pastry shell, adding in egg yolks and common spices with apple juice.

81. To prepare a plain white tourte.[81.1]

Grind or grate two pounds of fresh provatura and as much again of fresh ricotta, one pound of a creamy cheese and six ounces of grated Parmesan. When everything is ground up, add in fifteen egg whites or else four cream tops, three ounces of rosewater, four ounces of raisins, half an ounce of ginger and an ounce of cinnamon. With that filling make a tourte with a pastry shell and a twist around it, or else without a shell. Bake it in an oven, making its sugar glazing and giving it a glaze[81.2] before taking it out of the oven. When it is served, you can put beaten gold and[81.3] silver on it.

82. To prepare a white tourte with breadcrumb.

Cut a pound of breadcrumb and put it to soak in two and two-thirds litres[82.1] of goat's or cow's milk; boil it gently in that milk with a pound of fresh butter.

---

[80] ... *quale usava Papa Giulio III*: Giovanni Ciocchi del Monte was bishop cardinal of Palestrina, the pope (1550–5) whose election Scappi describes so closely in his appended account of the conclave following the death of Paul III. Scappi seems to be familiar with del Monte's habitual daily taste in food.

[81.1] A similar recipe is found in Lancelot de Casteau's *Tourte blanche a la Romaine* (*Ouverture de cuisine*, 44.) In Casteau's recipes the same qualification, 'in the manner of Rome,' echoes Scappi's Recipes 88 and 112, below. For his *Tourte blanche* Casteau uses a 'white creamy cheese,' butter, egg whites, ginger and, unlike Scappi, basil.

[81.2] In the previous recipe this *lustro* is produced by egg whites.

[81.3] As always, given the optional nature of the direction, this 'and' may be understood as 'or.'

[82.1] *un boccale.*

When it is cooked, so that it is more thick than thin, put it into a strainer and let the thin liquid[82.2] drain away on its own; then put it through the strainer. Get eight ounces of well ground provatura along with a pound of fresh ricotta, a pound and a half of sugar, half an ounce of ginger, a little salt and twelve egg whites or else eight eggs with both yolks and whites. With that filling make a tourte.

If you do not have any milk, cook the bread in a fat meat broth. If you want to colour it, put in common spices and a little grated cheese.

83. To make a white tourte with wafers and wafer cornets.

If the wafers or wafer cornets are made with sugar they will be better than any made with honey. For every three pounds of the cornets, get two pounds of fresh, creamy goat's or cow's milk and cook the cornets in it, adding in six ounces of fresh butter. And so that the wafers or cornets do not reduce to mush, boil the milk before putting them into it. When they are cooked put them into a filter and let them drain, then put them back into an earthenware or copper pot. With them put a pound and a half of fresh ewe's-milk ricotta, six ounces of grated creamy cheese, half an ounce of ginger, a pound and a half of sugar and twelve fresh egg whites. With that mixture fill a tourte pan that has a lower and upper pastry crust and a twist around it, the way the others are done. If you want it coloured put the yolks in with the whites, and instead of ginger use cinnamon.

84. To prepare a tourte of tagliatelle[84.1] or of lasagne cooked in a fat meat broth or in milk.[84.2]

Get tagliatelle or lasagne made with fine flour, eggs and either warm goat's milk or warm water; cook them in a fat meat broth or in goat's or cow's milk. When they are done, take them out and let them cool enough to be cut. Then have a tourte pan greased with butter and lined with a sheet of royal dough made with fine flour, rosewater, sugar and butter. Onto that dough set down a layer of provatura slices sprinkled with sugar, pepper and cinnamon, with a few lumps of fresh butter and grated Parmesan cheese; then put the bits of tagliatelle or lasagne on that, and on top of them make another layer of the same ingredients as are under them. You can make up several layers doing the same thing. Bake it, open-faced, in an oven or braise it. When it is almost done, sprinkle it with sugar and cinnamon. Be very generous with the butter.

In the same way you can do any sort of macaroni, made on an iron bar and cooked as described above. You can occasionally intersperse mint, marjoram and ground cloves of garlic with the pasta. Always serve it hot.

[82.2] *siero*, literally the whey.

[84.1] See another use of Scappi's *tagliatelli* (*sic*) in Recipe II,173.

[84.2] In his *Cooking in Europe 1250–1650*, 120, Albala suggests that Scappi's preparation is a forerunner of the modern dish, lasagna, though still without the tomato.

85.   To prepare a tourte with milk and a variety of fillings, popularly called 'Romagna Cups.'[85.1]

Get fifteen fresh eggs with three pounds of clotted cheese – that is, junket[85.2] – and half a creamy cheese, a pound of grated sugar, an ounce of cinnamon, an ounce of crumbled Neapolitan *mostaccioli*, half a pound of raisins and a suitable amount of salt. Then get an earthenware baking dish or a high-sided tourte pan[85.3] with boiling butter in it; put the above mixture into it, setting it over a low fire until you see that the mixture has thickened. When it has cooked, serve it hot or cold as you wish, garnished with sugar and rosewater.

The tourte can be made another way, by putting in fresh ricotta instead of junket, and instead of sugar, honey, along with slices of apple or quince and grated breadcrumb – but it will be more successful if you cook the grated bread in honey or must syrup. That tourte will turn out darker than the other one because of the honey in it, and it calls for more spices than the other. And you can make it in an earthenware baking dish;[85.4] in a deep tourte pan, do it with pastry under and over it.

86.   To make a crustless tourte, popularly called a *tartara*.[86.1]

Get six pounds of fresh goat's or cow's milk strained with twenty-five well beaten eggs; add in a little salt and saffron, two ounces of rosewater and a pound and a half of finely powdered sugar. Then get a high-sided tourte pan with six ounces of hot butter in it; put the mixture into it, stirring a little so all the sugar will not settle at the bottom. With that filling put in another six ounces of fresh butter in small bits, an ounce of well moistened[86.2] cinnamon and four ounces of

[85.1] *coppi romagnoli.* The Romagna was a province of the papal states in northeastern Italy. Its capital was Ravenna. For the name *coppi* see Recipe 49 where Scappi says that in Naples this is a generic term for *crostate*.

[85.2] Both terms that Scappi uses here, *lattaroli* and *giuncata*, refer to a clotted cheese. The latter term, designating pressed unsalted curds, derives from the word *giunco*, reed or rush, because the fresh cheeses were formed, set to drain, and stored in woven reed mats or baskets which patterned their surface. *Joncata, latte rapreso; da 'giunco' … perché si pone e si conserva su stoini di g.* (Battisti and Allesio, *Dizionario etimologico italiano*).

[85.3] The essential difference between a *tegame* (a pan or oven dish) and a *tortiera* (here qualified as *alta di sponde*: see Plate 9 of the engravings) is that the latter is usually metal.

[85.4] Again, the *tegame*.

[86.1] This is a sort of custard. The fourteenth-century *Libro per cuoco* uses almond butter for *tartare*. When Scappi uses the word again he means the 'pie' filling alone. See also Recipe 68, above.

[86.2] *stemperata.* The verb *stemperare* is generally used by Scappi in the sense of 'moisten,' although etymologically and in culinary history it indicated that the humoral temper of a foodstuff was altered or offset (*dis*-tempered) by the admixture of another ingredient.

currants that have been brought to a boil in wine or water. Cook it in an oven or braise it. When it is almost done, give it a glazing with sugar and cinnamon. When it is done, serve it hot.

With that *tartara* you can make another tourte by taking the *tartara* when it is cooked and putting it in a sieve, letting the thin liquid drain away. As it cooks, for every pound of it stir in six ounces of fresh ricotta, four ounces of creamy cheese, three ounces of ground pinenuts, an ounce of *mostaccioli*, three ounces of sugar, four eggs, six ounces of beet and spinach juice. With that mixture make a tourte with dough below and above and its twist around it. You can put elderflowers into that filling.

87. To prepare a rice tourte cooked in meat broth.[87]

Cook a pound of well cleaned rice in a fat meat broth. When it is done and is quite firm, take it out and let it drain; grind it in a mortar with a pound and a half of fresh provatura, a pound and a half of good Parmesan cheese, half a pound of creamy cheese, three-quarters of an ounce of pepper, an ounce of cinnamon, a pound and a half of sugar, four ounces of butter to keep it soft, and six fresh eggs. With that mixture make a tourte with dough below and above, and the twist around it. Bake it in an oven or braise it with its glazing on top.

You can do it with spelt the same way. And if you want it white, cook the rice in goat's milk. It is optional whether you strain it. Instead of the provatura, put in ricotta; instead of the spices, ground ginger and egg whites without the yolks, with more sugar and a little grated Parmesan cheese.

88. To prepare a tourte with coarse einkorn.[88]

Einkorn is a rather big grain, coarser than wheat; in Lombardy it is used quite a lot in cooking. Get it, clean it and soak it in warm water for four hours and wash it in several changes of warm water. Cook it in a good meat broth, as the rice and spelt are done, and make a tourte of it combined with the filling in the above recipe and following the directions given there.

89. To prepare a tourte of fresh peas, fava beans and haricot beans.[89.1]

Get four pounds of peas with a soft shell and half cook them in a good meat broth without shelling them. Take them out and grind them in a mortar. When

---

[87] The *Tourtes de ris* of Lancelot de Casteau (*Ouverture de cuisine*, 41) likewise has cinnamon, sugar, eggs and butter (though without Scappi's fat cheese as well as the butter).

[88] In his tourte recipes qualified as being 'in the Roman manner' Lancelot de Casteau has a *Tourte d'orge mondé à la Romaine* (*Ouverture de cuisine*, 44). It calls for Parmesan cheese (specifically), with egg yolks, sugar and cinnamon. His is a barley dish, the grains being cooked in 'a fat broth' and then ground in a stone mortar; Scappi's *formontone* (modern *frumentone* and *formentone*: maize) may well be Casteau's barley.

[89.1] A similar recipe is found in Lancelot de Casteau (*Ouverture de cuisine*, 40: *Tourtes de febves*), without the peas but with butter, eggs, cinnamon and sugar.

they are ground, put them through a sieve. When that is done, get a pound and a half of raw peas, ground and sieved – that is done so the tourte will be greener and tastier. Mix the cooked peas with the raw ones, along with a pound of fresh ricotta or fresh provatura ground up in the mortar, four ounces of fat Parmesan cheese, two ounces of crumbled musk-flavoured Neapolitan *mostaccioli*, three-quarters of an ounce of cinnamon, six ounces of fresh butter, half an ounce of pepper, three cream tops and six beaten egg yolks. With that mixture make a tourte – with a rather thick sheet of royal dough[89.2] on the bottom of the tourte pan because a runny tourte like that sometimes seeps through the dough. Bake it in an oven without an upper pastry crust, with only its glazing of sugar and cinnamon. Should you want to cover it with a sheet of dough, make the filling a little thicker, adding in more hard cheese. In that way you can make it with fresh fava beans, tender and shelled, and with fresh haricot beans. If the peas are not tender, soften them and cook them as directed above.

90. To prepare a tourte of artichoke and cardoon hearts.

Cook the artichoke in a meat broth or salted water, taking the best part of it which is the heart. When it is cleaned of its fuzz and any other dirt, beat it small with knives, and then fry it in butter. When that is done, add in a creamy cheese and a hard cheese, pepper, cinnamon, sugar, and beaten mint and marjoram. Into that you can add fresh field mushrooms because they are found at the same time of year. With that mixture make a tourte.

You can make it in the same way with the best parts of a cardoon, which are its stalk and the whitest ribs, when those, too, are cooked in a good broth.

91. To prepare a tourte of dry[91.1] peas, haricot beans or other legumes.

When the peas are cooked in a good meat broth, grind them in a mortar and put them through a strainer. For every pound of the strained peas add in six ounces of grated Parmesan cheese and six ounces of fresh ricotta or fresh provatura ground in a mortar, six ounces of goat's or cow's milk – and if you do not have milk get cold fat broth – a pound of sugar, six beaten egg yolks – or three with their whites – half an ounce of pepper and three ounces of fresh butter. With that mixture make a tourte with a shell of pastry dough beneath and above. Bake it in an oven and serve it hot with sugar and cinnamon over it.

You can do it the same way with haricot beans, having parboiled them first and then cooked them again in a meat broth. It is enough for split chickpeas to be cooked in a good broth, like brown chickpeas[91.2] and lentils. With split fava

---

[89.2] In the 1581 printing: *alquanto grassetto*: 'somewhat fat.' In the 1570 printing: *alquanto grossetto*: 'somewhat thick' – as in Recipe V,74.

[91.1] That is, preserved, as distinct from the fresh legumes two recipes above.

[91.2] These *ceci rossi* are perhaps the dried legume. They are also used later in Recipe 145.

beans, when they are well cooked, you can mix spring onions, beaten and sautéed, along with the other ingredients, putting in fewer eggs than are added to the other fillings.

92. To prepare a Lombard herb tourte.[92]

Chop chard greens small with knives and wash them in several changes of water, letting them drain by themselves in a colander because if you press them their juice will come out and that is their goodness. Then get a pound of grated fresh Parmesan cheese or else Ligurian cheese, an ounce of pepper and cinnamon combined, a quarter-ounce of cloves and nutmeg combined, four ounces of fresh butter and six eggs. When everything is mixed together, get a tourte pan, greased with butter and lined with a shell of dough made of wheat flour, rosewater, sugar, butter, egg yolks and warm water. Put the mixture into the pan, covering it with a rippled sheet of dough. Bake it in an oven or braise it, and serve it hot. It is optional whether you put sugar into the filling and over the top.

93. Another way to prepare an herb tourte during the winter.

Chop up chard greens as above and sauté them in butter. Then with that put grated dry cheese and grated creamy cheese, the same amount of each, along with very clean currants, a little finely chopped mint and marjoram, beaten fresh eggs, pepper, cinnamon, sugar, and a little goat's or cow's milk; the amount of each ingredient will depend on the amount of the greens. With that mixture make a tourte as above, with melted butter over it, poking the top with the tip of a knife to keep the pastry from deforming the tourte as it swells. If you have no milk use a fat meat broth.

94. To prepare a green tourte, popularly called *herbolata*.[94.1]

Get tender chard greens, the same amount of spinach and borrage and bugloss, and chop them up finely. Wash them in several changes of water and sauté them in butter.[94.2] Then get a creamy cheese, a firm grated cheese, and ricotta and fresh provatura ground in a mortar, pepper, cinnamon, beaten eggs and a little goat's or cow's milk. With all that make up a filling and make a tourte of it. Bake it the way

---

[92] Interestingly, Lancelot de Casteau offers a similar recipe for a green tourte which he qualifies as *cremoneze*, 'of Cremona' (*Ouverture de cuisine*, 36). It combines finely chopped spinach and mint, grated Parmesan (this specification from a resident of the Lowlands) cheese, sugar, cinnamon, nutmeg, butter and eggs.

[94.1] The *herbolata* goes far back into late-medieval cookery. See, for instance the *herbulata de maio*, Recipe 127 in the *Neapolitan Recipe Collection*.

[94.2] In 1614 Castelvetro (trans. Riley, 50–1) writes of spinach *tortelli* common at home in Modena: 'Spinach, a very good and wholesome garden plant, which we eat on its own or accompanied by other herbs, such as spinach beets, parsley and borage ... We often put this spinach mixture in tarts, and in *tortelli* which are fried in oil and butter and served with honey or, better still, sugar.'

the ones above are done. You can do it otherwise without a pastry shell, the way white tourtes are done,[94.3] having put more butter into the tourte pan and more milk into the filling. When it is baked, serve it hot. For the one that has no pastry shell, make a sugar glazing for it. A tourte like that is served in May more than at any other time.

95. To prepare another *herbolata* with herb juice.

Grind up fresh provatura, ricotta, a creamy cheese and a hard cheese – the same amount of each. For every two pounds of those ground cheeses, get a pound of sugar and a pound of juice drawn from chard greens and spinach, along with two pounds of goat's or cow's milk, ten beaten eggs, half an ounce of cinnamon, half an ounce of pepper, and a quarter-ounce of ground nutmeg and cloves together. With that mixture make up a tourte in a tourte pan without a pastry shell – that is, when the mixture is put in the pan, make sure the butter is hot so that the filling will not suddenly shrink and stick to the bottom of the pan. Give it heat beneath and above. When it is almost done, make its top glazing with sugar and cinnamon. When it is done, serve it hot.

96. To make a Bolognese herb tourte without eggs, baked on a copper sheet or braised in earthenware.[96]

When the chard greens have been chopped up small and washed, let them drain by themselves. Then, without crushing them, mix them with grated Parmesan cheese and *struccoli* – that is, cheese freshly made that day – along with pepper and cinnamon. Then get a copper baking sheet greased with a little butter and with a sheet of pastry dough on it; on that sheet gently put the filling to a height of a good three fingers. On the filling put little chunks of butter and cover it with another sheet of pastry, rippled or smooth, crimping it all around. Sprinkle it with plain water and brush it with butter: that is done so the pastry will rise. Bake it in an oven or braise it in earthenware vessel. When it is done, a tourte like that will have flattened so much that it is scarcely half a finger high. Serve it hot with sugar over it. Rather than on a sheet of copper you can also do it on an earthenware baking sheet or in tourte pans.

[94.3] See the *torta bianca comune* of Recipe 81, as well as other *torte bianche* before and after that one.

[96] Scappi's typesetter put *sul suolo di rame, o sul* [sic] *testo di terra*; later in the recipe he allows a *suolo di terra*, an earthenware sheet. That terracotta platter would act like a pizza stone today, radiating a relatively even heat. The use of a *testo* here would again indicate that a 'cooking bell' was any container which could braise its contents by both sitting on hot coals and holding them on a lid which was relatively flat.

97. To prepare a Genovese *gattafura*.

Get *struccoli*[97] or *agretti* – which are fresh, day-old, unsalted cheeses; when they have a bit of a nip to them they are considerably better. Grind them up in a mortar until they become like butter and mix them with ground chard greens, a little beaten mint and ground pepper. Then get a sheet of pastry dough and spread it out on a copper baking sheet that is greased with butter; on that dough put the filling so that it is no more than half a finger high. On that filling sprinkle sweet olive oil and cover it with another, very thin sheet of dough. Bake it as above. Serve it hot, because it is worthless cold, even though those tourtes are often reheated on a grill. They can also be done the same way in tourte pans.

98. To prepare Genovese onion *gattafura*.

Grind *struccoli* or fresh provatura or *provaggiole*[98.1] that are sour;[98.2] they should be so well ground up that they become like butter; add a little sweet olive oil to them. Get parboiled onions that have been well beaten with a knife, and mix the ground cheese and pepper with them. Get a baking sheet that is sprinkled with grated bread and has a sheet of dough on it made of fine flour, water and oil. On that pastry put the filling to a height of half a finger and, with a spoon, go on to sprinkle a little olive oil over it. Distribute the mixture on top in big pinches. Cover it over with another sheet of dough; splash that with plain water and sprinkle some oil on it with the spoon. Bake it by braising[98.3] or in an oven. Serve it hot with sugar over top. Instead of oil you can use butter.

99. To prepare an ordinary herb tourte.

Get tender chard greens, spinach tips, mint and marjoram, cut them up small, wash them and let them drain by themselves. Then get two pounds of fresh ricotta, a pound and a half of grated Parmesan cheese, six ounces of a fat cheese, six ounces of fresh butter, half an ounce of pepper, three-quarters of an ounce of cinnamon, a quarter-ounce of cloves, six fresh eggs, beaten, and six ounces of sugar; with all those things make up a filling. Have a tourte pan ready, lined with a sheet of royal dough and with its flaky-pastry twist around it. Put the filling into it and cover it with a rippled sheet of pastry. Bake it in an oven or braise it. Serve it hot. It is optional whether you make it deep or shallow.

---

[97] Defined in the previous recipe as cheeses made freshly that same day.

[98.1] The identity of this cheese is uncertain. Its name may derive from the Latin *profectus*, 'of use,' and Italian *proveccio*, 'use, benefit.'

[98.2] *acetose*: acidic, although Scappi's word means literally vinegary.

[98.3] *facciasi cuocere sotto il testo*: The *testo* is a pot designed to allow a controlled heat from both below and above, rather like a miniature oven. Tourte pan lids (illustrated in Plate 8, *tortera con il coperio*, and Plate 9, *coperchi per tortere*) are flat and may have an area to hold hot coals.

100. To prepare a tourte of fresh pea- or bean-leaves.

Get the leaves of those vegetables in the autumn or the winter because in those seasons the plants are not bearing anything. Chop them up small and put in everything that was used in the previous tourtes except for the herbs, stirring it all together with the leaves. Make a tourte, baking it the way set out above. If you want the tourte to be made with the juice but not the leaves, grind the leaves.

101. To prepare a tourte popularly called *nosetto*.[101]

Get a hundred or so walnuts, shell them and grind them in a morter with six ounces of breadcrumb soaked in a fat broth. To that add a pound of a fat cheese, half a pound of Parmesan cheese, four ounces of fresh provatura, a handful of mint, marjoram and a few chard greens chopped up small. Put half an ounce of pepper with that, three-quarters of an ounce of cinnamon, half an ounce of cloves and nutmeg together, eight ounces of very clean raisins, and eight egg yolks or else four eggs with their whites. When all that has been thoroughly mixed together, have a tourte pan ready with a rather thick lower shell of dough in it and its twist around it. Put the filling into it and cover it with another sheet of rippled dough or one made in strips like shutter louvres. Bake it in an oven or braise it. Serve it hot. If you want to put sugar into the filling, that is optional.

102. To prepare a lettuce or endive tourte.

Get the white part of lettuce and parboil it in water. Take it out, let it drain and beat it small on a table with knives; squeeze its juice out. Sauté it in butter, then add grated cheese to it, ground fresh provatura, sugar, eggs and spices. With that mixture make a tourte with a lower and upper crust shell as the previous ones. Bake it in an oven or braise it. Serve it hot with sugar over top.

You can do it with white endive that way. Instead of water you boil it in a meat broth.

103. To prepare a tourte of asparagus, cultivated or wild, and of hops.

Cultivated asparagus can be harvested between April and the end of October; wild asparagus, from the fall throughout April; hops, twice a year, in the fall and the spring. Of each of them take the tenderest part and parboil it in water, then take it out and squeeze the water out of it. Beat it small together with mint, marjoram and a little parsley, and sauté that in butter, adding in raisins. Then follow all the directions for making the tourte in the preceding recipe, and using the same ingredients.

---

[101] In Recipe II,199 this *nosetto* is compounded a little differently and is used as a stuffing. Here, as a pie filling, it gives its name to the pie itself.

104. To prepare a cauliflower[104] tourte.

Get the whitest part and parboil it in a fat broth. Beat it a little with knives, together with a little mint, marjoram and a grated old cheese and ground provatura, pepper, cinnamon, cloves and sugar; if you were to put a little saveloy stuffing in with it, that would not be bad, adding in eggs. With that mixture make a double-shelled tourte, the upper one being like jalousie louvres. Bake it an oven rather than braising it.

You can do it with the stalk of a Savoy cabbage the same way, putting more of the saveloy mixture with it than with the other one, and more spices and less sugar.

105. To prepare a tourte of kohlrabi.

Get a kohlrabi bulb that is not woody, peel it and cut it into slices; cook it in a fat broth. When it is done, take it out of the broth, let it drain and beat it with knives. For every pound of the beaten bulb, get half a pound of grated Parmesan cheese, three ounces of creamy cheese and three ounces of grated provatura, half an ounce of pepper, half an ounce of cinnamon, a quarter-ounce of cloves and nutmeg combined, six eggs and three ounces of butter. With all those things make up a filling and with that make a tourte with a lower shell and an upper one that is open.[105] Bake it in an oven rather than braising it. Serve it hot.

You can do it with head cabbage the same way. Note that any tourte made with cabbage needs to be baked in an oven rather than braised, and for that reason the last dough put on it always has to be open. Tourtes like that call for more spices than other sorts, and less sugar. And to decrease the smell of the cabbage you could always put in a clove of garlic.

106. To prepare a tourte of domestic pumpkin.

Scrape the domestic pumpkin, which should be tender and sweet. If it is big, take out its seeds; if small, there is no need to. Cook it in good fat broth. When it is done, take it out and squeeze the broth out of it. Then beat it with knives on a table that is not of walnut.[106] For every pound of beaten pumpkin put in six ounces of a grated creamy cheese, four ounces of fresh ricotta, three ounces of a

---

[104] Castelvetro seems never to have enjoyed this tourte, though he enthuses over the vegetable itself: 'For beauty and goodness [cauliflowers] take pride of place in the cabbage family. They … make an excellent dish, cooked in broth and served on slices of bread, with some of the broth poured over, and seasoned with grated mature cheese and pepper.' (Trans. Riley, 105.)

[105] *con un'altro di sopra aperto*: this upper shell presumably has an opening or openings, such as with the slatted arrangement previously referred to or some shape of opening cut through it. See a confirmation of this conjecture a little further on.

[106] While walnut is a suitably hard wood for kitchen work, there was some anxiety that it would contaminate the flavour of delicate foodstuffs. See also Recipes 107, below, and VI,87: a kitchen table may be of any wood, *eccettuando la noce che fa negro & amaro*.

soft creamy cheese, eight eggs, six ounces of sugar and an ounce of pepper and cinnamon together. Mix everything together and with that filling make a tourte with a rather thick lower shell and an upper one made like shutter louvres. Bake it in an oven or braise it. When it is almost done, give it a glazing with sugar and rosewater. When it is done, serve it hot.

You could do up any sort of pumpkin the same way. And you can put a little milk into the filling mixture.

107. To prepare a pumpkin-and-onion tourte.

Get the same amount of each and parboil them in water; take them out and squeeze the water out of them so that they end up quite dry. Beat them on a table that is not of walnut and sauté them in butter or lard. When they have cooled, for every two pounds of the fried pumpkin and onion, get a pound of fresh provatura, a pound of a creamy cheese ground up with the provatura, half a pound of grated Parmesan cheese, ten fresh eggs, a beaker of milk, a pound of sugar, three-quarters of an ounce of pepper, an ounce of cinnamon and a little saffron. With that mixture make up a tourte with a lower and upper shell and the flaky-pastry twist around it. Bake it in an oven or braise it. A tourte like that always needs to be served hot. In the filling you can put a handful of beaten herbs – that will depend on the taste of the person it is intended for.

108. To prepare a pumpkin tourte without a shell.

When the pumpkin is scraped, cook it in a good meat broth or else in salted water and butter. Then put it into a strainer and squeeze the broth out of it. Grind it in a mortar along with, for every two pounds of it, a pound of fresh ricotta and a pound of a creamy cheese that is not too salted. When everything is ground up, put it through a colander, adding in ten well beaten eggs, a pound of ground sugar, an ounce of ground cinnamon, a pound of milk, four ounces of fresh butter and half an ounce of ginger. Have a tourte pan ready with six ounces of very hot butter in it and put the filling into it. Bake it in an oven or braise it, giving it a glazing with sugar and cinnamon. Serve it hot.

You can do a midrib of lettuce in April the same way, after it has steeped thoroughly and been parboiled.

109. To prepare a eggplant tourte.

Get eggplants, skin them and parboil them in water, though they would be better done in a meat broth. When they are done, squeeze the broth out of them and beat them with knives. Sauté them in rendered fat or butter, and make a tourte of them with the same ingredients and in the same way as in the previous recipe.

110. To prepare a turnip tourte.[110.1]

Cook the turnip well under the coals, peel it and take the best part of it and beat it small with knives. Sauté it in butter or rendered fat and let it cool. To it add a pound of grated Parmesan cheese, a pound of a creamy cheese, six ounces of well ground fresh provatura or ricotta, a pound of sugar, three-quarters of an ounce of pepper, an ounce of ground cinnamon and eight eggs. With that mixture make a tourte with a lower and upper shell, baking it in an oven or braising it. When it is almost done, give it a glazing.[110.2] Serve it hot. If you do not have time to cook the turnip under the coals you can do it in a good broth, and follow the above directions.

111. To prepare a tourte of carrots or other roots, along with other ingredients.

Wash and scrape the carrots and parboil them in water. Take them out of the water and cook them in a good meat broth. When they are done, take them out and beat them small with knives, adding in mint and marjoram and, for every two pounds of beaten carrots, a pound of grated Ligurian Parmesan cheese,[111.1] a pound and a half of a creamy cheese, six ounces of provatura, an ounce of ground pepper, two ounces of ground Neapolitan *mostaccioli*, an ounce of cinnamon, two ounces of candied orange peel[111.2] cut up small, a pound of sugar, eight eggs and three ounces of butter. With that filling make up a tourte with a lower and upper shell and the flaky-pastry twist around it. Bake it in an oven or braise it, make the glazing for it of sugar, cinnamon and rosewater.

You can make a tourte of every sort of parsnip and parsley root the same way, when you have dug out their core.

112. To prepare a melon tourte.[112.1]

Get a melon with its rind and seeds removed, slightly unripe rather than ripe, and cut it up into small pieces. Sauté them gently in butter, stirring them

---

[110.1] Lancelot de Casteau's *Tourtes de naveaux* (*Ouverture de cuisine*, 40) likewise uses a soft, fat cheese (along with butter – his being a northern recipe), cinnamon and eggs.

[110.2] Scappi means the crisp upper surface of sugar and cinnamon that he often prescribes for a tourte.

[111.1] *cascio Parmigiano di Riviera*. See also the *cascio di Riviera* in Recipe 92, above.

[111.2] This *scorza di melangole condite* (seen also in Recipe 218, below) is a commonly available product. In his 1557 book *Le vray et parfaict embellissement de la face* the physician Michael Nostradamus, who practised many years in Italy, provides detailed recipes both for *Orengeat en succre ou en miel* (which uses orange peel) and for confecting orange peel (Part II, Chapters 3 and 4).

[112.1] The recipe for *Tourte de melon* of Lancelot de Casteau (*Ouverture de cuisine*, 43) is qualified as *a la Romaine*, 'in the manner of Rome.' Its first direction is to 'get a melon that is not too ripe'; its ingredients include 'good, fat' cheese, cinnamon, sugar and nutmeg. Although no mention is made here of eggs, see Recipe 88, above, where Casteau's 'Roman' recipe does include egg yolks.

continuously with a spoon. Take them out, let them cool and put them through a colander. For every two pounds of sautéed melon, add in six ounces of Parmesan cheese, six ounces of fresh, well ground ricotta or provatura, two ounces of a creamy cheese, two ounces of crumbled Neapolitan musk-flavoured *mostaccioli*, an ounce of cinnamon, half an ounce of pepper, six ounces of sugar and ten fresh egg yolks or else six eggs with their whites. Have a tourte pan greased with butter and with a rather thick sheet of pastry dough – made of fine flour, rosewater, egg yolks, butter and salt – and with the flaky-pastry twist around it. Put the filling into it and cover it with another sheet of dough made like shutter louvres. Bake it in an oven or braise it, with melted butter over its top. When it is almost done, make its glazing of sugar and cinnamon. When it is done, serve it hot[112.2] as you wish.

You can do a tourte of unripe peach, apricot and plum the same way.

113. To prepare a quince tourte.

Cook a quince in the coals or on a spit or else in a good broth. Then take the best part of it and grind that in a mortar. When it is ground up, sauté it in butter the way the melon above is done. Make a tourte of it following the same directions and with the same ingredients as for the melon tourte, though with fewer eggs.

114. To prepare a tourte of various sorts of big pears.

Peel bergamot pears, ricardo pears, Florentine pears, *caravella* pears or some other sort of pear that is quite excellent. Cut them up into small pieces. Cook them in butter or else in wine and sugar. When they are done, grind them in a mortar, putting with them the whole mixture of those ingredients that are put with the melon; however, less egg is put put in. The season for those pears is from September to the end of March. And instead of cooking them in wine, you can do them in a broth.

115. To prepare a tourte of muscatel pears.

Between May and the end of July get muscatel pears with their flower and stem cut off. They can be pared – though given that the skin is their goodness there is no need to. Stew them in wine, sugar and butter. When that is done, grind them in a mortar and make a tourte of them with the same ingredients and directions as above.

116. To prepare an apple tourte.

Get red apples[116] and roast them in the coals, then remove the burnt skin with wine and water. Cut the best part into thin slices, grinding them in a mortar

---

[112.2] The usual alternative option, cold, seems to have been forgotten.

[116] These *mele appie* are the commonly used apple in Scappi's kitchen. See other varieties in Recipe 61, above.

with two ounces of *mostaccioli* for every two pounds of apple slices, along with four ounces of grated cheese and six ounces of fresh provatura. When everything is ground up, add in six raw egg yolks and two eggs with their whites, half an ounce of ground cinnamon, half an ounce of pepper, cloves and nutmeg together, and eight ounces of sugar. With that mixture make a tourte in a tourte pan with a rather thick pastry shell and the twist around it. If you do not want to roast them, slice them and sauté them in butter or else stew them in sugar, wine and rosewater, following the procedure for baking the tourte in an oven or braising it, like the previous ones. A tourte like that can always be served cold or hot, as you like.

117. To prepare a medlar tourte.

Get ripe medlars, whose season begins in October and goes to the end of February. Clean away their stem and flower and stew them in wine, sugar and butter. Put them through a strainer or a colander because of the seeds. Then make the tourte with the same ingredients and procedure as for the melon in Recipe 112. Serve it hot or cold as you like. With fewer eggs, though.

118. To make a tourte of cherries,[118] visciola cherries and morello cherries.

Roman cherries are quite a bit better than the other varieties; they come into their season at the end of April, visciola cherries in the middle of May and morello cherries in June. In any case, get whichever variety when they are not too ripe and stew them in fresh butter. When they are done, strain them, adding in fresh ricotta, a creamy cheese and a little hard cheese, and crumbled Neapolitan *mostaccioli*, as well as pepper, cinnamon and beaten eggs – the amount of each depending on your judgement. With this mixture make a tourte with a lower and upper crust. Bake it in an oven or braise it, making a glazing for it with sugar and rosewater. Serve it hot.

In the same way you can do strawberries, which begin in May and go to the end of June, though in Rome they begin in April.

119. To prepare a muscat-grape tourte.

Seed the grapes, and for every two pounds of them put four ounces of breadcrumb with them and stew them in an earthenware or tinned copper pot with six ounces of butter. When they are done, strain them with eight ounces of fresh ricotta and ten egg yolks. When they are strained, add in four ounces of grated cheese, an ounce and a half of ground Neapolitan *mostaccioli*, six ounces of sugar, half an ounce of cinnamon and two ounces of orange juice or of candied orange peel cut up into small bits. With that filling make up a tourte with a rather thick bottom shell. Bake it in an oven or braise it, making its glazing with sugar and cinnamon. Serve it hot or cold as you like.

You can do it with gooseberries or verjuice grapes the same way.

---

[118] These *cerase* are unqualified and are probably the 'Roman' variety he describes at the beginning of his recipe.

120. To prepare a tourte of fresh or dried chestnuts.

You can get fresh chestnuts in August; they are quite a bit better when they are slightly unripe – that is, those that are just whitening. Boil them in a meat broth or in salted water. Peel off their outer and inner skins, then grind them in a mortar and put them through a filter or a colander. For every two pounds of the strained chestnuts add in a pound of fresh butter, half a pound of goat's or cow's milk, a pound of a creamy cheese, half a pound of a grated dry cheese, a pound of sugar, half a pound of fresh, well ground ricotta or provatura, an ounce of cinnamon, half an ounce of pepper and six uncooked egg yolks. When everything is blended together, make a tourte with a lower and upper shell and a twist around it. Bake it in an oven or braise it. When it is almost done, make a glazing on it with sugar, cinnamon and rosewater. When it is done, serve it hot. You can do it the same way with dried chestnuts, putting in more milk and fewer eggs.

Should it happen that you would like to make a tourte of blackberries[120.1] or acorns, that can be done, being sure the acorns are very clean and have soaked, and then are parboiled in a good broth. Acorns from a Turkey oak[120.2] are better than any other sort for that purpose.

121. To prepare a tourte with various ingredients, called *pizza* by Neapolitans.

Get six ounces of shelled Milanese almonds, four ounces of shelled, soaked pinenuts, three ounces of fresh, pitted dates, three ounces of dried figs and three ounces of seeded muscatel raisins; grind all that up in a mortar. Into it add eight fresh raw egg yolks, six ounces of sugar, an ounce of ground cinnamon, an ounce and a half of crumbled musk-flavoured Neapolitan *mostaccioli* and four ounces of rosewater. When everything is mixed together, get a tourte pan that is greased and lined with a sheet of royal pastry dough;[121.1] into it put the filling, mixed with four ounces of fresh butter, letting it come up to no more than a finger in depth. Without it being covered, bake it in an oven. Serve it hot or cold, whichever you like. Into that *pizza* you can put anything that is seasoned.[121.2]

How to make various twists, of flaky pastry or not, filled or not.

122. To prepare a filled twist.[122.1]

Make a dough of two pounds of fine flour with six fresh egg yolks, two

---

[120.1] These *triboli* (*Rubus fruticosus*) are also known as brambles.

[120.2] Turkey oak: *cerro*, scientifically a *Quercus cerris*.

[121.1] Recipe 84 indicates that 'royal dough' is a mixture of fine flour, rosewater, sugar and butter.

[121.2] *si puo mettere d'ogni sorte condite*. Scappi's verb *condire* could also include anything that is candied, as he uses it in the rubric to Recipe VI,210 for candied citrus peel.

[122.1] In his *Banchetti* of 1549 Messisbugo directs that a *tortiglione* be rolled up like a *cialdone* or rolled wafer, with two pounds of butter, inside and out, for two ropes. This present *tortiglione ripieno* is the treat today called *brioches con l'uvetta*. In Scappi's version the fruit in the optional

ounces of rosewater, an ounce of leaven[122.2] moistened with warm water, four ounces of either fresh butter or rendered fat that does not smell bad, and enough salt. That dough should be kneaded well for half an hour. Make a thin sheet of it, greasing it with either melted butter that is not too hot or with rendered fat. With the pastry wheel[122.3] cut the edges one after the other, which are always quite a bit thicker than the rest. Sprinkle the dough with four ounces of sugar and an ounce of cinnamon. Then get a pound of currants that have been brought to a boil in wine, a pound of dates cooked in that wine and cut up small, and a pound of seeded muscatel raisins that have been brought to a boil in wine; combine all those ingredients and mix them with sugar, cinnamon, cloves and nutmeg. Spread that mixture out over the sheet of dough along with a few little gobs of butter. Beginning at the long edge of the dough, roll it up like a wafer cornet, being careful not to break the dough. A twist like that needs only three rolls so it can cook well; it should not be too tight. Grease its surface with melted butter that is not too hot. Begin at one end to roll it up, not too tightly, so it becomes like a snail shell or a maze.[122.4] Have a tourte pan on hand lined with a rather thick sheet of the same dough greased with melted butter and gently put the twist on it without pushing it down. Bake it in an oven or braise it with a moderate heat, not forgetting to grease it occasionally with melted butter. When it is almost done, sprinkle sugar and rosewater over it. Serve it hot. The tourte pan in which the twists are baked has to be ample and with low sides.[122.5]

123. Another way to prepare a filled twist.

Roll out a sheet of dough made as above and grease it with melted butter that is not too hot; sprinkle it with sugar and cinnamon. On that dough put finely cut-up beef marrow and the same amount of fine saveloy mixture spread around. Roll the dough up making a twist of it; bake it as above. Serve it hot. You can put grated uncooked *salciccione* into it instead of the saveloy stuffing.

124. Another way to prepare a filled twist.

When you have made a sheet of dough like the one above, grease it with melted butter and sprinkle it with sugar and cinnamon. Then get hard-boiled egg yolks beaten small and mixed with steeped pinenuts and raisins, and scatter a few little bits of butter on top of that. Make the twist and bake it as above in an oven in a tourte pan.

---

filling includes dates as well as currants and muscatel raisins. These 'twists' are not merely for the decorative use we have so frequently seen in this Book V, but are edible treats in themselves. When baked on a bed of pastry in tourte pans, the preparation is a 'twist tourte.'

[122.2] This is a sourdough leavening, a yeast in which fermentation is active.

[122.3] See two sorts of *sperone* illustrated in the engravings of Plates 14 and 15.

[122.4] *a foggia … di laberinto.*

[122.5] Shallow *tortere* are illustrated at the top of Plate 9.

125. To prepare a flaky-pastry twist with the pastry leaves exposed.[125.1]

Roll out a sheet of dough that is somewhat longer than the previous one, grease it with rendered fat or melted, clarified butter and make a roll of it the size of a rolling pin;[125.2] let it cool. Get a tourte pan lined with a sheet of that same dough and with the flaky-pastry twist around it. With a warm knife cut the roll apart lengthwise. With your hands greased with hot butter so the dough will not stick to them as you handle it, take one of the halves and set it out in the pan with the edges of the layers upward; do the same with the other half, so filling the pan. Then brush melted butter that is not too hot over that. Bake it in an oven or braise it with more heat from the top than the bottom.[125.3] When it is done, serve it hot with fine sugar and rosewater over it.

If you want to do flaky *mostaccioli*, make the lump of dough a little larger.[125.4] When it has cooled, cut the roll into pieces the width of a fist;[125.5] split those pieces in two lengthwise with a warm knife. Put the halves into the tourte pan with the edges of the layers upwards, greased with either melted butter or rendered fat that is not too hot. Bake it in the oven as directed above. Serve it with fine sugar over top.

126. To prepare a twist with the pastry leaves concealed.

Make up a dough of two pounds of fine flour with six egg yolks, four ounces of breadcrumb that has soaked in either goat's milk or a fat broth, an ounce and a half of leaven moistened with rosewater, three ounces of fine sugar, a suitable amount of salt and four ounces of butter. Knead the dough well for half an hour. Then make a very thin sheet of it and trim its edges with a pastry wheel. Grease it with clarified butter, sprinkle it with sugar, cinnamon and powdered dry sweet fennel, along with a few little lumps of butter on top the size of hazelnuts. Make

---

[125.1] This and the following Recipe 126 are counterparts. The first version (*di sfogliatura aperta*) slices the roll of pastry so that the edges of all the thin layers are 'open' or exposed; then the first part of Recipe 126 (*di sfogliature serrata*) makes use of a whole, uncut *tortiglione* of 'closed' or concealed leaves, while the second part combines the two possibilities.

[125.2] The *bastone di pasta* that is seen being used in Plate 2 appears of the same diameter as, or slightly smaller than, a modern one.

[125.3] See the note about a *testo* in Recipe 98, above.

[125.4] The word printed just before *piu grossetto* (as in Recipe 44 also) is *pastone*, the initially kneaded lump of dough before it is further worked for a specific purpose. However, given that this present procedure is an alternative to what we have just read in the first paragraph, we may wonder whether Scappi meant the word to be *bastone*, the rolling pin whose size (*grossezza*) helps measure the diameter of the pastry roll: the roll of flaky pastry for the present procedure should be of a slightly larger diameter.

[125.5] More accurately, *un sommesso* was the width of a fist with the thumb extended: 16–18 centimetres. However, the use of the word in Recipe 127 suggests that for Scappi it measures only a 'fist.'

the twist four layers thick.[126.1] Have a tourte pan ready with a sheet of buttered pastry in it, and carefully begin to set out[126.2] the twist in it until the pan is almost full. Then, with the dry palm of your hand flatten the twist until the pan is filled, minding you do not break any of the pastry layers because then the tourte would not swell up. On it put melted butter that is not too hot. Bake it in an oven with a moderate heat.[126.3] When it is done serve it hot with sugar and rosewater over it.

If you want the twist in two ways – that is, with the pastry leaves both exposed and concealed: when the twist is rolled lengthwise in eight layers, cut it along the middle the way the exposed one[126.4] is done. For the one you want with concealed leaves, do it in four layers.[126.5] In the middle of a tourte pan with a sheet of dough on it, begin with the part of the twist with exposed leaves, making two circles, then with the twist with concealed leaves make two other circles, repeating that until the last one, around the outside of the pan, is with exposed leaves. The open-leaved one is not sprinkled with sugar and cinnamon, because sugar and cinnamon do not let pastry puff up.

[Flans and *pizze*]

127. To prepare small flans[127.1] filled with various ingredients.

Make up a dough out of two pounds of fine flour, three ounces of fresh butter, four ounces of rosewater, six egg yolks and the remainder warm goat's or cow's milk, and enough salt. With that make a thin sheet of pastry. Have a pound of parboiled calf's sweetbreads on hand, beaten small with knives and mixed with three ounces of beef marrow, two ounces of raisins that have been brought to a boil in wine, four hard-boiled egg yolks cut up into small bits, two uncooked egg yolks, four ounces of sugar, an ounce of cinnamon and two ounces of grated creamy cheese. Then cut the sheet of dough into several pieces more than a fist[127.2] in width and a handswidth and a half in length. On each piece put the

---

[126.1] In Recipe 122 Scappi indicates that a 'basic' *tortiglione* normally needs to be rolled up to only three thicknesses.

[126.2] Scappi uses only the verb *accommodare* here. More explicitly later he will direct that the pastry roll be laid down in a spiral.

[126.3] The word *fuoco* is set as *fooco* in the reprinting.

[126.4] That is, as in Recipe 125.

[126.5] This alternative rolled *tortiglione* will therefore be of a diameter similar to that of the split ('open' or 'exposed') one which is rolled to eight layers.

[127.1] See the *fiadoni* or flat cakes in Recipe 47. The *fiadoncelli* in the present recipe are smaller, more delicate varieties of them.

[127.2] See the note on *sommesso* in Recipe 125. It is difficult to explain the use here of both *sommesso* and *palmo* for roughly the same measurement.

filling to one side and roll it up in three turns, greasing it[127.3] between each turn; coat the grease with beaten egg whites so the layers of the roll will stick together. With the pastry wheel slash it three times on the side without going through. Bake it in an oven the way the flaky pastries are done, or else fry it in rendered fat. When they are done, serve them hot with sugar over them.

If you want to put various filling into the little flans, get all the fillings for *crostate*, tourtes and twists described previously, with the exception of those of herbs and *tartare*.[127.4]

128. To prepare flaky *pizza*, popularly called a dry napoleon.[128.1]

Get a sheet of dough that is rolled out thin and made as the previous one. Have a tourte pan ready, greased with melted butter, and on that pan put a rather thick sheet of that dough, and on that put ten more thin sheets, greased between each with butter and sprinkled with sugar and elderflower, dry or fresh. Bake it in an oven or braise it. When it is done, serve it hot with sugar and rosewater over it.

It can be done differently: when the dough is rolled out as above, grease it with melted butter and let it cool a while. Spread some more of that butter on it and sprinkle it with sugar. Make a twist with six rolls; when it is done grease it its full length and wind it around like a labyrinth[128.2] and put it into the pan which has another sheet of dough in it greased with butter. With a hand smeared with warm butter – so the dough will not stick to it – flatten it so it is no more than a finger deep, and with the heel of your hand press it down so that the trace of your hand is left.[128.3] Brush melted butter over it. Bake it in an oven with a low heat. Serve it hot with sugar and rosewater on it; if you do not want to put sugar and rosewater on it, put the sugar into the dough. To make it pretty you can make that *pizza* with a flaky-pastry twist around it.

[127.3] In other recipes butter has been used.

[127.4] The exceptions are in Recipes 99 and 86 respectively.

[128.1] *Sfogliata asciutta*. A 'plain' *sfogliata* is described in Recipe 217, below. Scappi will devote a group of five recipes to this sort of preparation; see also Recipe 216, below. The earliest appearance of a preparation called a *pizza* is in the so-called *Manoscritto Lucano*, ed. Michael Süthold, written in southern Italy at the beginning of Scappi's century: a colophon makes its origin definite: in Nerula, 3 August 1524. The manuscript contains four sorts of *pizza*: *Picza figliata* (Recipe 57), *Picza bianca* (Recipe 77), *Una altra picza* (Recipe 78), and *Picza riale* (Recipe 86; see Scappi's Recipe 73, above). None of those recipes seems to have made it into Scappi's collection unchanged; most have some sort of upper crust, whether plain or ornamental, like a tourte. See Riley's comments about the genre in *The Oxford Companion to Italian Food*, 410.

[128.2] Earlier, in Recipe 122, Scappi described this winding or twisting as giving the look of a snail's shell.

[128.3] Neither edition has a negative here. Despite the thinness of his dough, Scappi seems to want an irregular surface on it.

129. To prepare a flaky *pizza* with exposed leaves.

When the sheet of dough is rolled out as directed above, without sugar, make a roll the size of a large wooden pestle and let it cool. Then have a tourte pan ready with a buttered sheet of dough on its bottom and a twist around it. With a hot knife cut the rolled-up dough crosswise into several pieces, each two to three finger-widths wide.[129.1] Put one of those pieces into the tourte pan – the pan being of a proper size for the piece of dough, that is, neither too big nor too small. When it is in the pan, brush it with melted butter that is not too hot, and with the palm of your hand, greased with hot butter, set about spreading that piece out in the pan so that it ends up one finger thick. Bake it in an oven or braise it with more heat from above than below. Serve it hot.

It can be done differently: when the *pizza* has been cut carefully, spread it out a little with your hand, then brush it all around with beaten egg so it will not stick to the sides[129.2] as it cooks. Fry that *pizza* in rendered fat or melted butter that is not too hot. When it is done, serve it hot with fine sugar over it.

With that roll of flaky pastry you can make various preparations, fried or baked, depending on the judgement of the person doing them.

130. Another way to do *pizza*.

Get two pounds of fine flour and make up a dough with six ounces of Parmesan cheese that has been ground in a mortar, moistened with a fat broth and rosewater and strained; add in three ounces of sugar, six egg yolks, three ounces of breadcrumb soaked in a fat broth, half an ounce of cinnamon and half an ounce of cloves and nutmeg together. Knead the dough for an hour and make a thin sheet of it. Brush melted butter on it and make a twist of it with the sheet rolled in four layers lengthwise; brush it with melted butter that is not too hot. With that twist make several small cakes,[130] fry them in butter or rendered fat and bake them in an oven in a tourte pan just as twists are done. Serve them hot with sugar over them.

In another way you can make up dough from flour with a very fat broth that is boiling, adding in beaten egg yolks, sugar, rosewater, butter and the same spices. While it is still hot, knead the dough so it does not get too stiff. Divide it up into little four-ounce pieces and make a small cake of each one. Bake them with butter in an oven in a tourte pan. Serve them hot with sugar over them. Instead of a number of small *pizze* you could make one large *pizza*. Into that dough you can mix pinenuts that have steeped, are shelled and crushed, and leaven.

[129.1] *d'altezza di due i tre dita.*

[129.2] The *orlo* is apparently the rim or edge of the frying pan.

[130] These are *fuccacine* (later spelled *fucaccine*), a diminutive of the modern *focaccia* (origin of the French *fougasse* and *fouace*). See the note on the origin of 'flan' in Recipe 47.

131. Another way to prepare flaky *pizza*.

Make a dough of three pounds of fine flour with two ounces of leaven, four ounces of breadcrumb that has soaked in warm water, and a reasonable amount of salt. When the dough is made let it sit covered in a warm place until it has risen, as is done with bread. Then knead it again on a table for half an hour, gradually adding in two pounds of fresh butter. When it is kneaded enough that all of the butter has been worked into it and the dough has become soft, split it up into two or three parts and with each make a *pizza* in a tourte pan which has fresh butter in it. Bake it in an oven with melted butter over it. Make a few holes on top with the tip of a knife so it will not swell up. When it is almost done, sprinkle sugar and rosewater on it. A pastry dough like that should bake slowly. Serve it hot.

132. Another way to prepare round flaky *pizze* cooked in an oven on paper.

Get two pounds of fine flour and make dough of it with warm water, salt, an ounce and a half of leaven moistened with warm water and three ounces of fresh butter. When the dough is made in such a way that it is neither too thin nor too thick, let it sit in a white cloth in a warm place until it rises like bread. Knead it again on a table, using as little flour as possible as you knead it. Have two pounds of fresh butter ready in lumps the size of hazelnuts, which butter has steeped in cold water and then sat in rosewater. Take the dough and, with either the palm of your hand or a rolling pin, spread it out and make it round like a trencher[132.1] and as thick as a knife. Then get the little lumps of butter and put them on it one by one, leaving a good finger's width of the outer edge free of them. Brush that bare edge with beaten egg. Turn the sheet of dough back onto the butter on all four sides, so that the dough looks like a priest's biretta – that is, so the part brushed with egg comes together.[132.2] With your hand work it in such a way that it becomes round and gently flatten it out, watching you do not break the layers of dough, and giving it again the size and round shape it originally had. Repeat that several times until the butter is used up and it is incorporated into a ball like a round loaf. Have a sheet of thick paper ready, its middle greased with butter, and put the dough on it with the layered part downwards, having the smooth part upwards and colouring that with beaten eggs. Put it into an oven that is not too hot, with the heat mostly from below. As it begins to swell up, cover it with a sheet of rag paper so it will not get too browned and let it finish baking. When it is done, it should always be served hot.

If you want to do it differently, before the dough has been put on it divide it up into several small pieces, and out of those small pieces make round sheets the size of an ordinary trencher board and not larger than a tourte shell. Again brush around them with beaten egg and in their middle put the lumps of butter. On the

---

[132.1] A *tagliere* is a wooden cutting board, used either in a kitchen or on a dining table.

[132.2] The procedure will form four arched ridges, their middles joining at the centre of the *pizza*.

butter put another sheet of dough; repeat that process making eight or ten layers of dough, each on top of the other. Then, with the palm of your hand, flatten it all gently, being careful not to break them. This latter *pizza* can be baked in a tourte pan with a sheet of dough under it and a flaky-pastry twist around it to make it prettier. Always serve it hot with fine sugar over it. Again, you can colour it with egg yolks just as it is almost baked, sprinkling it with sugar.

133. To prepare a dough with which you can make various preparations[133] that are fried in rendered fat.

Make a dough of two pounds of fine flour with three ounces of sugar, three ounces of butter, six egg yolks, four ounces of rosewater and the rest warm water and salt or else warm goat's milk. When it has been kneaded for half an hour, make a sheet of it and use a small brush to spread white wine or rosewater or milk over that. Fold it back on itself, then cut it into strips with the pastry wheel and with those make lumps, braids and other pieces using white-metal moulds, depending on the cook's preferences. Fry them in rendered fat. When they are done, serve them with fine sugar over them. They can also be baked in an oven, first brushing them with egg white and then sprinkling them with sugar.

134. To prepare a dough with which you can make balls and various other preparations.

Make up a dough with two pounds of fine flour and as many fresh eggs as that amount of flour can hold, and three ounces of rosewater and enough salt. With that dough make a thin sheet, letting it rest for a quarter of an hour. Then cut it into round pieces a hand and a half across, and with the pastry wheel, slice those into strips a finger in width, sticking the strips all together on both sides.[134.1] With a round wooden skewer pick up strips at random.[134.2] Then have a cylindrical copper pan[134.3] ready with hot rendered fat in it and put the dough in it, minding that the last bit to go into the fat is what is on the skewer. Cover it quickly with a holed lid and let it cook. When it is done, take it out and put clarified honey[134.4] or sugar on it. Serve it hot or cold as you wish.

---

[133] Here and below, *lavorieri*: literally works or handiworks, pieces.

[134.1] *d'amendue le bande tutte insieme*. That will create a unit consisting of perhaps seven or eight layers, of diminishing length from the middle to the outside.

[134.2] The verb *pigliare* normally means 'get' or 'take'; here, 'stick them through,' 'pick them up' as with a knitting needle. The sense of the direction – *si pigliarà una lista sì, et l'altro* [sic] *nò* – seems intended to put irregular waves and folds within the multi-layered stack of pastry.

[134.3] This *bocculo*, apparently a sort of timbale for deep-frying, is mentioned only here.

[134.4] To clarify honey, see Recipe VI,205.

135. To prepare another sort of dough from which you can make *struffoli*[135.1] and other preparations.

Beat ten fresh eggs, laid that day, combine fine flour with that and make up a dough that is a little thinner than the one above. Knead it well for half an hour on a table, then roll it thinly as if you were going to make small *ciambelle*.[135.2] With a knife cut the rolls like dice. When there are a large number of them cut up, let them dry out a little. Then fry them in rendered fat that is not too hot, watching that they do not get too browned. With a holed spoon, take them out. Then make castles out of them and other fanciful things. Serve them cold.[135.3]

[Fritters]

136. To prepare various sorts of fritters, beginning with Venetian-style fritters.

Boil six pounds of goat's milk in a well tinned casserole pot along with six ounces of fresh butter, four ounces of sugar, four ounces of rosewater, a little saffron and a suitable amount of salt. As it boils up, gradually put in two pounds of flour, stirring continously with a wooden spoon until it is quite thick like bread dough. Take it out of the casserole and put it into a stone mortar and grind it for a quarter of an hour. Then take it out and put it into either a copper pot or an earthenware one, stirring with the wooden spoon or with your hand until it has cooled. Then have twenty-four fresh eggs on hand and put them in one by one, constantly stirring with the wooden spoon or your hand until the dough has liquified. When the eggs are all in, beat it for a quarter of an hour until it forms bubbles. Let it sit for a quarter of an hour in the pot, tightly covered, in a warm place. Beat it again. Then have a pan ready with hot rendered fat in it and take that mixture and put it on a trencher board and with the mouth of a carafe dipped in cold rendered fat, or else with a tube of white metal, cut the fritters and put them into the fat, giving them a low heat. Shake the pan from time to time, making the fritters move about in the fat, without touching them. When the fritters begin to be cooked they will crisp up because by nature they swell and begin to look like medlars. Often they roll over by themselves. When you see that they have

---

[135.1] Today these are small balls of pastry dough and honey, fried. See Book I, §44 for the circular piece of copper (?) equipment used by Scappi to make them: 'Rings for making *struffoli*, with a cover.' Domenico Romoli devotes Book V, Recipe 89 (the second recipe with that number) of his *Singolar dottrina* (1560; f. 183r in the Venice 1593 edition) to directions for making *Strufoli alla Romanesca*.

[135.2] *ciambellette*. These are small ring-shaped cakes or pastries: see Recipes 148 and 150, below. The dough is rolled up to form a long rope. What Romoli directs is that the rope of very smooth dough should be as fine as vermicelli and, when cut, should be cubic in shape rather than cylindrical.

[135.3] Romoli writes that the fried *struffoli* are coated in hot honey; they are made particularly at carnival time and for some time afterwards.

browned a little and are light, take them out with a holed spoon. Serve them hot with fine sugar on them.

With a syringe you can make a variety of preparations with that dough,[136] although it ought to be thicker than the fritter batter. After the dough is made up for a syringe, for it to be better leave it for half an hour in a oven that is not too hot. Serve it with fine sugar over it.

137. Another way to prepare milk fritters.

Get a pound of fine flour, two ounces of cold melted butter, two ounces of sugar, two ounces of rosewater, a little saffron, salt, eight eggs and a beaker of goat's milk; with all that make up a batter like well beaten glue. Let it sit in the same pot in a warm place for a quarter of an hour. Beat it again. Make fritters of it in the way described above. In that mixture you can put elderflowers or beaten mint and marjoram.

138. To make fritters called *frascate*.

Make up a batter of eight ounces of flour with ten fresh eggs, three ounces of melted butter, two ounces of sugar, a little saffron, enough salt and two ounces of rosewater; make especially sure that it be well beaten. Have a frying pan with hot rendered fat. Put some of that thick batter[138] into a holed spoon or into a medium-sized colander and, with another spoon without holes, push all of it through so that it takes up the whole pan. Just as soon as you see that it is swelling up, with great care turn it over so it will not brown too much, and take it out because that sort of batter cooks quickly. Pile up each of the pieces on top of one another sprinkled with sugar. If you want to hold them for a while, keep them in a moderately hot oven covered with rag paper.

139. To prepare another sort of fritter.[139.1]

Get a pound of grated creamy cheese[139.2] and four ounces of breadcrumb that has soaked in goat's milk, mix those together with ten well beaten eggs, two ounces of sugar, ten ounces of flour, a little fine flour and a little elderflower that has soaked in milk. Then make fritters as large or as small as you like, cooking them in rendered fat. Serve them with sugar over them.

---

[136] See one of these (*seringhe*) in Plate 13. Here Scappi's *pasta* could be understood as a relatively thick 'batter' rather than 'dough.'

[138] Scappi describes the mixture as a 'runny dough': *essa pasta liquida*.

[139.1] This elderflower fritter was known in popular cookery in Castelvetro's Modena: 'Toward the end of spring, the elder comes into bloom, and makes wonderful fritters. Mix the blossoms with ricotta, Parmesan, egg, and powdered cinnamon, and shape the mixture into little crescent shapes. Flour them lightly and fry them in butter, and send to table sprinkled with sugar' (trans. Riley, 72).

[139.2] See the note in Book I, §8.

140. Another way to prepare fritters.

Make a dough of two pounds of flour with a pound of warm goat's or cow's milk, two ounces of leaven moistened with six ounces of milk, six ounces of a grated creamy cheese, half an ounce of cinnamon, a little saffron, eight fresh eggs, four ounces of sugar, three ounces of butter and four ounces of fresh provatura ground in a mortar. Work the dough until it is like a well beaten glue. Let it stand for an hour, well covered, in a warm place. Then pound it down again. Make fritters of it with the mouth of a carafe or a white-metal tube, and fry them in rendered fat. Serve them hot with sugar on them. You can put raisins into that mixture.

141. To prepare fritters with chicken flesh.

When in a mortar you have ground up the breast meat of two chickens that have first been boiled, add in two pounds of *bazzotto* cheese,[141] half a pound of grated Parmesan cheese, three ounces of sugar, six eggs and half an ounce of cinnamon. Of that mixture make balls the size of a hard-boiled egg yolk. Have a pot on hand containing six beaten eggs with two ounces of flour and coat the balls in that one by one; just as soon as they are coated drop them into hot rendered fat and fry them. When they are done, serve them hot with sugar over them.

You can do calf's and goat-kid's brains, boiled, in the same way.

142. To prepare rice fritters.

Cook two pounds of rice in a fat meat broth or else in goat's or cow's milk and sugar so that it is quite thick. Take it out of the pot and let it cool. In a mortar grind four ounces of sugar and eight fresh eggs with one pound of creamy cheese. Make balls of that mixture; dredge them in fine flour, then fry them in rendered fat. When they are done, serve them hot with sugar on them.

143. To prepare elderflower fritters.

Get a pound of a creamy cheese and a pound of either fresh cheese or ricotta cheese. Grind those in a mortar, adding in three ounces of grated bread, four ounces of sugar, six eggs, a little saffron and three ounces of very clean elderflower that has soaked in milk. Then make balls of that mixture, dredging them in fine flour, and set them to fry in melted butter or rendered fat. When they are done, serve them hot with sugar on them.

144. To prepare another sort of fritter, commonly called *pappardelle*[144] by Romans.

Get fresh ewe's-milk ricotta and press out the whey through a strainer. For every pound of the ricotta get three eggs, three ounces of sugar and three ounces of

---

[141] This variety of plump, semi-soft cheese is used also in Recipes 47 and 150; in the latter place it is specifically of cow's milk.

[144] That is, 'gobble-ups.' Panunto's version of the *pappardelle* is similar (V,99).

breadcrumb soaked in warm goat's milk and then squeezed out. Make the mixture rather thick. Cut out fritters of it with a carafe mouth or a white-metal tube, and fry them in rendered fat or melted butter. When they are done, serve them hot with sugar on them.

145. To prepare fritters, popularly called *zeppolle*[145.1] by Romans.

Get one pound of brown chickpeas[145.2] that have steeped; when their outer skin is removed, boil them in a good meat broth with six ounces of shelled chestnuts. Then take them out of the broth, drain them and grind them in a mortar with six ounces of old shelled walnuts that are not rancid, adding in four ounces of sugar, an ounce of cinnamon and half an ounce of cloves and nutmeg together. Then have ready an ounce and a half of leaven that has been moistened with a beaker of warm white wine and a little rosewater; mix everything together, adding in mint, marjoram, burnet and wild thyme – all beaten with knives. Make balls of that mixture and fry them in rendered fat or butter. When they are done, brush them with rosewater. Serve them hot, dressed with sugar and cinnamon.

If, though, after the mixture has been made up it sits for an hour, covered, in a warm place, it will be quite a bit better because of the leaven. And if you do not have any leaven, instead of it you can use six egg whites.

146. To prepare a thin dough with which, using rosette irons, you can make various preparations called 'Sardinian fruit.'

Get a pound and a half of fine flour and make a batter of it like glue with two-thirds of a litre of cold goat's milk, four ounces of melted butter, two ounces of rosewater, enough salt and six uncooked egg yolks. When that batter is made up, beat it so it becomes thin like that from which wafer cornets are made. Get very clean rosette irons[146.1] and heat them in rendered fat, then dry them with a linen cloth: that is done so that what is on the iron will come off better. Have a pan with hot rendered fat ready and put the iron into it to heat up. When it is hot, dip it into the batter, not going higher than the mark, and fry it in the hot fat. When they are cooked serve them with sugar on them. They can be filled with whitedish, with yellowdish[146.2] and with other ingredients. When it is a little thicker, that batter mixture can be used for various preparations with a funnel and then fried.

[145.1] This word being a diminutive of *zeppa*, a wedge, an English translation of these fritters' name might be 'wedgies.'

[145.2] That is, dried, not fresh.

[146.1] See one of these, with a waffle pattern and a long handle, illustrated in Plate 15 of the engravings: *Per lavoreri di pasta*. The pot (of grease) that is shown will sit over the fire on a tripod.

[146.2] This is the *ginestrata* seen in Recipes II,160 and III,223.

147. To prepare Sienese *berlingozzi*.[147.1]

Make up a dough of three pounds of fine flour with sixteen well beaten eggs and a little salt, making it thin rather than thick. Then with that dough make a little round *ciambella*.[147.2] Brush both pieces[147.3] with beaten egg white so they stick together. Flour an oven peel[147.4] and put the *ciambella* on it, slitting it in three places. Colour it with beaten eggs, immediately sprinkle it with sugar and put it into a very clean oven that is rather warm. When it begins to rise and to brown, put a sheet of paper on it. When it is done, serve it hot, because when it cools it is not as good or as firm or as tasty.

148. To prepare large *ciambelle*[148.1] with eggs and milk.

Make a dough of three pounds of fine flour with eight fresh, beaten eggs, six ounces of sugar, three ounces of rosewater and the rest warm goat's milk, with a little salt. Make the dough so that it is not too thick, though it should be well kneaded. Make the large *ciambelle*[148.2] four ounces each and put them into a cauldron of boiling water. Leave them there until until they float, then take them out and let them cool and dry. Bake them in an oven on paper or on a floor that is very clean. When they are done, serve them hot or cold, whichever you wish. You can put dried sweet fennel or anise with that.

149. To prepare a mixture with which you can make various things with dough on a mould.

Get a pound of shelled Milanese almonds, three ounces of Neapolitan *mostac-cioli*, fifteen hard-boiled egg yolks and two pounds of sugar, and grind all that together with four ounces of rosewater. Have a rather thick sheet of dough ready, made with fine flour, egg yolks, sugar, rosewater and a reasonable amount of salt. Put a part of that dough[149.1] on a wooden or metal mould of moderately high

---

[147.1] These pasties, similar to modern Italian *croccanti*, may have been named after *Berlingaccio*, Carnival Thursday.

[147.2] This *ciambellotta* (a diminutive of *ciambella*) is a ring-shaped pasty for the making of which Scappi gives directions in the next recipe.

[147.3] *amendue le pizze*: Scappi's direction implies that a roll of dough has been made and its ends are to be joined to form a *ciambella*'s ring.

[147.4] See Plate 11 for a *pala per infornar*.

[148.1] *ciambelloni* differentiated from the smaller ones, *ciambellotte*, of the previous recipe.

[148.2] The shape of each *ciambella*, typically a ring or bagel form, is not specified, probably because it is so generally known. A modern *ciambella* has a short bar across its centre.

[149.1] See the next recipe. The whole procedure might have been a little clearer if the cook had been directed to cut out patches of the flattened dough roughly the size and shape of the mould; two of these will sandwich the almond-yolk-sugar mixture, with one of them imprinted on the mould.

relief, which mould should have been sprinkled with fine flour so the dough will not stick to it. On the dough put as much of the mixture as the mould will hold, cover the mixture over, having first brushed the dough all around with egg whites so that the sheet of dough that will be put on top will adhere well together with it. When it is moulded,[149.2] fry it in rendered fat that is not too hot, minding that you put the side with the impression downwards and that there is enough fat in the pot that the pastry will not sink to the bottom, because if it were to sink to the bottom the impression would be spoiled. When it is cooked, serve it hot with sugar over it.

If the dough is made with almond milk or pinenut milk, and sugar, without egg yolks, you can bake it in an oven with the impression upwards. And you can fry it, too.

150. To prepare filled *ciambelle*.

Get a pound of creamy, plump, moderately soft cheese[150.1] – that is, of cow's milk, without salt – a pound of grated Parmesan cheese, six ounces of fresh butter, twelve fresh eggs and a little saffron; mix all that together. Then make up a dough of three pounds of fine flour with ten ounces of warm goat's milk, four ounces of breadcrumb soaked in that milk, six egg yolks, four ounces of butter and enough salt. When the dough is well kneaded, gradually knead in a further four ounces of butter. Split the dough up into two-ounce lumps and with a pin roll them out making them round[150.2] and leaving them the thickness of a tourte shell. On one side of each round of that dough put two ounces of the above filling, rolling them up one and a half times and brushing them with melted butter. Then make them into little *ciambelle*, flattening them with the palm of your hand. Put them on butter-greased paper in a tourte pan and colour them as *offelle*[150.3] are coloured. Bake them in an oven. When they are done, serve them hot.

In a different way you can roll out a big sheet of the dough and, along its length put a ridge of the filling a finger in height. Make a roll of that, and bake it in a tourte pan in the oven with melted butter over it. With the same filling you can make lanterns and Brescian cascades,[150.4] and a thick soup of ravioli cooked in a good broth and using the same dough.

[149.2] This 'moulding' involves some pressure: Scappi writes that the pastry is *imprentata* or 'imprinted.'

[150.1] *cascio bazzotto grasso*: see Recipe 141.

[150.2] *tondi*. The 1581 typesetter read the word – or at least set it – as *mondi*, 'cleaned, pared.'

[150.3] See Recipe 48, above.

[150.4] *cascatelle alla Bresciana*. This preparation may be related to the *chalamoni Bresie* mentioned by Pantaleone da Confienza, 2, §10 (at p. 122 in the Naso edition). This latter is a variety of fondue making use of a Brescian-type cheese. Panunto describes *Casatelle* (sic, Recipe V,100) of ricotta, eggs, herbs, spices and sugar in pastry.

151. To prepare another sort of pastry filled with chicken.

With knives beat two capon breasts that have first been boiled or spit-roasted. To them add four ounces of Milanese almonds, shelled and ground in a mortar, two ounces of Neapolitan *mostaccioli*, four ounces of a creamy cheese, eight uncooked egg yolks, an ounce of cinnamon and a little saffron. With that filling make up little *ciambelle* using the same dough and following the same directions as in the previous recipe. Otherwise make little flans[151] of it. Fry them in rendered fat.

In the same way you can do a calf's kidney that has been roasted on a spit along with its tenderloin.

152. To prepare a filling with which you can make small *ciambelle* and small flans.

In butter stew four pounds of peeled apples cut into small pieces, along with an ounce of ground cinnamon. When they are done, take them out and let them cool. Add in an ounce and a half of ground *mostaccioli*, six ounces of a creamy cheese, four ounces of shelled, crushed pinenuts that have steeped, six raw egg yolks and six ounces of sugar. Use that filling to make small *ciambelle*, small flans, tortellini and other preparations fried in rendered fat. You can also make filled twists with it, baking them in a tourte pan in an oven. When they are done, they need to be served hot.

Pies[153] of several sorts of fish and other ingredients for a lean day.

153. Firstly, to make a sturgeon pie with thick dough for keeping or for serving hot.

Get a skinned sturgeon, cut up into six-pound pieces; let those sit for two hours coated in a mixture of pepper, cloves, cinnamon, ginger and crushed nutmeg, and verjuice or orange juice, with enough salt. Then have a sheet of dough ready, made of coarsely sieved flour as directed in the first recipe of this Book. However, if you want to make this pie's dough tender so that it can be eaten, make it up as for the shells in Recipe 2, but instead of the eggs put in a little Greek wine; and instead of the rendered fat, oil, with a little ground pepper and a suitable amount of salt. Roll it out to the thickness of a little finger, more or less, depending on the size of the piece of fish. On the dough sprinkle some of the same spice mixture

---

[151] For these *fiadoncelli* see Recipe 127.

[153] As at the beginning of this Book, some of the *pasticci* in the following recipes are varieties of pasty or turnover, *pasticci in sfoglio*, making use of a single sheet of pastry dough as a wrap over and around a relatively stable filling. Sometimes the phrase *in cassa* (*en croûte*) will qualify 'standing' pies; those have the structure of a normal pie, with a lower crust forming a base and sides, and optionally an upper crust, but are baked unsupported by an oven dish. And, of course, there are pies, generally more shallow, whose more or less mobile filling or fine pastry needs the support of some sort of pie plate.

that is used above. Put the piece of sturgeon on the dough, sprinkling the same spices over it. Close the pie over. Bake it in an oven. If you want to colour it with saffron-tinged water, that is up to you. When it is done, serve it hot or cold as you wish.

If a pie like that is to be served on a meat day, you can stick the piece of sturgeon with lardoons of salt pork belly, or else put pieces of mortadella or *salsiccioni* with the fish. Make the dough the way it is done for the ox tongue in the first recipe.

154. To prepare sturgeon pies *en croûte* for serving hot.

Take the sturgeon's belly, which is always the best part, skin it and cut it up into big or small pieces, depending on the size of pie you will be wanting to make. Let the pieces sit for an hour coated with the spices of the previous recipe. Put them into a pastry shell with prunes and dried visciola cherries during the winter and spring, and in summer with gooseberries and whole verjuice grapes. That shell should be made of sieved flour and water with no salt, and should be quite firm. If you want it to be made better, put eggs and butter into it; in Lent, though, you do not use eggs or butter, but only plain water. Cover the pie over and bake it. When it is done, it is served hot. No fat is put into that pie because sturgeon in itself is fat.

In the same way you can do all the parts of a sturgeon, except for the whole head.

155. To prepare sturgeon pies *en croûte* with fresh peas.

Get the umbilical part[155] of a sturgeon, skinned and cut up into small pieces the size of an egg. Let it sit an hour in a mixture of oil or melted butter, pepper, cinnamon and salt. Put it into a pastry shell with fresh peas, which shell should be made with sieved flour as above. Add in a little beaten fine herbs and saffron. Cover the pie over and bake it in an oven. Serve it hot. If you want to put a few slices of cheese into the pie that is optional, being careful to put less salt into the filling. And instead of fresh peas you can put in dried peas that have steeped and are half cooked.

In the same way you can do any part of a sturgeon except for the whole head.

156. To prepare sturgeon pies *en croûte* with a sauce in them.

Get a sturgeon, skinned however you wish,[156.1] cut it up as above and set it to steep for two hours in royal seasoning made of rose vinegar, malmsey, sugar, salt, pepper, cloves and nutmeg, with a little garlic to flavour it. Have some pastry

---

[155] See the note concerning the *bellicolo* in Recipe III,52.

[156.1] *di che lato si voglia* appears as *di che latte si voglia*, 'whichever milk you like.'

ready, somewhat firmer than the other ones,[156.2] and into it put the pieces of sturgeon with a little butter along with raisins or seeded muscatel raisins. Cover the pie over and bake it, making a little peak in its cover.[156.3] When it is almost done, make a hole at the peak. Then have a little of that same seasoning ready, tempered with sugar, saffron and beaten egg yolks, and put that into the pie through the hole on top, and finish off baking it. Serve it hot.

If it is for a day in Lent, though, you will not put any eggs into it.

157. To prepare pies of stuffed sturgeon flesh *en croûte*.

Get croquettes already cut and stuffed as is directed in Recipe 15 of the Book on Fish, and put them into a pastry shell with gooseberries or verjuice grapes in summer, or else raisins, prunes and dried visciola cherries in winter, adding in pepper, cinnamon and a little firm butter. Cover the pie over and bake it in an oven. It is optional whether you put a sauce made of roasted hazelnuts, raisins, *mostaccioli* and orange juice into that pie; if you do so, there will be no need to put in prunes and dried visciola cherries. Whenever you do not put in sauce you can also put some spring onions, sautéed with beaten pennyroyal, with that sturgeon flesh. When it is baked, it is served directly hot.

158. To prepare a pie of beaten sturgeon flesh *en croûte*.

Take part of the back flesh of a sturgeon and another part from the belly and, for every pound of that flesh, four ounces of desalted fat tuna belly, skinned and deboned. Beat everything together, adding in pepper, cinnamon, cloves, nutmeg, sugar and, in winter and spring, verjuice, in summer, verjuice grapes or gooseberries with a handful of fine herbs. With that filling make up pies, large or small, whether of flaky pastry or not. If, though, you want the filling not to be of so fine a texture, half cook the tuna belly and the sturgeon before it is beaten, and to that add butter or oil to keep it soft. I have found, however, that it is considerably better to put the filling into the pastry shell raw rather than cooked because it is tastier. Bake it in an oven, serving it hot.

159. To prepare pies of sturgeon milt and liver.

Get the milt and liver, with the gallbladder removed, and cut them into small pieces, dredging the pieces in the above spices with sugar, verjuice and oil. Put them into a pastry shell with the mixture with which they were coated. When they are almost baked, into the pie through the hole put a sauce made of egg yolks, sugar and orange juice; on fasting days instead of egg yolks, almonds ground

---

[156.2] Scappi is probably referring to the pastry shells specified in the preceding recipes. The more fluid filling in this present pie calls for a dough that will withstand the greater pressure from within.

[156.3] As in Recipe 2, the upper crust is slightly conical.

with *mostaccioli* and moistened with malmsey, sugar and orange juice. Finish off baking it. Serve it hot.

In that way you can also do sturgeon eggs after they have been boiled, increasing the spices, with various flavourings and other ingredients, depending on the taste of the person having them made. You can also do all the above pies with shad, swordfish or garfish much as with sturgeon.

160. To prepare big pies of sturgeon fingerlings[160.1] in shells for serving cold.

Get the sturgeon fingerlings fresh, gutted and skinned; if they are big they will be better. Cut them up into small pieces according to their size. Let them sit for half an hour coated with a spice mixture as is directed in the recipe above for sturgeon belly.[160.2] Put them in a sheet of dough and make the pie the way it is done for sturgeon.[160.3] Bake it the same way, and serve it hot or cold as you wish.

161. To prepare a pie of sturgeon fingerlings *en croûte* to be served hot.

Get the fingerlings gutted and skinned, and cut them into small pieces depending on their size. Let them sit for half an hour coated in a spice mixture as is said in the above recipe for sturgeon belly, and put them into a pastry shell with a little oil or butter, prunes, dried visciola cherries or gooseberries or verjuice grapes, depending on the time of year. Bake it in an oven. Serve it hot. You can also put a variety of seasonings into that pie, depending on the wishes of the person for whom it is being made.

162. To prepare big pies of umbra in a pastry wrap for keeping.

Get six-pound pieces of umbra with the scales removed. If they are from the back, lard them with salted tuna belly which has steeped; if from the belly there is no need for larding. Let them sit for an hour in the spice mixture given in Recipe 153. Put them on the sheet of pastry dough the way the sturgeon is done, and bake it in an oven. When it is done, serve it hot or cold, whichever you want.

163. To prepare pies of umbra *en croûte* for serving hot.

Get six-pound pieces of fresh, scaled umbra and let them sit for half an hour in a spice mixture and salt that is set out in the other recipes. Put them into a pastry shell with sautéed onions under and over them and verjuice grapes and a little butter. Cover the pie over. Bake it in an oven and serve it hot.

You can use that fish for making all the sorts of pies you make with sturgeon.

[160.1] *porcellette, cioè Storioncini piccolini*: 'small piglets – that is, tiny sturgeon.'

[160.2] The reference seems to be to Recipe 154 which, for its spices, refers back to Recipe 153.

[160.3] Recipe 153.

164. To prepare pies of tuna in a pastry wrap for keeping.

Get skinned pieces of tuna of whatever size you like, and let them sit in a mixture of pepper, cloves, cinnamon, nutmeg, ginger and salt, oil and either vinegar or verjuice. Follow the directions for making a sturgeon pie. You can also let them sit in a seasoning and then make pies of them with a sheet of dough as is directed for sturgeon in the above recipe. Bake it the same way, serving it hot or cold as you wish. You can also lard it with salted salmon that has steeped, putting less salt into the filling.

165. Various ways to make tuna pies *en croûte*.

Get a skinned tuna belly cut up into whatever sized pieces you like, and let them sit an hour in the above spice mixture and salt. Put them into a pastry shell made, as is directed in Recipe 154, of sieved flour, with prunes, dried visciola cherries and sautéed onions in it. Cover the pie over. Bake it in an oven. When it is done, serve it hot. With that tuna belly you can also put fresh peas and beans. And you can also put the belly into pastry only coated with spices; when it is half cooked, add in through the hole a sauce of prunes and visciola cherries. Alternatively, you can let the belly sit in a seasoning as is done with the sturgeon belly in Recipe 154. And you can make pies of it in all the ways the sturgeon belly is done.

Likewise you can make pies of skipjack tuna the way they are done with the sturgeon fingerlings in Recipe 161.

166. To prepare pies with whole sea bass and other sea fish in a pastry wrap for keeping.[166.1]

Get a sea bass that is no bigger than ten pounds and is fresh. If it is in January remove nothing but its bowel and gallbladder, through its mouth. Scale it, and with the tip of a knife puncture it in several places and let it sit for an hour coated with pepper, crushed nutmeg, cloves, cinnamon, ground ginger, salt, oil and vinegar. Put it, sprinkled with those same spices under and over it, onto a sheet of dough made of coarsely sieved flour. Bake it in an oven. When it is done it can be kept or served hot.

After it has been scaled you can also put it to steep in a royal seasoning[166.2] whole like that, sprinkling it afterwards with spices. Then put it onto a sheet of pastry. In that pie you can put mint and marjoram leaves which will give it an excellent flavour.

In the same way you can do small umbra, dentex, corb, gilthead, big sea bream and big saupe.

[166.1] Rather than *in sfoglio*, an apparent misprint has this rubric ending *per conservare il sfoglio*.

[166.2] See Recipes 156 and 188 for two compositions of 'royal seasoning.'

167. To prepare pies of big sea bass *en croûte* for serving hot.

When a sea bass is big it is gutted, scaled and cut up into four-pound pieces. Let it sit half an hour in the above spice mixture, then put it into a pastry shell made of finely sieved flour as is directed in Recipe 154, with prunes and dried visciola cherries, or else with beaten onions. Cover the pie over and bake it in an oven. You can also add in some flavourings made of ground raisins, muscatel raisins and ground *mostaccioli* moistened with Greek wine, sugar and orange juice.

If you wish to make pies of croquettes[167.1] of that large sea bass, cut them lengthwise and remove the fine bones in them. Then stuff them[167.2] with the bone-free flesh of another sea bass ground up with salted eel or else with salted tuna belly, along with mint and marjoram, adding in spices and raisins. When the croquettes are stuffed, make pies with them. Bake them like the sturgeon ones in Recipe 157.

168. To prepare pies of sea bass insides *en croûte* for serving hot.

Get the milt and liver, without the gallbladder, cutting everything up into little pieces, sprinkle them with pepper, cinnamon, cloves and sugar. Put them into a shell, whether of flaky pastry or not, along with salt, raisins or seeded muscatel raisins; you can put in a little beaten mint and marjoram, and a little butter if it is not during Lent. If it is in plum season, put some in with that liver and milt, for they will be excellent. When the pies are baked, serve them hot. Through the hole on top you can add a little saffron-tinged verjuice. And with the liver and milt you can also put the eggs of that sea bass.

169. To prepare pies of whole shad, to be served either hot or cold.

Get a shad and scale it; remove its bowels and gallbladder through its mouth, leaving the other guts. Puncture it several times with a knife tip and follow all the directions given for the pie of a whole sea bass in Recipe 166.[169] Serve it hot or cold as you like.

170. To prepare pies of grey mullet in a pastry wrap to be served hot or for keeping.

Get a grey mullet – that is to say, a large mullet[170.1] – scale it and gut it, and slash it several times with the tip of a knife. Coat it with pepper, cinnamon, cloves, nutmeg, vinegar and oil, and put it onto a sheet of dough with a few cloves of garlic, or with mint and marjoram. If you want to steep it first in a seasoning,

---

[167.1] As in Recipe 157 these *polpette* are slender, elongated slabs or fillets of fish flesh.

[167.2] In Recipe 157 Scappi refers back to Recipe III,15 where the flattened slabs of flesh contain their 'stuffing' by being rolled up.

[169] Both editions show *a cap. 153* here.

[170.1] *il cefalo, cioè muggine grosso.*

that is an option, providing you do not neglect to sprinkle it with spices. Bake it in the usual way and serve it hot or cold as you wish. If, however, you want to do it *en croûte,* cut it up into pieces and follow the directions given for the sea bass pie *en croûte* in Recipe 167.

You can do mackerel, horse mackerel,[170.2] big garfish[170.3] and fresh cod[170.4] the same way.

171. To prepare pies of red mullet in a pastry wrap for keeping or for serving hot.

Get a large red mullet, which is always better, scale it, and remove its little bowel through its umbilicus. Sprinkle it with ground pepper, cloves, cinnamon, nutmeg and ginger, and salt, and with that put leaves of mint and marjoram and a little wild thyme. Put it onto a sheet of dough with butter or else a little oil, and bake it the way the others are done. Serve it hot or cold, whichever you wish.

In the same way you can do goby and whole gurnard, having first removed their back bone.

172. To prepare pies with the flesh of mullet, goby, gurnard and other fish.[172]

Scale the mullet and take its flesh with the bones and skin removed; skin the gurnard and goby, and take their flesh with the bones removed. Beat the raw flesh of both with knives, adding in oil or butter (the latter depending on the day) with pepper, cinnamon, cloves, nutmeg and enough saffron. For every pound of that flesh, beat in two ounces of desalted tuna belly or else deboned anchovies, along with mint, marjoram, a little sugar and raisins. When everything has been mixed together with the goby's liver cut up into small pieces, make pastry-shell pies of it that are large or small, whichever you want. When they are almost baked, you can put a flavouring made of clear verjuice and sugar in through the hole on top. If it is in summer, though, mix gooseberries or verjuice grapes with the fish flesh. Pies like that should always be served hot. In spring you can put field mushrooms into those pies, and in the fall peeled truffles.

You can do the flesh of a sea bream, a gilthead, a dentex, sea and lake sardines and fresh anchovies.

173. To prepare pies of whole sardines in either a pastry wrap or a shell, for serving hot.

Get sardines[173.1] that are above all fresh and, without gutting them, scale them and let them steep for half an hour in the above-mentioned spices along with

---

[170.2] *suero.* See the note in Recipe III,67.

[170.3] Garfish or needle-fish, typeset as *angusella* in both 1570 and 1581. In Recipes III,87–9 the fish is spelled *augusella.* The name derives from *acus, acúcula, aguglia,* needle.

[170.4] Recipe 196 indicates that cod was available on the market in dried form also.

[172] These pies are *en croûte.*

[173.1] Scappi tends to use a singular when speaking generically: *la sarda.*

fennel flour, oil and verjuice or vinegar. Pile them on top of one another on a sheet of dough or in a shell, sprinkling them with that spice mixture and with a little pennyroyal and a few cloves of garlic. Bake the pie in an oven the way the others are done. Serve it hot or cold as you wish. It is optional whether you cut the head off the sardines.

In the same way you can do freshwater mullet, bream and every other small fish except for a poor cod.[173.2]

174. To prepare little pies, of flaky pastry or not, of a poor cod.

Get a poor cod that has been washed in warm water and then mixed with the above spices, adding in, for every pound of it, four ounces of tuna belly, steeped and cut up small, a little verjuice, sugar, a little spring onion, beaten and sautéed, mint and marjoram, and raisins; with that mixture fill the shells. Bake them in an oven the way the other pies are done.

You can do smelt and every other sort of boneless small fish that same way.

175. To prepare pies of turbot in a pastry wrap for keeping and for serving hot.

Get a turbot and gut it; skin it or else cut off the spines it has on its back. Let it sit for half an hour in a mixture of pepper, cloves, cinnamon, nutmeg, a little oil, and verjuice or vinegar. Put it onto a sheet of dough and make up the pie. Bake it in an oven. Serve it hot or cold as you wish.

If you want it in a pastry shell,[175.1] though, cut it up and sprinkle it with the above spices. Put it into a shell with a few thin slices of desalted tuna belly, mint and marjoram, and a few damson prunes in it. Bake it. You can also put it into a shell plain, without tuna belly, with a little sweet oil or butter. When it is almost cooked, through the hole in its top put in a flavouring made of orange juice, sugar, cinnamon and saffron; or else put in some lamprey sauce.[175.2]

In both of those ways you can also do a sole or a flounder when either of those fish is big and skinned, and also a John Dory after its outer barbs have been removed.

176. To prepare pies of rayfish in a pastry wrap for serving hot or for keeping.

Get a ray and skin it; if it is big, cut it into ten-pound pieces, more or less, depending on what you want. Take the thickest and best part, which is its back, and let that sit in the spice-and-verjuice mixture mentioned above, with more salt than is put in for the other fish. Put it onto a sheet of dough and bake it as the others are done. Before you put it into the pastry you can also let it steep in a

---

[173.2] See this *pesce ignudo* immediately below and in Recipes III,77 and V,204.

[175.1] *in cassa: en croûte.*

[175.2] This *sapore della lampreda* is probably the flavouring whose ingredients are listed in Recipe 178; Recipe 179 refers back to that composition. See also Recipes III,92 and 158.

seasoning of garlic and sprinkle it with the same spices. That pie is served hot or cold as you wish. In summer it can be kept for four days; in winter, for ten. If they are small rayfish, follow the directions for turbot in a pastry wrap in the previous recipe.

177. To prepare pies of rayfish *en croûte* for serving hot.

Get the pieces that have sat in the above spices or steeped in a seasoning, and put them into a pastry shell with some beaten spring onions in it along with mint and marjoram. In spring you put in gooseberries; in summer, verjuice grapes; in winter, prunes and dried visciola cherries, a little saffron and cinnamon. Cover the pie over and bake it as above. Serve it hot.

You can do all sorts of small and full-sized rayfish that way, as well as smooth hound and fresh cod after they have been skinned, cleaned and cut up into several pieces.

178. To prepare pies of large lampreys *en croûte* for keeping or for serving hot.

Get a lamprey and clean off its slime in warm water; remove its bowels and gallbladder, leaving in its liver; set its blood aside. Cut it up into rounds because they can go into the pie more easily; let them sit for an hour more or less, depending on the season, in a mixture of pepper, cloves, cinnamon, nutmeg, verjuice, sugar and salt, all ground up together, along with a little sweet-almond oil or olive oil. Put them into the pastry shell with chopped fresh dates and seeded muscatel raisins or ordinary raisins. Instead of oil you can use butter; and with that, beaten mint and marjoram. Cover the pie over and bake it in an oven. When it has been in the oven for half an hour, dilute the lamprey's blood with malmsey wine and orange juice, adding in more sugar, and put it into the pie through the hole on top, and let it finish baking. When it is done, it can be served hot or kept for a few days.

If you do not like the above flavouring, put in another one made of roasted almonds, well ground in a mortar with raisins, *mostaccioli* and sugar, moistened with malmsey and orange juice, all of that thoroughly mixed with the blood before it is put into the pie. When the lamprey is extremely large you can also half braise it in oil before putting it into the wrap.

In that way you can do every sort of young lamprey, as well as moray and conger eel.

179. To prepare pies of large or small squid *en croûte* for serving hot.

Take a large squid, clear away its barbs, the cartilage around its beak, its eyes and its mane which is often full of sand. Set aside the bladder which is full of a black ink-like liquid. After the squid has been well cleaned and washed, stuff it with the mixture described in Recipe 103[179] for stuffed squid, in the Book on

---

[179] In both printings, *nel cap. 102.*

Fish. Put it into a pastry shell containing solid butter, ordinary raisins, seeded muscatel raisins and sautéed spring onions, cooled, adding in pepper, cinnamon and saffron. If it is for a fasting day, though, instead of using butter coat the squid, after it has been stuffed, with oil and verjuice and sprinkle it with the above spices. Cover the pie over and bake it. When it is almost done, dilute the liquid in the squid's bladder with orange juice, malmsey wine and sugar, and put it into the pie through the hole on top. Finish off baking it. When it is done, serve it hot.

Instead of that flavouring, when the squid is not stuffed and there are no onions in the pie, you can also put lamprey sauce into it, mentioned in the previous recipe, its liquid being diluted instead of the lamprey's blood.

In all those ways you can do cuttlefish, stuffed or cut up, and octopus when it is cleaned inside and out, and every sort of small squid, too. I shall not write about scorpion fish or green wrasse because they are not much used, less than other fish, and it would take too much space to deal with them.

180. To prepare pies of land and sea turtles *en croûte*.

Get a tortoise,[180] which is quite a bit better than the sea turtle, and, because it is juicier, immediately after its head has been cut off, while still uncooked, remove its shell and its skin and claws and everything else that is dirty. Remove the gallbladder from the liver, and if the eggs have formed a shell, take that off them. Coat everything in pepper, cinnamon, cloves, nutmeg, salt, a little sugar, orange juice and saffron. Put it into a pastry shell, adding in ordinary raisins and seeded muscatel raisins, and either pennyroyal or spring onions beaten and sautéed in a little butter or oil. Cover the pie over and bake it. When it is almost done, put a flavouring into it of verjuice, sugar and a little orange juice; finish off baking it. Instead of that flavouring you can put in another made of almonds; and instead of almonds, in the springtime you can put field mushrooms into the pie. If you do not want to put the turtle raw into the pastry wrap, you can parboil it before its shell is removed, following the above directions for cleaning it.

If it is a sea turtle, which is quite tough, if it is taken out of its shell raw cut it up and let the pieces sit for at least four hours in a seasoning made of vinegar, must syrup, salt, strong spices and garlic. Take it out of the seasoning, coat it with the above spice mixture and put it into a pastry shell with beaten and sautéed spring onions under and over it, along with a little wild thyme and marjoram. Set it to bake as above. When it is almost done, get some of the seasoning in which the pieces have sat and put that into the pie through the hole on top; let it finish baking. Serve it hot.

In all those ways you can do the liver and eggs, without putting them into any seasoning. In that same way you can do a freshwater turtle, which has a tail.

---

[180] Literally, a 'land turtle.' Scappi distinguishes between his *tartarughe* only with the qualifications *di terra* and *di mare*. See Recipe III,165.

181. To prepare pies of lobsters or spiny lobsters[181.1] *en croûte.*

Get those lobsters and cook them in water with salt and pepper. Take them out and take the flesh from their tail and claws. If you want to do the tail whole, lard it all over with salted eel flesh; do the same with the claws if they are taken off whole. Sprinkle them with pepper, cloves, cinnamon and nutmeg and put them in a pastry shell with prunes and dried visciola cherries, and pennyroyal and spring onions, beated and sautéed. Cover the pie over and bake it in an oven. As soon as it has heated up, put a flavouring into it made of verjuice, sugar, cinnamon and saffron; finish baking it. You can also leave out the spring onions and the above flavouring, putting in a sauce made like the one for the lamprey.

If you want it differently, though, take the raw flesh and beat it, following the directions for making a pie of the flesh of a red mullet in Recipe 173.[181.2] Make the pies either of flaky pastry or not. However, if you want to beat the cooked flesh of those lobsters, follow directions such as are given for sturgeon flesh in Recipe 158. In those ways you can do every sort of domestic crayfish and some other sorts.

182. To prepare pies of tender crabs *en croûte.*

Get tender crabs[182] and put them in a pastry shell with beaten mint and marjoram, raisins, pepper, cinnamon, cloves, nutmeg, sugar, salt, either butter or sweet-olive oil, and either orange juice or verjuice. Cover the pie over and bake it. When it is almost done, through the hole in its top add in a little more saffron-tinged verjuice and sugar, or else a sauce made of raisins and *mostaccioli* moistened with orange juice. Finish off its baking. A pie like that is always served hot.

In that same way you can do crayfish that have shed their shell.

183. [To make pies of hermit-crab meat *en croûte,* served hot.][183]

Because, in Recipe 180 of the Book on Fish, I spoke about the hermit crab, which has no flesh except in the hollow of its legs, you can cook them in the manner outlined in that Recipe. Take whatever is meaty on their body and, together with the mixture that is made up in Recipe 181 to stuff its shell, make pies with that in the usual way. I do not consider other sorts of crabs to be good for making pies because they have very little flesh on them and are easier to suck than to bite.

[181.1] spiny lobsters: *locuste,* scientifically, *Palinurus vulgaris,* otherwise called sea crayfish.

[181.2] An error in numbering, copied in 1581, puts the red mullet (*triglia*) in Recipe 172.

[182] See Recipe III,161.

[183] A blunder was committed in the second printing: the rubric for *gongole* and *telline* that heads up Recipe 185 was reproduced here rather than the proper one for *granchio porro,* hermit crabs. However the Table that follows Book V was, of course, correctly copied, showing the 'name' of this recipe properly as *Per fare pasticci di polpa di granchiporri in cassa serviti caldi.*

Furthermore, the references to Book III erroneously read respectively Recipes 179 and 180 in both printings.

184. To prepare pies of oysters *en croûte* for serving hot.

Get oysters, removing them from their shell either after they have sat a little on a grill or while they are still raw. Set their water aside. Coat them with pepper and cinnamon, and put them in a pastry shell with a little butter or sweet-olive oil. Cover the pie over and bake it like the other ones. When it is almost done, have a flavouring made up of other oysters ground in a mortar, a little *mostaccioli* and spinach tips moistened in the water[184] and a little malmsey, orange juice and sugar; put all of that through the hole in the top of the pie. Finish off baking it.

You can also do them in pies with sautéed spring onions; and in the spring put field mushrooms with them. On meat days, instead of the other ingredients use the stuffing of fine saveloy. After they have been dug out of their shell you can also sauté them in butter with mint, marjoram and orange juice. When they have cooled, put them into the pastry shell with raisins, pepper and cinnamon; cover the pie over and finish baking it.

185. To prepare pies of cockles and telleen clams *en croûte* for serving hot.

Get cockles and plunge them, in a towel or net, into boiling water with salt and pepper. When they have opened, take them out of the water. Sauté them in butter or sweet-olive oil with beaten fine herbs and orange juice. Let them cool and put them into a pastry shell with ordinary raisins or seeded muscatel raisins, pepper and cinnamon. With that you can put the parboiled stems of artichokes or cardoons, cut up small. Cover the pie over and bake it in an oven. Serve it hot.

In all those ways you can do any sort of cockles, telleens, *poveraccie*[185] and limpets.

186. To prepare pies of shelled snails *en croûte*.

Get old snails, which are quite a bit better than new ones, and parboil them in water. Take them out of their shell and purge them with salt in the usual way.[186] Sauté them with spring onions or else with fine herbs as is done with cockles. Put them into a pastry shell with pepper, cinnamon and a clove of garlic, a little verjuice, must syrup, damson prunes and enough salt. Cover the pie over and bake it in an oven like other ones. Serve it hot.

You can also do them in all the ways oysters are done in a pie in Recipe 184, except that you do not grind them. And you can do the pies with flaky pastry.

---

[184] *con la sua acqua*: despite the singular of *sua*, this seems to be the oyster 'water' that was reserved.

[185] See Recipe III,193.

[186] See Recipe III,199 for this 'usual way.' See the same purging-by-salt operation again in Recipe V,208. Recipe III,197 describes a longer process that does not involve salt.

187. To prepare pies of trout or carp in a pastry wrap for keeping or for serving right away.

Get a trout and, if you want to do it whole, scale it and gut it. Give it a lengthwise slit on both sides. If it is big, puncture it a few times with a knife. Let it sit an hour coated with a mixture of crushed pepper, ground cloves, cinnamon and nutmeg, a little verjuice or vinegar, and salt. Have a sheet of dough ready made of coarsely sieved flour and put the trout on it with the spices under and over it, as well as a few slices of candied citron peel.[187.1] Cover the pie over and bake it in an oven the way the others are done. That sort of pie is kept for ten days in winter, and in summer four. It can be served directly from the oven.

You can do large and small salmon carp that way, as well as chub from the Tiber and from Lombardy,[187.2] and a large perch once it has been gutted and carefully scaled.

188. To prepare pies of big pike in a pastry wrap for serving hot or for keeping.

Get a big or medium-sized pike, scale and gut it. If you want to put it into a pie whole, let it sit for three hours in royal seasoning made of vinegar, salt, pepper, must syrup, coriander and cloves of garlic. Take it out and sprinkle it with the same spices used on the trout above. Put it onto a sheet of dough with chopped sweet olives and bake it in an oven the way the other ones are done. When it is finished it can be kept for eight days, or it can be served immediately.

If you want it *en croûte*, when the pike has been scaled cut it up into whatever pieces you like, sprinkle them with the spice mixture and put them into the pastry shell with prunes and dried visciola cherries. Bake it. When it is almost done, through the hole on top put in a white sauce made of almonds, breadcrumb and sugar moistened with verjuice and Greek wine or malmsey. Finish off baking it. When it is done, serve it hot. You can also do it in a pie with beaten and sautéed onions or with beaten herbs.

In all the above ways you can do carp[188] and a big pike. After it has been scaled it can be larded with desalted tuna belly or else desalted anchovies.

189. To prepare pies of stuffed tench in a pastry wrap.[189.1]

Get a big tench, scale and gut it, and stuff it with the mixture described in Recipe 140 for stuffed tench in the Book on Fish.[189.2] Sprinkle it with the same

---

[187.1] See Recipe VI,210 for this *limoncelli cedrati*.

[187.2] Scappi distinguishes two varieties of chub here depending on their origin. He names them, respectively, *squalme* and *cavedini*.

[188] Again, Scappi avails himself of two names to identify a carp: *pesce carpione, cioè raina*.

[189.1] The rubric should also have added 'or *en croûte*': the first procedure to be described is, in fact, *in cassa*.

[189.2] *cap. 140* is printed in both editions. Recipe III,140 has a stuffing in common with fish in preceding recipes. Recipe III,141 has a unique variant for stuffing tench.

spices the trout is sprinkled with in Recipe 187, and put it into a pastry shell with a few thin slices of apple on top of it. Bake it the way other pies are done. It can either be served hot or be kept.

You can also skin a tench, leaving the skin attached to its head and tail; then stuff it with the mixture that the tench skin is stuffed with in Recipe 140 of the Book on Fish.[189.3] When it is stuffed, sprinkle it with the same spices and sugar, and put it onto a sheet of dough made of fine flour, egg yolks, butter, salt and warm water: that is done so that the pastry can be eaten along with the tench. Cover the pie over and bake it in the oven. Serve it hot.

You can also do a pie of a large tench without stuffing it and without skinning it, though be very sure to remove the teeth of any tench because they make a preparation bitter. Before putting them into a wrap you can also heat up the stuffed ones in oil because they will cook much more quickly than if raw.

190. To prepare pies of tench with peas and other ingredients *en croûte* for serving hot.

Get a tench, scale it, take out its gallbladder but leave in the other organs, and remove its teeth. If it is big, cut it up; if you want, let it steep an hour in royal seasoning.[190] Then sprinkle it with pepper, cinnamon, cloves, nutmeg and salt. Put it into a pastry shell with prunes and dried visciola cherries, and onions sautéed in butter or oil. Cover the pie over and bake it as above. When it is almost done, through the hole on top add in a little verjuice tinged with saffron; finish off baking it. Serve it hot.

If you want it *en croûte* with fresh peas, there is no need to steep the tench in a seasoning, nor even to put the other ingredients with it, but only to sprinkle it with the above spices and with a few little pieces of cheese and butter. On meat days you can also bake the tench either whole or cut up with the stuffing for saveloy sausage under and over it, and truffles inside.

191. To prepare pies of large eels *en croûte* for serving hot or for keeping.

Get an eel, skin and gut it, cut off its head and tail and slice the rest of it in rounds. Let it sit an hour in royal seasoning; sprinkle it with the above spice mixture. Put it into a pastry shell with a little oil or butter, and bake it. In winter it will keep for eight days, although if you want to serve it directly from the oven there is no need to steep it in the seasoning – in that case sprinkle it with spices and in with it put sautéed onions and prunes and dried visciola cherries; in spring, gooseberries; in summer, verjuice grapes.

If you do not want to do it that way, you can do it like the lamprey in Recipe 178. You can do amberjack and burbot the same way.

[189.3] The reference printed in both editions, *cap. 139*, is clearly in error.

[190] Unfortunately the ingredients of the *adobbo reale* here and in the next recipe are not specified. See, however, Recipes V,156 and 188.

192. Several ways to prepare pies of frogs' legs *en croûte* for serving hot.

Get the frogs' legs[192] cut away from the body and set them for half an hour in a mixture of spring onions, beaten and sautéed, pepper, cinnamon, saffron and a little verjuice. Put them into a pastry shell with raisins and bake it. When it is almost done, get beaten egg yolks moistened with clear verjuice and put that in through the pie's hole; finish off baking it. Instead of raisins you can also put in gooseberries in the spring and verjuice grapes in the summer. And if you do not want onions, put in fine herbs without sautéing them. When the pie is done, serve it hot.

With that you can make flaky-pastry pies.

193. To prepare pies of deboned frogs *en croûte*.

Get frogs[193] and boil them in plain water. Then take the flesh from the thighs and mix it with sugar, the above spices and orange juice. Put that into a pastry shell with butter, and bake it. When it is almost done, have either a garlic sauce moistened with bouillon in which the frogs have been cooked and tinged with saffron, or else a white sauce of almonds moistened with its bouillon and a little verjuice; pour it in through the hole. Bake it. Serve it hot. If you do not want to put in those sauces, use whatever sauce you like.

194. To prepare pies of salted tuna belly *en croûte* for keeping or for serving hot.

Get skinned tuna belly that is not rancid, and steep it for six hours, changing the water; for two further hours steep it in wine, vinegar and must syrup. Then take it out and put it, sprinkled with spices and sugar, into a pastry shell; put beaten onions, and prunes and dried visciola cherries in with it. Bake it in an oven. When it is more than half done, through the hole on top put in a little of the seasoning in which it steeped; finish off baking it. Serve it hot.

If you want to keep it, there is no need to put any sauce into it. Also, instead of the seasoning used for steeping you can put in lamprey sauce[194] or some other sauce.

In the same way you can do preserved tuna, semi-salted sturgeon belly, salmon when they have steeped and been skinned, salted eel without steeping it, and any other salted fish.

---

[192] In his rubric Scappi writes only *pasticci di Rane*, frog pies. Here, though, he begins his recipe explicitly with *le coscie*, the thighs. See also Recipe III,162.

[193] Scappi uses the word *rane* alone, as he does in the rubric to this and the previous recipe. The legs will be of primary interest, though; other parts of a frog are cooked in Recipe 210.

[194] See Recipe III,158.

195. To prepare pies of large sardines and anchovies[195.1] *en croûte*.

Get one of the above-mentioned fish, wash it in wine, split it down the middle, removing its bones and sprinkle the halves with sugar, pepper, cinnamon, cloves and nutmeg. Put them into a small pastry shell interspersed with raisins and beaten fine herbs, and a little butter or oil. Cover the pie over and bake it. When it is half done, through the hole on top you can put in a sauce made of raisins and ground *mostaccioli*, moistened with orange juice and malmsey, and sugar. When it is baked, serve it hot. You can also do it with spring onions, prunes and dried visciola cherries the way the one above for salted tuna belly is done.

You can do salted herrings[195.2] the same way, after they have steeped, and salted shad and grey mullet.

196. To prepare pies of cod and other dried fish *en croûte*.

Get cod and steep it in warm water, skinning it. Cut up its flesh into small pieces and sauté them with spring onions and chopped fine herbs. When they have been sautéed, put them into a pastry shell with pepper, cinnamon, cloves, salt, ground nutmeg, raisins, orange juice and seeded muscatel raisins. Cover the pie over and bake it like the other ones. If you want to put a flavouring into it, that is up to you.

You can do dried pike the same way.

197. To prepare flaky-pastry pies of mullet caviar, smoked sturgeon back, herring back and salted caviar[197.1] *en croûte*.

Cut up the mullet caviar and the smoked sturgeon back into thin slices. The herring back is skinned; take its flesh, along with its milt or roe, all that likewise being cut into thin slices. Do the same with the salted caviar. In a small flaky-pastry shell[197.2] a first layer is made of salted caviar and raisins with beaten fine herbs; the next layer, of mullet caviar, sturgeon back and herring; go on like that, making three layers of it, so the last one is of salted caviar. Into it put a little oil or butter, and orange juice, sugar, cinnamon, pepper and cloves. Cover the little

---

[195.1] *di Sardoni, d'Alici, o d'Anchiughe*. In Recipe III,211 Scappi twice clarifies the meaning of *alici* by adding *cioè anghioie*, which latter name, he explains in III,76 (using the form *inghioiù*), is the Genoese and Milanese name for anchovy.

[195.2] These are *aringhe bianche*, white herrings – as distinct from red herrings which have been preserved by smoking. See Recipe III,210. Balducci Pegolotti (ed. Evans, 380) declares that the best *aringhe insalate* come from *Mare Miano* between England and Flanders; they should have been salted that year, have an outer colour he descibes as *rossetta*, pinkish, and have a good herring smell: *vogliono essere … di buono odore secondo odore d'aringhe*.

[197.1] This *caviale* is a preparation of sturgeon eggs, as distinct from the mullet caviar, *bottarghe*. See Recipe III,24. See also the *crostata* in Recipe 213, below, which uses similar ingredients.

[197.2] Not merely a *cassa* or a *cassetta* (as in Recipe 195), Scappi specifies a *cassettina*, a tiny shell or casing. Presumably its height made up for its small diameter.

shell over and bake it. Serve it hot with sugar on top. You can also make the pie of those ingredients with each thing separate from the other.[197.3]

[Lean *crostate* and tourtes]

198. To prepare a *crostata* of sturgeon liver and milt.

Get a sturgeon liver without the gallbladder, wash it and cut it into thin slices; do the same with the milt. Coat them with a mixture of pepper, cinnamon, cloves and sugar. Have a tourte pan ready, greased with oil or butter, lined with three sheets of extremely thin dough and, around it, its flaky-pastry twist made with fine flour, egg yolks, butter, rosewater, salt and either warm goat's milk or plain water. Butter should be brushed between each of the sheets of dough. On them sprinkle some of the same spice mixture with sugar, and on that put beaten mint and marjoram, gooseberries or raisins, and hard-boiled egg yolks broken up small. Then put the liver and milt on top along with, in spring fresh field mushrooms, in winter dried field mushrooms that have steeped. Over all that put some more of the same spice mixture again as was put underneath, along with orange juice. Cover the tourte pan over with another two sheets of dough brushed with butter, and on top of them a few strips of flaky pastry. Then, with a cutting knife that has a hot tip, slit the twist and brush it all around with melted butter; do the same with the strips of flaky pastry that were put on top. Bake it in an oven or under a cooking bell, doing the flaky-pastry twist the best. When it is done, serve it hot with sugar and rosewater on top.

You can sometimes put thin slices of fresh provatura into that *crostata*.

199. To prepare *crostate* of sturgeon liver and milt during Lent.

Get the liver and milt of a sturgeon, cut up as directed above; coat them with the same spices, along with beaten herbs and either gooseberries or raisins. For every two pounds of liver and milt, use one pound of semi-salted sturgeon belly, skinned, and boiled in salted water; cut it into thin slices. Then get a tourte pan, greased with sweet-almond oil or a good olive oil, and lined with three sheets of dough laid on one another and that oil between each – the dough being made with fine flour and a milk made from shelled pinenuts or almonds, with sugar, salt and a little oil. Follow the directions given above for incorporating those ingredients, adding in a little orange juice. Cover the tourte pan with three other sheets of dough. Bake it in an oven the way the ones above are done, having first brushed it with oil. You can fashion the top in various ways, that being at the cook's discretion.

Instead of sturgeon belly you can use thin slices of tuna belly, desalted and cooked. Also, instead of raisins you can put in seeded muscatel raisins and pinenuts steeped in water; in summer, gooseberries.

[197.3] The idea may perhaps be that the major ingredients need not be layered but merely set in the pie, apart, on a single level.

200. To prepare a tourte of sturgeon liver and milt.

Get the liver – the gallbladder removed – and the milt, which must be very clean, and bring them to a boil in salted water along with a little skinned belly from the same sturgeon. When they have boiled, take them out and let them cool. Beat them with knives, along with mint and marjoram, mixing everything together with uncooked egg yolks, very clean raisins and the same spices and sugar as were used in the previous recipe, along with a little grated fresh provatura and a little verjuice tinged with saffron, but without gooseberries. Then have a tourte pan ready, greased with butter, lined with a rather thick sheet of dough and with its twist, made of the same dough as is described in Recipe 108. Put the filling into the pan, being careful that the tourte does not come higher than a finger and a half. With another sheet of dough, fashioned like shutter slats or in any other manner, cover it over. Bake it in an oven or braise it. Serve it hot, sprinkled with sugar and rosewater.

If you want to make it for a day in Lent, instead of butter use oil. Instead of hen's eggs and provatura, use raw sturgeon eggs and pistachios, shelled and crushed, and dates cut up small. In all the above ways you can do the milt and liver of an umbra and a sea bass and any other normally eaten fish of either salt water or fresh.

201. To prepare a tourte of sturgeon flesh.

Get skinned sturgeon belly, which is the best part of it, and boil it in salted water. When it is cooked, take it out, let it cool and with knives beat it, along with mint, marjoram and a little green wild thyme, stirring in ground *mostaccioli*, dried figs chopped up small, raisins, fresh crushed pinenuts, ground pepper, cinnamon and cloves, sugar and enough salt, and raw egg yolks with a little grated Parmesan cheese. Have a tourte pan greased with butter and lined with a rather thick sheet of dough, and with its flaky-pastry twist around it. Put the filling into it with a little orange juice or verjuice so it will have a pleasant flavour, and a few little bits of butter in it to keep it soft. Cover it over with another sheet of dough. Bake it the way the ones above are baked. Serve it hot, sprinkled with sugar and rosewater.

If you want it for a day in Lent, instead of eggs and cheese, put in marzipan paste and the eggs of some other fish; and instead of butter, use oil.

In the same ways you can do a tourte of the flesh of every sea fish or freshwater fish that are eaten, provided only that they are skinned and deboned.

202. To prepare *crostate* of big lampreys.

Get a lamprey, remove its teeth, set its blood aside, clean it in hot water, cut it up into rounds and let them sit half an hour coated with a mixture of salt, pepper, cloves, nutmeg and sugar. Half roast them on a spit, then take them down and cut each of the rounds in half. Have a tourte pan greased with butter, lined with three very thin sheets of dough brushed with butter, and with its twist around it. On the sheets of dough make a layer of beaten mint and marjoram, fine, ground *mostaccioli*, fresh dates cut up small, raisins, small lumps of butter, sugar and some of the same spice mixture with which the lamprey was coated. On that layer place the pieces of lamprey, and on them put as much of the mixture again as was put under them, along with a little malmsey mixed with its blood and orange juice. Cover it over with two other sheets of dough and with a few flaky-pastry strips on top. Bake it in an oven or braise it. When it is done, serve it dressed with sugar and rosewater.

If you want it for a day in Lent, instead of butter, use oil.

In that way you can prepare young lamprey without their being roasted on a spit, and conger and eel whenever they are skinned and their middle bone removed, and moray eel when its slime is thoroughly cleaned off it and its bones are removed.

203. To prepare a *crostata* of fresh sardines.

Get fresh sardines, scale them, cut off their head; with a scraping knife[203.1] split them in half, removing their spine. Wash them and steep them in a mixture of pepper, cloves, cinnamon and dry sweet fennel, powdered, salt and either verjuice or orange juice. Have a tourte pan ready, greased with butter, lined with three very thin sheets of dough, each brushed with butter, and the twist around it. On those three sheets make a layer of beaten mint and marjoram, raisins, dry walnuts, shelled and crushed, and a few thin slices of fresh provatura, everything sprinkled with sugar, the same spice mixture and orange juice or verjuice. On those things arrange the sardines, making three layers of them interspersing each layer with the same ingredients. Should you want to put a sheet of dough, fried in butter or oil, in the middle,[203.2] there is no need to make more than a single layer of sardines under that fried dough and another layer over it. When the sardines are all arranged and the other ingredients above the fried sheet of dough, cover the pie over with two further very thin sheets of raw dough, or a single one with flaky-pastry strips. Bake it in an oven the way the other ones are done. Serve it hot with sugar and rosewater over it.

If you want it for a day in Lent, instead of butter, use oil; and instead of provatura, cloves of garlic that have first been boiled.

In the same way you can do the flesh of anchovies, red mullets, gurnards, gobies and the flesh of any other sort of fish with its scales, skin and bones removed. They should be cut up small. If you want to make a tourte of them, follow the direction for the sturgeon tourte in Recipe 201.

[203.1] *un coltello che rada*: see two *coltelli da raschiare* in Plate 13.

[203.2] See the same arrangement in Recipe 52, above, to make a *crostata doppia*.

204. To prepare a *crostata* of a poor cod.[204]

Get a poor cod that has been washed enough in warm water that its slime is all cleaned off. For every pound of it, get three ounces of raw, desalted salmon, pound it small and mix it with the poor cod. Have a tourte pan ready, greased with butter and lined with three sheets of dough like the ones above, and follow all the directions for making a *crostata* that are given in the previous recipe for sardines, and using the same ingredients.

In the same ways you can prepare all sorts of small fry once they are deboned. If you want to make a tourte of them, mix a little grated cheese and egg yolks in with them. On a day in Lent instead of cheese and egg yolks, use dry walnuts, shelled and ground, and breadcrumb soaked and ground up with the walnuts. Make the tourte in the ways directed above.

205. To prepare a *crostata* of large crayfish, of salt water and freshwater.

Get crayfish and cook them in wine, vinegar and pepper. Remove the flesh from the tail and claws; sea crayfish will have theirs cut into slices, while that of freshwater crayfish is left whole. If, though, you want to cut the tails lengthwise, first remove the little nerve. Sauté them in butter. When they are done, let them cool. Having prepared a butter-greased tourte pan lined with three very thin sheets of dough, each brushed with butter, and with its flaky-pastry twist around it, on that flaky-pastry crust set thin slices of fresh provatura sprinkled with pepper, nutmeg, cloves, cinnamon, sugar and orange juice; on top of that, put beaten mint, raisins and seeded muscatel raisins cut up small. Over all those ingredients put the sautéed crayfish meat, with as much again of the ingredients that were put underneath. If, as with the sardines in Recipe 203, you want to set in the middle a sheet of dough fried in butter, that is an option. Bake[205] it with the same amount again of thin slices of fresh provatura and bits of butter, and two very thin leaves of dough made as directed above. Bake it like the other ones. Serve it hot with sugar and rosewater over top.

If you want to serve it on a day in Lent, do not put any provatura into it; and, instead of butter, use oil of sweet almonds or olive oil. If you want to make a tourte of the crayfish, after the meat has been beaten small follow the directions for the sturgeon tourte in Recipe 201.

You can do the tails of prawns, small crayfish and squilla in the same ways.

206. To prepare a *crostata* of tender crabs and crayfish – that is, that have cast their shell off.

Take tender crabs and, to do them better, kill them in boiling wine with pepper. Take them out right away and let them cool. Then have a butter-greased

---

[204] For this fish, a *pesce ignudo*, see Recipes III,77, and 173 and 174 above.

[205] *Sic.*

tourte pan ready, lined with three sheets of dough buttered between each and with the flaky-pastry twist around it; onto those sheets put beaten mint and marjoram, and either artichoke hearts that have first been boiled and well beaten or else peeled truffles, along with pepper, cinnamon, cloves, nutmeg, sugar and little lumps of butter. Then put the crabs on top whole or in pieces and on them as much again of the mixture as before, along with orange juice or verjuice, and a suitable amount of salt. Cover the pan over with two more sheets of dough and a few strips of flaky pastry. Bake it in an oven the way the other ones are done. Serve them with sugar and rosewater over top.

For a day in Lent, instead of butter use sweet-almond oil or olive oil. If you want to make a tourte of them, beat the crabs or crayfish after they have been boiled, and follow the directions given in the previous recipe.

207. To prepare an oyster *crostata*.

Get shelled oysters, setting their water aside. If the oyster has been removed raw, take the whitest part and sauté it in butter; grind the rest of it in a mortar with a few roasted Milanese almonds, moistened with the reserved water and a little verjuice. Have a butter-greased tourte pan prepared with three leaves of dough as before, and on that shell have raisins and beaten mint and marjoram; sprinkle all that with pepper, cinnamon and sugar. Then put the oysters on that, and over them as much of the same mixture as under, and the flavouring on top.[207.1] Cover it over with two more thin sheets of dough and a few strips of flaky pastry. Bake it in an oven or braise it. Serve it hot with sugar and rosewater over it.

On Lenten days, instead of butter use oil. In with that you can also put six peeled truffles cut up small.

In the same way you can do oysters, both those that have steeped in a seasoning and salted ones, cockles of all sorts, razor clams and telleen clams, *poveraccie*,[207.2] limpets and mussels. Those *crostate* can be served as tourtes.

208. To prepare a *crostata* of shelled snails.

Get snails that have been thoroughly purged and boil them in water so they are well cooked. Remove them from their shell, taking the better part of them; wash them again and purge them with salt.[208] Then sauté them with beaten onions. Have a butter-greased tourte pan ready, lined with three sheets of very thin dough, brushed with butter between each, and with the flaky-pastry twist around it. In the shell put beaten mint and marjoram, raisins and seeded muscatel raisins cut up small; sprinkle everything with pepper, cloves, cinnamon, sugar and salt. Then

---

[207.1] The *compositione* or 'mixture' is the raisins and herbs; the *sapore* or 'flavouring' or 'sauce' is the sweet spice mixture.

[207.2] See Recipe III,193.

[208] See Recipe III,199.

put in the snails, with as much again of the mixture over them as is under them, and sprinkle that with the same spices. You can also put in a little grated Parmesan cheese, adding a little verjuice or orange juice. Cover it over with two more layers of dough with a few strips of flaky pastry on top. Bake it in an oven or braise it. Serve it hot, garnished with sugar and rosewater.

You can do tourtes the same way with snails, having beaten them before frying them. For a fasting day, instead of butter use oil, and instead of cheese, old walnuts, shelled and crushed.

209. To prepare a *crostata* of the viscera of any sort of turtle.

Get the liver without the gallbladder, and shell-less eggs. For every pound of them, get three ounces of salted eel flesh, cooked and ground in a mortar, with an ounce of fine *mostaccioli*. Sauté the liver and eggs a little in butter. Then have a tourte pan prepared with three sheets of dough like the ones above, and the flaky-pastry twist around it. In that shell put beaten mint and marjoram, raisins, pepper, cloves, sugar and cinnamon; on that mixture put the liver, eggs and ground eel, moistened with orange juice or verjuice, and then as much again of the mixture as was put beneath. Sprinkle on the same spices. Cover the pan over with two more sheets of dough and a few strips of flaky pastry. Bake it in an oven or braise it. Serve it with sugar and rosewater over top.

Instead of the eel you can grind up field mushrooms, moistening them with orange juice or verjuice, and put the mixture on top; and instead of the butter, oil of sweet almonds or of olives. If you want to make it with meat of the same turtle, boil the turtle until it is well done, then take the flesh and give it the same sautéing. Follow the directions above for making the *crostata*.

210. To prepare a *crostata* of frogs' liver and flesh.

Get the flesh and liver of frogs that must first be steeped in several changes of water; with the flesh raw and the liver with the gallbladder removed, sauté them in butter or oil. Then follow the directions given for the *crostata* of a sturgeon's viscera in Recipes 198 and 199.

211. To prepare a *crostata* of salted anchovies.

Get anchovies and wash them in wine. Split them in half lengthwise and remove their spine. Have a tourte pan prepared with the three sheets of dough and the twist; in the shell there should be beaten mint and marjoram, ordinary raisins and seeded muscatel raisins, sprinkled with pepper, cinnamon, cloves and nutmeg. Set out the anchovies, and on them put as much of the mixture as is put under them. You can separate them also with a sheet of dough fried in butter;[211] and if you want to put in thin slices of fresh provatura, that is up to you. Cover it

---

[211] See Recipe 52.

over with two more similar sheets of dough, with flaky-pastry strips on top. When it is baked it is served garnished with sugar and rosewater.

For a day in Lent, instead of the butter and provatura, use oil and shelled, crushed pinenuts.

212. To prepare a *crostata* of salted tuna belly or of other salted fish.

Get three pounds of salted tuna belly that is not rancid, and let it steep in several changes of water until most of its salt is gone. Boil it, changing the water again; when it is almost cooked, take it out. Cut it up into thin slices and let it sit in vinegar and must syrup. Have a buttered tourte pan prepared with the three sheets of dough like the ones above and with the flaky-pastry twist around it. On the shell put sugar, pepper, cloves, cinnamon, beaten mint and marjoram, raisins and seeded muscatel raisins, crushed pinenuts and pitted prunes that have first steeped. Then onto those ingredients put the thin slices of tuna belly with a few little lumps of butter, fresh provatura or some other unsalted cheese, and as much again of the same ingredients as are under the tuna belly. If you want to make more layers, that is an option. If you want to put a fried sheet of dough in the middle, making two layers with the same ingredients and the tuna belly, that can be done. Then cover it over with two more sheets of dough and a few strips of flaky pastry over the top. Bake it in an oven or braise it. Serve it hot, splashed with rosewater and sprinkled with sugar.

For a day in Lent, use oil instead of butter. You can also put in some spring onions, beaten and sautéed. If you want to make a tourte of it, beat the tuna belly very small, mix in the other ingredients, adding eggs and fresh ricotta. During Lent, instead of eggs and ricotta use marzipan paste and raw eggs of another fish.

In the same way you can do smoked tuna belly,[212] salmon and salted eel, and mullet after it has steeped and been scaled because mullet cannot be parboiled.

213. To prepare a *crostata* of mullet caviar, sturgeon back, smoked herring back and caviar.

Get a tourte pan lined with the three sheets of dough and the flaky-pastry twist around it; in that shell should be the same mixture and spices as are used in the preceding recipe for tuna belly. Then on that make a layer of thin slices of caviar and mullet caviar, some herring back with that fish's milt or eggs, and some sturgeon back, sprinkling that with sugar. On it put as much again of the same mixture as was put underneath, with orange juice. You repeat, making two layers like that; and if you want to put a fried sheet of dough in the middle, that is optional. Cover it over with two more sheets of dough with a few strips of flaky pastry on top. Bake it in an oven. When it is done, serve it hot, sprinkled with sugar and splashed with rosewater.

On a fasting day, instead of butter use sweet-almond oil or olive oil. On a meat day you can put thin slices of fresh, unsalted cheese into that *crostata*.

---

[212] This is the *sorra* seen in Recipes III,207 and 208.

214. To prepare a *crostata* of mushrooms for a day in Lent in the spring.

Get field mushrooms that have been scraped and are thoroughly cleaned of sand; wash them well. If they are big, cut them up into small bits. Sauté them in oil. Have a butter-greased tourte pan ready, lined with three sheets of dough in it made with fine flour, warmed almond milk or pinenut milk, and sugar.[214] On that shell spread the mushrooms mixed with beaten mint and marjoram, thin slices of parboiled desalted tuna belly and seeded muscatel raisins; sprinkle everything with pepper, cloves, cinnamon and sugar, and either orange juice or verjuice over top. Cover it with two more similar sheets of dough brushed with oil between them. Bake it in an oven or braise it.

You can do all sorts of fresh funghi the same way, as well as fresh, tender peas and beans. Serve it hot.

215. To prepare a *crostata* of prunes and dried visciola cherries and other things.

Get prunes and dried visciola cherries that have steeped and pit them. Then get clean dates, parboiled and cut up into bits, seeded muscatel raisins, currants, dried figs from barrels[215] cut up into bits, pinenuts and pistachios, shelled and steeped, pepper, cinnamon, cloves, nutmeg and sugar; mix all that together. There should be the same amount of each fruit. Then have a tourte pan prepared, brushed with almond oil and lined with three very thin sheets of dough made of fine flour, pinenut milk, oil, sugar and salt; between each of the sheets of dough, almond oil should be brushed. Put the filling into the pan. If you want to put a butter-fried sheet of dough the size of the pan in the middle, that is an option; that way you can make more layers. Cover it over with two more thin sheets of dough, and a third one fashioned in a variety of ways. Bake it in an oven or braise it, sprinkled with sugar. Serve it hot.

Into that you can put some truffles. If you want to make a tourte of it, mix raw fish eggs in with everything, and more herbs.

216. To prepare flaky-pastry *pizze* for a day in Lent.

Get two pounds of flour, warmed milk made from either six ounces of Milanese almonds or else one pound of shelled pinenuts, three ounces of sugar, two ounces of rosewater, one ounce of salt and two ounces of sweet-almond oil; mix all that together with the flour and make up a dough of it that is not too firm. Knead it well for a quarter of an hour, and make a long, thin sheet of it. Brush it with sweet-almond oil or olive oil, sprinkle it with sugar and cinnamon, and roll it up like a wafer cornet. When the twist is made, make tiny wheels[216.1] of it,

---

[214] And, of course, with olive oil (see the upper crust) brushed between each of the sheets of dough.

[215] It is not clear why Scappi should specify *fichi secchi di barili*.

[216.1] These *ruotoli picciolini* seem to be transverse slices of the twist, which – by what Scappi writes – are flattened without being turned on end.

and make *pizze* of those wheels by spreading them out with the heel of your hand. Those *pizze* can be baked in a tourte pan like tourtes, or else you can fry them in oil. Serve them hot with sugar over them.

With that sheet of dough you can make twists filled with sugar, cinnamon, wine-cooked raisins, crushed pinenuts and seeded muscatel raisins. Then bake them the way tourtes are done, or else fry them.

That dough can also be used to make small flans stuffed with a mixture made up as directed for the prune *crostata* in Recipe 215. As well you can use it for making large or small tortellini filled with marzipan paste,[216.2] and other preparations that have to be fried.[216.3]

217. To prepare plain napoleons[217.1] for a day in Lent.

Get a piece of dough made as above. With it make eight very thin sheets the size of the tourte pan you will be using, and one a little bigger than the other ones. Have the pan ready with a coating of oil and into it put the larger sheet of dough[217.2] and then the other eight sheets, each one brushed with sweet-almond oil and sprinkled with sugar and cinnamon. Into the last sheet bumps or some other design should be worked. Brush the top with oil. Bake it. When they are almost done, give it a glazing with sugar. Serve it hot.

Sometimes you can intersperse green or dry elderflowers between the sheets of dough.

218. To prepare a cinnamon tourte, or some other sort.

Get a pound of Milanese almonds and grind them with a pound of sugar, two ounces of Neapolitan *mostaccioli*, three ounces of pinenut paste, one ounce of cinnamon, four ounces of clarified honey,[218.1] two ounces of dried peaches that have steeped, and two ounces of candied orange peel. When everything has been ground up in a mortar, add in a beaker of rosewater to make the mixture thinner. Then have a tourte pan ready, lined with a rather thick sheet of dough made of fine flour, salt, oil, pinenut milk and sugar; put the filling into it. That tourte should not be too deep. Cover it over with another sheet of dough worked in any of a variety of ways. Bake it with a low heat, giving it a glazing of sugar and rosewater. Serve it hot or cold as you like.

[216.2] See the *tortelletti di Marzapane* in Recipe 229, below.

[216.3] Such pasties would include the small flans seen, for instance, in Recipes 19, 151 and 230 ff.

[217.1] *sfogliate semplici.* See Recipe 49, above.

[217.2] This larger, and perhaps thicker, round of dough will form the sides of the 'pie,' containing the multilayered sweet cinnamon puff.

[218.1] For the 1581 printing the typesetter confused two of the amounts: ... *mostaccioli Napoletani, tre oncie di mele monde, due oncie di pignoccati, & un'oncia di cannella, quattro oncie di mele monde* ...

In the same way you can make a marzipaned tourte[218.2] made of ground almonds, sugar and rosewater; or else marzipan paste. You can also make a tourte that same way with various candied fruits mixed with marzipan paste and pinenut paste ground up with them. And for a tourte that you want to have a slightly roasted flavour, put in orange juice or verjuice.

219. To prepare a tourte of spinach with fresh eel flesh for a day in Lent.

Get the tenderest parts of spinach, wash them well and sauté them in oil. When they are done, drain off the water they exude and beat them small with knives. With them put ordinary raisins, seeded muscatel raisins, steeped pinenuts, dates cooked in wine and cut up small, thick almond milk, dried figs cut up small, sugar, pepper, cinnamon, cloves and enough salt. Then have skinned eels cut into rounds, deboned, and boiled or roasted on a spit. Put that flesh, in small chunks, into the mixture. Have a tourte pan ready, greased with a good almond oil or olive oil, and lined with a rather thick sheet of dough made of fine flour, warm pinenut milk, rosewater, sugar and salt. Put the filling, neither too thick nor too thin, onto the dough in the pan. Cover it over with another sheet of dough made like a jalousie shutter or in some other fashion. Bake it in an oven. When it is almost done, give it a glazing of sugar and rosewater.

If you do not want the eel in small chunks, grind up the flesh in a mortar. If you cannot get fresh eel, take some salted eel that has steeped and parboiled. Serve it hot.

You can do the back flesh of a big grey mullet the same way, after its bones have been removed and it has boiled or roasted on a grill; and the flesh of a conger. The amount of each ingredient is at the discretion of the person doing the tourte.

220. To prepare a tourte of spinach and other aromatic herbs for a day in Lent.

Get tender spinach and sauté it in a very good oil. When that is done, strain the liquid away and beat the spinach small, adding in beaten mint, marjoram and burnet, raisins, seeded muscatel raisins, old nuts ground in a mortar along with caviar and water-soaked breadcrumb, and pepper, cinnamon, sugar and a little sautéed spring onion; the amount of each is at the cook's discretion. Have a tourte pan oiled and prepared with a rather thick sheet of dough; put the filling into it. Cover the tourte with another sheet of dough made like a jalousie or rippled. Bake it in an oven or braise it. When it is almost done, give it a glazing with sugar. Serve it hot.

Into that filling you can combine boiled crayfish tails, and[220] snails sautéed with spring onions, and also peeled field mushrooms, or else a few thin slices of apple, and many other sorts of ingredient, depending on the cook's judgement.

[218.2] Full directions for this *torta marzapanata* are given in Recipe VI,120.

[220] The *and*s in this sentence may be alternatives.

221. To prepare a tourte of cardoons for a day in Lent.

Get a cardoon, clean the best part of it and let it steep for two hours. Cut its heart into several slices and boil those in water, salt and sweet-almond oil. When they are done, beat them small with knives, adding in a handful of beaten fine herbs and, for every pound of that mixture, four ounces of truffles, peeled and cut up small, one and a half ounces of ground *mostaccioli*, two ounces of shelled pinenuts, steeped and crushed, three ounces of very clean currants, four ounces of sugar, half an ounce of cinnamon, half an ounce of pepper, enough salt, orange juice and three ounces of almond oil. Mix everything together. Make up a tourte with it using two sheets of dough. Bake it in an oven or braise it. When it is almost done, give it a glazing with sugar. Serve it hot.

You can do artichoke hearts, boiled and beaten, the same way, and Neapolitan palm branch shoots.[221]

222. To prepare a tourte of asparagus, cultivated and wild.

Get asparagus tips, parboil them and beat them small. Mix them into the filling of Recipe 220 above, except for the caviar. Make up a tourte with them as directed in that recipe.

223. To prepare a tourte of fresh funghi.

Get morels or else the mushroom that grows in the woods at the foot of chestnut trees and briar bushes, which is round and firm and tends toward an orange colour. The safest thing is to bring them to a boil in water, though they are much more flavourful raw. In any case, whether raw or cooked, peel them carefully, beat them small with a knife and sauté them in oil. Then get those ingredients that are used above in Recipe 222, adding in beaten and sautéed spring onions or else a small clove of garlic. Make up a tourte with them in the way outlined in the above recipe.

In the same way you can do any sort of salted fungus that has steeped and been parboiled.

224. To prepare a tourte of dried peas and other legumes.

Get dried peas that have steeped and cook them. When they are done, take them out of their bouillon and grind them in a mortar. For every pound of them, add four ounces of Milanese almonds into the mortar and grind them together. Put the mash through a colander[224.1] and add in a little of their fat broth,[224.2] four ounces of spring onion, beaten and sautéed, a handful of beaten fine herbs,

---

[221] The 1570 typesetter's *palmette* suffered a metathesis of the *a* and *l* when the book was again set in type in 1581: *plamette*.

[224.1] This *foratora* is pictured in Plates 9 and 10, this latter engraving showing a handle.

[224.2] This *brodo grasso* seems to refer to the peas' cooking water that still has particles of the peas in it.

four ounces of clean currants, an ounce of pepper, half an ounce of cinnamon, six ounces of sugar and enough saffron. Make up the tourte with the two sheets of dough and bake it in an oven or braise it. When it is almost done, give it a glazing with sugar and rosewater.

In the same way you can do it with dried chickpeas, haricot beans, lentils, common vetch or broad beans in their pod,[224.3] whenever they are cooked in the above manner.

225. To prepare a tourte with split chickpeas.

Get split chickpeas that are clean, well washed and cooked in water and oil. When they are done, put them through a strainer. For every pound of the strained chickpeas add in two ounces of ground fine *mostaccioli*, beaten fine herbs, a little sautéed spring onion, one ounce of pepper and cinnamon combined, eight ounces of sugar, a little saffron, and three ounces of almond oil to keep it soft. Then have an oiled tourte pan prepared with a rather thick sheet of dough in it, and put the filling into the pan. Cover it over with another sheet of dough made like a shutter's slats or in some other manner. Bake it in an oven or braise it, and give it a glazing. Serve it hot.

You can do the same with split broad beans.

226. To prepare a tourte of a gurnard.

Get the flesh of a gurnard that has first been boiled and deboned. For every two pounds of flesh, get a pound of shelled Milanese almonds, and grind all that in a mortar with a pound of sugar, six ounces of steeped pinenuts and two ounces of starch flour;[226] moisten everything with the bouillon in which the fish was cooked, strain it so the mixture is not too thin. Add six ounces of very clean currants in with that; if you want to put in a handful of beaten fine herbs, pepper and cinnamon, that is up to you. If you want it white, though, you will put in only ground ginger and salt. Then have a tourte pan ready, coated with almond oil and lined with a rather thick sheet of dough. Put the filling into it, and cover it over with a sheet fashioned like a jalousie or some other fancy work. Bake it in an oven or braise it. Serve it hot or cold as you like.

You can do the flesh of a sea bass the same way, and a pike, when they are boiled in water.

227. To prepare an almond-milk tourte.

Get a pound of Milanese almonds, grind them in a mortar with a pound of sugar, five ounces of starch flour and four ounces of steeped pinenuts; moisten all that with a pound and a half of pike bouillon that is not too salty and with three ounces of rosewater. If everything has been ground up thoroughly there is

---

[224.3] *fava di scorza.*

[226] *farina d'amido.* This traditional variety of thickener was made by drying steeped flour.

no need to strain it. Put it all into a casserole pot and cook the mixture, stirring it constantly with a wooden spoon. As it begins to thicken, take it off the fire and let it cool. Make a tourte of it with the two sheets of dough the way the previous ones are done.

You can also put that filling into a tourte pan without it being cooked, though for it not to have the flavour of the starch flour it is cooked first. If you want to alter the colour of that tourte, put in cinnamon, saffron and raisins and it will become yellow; if you want it green, spinach juice. That tourte is served hot or cold. When the filling is cooked in a casserole pot it can be served as a thick soup with sugar and cinnamon over it.

228. To prepare a tourte of starch for a day in Lent.

Get a pound of ground marzipan paste, three ounces of pinenut paste, four ounces of starch cooked in almond milk[228] and sugar. Mix all that together with three ounces of rosewater and with it make a tourte by following the directions for making a rather thick shell in a tourte pan that has been brushed with sweet-almond oil. Cover it over with another sheet of dough, either bumpy or like a shutter's slats. Bake it in an oven or braise it. Serve it hot or cold as you wish with sugar and rosewater over it.

[Lean tortellini, flans, *crostoli*, fritters]

229. To prepare tortellini of marzipan or various other fillings.

Get a pound of shelled Milanese almonds, four ounces of pinenut paste and one pound of sugar, and grind them together with three ounces of rosewater.[229.1] With that make large or small tortellini, in a pastry shell made as in the preceding recipe and cut with a pastry wheel or with a wooden dough-cutter,[229.2] and fry them in oil. When they are done serve them hot, garnished with sugar.

In the same way you can make tortellini with the fillings used in all the *crostate* and tourtes described above.

230. To prepare small flans with various fillings.

Get fine flour and make a dough of it with white wine, rosewater, sugar, salt, oil and saffron, ensuring, though, that there is more rosewater than white wine;

---

[228] This is the reading of the first printing: *pignoccati, oncie quattro d'amido cotto con latte d'amandole.* In the 1581 reprint, the ingredients are copied as *pignoccati, oncie quattro d'amandole,* 'pinenut paste, four ounces of almonds.'

[229.1] For Lancelot de Casteau's readers marzipan is exotic enough a preparation that he gives it a recipe: *Pour faire Marsepain (Ouverture de cuisine,* 58). This is a plain combination of ground almonds, sifted sugar and rosewater, but lacks Scappi's pinenuts.

[229.2] See the first implement, a *sperone,* in Plates 14 and 15; the second, a goblet-like *bussolo* for stamping out a circle of dough, in Plate 12.

everything should be warm. Make up the dough so that it is not too firm, and with it roll out a long, very thin sheet. Then get shelled, steeped pinenuts, dates parboiled in wine and cut up small, very clean currants parboiled in wine, and seeded muscatel raisins cut up small; mix all that together with sugar, cinnamon and a little beaten mint and marjoram. With that filling make small flans with a pastry shell as directed above. Fry them in very good oil. Serve them hot with sugar over them.

You can make small flans that way with all the above *crostate* and tourtes – that is, with their fillings. And with that dough you can make *crostoli*[230] and other pieces that are fried in oil.

231. To prepare small flans with the flesh of fresh eels.

Get a fresh, skinned eel that is cut in rounds and roasted on a spit. Split the rounds in half through the middle and remove the bone. Have a sheet of dough made up of flour, rosewater, white wine, salt and either olive oil or warm pinenut oil. Sprinkle the eel with pepper, sugar, cinnamon and cloves. Set two or three pieces of it onto the sheet of dough[231.1] which is thin and a palm in width; next, onto the eel put raisins and a little beaten mint and marjoram. Roll the dough up around the eel, making three layers like wafer cornets. When the small flan has been made, brush the dough[231.2] and pinch it together so none of the filling can come out. On each side of it give it three slashes with a pastry wheel. Fry them in oil. When they are done, serve them hot, garnished with sugar.

232. Various ways to make *crostoli* for a Lenten day.[232.1]

Get an ounce of leaven and a pound of flour. Make that up into dough with pinenut oil that is made with a little white wine, and rosewater, plain warm water, salt, sugar and oil; to colour it, a little saffron. When the dough is made, and not too stiff, roll it out into a thin sheet. With that you can make knots, tresses and other pieces, making use of it before making a *crostolo*.[232.2] Fry it in oil. When they are done, serve them in dishes garnished with honey and sugar.

---

[230] Scappi's term here and in Recipe 232 is *grostoli*. They are deep-fried bits of pastry for which directions are given in Recipe 232. In 1549 Messisbugo also described varieties of *grostoli*.

[231.1] Scappi might usefully have specified that the pieces be set at one of the narrower ends of the rolled-out dough.

[231.2] Presumably with eggwhite.

[232.1] Scappi's word, here and in Recipe 230, is *grostoli*. Zingarelli (*Vocabulario della lingua italiana*) defines the modern *crostoli*, cognate with *crosta*, 'crust,' as 'the name used in Trentino for *cenci*.' The same dictionary states: '*cencio*, a sweet of egg-dough cut in rounds, rectangles or strips and fried, typical of Carnival.'

[232.2] *addoppiandola prima che si faccia il grostolo*. This instruction seems to suggest that Scappi considers the frying of the dough to be the defining step in making his *grostoli*.

If you want to make balls with that dough, follow the directions given in Recipe 134. If you want them to come out white, change the oil with each ball. Serve them with honey and sugar over top of them. You can also make that dough without the pinenut oil, but with only wine, water, oil, sugar and salt.

233. To prepare a batter with which to make fritters and other pieces.

Get fine flour and put it into a glazed earthenware or tinned copper pot; make a batter of it with water, white wine, cool oil and salt, and tinge it with saffron. Beat it enough with a wooden spoon that it becomes like a runny glue. Then get casting moulds – that is, lions, eagles, knots and other fanciful shapes; heat the moulds up in oil, and follow the directions given for making the pieces in Recipe 145. Serve them hot, with sugar over them.

Those batter shapes are sometimes filled with various fillings. The batter can also be used for making fritters with bay leaves and sprigs of rosemary and sage, adding in dried grapes steeped in hot wine, and a little leaven and sugar. The batter will be quite a bit better for making fritters after it has sat in a hot place. Every sort of fritter needs to be served hot with sugar and honey over the top of it.

234. To prepare a batter with which you can make various sorts of fritter.

Get a pound of Milanese almonds and grind them in a mortar, moistening them with three pounds of warm water. Heat that milk up. Have two ounces of leaven moistened with warm water; put it into the almond milk along with a little salt, four ounces of sugar, eight ounces of white wine, four ounces of oil, two pounds of fine flour and a little saffron to colour it. Beat the batter for half an hour with a wooden spoon. Let it sit in a hot place for three hours. Beat it again with the spoon. Cover the pot over and let it sit for half an hour where it is moderately warm, then beat it one more time. Test it in hot oil and if the batter puffs up it will be exactly as it should be; otherwise beat it again and let it sit. Then with the spoon make the fritters, large or small as you wish. When they are done they need to be served hot from the pan with sugar on them. If you want to give them a sharp[234.1] flavour with herbs, make the batter thinner and put in finely chopped bitter herbs.

With that batter you can make fritters with parsnips after they have been parboiled. As well, you can make fritters of salted sardines and anchovies, apple slices and bryony[234.2] cut up into thin slices, boiled white leeks, boiled crayfish tails, sprigs of rosemary and sage, and other things. You can also make the batter without almond milk but with warm water alone and more flour.

[234.1] Scappi writes *amare* here and at the end of this sentence: 'bitter.'

[234.2] The *cocuzze marine* may be compared with the *zucche marine* in Recipes III,225 and 227.

235. To prepare rice fritters.

Get one pound of rice, clean it, wash it in several changes of water and put it on the fire with enough cool water to cover it. When it has absorbed the water, get milk made from a pound of almonds and half a pound of sugar; put half of it[235.1] in and add the rest gradually until it is well cooked and thick. When it is cooked spread it out on a small table and let it dry by itself. Then take it and make little balls of it the size of half a Florentine ball;[235.2] coat those little balls with a batter made of fine flour, water, salt, oil and white wine. Fry them in oil. When they are done, serve them hot with sugar on them.

You can do them differently: when the rice is dry, grind it in a mortar adding in the crumb of a loaf of bread soaked in the broth that the rice cooked in. Then make little balls of it as above, coat them in fine flour and fry them in oil. Serve them hot, garnished with sugar.

236. To prepare a piece made of batter with a syringe.

Get a pound of clear water, half a pound of wine, four ounces of oil, two ounces of sugar, one ounce of leaven moistened with that water, a little salt and saffron; boil everything in a casserole pot. As it is boiling, get fine flour and put it in gradually, stirring it with a wooden spoon until it thickens. Remove it and grind it in a mortar for a quarter of an hour. If that batter is too thick, add in a little wine and oil. Then have a pan with good olive oil hot in it. Put the paste into a syringe, and force it out into the hot oil. In that way you can make knots and other fanciful things. When it is cooked, take it out and serve it with sugar on it.

You can also do it without a syringe, only by rolling the dough out and forming it like *ciambelle*,[236] not putting any flour on it as you knead it but coating your hand with very good oil.

237. To prepare dainty biscuit morsels.[237.1]

Get two pounds of white breadcrumb and bake it a second time.[237.2] Grind it in a mortar and put it through a sieve so it becomes like flour. For every pound of that sieved substance, add as much again of fine flour, two and a half pounds of finely sieved sugar and four ounces of leaven ground in a mortar and moistened with fifteen fresh eggs; then everything should be mixed together with

---

[235.1] That is, the almond milk, added in stages as the rice cooks.

[235.2] We have been told in Recipe III,195 that a *palla Fiorentina* is roughly the size of sea urchin.

[236] That is, in rings or spirals.

[237.1] *morselletti di biscotti*: See also the recipe for *mostaccioli*, called *morselletti* as here, in Recipes VI,142 (where they are qualified as Milanese) and 143.

[237.2] Scappi's direction is *facciasi biscottare*. This verb is compiled of *bis* and *cotto*, reflecting the double cooking of, literally, a bis-cuit. Toward the end of this recipe Scappi will call it *pan biscottato*, 'double-baked bread.'

three-quarters of an ounce of raw anise ground into powder and four ounces of rosewater. When everything is thoroughly mixed and beaten together so that it looks like fritter batter, let it sit for two hours in a warm place. Beat it again, adding in four more eggs and an ounce of salt; then let it sit for another hour. Then have a buttered tourte pan and put the filling into it so it is a finger's width in depth. Put that into an oven that is not too hot. Leave it there until it is dry. Remove it and with a sharp knife cut it into little long rectangles, as wide or narrow as you like. Just as soon as they have been cut up, put them immediately into marzipan tourte pans,[237.3] set out apart with paper under them, and put them back into the oven with a very moderate heat. Leave them there for half an hour, turning them several times until they have firmed up. In order to keep them white, keep them covered with rag paper.

In that filling instead of wheat flour you could use the same amount of starch flour, though with more leaven and more eggs. You can also make biscuits like that with fine flour, eggs, sugar, coriander flour[237.4] and musk. And instead of flour you can do it with double-baked white bread, powdered, eggs, sugar and leaven. And when you put them into the tourte pan to cook them, instead of greasing the pan you put wafers or host wafers under them.

If you want to do it differently, see the Book titled On Convalescents, separate from this Fifth Book, at Recipe 142.

End of Book Five.

[237.3] *tortiere da marzapane* are shallow oven dishes.

[237.4] This *fior di coriandole* may well be understood as the cluster of seed pods contained in the 'coriander flower' and implying either the finely ground seeds, as seems generally to be the case with Scappi's 'fennel flower/flour,' or whole coriander seeds. Only in several of the menus in Book IV does Scappi write the word *coriandole*. For every other occurence of the spice, in some twenty recipes, Scappi writes *pitartamo*.

Book VI

Dishes for the Sick[i]

I t seems to me that I should have done nothing, after having in the five books instructed you[ii] about mastering various sorts of dishes suitable for healthy people, had I not shown you as well how to go about making prepared potions,[iii] broths, concentrates, pastes, barley dishes and many other preparations needed by the sick and convalescent, all of which preparations I have proved with many gentlemen when they have been indisposed, and above all with the Most Reverend Cardinal di Carpi, of blessed memory, during his long illness,[iv] as both you and they know. In this they can confidently take the word of his Excellency Federigo Donati, personal physician to Our Lord, and of the Reverend Alessandro Casale, His Holiness's Chamberlain. Those persons have urged me to agree to publish this present opuscule and to dedicate it, along with the other five books, to the Reverend Francesco Reinoso,[v] personal Steward of Our Lord. However, as occasion demands, you will be called on to serve one or another of these preparations, working with all the assiduity and dependability that I have always demonstrated to you.

---

[i] Properly, Scappi's title is 'On Convalescents': *Libro sesto et ultimo. De convalescenti.* There may be evidence, in this choice of term, of a reluctance to appear to usurp a physician's prerogative to prescribe therapeutics, including food, for those who are actually in the throes of some illness. Throughout this Book VI Scappi continually shows the greatest deference to the opinions of court physicians. Nevertheless, in the first sentence of this new book he does write of preparing food for *gl'infermi*, the sick.

In Recipe III,144 Scappi refers to the *libro de geli, et sapori*, the 'book on jellies and sauces.' That designation would appear to apply to those recipes from 186 of this present book to the book's end. In that designation is a hint of an earlier form of the diverse contents of Book VI.

[ii] Scappi is still addressing his 'apprentice,' Giovanni. See both the title page and the beginning of Book I where the intended reader is called Scappi's *discepolo*.

[iii] These *acque cotte*, literally 'cooked waters,' will constitute the opening section of Scappi's Book VI. In all cases the water does undergo a boiling. See Plate 12 for the basic operation.

[iv] Rodolfo Pio da Carpi, senior cardinal and dean of the Sacred College of Cardinals, died on 2 May 1564 after a four-month illness, in great pain and unable to eat or to speak. See Recipe 21, below.

[v] The dedication of Scappi's whole work is indeed to *Don Francesco Reinoso, Scalco et Cameriero secreto della Santità di N. S. Pio Quinto.*

535

[To make various sorts of prepared potions.^{v}]

As far as making decoctions of potions is concerned, my experience has shown that purified rainwater and water from cisterns^{vi} and from a few rivers such as the Tiber and the Po are excellent. The opposite are waters from lakes, ponds, snow-melts and ice-melts.^{vii}

1. To cook a plain potion.

Get one of the above waters and boil it in a clean pot either of glazed earthenware that has not been used for anything else, or else of tinned copper, until two-thirds of its quantity has boiled away. Then let it cool, putting it through a white cloth into another pot, watching that the scum – that is, any sediment – does not get poured off. If you want to cook it in a glass pot, something like a large double carafe,$^{1.1}$ when the flask is filled, it is put on a brick by the fire and let boil until it has reduced by three fingers. Take the carafe off the fire with great care, letting it cool by itself because there is a great risk of it breaking. When the water has cooled, follow the above direction for filtering it.

It will also cook another way. When the large glass carafe is filled, or else an earthenware pitcher,$^{1.2}$ get a cauldron with cold water in it on a tripod on the fire, and put the carafe or pitcher into that so that it is under the water up to its neck. Let the water in the cauldron boil until the water in the carafe or pitcher has reduced by three fingers. Take the pitcher$^{1.3}$ out and let it cool; take the carafe

---

^{v} The Table at the end of this Book VI shows a section heading that includes Recipes 1–10 and that reads *Per fare diverse acque cotte con piu materie*. We have chosen the word 'potion' to translate the prepared *acqua* that will be served up to an invalid, keeping 'water' for the raw material. Although the word 'cook' may seem a strange thing to do to water, we have kept it in the rubric to each of these recipes. Two 'waters' absent from this series of recipes are rosewater and musk water, perhaps because in Scappi's kitchen they had become flavourants – see Recipes 35, below: 'rosewater to give it flavour,' and 139 where rosewater and musk water are optional – and not primarily pharmaceutical.

The basic 'process' for making *acque cotte* is illustrated in the engraving at the foot of Plate 12.

^{vi} Scappi uses the same word *conserva* for the water tanks that can be seen in the first of the engraved plates accompanying his work. They seem to be the immediate source of water for most kitchen work.

^{vii} It is surprising that in this survey Scappi does not pass judgement on well water or spring water, which may, though, be the origin of supply for his *conserve*.

$^{1.1}$ *un caraffone doppio*: It was fairly common to use two glass flasks, the inner one containing a food to be cooked and the outer one with boiling water. In Plate 12 the larger flask on the hearth holds another in its mouth.

$^{1.2}$ A metal *cucumo* can be seen in Plate 10.

$^{1.3}$ The earthenware *cucumo* (here) and the glass *caraffone* (below) are to be handled differently.

out of the boiling water and put it into warm water. Filter[1.4] the water as above.

2. To cook a ferous potion.[2.1]

Get the water and boil it in an earthenware or copper pot for a quarter of an hour; put it into another pot to cool. Have pieces of steel[2.2] heated in the fire which you will dip into the water several times because, according to the Physician,[2.3] the more they are dipped all the more constipating the potion becomes. If you do not have any steel, get a worn-down iron horseshoe and heat it up instead of the steel. Let the water sit three hours, then filter it slowly through three layers of a white cloth where there is a large piece of white sponge.

You can filter it alternatively, though it will take more time: get a piece of white linen, put it completely into the water, then take a little of it out of the water; under that corner of the cloth you hold a fine receptacle to catch the water dripping from the cloth. The more times the water drips that way, even though with the strength of the fire it will still be slightly cloudy, the better it will be.

3. To cook a potion of anise, sugar and cinnamon.

Get whatever amount of water you want and boil it for more than half an hour in either a glazed earthenware pot or a large glass double carafe. For every two and two-thirds litres[3.1] of water, add in one ounce of anise. When it has boiled for another quarter of an hour, put in two ounces of fine sugar, carefully skimming it so the anise does not get pushed out. When it has boiled for another quarter of an hour, you will put in a quarter-ounce of whole cinnamon, immediately taking the pot off the fire and keeping the lid on it until it is half cooled: that is done so the water can pick up the essence[3.2] of the cinnamon. When it is cold, filter it through white cloths, though it would be better to put it through a filter cone[3.3] of coarse

---

[1.4] The typesetter's *tolisi* was corrected to *colisi* in subsequent editions.

[2.1] *acqua ferrata*.

[2.2] Scappi specifies *acciaro* here, not merely *ferro*, iron.

[2.3] The word *il Phisico* is normally set with a capital letter in this Book VI. If it is a particular individual to whom Scappi alludes (rather to a generic functionary), he may perhaps have in mind Federigo Donati, the pope's personal physician, whom he mentioned in the preamble above and whom Giovanni certainly knew.

[3.1] *per ogni boccale*.

[3.2] When Scappi uses the word *sustanza* here, it is clear that his thinking is influenced by physical and medical theory that was long established in Europe. To every physical entity, including foodstuffs, was attributed a set of properties that determined its essence or nature. For the most efficacious therapeutic use of a substance a physician (or cook) had to be aware of the essence of that substance and to know how best to extract it. Cinnamon was generally understood to be warm and dry in the third degree out of four, properties useful for combatting an indisposition marked by excessive cold and moisture.

[3.3] See an illustration of this *calzetta* in Plates 2 and 18.

white wool with a bit of sponge at its bottom. That potion will have a cinnamon colour to it.

4. To cook a cinnamon potion.

Get the amount of water you want and cook it as above. When it has boiled for half an hour and been reduced by three fingers, for every two and two-thirds litres of water put in a quarter of an ounce of whole cinnamon. Bring it to a boil with that, let it cool, keeping the pot sealed with cloths. Filter it the above way.

5. To cook a potion of dried figs, jujubes, currants and liquorice that is called pectoral.

Get the amount of water you will want and boil it in a glazed earthenware pot or in a large carafe as above, along with the above ingredients – that is, figs cut up into small pieces, whole jujubes,[5.1] raisins that are very clean or, preferably, washed; you will not put in the liquorice[5.2] until it has been boiled half an hour because it gives off a slight bitterness and too much colour. Skim it carefully. When it has cooked, filter it through a cloth or a filter cone as directed above. In summer it goes bad quickly; in winter it will not last more than three days. Sometimes hulled barley is thrown in with the other things, and Spanish honey or an excellent honey of some other origin. That will depend on the Physician's prescription.

6. To cook a mastic potion.[6]

Get five and a third litres of water, amounting to twelve pounds; for each two and two-thirds litres get a quarter-ounce of mastic and boil it slowly in one of the

---

[5.1] These dark-red, olive-sized berries, *giuggiole* in Scappi's text, are native to the Mediterranean. Long valued by Arabic physicians, the fruit enjoyed a pharmaceutical reputation and was traditionally associated with the plant eaten by Homer's lotus-eaters. See Alain Touwaide's study of the *ziziphus*, 'The Jujube Tree in the Eastern Mediterranean: A Case Study in the Methodology of Textual Archeobotany,' *Health and Healing from the Medieval Garden* (Woodbridge, Suffolk: The Boydell Press, 2008), 72–100. Aldobrandino da Siena (*Le Régime du corps*, ed. Landouzy and Pépin, 51) lists the berry among medicines with cold properties.

[5.2] Miguel Gual Camarena notes that the liquorice root that was produced in Spain for export was handled by English merchants as early as 1371: *Vocabulario del comercio medieval*, 403. It was used as both a sweetener and a medicine. An Anglo-Norman medical poem of the thirteenth century lists ground liquorice as part of a potion taken to ease a constricted chest: *La Novelle Cirurgerie*, ed. Constance B. Hieatt and Robin F. Jones (London: Anglo-Norman Text Society, 1990), 14, line 462. 'It is useful in treating hoarseness of the voice and throat; it is a diuretic; it cures constipation of the intestine and kidneys. It is good for the blood': *liquiritia*, f.42 in the Vienna *Tacuinum*, trans. Judith Spencer, *The Four Seasons of the House of Cerruti* (New York and Bicester: Facts On File, 1984), 83.

[6] Mastic, a culinary flavourant since the Middle Ages, is the resin of an evergreen shrub common to southern Europe. According to Gual Camarena (357) it was traded commercially in the fifteenth century particularly from the Ionian Islands.

pots mentioned above, skimming the white scum a little from on top. When it has boiled until it has reduced by three fingers, let it cool in that pot with a lid on. When it is cold, put it through a filter cone.

7. To cook a barley potion.[7]

Get a total of five and a third litres of water and one pound of hulled barley that has been thoroughly washed in warm water. Boil them together slowly over a low fire in one of the above-mentioned pots until the barley has burst. After it has cooled, filter it through white cloths or through a filter cone.

8. To cook a potion of non-hulled barley.

Get barley, sieve it to get rid of all dirt and wash it in cold water. Grind it in a mortar with a wooden pestle so that the hull and the bran come away. Take it out of the mortar, rub it in a coarse cloth. Do that several times, until it is left smooth and clean. For every pound of it use five and a third litres of water. Boil it slowly, watching that in boiling the barley does not escape because it naturally floats and makes a scum. When it is skimmed twice, the pot can be covered with an earthenware lid. It takes quite a bit more cooking than the previous ones. When the barley has burst, take it off the fire, let it cool and filter it as above. Physicians claim that that potion is better than the previous ones.

9. To cook a chicory potion.

Get chicory in the spring and boil it in an earthenware pot with water. When it is done, filter it hot like that through a white cloth. When it is wanted for drinking, you can put a little rose honey or sugar into it, depending on what the physician prescribes.

[10. To cook a potion with asparagus and hops.][10]

---

[7] The use of barley in medical therapy had a long history by Scappi's day. In the thirteenth century the physician Aldobrandino da Siena stated that, barley being recognized as temperately cool and dry, barley water was effective in treating a mild, sweaty fever.

[10] Following Recipe 9 the text of both the 1570 and 1581 printings of the *Opera* passes immediately to Recipe 11. The index at the end of this Book VI lists a recipe numbered 10, to be found on this same folio 393 (335 according to the 1581 index), bearing the rubric *Per cuocere acqua con sparagi, & lupoli*. That recipe was to be the last of the section devoted to potions. The omission of the asparagus-and-hops potion from *both* the first and second printings is rather surprising.

Castelvetro (trans. Riley, 50) provides us with a description of a medicinal hops potion which was likely close to what Scappi intended: 'Hops are an excellent herb for refreshing and purifying the blood. So those of us who are concerned about our health but do not wish to bother the doctor with trivial complaints, or fall into the hands of some grasping druggist, take a handful of hops and the same amount of fumitory, endive and borage, and boil them, well washed, in fresh water without salt. There should be at least two quarts of liquid which must be boiled and reduced by half. The leaves are then taken out and eaten as a salad. The following morning, on rising, we drink a glass of the liquid, tepid, and continue thus for seven or nine days. We then take a dose of senna or manna, or some other light purgative. In this way, we keep ourselves

To make concentrates from various meats, both fowl and quadruped.[viii]

11. To make a concentrate of capon.[11.1]

Get a capon that is meaty and not force-fed,[11.2] that is of middle age and neither young nor too old, because the young one does not give the required substance and the overly old one is too tough and takes too long to make a broth – even though it may make a more robust broth than the other ones – and its broth reduces, more quickly than the capon cooks. If you want to add water, the concentrate is not as good. So the capon should be of medium age and just killed – because the longer it has been dead the less strength the concentrate will have. As soon as it has been drawn, cut it up into small pieces; and if it is butchered, it will be better than if its neck is wrung, because its meat will stay whiter. And if you can do it without washing it, that would be better; though to make the thing cleaner and more delicate, wash it just once in water[11.3] without wringing it out, putting those little pieces into a glazed earthenware pot that does not smell bad. Keep them covered with water by four fingers. Boil it on a low fire and skim it carefully. When that's done, seal an earthenware cover onto the pot with dough all around, so that nothing can ooze out. Then put the pot on hot coals away from

---

fresh and healthy at very small cost. This medicine is particularly good for any unpleasant itching rash, which it clears up rapidly.' Castelvetro's *Brieve racconto di tutte le radici, di tutte l'herbe et di tutti i frutti, che crudi o cotti in Italia si mangiano* (1614) affords valuable perceptions of how an intelligent Italian of the time, who was neither a professional cook nor a physician, understood the gastronomic and medicinal values of certain foodstuffs. Scappi uses hops again in a slightly more substantial preparation in Recipe 104, below.

[viii] The Table at the end of this Book shows a sectional rubric that is slightly more accurate: *Per far brodi consumati di piu sorti, & altri sussidi.* It includes Recipes 11–29, the *sussidi* in some cases not being clearly distinguished from the *brodi consumati*. The *brodi consumati* suggest in some ways a modern consommé or thick broth; a *sussidio*, we learn later (Recipes 16 ff.), is a tonic. Its preparation involves the use of a press, a *torchietto* (see Plate 12), as a means to extract a food's essence.

It may be noted that the first recipes here, for chicken and capon, belong to the most venerable of traditional preparations for the sickly, sick and convalescent.

[11.1] The typesetter in the first printing correctly put 11 as the number of this recipe – as it must have been in the manuscript from which he was working – apparently without noticing that he had skipped Recipe 10. (See the note to Recipe [10], above.) The 1581 typesetter changed the number he read in the first printing, putting 10 for the present recipe, but numbers his next recipe correctly as 12.

[11.2] Scappi puts an identical injunction against the use of force-fed fowl in Recipes 32 and 202, below. But see also the common case of force-fed geese, Recipe II,150. Along with barley, various members of the domestic poultry family enjoyed a long-standing, solid pharmaceutical reputation.

[11.3] Scappi writes, here and in several of the next recipes, *in un'acqua sola* – that is, without changing the water for a rewashing.

the flame with a brick or some other weight on the lid so the boiling will not lift the lid. Boil it gently for three hours more or less, depending on the age of the chicken. For it to be good, two-thirds of it should boil away.[11.4] However, to be sure about that without having to uncover the pot so often, put the chicken's feet into another pot and boil them, too, in water with the pot well sealed; when the feet are cooked, then the broth will be reduced as it should be and properly made.[11.5] Put it through a filter or strainer. Present it for drinking with sugar or with some other ingredient depending on the Physician's prescription.

12. Another and quicker way to make a concentrate of hens and capons.

Get a pullet[12.1] of the goodness and size specified above, and killed that same day in the same way. Cut it up into pieces as small as you can and wash away its blood in a single basin of water. Put it into a pot with less water than for the one above and boil it for an hour, skimming it very thoroughly. Then take the pieces out and put them into a marble mortar and pound them three or four times with the pestle. Set them to boil again in the pot with the same broth; again skim off the thick white scum it will make. Add in a little cinnamon; boil it for another hour, keeping the pot sealed as above. Then, when you want to serve it for drinking, or to make thick broths,[12.2] filter it. I do not mention salt because it is optional.

13. To prepare a tasty concentrate of capon.

It will seem a wonderful thing to people that such a broth as this should be given to convalescents, but I have made it several times on Physicians' prescriptions. Get a capon cut up in pieces as above; boil it in a pot with water over a low fire until it is well skimmed. Keep the pot covered with an earthenware lid, letting it boil for an hour with a thin slice of prosciutto that is not rancid in it: that is done to give the broth a little flavour and to keep finicky people happy. Take the ham out after it has boiled the above length of time, and put in an eighth of an ounce of whole cinnamon. When it has boiled until it has reduced by half, put it through a strainer. You can make thick soups[13] with that broth, because it is more appropriate for thick soups and broths than for giving as a beverage.

[11.4] This genre of preparation, a *brodo consumato*, is properly a broth of which a major portion has been 'consumed' or boiled away. Scappi will offer several similar preparations.

[11.5] The same procedure is explained with a few more details in Recipe 23.

[12.1] The use of pullets and capons in this book of preparations for the sick is significant. Even when turkey meat is prepared, it is expressly the meat of turkey pullets (Recipe 27 and elsewhere) that is to enter the preparation. Chicken had since Antiquity enjoyed a reputation as an ideal food for the sick and sickly because of its humoural qualities of slightly moist and slightly warm. Those qualities tended to be assured in younger fowl.

[12.2] Scappi will offer recipes for several versions of this *brodetti* in Recipes 60 ff.

[13] *minestre*: See later in the present Book.

14. To prepare a concentrate of the above chickens with various other ingredients.

Get a big, meaty chicken with its fat cut off; cut it up into several pieces; above all, it should have been killed that very day. When those little pieces have been washed in water, only once, set them to boil in a pot with a piece of cinnamon as directed above until it has reduced by two-thirds. While still hot strain it through a filter. For every bowlful of it put in a fresh egg yolk, an ounce of sugar and either the juice of two oranges or a little verjuice.[14] Give it to the convalescent to drink. Physicians say that it is of great sustenance.

15. To prepare an impromptu[15.1] capon concentrate.[15.2]

Get a capon that has been carefully plucked and drawn, killed that day; half cook it in boiling water. Then put it into a very clean marble mortar and crush it up with a wooden pestle that does not have a bad smell to it. Put it into another, three-litre pot[15.3] with a little of the same broth in which it was cooked. Boil it, skimming off the thick scum it will make; let the broth reduce by two-thirds. Then filter it. With that broth you can make sops and thick broths, and it can be drunk.

16. Another way to do a broth of the above chickens.

Get a chicken cut into small pieces and wash it only once. In a basin mix the pieces with fat from that chicken and ground cinnamon, a little verjuice, malmsey, currants and a little salt. Put all of that into a pastry shell[16.1] whose dough is made of fine flour, eggs and water. Set it to bake in an oven, leaving it there for an hour and a quarter. Take the pie out of the oven. Take some of the broth that is in the shell and strain it through a colander.[16.2] With it you can make sops with thin

---

[14] Scappi's use of verjuice in these recipes for the sick is to be noted. '*Vers jus*,' writes Aldo-brandino, 'which is made from unripe grapes, and from vine tendrils and from chives and other bitter things, has the same property [as sour apples and vinegar], which is to cool warmth, and to check the stomach's overheating caused by bile, and to slake thirst caused by much heat, and to bind the belly and to check and control vomiting' (*Le Régime du corps de maître Aldebrandin de Sienne*, 119; my translation). Scappi's alternative to verjuice is often, as in the present recipe, orange juice, whose nature is similarly acerbic. If verjuice grapes are called for, an alternative can be gooseberries.

[15.1] *all'improvista* – that is, when the need has been unforeseen. The cook is suddenly called upon to make an appropriate dish, presumably because someone has suddenly fallen ill. We might say a 'quick' dish. See other such recipes at VI,76.

[15.2] The rubric reads only *brodo* but we should understand *brodo consumato*.

[15.3] *una pignatta di un boccale*.

[16.1] This is the solid, free-standing shell called a *cassa*.

[16.2] Scappi's word here, and elsewhere in Book VI, is *colatoro*. In Recipe 73, below, he writes in the same sense of a *foratoro*, two models of which are pictured in Plates 9 and 10. To this point in the recipe Scappi has provided an illustration of the concept of a pastry shell as merely a container for food as it cooks; see also Recipe 25 in this regard.

slices of bread; you can also drink it. That broth is called *sussidio*.[16.3]

17. Another way to prepare the chicken broth called *sussidio*.

Get a chicken as above, meaty, plucked whole and drawn; and another chicken killed that very day and cut up into pieces. With the pieces of the second stuff the first, the whole chicken, doing it in such a way that the stuffing cannot leak out. Bring it to a boil in hot water. Mount it on a spit and roast it slowly. When it is better than half cooked, put it under a small press[17.1] and with its pressure squeeze out its juice. With that juice you can make dips,[17.2] and you can give it as a drink with a little orange juice and sugar, having first warmed it up in a fine receptacle. If you do not have a press, you can put it hot into a mortar and with the pestle very quickly[17.3] pound it several times, having set out a strainer to squeeze it immediately so the juice comes out.

18. Another way to prepare the broth called *sussidio*.

Get two capons, killed that day, to make only a single bowl of broth. Beat one and a half of them with knives,[18] along with their bones. The remaining half you divide into several pieces and boil them in a pot with a litre and a third of water until it is well reduced. Then take the beaten capon and put it into a basin, stirring into it a little salt and a little ground cinnamon. Put everything into a well tinned tourte pan, giving it a gentle heat from below and above the way tourtes are baked, stirring it from time to time and putting in the reduced broth from the half capon. Let it braise until the beaten meat is cooked, then strain it and, in a fine receptacle, reboil it with a little sugar and orange juice or a little verjuice. With egg yolks that broth can be used to make thick broths and sops.

19. To prepare a chicken broth of great nourishment, reduced down to a jelly.

Get four meaty young capons with their necks and feet, clean of blood. Cut everything up small, including the bones, and boil it all in a new pot that does not have a bad smell to it, with enough water to cover it by four fingers; skim it

---

[16.3] The name of this broth for the sick (variations of which are seen in the next recipes) means relief or aid – 'first aid' as might have been said had it been made *all'improvista*. In medical terms it is a palliative or alleviative. In the present recipe only the juice of the meat is used; in the next recipe and Recipe 29 a press extracts that juice: see Plate 12 where *sussidio* is the label on a small press, as if the mechanism were designed or particularly used for extracting a food's goodness for the sick.

[17.1] A *torchietto*. For a *torchio* see Plate 23.

[17.2] *suppette*, diminutive of *suppa*, a sop. The modern expression *fare la zuppetta* is to dip bits of bread or biscuits into a liquid.

[17.3] The phrase *in fretta* is repeated: *in fretta in fretta*, 'immediately, right away.'

[18] To crush the meat and bones Scappi expects the cook to use not the flat blade of heavy knives but their spine.

carefully. When two-thirds of it has boiled away, take out the grease[19.1] and put it through a strainer. Set it to boil without the meat with a stick of cinnamon and the beaten white of an egg. Put it through a small woollen filter cone[19.2] that jelly is put through, and set it in a cold place to jell in beakers or other containers until it sets.

When you strain that broth you can add into it a little verjuice and a little finely ground sugar and salt. You can also make it without cinnamon. In the fall you can boil a little quince[19.3] with it, or else put some in when it goes through the filter cone. When the broth has cooled you can put in a little pomegranate wine,[19.4] which will give the jelled broth quite a pretty appearance. If you want it yellowish, you can colour it with a little saffron. That broth is given to convalescents when they are very thirsty – which was done in 1551 for the Most Illustrious and Most Reverend Cardinal Andrea Cornaro.[19.5]

20. To prepare a jelly with almond milk, which is served in dishes like junket[20.1] and is made from chicken broth.[20.2]

Get the broth that has been cooked as above but without cinnamon, and let it sit until it is no longer hot. Then get six ounces of ground Milanese almonds with an ounce of white starch flour[20.3] and three ounces of fine sugar, everything moistened with the broth. Strain it through a filter cone several times and put it in a cold place in dishes to jell.

[19.1] *il grasso*: should we understand the greasy scum?

[19.2] *calzetta di lana*: Being of wool fibres, this cone is literally of felt. The caption by the filter bag in Plate 2 reads, 'Jelly is being made.'

[19.3] Scappi will use quince in several of these preparations for those who are unwell. Castelvetro writes that quince 'are indispensable to the druggist because of their astringent properties. They are also used in wines and oils, and in the preparation of savories, jellies, sweetmeats and quince pastes, which are delights for all, not just for the sick' (trans. Riley, 118 and 120).

[19.4] Made from the juice of pomegranate seeds, this wine appears several times as an ingredient in Scappi's preparations for the sick. Pomegranates, writes Castelvetro, 'are a particularly good restorative for invalids. The juice assuages the violent thirst of the feverish. We make a beautiful-looking wine from its pretty seeds for that purpose' (trans. Riley, 127). Scappi also uses pomegranate wine to make a sauce for the sick (Recipe 264, below) as well as for ordinary dishes (Recipes II,264 and 270).

[19.5] The cardinal died on 30 January 1551.

[20.1] *giuncata*: see the note to Recipe V,85.

[20.2] In the Table this explicit rubric is a little simplified to *Per far consumato in gelo con latte di mandole*.

[20.3] See the note in I,§27.

21. To prepare a concentrate with an alambic.[21.1]

Get the flesh of two capon breasts, without skin or gristle, cut lengthwise like raw croquettes, the capon having been killed that very day and the flesh being unwashed but only wiped with a clean cloth. Place the pieces on top of one another in a squat glass flask with slices of lemon that has both the outer and inner layers of its peel removed,[21.2] leaving only the juicy flesh; put those slices between each piece of capon. Alternatively, instead of lemon you can put in sorrel and ground gold and various other things depending on what the Physician orders.[21.3] When the breasts and lemon flesh are arranged in the flask, fit the flask on the mouth of a copper kettle[21.4] full of water where there is only a small tube for ventilation. It should be like a water bottle.[21.5] The kettle is set to boil on a hearth where there is a low coal fire. The strength of that heat will make the breast begin to distil[21.6] when the flask is covered with its lid – that also of glass and sealed all around with bits of rag soaked in beaten egg white and flour so that no vapours can leak out. The top of the small flask – that is, its cap, where the liquid is to escape – will connect with the neck of a large carafe which will be packed around with rags so nothing can leak away. The ingredients will take at least four hours to distil. Physicians declare that concentrate to be of great nourishment; it is called a concentrate made in a double boiler,[21.7] although it can be made in various

---

[21.1] A still, in which a liquid is refined by being converted to a vapour and then condensed again to a liquid, was a well-known apparatus in late-medieval times, as was the theory about what took place in it. For alchemists and philosophers the process allowed the capture of the absolute, vital quality of a substance, its fifth or quint-essence, apart from but superior to the other four, its relative warmth, coolness, dryness or moistness. Some variety of elementary still was normally a possession of every wealthy household. See the *Neapolitan Recipe Collection*, Recipes 97 (*Cossa stillata*) and 98 (*Stillato de cossa ho de galina in caraffa*), for preparations similar to the present one.

The Table that follows Book VI again varies the rubric (*Per fare un Consumato a Lambicco*) that appears here: *Per far consumato a lambicco detto a bagno maria*. See later in the recipe.

[21.2] Scappi describes the second as a *la pellicola bianca*, the white membrane.

[21.3] The use of precious metals and gemstones in the preparation of medications was extensive at this time, particularly when distilling permitted their wonderful qualities to be extracted and absorbed by the invalid.

[21.4] See the various *caldari* illustrated in Plates 7 and 9. We may imagine that Scappi initially thinks of one of the smaller sizes at the foot of Plate 9. The base of the glass flask must sit snugly in the kettle's opening.

[21.5] For Scappi's *bottiglia*, his revised notion of what is needed for holding both the boiling water and the flask, see the *butiglia* at the top of Plate 10.

[21.6] *stillarsi* is the crucial word here. The vapours exuding from the capon flesh contain its essence.

[21.7] *consumato fatto a Bagno Maria*. The English name of this sort of double boiler still retains

other ways. That concentrate was made in 1564 at the end of April for the Most
Illustrious and Most Reverend Cardinal of Carpi, Ridolfo Pio.[21.8]

22. To prepare a concentrate of cockerels.

Get three male cockerels that are not too big, though meaty, and just killed,
plucked and drawn; remove their neck and feet, and wash them whole in water.
Cut them up small on a wooden table that is not of walnut,[22] put them in the glass
flask mentioned above and follow the same procedures as above. If you do not
have the means to do it as directed there, when the cockerels have been ground
up, including their bones, put them into a jug with a round, narrow mouth and boil
that in a cauldron as will be described in the following recipe. Let it boil for four
hours, then strain the concentrate which will be rather turbid and greasy. That
concentrate can be thickened with fresh egg yolks. Give it as a drink to whomever
needs it.

You can do it in the above ways with partridge, pheasant and peacock killed
that very day; and also, the meat of a calf killed the same day.

23. To prepare a concentrate of capon flesh.

Get the breast meat of three capons killed that very day, have it cut up into
small pieces and let them sit an hour in either malmsey or a cold lean broth –
that being as the Physicians will prescribe. With a needle threaded with scarlet
silk make several little strings of them with four to a string. Then have a round-
mouthed, glazed earthenware jug ready that is not too big; if you do not have a
jug, get a large glass double carafe. Inside the jug put the strings all around in
such a way that they do not reach the bottom; they should be tied close to the neck.
Stop up the mouth with a bit of clean cloth in several layers packed with tow so
that it is air-tight. Then put it into a cauldron containing cold water in such a way
that the mouth of the jug sticks not less than three fingers above the water. When
the cauldron is placed on a tripod with fire under it, put a weight on the mouth
of the jug to hold it steady and so the boiling will not turn it upside down. To be
more confident that it will not turn over, tie fine cords around the jug's neck, those
being fastened to the cauldron in a way they will not get scorched. Let it boil for
three hours. To be more sure, take a foot of that chicken and, tied with a string,
put it to boil in the cauldron; when that foot is cooked and is disintegrating, then
you can take the jug out and, with great care, remove the little strands of capon
meat. Take the liquor that has gone to its bottom and give it to the convalescent.

---

a French appellation, *bain Marie.* The origin of the designation is intriguing: it was popularly
believed that Miriam, the sister of Aaron and Moses, was an alchemist and that that particular
cooking apparatus was a special instrument in her science.

[21.8] As noted in Scappi's preamble to this book, Ridolfo Pio died on 2 May 1564.

[22] For an explanation of this caution see Recipe 87, below. See the same warning in Recipes
V,106 and 107.

If you want to do it in a double carafe – that being more risky, though – when the little strings of meat are arranged as was directed above and the mouth is stopped up with the same bit of cloth and with another covering of sheepskin[23.1] on top, put the large carafe into a cauldron with cold water in it; in the cauldron should also be hay or straw to protect the carafe from knocking against the sides of the cauldron. The neck of the carafe is tied with two fine cords to hold it and keep it from swinging about. Let it boil. Test it as before.[23.2]

That concentrate was made in 1548 for the Most Illustrious and Most Reverend Cardinal Pietro Bembo of Venice.[23.3]

With the above meat you can also make a distillate[23.4] with an alambic[23.5] or a glass flask as is normally used – that is, when the meat is sliced thinly and dried with a cloth, and interspersed with thin slices of white bread that has first been soaked in a reduced chicken broth.

24. To prepare a concentrated veal broth.

Get the brisket with its bones, and the meat from broken cannon bones along with the bones. When it is chopped up into small bits, put it to boil in a pot with enough lightly salted water to cover it by four fingers. Boil it only until it has been well skimmed,[24] then cover the pot with dough all around as was done with the capon one. When it is cooked, the broth being reduced by at least two-thirds, put it through a filter. That broth can be used for making thick broths and sops, and you can give it as a beverage as need be.

Should you not be able to get those cuts of veal, get some of its thigh with the bone because any cut of meat is better wherever there is a bone. Be advised, though, that that meat should be from a calf killed that day.

25. Another way to prepare a veal broth.

Get a part of the brisket and a part of the thigh with the hollow bone. Chop them up as small as you can, sprinkle that with cinnamon, a little salt and verjuice,

---

[23.1] This *carta pecorina* is a bit of prepared hide, smooth, thin and supple, suitable for writing upon. Scappi puts parchment to a similar use in Recipe 215, below.

[23.2] That is, cook a foot of the chicken in the water of the larger carafe.

[23.3] Pietro Bembo died on 19 January 1547 according to modern calendars. Scappi's dates for the month of January tend not to coincide with dating today. See the list below, Persons Mentioned in Scappi's *Opera*, for brief notes on the individuals named in his book. See also Recipe 28, below.

[23.4] *stillato*, an essence or liquor extracted from a substance.

[23.5] *campana*, literally, 'bell.' The *Vocabulario* of the Academia della Crusca (1612, 1623) has the following entry: *Campana dicesi pure un Vaso di terra, di cristallo, di piomba o di altra materia, fatto a guisa di una campana, per uso di distillare, con un beccuccio presso al fondo, lungo e torto, donde esce il liquore che si distilla.*

[24] That is, as in Recipe 13, until it no longer produces a scum.

and wash it[25.1] with malmsey; put a little finely ground sugar over it. Put all that into a pastry shell.[25.2] Bake it in an oven for two hours more or less, depending on how much there is of it. When it is done, take the broth that will be in the pastry and put it through a filter. With that broth you can make sops.

If you do not have flour for making the shell, get a cooking pot[25.3] and put those things into it. Cover it with its lid, sealed tightly all around with clay and egg white. Put it into an oven that is not too hot and leave it there for three hours, testing it several times without uncovering the pot.[25.4] And if you have neither a pot nor an oven, you can make it in stewpots[25.5] of well-tinned copper or earthenware, giving it more heat from above than below.

With that broth you can make stewed bread[25.6] and thick broths.

26. To prepare a broth of veal knuckles, reduced to a jelly.

Get ten pounds of veal knuckles – that is, from the knee joint to the other joint – cut up into several pieces. Wash it in several changes of water. Cook it in water that covers it by four fingers, in a new glazed pot that does not smell badly. When it has been skimmed well, add in a little salt. Cover the pot in the way described above, and let it boil until two-thirds of it has boiled away. To be on the safe side, you can test that broth in a beaker, letting it stand in cold water for half an hour: if the broth jells, take the pot off the fire and strain it into an earthenware pot. Remove the grease very thoroughly from it so the jelly will be clear. Put it into a smaller pot with four fresh, beaten egg whites, and half a pound of sugar if that is approved by the Physician,[26.1] along with a little verjuice or orange juice. Bring it to a boil and after that strain it several times through a filter cone until you see it as clear as amber.[26.2] If you want the broth coloured, follow the instructions for doing that with the capon broth in Recipe 19.

[25.1] *bagnisi*, literally 'bathe it,' generally used by Scappi in the sense either of dipping something in a liquid or of brushing it with a liquid.

[25.2] As in Recipe 16 this is a free-standing pie: veal *en croûte*.

[25.3] Several *pignatta*s can be seen in Plates 9 and 10.

[25.4] The text that has been set reads, somewhat mysteriously, *facendosi il saggio piu volte con la pignatta senza scoprirla*. Scappi may be thinking of the test he outlines in Recipe 11.

[25.5] *stufatore* (in the feminine). Several varieties of *stufatori* are illustrated in Plates 8 and 9.

[25.6] See other mentions of this *pane stufato* in Recipes 27, 41 and 62.

[26.1] A singular verb indicates that only the sugar must have a physician's sanction.

[26.2] In his *Pratica della mercatura*, 375, Pegolotti describes amber as *gialla in colore di fine oro, e chiara quanto più puot'essere, e che non tenga niente di torbido nè di ghiacciata*: a 'golden yellow colour, as clear as can be with no cloudiness or frostiness about it.'

27. To prepare a concentrated veal broth.[27.1]

Get six pounds of meat from the thigh of a calf that has been killed that very day, with the skin and ligaments[27.2] removed. Beat it small, the way greaseless sausage meat is beaten, and while you are beating it splash it with a little lean veal broth. Put it into a tinned tourte pan or an earthenware baking dish and give it heat from below and above, though more on the bottom than on top. Stir it around a little with a spoon. When it has braised an hour, put the broth through a straining cloth, squeezing the meat.

With that broth you can make stewed bread and a thick broth for drinking, adding sugar and orange juice to it on the Physician's orders. Sometimes raisins are put into the pan, and the meat is braised with them there. With the meat left in the strainer, by adding a little fat and gooseberries to it you can make a thick soup with egg yolks.

You can do it the same way using a wether's thigh, or a turkey pullet or capon – that is, with their breasts.

28. To prepare a broth of wether, called *sussidio*.[28.1]

Get the hind leg of a wether immediately after it has been killed and, without its being blanched[28.2] or larded, mount it raw on a spit and roast it slowly until it is more than half cooked. Catch the juice that drips from it. Take it down and cut it up while hot, with a dish under it catching the juice that flows from it. Put what is cut up, still hot, under a press and squeeze it, making its juice flow into a dish. While that is still hot, strain it through a colander or a strainer;[28.3] if it is not hot, heat it up. Then put it into a fine, clean pot with a little sugar and orange juice, and boil it until its colour changes because its first colour will be like blood and as it gets cooked it will become more tawny[28.4] and thick.

Generally this broth is given as a beverage. Sops can also be made with it. To provide more sustenance you can put in an egg yolk; that will depend on what

---

[27.1] The title of this recipe is identical with that of Recipe 24.

[27.2] These *nervi* likely include anything that is not meat, perhaps what the diner might call gristle.

[28.1] See other *sussidi* in Recipes 16–18, above, and the version of the present recipe that follows.

[28.2] Provided that Scappi means the meat to be plumped in water; otherwise, 'seared' if the preparatory operation is carried out directly over a flame – which is unlikely in this case: see, however, the next recipe. Scappi writes only *rifatto* in the present recipe.

[28.3] *stamigna*. See the shallow, colander-like pans pictured in Plate 11: *stamegna di rame*, a copper strainer, and *stamegna di ottone*, a brass strainer. A deep-bellied colander is shown in Plate 9: *foratoro*.

[28.4] *leonato*: literally the colour of a lion.

the Physician says. That *sussidio* was made in 1548 for the Most Illustrious and
Most Reverend Cardinal Jacomo Sadoleto, of Modena, in Rome.[28.5]

29. To prepare the above *sussidio* more quickly.

Get the meat of a wether's hind leg in little pieces the size of an egg. Mount
them on a spit and set them on the fire immediately so that their juice stays in
them. When they are half cooked, take them down quickly and put them under a
press, following the above procedure. If you do not have a press, just as soon as
they come off the spit put them into a mortar and pound them four or six times,
adding in a little reduced broth of that meat; put them through a strainer, following
the above directions, pressing the strainer hard.

If you do not have wether meat you can do it with veal, although Physicians
say that wether meat is better.

[To make several sorts of paste.][ix]

30. To prepare a paste[30.1] of capon flesh.

If you want the paste to be nourishing and white, get the breast meat of a
capon killed that day, half boiled in water without any salt, with the gristle and skin
removed. Grind it in a smooth, marble mortar: no other stone is good enough for
that purpose because the meat dries out and absorbs into it, especially travertines.
Grind it with a wooden pestle that is not acerbic, as walnut and other woods are.
With that meat grind a little breadcrumb[30.2] soaked in the lean broth in which the
capon was cooked, which bread should first be braised – which is done so the paste
will not have so meaty a flavour; with it put some finely ground sugar, moisten it
with the lean broth just mentioned, and put it through a strainer. Then heat it up
in a small kettle or a small pot on the mouth of a jug, which jug should have a
round mouth and be full of boiling water; and the small kettle or small pot should
be sealed. Whether it is made thick or thin will depend on the need.

It can also be made without bread. With it can be ground a few melon seeds
or Milanese almonds. For every chicken breast put in two ounces of sugar and
four almonds or else half an ounce of melon seeds. To decrease the meat smell,
you can boil a little marjoram in the broth, which you add in at the last because if
it were to boil with the paste it would darken it.

[28.5] Jacomo Sadoleto died on 19 October 1547. The cardinal was a close friend of Cardinal
Pietro Bembo, for whom also Scappi has written that he prepared a dish when the latter cardinal was ill (Recipe VI,23); he makes the same error of date, writing 1548 rather than 1547, the
year of death of both prelates.

[ix] This section heading does not appear here but before Recipe 30 in the Table at the end of this
Book VI.

[30.1] *pisto*, modern *pesto*, though not with the modern meaning.

[30.2] This *mollica di pane*, always translated with a singular, is from the part of a mound of bread
that is inside the crust.

31. To prepare a paste of spit-roasted capon.

Get a meaty capon that was killed that day and has been roasted on a spit with a calf's caul around it. Take the flesh of the breast, with bones, gristle, skin and fat removed, grind it in a mortar as directed above with a little breadcrumb that has first steeped in lean chicken broth, along with two ounces of fine sugar. Put it through a clean filter or strainer, making it as thin or as thick as you wish. A little orange juice and a drop of rosewater are often added in at the last.

You can do the same with pheasant breast or the breast of domestic pullets; for people who have less need of nourishment, use young pheasants and cockerels instead of capons. You can half cook the meat of those chickens, wrapped in damp paper, under hot coals, following the above directions.

32. To prepare a paste of chickens cooked in pastry.

Get the breast of a meaty chicken, not one that has been force-fed, but killed that day.[32.1] Boil it in slightly salted water until it is half cooked, then grind it in a mortar either with breadcrumb that has been braised or soaked in lean broth or else with four almonds, an ounce of melon seeds and three ounces of sugar. When all that is ground, having been moistened with lean broth of that chicken, if is has been thoroughly ground up there will be no need to strain it but only to add in a few currants and a little orange juice. Put everything into a pastry shell that is rather firm so as to hold the filling. Bake it in an oven with a low heat or braise it, without the pie being covered because it is enough for it to be a little thick.[32.2] Serve it hot because that's how it should be.

You can do the roasted meat of a pullet or pheasant the same way, and roasted or boiled veal, wether and goat kid.

33. To prepare a veal paste.

Get calf meat, what is under its shoulders and its loins, and cook it a little more than half. The calf must be killed that very day for it to be more nourishing. Grind it in a mortar with or without braised breadcrumb. When that is done, moisten it with lean broth in which the veal was cooked. Put it through a strainer

---

[32.1] Ken Albala points out that physicians held the flesh of captive animals and of cooped, force-fed fowl to be less nourishing and less readily digested than that of their free-ranging counterparts. He refers to the physician Thomas Moffett's *Healths Improvement*, written c.1595. Moffett puts a hypothetical question, 'Whether [the] penning up of birds, and want of exercise, and depriving them of light, and cramming them so often with strange meat, makes not their flesh as unwholsom to us as wel as fatr. To which I answer, that to cramb Capons, or any bird, and to deprive them of all light, is ill for them and us too' (London: Thomas Newcomb, 1655, 43). See Albala's *Eating Right in the Renaissance*, 135 and 142–3.

[32.2] Scappi's *percioche basta che habbia un poco di corpo* refers either to the adequate strength of the pie shell without an upper crust or to the pie's filling from which, uncovered, some moisture may boil away.

or colander. For every pound of meat that is to be ground, put in three ounces of sugar. Cook it like the other one.

You can do the meat of a wether and goat kid the same way, getting the meatiest and whitest parts as before.

34. To prepare a paste of spit-roasted veal.

Get a loin without bone or gristle and more than half cook it on a spit with a calf's caul around it. Just as soon as it is taken down, grind it without the caul but with braised breadcrumb, and moisten it with lean veal broth. Even though that paste will be somewhat greasy and cloudy, it will nevertheless be appetizing and very nourishing. Strain it and cook it the way the other one is done, though with a fine pot. At the end you can put in orange juice if the Physician prescribes it.

You can do a goat kid loin or wether loin the same way – and just so you'll know, the loin is what is next to the kidney and under the ribs. It is to be noted that quadrupeds generally have four of them, but the two that are by the kidneys are the good ones, and the two others that are above it and attached to the ridge of the spine are tougher and have more gristle and skin than the others.

35. To prepare a paste of the fish mentioned below.

Get a perch, pike, umbra or scorpion fish and boil it in salted water. Skin it, scale it, bone it and grind up its flesh in a mortar with a few hulled melon seeds, shelled Milanese almonds and sugar, and moisten it with pure water. Put it through a strainer and bring it to a boil in a very fine pot, adding in a drop of rosewater to give it flavour. Do not moisten it with the fish's broth because of its gelatinous nature and its smell. You can also do it without melon seeds[35] and without almonds, but only with the breadcrumb softened in water.

You can do the same with sea bream, red mullet and sardines, although sardines have only to be boiled. The sardine paste will become a little dark, but it will be tasty and good.

[To make various thick soups and stews of meat.][x]

36. To prepare a thick soup of boiled capon meat.

Get the breast meat of a capon cooked in salted water, and using knives beat it very small along with the kidney-fat of a calf or a goat kid, and mint, marjoram, sorrel and burnet, and, for every breast, two egg yolks with or without the whites; with that you can mix in gooseberries, verjuice grapes, seeded and peeled, raisins and sugar – that depending on the season. Then give that mixture the shape of a

---

[35] In the 1581 reprinting the word *forza* – perhaps an initial misreading of *senza* – was inserted into this alternative: *Si potrebbe ancho far forza senza seme di mellone.*

[x] *minestre e stufati di carne.* This sectional heading appears before Recipe 36 only in the Table at the end of this Book VI.

small soft cheese.[36] Have a good fat broth of capon boiling in a very clean pot, and into it put the mixture so that the broth floats it, because if there were not much broth the mixture would stick to the bottom. Boil it for an hour more or less, depending on the heat of the fire, keeping the pot covered. It is served hot with a little of the same broth over it.

37. Another way to prepare a thick soup of the meat of a capon breast.

Get the meat of a breast cooked in salted water and beat it small with knives along with either the fat from the capon's breast, the membrane removed from it, or else with the kidney-fat from a calf or goat kid, which is firmer than that of a capon and will always keep the mixture softer; and yet a capon's is healthier. When it is beaten, you can beat some of the above-mentioned fine herbs in with it, putting everything into a good capon broth and boiling it with either a few seeded, peeled verjuice grapes or else gooseberries or raisins, depending on the season. When it has boiled for half an hour at most, so that it has become rather thick, it can be served. It is optional whether you colour it with a little saffron. Into that mixture you can put a little fine sugar and two beaten egg yolks.

You can do any raw meat the same ways.

38. To make a thick soup of veal or goat-kid sweetbreads and a capon's breast meat.

Get the flesh of a meaty capon which has been half roasted on a spit, with its skin and little inside nerves removed. Beat it with knives, and with it the sweetbreads that have been half cooked – that is boiled in water – and kidney-fat of a calf or a goat kid, along with the above fine herbs, adding in fresh egg yolks, including half the whites, and sugar. Shape the mixture to look like the small soft cheese mentioned above or some other form. Cook it in fat broth. It is optional if you want to put verjuice grapes, gooseberries or raisins into it.[38.1]

With that same mixture you can make ravioli without a casing and cooked in broth.[38.2] You can do it likewise with the first mixture. And with the same mixture you can also make small pies, although it has to be kept rather runny if you want to do it in pies.

39. To stew a young cockerel.

Get a young cockerel that is not too tender, so it will be more nutritious, and boil it in capon broth if you want it to be more nourishing; if, though, you want it

---

[36] Scappi mentions the variety of soft, partially ripened cheese known as *casciotto* four times (here and in Recipes 38, 172 and 174, below), but always in reference to its size and shape: *in forma d'un casciotto, alla fogia … d'un casciotto, in forma di caschiotto*. See an article about this cheese in Riley, *The Oxford Companion to Italian Food*, 85.

[38.1] This sentence begins *se et vi si vorrà porre …* ; in later editions the initial *se* is dropped.

[38.2] See Recipe II,181 for the process for making this sort of ravioli.

plain, boil it in water with its neck and little gizzard. When it is almost done you can put in verjuice grapes or gooseberries. When you are ready to serve it, put in either two beaten egg yolks or else some finely chopped fine herbs with a little almond milk to thicken the broth. If it is in the fall or summer, though, instead of verjuice grapes put in damson plums or dried visciola cherries or raisins.

You can also prepare fat thrush the same way, and larks, fig-eaters, ortolans and other small birds; and also the sweetbreads of a goat kid and calf cut up into small pieces, and the testicles of a rooster and goat kid, and crests of large cockerels.[39]

40. To stew partridge and pheasant.[40]

Get a pheasant or a partridge, neither of which is old or hung overly long; draw it, remove its head and feet and blanch it in boiling water or sear it on the coals so it is more firm. Put it into a pot of well tinned copper or of glazed earthenware along with a broken calf's or cow's bone that has marrow in it – which is done to give it flavour. Put in enough water to cover that by three fingers, with a little bit of whole cinnamon, enough salt, a few pieces of quince, prunes and dried visciola cherrries. Boil it without skimming it, with the lid well sealed – though first, before sealing it, you can put in half a beaker of Greek wine or some other sort of wine with a little vinegar and sugar. Those things will depend on the physician's prescription. Cook it in the coals away from the flame.

In that way you can do turkey pullets and ordinary pullets and any other good fowl.

41. To stew goat kids' heads.

Get the goat kids' testicles, skinned, cleaned and white on both the outside and inside. Put them into a pot with a broken calf's bone with the marrow in it, and boil them with enough salted water to cover them by two fingers. When they are skimmed, add in a little verjuice and a little ground cinnamon and finish off cooking them with the pot sealed tightly.[41.1] With those heads you can also cook the odd piece of domestic squash[41.2] that is not bitter; and at the end you can add in some fine herbs. Serve them hot with a little of the same broth over them.

---

[39] Scappi explains in Recipe II,128 that these *galletti* are *pollastri piu grossi.*

[40] Both gamebirds were long established as medically approved ingredients in sickdishes. Of partridge flesh Aldobrandino of Siena (a highly respected physician who died at Troyes in 1287) wrote in French in his *Régime du corps* (1256): *Est caude tempreement, et sour toutes chars d'oiseaus ele est meudre, et fait milleur sanc, et por ce, le doivent user cil qui vuelent avoir milleur sanc, et leur cors en santé maintenir* (ed. Landouzy and Pépin, 130).

[41.1] Scappi writes 'so that it cannot breathe.'

[41.2] That is, some member of the *Cucurbitaceæ* family: pumpkin, gourd or vegetable marrow.

With that broth you can make stewed bread. If you should want to make a dainty pottage[41.3] of the eyes, ears and brain, follow the directions given for the feet. At the end, when you are ready to serve them, it is optional whether you put fresh egg yolks on them.

42. To prepare braised little balls of capon breast, the size of a *tommacella*.[42.1]

Get some of the same mixture as in Recipe 36 and of it make little balls that are more cubed than spherical. Then get a high-rimmed tourte pan with melted capon fat in it. Put the little balls into the pan, heating them very gently from below and above and stirring them until they are rather firm. Then put enough saffron-tinted chicken broth into the pan to cover them by a finger,[42.2] heating them very gently[42.3] from below and above, and cooking them with a low heat[42.4] as is described above. At the end add in a little verjuice or gooseberries and beaten fine herbs.

43. To prepare little balls with another mixture.

Get some of the mixture in Recipe 38 and make little balls of it, adding in a little fennel flower.[43] Cook them as above.

You can do the flesh of a pheasant and a partridge, raw or spit-roasted or boiled, the same way, and of any other fowl the Physician approves of.

44. To prepare *tommacelle* of the liver and meat of a chicken or capon.

Get the breast of a capon or hen that has been killed that day, raw or cooked, although it would be better if it were of a cockerel because it is tenderer. With knives beat it with veal fat and with its marrow, or else with fat of a goat kid and a few chicken livers, likewise raw, adding in fresh egg yolks, sugar, raisins, fennel flour, mint, marjoram and burnet, with a little ground cinnamon and salt. Make

---

[41.3] *pottaggino* here, but apparently equivalent to the *pottaggetto* that will be Scappi's usual designation of a pottage made of very delicate things – 'a dainty pottage' – in Recipes 48 ff. and 162 ff.

[42.1] Roughly the size of a sea urchin. See notes in Recipe II,107.

[42.2] The words 'heating them ... cover them by a finger' (*dandole foco ... che stiano coperte d'un dito di vantaggio*) are repeated in the text. If the repetition is deliberate and not a typesetter's *lapsus*, Scappi must mean that more broth is added at a mid-point in the cooking.

[42.3] The typesetter of the first printing shows the usual expression *pian piano*, as he had set Scappi's phrase three lines earlier, but the 1581 typesetter goes one better here with *pian pian piano*.

[42.4] *con foco lento*: 'with a slow heat.'

[43] That is, the dried seeds in the flower bulb, perhaps ground. Fennel's good reputation with physicians was popularly recognized: 'This herb has two good effects. One is that it improves the taste of bad wine ... The other virtue of fennel is that it warms a cold stomach, gets rid of wind, aids digestion and sweetens bad breath' (Castelvetro, trans. Riley, 78).

tommacelle of it with a goat-kid's or calf's caul, which caul should be tinged with saffron. Cook them in a tourte pan in melted chicken fat. Serve them hot with sugar and orange juice over them.

You can do the same thing with breast meat of a pheasant and turkey pullets, and with the liver of goslings. With it you can also stuff calf intestines that are thoroughly cleaned of all filth, which stuffed intestines have first to be boiled and then cooked on a grill; you can also first boil those intestines for a moment and then put them into cold water to be able to handle them better and to stuff them. Into that stuffing you can put some parboiled veal or goat-kid sweetbreads.

45. To prepare black pudding[45.1] with chicken liver.

Get the little livers without their gallbladder, heart and membranes;[45.2] above all they must be fresh. Before cooking them beat them with knives, along with capon, veal or goat-kid fat and fennel, mint, marjoram, burnet, sorrel,[45.3] raisins, fine sugar, fresh egg yolks with a few whites, and a little salt. That mixture is put into a small baking pan of tinned copper in which capon fat is melted. Apply heat to it, gently, top and bottom, adding in a little fat capon broth to keep it soft and being very careful that it does not stick on the bottom or sides. When you are ready to serve it, tip the pan over a dish. Garnish it with sugar and a little verjuice or orange juice.

With that mixture you can make *tommacelle* in a goat-kid's caul, and saveloy in a wether's caul, cooking them slowly in fat or else on a grill and turning them over frequently. Also, they can be used for tourtes with lower and upper pastry shells, and including various other ingredients. Along with the chicken livers you can beat some parboiled goat-kid sweetbreads.

46. To prepare braised veal bresaola.[46]

Get the loin that is under the kidney, the tenderest cut of veal, or from the thigh, skinned, and cut in thin slices the thickness of a knife blade. Beat them with the spine of a knife, sprinkle them with a drop of verjuice or vinegar, sprinkle them with fennel flour and salt. Put them into a tourte pan with a little beaten kidney-fat or melted capon fat, giving the pan heat from below and above and

---

[45.1] For the broad sense of *migliaccio* in past and present Italian cuisine, see Riley, *The Oxford Companion to Italian Food*, 327.

[45.2] *privi del fiele, & core, & pelliccine.*

[45.3] Scappi's Italian for sorrel is *herba acetosa*, and occasionally merely *acetosa*, literally 'acidic herb.'

[46] This dish is related to the modern *bresaola*, in more recent times made with a salted, dried beef. Scappi's *brisavoli* can begin with a variety of meats: see Recipes II,7, 14, 45, 66, 84, 99; III,16, 17, 39, 86, 151. The name was originally *brasavola* and derives from *brasare*, to cook on hot coals, i.e., to braise.

turning them over once. When they whiten they will be cooked. Serve them hot with the juice left in the tourte pan mixed with a little sugar.

You can also cook them on a grill without sprinkling verjuice or vinegar on them; grill them, though, over a low fire, basting them occasionally with melted capon fat. Serve them dressed with orange juice and sugar.

You can do it the same ways with the breast meat of turkey pullets, and also with a wether's loin and meat of a goat kid.

47. To prepare croquettes of stewed veal.

Get the loin, the tenderest cut of veal and slice it very thinly. Beat the slices with the spine of a knife and sprinkle them with salt and fennel flour. Stuff them with veal fat and beaten herbs, rolling them up like wafer cornets. Put them into a tourte pan or an earthenware pot with enough beaten fat and veal broth to half cover them. Cook them with heat below and above, turning them once and adding in gooseberries or verjuice grapes or raisins (depending on the season), and at the end a little beaten fine herbs. For the broth to be a little coloured, use saffron. If you want to stew them another way, follow the directions for partridge in Recipe 40.

You can do wether loin the same way. And you can cook them on a spit. Serve them with a little broth and orange juice over them.

48. To prepare a dainty pottage[48.1] of chicken[48.2] testicles.

Get a reduced broth of chicken or veal, with gooseberries or seeded verjuice grapes, beaten mint, marjoram, sorrel and burnet, and either a little grated bread or else almonds that have been shelled and ground to a slightly thick paste. Boil everything a little while with the rooster's testicles, stirring it several times with a spoon. That *pottaggetto* can be served on slices of bread.

You can do goat-kid testicles the same way.

49. To prepare a dainty pottage of the feet of a calf and goat kid, or of chickens.

Get a calf's feet or goat kid's feet with the skin cleaned off, washed and cut up into several small pieces. Put them into a glazed earthenware pot covered by four fingers with either water or veal or goat-kid broth that is not too salty. Boil it on coals away from the flame. When they are skimmed, put a bit of ground cinnamon in with them. When they are almost done, add in either gooseberries or peeled and seeded verjuice grapes, along with a little beaten fine herbs; in winter,

---

[48.1] The term *pottaggetto* designates a boiled, relatively thick preparation whose primary feature is that it is rich in exceptionally delicate ingredients. For that reason it is suitable sustenance for the sick. A *pottaggetto* can be served on sops, as in the present case. While largely developed in here and particularly later, Recipes 162 ff., Scappi has already used it in Recipes II,151 and III,179 and 211.

[48.2] In the recipe Scappi will change this *polli* (plural) to *gallo* (singular), a rooster.

instead of verjuice grapes use a little verjuice. It is optional whether you thicken the broth with beaten fresh egg yolks.

You can do chicken feet and wings the same way.

50. To prepare a dainty pottage of the testicles of a lamb or a suckling calf.

Get the testicles just as soon as the animal is killed; cut away the scrotum and, still raw, cut them crosswise into slices. Put those into a small saucepan or pot containing melted chicken fat that is not too hot; sauté them slowly, stirring them. When they have shrunk and firmed up, add in a little chicken or veal broth that is not too salty, a little cinnamon and saffron, and boil that. Then put in the ingredients used in the previous recipe.

You can do the udder of a suckling calf the same way.

To roast various fowls and meats.[xi]

51. To roast cockerels.

Get the tenderest and smallest cockerels and stuff them with their liver and – to keep them soft – veal fat or veal bone marrow, along with raisins, beaten fine herbs, either verjuice grapes or gooseberries, beaten fresh egg yolks and sometimes either damson prunes[51] or dried visciola cherries – depending on the season and the Physician's prescription. When they are stuffed, blanch them in boiling water so they will be more compact. Mount them on a spit with a calf caul or goat-kid caul around them, and a sheet of paper – which is done to keep them soft. Roast them over a low fire, more like the heat of coals than of a flame because a flame will scorch them and dry them out. When they are done, take them down off the spit and untie the paper and the caul from around them. On them put the juice that dripped from them into the dripping pan, mixed with orange juice and sugar or verjuice.

The same can be done with young partridge, young pheasant, ordinary pullets and turkey pullets, and with any fowl that is prescribed or ordered by the Physician.

52. To roast fowl that have not been drawn and have to be plucked dry, being those that follow.

Fig-eaters, nesting swifts, ortolans, *rigabbi*,[52] larks, turtledoves, thrush, blackbirds and quail: all those need to be cooked while fresh. A fig-eater and ortolan need to be cooked immediately, and when they are almost done they should be sprinkled with grated bread, sugar, fennel flour and salt. They can be

---

[xi] The section heading at this point incorporates the rubric for the first recipe in it by concluding with the words 'beginning with cockerels.'

[51] These *prugne damascene* may be fresh plums rather than prunes.

[52] The identity of this species of bird is not clear. Early Italian has a very old word, *gabbo*, meaning 'jest' or 'trick': this wildfowl may be a jay. Modern Italian calls a gull, *gabbiano*.

cooked wrapped in a goat kid's or wether's caul with fennel flour and salt. The others, however, are cooked on the spit with thin slices of caul and a few bay leaves between them. Their glazing is made of fennel flour, salt and sugar like the fig-eater's and ortolan's.

53. To prepare goat-kid or veal croquettes roasted on a spit.

Because a goat kid has quite a few more ligaments in its leg than a calf, get the leanest part of it, cut it into thin slices and beat them with a knife[53] along with kidney grease from the same animal, a little fine herbs, fresh egg yolks, fresh fennel flour and salt. Stuff them and roll them up like wafer cornets. Put them on a spit. When they are cooked, serve them hot, garnished with a few cooked raisins, orange juice and sugar.

In all those above ways, and others, you can do the breast meat of a capon, killed that day, turkey pullets and pheasants, although croquettes of those fowl, when you want to do them on a spit, are wrapped in the thinnest part of a goat kid's or calf's caul to keep them soft.

54. To do up a goat kid's head, boneless and stuffed.

Immediately the goat kid has been killed, get its head, with the hair removed and a little of the neck left on it. Wrap it in a white cloth and beat it all over well with a wooden pestle until all the bones are broken but not the skin. Dig out the bones and brains through the neck opening by turning the head inside out so that what is inside comes out. Wash it and shape it as it was.[54.1] Sew up the mouth so the stuffing cannot spill out. Have fat from a calf or from that same goat kid, and half-boiled goat-kid sweetbreads, beaten mint, marjoram and parsley, raisins, sugar, cinnamon, fresh eggs and salt; mix everything together and stuff the head with that, sewing up the neck opening again. Set it to boil in a small cooking pot[54.2] with a good broth of some other meat. When it is cooked, put in those fine herbs, beaten very small, either gooseberries or verjuice grapes, and a little saffron, depending on the season. When it is done, put it in a dish with some of that broth and serve it hot.

55. To do deboned, stuffed cockerels.

Get a cockerel or pullet killed that day. If plucked dry it will be better; mind that the skin is not broken. Draw it, put it in several layers of a white cloth and, with a pestle or some other chunk of wood, pound its bones except for the part ahead of its wings which cannot be cleaned out. Remove the bones through the

---

[53] Invariably it is the narrow back or spine of a knife that Scappi uses to beat a foodstuff, usually to break up its fibres.

[54.1] That is, turn it again right-side out.

[54.2] A *pignattina* is a smaller variety of the *pignatta*s seen in Plate 10.

area through which it was gutted, turn the chicken inside out as was directed for the boneless goat kid's head. Leave a part of the neck and carefully remove the crop so the skin is not broken, leaving its feet. When you have cleaned out all that can be cleaned out, make it look like it was originally and wash it. With a stuffing made of the raw breast meat of a cockerel, beaten with veal fat, aromatic fine herbs, raw eggs, sugar, cinnamon, raisins and gooseberries – depending on the season – and enough salt, stuff the cockerel. Sew up where the stuffing was put in, put the bird into a casserole pot[55.1] with cold water in it and boil it. When it comes to a boil take it out: that is done so it will return to its original shape and can be accommodated all the more easily in a stewpot or other pot. Cook it either in the broth of some other meat or just plain in salted water, deboned and its neck drained of blood. When it is done, serve it hot.

The bones can also be removed in another way, by cutting along the spine right to the haunch[55.2] and, with a small cutting knife, carefully lift the flesh from the bone, watching that you do not cut the skin. When all the flesh is lifted off, remove what is inside and the bones that are in the breast, thighs, wings and other places. Use the same mixture as above and stuff the bird. Sew it up inconspicuously; the thread will hold more firmly and better if the bird has been plucked dry. Cook it and serve it as above.

If you want it roasted, when it is taken out of the boiling water sprinkle it with fennel flour, salt and sugar, wrap it in the caul of a calf, wether or goat kid with some paper around that. Mount it on a spit and roast it, preferably over the heat of coals rather than over flames because a flame will dry it out and melt it. When it is done, serve it hot with orange juice and sugar over it. Be careful to remove the thread from the places where it was sewn.

You can also do dovecot squab and all other sorts, and capons and pullets, immediately they have been killed and plucked dry.

[To make barley gruel.][xii]

56. To prepare gruel of hulled barley.[56.1]

Get hulled barley that has first been well ground in a mortar so that the sheath around it is removed, and put it to soak in warm water. Leave it there an hour,

---

[55.1] See the two sizes of *cazzola* in Plate 10.

[55.2] Scappi's *cadrione* is the ilium.

[xii] Not in the text, this sectional rubric appears before Recipe 56 in this Book's Table.

[56.1] Barley had a long tradition as both a suitably nutritious food and an efficacious restorative for the sick. This *orzata* or barley porridge was recognized across Europe as a practical preparation of barley for that purpose. It was held so much to be a sort of universal remedy that Recipe 59 describes how to make a dose of it as a traveller's provision. See also Recipes 7 and 8, above, for barley potions.

rubbing it with your hand several times and changing the water. Put it into a new pot with two and two-thirds litres of water for every pound of barley. Cook it over a low fire, being careful not to touch it with any iron because that would make the barley go black and bitter. It needs to boil considerably more than barley water.[56.2] When the barley has cooked to a state of disintegration rather than otherwise – it being less flatulent that way – put it through a strainer or filter, at the same time adding in some of the same water in which it was cooked. Make it thin or thick, however you want to use it, heating it up again in a fine vessel with fine sugar in it. You can put melon-seed milk in with that barley gruel. You can also dilute it with a lean capon broth – depending on the use for it and the Physician's prescription.

57. To prepare barley gruel with ordinary barley.

Get the sort of barley that is given to horses; above all it has to be new and not smell bad. Grind it in a mortar and remove its hull the way that is done for the barley potion of Recipe 8. Boil it in water in a new pot that does not smell badly, skimming it with a wooden spoon and letting it finish cooking. Note that that sort of barley needs more cooking than the previous sort. You should know that sometimes a type of cracked barley,[57.1] which is yellowish and looks just like einkorn, is brought to Rome from German lands; of that barley, gruel and thick soups are made. The Sovereign Pontiff Pius IV used to take it often in '64.[57.2]

58. To prepare a thin barley gruel.

Get either of the above-mentioned barleys and clean it the same way. Cook it in a pot, with two and two-thirds litres of water for every pound of barley. Reduce it by two-thirds so that the remaining water is a tawny colour and thick. Put the barley into a filter cloth and immediately discard the water that comes through first. Carefully squeeze the cloth and tie it up; hang it over a nail and the water that oozes out[58.1] will, according to Physicians, be excellent. To that barley gruel[58.2] you can add melon seeds, reduced to milk, and sugar.

59. To prepare barley gruel for travelling.

Get the barley gruel made with hulled barley, strained and thick. Spread it out in tinned tourte pans; it should not be higher in the pans than the thickness of a knife. Put it into an oven after bread has come out, or else after the oven has been heated to the same moderate heat as when bread has finished baking, and

---

[56.2] See Recipe 8, above.

[57.1] *certo orzo ... rotto.*

[57.2] *nel 64*: Giovanni Angelo Medici died on 9 December 1565.

[58.1] *& quella che riuscirà ... .* The verb is a learned composite of *uscire*.

[58.2] 'Gruel' is normally the sense of the word *orzata* that Scappi writes here and in the rubric. However, in his recipe he refers several times to *acqua*.

leave it there until it has thoroughly dried out. Take it out of the tourte pans, set it on paper, pack it again in the pans and put it back in the oven. Leave it there until it can be reduced to powder. When it has been powdered, it is carried in boxes or leather pouches. When you want to use it, you take two ounces of it per bowl and moisten it with lean chicken broth; after it has sat soaking for a quarter of an hour, add sugar to it. If you want to strain it, that is optional; it can also be served without straining. You can also bring it to a boil with melon-seed milk.

To make various thick broths.[xiii]

60. To prepare a thick broth with chicken broth and fresh egg yolks.

Get chicken broth or veal broth that has been reduced by half and is cold. For every third of a litre[60.1] get three fresh egg yolks beaten with orange juice or verjuice and sugar; put that through a strainer because of lumps in the egg. Put everything into a small kettle or a small pot which is set on the mouth of a jug[60.2] that has a round mouth and is full of boiling water. The small kettle must be sealed up and left sitting for a quarter of an hour, more or less, depending on how much thick broth you are making. When you see that it is beginning to set, take it off the fire, stir it a couple of times with a spoon, and serve it hot.

You can also do it with the broth hot: that is, when the broth is boiling, quickly put the egg yolks in with the other ingredients. However, for it to be more delicate it is made with the broth cold.

61. To prepare a thick broth with fresh eggs.

Get fresh eggs and beat both the yolks and whites together. Then have a fine small pot with reduced chicken or veal broth boiling in it, with a little verjuice and sugar. Put the eggs into it, stirring with a wooden or silver spoon until it thickens. You can also cook it on a jug as is done above. Serve it hot on thin slices of bread.

62. To prepare a thick broth with beaten fine herbs.

Get chicken or veal broth with a little ground cinnamon in it, and gooseberries or verjuice grapes, seeded and peeled. Boil it for a quarter of an hour with beaten fine herbs, marjoram, burnet and parsley. Put in beaten eggs, stirring with a spoon until it darkens a little. You can make stewed bread with that thick broth when it

---

[xiii] This section heading incorporates the rubric for Recipe 60: *& prima per fare bro-detto con brodo di Pollo* ... (The 1581 typesetter put *brodetto di brodo di Pollo*.) The culinary genre *brodetto*, of which Scappi has grouped varieties here in Recipes 60–4, continues to live in modern Italian cuisine: see the entry 'brodetto' in Riley, *The Oxford Companion to Italian Food*, 77.

[60.1] *mezza foglietta.*

[60.2] See Plate 10 for a representation of a *cucumo*.

is clear,[62] the slices of bread being thin. If you want to serve it as a thick soup, let it thicken a little more. Serve it hot. In winter, rather than gooseberries put in verjuice.

63. To prepare a thick white broth with almond milk.

Get shelled Milanese almonds and make them into milk with cold lean capon broth. With that milk beat egg whites with verjuice and sugar. Put that through a filter into a very clean pot of well-tinned copper or earthenware. Cook it on a jug[63] the way the first one was done or else on the coals, stirring often with a spoon. When it is done, serve it hot, on thin slices of bread or not.

64. To prepare a thick broth called *zabaglione*.[64.1]

Get six uncooked fresh egg yolks without the whites, six ounces of sweet malmsey, three ounces of sugar, a quarter-ounce of ground cinnamon and four ounces of pure water; mix everything together. Put it through a sieve or a colander. Cook it in a small kettle[64.2] with boiling water – that is, get a copper cooking basin[64.3] – containing enough water that the kettle is sitting in three fingers of it; boil the water until the *zabaglione* thickens like a thick broth. You can put a little fresh butter with that *zabaglione* and, instead of the malmsey, a trebbiano from Pistoia or else some other sweet white wine. If you do not want the preparation so fumy, use less wine and more water. In Milan that preparation is given to pregnant women. Although it can be made with whites and yolks, you have to put it through a strainer because of the eggs' tread.[64.4] It is served hot.

65. To prepare a thick soup popularly called *vivarole* without cheese.[65.1]

Get fresh eggs beaten with chard juice and a little almond milk, and put that

---

[62] See the reference to *pane stufato* in Recipe 25, above.

[63] See Recipe 60.

[64.1] The preparation is spelled *zambaglione* in Scappi's *Opera* (Recipe 67, below, and II,64). Versions of this dish are still made: see Riley, *The Oxford Companion to Italian Food*, 588. The usual pronunciation of its name was *zabaglione* – even in the fifteenth century when a recipe for *zabaglione* is found jotted onto a flyleaf of a manuscript cookbook: see *The Neapolitan Recipe Collection*, Recipe 220.

[64.2] This *caldarina* is one of the smaller models of the *caldari* seen in Plate 9.

[64.3] A *bastardella* is a dished cooking pan, with a lid, somewhat like a modern paella pan and resembling the *concha* illustrated in Plate 9. In Book IV, folio 329r [f.276v], Scappi describes it as a *catino*, a basin.

[64.4] Scappi's term, *calatura*, is changed to *galatura*, 'fertilizing element,' in the reprinting.

[65.1] Versions of this egg dish have already been seen Recipes II,183 and III,285.

The rubric of this and a good number of the recipes in the present Book VI contains the specification that no cheese is included among the ingredients. The omission of cheese in a dish likely stems from medical concerns about the highly variable and often deleterious properties of different cheeses.

through a strainer. Put it into a pot or small kettle containing chicken or veal broth that is not too hot. Cook it on a jug[65.2] with a little melted chicken fat on top. If you do not want to cook it on a jug, do it on the coals, having the broth boiling first before putting the eggs in. Serve the soup hot.

66. A different way to prepare a *vivarole* thick soup.

Get fine herbs – that is, mint, marjoram, parsely, chard – beaten small, and put them into a pot with chicken or veal broth along with seeded verjuice grapes or gooseberries, and boil that for a quarter of an hour, and a little grated bread in with it. Then get beaten eggs and put them into the pot, giving it a stir with a spoon so they thicken. Serve it hot.

67. To prepare a *zabaglione* with almond milk.

Get six ounces of Milanese almonds and soak them in cold water for eight hours: that is done so they'll be tastier and whiter. When they have been shelled, grind them up and make them into milk with a lean chicken broth, cold. Put it through a strainer with ten fresh egg yolks and six ounces of sweet malmsey or else trebbiano from Pistoia or some other sweet white wine, along with four ounces of fine sugar, an eighth of an ounce of ground cinnamon and a little rosewater for flavouring. Cook it in a tinned copper pot away from the flame until it thickens, stirring continuously with a silver or wooden spoon. If you want to serve it as a thick soup, thicken it somewhat; but if you want to serve it as a beverage, make it thin. Physicians say that this and the previous one[67] are extremely nourishing.

68. To prepare purified goat's whey.

Get that hour's milk and put yellow bedstraw or wild cardoon[68.1] into it. When it has set, put it over a low fire away from the flame. When the milk begins to warm up, carefully remove the cheese, which in some places is called *struccoli*.[68.2] Then put a little vinegar or verjuice into it and boil it gently until it has made ricotta. Put it through a fixed strainer[68.3] and again through a small filter cone of woven cotton.[68.4] If you want the whey to be rose-flavoured, leave

---

[65.2] Scappi describes this procedure of cooking over the mouth of a pitcher or jug in Recipe 60.

[67] Presumably *l'antescritto* refers back to the first *zambaglione* of Recipe 64.

[68.1] *quaglio o presame*: these two plants yielded a vegetable rennin or curdling agent in use before the common reliance of cheesemakers upon rennet, the enzyme from a stomach lining of young ruminants. The first, also known as lady's bedstraw, is *Galium verum*; the initial element of the scientific name derives from the Greek for milk. The second, a wild cardoon or wild artichoke, is *Cynara cardunculus scolymus* or *Cynara humilis*, varieties of thistle.

[68.2] In Recipe V,96 Scappi defines *struccoli* as cheese freshly made that day.

[68.3] This *setaccio fisso* may be a fabric supported on some sort of frame. See the apparatus used in Recipe 143 also.

[68.4] *bombagina*.

it in an infusion for three hours, more or less depending on the use it will be put
to. When it has sat that long with roses, filter it again. It will be warmed in hot
water, then you can give it for drinking or for any other use that the Physician will
prescribe.

[To make various thick soups of bread and grains.]^{xiv}

69. To prepare a thick soup of bread pudding$^{69.1}$ for a meat or lean day.

Get day-old white breadcrumb, diced to the size of a hazelnut. Bathe it in
a boiling lean broth, leaving it there for a quarter of an hour: that is done so the
bread will be tastier and softer. Then remove it from that broth and put it into a
good, half-reduced capon broth that is not too salty and finish cooking it. Thicken
it a little with egg yolks so that it sets and has that rather rich yellow film over
top. In summer instead of eggs, grind hulled melon seeds, making milk of them
with some of the same lean broth. An eighth of an hour before you are to serve
it, put that milk into it. Do not let it boil because it will curdle. It is optional
whether you put fine sugar into that bread pudding. Instead of melon-seed milk
you can use almond milk, bringing it to a boil with the pudding. On Fridays and
Saturdays,$^{69.2}$ instead of the broth use fresh, washed butter;$^{69.3}$ and on fasting
days, sweet-almond oil.

You could do grated bread the same way.

70. To prepare bread pudding with almond milk.

Get breadcrumb as above, soak it in boiling water – which is done to remove
the bread's stickiness$^{70.1}$ and so the milk can penetrate it more easily, because if
you were to put the bread in dry like that the almond paste$^{70.2}$ would cook and the
bread in the middle would be dry. With the bread soaked, though, and the water
strained through a colander, put it into the almond milk; there should be fine sugar
and a little salt with that milk. Set it to boil for a quarter of an hour. It is optional

---

^{xiv} This section heading appears before Recipe 69 in the Table at the end of this book.

$^{69.1}$ Scappi's *panata* has had a long and widespread history in Italy. See Riley, *The Oxford Companion to Italian Food*, 355. This will initiate a series of four recipes for varieties of *panata*.

$^{69.2}$ These days were the lean days intended to cleanse one's body in preparation for the solemn feast day of Sunday. See the same substitution to be made in Recipe 80.

$^{69.3}$ The fresh butter – presumably unsalted – is washed in order perhaps to remove any remaining whey. Normally the washing of butter is intended to remove the preservative salt in it, as in Recipe 144 below where the butter is several days old.

$^{70.1}$ By *viscosità del pane* Scappi probably means the gluten or glutinousness of the flour.

$^{70.2}$ Scappi writes *mandolata* here for what will be the result of boiling sweetened and lightly salted almond milk (made from grinding almonds along with a liquid). It is a sort of pudding. In Recipe 170 of this book a filtering seems also to be involved in making it.

whether you make it thin or thick: the more it boils the thicker it gets and the less white. If at the end you want to put in a little melon-seed milk before you take it out and serve it, giving it a stir with a spoon, that is optional.

71. To prepare bread pudding with melon-seed milk.

Get breadcrumb that has been cut up as in the first recipe on bread puddings[71] and boil it in salted water. When it has boiled, put it through a colander. Have milk ready from melon seeds, with sugar, and put enough of it into the pudding that it will not be too runny. Put it into a small caudron or small pot and put that into a big caudron filled with boiling water, or on top of a round-mouthed jug full of boiling water; in doing that keep the container with the bread pudding covered. Mix the milk in with the bread. You will not let it boil, because if it were to it would become lumpy like ricotta. Serve it hot. That milk is made with either water or chicken broth.

72. To prepare a plain bread pudding, which can be used when someone has a chill.[72]

Get breadcrumb cut up as above. When it has soaked in boiling water for a quarter of an hour, drain off the water and cook the bread in water and sugar, without salt. Serve it hot.

73. To prepare grated bread.[73.1]

Grate white breadcrumb that is firm, because otherwise you would not be able to grate it with the cheese grater. While it is still dry like that, put it through a colander[73.2] whose holes should not be too fine. Take the finest part of it and put it into boiling chicken broth or veal broth that has been strained. To make the bread tastier, boil it slowly; some people say it should boil for two or three hours, though in my experience I have found that half an hour is quite enough. Afterwards you can thicken it with fresh egg yolks; otherwise you can serve it plain. On lean days instead of broth you can use fresh, washed butter; on fasting days, oil of sweet almonds. Whichever way it is made, you always have to mind this instruction, that you put it into broth or water that is boiling. Serve it hot.

74. To prepare grated bread with almond milk.

When the breadcrumb has been grated as above, and put through a colander, put it into boiling water and leave it there for a quarter of an hour. Then, with a

---

[71] Recipe 69.

[72] This is a rare instance in which Scappi seems to be prescribing a treatment for a specific medical condition, albeit a simple and common one.

[73.1] Scappi uses the phrase *pan grattato*, here and in the following recipe, as the name for a variety of thick soup composed mainly of that ingredient.

[73.2] See the *foratoro* in Plate 9.

filter or strainer, strain the water out of it. Put it, along with enough fine sugar, into milk made up of Milanese almonds, which milk should first be boiled; stir it with a spoon. Boil it for half a quarter of an hour. Then serve it. After the water has been strained from the bread, you can also immediately put almond milk and sugar into the same pot. And if, at the end, you would like to put in melon-seed milk, to make that thick soup more refreshing, that is up to you.

75. To prepare bread that has been filtered or strained.

When the bread pudding has been cooked in any of the above ways, strain the broth or milk. The smoothest and thickest part is put through a strainer or filter, putting it back into a tinned copper pot either with beaten egg yolks and fine sugar or with the oily part of cooked almond milk. Do no more than bring it a boil so that it does not curdle, stirring with a wooden or silver spoon. Serve it hot.

76. To prepare an impromptu thick white soup of breadcrumb.

Get white breadcrumb, cook it in goat's milk and put the firmest part of it through a strainer. Add in finely ground sugar and the breast meat of a capon boiled in water and then ground in a mortar. Put all that into into a casserole pot or a tinned cooking basin with a pound of sugar more or less, depending on the amount of bread you have. Set it on the fire, stirring with a wooden spatula until it thickens. When it is cooked it can be served hot or cold.

The same can be done with almond milk. These dishes are made when you cannot get rice flour or starch.

77. To prepare whitedish with goat's milk.

Get five pounds of that hour's milk from a goat, strained, eight ounces of fine rice flour, and the breast of a capon or young hen, boiled and then combed out like hair and[77.1] ground in a mortar. First put the milk and rice flour, along with a little white salt, into a casserole pot set on a tripod over a coal fire, stirring with a spatula. When you see it begin to thicken a little, put in the combed-out or ground breast, mixed with cold milk and enough fine sugar; finish cooking it. You can also put four fresh cream tops[77.2] in with the milk because that will make the whitedish more delicate. When you see that the whitedish is sticking to the spatula when you lift it up, it will be cooked then. Take it down off the fire and beat it with the spatula, adding in rosewater. Serve it hot or cold as you like.

78. To prepare whitedish with almond milk.

Get half a pound of flour made of washed, well-culled rice. For every ounce and a half of the flour get a pound of almond milk, made with water in which a

---

[77.1] Later the text will read *or*, indicating that these are alternative procedures.

[77.2] See Recipe 145 for the making of these *capi di latte*. That recipe suggests that each of the cream tops is the amount of cream yielded by a *boccale* (two and two-thirds litres) of milk.

pound of rice was cooked, and three ounces of sugar. Put all of that into a well-tinned casserole pot or cooking basin and cook it over a low coal fire, stirring with a spatula until it is thoroughly cooked – not failing to add in salt and rosewater. On a fasting day, if the Physician allows it, instead of the chicken you can put in boiled flesh of a scorpion fish, or boiled pike back. Then serve it hot or cold, as you wish, with sugar over it.

79. To prepare a thick starch soup with almond milk.

For every six ounces of white starch flour that is not old get four pounds of almond milk. Moisten everything and strain it into a well-tinned casserole pot with six ounces of finely ground sugar and a little white salt. Cook it the way the whitedish is done.[79] When it is done, take it off the fire and add in a little rosewater. If you want it like whitedish, keep it thick and put in more sugar. Serve it hot or cold as you wish.

80. To prepare a thick rice soup with chicken broth.

Get Milanese or Salernitan rice, which are the best, wash it in several changes of warm water and let it stand for an hour in the last warm water. Put it into a pot of glazed earthenware or well-tinned copper with chicken or veal broth, and boil it gently: that is done so the rice will swell up. Do not fail to add broth as it is needed during the cooking. The more vigorously and tightly sealed it boils, the more it will swell up and become white. It is optional whether you strain it; follow the directions given below in the recipe for strained spelt.[80] On a Friday or Saturday use fresh washed butter rather than broth. Serve it hot.

81. To prepare a thick rice soup with almonds.

Get rice that has been washed as above in several changes of warm water and has soaked. Set it in a colander in the heat of the sun or the fire, stirring it around only until it dries, because if you were to leave it too long in that heat it would darken. Put it into a pot of tinned copper or glazed earthenware with enough plain water to cover it by two fingers, and bring it to a boil. For every pound of rice get a pound of Milanese almonds made into milk; begin to add in the clearer part of the milk until the rice is half cooked. Put the other part of the milk, together with a pound of finely ground sugar, into the rice, boiling it gently with the pot covered until it has finished cooking. Mind that you do not stir it up with the spoon for fear you might break it and that it might become less white. If you want to strain it, follow the directions given below in the recipe for strained spelt. Serve it hot.

---

[79] In the previous recipe.

[80] Recipe 83.

82. To prepare a thick spelt soup with capon broth.

Get spelt that does not smell bad and wash it in several changes of warm water to remove any sand and the husk that rises to the surface. Put it into a small, very clean earthenware pot or one of well-tinned copper, along with enough capon or veal broth to cover it, and keep adding it in handfuls until you see it is cooked. You can blend in egg yolks and colour it with a little saffron. Serve it somewhat hot. On lean days instead of broth use fresh washed butter.

83. To prepare a thick soup of stewed, strained spelt.

Get clean spelt that has been washed as above and put it into an earthenware pot with enough capon broth to cook it; with that broth a calf's bone or else a piece of kidney, along with a raw capon breast and a little whole cinnamon. Seal up the pot with its lid rimmed round with dough, and boil it gently for three hours because spelt by nature needs a good cooking. When it is done, grind up the capon breast in a mortar and put it through a strainer together with the spelt. To make it more nourishing, when it has been strained you can add in fresh egg yolks and fine sugar. Serve it hot.

You can do hulled barley like that.

84. To prepare a thick soup of spelt with almond milk.

Get clean, washed spelt and bring it to a boil in plain water, sugar and a little salt, until it has thickened a little: that is done to make it cook better in the milk. Then put in almond milk moistened either with lean chicken or veal broth if it is a meat day or, if it is a lean day, with plain water. Boil it gently, stirring it occasionally with a spoon, until it is cooked. If you want to put it through a filter or strainer, you can follow the directions given above. When it has been strained, add melon-seed milk to it and warm it up with that milk. Then serve it somewhat hot with a few drops of rosewater and fine sugar over the top of it.

85. To prepare a thick soup of goat's milk, egg yolks and orange juice.

Beat twelve fresh egg yolks with a litre of goat's milk and six ounces of clear, semi-sweet orange juice;[85] strain it with a pound of finely ground sugar and four ounces of warm melted butter. Put everything into a pot or small copper kettle, greased with cold butter, and stir the pot. Set it to cook in a pot full of boiling water and leave it there until the mixture has firmed up. When it is thick, take it out. Serve it with sugar and rosewater over it. In April and May you could put some strawberries to cook with that.

86. To stuff a large loaf of bread.

Get a round, two-pound loaf, a day old, and make a round hole in the middle of the bottom crust. Dig out all the crumb so that only the crust is left, which

---

[85] *sugo di melangole di mezzo sapore chiare.* As in Recipe II,250 and VI,129, below, this dish is to be relatively sweet, without the bitter tang of normal orange juice.

should be scraped on the outside before the crumb is removed. Have a mixture made up of boiled capon breast ground in a mortar with hard-boiled egg yolks, marzipan paste and *mostaccioli*, everything mixed with raisins and beaten fine herbs, raw eggs, cinnamon and enough saffron. Fill the loaf and stop up the hole with the crust that was cut out. Put the loaf into a copper stewpot of a suitable size – that is, which is neither too big nor too small – with a fat broth. Cook it slowly for an hour and a half. When the loaf has swollen up and is cooked, pour the broth out of the pot and carefully place the loaf in a dish because otherwise[86] you could not get it out whole.

You can cook it differently, as follows. When the loaf is filled, put it into a towel or a piece of filter cloth. With the loaf filled like that and the towel tied up, put it into a cauldron of boiling broth and leave it to cook, though with a light cord attached on the towel so the loaf will not move this way and that with the boiling but rather stay still.

When it is cooked in one or the other of the above ways, serve it hot, garnished with sugar and cinnamon and a little fat broth. In that loaf you could cook small, drawn birds, and goat kid sweetbreads and testicles.

To make various thick soups of herbs.[xv]

87. Firstly: To prepare a thick borage soup with chicken broth.

Get tender borage without the stems,[87] washing it in several changes of water and boiling it in plain water for a quarter of an hour, being careful to put it into boiling water – because if you were to put it into cold water it would lose its colour and not be so tasty. When the borage has boiled, set it in a colander, leaving it there for a quarter of an hour without pressing it because the pressing would drive out its goodness. Then beat it small with knives on a very clean table of elm or some other wood, with the exception of walnut which turns things dark and bitter. Then have some half-reduced capon broth and put the borage into it; finish off its cooking without any other ingredients. On a lean day instead of the broth use fresh washed butter, and on fasting days, sweet-almond oil.

88. To prepare a thick borage soup with almond milk.

Get young, tender borage, the part in the middle – that is, the tender inner stalks – and get a sufficient amount of them; wash them in several changes of clear water. Then put all the stalks, tied together as broccoli is tied,[88.1] to boil

---

[86] Scappi's warning refers back to draining the broth from the pot before trying to remove the stuffed loaf from the pot.

[xv] This section heading appears both here in the text and in the Table at the end of this book.

[87] *senza le coste*. Normally the *coste* refer to the ribs in a leaf. Here and in the next recipe, however, it may be that Scappi has the flowerlets in mind.

[88.1] See Recipe III,237. As with broccoli, the *garzetto* of borage likely refers to the bud or centre of the flower, perhaps the berrylike seed receptacle with the stem still attached.

a short while[88.2] in hot water. When they are out of the water let them drain by themselves; finish off cooking them in a fat chicken broth. Have a milk of Milanese almonds ready, moistened with capon broth and with fine sugar; bring that milk to a boil in some other fine receptacle. Then remove the stalks from the broth where they have finished cooking and put them whole like that, but untying them, into the receptacle containing the milk, and boil them for a quarter of an hour until the milk with the stalks has thickened a little. Mind above all that it is not too salty. On a Friday or Saturday instead of broth use water.

You can do the above beaten borage the same way.

89. To prepare a thick soup of chard, borage, bugloss and mugwort[89] with chicken broth.

Get the greenest chard leaves because the brownish and black sort are not so good; grind them small with the other herbs after they have been washed well, just as you grind them up for tourtes, or else pick the leaves into bits. Put them into a copper cooking basin or into some other fine earthenware pot with very little chicken or veal broth. Cook them over a low heat, stirring often because they will make a broth by themselves. With them put a little dill to flavour them; and, when they are more than half cooked, put in gooseberries or verjuice grapes or raisins, those depending on the season. Once the herbs have been washed and parboiled they can also be immediately beaten with knives as directed in the recipe for chicory below. If you want it with almond milk, follow the directions given above for borage; and if you want it with butter or with sweet-almond oil, follow the directions contained in Recipe 84.

90. To prepare a thick spinach soup.

Get spinach in the spring, although in Rome you can find it at any time of the year. Wash it in several changes of water, taking the tenderest part. Sauté it in oil or butter or chicken fat. Then finish off cooking it in chicken broth and prunes. Serve it hot with its broth.

91. To prepare a thick lettuce soup with chicken broth.

Get lettuce from March to the end of May, that being its season; take the whitest part of it, after it has been washed, and set it to boil in hot water. Beat it, not too small, with a knife and without squeezing the moisture out of it. Cook it

---

[88.2] Scappi puts the phrase 'bring to a boil' into a plural, 'four boilings,' meaning for a some-what longer period than briefly but not as long as a time that could be measured as a fraction of an hour.

[89] *biete, borragine, buglosa, herba bianca*; the middle two, borage and alkanet, are related herbs. Messisbugo lists the *flowers* of borage, bugloss, mint and rosemary (*fiori di boragine, di buglosa, e di menta e di rosmarino*) in a paragraph apparently devoted to the possible ingredients of a salad (*Banchetti*, ed. Faccioli, *Arte della cucina*, I, 270).

in a good chicken broth. A quarter of an hour before you'll be wanting to serve it, thicken it with fresh egg yolks, taking it immediately off the fire so that it turns out as if it had set. You can put gooseberries in with that. It can be made without the eggs.

The same can be done with endive. If it is a lean day, instead of broth use fresh washed butter; if a fast day, sweet-almond oil.

92. To prepare a thick soup of lettuce ribs in any season.

Get the tenderest and whitest ribs of lettuce, with the leaves cut away. Chop them into small bits half a finger-width long and boil them as in the previous recipe. Recook them in a good broth. If you want to thicken it with beaten, fresh egg yolks and a little verjuice, you can do that following the directions about taking it off the fire in the other recipe;[92] and if you want to thicken it with almond milk, do what is written above in the recipe for borage.[92] If it is for a lean day, do as is directed in the other recipes. In the spring you can put gooseberries into lettuce soup; in summer, seeded and peeled verjuice grapes; in the fall and winter, currants and verjuice so it will be pleasantly sweetish. Those things can be put in any thick soup with the exception of any made with almond milk.

93. To prepare a thick chicory soup.

Get chicory in the spring, and in summer get the tips which are their tenderest part. Make bundles of them like asparagus and set them to boil in hot water for a quarter of an hour. Then take them out and let them sit in cold water for another quarter of an hour. When they are out of that, let them drain without pressing them; then cook them in a good chicken or veal broth. With them you can cook a few currants. Then serve them either on slices of bread or not, as you wish. If it is a lean day, instead of broth, fresh washed butter; if a fast day, sweet-almond oil.

94. Another thick chicory soup.

Get the stalk – that is, the middle of chicory – with the leaves cut away, and make clumps of it as above. Set them in cold water to boil for another[94] half-hour and then cook them in a good chicken broth. If you want the broth to be a bit thick, get a little grated bread and boil them together. You can also put in seeded muscatel raisins to boil. If it is a lean day or fast day, follow the directions given above.

---

[92] Recipe 91. The yolks must be put in immediately as the pot is taken off the fire.

[92] Recipe 88.

[94] It is not clear why the direction reads *un'altra mezz'hora*. Is the cook to add 30 minutes to the 15-minute boiling that tender chicory undergoes in the previous recipe?

95. A different way to prepare a thick chicory soup.

Get the tenderest leaves, wash them well and set them to boil in plain water for half an hour. Then take them out and put them into cold water for half a quarter of an hour. Then set them to drain in a copper colander or sieve, without pressing them. Beat them on a table; then, without pressing them, put them to cook in a clean pot with capon or veal broth in it, adding in some clean, washed raisins. If it is a lean day or a fast day, follow the directions for the other chicory dishes. The previous ones can likewise be beaten.

96. To prepare a thick soup of chicory roots.

Get a chicory root, scrape it well, dig out its core, and wash it in several changes of water. Boil it in plain water for an hour more or less, depending on how tough it is. Take it out of the boiling water and put it into cold water until it has cooled, beat it small with knives and cook it in a good chicken or veal broth. If you want to leave the root in small bits you can thicken it with almond milk, which milk should be made with a lean broth. If it is a lean day, instead of broth use fresh washed butter; if a fast day, sweet-almond oil. Serve it hot.

97. To prepare a thick soup of purslane.

Get purslane leaves,[97.1] which are fairly firm and smooth, and wash them well. Put them into hot water to boil for about a quarter of an hour. When you take them out of that water put them into cold water, changing it several times: that is done to keep them tender and more digestible. Then beat them with knives on a table. Cook that in fat chicken or veal broth. You can put raisins with it but generally it is served plain. You can also cook it without its having been beaten. It should be neither too thin nor too thick. For either a lean day or a fast day, follow the directions above.

You can also cook poppy[97.2] the same way.

98. To prepare a thick soup of mallow.

Get mallow in the spring and fall, in which two seasons it is more tender; in the spring take the tip which is popularly called 'mallow asparagus,'[98.1] and in the fall the tenderest leaves. Wash it well, bind it in bundles and set it in hot

---

[97.1] Aldobrandino (*Régime du corps*, ed. Landouzy and Pépin, 168) declared that purslane was cold in the third (i.e., very high) degree and moist in the second degree. He wrote: 'Its nature makes it more appropriate for countering diseases than for nourishing, because it is useful for people with an overheated stomach, bladder and kidney, and it lowers the great heat of fevers.'

[97.2] Scappi writes two names here, *herba paverina, cioè* [that is] *occhiale*. Because poppy is suggested as an alternative to purslane, it is the poppy's leaves, best when young and green, that Scappi means to be used. The *Opera* makes no other mention of poppy or its seeds.

[98.1] *sparago di malva* – that is, the seed tips or fruit, called 'cheeses' in English, which are here likened to asparagus tips.

water to boil. Take it out and put it into cold water for a quarter of an hour. Put it into chicken broth and finish off cooking it. Serve it with its broth. If you want to make a thick soup of its stalk and leaves, beat them small and follow the directions given for chicory in Recipe 93. Instead of using broth on a fast day cook them in plain water and butter or sweet-almond oil. If you want them in a salad with raisins, when they come to a boil in water, take them out and make a salad of them the same way as with asparagus.[98.2]

99. To prepare a thick soup of nettle.

Get small nettle in the spring or fall because it is better than the big sort, and take the tenderest part of it. Wash it in several changes of water and boil it in water for more than a quarter of an hour. Strain it through a colander, cooling it with cold water; beat it with knives. Cook it either in chicken broth or in butter or olive oil or sweet-almond oil – though according to Physicians it is much better ground like minor herbs immediately after being washed, then cooked in a little broth without having been parboiled; they say the same about mallow.

You can do tender bean leaves and pea leaves that way.

100. To prepare a thick soup of cauliflower.[100]

Get the flower, which is the firmest and whitest and best part, and wash it well. Then have water boiling and put the cauliflower into it, letting it boil for a quarter of an hour, with salt, because by nature cauliflower cooks quickly. It has branches like coral. To see whether it is done, try the rib. When it is done, put it dry into a dish with orange juice, prime olive oil or sweet-almond oil and a very little broth; cauliflower likes pepper.

You can cook broccoli in the spring that way. And instead of water, get chicken or veal broth.

101. To prepare a thick soup of rhubarb roots.[101.1]

When the roots are washed, bring them to a boil in water, from which you take them out to put them into cold water. They are cooked whole like that in chicken or veal broth. You can thicken the broth with fresh egg yolks and verjuice, following the directions set out for lettuce ribs. If you want to beat them with a knife before putting them into the broth, that is possible.

[98.2] Recipe 103 does not explicitly mention the possibility of serving asparagus in a salad.

[100] This is a version of Recipe III,239. See also Recipe II,195 where meat broth is the boiling medium.

[101.1] Rhubarb, *Rheum rhaponticum,* is a vegetable whose large rhizome had for a long time been valued by Chinese, Greek and Roman physicians. A comparison with sorrel led in relatively modern times to the use of rhubarb stalks for general consumption.

The same can be done with alexanders root.[101.2]

102. To prepare a thick soup of parsley – that is, its roots.

Clean the root, dig out the core, wash it well and parboil it in hot water until it is tender. Take it out and put it into cold water, leaving it there for half an hour. Then beat it with knives, or else divide it up into small pieces, cooking it in a fat broth of chicken or veal. You can thicken it with fresh egg yolks and verjuice, although without eggs it can be served with a little cinnamon over it.

103. To prepare a thick soup of wild or cultivated asparagus.[103.1]

Get the tenderest part and put it into hot water to boil until it becomes tender. Then finish off cooking it in a good capon or veal broth. It needs to be served with a very little of that broth. With wild asparagus you can cook some raisins. When the cultivated sort is cooked in the broth and has not disintegrated, you can serve it with orange juice, sugar and salt.[103.2] On a lean day or a fast day follow the directions for the other herbs.

104. To prepare a thick soup of hops.

Get the tenderest part of them, wash them well and put them into water to boil. When they are done, take them out and put them into cold water. When they have cooled, take them out, beat them with knives and cook them with chicken broth. Furthermore, you can cook them with a few raisins or gooseberries; you can also omit beating them, following the directions for asparagus. Sometimes you can put in a few melon seeds that have been made into milk. The same can be done with thick soups of beaten chicory.[104] If it is for a lean day, instead of broth use fresh washed butter; for a fast day, sweet-almond oil.

105. To prepare a thick soup of common squash.

Get a squash that is soft and sweet, being aware that some people claim that the hairy ones are softer and sweeter than any other sort. Scrape the soft one with a knife; remove the rind of a hard one. Cut up the best part of it into small chunks.

[101.2] *radica di macerone*. The stalks and leaves of the plant variously called alexanders, black lovage or horse-parsley (*Smyrnium olusatrum*) were long valued for their celery-like flavour in salads, soups and stews. The root had medicinal properties.

[103.1] Several recipes in this Book VI make use of asparagus, handled alternatively to mallow or hops (Recipes 98, 104) or in combination with hops (the missing Recipe 10). All three plants were held to be medicinally useful. '[In the spring] asparagus begins to appear, which is even better than hops as a vegetable or medicine ... Quite apart from being good to eat, asparagus is a most health-giving vegetable; it cannot harm any part of the human body and is positively helpful to those who find urinating painful' (Castelvetro, trans. Riley, 53).

[103.2] We may wonder whether Scappi means this preparation to amount to serving asparagus 'in a salad' as he indicated in Recipe 98, above.

[104] See Recipe 95, above.

A soft one is put into a very clean pot with chicken broth and boiled gently on a low fire, stirring it with a wooden spoon and adding in enough broth, because vigorously boiling squash will by nature make the broth more delicate and always somewhat thick. At the end you can add in gooseberries or verjuice grapes. To colour it a little, put in a small amount of saffron. It should be noted that you can thicken it with fresh beaten egg yolks. You can beat it small with knives on a table when it is more than half parboiled in salted water; then put it, beaten, into the broth. On a lean day or a fast day, do as directed above.

Sun-dried squash rinds, transported to Rome and elsewhere from Savona and Genova, can be done up in all the above ways after they have been parboiled in boiling water for half an hour and then left in cold water for a quarter of an hour. Moreover, after they have been floured you can fry them in oil or some other liquid. Serve them with various sauces over them.

106. To prepare a thick squash soup with almond milk.

Get some squash that is diced or cut in rounds, and boil it in plain water for a quarter of an hour. Then boil it again in chicken or veal broth until it has cooked. Have ready on hand, in a fine, clean pot, milk made of Milanese almonds and some of the broth in which the squash was cooked, along with a little verjuice; put the squash into it, boiling it until it curdles[106] and adding in enough fine sugar: that is done to make the soup more nutritious. Serve it hot, garnished with sugar. If it is for a lean day, use water instead of broth.

107. To prepare a thick soup of stuffed squash.

Get a squash that is rather long and not too big around.[107.1] When it is scraped cut it into pieces of a palm's width or less. Boil it in water until it softens. Then take it out and put it into cold water. Carefully remove the core on one side, doing it in such a way that the mixture will not escape on the other.[107.2] Then have a mixture ready of veal sweetbreads and goat-kid fat, both boiled and beaten with boiled cockerels' breast mixed with fresh eggs, gooseberries, mint, marjoram and burnet, a little saffron to colour it and enough salt. With that mixture fill the hollow in the squash. Then seal it up with a round of the squash a finger thick, reinforcing that with briar[107.3] skewers. Put it to cook in a copper or earthenware pan[107.4] with chicken or veal broth, keeping the vessel covered. When it is done,

---

[106] Or congeals: *venga quagliata.*

[107.1] The sixteenth-century Italian word *zucca* covered a range of *cucurbitæ* or gourds. In this recipe Scappi likely has in mind a sort of zucchini or courgette.

[107.2] A thin wall of the squash core is to be left on the bottom when the slabs of squash lie flat.

[107.3] The slender fibrous branches of a *scopa*, the briar bush that gave its name to the Italian word for a broom. See Scappi's *scopa* in Plate 25.

[107.4] See engravings of various sorts of *navicella* in Plates 6 and 8.

turn the squash over a couple of times. If you want to thicken the broth a little you can do that with beaten fresh egg yolks and verjuice. When the squash is served, it can be cut crosswise like *salsiccioni* or lengthwise, or else leave it whole. If it is a lean day make the stuffing with marzipan paste, eggs, bread soaked in water and sugar; on a fasting day put in a few pinenuts or hazelnuts, ground up, instead of the eggs, mixing mint, marjoram and fine herbs into the stuffing. In cooking it, follow the directions in the previous recipe for cooking with water.

108. To prepare a thick soup of stuffed lettuce.

Get stalks[108] of lettuce, the best part of them, and, still whole, bring them to a boil in hot water – because if you were to put them into cold water they would lose some of their goodness. When they have boiled for a quarter of an hour, put them into cold water, leaving them there until they are quite cold. Take them out and put them on a table, letting them drain by themselves. Have a mixture ready of a boiled capon breast and veal marrow, everything beaten together and mixed with fresh eggs, mint, marjoram, burnet, sorrel, gooseberries if it is summer, otherwise raisins, and sugar and grated bread with salt; with that mixture stuff the lettuce, interspersing the stuffing between the leaves so that it is quite full. Bind it up carefully with a little string, stalk by stalk, and cook it in chicken broth in a narrow pot, turning it over several times so that it cooks thoroughly. When it is done, untie it, either whole like that or split through the middle, lengthwise. Serve it in dishes with that broth over top. If you want the broth to be somewhat thickened, do it with beaten eggs and a little verjuice.

109. To prepare a thick soup of fresh peas.

Get fresh, tender peas and put them into a pot or tinned cooking basin with a very little fat chicken or veal broth and cook them, adding in beaten dill. If you want to give it a little flavour, put in a thin slice of prosciutto or mortadella. Cook it, putting in a little beaten herbs. Instead of the broth, on lean days use fresh washed butter and on fast days sweet-almond oil. If you would like to cook the pods, you could do them without the dill.

110. To prepare a thick soup of brown chickpeas.[110.1]

Get brown chickpeas, dry and wrinkled, which are the best sort; wash them in warm water, leaving them to soak in that warm water in a hot place for six hours, then take them out. If you want them done in chicken broth, put them into

---

[108] These *piedi* still include leaves: see further on.

[110.1] *minestra di ceci rossi.* Chickpeas enjoyed a history as a healthy foodstuff. In 1420 Savoy Chiquart was preparing the same sort of *Syseros* (Recipe 76 in his section of dishes for the sick), using sage as well as parsley root. Concerning sage, a Latin adage was couched as a question: 'Why should anyone whose garden produces sage ever die?' *Cur moritur homo cui salvia crescit in horto?*

a pot with enough cold broth to cover them by four fingers; cook them in that broth, keeping the pot closed. But if you want them done in water rather than that broth, cook them in the water they steeped in, with sprigs of rosemary or tips of sage, and either sweet-almond oil or olive oil. That broth will always be better as a beverage than the one made with meat broth.[110.2]

111. To prepare a thick soup of split chickpeas.

Get the split chickpeas – that is, shelled – and, having first cleaned them well, set them to cook in water, salt and oil. Boil them slowly and in a confined space rather than freely. You can sometimes put a little finely chopped pennyroyal with that. Serve it with a garnish of cinnamon.

[To make pies of various ingredients.][xvi]

112. To prepare little pies of small birds.

Get a little veal or wether meat with beef marrow, beat them small with knives[112.1] on a table and put that into a small pastry shell,[112.2] splashing a little verjuice on it and sprinkling it with cinnamon and salt. Then get the small birds, drawn, and put them on the beaten meat with prunes and dried visciola cherries if it is the fall or winter, and in summer with gooseberries or verjuice grapes and maybe an odd muscatel pear. Bake it in an oven. When it is almost done, through the hole on top you can put in a little broth slightly tinged with saffron, if the Physician approves.

In the same way you can do partridge, young pheasants, cockerels, thrush, quail and all sorts of small gamebirds as are prescribed by the Physician.

[110.2] Castelvetro's testimony supports Scappi's statement: 'White and red chickpeas, the latter being the most wholesome, are some of the healthiest vegetables you can find. Take a ladleful of the red chickpeas and boil them in unsalted water with plenty of oil, and when they are cooked squeeze lemon juice over them. The liquid from this is taken by sufferers from kidney stones, or other kidney complaints, to alleviate pain in urinating' (trans. Riley, 102).

[xvi] This section heading appears before Recipe 112 in the Table at the end of this book.

[112.1] The plural here is significant. As is normally the case, Scappi intends that the narrow spine of a relatively heavy knife be used for such beating. A knife in each of the cook's hands will shorten the work. Generally all of the ingredients in pies and, later, tourtes for the sick are carefully tenderized, in part in order to extract all of the elemental 'goodness' in a foodstuff that might benefit a patient.

[112.2] This _cassetta_, usually a small (round) box, is for a free-standing pie – that is, one unsupported by a pie plate or any baking dish – so commonly made in Book V. We might call the present recipe 'Small birds _en croûte_.' The later reference to a hole on top indicates that the pie is covered, as is explicitly the case in the next recipe. The next recipe states that the dough for a similar casing is made of fine flour, eggs and butter.

113. To prepare little pies with beaten veal.

Get veal, with the bones, gristle and skin removed, and boil it briefly in a pot with some other meat[113.1] until it is sealed.[113.2] Take it out and beat it small on a table. Elsewhere beat a veal kidney – that is, the kidney-fat, without its membrane. Mix everything together, along with either gooseberries or seeded verjuice grapes or raisins, depending on the season, and enough salt. Put all that into a small pastry shell made of fine flour, eggs and butter. When the pie is covered, bake it in a oven. When it is almost done, through the hole in the top add in a little broth tinged with saffron, and a little ground cinnamon if the Physician approves. Serve it hot.

You can do wether and goat-kid meat the same way, and raw breast of pheasant, hen, capon and partridge.

114. To prepare little pies of fish flesh.

Get pike and roast it on a grill. When it is half done, skin it, scale it and debone it. Take its flesh which you beat with knives. Have a pastry shell ready, made of fine flour, butter and fresh egg yolks; into it put the beaten fish flesh with butter, raisins, mint, marjoram, sugar, a little salt, and verjuice or gooseberries depending on the season. When it is covered over, bake it in an oven. When it is almost done, add in a little broth made with saffron-tinged butter. Serve it hot.

You can do the same with the flesh of umbra, perch, scorpion fish, red mullet and sea bream.

115. To prepare quince pies.

Get a quince and, with it wrapped in butter-greased paper, half roast it on a spit. Then take it down, carefully core it with a knife and clean its outside. Stuff the hole in the quince with beef marrow or with butter, sugar, a little cinnamon and whole cloves. Have a small pastry shell made up of fine flour, butter and egg yolks, which shell is of a size suitable for the quince; put the quince into it. Bake it in an oven. When it is done, it can be served either hot or cold.

You can also put raw quince into the pastry shell whole[115] or cut up, sometimes with muscatel raisins. You could do all sorts of fish that way, and raw apples, coring them through their stem end.

[113.1] It seems likely that the phrase should have read: 'with *the broth* of some other meat.' See Recipes 54 and 55 in this book, for instance.

[113.2] Scappi writes, literally, 'until the blood is dead': *fin'a tanto, che sia morto il sangue*.

[115] Whole, but not stuffed.

[To make various sorts of tourtes.][xvii]

116. To prepare a tourte of pheasant meat without cheese.[116.1]

Get the breast meat of two spit-roasted pheasants. Grind them in a mortar with six ounces of unpared apples, two ounces of *mostaccioli*, three ounces of marzipan paste, one ounce of candied pinenuts, three ounces of beef or veal marrow and six fresh egg yolks. When all that is ground up enough to go through a sieve or a colander, put in four ounces of sugar and an ounce of rosewater. Put it into a tourte pan lined with a sheet of dough made with fine flour, fresh egg yolks, butter, sugar and rosewater. Bake it in an oven or braise it with melted capon fat over it, and give it a glazing with sugar and rosewater. Serve it hot. That tourte should not be deeper than the thickness of a knife, and should be cooked like marzipan.[116.2]

117. To prepare a tourte of lobster[117.1] claws.

Get claws that have been boiled in water, shell them and grind them in a mortar with steeped pinenuts, fresh dates and marzipan paste; make a mixture of all that combined with sugar, fresh eggs, finely beaten mint, marjoram and burnet, as well as a little powdered *mostacciolo*, finely ground cinnamon and fresh butter, everything mixed together. With that mixture make up a tourte with a small sheet of pastry both beneath and above. On fast days instead of butter use sweet-almond oil, and instead of eggs, breadcrumb cooked in almond milk.

You can also make ravioli of it with or without a casing,[117.2] serving it dressed with sugar and cinnamon after it has been boiled. You could also make ravioli fried in oil – that is, encased in a dough made of fine flour, oil, white wine, salt and water.

118. To prepare a whitedish tourte without cheese.

Get two pounds of whitedish made in the way described in Recipe 76, and six ounces of pinenut paste,[118.1] six fresh egg whites and three cream tops.[118.2] After

---

[xvii] This section heading appears before Recipe 116 in the Table at the end of this Book VI.

[116.1] Egg yolks and cheese are two of the fundamental ingredients in the *torte* of Book V (Recipes 66 ff.). Here in Book 6, 'On Convalescents,' several tourte recipes (and the one *crostata*, Recipe 129) are composed expressly without cheese. A preparation that lacks cheese (and other dairy products and meat) might qualify for serving on fasting days, but Scappi's intention in offering such cheese-free tourtes may be as much medical as religious.

[116.2] See the so-called marzipanned tourte in Recipe 120.

[117.1] As in Recipe V,181 this crustacean is either a spiny lobster or a sea crayfish.

[117.2] See also the variation of Recipe 38, above; and directions for making casing-less ravioli in Recipe II,181.

[118.1] See Recipe 217, below.

[118.2] See Recipes 77 and 145.

it has all been ground up in the mortar, put it through a strainer. Put it into a tourte pan lined with a sheet of dough made of fine flour, egg yolks, butter, salt, sugar and rosewater, with another sheet of dough on top worked in various designs. Bake it in an oven or braise it, giving it a glazing with sugar and rosewater. Serve it hot or cold as you wish.

119. To prepare a tourte of cream tops.

Get twenty cream tops, one pound of pinenut paste ground in a mortar, three ounces of small marzipan biscuits[119] and eight fresh egg whites. When everything has been ground up, strain it with a little rosewater and a little white salt, adding in six ounces of fine sugar. Put it into a tourte pan lined with a sheet of dough made as above. Bake it in an oven or braise it, giving it a glazing of sugar and rosewater. Serve it hot or cold, whichever you want.

120. To prepare a marzipanned tourte.

Get a pound of shelled almonds and grind them thoroughly in a mortar. Then have a pound of melted sugar boiling in a casserole pot and put the almonds into it until they become a paste. Put it back into the mortar and grind it up again. When it has cooled, add in six egg whites and a beaker of milk made from melon seeds. Put all of that into a tourte pan lined with a sheet of dough as above. Bake it in an oven with its glazing of sugar and rosewater on it.

When you do not have time to grind the almonds, get some marzipan paste. And instead of the sheet of dough that is put under the tourte, get some wafers, having first greased the tourte pan with butter. You can also grease the pan with wax and then put moistened wafers on that.

121. To prepare a tourte of common squash without cheese.

Get tender, sweet squash, either scraped clean or without its rind. Take the best part of it and cook it in a good veal or chicken broth. Then with a filter cloth or some other cloth squeeze out all the broth from it and in a mortar grind what is left of the squash. For every pound of squash grind with it four ounces of pinenut paste, three ounces of breadcrumb that has cooked in a good broth, and six fresh egg whites: that is done so the tourte will turn out white. However, you could put the yolks in with the whites. When everything is ground up, put it through a sieve that is not too fine, adding in three ounces of sugar and two ounces of pinenuts that have sat for at least six hours in fresh water. Then make a tourte in a tourte pan with the same dough that is made up for the other ones. Follow the same directions for baking it. And instead of breadcrumb you can use ricotta made that very day of ewe's or cow's milk. If it is not a meat day, though, cook the squash in plain salted water. Make the same glazing of sugar and rosewater. Serve it hot or cold as you like.

---

[119] *biscotelli.*

122. To prepare a melon tourte without cheese.

Get the best part of a melon that is not too ripe, with the rind and seeds removed.[122] Cook it in butter. When it is done, strain it and to every pound of strained melon add four ounces of marzipan paste, ground in a mortar, an ounce and a half of ground *mostaccioli* and four fresh eggs. When that mixture is made up, put it into a tourte pan lined with a sheet of dough made of fine flour, egg yolks, sugar, salt, butter and rosewater. Bake it in an oven or braise it, giving it its glazing with sugar and rosewater. With the melon you can cook a few thin slices of Florentine pears. Serve it hot.

123. To prepare a quince tourte without cheese.

Get a whole quince and, without peeling it, put it on a spit with enough paper, greased with fresh butter, around it to cover it. Turn it slowly the way roasts are turned for two hours, more or less, depending on its size. When it is done, remove the paper from it, peel it, take the best part of it and grind it in a mortar. For every pound of quince get four ounces of marzipan paste, an ounce and a half of fine *mostaccioli*, three ounces of sugar, three fresh eggs and two ounces of fresh butter. When the mixture has been made up and strained in several passes,[123] put it into a tourte pan that is lined with a sheet of dough that is not too thin, made of fine flour, egg yolks, sugar and butter. Cover the tourte with the same dough made like shutter louvres or in other ways. Bake it in an oven or braise it, making its glazing of sugar and rosewater. Serve it hot or cold as you wish. In Lent instead of butter put in sweet-almond oil and, instead of eggs, breadcrumb cooked in almond milk; the dough will be made of pinenut milk, salt, almond oil and flour.

124. To prepare a tourte of quince and *caravella* pears.[124]

Get as many quince as pears, not paring them but only cleaning them of their down with a cloth. Grate them with a cheese grater and cook them slowly in butter in a pan, stirring them up from time to time. For every pound of the grated fruit, grind four ounces of marzipan paste, three ounces of candied citron, one ounce of candied orange peel, three ounces of sugar, three ounces of sugared pinenuts, one ounce of fine *mostaccioli* and three fresh eggs. When everything is ground up, get a tourte pan lined with a sheet of dough made of fine flour, egg yolks, sugar, salt, rosewater and butter; into it put the filling with bits of butter on top, covered with another sheet of dough in the form of shutter slats. Bake it in an oven or braise it, making its glazing with sugar and rosewater. Serve it however you like.

---

[122] Melons enjoyed a good medical reputation. 'Melons are marvellously refreshing to the system. They are excellent for those who are troubled with kidney stones and will cure burning urine between midday and starlight' (Castelvetro, trans. Riley, 88).

[123] *per piu respetti*: The *Dizionario etimologico del italiano* (V,3264a) glosses early senses of *rispetti* as 'relazione di quantità' and 'dilazione di tempo.'

[124] See the note in Recipe II,27.

125. To prepare a tourte of apples and Florentine pears without cheese.

Get those pears and apples, with no cheese; pare and core them and cut them into thin little slices. Cook them in fresh butter. It is optional whether you grind your filling mixture, although I find it is more delightful to leave the thin slices whole like that. Having lined a tourte pan with a sheet of dough, sprinkled with sugar and ground *mostaccioli*, carefully set down a layer of pears and apples, sprinkle them and repeat several times until the tourte pan is filled. Cover it over with a sheet of uncut dough with another on it cut however you like. Bake it in an oven or braise it, making its glazing of sugar and rosewater. If, however, you want to grind the apples and pears in a mortar, grind two ounces of *mostaccioli* in with them and, for every pound of the filling, four egg yolks. Serve it however you wish.

You can do any sort of pear and apple that way. And put a little cinnamon into what you sprinkle on them, and little lumps of butter.

126. To prepare an apple tourte without eggs, cheese or butter.

Get six ounces of unpared apples, four ounces of marzipan paste, three ounces of sugared pinenuts, an ounce and a half of *mostaccioli* and two ounces of fine sugar; grind all that together in a mortar with two ounces of breadcrumb soaked in almond milk. When that is done, put it into a tourte pan lined with a rather thick sheet of dough made with fine flour, sweet-almond oil, sugar, salt and warm pinenut milk. Bake it in an oven or braise it, making its glazing on top with sugar and rosewater. If you do not have sugared pinenuts, you can use pinenut paste; and if you do not have that, you can use pinenuts soaked in water along with more sugar. If you do not have marzipan paste, grind up some almonds and use that. On a meat day, instead of the oil, use butter or chicken fat. Serve it hot or cold, whichever you prefer.

127. To prepare a peach tourte.

Get clingstone peaches because they are always better, and follow the directions given for apples and Florentine pears in Recipe 125. The same can be done with apricots. If you want to make pies with peaches, if they are clingstone there is no need to pit them, but if they are freestone take out their pit and follow the directions for quince in Recipe 115. And note that a peach needs less cooking than a quince. Serve it however you like.

128. To prepare a visciola-cherry tourte without cheese.

Get visciola cherries, cook them in a little butter over a low fire, and strain the thickest part of them. Have ground marzipan paste ready, fresh egg yolks and *mostaccioli*, the amount of each at your discretion. When the filling is made up, have a tourte pan lined with a sheet of dough made from egg yolks, butter, sugar, rosewater, salt and fine flour; put the filling into it with a similar sheet of dough on top made like shutter slats.

The same can be done with fresh plums.

129. To prepare a strawberry *crostata* without cheese.

Get strawberries[129.1] in the spring up to the end of May, which is their season. Have a tourte pan ready lined with two sheets of dough, one on top of the other, between them sprinkled with sugar and cinnamon and brushed with fresh butter. When the foot of the strawberries is cut away and they are washed in wine and well drained, one-half of them is put on the first layer of dough,[129.2] sprinkled with sugar, cinnamon and semi-sweet orange juice. The other half is mixed with beaten fresh egg yolks, sugar and cinnamon. The same can be done with plums.[129.3] The pie is covered with two other sheets of dough like those on the bottom, and baked in an oven or braised.

You can do visciola cherries or morello cherries that way, having pitted them. You could do plums, too, after removing their pit and skin.

There will be no mention of strawberry sops because a strawberry is better eaten raw with sugar than used for making any sort of sops. In that way you could make the *crostata* with elderflower in the spring.

[To make various sops.][xviii]

130. To prepare muscatel pear sops.

Get muscatel pears as they come on the market[130] and pare them, leaving a finger-width of stem on them. Cook them in red wine, sugar, whole cinnamon and, for every two-thirds of a litre of wine, a pound of fine sugar. Have bread sautéed in butter and set out in dishes, and soaked in the pears' decoction. Set the pears there on end, sprinkling them with sugar and cinnamon.

If you want to make a tourte of them, follow the directions for pears and apples in Recipe 125. You could make apple sops that way.

131. To prepare sops of fresh plums, either whole or cut up.

Get plums that are not too ripe and leave them in boiling water until you see the skin wrinkling; take them out immediately. Put them into cold white wine and carefully skin them. Freestone ones will open in the middle; leave the other ones

---

[129.1] At the beginning of the following century Castelvetro still writes: 'Strawberries are one of the healthiest fruits to eat and would not even harm an invalid' (trans. Riley, 71).

[129.2] This pie being a *crostata*, in which the upper and lower crust are of flaky pastry, Scappi must mean *il primo sfoglio* as the double lower pie shell as a whole – to which unit he will refer for purposes of comparison when the upper crust is made up.

[129.3] This sentence anticipates an option mentioned later. We may wonder whether Scappi or his printer somehow substituted this sentence for a direction about what is to be done with the second half of the strawberries.

[xviii] This section heading appears before Recipe 130 in the Table at the end of this Book.

[130] *nel suo principio.*

whole. Have two-thirds of a litre of white wine ready, weighing a pound and a half, with a pound of fine sugar; bring that to a boil with the plums, watching that they do not get too cooked because a brief boiling is enough. If you want to put them in a dish, have thin slices of bread ready that have been braised and sautéed in butter, and pour some of the plums' cooking broth over them. Then onto the bread put the plums sprinkled with sugar and cinnamon. Serve them hot.

You could do apricots the same way, and slices of clingstone peaches[131] that are not too ripe.

132. To prepare prune sops.

Get damson prunes, which are the best, wash them in warm water and let them steep for a quarter of an hour. Cook them – depending on what the Physician prescribes – either in plain water and sugar or in water, wine and sugar. The same can be done with any sort of prune or dried visciola cherries. Serve them hot on thin slices of bread.

133. To prepare sops with dried dates.

Get dried dates that are not more than a year old, cut them through the middle and remove the white substance that is inside and the pit. Boil them in equal amounts of water and a sweet wine along with sugar. Have thin slices of braised bread set out in dishes and pour some of the decoction over them; put the dates on them. With the dates you can cook dried figs and seeded muscatel raisins. Serve it hot.

134. To prepare sops with new verjuice grapes.

Get whole verjuice grapes and cut them through their middle; peel them and seed them. Boil them, either in chicken broth and sugar or else in water and sugar, in such a way that they do not disintegrate. And because by nature verjuice broth turns white, you can tinge it with a little saffron. You can also put in beaten fine herbs. Then make up sops with braised bread.

You can do gooseberries that way. If you do not want sugar in it, it is optional whether you put in fresh beaten egg yolks. Serve it hot.[134]

---

[131] Castelvetro comments on the traditional suspicion that peaches had an unhealthy nature: 'For this reason they are steeped in good wine, which is supposed to draw out the harmful qualities. I very much doubt that these exist; I am sure that it is gluttony rather than hygiene that accounts for this practice. Peaches certainly taste much better with wine, and I notice that nobody ever throws away the wine that they have soaked in, or comes to any harm from drinking it' (trans. Riley, 109).

[134] These last three sentences are a single one in both of the 1570 versions, with commas only where the periods are inserted here.

135. To prepare sops with visciola cherries or morello cherries.

Get one or the other. They should be fresh and not too ripe and picked immediately before. For every two pounds of them get two-thirds of a litre of white wine, four ounces of fresh butter and four ounces of sugar. Bring that to a boil until the wine has coloured. Have slices of bread ready, braised and fried in butter and, when they are set out in dishes, pour some of the visciola cherry juice over them; then put the cherries on them with sugar.

If you want to make pies with them, have a small pastry casing ready, made with fine flour, egg yolks, butter and cold water. Put the visciola cherries or morello cherries into it with sugar, cinnamon and butter, and bake it in an oven. Serve it hot rather than cold. The sops can be made without butter.

If you want to preserve visciola cherries in syrup – I am not saying make a jelly of them – follow the directions below in the recipe for plums preserved in syrup, leaving the stem on them: they need to be done in small clusters.

136. To preserve fresh plums in syrup.

Skin the plums with a knife. Have clarified sugar[136.1] ready in a clean, well-tinned copper pot and, for every pound of sugar, six ounces of water. Boil it over a low fire with the plums in it, as many as can go into it without being too close together, until the plums are tender and the sugar has thickened. Then take that out of the pot, put it into dishes and let it cool.

The same can be done with apricots[136.2] and peaches. Bear in mind that a large clingstone peach can be cut up into pieces.

[136.1] Several of Scappi's recipes call for sugar that has been clarified (II,281, VI,152 and elsewhere). The process, involving water, egg whites, boiling and skimming, had been in use for a long time. The British Library, Harleian MS 2378, of the late-fourteenth or early-fifteenth century, offers detailed instructions for the operation:

'To clarifie suger. Take a quarte of fayre water & put it in a panne, & therto the whyte of iii egges; and take a brusche made of birchen bowes and bete the water and the egges to-gyddyr tyl it be resolued & kast a grete scome aboven. Than put away thi birchen and put therto ii pound of suger and medel all togyddyr. And than sette it over the fyre on a furnes, & whan it begynnyth to boyle wythdrawe thi fyr and lat it noght ryse. And so claryfye it wyth esy fyr. And whan it waxes fayr and clere in the myddell, take it fro the fyre and cole [*pour*] it thurgh a fayr streynour, and in the colyng holde thi brusche before the panne syde for comynge downe of the scome into the streynour. And wyth that suger thou may make all maner confectyons.' Constance B. Hieatt and Sharon Butler, ed., *Curye on Inglysch. English Culinary Manuscripts of the Fourteenth Century* (London: Oxford University Press, 1985), 'Goud Kokery,' p. 150, Recipe 11.

We see those egg whites in Scappi's Recipe 213, below.

[136.2] 'Apricots are usually eaten raw, but they make delicious and healthy sweetmeats when crystalized or preserved in syrup' (Castelvetro, trans. Riley, 84).

137. To prepare currant sops.

Get currants that are not at all old, wash them and clean them of any dirt. When they are cleaned and washed in several changes of water, let them drain in a colander. Boil a part of them in equal amounts of white wine and water, with sugar and a stick of whole cinnamon; grind the other part in a mortar, moistening it with the broth in which the currants were cooked, and straining that. Put everything together and bring it just to a boil and no more. Then make the sops the way the other was done. Whether it is made thin or thick is up to you. And you can do it plain without grinding it in a mortar. Serve it hot.

You can do muscatel raisins that way and other dried grapes once they are seeded.

138. To prepare *berlingozzi*.[138.1]

Get ten fresh, beaten eggs and make a dough of them with fine flour so that it turns out more on the thin side than thick. Let it sit for a quarter of an hour. Then make a round *ciambella*[138.2] and put three slashes in it. Put it into an oven that is hotter above than below; it should be very clean. When they have risen,[138.3] colour it with beaten egg yolk and rosewater, and quickly throw the sugar on them. When it is baked, serve them hot. You can colour them before it is put into the oven.

139. To prepare *zuccarini*[139.1] that look like *ciambelle*.

Get fine sugar that is reduced to powder. Get beaten fresh egg whites and put them into a shallow basin along with as much of that sugar as the eggs can hold – that is, so they form a thick paste. With that paste make up *ciambelle*, which you put into a tourte pan. They should be sprinkled with flour and brushed with white wax.[139.2] Bake them with little heat under them and somewhat more above. They need little cooking because the egg whites swell up in a lively way and end up light. Along with those ingredients you can put in a little rosewater or musk water if you like.

140. To prepare small *ciambelle* with eggs.

Get ten fresh eggs and six ounces of fine sugar and make a dough of them with as much fine flour as the eggs can hold; the dough should be thick. Knead it for an hour, taking care not to add any flour when you knead it or when you make

---

[138.1] See also Recipe V,147 for a Sienese variety of these confections.

[138.2] This is a variety of ring-shaped pastry, seen in Recipe V,148.

[138.3] *quando saranno alzati*: The pasty occasionally becomes plural in this recipe.

[139.1] The word is derived from *zuccaro*, sugar. One modern translation might be 'sugarplums,' although Scappi's confection is ring-shaped rather than a ball.

[139.2] The glazing with pure beeswax is noteworthy.

them, but rather greasing your hand with almond oil or Greek wine. When they are made, put them into boiling water and leave them boiling until they float up. Take them out with a holed spoon, put them into a basket to let them drain. When they have cooled, set them out in tourte pans of a big enough size, with edges that are not too high, and that have nothing on their bottom; arrange the *ciambelle* regularly in the pans. Bake them in a moderate oven which is hotter above than beneath. And before you take them out of the oven, make the rosette on them[140] with a feather dipped in fresh egg white. Serve them however you like.

141. To prepare rolled wafers with breadcrumb and sugar.

Get white breadcrumb, soak it in cold water and put it through a sieve. Make it into a dough with fine flour, rosewater, sugar, plain water, and fresh egg yolks because otherwise you could not make a wafer cornet. Make the batter either thin or thick, depending on the irons[141.1] you'll be using, by adding a little malmsey to it. Make the rolled wafer. If you want them filled with the breast meat of capon boiled in salted water, grind that meat in a marble mortar, moisting it with a little cold water and putting it through the sieve with the breadcrumb and mixing it in with the other ingredients. Roll up[141.2] the wafer cornets. They can also be made with almond milk and egg yolks.

142. To prepare dainty morsels[142.1] – that is, Milanese-style *mostaccioli*.[142.2]

Get fifteen fresh eggs, beat them in a casserole pot and strain them with two

---

[140] *si darà loro la rosa.*

[141.1] See the apparatus identified as *per fare cialde*, for making wafers, Plate 16.

[141.2] Scappi writes *faccianosi* here and twice before: 'make.' Cf., though, Recipe 53 where the verb is *revolganosi in sù*, 'roll up.'

[142.1] See also Recipe V,237. The present *morselletti* are a musk-flavoured variety of those small cakes. Elsewhere as ingredients Scappi calls for *mostaccioli muschiati* (Recipes II,249 and V,70 and 73) and for *mostaccioli Napolitani muschiati* (Recipes II,248 and V,64, 89, 112 and 121). Scappi usually attributes their origin to Naples; this present rubric is the only instance where Milan appears associated with them.

While Scappi gives no other recipe for what might be a 'plain' *mostaccioli*, a contemporary of his, Lancelot de Casteau, in Liege, an ecclesiastical centre, does offer directions for making that typically Italian confection. There is a striking resemblance between the two recipes. '*Pour faire monstachole* [*sic*], get a pound of skinned, ground almonds, a pound and a half of white flour, four ounces of cinnamon, half an ounce of nutmeg, finely ground cloves, ten grains of musk, two pounds of sifted white sugar, six egg yolks, two ounces of butter. Make a rather thick dough of that with a little rosewater, then shape your *monstacholes* in hollow moulds of whatever size you want, set them on wafers and paper and bake them in a moderately warm oven' (*Ouverture de cuisine*, 56).

[142.2] See Riley's observations on the *mostacciolo* (*The Oxford Companion to Italian Food*, 333). Sabban and Serventi (*A tavola nel Rinascimento*, 200) are not convinced that the name *mostacciolo* derives from *mosto*, must, there being no trace of must in any recipe they have seen for it. One might perhaps plausibly suggest that the name arises from its shape – a small snout, *mostac-*

and a half pounds of fine, powdered sugar, half an ounce of raw aniseed or else ground coriander, and a grain or two[142.3] of fine musk; with that put two and a half pounds of flour. Beat everything for three-quarters of an hour so that the dough becomes like fritter batter. Let it sit for a quarter of an hour, then beat it again. Then have greased sheets of paper ready, made like lamps,[142.4] or else high-sided tourte pans with, on the bottom, wafers that have not been moistened with anything; then put the batter into the lamps or tourte pans, filling them to no more than the thickness of a finger. Sprinkle them immediately with sugar and put them into a hot oven or, in the case of the ones in the tourte pans, bake them like tourtes.[142.5] When that batter has risen up and thoroughly dried out and is rather firm – that is, it should be like a soft focaccia[142.6] – take it out of the tourte pan or lamp. Right away with a broad, sharp knife cut them up into slices two fingers wide and as long as you like, and put them back into the oven on sheets of paper to bake again like biscuits,[142.7] turning them over often. The oven should not be as hot as before, though. When they have thoroughly dried out, take them out and set them aside because they are always better the second day than the first. They will last a month in their best state.

---

cio, or, perhaps, from its more modern sense, a mustache – rather than from its flavour – even though that is clearly indeed musty in both Scappi and Lancelot de Casteau. Today's *mostaccioli* are a sort of fruitcake made of flour, honey (or must syrup), raisins, dried figs, ground almonds and (a modern addition) chocolate. Sabban and Serventi offer a modernized rendition of Scappi's *Mostaccioli alla milanese*.

[142.3] This *grano* refers to an apothecary's unit of weight, roughly equivalent to .06 grams. The use of such a measurement indicates the exotic and pharmacological nature of musk. In any case, what Scappi means is a very small amount.

[142.4] The normal *lucerne* were covered, shallow, boat-like dishes, each upward-curving end of whose cover had a hole, one to fill the lamp with oil, the other for the wick and flame. Their shape was approximated by a priest's older-style two-pointed biretta – which, because of that similarity, was itself at one time popularly called a *lucerna*. These one-use moulds will produce a shallow curved cake.

[142.5] That is, with the tourte pan covered with a flat or concave lid that has hot coals or embers on it.

[142.6] This is the only place in which Scappi writes the word *focaccia*. (See Gillian Riley's commentary on this flatbread in *The Oxford Companion to Italian Food*, 215.) He refers, however, to a *fucaccina* (sic) in Recipes V,44 and 130.

[142.7] Scappi's verb here is *a biscottarsi*, literally 'to cook a second time.' The Italian term *biscotto* (seen in Recipe 143) and the English term *biscuit* (from the Old French) mean simply 'twice cooked.'

143. Another way to prepare dainty morsels – that is, *mostaccioli*.[143.1]

Get fine biscuits made with white bread,[143.2] grind them in a mortar and put them through a fixed sieve. Then get twelve fresh eggs and beat them well with two ounces of Greek wine or malmsey, two ounces of fresh leaven, two pounds of fine powdered sugar and ten ounces of the above ground and sieved biscuit. Beat everything for an hour, together with two grains of musk. Then follow the directions for making and baking given in the previous recipe. Be aware that they do not take such a sprightly fire. They will turn the colour of *mostaccioli*. Those biscuits are usually eaten in the winter with a good wine.

[Things to make with milk and other ingredients.][xix]

144. To prepare butter vermicelli.

Get fresh butter, which will be much better in May than in any other month, and put it through a syringe, splashing it with rosewater as it comes out. Serve it with finely ground sugar on it. If the butter is several days old, wash it[144] in several changes of cool water, and the last should be rosewater. Then grind it in a mortar with ten hard-boiled egg yolks for every pound of butter, and three ounces of sugar. When everything is ground up, put it through the syringe or through a colander. With that butter you can make various pieces of work with a syringe, at the Cook's discretion and of his design.

145. To prepare cream tops.

Get twenty-six litres of that day's cow's milk, warm it and then divide it up among various wooden or tinned-copper containers, each holding about two and two-thirds litres. Let them sit in a cool place until the cream separates – that is, with the film of cream on top. With a spoon lift off that film, which is the cream top, and put it in dishes. When you serve them, sprinkle them with fine sugar. Every time you want to lift that skin, warm the milk up and follow the directions given above for dividing it up in containers. If you want to carry those cream tops from place to place, put them into earthenware or glass pots, keeping them sealed in order to prevent the air from turning them brown and bitter.

[143.1] These, too, are musk-flavoured but not expressly Milanese in origin.

[143.2] See a recipe for such biscuits in V,237.

[xix] *Per far lavori di latte, & d'altre materie*: this sectional rubric appears before Recipe 144 in the Table at the end of this Book VI. Scappi's general term *lavori*, pieces, creations or products, literally 'works,' includes anything the cook can imagine to make up with certain materials at his disposal: artifacts, handiworks.

[144] According to Recipe 209, below, the present passage outlines the standard method of producing 'washed' butter.

146. To prepare ricotta cheeses with Milanese almonds and melon seeds.[146.1]

Grind two pounds of almonds, which have first steeped in cold water and been shelled, with four ounces of melon seeds, likewise hulled, and a pound and a half of fine sugar, moistening it with a reduced, clear broth made from fresh pike. If you do not have pike, use sea bass; and if you do not have any fish, get a broth of goat kid's feet. Strain it, then set it to cook the way starch is done in Recipe 79, adding in a little rosewater. When it is thick, put it into wicker ricotta moulds,[146.2] and put them into a cool place. The ones made of fish broth are served during Lent, and the ones made with goat kid's feet are served on meat days garnished with fine sugar and flowers.

[Various ways to cook eggs.][xx]

And firstly,

147. To cook eggs in hot water for drinking.

It is held that domestic hen's eggs are the best among those of all fowl, and all the more so when the hen is fed on grains rather than grasses. And if you want them for beverages they must be laid that very day. Get a pot of boiling water and put the eggs into it, and right away draw the pot back off the fire and take the eggs out. Make a small hole on a side of each egg, put them back into the pot and you will see the white coming out. When the eggs have been in for the time taken to say one *Credo*, take them out; touch the white that is outside the shell and if it is firm they are done. You can also use a knife to test whether they are done, by tapping them with the spine of the knife: if the eggs do not break and they stand the knocking they will be done; on the other hand, though, if they break, they will not be done. But the ones with the hole are the more sure.

You can also cook them by the heat of the fire, and when they draw their moisture[147] back into themselves, they are done.

148. To poach eggs in water.

Get an egg laid that day and carefully break it into a pot containing a little clear, cold water – that is done because if you put it into boiling water the egg will tend to sink to the bottom – and let it cover over[148] and the white congeal. When

---

[146.1] See Recipe III,219.

[146.2] This ersatz cheese – useful on a fasting day – will mimic the appearance of the soft new cheese (in English, 'junket') which, from the impression on it of the reed basket in which it sets, is called *giuncata* (Recipe V,85).

[xx] This section heading appears also in the Table at the end of this Book, before Recipe 147.

[147] Scappi calls this exuded moisture, 'sweat.'

[148] Scappi uses this verb *coprire* also in Recipe 154 to describe the way the outer film of protein around an egg turns white as the cold water is heated and the egg begins to cook.

it is covered such that it has become white, and the yolk is not broken, take the egg out with a flat spoon: that is done because if the spoon were holed the white would protrude into the holes and that would make it more difficult to be able to put them into the dish. Serve them with verjuice and sugar or orange juice over them. If you would like a few thin slices of buttered bread in the dish, you can do that.

149. A different way to poach eggs.

Get eggs cooked as above and have a dish ready with a few thin slices of braised bread; put the eggs on them. Then have a sauce made up of orange juice, verjuice, sugar, raisins and butter, all boiled together and tinged with saffron; put it over top of the eggs. In summer instead of verjuice use verjuice grapes, peeled and seeded; in spring instead of raisins, gooseberries. Serve them hot with sugar and cinnamon over them.

150. To poach eggs in goat's milk.

Get fresh, strained milk, bring it slowly to a boil and put eggs into it the way it is done above. Let them cook. Have dishes ready with thin slices of bread that have been dipped in leftover milk. Then on the bread put the eggs garnished with sugar and rosewater.

151. To poach eggs in white wine.

Get two and two-thirds litres of sweet white wine and set it boil in a pot of glazed earthenware or well-tinned copper along with a pound of sugar. Put fresh eggs to cook in it as described in Recipe 148. Dip thin slices of braised bread in the wine and a little fresh butter. With the eggs arranged on the bread, sprinkle them with sugar and cinnamon. That preparation is eaten more in winter than in any other season. It is served hot.

152. To poach eggs in sugar.

When some sugar has been clarified, put it into a silver or well-tinned copper saucepan, or into silver dishes, and heat it up. When the sugar is hot, put egg yolks into it along with a little rosewater. Give it heat from above with either a hot shovel or tourte pan lid.[152] Serve those eggs in the same pan with sugar and cinnamon over them. You can also cook the whites with them.

153. To do stuffed eggs.[153]

Get two-day-old eggs, because when fresh ones are cooked they are hard to shell and most of the egg sticks to the shell. Put them into hot water to cook

---

[152] As in Recipe III,269 and elsewhere the iron blade of this wooden-handled shovel or the copper pan cover will be heated for the purpose.

[153] See also Recipe III,273. Scappi's *uove ripiene* are a sort of devilled egg with a complex filling.

so they become hard. When they are done, put them into cold water and shell them. When that is done, cut them crosswise and remove their yolk, grinding it in a mortar with marzipan paste, raw egg yolks, sugar, cinnamon, mint, marjoram, burnet and water-cooked raisins. Fill the whites with that mixture, setting them in a tourte pan with the filling upwards. In that pan there should be melted capon fat or butter. Give it heat from below and above, turning them upside down. When you are ready to serve them, have a sauce ready made of Milanese almonds ground in a mortar and moistened with verjuice, and sugar; that sauce is cooked in a different, small saucepan with capon fat or butter. While it is still hot, pour it over the eggs. They can also be served without that sauce but with orange juice and sugar over them.

154. To do fried eggs.[154.1]

Get fresh eggs. Have fresh butter that is strained so that no sediment remains, and heat it up in a frying pan; hold the pan's handle up so the butter runs together and the eggs take on a good shape. Put the eggs into the butter when it is warm and let them cook slowly, splashing hot butter over the yolks with a spoon so they cover over.[154.2] With a sharp spoon take them out without breaking them. Serve them hot with orange juice and sugar over them.

You can do it with melted capon or goose fat. And with the same liquids you can cook them in a small saucepan of tinned copper or silver, or else in silver dishes, and serve them in those vessels.

155. To prepare small tubes of fresh eggs.

Beat ten eggs. Have a spoon that will hold only the amount of one egg and a frying pan[155.1] that is not too large and is greased with butter; put a spoonful of the egg into it, making an omelet the size of the pan. On the omelet put sugar, cinnamon and cooked raisins and roll it up like a rolled wafer. Do the others the same and stack them up, one on top of the other, sprinkled with sugar, cinnamon and orange juice. Cut off the tip of the tubes so they are all uniform[155.2] and stew them in butter, sugar, orange juice and rosewater between two dishes. Serve them hot.

156. To prepare a green omelet.

Beat eggs, put them through a colander with a beaker of chard and spinach juice and a little salt. Make an omelet in fresh butter, without turning it over so it

---

[154.1] *uove frittellate* are properly 'frittered eggs.'

[154.2] That is, so that the albumen whitens on top. See also Recipe 148.

[155.1] Scappi's *padella da frittate* is literally an omelet pan, clearly of a relatively small size. It should not be mistaken for the *padella per fare ovi frittolate* in Plate 8.

[155.2] That is – so that the ends align evenly.

will be softer. Use only a sharp spoon to draw it together in the pan, making it the same round size as the dish for which it is intended when cooked. Turn the pan over onto the dish. Serve it hot with a little orange juice and sugar over it.

You can do omelets that way without green juice, putting in a little water so they will be soft.

157. To prepare an almond omelet.

Grind shelled Milanese almonds in a mortar, moistening them with clear water, strain it so that what is strained is on the thick side. Stir it in with eggs, beating that very well and putting it all through a colander. Make the omelet in fresh butter. You can also put a little fine sugar into it if you like. Serve it hot with orange juice and sugar over it. You can also do it with capon flesh ground in a mortar, and ground pinenuts rather than almonds. That omelet needs plenty of butter so it will not stick to the pan.

158. To prepare an omelet with various fine herbs.

Get one-day-old eggs and beat them with a little salt; add in mint, marjoram, burnet, sorrel and parsley. Grind everything mixed together and make an omelet of it. Serve it hot like that, garnished with sugar. In the months of April and May, in place of the herbs you can put in fresh elderflowers.

159. To prepare an omelet in water.

Get one-day-old eggs, beat them and strain them with a beaker of juice from spinach tips and chard. Have a casserole pot or a cooking basin full of boiling salted water and butter; put the eggs into it and cover it over for a short while. Pick up the poached omelet with a spoon, make it into a ball and put the ball into a colander to let it drain. When it has drained, serve it in dishes with sugar and cinnamon over it. If you do not want it with the green juice, get mint, marjoram and burnet beaten small together with the eggs. You can do the omelet with eggs alone that way, and also with ground almonds with elderflowers.

160. To prepare goat's milk sops.

Get fresh goat's milk and, for every two-thirds of a litre of it, three ounces of finely ground sugar and three ounces of butter; bring them to a boil together. Then have breadcrumb, in slices, and set out in a dish and moistened twice with that milk until the bread has absorbed it. Then serve it with fine sugar and a drop of rosewater over top.

The same can be done with the milk of Milanese almonds.

161. To prepare sops with fresh butter, which are commonly called *butirata*.

This dish is made in May. Get thin slices of bread the thickness of a knife blade and three fingers wide; let them sit in an oven or in a tourte pan. Then get a somewhat dished silver plate, or else a small baking dish which is either silver or copper with its inside tinned, with butter in it. Set down a layer of bread slices sprinkled with fine sugar and as much again cold butter as before; repeat that for two or three layers. Then bake it with only a little heat below and above as is done with tourtes. Give it a glazing with sugar and rosewater.

[To make various dainty pottages.][xxi]

162. To prepare a dainty pottage with sea bass milt.

Get the milt of a sea bass along with its liver cut up into pieces; wash it thoroughly. Put them into a cooking basin or a small kettle with either sweet-almond oil or butter or excellent olive oil. Sauté that slowly, adding in enough unsalted broth of some other fish, or water, to cover it. Boil it with a little salt, adding in peeled, seeded verjuice grapes or else raisins with a little verjuice, and white wine and a little chopped fine herbs – that is, mint and marjoram – to give it colour.

If you do not have sea bass you can do it the same way with the milt and liver of an umbra or a sturgeon or pike. Likewise in a pottage you can do up any sort of fish that the Physician allows.

163. To prepare a dainty pottage of trout roe.

Get the freshest trout eggs you can, wash them and set them to boil for a quarter of an hour in water. Remove their membrane so that they become like peas, and make them into a little *pottaggino* as was done above, but leaving out the verjuice grapes and raisins; in place of them put in a little wine and a little verjuice. Serve them on thin slices of bread.

164. To prepare a dainty pottage of cockles and clams.

The cockles or clams you get must be fresh. Make them open on a shovel[164] or else plunge them into hot water in a net or towel, leaving them there until they have opened. Take them out of their shell, setting aside the water that is in there and straining it. Wash the cockles or clams because of the sand on them and put them into a small kettle or a cooking basin in almond oil or sweet-olive oil or butter, along with their water that has been set aside, and a little white wine, verjuice, saffron, cinnamon, a little ground almonds, and beaten mint, marjoram and parsley. Bring that to a boil and serve it hot.

The same can be done with telleens and limpets and with any other sort of shell fish.

[xxi] This sectional rubric, *Per far diversi pottaggetti*, appears before Recipe 162 in the Table at the end of Book VI. The term *pottaggino* that appears in Recipes VI,41 and 163 seems to be synonymous with *pottaggetto*.

[164] *pala*: Undoubtedly an iron-bladed fire shovel that can be heated in the coals, rather than a wooden oven peel. Causing the oysters of the next recipe to open *su le bragie* is likely the same operation as with *una pala*.

165. To prepare a dainty pottage of oysters.

Get fresh oysters, get them to open on the coals and set aside the water that is inside their shells. Take the tenderest, whitest part of them and put that into a small kettle or cooking basin with sweet-olive oil or sweet-almond oil. Sauté them gently, adding in the water that came from the shells and with it a little plain water, enough to cover them. Grind a few almonds with the darkest part of the oysters, the hinge muscle,[165] and put that through a colander with a little verjuice and white wine. Mix everything together with a little cinnamon and pepper, if the Physician agrees. Boil it for a quarter of an hour. Then serve it hot. It can also be done without almonds and with only a little beaten fine herbs.

166. To prepare a dainty pottage of snails.

Get snails that are closed up in their shell in the winter because they are cleaner during that season.[166.1] Boil them in water for two hours, take them out of their shell and wash them in salted water to remove their mucosity. Wash them again in several changes of cold water and cut them up or leave them whole. Follow the above directions for cooking them, putting a little mint, pepper and cinnamon with them because that sort of dish calls for them.[166.2] When they are cooked, add in a little verjuice. They are served on thin slices of bread. You can do them with their shell that way, having first dug them out, though, and cleaned them of any filth; afterwards they are put back into their shell.

167. To prepare a dainty pottage of deboned frogs.

Get eviscerated frogs from June throughout the fall and boil them in plain, lightly salted water. Take them out of the broth and put them into cold water. Take the meat and sauté it gently in oil or butter in a small pan, adding in water and enough salt, peeled and seeded verjuice grapes, mint, marjoram, burnet and parsley, those herbs beaten with a few ground almonds or grated bread to thicken the broth. Cook it all. Colour it with a little cinnamon and saffron. Instead of almonds and grated bread, you can thicken the broth with egg yolks, depending on the day. You can also beat the meat small after it is boiled, though because frogs' legs[167] are very small and by nature separate from one another, they are rarely beaten. Serve them hot.

---

[165] This is what Scappi calls the *sfogliatura.*

[166.1] Cf. otherwise, in Recipe III,197, the extensive process required in order to clean out snails.

[166.2] *percioche tal vivanda le richiede.* Snails are perceived as cold and moist creatures, requiring condiments, therefore, whose properties are markedly both warming and drying.

[167] This is the only instance in which Scappi writes *le coscie delle rane,* 'frogs' *legs.'* This passage implies that the whole recipe may have been dealing with the legs alone.

168. To prepare a dainty pottage of land tortoise.[168.1]

Get a tortoise at the time of year when grain is forming ears,[168.2] ideally throughout the fall, the female being better than the male. Cut its head off (experience will show you that the body lives for a day without the head). To make it more tender, set the tortoise on the fire in cold water, with the pot sealed, and boil it for two hours more or less, depending on its size. When it is cooked put it next into cold water, remove its shell and get the best parts, which are the eggs and liver. Make a pottage of them as is done with frogs – watching out for the gallbladder, though, because you can scarcely see it in the liver, it being in the big part.

You can also open the tortoise before it is cooked, right after the head has been cut off, and take the skinned meat and sauté it slowly in butter or oil, adding in a fish broth or water. Make a pottage of it as above, though it needs somewhat less cooking.

Often the eggs that are found in turtles are, with their shell, the size of a quail's egg and have a yolk and white like any other egg. They can also be fried in extremely good oil, first being floured. They are dressed with green sauce[168.3] or some other sauce. The same can be done with a snail, frogs and crayfish claws. Note that freshwater turtles are dark and have a tail and are not as good as the land sort which look like a checkerboard and have only a stub of a tail.

169. To prepare a dainty pottage of common field mushrooms.

In the spring get the sort of mushroom called agaric; that is their season. Clean them and wash them well because of the sand on them, and put them to sauté slowly in butter or olive oil in a cooking basin or some other pot, turning them from time to time, because they make a broth by themselves. In a mortar grind up a good bunch of them, as many as you can take in your hand, moistening them with hot water without making them too thin. Put them into a pot containing the whole, unground field mushrooms and boil them together with a little verjuice. Just before you want to serve them, put a few finely chopped herbs in with them. Then serve them hot on thin slices of bread. The reason why the mushrooms are ground in the mortar is so they will have more of their flavour, because when they are mixed with other ingredients they are not as good.

[168.1] See Recipe III,165.

[168.2] *nel tempo della spica.*

[168.3] See Recipe II,272.

170. To stew young lamprey from the Tiber.[170.1]

Get young lamprey in the spring, removing the slime on them with hot water so they end up thoroughly clean. Drain their blood with a little knife, and catch that blood,[170.2] putting the lamprey into a small pan with sweet-almond oil or olive oil and sautéing them slowly with heat from below and above; turn them over. When they have sautéed for a quarter of an hour, drain off most of the oil and leave the thick part that is in the bottom with the young lamprey. Then have roasted Milanese almonds that have been ground in a mortar with a little *mostaccioli*, sugar and raisins, moistening that with white wine and orange juice. Strain it so that it is thin, and mix it with both the blood that has been set aside and the thick oil that was left at the bottom. Put all of that with the lamprey, boiling it slowly until it has thickened a little. Serve them hot with a little cinnamon over them.

They can also be served without a flavouring. When they have been cooked in the above oil, drain off the oil. Dilute the blood with orange juice and pour it into the small saucepan with a little sugar, stirring it around with a spoon. Serve it hot.

You can also cook them on a grill, without their blood having been drained but only having washed them, turning them over and basting them with a sprig of rosemary dipped in oil. When they have cooked, serve them garnished with a little sugar and orange juice.

If you want them in little pies, when they are clean put them into a small pastry shell with a few raisins and a little butter. When they are almost baked, have the above sauce, made with roasted almonds, ready in the saucepan and put it in through the hole on top; finish off baking it. Serve it hot. They can also be done in pies with fine herbs, beaten mint, marjoram, sorrel and burnet, and either prunes or gooseberries.

171. To prepare a dainty pottage of fresh, deboned sardines.

Get fresh sardines, scaled and clean; take off their head and tail, split them through the middle and remove their bones. Put them into a small pan of tinned copper or earthenware with enough good olive oil, a little Greek wine and water to cover the sardines by a finger, and enough salt. Boil them. At the end put in mint, marjoram, burnet and whatever savory herbs you like. If you would like to put in a little almond milk, you can. In springtime you will put in a few gooseberries; in summer, verjuice grapes, peeled and seeded; and in winter, raisins and a little wine. You could also do them whole without the bones being removed.

[170.1] The 1581 printing: *Per fare stufate*; the first printing: *Per fare stufato*. Scappi gives his preparation the generic dish name *stufata* (or *stufato*), a stew. (See also the section heading before Recipe 36, above, and a mention of *stufatore*, stewpots, in Recipe 25.) Though the words suggest a cooking in a sealed pot, that seems not to be the case here.

[170.2] See the note in Recipe III,90 concerning the exceptional value of a lamprey's blood.

172. Another way to prepare a pottage of fresh sardines.

Get fresh sardines without their head, tail, scales and bones; wash them in several changes of water and let them sit for a quarter of an hour in hot water so that all of their skin can be removed and their white meat is left firm. Take them out of the hot water and let them drain. Grind them in a mortar with two ounces of breadcrumb soaked in hot almond milk and, for every pound of sardines, two ounces of marzipan paste and, if it is not a fasting day, two fresh eggs. When everything is ground up, put in two ounces of raisins or gooseberries or peeled, seeded verjuice grapes – depending on the season – and a handful of finely chopped herbs, and salt and saffron. When it has all been cooked again together, have a small kettle or cooking basin ready with saffron-tinged water, salt and boiling butter or oil; into that put the mixture made into a ball or in the shape of a small soft cheese.[172.1] Let it cook for half an hour. Then serve it dressed with that fish broth that is not too salty. Cook it in the cooking basin with fresh butter, stirring it continuously until it thickens. Then serve it hot.

With that mixture you could make ravioli without a casing,[172.2] and braised little balls made in the way described in the next recipe.

173. To prepare little balls of braised sardine flesh.

Get[173.1] fresh sardines without their head, tail, scales and bones, wash them and, still raw, cut them up small with knives along with fine herbs and fresh or dried fennel seeds, mixing orange juice or verjuice, a little salt, sugar and mild spices[173.2] in with that if the Physician approves. Out of that mixture make little balls the size of a hard-boiled egg yolk. Put them into a tourte pan containing sweet-almond oil or butter, and give them heat below and above as is done with tourtes. When they are sautéed, add in enough of another fish broth or saffron-tinged water to half cover them, and gooseberries or verjuice, and beaten fine herbs; finish off cooking them. When they are done, serve them with that broth.

They can be braised just with oil, orange juice and fennel flour, without beating them.

174. To prepare a dainty pottage of sea bream flesh.

Get a sea bream that is fresh, boil it in plain water but do not fully cook it. Take it out, drain it and carefully remove the skin and bones. Beat the flesh with knives on a table, along with mint, marjoram, burnet and other fine herbs,

---

[172.1] That is, thick, slightly flattened patties: *in forma di casciotto*. Cf. also Recipe 174.

[172.2] See Recipe II,181.

[173.1] The 1581 text reads *Pestinosi*, 'Grind up'; the earlier text shows (probably correctly) *Piglinosi*, 'Take' or 'Get.'

[173.2] The composition of these *spetierie dolci* is never described by Scappi. The mixture would likely include cinnamon and sugar but not pepper.

eggs, sugar and raisins, making it thick. Give it the shape of a large cheese or of ravioli. Cook it in a broth made of[174] butter and salt. However, if you want to do it like meat paste, use only raisins and verjuice grapes, seeded and peeled, or else gooseberries, depending on the season; to give it colour, a little saffron at the end. If it is a lean day but not a fast day, you can put in beaten egg yolks and fine herbs, although because the flesh of sea bream is by nature white, it looks better without herbs.

You can do the flesh of red mullet the same way, as well as sea bass, gilthead, trout, carp, perch and scorpion fish, because those are the least viscous fish; and yet you could also do pike, sturgeon and umbra. However, when the above fish are not bigger than between one and two pounds, they will be very viscous, especially if they have been caught in good waters and not in ponds or swamps. On fasting days, instead of butter use sweet-almond oil.

175. Various ways to make stuffed croquettes of sea bass, cooked on a spit.

Get fresh sea bass, scale it, then wash it and slice its flesh lengthwise with a slender knife in such a way that the skeleton is not touched; do not leave any bones in that flesh. If you want to be sure about bones, take the area between the tail and the umbilicus. When the flesh is sliced, beat it with the spine of a knife on the skinless side and sprinkle it with salt and fennel flour. Then turn each half over with the skin up and cover it either with a mixture composed of mashed sardines, as in Recipe 173 for the little balls, or else with the same flesh of a sea bass beaten with fine herbs and fresh or dried fennel seeds mixed with orange juice, salt and a small amount of mild spices. When they are covered, roll them up in such a way that the flesh is outward. Put them into a small copper pan with oil in it and heat them enough to close them up. Take them out and let them cool. Mount them on a slender spit with a sage or bay leaf between each and roast them over a rather sprightly fire, giving them a glazing of flour and sugar or grated bread. When they are done, serve them hot with a garnish of orange juice and sugar.

If you want them done on a grill, when they are spitted like that roast them, basting them occasionally with oil, vinegar and must syrup, turning them over often. When they are done, serve them with the same sauce.

If you want them done braised, though, when they are set out in the pan as above, heat them up until they have closed up, and turn them over, colouring them a little all around. Then put in enough fish broth which is not too salty but tinged with saffron, to half cover them; with that broth there should be gooseberries or verjuice grapes, and beaten fine herbs. Finish off cooking them the way a tourte is done. Then serve them hot with their broth. If you do not want them with broth, when they have coloured, finish off their cooking in a delicate sauce made of orange juice, sugar and verjuice. Serve them with that same sauce.

---

[174] We should probably read *fatto con* ('made with') rather than *fatto di*.

You could do large sea bream in each of those ways,[175] as well as corb, pike, trout and carp.

176. To prepare a dainty pottage of perch with Milanese almonds.

Get perch, a river fish and quite delicate, and boil it in salted water without its scales and bones, having deboned it thoroughly. Beat it very small with knives. Then have milk made up from Milanese almonds and plain water and sugar; put the beaten flesh into it and boil it over a low fire for a quarter of an hour. Then sereve it hot with a drop of rosewater.

The same can be done with the flesh of pike, umbra, sea bream and scorpion fish.

177. To prepare a pottage of crayfish tails and claws.

The claws of crayfish will always be more tender than their tails, yet take whichever you like. Boil a crayfish in water or wine, shell its tail and claws, remove the little ligament in its tail because that toughens it. Put them into a casserole pot or a cooking basin and sauté them with sweet-almond oil or olive oil or fresh butter. Grind up the body with its shell in a mortar, moistening it with the water the crayfish was cooked in. Strain it[177] and let it sit. Take the clearest part of that and put enough of it with the tails to cover them by two fingers. Boil them for half an hour more or less, depending on how much they need, with verjuice grapes or raisins depending on the season; if you put in raisins, put in verjuice, with a few fine herbs at the end when you are ready to serve. You can do it without grinding the crayfish body, though that is done to give it more flavour and aroma. The broth should be coloured, although from May to the end of August the tails and claws will make the broth more russet-coloured than at other times.

178. To prepare a pottage of the claws and tails of a spiny lobster.

Get a spiny lobster, boil it in salted water and wine, sealing the hole at the tail with a little cotton – that being done so the water will not get into the lobster, which water would make it woody and would take away its goodness. When it is cooked, take the claws, which are quite a bit more tender than the tail. Beat them small on a table the way veal is beaten, adding in some fresh eggs, though more yolks than whites, sugar and cinnamon, beaten mint, marjoram and burnet, and either gooseberries or whole verjuice grapes, peeled and seeded, or raisins,

---

[175] In Recipe III,49 Scappi stated that this *fragolino* (*frauolino* in the present recipe) has the driest flesh of any fish – *i pesci men viscosi*; he then added, *perciò nel libro de i convalescenti l'ho posto accommodato in molte vivande*. The logic for a physician or cook was straightforward: because of their habitat, fish possess by nature a cold, moist temperament; many diseases arise from, or occasion, the corrupting influence of moisture; for a person suffering such a disease, a fish with 'dry' flesh is clearly the least harmful. Other ways of preparing sea bream for the sick are found in Recipes VI,35, 114 and 174.

[177] That is, the filtered liquid.

depending on the season. Of that mixture make a ball like ricotta[178] and cook it in a broth of salted water and butter or almond oil. Serve it the way the sea bream are done in Recipe 174.

With that mixture you can make ravioli without a casing, serving it with sugar and cinnamon. When the tail of the above spiny lobster is shelled and the ligament cut out, you can cut it up into little bits and follow the above directions for the crayfish. You can also beat it with knives, and sauté it with oil or butter, adding in a fish broth or salted water, cinnamon and saffron, as well as all the other ingredients that are put into the other dishes except for the eggs. Then cook it so it stays like veal. With that mixture you can make little pies. The same can be done with lobster and with the hermit crab that is found in the Adriatic Sea.

179. Several ways to do tender crabs.[179.1]

Get a tender crab in the spring or fall, many of which are available in Rome, and in Venice, too, though only quite a bit smaller ones called shell-less crabs.[179.2] Flour them with fine flour, fry them in oil or in clarified butter. Serve them hot with orange juice over them. You can also cover them with green sauce instead of the juice. Another way of doing them is to make dainty pottages of them with oil or butter and fine herbs, with either gooseberries or seeded verjuice grapes or raisins, depending on the season.

You can do shell-less spiny lobsters and shell-less lobsters that same way, and any other sort of shell-less crayfish and shell-less crab.[179.3]

180. To grill pickerel.[180]

Get pickerel that are bigger than four ounces, put them on a grill without scaling them but having only gutted them through their mouth; baste them with a sprig of rosemary dipped in oil. Serve them hot, dressed with cooked raisins, sugar and vinegar. If you want to dress them with verjuice sauce, set them to cook without basting them. When you are ready to serve them, remove their skin so they are white, at which time you cover them with a verjuice sauce made with egg yolks, verjuice, sugar and rosewater. Otherwise cover them with green sauce.

You can do red mullet that way, as well as perch and any other fish that is under a pound, if the Physician allows it.

---

[178] Recipes III,219 and VI,146 refer to ricotta moulds, which must help produce a sphere.

[179.1] As Scappi explains in Recipe V,206, these are crustaceans that have *mutati* – that is, moulted or cast off their shell.

[179.2] Scappi calls these smaller crabs *mollecche*.

[179.3] In this last sentence Scappi qualifies each of these crustaceans, *locuste, gambari lioni, gambari* and *granchi* with the term *mutati* or *mutate*, hence his generic word *teneri* in the rubric to this recipe.

[180] These *luccetti* are a small pike and are not to be confused with the North American pickerel.

Several ways to cook fruits.[xxii]

181. To cook quince.[181.1]

Get a quince and roast it in the coals; otherwise, pare it with a knife; core it. Get the weight of the quince in sugar, moistened with clear water, and put that into a small kettle or a small pot in such a way that the quince is covered by two fingers – even though quince will by nature float; to keep it under, get a little stick and set it into one side of the quince so that it will be held on the bottom with that. That way you will be able to see how much of the sugar-water there is, because if the amount were little it would not be enough, and if there were too much of it the thing would not work.[181.2] You can do it differently: for every pound of fine sugar use a pound of clear water, boiling it slowly, skimming it with a wooden or silver spoon and carefully turning the quince over from one side to the other. If you want the decoction to jell, put little bits of another quince into it. Then serve it in dishes hot or cold, whichever you like, with its liquor over it.

182. To cook a rather firm quince.

Get a quince that has been peeled in one of the above ways. Set it to boil in the same amount of fine sugar as the quince's weight, and equal amounts of water and white wine along with a little whole, crushed cinnamon. To cook it, follow the directions given above, and serve it however you like.

In both of those ways[182] you can do bergamot pears, *caravella* pears and apples.

183. To cook a quince in a small pot.

Get a pared whole quince; if you do not want to pare it, roast it in hot coals, removing the discolouration with wine. Core it and put it into a small net or square of cloth.[183.1] Have a glazed earthenware pot ready, of eight-litre capacity,[183.2]

[xxii] This section heading, which appears before Recipe 181 in the Table at the end of the present Book, is incorporated into the rubric of the first recipe of this new section. It reads: *Per cuocere diversi frutti cominciando dal Cotogno.*

[181.1] Quince had long been recognized as a useful food to offer the sick, particularly for what were seen as their astringent qualities. 'The best quinces are large and full; they cheer the heart and stimulate the appetite ... Quinces, which are prepared in various ways, are not only suitable for the sick but useful and pleasing to the healthy ... ' (Spencer, *The Four Seasons of the House of Cerruti*, 71).

[181.2] *non riuscirebbe*: 'it would not succeed, turn out properly.' Presumably Scappi is referring to the whole recipe.

[182] *delli sudetti modi*: that is, by roasting or paring with a knife.

[183.1] In modern Italian a *fazzoletto* designates a headscarf (kerchief) or handkerchief.

[183.2] Scappi writes *tre boccali*. He has told us in Recipe 6, above, that one *boccale* weighs six pounds, or roughly 2.7 litres of water. Later, in Recipe 207, he will repeat that statement, quali-

and into it put one *boccale* of wine, six ounces of fine sugar, a quarter-ounce of whole cinnamon, four cloves, a little rosewater and a third of a nutmeg. Fasten the cloth or net containing the quince with a string to the peak of the pot's lid – and if it does not have a peak, make a hole in the centre of the lid and put the string through that hole, fastening it in such a way that the net cannot drop. Put it into the pot so that it does not touch the wine, being five fingers above it. Cover the pot over tightly and set it to boil on a low fire away from the flames for an hour more or less, depending on the size of the quince, because the quince has to be cooked by virtue of the wine's vapours as it boils. When it is done, it is served with sugar on it, hot or cold as you like. You can also cook it without sugar and without spices; and instead of wine you can use water.

Any quince to be done in water is placed in a silver dish or a pan of tinned copper or glazed earthenware along with half the quince's weight of sugar and two ounces of rosewater or plain water. Boil it for about a quarter of an hour. Serve it however you like.

When it is cooked in wine, you can even put more pieces of carefully peeled quince into the left-over decoction and cook them. They can be served or you can make a sauce out of them by straining or filtering them.

184. To spit-roast a quince.

Get a whole quince and core it without breaking it. Get a reed spit[184] the size of the hole in the quince – and if you do not have such a reed spit, mount the quince crosswise and fill the hole with sugar. Wrap two sheets of paper around the quince, greasing only the outside of the paper with butter. Cook it over a low fire. Then serve it hot or cold with sugar on it; if it is not peeled or if it is browned from the roasting, you peel it or clean it at that time. You can put a few sticks of cinnamon inside that quince.

You can also cut it in thick slices. After it is cooked you put it in silver dishes with sugar and rosewater over it, with a little heat under it. Alternatively, after they are more than half cooked on the spit finish off cooking them in sugar, water and wine in a pan or a small kettle.

185. To cook several quince in a pot.

Get a new pot rinsed with rosewater or white wine and put unpeeled, uncored quince into it – the number of quince depending on the size of the pot. Carefully sweep the ground where you will be setting the pot, so the quince will not get dirty, then turn the pot over on the ground, mouth down, and give it a moderate heat all around. Leave it like that for an hour and a half. When they are cooked,

---

fying the *boccale* by calling it a *boccale Romanesco*. Scappi is, of course, working in Rome with Roman measures.

[184] This sort of spit called a *cannuccia* is named after a slender hollow cane.

remove the fire and sweep all around the pot carefully so no dirt is left. Then take the quince out and peel them. Serve them whole in dishes with fine sugar and rosewater, heating them until the sugar is melted.

If you want to cook them differently, roast the quince on coals and, when they are cleaned, put them into a low-sided earthenware dish and set them to cook under the pot as above.[185.1] They can also be done under the coals wrapped in paper that is soaked in wine or water. In yet another way they can be done by putting the quince into a pot on the hot coals and covering the pot with a bowl full of water to its capacity of two-thirds of a litre;[185.2] when the water has boiled away the quince will be done.

To make various sauces and garnishes.[xxiii]

186. To prepare a raisin sauce.[186]

Get clean, washed raisins and grind them in a mortar along with, for every pound of them, three ounces of fine *mostaccioli*, three ounces of marzipan or thin slices of bread soaked in rose vinegar, and eight ounces of fine sugar. When everything is ground up together, strain it, having first moistened it with white vinegar and orange juice. Then serve it in dishes with sugar over it.

You can do seeded muscatel raisins and other dried grapes the same way.

187. To prepare a raisin-and-prune sauce.

Get a pound of raisins and another pound of prunes, both very clean and well washed. Cook them in wine and vinegar, together amounting to four litres,[187] along with three ounces of *mostaccioli*. When that is done, strain it. Whether you add in cinnamon and nutmeg, with a pound of finely ground sugar, is optional. Serve it in dishes. You should be aware that it will last for a few days.

[185.1] The pot will be upended onto the dish rather than onto the ground.

[185.2] That is, one *foglietta*.

[xxiii] This section heading appears before Recipe 186 in the Table that ends Book VI. It is partially reproduced in the text: *Per far diversi sapori, & prima.* Very generally speaking, *sapori* are cooking sauces, which may also be served up in a separate bowl as dipping sauces; they are dealt with in Recipes 186–8, 191, 196 and 201. On the other hand, *salze* seem to be primarily garnishes and are seen in Recipes 189, 190, 192–5, 197 and 200.

This is the last division within Book VI to be identified by means of a heading. The preparations between Recipe 202 and the end of the Book are a heterogeneity of jellies, *sapori* and confections.

[186] The word *sapore* here and in the following recipes is a flavouring or seasoning and, served in a side dish, can be a dipping sauce.

[187] *sei fogliette.*

188. To prepare a white sauce of Milanese almonds.

Grind a pound of Milanese almonds with white breadcrumb soaked in ver-juice; strain it, having moistened it with verjuice and lime juice. Add in six ounces of finely ground sugar and a little salt. Serve it freshly made because it goes bad quickly.

189. To prepare a pomegranate-wine[189.1] sauce.

Get clear pomegranate wine and, for every pound of wine, eight ounces of sugar. Boil that slowly in a casserole or pot, skimming it until it thickens to the point described in the directions for royal sauce in the second recipe below, which will be Recipe 192.[189.2]

190. To prepare red-currant sauce.[190.1]

Get red currants, which are like red grapes; seed them and take the best ones leaving aside any that are bruised; wash them. Set them in enough clear water to cover them by three fingers and boil them until the berries have burst. Strain the decoction while it is still hot, and filter it through a cone of coarse white twill until you can see it is as clear as a ruby. For every pound of that filtered decoction add in one pound two ounces of sugar. Boil it slowly in a casserole pot, stirring it constantly because of the sugar which will easily burn – which will happen with any other sauce when a person is not paying attention. When it has boiled for half an hour, test it; if it is beginning to get sticky[190.2] take it off the fire immediately, putting it into a glazed earthenware pot. When it has cooled you can make up beakers of it because it sets quite easily, just like jelly; for that reason it can more readily be called a jelly than a sauce.

191. To prepare a sauce with the solids of the above red currants.

Take what is left in the strainer and boil it for half an hour in water and wine with ground *mostaccioli*. Strain it, adding in sugar, a little salt and mild spices. Serve it however you like.

192. To prepare royal sauce.[192.1]

Get three pounds of fine sugar, two-thirds of a litre of white vinegar without any rosé in it, one-third of a litre of white wine and a little whole cinnamon; boil

---

[189.1] The manuscript in the Wellcome Institute for the History of Medicine contains a late-medi-eval *salsa de granato* at Recipe 277, but that one is based upon the unfermented juice. See also Scappi's other version of this pomegranate-wine sauce in Recipe II,264.

[189.2] Scappi wrote 191: *nel capitolo seguente, presso al prossimo, che sarà in cap. 191.* Clearly the reference should be to Recipe 192. Equally clearly, one or the other of the present Recipes 190 and 191 was inserted at some time after Scappi had written that reference.

[190.1] The text of this recipe is virtually identical with what was printed in Recipe II,265.

[190.2] The verb here is *invesciare*, in Recipe II,265 *viscare*.

[192.1] A similar recipe for royal sauce has also appeared at II,267.

all that in a new, glazed earthenware pot until it reaches a cooked stage. Keep the pot tightly covered. To tell whether it is done, put some on a plate and if it makes a globule that does not spread when you touch it, it is cooked. Then serve it, cold. Be careful not to let it burn because it has to be taken out just as soon as it makes that globule, as has just been said. When it is cooking it is optional whether you put in nutmeg and cloves. And rather than in an earthenware pot you can cook it in a casserole pot.[192.2]

193. To prepare a quince-juice sauce.

Grate an unpeeled quince lightly with a cheese grater and squeeze those gratings through a filter cloth until nothing more will come through. Put that into a large carafe and let it sit for six hours, until the solids have settled to the bottom. Take the clear liquid and put it into a casserole pot or a glazed earthenware pot along with, for every pound of juice, eight ounces of sugar and two ounces of vinegar or Greek wine.[193] Cook it the way the other ones are done.

194. To prepare apple-juice sauce.

Get apples and, unpeeled, grate them as above, and follow the same directions for making and clarifying the juice, adding in with it a little vinegar and white wine. Take the clearest liquid and, for every pound of the juice, add in eight ounces of sugar. Cook it as with the quince juice.

195. To prepare an orange-juice sauce.

Get the clear juice of either bitter or semi-sweet oranges along with, for every pound of it, four ounces of lemon juice; set the clearest liquid[195.1] to boil in a casserole pot with a pound and a half of fine sugar, cooking it as was directed in the previous recipe for pomegranate wine sauce,[195.2] so that it is reduced by two-thirds. It is optional whether you put rose vinegar into it.

196. To prepare new-verjuice sauce.

Get four pounds of new verjuice grapes, seeded and washed, and cook them in another beaker of new strained verjuice, adding in a little unmoistened breadcrumb. When it is thoroughly cooked, strain it. That sauce is served cold and will not last long because it goes bad quickly.

[192.2] *pignatta ... cazzuola*: See both the two sizes of *pignatta* and the *cazzolo con il manico sbusiato* in Plate 10.

[193] The text does not specify 'wine': *due oncie d'aceto, over greco*.

[195.1] That is, after any specks of pulp have settled out.

[195.2] Recipe 189.

197. To prepare green sauce.

Get parsley, spinach tips, sorrel, burnet, rocket and a little mint; chop everything up small and grind it in a mortar with thin slices of toast. If you wish to put in almonds or hazelnuts, they are optional, although for it to be greener it should be done without them. When it is all ground up, put in sugar and salt, moistening that with vinegar. And if it is done well, there should be no need to strain it.

You can do the same with vine sprouts – that is, the new tendrils of a grape vine.

198. To prepare verjuice sauce.[198]

Get new, strained verjuice and breadcrumb soaked in that verjuice, and put them through a strainer. Add in a little sugar and saffron. Cook it in such a way that it becomes like a thick broth. With that verjuice sauce you can cover fried dishes or serve some of it as a relish.

199. To prepare a sweet mustard.

Get a pound of grape juice, another pound of quince cooked in sugared wine, four ounces of apples cooked in sugared wine, three ounces of orange peel, two ounces of candied lime peel and half an ounce of candied nutmegs; in a mortar grind up all of the confections along with the quince and apples. When that is done, strain it together with the grape juice, adding in three ounces of clean mustard seed, more or less, depending on how strong you want it to be. When it is strained, add in a little salt, finely ground sugar, half an ounce of ground cinnamon and a quarter-ounce of ground cloves. It is optional just how mild or strong you make it. If you do not want to grind up the confections, beat them small. If you do not have any grape juice you can do it without, getting more quince and apples cooked as above.

200. To prepare visciola-cherry sauce.

Get two pounds of fresh visciola cherries with their stems off and put them into a pot of tinned copper or glazed earthenware. Boil them slowly in a beaker of white wine without stirring them. When they have burst open fully, strain them without pressure but to get only the juice that they will have yielded. For every pound of that juice get a pound of fine sugar and boil everything in a casserole pot, skimming it with a wooden or silver spoon and letting it continue to boil until it will form a globule: do the test as in the directions for royal sauce,[200] adding in a little salt. It is kept in a glazed earthenware pot and lasts a long time. If you want to put in the odd clove and a little whole cinnamon to boil, that can be done. It is served cold.

---

[198] This is a duplicate of Recipe II,273.

[200] Above, Recipe 192 and II,267.

It can be done another way: squeeze out the visciola cherries before they are cooked, filter the juice that comes out of the strainer and let it sit for three hours in an earthenware pot. Refilter it through a linen cone so it is clear with no pulp in it. For every pound of that juice, get a pound of fine sugar and cook that in a casserole pot, skimming it with a wooden or silver spoon. You can put a little whole cinnamon in to cook with it and, just before taking it off the fire, cloves bound up in a bit of cloth. Be careful it does not burn and does not overcook because it will darken. When it is done, let it cool. Put it away in a glazed earthenware pot, not having overlooked putting a little salt in it.

201. To prepare a quince sauce with orange juice.

Get a pound of peeled and cored quince, a pound of finely ground sugar and six ounces of clear water; cook the quince cut up into pieces. When that is done, test the decoction, and if it makes a globule that does not spread when you touch it, take the quince off the fire. Put three ounces of strong or diluted orange juice in with it and bring it to a boil, skimming it only once with a wooden or silver spoon. Take it off and serve it cold. You can put a stick of cinnamon and two cloves in to boil with that. That sauce is kept in glazed pots and lasts a year, though it becomes like jelly. If you want it thick, strain the pieces of cooked quince along with the decoction, adding in pepper, cloves, cinnamon and nutmeg.

[A miscellany of jellies, confections, ...]^{xxiv}

202. To prepare a jelly of finely chopped chicken with quince juice.

Get four capons, meaty and not force-fed, killed that day, plucked and drawn. Cut them up into small pieces with their feet and their necks drained of blood. Along with them get twenty goat kids' feet, cleaned and skinned. Boil everything in a glazed earthenware pot in enough clear water to cover it all; with the water put six pounds of verjuice – the better if it is new verjuice. When two-thirds of it has boiled away and it is well skimmed and the fat lifted off with a wooden or silver spoon, test it with a beaker the way it was done in Recipe 26 with the broth of veal knuckles reduced to a jelly. Then strain the decoction and put it back into the pot with two pounds of finely ground sugar, half an ounce of ground cinnamon, eight ounces of clear quince juice, four ounces of vinegar, six ounces of white wine, enough salt and three apples cut up small. With six fresh, beaten egg whites boil everything again until the egg whites come to the surface; then put it through a cone filter of white cloth several times, until it becomes amber in colour. Put that into beakers or dishes in a cool place to jell. You can put slivers of boiled capon under that jelly. If you do not have any quince, make apple juice; if you do not have goat kids' feet, get the same number of capons. When that jelly goes through the filter cone, you can put two ounces of fine *mostaccioli*, whole, into it.

---

^{xxiv} This sectional rubric is an invention of the translator.

203. To do morello cherries into a jelly.

Get ten pounds of fresh morello or visciola cherries, picked that day, that are not bruised; leave half of their stem on them and make up bunches of them with ten to a bunch. Have a casserole pot with a pound of clear water in it, and put the morello cherries into it. As they begin to heat up, put in ten pounds of finely ground and sieved sugar and boil that slowly, skimming it with a spoon. When the cherries have burst and are all of one colour, take them out and put them into a dish, letting them drain. Boil the decoction by itself so that it cooks – remembering to skim it, though, and to test it in a dish: if it forms a globule that does not spread, put it in a cool place to jell.

You can do visciola cherries the same way. And you can cook fresh damson plums in that same decoction.

204. To cook apples with sugar.

Roast apples, setting them under hot coals a little while. Take them out and pare them, leaving the brown part.[204.1] Have a casserole pot with melted, clarified sugar in it and put the apples into that. Boil it slowly, skimming it. When they are cooked, take them out of the sugar and put them on silver dishes. Let the decoction boil, testing it; if it makes a globule, take it off the fire. Pour it warm over the apples and put that into a cool place to set.[204.2]

You can do a variety of apples the same way. If you want to do pears, though, such as muscatel pears, boil them in water to begin with and then finish off cooking them in the sugar; then continue on as above.

205. To clarify honey, which can be used as a garnish.

Get ten pounds of good, clean honey with nine pounds of water. Beat those together. Then get four well-beaten egg whites and half a pound of water and put that in a pot on a tripod or on a brazier. Boil it over a low fire, letting it boil for a quarter of an hour with the scum it will make; then skim that off and put in more beaten egg whites. Immediately put it through a filter cone of cotton or of whatever is used to filter jelly. When that is done, put it back into the same copper pot to boil slowly, skimming it with a silver or wooden spoon until it has been reduced to ten pounds. Be careful that it does not burn because it would darken. Test it in a dish and if it makes a globule and is a golden colour, take it off the fire. Put it aside in a glass jar or a glazed earthenware pot. Serve it cold.[205]

[204.1] This *rosoletta* of the fruit just under the peel is the browned colour imparted by the brief roasting.

[204.2] 'to set': Scappi's verb here is the same that he uses for the setting of a gelatin: *congelare*.

[205] A recipe for a 'honey-water beverage' (*Aqua mellata per bevere*) is printed in Plate 18 of the engravings: 'For every pound of clarified honey, gently boil it with seven and a half pounds of clear fountain water or river water, then put it through a clean cloth filter or a cone of cotton fabric.'

206. To prepare oxymel.[206]

Get ten pounds of honey, twenty of water and four of vinegar, and mix them together with six egg whites beaten without any water. Cook it and put it through a filter cone the way the honey is done above. When it has been filtered put it back into a casserole pot and boil it slowly, skimming it, until it cooks. That liquid needs to be boiled slowly because of the vinegar. Whether the sweet or bitter dominates is up to you. If the honey is Spanish it will always be better than our domestic honey.

207. To clarify vinegar, both white and red, with which jelly and various other garnishes can be made.

Get strong vinegar and, for every Roman *boccale* – which weighs six pounds – of it, two fresh egg whites. Beat them together with a wooden spoon until the egg whites turn into foam, then pour everything into a glazed earthenware pot and bring it to a boil over coal that is burning without any flame. Strain everything through a white cloth cone like the one used to strain jelly. When that has been done two or three times at the most, it will be perfect for making what is outlined above. It can be kept for a full year. You can clarify any sort of wine the same way.

208. To draw oil out of almonds, both sweet and bitter.

With the outer, hard shell removed, clean them of any rust colour or dust with a bit of white cloth or canvas. Heat them up in a broad pan, stirring them around. When that is done, rub them again with another cloth. Then, while they are still hot, put them into a mortar and grind them lightly with a wooden pestle so they will turn oily all the more readily. Test that with your hand and, if you find the almonds are yielding oil, immediately put them into another cloth, which is hot, and quickly use a press[208] on the almonds in the cloth, squeezing them until the oil comes out of them. If you do not have a press, as the almonds are being ground sprinkle them with hot water; then follow the above directions for putting them in a hot cloth and twist the cloth with all the strength of your arms until the oil comes out.

You can also make that oil without heating the almonds on the fire but only by grinding them lightly and squeezing them in the press. In that way you can get the oil from domestic walnuts, from pinenuts and from pistachios. If you want to use any of those oils in foods, they have to be used fresh – that is, immediately

---

[206] *ossimele*: The syrup is medicinal, physicians often giving it the qualification 'pectoral.' Bartolomeo Sacchi (alias Platina) refers to it in his *De honesta voluptate et valetudine* (ed. Milham, I,20; II,14 and 25; 126, 154 and 166 respectively) only in a medical context. The word derives from the Greek for '[mixture of] vinegar, honey.' It has only a remote relationship to mead, which is fermented, though Platina does write also of *hydromel* in II,14.

[208] This *torchio* is illustrated in Plate 23.

after they have been made – because they go rancid quickly. Even so, walnut oil lasts quite a bit longer than the others.

209. To wash every sort of oil, especially olive oil.

Get oil that is not rancid. If olive oil is virgin – that is, from select olives – it will be considerably better than what is made from ordinary ones. Put it into an earthenware or copper pot that has a tiny hole in its bottom stopped up with wax on the outside; in the pot there should be about ten litres of water for every two and a half litres of oil.[209] Beat it for a quarter of an hour with a wooden spatula or a spoon. When that is done, open up the hole in the pot and let the water run out, because oil will by its nature always float on top. When you see that the water has run out, close up the hole and put in more cold water and beat it again. Repeat that several times until the oil is thoroughly washed and clarified.

You can do the same with every sort of oil. You could wash melted chicken fat that way. Butter is washed differently, though, as is set out in Recipe 144.

210. To prepare lime[210.1] peels and orange peels with sugar, with which peels various preserves can be made; also, how to set them aside together when they have been candied like that.

Get citron peels – the bigger they are the better. Most especially, they have to be fresh. When the peels have been cleaned of both the pulp on the inner side and the cotton-coloured part that is under the pulp,[210.2] let them steep for four days and nights, changing the water twice a day. Then take them out of that water and put them into boiling water, leaving them to boil until they become tender. Then take them out and put them into cold water, again changing it several times; let them steep two more days. Then have melted, clarified sugar ready, a pound and a half for every pound of peel; put the peel into the sugar. In a casserole pot boil it slowly for an hour, skimming it with a wooden spoon. Then take them off the fire, leaving them in that pot or in some other pot. Every day for eight days heat them up in their decoction so the sugar will penetrate into the peels all the better. At the end of eight days they can be set aside in an earthenware or glass jar.

---

[209] The text has a ratio of *quattro boccali* to one *boccale*.

[210.1] Scappi writes *limoncelli cedrate*, citrons, at the beginning of this recipe, but here in its rubric the typesetter put only *limoncelli*, limes. See the note in Recipe 212, below.

When they were candied, the peels of both citrons (or sour limes) and tart oranges yielded that bitter-sweet taste that was so favoured by the Italian palate of the time. See Pierre Laszlo, *Citrus: A History* (Chicago and London: University of Chicago Press, 2007), 117, 124, 176–7. At p. 179 the author renders an English recipe from T. Dawson, *The Good Huswifes Jewell* (1596), for candied strips (one-quarter inch wide) of citrus peel, and refers to another 'sucade of peeles of Lemmons' in John Partridge, *The Treasurie of Commodious Conceits, and Hidden Secrets* (1573).

[210.2] The cook has the peel, roughly cut away from around the fruit, in his hand. The qualifications *di color di bombasina* and *ch'è sotto la mollica* indicate the membrane between the outer peel proper and the fruit.

The same can be done with orange peels, although they need to steep longer in water and they need to be parboiled twice in water. When those peels are done they can be served as a garnish and for *crostate*.

If you want to make a preserve of them, though, when they have been thoroughly cleaned with hot and cold water as above, they are taken out of the hot or cold water and put on a cloth or in a sieve to press the water out of them. Then they are ground in a stone mortar with a wooden pestle. When that is done they are strained without adding anything. Then a pound and a half of melted, clarified sugar is made ready for every pound of what is strained, and the strained substance is put into it and cooked in it, being stirred continuously with a wooden spoon so that it thickens like quince jam. When it is almost cooked, test it; if it is not sweet enough, add in some sugar. When you take this preserve out of the pot you can put in with it a quarter of an ounce of cinnamon and half an ounce of cloves per pound. If you have citron[210.3] peel and orange peel together, it will be quite delicious.

211. To prepare a preserve of morello-cherry pulp.

Get ten pounds of not-overripe morello cherries; they must above all have been picked that day and not be bruised. Take their stem off and put them into a copper or earthenware pot, pressing them a little until their juice comes out. Cook them in that juice over a low fire. When they are done, remove the juice and put the pulp through a strainer. For every pound of the strained cherries, get a pound of melted sugar and cook the pulp in the sugar the way the strained peels above are done.

You can do visciola cherries that way, although those will always be darker.

212. To prepare various sorts of confections in sugar.[212]

First, to do muscatel pears in clarified sugar: get those pears and peel them carefully. Then have boiling water and put the pears into it, boiling them for a quarter of an hour. When they are done, take them out and let them drain. Then get clarified sugar – for every pound of pears eight ounces of sugar, more or less

---

[210.3] Again, *limoncelli*, limes, and not *limoncelli cedrati*, citrons, as at the beginning of the recipe.

[212] Scappi's list of fruits and vegetables that could be, and were, confected in mid-sixteenth-century Italy is surprisingly brief. Michael Nostradamus's *Le vray et parfaict embellissement de la face ... & la seconde partie, contenant la Façon et maniere de faire toutes confitures liquides, tant en succre, miel, qu'en vin cuit* (Antwerp: Christophe Plantin, 1557) likely reflects Italian practice and provides long recipes for confecting, inter alia, pears (Part II, Chapter 24), lemon peel and orange peel (Chapters 1, 3 and 4; see Scappi's Recipe 210, above), lemons and oranges (Chapter 18), gourds (Chapter 2), walnuts, almonds and pinenuts (Chapters 5, 14 and 26), romaine lettuce stalks (Chapter 7), tart cherries (*que les Italiens appellent 'amarenes'* [sic], Chapter 8), ginger (Chapter 11), quince (Chapters 19–22), and bugloss bark (Chapter 23). See below, however, in the Index, Part 1, 'candied, confected ingredients.'

as you think best, although enough for the pears to be covered. When they have boiled slowly in that sugar for half a quarter of an hour, take them off the fire but leave them in the casserole pot. For six consecutive days heat them up in their decoction. At the end of the six days, put them into an earthenware jar or into some other glazed pot.

You can do ricardo pears that way, and Florentine pears and other varieties.

213. To prepare ricotta with almond milk.

That ricotta is made with shelled Milanese almonds that have first steeped in cold water for twenty-four hours. Grind those almonds in a mortar with, for every pound of them, a pound of fine sugar moistened with three ounces of rosewater and four ounces of a decoction of finely ground fish flesh, that flesh having first been thoroughly washed in warm water and boiled slowly in a pot with eight pounds of clear water for every pound of flesh. As you moisten the almonds be careful that the decoction is not hot because that would give them a greenish-grey cast. When it is done, strain it so that it is not too runny and let it sit until it is quite cool. Then have ricotta moulds sprinkled with rosewater and into them put what you have strained, using your palm to press it into the shape of each mould. Put it in a cool place and let it sit there for four hours.

You can make eggs with the same mixture, although it is thinner. The yolk is made of a firmer mixture, or else with marzipan paste tinged with saffron. When the egg is filled with that mixture, with the yolk in the middle, it is set in a cold place.

[For] fish jelly, shiny and clear, made with sugar and honey: when the fish has been boiled as I instructed in Recipe 246 of the Book on Fish,[213.1] and is not overcooked, you take it out of its decoction and grind it in a mortar with fine cinnamon. Then put it back into the decoction to boil slowly, though constantly skimming it, for a quarter of an hour. Then strain the decoction through a fine filter and put it back to boil with sugar, a little honey and a little of the decoction of the finely ground fish mentioned above. Put that decoction through a bag filter[213.2] the way it is done for meat jelly. If you want to clarify it with egg whites, that is an option. That decoction can be used to make pyramids and eggs and other fanciful things at the Chief Cook's discretion, though they should be left to set in a cold place. That decoction can also be used to cover trout, dentex, gilthead and other excellent fish that have first been cooked in wine, vinegar, salt, water and spices.

[213.1] Recipe III,246 has nothing to do with either fish or jelly. See also a related error in Recipe III,144.

[213.2] *il sacco*: see Recipe II,239.

214. To prepare an uncooked[214] jelly with a decoction of finely ground fish flesh.

First make up a mixture of clear white wine, clear verjuice, clear vinegar and sugar. Bring all that to a boil along with a little cinnamon, then add in the decoction of finely ground fish along with a well beaten egg white and put it through a cone filter several times. It will be done then.

You can also do it with a very clear broth of ground-up fish alone put cold, not hot, into the above mixture and put through a bag filter.

215. To prepare barley beverage[215.1] with capon flesh.

Cook hulled Italian barley in water – German barley is better – the way I directed in Recipe 155 of the Book on Convalescents: that is, as soon as the barley has burst, take it out and take the water strained from it and put that into a large carafe with the flesh of a capon's breast, the fat cut away from it. Seal the carafe with a bit of cloth wrapped around tow and a sheepskin[215.2] on top to keep any vapour from escaping. Put the carafe into a cauldron of cold water and arrange it in such a way that it cannot touch the sides. With the carafe in it, boil the cauldron until half the decoction[215.3] has been reduced by half. Then take it out and strain it. Into that large carafe you can put other things the Physician may prescribe to restore a sick person's health. Serve it with sugar.

216. To prepare a barley beverage with honey.

Get some barley water that has been cooked in the way set out in Recipe 57 of the Book on Convalescents. Instead of the sugar use clarified honey.[216.1] Furthermore, Physicians have it cooked in the above barley beverages[216.2] for patients who have a dry cough.

217. To prepare a thick soup of pinenuts or pistachios.

That soup is made the way almond paste is done:[217] that is, after the shelled pinenuts have steeped for six hours they are ground up in a mortar with a very clean pestle, then moistened with water, and fine sugar is added in. That is strained and cooked like almond paste.

It can also be done in the way set out above for pistachios with only a few melon seeds.

---

[214] *gelo crudo*: after the fish broth has been added to sweetened and flavoured liquids, it is not further boiled.

[215.1] *orzata*: A proper English term for this long-established medicinal drink is orgeat.

[215.2] See this used for the same purpose in Recipe 23.

[215.3] The *decottione* is apparently the contents of the 'sealed' carafe.

[216.1] Directions for clarifying honey have just been given in Recipe 205.

[216.2] Both of the earliest printings show a plural: *nelle sopradette orzate*.

[217] The process for making *mandolata* has been seen in Recipe 70, above.

218. To prepare a thick soup of apples in any season.

Peel apples, cut them into four and particularly cut away the hard part inside. Right away, so they will not lose their colour or flavour, put them into an earthenware or copper pot with enough clear water to cover them by three fingers, along with enough fine sugar. When they have begun to boil, put in a sprig of dry sweet fennel and cook them. They take at least three hours of cooking because they have to boil slowly.

End of the sixth and last book of M. Bartolomeo Scappi.[xxv]

[xxv] In both printed volumes the *Tavola di tutte le cose che si contengono nel presente libro de Convalescenti* begins immediately after this conclusion. After six pages of that Table of recipe names and numbers in Book VI, and the folio number where each recipe is found, the printer in 1570 placed a *Registro* or full list of all the folio gatherings that compose Scappi's *Opera*. To conclude the book, toward the end of that last right-hand page of the last folio of a gathering is the printer's colophon: 'In Venice, at the shop of Michele Tramezzino, 1570.' The verso of that folio is left blank. In the 1581 printing, after the Table of Book VI the typesetter barely had space, at the foot of the left-hand page of the last folio in its gathering, to squeeze in the words, 'End of the Table.' There is neither *Registro* nor colophon. The next page in that printing is the recto of the first folio of Scappi's narrative of the papal funeral and subsequent conclave. (For this appended material see Appendix I, below.)

Appendices

Appendix I

The Funeral of Pope Paul III and the Subsequent Conclave[1]

[f. A1r]

Having in Book IV shown, with etchings and pictures, the various sorts of furnishings necessary for a kitchen and the utensils that are used also to serve a Conclave, both within it and without, I am loathe not to relate the sumptuous arrangements adopted in 1549 for the funeral of Paul III, of blessed memory, of the House of Farnese, along with the number of Cardinals living at that time which amounted to fifty-eight[2] – the ones who entered the Conclave

---

[1] This segment of Scappi's *Opera* is printed immediately after Book VI and, despite the opening phrases, is clearly an addendum to the *Opera* proper. The foliation does not continue that of the whole book but begins a distinct section with a new sequence of folio numbers at 'A 1.' The material with which this segment is concerned is not entirely reflected in the rubric Scappi has given it: *Discorso funerale che fu fatto nelle essequie di Papa Paulo III* – 'The funeral procedures during the obsequies of Pope Paul III.' For Scappi the major part of the obsequies proper consists of the cardinals' nine-day *novendialia* (from the 20th to the 29th of November 1549). In his narrative the conclave flows naturally from the ceremonies of the papal funeral. It is Scappi's professional interest that is particularly seized by the rigid procedures established for feeding the cardinals during the prolonged period of some seventy-one days. The engraved plates from 20 to 28 illustrate the materials and arrangements associated with lodging and feeding the cardinals who participated in that conclave.

In Scappi's account of the event we find that the rules, established in 1274, governing a conclave seem generally still to have been in effect; they will, again generally, remain so four and a half centuries later. Today a conclave begins within ten days of a pope's death; nine consecutive days of papal obsequies – the *novendialia* – end with a funeral oration. During the interregnum the cardinal camerlengo assumes a certain papal administrative authority; on the day the conclave is to begin, the cardinals attend a votive Mass of the Holy Spirit in the Pauline Chapel. The cardinals have separate *cellæ* and live together behind locked doors; except in the case of serious illness, no one may leave (under pain of excommunication). Each cardinal may have only one servant with him. Communication is by means of 'rotas' (see Plate 21); responsibility for the conclave's security is shared by two persons, the marshal and a palatine prelate. The senior cardinal dean announces the name of the elected pope; a High Mass and papal coronation are celebrated on the Sunday that follows his election.

[2] However, on f. A2v Scappi writes that fifty-nine chambers or cells were prepared for the cardinals. In fact in his account Scappi identifies only forty-seven cardinals by name, though modern historians have reckoned a total of fifty-one participants; he seems not to have identified four or five individuals, beyond the forty-seven in his account, who are known to have attended that conclave, specifically Giampietro Carafa, Hippolito II d'Este, Federico Cesi, Durante de Duranti

617

and the ones who came along to it after it was closed, and the ones who came
out sick and who died; along with the names of the Roman Barons who had the
keeping of the Conclave.³ The manner of serving that Conclave will furthermore
be described.

So I shall say that, on the 20th of November 1549, in Monte Quirinale, called
Monte Cavallo, in the palace where there is now the vineyard of the Most Illustrious
Hippolito da Este, Cardinal of Ferrara,⁴ Paul III of blessed memory expired, in
the fifteenth year and twenty-ninth day of his pontifical reign. In attendance were
the two Most Illustrious and Most Reverend Cardinals, Farnese and Sant' Angelo,
and Duke Horatio, with many others whom he created;⁵ Duke Ottavio was out of
Rome.⁶ The following morning his body was borne on a covered litter through
Trastevere by his usual Swiss Guard and light horse guard to Saint Peter's Palace
and into the Consistory Chamber. There, dressed in pontifical robes of white
vestments as if he were going to celebrate, he was laid out on a bier which was
draped with a silken pall of purple⁷ and gold with lettering which spelled out
Paulus III · Pont · Max. At his feet were two cardinal's mitres.

---

and Girolamo Verallo. The failure to record the presence of Cardinal Carafa, known to have attended the 1549–50 conclave, is particularly remarkable and is remotely suggestive of a bias on
the part of Scappi. Giampietro Carafa was born in Benevento 28 June 1476 into a Neapolitan ba-
ronial family; he became bishop of Chieti (Theate) in 1505, was named legate to Henry VIII in
1513, archbishop of Brindisi in 1518, nuncio in Flanders and Spain in 1515, bishop of Ostia and
Velletri, archbishop of Naples in February 1549; he was made cardinal by Paul III 22 December
1536; became dean of the Sacred College 1553; and was elected pope as Paul IV 23 May 1555
until his death in Rome 18 August 1559. The identity of another cardinal who is mentioned by
Scappi, a certain Vicatino (f. A3v), remains uncertain and may be either one of the five individuals just listed or perhaps an alias for Cardinal Nicolò Ridolfo.
   The use of initial capitals on a word in this translation merely echoes their use in Scappi's
text.

³ Scappi writes later that those Roman barons were entrusted with the keys by which the cardinals were locked into their conclave. He will name only two of the barons: Ostilio Savello and
Bonifatio Sermoneta.

⁴ It is surprising that Scappi does not mention the cardinal of Ferrara among those who participated in the conclave that he will describe. Hippolito d'Este was, in fact, the candidate strongly
promoted by the French faction, royal and ecclesiastical, during the polling.

⁵ 'Created' in the sense of elevated to the dignity of the cardinalate.

⁶ The first two of these persons were his grandsons Ranuccio and Alessandro. Ottavio, Duke of
Parma, and Orazio, Duke of Castro, were other grandsons. All four were children of his eldest
(natural) son Pier Luigi, for whom Pope Paul had obtained the duchies of Parma and Piacenza in
1545 and 1547. In 1546 Titian (Tiziano Vecelli, c. 1490–1576) painted Paul III with Alessandro
and Ottavio Farnese close on each side of him.

⁷ In these descriptions Scappi regularly writes 'peacock-coloured,' *paonazzo*; we translate this hue
as 'purple,' although conceivably it could represent anything from a 'peacock blue' to a shimmer-
ing blue-green.

In the evening at about 5 p.m.[8] the whole College of Cardinals having assembled there, with many Bishops and Prelates as well as the Canons of Saint John Lateran and of Saint Peter[9] in their surplices, he was borne into the Papal Chapel before the altar where the Bishops and other Prelates with other personages kissed his feet. Then at 6 p.m. he was borne by those Canons into Saint Peter's and laid before the Chapel of the Most Holy Sacrament with his Mace Bearers[10] in front of him carrying the Mace inverted – that is, with its head downwards. Accompanying him were the above Most Illustrious and Most Reverend Cardinals vested in purple: Trani, Dean at that time, Ridolfo, Pisano, England,[11] Santa Croce, Morone,[12] Sfondrato, Capo di Ferro, Medichino, la Queva, Burgos, Coria, Savello, Vicatino, Sermoneta, Cornaro, Crispo, Farnese, Santa Fiore, Visco, Armagnac,[13] Carpi, Crescentio, Veruli, Maffeo, [f. A1v] Gaddi, Medon and Santo Angelo. And so the ceremonies around the body were conducted by a Bishop Canon of Saint Peter's and certain canticles were sung; then he was borne into Christ Chapel where he lay for three days with his feet toward the iron grille, in full vestments as was said above, with many rope torches burning day and night and many Priests to watch over him. At the end of the three days[14] he was buried behind the organ of Saint Peter's where, during nine days fifteen torches of yellow wax burned continuously.

On the 19th of that month,[15] the above-mentioned Most Illustrious and Most Reverend persons[16] began the obsequies which they called a *Novendialia* because

---

[8] *su le 22 hore*: the hours in a day were measured from sunset.

[9] The Lateran Church of San Giovanni is the Cathedral of Rome, properly the papal cathedral church, not the church of San Pietro in the present-day Vatican.

[10] These *Mazzieri* held honorary appointments. The engraver Giovanni Bernardi (Castel Bolognese 1494–22 May 1553) was appointed mace bearer by Clement VII (1523–34) and confirmed in that position by Paul III, receiving 200 scudi for the service. He may well have been one of those leading Paul III's funeral cortege. Every cardinal also seems to have attended the conclave with his own personal mace – symbolic of power – and its bearer: see further on, f. A3v.

[11] *Inghilterra.*

[12] Cardinal Giovanni Pietro Carafa (1476–1559), was later, as Paul IV, to imprison Cardinal Giovanni Morone (1509–80) in the Castel Sant' Angelo for heresy.

[13] Scappi's printer set *Armignac*.

[14] That is, on 24 or 25 November.

[15] *Alli 19 del detto mese*: This date may be in error. November is the only month that has been mentioned – 20 November being the date of Paul III's death! Because Scappi will write later that the conclave was locked away between 29 November 1549 and 7 February 1550, he must mean the 20th as the beginning of the cardinals' so-called *Novendialia*.

[16] Scappi refers to the cardinals consistently as *Illustrissimi & Reverendissimi*, sometimes, as here, without the noun cardinals.

they last nine days.[17]   In the middle of the church in front of the altar of the Most Holy Sacrament a Catafalque was set up, a pyramid two pikes high, its top shaped like the battlements of a castle made with black-painted merlons. Every two-hands distance there was a strip of wood with long nails set half a hand apart; those strips ran from the first capital of the columns right to the top of the battlements. The Catafalque had four sides and that arrangement was on each side. On top of the battlements were four rope torches which rose up, when the Most Reverend persons entered the church, along with all the wood torches[18] fixed on the nails set in the above-mentioned strips; every wood torch weighed at least half a pound and there were more than 1,120 of them. On the lower capital there were six other similar rope torches on each side, and at every corner of the Catafalque was a banner of black taffeta, and likewise on the battlements. Around the lower moulding was a band of black taffeta two arms in height. The heraldic arms of the Pope, without the keys, were painted on every side of that along with lettering which read 'Pope Paul III,' as well as a bit of foliage in white and a few Angels painted in umber in various poses and forms. Beneath that band of Angels were twelve columns covered with black fabric which supported the Catafalque, or castle; on each column a coat of arms of the Pope was painted. The circumference was more than a hundred hands, and beneath was a funeral couch, six hands deep and ten wide, covered with sheet of gold brocade[19] with border embellishments of black velvet all around; at each corner were a very finely embroidered coat of arms of the Pope and two pillows in gold brocade. At the foot of the couch were two papal tiaras [f. A2r] of crimson velvet with their ribbons hanging right to the ground.[20]

Every morning during the obsequies two officials, dressed from head to foot in black and cowled in such a way that only a bit of their face could be seen, were appointed to fan continuously with two banners of black taffeta.

---

[17] Gregory X's 1274 constitution for a conclave required that the cardinals assemble at the papal palace within ten days of a pope's death. Scappi will show two other features of a conclave – the closing and guarding of the doors behind the cardinals and the prohibition against their departure (on pain of excommunication) until a new pope has been elected – steps decreed in order to ensure that the Roman see remain vacant – *in Sedia Vacante* as the legend in Plate 21 says – for as short a period as possible.

[18] Scappi distinguishes between two sorts of torch, *torcie* and *fiaccole*. The first is of twisted rope or tow impregnated with wax, tallow or resin; the second is of resinous wood smeared with a similarly combustible substance.

[19] *riccio sopra riccio*, literally 'curl-on-curl' or 'loop-on-loop.'

[20] These *cappelli Papali* that are touching the ground, perhaps symbolically here, are properly *infulæ*, *caudæ* or lappets, two long pieces of fabric that are pendant from the back of a papal tiara. Normally they are highly decorated and particularly bear the arms or emblem of the pope wearing the tiara, in the case of Paul III undoubtedly the arms of the Farnese family.

At that couch at 11 a.m.[21] the Most Reverend Cardinals began Mass in the Sistine Chapel[22] where the Canons of Saint Peter's currently officiate; the Mass was usually sung by a Cardinal from among those created by the late Pope. When the Mass is over, four Cardinals in black velvet copes appear along with the one who has sung the Mass. The Subdeacon, when he has sung the epistle, takes the Cross and, in regular order, acolytes and other servers[23] with the master of the ceremonies,[24] then the Most Reverend Cardinals after them, process around the Catafalque on which, as was said, so many wax candles are burning. All about the Catafalque are seated the Pope's family on benches, dressed head to foot in black, with their wood torches, large and small according to the rank and condition of the men, lit in their hand. In every corner of the Catafalque a stool, all in black, was set out on which the four vested Cardinals went to sit; the one who had sung the Mass sat in the middle of the side facing the altar of Saint Peter. The Most Reverend Cardinal who was to the right of the Priest began to asperse the funeral couch with Holy Water, then with incense, having first made a reverence to the Cross, which was set in front of the Priest, and then to each Cardinal. That done, he said a prayer, and so did all the four other Cardinals. Then the Choir returned to where the whole College of Cardinals was, in their hand wood torches which were lit and a rope torch which was not.

When that was over they went to Saint Peter's Sacristy and held a general congregation that usually lasted three or four hours. It must not be forgotten[25] that in Saint Catherine's Chapel, which in Saint Peter's has an iron grille, two chests of tawny red wax candles were distributed every morning, as were also all the other candles, wood torches of three or four ounces each.[26] The tribune gallery of the church was draped all around with black fabric with lettering that said, in the vernacular, Pope Paul III; in that gallery an infinite number of torches burned throughout the funeral, each lasting two hours, and that over a period of nine days.[27]

On the 29th of that month Cardinal Trani sang a solemn Mass of the Holy Spirit. [f. A2v] When that was over, that Most Reverend person, having been

---

[21] *alle 16 hore.* Again, the same procedure is followed each day during the *novendialia.*

[22] *nella capella di Sisto:* of Pope Sixtus IV, Francesco della Rovere (1414–85, pope from 1471).

[23] *ministri.* Interestingly, Scappi's tense, now the present, will vary.

[24] Scappi never identifies this *maestro di cerimonie* otherwise. We see later that by tradition his function entitles him to certain perquisites.

[25] *Non restaron di dire.*

[26] *facole di tre & quattro oncie per ciascheduna.* Those 'torches' are clearly a smaller variety of the 1,120 half-pound *facole* that burned around the catafalque.

[27] Scappi writes *per spatio di nove mattine:* for nine mornings.

divested of the papal vestments,[28] intoned the *Veni Creator Spiritus* and so, as the Cross moved along with the Mace Bearers and other servers and singers, all the Most Reverend Cardinals went into the Conclave, which remained open for all of that day.

The following forty-one Cardinals gathered during the funeral: the Most Reverend Trento, Salviati,[29] Chalon,[30] Mantua, Cibò, Monte, Doria, Urbino and Augusta. After the Conclave was closed the following, in order, went into it: on the 4th of December Pacecho arrived; on the 12th, Paris,[31] Vendôme, Castiglione, Guise[32] and Tournon;[33] on the 28th Bologna and Rouen[34] arrived and entered the Conclave; on the last day of December Lorraine arrived; on the 13th of January 1550 Bourbon arrived and entered the Conclave on the following day.

On the 4th of December Veruli came out of the Conclave sick and was carried to the Castle Sant' Angelo; there, on the 19th of December, he died. On the 20th of that month Santa Croce came out. On the 1st of January 1550 Bologna came out with gallstones. On the 20th Ridolfo came out, and died on the 31st. On the 23rd Cibò came out and on the 1st of February he returned back into the Conclave.

There were fifty-nine cells all told in the Conclave. Every cell was roughly sixteen and one-half feet wide by the same long. The cells of those Cardinals created by the late Pope were decorated with purple fabric, with the bedding and furnishings of the same colour, with silken fringes, bed curtains, covers, mattresses and pillows also of the same colour. For every cell there was also a table covered with the same fabric, a rack[35] with six or seven pegs, a small wooden lantern,[36] two stools – one of which, with a high knee-opening, was for taking with him into

---

[28] Cardinal Trani was, as Scappi said earlier, dean of the College of Cardinals. As such he functioned as vice-pope during the interregnum.

[29] See Hurtubise, 'La "table" d'un cardinal de la Renaissance,' 249–82. The study centres on Bernardo Salviati (1503–68), younger brother of the Cardinal Giovanni Salviati named by Scappi, and cousin of Caterina de' Medici, queen of France, for whom he became spokesman in Rome; he was made cardinal in 1561 and bishop of Clermont in Auvergne. In the footsteps of his brother, he had assumed the bishopric of Saint-Papoul in 1549, passing it in turn to his nephew, Antonio Maria Salviati, in 1561.

[30] *Cialon.*

[31] *Parigi.* This cardinal is Jean du Bellay for whom Scappi seems to have prepared a collation at Monte Cavallo: see Book IV, f. 304r [1581 f. 252v].

[32] *Ghisa.*

[33] *Tornone.*

[34] *Roan.*

[35] Scappi describes this clothes hanger as a ladder. An interesting hanger apparently for a single article of clothing is labelled *Per sostentare panni,* 'to hang clothes,' in Plate 26.

[36] This *lanterna piccola di legno* may be the rather elegant *candelieri* illustrated in Plate 27.

the polling hall,[37] the other, lower one was for sitting on,[38] a chamber pot,[39] a jar[40] holding about three litres with a locking copper lid and its key, and many other things needed and useful in the cell – everything, though, in purple and with the arms of the Cardinal who occupied the cell.

Then there was a hamper[41] for carrying foods to the wicket,[42] each side of which has the coat of arms of the Most Reverend Cardinal and each end two large iron rings though which a staff,[43] a hand in thickness and ten hands long, was inserted for carrying. It was used by those serving the Conclave when they took the prepared dishes to the wicket – that is, the prepared kitchen dishes. For the sideboard[44] there was a large lined tub[45] of embossed leather, russet or purple, made like a purse,[46] with purple draw-cords and fringe, and a decoration and the Cardinal's arms on both sides; they had two handles, one at either end, through which a staff, [f. A3r] much like the one for the kitchen hamper, was passed.

---

[37] *nella sala del scrutinio.*

[38] Scappi calls these two articles of furniture *scabelli*. At the top of Plate 26, however, two varieties of *banchetta* or bench are illustrated that seem to be what Scappi is cataloguing at this point. The larger one is, in fact, a workbench, a writing desk with a drawer: *Banchetta alta con cassetta per scuttinio*, a tall bench with a case for balloting. It is shown with the ink-stand and pen on it, items that are engraved a little larger at the foot of the Plate beside the word *Calamaro* ('ink,' literally 'squid'). Also on its surface are what appear to be two (coloured?) ribbons, perhaps for voting.

[39] This *porta mondezza* is shown in Plate 22, where it is called an *orinale* or urinal.

[40] Plate 24 shows two views of this handle-less, amphora-shaped *vettina* (they are called *vittine* by the engraver), presumably intended for drinking water. Distinct from the normal 'kitchen' variety seen in Plate 12, the cardinals' model is furnished with a lockable lid for security.

[41] See this oval, metal-bound wooden chest in Plates 23 and (probably for personal belongings) 27: *cornuta*. Its lid could be hinged at both the side and across the middle, and had a lockable hasp. Plate 21 shows how this chest (*Cornuta di cocina*) was borne in a procession.

[42] Scappi explains later that the *sportello* is the locked gate in the grille that protected the area where non-verbal communication with the conclave itself was possible.

[43] Scappi's engraver has been nothing if not meticulous in illustrating in Plate 25 not only these *bastoni per le cornute* but the *bastoni per le porta carafe*, staves for the carafe trays (see below).

[44] The *credenza* was not located in the dining area but outside the locked area of the conclave.

[45] Plate 21 gives an idea of the large size of the *sporta* that Scappi is describing. In this engraving we see, left to right, beverages (identified as *Bottigliaria*, the buttery or wine cellar), food from the sideboard in the present *sporta* (*Credenza*), and prepared dishes from the kitchen (*Cornuta di Cocina*).

[46] In Plate 27 two such containers, which show clearly an embossed decoration and a place for the owner's arms, are in fact called *borse di credenza*. The fringe that Scappi will mention is visible around the point where the flexible top joins the rigid side.

In that tub were put all the things that were served by the sideboard officer,[47] though what those were you can find out in the Book on Prepared Dishes and the engravings. However, if the Most Illustrious Cardinals were created by other than the late Pontiff, all the above things were in green rather than purple.

Every Cardinal had with him a Secretary, a Nobleman, a personal attendant[48] and no one else, except for those who were sick and had cells apart.

To return now to our subject matter: we have still to speak about the arrangements followed for serving the Conclave from the outside. I shall begin first with the Most Illustrious Lords the Roman Barons (who continuously hold the keys to the entrance[49] of the Conclave) and the guards of soldiers at the grille and at the Rota[50] by which the Cardinals were served morning and evening, and where the Lord Magistrates of Rome[51] are as well. You should know that at the gate[52] to the Conclave – that is, at the wicket – are to be found all the Archbishops and Bishops who are in Rome; the arrangement is, however, that those whose name is drawn serve at the entrance to the Conclave that day and the following night for things that are needed or might happen at any time. And every one of them attends continuously an hour or two at the most, then they change; and continuously there have to be four of them on duty. Their cells are near that entrance to the Conclave. Two other guard duties are filled by Roman Baron Lords, those being Bonifatio, the father of Cardinal Sermoneta, and Lord Ostilio – called Lord Barons of the Corridor where they serve and of which a guard corps of Italians makes use going along it to get to the entrance to the Conclave. Similarly the Captain of the Swiss Guard also had Swiss Guards who, along with the late Pope's Footmen, had also to accompany the Most Reverend Cardinals who came out of the Conclave sick, as far as the place where they went to be put up; the light horse guard of the late Pope did the same. The same procedure was followed whenever a Cardinal arrived late in Rome, and he was accompanied by those guards up to the entrance to the Conclave.

The procedure followed by the Lords Steward and other household officials in serving was this. First, at the grille where the four Bishops were stationed

---

[47] The *credentiero* exercised a very old and august function in a wealthy medieval household.

[48] *un Secretario, un Gentilhuomo, un Cameriere.*

[49] Rather than *della porta*, the 1581 printing shows *della parte*, 'on behalf of.'

[50] Plate 21 shows in its upper right two such revolving 'wheels' – under the caption *Ruota del Conclave* – by which those in the conclave communicated with the outside world and vice versa.

[51] *li Sig. Conservatori di Roma.*

[52] Scappi's word is *porta*, generally a 'door'; later we learn that it is a double gate or wicket in the grille.

were two Messengers[53] whose responsibility was to call the Cardinals' Stewards according to an order, posted at the grille, where all the Cardinals were recorded; and so it could be seen who was to be served first and who next. That list was always made up the evening before by drawing by lot – although at the top of the list were the names of any sick Cardinals – and the serving followed the order of the draw among the sick Cardinals as among the well ones. [f. A3v] Four copies of the list were made up in the evening for the following morning, as was said: one of them was within the Conclave; one was posted at the gateway where the Lord Magistrates were stationed; and the two others were in the hands of the two appointed Messengers, of whom one was stationed at the serving table by the gateway where the Lord Stewards entered with the prepared dishes. And so, according to the order of the list, he called out who was to be served first and went on down it to the last.

The Lord Stewards, as I said, had a hamper for the kitchen food and a tub for the credenza food, and they served that way. To begin with, each Steward had, in those two containers, carefully prepared and arranged every item of food – the normal test[54] having been carried out by the Assayer, Cook, Cellarer,[55] Charcutier and others who might have been involved in the handling of the food. His Mace Bearer with his Most Reverend master's Mace would lead off, followed by two Footmen with two staves painted the same colour as the hamper. Then came the Steward with four or six squires who bore carafes full of all sorts of wine and pure water;[56] among them walked the Cellarer carrying a small carafe of wine;[57] the carafes were all covered with oranges or flowers, and had labels on which the variety and quality of the wines were written. Then came two Footmen bearing the large tub with the Credenza foods.[58] Then there followed the Assayers with

---

[53] *Cursori.* It may well be that the 'order' – which will govern those messengers' work and determine the sequence in which those cardinals who were present day by day were served their meals – also served Scappi as he later composed his record of attendance in the Conclave.

[54] The word that Scappi uses here is *credenza*. In former days the piece of furniture that became known as a *credenza* functioned in the original, etymological sense of a 'proving' table, where food from the kitchen was set out and inspected for anything suspicious or harmful before being served to the master, his family and guests. The ultimate test consisted of proving samples of each preparation by mouth. See the note in Book I, §45 where *la credenza* is, likewise, an assay. In the present instance a wide assortment of individuals will have been required to 'make the test,' *fare la credenza* of each cardinal's food before it is passed, by the *rota*, into the conclave.

[55] Or wine steward, the sommelier.

[56] These are represented in Plate 21 by the pair of persons on the far left marked *Bottigliaria*, cellar or buttery. The carrying tray for bottles is engraved twice in Plate 27: *Cassette per Caraffe*.

[57] This personnage can be seen partly hidden behind the pair carrying the tub from the *Credenza*.

[58] In Plate 21 this part of the procession is labelled simply *Credenza*.

two other Footmen carrying the hamper.[59]   After them and accompanying the prepared dishes came a few nobles, too, of that Most Reverend Cardinal. When the Steward was sent, as was said, to the place where things were served up, he finds at the first grille the guard of the Lord Magistrates; right by the end of the two staircases, he finds the Italian guards and the Swiss Guards; he goes along the corridor where there is another grille with two gateways, one to enter by for serving, the other to come out by after having served. As he goes in through that grille there is another Italian guard and Swiss Guard who open and close;[60] here the two Messengers (as I have said) who, following the order on the list, summon the Stewards. Just past the grille there is a table fifteen hands long and about four hands deep. When the Steward reaches it he takes a very white napkin from the Assayer; in front of the aforementioned four Bishops[61] another napkin is spread out with two knives and a fork which those Reverend Prelates would take, and he immediately presents himself along with the squires, handing over the carafes of wine and water and removing from his tub the several sorts of salad, fruit and other things needed for [f. A4r] the sideboard.[62] Then the two other Footmen would come along with the hamper containing various and diverse prepared dishes from the kitchen, all of which were taken out by the Steward and presented to the Prelates who, when they had seen them, tested them with proper respect using the fork.[63] It was not possible to send in closed pastries or whole chickens, those being cut up and opened in the presence of the Bishops who were there; nor could anyone send in wine in any vessel but of glass, nor serviettes, cloths or anything else what was not first opened out and examined. Earthenware and glass vessels that were sent in never came back because they were considered perquisites of the master of ceremonies. Any foods left over were distributed to the servants of the Conclave – that is, barbers, masons, carpenters, apothecaries,[64] sweepers[65] and various other retainers. When the Steward has finished serving, he attends at the

---

[59] In Plate 21 the label is *Cornuta di cocina*. It is interesting that the sequence of Scappi's description does not follow the progress of the procession but rather the left-to-right representation in the engraving.

[60] The two pair, each armed with a pike and distinctively different sets of body armour, can be seen in the upper left of Plate 21 by the *Porta di Guardia* and at the bottom right of the plate. The exit gateway, through which the attendants will bear empty tubs and hampers, is ahead of them as they descend steps (labelled *Scala di ritorno*) toward the artist.

[61] As the engraving (Plate 21) shows, they are seated at the table.

[62] *cose necessarie alla Credenza*. Perhaps more likely: 'things that needed the assay.'

[63] From the hands of the assayer bishops, each item of food and drink is then passed, by means of the *ruota*, in to the cardinal and his three attendants in the inner hall.

[64] *spetiali*, literally 'spicers' but also functioning as pharmacists.

[65] *scoppatori*: see the broom (*scopa*) thoughtfully illustrated in Plate 25.

grille to see whether the Reverend Lord his master wishes the dishes exchanged. Returning, he goes out by the other gateway, as was said. Serving was done like that, evening and morning.[66]

As well as the above arrangement for serving there remains yet to speak about the guard of that palace – that is, at the outer wall of the main gate into the palace, and apart from those, a large number of soldiers, posted in the watchtower and in the middle of the piazza – there are twenty-six Swiss night and day.[67] There is an iron chain there, and a plank hut where the guards rest. Upon the wall to the left in the entranceway to the palace there was a projecting ravelin with eight gunners and eight pieces of heavy artillery constantly guarded by another company of Swiss Guards and two sentinels. A short distance away from the ravelin, just at the main gate, which was guarded by fifty Swiss, and a little farther on, in the entry to the palace, there were three pieces of artillery guarded continuously by three Swiss sentinels: that was to reinforce the guard on the gate. Then to the left of the gate under a loggia there was a wooden grille where a company of Italians was stationed who marched back and forth. Turning to the right, where the well of Julius III is today, at the entrance to the courtyard leading to the Borgia Tower, under the gate where a chain hangs, there was a large guard of Italians. On the right as you go in, close to a niche, was a portable Altar decorated with various tapestries and other things and an arrangement in anticipation of the Mass of the Holy Spirit, sung there every morning by the chapel singers; during that Mass [f. A4v] the iron gates were under guard. By that means all the orders of Priests and Monks, with the 'little orphans'[68] at the head, processed in, passing by all the lower Guard and by the place where Mass was being said. And while the procession was entering, the whole guard was armed as if they were about to have to fight, right up to the end of the procession in the main Courtyard where the artillery was drawn up in a tight circle. In the middle with the two Deacons, the

---

[66] The so-called morning meal is the *Pranzo*, generally served at close to noon.

[67] The substantial military presence – including the artillery installations that Scappi will mention – has an explanation that goes some way back in history. In 1378 a Roman mob brought pressure upon the cardinals to elect Bartolomeo Prignano, Urban VI. The Sacred College subsequently reversed itself, claiming the election was coerced, and proceeded to elect Robert of Geneva, Clement VII. The two allegedly improper elections were deemed at the origin of two distinct and separate papal successions, the Great Schism of 1378–1417. The rigidly enforced procedures, jail-like arrangements and military readiness that Scappi describes during this conclave went some way to protect the supreme authority of the church.

[68] These *Orfanelli* (printed with an initial capital) were likely brothers of the Confraternita degli Orfani, whose hospice was founded in the Church of Santa Maria in Aquiro to care for and educate the many orphans left following the Sack of Rome in 1527. Paul III had conveyed the church to the order in 1540 and in 1541 elevated the brotherhood to the status of an Arciconfraternita. The square on which the church is located was known as the *Piazza degli Orfanelli*. The little orphans to which Scappi refers were members of that brotherhood.

Priest, who was to sing the Mass and who was standing there with his face turned toward the Conclave, in a loud voice sang the Hymn *Veni Creator*, along with litanies and other prayers; and the Clergy responded likewise. Shortly after that was over,[69] the Canons of Saint Peter came with Prelates with their usual music. When those processions came to an end, at the sound of a little bell everyone left, and the guard disarmed, assured by that signal that polling was finished and that there was to be no new Pontiff that morning.

Such procedures and ceremonies lasted from the 29th of November 1549, on which the Conclave was shut away, up until the 7th of February 1550,[70] on which day the new Pontiff, Julius III,[71] was created at ten o'clock in the evening.[72] On the following day at 2 p.m.[73] that was declared by the Most Reverend Cardinal Cibò,[74] holding the Cross in his hand and accompanied by the Most Reverend Cardinal de Guise. And on the day of the Chair of Saint Peter,[75] the 22nd of that month of February, at 2 o'clock, the College of Cardinals, by the hand of the aforementioned Most Reverend Cibò, crowned him; who then, on the 24th of that month, opened the Holy Gates.

The End

---

[69] The 1570 printing has *finito ciò, di li à poco venivano*, for which the 1581 printer set *finito ciò, di lì venivano*.

[70] It is known that the English cardinal, Reginald Pole (1500–58), lost this election by a single vote, the French-Italian faction eventually carrying the very extended contest over the emperor's wishes. The presence and absence of cardinals in the conclave on any given day was, as Scappi and others realized, of material significance.

[71] Giovanni Maria del Monte, 1487–1555.

[72] *à tre hore di notte.*

[73] *à hore 19.*

[74] Cibò was the senior cardinal bishop.

[75] *giorno della Cathedra di San Pietro.*

Appendix II
The Engraved Plates

The engraved plates that were made for the Tramezzino brothers to accompany the 1570 publication of Bartolomeo Scappi's *Opera* are unique both in the wealth of information they contain about professional cookery in the middle of sixteenth-century Italy and in the remarkably fine, realistic detail that the engraver was able to achieve for the scenes and objects he represented. The sequence of plates, their themes and the particular images in them are closely related to the text of the *Opera*, illuminating matters with which Scappi specifically deals: the layout of an ideal kitchen in which the range of routine activities can most efficiently be accommodated (Book I), the utensils that must be available for different culinary procedures (Books II, III, V and VI), the equipment for an itinerant kitchen (Book IV), and the numerous special arrangements that had to be made and articles provided in the case of a conclave (Scappi's appended narrative).

In his set of engravings the artist displays an iconographic tour de force of technical and artistic skill. At the same time he bequeaths an abundant, eloquent archive of historic information.[1]

Plate 1: The Main Kitchen. The artist incorporates many details into this plate, all of which indicate the great range of activity for which provision must be made in this place: joints of meat and a three-wicked lamp suspended from a ceiling beam, trammels over the hearth, shelves with cloths, a stuffed bag stuck with knives, a low wall of chafing chambers (called 'stoves' in early English) with their circular port above, tables for working pastry, cutting meat and serving up preparations, a mortar on its pedestal and, under a single-wicked lamp mounted on a wall, a stone trough for piped water. The doorway on the right gives access to the *camerino per garzoni*, the scullions' small chamber. Only one person is depicted in this ideal kitchen – but he is at the heart of all its facilities – the perdurable spit-turner, his gesture clearly evoking how inadequately he is shielded from the blazing fire and the heat reverberating from the iron bars of the hearth's backplate. (Not included in this view of three walls is a source of ventilation, normally a very large window through which the flow of fresh air could be regulated by shutters.)

---

[1] For other reviews of the content of each of these twenty-seven plates, see Firpo, *Gastronomia del Rinascimento*, 59–68; and Di Schino and Luccichenti, *Il cuoco segreto dei papi*, 98–126. In the latter work the authors report (94) that Barbara Jatta, of the Gabinetto delle Incisioni della Biblioteca Apostolica Vaticana, has found a particularly close stylistic similarity between the work here of Tramezzino's anonymous artist and that of Ambrogio Brambilla, a respected engraver in Rome at this time.

Plate 2: The Room Next to the Kitchen. Additional activity is shown where preliminary work is carried out. The large central table is devoted to making pastry while elsewhere in the room men are straining a sauce, stirring a whitedish over a fire or bringing a plate of something from an adjoining part of the kitchen. The long peels leaning just past that individual mark the kitchen's oven. In the right rear of the room a cauldron simmers on a brick 'wall' while a mechanism of the same family as that seen in Plate 14 is at hand to help lift the large vessel. In the left rear two faucets supply water from a tank (*conserva*), likely of lead, mounted in or on the wall above a stone trough. A well, located in a wall, is fitted with a rope, pulley and bucket. Projecting slightly from both side walls are cabinets in which to safeguard valuable fabrics, silverware or foodstuffs. The open windows provide fresh air to the workers.

Plate 3: The Scullery. The area is identified as a *loggia*, an open-air space where the mundane labours of sharpening knives, washing dishes and cleaning(?) fish can be done. The 'half-well' on the left may share the wall that is seen on the left of the previous plate. Beyond it a pair of eviscerated animals hang under a shallow roof; opposite is a sheltered space in which such bulky necessities as baskets can be stored. The all-important grindstone is continuously moistened from a small barrel.

Plate 4: Cool Place for Dairy Products. A room devoted solely to work with milk (*lavoreri de latte*) had become advisable in a large establishment as animal milk became a more important ingredient in food. The engraver shows three jobs in process: bringing milk in a large skin; whipping creamy milk into milk snow (*neve* [*di latte*]); and churning honey milk (*latte mele*). The significance of the observer in the internal window is open to speculation.

Plate 5: Cooking under a Hood. The arrangement of a hearth on a raised deck, with a large metal hood immediately over it, may be designed both to produce a stronger draft for the fire and to leave the attendant, on the floor of the room, still relatively cooler. The exceptional draft in the upper reaches of the conical hood allows the use of a second sort of spit-turning mechanism, whose details the engraver illustrates meticulously.

Plate 6: A Field Kitchen. When a cook's master is travelling, it may be necessary to cook outdoors. The practical utility of a pair of articulated spit-holders (see also Plate 16) is demonstrated, as well as the need for a robust four-legged pot support (see Plate 7) which is likewise fitted with spit-holders – where neither a fireplace trammel nor a low fire-wall is available. The artist cannily scatters the foreground with a variety of other equipment which a cook would be wise to take abroad with him. The tent, built from the standing remnants of two trees, will protect the food and fire from rain but the spit-turner (lacking the protective shield seen in Plate 1) is still grimacing from the heat.

Plate 7: Various Vessels, 1. Scappi's methodical survey of kitchen equipment begins with pots and pans, vessels which heat foodstuffs that are more or less liquid. The six-*some* cauldron is evidently of wrought iron. The middle vessel on the right, to which three legs are rivetted, is of copper, likely tinned on its inner side, and is called an oven because it can sit in coals and have other coals placed on its flat lid. The remaining pots here are likely of copper also.

Plate 8: Various Vessels, 2. An earthenware stewpot in the upper left has three legs and a lid with a concave centre and a circular, concave channel to hold coals; if cool water were placed in the lid's concave ring, vapour from the food simmering in the pot could condense and return to the food. The flat lids of other vessels here could also hold coals and the vessels function as mini-ovens. The holed plate (*piastrello*) shown beneath several *navicelle* was designed both to hold coal or charcoal, which would provide a steady, moderate heat but which needed a good draft from beneath to burn well, and to let ash fall clear of the combustion.

Plate 9: Various Vessels, 3. Tourte pans are important enough in Scappi's kitchen to be shown in several varieties, some with sloping sides, some with a flat rim. Three lids of various sizes for tourte pans are also of different designs. The first two can take coals within a raised rim around the centre of the lid, which centre is itself raised to remove the heat a little from the food within the relatively shallow pan. A colander is recognizable. A jug (*pignatta*) and a three-legged stewpot (*stufator*), this latter somewhat squatter than the one pictured in Plate 8, are earthenware. An apparently oval pan (*padella ovata*) seems designed for cooking eggs; it has a handle with a leg, presumably so that the weight of the long iron handle does not tip the pan (see also the fish pan in Plate 11). The end of that handle has a hook whose circular shape is unlike those shown on utensils in the next plate and suggests that it might have been intended to break the eggs that went into the pan. A set of kettles illustrates the need to be able to cook foods in a wide range of quantities.

Plate 10: Various Utensils, 1. From vessels, Scappi and his engraver gradually move to other sorts of practical hardware. A small mortar (marble or bronze?), for which two pestles (wood, marble, bronze?) should be available, is of prime importance. A skimmer has the unmistakable shape of a dipper, even to the hooked handle; beside it is a cheese grater which can be fixed at any angle by means of an adjustable leg. Two sorts of dripping pan, rectangular and oval, have different names and different means to fix them to a spit mounted below the one that holds the roast.

Plate 11: Various Utensils, 2. The curious upside-down 'copper strainer' (*stamegna di rame*) engraved beside the fish pan may not be an error; it may be fastened, by the pin which is shown through an eye, over a container of the same diameter before the container is inverted; the *brass* strainer shown toward the bottom of the plate looks identical. The pastry cutter is double-ended in order to make a different sized circle of dough, with maybe a different notching around its circumference (see the pie dough in the second row of Plate 9). The arrangement of spice pouches is intriguing, though perhaps not wholly practical. Beneath the spices is an instrument to shred 'like vermicelli' – *i.e.* to julienne – turnip and squash.

Plate 12: Vessels, Apparatus. Two large jars occupy the top of this plate, along with a grindstone designed to obtain the juice from a fruit or vegetable. Beneath are two sizes of cutter likely intended to cut out rounds of rolled dough, perhaps for turnovers. A set of weigh scales would have been in continual use throughout a cook's day. The food press could squeeze a juice from a foodstuff; the tonic broth (*susidio*) of the label is a sickdish which uses the juice of meats (see Recipes VI,16–18 and 28-9). The *aque cotte* designates another sort of sickdish preparation consisting of a concentrated flavoured water (Recipes VI,1–10).

Plate 13: Various Knives. While forks, skewers, larding needles, a tripe scraper, a macaroni cutter and a syringe are reproduced in this plate, the number and variety of knives justifies the rubric the engraver set at its head. The knife holder, obviously much larger than its representation, afforded the cook (the fellow in the previous plate: see the fifth and sixth knives on the right of Plate 13) quick access to just the right blade for the job.

Plate 14: Kitchen Apparatus, 1. The obvious size and weight of the cast iron cauldron and the necessarily massive scale of the lifting beam, supports and wheeled cart suggest something of the generous size of the kitchen that housed such a cauldron and cart. It speaks, too, to the number of persons that such a kitchen might on occasion be called upon to feed. The small items in the lower half of the plate – pastry wheel and knife, an interlocking set of strainers, nutmeg and sugar graters, and two sorts of scrapers – introduce the utensils to be shown on the next two plates.

Plate 15: Kitchen Apparatus, 2. Pastry utensils continue at the top, and a little lower in the form of a crusta iron which, its lower face coated with batter, can be dipped into a pot of hot grease. Then there are varieties of andiron (one of which will hold spits close to the ground), hearth tools, two grills (of which one is fitted with wheels), a boxed set of small containers for powdered herbs or spices, a candle stand and a variety of spits.

Plate 16: Kitchen Apparatus, 3. Spatulas, dippers, wafer irons, meat hooks, a sieve, a bellows, three sorts of spit holder, a heavy trivet and, on the left, a 'shovel for *gattafura*' (see Recipes V,97-8).

Plate 17: Kitchen Apparatus, 4. This plate shifts the reader's attention from the permanent home kitchen to the travelling kitchen. In the upper half we see a serving vessel into which a food can be put and then covered with either a small or a large plate (the engraver meticulously shows the shoulders on which the plates will sit in the vessel), over which coals can be placed in order to keep the food warm. Next is a wooden receptacle in which fireplace implements can be carried. The long-handled pot is labelled 'Spanish-style casserole pot for making whitedish.' A carrying basket for kitchen odds and ends is illustrated both in use and empty; the label on the second view mentions the net closure.

Plate 18: Saddle and Filter. The saddle depicted here is a remarkable creation specifically to answer the needs of a cook whose master will travel. It incorporates a surprising number of pockets and pouches, all lockable, in which, as the note explains, 'a variety of both kitchen and sideboard foods [for the master] can be put on the road early on a strong horse ridden by the cook's assistant' so the master can eat on his arrival at the day's destination. The cone filter below is, on the other contrary, a commonplace apparatus in any noble kitchen. The recipe for 'Honeyed water as a beverage' reads: For every pound of purified honey boil it gently with seven and a half pounds of clean fountain or river water; then strain it through a clean cloth or a cotton (*bonbasina*) filter cone.

Plate 19: Mechanical Escapement to Turn Spits. This mechanism, though hardly designed for an ambulant kitchen, is an equal in ingenuity to the saddle of the previous plate. While the engraver has been able very cleverly to capture the train of the many interlocking gears – of varying diameters so that the three spits turn at different speeds – the delivery of power from the spring of the lowest drum remains unclear.

Plate 20: Foot Warmer (Conclave). The conclave that Scappi observed so closely, that elected Pope Julius III, took place between the end of November 1549 and the first week in February 1550 – that is, in midwinter. The cardinals sat a lot and probably shivered as much. The footwarmer detailed here likely eased some of their discomfort and was undoubtedly considered a valuable possession. The top engraving shows the warmer's parts from the outside to the core: an elongated wooden box; an iron sheath; a corrugated copper element; an iron bar, square in section. By means of a hook through a ring on the iron bar, a servant can withdraw the bar from its casing and place it into a fire to heat. The wooden cap for the casing will prevent an accidental contact with the hot bar by the user.

Plate 21: Food Service Procession (Conclave). This fold-out engraving of a procession of servitors is a faithful rendition of the formal operation according to Scappi's account of food service to the cardinals during the conclave of 1549–50 (see Appendix I, f. A3v). Each cardinal's food is prepared separately by his staff and, following the cardinal's mace-bearer (*mazziero*), is borne in three capacious hampers, tubs and trays: food cooked in the kitchen (*cornuta di cocina*), sideboard food (*credenza*) and wine and water from the cellarer (*bottigliaria*). In turn each of the cardinals' stewards (*scalchi*, one of whom is seen standing at the table) presents his master's food to the examiners (*riveditori* and *reveditori*) to be appraised for salubrity, proper dishware and perhaps illicit communications.[2] If approved, the preparations will be set on the empty plates that the attendant at the table holds out and he will then set them on the 'wheels' (*ruote del conclave*) in the rear wall, a half-turn of which will give the cardinal and his three personal attendants, in the conclave refectory beyond, their meal. The servitors then file down stairs to the exit. Both entrance and exit are closely guarded by a member each of the two corps, Italian and Swiss, whose duty is to ensure a secure and proper functioning of the conclave.

Plate 22: Chamber Furnishings (Conclave), 1. The cell of every cardinal is furnished with a bedstead, armchair, box chair and, lower right, a lidded urine bottle. A long-handled incense burner is also fitted into this plate, as is, rather curiously, a cheese grater.

Plate 23: Miscellaneous Equipment, 1. A lockable chest that contains disparate odds and ends of kitchen utensils is useful when travelling. A hearth-in-a-sandbox can readily be shifted to wherever modest heat is needed. Two types of candle are shown, one with its long wick trailing in oil or semi-liquid tallow. Chamber furnishings occupy the lower half of the engraving: an ornate bellows, an equally ornate ewer and tray, likely intended for handwashing, and on the table a lidded case (*stucio*) with compartments for personal toiletries, including scissors alongside, and an hour-glass in its protective drawstring bag.

Plate 24: Kitchen Equipment for Travelling. Two large lockable wooden chests dominate the top of this plate, in the middle is a lockable case (*forciera*) for slender skewers, while filling the bottom are two large lockable jars, for which a dipper is relegated to the upper left, and a carafe (*boccale*). Also depicted are a rolled-up reed mat, a small assortment of tools (*ferriera*) and a leather pouch which is closed with a buckle.

Plate 25: Miscellaneous Equipment, 2. Perhaps the most interesting item here is the bedwarmer (*scalda letto*) with its decorative lid and an ornately turned handle which is echoed in a broom beside it. A representation of a table and four carrying staves for a hamper and a wine case (see Plate 21) seems superfluous, although the pair of staves labelled *bastoni pontificali* – for delivering food to the papal table – justify their inclusion in this plate by showing what could be imagined to be papal arms painted on those staves. An ideal kitchen had plenty of headroom for adequate fresh air; the ladder might be necessary for reaching high shelves or cabinets in such a kitchen.

Plate 26: Chamber Furnishing (Conclave), 2. Two solid seats, a sturdy writing table (rather than one of the normal folding variety: Plate 25), a lockable

---

[2] See ff.A3v–4r of Scappi's account of food service to the conclave. In the same place he identifies the four examiners as bishops.

cabinet, a wall-mounted clothes hanger and two tubs (for bathing?). Of those furnishings the most interesting is the desk, which bears the label *banchetta alta con cassetta per scruttinio*: the 'small box' (*cassetta*) appears as a tray or modern drawer and would be taken by a cardinal from his cell into the general assembly. Its contents include the two (coloured) ribbons for voting (*scruttinio*). The ink-well and quill pen on the desk warrant an enlargement at the bottom of the plate.

Plate 27: Food Service (Conclave). This plate is devoted primarily to articles used to carry food. (See these containers in Plate 21 also.) Two views are afforded of each of the wooden hampers, lockable and with a hinged lid, used for kitchen preparations; of the wine-steward's tray; and of the tub for the sideboard foods. This last variety of container, oval with a drawstring cover and larger than the representation suggests, may be of wood covered with tooled leather; it bears the arms of its owner. The foot of the engraving is filled with a miscellany of articles: a dustpan, an oil-and-vinegar tray, a tray for cleaning knives, a fly trap (*moscarola*) with an aperture on top and a vertically sliding gate to clean it out, and a candle holder.

Plate 1: The Main Kitchen

Plate 2   **Appendix II. Engravings   637**

Plate 2: The Room Next to the Kitchen

Plate 3: The Scullery

Plate 4   Appendix II. Engravings   639

Plate 4: Cool Place for Dairy Products

Plate 5: Cooking under a Hood

Plate 6   Appendix II. Engravings   641

Plate 6: A Field Kitchen

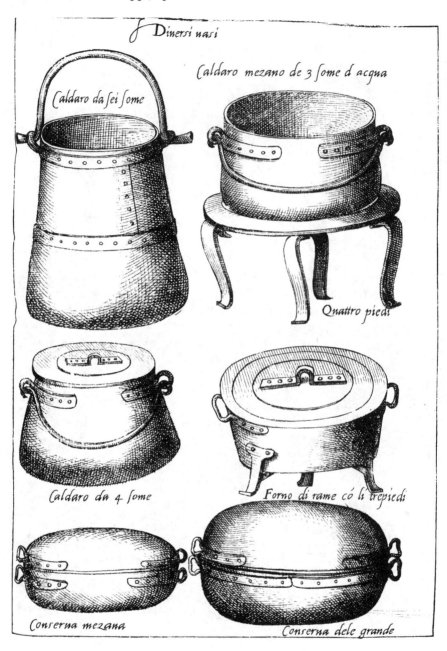

Plate 7: Various Vessels, 1

Plate 8

Appendix II. Engravings 643

Diuersi uasi

stufatoro

nauicella cō piastrelle et quatro piedi

nauicella cō piast relle et 4 piedi

Conserua

nauicella senza piedi

nauicella senza piedi

stufator ouato

Conserua bassa

Conserua grande

padella p fare oui frittolate

stufatoro largo

tortera con il coperto

nauicella bassa

conca

nauicella alta

Plate 8: Various Vessels, 2

Plate 9: Various Vessels, 3

Plate 10   Appendix II. Engravings   645

Plate 10: Various Utensils, 1

Plate 11: Various Utensils, 2

Plate 12   Appendix II. Engravings   647

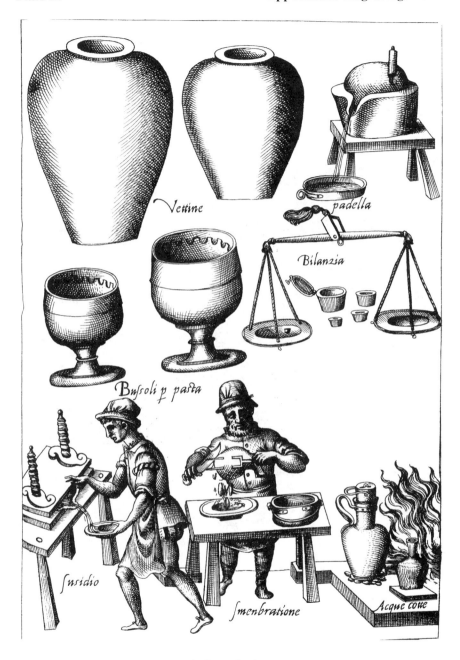

Plate 12: Vessels, Apparatus

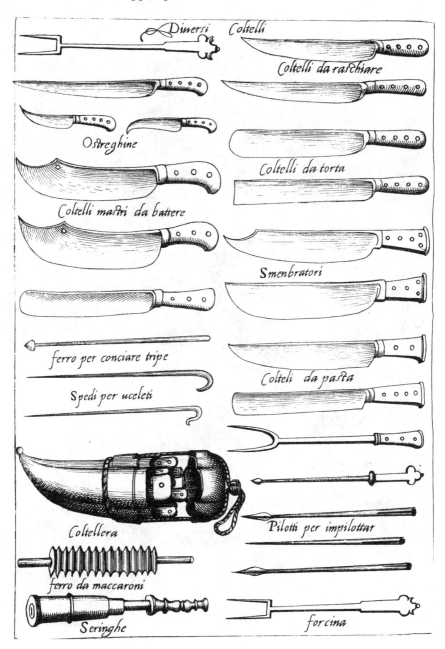

Diuersi   Coltelli

Coltelli da raschiare

Ostreghine

Coltelli da torta

Coltelli maestri da battere

Smenbratori

ferro per conciare tripe

Spedi per uceleti

Coltelli da pasta

Coltellera

Pilotti per impilottar

ferro da maccaroni

Seringhe   forcina

Plate 13: Various Knives

Plate 14   Appendix II. Engravings   649

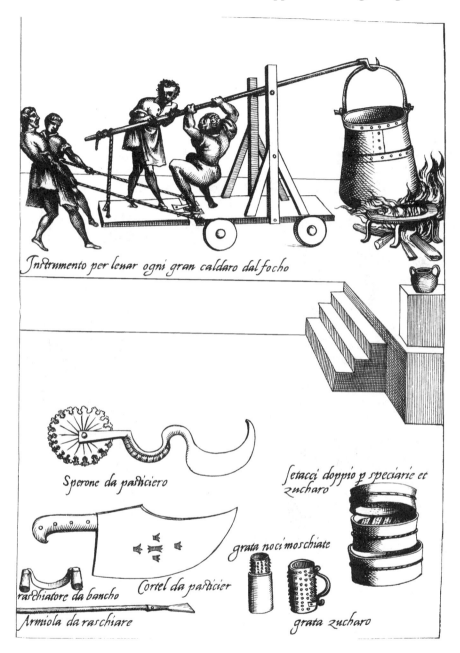

Plate 14: Kitchen Apparatus, 1

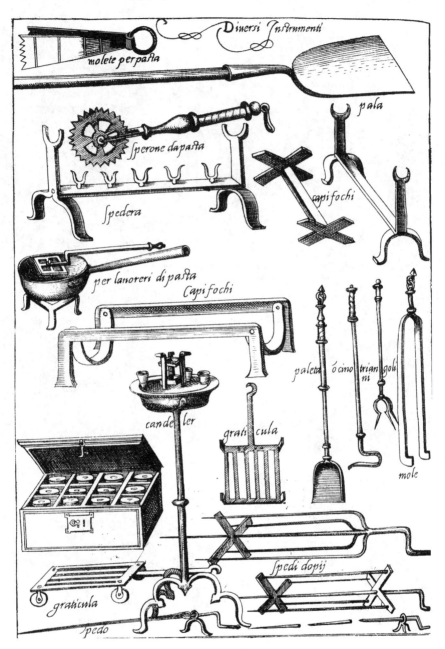

Plate 15: Kitchen Apparatus, 2

Plate 16   Appendix II. Engravings   651

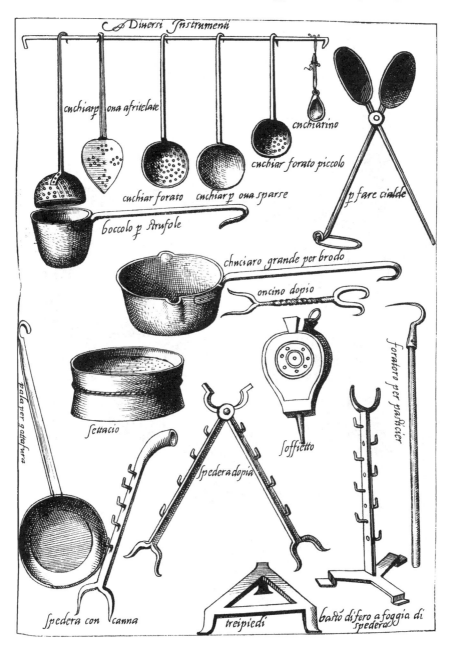

Plate 16: Kitchen Apparatus, 3

Schalda uinande con le sue piastrele

Bussuolo di legno có tre cerchi di ferro p ripore spedi et palle

Casola alla spagnola per far il magnar bianco

Ceste per uiaggio p portar massaritie

Cesta uota con la rete per portar massaritie

Plate 17: Kitchen Apparatus, 4

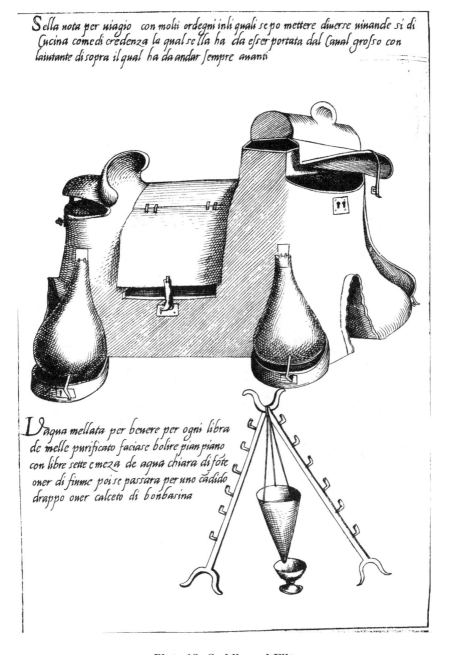

Sella nota per uiagio con molti ordegni inli quali se po mettere diuerse uiuande si di Cucina comedi credenza la qual sella ha da esser portata dal Caual grosso con laiutante di sopra il qual ha da andar sempre auanti

Uagua mellata per beuere per ogni libra de melle purificato faciase bolire pian piano con libre sette e meza de aqua chiara di fote oner di fiume poi se passara per uno cadido drappo oner calceto di bonbasina

Plate 18: Saddle and Filter

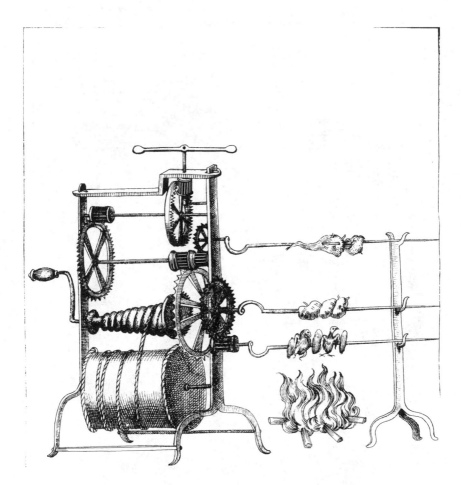

Molinello con tre spedi che si uolta dasse per forza de ruotte con il tempo a foggia di orologio come nella presente figura si dimostra

Plate 19: Mechanical Escapement to Turn Spits

Plate 20   Appendix II. Engravings 655

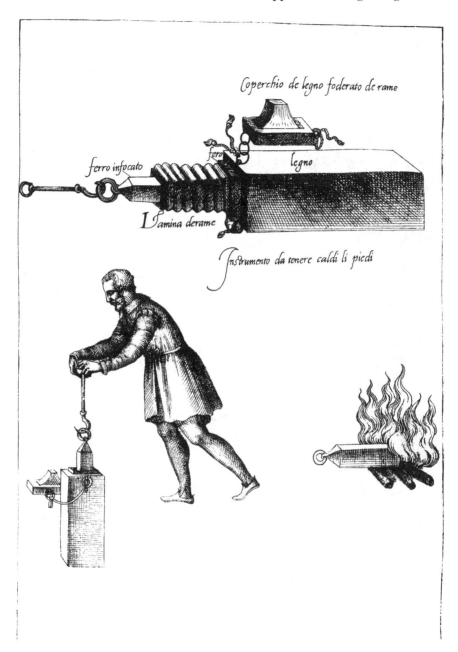

Coperchio de legno foderato de rame

ferro infocato *ferro* *legno*

Lamina derame

Instrumento da tenere caldi li piedi

Plate 20: Foot Warmer (Conclave)

Tavola, dove li scalchi precintano le vivande delli R.mi, Alli venditori

Rima del Conclave

Ruecchiori

Mazziero

Cucina di Cucina

Credenza

Scala di ritorno

Porta di Guardia

Bottigliaria

Ordine che si tiene in Sedia Vacante a servire gl'Ill.mi, et R.mi Cardinali al Conclave, si di robbe di Cucina, come di Credenza et di bottigliaria

Plate 21: Food Service (Conclave)

Plate 22   Appendix II. Engravings   657

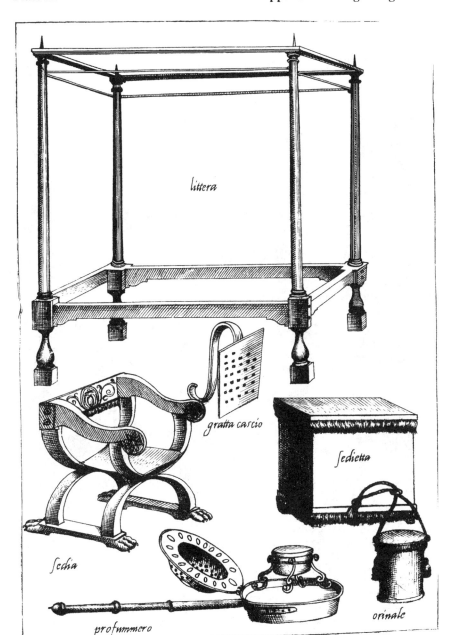

Plate 22: Chamber Furnishings (Conclave), 1

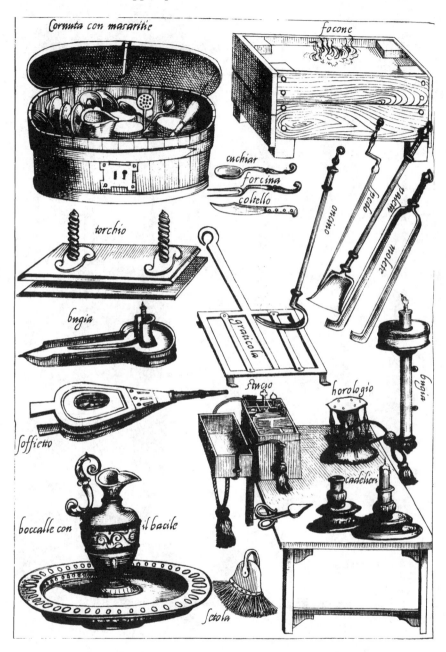

Cornuta con masaritie

focone

cuchiar
forcina
coltello

torchio

bugia

oncino
spedo

paletta

molette

la graticola

stucio

horologio

bugia

soffietto

candelieri

boccalle con   il bacile

setola

Plate 23: Miscellaneous Equipment, 1

Plate 24   Appendix II. Engravings   659

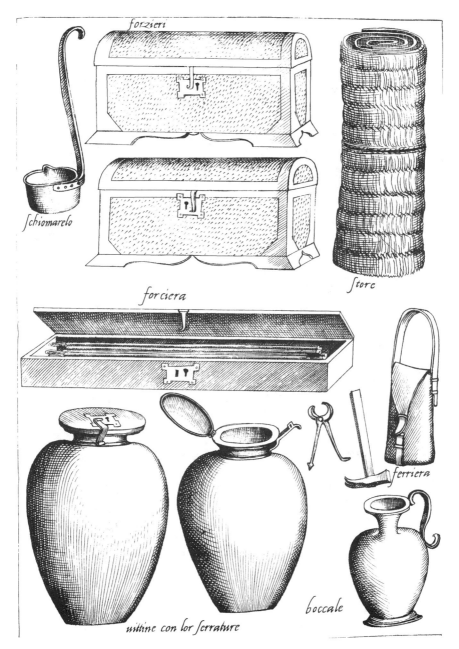

forzieri

schiomarelo

store

forciera

ferriera

uittine con lor serrature

boccale

Plate 24: Kitchen Equipment for Travelling

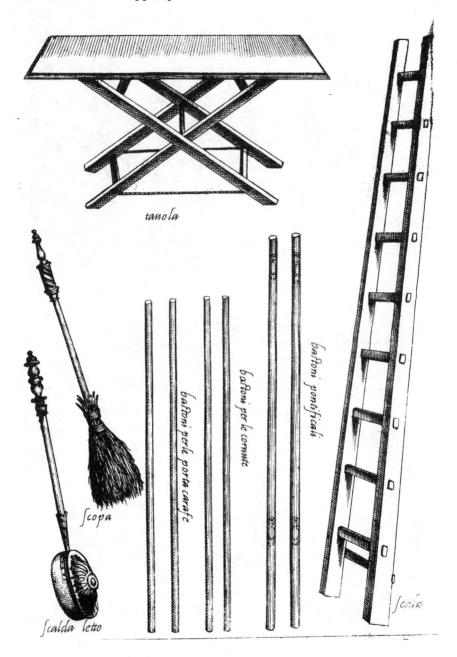

tauola

bastoni per le porta carafe

bastoni per le comute

bastoni pontificali

scopa

scalda letto

scala

Plate 25: Miscellaneous Equipment, 2

Plate 26   Appendix II. Engravings   661

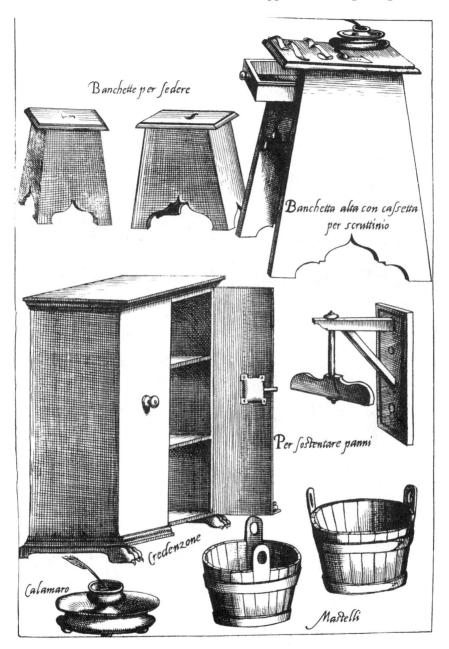

Plate 26: Chamber Furnishings (Conclave), 2

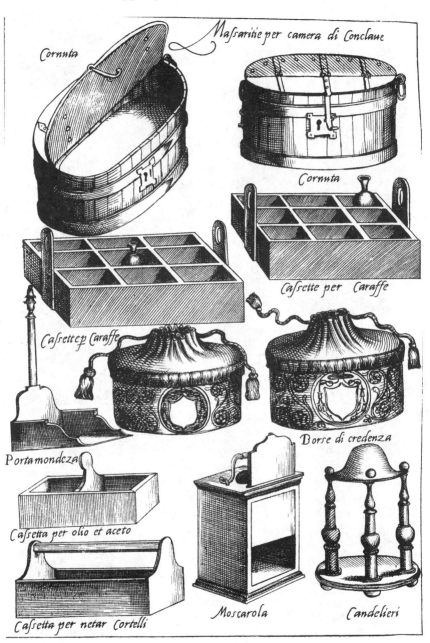

Massaritie per camera di Conclaue

Cornuta

Cornuta

Cassette per Caraffe

Cassette p Caraffe

Portamondeza

Borse di credenza

Cassetta per olio et aceto

Cassetta per netar Cortelli

Moscarola

Candelieri

Plate 27: Food Service (Conclave)

Appendix III

Household Functionaries

Several Italian writers in the sixteenth and seventeenth centuries offered advice about the household staffing proper for a noble (or affluent bourgeois) establishment, as well as job descriptions of the important functionaries in that household. A contemporary of Scappi was Domenico Romoli (alias Panunto), whose *Singolare dottrina* was first published in 1560.[1] At the beginning of his Book IV Panunto refers to meals whose menus he drew up in 1546; he must have been employed at that time in his full professional capacity. By 1560 and apparently retired, the ex-steward is ready to pass on his accumulated professional wisdom.

His book is addressed to a younger man, Francesco, a would-be *scalco* or steward in a wealthy household.[2] In Book I he outlines, in considerable detail and with an awareness of human weaknesses, not only the nature of the duties of a *scalco* but those as well of a *spenditore* (a purchasing agent or procurement officer), a *cuoco secreto*, a *credenziere* (a sideboard attendant), *bottigliere, dispensiere, panatiere, soprastante del piatto, gentilhuomini* and *camerieri*, for all of whom the steward is responsible. As a steward himself, Domenico Romoli was thoroughly familiar with the work of all of these household officers. It is his view of the personal or private cook that interests us most particularly, given that Panunto was working in the same ecclesiastical milieu as Scappi and at the same time.

> You should be aware of and keep a vigilant eye on everything that concerns your lord's food, and above all else you must order that the Kitchen, the Credenza and the Personal Provisioning Office[3] behave the way a miser watches his treasury ...
>
> I sometimes ponder how very important an individual is who is a personal officer of noble Princes since in the face of so many dangers they place their life in his hands. The Cook is one of the foremost of those officers, and I used to shudder when I held the office that you aspire to, and now give God the most heartfelt thanks for having seen me through it

---

[1] *La singolare dottrina.* The printing used for this translation is by Gio. Battista Bonfadino in Venice, 1593.

[2] The designation *scalco* is of Lombard origin, deriving from an Indo-European word for servant. Prefaced with the adjective 'old,' *sini*, a cognate word *seneschal* came to designate the senior retainer of a household.

A survey of the principal food-service officers, and others, in a wealthy house is presented by Andrea Manciulli, 'Le arti della tavola' in *Et coquatur ponendo*, 325–46.

[3] These are, respectively, *la cucina, credenza, & dispenza secreta.* The second is the table in the dining hall at which food intended for the master is tested or proved; the third is the domain of the provisioner or purchasing agent, whose primary concern is to procure foodstuffs for the master's board.

honourably. In truth it is one of the most care-racked offices that can be imagined, because you have constantly to keep your eyes wide open: in striving to do your duty and to avoid any mishap, you must always have your mind on the dangers around you. To exercise the function properly you have to arm yourself with a shield rich in charity, faith and dedication.

To get back to what we were saying, after having found a Provisioner you must next secure a good and worthy Cook, one who, like an old physician, has grown old in his art. Above all, have nothing to do with a drunkard, even if he were the most outstanding master cook in the world: for, rather than cooking the foods as you need to serve them, he will have cooked the main dishes before the appetizers. I warn you because it has often happened to me; so be careful. What goes on in a kitchen is supremely demanding, exhausting and exasperating, and for that reason an older person cannot stand it for long; you should give him a suitable young man, trained by him or by a colleague, as deputy cook.[4] The assistants should be experienced and the scullions clean[5] – with instruction you can insist on their being neat and clean. You will supply them amply with fine and coarse cloth and aprons. You will constantly require them to be clean-shaven, to have their hair closely trimmed, to have their white blouses tucked under their aprons, their clothing short, clean and snug. Mind that they are not snotty nor have pimples or pustules. They should not be quarrelsome but obedient, civil, cheerful and, as much as possible, Italian rather than foreigners.[6]

When their dishes are all prepared and you are ready to begin serving them, he will have them thoroughly clean the little table where their work will be dished up. He will also have them set out on it everything that is needed, both morning and evening, such as lemons, oranges, cheeses and candies, and the master's caddy of spiced candy. And he will have his clean knives and your serviette around a clean loaf of bread set out for the usual proving of dishes and sauces, and a medium-sized iron fork.

In particular you should keep the Cook cheerful, though not with that cheer that comes from too much drinking, as I said.

For now I shall leave off dealing with the activities of the rest of the officers, to advise you how you ought to direct and manage their work and yours.

After the evening meal have your Cook and Provisioner come to your room and together settle with them what foods they will be serving the next morning; that way the Provisioner will bring the foodstuffs into the storeroom early. As he may not have been able to find everything that he was sent out for, you have to get up very early and, setting aside all other duties, go to see him and, checking what he has brought in, reorder your foodstuffs, directing him to go back out for whatever is missing. When you have finished serving your master's dinner, you will go back to the kitchen and make arrangements for the supper, because often in the morning some odd things are left over that can be served cold at supper.

I should like to see you and your Cook take great pains to become thoroughly familiar with your master's taste because it is apparent that some masters do not like spices, or cheese, or sweet things, or bitter things. Likewise you should know what his fixed, usual

---

[4] *per sottocuoco*, literally 'undercook' or *sous-chef*.

[5] Panunto calls these kitchen workers *aitanti* and *garzoni*, respectively.

[6] *tramontani*, particularly French, German or of other nationalities from beyond the Alps.

hour for meals is, both morning and evening. Clearly, a gentleman's appetite is hard to determine, because in most cases it tends to be whimsical; but you have to be as assiduous as you can, for in this business a person must be more a diviner than a steward. When you cannot guess their meal times it is no wonder that they are badly served, because prepared dishes and appetizers dry out, sauces and soups are spoiled, boiled things get cold and roasted things get tough in the warming pans. But I tell you, if you know the set meal time you will not go wrong. You will have to watch that the small appetizers don't get overcooked – they'll be done while you are setting up the table; big roasts can be kept on the spit until serving time. That way your honour will not suffer and your master will be pleased at how good all your dishes are when they have been well prepared by that worthy Cook.

The *Libro dello scalco* of Cesare Evitascandalo[7] is again concerned primarily with that most senior individual in the hierarchy of such court servants, the steward. Francesco Reinoso was the personal *scalco* of Pius V and, as such, the superior to whom Scappi was immediately responsible and who exercised the most authority over his professional activities.

The Steward should know what a prepared dish is, and what it is made of, so that he can explain, if he is asked, whether a tangy garnish is made with vinegar or something else, or whether a sweet one is made with sugar or honey; in the roast course he should be able to tell the difference between a thrush and a blackbird, a suckling calf and a grazing calf, a fig-eater or some other small bird; and the same with a great many other fowl and animals, both wild and domestic. Whoever wishes to exercise that most honorable profession must have had long practical experience in kitchen matters and have taken pleasure at seeing and learning all that is associated with a good cook, so that he himself can organize and be competent. The Steward should mind that the cook has clean hands, without scabies or any other filth, and not have festering legs as many do from too much wine, which ruins the liver. In the evening after supper he will plan the dishes he wants made the following morning, both roasted dishes and boiled dishes, appetizers, potages, soups, pastries and every other prepared dish.

Following is the translation of an extract from Francesco Liberati, *Il perfetto maestro di casa*.[8] While *Il perfetto maestro* was written some three generations after Scappi's *Opera*, the book affords a broad, informative survey of an affluent household, whose hierarchic structure and clearly delineated responsibilities remained little changed from Scappi's time. In places Liberati's sardonic comments suggest that wholehearted devotion to the welfare of the house and its Master was sometimes not universal among the retainers.

---

[7] *Libro dello scalco* (Rome: Vullietti, 1609), 1–4, as reprinted in Maria Luisa Incontri Lotteringhi della Stufa, *Pranzi e conviti* (Florence: Olimpia, 1965), 167 f.

[8] *Il perfetto maestro di casa* (Rome: Hercole, 1670). The original text is likewise reproduced in Lotteringhi della Stufa, *Pranzi e Conviti*, 168–70. She writes that Liberati was in the service of various cardinals, including Cardinal Bichi of Siena.

The Cup Bearer[9] should be refined and trustworthy, with a gravity of person; he supervises wines, waters, cup mats,[10] beakers and containers in the wine cellar.

The Steward, because he has his Master's life in his hands, must be very careful that the dishes destined for his mouth be of the highest quality and that they pass through as few hands as possible, undergoing the usual test only by the Cook before being brought to the table.

The Carver,[11] young, hardy and handsome, while serving must be steady on his feet, making an effort not to touch the table with his waist or get his hands greasy, making free use of the serviette which he has firmly on his left arm during his work. He will make no noise with his knife on the meat or dishes, and even less will he make himself heard with sneezing or coughing. When his Master or some guest of his has been served he will cover the set of knives with a doily, wrapping the knives around with the small napkin they are sitting on; bowing, he will hand it over to whomever is close to him, and then he will stand by, right up until the end.

The Sideboard Attendant[12] must take his orders from the Steward and lay the sideboard and tables with the dishes to be set out, clean the silverware and vessels. When travelling he will carry the Master's cutlery on his own horse, leaving four or five hours ahead of him. He will also take the hand-washing basin and ewer, along with a pair of pouches containing towels, tablecloths, serviettes, knives, spoons, forks and skewers, and all the other minor things like sugar, spices and, often, bread, which on a trip can turn out not to be very good.

The Provisioner of foodstuffs will procure whatever is on the list that the Steward gives him every day, and he never leaves the house without notifying the Steward or the Major-Domo.[13]

The Sommelier[14] will never let his Master drink wines that are not perfectly healthy. He will be supremely clean;[15] he will not let anyone approach the little table and vessels he has prepared, and even less will he let anyone drink from the beakers from which the Master normally drinks. Whenever there are outside guests and banquets he will be careful to bring in several sorts of fresh wine and water, and to put fanciful beakers and a variety of small decanters and vessels on display. If the Master should go to eat in someone else's

---

[9] *Il Coppiere.*

[10] These *sottocoppe* are likely a sort of coaster. See the same article furnished by the *Cellarer* (*Il Bottigliere*) below.

[11] *Il Trinciante.* On this functionary see Vincenzo Cervio, *Il Trinciante* (Venice: the heirs of Michele Tramezzino, 1581); partially reprinted by Firpo, *Gastronomia*, 97–129; and in Faccioli, *Arte della cucina*, II, 67–118. Cervio dedicated his work to Cardinal Alessandro Farnese (1520–89), grandson of Paul III.

[12] *Il Credenziere.*

[13] *Il Maestro di Casa.*

[14] *Il Bottigliere.* A modern English cognate of that Italian word is butler.

[15] *esquisitamente polito.*

house, the Cellarer will bring along the cup mat, decanters and beakers inside a small hamper; he will do the same for a trip, bringing a locked chest full of the best wines.

The Dispenser will dispense nothing out of his stores without a prescription. Well furnished with counterpoise weigh scales and lever scales, he will be cautious in writing everything out and in weighing it, minding that he does not give an order to the bakery to make loaves under-weight, or make them by himself in order to appropriate the surplus. Let him remember that, apart from what is coming to him and his salary, he cannot take his Master's property; to do otherwise is what in Tuscan is called *rubare*.[16]

The Cellarer[17] handles a particular substance which is appreciated by many people, for which reason he will always have chums to help him dispose of it. If he cannot live off it by himself, the casks will quickly be depleted, so that when the tally does not add up he will be reduced to committing fraud and will be ruined. He must not allow revelry in the cellar. He himself must be temperate in his drinking, and should know about wines so as to keep them and distribute them. As he receives them he will sample each of the barrels, one by one, checking them against the sample.

The Personal Cook[18] serves the Prince's board and must be off in a kitchen separate from the common one of the household; that office is so important that neither the Steward or the Major-Domo can visit it if it is not convenient. In choosing him there must be information about his capability and his trustworthiness. It is advisable that the cook not be from a distant land – though, if he is, he should have lived for a long time with women in the Master's province. In the matter of cooking he needs to be experienced with pasta dishes, with jellies, plain boiled dishes,[19] broths, pastries, potages and everything else touching on his service. He must avoid consuming a greater amount of wood, coal, spices, fats and similar ingredients than is required by the job; and taking the leftovers for himself under the pretext of payment in kind – which is not permitted, and all the less so are ashes and used frying oil, because the frying pan is not refilled every time – those things being distributed, the ashes to the laundry, the frying oil to the kitchen lighting service, so saving both oil and candles. That office must be clean, and cleanliness lies not only with the person and dress but also in the kitchen and the equipment, by cleaning copperware, pewter, tables, spits and everything else. It is not for outsiders to come into the private kitchen, nor are cooks there allowed the number of scullery boys that are usually found in similar places, both for the sake of cleanliness and because of accidents that can happen with them.

---

16 'To rob, steal.'

17 *Il Canovaro o Cantiniere.*

18 *Il Cuoco segreto.*

19 *lavori … di bianco.*

Bibliography

The following Bibliography is in three parts. Part 1 contains a listing, by date of publication, of works about food printed in Italy up to the beginning of the seventeenth century; contemporary translations of those works are also placed here. This part includes the sequence of early publications of Scappi's *Opera*. Part 2 groups modern reprints and translations of the *Opera* followed by some fourteenth- and fifteenth-century manuscript recipe collections, whether with modern editions or not; the contents of those late-medieval works may possibly have had some influence upon Scappi's cookery. The latter items are in roughly chronological order. Part 3 offers a very limited selection of modern studies in the field of Renaissance food and cookery.

For ecclesiastical figures of the period, biographies touching upon them and histories of their times, see also the beginning of the listing, below, Persons Mentioned in Scappi's *Opera*. For several useful dictionaries, see the beginning of the Index.

Early Italian printed books on food

1477
Pantaleone da Confienza
Summa lacticiniorum. Torino, 1477. Ed. Irma Naso, *Formaggi del medioevo. La 'Summa lacticiniorum' di Pantaleone da Confienza*, Turin: Il Segnalibro, 1990.

1508
Michele Savonarola (d. 1464)
Libretto de lo Excellentissimo Physico maistro Michele Savonarola: de tute le cose che se manzano comunamente e più che comune: e di quelle se beveno per Italia: e de sei cose non naturale: e le regule per conservare la sanità de li corpi humani, con dubii notabilissimi. In Venetia, per Simone de Luere, MDVIII. [*Libreto de tute le cosse che se manzano. Un libro di dietetica di Michele Savonarola, medico padovano nel secolo XV*, ed. Jane Nystedt. Stockholm: Stockholms Universitets, 1982.]

1516
Giovanni de Rosselli[1]

---

[1] The *Epulario* of Rosselli is merely a reissuing of a recipe collection that had become in a sense traditional since it first appeared in the mid-1400s in the *Neapolitan Recipe Collection*.

Opera nova chiamata Epulario, quale tracta il mode de cucinare ogni carne, ucelli, pesci d'ogni sorte. Et fare sapori, torte, pastelli, al modo de tutte le province composta per maestro Giovanne de Rosselli. In Venetia, per Agostino Zanni da Portese, MDXVI.

[The same]. In Venetia per industria e spesa di Nicolo Zopino et Vincenzo compagni in la chasa de maistro Jacomo Penci da Lecho impressore acuratissimo. Nel M.D.XVII a di III del Mese di Aprile.

[The same] ... *Per maestro Gionne. Rosselli francese.* At the end: Stampato in Venetia, per Nic. Zopino et Vincenzo compagni, Nel M.D.XVII a di xx de Agosto.

[The same] ... *& molte altre gentilezze. Composto per Maestro Gioanne de Rosselli Francese.* Stampato in Venetia per Nicolo Zopino e Vincenzo compagni. Nel MDXVIII adi xxi di Agosto.

Epulario opera noua, la quale tracta il modo de cucinare ogni carne, ucelli, pesci, d'ogni sorte. Et fare sapori, torte, pastelli, al modo de tutte de provincie. Et molte altre gentilezze. Composta per Maestro Giouanne de Rosselli. Venetia (Bernardino Benalio), 1519.

[The same]. Venetia, per Nicolo Zoppino et Vincenzo compagni, in la chasa di maistro Alexandro de Bindoni, 1521.

[The same]. Venetia, Benedetto e Augustino Bindoni, 1525, adi 22 de Zanaro.

[The same]. Venetia, Aluise di Torti, 1534.

Epulario, il qual tratta del modo del cucinare ogni carne, uccelli, & pesci d'ogni sorte, et di piu insegna far sapori, torte, pastelli, al modo di tutte le provincie del mondo. Con la gionta di molte altre cose bellissime. Venetia, In Frezzaria al segno della Regina, 1579.[2]

1521

Teofilo Folengo (1496–1544)

Doctrinæ cosinandi viginti, Toscolano (Alessandro Paganini), 1521. [Twenty recipes embedded in Book 14 of a Latin chivalric romance.] Ed. and trans. Faccioli, *Arte della cucina*, I, 237–51.

1524

MS Lucano.

Michael Süthold, *'Manoscritto Lucano.' Ein unveröffentlichtes Kochbuch aus Süditalien vom Beginn des 16. Jahrhunderts*, Kölner Romanistische Arbeiten, 70, Geneva (Droz), 1994. [The manuscript contains a colophon that reads *Scripto in Nerula lo anno 1524 a di .3. de agusto.*]

---

[2] An English translation of Rosselli's work appeared at the end of the century: *Epulario, or, The Italian banquet: Wherein is shewed the maner how to dresse and prepare all kind of flesh, foules or fishes: as also how to make sauces, tartes, pies, &c., after the maner of all countries: with an addition of many other profitable and necessary things.* London, printed by A.I. for William Barley, 1598.

c. 1530

Giovanni, maestro di cucina[3]

Opera dignissima & utile per chi si diletta di Cucinare: con molti bellissimi
  secreti di componere: & conservare vivande: & molti altri secreti di piu cose:
  Composto per il valente Maestro Giovane de la Cucina de la Santtità dil nostro
  Summo Pontefice. Stampata nela magnifica Citta di Milano per Pietro Paulo
  Verini Fiorentino in la condrada delle bandiere al ballone, [c. 1515].

1541

Opera nuova intitolata Dificio di Ricetti ... nella quale si contengono tre utilissimi
  Ricettarii, Venice (Vavassore), 1541.

Dificio di ricette nel quale si contengono tre utilissimi ricettari. Nel primo si tratta
  di molte & diverse virtù. Nel secondo si insegna a comporre varie sorti di
  soavi et utilissi. odori. Nel terzo & ultimo si tratta di alcuini secreti medicinali
  necessari in risanar li corpi humani, come nella tavola si potria vedere, Venice
  (Francesco Rampazetto), [1553].[4]

1549

Cristoforo di Messisbugo [*or* Messi Sbugo][5]

Banchetti compositioni di vivande, et apparecchio generale, di Christoforo di
  Messisbugo, allo illustrissimo et reverendissimo signor il signor don Hippolito
  da Este, Cardinale di Ferrara. Con gratia et Privilegio. In Ferrara, per
  Giovanni de Buglhat et Antonio Hucher Compagni, nell' Anno M.D.XLIX.
  Reprinted Venice: Neri Pozza, 1960; Milan: Neri Possa, 1992. Ed. Faccioli,
  Arte della cucina, I, 263–312.

---

[3] This qualification, as well as the approximate date of the twenty-four-folio work, are applied
by the British Library to its copy. Giovanni's 133 recipes derive primarily from the *Neapolitan*-
Martino-Platina tradition. The pope for whom Giovanni presumably worked would have been Leo
X (1513–21) or perhaps Clement VII (1523–34), both of whom were Medici.

[4] The *Dificio di Ricetti* was translated into French, its title literally, as *Le Bastiment de receptes,*
nouvellement traduict de italien en langue françoyse, Lyon (A l'escu de Cologine), 1541; and
Bastiment des receptes contenant trois petites parties de receptaires. La premiere traicte de di-
verses vertus & proprietez des choses ... , Poitiers (Jacques Bouchet), 1544; Lyon (Benoist Ri-
gaud), 1559; Paris (Guillaume de Nyverd), [1560].

[5] Messisbugo (1500–48) was a noble steward at the Este ducal court of Ferrara from 1524 until
his death. His *Banchetti* was first published a year after his death, 1549. Its final section contains 323 relatively concise recipes in six divisions: pasta, cakes, soups, sauces, broths and dairy
products; the recipes are designed as memoranda for a steward, not instructions for a cook. The
younger brother of Duke Ercole (1508–59), Hippolito d'Este, cardinal of Ferrara (1509–72), for
whom Messisbugo worked, was a close friend of Ridolfo Campeggio, son of Cardinal Lorenzo
Campeggio (1474–1539), for whom Scappi himself was probably working in 1536. Scappi never
mentions Messisbugo, though, or his work. (On Ippolito d'Este, see the book by Hollingsworth,
The Cardinal's Hat.)

Libro novo nel quale s'insegna a far d'ogni sorte di vivanda secondo la diuersità de' tempi, così di carne come di pesci, e'l modo d'ordinar banchetti, apparecchiar tavole, fornir palazzi, & ornar camere per ogni gran Prencipe. Opera assai bella, e molto Bisognevole à maestri di Casa, à Scalchi, à Credenzieri, & à Cuochi. Composta per M. Christofaro di Messisbugo & hora di novo stampato, con la sua Tavola ordinata, ove agevolmente si trovarà ogni cosa. In Venetia, al segno di san Girolamo. At the end: In Venetia, ad instantia di Giovanni della Chiesa Pavese. Nell'anno MDLII.

[The same]. *... Composta per M. Cristofaro di Messisbugo & hora di novo corretta & ristampata. Aggiontovi di nuovo, il modo di saper tagliare ogni sorte di carne & uccellami. Con la sua Tavola ordinata, ove agevolmente si trovarà ogni cosa.* In Venetia, al signo di San Girolamo. At the end: In Venetia, ad instantia di Giovanni delia Chiesa Pavese nell'anno MDLVI.

Christofaro di Messisbugo: Libro Novo nel qual s'insegna a far d'ogni sorte di vivanda (...) Et il modo d'ordinar banchetti, apparechiar Tavole, fornir palazzi (...). In Venetia, MDLVII. At the end: In Vinegia [sic] per gli heredi di Giovanni Padovano MDLVII. Facsimile: Sala Bolognese (Arnaldo Forni), 1980.

[The same]. In Venetia, MDLIX.

[The same]. Venetia, 1576.

[The same]. In Frezzaria, al Segno della Regina, 1578.

[The same]. In Venetia, In Frezzaria, al Segno della Regina MDLXXXI.

[The same]. In Venetia, Appresso Giovanni Alberti. MDLXXXV.

[The same]. Vinegia, A. Salicato, 1589.

[The same]. In Venetia, Appresso Lucio Spineda, 1600.

1554

Giovannl Battista Scarlino

Nuovo Trattato della varietà, & qualità de Vini, che vengono a Roma. Co i nomi loro, dove nascono, & come si debbano secondo le stagioni bere: co'l modo di comporgli diversamente, e sanar con essi molte gravi infermità, & altri belli segreti, utili a gli huomini, & alle donne. E de i buoni, e cattivi effetti che dal Vino seguono. Composto in terza rima da m. Gio. Bat. Scarlino. At the end: In Roma per Valerio Dorico. The dedication is dated 1554.

c. 1559

Sante Lancerio

[A letter on the nature and quality of wine and on travels undertaken by Pope Paul III, addressed by Lancerio to Cardinal Guido Ascani Sforza. Published by Giuseppe Ferraro, 'I vini d'Italia giudicati da papa Paolo III (Farnese) e dal suo bottigliere Sante Lancerio,' in *La Rivista Europea*, 7 (1876): II, 87–116, 339–49; ed. Faccioli, *Arte della cucina*, II, 317–41.]

1560

Paulo Giovio

Libro di Mons. Paolo Giovio de' Pesci Romani tradotto in Volgare da Carlo Zancaruolo. In Venetia, appresso il Gualtieri, 1560.

1560

Domenico Romoli (alias Il Panunto)[6]

La singolare dottrina di M. Domenico Romoli sopranominato Panonto, dell'ufficio dello Scalco, de i condimenti di tutte le vivande, le stagioni che si convengono à tutti gli animali, uccelli, & pesci, Banchetti di ogni tempo, & mangiare da apparecchiarsi di dì in dì per tutto l'anno à Prencipe, con la dichiaratione della qualità delle carni di tutti gli animali, & pesci, & di tutte le vivande circa la sanità. Nel fine un breve trattato del reggimento della sanità. Opera sommamente utile à tutti. In Venetia per Michele Tramezzino, MDLX.

La singolare dottrina di M. Domenico Romoli sopranominato Panonto, dell'ufficio dello Scalco, de i condimenti di tutte le vivande, le stagioni che si convengono à tutti gli animali, uccelli, & pesci, Banchetti di ogni tempo (...). In Venetia per Michele Tramezzino, MDLXX.

La singolare dottrina. Dell'ufficio dello Scalco, de i condimenti di tutte le vivande, le stagioni che si convengono a tutti gli animali, uccelli, & pesci, Banchetti di ogni tempo (...). In Venetia, MDXCIII. Presso Gio. Battista Bonfadino.

1567

Costanzo Felici di Piobbico

Dell'insalata e piante che in qualunque modo vengono preparate per cibo dall'homo, 1567: *Lettera sulle insalate. Lectio nona de fungis,* Studi e testi, 6, ed. Enzo Cecchini, with Guido Arbizzoni, *et al.,* Urbino (Accademia Raffaelo), 1977; repr. 1996.

1570

Bartolomeo Scappi[7]

Opera di M. Bartolomeo Scappi, cuoco secreto di Papa Pio V. Divisa in sei libri, ... Col privilegio del sommo Pontefice Papa Pio V, & dell'Illustrissimo Senato Veneto per anni XX. [Colophon:] In Venetia, Appresso Michele Tramezzino,

---

[6] The menus of Book IV refer to the year 1546–7. The pope at that time was Paul III; there is a prevalence of Florentine taste in Panunto's recipes.

[7] In the segment below concerning the various printings of Scappi's *Opera,* the bibliographic references are to Katherine Golding Bitting, *Gastronomic Bibliography* (San Francisco: Trade Pressroom, 1939); Georges Vicaire, *Bibliographie gastronomique* (London: Holland Press, 1954); and Lord Westbury (Richard Morland Tollemache Westbury, Baron), *Handlist of Italian Cookery Books* (Florence: Olschki, 1963).

MDLXX. 440 folios, 27 plates. [Westbury, Scappi 1, 202; Vicaire, col. 771. Copy consulted for this translation: University of Toronto Library. Facsimile: see Part 2, below.]

Opera di M. Bartolomeo Scappi, cuoco secreto di Papa Pio Quinto, divisa in sei libri. … , Venetia (Michele Tramezzino), 1581. 372 folios, 27 plates. [Copy consulted for this translation: Harvard University Library]

Opera di M. Bartolomeo Scappi, cuoco secreto di Papa Pio Quinto divisa in sei libri … , Venetia (Alessandro Vecchi; ad instantia de Gio. Martinelli), 1596. 343 folios, 27 woodcuts. [Westbury, Scappi 2, 202; Vicaire, col. 773]

Opera di M. Bartolomeo Scappi, … , Venetia (Alessandro Vecchi), 1598. 311 folios, 27 woodcuts. [Westbury, Scappi 3, 202; Vicaire, col. 773]

Opera di M. Bartolomeo Scappi … Ristampata con due aggiunte, cioè; il Trinciante, & il Maestro di casa. Con le figure che fan bisogno nella cucina, & alli reverendissimi nel conclave, Venetia (Alessandro Vecchi), 1605. 310 folios, 27 woodcuts.[8] [Westbury, Scappi 4, 202; Bitting, 419; Vicaire, col. 773]

Opera di M. Bartolomeo Scappi dell'Arte del cucinare, con laquale si può ammaestrare quel si voglia Cuoco, Scalco, Trinciante, o Maestro di Casa: Divisa in sei libri: Nel primo libro … . Aggiontovi nuovamente il Trinciante, & il Maestro di Casa. Dedicate al Mag. M. Matteo Barbini Cuoco, e Scalco celeberrimo della Città di Venetia, Venetia (Alessandro Vecchi), 1610. 310 folios, 27 woodcuts. [Westbury, Scappi 5, 202; Vicaire, col. 774]

Opera di M. Bartolomeo Scappi dell'Arte del cucinare, … , Venetia (Alessandro Vecchi), 1622. 310 folios, 27 pl. [Westbury, Scappi 6, p. 203; Vicaire, col. 774]

M. Bortolomeo [sic] Scappi *dell'arte d'el cucinare, con il Maestro di casa e Trinciante*, Venetia (Combi), 1643. 636 pages, 27 woodcuts. [Westbury, Scappi 7, 203; Vicaire, col. 775]

M. Bartolomeo Scappi, *Dell'Arte del cucinare, con il Maestro di casa e Trinciante*, Venetia (Combi), 1646.

1581

Vincenzo Cervio

Il Trinciante di M. Vincenzo Cervio, ampliato, et ridotto a perfettione dal Cavallier Reale Fusoritto da Narni, Trinciante dell'Illust^{mo} e Rever^{mo} Signor Cardinal Farnese. In Venetia, appresso gli Heredi di Francesco Tramezini, MDLXXXI.

Il Trinciante di M. Vincenzo Cervio, ampliato et a perfettione ridotto dal Cavalier Reale Fusoritto da Narni (…) aggiuntovi nel fine un breve Dialogo detto il Mastro di Casa (…). Roma, 1593. Facsimile: Sala Bolognese (Arnaldo Forni), 1980.

---

[8] It may be noted that in this publication and several following it, *Il trinciante* is by V. Cervio and dated 1604; and *Il maestro di casa* is by C. Pandini.

Il trinciante. Ampliato et ridotto a perfettione dal cavalier Realle Fusoritto da Narni. Con una bellissima aggiunta fatta novamente dall'istesso cavalier Reale. Venetia (Heredi di G. Varisco), 1593.

1584
Giovanni Battista Rossetti

Dello scalco del Sig. Gio. Battista Rossetti, Scalco della Serenissima Madama Lucretia da Este Duchessa d'Urbino, Nel quale si contengono le qualità di uno Scalco perfetto, & tutti i carichi suoi, con diversi ufficiali à lui sottoposti: Et gli ordini di una casa da Prencipe, e i modi di servirlo, cosìin banchetti, come in tavole ordinarie. Con gran numero di banchetti alla Italiana, & alla Alemana, di varie, e bellissime inventioni, e desinari, e cene familiari per tutti i mesi dell'anno, … . In Ferrara appresso Domenico Mammarello, MDLXXXIIII.

1586
Castor Durante da Gualdo (1529–90)

Il Tesoro della sanità. Nel quale si da il modo da conservar la Sanità, & prolungar la vita, & si tratta della Natura de' Cibi, & de i Rimedii de i Nocumenti loro. Opera nuova di Castor Durante da Gualdo, Medico, & Cittadino Romano. In Roma, ad instantia di Iacomo Tornieri, & Iacomo Biricchia, appresso Francesco Zannetti, 1586. Facsimile: Rome (Julia), 1965. [The author's translation of his own *De bonitate et vitio alimentorum centuria.* Pesaro, 1565.]

1587
Baldassare Pisanelli

Trattato della natura de' cibi et del bere del Sig. Baldassare Pisanelli, medico bolognese. Nel quale non solo tutte le virtù, & i vitii di quelli minutamente si palesano; ma anco i rimedii per correggere i loro difetti copiosamente s'insegnano; tanto nell'apparecchiarli per l'uso, quanto nell'ordinare il modo di riceverli. Distinto in un vago, e bellissimo partimento, tutto ripieno della Dottrina de' più celebrati Medici, e Filosofi; con molte belle Historie Naturali. In Venetia, appresso Gio. Battista Uscio, MDLXXXVII.

1592
Alessandro Petronio

Del viver delli Romani, et di conservar la sanità di M. Alessandro Petronio da Civià Castellana libri cinque Dove si tratta del Sito di Roma, dell'Aria, de' Venti, delle Stagioni, dell'Acque, de' Vini, delle Carni, de' Pesci, de' Frutti, delle Herbe, e di tutte l'altre cose pertinenti al governo de gli Huomini, e delle Donne d'ogni età, e conditione. Opera utile, e necessaria non solo a Roma, ma ancora ad ogn'altro Paese. Con dui libri appresso dell'istesso autore, del mantenere il Ventre molle senza Medicine. Tradotti dalla lingua Latina[9] *nella Volgare, dall'Eccellente Medico M. Basilio Paravicino, da Como.* In Roma, appresso Domenico Basa, MDXCII.

1596
Andrea Bacci (1524–1600)
De naturali vinorum historia. Roma, a cura di Niccolò Muzi, 1596. [Complete trans. into Italian by G. Cometti in *Annali di viticoltura ed enologia*, 7 and 8 (1875), and 9 (1876). Partial reproduction and trans. by Faccioli, *Arte della cucina*, II, 120–33.]

1602–36 (uncertain)
Giovanni del Turco
Epulario nel quale s'insegna il modo di cucinare ogni vivanda secondo l'uso della città di Firenze e di mr. Bartolommeo Scappi e di altri cuochi eccellenti. [A manuscript work, largely an adaptation of Scappi's recipes, published in *Epulario e segreti vari, trattato di cucina toscana nella Firenze seicentesca (1602–1636).* Sala Bolognese: Arnaldo Forni, 1992.]

1604
Lancelot de Casteau (1546–1616)[10]
Ouverture de cuisine par Lancelot de Casteau, Montois, en son temps Maistre Cuisinier de trois Princes de Liege. A Liege, par Leonard Streel Imprimeur juré, MDCIIII. Facsimile in *Ouverture de Cuisine par Lancelot de Casteau*, presentation Herman Liebaers, mod. Fr. trans. Léo Moulin, commentary Jacques Kother. Antwerp and Brussels: De Schutter, 1983.

1614
Giacomo Castelvetro (1546–1616)
Brieve racconto di tutte le radici, di tutte l'erbe e di tutti i frutti, che crudi o cotti in Italia si mangiono, MSS in Cambridge, Trinity College R.14.19 (14 June 1614) and R.3.44 (28 June and 28 September 1614). [Modern editions by Luigi Firpo in *Gastronomia del Rinascimento* (Turin: Unione Tipografico-Editrice, 1974), 131–76, and by Emilio Faccioli, (Mantua, 1988); trans. Gillian Riley, *The Fruit, Herbs and Vegetables of Italy* (New York and London: Viking Press and British Museum, 1989).]

---

[9] The original Latin edition dates from 1581.

[10] On the title page the author's name is further qualified as *Maistre Cuisinier de trois Princes de Liege. Premierement a Monsieur Robert de Berghe, Conte de Walhain, Evesque de Liege. Secondement a Monsieur Gerard de Groisbeeck, Cardinal & Evesque de Liege. Tiercement a Noble & puissant Prince Ernest, Duc de Baviere, Archevesque de Cologne, Electeur, & Evesque de Liege, &c.* Although in French, the work – written in 1585 – shows a marked Italian influence.

1620
Mestre Robert
Libre de doctrina pera ben servir, de tallar, y del Art de Coch, ço est de qualsevol manera de potatges y salses; compost per lo diligent mestre Robert, coch del serenissimo senyor don Ferrando rey de Napols. Barcelona, 1520. [Contemporary trans. into Spanish as *Libro de cozina compuesto por maestro Ruberto de Nola cozinero que fue del serenissimo señor rey don Hernando de Napoles*, Toledo, 1525. Modern editions of both versions are listed below.]

Other publications of early Italian recipes

Translations and modern reprints of Scappi's *Opera*

Diego Granado Maldonado. *Libro de cozina en el cual se contiene el modo de guisar de comer en qualquier tiempo assi de carne como de pescado para sanos y enfermos y convalescientes: assi de pasteles, tortas y salsas como de conservas a la usanza española, italiana y tudesca de nuestras tiempos*, Madrid: Luis Sánchez, 1599.[11]

Magirus, Antonius. *Koocboec oft familieren Keuken-boec bequaem voor alle Jouffrouwen, die hun van keucken-handel off backen van Toertkens ende Taertkens willen verstaen. Gemaect Door M. Antonius Magirus*, Loven/Leuven: Jo. Christoph. Flavius, 1612; Antwerpen, 1655; Antwerpen, 1663.[12]

Scappi, Bartolomeo. *L'arte del cusinare; libro delle ricette per convalescenti, a cura di Ercole Vittorio Ferrario* (Collana medico-storica, 3) Milan: Edizioni Stedar, 1959.

Roversi, Giancarlo, ed. *Bartolomeo Scappi, Opera dell'Arte del cucinare* (Testi antichi di gastronomia, 12) Sala Bolognese: Arnaldo Forni, 1981; repr. 2002. [The book is a reprint of the Venice, 1570 edition, with an introductory essay by Roversi.]

Late-medieval recipe collections relating to Italy[13]

Anonimo Toscano. *Libro della cocina*, ed. Emilio Faccioli in *Arte della cucina, Libri di ricette, testi sopra lo scalco, il trinciante e i vini, dal xiv al xix secolo*, 2 vols., Milan (Il Polifilo), 1966; I, 19–57.

---

[11] This work incorporates parts of Scappi's *Opera* in Catalan. See Schildermans and Sels, 'Una traduzione olandese,' 69f.

[12] Eighty per cent of the 167 recipes in this work are adaptations of recipes in Scappi. See Schildermans and Sels, 'Una traduzione olandese,' below, where it is suggested that Magirus was *nato tra il 1567 e il 1572 da una buona famiglia della borghesia del Brabante e che si sia chiamato Antoon (De) Cock o Kok* (75).

[13] For a review of Italian recipe collections of this earlier period, see Bruno Laurioux, 'I libri di cucina' in *Et coquatur ponendo*, 249–310.

Anonimo Veneziano. *Libro per cuoco*, ed. Emilio Faccioli, ibid., I, 61–105.

Tractatus de modo preparandi et condiendi omnia cibaria, ed. Marianne Mulon, 'Deux traités inédits d'art culinaire médiéval' *Bulletin Philologique et Historique (jusqu'à 1610)*, 2 vols. 1968; publ. 1971. I, 380–95.

Liber de coquina ubi diversitates ciborum docentur, ed. Marianne Mulon, ibid. I, 396–420; ed. with German trans. Robert Maier, *Liber de Coquina: Das Buch der guten Küche*. Frankfurt am Main: F.S. Friedrich), 2005.

'Buone vivande': Domenico and Giacomo Zanichelli and Salomone Morpurgo, *LVII Ricette d'un libro di cucina del buon secolo della lingua* Bologna: Nicola Zanichelli, 1890.

Anonimo Meridionale. *Libro A* and *Libro B*, ed. Ingemar Boström, in *Anonimo Meridionale, Due libri di cucina* (Acta Universitatis Stockholmiensis, Romanica Stockholmiensia, 11) Stockholm: Almqvist and Wicksell, 1985; book 'A' 5–31 and book 'B' 32–48.

London, Wellcome Institute for the History of Medicine, WMS 211. [Untitled unpublished manuscript collection of 409 Italian recipes.]

Dilicate vivande. London, British Library, MS Add. 18165. [Unpublished manuscript collection of 114 Italian recipes.]

Chiquart. *Du fait de cuisine*, ed. and trans. Terence Scully, *The* On Cookery *of Master Chiquart (1420)* (Medieval and Renaissance Texts and Studies) Tempe, Ariz.: Arizona Center for Medieval and Renaissance Studies, [at press]; earlier edn. as 'Du fait de cuisine de Maistre Chiquart (1420). (Ms. S 103 de la bibliothèque Supersaxo, à la Bibliothèque cantonale du Valais, à Sion),' *Vallesia*, 40 (1985): 101–231.

Châlons-sur-Marne, Bibliothèque municipale, MS 319. [Untitled unpublished manuscript collection of 141 Latin recipes.]

Johannes von Bockenheim. *Registrum coquine*, ed. Bruno Laurioux, 'Le 'Registre de cuisine' de Jean de Bockenheim, cuisinier du pape Martin V,' *Mélanges de l'École française de Rome. Moyen Âge–Temps modernes*, 100 (1988): 709–60.

'De apereylar be de menyar': Barcelona, Biblioteca de Cataluña, MS 2112. [Catalan recipe collection of 167 recipes, partially published in the following work.]

Libre de sent soví. (Receptari de cuina), ed. Rudolf Grewe. Barcelona: Barcino, 1979.

Mestre Robert. *Libre del coch*, ed. Veronica Leimgruber. Barcelona: Curial Edicions Catalanes, 1982; edition of the Spanish version, *Libro de guisados*, ed. Dionisio Pérez (Los Claásicos Olvidados, 9). Madrid: Companía Ibero-Americana de Publicaciones, 1929; repr. Huesca: La Val de Onsera, 1994.

The Neapolitan Recipe Collection: Cuoco Napoletano, ed. and trans. Terence Scully. Ann Arbor: University of Michigan Press, 2000.

Maestro Martino. *Libro de arte coquinaria*. In Emilio Faccioli, *Arte della cucina*, 2 vols. Milan: Il Polifilo, 1966. I, 115–204. Also publ. as *Libro di Cucina del maestro Martino de Rossi*, ed. Aldo Bertoluzza. Trento: Edizioni U.C.T., 1993. [This recipe collection is a later copy of the preceding.]

Platina (i.e., Bartolomeo Sacchi), *De honesta voluptate et valitudine*, in ten manuscripts and first printed Rome (Ulrich Han ?), c. 1470. *Platina, On Right Pleasure and Good Health*, ed. and trans., Mary Ella Milham. (Medieval and Renaissance Texts and Studies, 168; Renaissance Society of America, Renaissance Texts Series, 17.) Tempe, Ariz.: Medieval and Renaissance Texts and Studies, 1998.

Casteau, Lancelot de. *Ouverture de cuisine*, 1585; first published Liège, 1604; facs. and mod. French trans. and comm., Herman Liebaers, Léo Moulin and Jacques Kother. Antwerp and Brussels: De Schutter, 1983.

Various studies

Albala, Ken. *Eating Right in the Renaissance*. Berkeley, Los Angeles and London: University of California Press, 2002.

— *Food in Early Modern Europe (1500–1800)*. Westport, Conn., and London: Greenwood Press, 2003.

— *Cooking in Europe 1250–1650*. Westport, Conn., and London: Greenwood Press, 2006.

— *The Banquet: Dining in the Great Courts of Late Renaissance Europe*. Urbana: University of Illinois, 2007.

Aldobrandino da Siena: *Le Régime du corps de Maître Aldebrandin de Sienne. Texte français du XIIIe siècle*, ed. Louis Landouzy and Roger Pépin. Paris: Champion, 1911.

Appunti di gastronomia. Milan: Condeco Editore, from 1989. [Managed by Claudio Benporat, this journal has offered several articles that present speculations on Scappi's life, for example, 'Bartolomeo Scappi. Ipotesi per una biografia,' 1 (990) 5–15 and 5 (1991) 14–16.; 'Bartolomeo Scappi e le sue origini bolognesi,' 9 (1992) 5–8.]

Bartolomeo Scappi il Lombardo Michelangelo della cucina. Atti della convegna internazionale, Luino, 22–23 maggio 1998, Milan: Accademia Italiana della Cucina, 1999. [This volume of conference papers by Montanari, Alberini, Cavarra, Rusconi and Frigerio is published in the series *I Cuaderni dell'Accademia*, 33.]

Benporat, Claudio. *Storia della gastronomia italiana*. Milan: Mursia, 1990.

— *Cucina e alimentazione nel mondo di Cristoforo Colombo*. Bologna: Arnaldo Forni, 1991.

— 'Bartolomeo Scappi, il mistero svelato.' *Appunti di gastronomia*, 46 (2005): 79–86.

— 'Bartolomeo Scappi, ipotesi per uno bibliografia.' *Appunti di gastronomia*, 5 (1991): 14.

— *Feste e banchetti. Convivialità italiana fra tre e quattrocento* (Biblioteca dell' 'Archivum Romanicum,' 302). Florence: Olschki, 2001.

— 'Evoluzione della cucina italiana alla fine del '500.' *Appunti di gastronomia*, 33 (2000): 35–43.

Capatti, Alberto, and Massimo Montanari. *La cucina italiana. Storia di una cultura.* Rome and Bari: Laterza, 1999. Translated as *Italian Cuisine: A Cultural History*. New York: Columbia University Press, 2003.

Cavarra, Angela Adriana. 'La corte papale di Roma nei giorni di Bartolomeo Scappi,' in *Bartolomeo Scappi il Lombardo Michelangelo della cucina* [see above], 35–59.

Cochrane, Eric (ed. Julius Kirshner). *Italy 1530–1630*. London and New York: Longman, 1988.

Cogliati Arano, Luisa. *The Medieval Health Handbook Tacuinum Sanitatis*. New York: George Braziller, 1976.

Davidson, Alan. *The Oxford Companion to Food*. Oxford and New York: Oxford University Press, 1999.

Delumeau, Jean. *Vie économique et sociale de Rome dans la seconde moitié du XVIe siècle*, 2 vols. Paris: E. de Boccard, 1957–9.

— *Rome au XVIe siècle*. Paris: Hachette, 1975. [This is a condensed version of the preceding work.]

Di Schino, June, and Furio Luccichenti. *Bartolomeo Scappi cuoco nella Roma del cinquecento*. Rome: (privately published), 2004.

— *Il cuoco segreto dei papi, Bartolomeo Scappi e la confraternita dei cuochi e dei pasticcieri*. Rome: Gangemi, 2008.

Et coquatur ponendo: cultura della cucina e della tavola in Europa tra Medioevo ed Età Moderna, ed. Allen J. Grieco and Giampiero Nigro. Prato: Istituto Datini, 1996.

Faccioli, Emilio. *Arte della cucina. Libri di ricette, testi sopra lo scalco, il trinciante e i vini*, 2 vols. Milan: Edizioni Il Polifili, 1966; reed. as *Arte della cucina in Italia*. Turin: Einaudi, 1987.[14]

Ferniot, Jean. *L'Europe à table*. Paris: Editions du Mécène [1993].

Firpo, Luigi. *Gastronomia del Rinascimento*. Turin: Unione Tipografico-Editrice Torinese, 1974.

FitzGibbon, Theodora. *Food of the Western World. An Encyclopedia of Food from North America and Europe*. New York: Quadrangle/New York Times Book, 1976.

Flandrin, Jean-Louis. *L'ordre des mets*, pref. Georges Carantino. Paris: Odile Jacob, 2002.

— and Odile Redon. 'Les livres de cuisine italiens des XIVe et XVe siècles.' *Archeologia Medievale*, 8 (1981): 393–408.

---

[14] References in the present work are to the first edition, of 1966.

— and Massimo Montanari, eds. *Histoire de l'alimentation*. Paris: Fayard, 1996; trans. Albert Sonnenfeld, *Food: A Culinary History*. London and New York: Penguin Books, 2000.

Fuenmayor, Antonio de. *Vida y hechos de Pío V*. Madrid: Luis Sánchez, 1595; repr. ed. Lorenzo Riber. Madrid: Aldus and Artes Gráficas, 1953.

Grewe, Rudolf. 'The Arrival of the Tomato in Spain and Italy.' *Journal of Gastronomy*, 3 (1987): 67–82.

Gual Camarena, Miguel. *Vocabulario del comercio medieval*. Barcelona: El Albir, 1976.

Héraud, Nathalie. 'Exotisme culinaire et représentations nationales dans les cuisines européennes du XVIe et du début du XVIIe siècle: le témoignage des livres de cuisine.' *Le Désir et le Goût*. Paris: Presses Universitaires de Vincennes, 2003. 119–33.

Hollingsworth, Mary. *The Cardinal's Hat: Money, Ambition and Housekeeping in a Renaissance Court*. London: Profile Books, 2004.

Hurtubise, Pierre. 'La "table" d'un cardinal de la Renaissance. Aspects de la cuisine et de l'hospitalité à Rome au milieu du XVIe siècle.' *Mélanges de l'École française de Rome. Moyen Âge–Temps modernes*, 92 (1980): 249–82.

— 'Une vie de palais: la cour du cardinal Alexandre Farnèse vers 1563.' *Renaissance and Reformation*, 16 (1992): 37–54.

— 'De honesta voluptate et l'art de bien manger à Rome pendant la Renaissance.' *Histoire, Économie, Société*, 13 (1994): 237–47.

Hyman, Philip and Mary. 'Les associations de saveurs dans les livres de cuisine français du XVIe siècle.' *Le Désir et le Goût*, ed. Odile Redon et al. Paris: Presses Universitaires de Vincennes, 2003. 135–50.

Kelly, John Norman Davidson. *The Oxford Dictionary of Popes*. Oxford: Oxford University Press, 1986.

Krondl, Michael. *The Taste of Conquest: The Rise and Fall of the Three Great Cities of Spice*. New York: Ballantine, 2007.

Laurioux, Bruno. 'Les livres de cuisine italiens à la fin du XVe et au début du XVIe siècle, expressions d'un syncrétisme culinaire méditerranéen,' in *La Mediterrània, àrea de convergència de sistemes alimentaris (segles V–XVIII)*. Palma: Institut d'Estudis Baleàrics, 1995. 73–87.

— 'I libri di cucina italiani alla fine del medioevo: un nuovo bilancio.' *Archivio Storico Italiano*, 154 (1996): 45–54.

— 'De Jean de Bockenheim à Bartolomeo Scappi. Cuisiner pour le pape entre le XVe et le XVIe siècle,' in *Offices et papauté, XIVe–XVIIe siècle: charges, hommes, destins*, ed. Armand Jamme and Olivier Poncet. Rome: École française de Rome. Moyen Âge–Temps modernes, 107 (2005): 303–32.

— *Gastronomie, humanisme et société à Rome au milieu du XVe siècle. Autour du* De honesta voluptate *de Platina*. Florence: Sismel–Edizioni del Galluzzo, 2006.

Lemaître, Nicole. *Saint Pie V*. Paris: Fayard, 1994.

Lopez, Robert S., and Irving W. Raymond. *Medieval Trade in the Mediterranean World. Illustrative Documents*. New York: Columbia University Press, 2001.

Malacarne, Giancarlo. *Sulla mensa del principe. Alimentazione e banchetti alla corte dei Gonzaga*. Mantua: Il Bulino, 2000.

Mariaux, P.A. *A tavola con il Principe. Une table princière au temps de la Renaissance italienne*. Vevey: Alimentarium, 1990.

Marini, Paolo, Paolo Rigoli and Aldo Dall'Igna. *Cucine, cibi e vini nell'età di Andrea Palladio*. Vicenza: Neri Possa, 1981.[15]

Montanari, Massimo. 'Note sur l'histoire des pâtes en Italie.' *Médiévales*, 16–17 (1989): 61–4.

— 'La cucina Italiana fra Medioevo e Rinascimento,' in *Bartolomeo Scappi il Lombardo Michelangelo della cucina* [see above]. 13–24.

Nicoud, Marilyn. 'Les médecins à la cour de Francesco Sforza ou comment gouverner le Prince (deuxième moitié du XVᵉ siècle),' in *Le Désir et le Goût*, ed. Odile Redon, et al. Paris: Presses Universitaires de Vincennes, 2003. 201–17.

Ory, Pascal. *Le discours gastronomique français des origines à nos jours*. Paris: Gallimard, Julliard, 1998.

Partner, Peter. *Renaissance Rome 1500–1559. A Portrait of a Society*. Berkeley, Los Angeles and London: University of California Press, 1976.

Pegolotti, Francesco Balducci. *La pratica della mercatura*, ed. Allan Evans. Cambridge, Mass.: Medieval Academy, 1936.

Pérez Samper, María de la Angeles. 'La integración de los productos americanos en los sistemas alimentarios mediterráneos,' in *La Mediterrània, àrea de convergència de sistemes alimentaris (segles V–XVIII)*. Palma: Institut d' Estudis Baleàrics, 1995. 89–148.

Perry, Charles. 'Couscous and Its Cousins,' in Rodinson et al., *Medieval Arab Cookery* [see below]. 233–8.

— 'Būrān: Eleven Hundred Years in the History of a Dish,' in Rodinson et al., *Medieval Arab Cookery* [see below]. 239–50.

Ray, John. *Travels through the Low Countries, Germany, Italy and France*. London, 1738. [Several pages from this diary are printed in Lord Westbury, *Handlist of Italian Cookery Books*, Florence (Olschki), 1963, xix–xxiii.]

Redon, Odile, and Bruno Laurioux. 'La constitution d'une nouvelle catégorie culinaire? Les pâtes dans les livres de cuisine italiens de la fin du Moyen Age.' *Médiévales*, 16–17 (1989): 51–60.

Riley, Gillian. *The Oxford Companion to Italian Food*. Oxford and New York: Oxford University Press, 2007.

---

[15] The compendium of Palladio (1518–80), *I quattro libri dell' Architettura*, was published in the same year as Scappi's *Opera*, 1570.

Rodinson, Maxime, A.J. Arberry and Charles Perry. *Medieval Arab Cookery. Essays and Translations*. Totnes, Devon: Prospect Books, 2001.

Rossi, A. 'I nomi dei pesci, dei crostacei e dei molluschi nei trattati cinquecenteschi in volgare di culinaria, dietetica e medicina.' *Studi di lessicografia italiana*, 6 (1984): 67–232.

Roversi, Giancarlo. *Bartolomeo Scappi, Opera dell'Arte del cucinare*. Sala Bolognese: Arnaldo Forni, 2002.

Sabban, Françoise, and Silvano Serventi. *A tavola nel Rinascimento. Con 90 ricette della cucina italiana*. Rome: Laterza, 1996.

Schildermans, Josef, and Hilde Sels. 'Una traduzione olandese dell'*Opera* di Bartolomeo Scappi.' *Appunti di gastronomia*, 42 (2003): 67–80; in English as 'A Dutch Translation of Bartolomeo Scappi's *Opera*.' *Petits Propos Culinaires*, 74 (2003): 59–70.[16]

Serventi, Silvano, and Françoise Sabban. *La pasta. Storia e cultura di un cibo universale*. Rome-Bari: Laterza, 2000.

Spencer, Judith. *The Four Seasons of the House of Cerruti*. New York and Bicester, U.K.: Facts on File, 1984.

Tacuina sanitatis: see Cogliati Arano and Spencer.

Tinto, Alberto. *Annali tipografici dei Tramezzino*. Venice and Rome: Istituto per la Collaborazione Culturale, originally 1966 but destroyed; repr. 1968.

Toussaint-Samat, Maguelonne. *History of Food*, trans. Anthea Bell. Cambridge, Mass. and Oxford: Blackwell, 1992.

---

[16] The authors call the *Koocboec* of Magirus 'una versione molto semplificata dell'*Opera* [of Scappi]' (78). See also: Hilde Sels, Josef Schildermans and Marleen Willebrands. *Lieve schat, wat vind je lekker? Het Koocboec van Antonius Magirus (1612) en de Italiaanse keuken van de renaissance*. Leuven: Davidsfonds, 2007.

Persons Mentioned in Scappi's *Opera*

The following is an alphabetical list of all the persons whose name appears in the *Opera*. The head word is the name that is most commonly printed in the 1570 edition (e.g., Pio IV rather than Pius IV or Medici). Any titles or qualifications that Scappi (or, perhaps in the preliminary material, his printer) associates with the person are reproduced here. The location of the mention in the *Opera* is given between brackets,[1] as are any additional data that might help to identify the individual.

The sketchy biographical details are distilled from a variety of sources which include, primarily, J.N.D. Kelly, *Oxford Dictionary of Popes* (Oxford and New York: Oxford University Press, 1986; siglum: Kelly); and Charles Berton, *Dictionnaire des Cardinaux* (Paris: J.-P. Migne, 1857; siglum: Berton; Berton's data are not uniformly reliable). The *Dizionario biografico degli Italiani* (Rome: Istituto della Enciclopedia Italiana, 1960– ; siglum: *DBI*). Of minor usefulness occasionally are also the following: *Dictionnaire d'histoire et de géographie ecclésiastique* (Paris: Letouzey et Ané, 1912– ; siglum: *DHGE*); Gaetano Moroni, *Dizionario di erudizione storico-ecclesiastica* (Venice: Tipographia Emiliana, 1840–61); and Ludwig von Pastor, *History of the Popes*, 40 vols. (London: Routledge and Kegan Paul, 1936–61); an Eng. tr. of *Geschichte der Päpste seit dem Ausgang des Mittelalters*, 16 vols. (Freiberg im Breisgau: Herder, 1886–1930). Of specific value is a variety of such monographs, touching upon families and individuals, as Giovanna R. Solari, *The House of Farnese*, trans. Simona Morini and Frederic Tuten (Garden City, N.J.: Doubleday, 1968). The internet website maintained by Salvador Miranda, 'The Cardinals of the Holy Roman Church,' www.fiu.edu/mirandas/cardinals.htm, is a rich mine of information about cardinals and conclaves from 1198 to the present.

A few of the popes whom Scappi will have known are presented cursorily in the Introduction.

Armignac: Illustrissimo et Reverendissimo Armignac [Conclave, f. a1r]. Georges d'Armagnac (1501–10 July 1585). A relative, the cardinal of Amboise, made him bishop of Rodez 1529; King Francis I sent him as ambassador to Venice 1541, then to Rome; made cardinal by Paul III 19 December 1544. (Berton, column 260)

---

[1] The notation 'Prelim.' refers to the various pages of authorization, privilege and dedication that appear before the beginning of Book I proper. 'Conclave' refers to Scappi's account – placed after his Book VI and translated here in Appendix I – of the death of Pope Paul III and the ensuing conclave.

Augusta: Reverendissimo Cardinal Augusta [Conclave, f.a2v]. Otto Truchess von Waldburg (d.2 April 1573). Bishop of Augsburg (*Augusta Vindelicorum*), Bavaria. Made cardinal by Paul III 19 December 1544.

Bellaia: Illustrissimo & Reverendissimo Cardinale Bellaia, residing in Rome at Monte Cavallo [IV,f.304r; 1581 f.252v]. Jean du Bellay (1492–16 February 1560). Bishop of Paris (1532–51) and Ostia, archbishop of Bordeaux, he fulfilled several ambassadorial tasks for Francis I. Made cardinal priest 1535; became dean of the Sacred College of Cardinals. (Berton, col. 485). See also Parigi, below, and Lemaître, *Saint Pie V*, 112 and 231.

Bembo: Illustrissimo & Reverendissimo Cardinal Pietro Bembo Venetiano [a concentrated broth prepared for him in 1548 (*sic*), VI,23]. Born of a patrician Venetian family (1470–19 January 1547); Venetian senator; intimate friend of Paul III. Curial cardinal 20 December 1538 (published 10 March 1539); priest 1539; bishop of Gubbio 1541, and of Bergamo 1544.

Bologna: Cardinal. Entered Conclave 28 December 1549; afflicted with gall-stones, he left it 1 January 1550 [Conclave, f.a2v]. Philippe de la Chambre (d.Rome 24 February 1550), Savoyard Benedictine, abbot of Saint-Pierre-de-Corbie. Bishop of Frascati and Bologna; cardinal priest 1533.

Bonifatio: see Sermoneta, Bonifatio.

Borbon: Cardinal; entered Conclave 13 January 1550 [Conclave, f.a2v]. Charles II de Bourbon-Vendôme (La Ferté-sous-Jouarre in Brie, 1523–9 May 1590). Son of Charles de Bourbon, duke of Vendôme; nephew of Cardinal 'Vendosme' (below). Bishop of Nevers 1540, then Saintes; made cardinal by Paul III (on recommendation of King Charles X) 9 January 1548; archbishop of Rouen 1550. (Berton, col. 585)

Burgos: Illustrissimo et Reverendissimo Cardinal Burgos [Conclave, f.a1r]. Juan Álvarez y Alva de Toledo (d. 15 September 1557). Bishop of Burgos; cardinal priest 20 December 1538.

Campeggio: Illustrissimo & Reverendissimo Cardinal Lorenzo Campeggio Bolognese [offered dinner (for which Scappi was responsible) to Emperor Charles V in Rome April 1536: IV, f.168v [1581 f.133v], 269r, 281v]. (Milan 1474–Rome 19 July 1539). Canonist. Bishop of Feltre; cardinal 1 July 1517. Legate to Henry VIII 1518, and to German states 1530. Afflicted with gout.

Capo di Ferro: Illustrissimo et Reverendissimo Cardinal Capo di Ferro [Conclave, f.a1r]. Girolamo (Recanati) Capo-di-Ferro (or Capodiferro, Capiferi) (Rome, 1502–59). Attendant to Alessandro Farnese (who became Pope Paul III); bishop of Nice; papal legate to the king of Portugal 1541, and to France 1541, 1544, 1547; cardinal 19 December 1544. Treasurer of the Apostolic Chamber. Died during the conclave following the death of Paul IV. (Berton, col. 615)

Carlo: Cesarea Maestà di Carlo Quinto Imperatore [received dinner offered by Cardinal Campeggio and prepared by Scappi, Rome, April 1536: IV,f.320r; 1581 f.269r]. Charles V, emperor of the Holy Roman Empire and king of

Spain (1500–58). Son of Philip of Burgundy and Juana, daughter of Ferdinand and Isabella.

Carpi: Sig. Gio. Lodovico, fratello del Card. di Carpi; offered a collation to Emperor Charles V at Montecavallo, 30 June [IV,f.331r; 1581 f.279r]. Giovanni Ludovico da Carpi.

Carpi: Illustrissimo & Reverendissimo Cardinal di Carpi, Ridolfo Pio (fe[lice] me[moria], Patrone nostro); desired that Scappi take Giovanni as an apprentice; owned a property called Montecavallo [I,f.1r; IV,f.331r; 1581 f.279r; VI,0; a distilled broth made for him 30 April 1564, VI,21; Conclave, f.a1r]. Rodolfo Pio da Carpi (Carpi 5 February 1500–Rome 2 May 1564). Of the house of the princes of Carpi (Modena); brother to Giovanni Ludovico. Bishop of Faenza 1528, Girgenti, Nole; archbishop of Salerno; cardinal priest 22 December 1536; bishop of Frascati 1553. A trusted adviser to Paul III; papal legate to France 1535–7; papal ambassador to Henry VIII 1536; intermediary between Francis I and Charles V, Nice 1539; governor of Ancona, in which post he effected humane social reforms; governor of Rome in the pope's absence 1543; cardinal protector of various religious orders; dean of the College of Cardinals. He possessed one of the richest libraries in Rome. Almost elected pope in 1559 but was felt too sympathetic to Imperial positions. A reformer, a highly respected, virtuous man who garnered much popular esteem and affection. (Berton, col. 1403)[2]

Casale: Reverendo Signor Alessandro Casale, (delli favori) maestro di Camera di sua Santità [Scappi and Giovanni owed obligation to: Book I,0; urged Scappi to publish his Book VI: VI,0.] Alessandro Cásale (d. Vigevano 1582); a native of Bologna, a Roman noble. Chief chamberlain of Pius V, 1566; bishop of Vigevano (near Milan) 1577. One of three executors named by Scappi in his first will of April 1571.

Castiglione: Cardinal Castiglione; entered conclave 12 December 1549 [Conclave, f.a2v]. Odet de Coligny de Châtillon (d. 13 April 1571). Administrator of Beauvais and Toulouse; cardinal 7 November 1533.

Cialon: Reverendissimo Cardinal Cialon [Conclave, f.a2v]. Robert de Lenoncourt (d. 4 February 1561). Bishop of Châlons-sur-Marne 1535; cardinal priest 20 December 1538; bishop of Metz; archbishop of Embrun, Arles. (Berton, col. 1132)

Cibò: Reverendissimo Cardinal Cibò; left conclave 23 January 1550, returned 1 February [Conclave, f.a2v, 4v]. Innocenzo Cibò (1492–April 1550). Grandson

---

[2] In Rome Rodolfo Pio lived first in the newly renovated Palazzo di Firenze but then in 1547 moved to the Via Tomacelli. See also C. Franzoni, G. Mancini, T. Previdi and M. Rossi, eds., *Gli inventori dell'eridità del cardinale Rodolfo Pio da Carpi* (Pisa: Edizione ETS, 2002); and Christiane Hoffmann, *Kardinal Rodolfo Pio da Carpi und seine Reform der Aegidianischen Konstitutionen* (Berlin: Duncker and Humbolt, 1989). A portrait of Rodolfo Pio (c. 1537) by Sebastiano del Piombo (c. 1485–1547) hangs in the Kunsthistorisches Museum of Vienna.

of Pope Innocent VIII, nephew of Pope Leo X. Administrator of Marseille; archbishop of Messina, Torino, Genova; governor of Florence 1537; made cardinal by Leo X 1513: senior cardinal in the Sacred College. He maintained the splendour of the Medici name; he was largely responsible for the election of Julius III. (Berton, col. 678)

Coria: Illustrissimo et Reverendissimo Cardinal Coria [Conclave, f. a1r]. Francisco Mendoza de Bobadilla (d. 1 December 1566). Bishop of Coria, Spain; made cardinal by Paul III 19 December 1544.

Cornaro: Illustrissimo et Reverendissimo Cardinal Andrea Cornaro [a jelled broth made for him in 1551, VI,19; Conclave, f. a1r]. (Venice 1509–Rome 30 January 1551.) Bishop of Brescia 1532; made cardinal deacon by Paul III 19 December 1544.

Crescentio: Illustrissimo et Reverendissimo Cardinal Crescentio [Conclave, f. a1r]. Marcello Crescenzi (d. 28 May 1552). Of a noble Roman family. Administrator of Conza; bishop of Marsico; cardinal 2 June 1542; legate to Bologna; protector of the order of Cîteaux; presided over the Council of Trent. (Berton, col. 777)

Crispo: Cardinal [Conclave, f. a1r]. Tiberio Crispo (d. 6 October 1566). Administrator of Amalfi; castellan of Castel Sant' Angelo 1542–5; bishop elect of Sessa Aurunca (Campania); made cardinal by Paul III 19 December 1544.

Donati: Eccell. Sig. Federigo Donati, medico secreto di N. S. [attended Cardinal di Carpi during his long illness, urged Scappi to publish his Book VI: VI,0]. Federico Donati (Corregio 1511–after 1570). Of a Paduan family, physician to Julius III (and perhaps also, according to Scappi's comment in the preamble to Book VI, to Pius IV and Pius V) and to Cardinal di Carpi. Known as the physician who attended Michelangelo during his final illness, in Rome 15–18 February 1564.

Doria: Reverendissimo Cardinal Doria [Conclave, f. a2v]. Girolamo Doria (b. Genoa, d. Genoa 25 March 1558). Bishop of Nebbi, Jacca, Huesca; archbishop of Tarragona; cardinal 20 December 1527. (Berton, col. 842)

Farnese: Illustrissimo et Reverendissimo Cardinal Farnese; attended Paul III at his death [Conclave, f. a1r]. Ranuccio Farnese (Venice 1530–29 October 1565), grandson of Paul III. Grand penitentary; bishop of Sabina; archbishop of Ravenna and Bologna; cardinal deacon (aged 15) 16 December 1545; patriarch of Constantinople. (Berton, col. 893) See also Santo Angelo, below.

Gaddi: Illustrissimo et Reverendissimo Cardinal Gaddi [Conclave, f. a1v]. Nicolò Gaddi (Florence 1490–16 January 1552). Bishop of Fermo 1521; cardinal 3 May 1527. (*DHGE*, XIX, 598b)

Ghisa: Cardinal; entered conclave 12 December 1549 [Conclave, f. a2v, 4v]. Charles de Lorraine-Guise (1525–74). Bishop of Toul, Metz, Verdun, Thérouane, Luçon and Valence; archbishop of Reims; abbot of Saint Denis, Fécamp, Cluny and Marmontier; cardinal priest 1547. (Berton, col. 652)

Giovanni: [suo discepolo: Title page; I, rubric]. Recommended by Cardinal Carpi (d. 1564) to Scappi as a pupil; accepted despite his youth. Giovanni Valfredo de Meldula.[3] See also Rinoso, below.

Giulio III: Pontefice 7 February 1550 [*torta bianca reale, quale usava Papa Giulio III*, V,80; Conclave, f. a4v]. Giovanni Maria Ciocchi del Monte, 1487–1555. (Kelly, 262) S.a. Monte.

Grimano: Illustrissimo et Reverendissimo Cardinal Marin Grimano (in Venetia) [II,149]. Marino Grimani (Venice 1488–Orvieto 28 September 1546). Bishop of Porto, Concordia, Ceneda (in Veneto) 1508; named patriarch of Aquileia, with the title of patriarch of Constantinople 1524; cardinal priest of S. Vitale, then of S. Maria in Trastevere 1527. A learned, eloquent man, patron of writers, artists; 'Sa vie privée ne fut guère exemplaire, ce qui était du reste le cas de la plupart des prélats de son temps' (, XXII, 262a).

Hippolito da Este: Illustrissimo. Cardinal di Ferrara [Conclave, f. a1r, but not mentioned as a participant]. Ippolito d'Este (1509–2 December 1572), second son of Alfonso I, duke of Ferrara, Modena, Reggio, and Lucrezia Borgia. Ordained priest 1564; archbishop of Milan 1519, Modena 1534, Lyon 1539 and Narbonne 1550; cardinal of Ferrara 20 December 1538 (published 5 March 1539).[4]

Hora: piu Illustriss. Sig. Hora [I,0]. Unidentified; superior to Scappi in Pius V's personal household, perhaps the kitchen clerk.

Horatio: Duca Horatio; attended Pope Paul III at his death [Conclave, f. a1r]. Orazio Farnese (1531–53), brother of Cardinals Alessandro (Santo Angelo) and Ranuccio Farnese, and Duke Ottavio Farnese; grandson of Alessandro Farnese (Paul III). Duke of Camerino. Married to Diane of France (1538–1619), natural daughter of Henry II (legitimized in 1547).

Inghilterra: Illustrissimo et Reverendissimo Cardinal Inghilterra [Conclave, f. a1r]. See Polo.

Julius III: see Giulio and Monte.

Lorena: Cardinal; entered conclave 31 December 1549 [Conclave, f. a2v]. Charles de Lorraine-Guise (d. 25 December 1575). Archbishop of Reims; made cardinal by Paul III 27 July 1547.[5] (Berton, col. 1105)

---

[3] The identification of Scappi's 'apprentice' is made by Scappi himself in a draft of his first testament (1571). See Di Schino and Luccichenti, *Bartolomeo Scappi*, 23 and note 28. The authors point out that Meldola lies twelve kilometres south of Forlì and (probably significantly) was a possession of the Carpi family at that time.

[4] See the finely documented biography by Mary Hollingsworth, *The Cardinal's Hat: Money, Ambition and Housekeeping in a Renaissance Court* (London: Profile Books, 2004).

[5] It is barely possible that this *Lorena* of Scappi is, rather, Jean de Lorraine (1498–10 May 1550) who was bishop of Metz, archbishop of Narbonne, Reims and Lyon, and who was made cardinal deacon by Leo X on 28 May 1518.

Maffeo: Illustrissimo et Reverendissimo Cardinal Maffeo [Conclave, f. a1r]. Bernardino Maffei (Rome 1514–16 July 1553). Humanist, secretary to Paul III, who made him bishop of Massa Maritima, Forimpopolo, Caserte; archbishop of Chieti; cardinal 8 April 1549. (Berton, col. 1176)

Mantua: Reverendissimo Cardinal Mantua [Conclave, f. a2v]. Ercole de Gonzaga-Mantua (1505–3 March 1563). Bishop of Mantua; archbishop of Tarragona; cardinal 3 May 1527. (Berton, col. 1022)

Medici: Cosmus Medices, Magnus Dux Hetruriæ, Florentiæ, et Senarum Dux II … [Prelim., f. a iii v]. Cosimo de' Medici (1519–74). Created first grand duke of Tuscany 1569, crowned by Pius V in the Vatican 5 March 1570.

Medichino: Illustrissimo et Reverendissimo Medichino [Conclave, f. a1r]. Giovanni Angelo Medici (1499–1565), Milanese (no relation to the Florentine Medicis). Physician and jurist. Archbishop of Ragusa 1545; made cardinal by Paul III 8 April 1549. Pope Pius IV (*q.v.*, below) 1559. (Kelly, 266)

Medon: Illustrissimo et Reverendissimo Medon [Conclave, f. a1v]. Antoine Sanguin de Meudon (d. 25 November 1559). Bishop of Orléans; archbishop of Toulouse; cardinal priest 19 December 1539 (as recommended by his aunt, the duchesse d'Étampes, mistress of Francis I); grand almoner of France 1543. (Berton, col. 1502)

Mondevi: see Paldeo.

Monte: Reverendissimo Cardinal Monte [Conclave, f. a2v, a4v]. Giovanni Maria Ciocchi del Monte (Rome 10 September 1487–23 March 1555). Bishop of Pavia 1520; vice-legate to Bologna 1524; bishop of Palestrina; archbishop of Mafredonia; cardinal 23 December 1543; pope as Julius III (7 February 1550). (Kelly, 262) S.a. Giulio III.

Morone: Illustrissimo et Reverendissimo Cardinal Morone [Conclave, f. a1r]. Giovanni Girolamo Morone (Milan 1527–1 December 1580). Papal nuncio to German lands 1542; cardinal 2 June 1542; legate to Bologna; presided over opening and closing of the Council of Trent. (Berton, col. 1251)

Ottavio: Duca Ottavio; absent from Rome at death of Paul III [Conclave, f. a1r]. Ottavio Farnese (d. 1586); son of Pier Luigi, first Duke of Parma and Piacenza, brother of Orazio and Cardinals Alessandro and Ranuccio, grandson of Pope Paul III. Duke of Parma (from 1547 and from 1549), and of Castro; married to Margherita of Austria, he was a son-in-law of the Emperor Charles; see Carlo.

Pacecho: Cardinal Pacecho; entered conclave 4 December 1549 [Conclave, f. a2v]. Pedro Pacheco de Montalvan (d. 5 March 1560). Of a noble Castillian family; bishop of Ciudad Rodrigo, then of Pamplona, Jaén, Sigüenza, Albano; made cardinal priest by Paul III 16 December 1545; viceroy of Naples.

Paldeo: Reveren. Prevosto del Mondevi, il Sig. Giovan Paldeo [IV,f. 168r; 1581 f. 133r].[6]

---

[6] Michele Ghislieri (Pius V from 1566), was bishop of the diocese of Mondevi, now Mondovi, in Piemonte from 1560.

Parigi: Cardinal Parigi; entered Conclave 12 December 1549 [Conclave, f. a2v]. Jean du Bellay (1492–16 February 1560). Bishop of Paris. S.a. Bellaia, above.

Paulo III, Papa, *di casa Farnese*, died in the fifteenth year and twenty-ninth day of his reign [Conclave, f. a1r, 1v, 2r]; *Paulus III · Pont · Max* [Conclave, f. a1r]. Alessandro Farnese (1468–1549). His sister Giulia was Pope Alexander VI's mistress. Cardinal deacon 1493; bishop of Parma 1509, Ferrara; priest 1519; dean of the Sacred College 1534; pope October 1534– November 1549. (Kelly, 261)

Pio: see Carpi.

Pio IV, Pontefice massimo [prelim.; 1564 (customarily ate fried frog's legs prepared for him by Scappi), III,163; Conclave, f. a1r, called Medichino; 1564 (customarily ate barley gruel), VI,57]. Giovanni Angelo Medici (unrelated to the Medicis of Florence) (Milan 31 March 1499–9 December 1565). Archbishop of Ragusa 1545; cardinal priest of Santa Pudenziana (province of Terni) 8 April 1549; pope 25 December 1559. (Kelly, 266) S.a. Medichino, above.

Pio V: Pius Quintus pontefice massimo [Prelim., f. a ii r, a iii v, a iv r]; *la seconda Incoronatione di Pio V*, 27 January 1567 [IV,f. 168v; 1581 f. 133v], *la seconda Incoronatione di Pio Quinto Pont. Opt. Max. in giorno di Venere*, 17 January 1566 [IV,f. 186r; 1581 f. 237v]. Antonio (he chose the name Michele) Ghislieri, saint (Bosco, near Alessandria 17 January 1504–1 May 1572). Studied at Bologna, ordained 1528, lectured at Pavia for sixteen years. Inquisitor for Como and Bergamo; commissary general of the Roman Inquisition, 1551.[7] Bishop of Nepi, Sutri 1556; cardinal 15 March 1557; inquisitor general 1558; bishop of Mondovi 1560; pope 7 January 1566–1 May 1572.

Pisano: Illustrissimo et Reverendissimo Cardinal Pisano [Conclave, f. a1r]. Francesco Pisani (d. 28 June 1570). Of a famous Venetian family. Apostolic protonotary; bishop of Padova, Albano, Frascati, Porto, Ostia; archbishop of Narbonne; cardinal 1 July 1517; dean of the College of Cardinals, protonotary apostolic, crowned popes Marcellus II and Paul IV (both in 1555). (Kelly, 268; Berton, col. 1405)

Polo: Illustriss. e Reverendiss. Card. Polo d'Inghilterra [III,206; *Inghilterra* Conclave, f. a1r]. Reginald Pole (1500–19 November 1558). A relative of and secretary of state to Queen Mary I (whose reign began July 1553). Archbishop of Canterbury; apostolic protonotary; cardinal deacon 22 December 1536;

---

[7] In 1542 Pope Paul III created the Holy Office, which became the Roman Inquisition, to enforce orthodoxy of faith throughout Christendom. Its six founding cardinals included Giovanni Pietro Carafa (1476–1559, patron of Ghislieri, Pope Paul IV 1555), Rodolfo Pio (see Carpi, above), Marcello Cervino and Juan de Toledo (see Burgos, above). Nicole Lemaître presents a detailed biography of Michele Ghislieri in *Saint Pie V*, 50–66; for a political, quasi-hagiographic biography by a contemporary, see Fuenmayor, *Vida y hechos de Pío V*.

lost election during conclave of 1549–50. Julius III (1550–55) appointed him legate to England; Pius IV divested him of this legateship.[8] (Berton, col. 1413)

Queva: Illustrissimo et Reverendissimo la Queva [Conclave, f. a1r]. Bartolomé de la Cueva de Albuquerque (d. 29 June 1562). Family of the diocese of Palestrina. Made cardinal by Paul III 19 December 1544.[9]

Ridolfo: Illustrissimo et Reverendissimo Cardinal Ridolfo; left the conclave, died 31 January 1550 [Conclave, f. a1r, 2v]. Nicolò Ridolfi. Nephew of Leo X, son of the Countess Medici and Ridolfo di Firenze. Apostolic protonotary; bishop of Orvieto, Vicenza, Forli, Imola, Viterbo; archishop of Florence, Salerno; cardinal 1 July 1517. Proposed as successor to Paul III. (Berton, col. 1460)

Rinoso: Reverend. Sig. Don Francesco (di) Rinoso (Reinoso, Reynoso), Scalco (et cameriero) secreto (della santità) di N. Sig. (Pio Quinto) [Prelim., f. a iv r; I,0; V,0; VI,0; Don Francisco IV,ff. 168r, 327r; 1581 ff. 133r, 275r]. Dedicatee of Scappi's *Opera*. Francisco Reinoso (Antillo, in Palencia, Spain 1534–Córdoba 23 August 1601). Scion of a destitute noble family, he studied arts and theology at Salamanca, went to Rome at the age of twenty. In 1557 he entered into the service of Cardinal Michele Ghislieri who, nine years later, became Pius V.[10] In an accounts book of the Ghislieri family before Pius V's pontificate (January 1566), a D. Francesco Brinoso (*sic*) is inscribed as *scalco segreto* alongside a most interesting entry for a *cuoco segreto* by the name of Giovanni.[11] Reinoso was named principal chamberlain and majordomo to Pius V, then archdeacon of Sepúlveda (Segovia) and Toledo. On the death of Pius V in 1572 he returned home to Spain where, as abbot of Husillos, he lived a sumptuous existence, then experienced a radical ascetic reform; bishop of Córdoba 1596–1601.

Roan: Cardinal Roan; entered conclave 28 December 1549 [Conclave, f. a2v]. Georges d'Amboise (d. 25 August 1550). Bishop of Montauban (at age fourteen); archbishop of Rouen; made cardinal priest by Paul III 16 December 1545. (Berton, col. 243)

Sadoleto: Illustrissimo et Reverendissimo Cardinal Jacomo Sadoleto, Modonese [broth prepared for him in 1548 (*sic*), VI,28]. (Modena 1477–Rome 19 October 1547). Humanist, close friend of Pietro Bembo; secretary to Cardinal Carafa

---

[8] See Thomas F. Mayer, *Reginald Pole: Prince and Prophet* (New York: Cambridge University Press, 2000).

[9] On one ballot at the 1559 conclave, Cardinal la Queva secretly curried a vote from each cardinal individually, confessing a longing to receive only one vote. His manœuvre was discovered.

[10] Fuenmayor writes that Reinoso accompanied the Cardinal into the conclave of 1566 in which Ghislieri was elected pope (*Vida y hechos de Pío V*, 48).

[11] See Firpo, *Gastronomia del Rinascimento*, 21, note 36.

in Rome; secretary with Bembo to Leo X 1513. Bishop of Carpentras; cardinal 22 December 1536. (Berton, col. 1487)

Salviati: Reverendissimo Cardinal Salviatti [Conclave, f. a2v]. Giovanni Salviati (Florence 1490–28 October 1553). Son of Jacomo Salviati and Lucrecia de' Medici, nephew of Leo X, patron of the arts, and of Caterina de' Medici, queen of France. Bishop of Oléron, Saint-Papoul (France), Ferrara, Fermo, Porto, Volterra; archbishop of Trani; cardinal 1 July 1517; proposed to succeed Paul III but Charles V was opposed. (Berton, col. 1500)

Santo Angelo: Illustrissimo et Reverendissio Cardinal Santo Angelo, Sant' Angelo; attended Pope Paul III at his death [Conclave, f. a1v]. Alessandro Farnese (1520–2 March 1589), son of the duke of Parma and Piacenza, grandson of Paul III. Bishop of Parma and Ostia; archbishop of Avignon 1535, and Monreale, Sicily 1556; patriarch of Jerusalem. Cardinal deacon 18 December 1534 (at age fourteen), dean of the College of Cardinals (vice-chancellor of the Church); served as papal legate to Francis I and Charles V. Vice-chancellor and cardinal protector of the Company of Cooks and Pastrymen of which Scappi was a member.[12] (Berton, col. 892)

S. Croce: Illustrissimo et Reverendissimo Cardinal S. Croce, left conclave 20 December 1549 [Conclave, f. a1r, 2v]. Marcello Cervini degli Spannochi (1501–30 April 1555). Scholar and bibliophile, apostolic protonotary 1534. Bishop of Nicastro 1539, Reggio Emilia 1540, Gubbio 1544; cardinal priest of Santa Croce 19 December 1539. Pope Marcellus II 9 April 1555. (Kelly, 264)

S. Fiore: Illustrissimo et Reverendissimo Cardinal S. Fiore [Conclave, A1r]. Guido Ascanio Sforza de Santa Fiore (Rome 26 November 1518–6 October 1564). Grandson of Paul III, son of Bosio Sforza, Count of Santa Fiore e Cotignola, and Costanza Farnese, brother of Cardinal Alessandro Sforza. Bishop of Montefiascone e Corneto 1528 (resigned 1548); cardinal deacon 18 December 1534 (at age sixteen); administrator of see of Parma 1535; legate in Bologna and Romagna 1536–40; camerlengo of the Church 1537–64. (Berton, col. 1521)

Savello: Illustrissimo et Reverendissimo Cardinal Savello [Conclave, f. a1r]. Giacomo Savelli (or de Sabellis) (d. 5 December 1587). Bishop of Nicastro, Albano, Porto; archbishop of Benevento; cardinal deacon 19 December 1539; apostolic protonotary; grand inquisitor. (Berton, col. 1505)

Savello: Ostilio Savello, Barone Romano [Conclave, A3r]. The Savelli (originally Sabelli) were a dominant noble family in Rome between the thirteenth and seventeenth centuries.

Scappi: magister Bartholomeo Scappi, *peritissimus Magister Bartolomeus Scapius, qui nunc profectus est nostris intimis Coquis* (Pius V, 29 March 1570);

---

[12] Di Schino and Luccichenti, *Il cuoco segreto dei papi*, 29.

præfectus est Coquorum Sanctissimi Domini nostri Pii Quinti Pontificis maximi librum de culina, ac de Architriclini officio, necnon de cibis ac medicamentis conficiendis, et convalescentibus certo modo (Cosmo de' Medici 1570) [Prelim., f. a ii r, a iii r, v, a iv v, a v r].

Sermoneta: Illustrissimo et Reverendissimo Sermoneta [Conclave, f. a1r, 3r]. Son of Bonifatio, according to Scappi. Niccolò (or Nicola) Caetani[13] di Sermoneta (1526–1 May 1585), son of Camillo, lord of Sermoneta and his second wife, Flaminia Savelli (see the two Savello, above). Archbishop of Capua; apostolic protonotary; made cardinal deacon (at age ten) by Paul III 22 December 1536 (published 13 March 1538). (Berton, col. 608; *DBI*, 16, 197)

Sermoneta: Bonifatio Sermoneta, Barone Romano, padre[14] del Card. Sermoneta [Conclave, f. a3r]. Bonifacio Caetani (1514–1 March 1574). First-born son of Camillo Gaetani, lord of Sermoneta and his first wife, Beatrice Gaetani d'Aragona; half-brother of cardinal Niccolò Sermoneta. In 1535 he married Caterina Pio di Savoia, daughter of Alberto, count of Carpi (see Carpi, above). A military man, he became captain of the guard for Henry II of France in 1550. (*DBI*, 16, 133)

Sfondrato: Illustrissimo et Reverendissimo Sfondrato [Conclave, f. a1r]. Francesco Sfondrati (Cremona 1493–Cremona 31 July 1550). Of a patrician family. Senator of Milan; counsellor to Emperor Charles V, sent by him to pacify Siena. Bishop of Sarno, Cremona; archbishop of Amalfi; legate to Charles V; nuncio to England 1544; made cardinal priest by Paul III 19 December 1544; received some votes during the 1549–50 conclave. (Berton, col. 1517)

Tornone: Cardinal Tornone; entered conclave 12 December 1549 [Conclave, f. a2v]. François de Tournon (Tournon en Vivarais; 1489–22 April 1562). Of an important Languedoc family. Archbishop of Embrun 1517, Auch, Bourges; abbot of Saint-Germain des Prés; cardinal 9 March 1530. Chief ambassador to secure release of Francis I in Madrid; legate to Henry VIII; arranged marriage of Caterina de' Medici with future Henry II of France. (Berton, col. 1572)

Tramezino: Franciscus et Michael (Michiel) Tramezinus, bibliopolæ Veneti [Prelim., f. a ii r, a iii r, v].

Trani: Illustrissimo et Reverendissimo Cardinal Trani, *all'hora Decano* [Conclave, f. a1r, 2r]. Giovanni Domenico de Cupis (d. 10 December 1553). Jurisconsult, apostolic protonotary. Bishop of Adria, Alba, Ostia, Palestrina; archbishop of Trani; cardinal 1 July 1517; dean of the Sacred College of Cardinals. Governor of Tivoli 1538. (Berton, col. 784)

---

[13] The name Gaetano was altered about 1530.

[14] The twelve-year difference in age between this, the elder Sermoneta, and his younger brother Niccolò, above, may have led Scappi or his source into an error here.

Trento: Reverendiss. Trento [Conclave, f. a2v]. Christoforo Madruzzi (d. 5 July 1578). Prince-bishop of Trento, bishop of Brixen; made cardinal by Paul III 2 June 1542 (published 1546).

Urbino: Reverendissimo Cardinal Urbino [Conclave, f. a2v]. Giulio Feltrio della Rovera (1535–3 September 1578). Administrator of Urbino. Bishop of Vienna; archbishop of Ravenna; made cardinal deacon by Paul III 27 July 1547. (Berton, col. 1481)

Vendosme: Cardinal Vendosme; entered conclave 12 December 1549 [Conclave, f. a2v]. Louis II de Bourbon de Vendôme (2 January 1493–13 March 1557); son of François de Bourbon, count of Vendôme, and Marie de Luxembourg, countess of Saint-Paul; uncle of Cardinal 'Borbon' (above). Bishop of Laon, France 24 April 1510–23 March 1552; made cardinal priest by Leo X 1 July 1517. (Berton, col. 585)

Veruli: Illustrissimo et Reverendissimo Veruli; sick, he left conclave 4 December 1549, died at Castel Sant' Angelo 19 December 1549 [Conclave, f. a1r, 2v]. Ennio Filonardi. Bishop of Veroli and Albano; prefect of the Castel Sant' Angelo, Rome; made cardinal by Paul III 22 December 1536.

Vicatino: Illustrissimo et Reverendissimo Cardinal Vicatino [Conclave, f. a1r]. It is conceivable that this person is Nicolò Ridolfo, who was the administrator of Vicenza and Trevico (Vicantinus), but the names Ridolfo and Vicatino appear in the same list on f. A1r.

Vintha: Franciscus Vintha [Prelim., f. a iii v]. Belisario di Francesco Vinta (1542–1613). Faithful and trusted legal agent of the Medici.[15]

Viseo: Illustrissimo et Reverendissimo Cardinal Visco [*sic*, perhaps a misprint; Conclave, f. a1r]. Miguel da Silva (d. 5 June 1556). Bishop of Viseu, Portugal; made cardinal by Paul III 19 December 1539.

Zambertus: Julius Zambertus, Duc. not. [prelim]. Zamberti was a respected Venetian family name.[16]

---

[15] Evidence of the high favour this Vinta enjoyed with the Medici can be seen in a particular well-known service he later provided the family. As a condition for a wedding with Eleanora de' Medici (1567–1611), virgin daughter of Grand Duke Francesco, a test was decreed by the College of Cardinals to determine the virility and potency of Vincenzo I Gonzaga (1562–1612), prince of Mantua. Vinta, then the Medici agent in Mantua, accompanied the virgin Julia Albizzi from her orphanage in Florence to Venice where he acted as observer and judge of the matter in question. For the text (dated 7 March 1584) see the internet website of the Medici Archive Project, Document for September 2001, www.medici.org/news/dom/dom092001.html: Kelley Helmstutler di Dio, 'Rising to the Occasion: Is Vincenzo I Gonzaga Impotent? The Mantuan Succession Hangs in the Balance.'

[16] The mathematician and humanist Bartolomeo Zamberti translated Euclid's *Elements* from Greek into Latin, the work being published in Venice, 1505.

Indices

The various listings in these Indices are designed primarily to help the reader find material that may be of interest in the English translation of Scappi's text. The opportunity is taken also to let the reader see the specific culinary term or terms, in sixteenth-century Italian, that Scappi has used to designate a thing or process.

The content of the menus of Book IV, whether reproduced there or not, is for the most part not indexed. The location of significant material from Book IV that can be found in various indices – that is, from the beginning and end sections of that book – as well as from those parts of Book I to which Scappi has *not* assigned a discrete number (which is indicated by § throughout the translation and commentary) is indexed, here and elsewhere, by reference to the folio number in the original printed edition of Venice, 1570; the corresponding place in the 1581 printing is also indicated by means of a folio number in brackets – for example: IV,f.330r [277v].

The content of Scappi's account of the conclave of 1549–50 is indexed separately here as Part 7.

The Indices of subject matter in the *Opera* proper are in six parts. The distribution was determined, rather arbitrarily in principle and in implementation, by a wish to make that matter as accessible as possible, and an Index as useful as practicable. Each Index is numbered: 1. Ingredients, 2. Prepared dishes, 3. Processes, 4. Kitchen hardware, 5. Measures, and 6. Miscellaneous terms.

Clearly the division into a number of parts gives rise to various difficulties. A few terms, and the things or actions they may represent, may well belong in several groupings, depending on the context. Such, for instance, is the case of ingredients in Scappi's cookery that are themselves preparations: prosciutto is prepared from hams of (generally) pigs and in a meal can quite normally be served cold from the sideboard in slices or diced; but prosciutto is also a common ingredient in dishes prepared in the kitchen. The same sort of equivocality exists with *mostaccioli*, the Neapolitan 'cake' that is crumbled into so many of Scappi's mixtures. The rough rule of thumb governing the distribution of items into the parts of this Index has been flexible, not to say, quite elastic. A few instances, if not the whole arrangement, may occasion disagreement.

The word 'passim' occasionally takes the place of a thorough listing or counting of all occurences of things (ingredients, utensils, dishes, procedures or merely 'terms') that Scappi writes frequently. If a number follows 'passim' it is intended as only a rough approximation of the total number of occurences of a term; that number may in a very general way serve as an indication of the relative importance of the thing in Scappi's text.

The following abbreviations are used as *sigla* in these Indices:

Bacci: Andrea Bacci, *De naturali vinorum historia* (Rome: Niccolò Muzi, 1596); ed. Faccioli, II, 119–33 (*see below*).

CID: Barbara Reynolds, *Cambridge Italian Dictionary* (Cambridge: Cambridge University Press, and Milan: Signorelli, c. 1985).

Cortelazzo: Manlio Cortelazzo, *Dizionario etimologico della lingua italiana*, 5 vols. (Bologna: Zanichelli, 1979–88); 2nd ed. rev. by Manlio Cortelazzo and Michele A. Cortelazzo, 1 vol. (Bologna: Zanichelli, 1999).

Crusca: Academia della Crusca, *Vocabulario degli accademici della Crusca* (Venice: Iacopo Sarzini, 1623); 5 vols. (Venice: Francesco Pitteri, 1741); 11 vols. (Florence: Tipografia Galleiana, 1863–1910); *Vocabulario degli accademici della Crusca, con tre indici delle voci, locuzioni, e proverbi latini, e greci, posti per entro l'opera* (Florence: Licosa Reprints, 1974).

DEI: Carlo Battisti and Giovanni Allesio, *Dizionario etimologico italiano*, 5 vols. (Firenze: Barbèra, 1975).

Faccioli: Emilio Faccioli, *Arte della cucina. Libri di ricette, testi sopra lo scalco, il trinciante e i vini*, 2 vols. (Milan: Il Polifilo, 1966).

Lancerio: a manuscript survey and evaluation of early-fifteenth-century wines, published by Giuseppe Ferraro, 'I vini d'Italia giudicati da papa Paolo III (Farnese) e dal suo bottigliere Sante Lancerio,' in *La Rivista Europea*, 7 (1876), pt. II, 87–116, 339–49; reprinted by E. Vizetelly, *I vini del mondo* (Turin, 1882); ed. Faccioli, I, 315–41 (*see above*).

Riley: Gillian Riley, *The Oxford Companion to Italian Food* (Oxford and New York: Oxford University Press, 2007). [This work offers informative commentary on ingredients and dishes with a brief history of their use in Italy.]

Rossi: Adriana Rossi, 'I nomi dei pesci, dei crostacei e dei molluschi nei trattati cinquecenteschi in volgare di culinaria, dietetica e medicina,' *Studi di Lessicografia Italiana a cura dell'Accademia della Crusca*, 6 (1984): 67–232.

Tommasini: Cesare Tommasini, *Vocabolario generale di pesca con le voci corrispondenti nei varii dialetti del Regno* (Turin: Paravia, 1906). (Only vol. 1, A–C, seems ever to have been published.)

Zingarelli: Nicola Zingarelli, *Lo Zingarelli 2002. Vocabolario della lingua italiana*, 12th ed. (Bologna: Zanichelli, 2002).

Of limited use are the following:

Francesco Alunno (d. 1556), *Le ricchezze della lingua volgare* (Vinegia: Aldo, 1543).

Giuseppe Baretti, *Dizionario delle lingue italiana ed inglese*, 2 vols. (Venezia: Pezzana, 1787).

Tullio di Mauro and Marco Marcini, *Garzanti Dizionario etimologico* (Milan: Garzanti Linguistico, c. 2000).

Gaetano Moroni, *Dizionario di erudizione storico-ecclesiastica*, 103 vols. (Venice: Tipographia Emilana, 1840–61).

Nicolò Tommaseo and Bernardo Bellini, *Dizionario della lingua italiana*, 20 vols. (Milan: Rizzoli, 1983).

1. Ingredients in the Recipes

animal:

    domestic: buffalo, cattle (bull, cow, steer, calf), goat (kid), guinea pig (hog, sow, suckling pig), sheep (wether, ewe, lamb)

    game: boar, chamois, deer (roe buck, doe), dormouse, hare, hedgehog, mountain goat, porcupine, rabbit, snails, stag, turtle (tortoise)

    viscera and products: blood, brisket, caul, intestines, kidney, lungs, marrow, pluck, spleen, sweetbreads, etc. (*see also* dairy products)

    preserved meats: preserved meat, pork jowl, pork rind, prosciutto, salami, sausage, blood sausage, saveloy (yellow, Milanese), sowbelly

fowl (unspecified): small birds

    domestic: dove (squab, Terni dove), duck, goose, peacock, poultry (capon, chicken, chick, cockerel, hen, pullet, rooster), swan, turkey (cock, cockerel, hen, pullet)

    game: bittern, blackbird, coot, crane, duck (wild, Muscovy, India, teal), figeater, wild goose, grouse, heron, jay, lapwing, lark, ortolan, partridge, pheasant, quail, redbreast, sparrow, starling, swift, thrush, turtledove, woodcock, wood pigeon

    their products: eggs (yolk, white)

seafood:

    fish: amberjack, anchovy, barbel, bass, sea bass, bonito, bream, brown meagre, burbot, carp, salmon carp, chub, cod (poor cod), conger, corb, cuttlefish, dentex, dogfish, eel (lamprey, moray), flounder, frog, garfish, gilthead, goby, grayling, green wrasse, gudgeon, gurnard (tub gurnard), herring, John Dory, leer fish, mackerel (horse mackerel), meagre, monkfish, mullet (red mullet, grey mullet, freshwater mullet), octopus, perch, pike, pilchard, rayfish, rudd, salmon, sardine, saupe, scorpion fish, sea snails, sea urchin, shad (freshwater shad, allis shad), shark, smelt, smooth hound, sole, squid, sturgeon, swordfish, tench, trout, tuna, turbot

    molluscs, crustaceans, etc.: clam (razor clam, striped Venus clam, telleen clam, wedge shell clam), cockle, crab (hermit crab, hog crab), crayfish (sea crayfish), limpet, lobster (spiny lobster), mussel, oyster, sea snail, squill fish (shrimp)

    fish products: eggs (roe) and milt, caviar, tripe

dairy products:

    butter, cheese (fresh and dry, new and old, salted and unsalted, bazzotto, curds, of ewe's milk, Ligurian, Maiorichino, March cheese, *caciocavallo*, mozzarella, Parmesan, provatura, Florentine raviggiolo, ricotta, Riviera, Romagna, Roman, Sardinian), cream, milk (of cow, ewe, goat), whey

grains and their products:

  barley, bran, bread, einkorn, flour, millet, foxtail millet, rice, semolina, spelt, starch, wafers, wheat

vegetables and herbs (unspecified): herbs

  above ground: alexanders, artichoke, asparagus, beans (broad, fava haricot), borage, broccoli, Brussels sprouts, bryony, bugloss, burnet, cabbage, capers, cardoon, cauliflower, chard, chickpea, chicory, cucumber, dill, eggplant, elderflower, endive, fennel, hops, juniper, kohlrabi, leek, lentils, lettuce, mallow, marjoram, mint, mugwort, myrtle, nettle, oregano, parsley, peas, pennyroyal, purslane, rape, rocket, rosemary, roses, sage, sorrel, spinach, squash (common, hairy, Genoese, Savona, Turkish), thistle, turnip greens, vetch, vine tendrils and leaves, wild thyme, yellow bedstraw

  below ground: carrots, elecampane, garlic, onion, parsnip, spignel, turnip

spices, etc., unspecified: spices (common, mild, Venetian)

  cinnamon, cloves, coriander, cumin, fennel seed, ginger, grains of paradise, mastic, musk, nutmeg, pepper, saffron

  colorants: orchil

  sweeteners: honey, sugar

  fungi: agaric, brittlegills, morel, parasol, *rossignoli*, truffle

fruit, nuts, seeds:

  acorns, almonds, anise, apples, apricots, azaroles, cherries (morello, Roman, visciola), chestnuts, citrons, dates, figs, gooseberries, grapes (Cesena, muscat, Slavonic, verjuice), hazelnuts, jujubes, limes, medlars, melons, mulberries, oranges, peaches (clingstone, freestone), pears (*acciole*, bergamot, caravella, Florentine, muscatel, moscarole, papal, riccardo, rough), pinenuts, pistachios, plums and prunes, pomegranates, poppy, pumpkin, quince, raisins (*passarina*, Slavonic) and currants (Corinthian, muscatel), rhubarb, sorb apples, strawberries, walnuts

liquids and fats:

  grape products: must, verjuice, vinegar (rose, white), wine (claret, French, Greek, Somma, Ischia, Lagrima, Magnaguerra, malmsey, muscatel, Roman, trebbiano)

  other liquids: bouillon, broth, juice (grape, lemon, lime, orange, pomegranate, quince, spinach), milk (almond, cow's, ewe's, goat's, melon-seed, pinenut), must (and must syrup), oil (linseed, olive), rendered lard, rosewater, spirits of fennel, water (and washwater)

This listing of the foodstuffs and condiments that Scappi calls for in his recipes is in three parts: the first – Plants, minerals, liquids – contains whatever is not flesh, or the product of a creature; the second – Animals, fowl – lists those creatures and their products; the third – Water creatures – is devoted to the flesh and products of fish, crustaceans and amphibians.

Plants, minerals, liquids

acorns II,131; V,120 *ghiande*

alexanders, black lovage, horse-parsley
Smyrnium olusatrum VI,101 *macerone* (Riley 11)

almonds, *Prunus amygdalus* I,23; passim 140 *mandole*; the quality of ~I,23; (sweet, mild, as distinct from bitter) Milanese ~ , *Prunus amygdalis dulcis* I,3; passim 60 *mandole ambrosine*; small (new) ~ IV,f.327v [275v] *mandorlette*; ~ oil I,3; II,153, 241; III,92, 148, 265, 266; V,178, 215; VI,69; passim *oglio, olio di mandole*; ~ milk I,2; IV,f.328v [276v] *latte di mandole, d'amandole; see also* milk, cheese in Animals and fowl, below

anise, aniseed, *Pimpinella anisum* VI,142; passim 8 *anici*; candied ~ II,140 *anici confetti*

apple I,20; IV, f.328r [275v] *mela, mele,* II,212, 281 *pomo*; red ~ III,259; IV, f.327v [275r]; V,61, 116; VI,194; passim 35 *mela appia, mele appie, mel'appie (see* the note in III,259); pink ~ IV,f.327v [275r]; V,61 *mele rose*; russet ~ IV,f.327v [275r]; V,61 *mele ruggini*; Spanish ~ II,245 *mele di Spagna; see also* sorb ~

apricots III,260; V,63, 112; IV,f.327v [275v]; VI,127, 131, 136 *arbicoccole*

artichoke, *Cynara scolymus* II,115, 120, 213; III,242, 263; IV,ff.134v, 327v [275v]; V,passim *carcioffolo, carciof-fano, carciofani*; ~ heart II,213; passim 13 *pedono, pedon, pedoni*

asparagus II,217; VI,[10], 93, 98, 104 *sparago, sparagi, sparigi*; cultivated ~ V,103 *sparagi domestici*; wild ~ II,217; V,103, 222 *sparagi salvatici*; wild or cultivated ~ III,247; V,222; VI,103 *sparagi salvatici & domestici*; tips (of ~) III,247 *mazzocchi; see also* mallow

azaroles, *Cratægus azarolus* III,260; IV,f.328r [275v] *lazzarole* (Riley 32)

barley II,185; III,222; V,47; VI,5, 7, 8, 56–9, 83 *orzo*; cracked ~ VI,57 *orzo rotto*; bran (of ~) VI,8 *risca*; hull, scale (of ~) VI,8, 57 *scaglia*

bean: broad ~ , fava ~ II,63; passim 22 *fava, fave*; broad ~ in their pod V,224 *fava di scorza*; split broad ~ V,225 *fava infranta*; haricot ~ II,152, 178, 180, 191, 201; III,253 *faggiolo, fagioli, faggiuoli; see also* legumes

biscuit: *see* Index 2, below

borage III,245, 248; VI,87–9, 92; passim 14 *borragine*; ribs (of ~) VI,87 *coste*; stems, stalks (of ~) VI,87 *cosie*; little stems, stalks (of ~) III,248 *caspetti; see also* stalk

bran I,15, 39; III,207, 216; V,1 *semola, semmola*

bread II,17; passim 270 *pane, pan*; white ~ II,176; passim 16 *pan bianco*; toast II,63; passim 26 *pane brustolito*; crumb(s), breadcrumb(s) II,116; passim 57 *mollica di pane*; a crustless loaf of ~ , breadcrumb III,243; V,235 *una mollica di pane; see also* biscuits in Index 2, below

brittlegills: *see* mushroom

III,246 *caspo della* ~; ~ tips, shoots
II,216; III,246, 248; VI,93 *cime, maz-
zocchi della* ~; ~ roots II,216; III,246;
VI,96 *radiche di* ~; *see also* endive

cinnamon I,26; II,42; *passim* 660 *canella,
cannella, canela*; candied ~ sticks
II,140 *cinamometti confetti*

citron (peel, candied) IV,f.327v [275r];
VI,124 *cedro, cedri (condito)*; *see also*
lime

clove I,26; VI,115; *passim* 143 *garo-
fano, garofani,* II,7; *passim* 94 *garofali,
garofoli*; whole ~ II,29, 38; *passim* 32
chiodo, chiodi di garafani

coriander II,6–8, 11, 13, 19, 44, 45, 61,
91, 100, 126, 130, 146; III,10, 36, 118,
V,188; VI,142 *pitartamo*; ground ~
II,99 *pitartamo pesto*; ~ flour V,237
fior di coriandole (cf. *fior di finocchio*)

crumb: *see* bread

cucumber II,218 *citriolo*

cumin II,193 *comino*

currant: red currant II,265, 266; VI,190
rebis; berry (of red ~) VI,190 *grano,
grani*; *see also* grape

date I,22; II,160; IV,f.327r [275r]; V,75
dattero, dattoli

dill VI,89 *aneto, aneti, herba aneta*

egg: *see* Animals and fowl, below

eggplant, aubergine, *Solanum melongena,
Solanum insanum* III,226, 229–33;
V,109 *molignana, molignane,* II,224
melanzane; also called *pomi sdegnosi*
(Riley 169)

einkorn (wheat), *Triticum monococcum*
II,185; V,47, 88; VI,57 *formentone,*
V,47 *formento grosso*; V,88 *formentone
grosso* (*Zingarelli* 'frumento grosso:
frumentone'; 'frumentone: (region.)
mais'; *DEI* 'formentone: grano sara-
ceno,' *Fagopyrum esculentum,* buckwheat); *see also* wheat

elderflower III,278, 279; V,77, 86, 128,
137, 139, 143, 217, 129, 158, 159 *fior,
fiori di sambuco, sambugo* (Riley 170)

elecampane (root), *Inula helenium* II,178
(radica di) enula

endive, escarole, Batavian endive, *Ci-
chorium endivia* (known as chicory
in U.S.; curled leaves, green) II,202;
III,245; V,102; VI,91 *endivia, indivia;*
V,102 *indivia bianca*; *see also* chicory

fava bean: *see* bean

fennel, *Fœniculum vulgare* I,5; II,6 *finocchio* (Riley 189); wild ~ III,243 *finocchi selvaggi*; sweet ~ , *Foeniculum
vulgare var. dulce* II,35; VI,218 *finnocchio dolce*; ~ sprout, shoot II,207, 209;
III,243 *germuglio, germugli, germoglio
di finocchio, di finocchi selvaggi*; separated ~ seeds II,46; V,37 *finocchio
sgranato*; I,10; II,25; III,46, 133 *grani
di finocchio*; sweet ~ seeds III,133
grani di finnocchio dolce; ~ panicle;
cluster of sweet ~ seeds II,137; V,36
pannocchie di finocchio dolce; cluster
of dry ~ seeds II,140, 198, 211 *pannocchie di finocchio secco*; ~ flour
(seeds ground up, or the flower[s]
containing the seeds, which may be
ground) I,39 (*see* the note there); II,7;
passim 148 *fior, fiori di finocchio*;
dried ~ flour II,66 *fior di finocchio
secco*; fresh or dried ~ flour II,229;
VI,173, 175 *fior di finocchio verde o
secco* (cf. II,7 and V,237 *fior di pitartamo, di coriandole*); fronds, feathery
tips (of wild ~) III,243 *barbe*

figs: fresh figs IV,f.327r [275v] *fichi fres-
chi*; dried ~ I,25; II,160; III,223, 257;
IV,f.327r [275r]; V,121, 201, 215, 219;
VI,5, 133 *fichi secchi*

flour (including the quality of every sort
of ~) I,27 *farina (di frumento)*; fine ~
II,18; V,1; *passim* 197 *fior di farina*;
coarse ~ V,1, *passim farina grossa,
farina di grano setacciata per il setaccio chiaro*; loose, excess ~ II,171–3

zinne; I,36; II,17, 23 *poppa, poppe*; teats II,17 *capitelli*; beef fat (salted) *ragnonatica*: its quality, to make and preserve it I,5; calf I,44; passim 270 *vitella, vitelle, vitello, vitelli,* veal V,7; passim *carne di vitella*; suckling calf, milk-fed veal II,7, 13, 23, 37 *vitella mongana,* II,38 *vitella mongana, cioè di latte,* II,24, 25 *vitella di latte,* VI,50 *vitella lattante*; weaned, newly weaned (calf) II,1, 30; III,38, 204 *seccaticcia, secaticcie*; free-ranging, grazing (calf) II,7, 13 *camporeccia, campareccia, see* II,23 for distinction between *mongane* and *campareccie*; calf's head VI,41, 54 *testicciuola, testicciuole,* nape of a calf's neck V,7, 22 *gnucca, gnocca,* chuck II,26 *coppa* (*Zingarelli* 'taglio di carne bovina, dietro il collo'), knuckles (of veal) VI,26, 202 *giunture,* shin (cut of veal) VI,24 *stinchi; see also* brisket, intestines, kidney, leg, loin, lungs, marrow, pluck, spleen, sweetbreads, tenderloin

caul, peritoneal membrane, mesentery, omentum (of kid, pig, wether) I,40; II,17; passim 52 *rete*

chamois (female) II,76 *camozza*

cheek, jowl (of boar) II,92, (of bull) V,3 *guancia*

cheese I,7, 8; passim 300 *cascio*; the quality of all ~ and to preserve them I,8; fresh ~ , made that day V,96–8; VI,68 *struccoli,* new and old ~ II,43 *cascio nuovo et vecchio*; fresh and salted ~ I,8 *casci freschi et salati*; fresh ~ II,116; V,97 *cascio fresco*; day-old, unsalted, pressed, slightly sour-tasting ~ V,97 *(struccoli overo) agretti*; old ~ II,28, 116 *cascio vecchio*; junket, curd, curdled (almond) milk V,85; VI,20 *giuncata*; a fat (creamy) ~ II,159; passim *cascio grasso*; moderately salted ~ II,77, 116, 159, 178, 225;

V,108 *casio (fresco, grasso) non troppo salato*; a small soft ~ VI,36, 38, 172, 174 *casciotto* (Riley 85); a plump, moderately soft ~ V,47, 141, 150 *(cascio) bazzotto (grasso)*; dry ~ II,116 *cascio secco*; *caciocavallo* I,8; IV,f.327v [275r] *cascio cavallo (fresco et secco)* (Riley 84); ewe's-milk ~ V,71 *cascio pecorino* (Riley 384); ewe's-milk ricotta II,168; V,77 *ricotta di pecora,* V,72, 79, 83, 92, 144; VI,121 *ricotta pecorino*; ewe's-milk curd V,73, 75 *fiorita di pecora,* V,74 *fiorita pecorina*; (ewe's-milk) curd ricotta IV,f.327v [275r] *ricotte fiorite*; varieties of clotted ~ V,85 *lattaroli (cioè giuncata)*; March ~ I,8; IV,f.327v [275r] *cascio marzolino, casci marzolini* (Riley 313); *see* the listing of varieties in I,8; IV,f.327v [275r]: *casci marzolini, raviggioli Fiorentini, Romanesco, Riviera, Maiorichino*; mozzarella (a milky buffalo cheese) IV,f.327v [275r] (Riley, *mozzarella di bufala,* 336); V,74 *mozzarelle (fresche)*; Parmesan II,22, 24; V,87; passim 45 *cascio Parmigiano* (Riley 361), *see also* Ligurian; *provaggiole*(?) V,98 *provaggiole*; provatura, a buffalo ~ II,22; V,165; passim 60 *provatura* (Riley 422); March provatura I,8; IV,f.327v [275r] *provatura, provature marzoline*; Florentine *raveggioli,* a small, soft, pressed, fresh ~ I,8; IV,f.327v [275r]; V,62 *casci raviggioli Fiorentini* (*Zingarelli* 'raveggiolo: formaggio tenero di latte di pecora o capra, in piccole forme schiacciate, da mangiare fresco'); ricotta ~ VI,71, 121, 178 *ricotta, recotta* (Riley 442); wicker ricotta moulds V,146 *forme delle ricotte fatte di vimini*; Ligurian ~ I,8; IV,f.327v [275r]; V,48, 92 *cascio di Riviera*; Ligurian Parmesan V,111 *cascio Parmigiano di Riviera*; Romagna

Water creatures and their products

2. Preparations

Few of Scappi's recipes have what we might call proper names, such as '*capiro-tata.*' Most either embody a common, generic name, such as 'sops of roasted almonds' or 'quince tourte,' or else simply the name of the foodstuff with perhaps some indication of the principal way in which it is prepared, such as 'To roast calf sweetbreads on a spit and on a grill.' The following Index includes the rubrics that Scappi wrote to all of the recipes and descriptions in his *Opera*, preceded by a succinct translation of each of those rubrics. The recipes are listed alphabetically (in English), primarily by their main ingredient, and secondarily by a limited number of common genres of preparation.

In a number of instances a recipe is listed in several places, particularly where Scappi's rubric mentions one or more generic dishes that can be prepared by means of that recipe. The recipe will appear under each of the relevant generic groupings, but Scappi's original (Italian) rubric is reproduced in only the place where the main ingredient falls according to its English name.

The reader should bear in mind that a good proportion of Scappi's recipes go beyond what the rubric indicates. To his recipes he frequently appends additional foodstuffs that can be handled by a similar process, or additional, variant preparations for which the principal ingredient is also suitable.

The menus of Book IV, and the dishes contained in them, are not specifically catalogued here.

For a general listing of all of the foodstuffs, major and minor, used in Scappi's kitchen, the reader should look in the preceding section, Index 1.

sudetti animali; ~ feet II,16 *Per cucinar li piedi di bove, o di vaccina in diversi modi*; ~ liver II,19 *Per cucinare il fegato di bove o di vaccina in diversi modi*; ~ loin, roasted another way II,9 *Per arrostire il sopradetto lombo ad un'altro modo*; ~ loin, roasted or stewed another way II,10 *Per arrostire, e stufare il lombo della vaccina, o del bove in altro modo*; ~ loin, spit-roasted or stewed II,8 *Per arrostire nello spedo, e stufare il lombo del bove, o di vaccina*; ~ loin, stewed in an oven or under a cooking bell II,11 *Per stufare in forno over sottestare il lombo del bove, o della vaccina*; ~ ribs, spit-roasted II,6 *Per arrostire nello spedo la schiena di bove o di vaccina*; ~ spleen II,21 *Per cucinar la milza di bove, o di vaccina in piu modi*; ~ tripe II,22 *Per cucinar le trippe di bove o di vaccina in diversi modi*; ~ , breast, boiled II,3 *Per alessare ogni agio, cioè parte delli sopradetti animali, cominciando dal petto*; ~ , brisket II,5 *Per cucinar la punta del petto, cioè il callo del bove, over vaccina in diversi modi*; ~ , lean, II,15 *Per cucinar la carne magra di vacca, o di bove in diversi modi*; ~ loin, stewed in the German fashion II,12 *Per stufare il lombo di bove alla Tedesca*; ~ loin, in a pasty V,4 *Per far pasticcio di Lombolo di Bove*; ~ upper hind leg in a pie V,5 *Per fare pasticcio di polpa di coscia di Bove*; ~ head II,1 *testa del bove in diversi modi*; ~ tongue, *en croûte* V,2 *Per fare la lingua di Bove in cassa*; ~ tongue, in a pastry wrap V,1 *Per far pasticcio di lingua di bove in sfoglio*; ~ or cow's tongue II,2 *Per cuocere la lingua del bove, & della vaccina in diversi modi*; ~ cheeks, eyes and snouts, in a pie V,3 *Per fare pasticcio di guancie, occhi, & grugni di Bove*; bull's

testicles, or those of other quadrupeds, in a pie V,35 *Per fare pasticcio di testicoli di Toro, & d'altri quadrupedi*; cow's lungs, blood, kidney and liver in a fricassee II,20 *Per far fricassea del polmone, del sangue, del rognone, & del fegato della vaccina*; ~ udder II,17 *Per cucinar la Zinna della vaccina in piu modi*; ~ udder, in a pasty V,6 *Per far pasticcio di zinna di Vaccina*; ~ udder, sautéed and in various fricassees II,18 *Per soffriggere, & far diverse fricassee di Zinna di Vaccina*; cow: *see also* goat's milk

berette: see II,175

berlingozzi VI,138 *Per fare Berlingozzi*; ~ , Sienese V,147 *Per fare Berlingozzi alla Senese*

birds, small, in little pies VI,112 *Per far pasticetti d'uccelletti*

biscuits: bread ~ V,237 *pan biscottato*; dainty morsels made of ~ V,237 *Per fare morselletti di biscotti*; *see also* marzipan ~ VI,119 *biscotelli di marzapane*; Pisan and Roman ~ IV,f.327r [275r] *biscotti Pisani et Romaneschi*

black pudding with chicken liver VI,45 *Per fare migliaccio di fegato di Pollo*; black pudding: *see also* II,110, 187; V,67, 68; and a small variety, *migliaccetti*, II,151

blood sausage from a domestic pig's blood II,110 *Per far sanguinacci di sangue di porco domestico*; *see also* V,67

boar (wild) II,91 *Per cuocere ogni sorte di carne porcina selvaggia*; ~ head, in wine, water, vinegar and spices II,92 *Per cuocere la testa del porco cignale con vino, acqua, aceto, e spetierie*; ~ leg (of a young, wild boar), or that of other swine, in a pastry wrap V,30 *Per fare pasticcio di zigotto di Rufalotto in sfoglio, & d'altri Porci*; ~ piglet

spedo & in altri modi il polletto cioè il pollastro piccolino; capons, hens and pullets, boiled in salted water, wrapped in a caul so they stay white II,118 *Per cuocere li sopradetti volatili, capponi, galline, & pollanche in un'altro modo con acqua & sale involte in rete, acciò rimangano bianchi*; capon, boiled and dressed variously II,121 *Per alessare ogni sorte di capponi, e servirli con diverse compositioni sopra*; ~ (boneless), boiled II,122 *Per alessare il cappone senz'osso*; ~ , boiled and done up II,123 *Per alessare & accommodare il cappone sopramentato*; ~ and hens (domestic), boiled II,117 *Per alessare ogni sorte di capponi & galline nostrali*; ~ , stewed II,120 *Per stufare ogni sorte di capponi in un'altro modo*; ~ and hens, stewed II,119 *Per stufare ogni sorte di capponi & galline nostrali*; ~ , parboiled and spit-roasted II,125 *Per arrostir nello spedo il cappone, che prima sia stato mezo alessato*; ~ , sautéed II,126 *Per soffriggere il cappone in diversi modi*; ~ , spit-roasted II,124 *Per arrostire il cappone nello spedo in diversi modi*; ~ , in a concentrate VI,11 *Per fare brodo consumato con Cappone*, ~ , in a thick soup VI,36 *Per fare minestra di polpe di Capponi lessate*; hens and capons, in a different, quicker concentrate VI,12 *Per fare brodo consumato con Galline, & Capponi in altro modo, & con brevità*; capon, in a tasty concentrate VI,13 *Per far brodo consumato di Cappone saporito*; ~ , in a concentrate VI,23 *Per fare un consumato di polpe di cappone*; ~ breast, in a tourte V,72 *Per fare torta di petto di Cappone*; ~ breast, in a thick soup VI,37 *Per far minestra di polpe di petto di Cappone in un altro modo*;

~ breast, in little balls, braised VI,42 *Per far pallotte sottostate di petto di cappone grosse quanto una tommacella*; ~ broth, impromptu VI,15 *Per fare all'improvista un brodo di Cappone*; ~ paste VI,30 *Per far pisto di polpe di Cappone*; ~ paste, spit-roasted VI,31 *Per fare pisto di Cappone rostito nello spedo*; cockerels, deboned, stuffed VI,55 *Per accommodate Pollastri ripieni senz'ossa*; cockerels, roasted VI,51 *Per far diversi volatili arrosti, & prima per rostir pollastri*; cockerels, in a concentrate VI,22 *Per fare un consumato di pollastri*; cockerels (young), stewed VI,39 *Per stufare un Pollastrino*; *see also* doves, liver

chickpeas (brown), in a thick soup VI,110 *Per far minestra di ceci rossi*; ~ (brown), in a thick soup III,250 *Per far minestra di Ceci rossi*; ~ (split), in a thick soup III,251 *Per far minestra di Ceci infranti*; ~ (split), in a thick soup with meat broth II,192 *Per far minestra di ceci infranti con brodo di carne, & altre materie*; ~ (split), in a tourte V,225 *Per fare torta di Ceci infranti*; ~ (split), in a thick soup VI,111 *Per far minestra di ceci franti*

chicory, in a thick soup III,246 *Per far minestra di Cicorea*; ~ , in a thick soup with meat broth II,216 *Per far minestra di cicorea con brodo di carne*; ~ , in a thick soup VI,93 *Per far minestra di Cicorea*; ~ , in a thick soup, differently VI,94 *Per fare un'altra minestra di Cicorea*; ~ , in a thick soup, differently VI,95 *Per far minestra di Cicorea in un'altro modo*; ~ root, in a thick soup VI,96 *Per far minestra di radiche di Cicorea*; ~ potion VI,9 *Per cuocere acqua con Cicoria* chub (prepared as a grey mullet) III,127 *Della statura e stagione del pesce Cavedine*

ciambelle, filled V,150 *Per fare ciambelle ripiene*; ~ (large) V,148 *Per fare Ciambelloni con ova, & latte*; ~ (small), with eggs VI,140 *Per fare ciambellette con uova*; ~: filling for small ~and flans V,152 *Per fare una compositione della quale se ne potrà fare ciambellette, & fiadoncelli*; *ciambelle, ciambellette, ciambellotta, ciambelloni: see also zuccarini*; III,88, 92, 93, 157; IV,f.327r [275r]; V,135, 147, 151, 236; VI,138

cianciarelle: see thick soups

cinnamon tourte, and others V,218 *Per fare torta cannellata, & d'altra sorte*; cinnamon potion VI,4 *Per cuocere acqua con cannella*

cipollata III,224 *Per far cipollata*

civiero, used as in II,248 II,249 *Per far civiero, ilquale potrà servire come il sopradetto*

clams (razor) III,192 *Per cuocere Cappe Lunghe in piu modi*; ~ and cockles III,190

cockerels: *see* chickens, doves

cockles and clams, in a dainty pottage VI,164 *Per fare un pottaggetto di gongole, e telline*; cockles and telleen clams *en croûte* to serve hot V,185 *Per fare pasticci di Gongole, & Telline in cassa per servire caldi*

cod (fresh) III,111 *Per cuocere Merluccie fresche in diversi modi*; ~ (dried) III,112 *Per cuocere Merluccie secche in piu modi*; ~ and other dried fish *en croûte* V,196 *Per fare pasticci di Merluccia, & altri pesci secchi in cassa*; *see also* poor cod

compote: compote of fennel and other fruit IV,f.327r [275r] *finocchio in composta, et d'altre frutte composte*

confections: sugar ~ VI,212 *A fare conditi in zuccaro di diverse sorti*; IV,f.327r [275r] *confettioni bianche, d'olive, et capparini di piu sorte*; *see also robbe condite, frutti conditi* IV,f.327r [275r]; V,121; VI,212; and candied in Index 1

conger: *see* eel

copper equipment, tinned on the inside I,44 *Masseritie di rame stagnate dentro coppete: see* goblets

corb (pieces), 'starched' III,30 *Per cuocere pezzi d'Ombrina in salda*; ~ *en croûte*, to serve hot V,163 *Per fare pasticci d'Ombrina in cassa per servili caldi*; ~ , in a Venetian pottage III,31 *Per far pottaggio di pezzi d'Ombrina alla Vinetiana*; ~ , in big pastry wraps, to serve cold V,162 *Per fare pasticci grossi d'Ombrina in sfoglio per conservare*; ~ head III,29 *Per cuocere la testa dell'Ombrina*; coucous, *succussu: see* wheat

court-bouillon: *see* III,64 *sapor bianco*, III,64 *cappone in bianco*, III,147 *luccio in bianco*

cow: *see* beef

crabs (tender), *en croûte* V,182 *Per fare pasticci di Granchi teneri in cassa*; ~ (tender), and crayfish, in a *crostata* V,206 *Per fare crostata di Granchi teneri, cioè mutati, & Gambari mutati*; ~ (tender), VI,179 *Per accommodare Granchi teneri in piu modi*; ~ (hermit), braised III,181 *Per sottestar Granchiporri*; ~ (hermit), in pies V,183 [erroneously: *Per fare pasticci di Gongole, & Telline in cassa per servire caldi*]

crane, spit-roasted and otherwise II,142 *Per arrostir nello spedo & cuocere in piu modi le grue*; cranes: *see also* gizzards

crayfish (freshwater), III,177 *Per cuocere Gambari d'acqua dolce in piu modi*; ~ (large), in a *crostata* V,205 *Per fare crostata di Gambari grossi, maritimi,*

& *d'acqua dolce*; ~ tails and claws, in
a pottage VI,177 *Per far pottaggio di
code, & zanche de Gambari*; ~: *see
also* crabs

cream tops VI,145 *Per fare capi di latte*;
~ , in a royal tourte V,78 *Per fare
torta di capi di latte, et altre materie,
Reale*; ~ , in a tourte VI,119 *Per far
torta di capi di latte*

croquettes: ~ and fingers from the lean
meat of a suckling calf's leg II,43
*Per far polpette, & polpettoni della
carne magra della sopradetta coscia di Vitella mongana*; ~ of stewed
veal VI,47 *Per far polpette di carne
di Vitella stufate*; *see also* fingers, and
II,14, 15, 44, 45, 71, 84, 102, 141;
III,15, 16, 37; VI,21, 53

crostate (*crostate, coppi, pan ghiotto*
and *sfogliate*; *see* the note in Recipe
II,229): ~ of anchovies (salted) V,211;
apples, in a ~ or pie V,61; artichoke-
or cardoon-hearts, in a ~ or pie V,59;
calf's brains and sweetbreads in a ~
(gourmand bread) II,231; calf's kidney, spit-roasted in a ~ (gourmand
bread) II,229 *Per far crostate, cioè
pan ghiotto con rognon di vitella arrostito nello spedo*; calf's kidney and
loin, spit-roasted, in a ~ V,52; ~ of
calf's tongue, etc. V,53; calf (suckling) sweetbreads in a ~ V,50; caviar
(cooked or raw) in a ~ III,265; ~ of
creamy cheese ('*butirata*') II,233;
cherries (visciola or morello), strawberries, gooseberries or fresh verjuice
grapes in a ~ V,64; cow's udder in a
~ ('*coppi*' and '*sfogliati*') V,49 *Per
fare diverse sorte di crostate, da Napoletani dette Coppi, & da Lombardi
Sfogliati principiando alla zinna di
vaccina*; crabs (tender), and crayfish in
a ~ V,206; ~ of large crayfish V,205;
doves' cruppers and flesh in a ~ V,54;

fig-eaters, ortolans and swifts in a ~
V,55; fresh-pea, in a ~ or pie V,60;
frogs' liver and flesh in a ~ V,210;
goat kid's sweetbreads, eyes, ears and
scrotum-and-testicles in a ~ V,51; ~ of
prosciutto V,56; ~ of large lampreys
V,202; mullet caviar, sturgeon back,
smoked herring back and caviar in a ~
V,213; ~ of common field mushrooms
V,57; ~ of mushrooms, in Lent in the
spring V,214; oyster ~ V,207; peach,
apricot or plum V,63; peas (fresh), in
a ~ or pie V,60; ~ of poor cod V,204;
pork jowl (salted) or prosciutto in a ~
(gourmand bread) II,230; prunes and
dried visciola cherries in a ~ V,215;
quince ~ V,62; ~ of fresh sardines
V,203; snails in a ~ V,208; ~ of strawberries, without cheese VI,129; ~ of
sturgeon liver and milt V,198; ~ of
sturgeon liver and milt, in Lent V,199;
truffles, etc., in a ~ and pies V,58; tuna
belly (salted), or other salted fish in
a ~ V,212; turnip ~ V,65; ~ of turtle
viscera V,209

crostoli, in Lent V,232 *Per fare grostoli
in diversi modi per giorno Quadragesimale*; *see also* V,230

crowns, imperial and royal, *corone Impe-
riali e Reali*: *see* V,45

cumin dish, Roman-style II,193 *Per fare
una cominata alla Romanesca*

currants: currant sops VI,137 *Per fare
zuppa d'uva passa di Corintho*; ~ (red)
sauce II,265 *Per far salza di Rebis*;
~ (red) sauce VI,190 *Per far salza di
Rebis*

cuttlefish, in a pottage III,105 *Per cuocere
la Seppa in pottaggio*

dates, at their best I,22 *Per conoscer la
bontà del Dattero*; ~ (dried), in sops
VI,133 *Per fare zuppa di Datteri secchi*

dentex, how cooked III,47

devilled eggs: *see* eggs

distillate, essence, liquor, *stillato*: *see* VI,23

double omelets: *see* omelets

dough (pastry), for moulding V,149 *Per fare una compositione della quale se ne potrà fare diversi lavori di pasta in forma*; ~ (thin), for making 'Sardinian fruit' with rosette irons V,146 *Per fare una pasta liquida, della quale se ne potran fare diversi lavorieri con forme da getto, dette frutte di Sardegna*; ~ for *struffoli*, etc. V,135 *Per fare un'altra sorte di pasta, della quale se ne potrà fare strufoli, & altri lavorieri* (*see* Plate 16, *boccolo per strufole*); ~ for balls, etc. V,134 *Per fare una pasta della quale se ne potrà fare palle, & diversi altri lavorieri*; ~ for fried preparations V,133 *Per fare una pasta, della quale se ne puo fare diversi lavorieri fritti nel strutto*; ~: *see also* pastry

doves, boiled, etc. II,130 *Per cuocere i soprascritti piccioni alessi ò in altro modo*; ~ (barnyard or dovecot), spit-roasted II,129 *Per arrostire allo spedo piccioni domestici ò di torre*; ~ or cockerel, in a pie V,41 *Per fare pasticci d'ogni sorte di Piccioni, e di Pollastri*; ~ , in a royal tourte ('lady's lips pizza') V,73 *Per fare torta reale di polpa di piccioni, da Napoletani detta pizza di bocca di Dama*; ~ cruppers and flesh, in a *crostata* V,54 *Per fare crostata di gropponi, & polpe di piccioni*

ducks (wild), spit-roasted and otherwise II,144 *Per arrostir nello spedo, & cuocere in piu modi anatre selvaggie*; ~ and geese tongues II,149 *Per accommodare in diversi modi le lingue d'anatre, & oche domestiche, & salvatiche*; ~ (poultry-yard): *see also* goose

earlets and little napoleons full of whitedish V,44 *Per fare orecchine, & sfogliatelle piene di bianco magnare*

eel (salted) III,213 *Per cuocere, & servire l'Angille salate*; ~ (salted), at its best I,12 *Per conoscer la bontà dell'Anguille salate*; ~ (of all sizes), fried, soused, in verjuice sauce and marinated III,159 *Per friggere, accarpionare, & mettere in agrestata, & marinare anguille grosse, mezane, & picciole*; ~ , braised and grilled III,157 *Per sottestare anguille, & cuocere su la graticola*; ~ , inside out III,158 *Per cuocere anguille grosse roverse con vino*; ~ (large), *en croûte*, to serve hot or cold V,191 *Per fare pasticci d'anguille grosse in cassa per servire caldi, & conservare*; ~ (large, salted), in a pottage III,214 *Per far pottaggio di Anguille grosse salate*; ~ , spit-roasted III,156 *Per arrostire Anguille nello spedo*; ~ (conger) spit-roasted III,99 *Per arrostire nello spedo il pesce Gongoro*; ~ (moray), braised III,97 *Per sottestar Morene*; mock ~ , stuffed, cooked in several ways III,160 *Per fare Anguille finte ripiene, cotte in piu modi*

eggplant, stuffed, in Lent III,230 *Per cuocere molignane ripiene in giorno quadragesimale*; ~ , in a thick soup with meat broth II,224 *Per far minestra di melanzane in diversi modi con brodo di carne*; ~ , in a thick soup, in Lent III,232 *Per far minestra di Molignane in giorno quadragesimale*; ~ (*pomi sdegnosi*), braised III,229 *Per sottestare Molignane cioè pomi sdegnosi*; ~ tourte V,109 *Per fare torta di molignane*

eggs (*uove*; *see also* omelet): ~ , hardboiled and fried III,272 *Per cuocere uove dure con butiro overo con oglio*; ~ , poached III,268 *Per cuocere l'uovo sparso in acqua semplice*; ~ , poached

sorte di fritelle; ~ , differently V,140
Per fare fritelle a un'altro modo; ~
called *'pappardelle'* V,144 *Per fare
un'altra sorte di frittelle, dal vulgo
Romano dette Pappardelle*; ~ called
'zeppolle' V,145 *Per fare frittelle,
dal vulgo Romano dette Zeppolle*; ~ ,
Venetian-style V,136 *Per fare varie
sorte di fritelle, & prima per fare frittelle alla Venetiana*; chicken ~ V,141;
elderflower ~ V,143; milk ~ V,137; rice
~ V,142; rice ~ V,235; *see also* II,55,
57, 148; III,77, 211, 248, 275; V,237;
VI,142
frogs, *en croûte*, to serve hot V,192 *Per
fare pasticci di Rane in piu modi in
cassa per servir caldi*; ~ (deboned),
en croûte V,193 *Per fare pasticci di
Rane senz'osso in cassa*; ~ (deboned),
in a dainty pottage VI,167 *Per fare
pottaggetto di Rane senza ossa*; ~ liver
and flesh, in a *crostata* V,210 *Per fare
crostata di fegato, & polpa di Rane*;
~ (deboned), in a thick soup III,164
Per far minestra di Rane senz'osso;
~ , fried, in verjuice sauce III,163 *Per
friggere, & accommodare in agrestata
le Rane*
fruit (fresh), in sops III,260 *Per far suppa
di diversi frutti freschi*; ~ (dried), in
sops III,257 *Per far suppe di diversi
frutti secchi*; ~ *crostate* and pies ...
V,57 *Per fare crostate, & pasticci di
diverse frutte* ...
funghi (fresh), in a tourte V,223 *Per fare
torte di Fonghi freschi*; *see also* mushrooms
galantine: *see* sauces
garfish, grilled or spit-roasted, braised or
fried III,88 *Per cuocere l'Augusella su
la graticola, o nello spedo, sottestata,
& fritta*; ~ , in pottages III,89 *Per fare
pottaggio di Auguselle in piu modi*
garlic, in a thick soup with meat broth
II,210 *Per far minestra d'aglio con*

brodo di carne, & altre materie; ~
sauce, with fresh walnuts and almonds
II,257 *Per fare agliata con noci fresche, & amandole*; *see also* garlic sauce
II,1, 4, passim 32
gattafura: Genovese ~ V,97 *Per fare
gattafura alla Genovese*; Genovese
onion ~ V,98 *Per fare gattafura di
cipolle alla Genovese*; *see also* I,44
gilded bread: *see* bread
gilded sops: *see* capirotata and sops
gilthead, grilled III,44 *Per cuocere Orate
su la graticola*; ~ , in a pottage III,45
*Per cuocere il pesce Orata in potag-
gio*; ~ , soused, marinated and preserved III,46 *Per accarpionare, &
marinare, & conservare in aceto Orate*
gizzards of goslings, geese, cranes, domestic peacocks and turkey hens,
spit-roasted, in fricassees II,148 *Per
arrostire allo spedo, & far diverse fricassee di magoni di papari, d'oche, di
grue, di pavoni nostrali, & di galline
d'India*
gnocchi: *see* macaroni; III,253, 255, 256
goat, kid (*capra, capretto*): goat and
chamois II,76 *Per cocinare ogni agio,
cioè ogni parte di Capra, & di Camozza*;
~ milk pie, with either sowbelly or
cow's udder V,46 *Per fare pasticcio di latte di capra, & sommata, ò
zinna di vaccina*; ~ milk sops VI,160
Per fare zuppa di latte di Capra; ~
milk, etc., in a thick soup VI,85 *Per
far minestra di latte di capra, rossi
d'ova, & sugo di melangole*; ~ milk
whey, purified VI,68 *Per fare siero di
latte di Capra purificato*; ~ kid, boiled
or roasted II,78 *Per alessare, & arrostire, & far molte vivande d'ogni agio,
cioè parte del capretto, eccettuando la
testa*; ~ kids (whole), spit-roasted or
braised II,77 *Per arrostire nello spedo,
& sottestare capretti intieri*; ~ kid or

~ tourte, Bolognese, without eggs V,96 *Per fare torte d'herbe alla Bolognese senz'ove, cotte sul suolo di rame, o sul testo di terra*; ~ tourte, Lombard-style V,92 *Per fare torta d'herbe alla Lombarda*; ~ in a thick soup with meat broth II,203 *Per far minestra di diverse herbette con brodo di carne, & altre materie*; ~ (fine), in a thick broth VI,62 *Per fare brodetto con herbicine battute*

herring: ~ (smoke-dried), at its best I,17 *Per conoscer la bontà dell'Arenghe secche al fumo*; ~ (white salted and smoke-dried) III,210 *Per cuocere Arenghe bianche salate, & secche affumate*

honey, at its best I,20 *Per conoscer la bontà del mele*; ~ , clarified, for a garnish VI,205 *Per chiarificare il mele, ilquale puo servire per sapore*

hops, fried III,248 *Per friggere Lupoli*; ~ , in a thick soup VI,104 *Per far minestra di Lupoli*

horse mackerel, how to cook it III,68 *Per cuocere il Suero in piu modi*

impromptu thick whitedish soup II,167 *Per far minestra di bianco magnare all'improvista*

jays, stockdoves, small coots, woodcocks and teal ducks, spit-roasted II,131 *Per arrostire nello spedo i piccioni di ghianda, palombelle, felicette, beccaci, & garganelli*

jelly: ~ of almond milk and chicken broth, served like junket VI,20; ~ of turbot III,82; ~ of nourishing chicken broth VI,19; ~ of cherries (morello) VI,203; ~ of cherries (morello) II,280; ~ of chicken, chopped, with quince juice VI,202; fish (marinated or jellied), at its best I,19; ~ (uncooked) of fish decoction VI,214; ~ (clarified) of fish II,246; ~ of goat kids' and

capons' parts II,240; ~ of pigs' snout, ears and feet II,242; ~ of pigs' feet, snout and ears, interspersed with slices of mock salami II,243; ~ of quince II,247; ~ of tench III,144; ~ of veal-knuckle broth VI,26; vinegar, clarified, for ~ , etc. VI,207; ~ of wethers' feet II,245; ~ of wether's and calf's feet II,239; ~ (quick) of wethers' and calf's feet II,244; ~ (for moulding) of wether's and calf's feet II,241; *see also* Slavonic jelly IV,f.327v [275r] *gelatina Schiavona*

John Dory, how to cook it III,84

junket, curd, curdled milk, cream, *giuncata*: *see* almond milk; II,169; V,85

kohlrabi, in a thick soup with meat broth II,194 *Per far minestra di caulo torsuto con brodo di carne, & altre materie, & cuocerlo in diversi modi*; ~ bulb, stuffed III,241 *Per cuocere la Rapa di Cauli torzuti ripieni*; ~ bulb, differently III,242 *Per cuocere la Rapa di caulo torzuto in un'altro modo*; ~ tourte V,105 *Per fare torta di cavoli torzuti*

lamprey (large), braised III,92 *Per sottestar Lamprede grosse*; ~ (large), spit-roasted III,91 *Per cuocere Lamprede grosse nel spedo*; ~ (large), en croûte, to serve cold or hot V,178 *Per fare pasticci di Lamprede grosse in cassa per conservare, & servire caldi*; ~ (large), in *crostate* V,202 *Per fare crostate di Lamprede grosse*; ~ (young), marinated and soused III,95 *Per marinare & accarpionare Lampredozze*; ~ (young), grilled III,93 *Per cuocere Lampredozze su la graticola*; ~ (young, river), braised III,94 *Per sottestare Lampredozze di fiume*; ~ (young, Tevere), stewed VI,170 *Per fare stufate di lampredozze del Tevere*

~ V,60; pheasant or partridge (young or old), or capon, gosling or duck, in a ~ V,38; ~ of whole shad, to serve hot or cold V,169; ~ with a cream filling V,45; poor cod, in little ~ V,174; prosciutto ~ V,31; quince ~ VI,115; rabbit (whole), in a ~ V,28; ~ of large *salsiccione* V,32; ~ of saveloy or fresh sausage V,34; ~ of whole shad, to serve hot or cold V,169; stag's leg, in a ~ V,26; sturgeon ~ in thick dough, to serve hot or cold V,153; ~ of sturgeon milt and sturgeon liver V,159; sturgeon fingerlings in big ~ shells, to serve cold V,160; *salsiccione* (large), in a ~ V,32; thrush, quail or other small birds, in a ~ V,39; truffles, etc., in *crostate* and ~ V,58; turkey pullet, in a ~ V,37; veal croquettes, stuffed, in a ~ V,17; wether's leg, in a ~ V,21; whitedish, in a ~ shell of flaky pastry or not V,43; ~: s.a pastry wrap, tourte

pig, pork (*porco*; *see also* boar): ~ belly II,101 *Per cocinar la pancia del porco in diversi modi*; ~ breast II,98 *Per cuocere il petto di porco domestico in diversi modi*; ~ jowl (salted) or prosciutto, in *crostate* (gourmand bread) II,230 *Per far crostate cioè pan ghiotto con barbaglia di porco, o presciutto*; ~ ribs II,99 *Per cucinare la schiena del porco domestico in diversi modi*; ~ tenderloin II,100 *Per fare il lomboletto di porco domestico in piu modi*; ~ blood, in a tourte ('blood pudding') V,67 *Per fare torta di sangue di porco domestico, dal vulgo detta migliaccio*; ~ blood, in another tourte ('white blood pudding') V,68 *Per Fare un'altra torta di sangue di Porco, dal vulgo detta migliaccio bianco*; ~ or kid's blood, in an omelet II,237 *Per far frittata di sangue di porco o di capretto*; ~ feet, snout and ears, in a jelly interspersed with slices of mock salami,

with a decoction made as before II,243 *Per far gelo di piedi, grugni, & orecchi di porco, tramezzato con fette di salame finto, fatta la decottione nel modo sopradetto*; ~ head II,96 *Per cuocere la testa del porco domestico in diversi modi*; ~ leg II,102 *Per cocinare il cigotto, cioè coscietto del porco domestico*; ~ leg-meat, in a mortadella wrapped in a caul II,103 *Per far mortatelle di carne magra di cigotto di porco domestico involte nella rete*; ~ liver, roasted II,106 *Per arrostire in diversi modi il fegato di porco domestico*; ~ neck and throat II,97 *Per cucinare in diversi modi il collo, & la scannatura del porco domestico*; ~ pluck II,105 *Per cuocere in diversi modi la coratella del porco domestico*; ~ snout, ears and feet, in a jelly II,242 *Per far gelo di grugni, orecchi, & piedi di porco*; ~ 'tasty morsels' II,104 *Per cuocere le bocche del porco saporite, dico del porco domestico*; ~ salami II,114 *Per cuocere ogni sorte di salami di carne di porco*; piglet (suckling, domestic or wild) II,83 *Per arrostire il porchetto domestico, & selvaggio*

pike, plain, etc. III,147 *Per cuocere il Luccio in bianco, et in altri modi*; ~ (large, salted and smoked) III,215 *Per cuocere il Luccio grosso salato, che sia stato nel fumo*; ~ , in a French-style pottage III,148 *Per cuocere il Luccio in pottaggio alla Francese*; ~ , fried III,150 *Del friggere il Luccio*; ~ (large), spit-roasted or grilled III,149 *Per cuocere il Luccio grosso nello spedo, & su la graticola*; ~ , in bresaola and croquettes III,151 *Per far brisavoli, & polpette di polpe di Luccio cotte in piu modi*; ~ (big), in a pastry wrap, to serve hot or cold

with meat broth II,204 *Per far mines-*
tra di spinaci con brodo di carne; ~ ,
sautéed, etc. III,244 *Per soffriggere*
Spinaci, & cuocerli in altri modi; ~
tourte with fresh eel, in Lent V,219
Per fare torta di Spinaci con polpa
d'Anguille fresche per giorno Quadra-
gesimale; ~ and herb tourte, in Lent
V,220 *Per fare torta di Spinaci, & al-*
tre herbe odorifere per giorno Quadra-
gesimale; see also ~ in the Florentine
fashion III,244 *all Fiorentina*
squash, in a thick soup in Lent III,225
Per far minestra di zucche nostrali in
giorno di quaresima; ~ , in a thick
soup VI,105 *Per far minestra di zuc-*
che nostrali; ~ , in a thick soup, with
almond milk VI,106 *Per far mines-*
tra di zucche con latte di mandole;
~ , in a thick soup with meat broth
II,218 *Per far minestra di zucche nos-*
trali con brodo di carne in diversi
modi; ~ and onions, in a thick soup
('*carabazzata*') II,219 *Per far mines-*
tra di zucche & cipolle in diversi
modi, dal vulgo detta carabazzata;
~ , stuffed, in Lent III,226 *Per empire*
zucche nostrali in giorno quaresimale;
~ (stuffed), in a thick soup VI,107
Per far minestra di zucche ripiene; ~
(whole), stuffed, boiled and oven-baked
II,221 *Per alessare & cuocere in forno*
le soprascritte zucche intiere piene di
diverse compositioni; ~ , fried III,227
Per friggere Zucche nostrali; ~ tourte,
without cheese VI,121 *Per far torta di*
zucche nostrali senza cascio; ~ rinds
('*zazzere*') III,228 *Per cuocere scorze*
di Zucche dal vulgo dette Zazzere
squid (large), in a pottage III,102 *Per*
far pottaggio di Calamari grossi; ~ ,
stuffed, in a pottage III,103 *Per far*
pottaggio di Calamari ripieni; ~ , fried
or in a pottage III,101 *Per friggere, &*

far pottaggio di Calamari; ~ (large or
small), *en croûte* for serving hot V,179
Per fare pasticci in cassa di Calamari
grossi, & piccoli per servire caldi
squill fish and saltwater shrimp, how to
cook them III,179
stag: ~ meat II,87 *Per cuocer la carne*
di cervo in diversi modi; ~ leg, in a
pie V,26 *Per fare pasticcio di coscia*
di Cervio; ~ , roebuck and fallow deer,
breast and ribs, in a larded broth II,85
Per far brodo lardiero del petto, &
delle coste delli sopradetti animali; ~
(young), roebuck and fallow deer leg,
shoulder and loin, roasted II,84 *Per*
arrostire il cigotto, spalla, & lombo
di Cervietto, di Capriolo, & di Dame;
~ (young), roebuck and fallow deer
liver, without the gall bladder II,86 *Per*
cuocere il fegato de i detti animali in
piu modi, i quali fegati non hanno fiele
starch, in a thick soup with meat broth
II,166 *Per far minestra di amido con*
brodo di carne; ~ , in a thick soup,
with almond milk III,220 *Per far*
minestra di amido con latte di man-
dole; ~ , in a thick soup, with almond
milk VI,79 *Per far minestra di amido*
con latte d'amandole; ~ tourte, in Lent
V,228 *Per fare torta d'Amido in giorno*
Quadragesimale
strawberry *crostata* without cheese VI,129
Per fare crostata di fragole senza cas-
cio
struffoli: see I,44; V,135 and Plate 16
stuffing for every sort of commonly eaten
animal, quadruped and fowl, for spit-
roasting II,115 *Per far diverse com-*
positioni, delle quali si potrà empire
ogni sorte d'animali usati, si quadru-
pedi come volatili che si voranno
arrostire nello spedo; stuffing for
quadruped members and fowl, those
to be boiled in salted water II,116
Per far varie compositioni, delle quali

chicory VI,93; ~ of chicory, differently
VI,94; ~ of chicory, differently VI,95;
~ of chicory root VI,96; ~ called *cianciarelle* II,182 *Per far minestra detta
cianciarelle*; ~ of cracked millet or
foxtail millet II,186; ~ of egg and
milk, differently III,286; ~ of eggplant
with meat broth II,224; ~ of eggplant,
in Lent III,232; ~ of wild fennel shoots
with meat broth II,207; ~ of wild
fennel III,243; ~ of flour and bread
('*millefanti*') II,171; ~ of boneless
frogs III,164; ~ of garlic with meat
broth II,210; ~ of dried haricot beans
III,253; ~ of herbs with meat broth
II,203; ~ of hops VI,104; impromptu
whitedish ~ II,167; ~ of kohlrabi
with meat broth II,194; ~ of leeks
and onions with meat broth II,209;
~ of dried lentils III,254; ~ of lettuce
II,202; ~ of lettuce with chicken broth
VI,91; ~ of lettuce ribs VI,92; ~ of
stuffed lettuce VI,108; ~ of lobster
III,172; Lombard-style ~ , with herb
tortellini II,179 *Per far minestra di
tortelletti d'herba alla Lombarda*; macaroni, in a ~ ('gnocchi') II,176; macaroni, in a ~ with an iron rod II,175;
macaroni, in a ~ , Roman-style II,174;
~ of mallow VI,98; ~ of melons with
meat broth II,222; ~ of Savoy and
Bolognese cabbage with meat broth
II,198; ~ of milk ('Hungarian Soup')
II,169; ~ of milk (goat's), etc. VI,85;
~ of common field mushrooms, etc.
II,215; ~ of salted mushrooms III,235;
nettle ~ VI,99; ~ of onions and leeks
together, in Lent III,234; ~ of parsley and other herbs ('Apostles' broth'
in Roman courts) II,206; ~ of parsley
root II,208; ~ of parsley root VI,102; ~
of fresh peas VI,109; ~ of fresh peas,
beans [or chickpeas] III,249; ~ of peas
or beans II,188; ~ of dried peas II,191;

~ of pinenuts or pistachios VI,217; ~
of purslane VI,97; ~ of quince with
meat broth II,223; ~ of rape greens
II,205; ~ of ravioli (without a casing)
II,181; ~ of rhubarb root VI,101; rice
flour, for hot ~ II,155; ~ of rice with
almond milk or oil III,221; ~ of rice
or spelt II,184; rice, in a Damascene ~
II,154; ~ of rice with almonds VI,81;
~ of rice with chicken broth VI,80;
~ of white ricotta II,168; semolina ~
II,170; spelt ~ VI,83; ~ of spelt with
almond milk VI,84; ~ of spelt with
capon broth VI,82; ~ of spinach VI,90;
~ of spinach with meat broth II,204; ~
of stuffed squash VI,107; squash and
onions in a ~ ('*carabazzata*') II,219;
~ of squash with meat broth II,218; ~
of squash in Lent III,225; ~ of squash
VI,105; ~ of squash with almond milk
VI,106; ~ of starch with meat broth
II,166; ~ of starch with almond milk
III,220; ~ of starch with almond milk
VI,79; ~ of sturgeon III,5; another ~
of sturgeon III,6; another ~ of sturgeon III,7; ~ of tagliatelli II,173; ~ of
truffles with chicks II,214; ~ of Turkish squash, in thick soups II,220; ~
of turnips and rapes II,211; turnip, in
a Venetian-style ~ II,212; ~ of veal
or goat-kid sweetbreads and capon's
breast VI,38; impromptu white ~
VI,76; ~ of whitedish II,162; ~ of
whitedish with breadcrumb, almonds
II,165; ~ of whitedish with starch,
pinenuts II,164; yellowdish, as a ~ or
meat garnish II,160; *see also vivarole*
thrush, blackbirds and larks, spit-roasted
and otherwise II,134 *Per cuocere nello
spedo, & in altri modi, tordi, merli,
& lodole*; thrush, quail or other small
birds, in a pie V,39 *Per fare pasticcio
di Tordi, & quaglie, & altri uccelletti
tommacelle*: ~ from pork liver II,107 *Per
far tommacelle di fegato di porco*; ~

from pork liver, in another way II,108 *Per far tommacelle di fegato di porco in un'altro modo*; ~ from a domestic pork liver and delicate tenderloin II,109 *Per far tommacelle di fegato, & lomboletti di porco domestico*; ~ of chicken or capon liver and meat VI,44 *Per far tommacelle di fegato, & polpa di pollo o cappone*; *see also* II,47, 50, 103, 115, 150; III,12–14, 153, 173, 175; VI,42, 45

tortoise, in a dainty pottage VI,168 *Per far pottaggetto di Tartarughe di terra*

tourte (*torta*): ~ called '*nosetto*' V,101 *Per fare torta dal vulgo detta Nosetto*; ~ called '*pizza*' V,121 *Per fare torta con diverse materie, da Napoletani detta pizza*; almond-milk ~ V,227; apple ~ V,116; apple ~ , without eggs, cheese or butter VI,126; apples and Florentine pears, in a ~ without cheese VI,125; artichoke- and cardoon-heart ~ V,90; asparagus and hops ~ V,103; asparagus ~ V,222; breadcrumb white ~ V,82; ~ of coarse buckwheat V,88; ~ of calf's brain and sweetbreads V,69; capon-breast ~ V,72; cardoon ~ , in Lent V,221; ~ of carrots or other roots V,111; cauliflower ~ V,104; ~ of visciola cherries, without cheese VI,128; ~ of Roman, visciola and morello cherries V,118; ~ of fresh or dried chestnuts V,120; split chickpeas in a ~ V,225; cinnamon ~ , and others V,218; cream tops, in a ~ VI,119; crustless ~ ('*tartara*') V,86 *Per fare torta senza pasta dal vulgo detta tartara*; eggplant ~ V,109; fresh funghi in a ~ V,223; green ~ ('*herbolata*') V,94 *Per fare torta verde, dal vulgo detta herbolata*; ordinary herb ~ V,99; herb ~ , in winter V,93; Bolognese herb ~ , without eggs V,96; Lombard-style herb ~ V,92; kohlrabi ~ V,105; lettuce or

endive ~ V,102; ~ of lobster claws VI,117; marzipanned ~ VI,120; medlar ~ V,117; melon ~ V,112; melon ~ , without cheese VI,122; milk ~ ('Romagna Cups') V,85; muscat-grape ~ V,119; muscatel-pear ~ V,115; omelet in water ('~ in water') III,279; ~ of fresh pea- or bean-leaves V,100; peach ~ VI,127; pear ~ V,114; ~ of fresh peas, fava beans and haricot beans V,89; ~ of dry peas, haricot beans or other legumes V,91; ~ of peas and other legumes (dried) V,224; pheasant ~ , without cheese VI,116; domestic pig's blood, in a ~ ('blood pudding') V,67; pigs blood, in another ~ ('white blood pudding') V,68; pumpkin ~ V,106; pumpkin-and-onion ~ V,107; pumpkin ~ without a shell V,108; quince ~ V,113; quince ~ , without cheese VI,123; ~ of quince and *caravella* pears VI,124; rice ~ V,87; ricotta ~ V,77; royal ~ , with various fillings V,75 *Per fare torta reale di varie compositioni*; royal white ~ V,80 *Per fare torta bianca reale, quale usava Papa Giulio III*; cream tops, in a royal ~ V,78; dove, in a royal ~ ('lady's lips pizza') V,73; royal ~ of pheasant and partridge V,70; pheasant and partridge, in another royal ~ V,71; royal ~ of pinenuts, almonds, etc. V,74; royal ~ of ricotta, a creamy cheese and apple juice V,79; royal ~ with various fillings V,75; whitedish, in a royal ~ V,76; scorpion-fish ~ V,226; ~ of spinach and herbs, in Lent V,220; spinach ~ , with fresh eel, in Lent V,219; squash ~ , without cheese VI,121; starch ~ , in Lent V,228; ~ of sturgeon liver and milt V,200; sturgeon ~ V,201; ~ of tagliatelli or lasagne V,84; turnip ~ V,110; veal ~ V,66; whitedish, in a ~ without cheese VI,118; white ~ , plain

Turkish squash, in thick soups II,220 *Per far diverse minestre di zucche Turchesche*

turnip, in a Venetian-style thick soup II,212 *Per far minestra di rape alla Venetiana con brodo di carne*; ~ , in a tourte V,110 *Per fare torta di Rape*; ~ *crostata* V,65 *Per fare crostata di rape*; ~ and rapes, in a thick soup II,211 *Per far minestra di rape, & navoni con brodo di carne in diversi modi*

turtledoves and quail, roasted and done up II,133 *Per arrostire, & accommodare tortore, & quaglie in piu modi*

turtle (sea), how to cook it III,166 *Per cuocere la Tartaruga marittima in piu modi*; ~ , various other ways III,168 *Per cuocere Tartarughe in diversi modi*; ~ (land and sea), *en croûte* V,180 *Per fare pasticci di Tartarughe di terra, & di mare in cassa*; ~ viscera, in a *crostata* V,209 *Per fare crostate d'interiori, di Tartarughe d'ogni sorte*

twists (*tortiglioni*): flaky-pastry ~ , with exposed leaves V,125 *Per fare tortiglione sfogliato di sfogliatura aperta*; flaky-pastry ~ , with concealed leaves V,126 *Per fare tortiglione di sfogliatura serrata*; ~ , filled V,122 *Per fare tortiglione ripieno*; ~ , filled, differently V,123 *Per fare tortiglione ripieno a un'altro modo*; ~ , filled, differently V,124 *Per fare tortiglione ripieno a un'altro modo*; *see also* dough

urchin (sea), how to cook it III,195

veal, calf, calves (*vitella*; *see also* beef): ~ braised, in bresaola VI,46 *Per fare Bresavoli sottostati di carne di Vitella*; ~ breast, boiled II,33 *Per alessare il petto della vitella*; ~ breast, stuffed and roasted on a spit or grill II,36 *Per arrostir nello spedo, & su la graticola il petto della detta vitella ripieno*; ~

loin, beaten, in pie shells V,19 *Per fare pasticci di lonza di Vitella battuta in cassa*; ~ (beaten), in little pies VI,113 *Per far pasticetti di Vitella battuta*; ~ (beaten), in a plain- or flaky-pastry shell V,18 *Per fare pasticci di polpa di vitella battuta in cassa, & sfogliati*; ~ paste VI,33 *Per far pisto di carne di Vitella*; ~ paste, spit-roasted VI,34 *Per far pisto di carne di vitella arrosta nello spedo*; ~ tourte V,66 *Per fare torta di carne Vitellina*; ~ croquettes, stuffed, in a pie V,17 *Per fare pasticcio di polpette di vitella ripiene in an'altro modo*; ~ sweetbreads, spit-roasted or grilled II,49 *Per arrostire l'animelle di vitella nello spedo, & su la graticola*; ~ or goat-kid sweetbreads and capon's breast, in a thick soup VI,38 *Per fare una minestra d'animelle di Vitella, overo di Capretto, & polpe di petto di Cappone*; ~-broth concentrate VI,24 *Per far brodo consumato di carne di Vitella*; ~-broth concentrate VI,27 *Per far brodo consumato di carne di Vitella*; ~-broth concentrate, differently VI,25 *Per far brodo di carne di Vitella in un'altro modo*; ~ blood II,59 *Per cuocere il sangue della sopradetta vitella in piu modi*; ~ brains and sweetbreads, in a tourte V,69 *Per fare torta di cervella, et animelle di Vitella*; ~ brains II,52 *Per cuocere le cervella CHECK di vitella in diversi modi*; ~ brains and sweetbreads, in *crostate* (gourmand bread) II,231 *Per far le dette crostate o pan ghiotto con cervelle, & animelle di vitella*; ~ liver, in a pie V,14 *Per fare pasticcio di fegato di Vitella*; ~ kidney, spit-roasted, in *crostate* (gourmand bread) II,229 *Per far crostate, cioè pan ghiotto con rognon di vitella arrostito nello spedo*; ~ kidney and loin, spit-roasted, in a *crostata* V,52 *Per far*

indorata, & su la graticola; ~ (suckling), head, spit-roasted II,25 *Per arrostir nello spedo la testa di vitella
di latte con pelle, & senza pelle*; ~
(suckling), kidney, spit-roasted II,41
*Per arrostire nello spedo il rognone
della vitella mongana*; ~ (suckling),
tripe II,57 *Per cuocere trippe di vitella
mongana in diversi modi*; ~ (suckling),
tripe, stuffed II,58 *Per riempir trippe
di vitella mongana*; ~ (suckling), leg,
spit-roasted, etc. II,42 *Per cuocere
nello spedo, & in diversi altri modi la
coscia della vitella mongana*; ~ (suckling) head (deboned) II,24 *Per cucinar
la testa della vitella di latte sanza osso
in piu modi*
verjuice sauce II,273 *Per fare una agrestata*;
    verjuice sauce VI,198 *Per fare agrestata*;
    verjuice (new) sauce VI,196 *Per far
    sapore d'agresto nuovo*
vetch: *see* beans (broad)
vinegar, clarified, for jelly, etc. VI,207
    *Per chiarificar l'aceto, sìbianco, come
    vermiglio, del quale se ne potrà fare
    geli, & diversi altri sapori*
viscera, cooked immediately after an an-
    imal's slaughter I,36 *De gl'interiori,
    che subito morto l'animale richiedono
    d'esser cucinati*
vivarole II,183 *Per far minestra di viva-
    role*; ~ III,285 *Per far minestra vol-
    garmente detta vivarole*; ~ , without
    cheese VI,65 *Per fare minestra volgar-
    mente chiamata vivarole sanza cascio*;
    ~ , differently VI,66 *Per far minestra
    di vivarole in un'altro modo*
wafers and wafer cornets, in a white
    tourte V,83 *Per fare torta bianca di
    cialde, & di cialdoni*; rolled wafers
    with breadcrumb and sugar VI,141 *Per
    fare cialdoni con mollica di pane, &
    zuccaro*; *see also cialde, cialdoni* II,14,
    43; V,83, passim and *ostie* V,237

walnut paste *nosetto, nosetti: see* cab-
    bage, tourtes
waters: *see* potions
wether: ~ breast II,61 *Per cuocere il
    petto di castrato in diversi modi*; ~
    breast, in a pottage II,62 *Per far pot-
    taggio di petto di castrato*; ~ breast,
    in another pottage II,63 *Per far pot-
    taggio di petto di castrato in un'altro
    modo*; ~ broth, ('sussidio') VI,28 *Per
    far brodo di Castrato detto Sussidio*;
    [~ broth] *sussidio*, more quickly VI,29
    *Per fare il soprscritto Sussidio con piu
    brevità*; ~ leg, boiled whole II,68 *Per
    alessare il Zigotto del castrato intiero*;
    ~ leg, spit-roasted whole II,70 *Per ar-
    rostir nello spedo il cigotto di castrato
    intiero*; ~ leg (stuffed), braised whole
    II,69 *Per sottestare il zigotto di cas-
    trato intiero ripieno*; ~ leg, in a pie
    V,21 *Per fare pasticcio di zigotti di
    castrato in piu modi*; ~ leg-meat II,71
    *Per accommodare in diversi modi la
    carne magra del cigotto di castrato*;
    ~ leg-meat, in a pottage II,72 *Per far
    pottaggio di carne magra del cigotto
    di castrato*; ~ leg-meat, in a pottage
    II,73 *Per far pottaggio di carne ma-
    gra di cigotto di castrato con latte di
    amandole*; ~ ribs II,66 *Per cuocere la
    schiena del castrato in diversi modi*; ~
    rump and tail, grilled II,67 *Per cuocere
    il groppone, & coda di castrato su la
    graticola in diversi modi*; ~ shoulder,
    spit-roasted or grilled II,64 *Per arro-
    stire nello spedo, & su la graticola la
    spalla di castrato*; ~ shoulder, wrapped
    in a mock caul, braised, grilled or spit-
    roasted II,65 *Per sottestare, & arrostire
    su la graticola, & nello spedo spalle di
    castrato involte in rete contrafatta*; ~
    feet, in a pottage II,74 *Per far pottagio
    di piede di castrato*; ~ feet, in a jelly
    II,245 *Per far gelo con piedi di cas-
    trato*; ~ and calf feet, in a jelly II,239

3. Procedures

Index 3 is concerned with actions relating to foodstuff production and transformation, and to kitchen work. Brackets around an infinitive indicate that only a participle or a finite form of the verb is found in the text.

to fail (to do something), neglect, over-look, forget II,51; passim 40 *mancare (di fare)*, III,122; VI,213; Con-clave,f.A2r *non* [*restare*] *(di fare)*

to feed, force-feed (poultry) I,39, II,127 *apastare, appastare*; force-fed (capon) VI,11, 32, 202 *pastare*

to fill: *see* to stuff

to finish off, use up V,22, 132 [*fornire*]: *non sia fornito di tagliare* (*DEI* 'XIV, finire, terminare')

to firm up, solidify, stiffen II,54, 55; passim *fermare*; to firm up, set (a mixture) II,24, 43; III,273 *appreso* [*apprendere*]; to firm up, tighten (a roll of dough) V,122 [*calcare*]; *see also* to set

to fit up, arrange, set in order I,2; II,140, 146; V,27, 36; VI,215 *congegnare*

to flatten, smooth out V,128 *spianare*

to flavour with musk II,248; III,280; passim *muschiare*

to flesh, remove, strip flesh from bone II,9 *scarnare*

to float II,3; passim 12 *stare, venire a gallo*, II,56, 246 *stare, venire a galla*

to flour II,5, 130; IV,f.329v [277v]; passim 80 *infarinare*

to fray, flay, draw into strands, reduce to threads, comb out (flesh) III,215 *sfilare*

to gather up II,9, 73; passim [*ricogliere*]

to gild (by means of egg yolk) II,5, 18, 28, 31, 35, 67, 79 *indorare*

to go mouldy, mildew III,24; V,15 *muffare*

to graze, feed II,77, 84; III,0 *pascolare*

to grease (with an oil, grease, butter) V,49; VI,120; passim 50 *ungere, ongere, onto*

to grind I,2, 27 *macinare*

to gut (a fish): gutted V,41 *privi de gli interiori*

to hang (meat) II,127 *affaggianare* (*DEI* 'preparare selvaggina come si fa dei faggiani'); to hang briefly or beat

(flesh, in order to tenderize the meat) I,32, II,84, 141, 170 *frollare, frolletto*

to hang (up), affix, adhere I,2; passim *appiccare*

to heat up, give heat (of fire) to II,91; VI,2 *focare*

to hole, make a hole II,153 [*sbusciare*], II,220, 226 [*busciare*]

to impress, imprint V,146, 149 [*improntare*]

to inform, realize, note, take note, mind, watch, warn *avertire, avvertire, adver-tire*

to insert between, alternate with (layers), intersperse II,121 *tramezzare, tramezare* (*Zingarelli* 'interporre, sepa-rare')

to jell: *see* to set

to keep, set aside, store, preserve I,2, 5; passim 90 *conservare*

to kill, slaughter I,32; II,23 *ammazzare*, III,91–3, 95, 168, 197; V,206 *fare morire*; *see also* to butcher

to knead (dough) II,176; VI,140 *rimenare*, I,2; V,1 *gramolare*

to lard, to stud (with garlic, cloves) *impil-lotare*; IV,f.330r [277v] *piegottar*

to leak, breathe (a vapour) II,26; passim 10 *fiatare*, I,33; VI,215 *rifiatare*, I,42; II,69; passim 10 *sfiatare*

to lean against I,42 *pontare* (*Zingarelli* 'premere sopra un punto solo')

to light, ignite (a flame) I,44; IV,f.328v [276r], v; V,11; Conclave,f.A1v, A2r, A3v *accendere, acceso*

to load onto a pack animal IV,f.329v [277v] *metter per soprasoma*

to look at, examine, check (on) V,11 *visitare*

to lower, drop (down), decrease, reduce, press down V,128; VI,26 [*calare*]

lumpy: to become lumpy II,153; III,5; VI,69 *agruppare*

to macerate, steep in a seasoning II,38; V,156 [*ponere, mettere, fare stare*] *in adobbo*

caldetta
to whip, flail, thrash (as grain) VI,8
[*frustare*]
to wind up, around II,80 [*innaspare*]

to work (together), mix thoroughly (together) *confettare*; to work, decorate
I,2; V,55; passim 18 *lavorare*; *see also*
to prepare

4. Kitchen Equipment for Handling, Cooking, Serving

Index 4 deals mostly with the hardware in Scappi's kitchen. It lists the things that a cook made use of as he handled foodstuffs and prepared dishes. The four subsections contain severally the larger fixtures, the receptacles, the handtools and the materials (cloths, metals, woods) of that work.

Fixtures, furnishings

alambic, distilling flask VI,21 *lambicco*, VI,21, 23 *campana (Crusca* 'campana dicesi pure un Vaso di terra, di cristallo, di piomba o di altra materia, fatto a guisa di una campana, per uso di distillare, con un beccuccio presso al fondo, lungo e torto, donde esce il liquore che si distilla')

andirons, firedogs I,42, 43; IV,f.330r [277v] *capifochi*, I,42 *cavedoni*

bars IV,f.328v [276v] *caiennacci (di ferro)*

bellows I,44; IV,f.329v [277v] *soffietto, soffietti*

benches (on which several persons sit) Conclave,f.A2r *bancchi*; (a row in a latrine, with several positions) I,2 *(un ordine di) banchi (con piu poste)*; *see also* workbench

board, table (board(s) on trestles) I,2; passim 79 *tavola, tavole, see* Plate 25; folding tables I,2 *tavole snodate*; portable, travelling tables I,44 *tavole snodate per viaggio*; dismantled table IV,f.329v [277v] *tavole disnodate*; small table, cutting board I,2; II,65; passim 16 *tavoletta, tavolette*; large table I,2 *tavolone*; round board, disk II,247, 267; III,276 *(un) tondo*

brackets (of iron) I,2 *staffe (di ferro)*

brazier II,160, 162; VI,205 *focone*

brick I,2; II,137, 146; VI,1, 11 *mattone, mattoni*

buttress, spur, projection (of wall) I,2 *sperone, speroni*

candle holders (iron, brass) IV,ff.327r [275r], 277r, 277v *candellieri (di ferro, d'ottone)*

chains (for folding tables) IV,f.329v [277r], 277v *catene*

closets, wardrobes I,2 *armarii*

cooking bell (earthenware) II,43, 47, 77, 187, 225; III,186; V,0, 50, 54, 55, 57, 60, etc; VI,32, 118, etc. *testo*; not mentioned in Book I or illustrated in Plates

cupboard: *see* sideboard

drains (from latrines) I,2 *condutti*

fireplace, hearth, chimney, breast of I,2, 42; III,14; IV,ff.328v [276r], 329r [277r] *camino, camini*

flue (of fireplace) I,2; IV,f.328v [276r] *canna*

folding, hinged, jointed, articulated *(snodato)*: *see* board, grater, grill, iron bars, spit-supports

grill, gridiron I,2; passim 170 *graticola, graticole*; folding round ~ I,43 *graticole da ruota snodate*

hinged: *see* folding

hook I,2, 42, 43; III,97; V,1, 21 *uncino, uncini*; set of hooks (fastened beneath a shelf) I,2 *(un' ordine di) rastelli*, Plate 2

iron fastenings, fittings I,2 *ferri congegnati*; hinged iron bars I,2 *ferri snodati*; iron rings (for dressing tripe) I,43 *ferri tondi (per acconciar trippe)* (the Venice 1581 printing shows *ferritondi*)

kneading trough I,2 *spartura*; I,2 *gramola*; dough tray I,2 *marva*

lip, I,44; VI,107 *navicella, navicelle,* Plates 6 (*navicela*) and 8, *see also* chafing dish; deep ~ (for poaching eggs) IV,f.329r [276v] *bolsonette (per far ove sparse),* Plate 10, *bolsoneto per far ova;* cylindrical copper ~ , timbale V,134 *bocculo; see also* tourte

pitcher, flask, jug (with neck and handle) I,44; II,163; VI,1, 22, 23, 30, 60, 61, 63, 65, 71 *cucumo, cucumi,* Plate 10

plate: *see* dish, tile

pot: *see* casserole, stewpot, vessel

stewpot, pot, cooking pot II,8; passim 110 *pignatta, pignata, pignate,* Plates 6 (*pignato*), 9 and 10; earthenware ~ II,17, 153; passim *pignatta di terra;* glazed earthenware ~ II,112, 268; VI,11, 26, 49, 183, 192, 193, 202 *pignatta di terra invetriata,* VI,207 *pignatta di terra vetriata;* copper ~ I,44; IV,f.329r [277r]; VI,40, 85 *pignatta di rame;* small ~ VI,30, 54, 60, 82 *pignattina, pignatina;* ~ II,43; III,2; VI,55 *stufatoro, stufatora:* Plate 8. *stufatoro, stufator ovato, stufatoro largo;* VI,25 *stufatore di rame*

tile, plate (with or without holes, used to hold coals beneath a chafing dish) I,44 *piastrella, piastrelle,* Plates 8, 10, 17

tub, case, receptacle Conclave,f.A2v, 3r, 3v *sporta;* large ~ , crates (partitioned, with lock) I,44; IV,f.328r [276r]; Conclave,f.A3v *sportone, sportoni (tramezzati);* small chest IV,f.328r [276r]; Conclave,f.A2v, 3r, 4r *sportello, sportine*

tourte pan II,28, 43; passim 184 *tortiera, tortiere,* Plate 9; copper ~ (shallow) III,94; small ~ II,235 *tortierette;* marzipan ~ V,237 *tortiere da marzapane*

vessel, container, pot I,3; passim 380 *vaso;* small pot III,183 *vassello;* pot (shallow and round-bottomed, lidded, copper) I,44; IV,f.329r [276v] *conserva, conserve,* Plates 7, 8; pot, jar,

flask (earthenware or glass) II,264, 274; VI,210, 212 *alberello, alberelli, albarel (di vetro, invetriati, di terra);* pots, jugs IV,f.329r [276v] *cucome* (1581 *cuogome*) (mod. cuccuma), Plate 10, *cucumo;* (Romagna) cups (a prepared dish, not a container) V,85 *coppi (romagnoli); see also* casserole, jar, stewpot

Utensils

aprons I,2 *grembiali;* long, coarse ~ IV,f.329r [276v] *zinnali (Zingarelli* 'zinale: ampio e lungo grembiule di tessuto rustico, indossato dalla massaia e dall'artigiano'); *see also* shirts, tunics

awl, drift, punch V,40 *puntarolo;* stylus II,81 *stile;* small (iron) stylus II,175 *stiletto (di ferro)*

baking sheet (of copper or earthenware) I,44; V,96, 97, 148 *suolo, suoli (di rame, di terra)*

baster I,43 *imbrattatoro*

bat, bludgeon, truncheon, club, stick (of iron) I,42; II,8; passim 22 *bastone, baston, bastoni (di ferro); see also* rolling pin

box: *see* cases

broom, whisk (of corn stalks) *mellica,* (of briar) V,223; VI,107 *scopa, scope;* sticks, stalks (component of a ~) VI,107 *stecchi (di scopa); see also* brush, toothpicks

brush: small brush, whisk V,133 *scopettina,* (for sprinkling with water) II,153 *granatino;* feather ~ (quill on end of a stick) V,11, 48 *pennello,* Plate 2 (at lower right: *penelo per indorar pastici*); bristle ~ II,55 *pennello di setole; see also* broom

cane I,43; II,137; III,51 *canna, canne*

case, box (esp. for serving candied nuts, seeds to table) IV,ff.194r [156v], 328r [276r], passim *casse* (Plate 6: *casse*

stylus: *see* awl

syringe, pastry tube I,44; II,241; IV,f.329v [277v]; V,136, 236; VI,144 *siringa, seringa, serenga, siringhe (di stagno)*; *Per fare un lavoriero di pasta fatto con la siringa*, Plate 13

thread III,158 *filo; see also* string

toothpicks, flavoured [mentioned in numerous menus that are not reproduced in this translation] *stecchi profumati*

trencher, cutting board, chopping board III,276; V,132, 136 *tagliero, tagliere*

tunics IV,f.328r [276r] *boricchi (Zingarelli* 'burrico: lunga vesta in lana in uso nel XVI e nel XVII sec.'); *see also* aprons, shirts

utensils for a master cook I,1 *delle circonstanze necessarie al mastro Cuoco*

wafer irons IV,f.329v [277v]; VI,141 *ferri da cialdoni*

Materials

(For metals see the lists in I,43, 44 and IV, ff.328r–30r.)

boxwood *busso, see* II,140; III,122

brass *ottone, see* candle holder, cutter, strainer

bristles (pig's), horsehair I,44; II,141, 155; IV,f.329v [277r] *setola, setole*; pig's ~ II,95 *setola porcina; see also* filter

bronze I,44; IV,f.329v [277r] *bronzo*

canvas, hemp cloth I,44; IV,ff.329r [276v], 329v [277r] *canovaccio, canovacci, cannovacci, canovaci*

clay VI,25 *creta*

cloth, fabric I,44 *tela*; I,35; II,243; passim *drappo, drappi*; ~ , clothing I,44; II,239; IV,f.329r [276v]; Conclave,f.A1v, 2v; passim *panno, panni*; coarse ~ II,161, 228; III,266 *drappo grosso*, I,44; II,140, 239; VI,8, 23 *panno grosso*; piece of (coarse, common) ~ , dusters, dust ~ I,2, 44; IV,f.327r [275r], 276v *mantili*; linen (~) I,5, 6, 39, 40; II,23, 24, 110, 122, 140; III,153; V,2, 7, 146, 200 *(drappo, pezza, tela, panno di) lino*, I,31 *drappolino*; broad linen ~ IV,f.329r [276v] *lenzuola*; coarse woollen ~ VI,3 *rascia* (*Zingarelli* 'tessuto spinato di grossa lana'); coarse twill II,265; VI,3, 190 *rascietta*; rag, bit of ~ VI,23, 208, 215 *pezza*; bits of rag VI,21 *pezzoline*; a rag, scrap ~ II,248 *un straccio*; fine ~ II,243 *drappo sottile*, I,2, 44; IV,f.327r [275r], 276v; Conclave,f.A4r *tovaglia, tovaglie*; table ~ IV,f.329r [276v], passim *(levata la) tovaglia, tovaglie ...* ; serving ~ , serviette I,44 *tovaglie per imbandire*; napkin, table runner I,2 *tovagliolo*; small square of ~ , (head)scarf VI,183 *fazzoletto*

copper *rame, see* basin, oven, strainer, stewpot, etc.; IV,f.329r [277r] *forni di rame, masseritie di rame stagnate dentro*, I,6 *vaso di rame*, I,44; II,153; IV,f.329r [277r]; VI,40 *pignatta di rame*, VI,82 *pignattina di rame*, II,163 *cazzuola di rame*, VI,21 *caldara di rame*, II,163; VI,85 *calderina di rame*, II,216; III,141; V,152, 183 *tegame di rame*, II,233, 269; VI,45, 154, 161, 171, 175 *tegametto di rame*, III,8, 94 *tortiera di rame*; II,17, 34,94, 120; III,2; VI,25, 86 *stufatoro di rame*, VI,107 *navicella di rame*, I,44 *stamigne di rame*, I,44; II,81 *foratoro di rame*, IV,f.329r [277r]; VI,95 *crivello di rame*, I,44 *cocchiare di rame*, I,44; II,221; V,96, 97 *suoli di rame*, I,44 *buttiglie di rame*, IV,f.329v [277v] *boccale di rame*; cast ~ II,154 *rame fonduta*, red copper, dark ~ II,152 *rame cupo*, tinned ~ II,163 *rame stagnato; see also* pewter

cotton cloth (for filter cone) VI,68 *bombagina, bombacina, bombasina; see* Plate 18, *bonbasina*

5. Measures

Subdivisions in this Index 5 include weights, volumes, sizes, times and heats.

Weights

grain V,74 *un grano di muschio*, VI,142
  un grano o due di, 143 *due grani di*
ounce I,5; passim *oncia, oncie*; half-~
  I,26; passim *meza, mez' oncia*
pound I,5; passim 600 *libra, libre*, abbr.
  II,111 *lib.*; Milanese ~ III,115, 138,
  146 *il peso Milanese, libre Milanesi*
  (che son di 28 oncie per libra)

Volumes (liquid and dry)

beaker, tumbler (one-half litre) II,227;
  VI,200 *bicchiere, bicchiero*; half a ~
  II,10 *mezo bicchiero*
bit, lump, chunk, dollop II,50; passim 16
  bocconi, II,20; III,5, 153, 156; passim
  64 *bocconcino, bocconcini*; small bits
  V,92, 219 *bocconcelli*, tiny bits III,275
  bocconcinelli
blob, globule, glob I,44; VI,192 *boccula,*
  boccule
bowlful II,154; VI,14, 18, 59, 185 *scodella*
caldaretta, a liquid measure I,43 *cal-*
  daretta
handful II,38; passim 16 *mano, man,*
  mani, II,62 *brancata*
jug, tankard I,45; II,162, 170, 187, 239,
  240, 242, 245, 244, 275; III,2, 10,
  82; V,82; VI,3, 4, 6–8, 15, 56, 58,
  145, 151, 183, 207, 209 *boccal, boc-*
  cale, III,30 *un boccale et mezo*; liquid
  measure of 2⅔ litres (or six pounds)
  II,162; VI,6, 131, 207; passim 35 *boc-*
  cale, boccal, boccali, VI,15 *una pig-*
  natta di un boccale; (silver) IV,f.327r
  [275r] *boccali d'argento*, (copper)
  IV,f.329v [277v] *boccali di rame*;

Roman *boccale* VI,207 *boccale Ro-*
manesco, Romaneschi (che pesa libre
sei), two weigh twelve pounds II,162;
liquid measure of two-thirds of a litre
(or 1½ pounds) I,44; II,119; passim
25 *foglieta, foglietta, fogliette*; weighs
1½ pound VI,131 *una foglietta laquale*
pesi una libra & mezza; liquid measure of about 90 litres *soma, some*:
I,2 a water tank holds 100 *some*; Conclave,f.A2v a flask holds three *some*
(originally a *soma* was the burden or
load that could be borne by a pack-
animal; *Zingarelli* 'unità di misura
per materiali e derrate, usata prima
dell'adozione del sistema metrico deci-
male, con valori variabili fra 66 e 145
litri'; *DEI* 'misura per vino o aceto
eguale a un quinto di gogno' [*Zin-*
garelli 'cogno: antica unità di misura
di capacità per liquidi, pari a circa 450
litri']; Faccioli, II,407, 91 litres)
pinches V,98 *pizzicotti*
tankard: *see* jug
the size of a hen's egg II,106; III,19
  grossezza d'un'uovo (di gallina)
the size of a walnut II,176, 181, 239
  quanto è una noce; the size of a hazelnut V,126, 132; VI,69 *la grossezza*
  d'una nocella

Sizes, quantities, distances

arm's length I,44; III,24; V,11 *braccio*
  (d'huomo), un braccio et mezo, (due)
  braccia
finger width, thickness II,14, 171, 181;
  passim 94 *dito, mezo dito, dita* fist,
  width of a fist (perhaps with thumb

extended) V,125, 127 *sommesso (Zingarelli* 'lunghezza del pugno col dito pollice alzato')

foot Conclave,A2v *piede*

handswidth, width of a palm I,2, 42; III,191; passim 50 *palmo, mezo palmo, palmi*

knife blade (its thickness as a measure) II,14; passim *una costa di coltello*

pike (unit of height) Conclave,f.A1v *(due) picche*

rod, perch (unit of measure, 16½ feet) *canna*; eight feet I,2 *meza canna*; thirty-three feet I,44 *tele lunghe due canne (per coprir carne)*

of a suitable size, amount I,2; II,218; V,42, 129; VI,115; passim 14 *proportionato*

spoonful V,2 *una cocciara*

Times

day, night, passim *giorno, giorni, notte*

one hour, several hours II,37, passim *un' hora, due, tre, quattro, sei hore*; a fraction of an hour: II,17, passim *meza, mez' hora*: III,142 *un terzo d'hora*; II,57, passim *un quarto d'hora*; V,2; VI,74; VI,172 *un mezzo quarto d'hora*; II,275; V,14; VI,142 *tre quarti d'hora*; I,3; II,38; VI,91 *un quinto d'hora*

length of time a liquid boils: briefly, merely brought to a boil *un bollo, boglio*; proportionately longer II,54; III,214; V,10; VI,113, 131 *due bolli*, III,153 *tre bolli*, III,102, 264; VI,88 *quattro bolli*

the length of time of a *Credo* III,267 *lo spatio d'un credo*

a short time, a while II,221 *un pezzo*, III,227 *un pezzuolo*

a short while, a moment VI,44 *un pezzotto*

Heats

fuel: coals, embers (glowing) I,2; II,10; passim 88 *(calor di, sotto le, su le) braccia, braccie, bracie, (alle) bragie*, III,250 *cinigie (Zingarelli* 'cinigia: cenere calda mescolata con brace'); hot ash I,44; II,28, 229; passim 25 *cenere, (sotto la) cenere calda, cinere, ceneri*

fuel: coal II,38, 239; V,75; VI,78, 207 *(fuoco di) carbone*

fuel: faggots III,197 *fassine*

fuel: tinder I,2 *esca*

heat I,2; II,27; passim 18 *calor, calore*

low heat, slight heat, warmth V,85, 138 *fuoco adagio*; II,38; III,91, passim *fuoco lento*; passim *lontan, lontano dalla fiamma*; I,32; II,114; III,273 *caldetto*; II,110; III,13; V,45 *(dare) una caldetta*

moderate heat II,9; V,122 passim *fuoco (ben) temperato*

too intense heat, V,15 *il fuoco troppo in pressa*

relative heats: VI,51 *a lento fuoco piu presto al calor di bracie che di fiamma*; VI,207 *al fuoco de cardone & non de fiamma*

sprightly, lively heat II,128 *fuoco gagliardo*; II43, 129 *fuoco gagliardetto*

6. Miscellaneous Terms

Index 6 is in a sense a catch-all: it groups terms that do not relate to Scappi's foodstuffs, recipes, cooking activities or kitchen equipment – that is, to any of the previous groupings. In this index are the names of places, people (common names only), meals and qualities that he mentions in the *Opera*.

bolognese, bolognesi; Bolgonese herb tourte V,96

Bolsena Lake (in SW Tuscany, NW of Viterbo; home of pike) III,75, 138, 146, 155 *lago di Bolsena*

Brescia (source of large crayfish) III,176; Brescian V,150 *(cascatelle alla) Bresciana*

Bromli, Gulf of III,83

Brondoli (port near Chiozza; source of flounder, many oysters) III,183

brown, reddish brown, deep red I,9; passsim 300 *rosso*; browned (the russet colour imparted by roasting) II,280, 281; V,65; VI,204 *rosolata, rosoletta*; *see also* russet, rust

bubbles V,136 *visiche*

Burgundy III,209 *Borgogna*

bush, woods (in the) II,23, 139 *(alla) foresta*

butcher I,35 *macello*

butchers I,43 *taglieri*

care, interest I,0, 44 *prudenza*; careful, conscientious I,1, 44 *prudente*; with learned skill I,0 *prudentemente*

Cesena (Romagna) II,274 (name given to a variety of grape)

chamberlain VI *maestro di camera*

Chiozza (town on coast near Venice) III,62, 79, 128, 183, 191

Cicoriali (where canes with edible tips are grown) (?) III,227 *cime de canne di valle, che sono portate ... nelle Pescarie di Roma da Cicoriali*

Civitavecchia (port for Rome; source of razor clams) III,54, 113, 114, 191 *Città Vecchia*

clean II,1; passim 140 *netto*; clean, white I,27, 35; II,91; V,232; passim 20 *candido*, cleaned of extraneous material II,72, 152; passim 45 *mondo*; *see also* neat, and to clean in Index 3

cleverness I,0; III,83, 175 *ingegno*

coarse (of strainer) I,44 *stamigne grosse (e sottili)*, V,1, 153 *chiaro*; (of flour, coarsely ground) V,2, 4, 5, 15, 21, 25, 27; passim *farina grossa*; (of cloth) VI,8 *panno grosso*; *see also* fine

Comacchio (port for Ferrara on the Adriatic, north of Ravenna) III,50, 53, 155, 213

common, local, home-grown *nostrale, nostrane*: ~ capon I,40; II,117, 119 *capponi nostrali*; ~ cockerel I,38 *pollastro d'India, et il nostrale*; ~ crayfish III,182; V,181 *gambari nostrali, et d'altra sorte*; ~ dove I,40 *piccioni nostrali*; ~ duck II,145 *anatra domestica, et d'India, laqual'Ł piu grossa, et piu nera della nostrale*; ~ goose II,145 *oche domestiche*; ~ gosling V,38 *paperi nostrali gioveni*; ~ hen II,112, 119, 127, 150; VI,147 *galline nostrale* (cf. I,40 *gallina d'India*); ~ honey VI,206 *mele di Spagna, sarà sempre migliore del nostrale*; ~ peacock I,39; II,140–2, 148; V,36, 37 *il pavon nostrale*; ~ pheasant I,39 *il faggiano nostrale*; ~ pullet II,127, 138; VI,31, 40, 51 *la pollanca nostrale [et] quella d'India*; ~ pumpkin V,106 *cocuzze nostrali*; ~ rabbit II,95; V,28, 29 *il coniglio d'India ... ha ... il pelo piu chiaro che il nostrale; il coniglio d'India, ... s'empie nel modo che s'empie il coniglio nostrale*; ~ raisins I,24 *uve passe, ma quella di Corinto è assai migliore che la nostrale; il zibibbo è migliore delle nostre uve grosse*; ~ squash II,128, 218, 220; III,226, 227; VI,41, 105, 121 *zucche nostrale* (cf. II,220 *zucca turchesca*); ~ walnuts VI,208 *noce nostrane (sic)*; *see also* domestic

Como Lake (home of big trout, shad) III,115, 120, 122, 124, 138, 146, 221 *lago di Como*

Consandolo (home of cranes; town between Ferrara and Ravenna on the

forked, split (of fish tail) III,39, 42, 48, 50, 65 *folcata, fulcata, forcata*

France III,130 *Francia*; French III,65, 148 *francese*; French word V,45 *vocabolo francese*; *see also* wine in Index 1, pottage in Index 2

fussy, finicky, fastidious, dainty (of people) III,282 *suogliatti, (persone) suogliate*

Garda Lake (source of salmon trout) III,121, 122, 124, 201

Genoa (many clams, mussels found on shore) III,40, 190, 193 *Genova*; *see also gattafura* in Index 2

German: ~ lands I,8; II,12, 197; III,119; VI,57 *(terra) tedesca, todesca*; in the ~ fashion III,119 *alla Tedesca*; ~ leather pouches IV,f.329v [277v] *borse di corame alla Tedesca*

glass workers, glass blowers IV,f.168v [133v] *vettrali*

Greek: *see* wine in Index 1

greenish-grey I,13; II,33; VI,213; (passim 13) *berettino, beretino*

greyish, brownish grey II,137, 138, 142; III,34, 60 *bigio*

Grigioni, Grisons (now a mountainous Swiss canton bordering the Tirol and Lombardy) II,137 *montagne de Grisoni*

guests IV,f.168r [123r] *convitati*, house guests IV,f.168v [123v] *convivanti*

harbingers, outriders, vanguard IV,f.328v [276r] *forieri*

harpoon, forked spear (for catching fish) III,83 *fossina*

horse IV,f.328r [276r] *cavallo*; mount I,44; IV,ff.328r [276r], [276v] *cavalcatura, cavalcature*

Hungarian II,169; V,42, 43 *minestra Ongaresco*

inclined to spoil, go bad I,1; II,140 *corruttibile*

inhabitants, residents (nearby) I,2 *convicini*

Italy II,141 *Italia*

Jews II,150 *Giudei*

juicy, succulent I,41 *sugoso*

knots, clumps (made of batter with a syringe) V,232, 233, 236 *gruppi*; *DEI groppo* 15th c. 'viluppo, nodo,' *gruppo* 16th c. 'nodo' from the Germanic *kruppa*

Lambro River (passes by Sant'Angelo and Marignano) III,123, 127 *l'Ambro*

lean II,2, 22; passim 70 *magro*

lean day: *see* day

Levant (source of the spice, orchil) II,246 *tornasone, ch'è pezza di levante*

Liguria, Ligurian region (around Gulf of Genoa, re cheese) I,8; IV,f.327v [275r]; V,48, 92, 111 *Riviera*

lodging IV,f.328v [276r], 276v, 277v *alloggiamento*

Lombardy II,205; III,125, 221 *Lombardia*; Lombard II,16, 22, 26, 121, 156, 179, 225, 226 156; III,155, 155, 162; V,49, 92 *lombardo*

lumber I,44 *schifi*

Maggiore Lake (home of big trout) III,115, 120, 125, 138, 146, 212, 216

Magnaguerra: *see* wine in Index 1

Majorcan IV,f.327v [275r] *Maiorichino*

Mantua III,130, 146 *Mantoa, Mantova*; Manua Lake (home of many carp) III,130 *lago di Mantoa*

Marca, La (La Marca Trevigiana, a province including Treviso, centred on the River Piave) II,136, 146 *La Marca*

marshland III,182 *valle*

master, employer, patron I,0 (f.1r); Conclave, f.A3v, 4r *patrone*

meal: noon, midday ~ , dinner IV,f.168v [133v], 330r [277v] *pranzo*; evening meal, supper IV,f.330r [133v]; passim *cena*; formal ~ IV,f.168v [133v], 327r [275r] *convito, conviti*; informal ~ , collation IV,f.168v [133v], f.155r, f.252v *collatione, colationi* (*Zingarelli* 'colazione: ant. fr. *colation*, dal lat.

7. Terminology in Reference to the Conclave

Given that Scappi published his account of the 1549–50 conclave as an addendum to his *Opera*, Index 7 is devoted solely to significant terms that Scappi used in that account, terms referring to any subject that a modern reader might conceivably find of interest. A translation of that text is above in Appendix I. Some of the things and persons mentioned in those pages will, of course, appear in the main body of the *Opera* as well.

The subdivision here into four segments is arbitrary but may be helpful: Cooking and eating, Persons (common names only), Places and Other things.

Cooking and eating

assay A3v *Credenza*

bottles A3v, 4r *vasi (di vetro, di terra)*; *see also* jug

carafe A3v *caraffe*; small ~ A3v *caraffetta*

common coarse fabric A4r *drappi*

fine table cloths A4r *tovaglie*

food A2v, 3r, 3v, 4r *vivanda, vivande*

fork A3v *forcina*

fruit A3v *frutti*

furnishings, equipment (of kitchen) A1r *massaritie*

hamper A2v, 3r, 3v, 4r *cornuta*; *see* Plates 23, 27

jug, jar (large) A2v *vettina*; *see* Plates 12, 24

kitchen A2v, 3v *cucina*

knives A3v *coltelli*

napkin, serviette A3v *salvietta*

oranges A3v *melangole*

pouch, purse A2v, 3v *borsa*; Plate 27

salad, pickled foods A3v *insalata*; *see* Index 2

sideboard A2v, 3v, 4r *credenza*

tub A2v, 3r, 3v *sporta*; large tub A3v *sportone*

utensils A1r *istrumenti*

Persons

acolytes A2r *accoliti*

apothecaries, pharmacists, spicers A4r *spetiali*

archbishops A3r *Arcivescovi*

assayer, tester A3r, 3v *credentiero, credentiere*; *see also* sideboard officer

barbers, rudimentary surgeons A4r *barbieri*

bishops A1r, 3r *vescovi*; bishop canon (of St Peter's) A1v *vescovo canonico (di Santo Pietro)*

canon (of St Peter's) A1r, 1v, 2r, 4v *Canonico, Canonici (di Santo Pietro)*

cannoneers A4r *canoniere*

cantors A2v, 4r *cantori (di capella)*

cardinals created (by a pope) A1r, 2r *creature*

carpenter, woodworker A4r *falignami* (*DEI* 'falegname: chi lavora il "legname", legnaiuola')

cellarer, sommelier, butler A3v *bottigliero*

charcutier, keeper or supplier of cured meats A3v *salcicciero*

clergy A4v *clero*

cook A3v *cuoco*

credenza officer: *see* assayer, sideboard officer

deacons A4v *Diaconi*

dean A1r *decano*

Dominicans, *Ordo Praedicatorum* A4v *Orfanelli*

to embroider A1v [*ricamare*]

torch: (waxed) rope ~ A1v, 2r *torcia, torcie (di cera gialla)* (*Zingarelli* 'torcia: fiaccola di funi ritorte e stoppa, impregnata di resina, sebo, cera'); wood ~ A1v, 2r *facola, facole*; A2r *fiaccole* (*Zingarelli* 'fiaccola: fusto di legno resinoso o sim. spalmato di materiale infiammabile')

to summon A3v [*addimandare*]

velvet A1v, 2r *veluto*

vestments A1r, 2v *paramenti*

wall (outer, usually with moat) A4r *trincera* (*Zingarelli* 'trincea, trincera opera di fortificazione campale composta da un fosso, con parapetto rivolto verso il nemico')

wax, ~ candle A2r *cera*; yellow ~ A1v *cera gialla*; tawny red ~ A2r *cera roscia*

wicket, grille, gate A2v, 3r, 4r *sportello* (*DEI* 'piccolo porta nell'uscio')

wood (the material) A2v, 4r *legno*; lumber A1v *legname*